AutoCAD
and its applications

B A S I C S

W9-BEO-252

by

Terence M. Shumaker
Chairperson, Drafting Technology
Director, Autodesk Premier Training Center
Clackamas Community College, Oregon City, Oregon

David A. Madsen
Faculty Emeritus
Former Chairperson
Drafting Technology
Autodesk Premier Training Center
Clackamas Community College, Oregon City, Oregon

Former Board of Director
American Design Drafting Association

Publisher
The Goodheart-Willcox Company, Inc.
Tinley Park, Illinois

Library of Congress Catalog Card Number
International Standard Book Number 1-56637-800-1

1 2 3 4 5 6 7 8 9 10   01   05 04 03 02 01 00

Library of Congress Cataloging-in-Publication Data

Shumaker, Terence M.
  AutoCAD and applications : basics, AutoCAD 2000/2000i /
by Terence M. Shumaker, David A. Madsen.

    p. cm.

  Includes index
  ISBN 1-56637-800-1
  1. Computer graphics. 2. AutoCAD I. Madsen, David A.
II. Title

T385.S46147 2000
604.2'0285'5369--dc21   99-26502
                                                  CIP

Introduction

AutoCAD and its Applications—Basics is a text that provides complete instruction in mastering AutoCAD 2000 and AutoCAD 2000i commands and drawing techniques. Typical applications of AutoCAD are presented with basic drafting and design concepts. The topics are covered in an easy-to-understand sequence and progress in a way that allows you to become comfortable with the commands as your knowledge builds from one chapter to the next. In addition, *AutoCAD and its Applications—Basics* offers the following features:

- Step-by-step use of AutoCAD commands.
- In-depth explanations of how and why commands function as they do.
- Extensive use of font changes to specify certain meanings.
- Examples and discussions of industry practices and standards.
- Actual screen captures of AutoCAD and Windows features and functions.
- Professional tips explaining how to use AutoCAD effectively and efficiently.
- Over 200 exercises to reinforce the chapter topics. These exercises also build on previously learned material.
- Chapter tests for review of commands and key AutoCAD concepts.
- A large selection of drafting problems supplement each chapter. Problems are presented as 3D illustrations, actual plotted industrial drawings, and engineering sketches.

With *AutoCAD and its Applications—Basics* you learn AutoCAD commands and become acquainted with information in other areas:

- Office practices for firms using AutoCAD systems.
- Preliminary planning and sketches.
- Linetypes and their uses.
- Drawing geometric shapes and constructions.
- Special editing operations that increase productivity.
- Making multiview drawings (orthographic projection).
- Dimensioning techniques and practices, based on accepted standards.
- Drawing section views and designing graphic patterns.
- Creating shapes and symbols for different uses.
- Creating and managing symbol libraries.
- Sketching with AutoCAD.
- Basic 3D drawing and display.
- Plotting and printing drawings.
- Using Windows Explorer for organizing and managing files and directories.
- Digitizing existing drawings.
- Accessing and working with the Internet.

Fonts Used in This Text

Different typefaces are used throughout this text to define terms and identify AutoCAD commands. Important terms always appear in **bold-italic face, serif** type. AutoCAD menus, commands, variables, dialog box names, and toolbar buttons are printed in **bold-face, sans serif** type. File names, directory folder names, paths, and keyboard-entry items appear in the body of the text in Roman, sans serif type. Keyboard keys are shown inside of square brackets [ ] and appear in Roman, sans serif type. For example, [Enter] means to press the Enter key.

Prompt sequences are set apart from the body text with space above and below, and appear in Roman, sans serif type. Keyboard entry items in prompts appear in **BOLD-FACE, SANS-SERIF** type, capital letters. In prompts, the [Enter] key is represented by the ↵ symbol.

In addition, commands, menus, and dialog boxes related to Microsoft® Windows® appear in Roman, sans serif type.

Checking the AutoCAD Reference Manuals

For 2000i Users...

No other reference should be needed when using this text. However, the authors have referenced relevant topic areas to the *AutoCAD User's Guide* and the *AutoCAD Customization Guide*. An icon in the margin identifies the specific chapter within the reference where additional information can be found. For example, the icon next to this paragraph tells you that you can find more information in chapter 5 of the *AutoCAD User's Guide*.

The *AutoCAD User's Guide* and *AutoCAD Customization Guide* are part of the help file installed with AutoCAD. To reference these materials, select **AutoCAD Help** from the **Help** pull-down menu.

The AutoCAD help also includes the *AutoCAD Command Reference*. Commands and variables are presented in alphabetical order in this manual. Refer to it for additional information on specific commands and system variables.

Other Text References

For additional information, standards from organizations such as ANSI (American National Standards Institute) and ASME (American Society of Mechanical Engineers) are referenced throughout the text. These standards are used to help you create drawings that follow industry, national, and international practices. Appendix J lists many of these standards.

Also for your convenience, other Goodheart-Willcox textbooks are referenced. Textbooks that are referenced include *AutoCAD and its Applications—Advanced*; *AutoLISP Programming—Principles and Techniques*; *Geometric Dimensioning and Tolerancing*; and *Process Pipe Drafting*. All of these textbooks can be ordered directly from Goodheart-Willcox.

Introducing the AutoCAD Commands

There are several ways to select AutoCAD drawing and editing commands. Selecting commands from the toolbars, pull-down menus, or the digitizer tablet template menu is slightly different than entering them from the keyboard. All AutoCAD commands and related options in this text are introduced by providing all of the commonly active command entry methods.

In many examples, command entries are shown as if they were typed at the keyboard. This allows the text to present the keyboard shortcuts, full command name, and prompts that appear on screen. Commands, options, and values you must enter are given in bold text, as shown on the next page. The available keyboard shortcuts are given first to reinforce the quickest way for you to enter commands at the keyboard. Pressing the [Enter] (return) key is indicated with the ↵ symbol.

```
Command: L or LINE↵
From point: 2,2↵
To point: 4,2↵
To point: ↵
```

General input, such as picking a point or selecting an object, is presented in *italic, serif font*, as shown below.

```
Command: L or LINE↵
From point: (pick a point)
To point: (pick another point)
To point: ↵
```

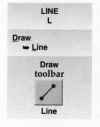

LINE
L

Draw
→ Line

Draw
toolbar

Line

The command line, pull-down menu, and toolbar button menu entry methods are presented throughout the text. When a command is introduced, these methods are illustrated in the margin next to the text reference. The toolbar in which the button is located is also identified. The example in the margin next to this paragraph illustrates the various methods of initiating the **LINE** command.

Some commands and functions are handled more efficiently by picking a toolbar button or a menu command. Many of these procedures are described in numbered, step-by-step instructions.

The AutoCAD digitizer tablet template is presented in Appendix M. This gives you the opportunity to become familiar with other input formats before using the template menu. Experiment with all command entry methods to find the most convenient way for *you* to enter commands.

Note for AutoCAD 2000i Users

For 2000i Users...

AutoCAD 2000 and AutoCAD 2000i are very similar programs. This text is designed to be used with either version of AutoCAD. When discussing features that differ between the two versions, a special note is provided for AutoCAD 2000i users. A sample of these notes is shown in the margin next to this paragraph. The note identifies how AutoCAD 2000i is different from AutoCAD 2000 with regards to the specific feature. Features unique to AutoCAD 2000i requiring expanded coverage are detailed in *Appendix A, AutoCAD 2000i Features and Express Tools*.

> These notes identify features unique to AutoCAD 2000i. If the feature is discussed in Appendix A, the note includes a reference to the page on which the discussion begins.

Flexibility in Design

Flexibility is the key word when using *AutoCAD and its Applications—Basics, AutoCAD 2000*. This text is an excellent training aid for individual instruction, as well as classroom instruction. *AutoCAD and its Applications—Basics, AutoCAD 2000* teaches you how to apply AutoCAD to common drafting tasks. It is also an invaluable resource for any professional using AutoCAD.

When working through the text, you will see a variety of notices. These notices include Professional Tips, Notes, and Cautions that help you develop your AutoCAD skills.

PROFESSIONAL TIP   These ideas and suggestions are aimed at increasing your productivity and enhancing your use of AutoCAD commands and techniques.

NOTE   A note explains important aspects of a command, menu, or activity. These aspects should be kept in mind while you are working through the text.

CAUTION

A caution alerts you to potential problems if instructions or commands are used incorrectly, or if an action can corrupt or alter files, folders, or disks. If you are in doubt after reading a caution, always consult your instructor or supervisor.

AutoCAD and its Applications—Basics provides several ways for you to evaluate your performance. Included are the following:

- **Exercises.** Each chapter contains in-text Exercises. These Exercises instruct you to perform tasks that reinforce the material just presented. You can work through the Exercises at your own pace.
- **Chapter Tests.** Each chapter includes a written test at the end of the chapter. Questions require you to give the proper definition, command, option, or response.
- **Drawing Problems.** There are a variety of drafting and design problems at the end of each chapter. These are presented as real-world CAD drawings, 3D illustrations, and engineering sketches. The problems are designed to make you think, solve problems, use design techniques, research and use proper drawing standards, and correct errors in the drawings or engineering sketches. Each drawing problem deals with one of seven technical disciplines. Although doing all of the problems will enhance your AutoCAD skills, you may be focusing on a particular discipline. The discipline related to a problem is indicated by a graphic in the margin next to the problem. Each graphic and its description is as follows:

 These problems address *mechanical* drafting and design applications, such as manufactured part designs.

 These problems address *architectural* and *structural* drafting and design applications, such as floor plans and presentation drawings.

 These problems address *electronics* drafting and design applications, such as electronic schematics, logic diagrams, and electrical part design.

 These problems address *civil* drafting and design applications, such as plot plans, plats, and landscape drawings.

 These problems address *graphic design* applications, such as text creation, logos, title blocks, and page layout.

 These problems address *piping* drafting and design applications, such as piping flow diagrams, pump design, and pipe layout.

 These problems address a variety of *general* drafting and design applications.

<table>
<tr>
<td>

NOTE

</td>
<td>

Some problems presented in this text are given as engineering sketches. These sketches are intended to represent the type of materials a drafter is expected to work from in a real-world situation. As such, engineering sketches often contain errors or slight inaccuracies, and are not drawn according to proper drafting conventions and applicable standards. Errors in these problems are *intentional* to encourage you to apply appropriate techniques and standards in order to solve the problem. As in real-world applications, sketches should be considered to be preliminary layouts. Always question inaccuracies in sketches and designs, and consult the engineer, designer, instructor, applicable standards, or other resources.

</td>
</tr>
</table>

Disk Supplements

To help you develop your AutoCAD skills, Goodheart-Willcox offers a disk supplement package to use with *AutoCAD and its Applications—Basics*. The AutoCAD 2000 or AutoCAD 2000i software is required for Goodheart-Willcox software to operate properly.

The *Student Work Disks* contain additional AutoCAD pull-down menus with a variety of activities. These activities are intended to be used as a supplement to the exercises and activities found in the text. These activities allow you to progress at your own pace. The student work disks can be purchased from Goodheart-Willcox.

ABOUT THE AUTHORS

Terence M. Shumaker is the Chairperson of the Drafting Technology Department and Director of the Autodesk Premier Training Center at Clackamas Community College. Terence has been teaching at the community college level since 1977. He has professional experience in surveying, civil drafting, industrial piping, and technical illustration. He is the author of Goodheart-Willcox's *Process Pipe Drafting*, and is coauthor of the *AutoCAD and its Applications* series (Release 10, 11, 12, 13, and 14 editions) and *AutoCAD Essentials*.

David A. Madsen is the former Chairperson of Drafting Technology and the Autodesk Premier Training Center at Clackamas Community College. David was an instructor/department chair at Clackamas Community College for nearly 30 years. In addition to community college experience, David was a Drafting Technology instructor at Centennial High School in Gresham, Oregon. David also has extensive experience in mechanical drafting, architectural design and drafting, and construction practices. He is the author of several Goodheart-Willcox drafting and design textbooks, including *Geometric Dimensioning and Tolerancing*, and is coauthor of the *AutoCAD and its Applications* series (Release 10, 11, 12, 13, and 14 editions) and *AutoCAD Essentials*.

NOTICE TO THE USER

AutoCAD and its Applications—Basics covers basic AutoCAD applications. For a text that covers the advanced AutoCAD applications, please refer to *AutoCAD and its Applications—Advanced*. Copies of any of these texts can be ordered directly from Goodheart-Willcox.

ACKNOWLEDGMENTS

The authors and publisher would like to thank the following individuals and companies for their assistance and contributions.

Special Recognition

Special thanks to Rod Rawls for his professional expertise in providing in-depth research and testing, technical assistance, reviews, and development of new materials for use throughout the text. Rod is an AutoCAD consultant and full-time instructor at the Autodesk Premier Training Center, Clackamas Community College. He is also the coauthor of *AutoLISP Programming: Principles and Techniques* published by Goodheart-Willcox.

Technical Assistance and Contribution of Materials

Margo Bilson of Willamette Industries, Inc.
Fitzgerald, Hagan, & Hackathorn
Bruce L. Wilcox, Johnson and Wales University School of Technology

Contribution of Photographs or Other Technical Information

Arthur Baker
Autodesk, Inc.
CADalyst magazine
CADENCE magazine
Chris Lindner
EPCM Services Ltd.
Harris Group, Inc.

International Source for Ergonomics
Jim Webster
Kunz Associates
Myonetics Inc.
Norwest Engineering
Schuchart & Associates, Inc.
Willamette Industries, Inc.

Technical Assistance and Reviews

Rod Rawls, Autodesk Premier Training Center, Clackamas Community College
Eugene O'Day, Ron Palma, Glynnis Patterson, Trevor Taylor, KETIV Technologies
Keith McDonald, FLIR Systems, Inc.

TRADEMARKS

Autodesk, the Autodesk logo, 3D Studio MAX, 3D Studio VIZ, AutoCAD, Heidi, and *WHIP!* are registered trademarks, and AutoCAD DesignCenter, AutoCAD Learning Assistance, AutoSnap, and AutoTrack are trademarks of Autodesk, Inc. in the U.S.A. and/or other countries.

Microsoft, Windows, Windows NT, Windows 95 andVisual Basic are trademarks of Microsoft Corporation.

TextPad is a registered trademark of Helios Software Solutions.

Contents

DRAWING AND PRINTING WITH AUTOCAD

EDITING THE DRAWING

AUTOCAD APPLICATIONS

DIMENSIONING AND TOLERANCING

ADVANCED DRAWING CONSTRUCTION

BASIC 3D DRAWING AND ADVANCED APPLICATIONS

CHAPTER 1

Introduction to AutoCAD Features

Learning Objectives

After completing this chapter, you will be able to:

- Describe the methods and procedures used in computer-aided drafting.
- Explain the value of planning your work and system management.
- Describe the appropriate locations for saving drawing files.
- Load AutoCAD from the Windows desktop.
- Describe the AutoCAD screen layout and user interface.
- Describe the function of dialog boxes.
- Use the keyboard and an input device to select commands, enter text, and pick locations on the screen.
- Identify the function of the **AutoCAD DesignCenter** and the **Properties** window.
- Use the **HELP** command for online assistance.
- Use the features found in the **Help Topics** dialog box.
- Access help while a command is active.
- Review the AutoCAD Learning Assistance and the AutoCAD Support Assistance.
- Define the use of function, control, and shortcut keys.

THE TOOLS OF CAD

The computer and software are the principal components of the present-day design and drafting workstation. These tools make up a *system* referred to as *CAD*—computer-aided design, or computer-aided drafting. CAD is used by drafters, designers, and engineers to develop designs and drawings, and to plot them on paper or film. Additionally, drawings and designs can be displayed as 3D models and animations, or used in analysis and testing.

CAD has surpassed the use of manual drafting techniques because of its speed, power, accuracy, and flexibility, but is not totally without its attendant problems and trade-offs. Although the uses of CAD designs are limited only by the imagination, it should be remembered that the computer hardware is sensitive to the slightest electrical impulses, and the human body is sensitive to the repetitive motions required when using the tools.

THE AUTOCAD TOOLBOX

Drawings and models are constructed in AutoCAD using XYZ coordinates. The *Cartesian (rectangular)* coordinate system is used most often, and is discussed in Chapter 4. Angular layouts are created by measuring angles in a counterclockwise direction. Drawings can be annotated with text and described with a variety of dimensioning techniques. In addition, objects can be given colors, patterns, and textures. AutoCAD also provides you with the tools to create basic pictorial drawings called *isometrics*, and powerful 3D surface models and solids.

THE APPLICATIONS OF AUTOCAD

Using AutoCAD software and this text, you will learn how to construct, lay out, dimension, and annotate two-dimensional drawings. Should you wish to continue your study into 3D modeling, 3D rendering, and customization, *AutoCAD and its Applications—Advanced* provides you with detailed instruction. Your studies will enable you to create a wide variety of drawings, designs, and 3D models in any of the drafting, design, and engineering disciplines.

The drawings can have hundreds of colors and *layers*, which contain different kinds of information. Objects can also be shown as exploded assemblies or displayed in 3D. See Figure 1-1.

In addition, objects in the drawing can be given "intelligence" in the form of **attributes**. These attributes are various kinds of data that turn a drawing into a graphical database. You can then ask questions of your drawing and receive a variety of information.

Using AutoCAD, you have the ability to construct 3D models that appear as wireframes or have surface colors and textures. The creation of solid models that have mass properties and can be analyzed is also possible with AutoCAD. The display in Figure 1-2 is an example of a solid model created in AutoCAD. 3D drawings and models can be viewed in several ways. These models can also be colored and shaded, or **rendered**, to appear in a realistic format.

Figure 1-1.
A nozzle shown as a 2D drawing and as a 3D model. (Autodesk, Inc.)

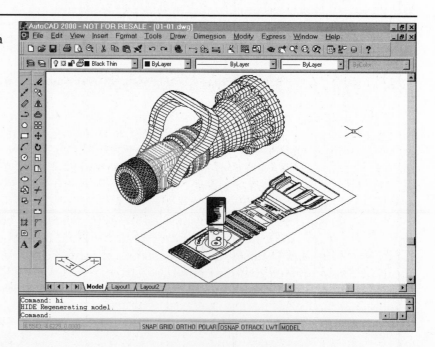

Figure 1-2.
A 3D model of
a connecting rod.
A—Model shown as
a wireframe with
edges marked by
lines. B—Color and
shading are added
when the model is
rendered.
(Autodesk, Inc.)

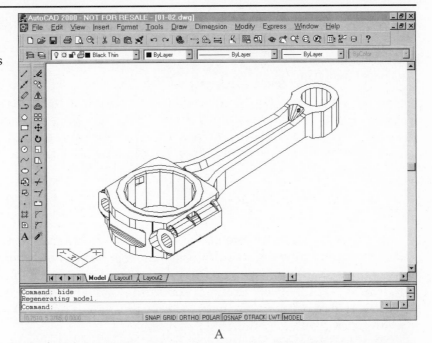

A

B

A powerful application of CAD software and 3D models is animation. The simplest form of animation is to dynamically rotate the model in order to view it from any direction. See Figure 1-3. Drawings and models can also be animated so that the model appears to move, rotate, and even explode into its individual components. An extremely useful form of animation is called a *walkthrough*. Using specialized software, you can plot a path through or around a model and replay it just like a movie. The logical next step in viewing the model is to actually be inside it and have the ability to manipulate and change the objects in it. This is called *virtual reality*, and is achieved through the use of 3D models and highly specialized software and hardware.

Figure 1-3.
This 3D piping model can be rotated and viewed from any location in 3D space. (Autodesk, Inc.)

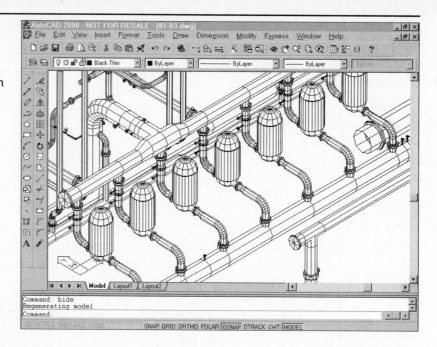

ESTABLISHING AN AUTOCAD DRAWING METHOD

All aspects of the project must be considered when developing a drawing plan. This requires careful use of the CAD system and detailed standards for the planning and drawing process. Therefore, it is important for you to be familiar with the AutoCAD tools and to know how they work and when they are best suited for a specific job. There is no substitute for knowing the tools, and the most basic of these is the Cartesian coordinate system.

Learn the XYZ Coordinate System

The XYZ coordinate system is the basic building block of any CAD drawing. The locations of points are described with XYZ coordinate values. These values are called *rectangular coordinates* and locate any point on a flat plane, such as a sheet of paper. The *origin* of the coordinate system is the lower-left corner. See Figure 1-4. A distance measured horizontally from the origin is an X value. A distance measured vertically from the origin is a Y value.

Rectangular coordinates can also be measured in three-dimensional space. In this case, the third dimension rises up from the surface of the paper and is given the Z value. See Figure 1-5. When describing coordinate locations, it is proper to give the X value first, the Y value second, and the Z value third. Each number is separated by a comma. For example, the value of 3,1,6 represents three units from the X origin, one unit from the Y origin, and six units from the Z origin. A detailed explanation of rectangular coordinates is provided in Chapter 4.

Figure 1-4.
The 2D rectangular coordinate system.

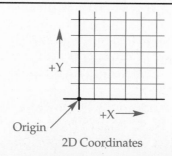

Origin

+Y

+X

2D Coordinates

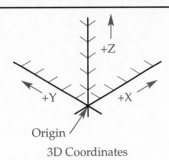

Figure 1-5.
The 3D rectangular
coordinate system.

Origin

3D Coordinates

Planning Your Drawing

Drawing planning involves looking at the entire process or project that you are involved in. A plan determines how a project is going to be approached. It includes the drawings to be created, how they will be titled and numbered, the information to be presented, and the types of symbols needed to show the information.

More specifically, drawing planning applies to how you create and manage a drawing or set of drawings. This includes which view or feature you draw first and the coordinates and AutoCAD commands you use to draw it.

Drafters who begin constructing a drawing from the seat of their pants—creating symbols and naming objects, shapes, and views as they go—do not possess a good drawing plan. Those who plan, use consistent techniques, and adhere to school or company standards are developing good drawing habits.

Throughout this text you will find aids to help you develop good drawing habits. One of the first steps in developing your skills is to learn how to plan your work. The importance of planning cannot be emphasized enough. There is no substitute.

Using Drawing Standards

Standards are guidelines for operating procedures, drawing techniques, and record keeping. Most schools and companies have established standards. It is important that standards exist and are used by all CAD personnel. Drawing standards may include the following items:
- Methods of file storage: location and name.
- Dimensioning techniques.
- File naming conventions.
- Text styles.
- Drawing sheet sizes and title blocks to be used.
- Linetypes.
- Drawing symbols.
- Color schemes for plotting.
- File backup methods and times.

Your standards may vary in content, but the most important aspect of standards is that they are used. When standards are used, your drawings are consistent, you become more productive, and the classroom or office functions more efficiently.

Planning Your Work

Study the planning pyramids in Figure 1-6. The horizontal axes of the pyramids represent the amount of time spent on the project. The vertical axes represent the life of the project. The top level is the planning stage and the bottom level is the final execution of the project.

The pyramid on the right is pointed at the top and indicates a small amount of planning. As the project progresses, more and more time is devoted to planning and less time is available for other tasks. This is *not* an ideal situation. The inverted

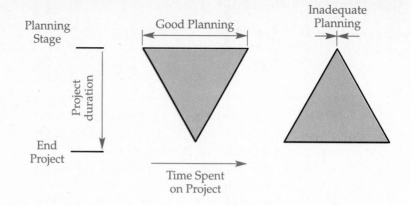

Figure 1-6.
Planning pyramids illustrate time required for well-planned and poorly-planned projects.

pyramid on the left shows a lot of time devoted to initial planning. As the project advances, less planning time is needed, thus freeing more time for tasks related to the completion of the project.

As you begin your CAD training, plan your drawing sessions thoroughly to organize your thoughts. Sketch the problem or design, noting size and locations of features. List the drawing commands needed in the order they are to be used. Schedule a regular time to use the computer and adhere to that time. Follow the standards set by your school or firm. These might include specific drawing names, project planning sheets, project logs, drawing layout procedures, special title blocks, and a location for drawing storage. Standards and procedures must be followed by everyone using the computers in your school or company. Confusion may result if your drawings do not have the proper name, are stored in the wrong place, or have the wrong title block.

Develop the habit of saving your work regularly—at least every 10 to 15 minutes. The **SAVETIME** system variable can be set to automatically save your drawings at predetermined intervals. **SAVETIME** is covered in detail in Chapter 3. Drawings may be lost due to a software error, hardware malfunction, power failure, or your own mistakes. This is not common, but you should still be prepared for such an event.

You should develop methods of managing your work. This is critical to computer drafting and is discussed throughout the text. Keep the following points in mind as you begin your AutoCAD training.

✓ Plan your work and organize your thoughts.
✓ Learn and use your classroom or office standards.
✓ Save your work often.

If you remember to follow these three points, your grasp of the tools and methods of CAD will be easier. In addition, your experiences with the computer will be more enjoyable.

Remember the planning pyramids as you begin your study of AutoCAD. When you feel the need to dive blindly into a drawing or project, restrain yourself. Take the time needed for development of the project goals. Then proceed with the confidence of knowing where you are heading.

During your early stages of AutoCAD training, write down all of the instructions needed to construct your drawing. Do this especially for your first few assignments. This means documenting every command and every coordinate point (dimension) needed. Develop a planning sheet for your drawings. Your time spent at the computer with AutoCAD will be more productive and enjoyable.

Using Drawing Plan Sheets

A good work plan can save drawing time. Planning should include sketches. A rough preliminary sketch and a drawing plan can help in the following ways:
- Determines the drawing layout.
- Sets the overall size of the drawing by laying out the views and required free space.
- Confirms the drawing units based on the dimensions provided.
- Predetermines the point entry system and locates the points.
- Establishes the Grid and Snap settings.
- Presets some of the drawing variables, such as layers, linetypes, and linewidths. (These items are explained in Chapter 4.)
- Establishes how and when various activities are to be performed.
- Determines the best use of AutoCAD.
- Results in an even workload.
- Provides maximum use of equipment.

Planning Checklist

In the early stages of your AutoCAD training, it is best to plan your drawing projects carefully. There is a tendency to want things to happen immediately—for things to be "automatic." But if you hurry and do little or no planning, you will become more frustrated. Therefore, as you begin each new project, step through the following planning checklist so that the execution of your project goes smoothly.
- ✓ Analyze the problem.
- ✓ Study all engineering sketches.
- ✓ Locate all available resources and list for future use.
- ✓ Determine the applicable standards for the project.
- ✓ Sketch the problem.
- ✓ Decide on the number and kind of views required.
- ✓ Determine the final plotted scale of the drawing, and of all views.
- ✓ Determine the drawing sequence, such as lines, features, dimensions, and notes.
- ✓ List the AutoCAD commands to be used.
- ✓ Follow the standards and refer to resources as you work.

PROFESSIONAL TIP

AutoCAD is designed so that you can construct drawings and models using the actual dimensions of the object. *Always draw in full scale.* The proper text and dimension size is set using scale factors. This is covered in detail in later chapters. The final scale of the drawing should be planned early, and is shown on the plot. Always plot the drawing to a specific scale if plotting a model space layout. Always plot the drawing at a scale of 1:1 if plotting a paper space layout.

Working Procedures Checklist

As you begin learning AutoCAD, you will realize that several skills are required to become a proficient CAD user. The following list provides you with some hints to help you become comfortable with AutoCAD. They will also allow you to work quickly and efficiently. The following items are discussed in detail in later chapters.
- ✓ Plan all work with pencil and paper before using the computer.
- ✓ Check the **Object Properties** toolbar at the top of the display screen and the status bar at the bottom to see which layer(s) and drawing aid(s) are in effect.

✓ Read the command line at the bottom of the display screen. Constantly check for the correct command, instructions, or proper keyboard entry of data.

✓ Read the command line after keyboard entry of data before pressing the [Enter] key. Backspacing to erase incorrect typing is quicker than redoing the command.

✓ If using a multibutton puck, develop a good hand position that allows easy movement. Your button-pressing finger should move without readjusting your grip of the puck.

✓ Learn the meanings of all the buttons on your puck or mouse and use them regularly.

✓ Watch the disk drive lights to see when the disks are being accessed. Some disk access may take a few seconds. Knowing what is happening will lessen frustration and impatience.

✓ Think ahead. Know your next move.

✓ Learn new commands every day. Don't rely on just a few that seem to work. Find commands that can speed your work and do it more efficiently.

✓ Save your work every 10 to 15 minutes in case a power failure or system crash deletes the drawing held in computer memory.

✓ If you are stumped, ask the computer for help. Use the online help to display valuable information about each command on the screen. Using AutoCAD's online help is discussed in detail later in this chapter.

EXERCISE 1-1

❑ Make a sketch similar to Figure 1-4. Label the origin, +X axis, and +Y axis. Sketch a dot located at the intersection of 3 units in the +X axis and 3 units in the +Y axis.

❑ Provide a short discussion about why it is important to plan your work before you start a drawing in AutoCAD. Why should a sketch be part of your preliminary planning?

AutoCAD User's Guide 2

STARTING AUTOCAD

AutoCAD 2000 and AutoCAD 2000i are designed to operate with Windows 2000, Windows 98, Windows NT, and Windows 95. Each of these interfaces are nearly identical. If you see illustrations in this text that appear to be NT, do not be concerned, for the 95 or 98 version of the AutoCAD feature is the same.

When AutoCAD is first installed, Windows creates a *program icon* that is displayed on the desktop. An *icon* is a small picture that represents an application, accessory, file, or command. In addition to the icon, the program name is listed as an item in the Start menu under the Programs item.

> **NOTE**
>
> AutoCAD must first be installed properly on the computer before it can be used. Refer to Appendix D for detailed instructions on AutoCAD installation and configuration of peripheral devices such as plotters, printers, and digitizers.

AutoCAD can be started using three different techniques. The quickest way to start AutoCAD is to double-click on the AutoCAD 2000 icon on the Windows desktop. See Figure 1-7.

Figure 1-7.
Double-click the
AutoCAD 2000 icon
on the Windows
desktop to start
AutoCAD.

AutoCAD 2000
icon

The second method for starting AutoCAD is to pick the Start button at the lower-left of the Windows desktop. This displays the Start menu. Next, move the pointer to Programs and either hold it there or pick to display the Programs menu. Now move the pointer to the AutoCAD 2000 item and click. This displays all the items in the AutoCAD 2000 program group. Pick on AutoCAD 2000 to load the software. See Figure 1-8.

These five items are listed in the AutoCAD 2000 menu:

- **AutoCAD 2000.** Loads the AutoCAD 2000 program.
- **AutoCAD 2000 License Agreement.** Allows you to review the AutoCAD 2000 license agreement at anytime.
- **AutoCAD 2000 Online Help.** This provides access to all the online documentation for AutoCAD 2000. This feature is discussed later in this chapter.
- **AutoCAD 2000 Readme.** Opens a text file that gives information on important items that may not be covered in the printed documentation or the online help files. Also provides links to other topics such as "What's New in AutoCAD 2000."

For 2000i Users...

The AutoCAD 2000i menu contains only two items: AutoCAD 2000i and Batch Plot Utility.

NOTE

A Windows *link* is identified by green, underlined text. The pointer changes to a hand icon when it is moved over link text. A new page of information is displayed when you pick a link.

- **Batch Plot Utility.** This temporarily loads AutoCAD and enables you to plot a group of files at one time. You cannot edit drawings with this utility. It can run in the background while you do other work. This is discussed in Chapter 10.

Figure 1-8.
Pick AutoCAD 2000 in the Programs menu to load AutoCAD.

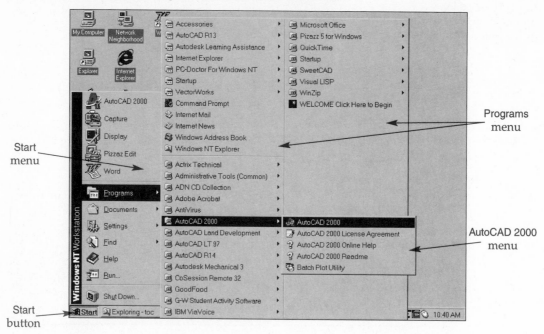

The third method for loading AutoCAD is the most difficult, and is the same process used to install software. You must locate and run the acad.exe file when using this method. Begin this process as follows:

1. Pick the Start button then pick Run... to display the Run dialog box. See Figure 1-9.
2. Enter the drive and directory location of the acad.exe file in the Open: text box.
3. Pick the OK button or press [Enter]. If you do not know the exact location of the acad.exe file, use the Browse... button. The acad.exe file is always located in the main AutoCAD directory folder. If the defaults were used during installation, this folder should be named AutoCAD 2000.

   AutoCAD is loaded and the **Startup** dialog box is displayed as shown in Figure 1-10. The functions of this dialog box are discussed thoroughly in Chapter 2. Pick the **Cancel** button to clear the dialog box.

For 2000i Users...

In AutoCAD 2000i, the **AutoCAD Today** window is displayed when AutoCAD loads. The **AutoCAD Today** window is discussed on page 961.

NOTE

After installing AutoCAD 2000, you have 30 days to register your software and obtain an authorization code. If the authorization code has not yet been entered, AutoCAD displays the **Authorization Wizard** dialog box, which allows you to either submit an authorization request or bypass the authorization and start working in AutoCAD. The **Authorization Wizard** provides simple step-by-step guidance for contacting Autodesk by e-mail, telephone, fax, or the World Wide Web. However, if it has been more than 30 days since the installation, you cannot work in AutoCAD until you obtain a valid authorization code from Autodesk. See Appendix D for a complete discussion of installing and authorizing AutoCAD.

Figure 1-9.
The Run dialog box allows you to load programs such as AutoCAD.

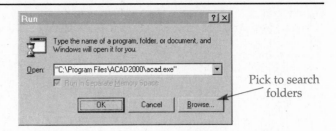

Pick to search folders

Figure 1-10.
The **Startup** dialog box is displayed when AutoCAD is loaded.

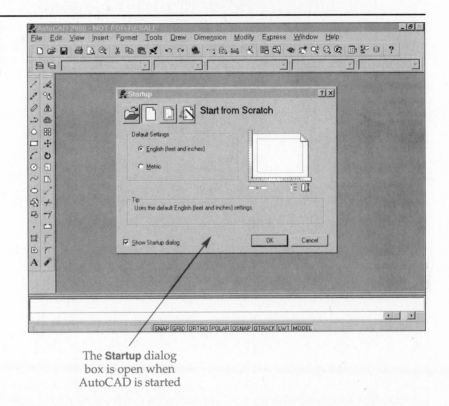

The **Startup** dialog box is open when AutoCAD is started

THE AUTOCAD GRAPHICS WINDOW

AutoCAD User's Guide 2

The AutoCAD graphics window is similar to any other window within the Windows operating system. Picking the small control icon in the upper-left corner displays a standard window control menu, and the icons in the upper-right corner are used for minimizing, maximizing, and closing the program window or individual document windows. See Figure 1-11.

Window sizing operations are done as with any other window. AutoCAD uses the familiar Windows style interface, with buttons, pull-down menus, and dialog boxes. Each of these items are discussed in detail in this chapter. Learning the layout, appearance, and proper use of these features allows you to master AutoCAD quickly.

Standard Screen Layout

The standard screen layout provides a large graphics, or drawing, area. The drawing area is bordered by *toolbars* at the left and top, and by the *floating command window* at the bottom. Look at your screen now and study the illustration in Figure 1-11. Note that the proportional size of the AutoCAD graphics window features may vary depending on the display resolution of your computer system.

Many of the elements of the AutoCAD graphics window are referred to as *floating*. This means that the item can be freely resized or moved about the screen into new positions. Floating features are contained within a standard Windows

Figure 1-11.
The standard AutoCAD graphics window.

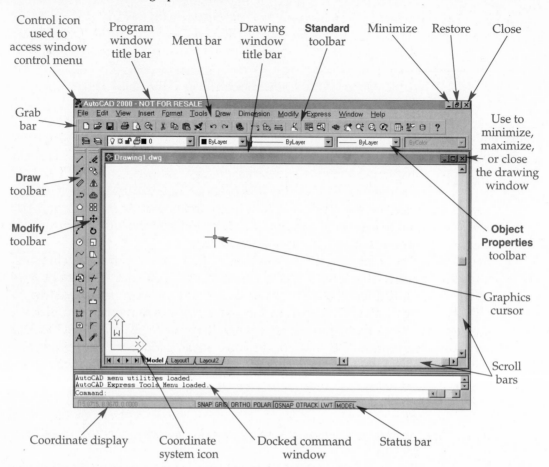

border and display a title bar at the top. When you run AutoCAD for the first time, the AutoCAD program window is displayed in a floating position on the desktop. A smaller window inside of the AutoCAD program window displays the drawing area for the currently open drawing file. Floating windows are moved and adjusted for size in the same manner as any other window, however, the drawing windows can only be adjusted and positioned within the AutoCAD program window.

Some floating features, such as toolbars, can also be *docked* around the edges of the graphics window. The toolbars displayed initially after installing AutoCAD are docked by default, and do not display a title bar. To place a docked toolbar in a floating position, you can either double-click the grab bar, or press and hold the pick button while pointing at the grab bar then move your mouse to drag the toolbar away from the edge of the window. The term *grab bar* refers to the two thin bars at the top or left edge of a docked toolbar. To dock a floating toolbar, double-click on the title bar or press and hold the pick button while pointing at the title bar and drag it to the edge of the graphics window (top, bottom, left, or right), then release the pick button. When the item is docked, it loses its border and title bar and becomes a part of the graphics window. Objects may be moved or docked at any time as needed.

Become familiar with these unique areas of the graphics window and the information provided by each. The following list describes the function of each area. Each of these features will be discussed in detail later in this text.

- **Floating command window.** In its default position, this window is docked at the bottom of the graphics window. It displays the Command: prompt and reflects any command entries you make. It also displays prompts that supply information to you or request input. This is where your primary communications with AutoCAD are displayed, so watch for any information shown on this line.

- **Menu bar.** The menu bar appears just below the title bar and displays a number of menu names. As with standard Windows menus, use the cursor to point at a menu name and press the pick button. This causes a *pull-down menu* to be displayed. Any time you pick an item followed by an *ellipsis* (...), a dialog box is displayed. A *dialog box* is a rectangular area that appears on the screen after you type or select certain commands. It contains a variety of options related to a specific command or function, and provides a convenient means of supplying information to AutoCAD.

- **Scroll bars.** The scroll bars allow you to adjust your view of the drawing area.

- **Graphics cursor.** This is your primary means of pointing to objects or locations within a drawing. The length of the graphics cursor crosshairs can be quickly changed. Pick **Options...** in the **Tools** pull-down menu, then pick the **Display** tab. Move the slider bar or change the number in the **Crosshair size** text box at the bottom of the tab to suit your needs. A 5% setting is default, and a 100% value extends the crosshairs to the limits of the graphics window.

- **Coordinate system icon.** This indicates the current coordinate system and helps to determine point locations.

- **Floating toolbar.** Floating toolbars contain various buttons that activate AutoCAD commands. These toolbars can be moved, resized, modified, hidden, or docked as needed.

- **Status bar.** This contains several buttons that display the current state of specific drawing control features and allow access for changing their settings. When a pull-down menu item is highlighted or you are pointing at a toolbar button, a brief explanation of the item is shown along the left side of the status bar.

- **Coordinate display.** This display field, found on the status bar, shows the XYZ cursor location according to the current settings.

- **Standard toolbar.** In the default AutoCAD screen configuration, the **Standard** toolbar appears just above the **Object Properties** toolbar. When you move your pointing device to the toolbar, the crosshairs change to the familiar Windows arrow pointer. As you move your cursor across a toolbar button, a 3D border is displayed around the previously flat button. The term *coolbar* is used to describe this animated behavior. Holding the cursor motionless over a button for a moment displays a *tooltip*, which shows the name of the button in a small box at the cursor location. While the tooltip is visible, a brief explanation of what the button does is displayed along the status bar at the bottom left edge of the window.

  Some buttons show a small black triangle in the lower-right corner. These buttons are called *flyouts*. Press and hold the pick button while pointing at a flyout to display a set of related buttons. The **Standard** toolbar contains a series of buttons that provide access to several of AutoCAD's drawing setup and control commands. Each of these features is identified and briefly described in Figure 1-12. These features are discussed in detail later in this text.

Figure 1-12.

The **Standard** toolbar and its components.

A — **Grab Bar.** A "grab" handle used for relocating toolbars.

B — **New.** Begins a new drawing.

C — **Open.** Opens an existing drawing for editing and revision.

D — **Save.** Writes the drawing information currently in memory to a file.

E — **Print.** Sends drawing information to a hardcopy device, such as a printer or plotter.

F — **Print Preview.** Displays a preview of the drawing layout prior to printing.

G — **Find and Replace.** Finds, replaces, selects, or zooms to a specified text item.

H — **Cut to Clipboard.** "Cuts" (removes) a specified portion of your drawing geometry, storing it in the Windows clipboard.

I — **Copy to Clipboard.** Copies a specified portion of your drawing geometry, storing it in the Windows clipboard.

J — **Paste from Clipboard.** "Pastes" (inserts) the contents of the Windows clipboard to a specified location in your drawing.

K — **Match Properties.** Copies the properties from one object to one or more objects.

L — **Undo.** Cancels the effects of the last command or operation.

M — **Redo.** Can be used after **Undo** to redo the previously canceled operation.

N — **Insert Hyperlink.** Attaches a hyperlink to an object or modifies an existing hyperlink.

O — **Object Snap Flyout.** Presents a series of buttons that activate tracking and object snap tools for accessing specific geometric points within a drawing.

P — **UCS Flyout.** Presents a series of buttons that activate various drawing inquiry commands.

Q — **Inquiry Flyout.** Presents a series of buttons that activate various coordinate system options.

R — **Redraw All.** Redraws the display in all viewports.

S — **Display Viewports Dialog.** Displays the Viewports dialog box for working with drawing viewports.

T — **Named Views Flyout.** Various options for changing the current view of your drawing are presented by this flyout

U — **3D Orbit.** Starts the **3DORBIT** command for interactive 3D viewing of objects in the current viewport.

V — **Pan Realtime.** Displays the hand cursor and moves the display in the current viewport dynamically in real time.

W — **Zoom Realtime.** Displays the zoom cursor and increases or decreases the displayed size of objects in the current viewport.

X — **Zoom Flyout.** Displays a series of buttons that activate **ZOOM** command options.

Y — **Zoom Previous.** Returns the previous display to the graphics area.

Z — **AutoCAD DesignCenter.** Activates the AutoCAD DesignCenter, allowing drawing information to be shared between multiple drawings.

AA—**Properties.** Displays the Properties window where you can set properties for new objects and modify the properties of existing objects.

AB—**dbConnect.** Provides an AutoCAD interface to external database tables.

AC—**Help.** Activates AutoCAD's online help facility.

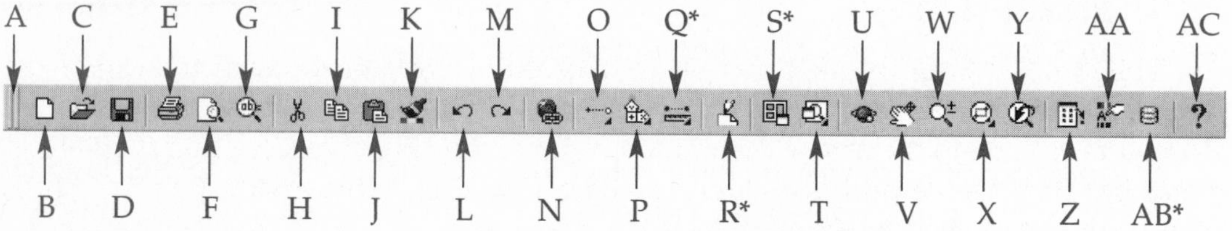

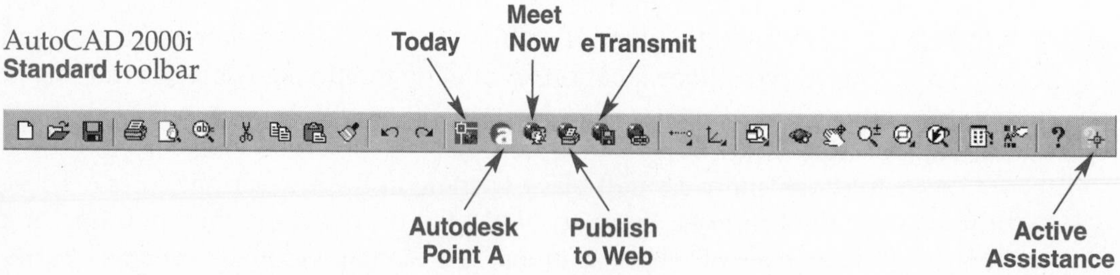

For 2000i Users...

The **Standard** toolbar in AutoCAD 2000i is slightly different from the **Standard** toolbar in AutoCAD 2000. The **Inquiry** flyout, **Redraw All**, **Display Viewports Dialog**, and **dbConnect** buttons have been replaced with the **Today, Autodesk Point A, Meet Now, Publish to Web, eTransmit**, and **Active Assistance** buttons.

A   C   E   G   I   K   M   O   Q*   S*   U   W   Y   AA   AC

B   D   F   H   J   L   N   P   R*   T   V   X   Z   AB*

* Available in AutoCAD 2000 only

AutoCAD 2000i
Standard toolbar

Today   Meet Now   eTransmit

Autodesk Point A   Publish to Web   Active Assistance

• **Object Properties toolbar.** In the default AutoCAD screen configuration, the **Object Properties** toolbar appears just above the graphics area with the **Standard** toolbar. This toolbar contains buttons and display fields for setting and adjusting the properties of objects in a drawing. Each of these features is identified and briefly explained in Figure 1-13.

Figure 1-13.
The **Object Properties** toolbar and its components.

A — **Grab Bar.** A "grab" handle used for relocating toolbars.

B — **Make Object Layer Current.** Allows selection of a drawing object to change the current layer to that of the selected object.

C — **Layers.** Accesses the **Layer Properties Manager** dialog box where you can create and manage drawing layers.

D — **Layer Control.** Shows the current layer and its properties. Picking the down arrow on the right side of the **Layer Control** field shows information on all drawing layers and provides a handy shortcut to common layer control options.

E — **Color Control.** Displays the current object creation color and when picked displays the four most recently used colors and the seven standard colors. Also allows access to the **Select Color** dialog box.

F — **Linetype Control.** Displays the current object linetype. Clicking on the down arrow to the right allows you to select a new linetype from the currently loaded linetypes. Also allows access to the **Linetype Manager** dialog box.

G — **Lineweight Control.** Displays the current object lineweight. Clicking on the down arrow to the right allows you to select a new lineweight from the list.

H — **Plot Style Control.** Displays the current object plot style. Clicking on the down arrow to the right allows you to select a new plot style from the list. Also allows access to the Current Plot Style dialog box.

EXERCISE 1-2

❑ Start AutoCAD.
❑ Select **Start from Scratch** from the **Startup** dialog box.
❑ Select **English (feet and inches)**.
❑ Pick the **OK** button.
❑ Look at all the features of the screen layout as shown in Figure 1-11.
❑ Keep AutoCAD open for the next exercise. If you must quit, pick **Exit** in the **File** pull-down menu and then pick **No** in the AutoCAD alert box.

Pull-Down Menus

The AutoCAD pull-down menus are located on the menu bar at the top of the screen. As with a toolbar, when you move your pointing device to the menu bar, the crosshairs change to the arrow pointer. From Figure 1-14, you can see that the default menu bar has twelve pull-down menu items: **File**, **Edit**, **View**, **Insert**, **Format**, **Tools**, **Draw**, **Dimension**, **Modify**, **Express**, **Window**, and **Help**.

Figure 1-14.
The AutoCAD menu bar. Pull-down menus are accessed by picking the words in this bar.

| File | Edit | View | Insert | Format | Tools | Draw | Dimension | Modify | Express | Window | Help |

For 2000i Users...

Express Tools are not provided with AutoCAD 2000i but can be downloaded from the Autodesk Point A Web site. The Express Tools discussed in this text are those provided with AutoCAD 2000.

NOTE

The **Express** pull-down menu is only available if a complete installation of AutoCAD was performed. If a typical or custom installation is performed, this pull-down menu may not have been loaded. See Appendix D for installation information.

Most of the available menu selections can be found in both the toolbars and the pull-down menus system. Some menu selections, however, are found in one of these two menu areas—so it is important to be familiar with the layout and use of both toolbars and pull-down menus. To see how a pull-down menu works, move your cursor to the **View** menu and press the pick button. A pull-down menu appears below **View**, Figure 1-15A. Commands are easily selected by picking a menu item with your pointing device.

Notice that several of the commands in the **View** pull-down menu have a small arrow to the right. When one of these items is selected, a *cascading menu* appears. A cascading menu has additional options for the previous selection, Figure 1-15B.

Some of the menu selections are followed by an ellipsis (...). If you pick one of these items, a dialog box is displayed. If you pick the wrong pull-down menu, simply move the cursor to the one you want. The first menu is removed and the new menu is displayed. The pull-down menu disappears after you pick an item in the menu, pick a point in the drawing area, or type on the keyboard.

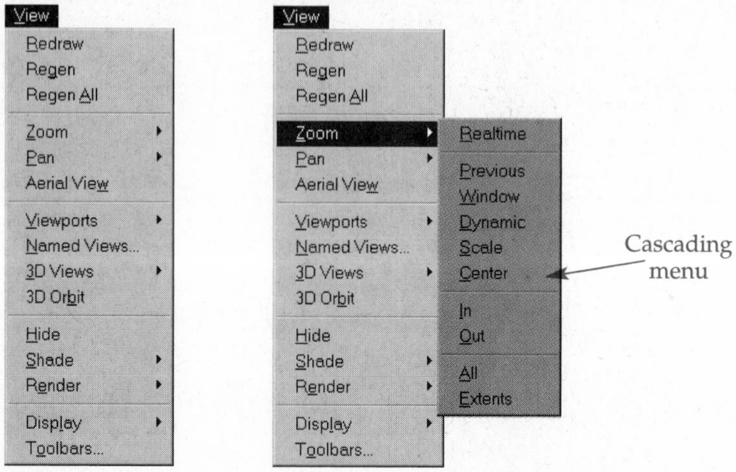

Figure 1-15.
Using the pull-down menus.
A—When you pick **View**, this pull-down menu is displayed.
B—A pull-down menu item followed by an arrow indicates a cascading menu. Selecting the item displays the cascading menu (shown here highlighted).

PROFESSIONAL TIP
You can also select a pull-down menu item by holding the pick button down while moving the pointer to the desired selection and releasing the pick button.

Accessing pull-down menus from the keyboard

As you move through the pull-down menus, note that one character of each pull-down menu title is underlined. This allows access to any pull-down menu selection using an [Alt]+[*key*] combination on the keyboard. For instance, the **File** menu can be accessed by pressing [Alt]+[F]. Pressing [Alt]+[D] accesses the **Draw** menu, and so on.

Once a pull-down menu is displayed, a menu item can be selected using a single character key. For example, suppose you want to zoom in closer to your work. Referring once again to Figure 1-15B, first press [Alt]+[V] to access the **View** menu. Then, press Z to select the **Zoom** command. Finally, press I to select the **In** option. These shortcut keystrokes for accessing pull-down menu items are called *menu accelerator keys*.

EXERCISE 1-3

❑ Continue from Exercise 1-2 or start AutoCAD as instructed in Exercise 1-2.
❑ Open each pull-down menu and read the options found in each menu without picking any options.
❑ Use each of the methods explained in the previous discussion to open pull-down menus.
❑ Keep AutoCAD open for the next exercise. If you must quit, pick **Exit** in the **File** pull-down menu and then pick **No** in the AutoCAD alert box.

Dialog Boxes

One of the most important aspects of AutoCAD is the graphical user interface (GUI) offered by the Microsoft Windows operating environment. A *graphical user interface* is how information, options, and choices are displayed for you by the software. The most common component of the GUI is the dialog box. A *dialog box* is a box that may contain a variety of information. You can set variables and select items in a dialog box using your cursor. This eliminates typing, saving time and increasing productivity.

A pull-down selection that is followed by an ellipsis (...) displays a dialog box when picked. An example of a simple dialog box is shown in Figure 1-16. This dialog box is displayed when you pick **Open...** from the **File** pull-down menu.

Buttons in a dialog box that are followed by an ellipsis (...) display another dialog box when they are picked. The second dialog box is displayed on top of the original dialog box, much like laying a sheet of paper on top of another. You must make a selection from the second dialog box before returning to the original dialog box.

There are standard parts to all dialog boxes. If you take a few minutes to review the following brief descriptions, you will find it much easier to work with the dialog boxes. Detailed discussions are provided in later chapters. You can become efficient in your use of dialog boxes by remembering two things—pick a button and enter text in a text box.

- **Command buttons.** When you pick a command button, something happens immediately. The most common buttons are **OK** and **Cancel**. Another common button is **Help**. See Figure 1-17. If a button has a dark border, it is the default. Pressing the [Enter] key accepts the default. If a button is "grayed-out" it cannot be selected. Buttons can also lead to other things. A button with an ellipsis (...) leads to another dialog box. A button with an arrow symbol (<) requires that you make a selection in the graphics window.

Figure 1-16.
A dialog box is displayed when you pick an item that is followed by an ellipsis. The dialog box shown here appears after you select **Open...** from the **File** pull-down menu.

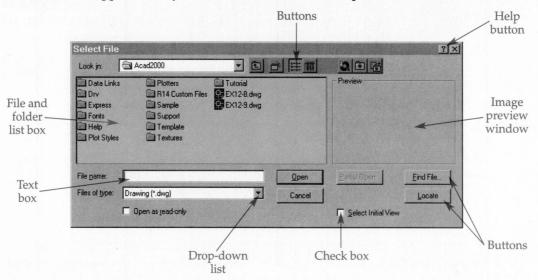

Buttons

Help button

File and folder list box

Image preview window

Text box

Drop-down list

Check box

Buttons

Figure 1-17.
When you select a button, something immediately happens. Three common buttons found in dialog boxes are the **OK**, **Cancel**, and **Help** buttons. Note the dark border around the **OK** button. This means that this is the default button.

- **Radio buttons.** When you press a selector button on your car radio, the station changes. Only one station can play at a time. Likewise, only one item in a group of radio buttons can be highlighted or active at one time. See Figure 1-18.
- **Check box.** A check box, or toggle, displays a "✓" when it is on (active). If the box is empty, the option is off. See Figure 1-18.
- **List box.** A list box contains a list of items or options. You can scan through the list using the scroll bar (if present) or the keyboard arrow keys. Either highlight the desired item with the arrow keys and press [Enter], or simply select it using your pointing device. See Figure 1-19.

Figure 1-18.
Only one radio button in a group can be highlighted at a time. A "✓" in a check box indicates that the item is active (on). Any number of check boxes can be active in a given group.

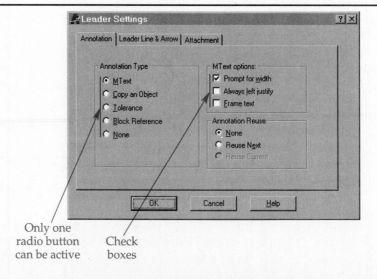

Only one radio button can be active

Check boxes

Figure 1-19.
A list box contains a list of items related to the dialog box. Here, the list shows the views
defined for the current drawing.

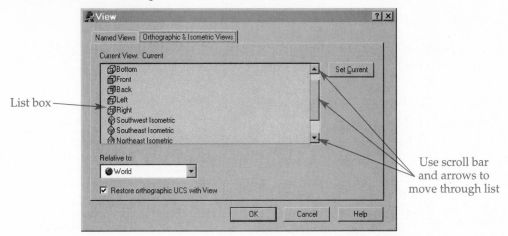

List box

Use scroll bar
and arrows to
move through list

- **Drop-down list box.** The drop-down list box is similar to the standard list box, except only one item is initially shown. The remaining items are hidden until you pick the drop-down arrow. When you pick the drop-down arrow, the drop-down list is displayed below the initial item. You can then pick from the expanded list, or use the scroll bar to find the item you need. See Figure 1-20.
- **Text box.** You can enter a name or single line of information using the text box. See Figure 1-21. When the currently selected text box is empty, the cursor appears as a flashing vertical bar positioned at the far left side of the box. If there is existing text in the box, that text appears highlighted. Any characters you then type will replace the highlighted text. Pressing either the [Backspace] key, space bar, or the [Delete] key deletes all the highlighted text. You can edit existing text using the cursor keys [Home], [End], right arrow, and left arrow. The [Home] key moves the cursor to the beginning of the line of text and the [End] key moves to the end of the line. The right arrow and left arrow keys move the cursor one character to the right or to the left, respectively. By using the [Ctrl] key in conjunction with the right arrow or left arrow key, you can move the cursor to the next word or the previous word, respectively.
- **File dialog.** The file dialog provides a simple means of locating and specifying file names using the familiar Windows style dialog. The example in Figure 1-22 shows a file dialog for selecting one or more drawing file names to open for editing. By *double-clicking* a folder name in the list, you can "open" it.

Figure 1-20.
A drop-down list
box is displayed
when you pick the
drop-down arrow.

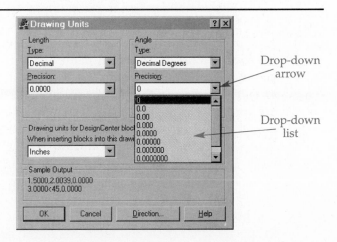

Drop-down
arrow

Drop-down
list

Figure 1-21.
You can enter a name, number, or single line of information in a text box. Several text boxes are shown here highlighted.

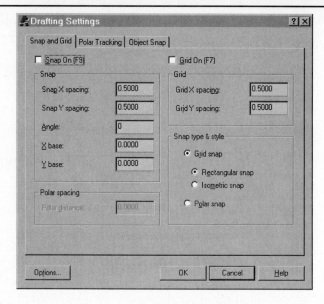

Figure 1-22.
The file dialog provides a simple means of locating files. The list box of this dialog box is highlighted.

For 2000i Users...

The **Select File** dialog box has been updated for AutoCAD 2000i. Refer to *Select File Dialog Box* on page 966 for details.

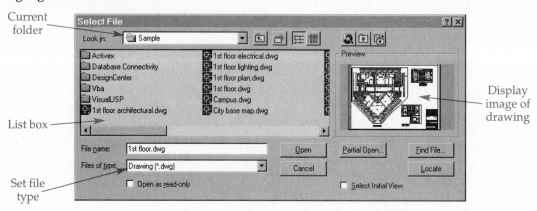

Current folder

List box

Set file type

Display image of drawing

Its contents are then displayed in the list box where items can be selected. The **Look in:** drop-down list displays the directory tree and allows you to browse for a storage device or a folder. The **Files of type:** drop-down list is used to specify the type of file being searched for. Once a file name is selected in the list box, it appears in the **File name:** text box, and its image appears in the **Preview** box. When selecting more than one file name, each file name appears in the **File name:** text box in quotation marks.

The four buttons above the upper-right corner of the list box allow you to back up one folder level, view your desktop, create a new folder, and display the files as a list of icons and names or with all file details. The three buttons above the preview box allow you to search the Web, display folders defined as favorites, or add the current folder to your list of favorites. The **Find File...** button allows you to search your computer or network for a specified file name, or simply browse through folders viewing the drawing previews. When a file name is known but the folder location is not, you can type the name in the **File name:** text box and pick the **Locate** button. AutoCAD then searches through its Support File Search Path as specified in the **Options** dialog box. If the path and the file name are already known, type it in the **File name:** text box and pick **Open** or press [Enter]. The **Partial open...** button allows you to specify what areas and elements of the drawing file information to load.

- **Scroll bars and buttons.** The scroll bar can be compared to an elevator sitting next to a list of items. The top arrow, or scroll button, points to the top floor, and the bottom arrow points to the basement. The box in the middle is the elevator. If you pick the elevator and hold down the pick button, you can move the box up or down. This displays additional items in the upper or lower floors of a list box. Pick the blank area above the elevator box to scroll up one page. Pick below the elevator box to scroll down one page. If you want to scroll up or down one file at a time, simply pick the up or down arrows. Horizontal scroll bars and buttons operate in the same manner. See Figure 1-23.
- **Preview box or image tile.** A preview box is an area of a dialog box that displays a "picture" of the item you select, such as a hatching style, linetype, or text font. See Figure 1-24. For many image tiles, picking anywhere on the image changes the associated setting and updates the image accordingly.
- **Tab.** A dialog box tab is much like an index tab used to separate sections of a notebook, or like the label tabs on the top of a manila file folder. Many dialog boxes in AutoCAD contain two or more "pages" or "panels", each with a tab at the top. Each tab displays a new set of related options. While the dialog box is displayed, you can pick any number of tabs in order to select options. The dialog box will only be dismissed when the **OK** button is picked. See Figure 1-25.
- **Alerts.** Alerts can be displayed in two forms. A note may appear in the lower-left corner of the original dialog box or a separate alert dialog box may appear. See Figure 1-26.
- **Help.** If you are unsure of any features of a dialog box, pick the question mark button in the upper-right corner of the dialog box. When the question mark appears next to your cursor, you can pick any feature in the dialog box to see a description of what it does. Figure 1-27 shows how this feature is used.
- **... (Ellipsis button).** Some dialog box features have an ellipsis button. The ellipsis button provides access to a related dialog box. See Figure 1-28.

Figure 1-23.
Use scroll bars and buttons to scroll through a listing or to view sections of a drawing.

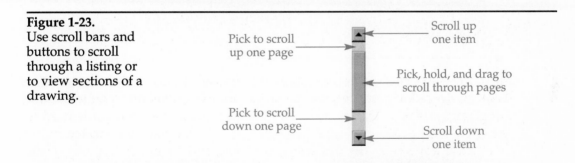

Figure 1-24.
An image tile displays the selected setting. Many image tiles, such as the ones shown here, can be picked to change the setting.

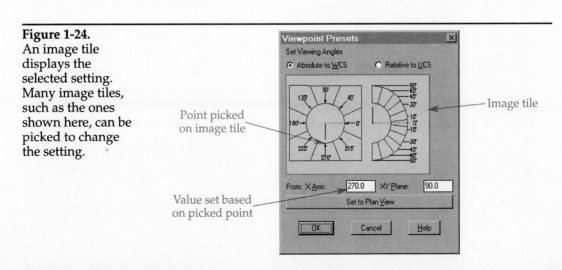

Figure 1-25.
A dialog box tab is much like an index tab used to separate sections of a notebook. Each tab displays a new set of related options.

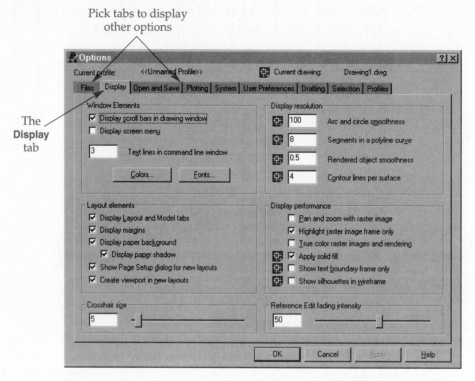

Figure 1-26.
An alert may appear as a separate dialog box.

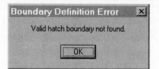

Figure 1-27.
Using the question mark button. A—Pick the question mark button and a question mark appears next to the cursor. B—Pick any feature in the dialog box and a brief description is displayed.

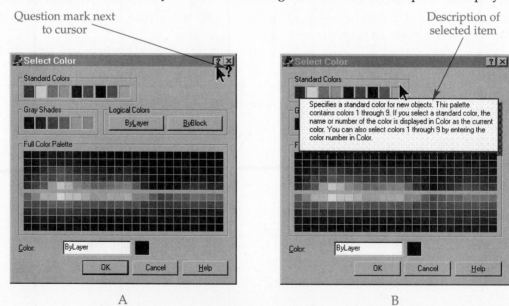

A

B

Figure 1-28.
The ... (ellipsis)
button displays a
dialog box providing
additional options
related to the dialog
feature it is next to.
The ellipsis button
shown here is picked
to display a dialog box
for defining and
modifying text styles.

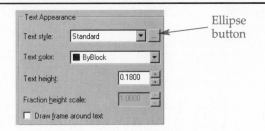

NOTE	Another method for displaying information about features in a dialog box is to point at the feature and right-click. If help information is available, the shortcut menu displays the **What's This?** option, which displays a description of the feature.

EXERCISE 1-4

❑ Continue from Exercise 1-3 or start AutoCAD as instructed in Exercise 1-2.
❑ Open a variety of dialog boxes to observe the features found in dialog boxes as identified in the previous discussion.
❑ You may make selections or change options in the dialog boxes, if you wish, but this is not required. This is just a chance for you to see what different dialog boxes contain.
❑ Keep AutoCAD open for the next exercise. If you must quit, pick **Exit** in the **File** pull-down menu and then pick **No** in the AutoCAD alert box.

Shortcut Menus

AutoCAD makes extensive use of shortcut menus to simplify and accelerate command entries. Sometimes referred to as *cursor menus* because they are displayed at the cursor location, these context sensitive menus are accessed by right-clicking. Because they are context sensitive, the shortcut menu content varies based on the location of the pointer when you right-click, and conditions such as whether a command is active or an object is selected.

When you right-click in the drawing area with no command active, the first item displayed on the shortcut menu is typically an option to repeat the previously used command or operation. See Figure 1-29A. If you right-click while a command is active, the shortcut menu contains options for the command. See Figure 1-29B.

NOTE	Shortcut menus are discussed where applicable throughout the text. To help familiarize yourself with this powerful AutoCAD feature, try clicking the right mouse button at different times while you are learning to use new AutoCAD commands or when practicing various dialog box operations. You can significantly increase your productivity in AutoCAD by learning to use these features effectively.

Figure 1-29.
The context sensitive shortcut menus in AutoCAD provide instant access to commands and options related to what you are doing at the time.
A—If a command is not currently active, the top menu pick repeats the previous command.
B—This menu displays options for the **ZOOM** command. This is accessed by right-clicking after the **ZOOM** command is activated.

A   B

AutoCAD Tablet Menu

A digitizer tablet can accept an overlay or menu that contains a large selection of AutoCAD's commands. Other specialized programs that operate with AutoCAD may have similar menus.

This text presents commands as if they are typed at the keyboard or selected from menus, dialog boxes, or toolbars. If you want to use a digitizer tablet to pick commands, the tablet must first be configured (arranged) before the menu can be used. See Appendix M for information on tablet configuration.

When you use a digitizer with AutoCAD, the cursor can only be moved within the active drawing area on-screen. Therefore, menu selections can only be made from the tablet menu overlay. Since all the AutoCAD commands do not fit on the tablet, you will still need to select toolbar buttons or make selections from the pull-down menus. In addition, using the tablet requires that you take your eyes off the screen and look down at the overlay. After picking a tablet command, look at the command line to be sure you picked what you desired.

The AutoCAD tablet menu is shown in Figure 1-30. If you plan on using a digitizer with a tablet menu, take some time and study its arrangement. Become familiar with the command groups and try to remember where each command is located. The quicker you learn the layout of the menu, the more efficient your drawing sessions will be.

Figure 1-30.
The AutoCAD tablet menu. (Autodesk, Inc.)

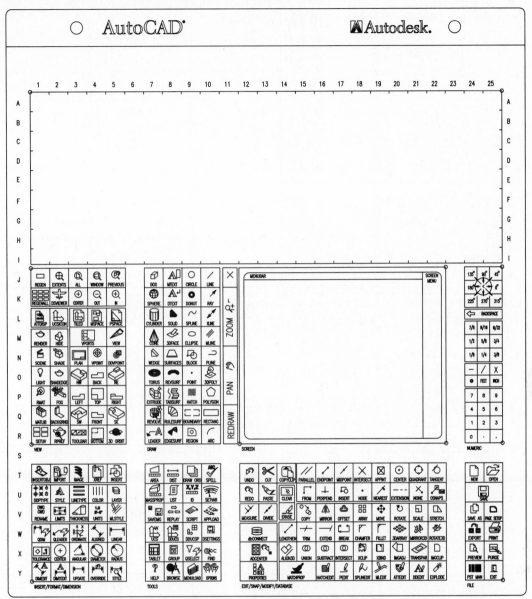

> **NOTE**
>
> Certain types of digitizer tablets can be configured to work both as a Windows system pointer (a mouse) and a digitizer. This type of configuration is called *absolute mode.* In order to operate in absolute mode, you must have a Wintab Compatible Digitizer. Windows NT requires both a Wintab System driver and an ADI Wintab driver to function. See the *AutoCAD Installation Guide* for more information.

Image Tile Menus

An image tile appears similar to a preview box, and displays an image of the object, pattern, or option that is available. AutoCAD uses several menus composed of images. See Figure 1–31. To choose the object you want to use, simply pick the image tile or text label in the list box. Image tile menus allow for easy selection, since you can see the shape or item represented by the image. To select an image, move your pointing device to it and pick.

Figure 1-31.
Image tile menus graphically display options or selections.

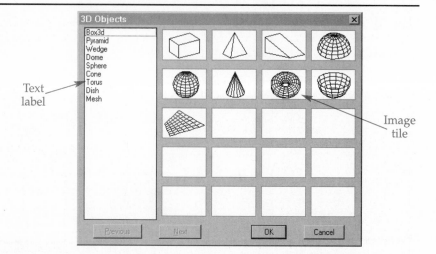

Text label

Image tile

Other AutoCAD Windows

Some AutoCAD features are presented in a special type of window that is sometimes referred to as a *modeless* dialog box. Features displayed in this manner include **AutoCAD DesignCenter**, the **Properties** window, and the **dbConnect Manager**. Unlike standard dialog boxes, these windows can be docked or resized, and they do not need to be dismissed in order to enter commands and work within the drawing.

AutoCAD DesignCenter

The **AutoCAD DesignCenter**, also known as **DesignCenter**, is a powerful drawing information manager that provides a simple tool for effectively reusing and sharing drawing content. One of the primary productivity benefits of using CAD is that once something has been created you can use it repeatedly in any number of drawings or drawing projects. Many types of drawing elements are similar or the same in numerous drawings, such as common drawing details, frequently used subassemblies or parts, and drawing layouts. **AutoCAD DesignCenter** lets you conveniently "drag and drop" drawing content to copy it from one drawing to another. *Drag and drop* is a feature that allows you to perform tasks by picking and holding the pick button while you drag the item to where you want it and release the pick button to drop it in the desired location.

When you first start **DesignCenter**, it is docked at the left side of the AutoCAD program window, Figure 1-32A. Figure 1-32B shows **DesignCenter** in a floating state. Double-click on the grab bar to use the floating state or double-click on the title bar to return to the docked position. The use of this powerful information management system is discussed throughout the text where it applies.

Figure 1-32.
AutoCAD DesignCenter. A—When you first start **DesignCenter**, it is docked at the left side of the AutoCAD program window. The grab bar along the top can be used to "float" **DesignCenter**. B—**DesignCenter** in a floating state.

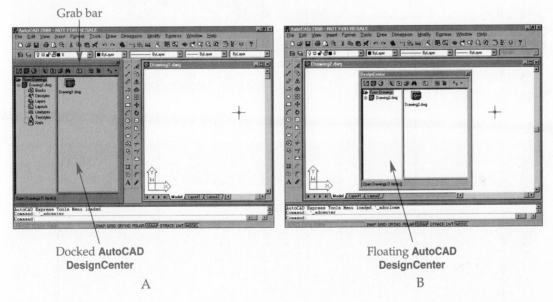

Grab bar

Docked **AutoCAD DesignCenter**

A

Floating **AutoCAD DesignCenter**

B

Properties window and dbConnect Manager

The **Properties** window lets you manage the properties of new and existing objects in a drawing, and the **dbConnect Manager** provides an easy way to access external database information.

These special windows can only be docked on the left or right side of the AutoCAD program window. Figure 1-33A shows both **DesignCenter** and the **Properties** window docked side-by-side. They can also be docked in a vertical arrangement, as shown in Figure 1-33B. When docked horizontally or vertically, a resizing bar allows you to adjust the size of each window to suit your needs. The actual use of the **Properties** window is explained where it applies throughout this text, and the **dbConnect Manager** is explained in *AutoCAD and its Applications—Advanced*.

Figure 1-33.
A—**DesignCenter** and the **Properties** window are docked side-by-side.
B—They can also be docked in a vertical arrangement.

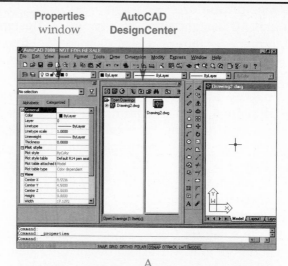

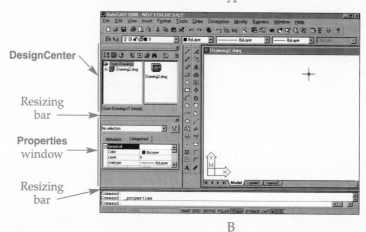

A

B

SELECTING AUTOCAD COMMANDS

AutoCAD commands may be selected in these four different ways:
- Executed by picking a toolbar button or icon.
- Selected from one of the pull-down or shortcut menus (or screen menus, if so configured).
- Selected from the digitizer tablet menu overlay.
- Typed at the keyboard.

The advantage of using toolbar buttons and on-screen menus is that you do not need to remove your eyes from the screen. Typing commands may not require that you turn your eyes from the screen. You can also learn commands quickly by typing them. However, when using a digitizer tablet, you must look down to pick tablet menu commands. On the other hand, a tablet menu overlay can show almost every command. Also, when configured as both a windows pointer and a digitizer (absolute mode), a tablet is a powerful and efficient input device.

NOTE

The examples shown in this text illustrate each of the AutoCAD commands as they appear when typed at the Command: prompt and when picked from toolbars and pull-down menus.

Using the Command Line

Commands and options can be entered directly into the floating command window. AutoCAD commands can only be typed when the floating command window displays the Command: prompt. When a command is started, whether from a menu selection or by typing, AutoCAD either performs the specified operation or prompts you for any additional information. AutoCAD commands have a standard format structured as follows:

Command: **COMMANDNAME**↵
Current settings: Setting1 Setting2 Setting3
Instructional text [Option1/oPtion2/opTion3/...] <default option or value>:

If the command has associated settings, these are displayed as shown. The instructional text indicates what you should do at this point, and all available options are shown within the square brackets. Each option has a unique combination of uppercase characters that can be typed rather than typing the entire option name. If a default option is displayed in the angle brackets, you can press the [Enter] key to accept it.

AutoCAD provides you with the ability to select previously used commands by using the up and down arrow keys. For example, if you wanted to use the **CIRCLE** command that was used a few steps prior to your present position, press the up arrow key on the keyboard until the command you need is displayed on the Command: line, then press [Enter] to activate it. This capability can be used to execute a typed command that is misspelled. For example, suppose you type LINE\ and press [Enter]. The following message appears:

Unknown command "LINE\". Press F1 for help.

Just press the up arrow key, then press [Backspace] to delete the backslash (\) and press [Enter] to execute the **LINE** command. This is a time-saving feature if you like to type commands at the Command: prompt.

The shortcut menu displayed when you right-click in the floating command window offers a cascading menu that shows a list of commands you have used recently. See Figure 1-34. This list shows up to six recently used command names. Pick a command name from the list to use that command again.

Figure 1-34.
The shortcut menu displayed when you right-click in the floating command window offers a cascading menu listing commands you have used recently.

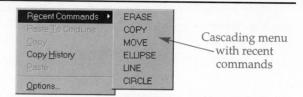

Cascading menu with recent commands

EXERCISE 1-9

❏ Continue from Exercise 1-8 or start AutoCAD as instructed in Exercise 1-2.
❏ Type the following command and follow the instructions:

> Command: **LINE**↵
> Specify first point: *(pick a point in the graphics window)*
> Specify next point or [Undo]: *(pick another point away from the first point)*
> Specify next point or [Undo]: ↵
> Command:

❏ Use the up and down arrows in the command window to access previously issued commands and then return to the current Command: prompt.
❏ Right-click in the command window to see the shortcut menu.
❏ Keep AutoCAD open for the next exercise. If you must quit, pick **Exit** in the **File** pull-down menu and then pick **No** in the AutoCAD alert box.

GETTING HELP

If you need help with a specific command, option, or program feature, AutoCAD provides a powerful and convenient online help system. There are several ways to access this feature. The fastest method is to press the [F1] function key. This displays the **Help Topics** dialog box. The first time you use the help system, the **Contents** tab lists the names of the available online reference guides for the AutoCAD help system, Figure 1-35. You can also display the **Help Topics** dialog box by selecting the question mark icon at the right end of the **Standard** toolbar, by picking **AutoCAD Help** from the **Help** pull-down menu, or by typing ? or HELP at the Command: prompt.

For 2000i Users...

The help system has been modified for AutoCAD 2000i. Refer to *Getting Help in AutoCAD 2000i* on page 957 for a complete discussion.

Figure 1-35. The **Help Topics** dialog box is displayed when you select **AutoCAD Help** from the **Help** pull-down menu or press the [F1] function key.

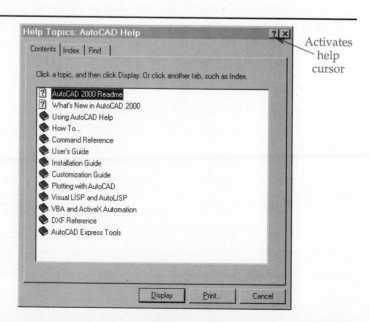

Activates help cursor

It is not necessary that AutoCAD be running in order to get help. The online help facility is available directly from the Windows desktop. Pick the Start button, pick Programs, pick AutoCAD 2000, and finally select AutoCAD 2000 Online Help. This also displays the **Help Topics** dialog box.

PROFESSIONAL TIP If you are unfamiliar with how to use a Windows help system, it is suggested that you spend time now exploring all the topics under Using AutoCAD Help in the **Contents** tab of the **Help Topics** dialog box.

Exploring the Contents of Help

The **Contents** tab displays a list of book icons and topic names. The book icons represent the organizational structure of books, chapters, and groupings of topics within the AutoCAD documentation. See Figure 1-36A. Topics contain the actual help information; the icon used to represent a topic is a sheet of paper with a question mark. The first book, Using AutoCAD Help, provides you with detailed information on using the Windows help system. To open a book or a help topic, double-click on its name or icon. Figure 1-36B shows the list of items displayed when the Using AutoCAD Help book is opened. Double-click on the Navigation Tips topic to display a window with a discussion of this topic. See Figure 1-37. Step-by-step instructions are provided in this window, as well as useful tips. These four buttons are located near the top of this window:

- **Help Topics.** Returns to the **Help Topics** dialog box.
- **Back.** Flips back to the previous help page. If no pages were previously displayed, this button is grayed-out.

Figure 1-36.
Using help. A—Double-click the book icon to open it and reveal the topics. B—Double-clicking the Using AutoCAD Help item presents another list of help topics

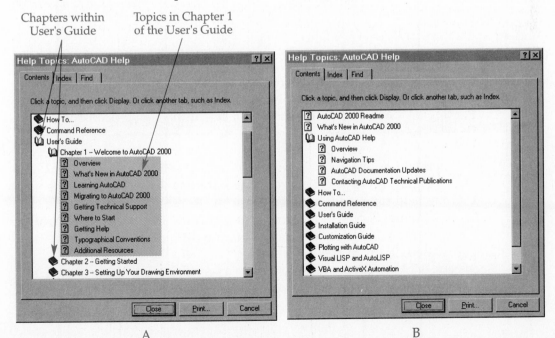

Figure 1-37.
Opening a topic
displays a help
window.

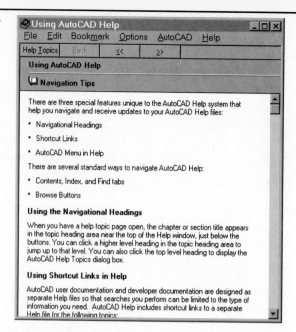

- **≪ and ≫.** These two buttons step forward and backward through the help documents sequentially, like turning to the next or previous page in a book.

The pull-down menus in the **Help Topics** dialog box provide several useful options, including:

- **File > Print topic.** Displays the **Print** dialog box, allowing you to send the contents of the current help dialog box to a printer.
- **Edit > Copy.** Copies the entire content of the current help dialog box to the Windows Clipboard. If you wish to copy only specific text, select it first and then use **Copy**.

NOTE

Remember, the key combinations [Ctrl]+[C] and [Ctrl]+[V] can be used to quickly execute the **Copy** and **Paste** commands, respectively.

PROFESSIONAL TIP

All the text inside the current help dialog box can be copied to the Clipboard by pressing the [Ctrl]+[Insert] keys. Use the paste function to insert this text into a new document.

- **Edit > Annotate.** Allows you to write a note that relates to the current help topic. See Figure 1-38. Picking **Save** in the **Annotate** dialog box attaches your note to the help topic with a paper clip icon. To read your annotation, click once on the paper clip. This note can also be copied to another document, or text from another document can be pasted into this note. When the note is no longer needed, it can be deleted.
- **Bookmark.** Bookmarks take you instantly to a specific page in the help system. A list of currently defined bookmarks appears on this menu, along with the **Define...** option, which lets you assign a named bookmark to the current help page.

Figure 1-38.
Using the **Annotate** option. A—You can write a note in the **Annotate** dialog box. B—The
paper clip icon appears when there is a note associated with a topic.

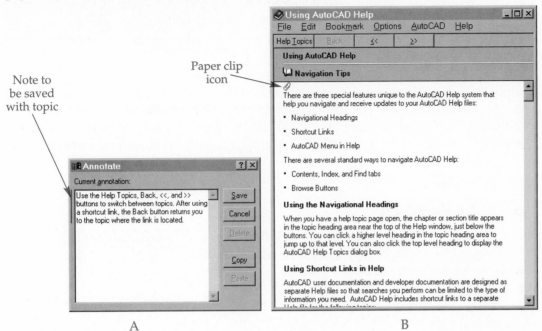

Note to
be saved
with topic

Paper clip
icon

A   B

CAUTION

In many AutoCAD help windows a **Bookmark** menu item is
displayed. Setting a bookmark in Windows was intended to
be a convenient tool for quickly recalling specific help topics.
However, this feature does not work as intended in
AutoCAD and other software that contains several documentation manuals. The AutoCAD help is composed of
eleven manuals, so there are eleven separate help files. When
a bookmark is set in one of the manuals, it will not be listed
when help from another manual is displayed. In other
words, in the current release of AutoCAD, bookmarks are not
added to a single list to reference all manuals quickly. Using
the **Index** and **Find** tabs (discussed later in this chapter) are
the best methods of locating topics.

- **Options > Keep Help on Top.** Displays a cascading menu with options that
  control how the help window is displayed in relationship to other windows.
  On Top indicates that the help window is always displayed in front of all other
  windows. Some help windows are always on top by default. The **Default**
  option means that the windows are displayed using the standard help system
  settings. The **Not on Top** setting means that help windows normally kept on
  top now remain in the selected order of open windows on the desktop.
- **Options > Display History Window.** Displays a small window listing previously
  viewed help pages. Pick the name of the previously viewed page to immediately return to that page.
- **Options > Font.** Allows you to select between small, normal, and large fonts
  for the display of the **Help Topics** dialog box text.
- **Options > Use System Colors.** Returns the help windows to the default
  Windows system colors.

PROFESSIONAL TIP

While a help window is displayed, pressing the right mouse button displays a shortcut menu that contains many of the items found in the pull-down menus.

The How To... book listed in the **Contents** tab shown in Figure 1-35 provides a variety of topics to assist you in understanding and using AutoCAD drawing concepts and techniques. The rest of the topics in the **Contents** tab provide an online version of the printed *AutoCAD 2000 Documentation Pack*, of which only the *Installation Guide* and the *User's Guide* are shipped with the software. Printed copies of the *Command Reference, Customization Guide*, and other available references must be ordered through your Authorized Autodesk Dealer or Reseller.

Using the **Index** Tab

Although the **Contents** tab of the **Help Topics** dialog box is useful for displaying all the topics in an expanded table of contents manner, it is not very useful when searching for a specific item. In this case, most people refer to the index. This is the function of the **Index** tab. See Figure 1-39.

The index can be used in two ways. The first is to scroll through the alphabetical list of items in the list box. This takes time because the list is lengthy. The second way is to follow the instructions above the text box: Type the first few letters of the word you're looking for. As you type each new character, the lower list changes to match your entry as close as possible. Test this by slowly typing the letters lin and notice the entry that appears highlighted at the top of the list. See Figure 1-40. If you were searching for information on drawing lines, you could now double-click on the specific item in the list.

Some items refer to several topics. In this case, the **Topics Found** dialog box is displayed. See Figure 1-41. Click on the topic you wish to see and pick the **Display** button. When you display the topic, a help screen is presented that may include text, hyperlinks, and graphics.

AutoCAD help screens that display information about a command also include a section at the bottom titled SEE ALSO. This section provides hyperlinks to related

Figure 1-39.
The **Index** tab displays an index listing.

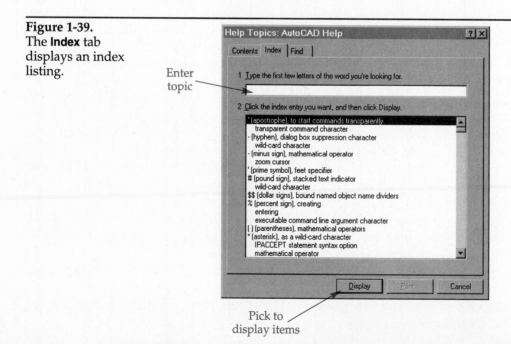

Figure 1-40.
The **Index** tab with lin entered in the text box. AutoCAD begins to give you help topics related to the text you are typing.

Entered text

AutoCAD selects topic that most nearly matches entry

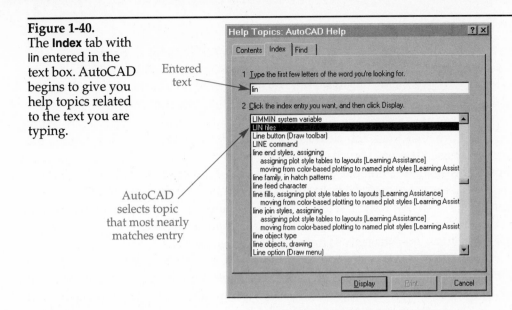

Figure 1-41.
The **Topics Found** dialog box.

Select topic

Pick to display topic

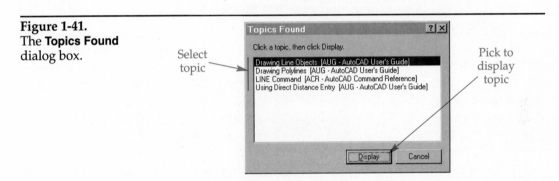

help topics. A *hyperlink* is green underlined text. If a hyperlink is selected, it automatically displays the help screen it is linked to. When the cursor is on hyperlink, it becomes a hand as shown in Figure 1-42. Picking with the hand displays specific help related to the hyperlink.

Figure 1-42.
The hand cursor appears as the cursor passes over a hyperlink.

Hand cursor identifies hyperlink

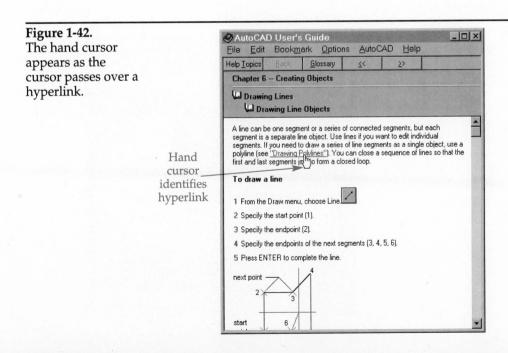

Using the Find Tab

The **Find** tab lets you conduct a detailed search based on one or more words. This should be your third choice for help after using the **Contents** and **Index** tabs. It is a more detailed search process because **Find** bases its search on words and word combinations. Therefore, it must first create its own word list, much like a super index.

The first time you select the **Find** tab, you are presented with the **Find Setup Wizard**. See Figure 1-43. Pick the **Next** button to accept the defaults. This creates the minimum database size.

When the word list is created, the display in the **Find** tab changes to that shown in Figure 1-44. This is a powerful help tool. Use **Find** in the following manner:

1. Begin your search by typing the topic you are looking for. Unlike the **Index** help, you can type more than one word. For example, suppose you want to know how to erase lines. Just type erasing lines and watch the displays change. See Figure 1-45.
2. Select any of the additional modifying words in the list box at the center of the dialog box. All the items in this box are highlighted and are deselected when you pick one. Hold the [Shift] key down if you want to add words to the selected list.
3. Look in the bottom list box for the final list of contestants. Select the one that appears most appropriate, and pick the **Display** button or press [Enter] to read about the topic.

Figure 1-43.
The **Find Setup Wizard** creates a database to be used to find help.

Figure 1-44.
The **Find** tab allows you to conduct a detailed search.

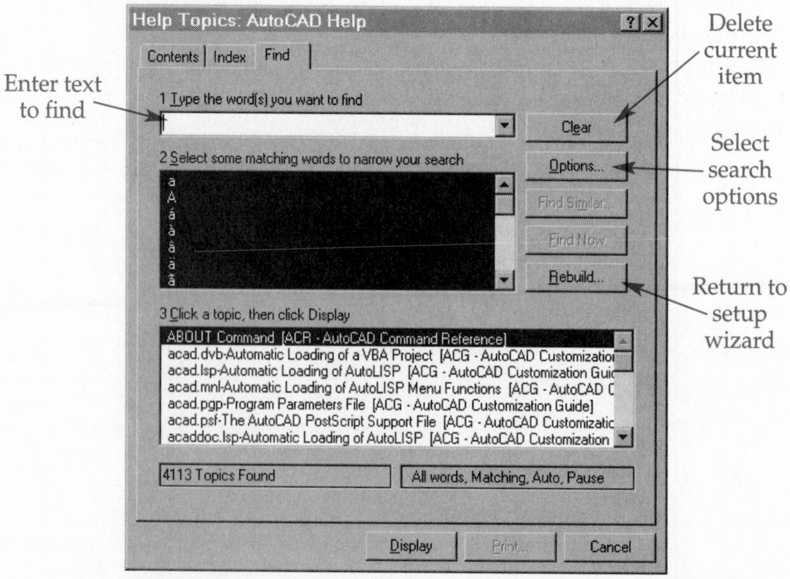

Figure 1-45.
Enter the topic you
wish to search for in
the text box.

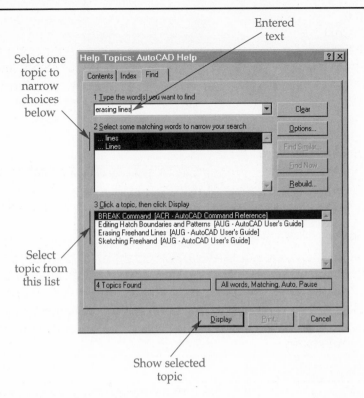

NOTE Creating a minimized version of the word list does not lessen your ability to search for words in the AutoCAD documentation. It just keeps the size of the word list file small until further additions are needed. If a **Find** search does not locate the specific topic you need, pick on the **Rebuild** button in the **Find** tab and the word list will be rebuilt.

Find is set for optimal searching, and like **Index**, immediately displays characters and words as you type them. The words also do not have to be typed in a logical order. You could have entered lines erasing in the previous example and the topics displayed would have been the same.

The **Find** utility, by default, searches through all the AutoCAD documentation. As a result, a wide variety of items may be displayed as a result of the search. You can limit the search to just the documents you need by picking the **Options...** button in the **Find** tab. This displays the **Find Options** dialog box. Pick the **Files...** button and the **File Options** dialog box lists all the files to be searched. Deselect any of the references that do not need to be included in the search. Pick **OK** in both dialog boxes when done.

Using the Glossary

The glossary is a list of AutoCAD terms. It can be accessed from any main help screen by picking the **Glossary** button. All the items in the glossary are displayed on one long page. Glossary topics can be accessed by scrolling through the list, or by picking one of the alphabet buttons above the list. Glossary definitions can be useful for obtaining a quick definition of an unfamiliar term. See Figure 1-46.

Figure 1-46.
The AutoCAD
glossary window.

Pick a
letter to
view terms
that begin
with that
letter

Use scroll
bar to
navigate
through
terms

Hyperlink

PROFESSIONAL TIP

AutoCAD's help function can also be used while you are in the process of using a command. For example, suppose you are using the **ARC** command and forget what type of information is required by AutoCAD for the specific prompts that are on screen. Get help by pressing the [F1] function key and the help information for the currently active command is displayed. This *context oriented help* saves valuable time, since you do not need to scan through the help contents or perform any searches to find the information.

EXERCISE 1-10

❏ Continue from Exercise 1-9 or start AutoCAD as instructed in Exercise 1-2.
❏ Access each of the **Help Topics** dialog box tabs and search out help topics of your choice to see how each option works.
❏ Pick the **Glossary** button in one of the help screens to see the AutoCAD glossary.
❏ Keep AutoCAD open for the next exercise. If you must quit, pick **Exit** in the **File** pull-down menu and then pick **No** in the AutoCAD alert box.

Finding out What's New

If you are familiar with the previous release of AutoCAD and are curious about the changes that were made for AutoCAD 2000, pick **What's New...** from the **Help** pull-down menu. This displays a listing of five different categories. Picking one of the categories displays a page of feature listings with brief descriptions and links to related help file pages. See Appendix A for a discussion of the new features in AutoCAD 2000.

AutoCAD Learning Assistance

AutoCAD provides a powerful learning tool called AutoCAD Learning Assistance™. This is accessed by selecting **Learning Assistance** in the **Help** pull-down menu. Learning Assistance is an interactive, multimedia facility composed of three parts: **Tutorials**, **Concepts**, and **Fast Track to AutoCAD 2000**. Each section contains a wide variety of presentations complete with text, graphics, sound, and animations. They are highly informative, and will satisfy the needs of persons with different learning styles.

The first time **Learning Assistance** is selected, it is installed on your hard drive. You can use the default folder name or create one yourself. Once **Learning Assistance** is installed on the hard drive, pick Programs in the Start menu, then pick AutoCAD Learning Assistance. It is suggested that you pick the **Autodesk Learning Assistance** selection at the top of the **Contents** tab, then pick the **How to Use** link and take a few minutes to familiarize yourself with how this learning tool functions.

NOTE   The *Learning Assistance CD* must be in the CD-ROM drive of your computer for you to view the video segments or listen to the audio clips within Learning Assistance. Text-only content can be viewed even if the CD is not present. AutoCAD does not need to be loaded for Learning Assistance to work.

After viewing and using these tools you can immediately apply them to your work. As you work through this text you can increase your AutoCAD skills by using **Learning Assistance**.

Using the AutoCAD Support Assistance

AutoCAD Support Assistance is a comprehensive support tool provided with AutoCAD 2000. It is accessed by picking **Support Assistance** in the **Help** pull-down menu. This powerful support tool features a knowledge base of information designed to help you find fast answers to questions, solutions for problems, and guidance for finding additional support and technical assistance.

USING THE EXPRESS TOOLS

For 2000i Users...

Express Tools are not provided with AutoCAD 2000i but can be downloaded from the Autodesk Point A Web site. The Express Tools discussed in this text are those provided with AutoCAD 2000.

This release of AutoCAD includes a set of features called Express Tools. These tools are not included in a typical installation but are included in a full installation of AutoCAD.

If the Express Tools are installed, an **Express** pull-down menu is included in the menu bar. Most of the Express Tools are AutoLISP routines or ObjectARX applications designed to improve productivity. The tools allow you to use a single command in a situation where several commands are normally needed.

AutoLISP is a programming language that is used to customize AutoCAD. An introduction to AutoLISP is covered in *AutoCAD and its Applications—Advanced*. Refer to *AutoLISP Programming*, available from Goodheart-Willcox, for complete coverage of AutoLISP programming. *ObjectARX* is internal applications, such as the **Multiline Text Editor**, and third-party applications. ARX applications are covered where they are used. *Third-party applications* are applications that are developed to work with AutoCAD.

Individual tools are referenced in appropriate locations throughout this text. For a full discussion of all the Express Tools, refer to Appendix A.

KEYS AND BUTTONS

AutoCAD provides several ways of performing a given task. A variety of keys on the keyboard allow you to quickly perform many functions. In addition, multibutton pointing devices also use buttons for AutoCAD commands. Become familiar with the meaning of these keys and buttons to help improve your performance with AutoCAD.

The [Esc] Key

Any time it is necessary to cancel a command and return to the Command: prompt, press the *escape key* [Esc] on your keyboard. This key is found on the upper-left corner of most keyboards and is typically labeled Esc. Some command sequences may require the [Esc] key to be pressed twice to completely cancel the operation.

Control Keys

Most computer programs use *control key* functions to perform common tasks. Control key functions are used by pressing and holding the [Ctrl] key while pressing a second key. These are also called *accelerator keys*.

Keep the following list close at hand and try them occasionally. If a command or key is noted as a "toggle," it is either on or off—nothing else.

Key Combination	Result
[Ctrl]+[A]	Group Selection mode (toggle)
[Ctrl]+[B]	Snap mode (toggle)
[Ctrl]+[C]	**COPYCLIP** command
[Ctrl]+[D]	Coordinate display on status line (toggle)
[Ctrl]+[E]	Crosshairs in isoplane positions left/top/right (toggle)
[Ctrl]+[F]	Osnap mode (toggle)
[Ctrl]+[G]	Grid mode (toggle)
[Ctrl]+[H]	Same as [Backspace]
[Ctrl]+[J]	Same as [Enter]
[Ctrl]+[K]	**HYPERLINK** command
[Ctrl]+[L]	Ortho mode (toggle)
[Ctrl]+[M]	Same as [Enter]
[Ctrl]+[N]	**NEW** command
[Ctrl]+[O]	**OPEN** command
[Ctrl]+[P]	**PLOT** (Print) command
[Ctrl]+[R]	Toggle viewport
[Ctrl]+[S]	**SAVE** command
[Ctrl]+[T]	Tablet mode (toggle)
[Ctrl]+[U]	Polar mode (toggle)
[Ctrl]+[V]	**PASTECLIP** command
[Ctrl]+[W]	Object Snap Tracking (toggle)
[Ctrl]+[X]	**CUTCLIP** command
[Ctrl]+[Y]	**REDO** command
[Ctrl]+[Z]	**UNDO** command
[Ctrl]+[1]	**Properties** window (toggle)
[Ctrl]+[2]	**AutoCAD DesignCenter** (toggle)
[Ctrl]+[6]	**dbConnect Manager** (toggle)

"Alt" Keys

Keystrokes using an [Alt]+[*key*] combination are typically reserved for Windows purposes such as menu access through the keyboard and shortcut keys that run a specified program. These are the two [Alt]+[*key*] combinations assigned to AutoCAD commands:

Key Combination	Result
[Alt]+[F8]	**VBARUN** command
[Alt]+[F11]	**VBAIDE** command

PROFESSIONAL TIP

Computer users who are experienced in working with MS-DOS or those who have used previous versions of AutoCAD may be familiar with using the [Ctrl]+[C] key combination as a **Cancel** command. In AutoCAD 2000, the [Ctrl]+[C] key combination activates the **COPYCLIP** command. If you want to use the [Ctrl]+[C] key combination so that it activates the **Cancel** command, pick **Options...** in the **Tools** pull-down menu, and then pick the **User Preferences** tab. In the **Windows Standard Behavior** area, remove the checkmark from **Windows standard accelerator keys**, then pick **OK**. You can now use [Ctrl]+[C] to cancel. See *AutoCAD and its Applications—Advanced* for information on customizing preferences.

Function Keys

Function keys provide instant access to commands. They can also be programmed to perform a series of commands. The function keys are located along the top of the keyboard. Depending on the brand of keyboard, there will be either 10 or 12 function keys. These are numbered from [F1] to [F10] (or [F12]). AutoCAD uses eleven function keys. These are listed below. As you become proficient with AutoCAD, you might program the function keys to do specific tasks using other computer programs.

Function Key	Result
[F1]	**HELP** command
[F2]	Flip screen from graphics to text (toggle).
[F3]	Object Snap mode (toggle)
[F4]	Tablet mode (toggle)
[F5]	Isoplane mode (toggle)
[F6]	Coordinate display (toggle)
[F7]	Grid mode (toggle)
[F8]	Ortho mode (toggle)
[F9]	Snap mode (toggle)
[F10]	Polar mode (toggle)
[F11]	Object Snap Tracking (toggle)

Button Functions

If you are using a multibutton pointing device, you can select control key functions by pressing a single button. The default settings of the pointing device buttons are as follows:

Button	Result
0	Pick
1	Return
2	**Object Snap** shortcut menu
3	Cancel
4	Snap mode (toggle)
5	Ortho mode (toggle)
6	Grid mode (toggle)
7	Coordinate display (toggle)
8	Crosshairs isoplane positions top/left/right (toggle)
9	Tablet mode (toggle)

EXERCISE 1-13

❏ Continue from Exercise 1-12 or start AutoCAD as instructed in Exercise 1-2.
❏ Use some of the control keys, alt keys, and function keys to become comfortable with how they work.
❏ If you are using a digitizer tablet and puck, use the button functions to see how they work.
❏ Exit AutoCAD by picking **Exit** in the **File** pull-done menu. Pick the **No** button in the AutoCAD alert box.

Understanding Terminology

The following terms are used throughout the text and will help you select AutoCAD functions. You should become familiar with them:

- **Default.** A value that is maintained by the computer until you change it.
- **Pick or click.** Use the pointing device to select an item on the screen or tablet.
- **Button**. One of the screen toolbar or pointing device (puck) buttons.
- **Key.** A key on the keyboard.
- **Function key.** One of the keys labeled [F1]–[F12] (or [F1]–[F10]) along the top or side of the keyboard.
- **[Enter] (↵).** The [Enter] or [Return] key on the keyboard.
- **Command.** An instruction issued to the computer.
- **Option.** An aspect of a command that can be selected.

AVOIDING "DISK FULL" PROBLEMS

When you save a drawing, AutoCAD allows you to specify a name and a location for the drawing file. The drawing will be saved in the AutoCAD program folder Acad2000 unless you specify a new one. You can also select the disk drive in which to save the drawing. The hard disk that contains the AutoCAD program folder is the default. New users to AutoCAD often want to save their drawings on a 3.5" disk instead of on the hard drive.

Saving a drawing to the 3.5" disk during a working session is not the most efficient way to operate AutoCAD. These drives are slow to store and access data. In addition, limited space on the 3.5" disk can soon lead to a Not enough space on disk error. If you save your drawing directly to these disks, AutoCAD also places a backup drawing file with the same name in the same location as the original file. Each time you save the original drawing, the backup file is updated. Therefore, you actually have two drawing files instead of one. For additional information see Chapter 14.

Always save your work to the hard disk on a regular basis—*every 10 to 15 minutes*. If you must save a drawing to a 3.5" disk, make it the last thing you do before you exit AutoCAD. You can also use the Windows Explorer at any time to quickly see if drawings will fit on your disk, and then copy them to the disk. Refer to Chapter 15 for a discussion of using the Windows Explorer. Chapters 2 and 3 discuss the techniques of starting and saving drawings properly.

PROFESSIONAL TIP

To ensure that your work is being saved on a regular basis, use the **SAVETIME** variable. Just enter **SAVETIME** at the Command: prompt, then enter the number of minutes between each automatic save. By default, your automatically saved drawing file is saved with the same name as the drawing, with a numeric suffix generated by AutoCAD and a file extension of auto.sv$. If for any reason the drawing file is damaged, this file can be renamed to a drawing file (.dwg) and loaded into AutoCAD.

NOTE

Most 3.5" disks are sold preformatted. But if you purchase unformatted disks, they must be formatted before they can be used by the computer. This process divides the disk into pie-shaped sectors, checks it for defects, and creates a file directory on the disk. This process is also useful for deleting all data from used disks. See Chapter 14 for a complete discussion on this process.

Chapter Test

Answer the following questions on a separate sheet of paper.

1. What system is used to construct drawings and models in AutoCAD?
2. Basic pictorial drawings are called _____.
3. How would you write the proper notation of the following values using the system referred to in Question 1: Z=4, X=2, Y=5?
4. What is *drawing planning*?
5. Why is drawing planning important?
6. What is the first thing you should do as part of your planning checklist?
7. Why should you save your work every 10 to 15 minutes?
8. What are standards?
9. What scale should you use to draw in AutoCAD?
10. Why should you read the command line at the bottom of the screen?
11. How is AutoCAD represented on the Windows desktop?
12. What is the quickest method for starting AutoCAD?
13. What is a hyperlink?
14. List four of the areas that compose the AutoCAD graphics window.
15. Which area displays the communication between you and AutoCAD?
16. What is the difference between a docked toolbar and a floating toolbar?
17. What are menu accelerator keys? How are they used? Give an example.
18. What is an option?
19. List the AutoCAD pull-down menus.
20. What is a flyout menu?
21. What is the function of tabs in a dialog box?
22. What must you do to the tablet before it can be used?
23. What are the functions of the following control keys?
    A. [Ctrl]+[B]
    B. [Ctrl]+[C]
    C. [Ctrl]+[D]
    D. [Ctrl]+[G]
    E. [Ctrl]+[O]
    F. [Ctrl]+[S]
24. Name the function keys that execute the same task as the following control keys.
    A. [Ctrl]+[B]
    B. [Ctrl]+[D]
    C. [Ctrl]+[G]
    D. [Ctrl]+[L]
    E. [Ctrl]+[T]
25. What is the difference between a *button* and a *key*?
26. What do you call a value that is maintained by the computer until you change it?
27. What type of pull-down menu item has an arrow to the right?
28. What type of menu contains a group of symbols or patterns?

29. What is an image tile?
30. What is *context oriented help* and how is it accessed?
31. How do you open a folder in a file dialog box in order to see its contents?
32. What is the area in a dialog box that displays a "picture" of the item you select?
33. What is the function of the ... (ellipsis) button?
34. How do you access a shortcut menu?
35. What is the purpose of a shortcut menu?
36. Why are shortcut menus considered context sensitive?
37. Name a powerful drawing information manager that provides a simple tool for efficiently reusing and sharing drawing content.
38. Name the window that lets you manage the properties of new and existing objects in a drawing.
39. How do you access previously used commands?
40. Identify the quickest way to access the **Help Topics** dialog box.
41. What happens to the cursor when you pick the question mark in the upper-right corner of a dialog box?
42. What is the purpose of the cursor mentioned in Question 41?
43. Describe the purpose of the book icons in the **Contents** tab of the **Help Topics** dialog box.
44. How do you use the **Index** tab of the **Help Topics** dialog box to find information on a topic?
45. Identify the tab in the **Help Topics** dialog box that allows you to do a detailed search based on one or more words.
46. How do you access help regarding a currently active command?
47. Name the pull-down menu and its option that gives you information about what is new in AutoCAD 2000.
48. How do you access the interactive, multimedia learning tool in AutoCAD?
49. What is AutoCAD Support Assistance?
50. What is the purpose of the Express Tools and when are they available?

Problems

1. Interview your drafting instructor or supervisor and try to determine what type of drawing standards exist at your school or company. Write this down and keep it with you as you learn AutoCAD. Make notes as you progress through this text on how you use these standards. Also note how the standards could be changed to match the capabilities of AutoCAD.

2. Research your drafting department standards. If you do not have a copy of the standards, acquire one. If AutoCAD standards have been created, make notes as to how you can use these in your projects. If no standards exist in your department or company, make notes as to how you can help develop standards. Write a report on why your school or company should create CAD standards and how they would be used. Discuss who should be responsible for specific tasks. Recommend procedures, techniques, and forms, if necessary. Develop this report as you progress through your AutoCAD instruction, and as you read through this book.

3. Develop a drawing planning sheet for use in your school or company. List items that you think are important for planning a CAD drawing. Make changes to this sheet as you learn more about AutoCAD.

4. Load AutoCAD from the Windows desktop using one of the three methods discussed in the chapter. Perform the following tasks:
   A. Pick the **OK** button at the **Startup** dialog box.
   B. Pick the minimize button at the upper-right of the AutoCAD graphics window.
   C. Pick the Start button on the Windows task bar, then pick <u>P</u>rograms. Next, pick the AutoCAD 2000 item, then pick AutoCAD 2000 Online Help.
   D. Pick the **Contents** tab if it is not displayed. Double-click the User's Guide item, then double-click Chapter 1 — Welcome to AutoCAD 2000. Double-click Getting Help.
   E. Pick the green hyperlink HELP and read the next help window.
   F. Dismiss the help window by picking the "X" close button at the upper-right of the dialog box.
   G. Restore AutoCAD by picking the AutoCAD button on the task bar.
   H. Close AutoCAD by picking the control icon at the upper-left of the AutoCAD graphics window.

5. Load AutoCAD by selecting the proper items using the Start button on the Windows task bar.
   A. Pick the **OK** button at the **Startup** dialog box.
   B. Move the pointer to a space between two buttons in the **Standard** toolbar and read the note on the status bar at the bottom of the screen.
   C. Move the pointer to a space to the left of the **Color Control** drop-down list box and read the note on the status bar.
   D. Slowly move the pointer over each of the buttons on the **Standard** toolbar and **Object Properties** toolbar and read the tooltips. Do the same on the **Draw** and **Modify** toolbars at the left of the screen.
   E. Pick the **<u>F</u>ile** pull-down menu to display it. Using the right arrow key, move through all the pull-down menus. Use the left arrow key to return to the **<u>D</u>raw** pull-down menu. Use the down arrow key to move to the **<u>C</u>ircle** command, then use the right arrow key to display the **Circle** options in the cascading menu.
   F. Press the [Esc] key to dismiss the menu.
   G. Close AutoCAD by picking **E<u>x</u>it** in the **<u>F</u>ile** pull-down menu.

6. Draw a freehand sketch of the screen display. Label each of the screen areas. To the side of the sketch, write a short description of each screen area's function.

Starting and Setting Up Drawings

Learning Objectives

After completing this chapter, you will be able to:

- Plan an AutoCAD drawing.
- Use the AutoCAD **Quick Setup** wizard.
- Use the AutoCAD **Advanced Setup** wizard.
- Use an AutoCAD template.
- Start a drawing from scratch.
- Manage drawings in the Multiple Design Environment (MDE).
- Use the **UNITS** and **LIMITS** commands to change drawing settings.
- Open an existing drawing.

PLANNING YOUR AUTOCAD DRAWING

AutoCAD User's Guide 2

Effective planning can greatly reduce the amount of time it takes to set up and complete a drawing. Drawing setup involves many factors that affect the quality and accuracy of your final drawing. AutoCAD helps make this planning process easy by providing a variety of automated setup options that help you begin a drawing. Even with these options, you still need to know the basic elements that make up your drawing. Some basic planning decisions include the following:

- The sheet size on which the drawing will be plotted.
- The units of measure being used.
- The precision required for the drawing.
- The name of the drawing.

This chapter discusses all of these AutoCAD setup options. It also provides an opportunity to experiment with them.

NEW
[Ctrl]+[N]

File
→ **New...**

Standard toolbar

New

For 2000i Users...

In AutoCAD 2000i, the **NEW** command displays the **AutoCAD Today** window. The options for starting a new drawing are found in the **Create Drawings** tab of the **My Drawings** area. Refer to *Creating Drawings* on page 963 for details.

When AutoCAD is first started, the **Startup** dialog box is automatically displayed. See Figure 2-1. This dialog box provides several methods of selecting settings for your drawing. If you are already in an AutoCAD session, you can start a new drawing using the **NEW** command. Access this command by picking **New...** from the **File** pull-down menu, pressing the [Ctrl]+[N] key combination, or typing NEW at the Command: prompt. This displays the **Create New Drawing** dialog box, which is identical to the **Startup** dialog box.

A row of four buttons near the top of the dialog box presents each of the available startup options. Hold your cursor on a button to see its name displayed in a tooltip. The following options are available:

- **Open a Drawing.** Select this option to open an existing drawing.
- **Start from Scratch.** This setup option starts a new drawing based on the initial default settings contained in the acad.dwt (English) or acadiso.dwt (metric) template. You can then set up all other drawing specifications.
- **Use a Template.** This setup option starts a new drawing based on a template. A *template* is a file that contains standard settings, which are applied to the new drawing. AutoCAD offers a selection of templates based on accepted industry standards, but you can also create your own templates or use any existing drawing file as a template.
- **Use a Wizard.** The startup wizard provides a step-by-step method of defining the drawing settings.

These startup options define the drawing appearance by setting items such as dimensioning features, pattern scales, and text size to match the selected drawing units and drawing area. The option you select in the **Startup** dialog box is presented as the default option for the next use of the **Startup** dialog box.

Figure 2-1.
The **Startup** dialog box opens when you begin AutoCAD. This dialog box can be turned off and AutoCAD will automatically start with the drawing setup based on the template file acad.dwt.

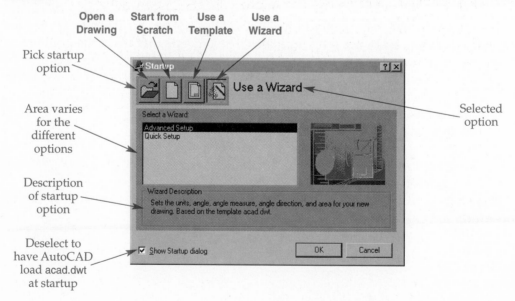

In Figure 2-1, the **Use a Wizard** option is currently selected. A *wizard* consists of AutoCAD setup options that automatically control scale factors for dimension settings, text height, and other drawing settings based on the information you provide. Two setup options are found in the **Select a Wizard:** list. The two wizard setup options are as follows:

- **Quick Setup.** This setup option allows a drawing to be quickly started by defining the drawing area and the required unit of measure.
- **Advanced Setup.** This setup option provides the same options found in the **Quick Setup** but with additional control and flexibility.

Highlight the desired setup option by picking either **Quick Setup** or **Advanced Setup**. **Advanced Setup** is the default option. A description of the highlighted wizard is given in the **Wizard Description** area. Look in this area for information provided by AutoCAD about any setup option chosen.

NOTE

To view additional information about of any features in these dialog boxes, select the **?** button in the upper-right corner and then pick the feature to see a brief description.

NOTE

AutoCAD provides a *Multiple Document Environment* (MDE). This means that AutoCAD can have many different drawings open at the same time. Each open drawing occupies an individual drawing window within the AutoCAD program window. An introduction to managing the MDE is provided later in this chapter.

In this chapter, you will start several new drawings. When you start a new drawing, AutoCAD assigns a temporary name of Drawing1.dwg. The second drawing you start is given a temporary name of Drawing2.dwg, the third is named Drawing3.dwg, and so on. You can assign a different name when you save the drawing file. Saving drawings is introduced in Chapter 3. If you exit from AutoCAD, you may be asked if you want to save each of the drawings that you started. For the discussion in this chapter, you should answer **No** to each prompt.

Using the **Quick Setup** Wizard

The following discussion explains how to start a new drawing using the **Quick Setup** option. To access this option in the **Startup** dialog box, double-click on **Quick Setup** in the **Select a Wizard:** list, or highlight **Quick Setup** and pick **OK** or press [Enter].

The **QuickSetup** dialog box shown in Figure 2-2 is displayed. The drawing units are set in the **Units** page of the **QuickSetup** dialog box, and the initial size of the drawing area is set in the **Area** page. Use the **Next >** and **< Back** buttons to display the needed page. A list along the left edge of the dialog box shows the names of the pages and displays a small arrow next to the name of the currently displayed page. When you have made all desired settings, pick the **Finish** button from the last page of the wizard.

For 2000i Users...

In AutoCAD 2000i, the **Quick Setup** wizard is accessed from the **Create Drawings** tab of the **My Documents** area of the **AutoCAD Today** window. Refer to *Creating Drawings* on page 963 for details.

Figure 2-2.
The **QuickSetup** dialog box contains two pages. The **Units** page, displayed first, uses an initial default of **Decimal** units.

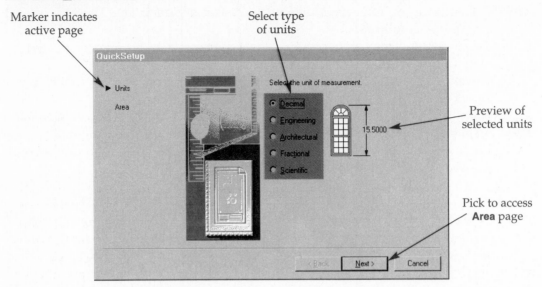

Marker indicates active page

Select type of units

Preview of selected units

Pick to access **Area** page

Setting units of measure

There are several options for setting drawing units in the **Units** page of the **QuickSetup** dialog box. The initial default setting is **Decimal** units using four decimal place precision. The default units, precision, and drawing area settings are based on the current settings found in the acad.dwt template. An example of the current units and precision settings is displayed in the preview image on the right. The units setting can be changed by picking the desired radio button. When a radio button is picked, the selected option becomes active. An example of the new active option is then displayed in the preview image. The units options are as follows:

- **Decimal.** These units are used to create drawings in decimal inches or millimeters. Decimal units are normally used on mechanical drawings for manufacturing. This option conforms to the ASME Y14.5M dimensioning and tolerancing standard. The initial default precision is four decimal places.
- **Engineering.** These units are often used in civil drafting projects such as maps, plot plans, dam and bridge construction, and topography. The initial default precision is four decimal places. The example from the preview image is shown in Figure 2-3A.
- **Architectural.** Architectural, structural, and other drawings use these units when measurements are in feet, inches, and fractional inches. The initial default precision is 1/16". The example from the preview image is shown in Figure 2-3B.
- **Fractional.** This option is used for drawings that have fractional parts of any common unit of measure. The initial default precision is 1/16. The example from the preview image is shown in Figure 2-3C.
- **Scientific.** These units are used when very large or small values are applied to the drawing. These applications take place in industries such as chemical engineering and astronomy. The initial default precision is four decimal places. The preview image in Figure 2-3D shows 1.5500E+01. The E+01 means that the base number is multiplied by 10 to the first power.

After selecting the type of units applicable to the drawing, pick the **Next** button to access the **Area** page.

AutoCAD and its Applications—Basics

Figure 2-3.
In addition to decimal, other types of units are available. Select the units appropriate for your drawing.

Engineering	Architectural	Fractional	Scientific
A	B	C	D

EXERCISE 2-1

❑ Open AutoCAD and look at the **Startup** dialog box. If AutoCAD is already running, access the **Create New Drawing** dialog box.

❑ Pick the **?** button and read the information about each of the different features of this dialog box.

❑ Pick the **Use a Wizard** button.

❑ Access the **QuickSetup** dialog box.

❑ Study the preview image. Pick each of the unit options and notice how the preview image changes.

❑ Pick the **Cancel** button.

NOTE

You can pick the **Cancel** button in any of the **Startup** dialog boxes to skip the setup process and go directly to the AutoCAD graphics window. This starts the drawing session using the current **Start from Scratch** default settings. You can then adjust these settings as needed. If you want to leave AutoCAD, pick **Exit** in the **File** pull-down menu and pick **No** when asked if you want to save changes.

Setting the drawing area

AutoCAD refers to the drawings you create as *models*. Models are drawn full-size in *model space*. Model space is active when the **Model** tab is selected, Figure 2-4. When you finish drawing the model, you then switch to *layout space*, where the drawing layout is organized as needed to be printed on paper. Model space and layout space are fully explained in Chapter 10 of this text. All text material prior to Chapter 10 is presented based on model space being active.

An AutoCAD drawing is created actual size using the desired unit of measure. If you are drawing an object that is measured in feet and inches, then you draw using feet and inches in AutoCAD. If you are creating a mechanical drawing for manufacturing, the drawing is full-size using decimal inches or millimeters. You draw the objects full-size regardless of the type of drawing, the units used, or the size of the final layout on paper. AutoCAD allows you to specify the size of the actual area required for your drawing, and refers to this as the *model space drawing limits*. The model space drawing limits can be changed at any time during the drawing process.

Now you are ready to set the drawing area, or model space drawing limits. The **Area** page of the **QuickSetup** dialog box is accessed by picking the **Next** button on the **Units** page. See Figure 2-5. There is a **Width:** and **Length:** text box with default sheet size settings of 12″ × 9″.

Change the width and length as desired by entering new values in the text boxes. The drawing area is set in full-scale units and should be large enough for the model being created. For example, if you are designing a 50′ × 30′ building, your drawing

Figure 2-4.
Model space is
active when the
Model tab is
selected.

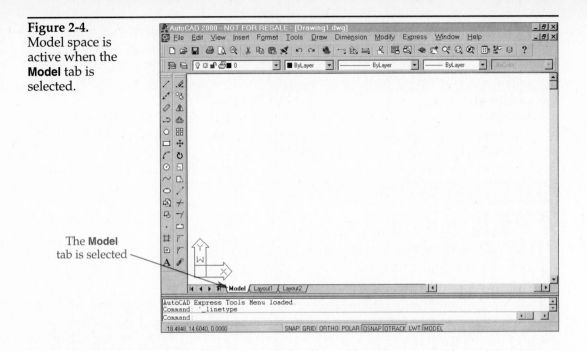

The **Model**
tab is selected

Figure 2-5.
The **Area** page of the **QuickSetup** dialog box. The model space drawing limits, or drawing
area default setting, is 12 × 9 units.

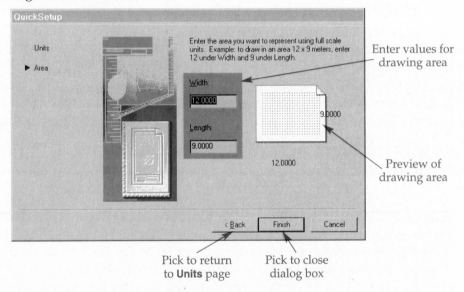

Enter values for
drawing area

Preview of
drawing area

Pick to return
to **Units** page

Pick to close
dialog box

area will need to be larger than 50′ × 30′ to allow room for dimensions, notes, and
other features. The preview image displays the orientation and dimensions of the
specified drawing area. Pick the **Finish** button when done.

Keep in mind that the size of your drawing area does not need to conform to
standard sheet sizes, because the sheet size is specified when you define the drawing
layout. Additionally, you can change the drawing limits at any time if more or less
space is required to complete the drawing. This is accomplished with the **LIMITS**
command.

The following list provides some professional guidelines that you can use to set
the drawing area width and length based on different units:
- **Inch and Metric drawings.** Calculate the total width and length of the objects
  included in all views with extra space between views and room for dimensions and notes. Use these values for your drawing area settings.

- **Architectural drawings.** The actual size of architectural drawings is based on feet and inch measurements. If you are drawing the floor plan that is 48′ × 24′, allow 10′ on each side for dimensions and notes to make a total drawing area 68′ × 44′. When you select architectural units, AutoCAD automatically sets up the drawing for you to draw in feet and inches.
- **Civil drawings.** The actual size of civil drawings used for mapping is often measured in units of feet. This allows you to set up the drawing limits similar to the architectural application just discussed. Civil drawings often represent very large areas, such as a plot plan that requires 200′ × 100′ to accommodate all the property lines, dimensions, and notes.

EXERCISE 2-2

❑ Start AutoCAD if it is not already started. Access the **QuickSetup** dialog box.
❑ Pick the **Next** button to go to the **Area** page in this wizard.
❑ Read the instructions at the top of the page.
❑ The default limits are 12 × 9. Change the width to 17, the length to 11, and notice the change in the preview image.
❑ Change the width to 8.5 and notice the difference in the preview image size and orientation.
❑ Pick the **Finish** button.

Using the Advanced Setup Wizard

The **Advanced Setup** wizard provides more options and flexibility than the **Quick Setup** wizard. In the **Startup** or **Create New Drawing** dialog box, double-click on **Advanced Setup,** or highlight **Advanced Setup** and pick the **OK** button or press [Enter]. The **Advanced Setup** dialog box is shown in Figure 2-6. This dialog box has five pages. Use the pages in progressive order or as needed to set up your drawing.

The first page (**Units**) is similar to the **Units** page in the **Quick Setup** wizard discussed earlier. Unlike the **QuickSetup**, the unit precision can be set using the **Precision:** drop-down list. The last page (**Area**) is the same as in the **Area** page in the **QuickSetup** dialog box. The other pages are described in the following sections.

For 2000i Users...

In AutoCAD 2000i, the **Advanced Setup** wizard is accessed from the **Create Drawings** tab of the **My Documents** area of the **AutoCAD Today** window. Refer to *Creating Drawings* on page 963 for details.

Figure 2-6.
The **Advanced Setup** dialog box has five pages. This **Units** page is the same as the **Units** page in the **QuickSetup** dialog box with the addition of the **Precision:** drop-down list.

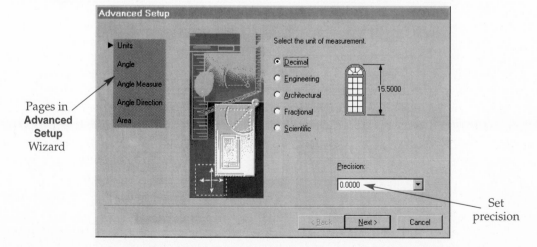

Pages in **Advanced Setup** Wizard

Set precision

Setting angular units

Use the **Angle** page to select one of five angular unit options and the precision (display accuracy) of angles. Figure 2-7 shows the **Angle** page. The angle measurement options are accessed by picking the desired radio button. The preview image shows a representation of units, and you can use the **Precision** drop-down list to set the precision. These options are available:

- **Decimal Degrees.** This is the initial default setting. It is normally used in mechanical drafting where degrees and decimal parts of a degree are commonly used.
- **Deg/Min/Sec.** This style is sometimes used in mechanical, architectural, structural, and civil drafting. The preview image in Figure 2-8A shows 90d, where the d is degrees. There are 60 minutes in one degree and 60 seconds in one minute.
- **Grads.** *Grads* is the abbreviation for *gradient*. The angular value is followed by a g as shown in the preview image, Figure 2-8B. Gradients are units of angular measure based on one-quarter of a circle having 100 grads. A full circle has 400 grads.
- **Radians.** A *radian* is an angular unit of measure where 2π radians = $360°$, and π radians = $180°$. For example, a $90°$ angle has $\pi/2$ radians and an arc length of $\pi/2$. The preview image in Figure 2-8C gives the default value of a $90°$ angle as 2r (1.5708 displayed with 0 decimal places). Changing the precision displays the radian value rounded to the specified decimal place.
- **Surveyor.** Surveyor angles are measured using bearings. A *bearing* is the direction of a line with respect to one of the quadrants of a compass. Bearings are measured clockwise or counterclockwise (depending on the quadrant), beginning from either north or south. Bearings are measured in degrees, minutes, and seconds. An angle measured 55°45'22" from north toward west is expressed as N55°45'22"W. An angle measured 25°30'10" from south toward east is expressed as S25°30'10"E. Figure 2-8D shows the preview as N0dE. Use the **Precision:** drop-down list to set measurement to degrees, degrees/minutes, degree/minutes/seconds, or to set decimal display accuracy of the seconds part of the measurement.

Once you have selected the units and precision for angular measurement, pick the **Next** button to go to the **Angle Measure** page, Figure 2-9. The orientation of the compass directions is the same as when you look at a map, with north at the top of the screen, east at the right, west at the left, and south at the bottom. Setting the angle measure establishes the direction for angle $0°$. The AutoCAD default is **East**, or on the right side of the screen. The **North**, **West**, and **South** radio buttons are used to place $0°$

Figure 2-7.
The **Angle** page is used to set the type of angular units. **Decimal degrees** is the initial default.

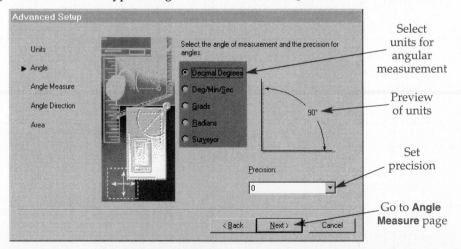

Figure 2-8.
In addition to decimal degrees, other types of angular units are available. Select the units appropriate for your drawing. All units are shown with the default precision.

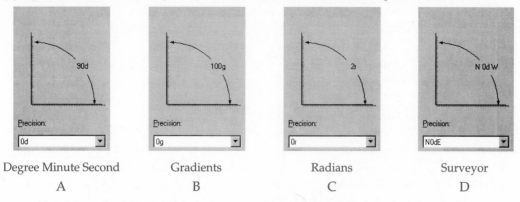

Degree Minute Second	Gradients	Radians	Surveyor
A	B	C	D

Figure 2-9.
In the **Angle Measure** page, the default angle zero direction is **East**.

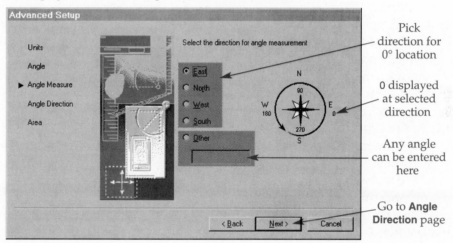

at those orientations. The **Other** option requires that you type a desired starting angle. After selecting the orientation for angular measurement, pick the **Next** button to go to the **Angle Direction** page.

The **Angle Direction** page allows you to select **Counter-Clockwise** or **Clockwise** angle direction. The angle direction originates from the compass position set in the **Angle Measure** page. The default angle direction is **Counter-Clockwise**. Figure 2-10 shows the default setting and related preview image.

NOTE

The values in the **Precision** lists affect coordinate displays for units and angular measure but have no effect on the accuracy of your drawing. The high accuracy of AutoCAD is maintained regardless of the display precision.

Figure 2-10.
The **Angle Direction** page determines the positive direction of angle measurement from the direction specified in the **Angle Measure** page. The default angle direction is **Counter-Clockwise**.

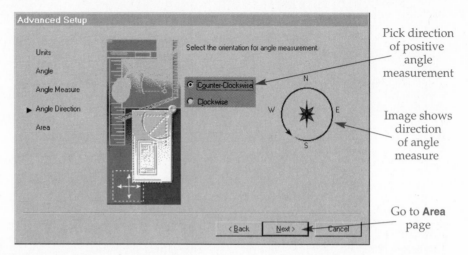

Pick direction of positive angle measurement

Image shows direction of angle measure

Go to **Area** page

EXERCISE 2-3

❑ Start AutoCAD if it is not already started. Use the **Startup** or the **Create New Drawing** dialog box and select **Advanced Setup**.

❑ Review the features found in the **Units** page that were previously covered in Exercise 2-1.

❑ Access the **Angle** page. Change the precision to different settings. Look at the preview image as you pick each of the angle unit options. Now, pick **Decimal Degrees**.

❑ Access the **Angle Measure** page. Pick each of the four compass orientation options. Notice how the preview image changes. Now, pick the **East** option.

❑ Access the **Angle Direction** page and notice the preview image for the default **Counter-Clockwise** option. Pick the **Clockwise** option and see the change in the image. Now, pick **Counter-Clockwise**.

❑ Review the features found in the **Area** tab.

Using an AutoCAD Template

For 2000i Users...

In AutoCAD 2000i, templates are selected from the **Create Drawings** tab of the **My Documents** area of the **AutoCAD Today** window. Pick **Templates** from the **Select how to begin** drop-down list, and then pick the template from the list provided.

In AutoCAD, templates store standard drawing settings and may contain predefined drawing layouts, title blocks, and other common drawing components. When you begin a drawing using a template, all the settings and contents of the template file are added to the new drawing. Using a template means that the drawing setup process is already complete and you are ready to begin drafting immediately. In addition to reducing drawing setup time, templates also help to maintain consistent standards in each of your drawings.

AutoCAD also allows you to start a new drawing based on an existing drawing file. A drawing file that is used as a template is also referred to as a *prototype drawing*.

A variety of templates conforming to accepted industry standards are included with AutoCAD. These templates are accessed by picking the **Use a Template** button in the **Startup** or **Create New Drawing** dialog box. The dialog box changes to show the **Use a Template** options, Figure 2-11. The **Select a Template** list shows the names of the template files found in the current drawing template file location specified in the **Files** tab in the **Options** dialog box. The .dwt file extension stands for *drawing template*.

Figure 2-11.
In the **Use a Template** startup option, the selected template is displayed in the preview image and a description is provided.

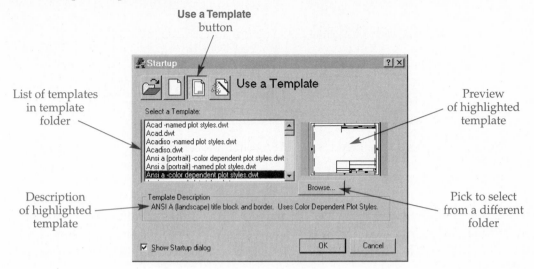

When a template is highlighted in the **Select a Template** list, a preview image is displayed and a description is given in the **Template Description** area. To start a drawing using a template, double-click on a template or highlight the template and pick the **OK** button or press [Enter].

The template files provided with AutoCAD use a naming system indicating the drafting standard referenced, the size of the title block in the preset layout, and the plot style settings used. Plot styles are introduced in Chapter 10.

Drafters often think of the drawing size as sheet size. The *sheet size* is the size of the paper that you use to layout and plot the final drawing. The sheet size takes into account the size of the drawing and added space for dimensions, notes, and clear area between the drawing and border lines. The sheet size also includes the title block, revision block, zoning, and an area for general notes. In AutoCAD, the sheet size is specified in the **Page Setup** wizard when defining your drawing layout. The **Page Setup** wizard is discussed in Chapter 10.

ASME/ANSI standard sheet sizes and format are specified in the documents ANSI Y14.1, *Drawing Sheet Size and Format* and ASME Y14.1M, *Metric Drawing Sheet Size and Format*. The proper presentation of engineering changes is given in ASME Y14.35M, *Revision of Engineering Drawings and Associated Documents*. ANSI Y14.1 lists sheet size specifications in inches as follows:

Size Designation	Size (in inches)
A	8 1/2 × 11 (horizontal format) 11 × 8 1/2 (vertical format)
B	11 × 17
C	17 × 22
D	22 × 34
E	34 × 44
F	28 × 40
Sizes G, H, J, and K are roll sizes.	

ASME Y14.1M provides sheet size specifications in metric units. Standard metric drawing sheet sizes are designated as follows:

Size Designation	Size (in millimeters)
A0	841 × 1189
A1	594 × 841
A2	420 × 594
A3	297 × 420
A4	210 × 297

Longer lengths are referred to as *elongated* and *extra-elongated* drawing sizes. These are available in multiples of the short side of the sheet size. Figure 2-12 shows standard ANSI/ASME sheet sizes.

All the ANSI templates and generic templates provided with AutoCAD are based on decimal inches as the unit of measure. The architectural templates are set up for the feet and inches measurements typically used in architectural applications. **Din**, **Iso**, and **Jis a0** through **Jis a4** template files are based on metric measurement settings.

NOTE *DIN* refers to the German standard *Deutsches Institut Für Normung*, which is established by the German Institute for Standardization. *ISO* is the International Organization for Standardization, and *JIS* is the Japanese Industry Standard.

The ANSI, DIN, ISO, and JIS templates provide a layout with the title block located in the lower-right corner. The architectural templates provide a title block on the right side of the sheet, which is common in the architectural industry.

The **Select a Template** list also contains the acad.dwt option for starting a drawing using feet and inches, and the acadiso.dwt option for using metric units. These options do not have layouts or title blocks already set up. Additional options for finding and using templates are discussed in Chapter 3.

When using a setup wizard, you enter values that define the drawing settings. When using a template, these values are automatically set. Templates usually have values for the following drawing elements:

✓ Standard layouts with a border and title block.
✓ Grid and snap settings.
✓ Units and angle values.
✓ Text standards and general notes.
✓ Dimensioning settings.

The **Use a Template** option lets you start a drawing project with little or no drawing setup being required. Sometimes, you may use a template that starts you with some or most of the required settings for the new drawing. After referencing the desired template, you can then adjust your drawing settings as needed for the type of drawing being created. When going through this text, you will discover many ways to adjust AutoCAD to match individual needs and professional applications. Each of these applications can be used to build customized templates.

Figure 2-12.
A—Standard drawing sheet sizes (ANSI Y14.1) B—Standard metric drawing sheet sizes
(ASME Y14.1M).

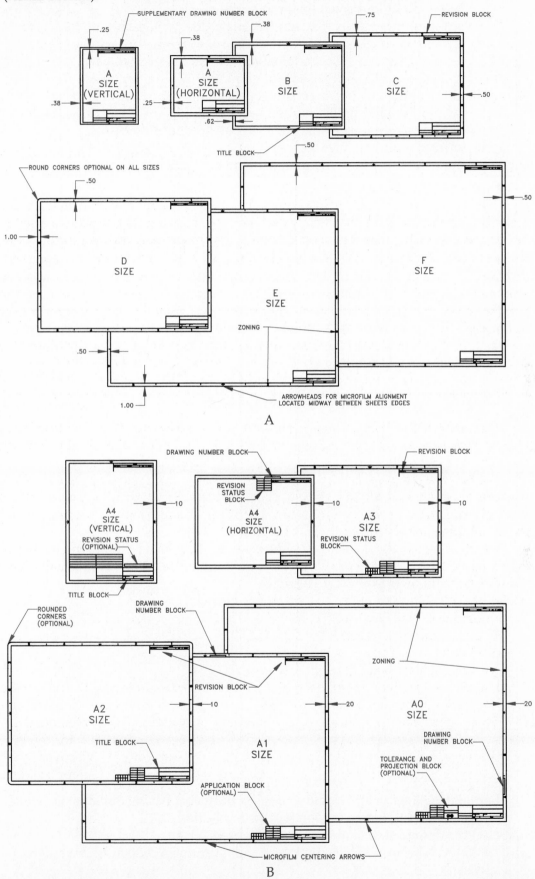

❑ Start AutoCAD if it is not already started. Use the **Startup** or **Create New Drawing** dialog box and pick the **Use a Template** button.

❑ While scrolling through the **Select a Template:** list, pick each template. Notice how the preview image and description change to represent each template.

❑ Pick a template from the **Select a Template:** list that interests you and start a new drawing. For example, pick an **Ansi b** template if you are interested in a B-size mechanical drawing, or one of the architectural templates for architectural drawings. Double-click on the desired option or highlight it and press [Enter].

❑ The AutoCAD screen now displays the layout, border, and title block as defined in the selected template.

❑ Pick the **Model** tab to make model space active.

Using the Start from Scratch Option

For 2000i Users...

To start a drawing from scratch, access the **Create Drawings** tab of the **My Documents** area of the **AutoCAD Today** window. Then pick **Start from Scratch** from the **Select how to begin** drop-down list.

The **Start from Scratch** button in the **Startup** and **Create New Drawing** dialog boxes is used if you want to set up a drawing on your own. When it is picked, AutoCAD displays the **Default Settings** options where either **English (feet and inches)** or **Metric** units can be selected. The preview image does not change but the **Tip** area reflects the current selection. The appearance of this dialog box for both English and metric settings is shown in Figure 2-13. When a drawing is started from scratch, settings such as limits and units must be established after the drawing has been started. This is discussed later in the chapter.

Figure 2-13.
In the **Start from Scratch** startup option, select the types of units.

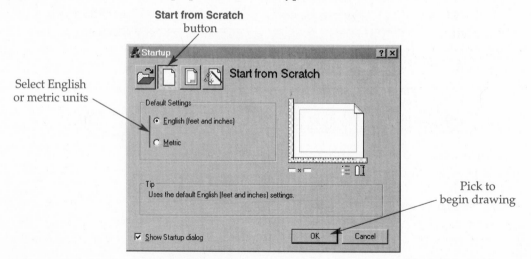

EXERCISE 2-5

❑ Start AutoCAD if it is not already started. Use the **Startup** or **Create New Drawing** dialog box and pick the **Start from Scratch** button.

❑ Highlight the **English** and **Metric** settings in the **Select Default Settings:** list while you watch the **Tip** change to represent each selection.

❑ Select the desired setting, then pick **OK** or press [Enter].

❑ The AutoCAD screen is now displayed and all AutoCAD defaults are automatically set.

Which Startup Option Should I Use?

Before starting an AutoCAD drawing, there should be some consideration of which startup option to use. Consider the following:

- **Wizards.** Wizards are often the best option when using AutoCAD as a design tool. In the design phase of a project, it may be too soon to be concerned about what the final drawing layout will look like. This option allows the size of the drawing area to be set up, including several of the drawing environment settings. It does not place a title block or border.
- **Templates.** Templates can be incredible productivity boosters. The provided template files may meet some personal needs, but creating new templates is where the greatest benefit is found. This allows you to use an existing drawing as a starting point for any new drawing. This option is extremely valuable for ensuring that everyone in a department, class, school, or company uses the same standards within their drawings.
- **Starting from scratch.** Use this option to "play it by ear" when just sketching or when the start or end of a drawing project is unknown. This is more frequently used by experienced AutoCAD users who are familiar with the settings that they like.

Disabling the **Startup** Dialog Box

In the lower-left corner of the **Startup** dialog box is the **Show Startup dialog** check box. It is checked by default, and the **Startup** dialog box appears every time AutoCAD is started. Click on the check box to turn this dialog box off. To turn the dialog box back on, select **Options...** from the **Tools** pull-down menu to access the **Options** dialog box. You can also right-click in the drawing area and select **Options...** from the shortcut menu to access this dialog box. Select the **System** tab and pick the **Show Startup dialog** check box in the **General Options** area.

If the **Startup** dialog box is disabled, launching AutoCAD automatically starts a new drawing using the template acad.dwt. If all the drawings you create are based on this template, there is no need to display the **Startup** dialog box every time you begin a new drawing.

For 2000i Users...

In AutoCAD 2000i, the startup behavior is set in the **System** tab of the **Options** dialog box using the **Startup** drop-down list in the **General Options** area. Refer to *Deactivating the AutoCAD Today Window* on page 965 for details.

MULTIPLE DESIGN ENVIRONMENT (MDE)

AutoCAD allows you to have multiple drawings open at the same time. This feature is referred to as the *Multiple Design Environment (MDE)* (sometimes called a *multiple document interface*, or *MDI*).

Most drafting projects are composed of a number of drawings, each presenting different aspects of a project. For example, in an architectural drafting project, required drawings might include a site plan, floor plan, electrical and plumbing plans, plus assorted detail drawings. Or consider a mechanical assembly composed of several unique parts. The required drawings might include an overall assembly view plus individual detail drawings of each component part. The drawings in such projects are closely related to one another. By opening two or more of these drawings at the same time, you can easily reference information contained in existing drawings while working in a new drawing. AutoCAD even allows you to directly copy all or part of the contents from one drawing directly into another using a simple drag-and-drop operation.

There are many ways to increase your drafting productivity through effective use of the MDE. These more advanced topics are covered throughout the text where they apply to the discussion material. The following information introduces the basic features and behaviors of the MDE.

Controlling Drawing Windows

Each drawing you open or start in AutoCAD is placed in its own drawing window. Based on AutoCAD's initial default behavior, drawing windows are displayed in a floating state. This means that the drawing area is displayed within a smaller window inside of the main AutoCAD program window. When multiple drawings are open at the same time, they are placed in a cascading arrangement by default. The name of each drawing is displayed on the left side of its title bar.

AutoCAD's drawing windows have the same control options as program windows on your desktop. They can be resized, moved, minimized, maximized, restored, and closed using the same methods used for program windows on your desktop. Figure 2-14 shows a summary of the standard window control functions available for drawing windows.

The drawing windows and the AutoCAD program window have the same relationship as program windows do with the Windows desktop. When a drawing window is maximized, it fills the available area in the AutoCAD program window. Minimizing a drawing window displays it as a reduced size title bar along the bottom of AutoCAD's drawing window area. Drawing windows cannot be moved outside the AutoCAD program window. Figure 2-15 illustrates drawing windows in a floating state and minimized.

To work on any currently open drawing, just pick its title bar if it is visible. You can quickly cycle through all open drawings in sequence by pressing either the [Ctrl]+[F6] or [Ctrl]+[Tab] key combination. To go directly to a specific drawing when the title bars are not visible, access the **Window** pull-down menu in AutoCAD. The name

Figure 2-14.
Drawing window control options.

Window Control Buttons		
Button	**Function**	**Description**
	Minimize	Displays window as a button along bottom of drawing window space in AutoCAD window.
	Restore	Returns window to floating state, at previous size and position, displays title bar.
	Maximize	Displays window at largest possible size, hides title bar.
	Close	Closes drawing, provides option to save drawing if any changes remain unsaved.
	Display window control menu	Display pull-down menu with window control options.

Resizing Controls		
Cursor	**Function**	**Usage**
 ↕	Size window vertically	Press and hold pick button while pointing at top or bottom border of window, then move mouse.
 ↔	Size window horizontally	Press and hold pick button while pointing at left or right border of window, then move mouse.
 ↘	Size window diagonally	Press and hold pick button while pointing at any corner on border of window, then move mouse.
 ✛	Move window	Press and hold pick button while pointing at title bar of window, then move mouse.

Figure 2-15.
Drawing windows can be displayed in several ways. A—By default, drawings are displayed in floating windows. When multiple drawings are open, the windows are placed in a cascading arrangement. B—Minimized drawing windows are displayed as a reduced size title bar. Pick the title bar to display a window control menu.

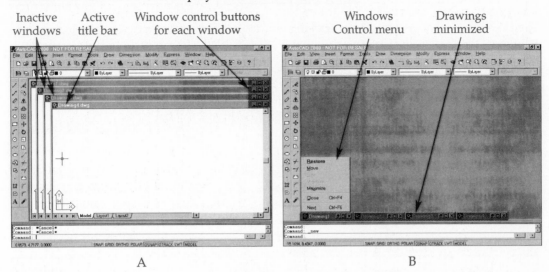

A

B

of each open drawing file is displayed, and the active drawing shows a checkmark next to it. See Figure 2-16A. Pick the name of the desired drawing to make it current. Up to nine drawing names are displayed on this menu. If more than nine drawings are open, a **More Windows...** selection is displayed. Picking this displays the **Select Window** dialog box, shown in Figure 2-16B.

The additional control options available in the **Window** pull-down menu include:

- **Cascade.** Drawing windows that are not currently minimized are arranged in a cascade of floating windows, with the active drawing placed at the front.
- **Tile Horizontally.** Drawing windows that are not currently minimized are tiled in a horizontal arrangement with the active drawing window placed in the top position.
- **Tile Vertically.** Drawing windows that are not currently minimized are tiled in a vertical arrangement with the active drawing window placed in the left position.
- **Arrange Icons.** Arranges minimized drawings neatly along bottom of AutoCAD drawing window area.

For 2000i Users...

In AutoCAD 2000i, the **Window** pull-down menu includes two additional options. Pick **Close** to close the active drawing or **Close All** to close all drawings.

Figure 2-16.
Selecting the active drawing window.
A—Pick the name of a drawing displayed on the **Window** pull-down menu to make it current. This menu also offers additional drawing window control options.
B—When more than nine drawings are open, pick **More Windows...** from the **Window** pull-down menu to display the **Select Window** dialog box.

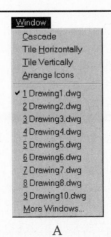

A

B

The effects of tiling the drawing window display varies based on the number of windows being tiled and whether they are tiled horizontally or vertically. See Figure 2-17.

Figure 2-17.
Tiled drawing windows. A—Three drawing windows, tiled horizontally. B—Three drawing windows, tiled vertically. C—Four drawing windows, tiled either horizontally or vertically.

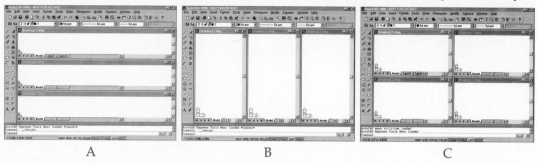

A   B   C

NOTE

Typically, you can change the active drawing as desired. There are some situations, however, when you cannot switch between drawings. For example, you cannot switch drawings during a dialog session. You must either complete or cancel the dialog box before switching is possible.

EXERCISE 2-6

❑ Start AutoCAD if it is not already started. Use the **Startup** or **Create New Drawing** dialog box and pick the **Start from Scratch** button.

❑ Pick the **Window** pull-down menu. Check to see how many drawing files are currently open.

❑ Start new drawings using the **Start from Scratch** option until you have at least ten drawings open at the same time.

❑ Use the **Window** pull-down menu to switch between drawings. Use the [Ctrl]+[F6] and the [Ctrl]+[Tab] key combinations to cycle between drawings.

❑ Pick the **Cascade** option from the **Window** pull-down menu to cascade the currently open drawing windows. Pick the **Tile Horizontally** and **Tile Vertically** options and observe the results of each action.

❑ Use the **Close** button to close all except four drawing windows without saving any changes. Pick the **Tile Horizontally** and **Tile Vertically** options and observe the results. Close one more drawing, repeat the tile operations, and observe the results.

❑ Minimize the remaining three drawings. Move the minimized drawings to different locations in the drawing window. Pick the **Arrange Icons** option and notice the new placement of the icons.

❑ Maximize one of the three drawing windows. Switch to another drawing using any desired method.

❑ Close two of the drawing windows without saving changes. Use the **Restore** button to place the drawing in a floating state. Resize the drawing window and move it to a new location. Double-click on the title bar of the drawing window.

❑ Close the last drawing window without saving changes.

After setting up AutoCAD, you are ready to begin drawing. The **Quick Setup** and **Advanced Setup** options provide a convenient way to initially set the drawing units and limits. However, these settings may need to be changed while working on the drawing or when the drawing is finished. The drawing units may be changed at any time with the **UNITS** command, and the model space drawing limits can be changed with the **LIMITS** command.

Changing Units

The **UNITS** command is the quickest way to set the units and angles. The **UNITS** command opens the **Drawing Units** dialog box for easy control of the settings. This command can be accessed by picking **Units...** in the **Format** pull-down menu or by typing UN or UNITS at the Command: prompt. The **Drawing Units** dialog box is shown in Figure 2-18.

Linear units are specified in the **Length** area of the **Drawing Units** dialog box. The established units in the current drawing are presented as the default values. Select the desired linear units format from the **Type:** drop-down list and use the **Precision:** drop-down list to specify the linear units precision. Access the **Type:** and **Precision:** drop-down lists located in the **Angle** area of the **Drawing Units** dialog box to set the desired angular units format and precision. Selecting the **Clockwise** check box changes the direction for angular measurements to clockwise from the default of counterclockwise.

Pick the **Direction...** button to access the **Direction Control** dialog box, Figure 2-19. The standard **East**, **North**, **West**, and **South** options are offered as radio buttons. Pick one of these buttons to set the compass orientation. The **Other** radio button activates

UNITS
UN

Format
➡ Units...

Figure 2-18.
The **UNITS** command accesses the **Drawing Units** dialog box

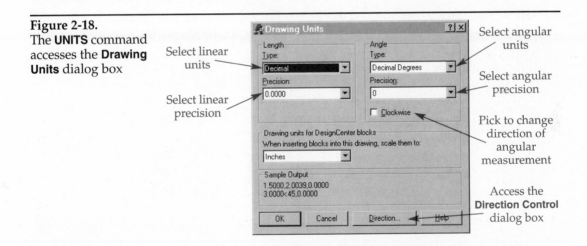

Select linear units

Select linear precision

Select angular units

Select angular precision

Pick to change direction of angular measurement

Access the **Direction Control** dialog box

Figure 2-19.
Picking the **Direction...** button in the **Drawing Units** dialog box displays the **Direction Control** dialog box.

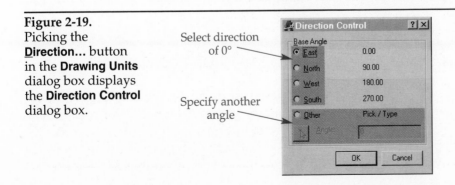

Select direction of 0°

Specify another angle

the **Angle:** text box and the **Angle** button. The **Angle:** text box allows an angle for zero direction to be entered. The **Angle** button allows two points on the screen to be picked for establishing the angle zero direction.

Unit-related values can also be set at the command line using the **-UNITS** command. Entering -UNITS at the Command: prompt opens the **AutoCAD Text Window**. You can then specify the same linear and angle unit settings available in the **Drawing Units** dialog box. When finished, press [F2] or pick the X button in the upper-right corner to close the **AutoCAD Text Window**.

Changing Limits

LIMITS

Format
➥ Drawing
Limits...

The model space drawing limits can be changed using the **LIMITS** command. The **LIMITS** command is accessed by entering LIMITS at the Command: prompt or by picking **Drawing Limits** in the **Format** pull-down menu.

The **LIMITS** command asks you to specify the coordinates for the lower-left corner and the upper-right corner of the drawing area. The lower-left corner is usually 0,0 but you can specify something else. Press [Enter] to accept the 0,0 value for the lower-left corner default, or type a new value. The upper-right corner usually identifies the upper-right corner of the drawing area. If you want a 17″ × 11″ drawing area, then the upper-right corner setting is 17,11. The first value is the horizontal measurement and the second value is the vertical measurement of the limits. Each value is separated by a comma. The command works like this:

Command: **LIMITS**⏎
Reset Model space limits:
Specify lower left corner or [ON/OFF] <0.0000,0.0000>: ⏎
Specify upper right corner <12.0000,9.0000>: **17,11**⏎
Command:

The **LIMITS** command can also be used to turn the limits on or off by typing ON or OFF at the prompt. When the limits are turned on, AutoCAD restricts you from drawing outside of the rectangular area defined by the limits settings. Limits are typically turned off for most drafting applications.

EXERCISE 2-7

❑ Open AutoCAD if it is not already open. Use the startup option of your choice.
❑ Access the AutoCAD graphics window.
❑ Open the **Drawing Units** dialog box and make the linear units architectural, angular measure decimal degrees, number of places for display of angles = 3, direction for angle 0 = 3 o'clock, with angles measured counterclockwise.
❑ Pick **OK** to exit the **Drawing Units** dialog box.
❑ Read through all the prompts for the **-UNITS** command and accept the default settings.
❑ Use the **LIMITS** command to turn the limits on and off.

AutoCAD
User's
Guide **2**

OPENING AN EXISTING DRAWING

Creating and saving drawings is discussed in detail in Chapter 3 of this text. Drawings that have been saved can be opened for additional work or for revisions. In the **Startup** dialog box there is an **Open a Drawing** button. Pick this button to access the **Open a Drawing** options. See Figure 2-20. The last four files opened are listed in the **Select a File:** list. Any one of the files listed can be opened by double-clicking on it.

Figure 2-20.
In the **Open a Drawing** option of the **Startup** dialog box, the **Select a File:** list contains the names of the last four files opened. Pick the **Browse...** button to display the **Select File** dialog box.

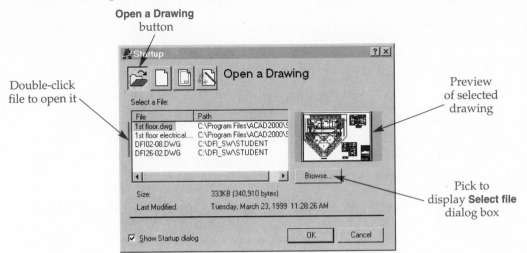

For 2000i Users...

In AutoCAD 2000i, the **AutoCAD Today** window replaces the **Startup** dialog box of AutoCAD 2000. Opening a drawing from the **AutoCAD Today** window is detailed in *Opening Drawings* on page 961.

To open a drawing file that is not listed, select the **Browse...** button to access the **Select File** dialog box, Figure 2-21. The **Select File** dialog box displayed by picking the **Browse...** button in the **Startup** dialog box allows you to select a single drawing file to open.

After you exit the **Startup** dialog box, a **Select File** dialog box can also be accessed by picking the **Open** button in the **Standard** toolbar, picking **Open...** in the **File** pull-down menu, using the [Ctrl]+[O] key combination, or entering OPEN at the Command: prompt. The **Select File** dialog box displayed by the **OPEN** command allows you to select any number of drawing files to open. Figure 2-22 shows multiple drawing files being selected for opening. The [Ctrl] and [Shift] keys are used when picking to select more than one file.

The default folder shown in the **Look in:** text box is Acad2000. Other folders and additional files can be accessed by double-clicking on a folder in the file and folder list. If you highlight a single drawing file, a preview of the drawing is shown. To open a file, double-click on it, or highlight it and pick the **Open** button.

OPEN
[Ctrl]+[O]

File
→ Open...

Standard toolbar

Open

Figure 2-21.
The **Select File** dialog box.

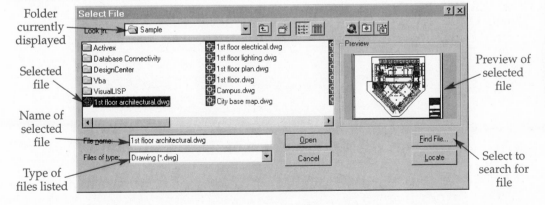

For 2000i Users...

The **Select File** dialog box has been updated for AutoCAD 2000i. Refer to *Select File Dialog Box* on page 966 for details.

Figure 2-22.
The **Select File** dialog box displayed by the **OPEN** command allows any number of drawings to be opened in a single operation. Use the [Ctrl] and [Shift] keys when picking to select multiple files.

Use [Ctrl] and [Shift] keys to select multiple files

Names of selected drawings

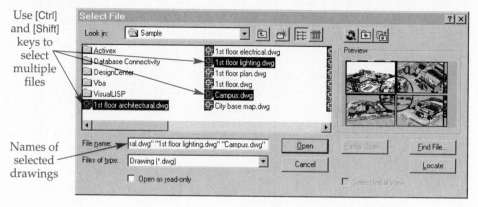

NOTE

If the file name and location are unknown, the **Find File...** button can be used to search for the file. Picking the **Find File...** button accesses the **Browse/Search** dialog box. In this dialog box, folders can be searched for specific files. This dialog box is discussed in Chapter 3 of this text.

To access additional drives, pick the drop-down arrow next to the **Look in:** text box. The **Look in:** drop-down list appears as shown in Figure 2-23. Pick any of the drives shown in this list to see the folders and files it contains. Access the desired folder or file, or close the dialog box.

When a drawing is open in the graphics window, you have the following options:

- Work on the drawing.
- Begin a new drawing by accessing the **NEW** command.
- Open another existing drawing.
- Exit AutoCAD by picking **Exit** in the **File** pull-down menu, or typing EXIT at the Command: prompt.

Figure 2-23.
Open the **Look in:** drop-down list to see the available drives and opened folders.

Pick to access drop-down list

Select drive and folder to view

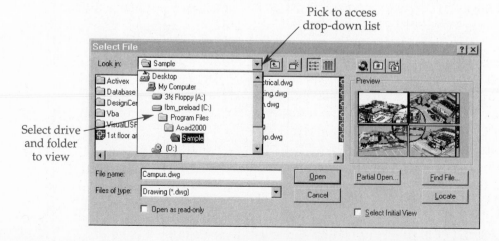

❏ Open AutoCAD if it is not already open.
❏ Access the **Select File** dialog box.
❏ In the Acad2000\Sample folder, pick one of the files such as 1st floor.dwg. Display it in the **Preview** image tile. Open the file for display in the graphics window.
❏ Access the **Select File** dialog box again.
❏ Open the Sample folder again. Pick each of the sample AutoCAD drawings. Look at the image of each in the **Preview** image tile.
❏ Open one of the sample drawings in the graphics window.
❏ Continue to use the **OPEN** command and look at different files.
❏ Exit AutoCAD when finished. Do not save changes to any of the drawings you opened.

Chapter Test

Answer the following questions on a separate sheet of paper.

1. Identify at least four basic planning decisions that need to be made before beginning a drawing.
2. How do you keep the **Startup** dialog box from being displayed when you start AutoCAD?
3. When in the **Startup** dialog box, how can you immediately close the box and enter the AutoCAD graphics window?
4. How do you return to the setup options if you are in the AutoCAD graphics window?
5. What are AutoCAD wizards?
6. Name the setup option that allows you to quickly start a drawing by defining the drawing area and units.
7. Name the setup option that provides units and angle control.
8. What is a template when used in AutoCAD?
9. Name the setup option that allows you to select from a list of files that store standard drawing settings and which may contain predefined drawing layouts, title blocks, and other common drawing components.
10. Name the setup option that asks you to select either English or metric units before opening the AutoCAD graphics window.
11. How do you open the **Startup** dialog box?
12. How do you open the **Create New Drawing** dialog box?
13. How do you open one of the wizards?
14. What is the purpose of the **?** button on the title bar of the **Startup** dialog box?
15. List the options found in the **Units** page of the **QuickSetup** dialog box.
16. This is an example of which type of units: 15.500?
17. This is an example of which type of units: 1'-3 1/2"?
18. This is an example of which type of units: 15 1/2?
19. What are the purposes of the **< Back** and **Next >** buttons?
20. An AutoCAD drawing is created _____ size using the units you select.
21. What is sheet size?
22. AutoCAD refers to the drawing area as _____.
23. What are the dimensions of an ANSI/ASME B size sheet?
24. Is the size of an ANSI/ASME A2 sheet specified in inches or millimeters?
25. What is the purpose of layout space?
26. 90.00° is an example of which angle units option?
27. 90°30'15" is an example of which angle units option?
28. N45°30'15"W is an example of which angle units option?

29. What is the AutoCAD default direction and compass orientation for measuring angles?
30. Which of the standard AutoCAD template files provides a border on the right side of the sheet for architectural applications?
31. What does the .dwt file extension stand for?
32. List at least four types of values or drawing elements found in templates.
33. What command opens the **Drawing Units** dialog box?
34. What happens when you enter -UNITS at the Command: prompt?
35. What is the upper-right corner limit for an architectural drawing using a C-size (22 × 17) sheet and a scale of 4 feet per inch when plotted if the lower-left corner limit is 0,0?
36. Name the pull-down menu that contains the **LIMITS** command.
37. The display of a measurement will change when a different number of digits to the right of the decimal point is specified. If a 1.6250 dimension is to be displayed, and the number of digits to the right of the decimal point is as follows, what is actually displayed?
   A. One digit.
   B. Two digits.
   C. Three digits.
   D. Four digits.
38. Give the commands and coordinate entries to set the model space drawing limits to 22 × 17:
   A. Command: _____
       Reset Model space limits:
   B. Specify lower left corner or [ON/OFF] <*current*>: _____
   C. Specify upper right corner <*current*>: _____
39. What is a purpose of the MDE?
40. How do you quickly cycle through all of the currently open drawings in sequence?

Drawing Problems

The following problems can be saved as templates for future use. You will be given instructions for saving, but saving drawings and templates is fully covered in Chapter 3 of this text. For Problems 1–3, use the Quick Setup wizard.

1. Create a template with 11″ × 8.5″ area and decimal units. Name it QK A SIZE (H) INCHES.dwt and include QUICK A SIZE (H) SETUP for its description. You now have a template for doing inch drawings on 11 × 8.5 (horizontal) sheets.

2. Create a template with an 8.5″ × 11″ area and decimal units. Name it QK A SIZE (V) INCHES.dwt and include QUICK A SIZE (V) INCHES SETUP for its description. You now have a template for doing inch drawings on 11″ × 8.5″ (vertical) sheets.

3. Create a template with a 594 × 420 area and decimal units. Name it QK A2 SIZE METRIC.dwt and include QUICK A2 SIZE METRIC SETUP for its description. You now have a template for doing metric (millimeters) drawings on 594 × 420 (A2) sheets.

For Problems 4–6, use the Advanced Setup wizard.

4. Create a template with a 17″ × 11″ area, decimal units with 0.000 precision; decimal degrees with 0.0 precision; default angle measure and orientation. Name it ADV B SIZE INCHES.dwt and include ADVANCED B SIZE INCHES SETUP for its description. You now have a template for doing inch drawings on 17 × 11 (B) sheets.

5. Create a template with a 420 × 297 (metric) area; decimal units with 0.0 precision; decimal degrees with 0.0 precision; default angle measure and orientation. Name it ADV ISO A3 SIZE MM.dwt and include ADVANCED ISO A3 SIZE MILLIMETERS SETUP for its description. You now have a template for doing metric (millimeters) drawings on 420 × 297 (A3) sheets.

In Problems 6–8, create a new template using an existing template as a model.

6. Begin a new drawing and select the Ansi c -color dependent plot styles.dwt template. Use the **UNITS** command to set decimal units with 0.000 precision and decimal angles with 0.0 precision. The direction control should be set to the default values. Set the limits to 0,0; 17,11. Name the drawing TEMP ANSI B.dwt and include ANSI B TEMPLATE SETUP for its description. You now have a template for doing inch drawings on 17 × 11 sheets with border and title block.

7. Begin a new drawing and select the Iso a4 -color dependent plot styles.dwt template. Use the **UNITS** command to set decimal units with 0.000 precision and decimal angles with 0.0 precision. The direction control should be set to the default values. Set the limits to 0,0; 420,297. Name the drawing TEMP ISO A3.dwt and include ISO A3 TEMPLATE SETUP for its description. You now have a template for doing metric (millimeters) drawings on 420 × 297mm sheets with border and title block.

8. Begin a new drawing and select the Architectural, english units -color dependent plot styles.dwt template. Use the **UNITS** command to set architectural units with 1/16″ precision and degrees/minutes/seconds angles with 0d00′00″ precision. The direction control should be set to the default values. Set the limits to 0,0; 22,17. Name the drawing TEMP ARCH.dwt and include ARCHITECTURAL TEMPLATE SETUP for its description. You now have a template for doing architectural drawings on 22 × 17 sheets with border and title block.

In Problems 9 and 10, create templates from scratch.

9. Begin a new drawing and select the **Start from Scratch** button. Select 0.00 as decimal units, 0.00 as decimal degrees, and 90° (North) for direction of the 0° angle. Make angles measure counterclockwise. Set the limits to 0,0; 17,11. Save as a drawing template named SFS B SIZE INCHES and include START FROM SCRATCH B SIZE INCHES SETUP for its description. You now have a template for doing inch drawings on 17 × 11 sheets.

10. Begin a new drawing and select the **Start from Scratch** button. Select 0.00 as decimal units, 0.00 as decimal degrees, and 0° (East) for direction of the 0° angle. Make angles measure counterclockwise. Set the limits to 0,0; 420,297. Save as a drawing template named SFS A3 SIZE METRIC and include START FROM SCRATCH A3 METRIC SETUP for its description. You now have a template for doing metric (millimeters) drawings on 420 × 297mm sheets.

AutoCAD includes many standard templates. These templates include settings and title blocks for many standardized sheet sizes. Three such templates are shown here.

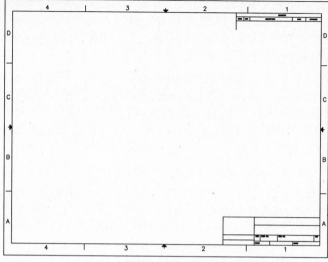

ANSI C Title Block

Architectural Title Block

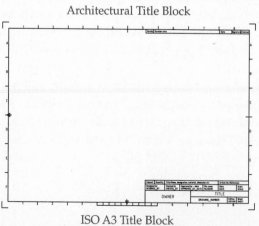

ISO A3 Title Block

CHAPTER 3

Introduction to Drawings, Saving Drawings

Learning Objectives

After completing this chapter, you will be able to:

- Display a grid of dots in the drawing area.
- Use the **LINE** command to draw several different geometric shapes.
- Cancel a command.
- Adjust grid and snap settings.
- Create a template drawing.
- Identify the function of the **FILEDIA** system variable.
- Save a drawing under a different name.
- Explain the difference between the **QSAVE**, **SAVEAS**, and **SAVE** commands.
- Specify how often your work is automatically saved.
- Save AutoCAD 2000 drawings for older releases.
- Save and open AutoCAD 2000 drawings in a DXF format.
- Open a saved drawing.
- Search for AutoCAD files.
- Explain how to open an AutoCAD drawing using the Windows Explorer.
- Use the **Partial Open** option and the **Partial Load** command.
- Use the **CLOSE** and **EXIT** commands.
- Determine the status of drawing parameters.

AutoCAD provides aids that help prepare the drawing layout, increase speed and efficiency, and ensure accuracy. These *drawing aids* include Grid mode and Snap mode. This chapter discusses each of these aids and how they are used to assist your drawing. AutoCAD automatically provides default drawing aids when you start a drawing, but you can change them to fit your own needs.

AutoCAD can be used to view and edit many formats of existing drawings, including drawing files found on the Internet. This chapter discusses the many different options available for opening existing drawings. This chapter also covers the different methods of saving the data you create with AutoCAD.

AutoCAD provides a grid or pattern of dots on the screen to help you lay out the drawing. When the Grid mode is activated, a pattern of dots appears in the drawing area as shown in Figure 3-1. The grid pattern shows only within the drawing limits to help clearly define the working area, and the spacing between dots can be adjusted.

Figure 3-2 shows the **Grid and Snap** tab of the **Drafting Settings** dialog box. This dialog box can be used to turn the grid on and off and to set the grid spacing. To access the **Drafting Settings** dialog box, select **Drafting Settings...** from the **Tools** pull-down menu, right-click on the **GRID** or **SNAP** button in the status bar and select **Settings...** from the shortcut menu, or type DSETTINGS, DS, SE, or RM at the Command: prompt.

Figure 3-1.
The grid spacing is represented by dots.

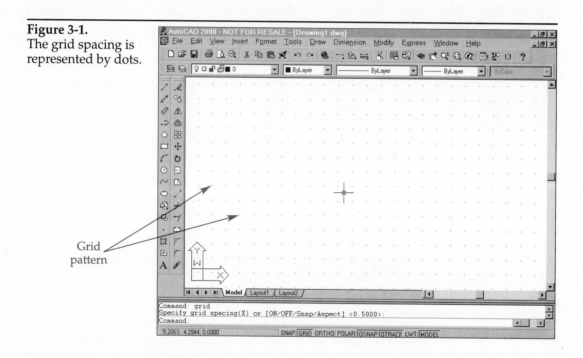

Grid pattern

Figure 3-2.
Grid setting can be made in the **Snap and Grid** tab of the **Drafting Settings** dialog box.

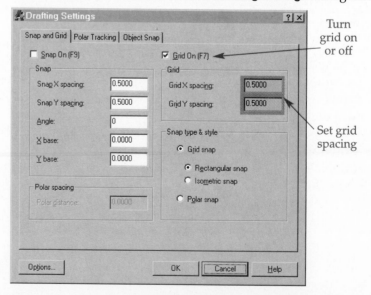

Turn grid on or off

Set grid spacing

AutoCAD and its Applications—Basics

The grid can be turned on (displayed) or off (not displayed) by selecting the **Grid On** check box. Other methods for turning the grid on and off include using the **ON** and **OFF** options of the **GRID** command, picking the **GRID** button on the status bar, using the [Ctrl]+[G] key combination, pressing the [F7] function key, or using pick button 6.

The grid spacing can be set in the **Grid** area of the dialog box. You can also set the grid spacing using the **GRID** command. Entering GRID at the Command: prompt provides the following prompt:

> Command: **GRID**↵
> Specify grid spacing(X) or [ON/OFF/Snap/Aspect] <*current*>: **.25**↵

You can press [Enter] to accept the default spacing value shown in brackets, or enter a new value as shown. If the grid spacing you enter is too close to display on the screen, you get the "Grid too dense to display" message. In this case, a larger grid spacing is required.

Setting a Different Horizontal and Vertical Grid

To set different values for horizontal and vertical grid spacing, enter the appropriate values in the **Grid X spacing:** and **Grid Y spacing:** text boxes in the **Drafting Settings** dialog box. This can also be done using the **GRID** command. Type A (for the **Aspect** option) to set different values for the horizontal and vertical grid spacing. For example, suppose you want a horizontal spacing of 1 and a vertical spacing of .5. Enter the following:

> Command: **GRID**↵
> Specify grid spacing(X) or [ON/OFF/Snap/Aspect] <0.2500>: **A**↵
> Specify the horizontal spacing(X) <0.2500>: **1**↵
> Specify the vertical spacing(Y) <0.2500>: **.5**↵

This **Aspect** option provides the grid spacing shown in Figure 3-3.

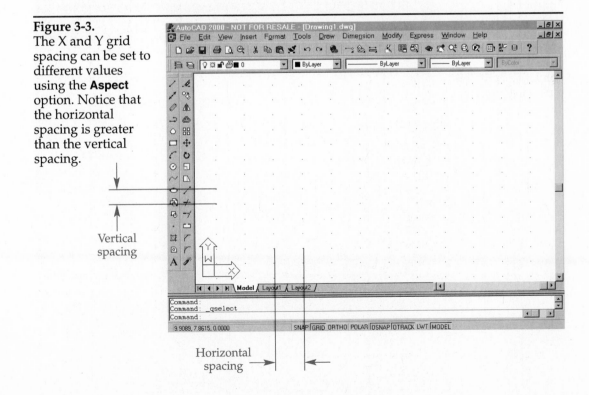

Figure 3-3.
The X and Y grid spacing can be set to different values using the **Aspect** option. Notice that the horizontal spacing is greater than the vertical spacing.

INTRODUCTION TO DRAWING LINES

This section gives a brief introduction to drawing lines so you can get started with AutoCAD drawing commands. You will see how the different drawing setup options affect the speed and accuracy of drawing lines. There are several ways to use the **LINE** command, but for now only one method is discussed. The **LINE** command is explained in detail in Chapter 4 of this text. Type L or LINE at the Command: prompt.

> Command: **L** *or* **LINE**↵
> Specify first point: *(move the screen cursor to any position on the screen and pick that point)*
> Specify next point or [Undo]: *(move the screen cursor to another location and pick a point)*

Notice that a line has been drawn between the two points. A "rubber band" line is attached to the last point selected and the cursor. The "rubber band" shows where the line will be drawn if you pick the current cursor location. The next prompt is:

> Specify next point or [Undo]: *(pick the next point)*

You can continue to draw connected lines until you press the [Enter] key or space bar to exit the **LINE** command. The following command sequence is displayed in Figure 3-4.

> Command: **L** *or* **LINE**↵
> Specify first point: *(pick Point 1)*
> Specify next point or [Undo]: *(pick Point 2)*
> Specify next point or [Undo]: *(pick Point 3)*
> Specify next point or [Close/Undo]: *(pick Point 4)*
> Specify next point or [Close/Undo]: ↵
> Command: *(meaning AutoCAD is ready for a new command)*

Figure 3-4.
Using the **LINE** command. Select the points in order from Point 1 to Point 4 to draw this three-segment line.

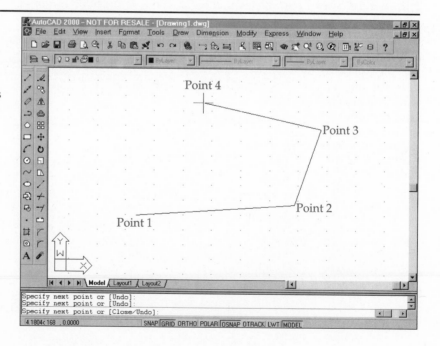

CANCELING A COMMAND

If you press the wrong key or misspell a word when entering a command or answering a prompt, use the [Backspace] key to correct the error. This only works if you notice your mistake *before* the [Enter] key is pressed. If you do enter an incorrect option or command, AutoCAD usually responds with an error message. You are then given another chance to enter the correct information or return to the Command: prompt. If you are not sure what has happened, reading the error message should tell you what you need to know.

Previous messages displayed in the floating command window are not always visible. Press the function key [F2] to display AutoCAD's text screen. This allows you to read the entire message. Also, you will be able to review the commands and options you entered. This may help you better understand what happened. You can press the [F2] key again to return to the graphics screen, or use your cursor to pick any visible portion of the graphics screen to make it current again.

It is often necessary to stop the currently active command and return to AutoCAD's Command: prompt to either reenter a command or use another command. This can occur if an incorrect entry is made and you need to restart the command using the correct method, or even if you simply decide to do something different. Some commands, such as the **LINE** command, can be discontinued by pressing the [Enter] key or the space bar. This exits the command and returns to the Command: prompt, where AutoCAD awaits a new command entry. However, there are many situations where this does not work. One example of this is using the **Window** option of the **ZOOM** command. Pressing [Enter] does not discontinue the command. In this case, you must cancel the command. (The **ZOOM** command is discussed in detail in Chapter 9.)

You can cancel any active command or abort any data entry and return to the Command: prompt by pressing the [Esc] key. This key is usually located in the upper-left corner of your keyboard. It may be necessary to press the [Esc] key twice to completely cancel certain commands. Many multibutton digitizer pucks use button number 3 to cancel a command. Additionally, most of the toolbar buttons and pull-down menu options automatically cancel any currently active command before entering the new command. So, in a case where you wish to abort the current command and start a new one, simply pick the appropriate pull-down menu option or toolbar button.

PROFESSIONAL TIP

Some old versions of AutoCAD use the keystroke combination of [Ctrl]+[C] to cancel an operation. By default, [Ctrl]+[C] activates the COPYCLIP command in AutoCAD 2000. If you would like to use [Ctrl]+[C] to cancel a command, you can take the check mark out of the **Windows standard accelerator keys** option in the **User Preferences** tab of the **Options** dialog box. The **Options** dialog box can be accessed by selecting **Options...** from the **Tools** pull-down menu.

❏ Start AutoCAD and use one of the startup options discussed in Chapter 2.
❏ Set the grid spacing at .5.
❏ Use the **LINE** command to draw two sets of four connected line segments.
❏ Turn off the grid and draw two sets of three connected line segments. Notice how having the grid on provides some guidance for locating points.
❏ Enter the **LINE** command and then cancel the command before picking a point.
❏ Enter the **LINE** command, pick the first point, and then cancel the command.
❏ Enter the **LINE** command, pick the first and second points, and then cancel the command.
❏ Type SAVE at the Command: prompt. When the **Save Drawing As** dialog box appears, type EX3-1 in the **File name:** box to save this exercise on your hard disk. Press [Enter] or pick the **Save** button.
❏ If you want to exit AutoCAD, select **Exit** from the **File** pull-down menu.

SETTING INCREMENTS FOR CURSOR MOVEMENT

AutoCAD User's Guide **3**

When you move your pointing device, the cursor crosshairs move freely on the screen. Sometimes it is hard to place a point accurately. You can set up an invisible grid that allows the cursor to move only in exact increments. This is called the *snap grid* or *snap resolution*. The snap grid is different than using the **GRID** command. The snap grid controls the movement of the crosshairs. The grid discussed in the previous section is only a visual guide. However, the snap grid and grid settings can be used together. The AutoCAD defaults provide the same settings for both.

Properly setting the snap grid can greatly increase your drawing speed and accuracy. The snap grid spacing can be set in the **Snap and Grid** tab of the **Drafting Settings** dialog box. See Figure 3-5. Enter the snap spacing values in the **Snap X spacing:** and **Snap Y spacing:** text boxes.

The **SNAP** command can also be used to set the invisible snap grid. Entering SNAP gives you the following prompt:

Command: **SNAP**↵
Specify snap spacing or [ON/OFF/Aspect/Rotate/Style/Type] <*current*>:

Figure 3-5.
Snap grid settings can be made in the **Snap and Grid** tab of the **Drafting Settings** dialog box.

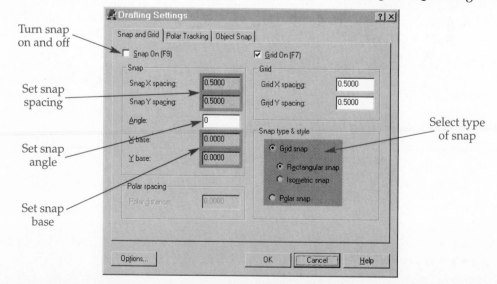

Pressing [Enter] accepts the value shown in brackets. The value that you set remains the same until changed.

The **OFF** option turns snap off, but the same snap spacing is again in effect when you turn snap back on. The snap spacing can be turned on or off at any time by clicking the **SNAP** button on the status bar, pressing [Ctrl]+[B], pressing function key [F9], deselecting the **Snap On (F9)** check box in the **Drafting Settings** dialog box, or pressing puck button 4.

Different Horizontal and Vertical Snap Grid Units

The snap grid is usually set up with equal horizontal and vertical snap grid units. However, it is possible to set different horizontal and vertical snap grid units. To do this, enter different values in the **Snap X spacing:** and **Snap Y spacing:** text boxes in the **Drafting Settings** dialog box. This can also be done using the **Aspect** option of the **SNAP** command:

    Command: **SNAP**↵
    Specify snap spacing or [ON/OFF/Aspect/Rotate/Style/Type] <0.5000>: **A**↵
    Specify horizontal spacing <0.5000>: **.5**↵
    Specify vertical spacing <0.5000>: **.25**↵

PROFESSIONAL TIP
The most effective use of the Snap mode quite often comes from setting an equal X and Y spacing to the lowest, or near lowest, increment of the majority of the feature dimensions. For example, this might be .0625 units in a mechanical drawing or 6″ in an architectural application. If many horizontal features conform to one increment and vertical features to another, then a corresponding snap grid can be set up using different X and Y values.

Rotating the Snap Grid

AutoCAD User's Guide 7

The normal snap grid pattern consists of horizontal rows and vertical columns. However, another option is to rotate the snap grid. This technique is helpful when drawing an auxiliary view at an angle to other views of the drawing. When the snap grid is rotated, you are given the option of setting a new base point. The base point is the pivot that the snap grid is rotated around. The base point of a normal snap grid is the lower-left corner. It may be more convenient to set the base point at the location where you will begin the view.

Using the **Drafting Settings** dialog box, enter the snap angle in the **Angle:** text box and the new base point in the **X base:** and **Y base:** text boxes. These values can also be set using the **Rotate** option of the **SNAP** command as follows:

    Command: **SNAP**↵
    Specify snap spacing or [ON/OFF/Aspect/Rotate/Style/Type] <A>: **R**↵
    Specify base point <0.0000,0.0000>:*(press* [Enter], *type a new coordinate value,*
       or pick a new base point)
    Specify rotation angle <0>: **45**↵

The grid automatically rotates counterclockwise about the base point when a positive rotation angle is given, and clockwise when a negative rotation angle is given. Figure 3-6 shows the relationship between the regular and rotated snap grids. Remember, the snap grid is invisible.

Figure 3-6.
The snap grid is usually horizontal rows and vertical columns. However, it can be rotated to help you draw. Notice the angle of the crosshairs. (The snap grid is invisible, but represented here by dots.)

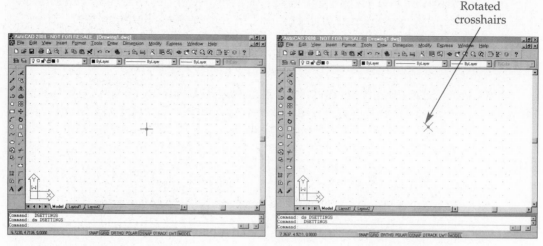

Default Snap Grid   Rotated Snap Grid

Setting the Snap Type and Style

The **Snap type & style** area of the **Drafting Settings** dialog box allows you to select one of two types of snap grids: grid snap or polar snap. Polar snap allows you to snap to precise distances along alignment paths when using polar tracking. Polar tracking is discussed in Chapter 6. Grid snap has two styles: rectangular and isometric. Rectangular is the standard style. The isometric pattern is useful when doing isometric drawings (discussed in Chapter 26). Select the radio button(s) for the snap type and style you desire and pick the **OK** button.

You can also use the **Type** and **Style** options of the **SNAP** command to change these settings. Use the **Type** option to select polar or grid snap and use the **Style** option to select standard (rectangular) or isometric.

Setting the Grid Spacing Relative to the Snap Spacing

The visible grid can be set to coincide with the invisible snap grid by choosing the **Snap** option after entering the **GRID** command. You can also set the dot spacing as a multiple of the snap units by entering the number of snap units between grid points. For example, 2X places grid points at every other snap unit. If the snap spacing is .25 and you specify 2X at the Grid spacing: prompt, the grid spacing will be .5 units.

    Command: **GRID**↵
    Specify grid spacing(X) or [ON/OFF/Snap/Aspect] <0.5000>: **2X**↵

❏ Start AutoCAD and use one of the startup options discussed in Chapter 2.
❏ Set the units to decimal, with precision two digits to the right of the decimal point.
❏ Set the angular measure to decimal, one fractional place, 0 direction, and counterclockwise.
❏ Set the limits to an A-size (12 x 9) sheet (lower-left corner: 0,0; upper-right corner: 12,9).
❏ Set the grid spacing to .5.
❏ Set the snap spacing to .25.
❏ Use the **LINE** command to draw two sets of four connected line segments.
❏ Turn Snap mode off and draw two sets of three connected line segments. Notice that when the Snap mode is activated, the cursor "jumps" exactly at .25 intervals.
❏ Type SAVE at the Command: prompt. Type EX3-2 in the **File name:** box. Pick the **Save** button or press the [Enter] key.
❏ If you want to exit AutoCAD, select **Exit** from the **File** pull-down menu.

PROFESSIONAL TIP  The Snap and Grid modes may be set at different values to complement each other. For example, the grid may be set at .5 and the snap at .25. With this type of format, each plays a separate role in assisting drawing layout. This may also keep the grid from being too dense. You can quickly change these values at any time to have them best assist you.

Factors to Consider When Setting Drawing Aids

The following factors will influence drawing aid settings:

✓ **The drawing units.** If the units are decimal inches, set the grid and snap values to standard decimal increments such as .0625, .125, .25, .5, and 1 or .05, .1, .2, .5, and 1. For architectural units, use 1, 6, and 12 inches, or 1, 2, 4, 5, and 10-foot increments.

✓ **The drawing size.** A very large drawing might have a 1.00 grid spacing, while a small drawing may use a .5 spacing or less.

✓ **Value of the smallest dimension.** If the smallest dimension is .125, then an appropriate snap value would be .125, with a grid spacing of .25.

✓ **Changing settings.** You can change the snap and grid values at any time without changing the location of points or lines already drawn. This should be done when larger or smaller values would assist you with a certain part of the drawing. For example, suppose a few of the dimensions are in .0625 multiples, but the rest of the dimensions are .250 multiples. Change the snap spacing from .250 to .0625 when laying out the smaller dimensions.

✓ **Always prepare a sketch before starting a drawing.** Use the visible grid to help you place views and lay out the entire drawing.

✓ **Be efficient.** Use whatever method works best and fastest when setting or changing the drawing aids.

❏ Start AutoCAD and use one of the startup options discussed in Chapter 2.
❏ Set decimal units precision three digits to the right of the decimal point.
❏ Set the angular measure to degrees/minutes/seconds, one fractional place, and default values for the rest of the options.
❏ Set the limits to 17,11 (lower-left corner at 0,0 and upper-right corner at 17,11).
❏ Zoom the screen using the **ZOOM All** option. To do this, type ZOOM at the Command: prompt, then enter A for the **ALL** option.
❏ Set the grid spacing at .5 units.
❏ Set the snap spacing at .25 units.
❏ Use the **LINE** command to draw two sets of eight connected line segments.
❏ Change the snap value to .125 and the grid spacing to .25. Draw several more lines and see what happens.
❏ Change the snap value to .5 and the grid spacing to 1. Draw several more lines and observe the results.
❏ Save the drawing as EX3-3.
❏ If you want to exit AutoCAD, select **Exit** from the **File** pull-down menu.

AutoCAD
User's
Guide   **2**

CREATING AND USING DRAWING TEMPLATES

Depending on the types of drawing projects you work with, there are many settings that are the same from one drawing to the next. This can include snap and grid settings, as well as many others. With most companies, standard borders and title blocks are used in all drawings. To save drawing setup time, templates are used.

The word *template* is defined as a model on which something is based. In AutoCAD, a *drawing template* is a model upon which other drawings are based. Templates were introduced in Chapter 2 with regard to starting an AutoCAD drawing. This discussion is a review of creating and using drawing templates. Depending on your specific needs, you can select from a number of predefined templates, or create your own.

When you use a template, all the settings saved in the template are applied to your new drawing. The template file can supply any information that is normally saved in a drawing file, including settings and drawing objects. Many of the templates already have standard borders and title blocks, which are then created in your new drawing. The template drawing contains the setup options that you choose plus any snap and grid setting that you use. As you continue through this text, you can add items to your templates, such as layer settings, company information, logos, text styles, dimension styles, and bills of material. All these settings are designed to your company or school specifications and based on your drawing applications.

Using an Existing AutoCAD Drawing Template

For 2000i Users...

To use a template to create a new drawing from the **AutoCAD Today** window, pick the **Template** option in the **Create Drawings** tab. Refer to *Creating Drawings* on page 963 for details.

To use a template to create a new drawing, select the **Use a Template** button in the **Startup** or **Create New Drawing** dialog box. The **Create New Drawing** dialog box is shown in Figure 3-7.

A number of predefined templates are available in the **Select a Template:** list box. When you highlight a template name, a brief description is provided in the **Template Description** area. These templates are based on different standards, including ANSI, ISO, DIN, and JIS. Two "normal" templates are provided: acad.dwt for English units and acadiso.dwt for metric units. A generic template and an architectural template are also listed. If you need to access an existing template that is not listed, pick the **Browse...** button to display the **Select Template** dialog box. This dialog box allows you to look in other directory folders to find a template.

Figure 3-7.
Templates make starting a new drawing more efficient. Pick the **Use a Template** button to list existing templates.

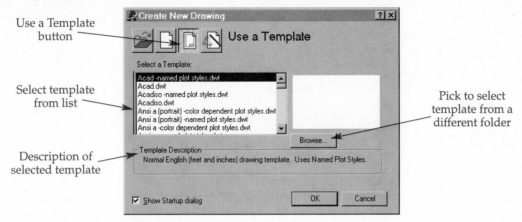

Use a Template button

Select template from list

Description of selected template

Pick to select template from a different folder

Creating Your Own Templates

If none of the predefined templates meet your needs, you can create and save your own custom templates. AutoCAD allows you to save *any* drawing as a template. A drawing template should be developed whenever a number of drawing applications require the same setup procedure. The template then allows the setup to be applied to any number of future drawings. Creating templates increases drafting productivity by decreasing setup requirements.

Some existing AutoCAD templates may be close to what you need and may simply need fine tuning. If the existing AutoCAD templates do not fit your needs, you may want to use a wizard to establish basic settings or even start from scratch. Some basic parameters that can be specified in a drawing template include units, limits, snap, and grid. You can also draw your own border and title block. Review Chapter 2 for a complete discussion about setting up a drawing with a wizard or by scratch.

As you learn more about working with AutoCAD, you will find many other settings that can be included in your drawing templates. When you have everything in the template that is needed, it is ready to save. Use the **SAVEAS** command to save a drawing template. The **SAVEAS** command is accessed by picking **Save As...** from the **File** pull-down menu, or by typing SAVEAS at the Command: prompt. This command displays the **Save Drawing As** dialog box, as shown in Figure 3-8. To specify that the drawing is to be saved as a drawing template, pick AutoCAD Drawing Template File(*.dwt) from the **Save as Type:** drop-down list. The file list window then shows all the drawing templates currently found in the Template folder. You can store custom templates in another location, but it is recommended that they be stored in the Template folder. This folder is displayed by default when the **Use a Template** option is selected in the **Create New Drawing** or **Startup** dialog box.

After specifying the name and location for the new template file, pick the **Save** button in the **Save Drawing As** dialog box. The **Template Description** dialog box is now displayed, as shown in Figure 3-9. Use the **Description** area to enter a brief description of the template file you are saving. You can enter up to 200 characters, but a brief description usually works best. Under the **Measurement** drop-down list, specify whether the units used in the template are English or metric and then pick the **OK** button.

The template name should relate to the template, such as Mechanical A size, for a mechanical drawing on an A-size sheet. The template might be named for the drawing application, such as Architectural floor plans. The template name might be as

For 2000i Users...

All file selection dialog boxes, including the **Save Drawing As** dialog box, have been updated for AutoCAD 2000i. The features of the updated **Save Drawing As** dialog box are outlined in *Select File Dialog Box* on page 966.

Figure 3-8.
Saving a template.

Folder where template will be saved

Enter name for template

Change type to save as template

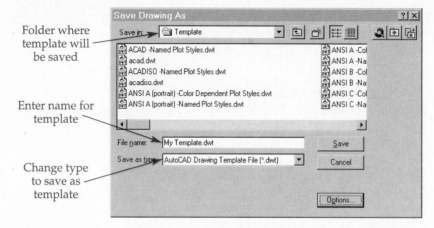

Figure 3-9.
Enter a description of the new template in the **Template Description** dialog box.

Enter description for template

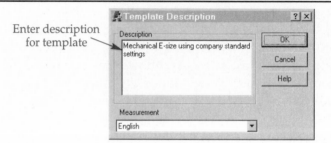

simple as Template 1. The name should be written in a reference manual along with documentation about what is included in the template. This provides future reference for you and other users. The template drawing you create is saved for you to open and use whenever it is needed.

Now, you can exit AutoCAD and when you start up again, the template you created is ready for you to use for preparing a new drawing.

PROFESSIONAL TIP

Generalized templates that set the units, limits, snap, and grid to specifications are useful, but keep in mind that you can create any number of drawing templates. Templates that contain more detailed settings can dramatically increase drafting productivity. As you refine your setup procedure, you can revise the template files. When using the **SAVE** command, you can save a new template over an existing one, or use the **SAVEAS** command to save a new template from an existing one.

EXERCISE 3-4

❑ Start AutoCAD to access the **Startup** dialog box, or pick **New...** from the **File** pull-down menu to open the **Create New Drawing** dialog box.

❑ Pick **Use a Template**.

❑ Create one of the following templates based on the type of drawing that you prefer:

> 1. Name: MECHANICAL-IN-A
> Use: Mechanical drawings in inches on A-size sheet.
> Template: Ansi a -color dependent plot styles.dwt
> Grid = .25
> Snap = .125
>
> 2. Name: MECHANICAL-IN-B
> Use: Mechanical drawings in inches on B-size sheet.
> Template: Ansi b -color dependent plot styles.dwt
> Grid = .5
> Snap = .25
>
> 3. Name: MECHANICAL-MM-A3
> Use: Mechanical drawings in metric on A3-size sheet.
> Template: Iso a3 -color dependent plot styles.dwt
> Grid = 10
> Snap = 5
>
> 4. Name: MECHANICAL-MM-A2
> Use: Mechanical drawings in metric on A2-size sheet.
> Template: Iso a2 -color dependent plot styles.dwt
> Grid = 20
> Snap = 10
>
> 5. Name: ARCHITECTURAL-D
> Use: Architectural drawings on D-size sheet.
> Template: Architectural, english units - color dependent plot styles.dwt
> Grid = 24
> Snap = 6

❑ Save the drawing template as explained in the previous discussion.

❑ Record the information about your template in a notebook.

❑ Create another new drawing template based on one of the previous options, but this time, design the template without a border and title block by using a setup wizard.

❑ Save the drawing template as explained in the previous discussion.

❑ Record the information about your template in a notebook.

SAVING DRAWINGS

Whether you start a new drawing from scratch or use a template, you need to assign a name for the new drawing and save it. The following discussion provides you with detailed information about saving and quitting a drawing.

When saving drawing files using either the **SAVE** or **SAVEAS** command, you can use a dialog box or type everything at the Command: prompt. Dialog boxes are controlled by the **FILEDIA** system variable. A *system variable* is a setting that lets you change the way AutoCAD works. These variables are remembered by AutoCAD and remain in effect until you change them again.

There are two **FILEDIA** system variable settings. The default is 1, which displays dialog boxes at the appropriate times. When **FILEDIA** is set to 0, dialog boxes do not appear. You must then type the desired information at the prompt line. You can quickly change the **FILEDIA** system variable as follows:

    Command: **FILEDIA**↵
    Enter new value for FILEDIA <1>: **0**↵

In the following discussion, the **FILEDIA** variable is set to 1, unless otherwise specified.

Naming Drawings

Drawing names may be chosen to identify a product by name and number, for example, VICE-101, FLOORPLAN, or 6DT1005. Your school or company probably has a drawing numbering system that you can use. These drawing names should be recorded in a part numbering or drawing name log. This helps serve as a valuable reference long after you forget what the drawings contained.

It is important to set up a system that allows you to determine the content of a drawing by the drawing name. Although it is possible to give a drawing file an extended name, such as Details for Top Half of Compressor Housing for ACME, Inc., Part Number 4011A, Revision Level C, this is normally not a practical way of sorting drawing information. Drawing titles should be standardized and may be most effective when making a clear and concise reference to the project, part number, process, sheet number, and revision level.

When a standardized naming system exists, a shorter name like ACME.4011A.C provides all the necessary information. If additional information is desirable for the easier recognition, it can be added to the base name, for example: ACME 4011 A.C Compressor Housing.Top.Casting Details. Always record drawing names and provide information related to the drawings.

The following rules and restrictions apply to naming all files, including AutoCAD drawings:

- A maximum of 256 characters can be used.
- Alphabetical and numeric characters and spaces, along with most punctuation symbols can be used.
- The following characters cannot be used: quotation mark ("), asterisk (*), question mark (?), forward slash (/) and backslash (\).

Saving Your Work

You must save your drawing periodically to protect your work by writing the existing status of your drawing to disk while remaining in the graphics window. While working in the graphics window, you should save your drawing every 10 to 15 minutes. This is very important! If there is a power failure, a severe editing error, or other problems, all the work saved prior to the problem will be usable. If you save only once an hour, a power failure could result in an hour of lost work. Saving your drawing every 10 to 15 minutes results in less lost work if a problem occurs.

There are three commands that allow you to directly save your work: **QSAVE**, **SAVEAS**, and **SAVE**. Also, any command or option that ends the AutoCAD session provides a warning that asks if you want to save changes to the drawing. This gives you a final option to either save or not save changes to the drawing.

Using the **QSAVE** Command

QSAVE
[Ctrl]+[S]

File
↳ Save

Standard
toolbar

Save

Of the three available saving commands, the most frequently used is the **QSAVE** command. **QSAVE** stands for *quick save*. The **QSAVE** command is accessed by picking the **Save** button from the **Standard** toolbar, picking the **Save** option from the **File** pull-down menu, typing QSAVE at the Command: prompt, or by pressing [Ctrl]+[S].

The **QSAVE** command response depends on whether the drawing already has a name. If the current drawing has a name, the **QSAVE** command updates the file based

AutoCAD and its Applications—Basics

on the current state of the drawing. In this situation, **QSAVE** issues no prompts and displays no messages.

If the current drawing has not yet been named, the **QSAVE** command displays the **Save Drawing As** dialog box, Figure 3-10. You must complete three steps in order to save your file:

1. Select the folder in which the file is to be saved.
2. Select the type of file to save, such as drawing (.dwg) or template (.dwt).
3. Enter a name for the file.

When selecting the folder in which the file will be stored, first select the disk drive from the **Save in:** drop-down list. Using this option, you can save to any available hard disk, floppy disk, or network drive. To move upward from the current folder, pick the **Up One Level** button. To create a new folder in the current location, pick the **Create New Folder** button and type the name for the folder.

The file listing area shows any folders or other drawing files found in the current folder. The default display style for the file dialog box is **List**. Pick the **Details** button to display additional file information, such as when it was last modified, file size, and file type. If some of the information is hidden, use the horizontal scroll bar to see more information. When the **Details** view is active, picking the **Name** label sorts the listing alphabetically in ascending order. Pick it again to change to a descending order. The **Size**, **Type**, **Modified**, and **Attributes** labels can also be used this way to sort the listing in the format identified by the title of the label.

The **Search the Web** button displays the **Browse the Web** dialog box, from which you can store AutoCAD files on the Internet. See *AutoCAD and its Applications—Advanced* for information on using AutoCAD with the Internet.

To go to your Favorites folder, pick the **Look in Favorites** button. By picking the **Add to Favorites** button, AutoCAD creates a shortcut to the selected file or folder and adds that shortcut to your system's Favorites folder.

The **Save as type:** drop-down list offers options to save the drawing file in alternate formats. For most applications, this should be set to AutoCAD 2000 Drawing (*.dwg) when saving drawings. When saving a template file, this is set as AutoCAD Drawing Template File (*.dwt).

If the drawing has not yet been named, the name Drawing1 appears in the **File name:** text box. Change this to the desired drawing name. You do not need to include the .dwg extension.

For 2000i Users...

All file selection dialog boxes, including the **Save Drawing As** dialog box, have been updated for AutoCAD 2000i. The features of the updated **Save Drawing As** dialog box are outlined in *Select File Dialog Box* on page 966.

Figure 3-10.
The **Save Drawing As** dialog box.

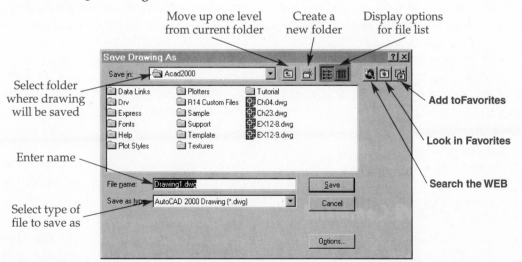

Once you have specified the correct location and file name, pick the **Save** button to save the drawing file. Keep in mind that you can either pick the **Save** button or you can just press the [Enter] key to activate the **Save** button and save the drawing.

Using the **SAVEAS** Command

The **SAVEAS** command is used in the following situations:
- When the current drawing already has a name and you need to save it under a different name.
- When you need to save the current drawing in an alternate format, such as a drawing file for AutoCAD Release 14, an AutoCAD LT drawing, or a drawing template file.
- When you open one of your drawing template files and create a drawing. This leaves the drawing template unchanged and ready to use for other drawings.

SAVEAS

File
↪ Save As...

The **SAVEAS** command is accessed by picking **Save As...** from the **File** pull-down menu or by typing SAVEAS at the Command: prompt. This command always displays the **Save Drawing As** dialog box. If the current drawing has already been saved, the current name and location are displayed. Confirm that the **Save in:** box displays the current drive and directory folder you want, and the **Save as type:** box displays the desired file type. Type the new drawing name in the **File name:** box and pick the **Save** button.

Using the **SAVE** Command

The third command provided for directly saving a drawing is the **SAVE** command. The **SAVE** command is not commonly used and is only available at the command line by typing SAVE. The **SAVE** command displays the **Save Drawing As** dialog box, regardless of whether or not the drawing has been previously saved. Because of this, the **QSAVE** command is better for saving a drawing in progress, and the **SAVEAS** command is better for saving a drawing with a new name or location.

If you try to save the current drawing using the same name and location as another drawing file, AutoCAD issues a warning message in an alert box and allows you to cancel the operation or replace the current drawing with the one you are working on. If you actually need to replace the existing file, pick the **Yes** button to overwrite the file with the information in the current drawing. If you do not wish to overwrite the file pick the **No** button to return to the **Save Drawing As** dialog box. To cancel the operation pick the **Cancel** button. Be very careful—if you pick the **Yes** button, the current drawing replaces the other drawing.

NOTE When saving a drawing to a different name, the **SAVE** command saves the drawing file with a different name but leaves you in the current drawing. The **SAVEAS** command discards all changes to the original drawing file up to the last save. Before using the **SAVEAS** command, close the drawing file and then reopen it to make sure that all changes remain.

Saving Your Work Automatically

AutoCAD provides you with an automatic work-saving tool called automatic save (autosave). All you need to do is enter the amount of time (in minutes) between saves in the **Open and Save** tab of the **Options** dialog box. This dialog box can be accessed by selecting **Options…** from the **Tools** pull-down menu. The value is entered in the **Minutes between saves** text box in the **File Safety Precautions** area. See Figure 3-11, which shows a setting of 15 minutes.

The autosave timer starts as soon as a change is made to the drawing. The timer is reset when the **SAVE**, **QSAVE**, or **SAVEAS** command is used.

Figure 3-11.
Use the **Open and Save** tab in the **Options** dialog box to set the autosave timer value.

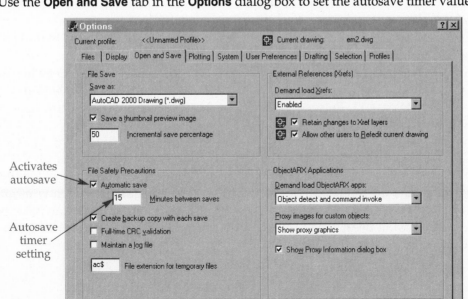

The drawing is saved when the first command is given after the autosave timer has been reached. For example, if you set the timer to 15, work for 14 minutes, and then let the computer remain idle for 5 minutes, an automatic save is not executed until the 19 minute interval, when you perform a command. Therefore, be sure to manually save your drawing if you plan to be away from your computer for an extended period of time.

The autosave drawing is always saved with the name of *DrawingName_n_n_nnnn*.sv$. If you need to use the autosaved file, it can be renamed with a .dwg file extension using the Windows Explorer. Refer to Chapter 14 for more information on the Windows Explorer.

PROFESSIONAL TIP

While an automatic save is a safeguard, it is inconvenient to rename the *DrawingName_n_n_nnnn*.sv$ file. Use the **QSAVE** command to continually save work in progress. A quick shortcut to the **QSAVE** command is the [Ctrl]+[S] key combination.

Where to Save the Drawing

As discussed earlier in this chapter, the first step when saving a drawing is to determine where the file should be saved. While your assignments should be saved in a file on the hard drive, you can save to a floppy disk for storage or transport to a remote system. The term *remote system* refers to a system that cannot be reached through a local network or an Internet connection.

Unless otherwise specified by your instructor or CAD manager, it is best to do your assignment on the hard drive and then save to a floppy disk. In fact, save your work to two floppy disks so you have a backup in case something happens to one disk. After you save your work to a floppy disk and quit the drawing session, you will need to transfer the previous work from the floppy disk to the hard disk.

Saving AutoCAD 2000 Drawings as Older Releases

Your AutoCAD 2000 drawings can be saved in Release 13 and Release 14 formats. This allows you to send AutoCAD 2000 drawings to businesses where older releases of AutoCAD are being used. This is also useful if you use AutoCAD 2000 at work or school and have Release 13 or 14 at home.

For 2000i Users...

Files saved in AutoCAD 2000 and AutoCAD 2000i are 100% compatible—a file saved in either version can be opened in the other.

To save as an older release, use the **SAVEAS** command. The **Save Drawing As** dialog box appears. Using the **Save as type:** drop-down list, indicate whether you need to save as a Release 13, Release 14, or AutoCAD LT drawing by selecting one of the following options:

AutoCAD R14/LT 98/LT 97 Drawing (*.dwg)
AutoCAD R13/LT 95 Drawing (*.dwg)

Next, specify the file name and location as previously discussed. When you save a version of a drawing in an earlier format, be sure to give it a different name than the AutoCAD 2000 version uses. This prevents you from accidentally overwriting your working drawing with the older format.

Saving AutoCAD 2000 Drawings in a DXF format

Your AutoCAD 2000 drawings can be saved in Release 12, Release 13, Release 14, and AutoCAD 2000 DXF formats. The DXF (drawing interchange file) format is used by AutoCAD users who may need to exchange files with other programs or import other software files into AutoCAD. The use of DXF files is explained fully in Chapter 14. This format allows you to send DXF drawings to businesses where older releases of AutoCAD are being used, or if a business requires a DXF formatted file.

To save as a DXF format, use the **SAVEAS** command. The **Save Drawing As** dialog box appears. Using the **Save as type:** drop-down list, select from the following options:

> AutoCAD 2000 DXF (*.dxf)
> AutoCAD R14/LT 98/LT 97 DXF (*.dxf)
> AutoCAD R13/LT 95 DXF (*.dxf)
> AutoCAD R12/LT 2 DXF (*.dxf)

Next, specify the file name and location as previously discussed. When you save a version of a drawing in an DXF format, be sure to give it a different name than the AutoCAD 2000 drawing file version uses. This prevents you from accidentally over-writing your working drawing with the DXF format. To find out more on DXF formats and their uses, see Chapter 14.

EXERCISE 3-5

❏ Start AutoCAD and use the template you developed in Exercise 3-4.
❏ Use the **LINE** command to draw a simple object of your own design.
❏ Use the **SAVEAS** command to save the drawing with the name EX3-5.
❏ Draw another simple object of your own design.
❏ Use the **QSAVE** command.
❏ Draw another object and use the **QSAVE** command again.
❏ Put a floppy disk in the 3 ½″ disk drive and use the **SAVEAS** command to save your drawing to the floppy disk.

OPENING EXISTING DRAWINGS

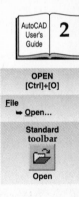

AutoCAD User's Guide 2

OPEN [Ctrl]+[O]

File
↳ **Open...**

Standard toolbar

Open

An existing drawing is one that has been previously saved. You can easily access any existing drawing with the **OPEN** command. To use the **OPEN** command, pick the **Open** button on the **Standard** toolbar, pick **Open...** from the **File** pull-down menu, press the [Ctrl]+[O] key combination, or type OPEN at the Command: prompt. If you are just starting AutoCAD, pick the **Open a Drawing** button in the **Startup** dialog box and click on the **Browse...** button. The **Select File** dialog box appears, Figure 3-12.

The **Select File** dialog box contains folder and file lists, just as in the **Save Drawing As** dialog box. Double-click on a file folder to open it and then double-click on the desired file to open it. The Acad2000\Sample folder is open with the sample drawings displayed in Figure 3-12. You can also type the file name in the **File Name:** text box and pick the **Open** button (or press [Enter]) to open the file.

When you pick an existing drawing that was created in AutoCAD 2000, Release 14, or Release 13, a picture of the drawing is displayed in the **Preview** image tile. This is an easy way for you to get a quick look at the drawing without loading the files into the AutoCAD graphics editor. You can view each drawing until you find the one you want.

After picking a drawing file name to highlight it, you can quickly highlight another drawing in the list by using the keyboard arrow keys. Use the up and down arrow keys to move vertically between files and use the left and right arrow keys to move horizontally. This enables you to scan through the drawing previews very quickly.

For 2000i Users...

The **Select File** dialog box has been updated for AutoCAD 2000i. Refer to **Select File** Dialog Box on page 966 for details.

Figure 3-12.

The **Select File** dialog box is used to select a drawing to open. Notice the 1st floor drawing has been selected from the file list box and appears in the **File Name:** text box.

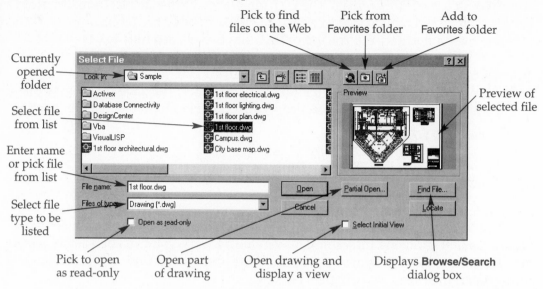

An easy way to become familiar with the **Preview** image tile feature is to look at the sample drawings that come with AutoCAD. To do the following exercise, the sample drawings must have been loaded during the AutoCAD installation process.

EXERCISE 3-6

❏ Start AutoCAD and use the setup option of your choice.
❏ Pick **Open...** from the **File** pull-down menu to access the **Select File** dialog box.
❏ Double-click on the directory that contains AutoCAD 2000 drawings, such as Acad2000, if it is not already open.
❏ Double-click on Sample.
❏ The file list should display all the sample AutoCAD drawing files.
❏ Pick any sample drawing and look at the **Preview** image tile. Pick as many as you like to preview. Use the cursor keys on your keyboard to scroll through the available files. Use the scroll bar to move the list from left to right as needed to display hidden files.
❏ Pick the **Cancel** button.
❏ If you want to exit AutoCAD, select **Exit** from the **File** pull-down menu.

For 2000i Users...

In AutoCAD 2000i, the **Favorites** button is located in the Places List.

Using the Search the Web and Favorites Buttons

When you pick the **Search the Web** button, AutoCAD displays the **Browse the Web** dialog box, from which you can open AutoCAD files from the Internet. The **Browse the Web** dialog box is explained in more detail later in this chapter.

AutoCAD allows you to store and retrieve locations on your hard drive or network drive as your Favorites folder. A Favorites folder can be a folder that holds project files or files that are used continuously. The **Look in Favorites** button allows you to go to your Favorites folder. The **Add to Favorites** button allows you to create a shortcut to the selected file or folder and adds that shortcut to your system's Favorites folder.

Using Initial View and Read-Only

When the **Select Initial View** check box in the **Select File** dialog box is activated, you can select a named view to be displayed when you open the drawing. This feature is discussed in detail in Chapter 9, when you learn to establish different views of your drawing.

The **Open as read-only** check box will open the drawing as *read-only*. When this is active, any changes or modifications made to the drawing cannot be saved. In other words, the drawing can only be used for viewing purposes. This is one way to protect your drawing file from any changes made by an unauthorized user. You can also use this mode if you want to practice on your drawing without fear of altering it. If you make changes that you want to save, you can still use the **SAVEAS** command to save under a different file name.

Searching for Files

There may be instances when you need to edit an existing drawing file, but you cannot remember the drawing name or where the drawing resides on disk. A drawing file (or any other AutoCAD file type) may be located by its name, type, date created, or time created.

Pick the **Find File...** button in the **Select File** dialog box to display the **Browse/Search** dialog box. There are two sections to this dialog available by selecting the appropriate tab. When you are looking for a specific file, select the **Search** tab, as shown in Figure 3-13.

Set the **Search Pattern:** to look for the file you need. Either a complete file name can be specified or a partial name can be used with standard "wildcard" characters. For example, the default specification of *.dwg finds all files that have a .dwg file extension. The asterisk can be used alone, or after other characters. The file specification of floor*.dwg finds all drawing files that have the first five characters of floor. It would find floor_01.dwg, floor.dwg, and floorpln.dwg. Question marks can also be used to position wildcards in single character positions. For example, the specification fl??r.dwg would find floor.dwg and flyer.dwg, but not floor_01.dwg. Wildcard combinations can be used. For example, the specification fl??r*.dwg would find floor.dwg, flyer.dwg, floorpln.dwg, and floor_01.dwg.

The **File Types:** drop-down list displays the available options of file types for the current operation. Since you are opening a drawing, the only file types available are dwg, dwt, and dxf.

For 2000i Users...

The **Browse/Search** dialog box of AutoCAD 2000 has been replaced with the **Find:** dialog box in AutoCAD 2000i. To access this dialog box, pick the **Tools...** button and then **Find...** in the **Select File** dialog box. Refer to *Finding Files* on page 967.

Figure 3-13.
The **Browse/Search** dialog box. To search for a file, select the **Search** tab. Search parameters can include drives, folders, and file types, and can be limited by the date or time the files were created.

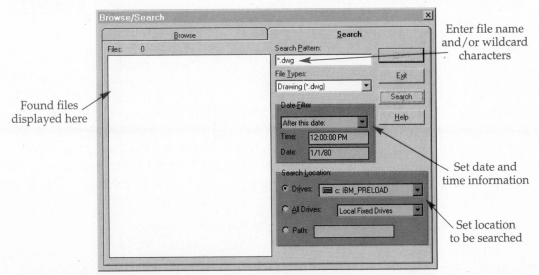

The **Date Filter** area can be used to limit the search to files created within a specific date range. Selecting the drop-down list allows you to specify whether the search should include only files last edited before or after the date specified below. Note that the format for specifying time and date must be as follows:

Date: mm/dd/yy
Time: hh:mm or hh:mm:ss

The **Search Location** area allows you to limit your search to specific drives or directory paths. First, select the appropriate radio button, then set the required specifications. For example, to limit your search to the contents of one disk drive, you must first select the **Drives:** radio button, then use the drop-down list to select the disk drive to search. Selecting the **All Drives:** drop-down list displays the options of searching only local fixed drives (hard disks) or searching all drives. Searching all drives will search all available hard and floppy disks, plus all available network drives.

If you wish to limit your search to specific directory paths, select the **Path:** radio button. For a single path, type your entry directly into the edit box. Finally, pick the **Search** button to begin the search. A dynamic display above the **Files:** window counts the number of files found matching the current search criteria, while the path names of the folders being searched are displayed below. The **Search** button changes to a **Stop Search** button, and can be pressed at any time to halt the search.

Once the search is complete, the found files and their locations are displayed in the **Files:** window. Only Release 13, Release 14, and AutoCAD 2000 drawing files are displayed graphically; files from earlier releases are shown only as a rectangle with an "X" shape and the directory path location of the file. The scroll bars can be used to display the entire path or more file listings. To open a drawing from the **Files:** window, double-click on the desired file.

Browsing through Drawing Files

When the file name is not known and you would like to look through your drawing files to find a specific drawing, select the **Browse** tab. See Figure 3-14. This allows you to select folders and look through the drawing files found there. To browse through a folder of drawings, use the following procedure:

1. Use the **Directories:** window to navigate to the desired folder. Double-click on the folder you want to look through. If you need to change the current disk drive

---

Figure 3-14.
When the file name is not known, select the **Browse** tab in the **Browse/Search** dialog box. Each individual drawing can be viewed.

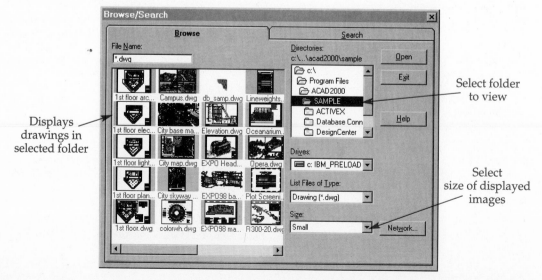

first, select the **Drives:** drop-down list and pick the appropriate disk drive. The **List Files of Type:** drop-down list shows only dwg, dwt, and dxf files since the active command is **Open**.

2. The **File Name:** edit box can be used to indicate specific files to display. Wildcard characters can be used here as well. For example, a*.dwg displays only drawing files that have a file name beginning with an *a*.

3. Use the scroll bar to view more files. To open a file from the **Browse** tab, double-click on the drawing image, or pick the image and then pick the **Open** button. If you need to view another folder, simply double-click on the new folder, and the drawing files contained there are displayed. The browser displays only the contents of a single directory.

4. To change the size of the drawing image displayed, pick the **Size:** drop-down list. Selecting **Small** allows up to 30 drawings to be displayed at one time. However, there will be very little detail since they are so small. The **Medium** setting completely displays 9 to 12 files. The **Large** setting provides the best image, but only one drawing is completely displayed.

Opening Release 12, Release 13, and Release 14 Drawings

You can open AutoCAD Release 12, Release 13, and Release 14 drawings in AutoCAD 2000. When you open a drawing from a previous release and work on it, AutoCAD automatically updates the drawing to AutoCAD 2000 standards when you save. After the previous release drawing is saved in AutoCAD 2000, it can be viewed in the **Preview** image tile during future applications.

Opening a Drawing from the File Pull-Down Menu List

AutoCAD stores the names and locations of the last four drawing files opened in the graphics window. These file names are listed at the bottom of the **File** pull-down menu, as shown in Figure 3-15. Any one of these files can be quickly opened by picking the file name.

If you try to open one of these drawing files after it has been deleted or moved to a different drive or directory, AutoCAD is unable to locate it. AutoCAD displays the message Cannot find the specified drawing file and opens the **Select File** dialog box.

For 2000i Users...

In AutoCAD 2000i, the number of previously opened drawings listed in the **File** pull-down menu can be specified in the **Open and Save** tab of the **Options** dialog box. The **Options** dialog box can be accessed by picking **Options...** from the **Tools...** pull-down menu. Enter the desired number in the **Number of recently-used files to list** text box in the **File Open** area.

Figure 3-15.
The **File** pull-down menu contains a list of the last four edited drawings.

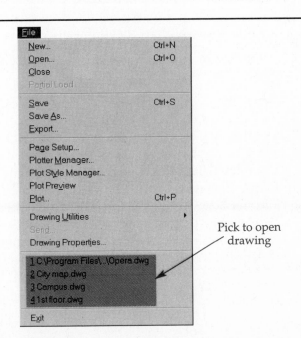

Pick to open drawing

Using Windows Explorer to Open Drawings

You can open drawing files through the Windows Explorer program. This is done two ways. You can double-click on the file and it will open in AutoCAD. If AutoCAD is not already loaded, AutoCAD will load and the file will be opened. You can also drag-and-drop a file to the AutoCAD command line and AutoCAD will open it. If AutoCAD is not open, you can drag-and-drop the file to the AutoCAD icon on your desktop. AutoCAD will then load and open the drawing file. For more information about the Windows Explorer, see Chapter 14.

Opening DXF Files

You can open AutoCAD Release 12, Release 13, Release 14 and AutoCAD 2000 DXF files in AutoCAD 2000. When you open a DXF file and work on it, AutoCAD automatically updates the DXF file to AutoCAD 2000 DXF standards when you save. After the previous release DXF is saved in AutoCAD 2000, it can be viewed in the **Preview** image tile during future applications. To open a DXF file, use the **OPEN** command and select DXF (*.dxf) in the **Files of type:** drop-down list. See Chapter 14 for more information on DXF files.

NOTE You can also use AutoCAD to open and save files on the Internet using the **Browse the Web** dialog box. This dialog box is accessed by picking the **Search the Web** button in the **Select File** and **Save Drawing As** dialog boxes. See *AutoCAD and its Applications—Advanced* for information on using AutoCAD with the Internet.

EXERCISE 3-7

❑ Start AutoCAD and pick the **Open a Drawing** button in the **Startup** dialog box. Notice the last opened drawings displayed in the **Select a File:** list. Pick on one or more of the files and notice the **Preview** image displayed. Pick the **Cancel** button to close the **Startup** dialog box.

❑ Select the **File** pull-down menu and notice the last opened drawings displayed near the bottom of the menu. Pick on one of the files to open the drawing.

❑ Open the **Select File** dialog box and pick the **Find File...** button.

❑ Open the **Search** tab in the **Browse/Search** dialog box. The **Search Pattern:** should be *.dwg, the **File Types:** should be Drawing (*.dwg), and the **Search Location:** should be C: or the drive where the AutoCAD sample drawings are located.

❑ Pick the **Search** button and see the results.

❑ Double-click on any desired AutoCAD sample file to open it, or pick the desired file followed by picking the **Open** button.

❑ Open the **Select File** dialog box and pick the **Find File...** button again.

❑ Find the directory with the AutoCAD sample drawings.

❑ Use the **Size:** list to pick the **Medium** and **Large** options to notice the difference. Pick the **Small** option again.

❑ Double-click on any desired AutoCAD sample file to open it.

❑ If you want to exit AutoCAD, select **Exit** from the **File** pull-down menu.

Opening Part of a Drawing

When working with large drawings, you can use the **Partial Open** option to open only part of a drawing. You can select only certain views and within those views, only specific layers. All views and layers that are not opened do not appear in the drawing area. For complex drawing, this can make editing much easier.

To partially load a drawing, first access the **OPEN** command, select the drawing, and then pick the **Partial Load** button in the **Select File** dialog box. This displays the **Partial Open** dialog box, Figure 3-16. This dialog box displays the drawing views and layers in the selected drawing.

The drawing views are listed in the **View geometry to load** area. Views are discussed in Chapter 9. Select a view, or select *Extents* or *Last*. The *Extents* option will load objects on the selected layers within the drawing extents. The *Last* option loads objects on the selected layers within the last saved view.

Select layers to be loaded in the **Layer geometry to load** area. Pick in the square next to the layer name to place a "✓" in the box. Only the checked layers can be loaded, and only the objects on those layers within the selected view will be loaded.

For 2000i Users...

To access the **Partial Open** dialog box in AutoCAD 2000i, pick the drop-down arrow next to the **Open** button and then select **Partial Open**.

Figure 3-16.
The **Partial Open** dialog box.

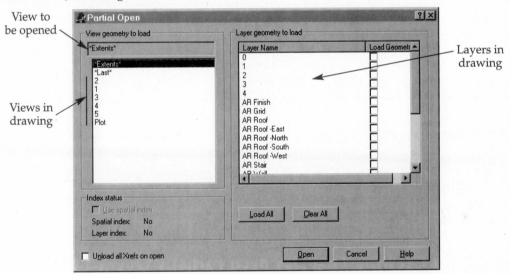

View to be opened

Views in drawing

Layers in drawing

NOTE

Many of the topics identified in the previous and following discussions are explained in detail later in this text. Layers are discussed in Chapter 4. Creation and use of views is covered in Chapter 9.

Using the Partial Load Command

After a drawing is partially open, you can load additional geometry from a view, selected area, or layers into the drawing using the **PARTIALOAD** command. You cannot unload any information that is currently loaded in the drawing. You can access the **PARTIALOAD** command by picking **Partial Load** from the **File** pull-down menu or by typing PARTIALOAD at the Command: prompt.

The **Partial Load** dialog box displays the views and layers available for specifying additional geometry to load into a partially open drawing. See Figure 3-17. This dialog box is nearly identical to the **Partial Open** dialog box. You can select additional views and layers to load into the drawing.

In addition to the features found in the **Partial Open** dialog box, the **Partial Load** dialog box also contains a **Pick a window** button. This button allows you to select a window to define the area from which objects should be loaded. All objects on the selected layers within the window are loaded.

Figure 3-17.
The **Partial Load** dialog box.

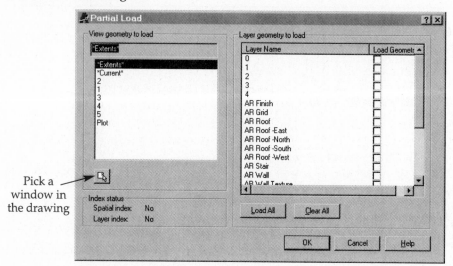

Pick a
window in
the drawing

Opening a Drawing That Has Been Partially Opened Before

When you partially open a drawing, make changes, and then save and close the drawing, AutoCAD "remembers" that the file had been only partially opened. When you open the drawing again, one of the dialog boxes in Figure 3-18 appears. The following options are available:

- **Fully Open.** Pick this button to load all views and layers in the drawing.
- **Restore.** Pick this button to load only the views and layers that had been previously loaded.
- **Specify.** Pick this button to specify the views and layers to be loaded.

> **NOTE**
>
> The **INDEXCTL** system variable controls whether layer and spatial indexes are saved with the drawing file. A spatial index organizes objects based on their location in space. A layer index is a list showing which objects are on which layers. Entering a value of 0 and no index is created. A value of 1 creates a layer index. A value of 2 creates a spatial index. And a value of 3 creates a layer and spatial index. The default value is 0.

Figure 3-18.
AutoCAD "remembers" if a file was previously partially opened. When you open the drawing again, one of these dialog boxes provides opening options. A—Using the **OPEN** command. B—Using the **Partial Open** option.

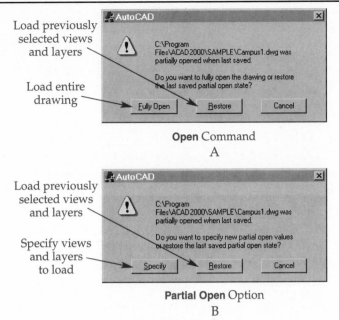

Load previously selected views and layers

Load entire drawing

Open Command
A

Load previously selected views and layers

Specify views and layers to load

Partial Open Option
B

EXERCISE 3-8

❑ Start AutoCAD and use the **Open** option in the **Startup** dialog box.
❑ In the **Select File** dialog box, find the AutoCAD sample folder.
❑ Select the City base map file then pick the **Partial Open...** button.
❑ In the **Partial Open** dialog box, select Extents in the **View geometry to load** area.
❑ In the **Layer geometry to load** area, select the following layers: 0, Street Curbs, and Border and Title Information, then pick **Open** button.
❑ Use the **RECTANG** command to draw a rectangle at the following coordinates: 4700,3900 and 16800,10300.
❑ Pick the **Partial Load** command from the **File** pull-down menu.
❑ In the **Partial Load** dialog box, select the **Pick a Window** button. At the Specify first corner: prompt, select the lower-left corner of the rectangle. At the Specify opposite corner: prompt, pick the upper-right corner of the rectangle.
❑ In the **Layer geometry to load** area, select the following layers: Freeways, Street Names, and Text Labels and Directions, then pick the **OK** button.
❑ Use the **SAVEAS** command to save the file as EX3-8.
❑ If you want to exit AutoCAD, select **Exit** from the **File** pull-down menu.

CLOSING A DRAWING

CLOSE

File
↳ Close

The **CLOSE** command is the primary way to exit out of a drawing file without ending the AutoCAD session. You can close the current drawing file by picking **Close** from the **File** pull-down menu, or by typing CLOSE at the Command: prompt. If you enter the **CLOSE** command before saving your work, AutoCAD gives you a chance to decide what you want to do with unsaved work. The AutoCAD alert box shown in Figure 3-19 appears. Press [Enter] to activate the highlighted **Yes** button. This saves the drawing. If the drawing is unnamed, the **Save Drawing As** dialog box appears. You can also pick the **No** button if you plan to discard any changes made to the drawing since the previous save. Pick the **Cancel** button if you decide not to close the drawing and want to return to the graphics window.

For 2000i Users...

The **CLOSEALL** command closes all drawings. This command and the **CLOSE** command can be selected from the **Window** pull-down menu.

Figure 3-19.
This AutoCAD alert box is shown if you try to exit AutoCAD or close a drawing file without saving the work. This is an opportunity to decide what will be done with unsaved work.

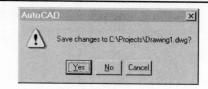

EXIT
QUIT

File
➥ E**x**it

EXITING AUTOCAD

The **EXIT** command is the primary way to end an AutoCAD session. You can close the program by picking **Ex**it from the **File** pull-down menu or typing EXIT or QUIT at the Command: prompt.

If you attempt to exit before saving your work, AutoCAD gives you a chance to decide what you want to do with unsaved work. The AutoCAD alert box shown in Figure 3-19 appears.

STATUS

Tools
➥ **Inquiry**
  ➥ **Status**

DETERMINING THE DRAWING STATUS

While working on a drawing, you may want to refresh your memory about some of the drawing parameters, such as the limits, grid spacing, or snap values. All the information about a drawing can be displayed using the **STATUS** command. Access this command by typing STATUS at the Command: prompt or selecting **Status** from the **Inquiry** cascading menu in the **Tools** pull-down menu. The graphics window automatically flips to the **AutoCAD Text Window** to display drawing information. See Figure 3-20.

The number of objects in a drawing refers to the total number of objects—both erased and existing. Drawing aid settings are shown, along with the current settings for layer, linetype, and color. These topics are discussed in later chapters of this text. Free disk space represents the space left on the drive containing your drawing file.

Figure 3-20.
The **AutoCAD Text Window** displays drawing information listed by the **STATUS** command.

AutoCAD and its Applications—Basics

When you have completed reading the status information in the text window, press the [F2] function key to flip back to the graphics window. This action automatically closes the text window and restores the inactive graphics window. You can also switch to the graphics window without closing the text window by clicking anywhere inside the graphics window.

> **NOTE**
>
> Another way to move between the graphics window and the text window is provided with the AutoCAD commands **GRAPHSCR** and **TEXTSCR**. Typing TEXTSCR at the Command: prompt flips to the text window. Typing GRAPHSCR flips to the graphics window. You can also flip to the text window from the graphics window by selecting **Text Window** from the **Display** cascading menu in the **View** pull-down menu.

Refer to the **STATUS** command periodically to see how much "free disk" space is available. If this free disk space becomes dangerously low, you may be unable to complete and save the drawing. This has been known to cause severe problems. AutoCAD automatically saves your work and ends the drawing session if it runs out of disk space.

EXERCISE 3-9

❑ Start AutoCAD and open the drawing you developed in Exercise 3-5.
❑ Use the **STATUS** command and read all the items displayed in the **AutoCAD Text Window**.
❑ Press the [F2] function key to return to the graphics window.
❑ Exit AutoCAD.

Chapter Test

Answer the following questions on a separate sheet of paper.
1. How do you set a grid spacing of .25?
2. How do you set a snap spacing of .125?
3. Name the command used to place a pattern of dots on the screen.
4. Identify the pull-down menu selection that accesses a dialog box used to select drafting settings.
5. How do you activate the snap grid so the screen cursor will automatically move in precise increments?
6. How do you set different horizontal and vertical snap units?
7. Name three ways to access the **Drafting Settings** dialog box.
8. Describe a template drawing.
9. Identify the command that you use to exit a drawing without saving.
10. What command would you use to save an existing drawing with a different name?
11. Explain how to cancel a command.
12. How do you change the name of a drawing while in the graphics window?
13. How often should work be saved?

14. Name the command that allows you to quickly save your work without displaying the dialog box.
15. The status of an AutoCAD drawing is currently displayed in the **AutoCAD Text Window**. List one method to get back to the graphics editor.
16. Name the system variable that allows you to control the dialog box display.
17. List the settings for the system variable described in the previous question that is used to achieve the following results:
    A. Dialog boxes displayed.
    B. Dialog boxes not displayed.
18. Why is it important to record drawing names in a log?
19. List at least three rules and restrictions for drawing names.
20. Name the pull-down menu where the **SAVE**, **SAVEAS**, and **OPEN** commands are located.
21. How do you exit AutoCAD without saving your work?
22. How do you set AutoCAD to automatically save your work at designated intervals?
23. Explain how you can obtain a list of existing drawing templates to select one for opening.
24. What command do you use to save a drawing to a floppy disk?
25. Give the keyboard shortcuts for the **DSETTINGS** command.
26. How do you turn the grid on and off at the status bar?
27. What is the result of pressing the [Ctrl]+[B] key combination or the [F9] function key?
28. Name the command that is accessed when you pick the **Save** button in the **Standard** toolbar.
29. Which option in the **Save as type:** list in the **Save Drawing As** dialog box should be used when saving a drawing file?
30. If a drawing has been previously saved, what is the difference between using the **QSAVE** or **SAVE** commands?
31. When you save a version of a drawing in an earlier format, why is it a good idea to give it a different name than the AutoCAD 2000 version uses?
32. What happens if you pick the **Find File...** button in the **Select File** dialog box?
33. What happens in the **Search** tab of the **Browse/Search** dialog box, if the **Search Pattern:** is *.dwg and the **File Types:** is Drawing (*.DWG), and you pick the **Search** button?
34. How do you open a file in the **Files:** window of the **Search** tab in the **Browse/Search** dialog box?
35. What is the purpose of the **Browse** tab in the **Browse/Search** dialog box?
36. What happens when you pick the different options in the **Size:** drop-down list in the **Browse** tab of the **Browse/Search** dialog box?
37. What command do you use if you want to refresh your memory about the drawing parameters?
38. What is a DXF file used for?
39. What is the Favorites folder?
40. Briefly explain the two ways to open an AutoCAD drawing using the Windows Explorer.
41. What is the purpose of the **Partial Open** option?
42. What command is used to load additional objects into a partially opened drawing?
43. Identify the command that you would use if you want to exit a drawing file but remain in the AutoCAD session.
44. What happens if you use the **CLOSE** command before saving your work?

Drawing Problems

1. Open one of your templates from Chapter 2 or Exercise 3-4. Draw the specified objects as accurately as possible with grid and snap turned off. Use the **LINE** command and draw on the left side of the screen only:
   - Right triangle
   - Isosceles triangle
   - Rectangle
   - Square
   Save the drawing as P3-1.

2. Draw the same objects specified in Problem 1 on the right side of the screen. This time, make sure the snap grid is turned on. Observe the difference between having snap on in this problem and off in the previous problem. Save the drawing as P3-2.

The following problems can be done if the AutoCAD Sample *file folder is loaded. In the following problems, use the **Browse/Search** dialog box to locate and open the specified drawing files, if needed, and complete the requested information:*

3. Locate and preview or open the Campus drawing. Describe the drawing in your own words.

4. Locate and preview or open the Watch drawing. Describe the drawing in your own words.

5. Locate and preview or open the 1st floor drawing. Describe the drawing in your own words.

6. Locate and preview or open the Tablet 2000 drawing. Describe the drawing in your own words.

7. Locate and preview or open the Truck model drawing. Describe the drawing in your own words.

8. Locate and preview or open the Opera drawing. Describe the drawing in your own words.

Foundation Plan. (Steve D. Bloedel)

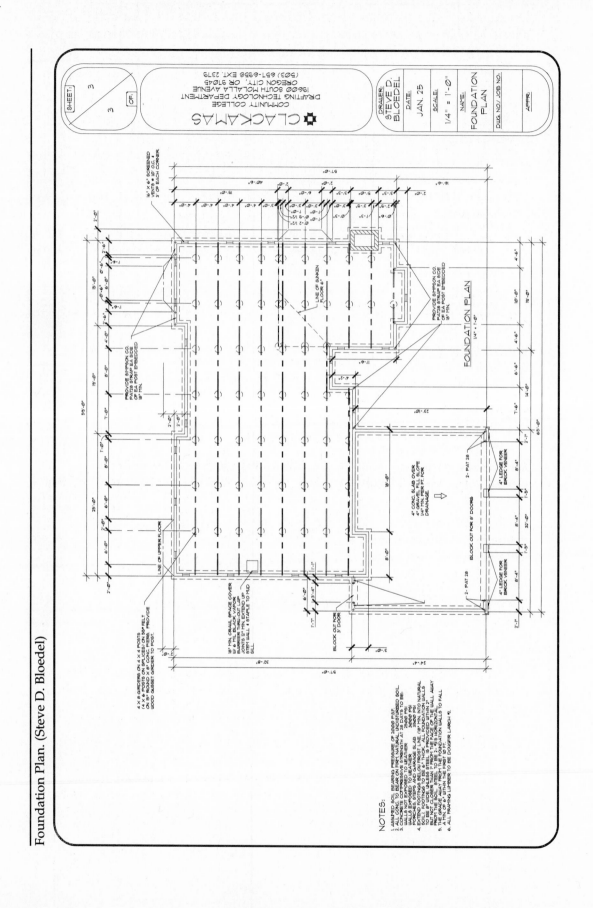

CHAPTER 4

Drawing Lines, Erasing Objects, Using Layers, and Making Prints

Learning Objectives

After completing this chapter, you will be able to:

- Use a variety of linetypes to construct an object.
- Select the **LINE** command to draw given objects.
- Use absolute, relative, and polar coordinate point entry systems.
- Use the screen cursor for point entry.
- Use the **MULTIPLE** command modifier.
- Use the Ortho mode and polar tracking.
- Use direct distance entry.
- Make revisions to objects using the **ERASE** command and its options.
- Make selection sets using the **Window**, **Crossing**, **WPolygon**, **CPolygon**, and **Fence** options.
- Remove and add objects to the selection set.
- Clean up the screen with the **REDRAW** command.
- Use the **OOPS** command to bring back an erased object.
- Use the **U** command to undo a command.
- Select stacked objects.
- Draw objects on separate layers using the **LAYER** command.
- Create and manage drawing layers.
- Draw objects with different colors, linetypes, and lineweights.
- Filter the list of layers.
- Use the **Properties** window to change layers, colors, linetypes, and lineweights.
- Use the **AutoCAD DesignCenter** to copy layers and linetypes between drawings.
- Make a print of your drawing.

Drafting is a graphic language that uses lines, symbols, and words to describe products to be manufactured or constructed. Line conventions are standards based on line thickness and type, which are designed to enhance the readability of drawings. This chapter introduces line standards and shows you how to use the AutoCAD drawing editor to perform basic drafting tasks.

LINE CONVENTIONS

The American National Standards Institute (ANSI) recommends two line widths to establish contrasting lines on a drawing. Lines are described as thick and thin. For manual drafting, thick lines are twice as thick as thin lines, with recommended widths of 0.6mm and 0.3mm, respectively. However, a single line width for all types of lines is acceptable on drawings prepared on a CAD system. Figure 4-1 shows recommended line width and type as taken from ANSI Y14.2M, *Line Conventions and Lettering*.

Figure 4-1.
Line conventions. (ANSI Y14.2M)

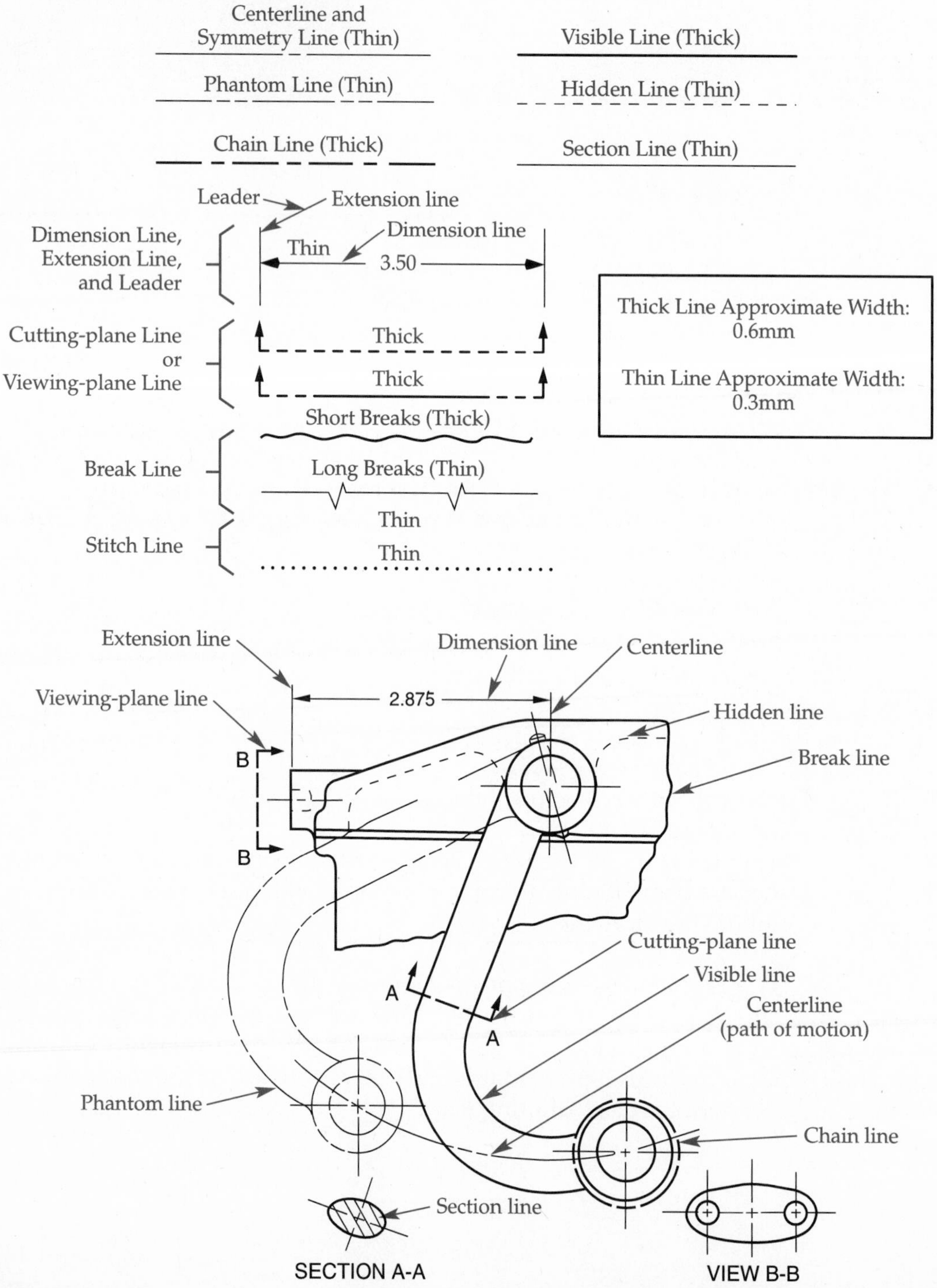

Object Lines

Object lines, also called *visible lines*, are thick lines used to show the outline or contour of an object, Figure 4-2. Object lines are the most common type of lines used on drawings. These lines should be twice as thick as thin lines.

Hidden Lines

Hidden lines, often called *dashed lines*, are used to represent invisible features of an object, as shown in Figure 4-2. Hidden lines are drawn thin so they clearly contrast with object lines. When properly drawn at full size, the dashes are .125" (3mm) long and spaced .06" (1.5mm) apart. Be careful if the drawing is to be greatly reduced or scaled down during the plotting process. Reduced dashes may appear too small.

Figure 4-2.
Object lines and
hidden lines.

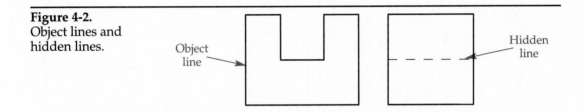

Centerlines

Centerlines locate the centers of circles and arcs and show the axis of a cylindrical or symmetrical shape, as shown in Figure 4-3. Centerlines are thin lines consisting of alternately spaced long and short dashes. The recommended dash lengths are .125" (3mm) for the short dashes and .75" to 1.5" (19mm to 38mm) for the long dashes. These lengths can be altered depending on the size of the drawing. The dashes should be separated by spaces approximately .06" (1.5mm) long. The small centerline dashes should cross only at the center of a circle.

Extension Lines

Extension lines are thin lines used to show the "extent" of a dimension, as shown in Figure 4-3. Extension lines begin a small distance from the object and extend .125" (3mm) beyond the last dimension line. Extension lines may cross object lines, hidden lines, and centerlines, but they may not cross dimension lines. Centerlines become extension lines when they are used to show the extent of a dimension. When this is done, there is no space where the centerline joins the extension line.

Figure 4-3.
This simple
drawing shows
centerlines,
extension lines,
dimension lines,
and leader lines.

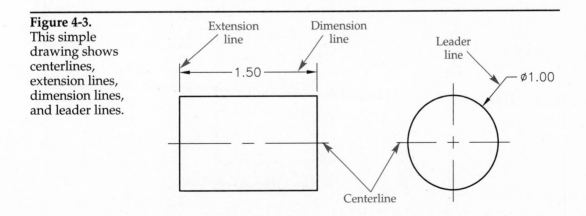

Dimension Lines

Dimension lines are thin lines placed between extension lines to indicate a measurement. In mechanical drafting, the dimension line is normally broken near the center for placement of the dimension numeral, as shown in Figure 4-3. The dimension line normally remains unbroken in architectural and structural drawings. The dimension numeral is placed on top of an unbroken dimension line. Arrows terminate the ends of dimension lines, except in architectural drafting where slashes or dots are often used.

Leader Lines

Leader lines are thin lines used to connect a specific note to a feature on a drawing. A leader line terminates with an arrowhead at the feature and has a small shoulder at the note, Figure 4-3. Dimension and leader line usage is discussed in detail in Chapters 18 and 19.

Cutting-Plane and Viewing-Plane Lines

Cutting-plane lines are thick lines that identify the location of a section. *Viewing-plane lines* are drawn in the same style as cutting-plane lines, but identify the location of a view. Cutting-plane and viewing-plane lines may be drawn one of two ways, as shown in Figure 4-1. The use of viewing-plane and cutting-plane lines is discussed in detail in Chapter 6 and Chapter 22.

Section Lines

Section lines are thin lines drawn in a section view to show where material has been cut away, as shown in Figure 4-4. Types of section lines and applications are discussed in Chapter 22.

Break Lines

Break lines show where a portion of an object has been removed for clarity or convenience. For example, the center portion of a very long part may be broken out so the two ends can be moved closer together for more convenient representation. There are several types of break lines shown in Figure 4-5.

Figure 4-4.
Section lines and the cutting-plane lines.

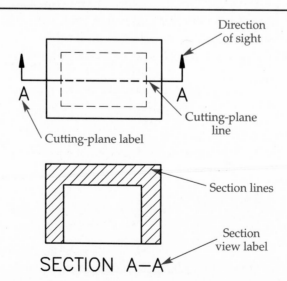

AutoCAD and its Applications—Basics

Figure 4-5.
Standard break lines.

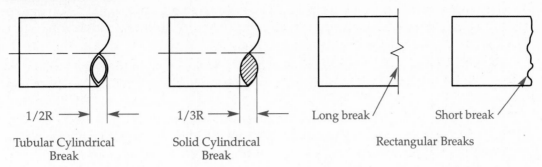

1/2R

Tubular Cylindrical
Break

1/3R

Solid Cylindrical
Break

Long break

Rectangular Breaks

Short break

Phantom Lines

Phantom lines are thin lines with two short dashes alternately spaced with long dashes. The short dashes are .125″ (3mm) long and the long dashes range from .75″ to 1.5″ (19mm to 38mm) in length, depending on the size of the drawing. Spaces between dashes are .06″ (1.5mm). Phantom lines identify repetitive details, show alternate positions of moving parts, and locate adjacent positions of related parts, Figure 4-6.

Chain Lines

Chain lines are thick lines of alternately spaced long and short dashes. They show that the portion of the surface next to the chain line has special features or receives unique treatment. See Figure 4-7.

Figure 4-6.
Phantom lines.

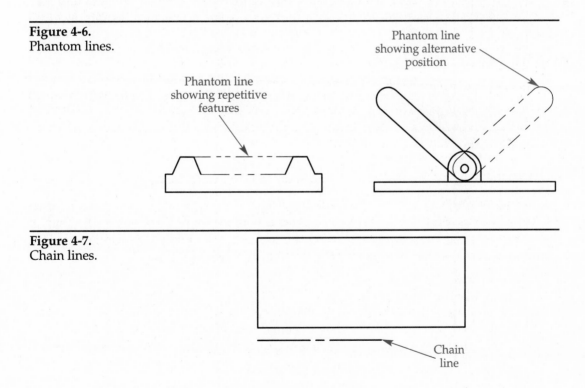

Phantom line
showing alternative
position

Phantom line
showing repetitive
features

Figure 4-7.
Chain lines.

Chain
line

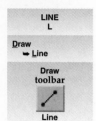
LINE
L

Draw
↳ Line

Draw
toolbar

Line

Individual line segments are drawn between two points on the screen. This is referred to as *point entry*. Point entry is the simplest form of drafting. After selecting the **LINE** command, simply enter the endpoints of the line.

The **LINE** command is accessed by picking the **Line** button in the **Draw** toolbar, by picking **Line** in the **Draw** pull-down menu, or by typing L or LINE at the Command: prompt.

When you use the **LINE** command, a prompt asks you to select a starting point. When the first point is selected (From point:), you are asked for the second point (To point:). When the next To point: prompt is given, continue selecting additional points if you want to connect a series of lines. When finished, press the [Enter] key or the space bar to get back to the Command: prompt.

The following command sequence is used for the **LINE** command:

Command: **L** *or* **LINE**↵
Specify first point: *(select the first point)*
Specify next point or [Undo]: *(select the second point)*
Specify next point or [Close/Undo]: *(select the third point, press* [Enter] *or the space bar to finish)*
Command: *(this appears if you pressed* [Enter] *or the space bar at the previous prompt)*

PROFESSIONAL TIP

AutoCAD provides a set of abbreviated commands called *command aliases*. Command aliases are also called *keyboard shortcuts* because they reduce the amount of typing needed when entering a command at the keyboard. Using command aliases allows you to enter commands more quickly. For example, instead of typing LINE at the Command: prompt, it is faster to type L. Becoming familiar with the available command aliases can help you become more productive with AutoCAD.

AutoCAD
User's
Guide

5

Responding to AutoCAD Prompts with Numbers

Many of the AutoCAD commands require specific types of numeric data. Some of AutoCAD's prompts require you to enter a whole number. For example, later in this book you will learn how to draw a polygon using the **POLYGON** command. This command requires that you specify the number of sides as follows:

Command: **POLYGON**↵
Enter number of sides <*current*>: **6**↵
Specify center of polygon or [Edge]: *(pick the center of the polygon)*
Enter an option [Inscribed in circle/Circumscribed about circle] <I>: ↵
Specify radius of circle: **2**↵
Command:

The Number of sides: prompt illustrates the simplest form of numeric entry, in which any whole number may be used. Other entries require whole numbers that may be positive or negative. A number is understood to be positive without placing the plus (+) sign before the number. However, a negative number must be preceded by the minus (-) sign.

Much of your data entry may not be whole numbers. In these cases, any real number can be used, and can be expressed as decimals, fractions, or scientific notation. They may be positive or negative. Here are some examples of acceptable real numbers:

4.250
-6.375
1/2
1-3/4
2.5E+4 *(25,000)*
2.5E-4 *(0.00025)*

When entering fractions, the numerator and denominator must be whole numbers greater than zero. For example, 1/2, 3/4, and 2/3 are all acceptable fraction entries. Fractional numbers greater than one must have a dash between the whole number and the fraction. For example, 2-3/4 is entered for two and three quarters. The dash (-) separator is needed because a space acts just like pressing [Enter] and automatically ends the input. The numerator may be larger than the denominator, as in 3/2, *only* if a whole number is not used with the fraction. For example, 1-3/2 is not a valid input for a fraction.

When you enter coordinates or measurements, the value used depends on the units of measure.

- Values on inch drawings are understood to be in inches without placing the inch marks (″) after the numeral. For example, 2.500 is automatically understood to be 2.500 inches.
- When your drawing is set up for metric values, any entry is automatically expressed as millimeters.
- If you are working in an engineering or architectural environment, any value greater than one foot is expressed in inches, feet, or feet and inches. The values can be whole numbers, decimals, or fractions.
  - For measurements in feet, the foot symbol (′) must follow the number, as in 24′.
  - If the value is in feet and inches, there is no space between the feet and inch value. For example, 24′6 is the proper input for the value 24′-6″.
  - If the inch part of the value contains a fraction, the inch and fractional part of an inch are separated by a dash, such as 24′6-1/2.

Never mix feet with inch values greater than one foot. For example, 24′18″ is an invalid entry. In this case, you should enter 25′6.

PROFESSIONAL TIP Placing the inch mark (″) after an inch value at the prompt line is acceptable, but not necessary. It takes more time and reduces productivity.

Point Entry Methods

There are several point entry techniques for drawing lines. Being familiar and skillful with these methods is very important. A combination of point entry techniques should be used to help reduce drawing time.

Each of the point entry methods uses the Cartesian, or rectangular, coordinate system. The *Cartesian coordinate system* is based on selecting distances from three intersecting axes. A *location* is defined by its distance from the intersection point, called the *origin*, in respect to each of these axes. In standard two-dimensional (2D) drafting applications, objects are drawn in the XY plane and the Z axis is not referenced. Using the Z axis is discussed in Chapter 27 with three-dimensional (3D) drafting.

In 2D drafting, the origin divides the coordinate system into four quadrants within the XY plane. Points are located in relation to the origin, where X = 0 and Y = 0, or (0,0). Figure 4-8 shows the X,Y values of points located in the Cartesian coordinate system.

When using AutoCAD, the origin (0,0) is usually at the lower-left corner of the drawing. This point also coincides with the lower-left corner of the drawing limits. This setup places all points in the upper-right quadrant, where both X and Y coordinate values are positive, Figure 4-9. Methods of establishing points in the Cartesian coordinate system include absolute coordinates, relative coordinates, and polar coordinates.

Using absolute coordinates

Points located using the absolute coordinate system are measured from the origin (0,0). For example, a point with X = 4 and Y = 2 (4,2) is located 4 units horizontally and 2 units vertically from the origin, as shown in Figure 4-10. The coordinate display on the status bar registers the location of the selected point in X, Y, and Z coordinates.

Figure 4-8.
The Cartesian coordinate system.

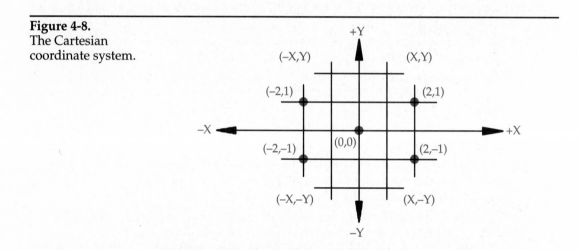

Figure 4-9.
The XY coordinate axes on the screen.

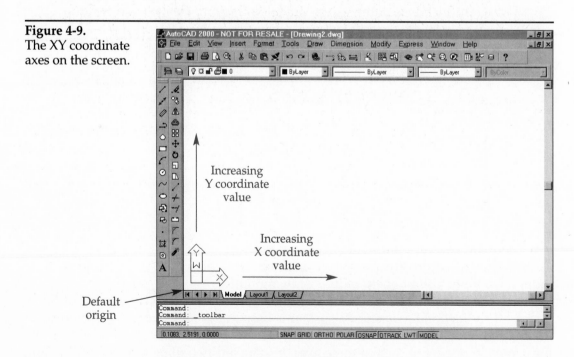

AutoCAD and its Applications—Basics

The discussion and examples in this chapter reference only the X,Y coordinates for 2D drafting. Also note that the coordinate display reflects the current system of working units. Remember, when the absolute coordinate system is used, each point is located from 0,0. Follow through these commands and point placements at your computer as you refer to Figure 4-11.

Command: **L** *or* **LINE**↵
Specify first point: **4,2**↵
Specify next point or [Undo]: **7,2**↵
Specify next point or [Undo]: **7,6**↵
Specify next point or [Close/Undo]: **4,6**↵
Specify next point or [Close/Undo]: **4,2**↵
Specify next point or [Close/Undo]: ↵
Command:

Figure 4-10.
Locating points with absolute coordinates.

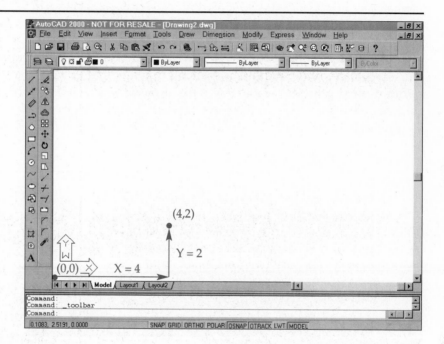

Figure 4-11.
Drawing simple shapes using the **LINE** command and absolute coordinates.

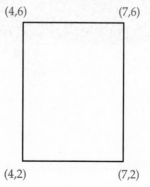

❏ Start a new drawing or use one of your templates.
❏ Given the absolute coordinates in the chart below, use the **LINE** command to draw the object.
❏ Save the drawing as EX4-1.

Point	Coordinates	Point	Coordinates
1	0,0	5	0,2
2	9,0	6	0,1.5
3	9.5,.5	7	.25,.5
4	9.5,2	8	0,0

Using relative coordinates

Relative coordinates are located from the previous position, rather than from the origin. The relationship of points in the Cartesian coordinate system shown in Figure 4-8 must be clearly understood before using this method. For relative coordinates, the @ symbol must precede your entry. This symbol is selected by holding the [Shift] key and pressing the [2] key at the top of the keyboard. Follow through these commands and relative coordinate point placements as you refer to Figure 4-12.

> Command: **L** *or* **LINE**↵
> Specify first point: **2,2**↵
> Specify next point or [Undo]: **@6,0**↵
> Specify next point or [Undo]: **@2,2**↵
> Specify next point or [Close/Undo]: **@0,3**↵
> Specify next point or [Close/Undo]: **@-2,2**↵
> Specify next point or [Close/Undo]: **@-6,0**↵
> Specify next point or [Close/Undo]: **@0,-7**↵
> Specify next point or [Close/Undo]: ↵
> Command:

Figure 4-12.
Drawing a simple shape using the **LINE** command and relative coordinates. Notice that the coordinates are entered counterclockwise from the first point (2,2).

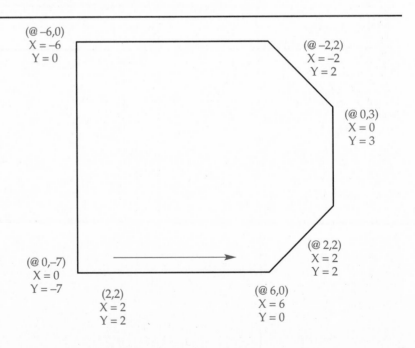

❑ Start a new drawing or use one of your templates.
❑ Use the **LINE** command to draw the object with the relative coordinates given in the chart below.
❑ Save the drawing as EX4-2.

Point	Coordinates	Point	Coordinates
1	1,1	5	@-9.5,0
2	@9,0	6	@0,-.5
3	@.5,.5	7	@.25,-1
4	@0,1.5	8	@-.25,-.5

Using polar coordinates

A point located using *polar coordinates* is based on the distance from a fixed point at a given angle. First the distance is entered, then the angle. The two values are separated by a < symbol.

The angular values used for the polar coordinate format are shown in Figure 4-13. Consistent with standard AutoCAD convention, 0° is to the right, or east. Angles are then measured counterclockwise.

When preceded by the @ symbol, a polar coordinate point is measured from the previous point. If the @ symbol is not included, the coordinate is located relative to the origin. If you want to draw a line 4 units long from point 1,1 at a 45° angle, the following information must be typed:

```
Command: L or LINE↵
Specify first point: 1,1↵
Specify next point or [Undo]: @4<45↵
Specify next point or [Undo]: ↵
```

Figure 4-14 shows the result of this command. The entry @4<45 means the following:

- **@.** Tells AutoCAD to measure from the previous point. This symbol must precede all relative coordinate inputs.
- **4.** Gives the distance from the previous point.
- **<.** Establishes a polar or angular increment to follow.
- **45.** Determines the angle, as 45° from 0°.

Figure 4-13.
Angles used in the polar coordinate system.

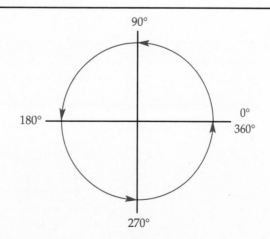

Figure 4-14.
Using polar
coordinates for the
LINE command.

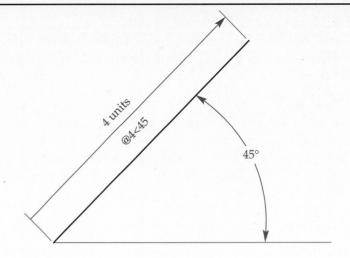

Now, follow through these commands and polar coordinate points on your computer as you refer to Figure 4-15.

```
Command: L or LINE↵
Specify first point: 2,6↵
Specify next point or [Undo]: @2.5<0↵
Specify next point or [Undo]: @3<135↵
Specify next point or [Close/Undo]: 2,6↵
Specify next point or [Close/Undo]: ↵
Command: ↵
LINE Specify first point: 6,6↵
Specify next point or [Undo]: @4<0↵
Specify next point or [Undo]: @2<90↵
Specify next point or [Close/Undo]: @4<180↵
Specify next point or [Close/Undo]: @2<270↵
Specify next point or [Close/Undo]: ↵
Command:
```

Figure 4-15.
Using polar
coordinates to draw.

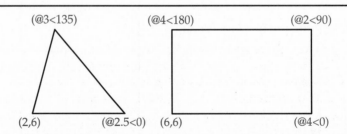

         AutoCAD and its Applications—Basics

Picking points using the screen cursor

The pointing device can be used to move the crosshairs and pick points. The Grid and Snap modes normally should be turned on for precise point location. This assists in drafting presentation and maintains accuracy when using a pointing device. With Snap on, the crosshairs move in designated increments without any guesswork.

When using a pointing device, the command sequence is the same as using coordinates. Points are picked when the crosshairs are at the desired location. After the first point is picked, the distance to the second point and the point's coordinates are displayed on the status line for reference. When picking points in this manner, there is a "rubberband" line connecting the "first point" and the crosshairs. The rubberband line moves as the crosshairs are moved, showing where the new line will be placed.

Drawing Multiple Lines

The **MULTIPLE** command is used to automatically repeat commands issued at the keyboard. This technique can be used to draw repetitive lines, polylines, circles, arcs, ellipses, or polygons. For example, if you plan to draw several sets of line segments, type MULTIPLE at the Command: prompt, press the space bar to add a space, and then type L or LINE. AutoCAD automatically repeats the **LINE** command until you have finished drawing all the desired lines. You must cancel to get back to the Command: prompt. The **MULTIPLE** command is used as follows:

```
Command: MULTIPLE↵
Enter command name to repeat: L or LINE↵
Specify first point: (pick the first point)
Specify next point or [Undo]: (pick the second point)
Specify next point or [Undo]: (pick the third point, or press [Enter])
Specify next point or [Close/Undo]: ↵
LINE Specify first point: (pick the first point)
Specify next point or [Undo]: (pick the second point)
Specify next point or [Undo]: (pick the third point, or press [Enter])
Specify next point or [Close/Undo]: ↵
LINE Specify first point: (press [Esc] to cancel) *Cancel*
```

As you can see, AutoCAD automatically reissues the **LINE** command so you can draw another line (or lines). Press [Esc] to cancel the repeating command.

The Coordinate Display

The area to the left side of the status bar shows the coordinate display window. The number of places to the right of the decimal point is determined by the units setting. The coordinate display changes to represent the location of the cursor in relation to the origin. Each time a new point is picked or the pointing device moved, the coordinates are updated.

The coordinate display is turned on and off by picking the coordinate display in the status bar, pressing the [Ctrl]+[D] key combination, function key [F6], or puck button 7. With coordinates on, the coordinates constantly change as the crosshairs move. With coordinates off, no coordinates are displayed.

There are three coordinate modes and they are controlled by the **COORDS** system variable. Set this variable to 0 for a static display. This displays coordinates only when points are selected. Set the **COORDS** variable to 1 for a dynamic absolute display. Set the variable to 2 for a dynamic length/angle (polar) display. A typical absolute coordinate display gives X, Y, and Z coordinates such as 6.2000,5.9000,0.0000. A polar coordinate display shows the distance and angle from the last point and the Z axis distance, such as 3.4000<180, 0.0000.

Drawing in Ortho Mode

The term *ortho* comes from "orthogonal," which means "at right angles." The Ortho mode constrains points selected while drawing and editing to be only horizontal or vertical. The directions are in alignment with the current Snap grid.

The Ortho mode has a special advantage when drawing rectangular shapes because all corners are guaranteed to be square. See Figure 4-16. Ortho mode can be turned on or off by picking the **ORTHO** button on the status bar, using function key [F8], puck button 5, or [Ctrl]+[L] key combination, or typing ORTHO at the Command: prompt.

Figure 4-16.
Using Ortho mode.
A—Angled lines cannot be drawn with a pointing device while Ortho mode is turned on.
B—With Ortho mode turned off, angled lines can be drawn.

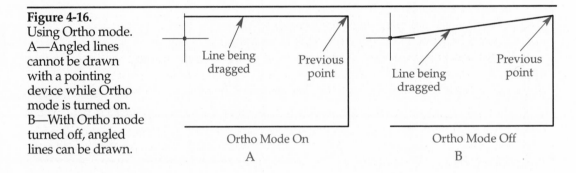

| Ortho Mode On
A | Ortho Mode Off
B |

AutoCAD User's Guide 5

Using Direct Distance Entry

Direct distance entry is a method of entering points that allows you to use the cursor to specify the direction and keyboard entry to specify a distance. To draw a line using this point entry method, drag the cursor in any desired direction from the first point of the line. Then type a numerical value that indicates the distance from that point.

The direct distance entry method works best in combination with the Ortho mode or polar tracking. Figure 4-17 shows how to draw a rectangle using direct distance entry. Note that the Ortho mode is on for this example:

Command: **L** *or* **LINE**↵
Specify first point: **2,2**↵
Specify next point or [Undo]: *(drag the cursor horizontally, type* 3*, and press* [Enter]*)*
Specify next point or [Undo]: *(drag the cursor vertically, type* 2*, and press* [Enter]*)*
Specify next point or [Close/Undo]: *(drag the cursor horizontally, type* 3*, and press* [Enter]*)*
Specify next point or [Close/Undo]: *(drag the cursor vertically, type* 2*, and press* [Enter]*)*
Command:

Figure 4-17.
Using direct
distance entry to
draw lines a
designated distance
from a current
point. With Ortho
mode on, move the
cursor in the desired
direction and type
the distance.

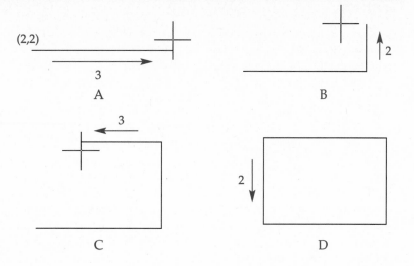

PROFESSIONAL TIP

Direct distance entry is a convenient way to find points quickly and easily with a minimum amount of effort. Use direct distance entry with Ortho mode or Snap mode to draw objects with perpendicular lines. Direct distance entry can be used whenever AutoCAD expects a point coordinate value, including both drawing and editing commands.

Using Polar Tracking

Polar tracking is similar to Ortho mode, except that you are not limited to 90 degree angles. With polar tracking toggled on, you can cause the drawing crosshairs to "snap" to any predefined angle increment. To turn on polar tracking, pick the **POLAR** button on the status bar or use the [F10] function key. Polar tracking provides visual aids. As you move the cursor in the desired direction, AutoCAD displays an alignment path and tooltip when the cursor crosses the default polar angle increment of 0, 90, 180, or 270 degrees. Setting different polar alignment angles is explained in Chapter 6.

After you start the **LINE** command and move the cursor in alignment with a polar tracking angle, all you have to do is type the desired distance value and press [Enter] to have the line drawn. Polar tracking is used as follows to draw the lines shown in Figure 4-18:

> Command: **L** or **LINE**↵
> Specify first point: **2,2** ↵
> Specify next point or [Undo]: **2** (drag the crosshairs while watching the tooltip; at 0 degrees, press [Enter])
> Specify next point or [Undo]: **3** (drag the crosshairs while watching the tooltip; at 90 degrees, press [Enter])
> Specify next point or [Close/Undo]: ↵

Polar tracking is discussed in detail in Chapter 6.

Figure 4-18.
Using polar tracking to draw lines at predefined angle increments.

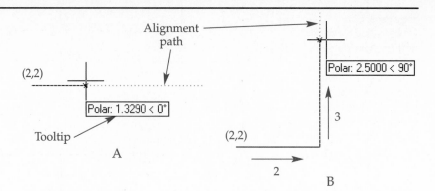

PROFESSIONAL TIP

Practice using the different point entry techniques and decide which method works best for certain situations. Keep in mind that you may mix methods to help enhance your drawing speed. For example, absolute coordinates may work best to locate an initial point or to draw a simple shape. These calculations are easy. Polar coordinates may work better to locate features in a circular pattern, or at an angular relationship. Practice with Ortho mode, polar tracking, and Snap settings to see the advantages and disadvantages of each. Change the Snap settings to assist in drawing layout accuracy.

Using the Close Line Option

A *polygon* is a closed plane figure with at least three sides. Triangles and rectangles are examples of polygons. Once you have drawn two or more line segments of a polygon, the endpoint of the last line segment can be connected automatically to the first line segment using the **Close** option. To use this option, type C or CLOSE at the prompt line. In Figure 4-19, the last line is drawn using the **Close** option as follows:

Command: **L** *or* **LINE**↵
Specify first point: *(pick Point 1)*
Specify next point or [Undo]: *(pick Point 2)*
Specify next point or [Undo]: *(pick Point 3)*
Specify next point or [Close/Undo]: *(pick Point 4)*
Specify next point or [Close/Undo]: **C**↵
Command:

Figure 4-19.
Using the **Close** option to complete a box.

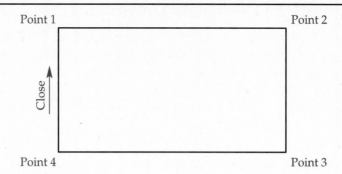

Using the Line Continue Option

Suppose you draw a line, then exit the **LINE** command, but decide to go back and connect a new line to the end of the previous one. Type L to begin the **LINE** command. Then, at the From point: prompt, simply press the [Enter] key or the space bar. This action automatically connects the first endpoint of the new line segment to the endpoint of the previous one, as shown in Figure 4-20. The **Continue** option can also be used for drawing arcs, as discussed in Chapter 5. The following command sequence is used for continuing a line:

Command: **L** or **LINE**↵
Specify first point: *(press* [Enter] *or space bar and AutoCAD automatically picks the last endpoint of the previous line)*
Specify next point or [Undo]: *(pick the next point)*
Specify next point or [Undo]: *(press* [Enter] *to exit the command)*
Command:

Figure 4-20.
Using the **Continue** option.

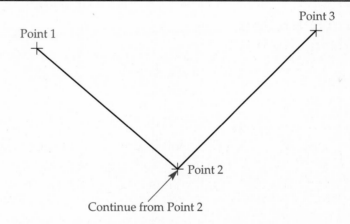

PROFESSIONAL TIP Pressing the space bar or [Enter] repeats the previous command. If no other commands have been used since the line to be continued was drawn, pressing the space bar or [Enter] repeats the **LINE** command.

Undoing the Previously Drawn Line

When drawing a series of lines, you may find that you made an error. To delete the mistake while still in the **LINE** command, type U at the Specify next point: prompt and press [Enter]. Doing this removes the previously drawn line and allows you to continue from the previous endpoint. You can use the **Undo** option repeatedly to continue deleting line segments until the entire line is gone. The following prompt sequence is shown in Figure 4-21.

> Command: **L** *or* **LINE**↵
> Specify first point: *(pick Point 1)*
> Specify next point or [Undo]: *(pick Point 2)*
> Specify next point or [Undo]: *(pick Point 3)*
> Specify next point or [Close/Undo]: *(pick Point 4)*
> Specify next point or [Close/Undo]: **U**↵
> Specify next point or [Close/Undo]: **U**↵
> Specify next point or [Undo]: *(pick Point 5)*
> Specify next point or [Close/Undo]: *(press* [Enter] *to exit the command)*
> Command:

Figure 4-21.
Using the **Undo** option while in the **LINE** command. Notice that the original Points 3 and 4 remain as blips until the screen is redrawn.

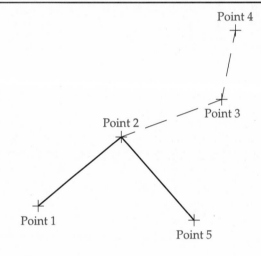

NOTE	When AutoCAD is configured to display screen menus, the **Close**, **Continue**, and **Undo** options appear in the **LINE** screen menu.

EXERCISE 4-6

❏ Start a new drawing, use one of your templates, or open a previous exercise.
❏ Experiment drawing lines using the following guidelines and options:
  ❏ Draw one triangle and one rectangle using the **Close** option.
  ❏ Draw two connected lines and end the **LINE** command. Then, repeat the **LINE** command and use the **Continue** option to draw additional lines.
  ❏ Draw eight connected lines. Then use the **Undo** option to remove the last four lines while remaining in the **LINE** command. Finally, draw four new connected lines.
❏ Save the drawing as EX4-6.

Editing is the procedure used to correct mistakes or revise an existing drawing. There are many editing functions that help increase productivity. The basic editing operations **ERASE**, **OOPS**, and **U** are introduced in the next sections.

To edit a drawing, you must select items to modify. The Select objects: prompt appears whenever you need to select items in the command sequence. Whether you select only one object or hundreds of objects, you create a *selection set*. You can create a selection set using a variety of selection options, including the following:

- Window selection
- Crossing selection
- Window polygon selection
- Crossing polygon selection
- Selection fence

When you become familiar with the selection set options, you will find that they increase your flexibility and productivity.

In the discussion and examples that follow, several of the selection set methods are introduced using the **ERASE** command. Keep in mind, however, that these techniques can be used with most of the editing commands in AutoCAD whenever the Select objects: prompt appears. Any of the selection set methods can be enabled from the prompt line.

Using the **ERASE** Command

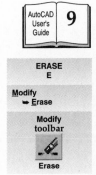

The **ERASE** command is similar to using an eraser in manual drafting to remove unwanted information. However, with the **ERASE** command you have a second chance. If you erase the wrong item, it can be brought back with the **OOPS** command. Access the **ERASE** command by picking the **Erase** button in the **Modify** toolbar, picking **Erase** in the **Modify** pull-down menu, or by typing E or ERASE at the Command: prompt.

When you enter the **ERASE** command, you are prompted to select an object to be erased as follows:

> Command: **E** *or* **ERASE**↵
> Select objects: *(select the object(s) to be erased)*
> Select objects: ↵
> Command:

When the Select objects: prompt appears, a small box replaces the screen crosshairs. This box is referred to as the *pick box*. Move the pick box over the item to be erased and pick it. The object is highlighted. Then, press the [Enter] key or the right mouse button and the object is erased.

NOTE 	The terms *entity* and *object* are interchangeable in AutoCAD. An entity or object is a predefined element that you place in a drawing by means of a single command. For example, a line, circle, arc, or single line of text is an entity or object.

After you pick the first object, the Select objects: prompt is redisplayed. You can then select another object to erase, as shown in Figure 4-22. If you are finished selecting objects, press the [Enter] key at the Select objects: prompt to "close" the selection set. The **ERASE** operation is completed and you are returned to the Command: prompt.

Figure 4-22.
Using the **ERASE** command to erase a single object.

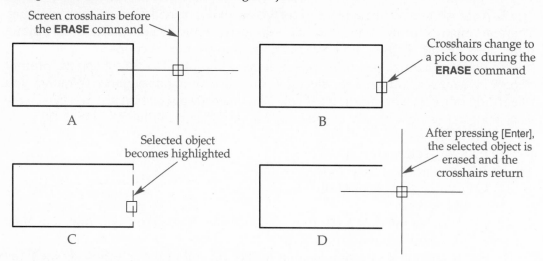

Screen crosshairs before the **ERASE** command

Crosshairs change to a pick box during the **ERASE** command

A

B

Selected object becomes highlighted

After pressing [Enter], the selected object is erased and the crosshairs return

C

D

Making a single selection automatically

Normally, AutoCAD lets you pick as many items as you want for a selection set, and selected items are highlighted to let you know what has been picked. You also have the option of selecting a single item and having it automatically edited without first being highlighted. To do this, enter SI (for single) at the Select objects: prompt. To select several items with this method, use the **Window** or **Crossing** selection options (discussed later in this chapter). The command sequence is as follows:

Command: **E** *or* **ERASE**↵
Select objects: **SI**↵
Select objects: (*pick an individual item, or use the* **Window** *or* **Crossing** *option to pick several items*)
Command:

Note that the Select objects: prompt did not return after the items were picked. The entire group is automatically edited (erased in this example) when you press [Enter] or pick the second corner of a window or crossing box.

PROFESSIONAL TIP

The **SI** (single) selection option is not commonly used as a command line option. This is because picking an object and pressing [Enter] requires less keystrokes than typing SI and pressing [Enter]. The **SI** option is most commonly used when developing menu macros that require single object selection.

Using the Last selection option

The **ERASE** command's **Last** option saves time if you need to erase the last entity drawn. For example, suppose you draw a line and then want to erase it. The **Last** option will automatically select the line. The **Last** option can be selected by typing L at the Select objects: prompt:

Command: **E** *or* **ERASE**↵
Select objects: **L**↵
1 found
Select objects: ↵
Command:

Keep in mind that using the **Last** option only highlights the last visible item drawn. You must press [Enter] for the object to be erased. If you need to erase more than just the last object, you can use the **ERASE** command and **Last** option repeatedly to erase items in reverse order. However, this is not as quick as using the **ERASE** command and selecting the objects.

EXERCISE 4-7

❏ Start a new drawing, use one of your templates, or open a previous exercise.
❏ Use the **LINE** command to draw a rectangle similar to the object in Figure 4-22.
❏ Type ERASE at the Command: prompt and erase two of the lines.
❏ Draw another rectangle, similar to the previous one.
❏ Type ERASE at the Command: prompt and enter L at the Select objects: prompt.
❏ Press [Enter] again and enter L to erase one more line.
❏ Save the drawing as EX4-7.

Using the Window selection option

The **W** or **Window** option can be used at any Select objects: prompt. This option allows you to draw a box or "window" around an object or group of objects to select for editing. Everything entirely within the window can be selected at the same time. If portions of entities project outside the window, they are not selected. The command sequence looks like this:

> Command: **E** *or* **ERASE**⏎
> Select objects: *(select a point below and to the left of the object(s) to be erased)*

When the Select objects: prompt is shown, select a point clearly below and to the left of the object to be erased. After you select the first point, the screen crosshairs change to a box-shaped cursor. It expands in size as you move the pointing device to the right. The box is a solid line. The next prompt is:

> Specify first corner: Specify opposite corner: *(pick the other corner to the right of the object(s) to be erased)*
> Select objects: ⏎
> Command:

When the Specify opposite corner: prompt is shown, move the pointing device to the right so the box totally encloses the object(s) to be erased. Then pick to locate the second corner, as shown in Figure 4-23. All objects within the window become highlighted. When finished, press [Enter] or pick the right mouse button to complete the **ERASE** command.

Figure 4-23.
Using the **Window** selection option with the **ERASE** command.

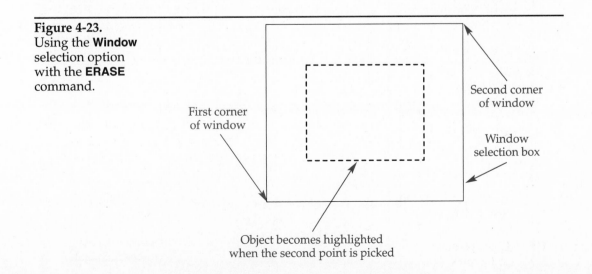

First corner of window

Second corner of window

Window selection box

Object becomes highlighted when the second point is picked

You can also manually specify the **Window** selection option from the command line. You need to do this if the **PICKAUTO** variable (discussed later in this chapter) is set to 0. The command sequence is as follows:

Command: **E** *or* **ERASE**⏎
Select objects: **W**⏎
Specify first corner: *(select a point outside of the object)*
Specify opposite corner: *(pick the other corner)*
Select objects: ⏎
Command:

When you manually enter the **Window** option, you do not need to pick the first point to the left of the object(s) being erased. The "box" remains the **Window** box whether you move the cursor to the left or right.

Using the **Crossing** selection option

The **Crossing** selection option is similar to the **Window** option. However, entities within and those *crossing* the box are selected. The **Crossing** box outline is dotted to distinguish it from the solid outline of the **Window** box. The command sequence for the **Crossing** option is as follows:

Command: **E** *or* **ERASE**⏎
Select objects: *(pick a point to the right of the object(s) to be erased)*

When the Select objects: prompt is shown, select a point to the right of the object to be erased. After you select the first point, the screen crosshairs change to a box-shaped cursor. It expands in size as you move the pointing device to the left. The next prompt is:

Specify first corner: Specify opposite corner: *(move the cursor to the left so that the box encloses or crosses the object(s) to be erased and pick)*
Select objects: ⏎
Command:

Remember, the crossing box does not need to enclose the entire object to erase it as the window box does. The crossing box need only "cross" part of the object. Figure 4-24 shows how to erase three of four lines of a rectangle using the **Crossing** option.

You can also manually specify the **Crossing** option from the command line. You need to do this if the **PICKAUTO** variable (discussed later in this chapter) is set to 0. The command sequence is as follows:

Command: **E** *or* **ERASE**⏎
Select objects: **C**⏎
Specify first corner: *(pick a point outside of the object)*
Specify opposite corner: *(pick the other corner)*
Select objects: ⏎
Command:

Figure 4-24.
Using the **Crossing** box to erase objects.

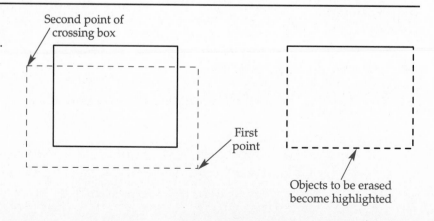

Second point of crossing box

First point

Objects to be erased become highlighted

AutoCAD and its Applications—Basics

When you manually enter the **Crossing** option, you do not need to pick the first point to the right of the object(s) being erased. The "box" remains the **Crossing** box whether you move the cursor to the left or right.

Using the PICKAUTO system variable

The **PICKAUTO** system variable controls automatic windowing when the Select objects: prompt appears. The **PICKAUTO** settings are: ON = 1 (default) and OFF = 0. Change the **PICKAUTO** value by typing PICKAUTO at the Command: prompt and then entering the new value. By default, **PICKAUTO** is set to 1. At this setting, you can automatically use the **Window** or **Crossing** selection process.

With **PICKAUTO** set to 1, pick any left point outside the object and then move the cursor to the right for a **Window** selection. The **Window** box outline is a solid line. Pick any right point outside the object and move the cursor to the left for a **Crossing** selection. The **Crossing** box is a dashed line.

You can use the automatic **Window** or **Crossing** option even if **PICKAUTO** is 0 (off). To do this, enter AU (for auto) at the Select objects: prompt, and then proceed as previously discussed.

Using the Box selection option

Another way to begin the window or crossing selection option is to type BOX at the Select objects: prompt. You are then prompted to pick the first corner, which is the left corner of a **Window** box or the right corner of a **Crossing** box. The command sequence is as follows:

Command: **E** *or* **ERASE**↵
Select objects: **BOX**↵
Specify first corner: *(pick the left corner of a **Window** box or the right corner of a*
    Crossing *box)*
Specify opposite corner: *(pick the opposite corner)*
Select objects: ↵
Command:

EXERCISE 4-8

❏ Start a new drawing, use one of your templates, or open a previous exercise.
❏ Set the **PICKAUTO** system variable to 0 (off).
❏ Draw a square using the **LINE** command with relative coordinates and the **Close** option.
❏ Type ERASE at the Command: prompt and use the **Window** selection option. Place the window around the entire square to erase it.
❏ Draw a rectangle using the **LINE** command, Ortho mode, and direct distance entry.
❏ Now, erase three of the four lines using the **Crossing** selection.
❏ Set the **PICKAUTO** system variable to 1 (on).
❏ Draw a rectangle using the **LINE** command and Snap mode.
❏ Now, enter ERASE and automatically erase the square using a window.
❏ Draw a rectangle using the **LINE** command and absolute coordinates.
❏ Enter ERASE and erase three sides of the square using the automatic **Crossing** selection.
❏ Save the drawing as EX4-8.

Using the WPolygon selection option

The **Window** selection option requires that you place a rectangle completely around the entities to be erased. Sometimes it is awkward to place a rectangle around the items to erase. When this situation occurs, you can place a polygon (closed figure with three or more sides) of your own design around the objects with the **WPolygon** selection option.

To use the **WPolygon** option, type WP at the Select objects: prompt. Then, draw a polygon that encloses the objects. As you pick corners, the polygon drags into place. The command sequence for erasing the five middle squares in Figure 4-25 is as follows:

  Command: **E** *or* **ERASE**↵
  Select objects: **WP**↵
  First polygon point: *(pick Point 1)*
  Specify endpoint of line or [Undo]: *(pick Point 2)*
  Specify endpoint of line or [Undo]: *(pick Point 3)*
  Specify endpoint of line or [Undo]: *(pick Point 4)*
  Specify endpoint of line or [Undo]: ↵
  Select objects: ↵
  Command:

If you do not like the last polygon point you picked, use the **Undo** option by entering U at the Specify endpoint of line or [Undo] prompt.

Figure 4-25.
Using the **WPolygon** selection option to erase objects.

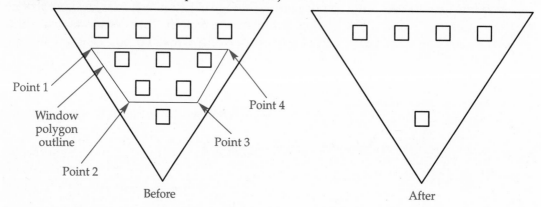

Point 1

Window polygon outline

Point 2

Point 4

Point 3

Before

After

Using the CPolygon selection option

The **Crossing** selection option lets you place a rectangle around or through the objects to be erased. Sometimes it is difficult to place a rectangle around or through the items to be erased without coming into contact with other entities. When you want to use the features of the **Crossing** selection option, but prefer to use a polygon instead of a rectangle, enter CP at the Select objects: prompt. Then, proceed to draw a polygon that encloses or crosses the objects to erase. As you pick the points, the polygon drags into place. The **CPolygon** line is a dashed rubberband cursor.

Suppose you want to erase everything inside the large triangle in Figure 4-26 except for the top and bottom horizontal lines. The command sequence to erase these lines is as follows:

  Command: **E** *or* **ERASE**↵
  Select objects: **CP**↵
  First polygon point: *(pick Point 1)*
  Specify endpoint of line or [Undo]: *(pick Point 2)*
  Specify endpoint of line or [Undo]: *(pick Point 3)*
  Specify endpoint of line or [Undo]: *(pick Point 4)*
  Specify endpoint of line or [Undo]: ↵
  Select objects: ↵
  Command:

If you want to change the last point you picked, enter U at the Undo/⟨Endpoint of line⟩: prompt.

Figure 4-26.
Using the **CPolygon** selection option. Everything enclosed within and crossing the polygon is selected.

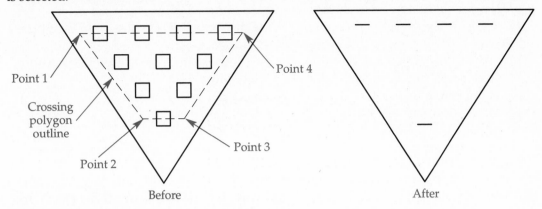

Before

After

PROFESSIONAL TIP

When using **WPolygon** or **CPolygon**, AutoCAD does not allow you to select a point that causes the lines of the selection polygon to intersect each other. Pick locations that do not result in an intersection. Use the **Undo** option if you need to go back and relocate a preceding pick point.

Using the Fence selection option

Fence is another selection option used to select several objects at the same time. When using the **Fence** option, you simply need to place a fence through the objects you want to select. Anything that the fence passes through is included in the selection set. The fence can be straight or staggered, as shown in Figure 4-27. Type F at the Select objects: prompt as follows:

  Command: **E** *or* **ERASE**↵
  Select objects: **F**↵
  First polygon point: *(pick Point 1)*
  Specify endpoint of line or [Undo]: *(pick Point 2)*
  Specify endpoint of line or [Undo]: *(pick Point 3)*
  Specify endpoint of line or [Undo]: *(pick Point 4)*
  Specify endpoint of line or [Undo]: *(pick Point 5)*
  Specify endpoint of line or [Undo]: *(pick Point 6)*
  Specify endpoint of line or [Undo]: ↵
  Select objects: ↵
  Command:

Figure 4-27.
Using the **Fence** selection option to erase entities. The fence can be either straight or staggered.

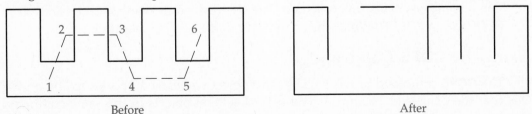

Before

After

Removing from and adding to the selection set

When editing a drawing, a common mistake is to accidentally select an object that you do not want to select. The simplest way to remove one or more objects from the current selection set is by holding down the [Shift] key and reselecting the objects. This is possible only for individual picks and implied windows. For an implied window, the [Shift] key must be held down while picking the first corner, and then can be released for picking the second corner. If you accidentally remove the wrong object from the selection set, release the [Shift] key and pick it again.

To use other methods for removing objects from a selection set, or for specialized selection needs, you can switch to the Remove objects mode by typing R at the Select objects: prompt. This changes the Select objects: prompt to Remove objects: as follows:

Command: **E** *or* **ERASE**↵
Select objects: *(pick several objects using any technique)*
Select objects: **R**↵
Remove objects: *(pick the objects you want removed from the selection set)*
Remove objects: ↵

Switch back to the selection mode by typing A, for Add, at the Remove objects: prompt. This restores the Select objects: prompt and allows you to select additional objects. This is how the **Add** feature works:

Remove objects: **A**↵
Select objects: *(continue selecting objects as needed)*
Select objects: ↵
Command:

Cleaning Up the Screen

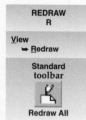

After you draw and edit a number of objects, the screen is cluttered with small crosses or markers called *blips*. In addition, many of the grid dots may be missing. This can be distracting.

The **REDRAW** command cleans the screen in the current viewport. To access the **REDRAW** command, pick **Redraw** from the **View** pull-down menu, or type R or REDRAW at the Command: prompt. The **Redraw All** button on the **Standard** toolbar can also be used to redraw the screen.

The screen goes blank for an instant, and the cleaned drawing and screen return. The **REDRAW** and **REDRAWALL** commands are discussed in Chapter 9.

Using the OOPS Command

The **OOPS** command brings back the last object you erased. It is issued by typing OOPS at the Command: prompt. If you erased several objects in the same command sequence, all are brought back to the screen. Only the objects erased in the most recent erase procedure can be returned using **OOPS**.

Using the U Command

While the **OOPS** command brings back the last object you erased, the **U** command undoes the last command. The **U** command is issued by typing U at the Command: prompt, or by using the [Ctrl]+[Z] key combination. **OOPS** can only be used one time in sequence, while **U** can be issued until every command used since the editing session began has been undone. Even **OOPS** can be undone with the **U** command.

Using the Previous Selection

The object selection options given to this point in the chapter have used the example of the **ERASE** command. These selection options are also used when moving objects, rotating objects, and performing other editing functions. These basic editing commands are explained in Chapter 11.

Often, more than one sequential editing operation needs to be carried out on a specific group of objects. In this case, the **Previous** selection option allows you to select the same object(s) you just edited for further editing. You can select the **Previous** selection set by typing P at the Select objects: prompt. In the following example, a group of objects is erased and the **OOPS** command is used to recover them. Then, the **ERASE** command is issued again, this time using the **Previous** selection option to access the previously selected objects:

Command: **E** or **ERASE**⏎
Select objects: (pick several items using any selection technique)
n found, n total
Select objects: ⏎
Command: **OOPS**⏎
Command: **E** or **ERASE**⏎
Select objects: **P**⏎
n found
Select objects: ⏎
Command:

Selecting All Objects in a Drawing

Sometimes you may want to select every object in the drawing. To do this, type ALL at the Select objects: prompt as follows:

Command: **E** or **ERASE**⏎
Select objects: **ALL**⏎
Select objects: ⏎
Command:

This procedure erases everything on the drawing. You can use the **Remove** option at the second Select objects: prompt to remove certain objects from the set. You can also enter ALL after typing R to remove all objects from the set.

EXERCISE 4-10

❑ Start a new drawing, use one of your templates, or open a previous exercise.
❑ Draw an object similar to the one shown in Figure 4-27.
❑ Use the **SI** selection option to erase one line.
❑ Use the **SI** selection option with a fence to erase any two lines.
❑ Experiment using the **Remove** and **Add** selection options by selecting six items to erase, removing two of the items from the selection set, and then adding three new entities.
❑ Use the **REDRAW** command to clean up the screen.
❑ Use the **ALL** selection option to erase everything from the drawing.
❑ Use the **U** or **OOPS** command to get everything back that you erased.
❑ Save the drawing as EX4-10.

Using the Multiple Selection Option

The **Multiple** option provides easy access to stacked objects. *Stacked objects* occur when one feature, such as a line, overlays another in a 2D drawing. These lines have the same Z values, so one is no higher or lower than the other. However, the last object drawn appears to be on top of all others.

When a point on an object is picked in select mode, the database is scanned and the first object found is the object selected. Additional picks will only duplicate the original results. Unless **Window**, **Crossing**, **Fence**, or **Multiple** is used, the underlying objects are inaccessible.

Using the **Multiple** option allows multiple picks at the same point. The first pick finds the first object. A second pick in the same place ignores the already selected object and finds the next object. This process continues for each pick made. The **Multiple** option is used by typing M at the Select objects: prompt. The command sequence used to erase two stacked lines with the **Multiple** option is as follows:

```
Command: E or ERASE↵
Select objects: M↵
Select objects: (pick the stacked objects twice, then press the [Enter] key)
2 selected, 2 found
Select objects: ↵
Command:
```

Notice that the *n* selected, *n* found prompt (in which *n* represents the number reported by AutoCAD) does not appear until you press the [Enter] key. This may make it difficult to select all overlapping objects if you do not know how many are there.

PROFESSIONAL TIP

When objects are selected using the **Multiple** option, the selected objects are not highlighted until the [Enter] key is pressed. This can speed up the selection process for text and other complex objects on workstations with slower display systems.

Often, you may want to modify an object underlying another without affecting the "top" object. To do this, enter the **Multiple** mode as previously discussed. For the previous example, pick a point on the object twice. Press [Enter] to end the multiple mode. AutoCAD tells you that both objects are selected. Now, use the **Remove** option and select the same point again. The "top" object is now removed from the selection set.

NOTE

When selecting objects to be erased, AutoCAD only accepts qualifying objects. *Qualifying object* refers to an object that is not on a locked layer and that passes through the pick box area at the point selected. Layers are discussed later in this chapter.

Cycling Through Stacked Objects

Another way to deal with stacked objects is to let AutoCAD cycle through the overlapping objects. *Cycling* is repeatedly selecting one item from a series of stacked objects until the desired object is highlighted. This works best when several objects cross at the same place or are very close together. To begin cycling through objects, hold down the [Ctrl] key while you make your first pick.

For the objects in Figure 4-28, pick the point where the four circles intersect. If there are two or more objects found crossing through the pick box area, the top object is highlighted. Now, you can release the [Ctrl] key. When you pick again, the top object returns and the next one is highlighted. Every time you pick, another object becomes highlighted. In this way, you cycle through all of the objects. When you have the desired object highlighted, press [Enter] to end the cycling process and return to the Select objects: prompt. Press [Enter] again to return to the Command: prompt.

The following command sequence is used to erase one of the circles in Figure 4-28, but you can use this for any editing function:

> Command: **E** *or* **ERASE**↵
> Select objects: *(hold down the* [Ctrl] *key and pick)* ⟨Cycle on⟩ *(pick until you highlight the desired object and press* [Enter]*)*
> <Cycle off>1 found
> Select objects: *(select additional objects or press* [Enter]*)*
> Command:

Figure 4-28.
Cycling through a series of stacked circles until the desired object is highlighted.

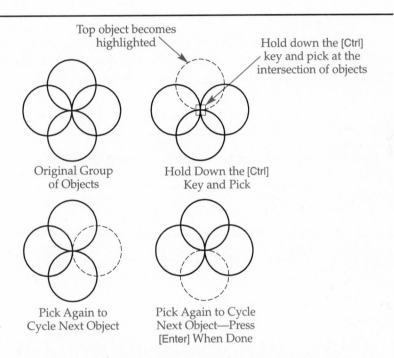

Top object becomes highlighted

Hold down the [Ctrl] key and pick at the intersection of objects

Original Group of Objects

Hold Down the [Ctrl] Key and Pick

Pick Again to Cycle Next Object

Pick Again to Cycle Next Object—Press [Enter] When Done

AN INTRODUCTION TO LAYERS

AutoCAD User's Guide **10**

In drafting, different elements or components of drawings might be separated by placing them on different sheets. You have an overlay system if each sheet is perfectly aligned with the others. This overlay system is referred to as *layers*. All the layers can be reproduced together to reflect the entire design drawing. Individual layers might also be reproduced to show specific details or components of the design. Using layers increases productivity in several ways:

✓ Specific information can be grouped on separate layers. For example, the floor plan can be drawn on one layer, the electrical plan on another, and the plumbing plan on a third layer.

✓ Several plot sheets can be referenced from the same drawing file by modifying layer visibility.

✓ Drawings can be reproduced by individual layers or combined in any desired format. For example, the floor plan and electrical plan can be reproduced together and sent to an electrical contractor for a bid. The floor plan and plumbing plan can be reproduced together and sent to the plumbing contractor.

✓ Each layer can be assigned a different color, linetype, or lineweight to help improve clarity.

✓ Each layer can be plotted in a different color or pen width, or not plotted at all.

✓ Selected layers can be turned off or frozen to decrease the amount of information displayed on the screen or to speed screen regeneration.

✓ Changes can be made to a layer promptly, often while the client watches.

Layers Used in Different Drafting Fields

In mechanical drafting, views, hidden features, dimensions, sections, notes, and symbols might be placed on separate layers. In architectural or civil drafting, there may be over one hundred layers. Layers can be created for floor plans, foundation plans, partition layouts, plumbing, electrical, structural, roof drainage, reflected ceiling, and HVAC systems. Interior designers may use floor plan, interior partition, and furniture layers. In electronics drafting, each level of a multilevel circuit board can be drawn on its own layer.

Current Layer

As you have worked through the exercises in this book, you may have noticed that "0" appears in the **Layer Control** box on the **Object Properties** toolbar. See Figure 4-29. Layer 0 is the AutoCAD default layer. Until another layer is defined and activated, all drawing is done on the 0 layer.

Figure 4-29.
0 appears in the **Layer Control** box on the **Object Properties** toolbar. Layer 0 is the AutoCAD default layer.

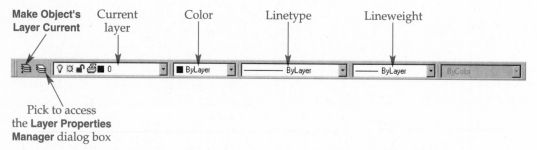

Pick to access the **Layer Properties Manager** dialog box

Naming Layers

Layers should be given names to reflect what is drawn on them. Layer names can have up to 255 characters and can include letters, numbers, and certain special characters including spaces. Typical mechanical, architectural, and civil drafting layer names are as follows:

Mechanical	Architectural	Civil
Object	Walls	Property Line
Hidden	Windows	Structures
Center	Doors	Roads
Dimension	Electrical	Water
Construction	Plumbing	Contours
Hatch	Furniture	Gas
Border	Lighting	Elevations

For very simple drawings, layers can be named by linetype and color. For example, the layer name Object-White may have a continuous linetype drawn in white. The linetype and color number, such as Object-7, can also be used. Another option is to assign the linetype a numerical value. For example, object lines can be 0, hidden lines 1, and centerlines 2. If you use this method, keep a written record of the numbering system for reference.

Layers can also be given more complex names. The name might include the drawing number, color code, and layer content. The name Dwg100-2-Dimen could refer to drawing DWG100, color 2, and the Dimen layer.

PROFESSIONAL TIP

In releases of AutoCAD prior to AutoCAD 2000, layer names could be no longer than 31 characters and could not contain spaces. If you save an AutoCAD 2000 drawing to the format of an earlier release, AutoCAD replaces any disallowed characters with underscores (_) and shortens the layer names to 31 characters.

INTRODUCTION TO THE LAYER COMMAND

AutoCAD User's Guide **10**

LAYER
LA

Format
➥ Layer...

Object Properties toolbar

Layers

The **LAYER** command opens the **Layer Properties Manager** dialog box shown in Figure 4-30. To display this dialog box, pick the **Layers** button from the **Object Properties** toolbar, select **Layer...** from the **Format** pull-down menu, or type LA or LAYER at the Command: prompt.

Only one layer is required in an AutoCAD drawing. That layer is named 0 and cannot be renamed or purged from the drawing. However, as discussed earlier, it is often useful to have more than one layer in a drawing. The most important layer is the *current layer* because whatever you draw is placed on this layer. It is useful to think of the current layer as the *top* layer.

Figure 4-30.
The **Layer Properties Manager** dialog box.

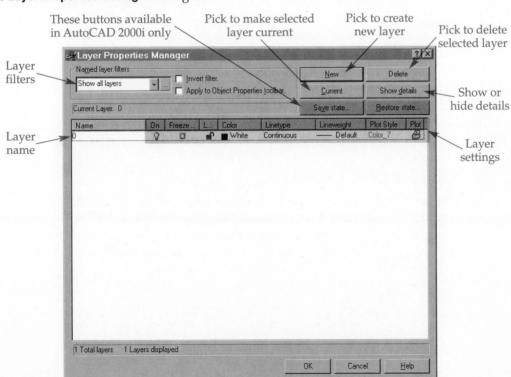

For 2000i Users...

The **Save state...** and **Restore state...** buttons are available in AutoCAD 2000i only. These buttons are explained in *Layer States*, beginning on page 968.

Creating Layers

Layers should be added to a drawing to meet the needs of the current drawing project. To add a new layer, pick the **New** button. A new layer listing appears, using a default name of Layer1. See Figure 4-31. The layer name is highlighted when the listing appears, allowing you to type in a new name.

You can also enter several new layer names at the same time. This is done by typing a layer name followed by pressing the comma key. This drops the Layer1 listing below the previously entered name. Entering several layer names in this manner is much faster, because it keeps you from having to pick the **New** button each time. Pick the **OK** button when finished typing the new layer names. When you reopen the **Layer Properties Manager** dialog box, the new layer names are alphabetized, as shown in Figure 4-32.

Figure 4-31.
A new layer is named Layer1 by default.

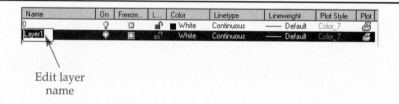

Edit layer name

Figure 4-32.
Layer names are automatically placed in numerical and alphabetical order.

Name	On	Freeze...	L...	Color	Linetype	Lineweight	Plot Style	Plot
0	♀	☼	⌐	■ White	Continuous	—— Default	Color_7	🖨
1	♀	☼	⌐	■ White	Continuous	—— Default	Color_7	🖨
2	♀	☼	⌐	■ White	Continuous	—— Default	Color_7	🖨
3	♀	☼	⌐	■ White	Continuous	—— Default	Color_7	🖨
Electrical	♀	☼	⌐	■ White	Continuous	—— Default	Color_7	🖨
Judy	♀	☼	⌐	■ White	Continuous	—— Default	Color_7	🖨
Plumbing	♀	☼	⌐	■ White	Continuous	—— Default	Color_7	🖨
Walls	♀	☼	⌐	■ White	Continuous	—— Default	Color_7	🖨

NOTE

Sorting can be controlled by selecting the headings in the layer names window. However, each time the **Layer Properties Manager** dialog is reopened, layers default to alphanumeric sorting.

Deleting Layers

Deleting a layer that is no longer in use is a simple process. First, select the layer. Then, pick the **Delete** button. The layer is erased from the list box.

Setting the Current Layer

You can set a new current layer by double-clicking the layer name or highlighting the layer name in the layer list and then picking the **Current** button. To highlight the layer name, simply pick it. The current layer is specified in the status line above the layer list in the **Layer Properties Manager** dialog box and in the **Object Properties** toolbar.

❑ Start a new drawing or open one of your templates.
❑ Open the **Layer Properties Manager** dialog box.
❑ Start a list of layer names similar to Figure 4-32 but in a different random order, or use other names of your own choosing. Enter a couple of the names by picking the **New** button after each entry.
❑ Continue the list of new layer names by pressing the comma key to enter several names.
❑ Pick the **OK** button when done.
❑ Open the **Layer Properties Manager** dialog box again and see how AutoCAD automatically lists the layer names in alphabetical order.
❑ Close the dialog box.
❑ Save as EX4-11.

NOTE

You can view context specific help by picking the **Help** button at the top right corner of the **Layer Properties Manager** dialog box and then picking the area of the dialog where you want help.

Viewing the Status of Layers

The status of each layer is displayed with icons to the right of the layer name. See Figure 4-33. If you position the pointer over an icon for a moment, a tooltip appears and tells what the icon refers to. Layer settings can be changed by picking the related icon.

- **Changing the layer name.** The layer name list box contains all the layers in the drawing. To change an existing name, pick the name once to highlight it, pause for a moment, then pick it again. When you pick the second time, the layer name is highlighted with a text box around it and a cursor for text entry to allow you to type a new layer name. Layer 0 cannot be renamed.

Figure 4-33.
Layer settings can be changed by picking the icons in the **Layer Properties Manager** dialog box.

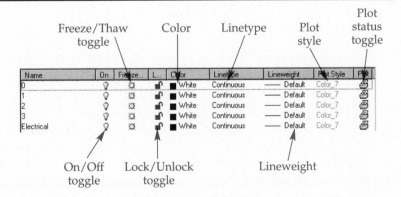

- **Turning layers on and off.** The lightbulb shows whether a layer is on or off. The yellow lightbulb means the layer is on; objects on that layer are displayed on-screen and can be plotted. If you pick on a yellow lightbulb, it turns gray, turning the layer off. If a layer is off, the objects on it are not displayed on-screen and are not plotted. Objects that are on a layer that has been turned off can still be edited when using advanced selection techniques, and are regenerated when a drawing regeneration occurs.

On   Off

Thawed   Frozen

- **Thawing and freezing layers.** Layers are further classified as thawed or frozen. Similar to the off setting, layers that are frozen are not displayed and do not plot. However, objects on a frozen layer cannot be edited and are not regenerated when the drawing regenerates. Freezing layers that contain objects that do not need to be referenced for current drawing tasks can greatly speed up your system performance. The snowflake icon is displayed when a layer is frozen. Layers are normally thawed, which means that objects on the layer are displayed on-screen. The sun icon is displayed for thawed layers. Picking the sun/snowflake icon toggles it to the other icon.

> **NOTE**
>
> It is important to note that objects on layers that are frozen cannot be modified, but objects residing on layers that are turned off can be modified. For example, if you turn off half your layers and use the **All** selection option with the **ERASE** command, even the objects on layers turned off will be erased!

Locked   Unlocked

- **Unlocked and locked layers.** The unlocked and locked padlock symbols are for locking and unlocking layers. Layers are unlocked by default, but you can pick on the unlocked padlock to lock it. A layer that is locked remains visible, but objects on that layer cannot be edited. New objects can be added to a locked layer.
- **Layer color.** The color swatch shows the current default color for objects created on each layer. When you need to change the color for an existing layer, pick the swatch to display the **Select Color** dialog box. Working with colors is discussed later in this chapter.
- **Layer linetype.** The current linetype setting for each layer is shown in the **Linetype** list. Picking the linetype name opens the **Select Linetype** dialog box, where you can specify a new linetype. Working with linetypes is discussed later in this chapter.
- **Layer lineweight.** The current lineweight setting for each layer is shown in the **Lineweight** list. Picking the lineweight name opens the **Lineweight** dialog box, where you can specify a new lineweight. Working with lineweights is discussed later in this chapter.
- **Layer plot styles.** This setting changes the plot style associated with the selected layers. The plot style setting is disabled when you are working with color-dependent plot styles (the **PSTYLEPOLICY** system variable is set to 1). Otherwise, picking the plot style displays the **Select Plot Style** dialog box. Plot styles are discussed in Chapter 10.

Plot   No Plot

- **Layer plot/no plot.** Select this toggle to turn off plotting for a particular layer. The "no plot" symbol is displayed over the printer image when the layer is not available to be plotted. The layer is still displayed, but not plotted.

The following layer options appear only in paper space layout mode, which is discussed in Chapter 10:

- **Thawing and freezing layers in active and new viewports.** These settings, for floating model space views on layouts, are detailed in Chapter 24. The options are visible only when a layout tab is active.

Working with Layers

Any setting that is changed affects all layer names that are currently highlighted. Highlighting layer names employs the same techniques used in file dialog boxes. You can highlight a single name by picking it. Picking another name deselects the previous name and highlights the new selection. You can use the [Shift] key to select two layers and all layer names between them on the listing. Holding the [Ctrl] key while picking layer names highlights or deselects each selected name without affecting any other selections.

A shortcut menu is also available while your cursor is in the layer list area of this dialog box. Press the right mouse button to display the shortcut menu shown in Figure 4-34. The options available on this menu are:

- **New Layer.** Creates a new layer.
- **Select All.** Selects all layers.
- **Clear All.** Deselects all layers.
- **Select all but current.** Selects all layers except the current layer.
- **Invert selection.** Deselects all selected layers and selects all deselected layers.
- **Invert layer filter.** Inverts the current filter setting. Filters are discussed later in this chapter.
- **Layer filters.** Displays a submenu with predefined filters. The choices are:
    - **Show all layers.**
    - **Show all used layers.**
    - **Show all Xref dependent layers.**

Figure 4-34.
Right-clicking in the list box of the **Layer Properties Manager** dialog box produces this shortcut menu. If a single layer is selected, a **Make Current** option is also available.

For 2000i Users...

In AutoCAD 2000i, this menu includes a **Save layer states...** option. The use of this option is explained in *Layer States*, beginning on page 968.

Setting the Layer Color

The number of layer colors available depends on your graphics card and monitor. Color systems usually support at least 256 colors, while many graphics cards support up to 16.7 million colors. Layer colors are coded by name and number. The first seven standard color numbers are listed below:

Number	Color
1	Red
2	Yellow
3	Green
4	Cyan
5	Blue
6	Magenta
7	White

Color settings affect the appearance of plotted drawings. Lineweights are associated with drawing colors. This is discussed in Chapter 10. Colors should also highlight the important features on the drawing and not cause eyestrain.

To change layer color, select the desired layer name or names and then pick the color swatch for one of the highlighted layer names. This displays the **Select Color** dialog box, as shown in Figure 4-35. The **Select Color** dialog box allows you to specify the default color for each layer.

To select a color, you can either pick the color swatch that displays the desired color or type the color name or number in the **Color:** text box. The first seven basic colors were listed previously in the table. The color white (number 7) refers to white if the graphics screen background is black, and black if the background is white. All other colors can be accessed by their ACI (AutoCAD Color Index) number.

Figure 4-35.
The **Select Color** dialog box.

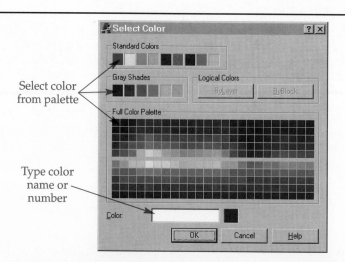

Select color from palette

Type color name or number

An easy way to investigate the ACI numbering system is to pick a color swatch and see what number appears in the **Color:** text box. After selecting a color, pick the **OK** button when ready. The color you picked is now displayed as the color swatch for the highlighted layer name in the **Layer Properties Manager** dialog box.

Setting the Layer Linetype

Earlier in this chapter you were introduced to line standards. AutoCAD provides standard linetypes that can be used at any time to match the ANSI standards or the standards for other drafting applications that you are using. You can also create your own custom linetypes. In order to achieve different line widths, it is necessary to assign a lineweight.

AutoCAD linetypes

AutoCAD maintains its standard linetypes in an external file named acad.lin. Before any of these linetypes can be used, they must be loaded and then set current, or assigned to a layer. Three of AutoCAD's linetypes are required and cannot be deleted from the drawing. The Continuous linetype represents solid lines with no breaks. ByLayer and ByBlock are logical linetypes and represent the linetype assigned to an AutoCAD layer or block insertion. ByLayer and ByBlock are assigned to objects in the drawing and cannot be assigned to layers because they already represent the linetypes assigned to individual layers. ByLayer means "use the linetype, color, or lineweight of the object's layer." ByBlock means "use the linetype assigned to the block insertion."

The AutoCAD linetypes are shown in Figure 4-36.

PROFESSIONAL TIP   Two linetype definition files are available, acad.lin and acadiso.lin. The ISO linetypes found in both files are identical, but the non-ISO linetype definitions are scaled up 25.4 times in the acadiso.lin file. The scale factor of 25.4 is used to convert from inches to millimeters. The ISO linetypes are for metric drawings.

Figure 4-36.
The AutoCAD linetype library contains ISO, standard, and complex linetypes.

Continuous —————————

Border — — — — —

Border2 — — — — — —

Borderx2 ——— ——— ———

Center ——— — ——— — ———

Center2 —— · — · —— · — ·

Centerx2 ——— — ———

Dashdot — · — · — · —

Dashdot2 — · — · — · — · —

Dashdotx2 ——— · ——— · ———

Dashed — — — — — —

Dashed2 — — — — — — — —

Dashedx2 ——— ——— ——— ———

Divide — · · — · · — · · —

Divide2 — · · — · · — · ·

Dividex2 ——— · · ——— · · ———

Dot · · · · · · · · · ·

Dot2 · · · · · · · · · · · ·

Dotx2 · · · · · · ·

Hidden — — — — — — —

Hidden2 — — — — — — — — —

Hiddenx2 ——— ——— ——— ———

Phantom — — — — — — —

Phantom2 — — — — — — — —

Phantomx2 ——— — — ———

Acad_iso02w100 — — — — — —

Acad_iso03w100 —   —   —   —

Acad_iso04w100 ——— · ——— · ———

Acad_iso05w100 ——— · · ——— · ·

Acad_iso06w100 ——— — — ———

Acad_iso07w100 · · · · · · · · · · · · ·

Acad_iso08w100 ——— — ——— — ———

Acad_iso09w100 ——— — — ——— — —

Acad_iso10w100 — · — · — · — ·

Acad_iso11w100 ——— · ——— · ———

Acad_iso12w100 — · · — · · — · · —

Acad_iso13w100 ——— · · ——— · · ———

Acad_iso14w100 — · — · — · —

Acad_iso15w100 — · · — · · — · ·

Fenceline1 —o———o———o—

Fenceline2 —□———□———□—

Gas_line ——— GAS ——— GAS ———

Hot_water_supply ——— HW ——— HW ———

Tracks ++++++++++++++++

Zigzag /\/\/\/\/\/\/\

Batting ∞∞∞∞∞∞∞∞∞∞∞

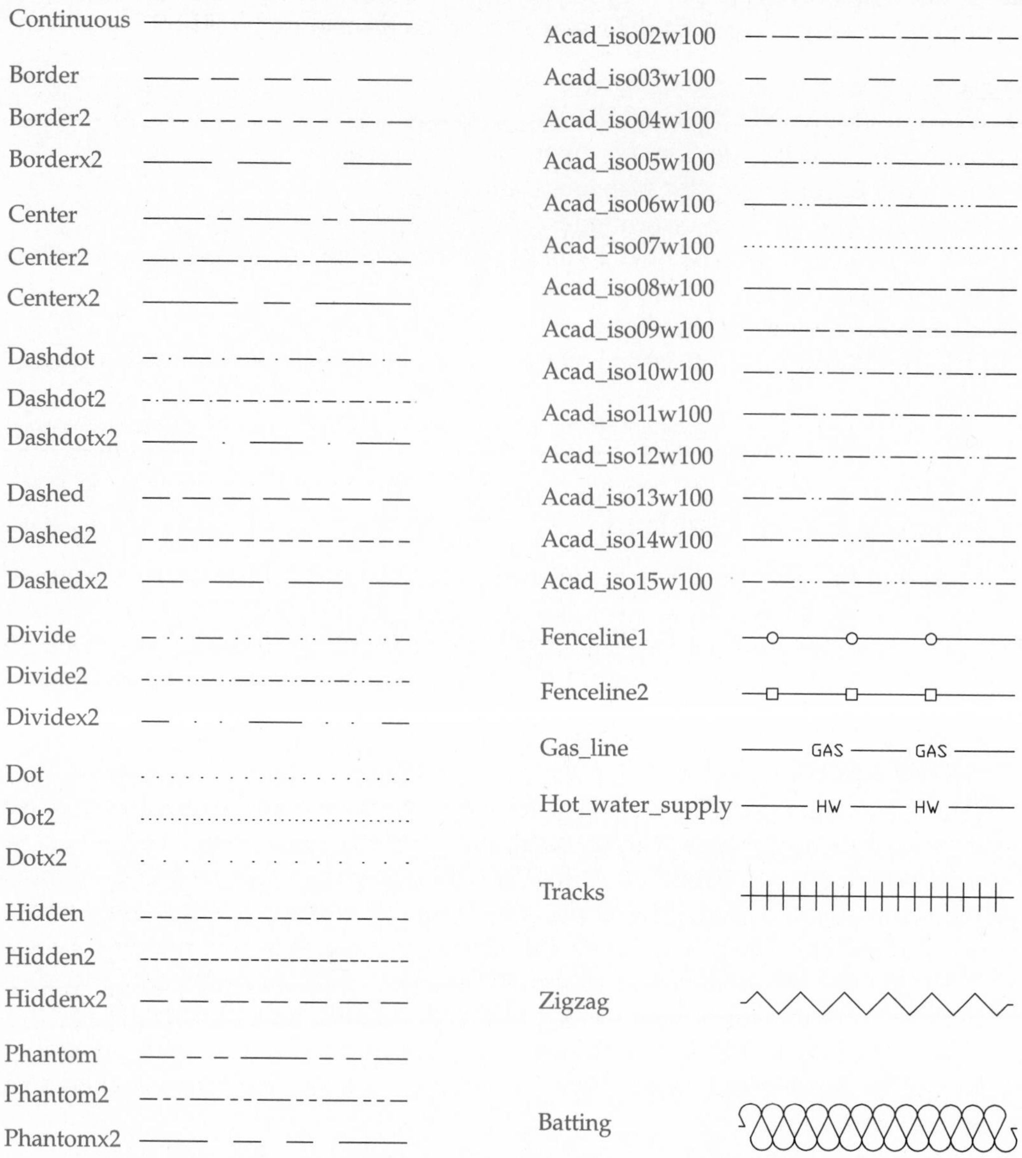

Changing linetype assignments

To change linetype assignments, select the layer name you want to change and pick its linetype name. This displays the **Select Linetype** dialog box shown in Figure 4-37. The first time you use this dialog box, you may find only the Continuous linetype listed in the **Loaded linetypes** list box. You need to load any other linetypes to be used in the drawing.

If you need to add linetypes that are not included in the list, pick the **Load...** button to display the **Load or Reload Linetypes** dialog box, shown in Figure 4-38. The ISO, standard, and complex linetypes are named and displayed in the **Available Linetypes** list. Standard linetypes use only dashes, dots, and gaps. Complex linetypes can also contain special shapes and text.

Use the down arrow to look at all the linetypes. Select the linetypes you want to load. Pick the **OK** button to return to the **Select Linetype** dialog box, where the linetypes you selected are listed as shown in Figure 4-39.

Figure 4-37.
The **Select Linetype** dialog box.

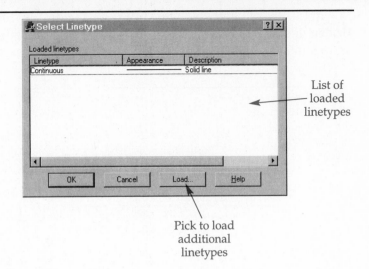

List of loaded linetypes

Pick to load additional linetypes

Figure 4-38.
The **Load or Reload Linetypes** dialog box.

Select file where linetype definitions are stored

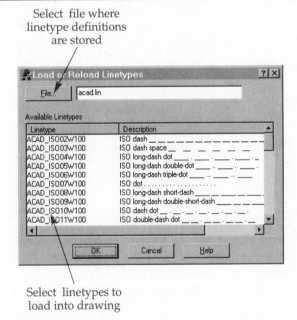

Select linetypes to load into drawing

Figure 4-39.
Linetypes loaded from the **Load or Reload Linetypes** dialog box are added to the **Loaded linetypes** list box.

Loaded linetypes

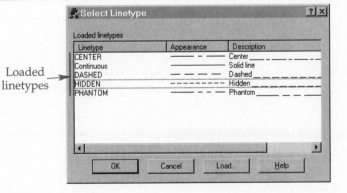

In the **Select Linetype** dialog box, pick the desired linetype and then pick **OK**. The Hidden linetype selected in Figure 4-39 is now the linetype assigned to the 2 layer, as shown in Figure 4-40.

Figure 4-40.
Objects drawn on the 2 layer will now have a Hidden linetype.

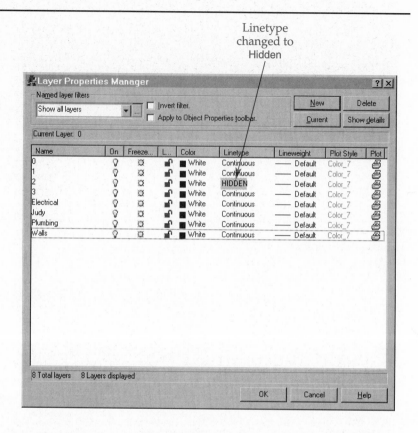

NOTE

The acad.lin file is used by default. You can switch to the ISO library by picking the **File...** button. This displays the **Select Linetype File** dialog box, where you can select the acadiso.lin file.

Managing linetypes

The **Linetype Manager** dialog box is a convenient place to load and access linetypes. This dialog box can be accessed by selecting **Linetype...** from the **Format** pull-down menu, by selecting **Other...** in the **Linetype Control** box in the **Object Properties** toolbar, or by typing LT or LINETYPE at the Command: prompt. See Figure 4-41.

This dialog box is similar to the **Layer Properties Manager** dialog box. Picking the **Load...** button opens the **Load or Reload Linetypes** dialog box. Picking the **Delete** button will delete any selected linetypes.

Changing lineweight assignments

Like linetype, objects can also have lineweight. *Lineweight* adds width to objects for display and plotting. Lineweights can be set for objects or assigned to layers. Assigning lineweights to layers allows you to have the objects on specific layers set to their own lineweights. This allows you to control the display of line thickness to match ANSI or other standards related to your drafting application.

The layer lineweight settings are displayed on the screen when the lineweight is turned on. To toggle screen lineweights, click the **LWT** button on the status bar, or right-click on the **LWT** button and pick the **On** or **Off** option from the shortcut menu.

Figure 4-41.
The **Linetype Manager** dialog box.

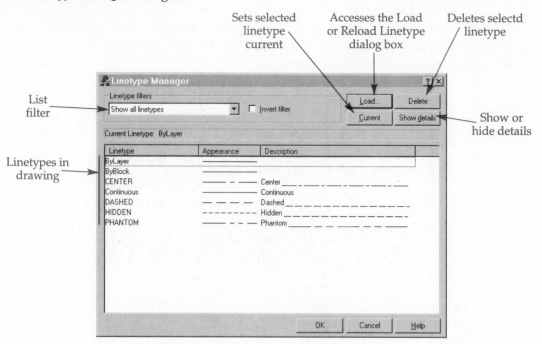

Sets selected linetype current

Accesses the Load or Reload Linetype dialog box

Deletes selectd linetype

List filter

Linetypes in drawing

Show or hide details

To change lineweight assignments in the **Layer Properties Manager**, select the layer name you want to change and pick its lineweight setting. This displays the **Lineweight** dialog box, shown in Figure 4-42. Scroll through the **Lineweight** list to select the desired lineweight. The **Lineweight** dialog box displays fixed lineweights available in AutoCAD for you to apply to the selected layer. The **Default** lineweight is the lineweight initially assigned to a layer when it is created.

The area near the bottom of the **Lineweight** dialog box displays **Original:**, which is the lineweight previously assigned to the layer, and **New:**, which is the new lineweight assigned to the layer. In Figure 4-42, the **Original:** and **New:** specifications are the same, because the initial layer lineweight has not been changed from the default.

Figure 4-42.
The **Lineweight** dialog box.

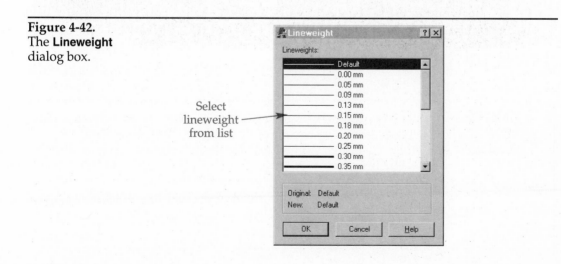

Select lineweight from list

Setting the current lineweight

Current lineweights are set in the **Lineweight Settings** dialog box shown in Figure 4-43. The **Lineweight Settings** dialog box can be accessed by picking **Lineweight...** from the **Format** pull-down menu, by typing LW or LWEIGHT at the Command: prompt, or by right-clicking on the **LWT** button on the status bar and then selecting **Settings...** in the shortcut menu.

LINEWEIGHT
LW

Format
⮕ Lineweight...

Figure 4-43.
The **Lineweight Settings** dialog box.

Select units

Lineweight display

Default lineweight setting

Display scale

Select lineweight

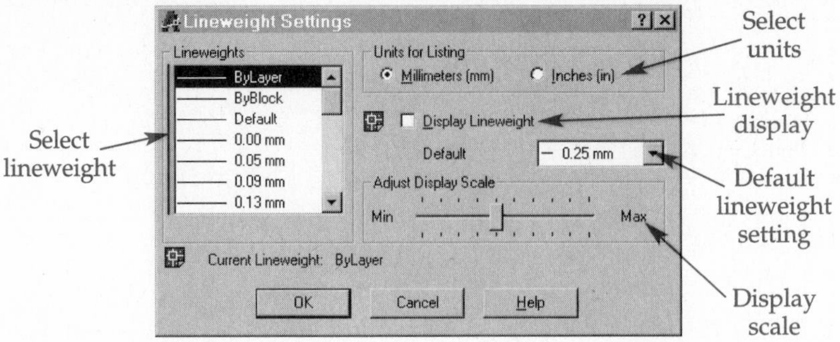

The following describes the features of the **Lineweight Settings** dialog box:
- **Lineweights.** Set the current lineweight by selecting the desired setting from the list. If lineweight is set ByLayer, the object lineweight corresponds to the lineweight of its layer. The Default option lineweight width is controlled by the Default list options. Settings other than ByLayer, ByBlock, or Default are used as overrides for lineweights of objects drawn with the selected option.
- **Units for Listing.** This area allows you to set the lineweight thickness to millimeters or inches.
- **Display Lineweight.** This is another way to turn lineweight thickness on or off. Check this box to turn lineweight on.
- **Default.** Select a lineweight default value from the drop-down list. This becomes the default lineweight for layers. The initial default setting is 0.01" or 0.25 mm. This is also controlled by the **LWDEFAULT** system variable.
- **Adjust Display Scale.** This scale allows you to adjust the lineweight display scale to improve the appearance of different lineweight widths. Adjustment of the lineweight display scale toward the **Max** value can reduce AutoCAD performance. A setting near the middle of the scale or toward **Min** may be preferred.
- **Current Lineweight.** This indicates the current lineweight setting.

For 2000i Users...

In AutoCAD 2000i, layer settings and properties can be saved as layer states. This allows you to save the settings for multiple layers, and then easily restore the settings in the future. This topic is thoroughly covered in *Layer States*, beginning on page 968.

NOTE

Object properties, such as color, linetype, and lineweight can be assigned "by layer" or "by object". It is important to note that "by object" overrides "by layer". For example, if a line's color property is ByLayer, then that line takes its color from the color of its layer. However, if that same line's color is changed "by object" to green, then that line is green regardless of layer color. This is also true for linetype and lineweight.

❏ Open EX4-11 if it is not already open.
❏ Open the **Select Linetype** dialog box and notice the default linetype.
❏ Pick the **Load...** button and load ISO02w100, Center, Dashed, Hidden, and Phantom.
❏ Pick the **OK** button.
❏ Apply the Hidden, Center, and Phantom linetypes to the layers of your choice.
❏ Apply the lineweight of 0.60mm to the Walls layer.
❏ Open the **Lineweight Settings** dialog box and experiment with lineweight settings. Draw a few lines after each setting to see the results.
❏ Save your work and exit AutoCAD, or keep this drawing open for the next exercise.

Using Layer Details

The **Layer Properties Manager** dialog box contains a **Show details** button. When selected, a new area is displayed at the bottom of the existing dialog box as shown in Figure 4-44, and the **Show details** button changes to a **Hide details** button. The features of the **Details** area are disabled unless one or more of the layers in the layer list are highlighted. The **Details** area provides an alternate way of entering the same information that can be entered in the upper area.

Figure 4-44.
The **Details** area of the expanded **Layer Properties Manager** dialog box.

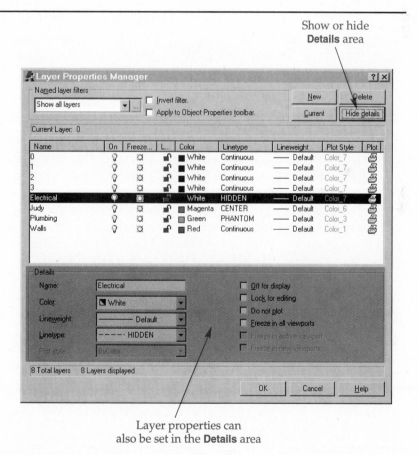

Show or hide **Details** area

Layer properties can also be set in the **Details** area

Layer Filters

In some applications, large numbers of layer names may be used to assist in drawing information management. Having all layer names showing at the same time in the layer list can make it more difficult to work with your drawing layers. *Layer filters* are used to screen, or filter, out any layers that you do not want displayed in the **Layer Properties Manager** dialog box. The **Named layer filters** area of the **Layer Properties Manager** provides options for filtering out unwanted layer names. See Figure 4-45. The default options are explained below:

- **Show all layers.** This is the default option, and shows all defined layer names.
- **Show all used layers.** The current layer and any layers that contain drawing objects are displayed.
- **Show all Xref dependent layers.** Xrefs are discussed in Chapter 24. This displays all layers brought in with externally referenced drawings.
- **Invert filter.** In addition to the default layer filter options, you can also invert, or reverse, the layer filter setting. For example, there is a choice to show all used layers, but what if you want to show all unused layers? In this case, you would check the **Invert filter** toggle to invert, or reverse, your choice.
- **Apply to Object Properties toolbar.** Check this toggle if you want only the layers that match the current filter displayed in the **Object Properties** toolbar. The **Layer Control** box tooltip shows when a filter is active.

Figure 4-45.
The **Named layer filters** area provides options for filtering layers.

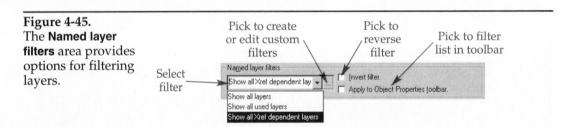

Select filter

Pick to create or edit custom filters

Pick to reverse filter

Pick to filter list in toolbar

Perhaps the most powerful aspect of **Named layer filters** area is the feature that allows you to create and save custom filters. To create or edit a custom layer filter, select the **...** (ellipsis) button to the right of the drop-down arrow. Picking this button displays the **Named Layer Filters** dialog box, shown in Figure 4-46. For example, you could define a filter that displays only layers whose names begin with "a" or "b" but also must be red or green and must be thawed and turned on. To create a layer filter with these properties, display the **Named Layer Filters** dialog box and type the values displayed in Figure 4-46. Click the **Add** button when finished.

You can select the layer filter named a b green red on thawed whenever you want to hide layers that do not meet these requirements. Following is an explanation of the various features of the **Named Layer Filters** dialog box:

- **Filter name.** Filter names are saved in this list. To create a new filter, type a name in the text box and pick the **Add** button. To delete an existing filter, select the name in the list and press the **Delete** button. Use the **Reset** button to clear all user-defined filter settings.
- **Layer Name.** Use this filter to display layers by name. For example, a single layer name can be entered in this text box if that is the only layer to be listed. Wildcard characters can be used to filter a specific group of layers. For example, the layer name W* would filter all layers beginning with *W*, such as Wall01, Wall02, and Wall03. An entry of Door,Window,W* would display the Door and Window layers, plus all layers beginning with *W*.
- **On/Off.** Use this filter to display only layer names that are on or off. The default for this setting is to display Both cases.
- **Freeze/Thaw.** Use this filter to display only layer names that are frozen or thawed.

Figure 4-46.
The **Named Layer Filters** dialog box.

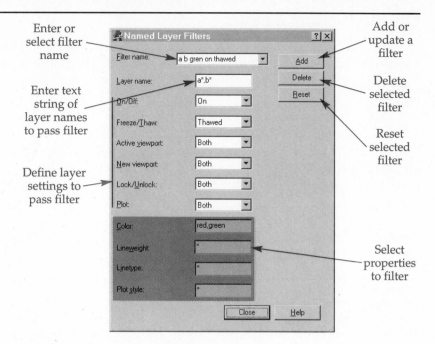

Enter or select filter name

Enter text string of layer names to pass filter

Define layer settings to pass filter

Add or update a filter

Delete selected filter

Reset selected filter

Select properties to filter

- **Active viewport.** Use this filter to display layer names frozen or thawed in the current viewport. (Viewport concepts are discussed in Chapter 10)
- **New viewports.** Use this filter to display layer names frozen or thawed in new viewports.
- **Locked/Unlocked.** Use this filter to display only layer names which are locked or unlocked.
- **Plot.** Use this filter to display layer names which plot or do not plot.
- **Color.** Use this filter to display layer names by color designation. Use color numbers or names. For example, you can use red or 1.
- **Linetype.** Use this filter to display layer names by linetype.
- **Lineweight.** Use this filter to display layer names by lineweight designation.
- **Plot style.** Use this filter to display layer names by plot style.

EXERCISE 4-16

❏ Open EX4-11 if it is not already open.
❏ Add a layer named A with color green, and a layer named B with color red.
❏ Create a named layer filter with the following specifications:

Filter name:	a b green red on thawed
Layer name:	a*,b*
On/Off:	On
Freeze/Thaw:	Thawed
Active viewport:	Both
New viewport:	Both
Lock/Unlock:	Both
Plot:	Both
Color:	red,green
Lineweight:	*
Linetype:	*
Plot style:	*

❏ Select the **Apply to Object Properties toolbar** check box and see the results in the **Object Properties** toolbar layer list. Deselect the **Apply to Object Properties toolbar** check box and look at the results in the **Object Properties** toolbar layer list.
❏ Save the exercise as EX4-16.

Quickly Setting a Layer Current

You can quickly make another layer current by using the **Layer Control** drop-down list located in the **Object Properties** toolbar. The name of the current layer is displayed in the box. Pick the drop-down arrow and a layer list appears, as shown in Figure 4-47.

Pick a layer name from the list and that layer is set current. When many layers are defined in the drawing, the vertical scroll bar can be used to move up and down through the list. Selecting a layer name to set as current automatically closes the list and returns you to the drawing editor. When a command is active, the drop-down button is grayed-out and the list is not available. You can also use the **CLAYER** system variable to make a layer current.

The **Layer Control** drop-down list has the same status icons as the **Layer Properties Manager** dialog box. By picking an icon, you can change the state of the layer.

For 2000i Users...

In AutoCAD 2000i, the **Layer Control** drop-down list also includes an icon for freezing and thawing in the current viewport. This setting is detailed in Chapter 24.

Figure 4-47.
The **Layer Control** drop-down list is located at the left side of the **Object Properties** toolbar. All layers are listed with icons representing their state and color. Double-click on a layer name to make it current.

Select icons to change layer status

Pick new current layer

PROFESSIONAL TIP   Layers are meant to simplify the drafting process. They separate different details of the drawing and can reduce the complexity of what is displayed. If you set color and linetype by layer, do not reset and mix entity linetypes and color on the same layer. Doing so can mislead you and your colleagues when trying to find certain details. Always maintain accurate records of your template drawings.

Making the Layer of an Existing Object Current

Object Properties toolbar

Make Object's Layer Current

Another quick way to set the current layer is to use the **Make Object's Layer Current** button in the **Object Properties** toolbar. When you pick this button, AutoCAD asks you to select an object on the layer you want to make current:

Command: (ai_molc)
Select object whose layer will become current: *(pick an object to make its layer current)*
Plumbing is now the current layer.
Command:

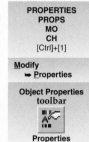

You should always draw objects on an appropriate layer, but layer settings are not permanent. You can change an object's layer if needed. You can also change other properties of the object, such as color and linetype. These properties can be modified using the **Object Properties** toolbar or by using the **Properties** window.

To modify properties using the **Object Properties** toolbar, select the object and then use the drop-down lists in the appropriate control boxes to change the property. After you have changed the properties, press [Esc] twice to deselect the object.

To modify an object's properties using the **Properties** window, pick the **Properties** button in the **Standard** toolbar, select <u>P</u>roperties from the <u>M</u>odify pull-down menu, or type PROPS, CH, MO, or PROPERTIES at the Command: prompt. If an object has been selected, you can also right-click and pick **Propertie<u>s</u>** from the shortcut menu. When you do this, AutoCAD displays the **Properties** window, shown in Figure 4-48.

The properties of the selected object are listed in the **Properties** window. The specific properties listed vary, depending on the type of object selected. Properties such as layer, linetype, and color are listed in the **General** category when the **Categorized** tab is selected.

To modify a particular object property, first find the property in the **Properties** window and select its value. Depending on the type of value, a specific editing method will be activated. Use this tool to change the value. For example, if you want to change an object's layer, pick **Layer** to highlight it as in Figure 4-48. A drop-down arrow is displayed to the right of the layer name. Pick the arrow to access the **Layer** drop-down list. Pick the layer name that you want to use for the selected object's layer. You can use this same process to change the color, linetype, or lineweight of a selected object or objects.

You can work in AutoCAD with the **Properties** window open and available for use. You can move the **Properties** window by picking and holding on the title bar while you move the mouse. If you want to close the **Properties** window, select the X at the upper-right corner of the window.

PROPERTIES
PROPS
MO
CH
[Ctrl]+[1]

<u>Modify</u>
➥ <u>P</u>roperties

Object Properties
toolbar

Properties

For 2000i Users...

In AutoCAD 2000i, double-click on an object to select the object and open the **Properties** window.

Figure 4-48.
The **Properties** window is used to modify the properties of the selected object.

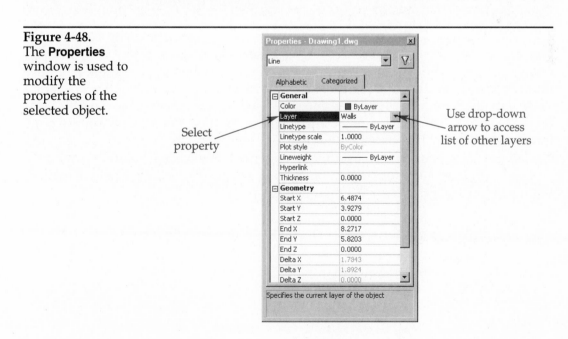

Select property

Use drop-down arrow to access list of other layers

PROFESSIONAL TIP

Several advanced layer commands are available in the **Layers** cascading menu in the **Express** pull-down menu. See Appendix A for Express Tools information.

EXERCISE 4-17

❏ Open EX4-11 if it is not already open.
❏ Use the **Layer Control** drop-down list in the **Object Properties** toolbar to experiment with making different layers current. Draw an object each time you change to a new current layer. Draw objects based on what you have already learned, such as line segments.
❏ Use the **Make Object's Layer Current** button to select an object in the drawing to make its layer current. Be sure the object you select is not on the current layer.
❏ Select an object and change its layer. Do this again, but this time select more than one object and change the layer in the **Properties** window.
❏ Use the **Properties** window to make other changes to objects, such as color and linetype.
❏ Save your work and exit AutoCAD, or keep this drawing open for the next exercise.

OVERRIDING LAYER SETTINGS

Color, linetype, and lineweight settings reference layer settings by default. This means that when you create a layer, you also establish a color, linetype, and lineweight to go with the layer. This is what it means when the color, linetype, and lineweight are specified as ByLayer. This is the most common method for managing these settings. Sometimes, however, you may need objects to reference a specific layer but have specific color, linetype, or lineweight properties that are different than the layer settings. In such a situation, the color, linetype, and lineweight can be set to an *absolute* value, and current layer settings are ignored. The term *absolute*, as used here and in future content, refers to an object being assigned specific properties that are not reliant on a layer or block for their definition.

❑ Start a new drawing or use one of your templates.
❑ Set up seven new layers using the **Layer Properties Manager** dialog box. Use the following settings:

Layer name	Linetype	Color
Object	Continuous	White
Hidden	Hidden	Red
Center	Center	Yellow
Electric	Continuous	Green
Phantom	Phantom	Cyan
Dot	Dot	Blue
Dim	Continuous	Magenta

❑ Establish a new template with the specified layers by saving with a name of your choice. Record the template name and the settings in a notebook for future reference.
❑ Draw the objects shown below. Place objects on the layer that has their linetype. The dimension layer will not be used at this time.

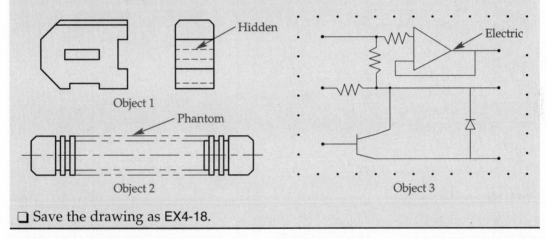

❑ Save the drawing as EX4-18.

Setting Color

The current object color can be easily set by selecting the **Color Control** drop-down list from the **Object Properties** toolbar. See Figure 4-49. The default setting is ByLayer. This is the recommended setting for most applications. To change this setting, pick another color from the list. If the color you want is not on the list, pick the item at the bottom of the list, labeled **Other...** to display the **Select Color** dialog box, or you can type COL or COLOR at the Command: prompt. Once an absolute color is specified, all new objects are drawn in the specified color, regardless of the current layer settings.

Figure 4-49.
The current object color is easily set by opening the **Color Control** drop-down list in the **Object Properties** toolbar. This control box is also used to change the color of select objects.

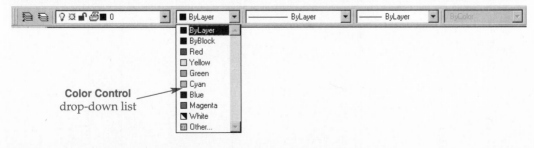

Another way to set the current object color is by using the **CECOLOR** system variable. **CECOLOR** stands for *current entity color*. This variable is set as follows:

> Command: **CECOLOR**↵
> New value for CECOLOR <BYLAYER>: *(enter new color value)*

Setting Lineweight

Similar to the current object linetype, you can set the current object lineweight to differ from the layer settings. To set the current object lineweight, pick the **Lineweight Control** drop-down list from the **Object Properties** toolbar and select the desired linetype. See Figure 4-50. You can also directly adjust the system variable that controls the current object linetype. This variable is called **CELWEIGHT**. Set the **CELWEIGHT** system variable in similar manner as the **CECOLOR** system variable. If ByLayer is desired, you must enter –1.

Figure 4-50.
The current object lineweight is easily set by opening the **Lineweight Control** drop-down list in the **Object Properties** dialog box.

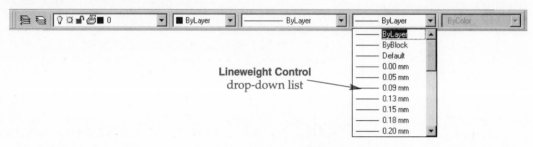

Lineweight Control drop-down list

Setting Linetype

Similar to the current object color, you can set the current object linetype to be separate from any layer settings. To set the current object linetype, pick the **Linetype Control** drop-down list from the **Object Properties** toolbar and select the desired linetype. See Figure 4-51. If the linetype that you want has not been loaded into the current drawing yet, it will not appear in the listing.

You can also directly adjust the system variable that controls the current object linetype. This variable is called **CELTYPE**, for *current entity linetype*. Set the **CELTYPE** system variable in the same manner as the **CECOLOR** system variable.

Figure 4-51.
The current object linetype is easily set by opening the **Linetype Control** drop-down list in the **Object Properties** dialog box.

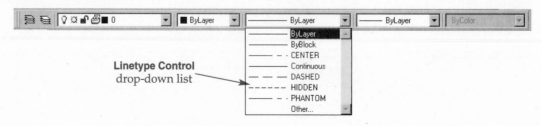

Linetype Control drop-down list

Colors, linetypes, and lineweights are often set as ByLayer. ByLayer is known as a *logical color*, while red, for instance, is known as an *explicit color*. If an object uses ByLayer as its color, then its color is displayed as the color assigned to the layer the object resides on. However, explicit properties override logical properties. Therefore, if an object's color is set *explicitly* to red, then it will appear red regardless of the layer it resides on. Change its color to ByLayer and it will use the layer color. It is a common AutoCAD mistake for users to set **CECOLOR**, **CELTYPE**, or **CELWEIGHT** to some value other than ByLayer and then wonder why new objects do not use the color of the current layer!

The **-LINETYPE** command allows you to load different linetypes, change the current linetype, and create custom linetypes at the Command: prompt. The command is accessed by typing -LT or -LINETYPE (a hyphen (-) typed before LINETYPE). The **-LINETYPE** command has several options:

- **?.** Lists the linetypes defined in a specified library file.
- **Create.** Allows creation of a new linetype and stores it in a specified library file.
- **Load.** Loads one or more linetypes from a specified library file.
- **Set.** Sets the current linetype used for newly drawn objects.

Setting the linetype scale

The linetype scale sets the length of dashes and spaces in linetypes. When you start AutoCAD with a wizard or template, the global linetype scale is automatically set to match the units you select. However, the global linetype scale can be overridden at the object level. *Global* means that the change affects everything in the current drawing.

The default object linetype scale factor is 1.0. As with layers, the linetype scale can be changed at the object level. One reason for changing the default linetype scale is to make your drawing more closely match standard drafting practices.

Earlier, you were introduced to the **Properties** window. When a line object is selected to modify, a **Linetype scale** property is listed. You can change the linetype scale of the object by entering a new value in this field. A value less than 1.0 makes the dashes and spaces smaller than that of the global setting, while a value greater than 1.0 makes the dashes and spaces larger. Using this, you can experiment with different linetype scales until you achieve the desired results. Be careful when changing linetype scales to avoid making your drawing look odd, with a variety of line formats. Figure 4-52 shows a diagram comparing different linetype scale factors.

Figure 4-52.
Drawing the same
linetype at different
linetype scales.

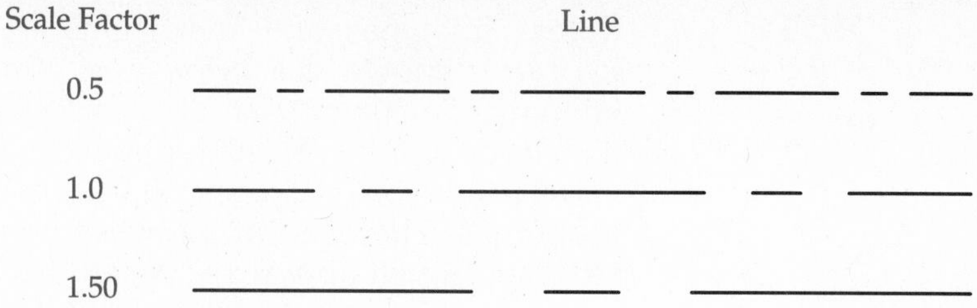

Scale Factor	Line
0.5	— — — — — — — — —
1.0	— — — — —
1.50	— — —

Changing the global linetype scale

The **LTSCALE** variable can be used to make a global change to the linetype scale. The default global linetype scale factor is 1.0. Any line with dashes initially assumes this factor.

To change the linetype scale for the entire drawing, type **LTSCALE** at the Command: prompt. The current value is listed. Enter the new value and press [Enter]. A Regenerating drawing message appears as the global linetype scale is changed for all lines on the drawing.

EXERCISE 4-19

❏ Start a new drawing, use one of your templates, or open a previous exercise.
❏ Draw the two objects shown below to approximate size.
❏ Change the linetype scale to .5, to 1.5, and then back to 1. Observe the effect each time it is changed.
❏ Change the linetype scale of only the hidden line to .5, to 1.5, and then back to 1.
❏ Change the linetype scale of only the centerline to .5, to 1.5, and then back to 1.
❏ Experiment with other linetype scales if you wish and then change back to 1.

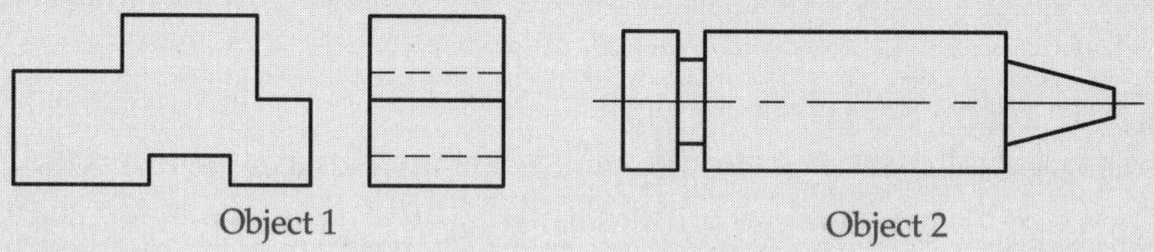

Object 1   Object 2

❏ Save the drawing as EX4-19.

AutoCAD User's Guide **14**

REUSING DRAWING CONTENT

In nearly every drafting discipline, individual drawings created as part of a given project are likely to share a number of common elements. All the drawings within a specific drafting project generally have the same set of standards. Drawing features such as the text size and font used for annotation, standardized dimensioning methods and appearances, layer names and properties, drafting symbols, drawing layouts, and even typical drawing details are often duplicated in many different drawings. These, and other components of CAD drawings, are referred to as *drawing content*. One of the most fundamental advantages of computer-aided drafting systems is the ease with which content can be shared between drawings. Once a commonly used drawing feature has been defined, it can be used again as needed, in any number of drawing applications.

The creation and use of drawing template files was covered in Chapter 2 and Chapter 3. Drawing templates represent one way to reuse drawing content that has already been defined. Creating your own customized drawing template files provides an effective way to start each new drawing using standard settings.

However, drawing templates provide only a starting point. During the course of a drawing project, you may need to add content to the current drawing that has been defined previously in another drawing. Some drawing projects may require that you revise an existing drawing rather than start a completely new drawing. For other projects, you may need to duplicate the standards used in a drawing supplied by a client.

AutoCAD 2000 provides a powerful drawing content manager called **AutoCAD DesignCenter**. **AutoCAD DesignCenter** allows you to reuse drawing content that has already been defined in previous drawings by using a drag-and-drop operation. **DesignCenter** was introduced in Chapter 1.

DesignCenter is used to manage several categories of drawing content, including blocks, dimension styles, layers, layouts, linetypes, text styles, and externally referenced drawings. Layers and linetypes are discussed in this chapter, but the other content types are introduced in the chapters where they apply. The following discussion details the features of the **DesignCenter** and shows how layer and linetype content found in existing drawings can be reused in other drawing projects.

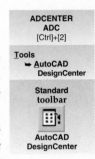

Using **DesignCenter** to Copy Layers and Linetypes

DesignCenter is activated by picking the **AutoCAD DesignCenter** button on the **Standard** toolbar, picking **AutoCAD DesignCenter** from the **Tools** pull-down menu, typing ADC or ADCENTER, or using the [Ctrl]+[2] key combination. This displays the **DesignCenter**, Figure 4-53.

It is not necessary to open a drawing in AutoCAD in order to view or access its content. **DesignCenter** allows you to directly load content from any accessible drawing. You can also use **DesignCenter** to browse through existing drawing files and view their content, or you can use its advanced search tools to look for specific drawing content.

Figure 4-53.
The **AutoCAD DesignCenter** is used to copy content from one drawing to another.

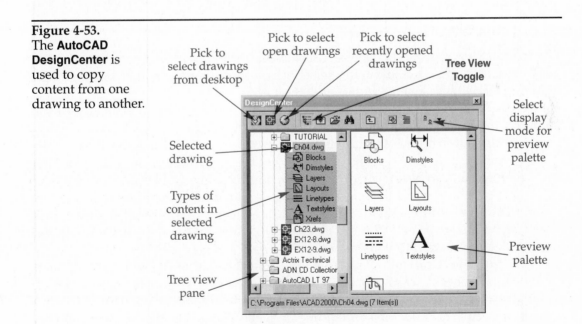

DesignCenter allows you to easily share content between drawings that are currently open in AutoCAD. To copy content, first select the drawing from which the content is to be copied. The drawing is selected from the tree view pane. If the tree view is not already visible, toggle it on by picking the **Tree View Toggle** button in the **DesignCenter** toolbar. The first three buttons on the **DesignCenter** toolbar control the tree view display:

- **Desktop.** Pick this button to display the folders and files found on the hard drive and network.
- **Open Drawings.** Pick this button to list only the currently opened drawings.
- **History.** Pick this button to list recently opened drawings.

Pick the plus sign (+) next to a drawing icon to view the content categories for that drawing. Each category of drawing content is listed with a representative icon. Pick the Layer icon to load the palette with the layer content found in the selected drawing. The preview palette now displays all of the available layer content, Figure 4-54.

Figure 4-54.
Displaying the layers found in a drawing using **DesignCenter**.

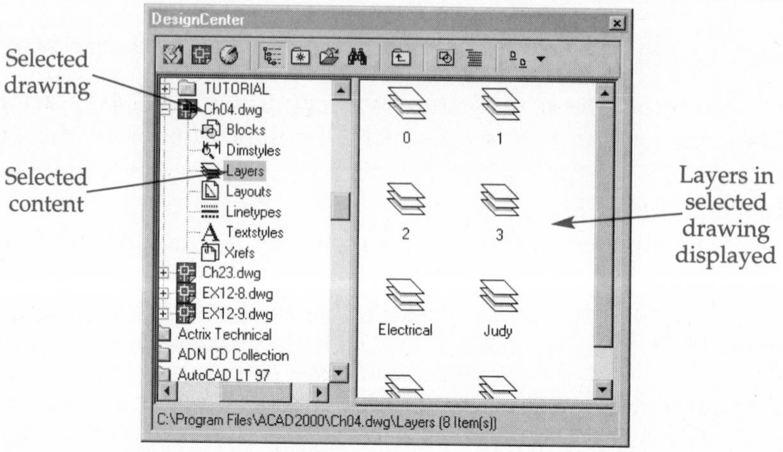

To select layers from the palette, use standard Windows selection methods. The [Shift] and [Ctrl] keys are used for selecting multiple items. In this example, the Ch04.dwg drawing is selected first, and the Layers content is picked. The preview palette displays the available content. Select the desired layers and use one of the following options to import them into the current drawing:

- **Drag-and-drop.** Move the cursor over the top of the desired icon in the preview palette. Press and hold down the pick button on your pointing device, and drag the cursor to the opened drawing. See Figure 4-55. Release the pick button and the selected content is added to your current drawing file.
- **Add from shortcut menu.** Select the desired icon(s) in the preview palette and right-click to open the shortcut menu. Pick the **Add** option and the selected content is added to your current drawing.
- **Copy from shortcut menu.** This option is identical to the add from shortcut menu option, except you select **Copy** from the shortcut menu instead of **Add**. Now, move the cursor to the drawing where you want the content added and right-click to open the shortcut menu. Select **Paste** and the selected contents are added to the current drawing.

To select more than one icon at one time, hold down the [Shift] key and pick the first and last icon in a group, or hold down the [Ctrl] key to select multiple icons individually.

The copied layers are now available in the active drawing, Figure 4-56. If a layer name that is being loaded already exists in the destination drawing, that layer name and its settings are ignored. The existing settings for the layer are preserved and a message is displayed at the command line indicating that the duplicate settings were ignored.

AutoCAD and its Applications—Basics

Figure 4-55.
To copy layers shown in **DesignCenter** into the current drawing, first select the layers to be copied, then drag-and-drop them into the drawing area of the current drawing.

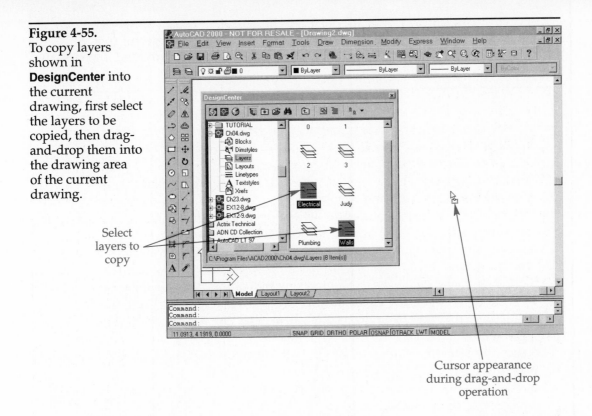

Select layers to copy

Cursor appearance during drag-and-drop operation

Figure 4-56.
The copied layers now appear in the **Layer Control** drop-down list of the current drawing.

Linetypes can be copied using the same procedure. In the tree view, select the drawing containing the linetypes to be copied. Then, select Linetypes to display the linetypes in the preview palette. See Figure 4-57. Select the linetypes to be copied, and then use drag-and-drop or the shortcut menu to add the linetypes to the current drawing.

Figure 4-57.
Linetypes can also be displayed in the preview palette.

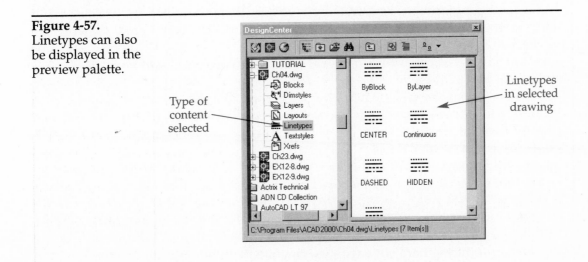

Type of content selected

Linetypes in selected drawing

| NOTE | The **AutoCAD DesignCenter** is a very powerful tool. Specific applications of the **DesignCenter** are provided throughout this text. |

EXERCISE 4-20

❏ Open EX4-18 for editing.
❏ Keep EX4-18 open while you start a new drawing from scratch.
❏ Activate the **AutoCAD DesignCenter**.
❏ Pick the **Open Drawings** button to list the open drawings in the tree view. Load the palette with the layer content from EX4-18.dwg.
❏ Select all the layer names shown in the palette, then drag-and-drop them into the new drawing.
❏ Notice the message on the command line indicating that duplicate layer names were ignored. Open the **Layer Control** drop-down list and view the layers now defined in the new drawing to confirm that the layers from EX4-18 were imported as expected.
❏ Select the **Desktop** button to display the desktop hierarchy in the tree view. Navigate to the Acad2000\Sample folder.
❏ In the tree view window, select the Wilhome drawing file and load the linetype content into the palette.
❏ Select the TINYDASH and THREEDOT linetypes, load them into the new drawing.
❏ Save the new drawing as EX4-20.

AutoCAD User's Guide 16

INTRODUCTION TO PRINTING AND PLOTTING

A drawing created with CAD can exist in two distinct forms: hard copy and soft copy. The term *hard copy* refers to a physical drawing produced on paper by a printer or plotter. The term *soft copy* refers to the computer software version of the drawing, or the actual data file. The soft copy can only be displayed on the computer monitor, making it inconvenient to use for many manufacturing or construction purposes. If the power to the computer is turned off, then the soft copy drawing is gone.

A hard copy drawing is extremely versatile. It can be rolled up or folded and taken down to the shop floor or out to a construction site. A hard copy drawing can be checked and red-lined without a computer or CAD software. Although CAD is the standard throughout the world for generating drawings, the hard copy drawing is still a vital tool in industry.

AutoCAD supports two types of hard copy devices—printers and plotters. Printers and plotters take the soft copy images that you draw in AutoCAD and transfer them onto paper. There are several types of *printers*, including dot matrix, inkjet, laser, and thermal transfer. Dot matrix printers are normally used to make low-quality check prints, while the better quality inkjet, laser, and thermal printers may be used for quick check prints of formal drawings. Print size for most of these printers is 8.5″ × 11″ or 8.5″ × 14″.

Large format hard copy devices are commonly referred to as *plotters*. These include inkjet, thermal, electrostatic, pen, and pencil plotters. These plotters are capable of producing hard copy with varying line widths and color output. Pen plotters have been the industry standard for preparing large format hard copy. They are called pen plotters because they use liquid ink, fiber tip pens, or pens with pencil lead. Multipen plotters can provide different line thickness and colors. Even though pen plotters can plot very fast, it takes quite some time to plot a large, complex drawing. Since plotting with pen plotters can often be time-consuming, they are rapidly being replaced in industry by inkjet, thermal transfer, and laser plotters.

Laser printers and plotters draw lines on a revolving plate charged with high voltage. The laser light causes the plate to discharge while an ink toner adheres to the laser-drawn image. The ink is then bonded to the paper by pressure or heat. The quality of the laser printer or plotter depends on the number of dots per inch (dpi). Laser printers are commonly 600 and 1200 dpi.

Thermal printers use tiny heat elements to burn dots into treated paper. The electrostatic process uses a line of closely spaced, electrically charged wire nibs to produce dots on coated paper. Inkjet plotters spray droplets of ink onto the paper to produce dot-matrix images.

The information found in this chapter is provided to give you only the basics so you can make your first plot. Chapter 10 explores the detailed aspects of printing and plotting.

Prints and plots are made using the **Plot** dialog box. Access this dialog box by selecting **Plot...** in the **File** pull-down menu, picking the **Plot** button in the **Standard** toolbar, pressing the [Ctrl]+[P] key combination, or typing PLOT at the Command: prompt. You can also right-click on a **Model** or **Layout** tab and select **Plot...** from the shortcut menu.

The first step in making an AutoCAD drawing is to create a model. The *model* is composed of various objects, such as lines, circles, and text. The model is created using the **Model** tab at the bottom of the drawing area. See Figure 4-58. The model is created in an environment called *model space.*

Once the model is completed, a layout can be created. A *layout* can contain various views of the model, a title block, and other annotations. In addition, the layout includes page setup information (such as paper size and margins) and plotter configuration data (information related to the specific model of printer or plotter being used). Layouts are created using the **Layout** tabs at the bottom of the drawing area. Layouts are created in an environment called *paper space*, and a single drawing can have multiple layouts.

Drawings can be plotted from the **Model** tab of the drawing area or from one of the **Layout** tabs. The following discussion will address plotting from the **Model** tab only. Creating and plotting layouts is addressed in Chapter 10.

Figure 4-58.
The **Model** and **Layout** tabs at the bottom of the drawing area are used to access the model space and paper space environments.

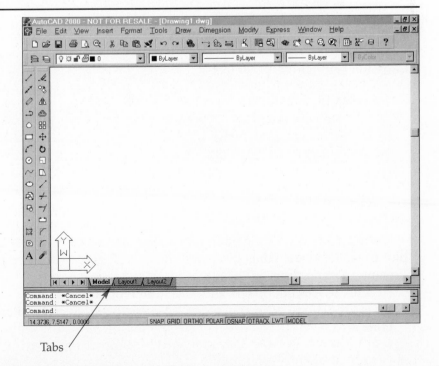

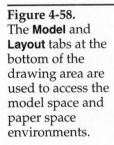

Tabs

Plot Device Tab

The **Plot** dialog box is shown in Figure 4-59 with the **Plot Device** tab displayed. The features of this tab will be discussed in detail in Chapter 10. The following is a brief introduction to some of the features:

- **Plotter configuration.** This area displays the name of the currently selected plotter and allows you to select a different plotter or printer. For now, it is assumed that your instructor or CAD system manager has taken care of the plotter configuration.
- **Plot style table (pen assignments).** All objects created in AutoCAD have a plot style property, just as all objects have a layer and color property. The plot style property determines how the object is plotted. The plot style table contains definitions for a collection of plot styles. This area displays the name of the currently selected plot style table and allows you to select a different table. This topic is described in detail in Chapter 10.
- **What to plot.** The **Current tab** option is used to plot from the **Model** tab. You can adjust the **Number of copies** setting to make multiple plots.
- **Plot to file.** If you select the **Plot to file** check box, you can write your plot to a file, rather than to a printing device. This is useful because many graphics programs can import and convert drawing information in the form of plot files.

Figure 4-59.
The **Plot** dialog box with the **Plot Device** tab selected.

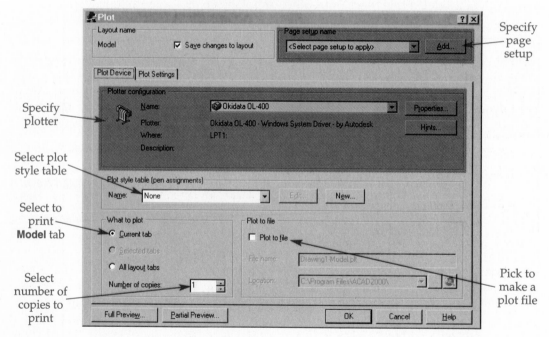

Making a Plot

There are many plotting options available. In this section, one method of creating a plot from the **Model** tab is discussed. Refer to Figure 4-60 as you read through the following plotting procedure:

1. Access the **Plot** dialog box and select the **Plot Settings** tab.
2. Check the plot device and paper size specifications in the **Paper size and paper units** area.

Figure 4-60.
The **Plot** dialog box with the **Plot Settings** tab selected.

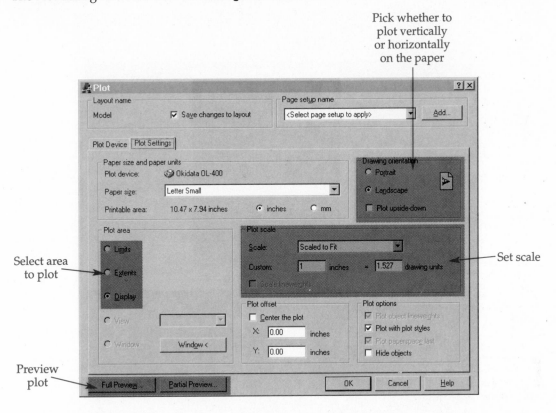

3. Select what is to be plotted in the **Plot area** area. The following options are available:
   - **Limits.** This option plots everything inside the defined drawing limits.
   - **Extents.** This option plots only the area of the drawing where objects are drawn.
   - **Display.** This option plots the current screen display.
   - **Window.** Pick the **Window** button to manually select a rectangular area of the drawing to plot. When you pick this button, the drawing window returns and you can select the window. After you select the second corner of the window, the **Plot** dialog box returns.
4. Select an option in the **Drawing orientation** area. Choose **Portrait** or **Landscape** to orient your drawing vertically (portrait) or horizontally (landscape). The **Plot upside-down** option rotates the paper 180 degrees.
5. Set the scale in the **Plot scale** area. Because you draw full-scale in AutoCAD, you typically need to scale drawings either up or down to fit the paper. Scale is measured as a ratio of either inches or millimeters to drawing units. Select a predefined scale from the **Scale** drop-down list, or enter your own values into the **Custom** fields. Choose Scale to fit from the **Scale** drop-down list to let AutoCAD automatically shrink or stretch the plot area to fill the paper.
6. If desired, use the **Plot offset** area to set additional left and bottom margins around the plot or to center the plot.
7. Preview the plot. Pick the **Full Preview** button to display the sheet as it will look when plotted, Figure 4-61. The cursor appears as a magnifying glass with a + and – symbol. The plot preview image zooms if you hold the left mouse button and move the cursor. Press [Esc] to exit the preview. The **Partial Preview** button displays the **Partial Plot Preview** dialog box, Figure 4-62. This shows the area of the paper and the area of the plotted drawing.
8. Pick the **OK** button in the **Plot** dialog box to send the data to the potting device.

Figure 4-61.
A full preview of the plot shows exactly how the drawing will appear on the paper.

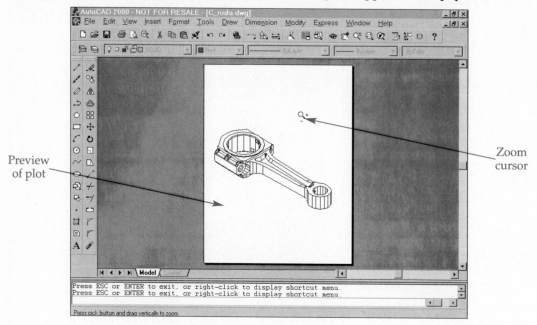

Preview
of plot

Zoom
cursor

Figure 4-62.
The **Partial Plot Preview** dialog box shows the location of the paper margins and the area covered by the drawing.

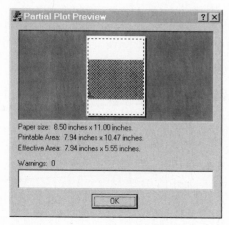

Before you pick the **OK** button to send your drawing to the plotter, there are several items you should check:

✓ Printer or plotter is plugged in.
✓ Cable from your computer to printer or plotter is secure.
✓ Printer has paper.
✓ Paper is properly loaded in the plotter and grips or clamps are in place.
✓ Ink cartridges or plotter pens are inserted correctly.
✓ Plotter area is clear for paper movement.

EXERCISE 4-21

❏ Open any of your previous drawings.
❏ Access the **Plot** dialog box.
❏ Set the plot scale to Scale to Fit, and set the plot area to **Display**.
❏ Pick the **Partial Preview** button and observe the display. Press the [Esc] key.
❏ Pick the **Full Preview** button and observe the results. A full representation of your drawing should be displayed as it will appear when printed on the paper. Press the [Esc] key.
❏ Experiment by changing the drawing orientation followed by a full preview after each change.
❏ Select the **Window** button and window a small portion of your drawing.
❏ Do another full preview to see the results. End the preview.
❏ Set the plot area to **Display** and preview the drawing. Make a print if a printer is available for your use.
❏ Exit AutoCAD.

Chapter Test

Answer the following questions on a separate sheet of paper.

1. Give the commands and entries to draw a line from Point A to Point B to Point C, and back to Point A. Then, return to the Command: prompt:
   A. Command: _____
   B. Specify first point: _____
   C. Specify next point or [Undo]: _____
   D. Specify next point or [Undo]: _____
   E. Specify next point or [Close/Undo]: _____
   F. Specify next point or [Close/Undo]: _____

2. Give the command and actions needed to quickly connect a line to an existing line, and then undo it as if it were wrong:
   A. Command: _____
   B. Specify first point: _____
   C. Specify next point or [Undo]: _____
   D. Specify next point or [Undo]: _____
   E. Specify next point or [Close/Undo]: _____

3. Give the command sequence used to erase a group of objects at the same time and then bring them all back:
   A. Command: _____
   B. Select objects: _____
   C. First corner: _____
   D. Specify opposite corner: _____
   E. Select objects: _____

4. Give the command necessary to refresh the screen.
5. Identify the following linetypes:

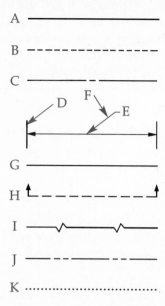

6. List two ways to discontinue drawing a line.
7. Name five point entry methods.
8. Identify three ways to turn on the coordinate display.
9. What does a coordinate display of 2.750<90 mean?
10. What does the coordinate display of 5.250,7.875 mean?
11. List four ways to turn on the Ortho mode.
12. Identify how you can continue drawing another line segment from a previously drawn line.
13. Define stacked objects.
14. How do you automatically use the **Window** selection method when you want to erase a group of objects?
15. How do you automatically use the **Crossing** selection option when you want to erase three out of four lines of a square?
16. How does the appearance of a window and crossing box differ?
17. Name the command that is used to bring back the last object(s) erased before issuing another command.
18. List at least five ways to select an object to erase.
19. Explain in general terms how direct distance entry works.
20. What is the default linetype in AutoCAD?
21. Name at least ten of AutoCAD's standard linetypes.
22. List the seven standard color names and numbers.
23. How are new layer names entered when creating several layers at the same time without using the **New** button in the **Layer Properties Manager** dialog box?
24. Which pull-down menu contains the **Layer...** option?
25. Identify three ways to access the **Layer Properties Manager** dialog box.
26. What condition must exist before a linetype can be used in a layer?
27. How do you make another layer current in the **Layer Properties Manager** dialog box?
28. How do you change a layer's linetype in the **Layer Properties Manager** dialog box?
29. How is the **Select Color** dialog box displayed from the **Layer Properties Manager** dialog box?
30. How do you load several linetypes at the same time from the **Load or Reload Linetypes** dialog box?

31. What is the state of a layer that is *not* displayed on the screen and *not* calculated by the computer when the drawing is regenerated?
32. Describe the purpose of locking a layer.
33. Are locked layers visible?
34. How do you easily select all the layers in the **Layer Properties Manager** dialog box list at the same time?
35. How do you know if a layer is off, thawed, or unlocked in the **Layer Properties Manager** dialog box?
36. Describe the purpose of layer filters.
37. Identify two ways to directly access property options for changing the layer, linetype, or color of an existing object.
38. Identify the following layer status icons:

A.   B.

C.   D.

E.   F.

39. How do you make the layer of an existing object current?
40. How do you make another layer current by using the **Object Properties** toolbar?
41. Why is ByLayer referred to as a logical color, linetype, and lineweight?
42. Define a global change.
43. Name the AutoCAD feature that allows you to use drag-and-drop to reuse drawing content that has already been defined in previous drawings.
44. In the tree view area of the **AutoCAD DesignCenter**, how do you view the content categories of one of the listed open drawings?
45. Briefly explain how drag-and-drop works.
46. How do you display all of the available layer content from a drawing in the **AutoCAD DesignCenter** preview palette?
47. Define hard copy and soft copy.
48. Identify four ways to access the **Plot** dialog box.
49. Describe the difference between the **Display** and **Window** options in the **Plot area** section of the **Plot** dialog box.
50. What is a major advantage of doing a plot preview?

Drawing Problems

Before beginning these problems, set up template drawings with layer names, colors, linetypes, and lineweights for the type of drawing you are creating. Review this chapter for information about setting up layering systems for different types of drawings. A basic layering format similar to the following can be used for some of the drawings:

Layer name	Color	Linetype
Object	White	Continuous
Hidden	Blue	Hidden
Center	Green	Center

Do not draw dimensions. Be sure to do preliminary planning for each drawing as discussed in this chapter.

1. Draw an object by connecting the following point coordinates. Save your drawing as P4-1. Make a print of your drawing if a printer is available.

Point	Coordinates	Point	Coordinates
1	2,2	8	@-1.5,0
2	@1.5,0	9	@0,1.25
3	@.75<90	10	@-1.25,1.25
4	@1.5<0	11	@2<180
5	@0,-.75	12	@-1.25,-1.25
6	@3,0	13	@2.25<270
7	@1<90		

2. With the absolute, relative, and polar coordinate entry methods, draw the following shapes. Set the limits to 22,17, units to decimal, Grid to .5, and Snap to .0625. Draw Object A three times, using a different point entry system each time. Draw Object B once each using at least two methods of coordinate entry. Do not draw dimensions. Save your drawing as P4-2. Make a print of your drawing if a printer is available.

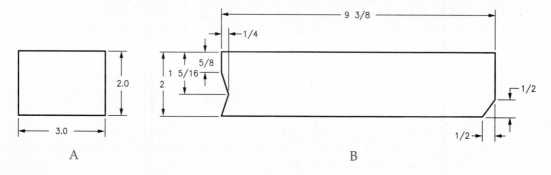

A   B

3. Draw the front elevation of this house. Create the dimensions proportional to the given drawings. Save the drawing as P4–3.

4. Draw the objects shown at A and B below using the following instructions:
   A. Draw each object using the **LINE** command.
   B. Start each object at the point shown and then discontinue the **LINE** command where shown.
   C. Complete each object using the **Continue** option.
   D. Do not draw dimensions.
   E. Save the drawings as P4-4.
   F. Make a print of your drawing if a printer is available.

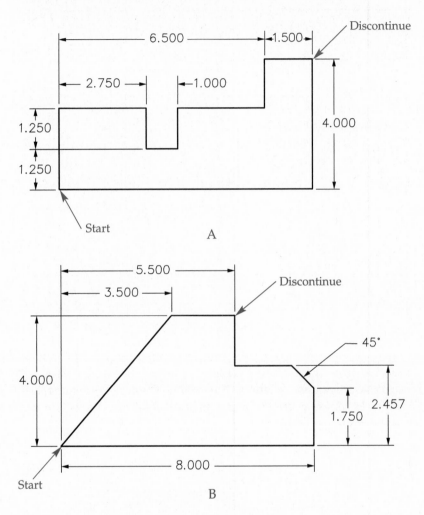

5. Draw the plot plan shown below. Use the linetypes shown, which include Continuous, Hidden, Phantom, Centerline, Fenceline2, and Gas_line. Make your drawing proportional to the example. Save the drawing as P4-5.

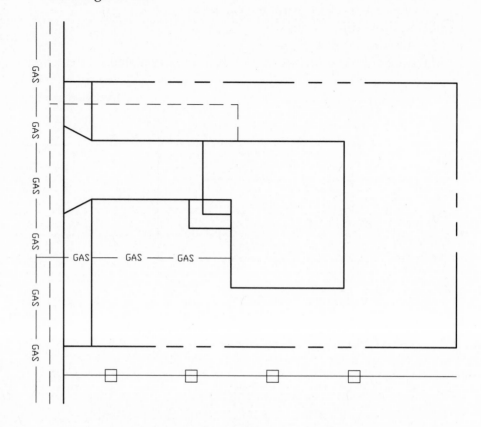

6. Draw the line chart shown below. Use the linetypes shown, which include Continuous, Hidden, Phantom, Centerline, Fenceline1, and Fenceline2. Make your drawing proportional to the given example. Save the drawing as P4-6.

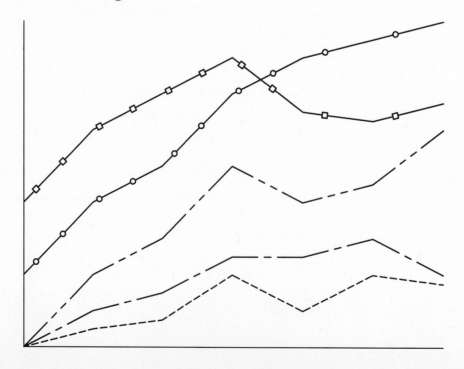

7. Draw the chart for the window schedule. Make the measurements for the rows and columns approximately the same as shown. Do not draw the hexagons or text. They will be added in Chapter 8. Save the drawings as P4-7.

WINDOW SCHEDULE

SYM.	SIZE	MODEL	ROUGH OPEN	QTY.
Ⓐ	12 x 60	JOB BUILT	VERIFY	2
Ⓑ	96 x 60	W4N5 CSM.	8'-0 3/4" x 5'-0 7/8"	1
Ⓒ	48 x 60	W2N5 CSM.	4'-0 3/4" x 5'-0 7/8"	2
Ⓓ	48 x 36	W2N3 CSM.	4'-0 3/4" x 3'-6 1/2"	2
Ⓔ	42 x 42	2N3 CSM.	3'- 6 1/2" x 3'-6 1/2"	2
Ⓕ	72 x 48	G64 SLDG.	6'-0 1/2" x 4'-0 1/2"	1
Ⓖ	60 x 42	G536 SLDG.	5'-0 1/2" x 3'-6 1/2"	4
Ⓗ	48 x 42	G436 SLDG.	4'-0 1/2" x 3'-6 1/2"	1
Ⓙ	48 x 24	A41 AWN.	4'-0 1/2" x 2'-0 7/8"	3

8. Draw the chart for the door schedule. Make the measurements for the rows and columns approximately the same as in the given problem. Do not draw the text. The text will be added in Chapter 8. Save the drawing as P4-8.

DOOR SCHEDULE

SYM.	SIZE	TYPE	QTY.
①	36 x 80	S.C. RP. METAL INSULATED	1
②	36 x 80	S.C. FLUSH METAL INSULATED	2
③	32 x 80	S.C. SELF CLOSING	2
④	32 x 80	HOLLOW CORE	5
⑤	30 x 80	HOLLOW CORE	5
⑥	30 x 80	POCKET SLDG.	2

9. Draw the chart for the interior finish schedule. Make the measurements for the rows and columns approximately the same as in the given problem. Do not draw the solid circles or the text. They will be added in Chapter 8. Save the drawing as P4-9.

INTERIOR FINISH SCHEDULE											
ROOM	FLOOR					WALLS				CEILING	
	VINYL	CARPET	TILE	HARDWOOD	CONCRETE	PAINT	PAPER	TEXTURE	SPRAY	SMOOTH	BROCADE	PAINT
ENTRY					•							
FOYER			•			•			•			•
KITCHEN			•					•		•		
DINING				•		•			•		•	•
FAMILY		•				•			•		•	•
LIVING		•				•		•			•	•
MSTR. BATH			•			•				•		•
BATH #2			•			•			•	•		
MSTR. BED		•				•		•			•	•
BED #2		•				•			•		•	•
BED #3		•				•			•		•	•
UTILITY	•					•			•	•		•

10. Draw the integrated circuit block diagram. Make your drawing proportional to the given problem. Do not draw the circle, line connections, or text. Save the drawing as P4-10.

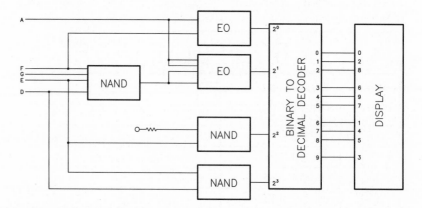

11. Draw the robotics system block diagram. Make your drawing proportional to the given problem. Do not draw the arrowheads or text. Save the drawing as P4-11.

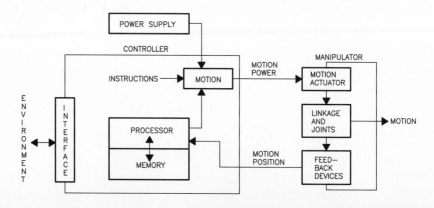

CHAPTER 5

Drawing Basic Shapes

Learning Objectives

After completing this chapter, you will be able to:

- Use **DRAGMODE** to observe an object drag into place.
- Draw circles using the **CIRCLE** command options.
- Identify and use the @ symbol function.
- Draw arcs using the **ARC** command options.
- Draw an arc extending from a previously drawn arc.
- Draw an arc extending from a previously drawn line.
- Use the **ELLIPSE** command to draw ellipses and elliptical arcs.
- Draw polygons.
- Draw rectangles.
- Draw rectangles with line width.
- Draw rectangles with chamfered and rounded corners.
- Draw donuts.
- Preset polygon and donut specifications.

The decisions you make when drawing circles and arcs with AutoCAD are similar to those made when drawing the items manually. AutoCAD provides many ways to create circles and arcs using the **CIRCLE** and **ARC** commands. These include the center location and radius or diameter, or where the outline of the circle or arc should be located. AutoCAD also provides the **ELLIPSE**, **POLYGON**, **RECTANG**, and **DONUT** commands. These commands can be used to draw a wide variety of shapes.

WATCHING OBJECTS DRAG INTO PLACE

Chapter 4 showed how the **LINE** command displays an image that is "dragged" across the screen before the second endpoint is picked. This image is called a *rubberband*. The **CIRCLE**, **ARC**, **ELLIPSE**, **POLYGON**, and **RECTANG** commands also display a rubberband image to help you decide where to place the object.

For example, when you draw a circle using the **Center, Radius** option, a circle image appears on the screen after you pick the center point. This image gets larger or smaller as you move the pointer. When the desired circle size is picked, the dragged image is replaced by a solid-line circle. See Figure 5-1.

Figure 5-1.
Dragging a circle to
its desired size.

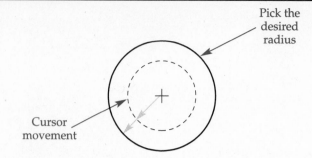

Pick the
desired
radius

Cursor
movement

The **DRAGMODE** system variable affects the visibility of the rubberband. The **DRAGMODE** can be set to be on, off, or automatic by typing DRAGMODE at the Command: prompt and pressing [Enter] as follows:

Command: **DRAGMODE**↵
Enter new value [ON/OFF/Auto] <Auto>: *(type ON, OFF, or A and press [Enter])*

The current (default) mode is shown in brackets. Pressing the [Enter] key keeps the existing status. When **DRAGMODE** is on, you must enter DRAG during a command sequence to see the objects drag into place. The following command sequence shows you how to activate the **DRAGMODE** while in the **CIRCLE** command.

Command: **CIRCLE**↵
Specify center point for circle or [3P/2P/Ttr (tan tan radius)]: *(pick a center point)*
Specify radius of circle or [Diameter]: **DRAG**↵ *(the circle will drag into place as you pick the desired radius)*
Command:

Selecting **OFF** disables **DRAGMODE**. This means that you will not see the objects drag into place. Even if you enter DRAG, AutoCAD ignores the request. When you set **DRAGMODE** to **Auto**, you see objects automatically dragged into place for all commands that support dragging. This is the default setting. Many users prefer to have the **DRAGMODE** set to **Auto**. However, some computer configurations slow down the drag process. When this occurs, you may prefer to turn **DRAGMODE** on or off.

AutoCAD
User's
Guide 6

CIRCLE
C

Draw
➡ Circle

Draw
toolbar

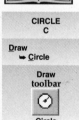

Circle

DRAWING CIRCLES

The **CIRCLE** command is used by picking the **Circle** button in the **Draw** toolbar, selecting **Circle** from the **Draw** pull-down menu, or entering C or CIRCLE at the Command: prompt. The options available in **Circle** cascading menu are shown in Figure 5-2.

Drawing a Circle by Radius

A circle can be drawn by specifying the center point and the radius. The *radius* is the distance from the center to the circumference of a circle or arc. The *circumference* is the perimeter or distance around the circle.

After accessing the **Center, Radius** option, you are asked to pick the center point followed by the radius. If the radius is picked on the screen, watch the coordinate display to help you locate the exact radius. The following command sequence is used to draw the circle in Figure 5-3:

Command: **C** *or* **CIRCLE**↵
Specify center point for circle or [3P/2P/Ttr (tan tan radius)]: *(select a center point)*
Specify radius of circle or [Diameter]: *(drag the circle to the desired radius and pick, or type the radius size and press [Enter])*

Draw
➡ Circle
➡ Center,
Radius

Figure 5-2.
The **Circle** cascading
menu in the **Draw**
pull-down menu.

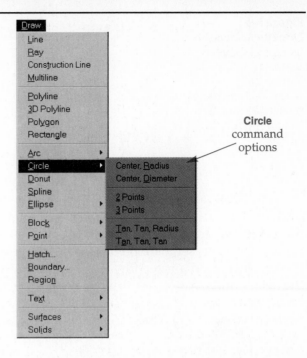

Circle
command
options

Figure 5-3.
Drawing a circle
specifying the
center point and
radius.

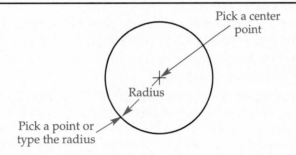

Pick a center
point

Radius

Pick a point or
type the radius

 NOTE

The radius value you enter is stored as the **CIRCLERAD** system variable. This system variable is the default radius setting the next time you use the **CIRCLE** command. If **CIRCLERAD** is set to zero, no default radius is provided in the **CIRCLE** command prompts.

Drawing a Circle by Diameter

A circle can be drawn by specifying the center point and the diameter. The command sequence for the **Center, Diameter** option is as follows:

Draw
➥ Circle
➥ Center,
Diameter

Command: **C** *or* **CIRCLE**↵
Specify center point for circle or [3P/2P/Ttr (tan tan radius)]: *(select a center point)*
Specify radius of circle or [Diameter]: **D**↵
Specify diameter of circle: *(drag the circle to the desired diameter and pick, or type the diameter size and press* [Enter]*)*

Watch the screen carefully when using the **Center, Diameter** option. The pointer measures the diameter, but the circle passes midway between the center and the cursor. See Figure 5-4. The **Center, Diameter** option is convenient because most circle dimensions are given as diameters.

Figure 5-4.
Drawing a circle using the **Center, Diameter** option. Notice that AutoCAD calculates the circle's position as you move the cursor.

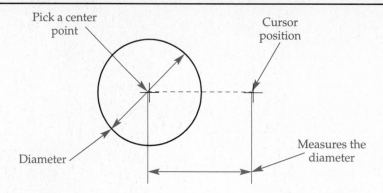

After you draw a circle, the selected radius becomes the default for the next circle (if **CIRCLERAD** is set to 0). If you use the **Diameter** option, the previous default setting is converted to a diameter. If you use the **Radius** option to draw a circle after using the **Diameter** option, AutoCAD changes the default to a radius measurement based on the previous diameter. If you set **CIRCLERAD** to a value such as .50, then the default for a circle drawn with the **Diameter** option is automatically 1.00 (twice the default radius).

Drawing a Two-Point Circle

A two-point circle is drawn by picking two points on opposite sides of the circle. See Figure 5-5. The **2 Point** option is useful if the diameter of the circle is known, but the center is difficult to find. One example of this is locating a circle between two lines. The command sequence is as follows:

> Command: **C** *or* **CIRCLE**↵
> Specify center point for circle or [3P/2P/Ttr (tan tan radius)]: **2P**↵
> Specify first end point of circle diameter: *(select a point)*
> Specify second end point of circle diameter: *(select a point)*

AutoCAD automatically calculates the radius of the created circle. This is the default radius the next time the **CIRCLE** command is used.

Figure 5-5.
Drawing a circle by selecting two points.

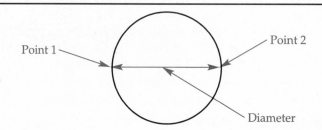

Drawing a Three-Point Circle

If three points on the circumference of a circle are known, the **3 Point** option is the best method to use. The three points can be selected in any order. See Figure 5-6. The command sequence is as follows:

> Command: **C** *or* **CIRCLE**↵
> Specify center point for circle or [3P/2P/Ttr (tan tan radius)]: **3P**↵
> Specify first point on circle: *(select a point)*
> Specify second point on circle: *(select a point)*
> Specify third point on circle: *(select a point)*

AutoCAD automatically calculates the radius of the created circle. This is the default radius used the next time the **CIRCLE** command is used.

Figure 5-6.
Drawing a circle given three points on the circle.

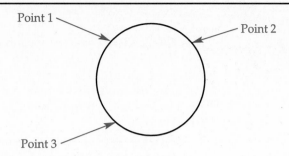

Drawing a Circle Tangent to Two Objects

The term *tangent* refers to a line, circle, or arc that comes into contact with an arc or circle at only one point. That point is called the *point of tangency*. A line drawn from the circle's center to the point of tangency is perpendicular to the tangent line. A line drawn between the centers of two tangent circles passes through the point of tangency. You can draw a circle tangent to given lines, circles, or arcs.

The **Tan, Tan, Radius** option is used to draw a circle tangent to two of these objects and to a specific radius. Once the **Tan, Tan, Radius** option is selected, select the lines, or line and arc, that the new circle will be tangent to. The radius of the circle is also required. To assist you in picking the three objects, AutoCAD uses the **Deferred Tangent** object snap by default. (Object snap modes are covered in Chapter 6.) When you see the **Deferred Tangent** symbol, move it to the objects that you want to pick. The command sequence is as follows:

> Command: **C** *or* **CIRCLE**↵
> Specify center point for circle or [3P/2P/Ttr (tan tan radius)]: **T**↵
> Specify point on object for first tangent of circle: *(pick the first line, circle, or arc)*
> Specify point on object for second tangent of circle: *(pick the second line, circle, or arc)*
> Specify radius of circle <current>: *(type a radius value and press [Enter])*

If the radius entered is too small, AutoCAD gives you the message: Circle does not exist. AutoCAD automatically calculates the radius of the created circle. This is the default radius used the next time the **CIRCLE** command is used. Two examples of this option are shown in Figure 5-7.

Figure 5-7.
Two examples of drawing circles tangent to two given objects using the **Tangent, Tangent, Radius** option.

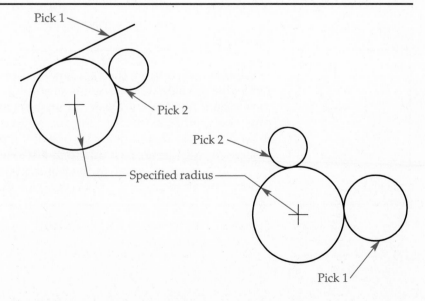

Drawing a Circle Tangent to Three Objects

Draw
➥ Circle
➥ Tan, Tan, Tan

The **Tan, Tan, Tan** option allows you to draw a circle tangent to three existing objects. This option creates a three-point circle using the three points of tangency. See Figure 5-8. Selecting the pull-down option is the same as using the **3 Point** option at the Command: prompt with the **TAN** object snap:

Command: **C** or **CIRCLE**↵
Specify center point for circle or [3P/2P/Ttr (tan tan radius)]: **3P**↵
Specify first point on circle: **TAN**↵
to (*pick an object*)
Specify second point on circle: **TAN**↵
to (*pick an object*)
Specify third point on circle: **TAN**↵
to (*pick an object*)
Command:

Figure 5-8.
Two examples of drawing circles tangent to three given objects.

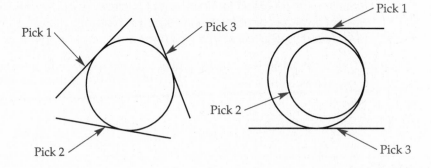

Using the @ Symbol to Specify the Last Coordinates

The @ symbol can be used to input the coordinates last entered. For example, suppose you want to draw a circle with a center at the end of the line just drawn. Enter the @ symbol when asked for a center point. The command sequence is as follows:

Command: **L** *or* **LINE**↵
Specify first point: **4,4**↵
Specify next point or [Undo]: **8,4**↵
Specify next point or [Undo]: ↵
Command: **C** *or* **CIRCLE**↵
Specify center point for circle or [3P/2P/Ttr (tan tan radius)]: **@**↵

The @ symbol automatically issues the coordinate 8,4 (end of the last line) as the center of the circle. The 8,4 value is saved in the **LASTPOINT** system variable. The @ symbol retrieves the **LASTPOINT** value.

Another application of the @ symbol is drawing concentric circles (circles with the same center). To do this, draw a circle using the **Center, Radius** or **Center, Diameter** options. Then, enter the **CIRCLE** command again and type @ when asked for the center point. This automatically places the center of the new circle at the center of the previous circle.

EXERCISE 5-1

❑ Begin a new drawing or use one of your templates.
❑ Set the **CIRCLERAD** system variable to 0.
❑ Use the **Center, Radius** option of the **CIRCLE** command to draw a circle similar to the one shown in Figure 5-3.
❑ Use the **Center, Diameter** option of the **CIRCLE** command to draw the circle shown in Figure 5-4.
❑ Draw two vertical parallel lines two units apart. Then use the **2 Point** option of the **CIRCLE** command to draw a circle tangent to the two lines.
❑ Use the **3 Point** option of the **CIRCLE** command to draw the circle shown in Figure 5-6.
❑ Use the **Tangent, Tangent, Radius** option of the **CIRCLE** command to draw the circles shown in Figure 5-7.
❑ Use the **Tan, Tan, Tan** option to draw circles tangent to the existing objects as in Figure 5-8.
❑ Draw a line. Use the **Center, Radius** option of the **CIRCLE** command and the @ symbol to place the circle's center at the endpoint of the line.
❑ Draw three concentric circles using @ and the **CIRCLE** command.
❑ Set **CIRCLERAD** to .5 and draw circles using each **CIRCLE** command option. Compare the prompts to those from the first circles drawn in this exercise.
❑ Save the drawing as EX5-1.

DRAWING ARCS

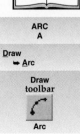

An *arc* is defined as any part of a circle or curve. Arcs are commonly dimensioned with a radius, but can be drawn by a number of different methods. The **ARC** command can be accessed by selecting **Arc** from the **Draw** pull-down menu. There are eleven arc construction options accessible in the **Arc** cascading menu, Figure 5-9. This is the easiest way to access the **ARC** command and an arc option. However, the **ARC** command and its options also can be accessed by picking the **Arc** button in the **Draw** toolbar, or by typing A or ARC at the Command: prompt. The **3 Points** option is the default when using the toolbar button or the Command: prompt.

Figure 5-9.
The **Arc** cascading
menu in the **Draw**
pull-down menu.

Arc
command
options

It is easiest to select the desired **ARC** option using the **Arc**
cascading menu in the **Draw** pull-down menu. When an **ARC**
option is selected, AutoCAD automatically prompts you for
the next required input.

Drawing a Three-Point Arc

The **3 Points** option asks for the start point, second point along the arc, and then
the endpoint. See Figure 5-10. The arc can be drawn clockwise or counterclockwise,
and is dragged into position as the endpoint is located. The command sequence is as
follows:

Draw
↳ **Arc**
　↳ **3 Points**

Command: **A** *or* **ARC**↵
Specify start point of arc or [CEnter]: *(select the first point on the arc)*
Specify second point of arc or [CEnter/ENd]: *(select the second point on the arc)*
Select end point of arc: *(select the arc's endpoint)*
Command:

Figure 5-10.
Drawing an arc by
picking three points.

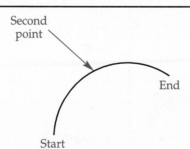

Second
point

End

Start

Drawing Arcs Using the **Start, Center, End** Option

Use the **Start, Center, End** option when you know the start, center, and endpoints. Picking the start and center points establishes the arc's radius. The point selected for the endpoint determines the arc length. The selected endpoint does not have to be on the radius of the arc. See Figure 5-11. The command sequence is as follows:

> Command: **A** *or* **ARC**↵
> Specify start point of arc or [CEnter]: *(select the first point on the arc)*
> Specify second point of arc or [CEnter/ENd]: **C**↵
> Specify center point of arc: *(select the arc's center point)*
> Specify end point of arc or [Angle/chord length]: *(select the arc endpoint)*
> Command:

Figure 5-11.
Using the **Start, Center, End** option. Notice the endpoint does not have to be on the arc.

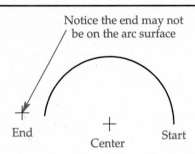

Notice the end may not be on the arc surface

End   Center   Start

Drawing Arcs Using the **Start, Center, Angle** Option

When the arc's included angle is known, the **Start, Center, Angle** option may be the best choice. The *included angle* is an angle formed between the center, start point, and endpoint of the arc. The arc is drawn counterclockwise, unless a negative angle is specified. See Figure 5-12. The following shows the command sequence with a 45° included angle:

> Command: **A** *or* **ARC**↵
> Specify start point of arc or [CEnter]: *(select the first point on the arc)*
> Specify second point of arc or [CEnter/ENd]: **C**↵
> Select center point of arc: *(select the arc center point)*
> Specify end point of arc or [Angle/Chord Length]: **A**↵
> Specify included angle: **45**↵
> Command:

Figure 5-12.
How positive and negative angles work with the **Start, Center, Angle** option.

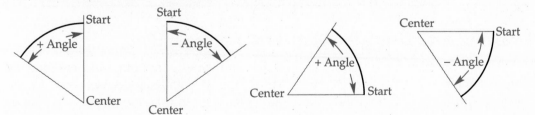

Drawing Arcs Using the **Start, Center, Length** Option

Draw
→ Arc
→ Start, Center, Length

The chord length can be determined using a chord length table (see Appendix L). A one-unit radius arc with an included angle of 45° has a chord length of .765 units. Arcs are drawn counterclockwise. Therefore, a positive chord length gives the smallest possible arc with that length. A negative chord length results in the largest possible arc. See Figure 5-13. The following shows the command sequence with a chord length of .765:

> Command: **A** *or* **ARC**↵
> Specify start point of arc or [CEnter]: *(select the first point on the arc)*
> Specify second point of arc or [CEnter/ENd]: **C**↵
> Specify center point of arc: *(select the arc center point)*
> Specify end point of arc or [Angle/Chord Length]: **L**↵
> Specify length of chord: *(type* **.765** *for the smaller arc or* −**.765** *for the larger arc, and press* [Enter]*)*
> Command:

Figure 5-13.
How positive and negative chord lengths work with the **Start, Center, Length** option.

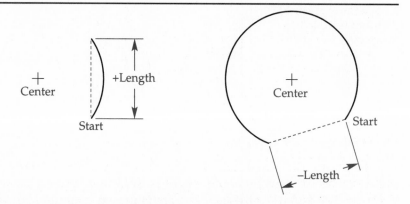

EXERCISE 5-2

❑ Begin a new drawing or use one of your templates.
❑ Use the **3 Points** option of the **ARC** command to draw arcs similar to those shown in Figure 5-10.
❑ Use the **Start, Center, End** option of the **ARC** command and draw the arc shown in Figure 5-11.
❑ Use the **Start, Center, Angle** option of the **ARC** command and draw the arcs shown in Figure 5-12.
❑ Use the **Start, Center, Length** option of the **ARC** command and draw the arcs shown in Figure 5-13.
❑ Save the drawing as EX5-2.

Drawing Arcs Using the **Start, End, Angle** Option

Draw
→ Arc
→ Start, End, Angle

An arc can also be drawn by picking the start point, endpoint, and entering the included angle. A positive included angle draws the arc counterclockwise, while a negative angle produces a clockwise arc. See Figure 5-14. The command sequence is as follows:

> Command: **A** *or* **ARC**↵
> Specify start point of arc or [CEnter]: *(select the first point on the arc)*
> Specify second point of arc or [CEnter/ENd]: **E**↵
> Specify end point of arc: *(select the arc endpoint)*
> Specify end point of arc: **A**↵
> Specify included angle: *(type a positive or negative angle and press* [Enter]*)*
> Command:

Figure 5-14.
How positive and
negative angles
work with the **Start,
End, Angle** option.

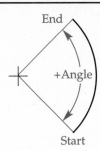
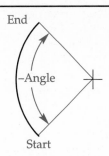

Drawing Arcs Using the **Start, End, Radius** Option

A positive radius value for the **Start, End, Radius** option results in the smallest possible arc between the start point and endpoint. A negative radius gives the largest arc possible. See Figure 5-15. Arcs can only be drawn counterclockwise with this option. The command sequence is as follows:

Draw
↦ Arc
  ↦ Start, End,
    Radius

> Command: **A** *or* **ARC**↵
> Specify start point of arc or [CEnter]: *(select the first point on the arc)*
> Specify second point of arc or [CEnter/ENd]: **E**↵
> Specify end point of arc: *(select the arc endpoint)*
> Specify center point of arc or [Angle/Direction/Radius]: **R**↵
> Specify radius of arc: *(pick, or type a positive radius or negative radius and press* [Enter])

Figure 5-15.
Using the **Start, End,
Radius** option with
a positive and
negative radius.

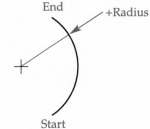
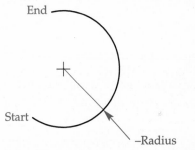

Drawing Arcs Using the **Start, End, Direction** Option

An arc can be drawn by picking the start point, endpoint, and entering the direction of rotation in degrees. The distance between the points and the number of degrees determines the arc's location and size. The arc is started tangent to the direction specified, as shown in Figure 5-16. The command sequence is as follows:

Draw
↦ Arc
  ↦ Start, End,
    Direction

> Command: **A** *or* **ARC**↵
> Specify start point of arc or [CEnter]: *(select the first point on the arc)*
> Specify second point of arc or [CEnter/ENd]: **E**↵
> Specify end point of arc: *(select the arc endpoint)*
> Specify center point of arc or [Angle/Direction/Radius]: **D**↵
> Specify tangent direction for the start point of arc: *(pick the direction from the start point, or type the direction in degrees and press* [Enter])
> Command:

Figure 5-16.
Using the **Start, End, Direction** option.

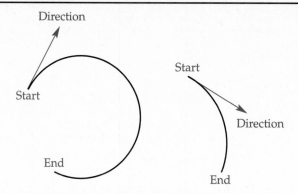

Drawing Arcs Using the **Center, Start, End** Option

Draw
➥ Arc
➥ Center, Start, End

The **Center, Start, End** option is a variation of the **Start, Center, End** option. See Figure 5-17. Use the **Center, Start, End** option when it is easier to begin by locating the center. The command sequence is as follows:

Command: **A** *or* **ARC**⏎
Specify start point of arc or [CEnter]: **C**⏎
Specify center point of arc: *(pick the center point)*
Specify start point of arc: *(pick the start point)*
Specify end point of arc or [Angle/Chord/Length]: *(pick the arc's endpoint)*
Command:

Figure 5-17.
Using the **Center, Start, End** option. Note that the endpoint does not have to be on the arc.

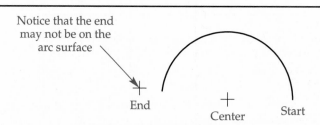

Notice that the end may not be on the arc surface

End   Center   Start

EXERCISE 5-3

❏ Begin a new drawing or use one of your templates.
❏ Use the **Start, End, Angle** option of the **ARC** command to draw arcs similar to those shown in Figure 5-14.
❏ Use the **Start, End, Radius** option of the **ARC** command to draw the arcs shown in Figure 5-15.
❏ Use the **Start, End, Direction** option of the **ARC** command to draw the arcs shown in Figure 5-16.
❏ Use the **Center, Start, End** option of the **ARC** command to draw the arc shown in Figure 5-17.
❏ Save the drawing as EX5-3.

Drawing Arcs Using the **Center, Start, Angle** Option

Draw
→ Arc
→ Center, Start, Angle

The **Center, Start, Angle** option is a variation of the **Start, Center, Angle** option. Use the **Center, Start, Angle** option when it is easier to begin by locating the center. Figure 5-18 shows how positive and negative angles work with this option. The command sequence is as follows:

Command: **A** *or* **ARC**↵
Specify start point of arc or [CEnter]: **C**↵
Specify center point of arc: *(pick the center point)*
Specify start point of arc: *(pick the start point)*
Specify end point of arc or [Angle/Length of chord]: **A**↵
Specify included angle: *(pick the included angle or type a positive angle or negative angle and press [Enter])*
Command:

Figure 5-18.
How positive and negative angles work with the **Center, Start, Angle** option.

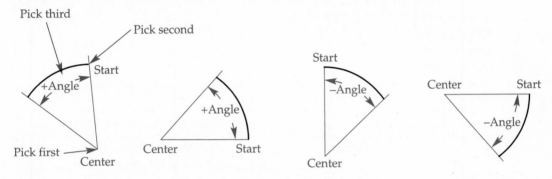

Drawing Arcs Using the **Center, Start, Length** Option

Draw
→ Arc
→ Center, Start, Length

The **Center, Start, Length** option is a variation of the **Start, Center, Length** option. Use the **Center, Start, Length** option when it is easier to begin by locating the center. Figure 5-19 shows how positive and negative chord lengths work with this option. The command sequence is as follows:

Command: **A** *or* **ARC**↵
Specify start point of arc or [CEnter]: **C**↵
Specify center point of arc: *(pick the center point)*
Specify start point of arc: *(pick the start point)*
Specify end point of arc or [Angle/Cord/Length]: **L**↵
Specify length of chord: *(pick, or type the chord length and press [Enter])*
Command:

Figure 5-19.
How positive and negative chord lengths work with the **Center, Start, Length** option.

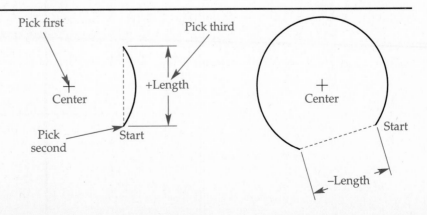

Continuing Arcs from a Previously Drawn Arc or Line

Draw
→ Arc
→ Continue

An arc can be continued from the previous arc or line. To do so, pick **Continue** from the **Arc** cascading menu in the **Draw** pull-down menu. The **Continue** option can also be accessed by beginning the **ARC** command and then pressing the [Enter] key, pressing the space bar, or selecting **Enter** from the shortcut menu.

When a series of arcs are drawn in this manner, each consecutive arc is tangent. The start point and direction are taken from the endpoint and direction of the previous arc. See Figure 5-20.

The **Continue** option can also be used to quickly draw an arc tangent to the endpoint of a previously drawn line. See Figure 5-21. The command sequence is as follows:

Command: **L** *or* **LINE**↵
Specify first point: *(select a point)*
Specify next point or [Undo]: *(select a second point)*
Specify next point or [Undo]: ↵
Command: **A** *or* **ARC**↵
Specify start point of arc or [CEnter]: *(press space bar or* [Enter] *to place start point of the arc at end of the previous line)*
Specify end point of arc: *(select the endpoint of the arc)*
Command:

Figure 5-20.
Using the **Continue** option to draw three arcs.

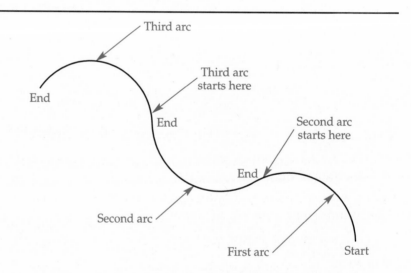

Figure 5-21.
An arc continuing from the previous line. Point 2 is the start of the arc and Point 3 is the end of the arc.

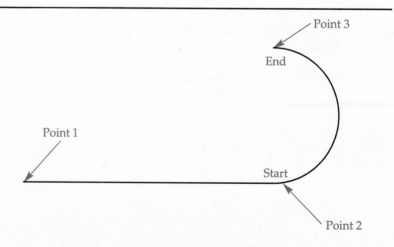

AutoCAD and its Applications—Basics

❑ Begin a new drawing or use one of your templates.
❑ Use the **Center, Start, Angle** option of the **ARC** command to draw arcs similar to those shown in Figure 5-18.
❑ Use the **ARC** command and the **Continue** option to draw the arcs shown in Figure 5-20.
❑ Use the **ARC** command and the **Continue** option as described in the text to draw an arc connected to a previously drawn line as shown in Figure 5-21.
❑ Save the drawing as EX5-4.

DRAWING ELLIPSES

When a circle is viewed at an angle, an elliptical shape is seen. For example, a 30° ellipse is created if a circle is rotated 60° from the line of sight. The parts of an ellipse are shown in Figure 5-22. The **ELLIPSE** command can be accessed by selecting **Ellipse** from the **Draw** pull-down menu, picking the **Ellipse** button in the **Draw** toolbar, or entering EL or ELLIPSE at the Command: prompt. An ellipse can be drawn using different options of the **ELLIPSE** command.

Figure 5-22.
Parts of an ellipse.

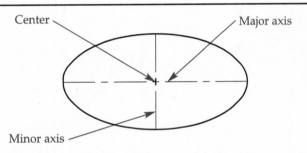

Center · Major axis · Minor axis

Drawing an Ellipse Using the **Axis, Endpoint** Option

The **Axis, Endpoint** option establishes the first axis and one endpoint of the second axis. The first axis may be either the major or minor axis, depending on what is entered for the second axis. The longer of the two axes is always the major axis. After you pick the first axis, the ellipse is dragged by the cursor until the point is picked. The command sequence for the ellipses in Figure 5-23 is as follows:

Command: **EL** *or* **ELLIPSE**↵
Specify axis endpoint of ellipse or [Arc/Center]: *(select an axis endpoint)*
Specify other endpoint of axis: *(select the other endpoint of the axis)*
Specify distance to other axis or [Rotation]: *(select a distance from the midpoint of the first axis to the end of the second axis and press* [Enter]*)*

If you respond to the Specify distance to other axis or [Rotation]: prompt with R for rotation, AutoCAD assumes you have selected the major axis with the first two points. The next prompt requests the angle that the ellipse is rotated from the line of sight. The command sequence is as follows:

Command: **EL** *or* **ELLIPSE**↵
Specify axis endpoint of ellipse or [Arc/Center]: *(select a major axis endpoint)*
Specify other endpoint of axis: *(select the other endpoint of the major axis)*
Specify distance to other axis or [Rotation]: **R**↵
Specify rotation around major axis: *(type a rotation angle, such as* 30 *and press* [Enter]*)*

Figure 5-23.
Constructing the same ellipse by choosing different axis endpoints.

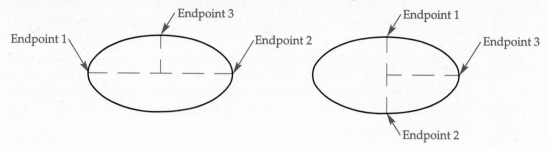

The **30** response draws an ellipse that is 30° from the line of sight. A **0** response draws an ellipse with the minor axis equal to the major axis. This is a circle. Any rotation angle between 89.42° and 90.57° or 269.42° and 270.57° is rejected by AutoCAD. Figure 5-24 shows the relationship between several ellipses having the same major axis length but different rotation angles.

Figure 5-24.
Ellipse rotation angles.

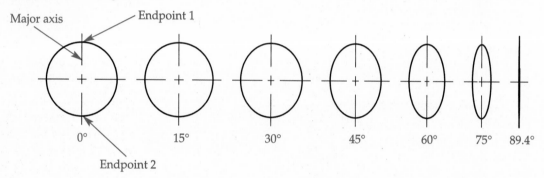

Drawing an Ellipse Using the **Center** Option

Draw
➥ **Ellipse**
  ➥ **Center**

An ellipse can also be constructed by specifying the center point and one endpoint for each of the two axes. See Figure 5-25. The command sequence for this option is as follows:

> Specify axis endpoint of ellipse or [Arc/Center]: **C**⏎
> Specify center of axis: *(select the ellipse center point)*
> Specify endpoint of axis: *(select the endpoint of one axis)*
> Specify distance to other axis or [Rotation]: *(select the endpoint of the other axis)*

The rotation option can be used instead of selecting the second axis endpoint.

Figure 5-25.
Drawing an ellipse by picking the center and endpoint of two axes.

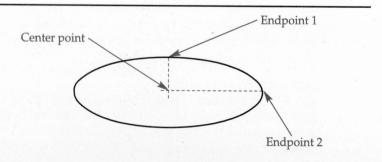

Drawing Elliptical Arcs

The **Arc** option of the **ELLIPSE** command is used to draw elliptical arcs. The command sequence for the **Arc** option is as follows:

Draw
→ Ellipse
→ Arc

```
Command: EL or ELLIPSE↵
Specify axis endpoint of ellipse or [Arc/Center]: A↵
Specify axis endpoint of elliptical arc or [Center]: (pick the first axis endpoint)
Specify other endpoint of axis: (pick the second axis endpoint)
Specify distance to other axis or [Rotation]: (pick the distance for the second axis)
Specify start angle or [Parameter]: 0↵
Specify end angle or [Parameter/Included angle]: 90↵
Command:
```

Once the second endpoint of the first axis is picked, you can drag the shape of a full ellipse. This can be used to help you visualize the other axis. The distance for the second axis is from the ellipse center to the point picked. Then enter a start angle. The start and end angles are the angular relation between the ellipse center and where the arc begins. The angle of the elliptical arc is established from the angle of the first axis. A 0° start angle is the same as the first endpoint of the first axis. A 45° start angle is 45° counterclockwise from the first endpoint of the first axis. End angles are also established counterclockwise from the start point. Figure 5-26 shows the elliptical arc drawn with the previous command sequence, and displays samples of different start and end angle arcs.

Figure 5-26.
Drawing elliptical arcs with the **Arc** option. Note the three examples at the bottom using three different angle settings.

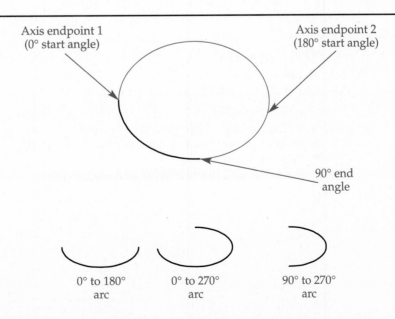

Axis endpoint 1
(0° start angle)

Axis endpoint 2
(180° start angle)

90° end angle

0° to 180° arc   0° to 270° arc   90° to 270° arc

Using the Parameter option

The **Parameter** option requires the same input as the other arcs until the Specify start angle or [Parameter]: prompt. The difference is that AutoCAD creates the elliptical arc using a different means of vector calculation. The results are similar, but the command sequence is as follows:

> Specify start angle or [Parameter]: **P**↵
> Specify start parameter or [Angle]: *(pick the start point)*
> Specify end parameter or [Angle/Included angle]: *(pick the end point)*
> Command:

Using the Included option

The **Included** option establishes an included angle beginning at the start angle. An included angle is an angle that is formed by two sides, or in this case, an angle that is formed as a number of degrees from the start angle. This option requires the same input as the other arcs until the Specify end angle or [Parameter/included angle]: prompt. The command sequence is as follows:

> Specify end angle or [Parameter/Included angle]: **I**↵
> Specify included angle for arc <*current*>: **180**↵
> Command:

Rotating an ellipse arc around its axis

The **Rotation** option for drawing an elliptical arc is similar to the **Rotation** option when drawing a full ellipse discussed earlier. This option allows you to rotate the elliptical arc about the first axis by specifying a rotation angle. Refer back to Figure 5-24 for examples of various rotation angles. This option requires the same input as the other arcs until the Specify distance to other axis or [Rotation]: prompt. The command sequence is as follows:

> Specify distance to other axis or [Rotation]: **R**↵
> Specify rotation around major axis: *(enter rotation value)*
> Specify start angle or [Parameter]: *(enter start angle)*
> Specify end angle or [Parameter/Included angle]: *(enter end angle)*
> Command:

Drawing an elliptical arc using the Center option

The **Center** option for drawing an elliptical arc lets you establish the center of the ellipse. See Figure 5-27. This option requires the same input as the other arcs until the Specify axis endpoint of elliptical arc or [Center]: prompt. The command sequence is as follows:

> Specify axis endpoint of elliptical arc or [Center]: **C**↵
> Specify center of elliptical arc: *(select the ellipse center point)*
> Specify endpoint of axis: *(select endpoint of axis)*
> Specify distance to other axis or [Rotation]: *(select the endpoint of the other axis)*
> Specify start angle or [Parameter]: **0**↵
> Specify end angle or [Parameter/Included angle]: **180**↵
> Command:

Figure 5-27.
Drawing elliptical
arcs with the **Center**
option.

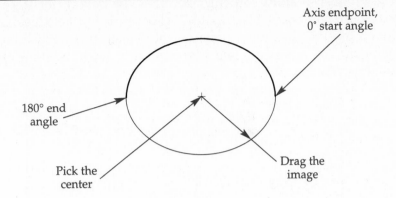

Axis endpoint,
0° start angle

180° end
angle

Drag the
image

Pick the
center

NOTE

The setting of the **PELLIPSE** system variable affects the way
an ellipse can be edited. An ellipse drawn while **PELLIPSE** is
set at 0 is a true elliptical object, while an ellipse drawn while
PELLIPSE is set at 1 is a polyline ellipse. A true elliptical
object maintains its elliptical shape during grip editing. (Grip
editing is discussed in Chapter 12 of this text.) The vertices of
a polyline ellipse can be moved out of the elliptical shape.
The **Arc** option of the **ELLIPSE** command is not available
when **PELLIPSE** is set to 1.

EXERCISE 5-6

- ❑ Begin a new drawing or use one of your templates.
- ❑ Use the **Arc** option of the **ELLIPSE** command to draw the following elliptical arcs:
  - ❑ Use axis endpoints, axis distance, start angle = 0, and end angle = 90; similar to Figure 5-26.
  - ❑ Use the same options as in the previous instructions to draw a 0° to 180° arc, 0° to 270° arc, and a 90° to 270° arc similar to the samples in Figure 5-26.
  - ❑ Use the **Parameter** option to draw an elliptical arc of your own design.
  - ❑ Use the **Rotation** option to rotate an elliptical arc 45° about its axis.
  - ❑ Use the **Included** option to draw an elliptical arc with a 180° included angle and another with a 90° included angle.
  - ❑ Use the **Center** option to draw an elliptical arc of your own design.
- ❑ Save the drawing as EX5-6.

DRAWING REGULAR POLYGONS

A *regular polygon* is any closed-plane geometric figure with three or more equal
sides and equal angles. For example, a hexagon is a six-sided regular polygon. The
POLYGON command is used to draw any regular polygon with up to 1024 sides.

The **POLYGON** command can be accessed by selecting **Polygon** from the **Draw**
pull-down menu, picking the **Polygon** button in the **Draw** toolbar, or entering POL or
POLYGON at the Command: prompt. Regardless of the method used to select the
command, you are first prompted for the number of sides. If you want an octagon
(polygon with eight sides), enter 8 as follows:

```
Command: POL or POLYGON↵
Enter number of sides <current>: 8↵
```

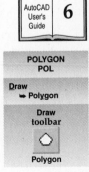

AutoCAD
User's
Guide **6**

**POLYGON
POL**

Draw
➥ Polygon

**Draw
toolbar**

Polygon

The number of sides you enter becomes the default for the next time you use the **POLYGON** command. Next, AutoCAD prompts for the edge or center of the polygon. If you reply by picking a point on the screen, this point becomes the center of the polygon. You are then asked if you want to have the polygon inscribed within, or circumscribed outside of, an imaginary circle. See Figure 5-28.

A polygon is *inscribed* when it is drawn inside a circle and its corners touch the circle. *Circumscribed* polygons are drawn outside of a circle where the sides of the polygon are tangent to the circle. You must then specify the radius of the circle. The command continues as follows:

> Specify center of polygon or [Edge]: *(pick center of polygon)*
> Enter an option [Inscribed in circle/Circumscribed about circle] *<current>*: *(respond with I or C and press* [Enter]*)*
> Specify radius of circle: *(type the radius, such as 2, and press* [Enter]*, or pick a point on the screen at the desired distance from the center)*

The **I** or **C** option you select becomes the default for the next polygon. The Specify center of polygon or [Edge]: prompt allows you to pick the center or specify the edge. Notice that picking the center is the default. If you want to draw the polygon on an existing edge, specify the **Edge** option and pick edge endpoints as follows:

> Specify center of polygon or [Edge]: **E⏎**
> Specify first endpoint of edge: *(pick a point)*
> Specify second endpoint of edge: *(pick second point)*

After you pick the endpoints of one side, the rest of the polygon sides are drawn counterclockwise.

Polygons are polylines and can be easily edited using the **PEDIT** (polyline edit) command, which is discussed in Chapter 16 of this text. For example, a polygon can be given width using the **Width** option of the **PEDIT** command.

Hexagons (six-sided polygons) are commonly drawn as bolt heads and nuts on mechanical drawings. Keep in mind that these features are normally dimensioned across the flats. To draw a polygon to be dimensioned across the flats, circumscribe it. The radius you enter is equal to one-half the distance across the flats. The distance across the corners (inscribed polygon) is specified when the polygon must be confined within a circular area. One example is the boundary of a swimming pool deck in architectural drafting. Notice the distance across the flats and the distance across the corners in Figure 5-29.

Figure 5-28.
Drawing an inscribed and a circumscribed polygon.

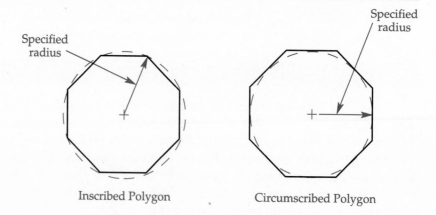

Inscribed Polygon   Circumscribed Polygon

Figure 5-29.
Specifying the
distance across the
flats and between
the corners of a
polygon.

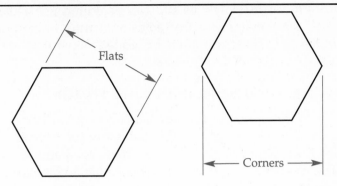

Flats

Corners

Setting the Number of Polygon Sides

AutoCAD allows you to set the default number of polygon sides with the **POLYSIDES** system variable. This value can be set in your template for future use, but is automatically reset to 4 in a new drawing. Type POLYSIDES at the Command: prompt and enter the number of default sides for the **POLYGON** command. The value you specify for the default is used until you change the value again using the **POLYSIDES** system variable or the **POLYGON** command.

EXERCISE 5-7

❑ Begin a new drawing or use one of your templates.
❑ Draw a hexagon with a distance of three units across the flats. Then draw another hexagon measuring three units across the corners.
❑ Draw an octagon with a horizontal edge that is 1.75 units long.
❑ Draw a pentagon circumscribed about a circle having a 2.25 diameter.
❑ Save the drawing as EX5-7.

DRAWING RECTANGLES

AutoCAD
User's
Guide **6**

RECTANG
RECTANGLE
REC

Draw
➡ Rectangle

Draw
toolbar

Rectangle

AutoCAD's **RECTANG** command allows you to easily draw rectangles. When using this command, pick one corner and then the opposite corner. See Figure 5-30. The **RECTANG** command can be accessed by picking **Rectangle** in the **Draw** pull-down menu, by picking the **Rectangle** button in the **Draw** toolbar, or entering REC, RECTANG, or RECTANGLE at the Command: prompt:

Command: **REC, RECTANG,** *or* **RECTANGLE.**↵
Specify first corner point or [Chamfer/Elevation/Fillet/Thickness/Width]: *(select the first corner of the rectangle)*
Specify other corner point: *(select the second corner)*
Command:

Figure 5-30.
Using the **RECTANG**
command. Simply
pick opposite
corners of the
rectangle.

Other
corner

First
corner

Rectangles are polylines and can be edited using the **PEDIT** command. Since a rectangle is a polyline, it is treated as one entity until exploded. After it is exploded, the individual sides can then be edited separately. The **EXPLODE** command is discussed in Chapter 16 of this text.

Drawing Rectangles with Line Width

The **Width** option of the **RECTANG** command is used to adjust the width of the rectangle in the XY plane. Setting line width for rectangles is similar to setting width for polylines, which is discussed in Chapters 15 and 16.

The following sequence is used to create a rectangle with .03 wide lines:

Command: **REC**, **RECTANG**, *or* **RECTANGLE**.↵
Specify first corner point or [Chamfer/Elevation/Fillet/Thickness/Width]: **W**.↵
Specify line width for rectangles *<current>*: **.03**.↵

You can press [Enter] at the Specify line width for rectangles: prompt to have the rectangle polylines drawn with the default polyline width. If you enter a value at this prompt, the polylines are drawn with that additional width.

After setting the rectangle width, you can either select another option or draw the rectangle. Continue selecting options until you have set the characteristics correctly, then draw the rectangle.

Drawing Chamfered Rectangles

A *chamfer* is an angled corner on an object. Drawing chamfers is covered in detail in Chapter 11 of this text. This is a brief introduction to drawing chamfers on rectangles. To draw chamfers on rectangles, use the **Chamfer** option of the **RECTANG** command. The rectangle created will have chamfers drawn automatically.

After you select the **Chamfer** option, you must provide the chamfer distances, Figure 5-31. The command sequence is as follows:

Command: **REC**, **RECTANG**, *or* **RECTANGLE**.↵
Specify first corner point or [Chamfer/Elevation/Fillet/Thickness/Width]: **C**.↵
Specify first chamfer distance for rectangles *<current>*: *(enter the first chamfer distance)*
Specify second chamfer distance for rectangles *<current>*: *(enter the second chamfer distance)*
Specify first corner point or [Chamfer/Elevation/Fillet/Thickness/Width]:

After setting the chamfer distances, you can either draw the rectangle or select another option. If you select the **Fillet** option, the chamfers will not be drawn.

The default chamfer distances are the chamfer distances or fillet radius used to draw the previous rectangle. If the default for the first chamfer distance is zero and you enter a different value, the new distance becomes the default for the second chamfer distance. However, if the default chamfer distances are nonzero values, a new value entered for the first distance does *not* become the default for the second distance.

Figure 5-31.
A chamfer is an angled corner. An example of chamfer distance.

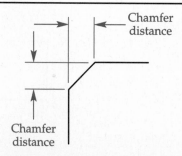

Drawing Filleted Rectangles

A *fillet* is a rounded corner on an object, Figure 5-32. Drawing fillets is covered in detail in Chapter 11 of this text. This is a brief introduction to drawing fillets on rectangles.

Fillets are automatically drawn on rectangles using the **Fillet** option of the **RECTANG** command. After selecting the option, you must enter the fillet radius:

> Command: **REC, RECTANG,** *or* **RECTANGLE.⤶**
> Specify first corner point or [Chamfer/Elevation/Fillet/Thickness/Width]: **F⤶**
> Specify fillet radius for rectangles <*current*>: *(enter a fillet radius or press* [Enter] *to accept the default)*
> Specify first corner point or [Chamfer/Elevation/Fillet/Thickness/Width]:

The default fillet radius is the radius of the previously drawn rectangle. Once a fillet radius is specified, the **RECTANG** command will automatically draw fillets on rectangles. In order to draw rectangles without fillets, the fillet radius must be set to 0. Figure 5-33 shows examples of rectangles drawn with chamfers and fillets.

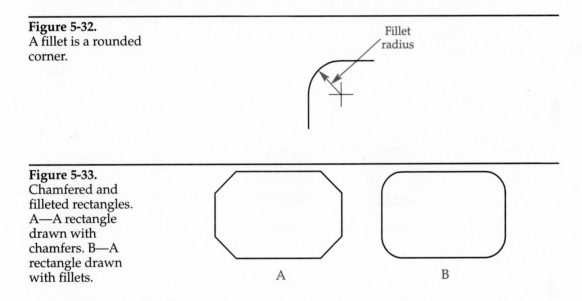

Figure 5-32.
A fillet is a rounded corner.

Figure 5-33.
Chamfered and filleted rectangles. A—A rectangle drawn with chamfers. B—A rectangle drawn with fillets.

A   B

Additional RECTANG Options

There are two other options available when using the **RECTANG** command. These options remain effective for multiple uses of the command:

- **Elevation.** This option sets the elevation of the rectangle along the Z axis. The default value is 0.
- **Thickness.** This option gives the rectangle depth along the Z axis (into the screen). The default value is 0.

A combination of these options can be used to draw a single rectangle. For example, a rectangle can have fillets and a .03 line width.

EXERCISE 5-8

❑ Begin a new drawing or use one of your templates.
❑ Use the **RECTANG** command to draw a rectangle.
❑ Use the **RECTANG** command to draw a rectangle with .03 line width.
❑ Use the **RECTANG** command to draw rectangles similar to Figure 5-33.
❑ Save the drawing as EX5-8.

DONUT
DOUGHNUT
DO

Draw
➡ Donut

Donuts drawn in AutoCAD are actually polyline arcs with width. Drawing polylines is introduced in Chapter 15, and is covered in detail in Chapter 16. The DONUT command allows you to draw a thick circle. It can have any inside and outside diameter, or be completely filled. See Figure 5-34.

The **DONUT** command can be accessed by selecting **Donut** from the **Draw** pull-down menu, or by entering DO, DONUT, or DOUGHNUT at the Command: prompt as follows:

Command: **DO**, **DONUT**, *or* **DOUGHNUT**.↵
Specify inside diameter of donut *<current>*: *(enter inside diameter)*
Specify outside diameter of donut *<current>*: *(enter outside diameter)*
Specify center of donut or <exit>: *(select the donut center point)*
Specify center of donut or <exit>: *(select the center point for another donut, or press* [Enter] *to discontinue the command)*

The current diameter settings are shown in brackets. New diameters can be entered, or press the [Enter] key to keep the current value. A 0 inside diameter produces a solid circle.

After selecting the center point, the donut appears on the screen. You may pick another center point to draw the same size donut in a new location. The **DONUT** command remains active until you press [Enter] or cancel by pressing [Esc].

When the **FILL** mode is turned off, donuts appear as segmented circles or concentric circles. **FILL** can be used transparently by entering 'FILL while inside the **DONUT** command. Then, enter ON or OFF as needed. The fill in previously drawn donuts remains on until the drawing is regenerated.

Figure 5-34.
Examples of doughnuts.

Fill on

Fill on,
ID = 0

Fill off

Fill off,
ID = 0

NOTE

The setting for the inside diameter and outside diameter of donuts are stored in the **DONUTID** and **DONUTOD** system variables, respectively. If the value of **DONUTID** is greater than the value of **DONUTOD**, the values are switched when the next donut is drawn.

EXERCISE 5-9

❑ Begin a new drawing or use one of your templates.
❑ Draw a donut with a .5 inside diameter and a 1.5 outside diameter.
❑ Draw a donut with a 0 inside diameter and a 1.5 outside diameter.
❑ Turn the **FILL** mode off and enter REGEN to see what happens to the donuts.
❑ Set **DONUTID** to .25 and **DONUTOD** to .75.
❑ Enter DONUT at the Command: prompt and draw a donut using the defaults.
❑ Use a transparent **FILL** command ('FILL) to turn **FILL** on while in the **DONUT** command. Now, draw two more donuts.
❑ Select **Donut** from the **Draw** pull-down menu and draw three more donuts. Notice the inside and outside presets you set earlier are automatically used.
❑ Save the drawing as EX5-9.

Chapter Test

Answer the following questions on a separate sheet of paper.

1. Give the command, entries, and actions required to draw a circle with a 2.5 unit diameter:
   A. Command: _____
   B. Specify center point for circle or [3P/2P/Ttr (tan tan radius)]: _____
   C. Specify radius of circle or [Diameter]: _____
   D. Specify diameter of circle: _____

2. Give the command, entries, and actions to draw a 1.75 unit radius circle tangent to an existing line and circle:
   A. Command: _____
   B. Specify center point for circle or [3P/2P/Ttr (tan tan radius)]: _____
   C. Specify point on object for first tangent of circle: _____
   D. Specify point on object for second tangent of circle: _____
   E. Specify radius of circle: _____

3. Give the command, entries, and actions needed to draw a three-point arc:
   A. Command: _____
   B. Specify start point of arc or [CEnter]: _____
   C. Specify second point of arc or [CEnter/ENd]: _____
   D. Specify end point of arc: _____

4. Give the command, entries, and actions needed to draw an arc, beginning with the center point and having a 60° included angle:
   A. Command: _____
   B. Specify start point of arc or [CEnter]: _____
   C. Specify center point of arc: _____
   D. Specify start point of arc: _____
   E. Specify end point of arc or [Angle/Chord Length]: _____
   F. Specify included angle: _____

5. Give the command, entries, and actions required to draw an arc tangent to the endpoint of a previously drawn line:
   A. Command: _____
   B. Specify start point of arc or [CEnter]: _____
   C. Specify end point of arc: _____

6. Give the command, entries, and actions needed to draw an ellipse with the **Axis, End** option:
   A. Command: _____
   B. Specify axis endpoint of ellipse or [Arc/Center]: _____
   C. Specify other endpoint of axis: _____
   D. Specify distance to other axis or [Rotation]: _____

7. Give the command, entries, and actions necessary to draw a hexagon measuring 4" (102mm) across the flats:
   A. Command: _____
   B. Enter number of sides: _____
   C. Specify center of polygon or [Edge]: _____
   D. Enter an option [Inscribed in circle/Circumscribed about circle]: _____
   E. Specify radius of circle: _____

8. Give the responses required to draw two donuts with a .25 inside diameter and a .75 outside diameter:
   A. Command: _____
   B. Specify inside diameter of donut: _____
   C. Specify outside diameter of donut: _____
   D. Specify center of donut or <exit>: _____
   E. Specify center of donut or <exit>: _____
   F. Specify center of donut or <exit>: _____

Chapter 5   Drawing Basic Shapes

9. Describe why the @ symbol can be used by itself for point selection.
10. Define the term *included angle*.
11. List the three input options that can be used to draw an arc tangent to the endpoint of a previously drawn arc.
12. Given the distance across the flats of a hexagon, would you use the **Inscribed** or **Circumscribed** option to draw the hexagon?
13. Describe how a solid circle can be drawn.
14. Identify how to access the option that allows you to draw a circle tangent to three objects.
15. Identify two ways to access the **Arc** option for drawing elliptical arcs.
16. Name the AutoCAD system variable that lets you draw a true ellipse or a polyline ellipse with the **ELLIPSE** command.
17. Name the pull-down menu where the **RECTANG** command is found.
18. What is the default option if the **ARC** command is typed at the Command: prompt?
19. Give the easiest keyboard shortcut for the following commands:
    A. **CIRCLE**
    B. **ARC**
    C. **ELLIPSE**
    D. **POLYGON**
    E. **RECTANG**
    F. **DONUT**
20. Name the command option that is designed specifically for drawing rectangles with line width.
21. Name the command option that is used to draw rectangles with rounded corners.
22. Describe how you would draw a rectangle with different chamfer distances at each corner.
23. What is the **ELLIPSE** rotation angle that causes you to draw a circle?
24. Explain how to turn the **FILL** mode off while inside the **DONUT** command.
25. Name the system variable used to set the default radius when drawing circles.
26. Name the system variables used to preset the inside and outside donut diameters.
27. Name the system variable used to set the default number of polygon sides.

Drawing Problems

Start AutoCAD and use one of the setup options or use a template. Do not draw dimensions or text. Use your own judgment and approximate dimensions if needed.

1. You have just been given the sketch of a new sports car design (shown below). You are asked to create a drawing from the sketch. Use the **LINE** command and selected shape commands to draw the car. Do not be concerned with size and scale. Consider the commands and techniques used to draw the car, and try to minimize the number of entities. Save your drawing as P5-1.

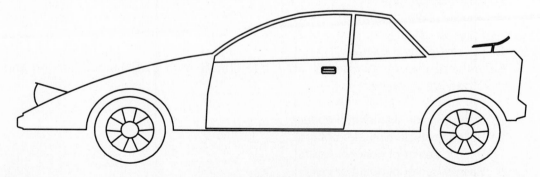

2. Use the **LINE** and **CIRCLE** command options to draw the objects below. Do not include dimensions. Save the drawing as P5-2.

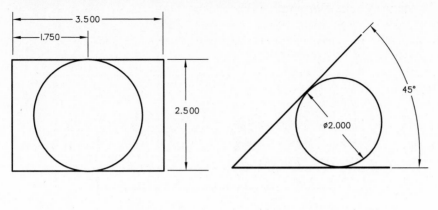

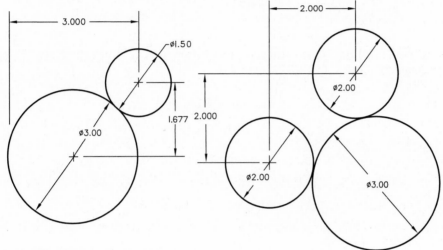

3. Draw the following object. Do not include dimensions.

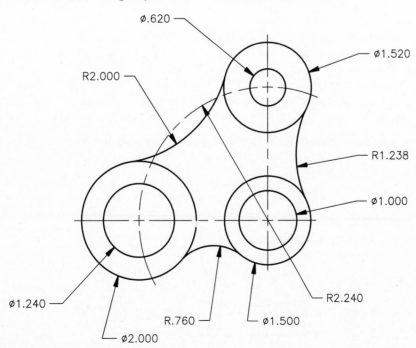

(Art courtesy of Bruce L. Wilcox)

4. Draw the pressure cylinder shown below. Use the **Arc** option of the **ELLIPSE** command to draw the cylinder ends. Do not draw the dimensions. Save the drawing as **P5-4**.

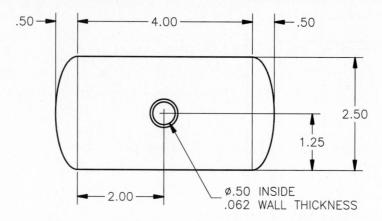

5. Draw the hex head bolt pattern shown below. Do not draw dimensions. Save the drawing as **P5-5**.

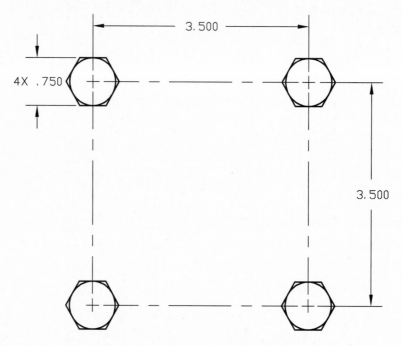

6. Draw the spacer below. Do not draw the dimensions.

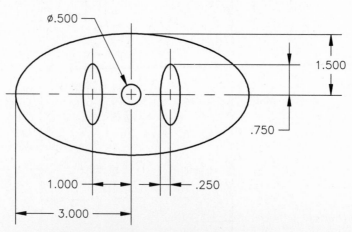

7. Draw the following object. Do not include dimensions.

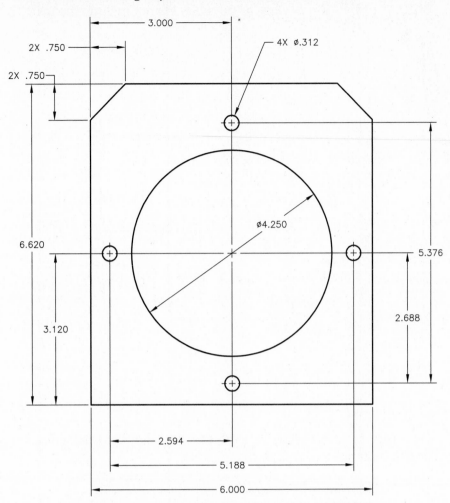

8. Draw the following object. Do not include dimensions.

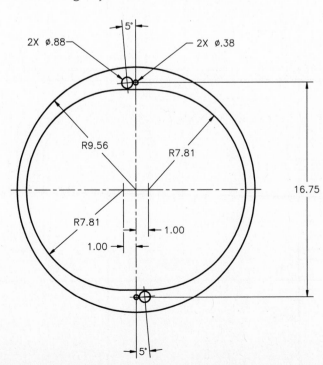

9. Create this controller integrated circuit diagram. Use a rule or scale to keep the proportion as close as possible. Do not include the text.

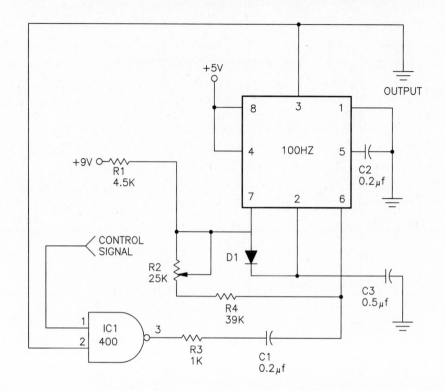

10. Draw this elevation using the **ARC**, **CIRCLE**, and **RECTANG** commands. Do not be concerned with size and scale.

CHAPTER 6

Object Snap, Geometric Constructions, and Multiview Drawings

Learning Objectives

After completing this chapter, you will be able to:

- Use object snap modes to create precision drawings.
- Use object snap overrides for single point selections.
- Set running object snap modes for continuous use.
- Use the AutoSnap features to speed up point specifications.
- Adjust aperture size based on point selection needs.
- Use temporary tracking and AutoTrack modes to locate points relative to other points in a drawing.
- Use polar tracking and polar snap.
- Use the **OFFSET** command to draw parallel lines and curves.
- Divide existing objects into equal distances using the **DIVIDE** command.
- Use the **MEASURE** command to set designated increments on an existing object.
- Create orthographic multiview drawings.
- Adjust snap grid and UCS settings to construct auxiliary views.
- Use construction lines to assist in drawing multiviews and auxiliary views.

This chapter explains how the powerful **OSNAP** command features are used when creating and editing your drawing. **OSNAP** means *object snap*. Object snap allows you to instantly locate exact points relative to existing objects. A feature called *AutoSnap™* can be used to visually preview and confirm snap point options prior to point selection. Other point selection methods, such object snap tracking, polar tracking, and X and Y coordinate filters, allow you to locate points relative to existing points. This chapter continues with an explanation of how to create parallel offset copies, divide objects, and place point objects. Creating multiview drawings using orthographic projection and construction lines is also covered.

SNAPPING TO SPECIFIC FEATURES

AutoCAD User's Guide 7

Object snap is one of the most useful tools found in AutoCAD. It increases your drafting ability, performance, and productivity. The term *object snap* refers to the cursor's ability to "snap" exactly to a specific point or place on an object. The advantage of object snap is that you do not have to pick an exact point.

The AutoSnap feature is enabled by default. With AutoSnap active, visual cues are displayed while using object snap. This helps you in visualizing and confirming object snap candidate points.

These visual cues appear as *markers* displayed at the current selection point. Figure 6-1 shows two examples of visual cues provided by AutoSnap. The endpoint of a line object is being picked in Figure 6-1A. The visual cue for an **Endpoint** object snap is shown as a square when the cursor is placed close to the line object. After a brief pause, a tooltip is displayed, indicating the object snap mode. In Figure 6-1B, a point that is tangent to an existing circle is being selected. The AutoSnap symbol for a tangency point is shown as a circle with a tangent horizontal line.

Another visual clue that is displayed with some object snaps and also with AutoTrack options is an alignment path. An *alignment path* is a dashed line that shows the path upon which an object would be drawn if aligned as desired with another object. For example, you will see a parallel alignment path created when drawing parallel objects using the parallel object snap. An *extension path* is a type of alignment path that is displayed when using the **Extension** object snap to find the imaginary extension of an existing object.

The default settings for AutoSnap are used for this discussion of the object snap features. Changing AutoSnap settings and features is discussed later in this chapter.

Figure 6-1.
AutoSnap displays markers and related tooltips for object snap modes.

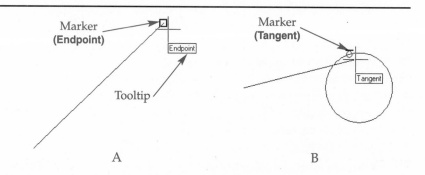

OBJECT SNAP MODES

Object snap modes determine the point to which the cursor snaps. These modes can be activated using one of several different methods. An object snap override can be typed at the prompt line or selected from the **Object Snap** shortcut menu shown in Figure 6-2. This menu is activated by first holding down the [Shift] key and then right-clicking your mouse or picking the [Enter] button on your puck. Object snap overrides are also available as buttons in the **Object Snap** toolbar, Figure 6-3.

To activate the **Object Snap** toolbar, select **Toolbars...** from the **View** pull-down menu. Then, select **Object Snap** in the **Toolbars** dialog box. Pick the **Close** button to close the **Toolbars** dialog box. You can keep the **Object Snap** toolbar floating, or you can dock it in a place at the edge of the graphics window that is convenient for your access.

Object snap override refers to the entry of an object snap mode at a point specification prompt. A *point specification prompt* is any prompt that asks you to enter or pick a point coordinate. Object snap overrides are active for one point specification only, and they override any previously set object snap modes for that one entry.

A *running object snap* stays active for all point selections until it is changed. Running object snap modes are discussed later in this section.

Figure 6-2.
The **Object Snap** shortcut menu provides quick access to object snap overrides.

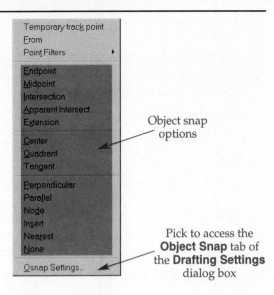

Object snap options

Pick to access the **Object Snap** tab of the **Drafting Settings** dialog box

Figure 6-3.
The **Object Snap** toolbar.

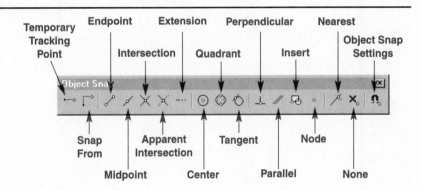

NOTE

When AutoCAD is configured to display screen menus, the object snap modes screen menu can be accessed by picking "****" near the top of the current screen menu.

The table in Figure 6-4 summarizes the object snap modes. Included with each mode is the marker that appears on-screen and its button from the **Object Snap** toolbar. Each object snap mode selects a different portion of an object. When activated from the prompt line, only the first three letters are required.

PROFESSIONAL TIP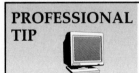

Remember that object snap overrides are not commands, but are used in conjunction with commands. If you type MID or PER at the Command: prompt, AutoCAD displays an "Unknown Command" error message.

Practice with the different object snap options to find which works best in various situations. Object snap can be used during many commands, such as **LINE**, **CIRCLE**, **ARC**, **MOVE**, **COPY**, and **INSERT**. The most common object snap uses are discussed in the following sections.

Figure 6-4.
The object snap modes.

Object Snap Modes			
Mode	**Marker**	**Button**	**Description**
Endpoint	□		Finds the nearest endpoint of a line, arc, elliptical arc, spline, ellipse, ray, solid, or multiline.
Midpoint	△		Finds the middle point of any object having two endpoints, such as a line, arc, elliptical arc, spline, ellipse, ray, solid, xline, or multiline.
Center	○		Locates the center point of a radial object, including circles, arcs, ellipses, elliptical arcs, and radial solids.
Quadrant	◇		Picks the closest of the four quadrant points that can be found on circles, arcs, elliptical arcs, ellipses, and radial solids. (Not all of these objects may have all four quadrants.)
Intersection	×		Picks the closest intersection of two objects.
Apparent Intersection	⊠		Selects a visual intersection between two objects that appear to intersect on screen in the current view, but may not actually intersect each other in 3D space.
Extension	+		Find a point along the imaginary extension of an existing line or arc.
Insertion	⌐⌐		Finds the insertion point of text objects and blocks.
Perpendicular	⌐		Finds a point that is perpendicular to an object from the previously picked point.
Parallel	∥		Used to find any point along an imaginary line parallel to an existing line or polyline.
Tangent	⊼		Finds points of tangency between radial and linear objects.
Nearest	⊠		Locates the point on an object closest to the crosshairs.
Node	⊗		Picks a point object drawn with the **POINT** command.
None			Turns running object snap off.

Endpoint Object Snap

In many cases, you need to connect a line, arc, or center point of a circle to the endpoint of an existing line or arc. Select the **Endpoint** object snap option and move the cursor past the midpoint of the line or arc toward the end to be picked. A small square marks the endpoint that will be picked.

In Figure 6-5, the following command sequence is used to connect a line to the endpoint of an existing line:

    Command: **L** or **LINE**↵
    Specify first point: (pick a point)
    Specify next point or [Undo]: (pick the **Endpoint** button, type END, or pick **Endpoint**
        from the **Object Snap** shortcut menu)
    of (move the cursor near the end of the line and pick)
    Specify next point or [Undo] ↵
    Command:

AutoCAD and its Applications—Basics

Figure 6-5.
Using **Endpoint** object snap.

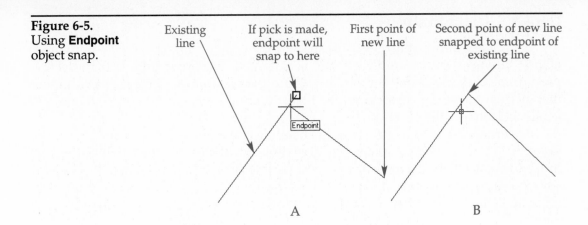

The **Endpoint** object snap can be used to quickly select the endpoints of all types of lines and arcs. It is often selected as a running object snap.

Midpoint Object Snap

The **Midpoint** object snap mode finds and picks the midpoint of a line, polyline, or arc. Type MID at the prompt, pick the **Midpoint** button, or select **Midpoint** from the **Object Snap** shortcut menu to activate this object snap. Then position the cursor near the midpoint of the object, and a small triangle marks the midpoint where the line will snap. See Figure 6-6.

Figure 6-6.
Using **Midpoint** object snap.

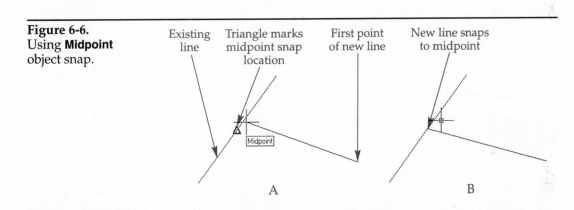

EXERCISE 6-1

❏ Start AutoCAD and use the setup option of your choice.
❏ Use the **Endpoint** and **Midpoint** object snap modes to draw the object shown below. Draw Line 1, then Line 2 connecting to the endpoint of Line 1. Draw Line 3 from the endpoint of Line 2 to the midpoint of Line 1. Draw Arc A with one end connected to the endpoint of Line 1.
❏ Save the drawing as EX6-1.

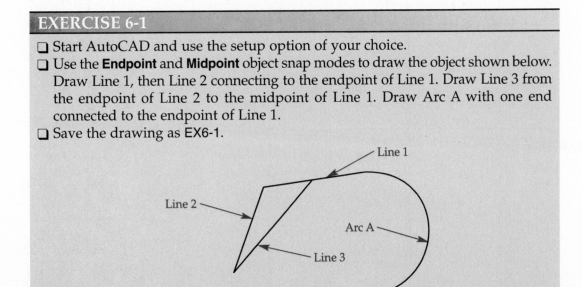

Center Object Snap

The **Center** option allows you to snap to the center point of a circle, doughnut, ellipse, elliptical arc, or arc. The mode is activated by typing CEN at the selection prompt, picking the **Center** button, or picking **Center** from the **Object Snap** shortcut menu. Then move the cursor onto the object whose center point is to be located. A small circle marks the center point.

Be sure to move the cursor near the object, not the center point of the object. For example, when locating the center of a large circle, the **Center** object snap mode will *not* locate the center if the cursor is not near the perimeter of the circle. Even if the cursor is over the center of the circle, it may not be near enough to the circle to activate the snap point. In Figure 6-7, the **Center** object snap is used to draw a line to the center of a circle.

Figure 6-7.
Using **Center** object snap.

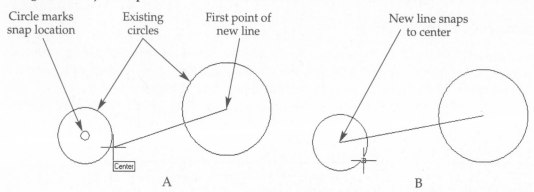

Quadrant Object Snap

A *quadrant* is a quarter section of a circle, doughnut, ellipse, elliptical arc, or arc. The **Quadrant** object snap mode finds the 0°, 90°, 180°, and 270° positions on a circle, doughnut, or arc, Figure 6-8.

When picking quadrants, locate the aperture on the circle, doughnut, or arc near the intended quadrant. For example, Figure 6-9 illustrates use of the **Quadrant** object snap mode to locate the center point of a new circle at the quadrant of an existing circle. The command sequence is as follows:

> Command: **C** *or* **CIRCLE**⏎
> Specify center point for circle or [3P/2P/Ttr (tan tan radius)]: *(pick the* **Quadrant**
>   *button, type QUA, or pick* **Quadrant** *from the* **Object Snap** *shortcut menu)*
> of *(move the cursor near the desired quadrant and pick)*
> Specify radius of a circle or [Diameter]: *(pick a radius)*

Figure 6-8.
The quadrants of
a circle.

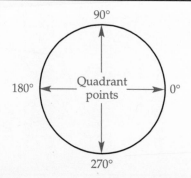

AutoCAD and its Applications—Basics

Figure 6-9.
Using **Quadrant**
object snap.

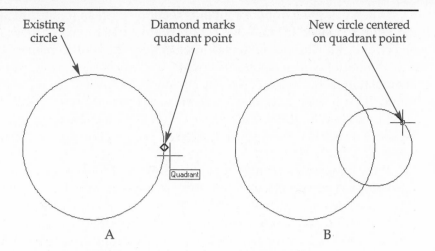

Existing circle

Diamond marks quadrant point

New circle centered on quadrant point

Quadrant

A   B

NOTE

Quadrant positions are unaffected by the current angle zero direction, but always coincide with the current WCS (World Coordinate System). The WCS is discussed later in this chapter. The quadrant points of a circle, doughnut, or arc are at the top, bottom, left, and right, regardless of the rotation of the object. However, the quadrant points of ellipses and elliptical arcs rotate with the object.

EXERCISE 6-2

❑ Start AutoCAD and use the setup option of your choice.
❑ Use the **Center** and **Quadrant** object snap modes for the following:
  ❑ Draw two separate circles and refer to the one on the left as Circle A and the other as Circle B.
  ❑ Draw a line from the center of Circle A to the 180° quadrant of Circle B.
  ❑ Draw a line from the center of Circle B to the 270° quadrant of Circle B to the 270° of Circle A, and finally to the center of Circle A.
❑ Save the drawing as EX6-2.

Intersection Object Snap

The **Intersection** object snap is used to snap to the intersection of two or more objects. This mode is activated by typing INT at the selection prompt, picking the **Intersect** button, or picking **Intersection** from the **Object Snap** shortcut menu. Then move the cursor near the intersection. A small "X" marks the intersection. See Figure 6-10.

Figure 6-10.
Using **Intersection**
object snap.

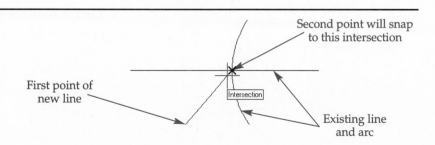

Second point will snap to this intersection

First point of new line

Intersection

Existing line and arc

When picking a point for an **Intersection** object snap, the "X" appears only when the cursor is close to the intersection point of two objects. If the cursor is near an object, but not close to an actual intersection, the tooltip reads Extended Intersection, and the AutoSnap marker is followed by an ellipsis (…). When using **Extended Intersection**, you can select the objects one at a time and then the intersection point is found. This is especially useful when two objects do not actually intersect, and you need to access the point where these objects would intersect if they were extended. Figure 6-11 shows the use of **Extended Intersection** to find an intersection point between a line and an arc.

If the intersection point is not in the currently visible screen area, then the AutoSnap marker is not displayed when pointing to the second object. However, AutoSnap still allows you to confirm the point before picking. Keeping the cursor motionless for a moment still displays the tooltip, and this supports the fact that the two objects do actually intersect somewhere beyond the currently visible area. When selecting two objects that could not intersect, no AutoSnap marker or tooltip is displayed, and no intersection point is found if the pick is made.

Apparent Intersection Object Snap

The *apparent intersection* is the point where two objects created in 3D space appear to intersect based on the current view. Three-dimensional objects that are far apart may appear to intersect when viewed from certain angles. Whether they intersect or not, this option returns the coordinate point where the objects appear to intersect. This is a valuable option when working with 3D drawings. Creating and editing 3D objects is discussed in Chapter 27 and in *AutoCAD and its Applications—Advanced, AutoCAD 2000*.

Figure 6-11.
Finding the extended intersection of two objects. A—Select the first object. B—When the second object is selected, the extended intersection becomes the snap point. C—The completed line.

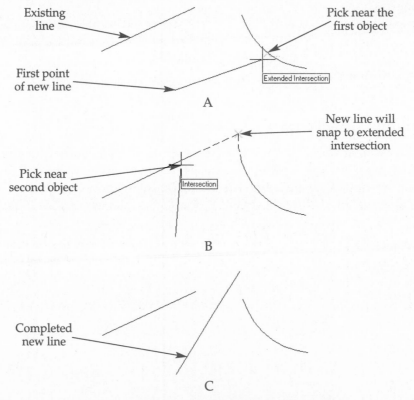

AutoCAD and its Applications—Basics

Extension Object Snap

The **Extension** object snap is used to find any point along the imaginary extension of an existing line or arc. This mode is activated by typing EXT at the selection prompt, picking the **Extension** button, or picking **Extension** from the **Object Snap** shortcut menu. The extension object snap differs from most other snaps because it requires more than one selection point. The initial point(s), called the *acquired point,* is not selected in the typical manner but is found by simply moving the cursor over the surface of the line or arc from which the new entity is to be extended. When the object is found, a (+) symbol marks the location. The last point, which is the actual snap point, is located anywhere along the extension path. The *extension path,* represented by a dashed line or arc, extends from the acquired point to the current location of the mouse.

Figure 6-12 shows an example of the **Extension** object snap being used on both the arc and the rectangle. The first acquired point is found by moving the cursor directly over the endpoint of the arc. When the tooltip for Endpoint is displayed, the (+) marker becomes visible at the end of the arc. The second acquired point is found in the same manner at the corner of the rectangle. Dragging the cursor slowly from left to right allows the intersection of both extension paths to be displayed as dashed lines as shown in Figure 6-12.

The **Extension** object snap can also be used in a manner similar to temporary tracking and the **From** object snap, which are discussed later in this chapter. In Figure 6-12, Line B is started 1 unit away from the corner of the rectangle through use of the **Extension** snap and direct distance entry.

Figure 6-12.
The **Extension** object snap being used on an arc and rectangle.

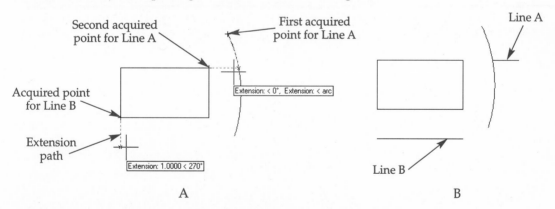

EXERCISE 6-3

❏ Start AutoCAD and use the setup option of your choice.
❏ Draw a rectangle with an arc to the right of the rectangle similar to Figure 6-12A.
❏ Use the **Extension** object snap mode to draw Line A and Line B similar to those in Figure 6-12B.
❏ Save the drawing as EX6-3.

Perpendicular Object Snap

A common geometric construction is to draw one object perpendicular to another. This is done using the **Perpendicular** object snap mode. This mode is activated by typing PER at the selection prompt, picking the **Perpendicular** button, or picking **Perpendicular** from the **Object Snap** shortcut menu. A small right-angle symbol appears at the snap point. This mode can be used with arcs, elliptical arcs, ellipses, splines, xlines, multilines, solids, traces, or circles.

Figure 6-13 shows an example of the **Perpendicular** object snap being used for the endpoint of a line. The endpoint is located so the new line is perpendicular to the existing line. In Figure 6-14, the first point of the line is selected with the **Perpendicular** object snap. The tooltip reads Deferred Perpendicular. The term *deferred perpendicular* means that the calculation of the perpendicular point is delayed until another point is picked. The second endpoint determines the location of the first endpoint.

It is important to understand that perpendicularity is calculated from points picked, and not as a relationship between objects. Also, perpendicularity is measured at the point of intersection, so it is possible to draw a line that is perpendicular to a circle or an arc.

Figure 6-13.
Drawing a line from a point perpendicular to an existing line. The **Perpendicular** object snap mode is used to select the second endpoint.

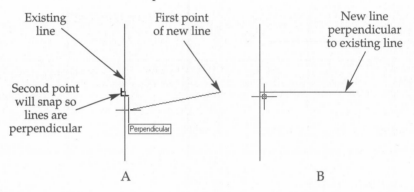

Figure 6-14.
Deferring the perpendicular location until the second point is selected. The **Perpendicular** object snap mode is used to select the first endpoint.

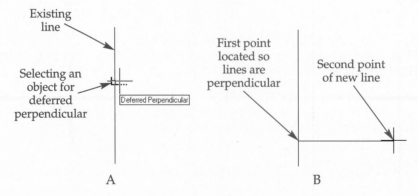

Tangent Object Snap

The **Tangent** object snap is similar to the **Perpendicular** object snap. However, instead of aligning the objects perpendicularly, it aligns objects tangentially. This mode is activated by typing TAN at the selection prompt, picking the **Tangent** button, or picking **Tangent** from the **Object Snap** shortcut menu. A small circle with a horizontal line appears at the snap point.

In Figure 6-15, the endpoint of a line is located using the **Tangent** mode. The first point is selected normally. Then the **Tangent** mode is activated and the cursor is placed near the tangent point on the circle. AutoCAD determines the tangent point and places the snap point (and the endpoint) there.

When creating an object that is tangent to another object, multiple points may be needed to fix the tangency point. For example, the point where a line is tangent to a circle cannot be found without knowing the locations of both ends of the line. Until both points have been specified, the object snap specification is for *deferred tangency.* Once both endpoints are known, the tangency is calculated and the object is drawn in the correct location. In Figure 6-16, a line is drawn tangent to two circles. The command sequence is as follows:

Command: **L** *or* **LINE**↵
Specify first point: *(pick the* **Tangent** *button, type* TAN, *or pick* **Tangent** *from the* **Object Snap** *shortcut menu.)*
tan to *(pick the first circle)*
Specify next point or [Undo]: *(pick the* **Tangent** *button, type* TAN, *or pick* **Tangent** *from the* **Object Snap** *shortcut menu.)*
tan to *(pick the second circle)*
Specify next point or [Undo]:* ↵
Command:

Figure 6-15.
Using **Tangent** object snap.

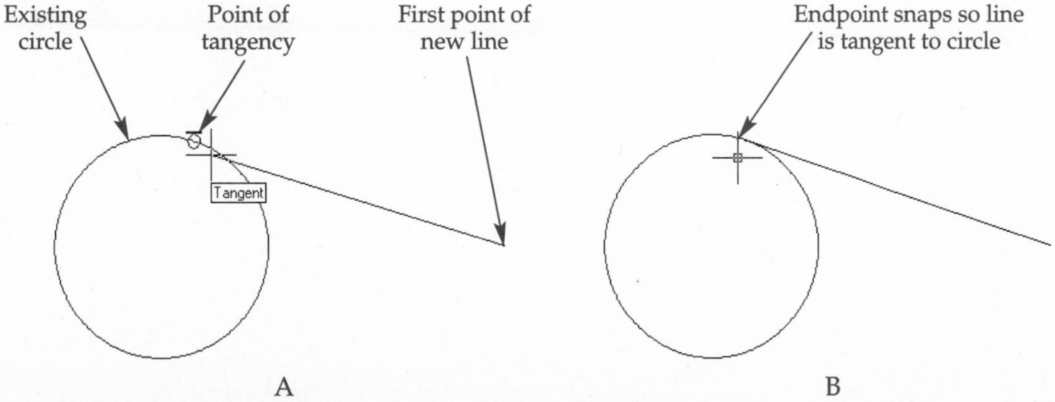

Existing circle
Point of tangency
First point of new line
Endpoint snaps so line is tangent to circle

A   B

Figure 6-16.
Drawing a line
tangent to two
circles.

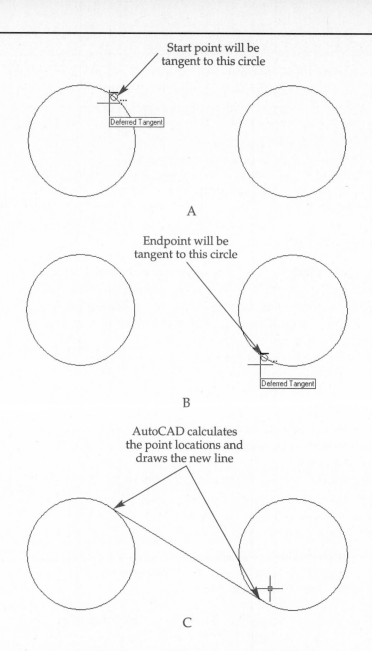

Start point will be
tangent to this circle

Deferred Tangent

A

Endpoint will be
tangent to this circle

Deferred Tangent

B

AutoCAD calculates
the point locations and
draws the new line

C

EXERCISE 6-5

❏ Start AutoCAD and use the setup option of your choice.
❏ Draw a line tangent to an existing circle.
❏ Draw two circles and then draw a line tangent to both of the circles.
❏ Use the **Tangent** object snap to draw two lines that are tangent to the circles but do not cross.
❏ Save the drawing as EX6-5.

Parallel Object Snap

The process of drawing, moving, or copying objects that are not horizontal or vertical is improved with the **Parallel** object snap mode. This option is used to find any point along an imaginary line that is parallel to an existing line or polyline. (Polylines are discussed in Chapter 15.) The parallel object snap is activated by typing PAR at the selection prompt, picking the **Parallel** button, or picking **Parallel** from the **Object Snap** shortcut menu.

The parallel object snap is similar to the **Extension** object snap because it requires more than one selection point. The first point, called the acquired point, is found by pausing the cursor above the line to which the new object is to be parallel. When the object is found and you move the cursor in a direction parallel to the existing line, a (//) symbol marks the existing line. The last point, which is the actual snap point, is located anywhere along the *parallel alignment path*, which is represented by a dashed line. When the alignment path is displayed, the **Parallel** snap marker will also display on the line from which the parallel is used. Now you pick the second point of the parallel line. Figure 6-17 shows an example of the **Parallel** object snap being used to draw a line parallel to an existing line. The following command sequence is used:

Command: **L** *or* **LINE**↵
Specify first point: *(pick the first point of the new line)*
Specify next point or [Undo]: **PAR**↵
par to *(move the cursor over the existing line until you see the acquired point symbol. Then move the cursor near the first endpoint of the new line. At this time the parallel alignment path and the Parallel snap marker are displayed. Pick the endpoint of the new line.)*
Specify next point or [Undo]: ↵
Command:

Figure 6-17.
Using the **Parallel** object snap option to draw a line parallel to an existing line. A—Select the first endpoint for the new line, then move the crosshairs near the existing line to acquire a point. B—After the parallel point is acquired, move the crosshairs near the location of the parallel line, and an extension path appears.

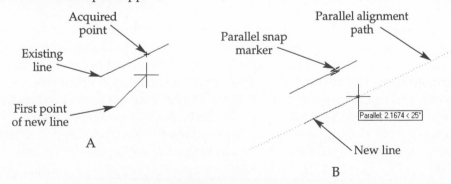

Node Object Snap

Point objects can be snapped to using the **Node** object snap mode. In order for object snap to find the point object, the point must be in a visible display mode. Controlling the point display mode is covered later in this chapter.

Nearest Object Snap

When you need to specify a point that is on an object but cannot be located with any of the other object snap modes, the **Nearest** mode can be used. This object snap locates the point on the object closest to the crosshair location. It should be used when you want an object to touch an existing object, but the location of the intersection is not critical.

Consider drawing a line object that is to end on another line. Trying to pick the point with the crosshairs is inaccurate because you are relying only on your screen and mouse resolution. The line you draw may fall short or extend past the line. Using **Nearest** ensures that the point is precisely on the object.

PROFESSIONAL TIP

When AutoCAD uses object snap modes, it searches the entire drawing database for the specified type of point nearest to the crosshairs. When working on complex drawing, you may want to use the **Quick** mode, which selects the first point satisfying the snap mode. The **Quick** mode must be activated at the Command: prompt, and is only effective for a single selection. It is activated by preceding the object snap mode with QUI and a comma. For example, the following command sequence would be used to activate the **Tangent** object snap mode in **Quick** mode:

Command: **L** *or* **LINE**↵
Specify first point: **QUI,TAN**↵

AutoCAD User's Guide 7

DDOSNAP
OSNAP
OS

Tools
➡ Drafting Settings...

Object Snap toolbar

Object Snap Settings

SETTING RUNNING OBJECT SNAPS

The previous discussion explained how to use object snaps by activating the individual mode at the selection prompt. However, if you plan to use object snaps continuously, you can set *running object snaps*. You preset the running object snap modes, and AutoCAD automatically activates them at all point selection prompts.

You can set a running object snap using the **Object Snap** tab in the **Drafting Settings** dialog box. Pick **Drafting Settings...** from the **Tools** pull-down menu, pick the **Object Snap Settings** button from the **Object Snap** toolbar, right-click on the **OSNAP** or **OTRACK** button on the status bar and select **Settings...** from the shortcut menu, or type OS, OSNAP, or DDOSNAP at the Command: prompt. You can also type DSETTINGS at the Command: prompt to access the **Drafting Settings** dialog box.

The **Object Snap** tab of the **Drafting Settings** dialog box is shown in Figure 6-18. Notice that the **Endpoint**, **Intersection**, **Extension**, and **Parallel** modes are active. You can use this dialog box at any time to discontinue a running object snap or to set additional modes.

Toggling, Disabling, and Overriding Running Object Snap

Running object snap is active at all point selection prompts, but is temporarily suspended when an object snap override is entered. The override is temporary, and is active for a single point selection only. Any currently running object snap mode is reactivated for the next pick.

AutoCAD and its Applications—Basics

Figure 6-18.
Running object snap modes can be set in the **Drafting Settings** dialog box.

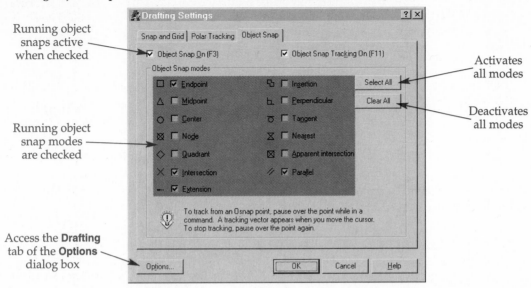

Running object snaps active when checked

Running object snap modes are checked

Access the **Drafting** tab of the **Options** dialog box

Activates all modes

Deactivates all modes

To make a single point selection without the effects of any running object snap modes, enter the **None** object snap mode. When you need to make several point specifications without the aid of object snap, you can toggle it off by clicking the **OSNAP** button on the status bar at the bottom of the AutoCAD window. The advantages of this method are that you can make several picks, and you can restore the same running object snap modes by clicking **OSNAP** again. You can also right-click on the **OSNAP** button and pick **Off** from the shortcut menu, pick the **Object Snap On (F3)** check box in the **Drafting Settings** dialog box, or press the [F3] key on your keyboard. Turn running object snaps back on using any of these options.

You can remove the active checks in the **Drafting Settings** dialog box as needed to disable running object snaps. You can also pick the **Clear All** button to disable all running modes. Select desired running object snaps by picking the associated box or pick the **Select All** button to activate all object snaps.

Using Multiple Object Snap Modes

As shown with the examples of running object snap, more than one object snap mode can be made active at once. When multiple modes are running at the same time, each of the modes is checked for possible points, and the closest point is selected.

For example, assume the **Endpoint** and **Midpoint** object snap modes are active. The AutoSnap marker locates either an endpoint or the midpoint of a line, depending on which is closest to the crosshairs location. This can cause conflicts between some object snap modes. For example, no matter where you pick a circle, the closest quadrant point is always closer than the center of the circle. This means that when **Quadrant** and **Center** are both active, a quadrant point is always selected.

The **Nearest** object snap mode causes conflicts with almost every other mode. The nearest mode does not move the selection point to a nearby feature of an object, but picks the point on the object closest to the current cursor location. This means that the **Nearest** mode always locates the closest point.

The [Tab] key on your keyboard can be used to cycle through available snap points. This works well when multiple object snap modes are active. For example, use this feature if you are trying to select the intersection between two objects where several other objects intersect nearby. To use this feature, when the AutoSnap marker appears, press the [Tab] key until the desired point is marked.

EXERCISE 6-7

❑ Start AutoCAD and use the setup option of your choice.
❑ Set the **Endpoint**, **Midpoint**, and **Perpendicular** running object snaps and practice using them in at least two situations. Drawings similar to Figure 6-5, Figure 6-6, and Figure 6-13 can be used.
❑ Change the running object snap to **Center** and **Tangent**, and use each twice in creating a simple drawing. Drawings similar to Figure 6-7 and Figure 6-16 can be used.
❑ Discontinue the running object snaps.
❑ Save the drawing as EX6-7.

AutoCAD User's Guide 7

AUTOSNAP SETTINGS

The AutoSnap feature makes object snap much easier to use. However, if you do not wish to have the additional visual cues while using object snap, you can turn the AutoSnap feature off. AutoCAD also allows you to customize the appearance and functionality of the AutoSnap feature by picking the **Options...** button in the **Object Snap** tab of the **Drafting Settings** dialog box to access the **Drafting** tab of the **Options** dialog box. This tab is shown in Figure 6-19. The settings are described as follows:

- **Marker.** Toggles the AutoSnap marker display.
- **Magnet.** Toggles the AutoSnap magnet. When active, the magnet snaps the cursor to the object snap point.
- **Display AutoSnap tooltip.** Toggles the tooltip display.
- **Display AutoSnap aperture box.** Toggles the display of the aperture.

The marker size and color can also be adjusted to suit your needs. For example, the default marker color is yellow, but this is difficult to see if you have the graphics screen background set to white. Pick the down arrow to access the **AutoSnap marker color:** drop-down list, and select the desired color. At higher screen resolutions, a larger marker size improves visibility. Move the slider at the **AutoSnap Marker Size:** area to change the size.

Figure 6-19.
Setting AutoSnap features.

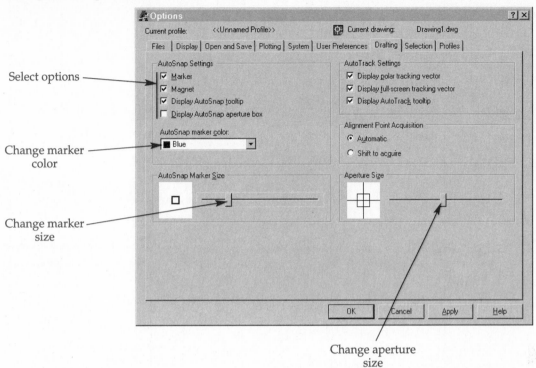

Select options ——

Change marker color ——

Change marker size ——

Change aperture size

The **AUTOSNAP** system variable controls the display of the AutoSnap marker and AutoSnap tooltip and turns the AutoSnap magnet on or off. The **OSMODE** system variable uses bit codes to set object snap modes.

EXERCISE 6-8

❏ Start AutoCAD and use the setup option of your choice.
❏ Open the **Drafting Settings** dialog box and then the **Options** dialog box.
❏ Move the **AutoSnap Marker Size** slider and watch the image change to represent the marker size.
❏ Change the marker color to red.
❏ Use the newly revised marker size and color to draw objects of your choice with the object snaps.
❏ Save the drawing as EX6-8.

Changing the Aperture Size

When selecting a point using object snaps, the cursor must be within a specific range of a candidate point before it is located. The object snap detection system finds everything within a square area centered at the cursor location. This square area is called the *aperture* and is invisible by default.

To display the aperture, open the **Drafting Settings** dialog box and pick the **Options...** button from the **Object Snap** tab. The **Drafting** tab of the **Options** dialog box appears. Activate the **Display AutoSnap aperture box** check box. Having the aperture visible may be helpful when you are first learning to work with object snap. The **APBOX** system variable turns the AutoSnap aperture box on or off.

To change the size of the aperture, move the slider in the **Aperture Size** area. Various aperture sizes are shown in Figure 6-20. The aperture size can also be set by typing APERTURE at the Command: prompt.

Figure 6-20.
Aperture box size is measured in pixels. The three examples here are not shown at actual size, but are provided to show the size relationship between different settings.

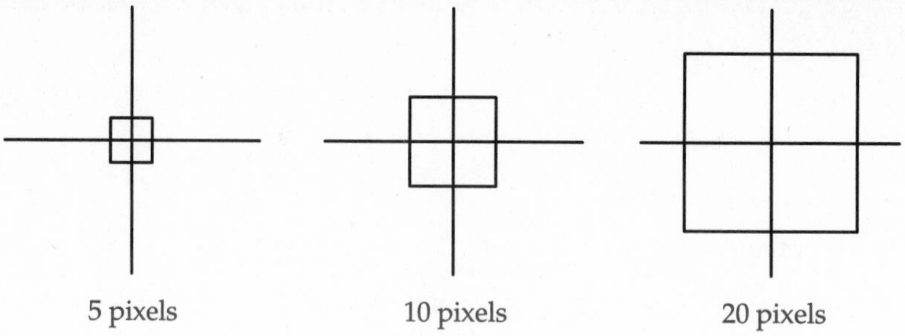

5 pixels   10 pixels   20 pixels

The size of the aperture is measured in *pixels*. Pixels are the dots that make up a display screen.

Keep in mind that the *aperture* and the *pick box* are different. The aperture is displayed on the screen when object snap modes are active. The pick box appears on the screen for any command that activates the Select objects: prompt.

EXERCISE 6-9

❏ Open EX6-7.
❏ Display the aperture.
❏ Change the aperture size to 5 pixels. Draw lines to existing objects using the object snap modes of your choice.
❏ Change the aperture size to 20 pixels. Again, draw lines to the existing objects using the object snap modes of your choice.
❏ Observe the difference in aperture size. Determine your personal preference between the 5 and 20 pixel sizes as compared to the AutoCAD default of 10 pixels.
❏ Save the drawing as EX6-9.

AutoCAD
User's
Guide **7**

USING TEMPORARY TRACKING TO LOCATE POINTS

Tracking is a system that allows you to visually locate points in a drawing relative to other points. Tracking creates a new point using the X coordinate of one tracking point and the Y coordinate of another. The tracking feature can be used at any point specification prompt, just like object snap. Tracking can also be used in combination with object snap.

To activate temporary tracking, pick the **Temporary Tracking Point** button from the **Object Snap** toolbar, type TT, or pick **Temporary track point** from the **Object Snap** shortcut menu.

As an example, tracking can be used to place a circle at the center of a rectangle. See Figure 6-21. The center of the rectangle corresponds to the X coordinate of the midpoint of the horizontal lines. The Y coordinate corresponds to the Y coordinate of the vertical lines. Temporary tracking can be used to combine these two points to find the center of the rectangle using this sequence:

TT

Object Snap toolbar

Temporary Tracking Point

Command: **C** *or* **CIRCLE**↵
Specify center point for circle or [3P/2P/Ttr (tan tan radius)]: **TT**↵
Specify temporary OTRACK point: **MID**↵
of (*pick one of the vertical lines and move the cursor horizontally*)
Specify center point for circle or [3P/2P/Ttr (tan tan radius)]: **TT**↵
Specify temporary OTRACK point: **MID**↵
of (*pick one of the horizontal lines and move the cursor vertically*)
Specify center point for circle or [3P/2P/Ttr (tan tan radius)]: (*select the point where the two alignment paths cross intersect*)
Specify radius of circle or [Diameter] <*current*>: ↵
Command:

Figure 6-21.
Using temporary tracking to locate the center of a rectangle. A—The midpoint of the left line is acquired. B—The midpoint of the bottom line is acquired. C—The center point of the circle is located at the intersection of the alignment paths.

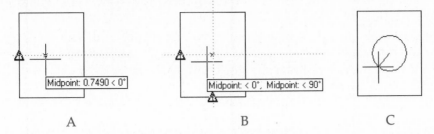

A   B   C

The direction of the orthogonal line determines whether the X or Y component is used. In the previous example, after picking the first tracking point, the cursor is moved horizontally. This means that the Y axis value of the previous point is being used and tracking is now ready for an X coordinate specification.

After moving the cursor horizontally, you may notice that movement is locked in a horizontal mode. If you need to move the cursor vertically, move the cursor back to the previously picked point and then drag vertically. Use this method anytime you need to switch between horizontal and vertical movement.

Using the **From** Point Selection Option

The **From** point selection mode is another tracking tool that can be used to locate points based on existing geometry. The **From** point selection mode allows you to establish a relative coordinate, polar coordinate, or direct distance entry from a specified reference base point. Access the **From** option by selecting the **Snap From** button in the **Object Snap** toolbar, select **From** in the **Object Snap** shortcut menu, or type FRO at a point selection prompt. The example in Figure 6-22 shows the center point for a circle being established as a polar distance from the midpoint of an existing line. The command sequence is shown here:

> Command: **C** *or* **CIRCLE**↵
> Specify center point for circle or [3P/2P/Ttr (tan tan radius)]: **FRO**↵
> Base point: **MID**↵
> of *(pick line)*
> <Offset>: **@2<45**↵
> Specify radius of circle or [Diameter] <*current*>: **.75**↵
> Command:

Figure 6-22.
Using the **From** point selection mode following the command sequence given in the text.

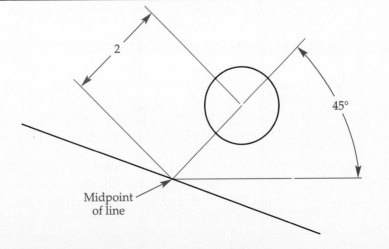

2

45°

Midpoint
of line

❏ Start AutoCAD and use the setup option of your choice.
❏ Draw a rectangle similar to the one in Figure 6-21.
❏ Use tracking to locate the center of the rectangle and draw a circle with its center at that location.
❏ Draw a line with a length and angle similar to Figure 6-22.
❏ Use the **From** point selection option to draw a φ.75 circle with its center 2 units and 45° from the midpoint of the line, similar to Figure 6-22.
❏ Save the drawing as EX6-10.

USING AUTOTRACKING TO LOCATE POINTS

The temporary tracking mode, discussed earlier, allows the relative placement of a point for a single task. The AutoTrack™ mode enables this feature to be activated at all times, similar to running object snaps. The purpose of AutoTracking is to reduce the need for construction lines and keyboard entry.

There are two AutoTrack modes: object snap tracking and polar tracking. Both modes provide alignment paths to aid in precise point location relative to existing points. Any command requiring a point selection, such as the **COPY**, **MOVE**, or **LINE** command, can make use of these modes.

Object Snap Tracking

Object snap tracking is always used in conjunction with object snaps. When this mode is active, placing the crosshairs near an AutoSnap marker will acquire the point. Once a point is acquired, horizontal and vertical alignment paths are available for locating points.

Object snap tracking is toggled on and off with the [F11] function key or the **OTRACK** button on the status bar. This mode is only available for points selected by the currently active object modes. When running object snaps are active, all selected object snap modes are available for object snap tracking. However, these modes are not available for object snap tracking if running object snaps are deactivated.

In Figure 6-23, object snap tracking is used in conjunction with the **Perpendicular** and **Midpoint** running object snaps to draw a line that is 2 units long and perpendicular to the existing, slanted line. The running object snap modes are set before the following command sequence is initiated, and the **OSNAP** and **OTRACK** buttons on the status are active.

Command: **L** *or* **LINE**↵
Specify first point: *(select the midpoint of the existing line, pausing the crosshairs to acquire the point)*
Specify next point or [Undo]: *(position crosshairs as shown in Figure 6-23A to activate perpendicular alignment path)* **2**↵
Specify next point or [Undo]: ↵
Command:

PROFESSIONAL TIP

AutoTracking is similar in performance to the **Extended** object snap. Experiment with a combination of just the **Endpoint** object snap mode and AutoTracking. Then try a combination of **Endpoint** and **Extended** object snap modes without AutoTracking to see the difference. Notice that without object snap tracking, you cannot drag in a direction perpendicular to an endpoint.

Figure 6-23.
Using object snap tracking to draw a line. A—First endpoint located at midpoint of existing line. The alignment path is displayed when the crosshairs are near. B—The completed line, with the second endpoint identified using direct distance entry along the alignment path.

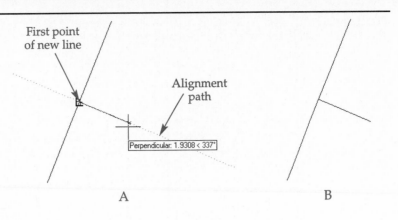

First point of new line

Alignment path

Perpendicular: 1.9308 < 337°

A   B

EXERCISE 6-11

❑ Start AutoCAD and use the setup option of your choice.
❑ Set the **Midpoint** and **Perpendicular** running object snaps.
❑ Draw a line at an angle similar to the line in Figure 6-23A.
❑ Use object snap tracking to draw a new line perpendicular to the midpoint of the first line and 5 units away, similar to Figure 6-23B.
❑ Save the drawing as EX6-11.

Polar Tracking

The Ortho mode, discussed in Chapter 4, forces the cursor movement to orthogonal (horizontal and vertical) orientations. When Ortho is turned on and the **LINE** command is in use, all new line segments are drawn at either 0°, 90°, 180°, or 270°. Polar tracking works in much the same way, but allows for a greater range of angles.

Polar tracking can be turned on and off by selecting the **POLAR** button from the status bar or by using the [F10] function key. AutoCAD automatically turns Ortho off when polar tracking is on, and turns polar tracking off when Ortho is on. You cannot use polar tracking and Ortho at the same time.

When the polar tracking mode is turned on, the cursor snaps to preset incremental angles when a point is being located relative to another point. For example, when using the **LINE** command, polar tracking is not active for the first endpoint selection, but is available for the second and subsequent point selections. Polar alignment paths are displayed as dashed lines whenever the cursor comes into alignment with any of these preset angles.

To set incremental angles, use the **Polar Tracking** tab in the **Drafting Settings** dialog box. To access this dialog box, right-click on the **POLAR** button from the status bar and then select **Settings...**, pick **Drafting Settings...** from the **Tools** pull-down menu, or type DSETTINGS at the Command: prompt. Figure 6-24 shows the **Polar Tracking** tab of the **Drafting Settings** dialog box.

The following features are found in the **Polar Tracking** tab:

• **Polar Tracking On (F10).** Check this box, press the [F10] key, or pick the **POLAR** button on the status bar to turn polar tracking on.

• **Polar Angle Settings area.** This area of the dialog box allows you to set the desired polar angle increments. It contains the following items:

  • **Increment angle.** This drop-down list is set at 90.0 by default. This setting provides angle increments every 90°. Open the drop-down list to use a variety of preset angles. The angle set in Figure 6-24 is 30.0, which sets polar tracking in 30° increments.

Figure 6-24.
The **Polar Tracking** tab of the **Drafting Settings** dialog box.

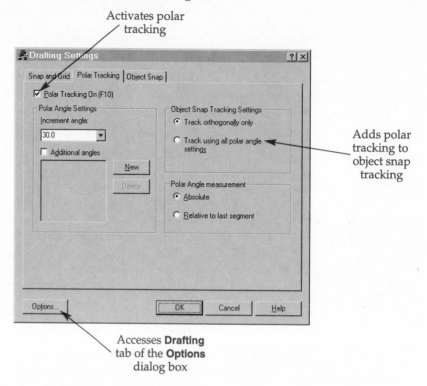

Activates polar tracking

Adds polar tracking to object snap tracking

Accesses **Drafting** tab of the **Options** dialog box

- **A̲dditional angles.** This check box activates your own angle increments. To do this, pick the **N̲ew** button to open a text box in the window. Type the desired angle. Pick the **N̲ew** button each time you want to add another angle. The additional angles are used together with the incremental angle setting when you use polar tracking. Use the **Delete** button to remove angles from the list. You can make the additional angle(s) inactive by turning off the **A̲dditional angles** check box.

- **Object Snap Tracking Settings area.** This area is used to set the angles available with object snap tracing. If **Track orthogonally only** is selected, only horizontal and vertical alignment paths are active. If **Track using all polar angle settings** is selected, alignment paths for all polar snap angles are active.

- **Polar Angle measurement area.** This setting determines if the polar snap increments are constant or relative to the previous segment. If **A̲bsolute** is selected, the polar snap angles are measured from the base angle of 0° set for the drawing. If **R̲elative to Last Segment** is checked, each increment angle is measured from a base angle established by the previously drawn segment.

The system variables that control polar tracking settings are **POLARANG** and **POLARADDANG**.

Figure 6-25 shows an example using polar tracking with 30° angle increments to draw a parallelogram by using the following command sequence:

Command: **L** *or* **LINE**↵
Specify first point:*(select the first point)*
Specify next point or [Undo]: *(drag the cursor to the right while the polar alignment path indicates <0°)* **3**↵
Specify next point or [Undo]: *(drag the cursor to the 60° polar alignment path)* **1.5**↵
Specify next point or [Close/Undo]: **3**↵
Specify next point or [Close/Undo]: **C**↵
Command:

AutoCAD and its Applications—Basics

Figure 6-25.
Using polar tracking with 30° angle increments to draw a parallelogram. A—After the first side is drawn, the alignment path and direct distance entry are used to create the second side. B—Horizontal alignment path is used for the third side. C—Parallelogram completed with the **Close** option.

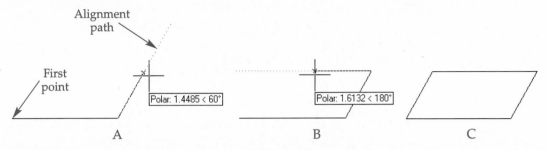

EXERCISE 6-12

❑ Start AutoCAD and use the setup option of your choice.
❑ Open the **Polar Tracking** tab of the **Drafting Settings** dialog box and set the increment angle to 30.
❑ Use polar tracking to draw a parallelogram similar to Figure 6-25.
❑ Save the drawing as EX6-12.

Polar tracking with polar snaps

Polar tracking can also be used in conjunction with polar snaps. If polar snaps are used when drawing the parallelogram in Figure 6-25, there would be no need to type the length of the line, because you set both the angle increment and a length increment. The desired angle and length increment are established in the **Snap and Grid** tab of the **Drafting Settings** dialog box. You can open this dialog box as previously described, or you can right-click on the status bar **SNAP** button and pick **Settings...** from the shortcut menu. This opens the **Drafting Settings** dialog box as shown in Figure 6-26.

Figure 6-26.
The **Snap and Grid** tab of the **Drafting Settings** dialog box is used to set the polar snap spacing.

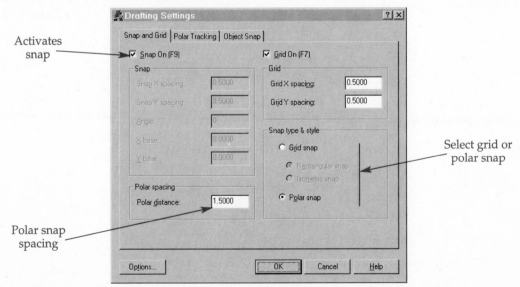

Figure 6-27.
Drawing a parallelogram with polar snap.

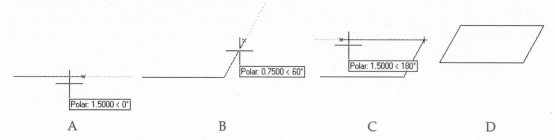

| A | B | C | D |

Polar snap is activated by picking the **Polar snap** button in the **Snap type & style** area of the dialog box. Picking this button activates the **Polar spacing** area and deactivates the **Snap** area. The length of the polar snap increment is set in the **Polar distance:** box. If the **Polar distance:** setting is 0, the polar snap distance will be the orthogonal snap distance.

Figure 6-27 shows a parallelogram being drawn with 30° angle increments and .75 length increments. The lengths of the parallelogram sides are 1.5 and .75.

Using polar tracking overrides

It takes some time to set up the polar tracking and the polar snap options, but it is worth the effort if you have several objects to draw that can take advantage of this feature. If you want to perform polar tracking for only one point, you can use the polar tracking override to do this easily. This works for the specified angle if polar tracking is on or off. A polar tracking override is done by entering a left angle bracket (<) followed by the desired angle when AutoCAD asks you to specify a point. The following command sequence uses a 30° override to draw a line 1.5 units long:

```
Command: L or LINE↵
Specify first point: (pick a start point for the line)
Specify next point or [Undo]: <30↵
Angle override: 30
Specify next point or [Undo]: (move the cursor in the desired 30° direction) 1.5↵
Specify next point or [Undo]: ↵
Command:
```

EXERCISE 6-13

❑ Start AutoCAD and use the setup option of your choice.
❑ Open the **Polar Tracking** tab of the **Drafting Settings** dialog box and set the increment angle to 60.
❑ Open the **Snap and Grid** tab of the **Drafting Settings** dialog box to set the polar distance at .75.
❑ Use polar snap to draw a parallelogram similar to Figure 6-27.
❑ Use the polar tracking overrides to draw the following connected lines:
  ❑ Start from a point of your choice and draw a line at a 67° angle and 1.125 units long.
  ❑ Continue 293° and 1.125 long.
  ❑ Continue 67° and 1.125 long.
  ❑ Continue 293° and 1.125 long.
  ❑ Exit the **LINE** command.
❑ Save the drawing as EX6-13.

AutoTrack Settings

The settings that control the function of AutoTracking can be accessed through the **Options...** button on the **Drafting Settings** dialog box. This opens the **Options** dialog box to the **Drafting** tab. This tab was illustrated in Figure 6-19.

The following options are available in the **AutoTrack Settings** area:

- **Display polar tracking vector.** When this feature is selected, the alignment path is displayed. When this option is off, no polar tracking path is displayed.
- **Display full-screen tracking vector.** When this option is selected, the alignment path for object snap tracking extends across the length of the screen. If not checked, the alignment paths are shown only between the acquired point and the cursor location. Polar tracking vectors always extend from the original point to the extents of the screen.
- **Display AutoTrack tooltip.** When this box is checked, a temporary tooltip is displayed with the AutoTrack alignment paths.

The options in the **Alignment Point Acquisition** area determine how the object snap tracking alignment paths are selected:

- **Automatic.** When this option is selected, points are acquired whenever the cursor is paused over an object snap point.
- **Shift to acquire.** When this option is selected, the [Shift] key must be pressed to acquire an object snap point and use object snap tracking. AutoSnap markers are still displayed and normal object snap can be used without pressing the [Shift] key. If many running object snaps are set, it may be useful to use this option to reduce the number of paths displayed across the screen.

The **TRACKPATH** system variable stores the alignment path display settings, and the **POLARMODE** system variable stores the alignment point acquisition method.

Point Filters

Tracking allows you to combine the X coordinate of one point and the Y coordinate of another point to locate a new point. You can also directly access the X or Y coordinates of a point by using point filters. *Filters* allow you to select any aspect of an object while filtering out other objects, items, or features.

There are many uses for filters. Filters used for layer control were introduced in Chapter 4. Point filters and object selection filters are completely discussed in Chapter 7.

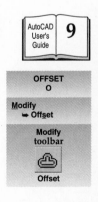

AutoCAD User's Guide **9**

OFFSET
O

Modify
↳ Off**s**et

Modify
toolbar

Offset

DRAWING PARALLEL LINES AND CURVES

The **OFFSET** command is used to draw concentric circles, arcs, curves, polylines, and parallel lines. This command is accessed by picking **Offset** in the **Modify** pull-down menu, picking the **Offset** button in the **Modify** toolbar, or typing O or OFFSET at the Command: prompt. When selected, the command produces the following prompt:

    Command: **O** *or* **OFFSET**↵
    Offset distance or [Through] <*current*>:

Type a distance or pick a point for the parallel object to be drawn through. The last offset distance used is shown in brackets. If you want to draw two parallel circles a distance of .1 unit apart, use the following command sequence. Refer to Figure 6-28.

    Command: **O** *or* **OFFSET**↵
    Specify offset distance or [Through] <*current*>: **.1**↵
    Select object to offset or <exit>: *(pick the object)*
    Specify point on side to offset: *(pick the side of the object for the offset to be drawn)*
    Select object to offset or <exit>: *(select another object or press* [Enter]*)*

Figure 6-28.
Drawing an offset using a designated distance.

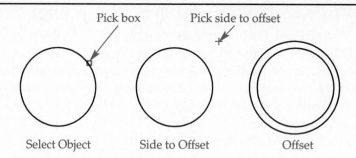

When the Select object to offset prompt first appears, the screen cursor turns into a pick box. After the object is picked, the screen cursor turns back into crosshairs. No other selection option (such as window or crossing) works with the **OFFSET** command.

The other option is to pick a point that the offset is drawn through. Type T as follows to produce the results shown in Figure 16-29:

Command: **O** *or* **OFFSET**↵
Specify offset distance or [Through] <*current*>: **T**↵
Select object to offset or <exit>: *(pick the object)*
Specify through point: *(pick the point that the offset will be drawn through)*
Select object to offset or <exit>: ↵

Object snap modes can be used to assist in drawing an offset. For example, suppose you have a circle and a line and want to draw a concentric circle tangent to the line. Refer to Figure 6-30 and the following command sequence:

Command: **O** *or* **OFFSET**↵
Specify offset distance or [Through] <*current*>: **QUA**↵
of *(pick the existing circle)*
Specify second point: **PER**↵
to *(pick the existing line)*
Select object to offset or <exit>: *(pick the existing circle)*
Specify point on side to offset: *(pick between the circle and line)*
Select object to offset or <exit>: ↵
Command:

Figure 6-29.
Drawing an offset through a given point.

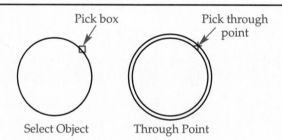

Figure 6-30.
Using **OFFSET** to draw a concentric circle tangent to a line.

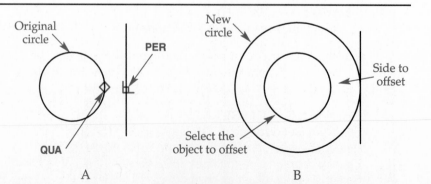

❏ Start AutoCAD and use the setup option of your choice.
❏ Draw two circles and two objects made up of line and arc segments.
❏ Use the **OFFSET** command to draw parallels a distance of .2 units on the inside of one circle and one arc-line object.
❏ Use the **OFFSET** command again, this time specifying **Through** point on the outside of the other circle and arc-line object.
❏ Save the drawing as EX6-14.

DIVIDING AN OBJECT

AutoCAD User's Guide 7

DIVIDE
DIV

Draw
➥ P**o**int
➥ **D**ivide

A line, circle, arc, or polyline can be divided into an equal number of segments using the **DIVIDE** command. To start the **DIVIDE** command, select **D**ivide from the **P**oint cascading menu of the **D**raw pull-down menu, or type DIV or DIVIDE.

The **DIVIDE** command does not physically break an object into multiple parts. It places point objects or blocks at the locations where the breaks would occur if the object were actually divided into multiple segments.

Suppose you have drawn a line and want to divide it into seven equal parts. Enter the **DIVIDE** command and select the object to divide. Then, enter the number of segments. Refer to Figure 6-31. The procedure is as follows:

Command: **DIV** *or* **DIVIDE**↵
Select object to divide: *(pick the object)*
Enter the number of segments or [Block]: **7**↵
Command:

The **Block** option of the **DIVIDE** command allows you to place a block at each division point. To initiate the **Block** option, type B at the prompt. You are then asked if the block is to be aligned with the object. A *block* is a previously drawn symbol or shape. Blocks are discussed in detail in Chapter 23 of this text.

After the number of segments is given, the object is divided with points. However, by default, points are displayed as dots, which may not show very well. Notice in Figure 6-31 that the appearance of the marks has been changed by changing the point style. This can be done by selecting **P**oint Style... from the **Fo**rmat pull-down menu and selecting a new point style from the **Point Style** dialog box. Drawing points and setting point style is discussed later in this chapter.

Figure 6-31.
Using the **DIVIDE**
command. Note
that the default
marks (points) have
been changed to X's.

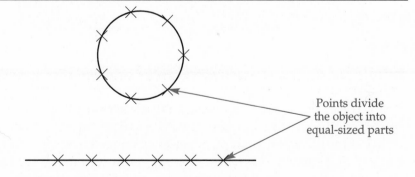

Points divide
the object into
equal-sized parts

MEASURE
ME

Draw
➥ P**o**int
➥ **M**easure

DIVIDING OBJECTS AT SPECIFIED DISTANCES

Unlike the **DIVIDE** command, where an object is divided into a specified number of parts, the **MEASURE** command places marks a specified distance apart. The **MEASURE** command is accessed by picking **Measure** from the **Point** cascading menu of the **Draw** pull-down menu, or by typing ME or MEASURE at the Command: prompt. The line shown in Figure 6-32 is measured with .75 unit segments as follows:

Command: **ME** *or* **MEASURE**↵
Select object to measure: *(pick an object)*
Specify length of segment or [Block]: **.75**↵

Measuring begins at the end closest to where the object is picked. All increments are equal to the entered segment length except the last segment, which may be shorter. The point style determines the type of marks placed on the object, just as it does with the **DIVIDE** command. Blocks can be inserted at the given distances using the **Block** option of the **MEASURE** command.

Figure 6-32.
Using the **MEASURE** command. Notice that the last segment may be shorter than the others, depending on the total length of the object.

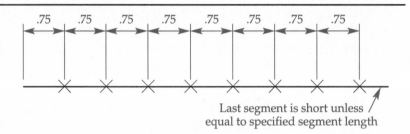

.75 .75 .75 .75 .75 .75 .75 .75

Last segment is short unless equal to specified segment length

EXERCISE 6-15

❏ Start AutoCAD and use the setup option of your choice.
❏ Select the X point style from the **Point Style** dialog box.
❏ Draw two circles of any diameter and two lines of any length.
❏ Use the **DIVIDE** command to divide one circle into 10 equal parts and one line into 5 equal parts.
❏ Use the **MEASURE** command to divide the other circle into .5 unit parts and the other line into .75 unit parts.
❏ Draw two parallel vertical lines. Make each line 3" (75mm) long and space them 4" (100mm) apart. Use the **DIVIDE** command to divide the line on the left into 10 equal increments. Draw horizontal parallel lines from each division on the left line over to the right line. Use the **Node** and **Perpendicular** object snap options to assist you.
❏ Save the drawing as EX6-15.

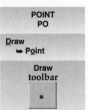

AutoCAD User's Guide 6

POINT
PO

Draw
➥ P**o**int

Draw toolbar

Point

DRAWING POINTS

You can draw points anywhere on the screen using the **POINT** command. This command is accessed by picking the **Point** button from the **Draw** toolbar, typing PO or POINT at the Command: prompt, or selecting one of the options from the **Point** cascading menu in the **Draw** pull-down menu. The appearance of the point is controlled by the point style, which is set in the **Point Style** dialog box. The command sequence is as follows:

Command: **PO** *or* **POINT**↵
Current point modes: PDMODE=0   PDSIZE=0.0000
Specify a point: *(type point coordinates or pick with pointing device)*
Command:

When the **POINT** command is used, the current point modes are listed at the command line. The **PDMODE** system variable specifies the type of point marker, and the **PDSIZE** system variable specifies the size of the point marker. Point style is discussed later in the chapter.

When all you need to do is place a single point object, type PO or POINT at the Command: prompt or select the **Single Point** option from the **Point** cascading menu. After drawing a single point, you are returned to the Command: prompt. When you need to draw multiple points, use the **Point** button or pick **Multiple Point** from the **Point** cascading menu. Press [Esc] to exit the command.

NOTE   If the point style is set as dots and blips are active, the blip covers the dot when the point is selected. Enter REDRAW at the Command: prompt and press [Enter] to erase the blip.

Setting Point Style

The style and size of points are set using the **Point Style** dialog box, Figure 6-33. This dialog box is accessed by selecting **Point Style...** from the **Format** pull-down menu or by entering DDPTYPE at the Command: prompt.

The **Point Style** dialog box contains twenty different point styles. The current point style is highlighted. To change the style, simply pick the graphic image of the desired style.

DDPTYPE

Format
➥ Point Style...

Figure 6-33.
The **Point Style** dialog box. This is a quick way to select the point style and to change the point size.

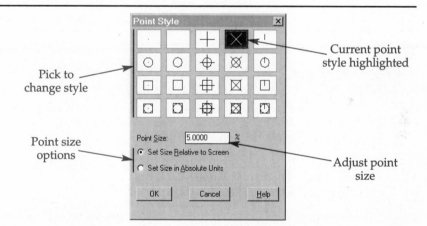

Current point style highlighted

Pick to change style

Point size options

Adjust point size

NOTE The point style is stored in the **PDMODE** system variable. This variable can be changed at the Command: prompt. The **PDMODE** values of the point styles shown in the top row of the **Point Style** dialog box are 0 through 4, from left to right. These are the basic point styles. Add a circle (second row in dialog box) by adding 32 to the basic **PDMODE** value. Add 64 to draw a square (third row), and add 96 to draw a circle and square (bottom row). For example, a point display of an X inside a circle has a **PDMODE** value of 35. That is the sum of the X value of 3 and the circle value of 32.

Set the point size by entering a value in the **Point Size:** text box of the **Point Style** dialog box. Pick the **Set Size Relative to Screen** option button if you want the point size to change in relation to different display options. Picking the **Set Size in Absolute Units** option button makes the points appear the same size no matter what display option is used. The effect of these options is shown in Figure 6-34.

Figure 6-34.
Points sized with the **Relative to Screen** setting change size as the drawing is zoomed. Points sized with the **Absolute Units** setting remain a constant size.

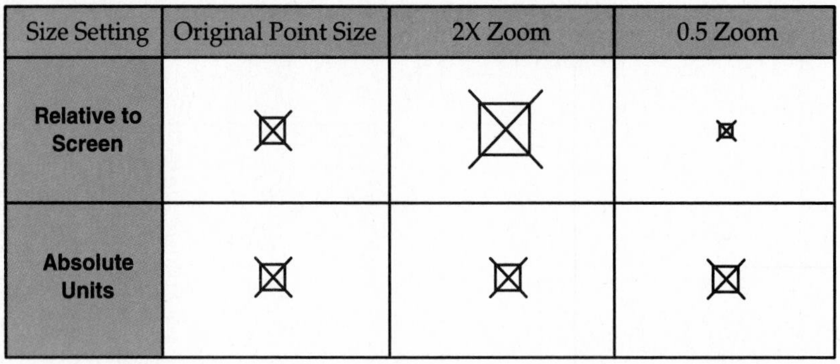

Size Setting	Original Point Size	2X Zoom	0.5 Zoom
Relative to Screen	⊠	⊠	⊠
Absolute Units	⊠	⊠	⊠

NOTE

The point size and relative/absolute setting can also be modified using the **PDSIZE** (point display size) system variable. Positive **PDSIZE** values change size in relation to different display options (relative to screen). Negative **PDSIZE** values make the points appear the same size no matter how much you **ZOOM** the drawing (absolute units).

EXERCISE 6-16

❑ Start AutoCAD and use the setup option of your choice.
❑ Draw single points by entering PO at the Command: prompt.
❑ Pick the **Point** button from the **Draw** toolbar and draw several points.
❑ Access the **Point Style** dialog box to change the point style.
❑ Save the drawing as EX6-16.

ORTHOGRAPHIC MULTIVIEW DRAWINGS

Each field of drafting has its own method to present views of a product. Architectural drafting uses plan views, exterior elevations, and sections. In electronics drafting, symbols are placed in a schematic diagram to show the circuit layout. In civil drafting, contour lines are used to show the topography of the land. Mechanical drafting uses *multiview drawings*.

This section discusses multiview drawings. Multiview drawings are based on the standard ANSI Y14.3. Also explained is the use of construction lines for view alignment and use in geometric construction.

Multiviews are made using orthographic projection. *Orthographic projection* involves projecting object features onto an imaginary plane. This imaginary plane is called a *projection plane*. The imaginary projection plane is placed parallel to the object. Thus, the line of sight is perpendicular to the object. This results in views that appear two-dimensional, Figure 6-35.

Six two-dimensional views show all sides of an object. The six views are the front, right side, left side, top, bottom, and rear. The views are placed in a standard

Figure 6-35.
Obtaining a front view with orthographic projection.

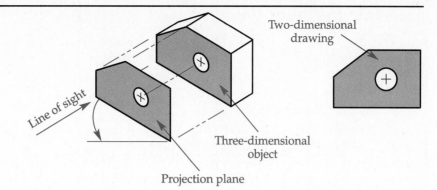

arrangement so others can read the drawing. The front view is the central, or most important view. Other views are placed around the front view, Figure 6-36.

There are very few products that require all six views. The number of views needed depends on the complexity of the object. Use only enough views to completely describe the object. Drawing too many views is time-consuming and can clutter the drawing. In some cases, a single view may be enough to describe the object. The object shown in Figure 6-37 needs only two views. These two views completely describe the width, height, depth, and features of the object.

Figure 6-36.
Arrangement of the six orthographic views.

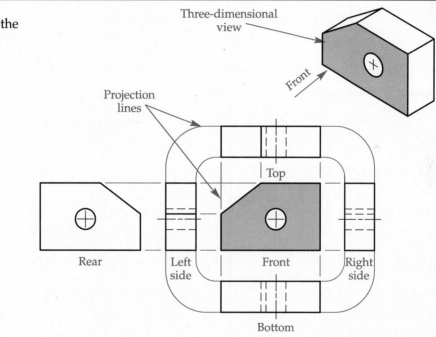

Figure 6-37.
The views you choose to describe the object should show all height, width, and depth dimensions.

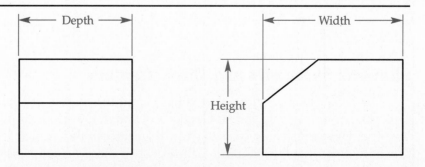

Selecting the Front View

The front view is usually the most important view. The following guidelines should be considered when selecting the front view:

- ✓ Look for the best shape or most contours.
- ✓ Show the most natural position of use.
- ✓ Display the most stable position.
- ✓ Provide the longest dimension.
- ✓ Contain the least hidden features.

Additional views are selected relative to the front view. Remember, choose only the number of views needed to completely describe the object's features.

Showing Hidden Features

Hidden features are parts of the object not visible in the view you are looking at. A visible edge appears as a solid line. A hidden edge is shown with a hidden line. Hidden lines were discussed in Chapter 4. Notice in Figure 6-38 how hidden features are shown as hidden lines. Hidden lines are thin to provide contrast to object lines.

Figure 6-38.
Hidden features are shown with hidden lines.

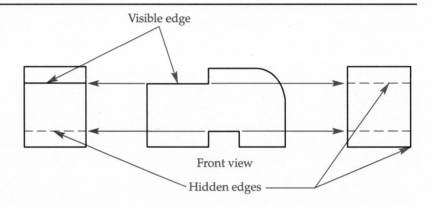

Visible edge

Front view

Hidden edges

One-View Drawings

In some instances, an object can be fully described using one view. A thin part, such as a gasket, can be drawn with one view. See Figure 6-39. The thickness is given as a note in the drawing or in the title block. A cylindrical object can also be drawn with one view. The diameter dimension is given to identify the object as round.

Figure 6-39.
A one-view drawing of a gasket. The thickness is a given in a note.

Thickness 1.5mm

Showing Symmetry and Circle Centers

The centerlines of symmetrical objects and the centers of circles are shown using centerlines. For example, in one view of a cylinder, the axis is drawn as a centerline. In the other view, centerlines cross to show the center in the circular view. See Figure 6-40. The only place that the small centerline dashes should cross is at the center of a circle.

Figure 6-40.
Drawing
centerlines. A—For
a cylinder. B—For a
round hole.

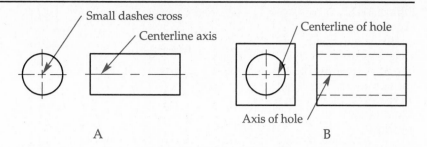

A   B

DRAWING AUXILIARY VIEWS

In most cases, an object is completely described using a combination of one or more of the six standard views. However, sometimes the multiview layout is not enough to properly identify some object surfaces. It may then be necessary to draw auxiliary views.

Auxiliary views are typically needed when a surface on the object is at an angle to the line of sight. These slanted surfaces are *foreshortened*, meaning they are shorter than the true size and shape of the surface. To show this surface in true size, an auxiliary view is needed. Foreshortened dimensions are not recommended.

Auxiliary views are drawn by projecting lines perpendicular (90°) to a slanted surface. Usually, one projection line remains on the drawing. It connects the auxiliary view to the view where the slanted surface appears as a line. The resulting auxiliary view shows the surface in true size and shape. For most applications, the auxiliary view need only show the slanted surface, not the entire object. This is called a *partial auxiliary view* and is shown in Figure 6-41.

In many situations, there may not be enough room on the drawing to project directly from the slanted surface. The auxiliary view is then placed elsewhere, Figure 6-42. A viewing-plane line is drawn next to the view where the slanted surface appears as a line. The *viewing-plane line* is drawn with a thick dashed or phantom line in accordance with ANSI Y14.2M. It is terminated with bold arrowheads that point toward the slanted surface.

Figure 6-41.
Auxiliary views
show the true size
and shape of an
inclined surface.

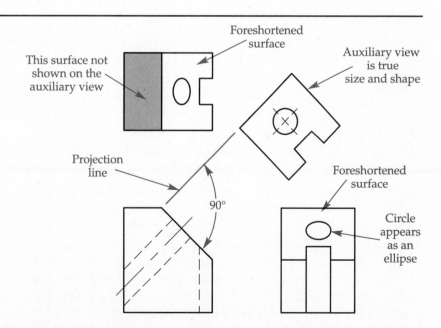

Figure 6-42.
Identifying an auxiliary view with a viewing-plane line. If there is not enough room, the view can be moved to a different location.

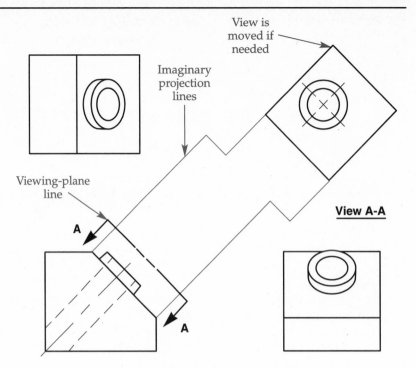

Each end of the viewing-plane line is labeled with a letter. The letters relate the viewing-plane line with the proper auxiliary view. A title such as VIEW A-A is placed under the auxiliary view. When more than one auxiliary view is drawn, labels continue with B-B through Z-Z (if necessary). The letters *I*, *O*, and *Q* are not used because they may be confused with numbers. An auxiliary view drawn away from the multiview retains the same angle as if it is projected directly.

PROFESSIONAL TIP

Changing the rotation angle of the snap grid is especially useful for drawing auxiliary views. After the views have been drawn, access the **SNAP** command. Then, pick the base point for rotation on the line that represents the slanted surface. Enter the snap rotation angle equal to the angle of the slanted surface. If you do not know the angle, use object snap modes and pick points on the slanted surface to define the angle. Rotating the snap grid is discussed completely in Chapter 3.

Using the User Coordinate System for Auxiliary Views

All the features on your drawing originate from the *World Coordinate System (WCS).* This is the X, Y, and Z coordinate values measured from the origin (0,0,0). The WCS is fixed. The *User Coordinate System (UCS),* on the other hand, can be moved to any orientation. The UCS is discussed in detail in *AutoCAD and its Applications, Advanced—AutoCAD 2000.*

In general, UCS allows you to set your own coordinate origin. The UCS 0,0,0 origin has been in the lower-left corner of the screen for the drawings you have done so far. In many cases this is fine, but when drawing an auxiliary view it is best to have the measurements originate from a corner of the view. This, in turn, makes all auxiliary view features and the coordinate display true as measured from the corner of the view. This method makes it easier to locate and later dimension the auxiliary view features.

Figure 6-43 shows an example of aligning the UCS to the auxiliary view. First, draw the principal views, such as the front, top, and right side. Then, move the UCS origin to a location that coincides with a corner of the auxiliary view using this command sequence (refer to Figure 6-43):

```
Command: UCS⤶
Current ucs name: *WORLD*
Enter an option [New/Move/orthoGraphic/Prev/Restore/Save/Del/Apply/?/World]
    <World>: N⤶
Specify origin of new UCS or [ZAxis/3point/OBject/Face/View/X/Y/Z] <0,0,0>: 3⤶
Specify new origin point <0,0,0>: (select Point A as shown in Figure 6-43)
Specify point on positive portion of X-axis <current>: (select Point B)
Specify point on positive-Y portion of the UCS X-Y plane <current>: (select Point C)
Command:
```

The icon is rotated and moved as shown in Figure 6-43B. If you want the UCS displayed in the lower-left corner of the drawing area, select **Named UCS...** from the **Tools** pull-down menu. This displays the **UCS** dialog box. On the **Settings** tab, deactivate the **Display at UCS origin point**.

Before you begin drawing the auxiliary view, use the **Save** option of the **UCS** command to name and save the new UCS:

```
Command: UCS⤶
Current ucs name: *NO NAME*
Enter an option [New/Move/orthoGraphic/Prev/Restore/Save/Del/Apply/?/World]
    <World>: S⤶
Enter name to save current UCS or [?]: AUX⤶
Command:
```

Now, proceed by drawing the auxiliary view. When you have finished, use the default **World** option to reset the UCS back to the WCS origin:

```
Command: UCS⤶
Current ucs name:  *WORLD*
Enter an option [New/Move/orthoGraphic/Prev/Restore/Save/Del/Apply/?/World]
    <World>: ⤶
Command:
```

Figure 6-43.
Relocating the origin and rotating the Z axis of the UCS system. A—Rotating the UCS to align with the auxiliary view angle. B—The UCS icon displayed at the current UCS origin at the corner of the auxiliary view.

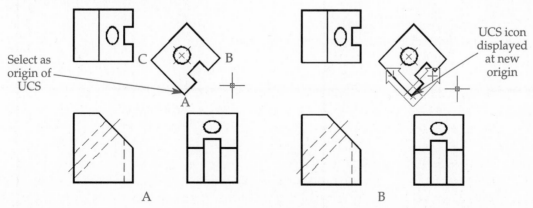

DRAWING CONSTRUCTION LINES

In drafting terminology, *construction lines* are lines used for layout purposes. They are not part of the drawing. In manual drafting, they are either drawn very lightly or removed so they do not reproduce.

AutoCAD has construction lines and rays that can be used for such purposes. For example, you can use construction lines and rays to project features between views for accurate placement, for geometric constructions, or to coordinate geometric locations for object snap selections. The AutoCAD command that lets you draw construction lines is **XLINE**, while rays are drawn with the **RAY** command. Both commands can be used for similar purposes, however, the **XLINE** command has more options and flexibility than the **RAY** command.

Using the XLINE Command

The **XLINE** command creates xline objects. An *xline object* is an infinite length line designed for use as a construction line. Although these lines are infinite, they do not change the drawing extents. This means that they have no effect on zooming operations.

The xlines can be modified by moving, copying, trimming, and other editing operations. Editing commands such as **TRIM** or **FILLET** change the object type. For example, if one end of an xline is trimmed off, it becomes a ray object. A *ray* is considered semi-infinite because it is infinite in one direction only. If the infinite end of a ray is trimmed off, then it becomes a line object.

Construction lines and rays are drawn on the current layer and plot the same as other objects. This may cause conflict with the other lines on that layer. A good way to handle this problem is to set up a special layer just for construction lines.

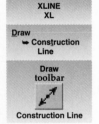

XLINE
XL

Draw
➥ Construction
Line

Draw
toolbar

Construction Line

The **XLINE** command can be accessed by picking the **Construction Line** button in the **Draw** toolbar, by picking **Construction Line** in the **Draw** pull-down menu, or by typing XL or XLINE at the Command: prompt. The **XLINE** command sequence appears as follows:

Command: **XL** *or* **XLINE**↵
Specify a point or [Hor/Ver/Ang/Bisect/Offset] :

The following **XLINE** options are available:

- **From point.** This **XLINE** default allows you to specify two points that the construction line passes through. The first point of an xline is called the *root point.* After you pick the first point, the Through point: prompt allows you to select as many points as you like. Xlines are created between every point and the root point. Use the object snap modes to accurately pick points:

> Command: **XL** *or* **XLINE.**↵
> Specify a point or [Hor/Ver/Ang/Bisect/Offset]: *(pick a point)*
> Specify through point: *(pick a second point)*
> Specify through point: *(pick another second point)*
> Specify through point: *(draw more construction lines or press [Enter])*
> Command:

Figure 6-44 shows how construction lines can be used to help project features between views.

- **Hor (H).** This option draws a horizontal construction line through a single specified point. It serves the same purpose as the default option, but the line is automatically drawn horizontally and you only have to pick one point.
- **Ver (V).** This option draws a vertical construction line through the specified point.

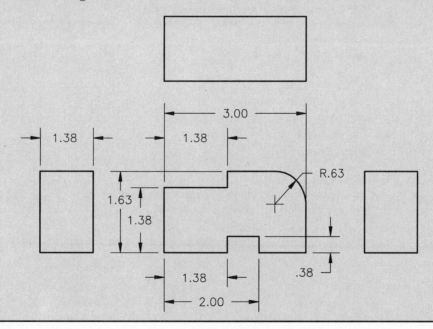

EXERCISE 6-17

❑ Start AutoCAD and use the setup option of your choice. One of your templates may already have proper layers and linetypes.
❑ Set up layers and linetypes as needed. Review Chapter 4 if necessary.
❑ Draw the four views of the object shown below. Do not draw dimensions.
❑ The top and side views are currently incomplete. Use construction lines to help you complete all views by adding the missing lines.
❑ Save the drawing as EX6-17.

Figure 6-44.
Using the **XLINE** command default option. You can also use the **XLINE Hor** option.

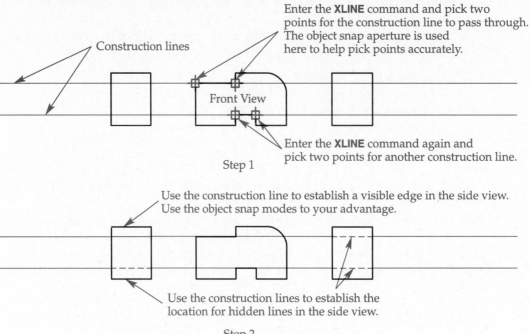

Construction lines

Enter the **XLINE** command and pick two points for the construction line to pass through. The object snap aperture is used here to help pick points accurately.

Front View

Enter the **XLINE** command again and pick two points for another construction line.

Step 1

Use the construction line to establish a visible edge in the side view. Use the object snap modes to your advantage.

Use the construction lines to establish the location for hidden lines in the side view.

Step 2

- **Ang.** This option draws a construction line at a specified angle through a specified point. The default lets you specify an angle and then pick a point for the construction line to be drawn through. This works well if you know the angle, or you can pick two points in the drawing to describe the angle:

> Command: **XL** *or* **XLINE**↵
> Specify a point or [Hor/Ver/Ang/Bisect/Offset]: **A**↵
> Enter angle of xline (0) or [Reference]: *(enter an angle, such as* 45*)*
> Specify through point: *(pick a point)*
> Specify through point: *(draw more construction lines or press* [Enter]*)*
> Command:

A reference angle from the angle of an existing line object can be specified by using the **Reference** option. This can be used when you do not know the angle of the construction line, but you know the angle between an existing object and the construction line:

> Command: **XL** *or* **XLINE**↵
> Specify a point or [Hor/Ver/Ang/Bisect/Offset]: **A**↵
> Enter angle of xline (0) or [Reference]: **R**↵
> Select a line object: *(pick a line)*
> Enter angle of xline <*current*>: **90**↵
> Specify through point: *(pick a point)*
> Specify through point: *(draw more construction lines or press* [Enter]*)*
> Command:

Figure 16-45 shows the **Ang** option used to draw construction lines establishing the location of an auxiliary view.

Both the **RAY** command and the **XLINE** command allow the creation of multiple objects. You must press [Enter] to end the command.

EDITING CONSTRUCTION LINES AND RAYS

The construction lines that you create using the **XLINE** and **RAY** commands can be edited and modified using standard editing commands. These commands are introduced in Chapter 11 and Chapter 12. The construction lines will change into a new object type when infinite ends are trimmed off. A trimmed xline becomes a ray. A ray that has its infinite end trimmed becomes a normal line object. Therefore, in many cases, your construction lines can be modified to become part of the actual drawing. This approach can save a significant amount of time in many drawings.

Chapter Test

Answer the following questions on a separate sheet of paper.

1. Give the command and entries needed to draw a line to the midpoint of an existing line:
   A. Command: _____
   B. Specify first point: _____
   C. Specify next point or [Undo]: _____
   D. of _____
2. Give the command and entries needed to draw a line tangent to an existing circle and perpendicular to an existing line:
   A. Command: _____
   B. Specify first point: _____
   C. to _____
   D. Specify next point or [Undo]: _____
   E. to _____
3. Give the command sequence required to draw a concentric circle inside an existing circle at a distance of .25:
   A. Command: _____
   B. Specify offset distance or [Through] <*current*>: _____
   C. Select object to offset or <exit>: _____
   D. Specify point on side to offset: _____
   E. Select object to offset or <exit>: _____
4. Give the command and entries needed to divide a line into 24 equal parts:
   A. Command: _____
   B. Select the object: _____
   C. Enter the number of segments or [Block]: _____
5. Define object snap.
6. Define quadrant.
7. Define running object snap.
8. How do you set running object snaps?
9. How do you access the **Drafting Settings** dialog box to change object snap settings?
10. Describe the object snap override.
11. How do you change the aperture size?
12. What value would you specify to make the aperture half the default value?
13. How is the running object snap discontinued?
14. List two ways to establish an offset distance using the **OFFSET** command.
15. What is the difference between the **DIVIDE** and **MEASURE** commands?
16. If you use the **DIVIDE** command and nothing appears to happen, what should you do?

17. How do you access the **Point Style** dialog box?
18. How do you change the point size in the **Point Style** dialog box?
19. How do you activate the **Object Snap** shortcut menu?
20. Define AutoSnap.
21. What is an AutoSnap tooltip?
22. Name the following AutoSnap markers:

A. B. C.

D. E. F.

G. H. I.

J. K. L.

23. What does it mean when the tooltip reads Deferred Perpendicular?
24. What is the situation when the tooltip reads Extended Intersection?
25. What conditions must exist for the tooltip to read Tangent?
26. What is a deferred tangency?
27. Which object snaps depend on "acquired points" to function?
28. If you are using running object snaps and you want to make a single point selection without the effects of the running object snaps, what do you do?
29. If you are using running object snaps and you want to make several point specifications without the aid of object snap, but you want to continue the same running object snaps after making the desired point selections, what is the easiest way to temporarily turn the running object snaps off?
30. What do you do if there are multiple AutoSnap selection possibilities within range of the cursor and you want to select a specific one of the possibilities?
31. Define AutoTracking.
32. Which feature should be used in conjunction with AutoTracking?
33. How do you turn AutoSnap off?
34. How do you change the color of the AutoSnap marker?
35. How do you draw a single point and how do you draw multiple points?
36. Provide at least four guidelines for selecting the front view of an orthographic multiview drawing.
37. When can a part be shown with only one view?
38. When is an auxiliary view needed and what does an auxiliary view show?
39. What is the angle of projection from the slanted surface into the auxiliary view?
40. Name the AutoCAD command that allows you to draw construction lines.
41. What is the difference between the construction lines drawn with the command identified in Question 40 and rays drawn with the **RAY** command?
42. Why is it a good idea to put construction lines on their own layer?
43. Name the option that can be used to bisect an angle with a construction line.

Drawing Problems

Load AutoCAD for each of the following problems and use one of your templates or start a new drawing using your own variables.

1. Draw the object below using the object snap modes. Save the drawing as P6-1 (omit dimensions).

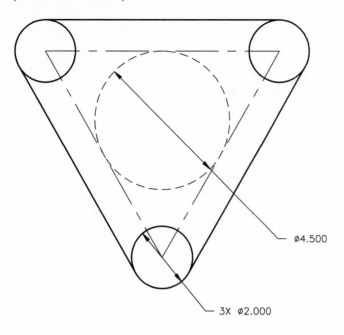

ø4.500

3X ø2.000

2. Draw the object below using the object snap modes indicated. Save the drawing as P6-2.

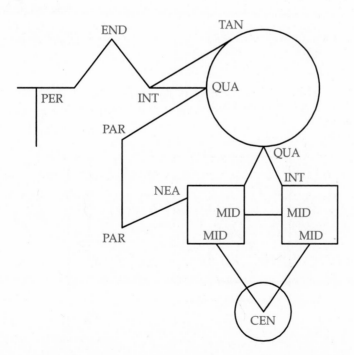

3. Draw the object below using **Endpoint**, **Tangent**, **Perpendicular**, and **Quadrant** object snap modes. Save the drawing as P6-3.

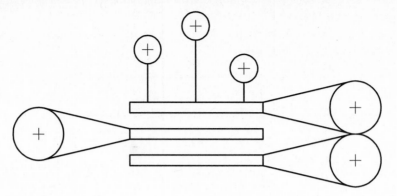

4. Use the **Midpoint**, **Endpoint**, **Tangent**, **Perpendicular**, and **Quadrant** object snap modes to draw these electrical switch schematics. Do not draw text or arrowheads. Save the drawing as P6-4.

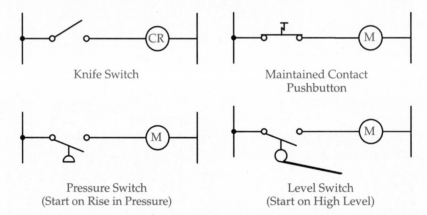

Knife Switch

Maintained Contact
Pushbutton

Pressure Switch
(Start on Rise in Pressure)

Level Switch
(Start on High Level)

5. Draw the front and side views of this offset support. Use construction lines. Do not draw the dimensions. Save your drawing as P6-5.

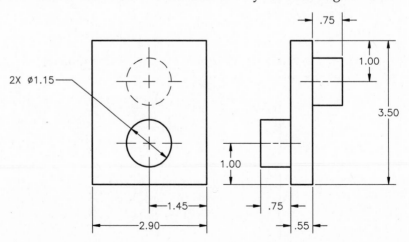

6. Draw the top and front views of this hitch bracket. Use construction lines. Do not draw the dimensions. Save your drawing as P6-6.

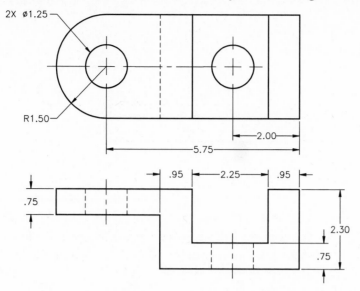

7. Draw this aluminum spacer. Use object snap modes and construction lines. Do not draw dimensions. Save the drawing as P6-7.

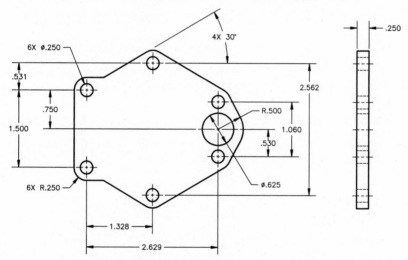

8. Draw the spring using the **OFFSET** command for material thickness. Do not draw dimensions. Save the drawing as P6-8.

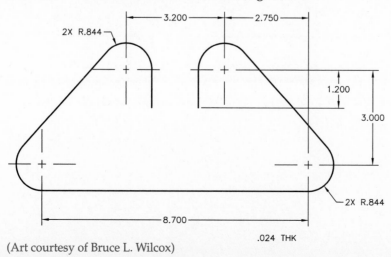

(Art courtesy of Bruce L. Wilcox)

9. Draw the gasket without dimensions. Save the drawing as **P6-9**.

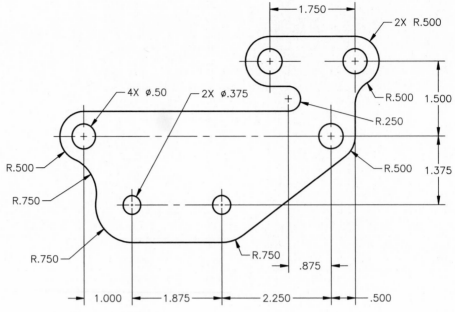

(Art courtesy of Bruce L. Wilcox)

10. Draw the sheet metal chassis without dimensions. Use object snap tracking and polar tracking to your advantage. Save the drawing as **P6-10**.

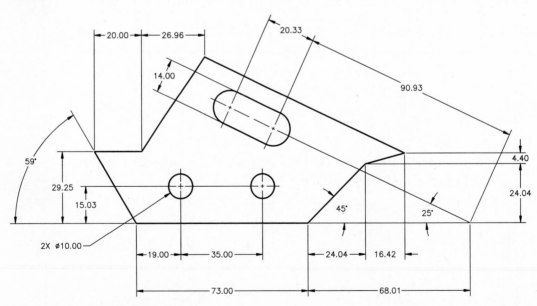

(Art courtesy of Bruce L. Wilcox)

In Problems 11 through 15, draw the views needed to completely describe the objects. Use object snap modes, AutoTrack modes, and construction lines as needed. Do not dimension. Save the drawings as P6-(problem number), such as P6-11, P6-12, etc.

11.

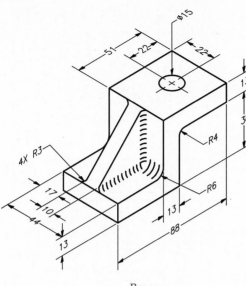

Brace

12.

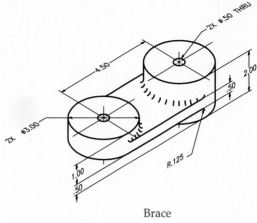

Brace

13.

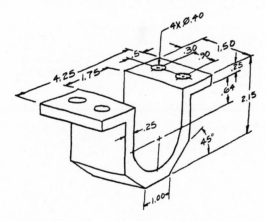

Journal Bracket

14.

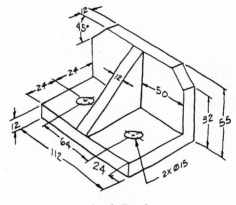

Angle Bracket
(Metric)

15.

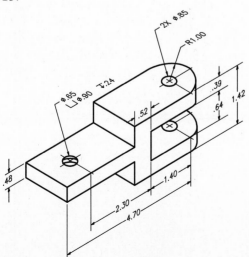

Hitch Bracket

---

16. Draw the views of this pillow block, including the auxiliary view. Use construction lines. Do not draw the dimensions. Save your drawing as P6-16.

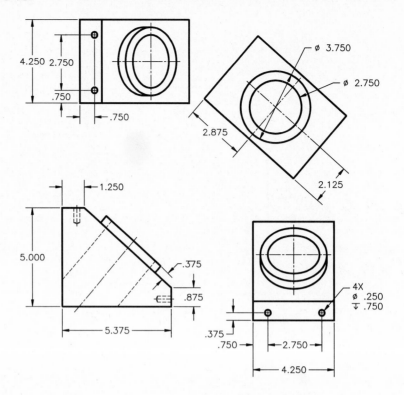

17. Use object snap modes to draw this elementary diagram. Do not draw the text. Save the drawing as P6-17.

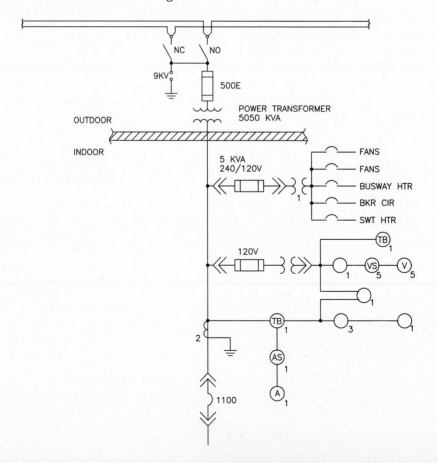

CHAPTER 7

Using the Geometry Calculator and Filters

Learning Objectives

After completing this chapter, you will be able to:
- Use the geometry calculator to make mathematical calculations.
- Make calculations and use information based on existing drawing geometry.
- Add objects to drawings using the geometry calculator and object snaps.
- Make point selections using point filters.
- Use selection set filters to create custom selection sets according to object types and object properties.

AutoCAD commands require precise input. Often, the input is variable and based on objects or locations within a drawing. AutoCAD provides a feature known as the *geometry calculator* to help find and use this type of information.

The geometry calculator and its use is explained in this chapter. Fundamental math calculations and drafting applications are presented. Complex mathematical calculations are also possible. Also covered in this chapter is the **FILTER** command, which allows you to customize a selection set by filtering objects based on object type and object properties.

USING THE GEOMETRY CALCULATOR

AutoCAD's geometry calculator allows you to extract and use existing information in your drawing. The geometry calculator also allows you to perform basic mathematical calculations at the command line or supply an expression as input to a prompt.

The geometry calculator is accessed by typing CAL at the Command: prompt. You are then prompted for an expression. After you type the mathematical expression and press [Enter], AutoCAD automatically simplifies the expression, as shown in the following example:

CAL

```
Command: CAL↵
>> Expression: 2+2↵
4
Command:
```

Basics of the Geometry Calculator

The geometry calculator is more powerful than most hand-held calculators because it can directly access drawing information and can supply input to an AutoCAD prompt. The types of expressions that can be entered include numeric expressions and vector expressions. A *numeric expression* refers to a mathematical process using numbers, such as the expressions solved using normal calculators. A *vector expression* is an expression involving a point coordinate location.

To use the geometry calculator, you must understand the ordering and format of an expression. The geometry calculator evaluates expressions according to the standard mathematical rules of precedence. This means that expressions within parentheses are simplified first, starting with the innermost set and proceeding outward. Mathematical operators are evaluated in the standard order: exponents first, multiplication and division next, followed by addition and subtraction. Operators of equal precedence are evaluated from left to right.

Making Numeric Entries

The same methods of entering numbers used at AutoCAD prompts are also acceptable for calculator expressions. When entering feet and inches, either of the accepted formats can be used. This means that 5'-6" can also be entered as 5'6". The 5'-6" value can also be entered as inches (66). When a number expressed in feet and inches is entered, AutoCAD automatically converts to inches:

> Command: **CAL**↵
> >> Expression: **24'6"**↵
> 294.0

NOTE   An entry at the Expression: prompt must be completed by pressing [Enter]. Pressing the space bar adds a space to your entry; it does not act as a return at this prompt.

Using Basic Math Functions

The basic mathematical functions used in numeric expressions include addition, subtraction, multiplication, division, and exponential notation. Parentheses are used to group symbols and values into sets. The symbols used for the basic mathematical operators are shown in the following table:

Symbol	Function	Example
+	Addition	3+26
-	Subtraction	270-15.3
*	Multiplication	4*156
/	Division	256/16
^	Exponent	22.6^3
( )	Grouped expressions	2*(16+2^3)

The following examples use the **CAL** command to solve each of the types of mathematical functions shown in the previous table:

> Command: **CAL**↵
> >> Expression: **17.375+5.0625**↵
> 22.4375

```
Command: CAL↵
>> Expression: 17.375-5.0625↵
12.3125


Command: CAL↵
>> Expression: 12*18.25↵
219.0


Command: CAL↵
>> Expression: 27'8"/4↵
83.0
Command: CAL↵
>> Expression: 9^2↵
81.0


Command: CAL↵
>> Expression: (17.375+5.0625)+(4.25*3.75)-(18.5/2)↵
29.125
```

PROFESSIONAL TIP

The geometry calculator has limits when working with integer values. (An *integer* is a number with no decimal or fractional part.) Numeric values that are greater than 32,767 or less than –32,768 must be presented as real numbers. When working with values outside this range, type a decimal point and a zero (.0) after the value.

EXERCISE 7-1

❑ Open a drawing and use the **CAL** command to make the following calculations:
  ❑ A. 28.125+37.625
  ❑ B. 16.875-7.375
  ❑ C. 6.25+3.5
  ❑ D. (25.75÷4)+(5.625×3)
  ❑ E. 3.625 squared
  ❑ F. (12.125×3)+(24÷3+5.25)-(3.75÷1.5)

Making Unit Conversions

The calculator has a **CVUNIT** function that lets you convert one type of unit into another. For example, inches can be converted to millimeters, or liters can be converted to gallons. The order of elements in the **CVUNIT** function is:

    CVUNIT(value,from_units,to_units)

The following example converts 4.7 kilometers to the equivalent number of feet:

```
Command: CAL↵
>> Expression: CVUNIT(4.7,kilometers,feet)↵
15419.9
```

If the units of measure you specify are either incompatible or are not defined in the acad.unt file, the message >> Error: CVUNIT failed to convert units is displayed and the prompt is reissued.

The **CVUNIT** function can work with units of distance, angles, volume, mass, time, and frequency. The units available for conversion are specified in the file acad.unt found in the Acad2000\Support directory folder. This file can be edited to include additional units of measure if needed.

Point Entry

While the numeric functions of the calculator provide many useful capabilities, the most powerful use of the geometry calculator is its ability to find and use geometric information. Information such as point coordinates can be entered as input to the geometry calculator.

A point coordinate is entered as two or three numbers enclosed in square brackets and separated by commas. The numbers represent the X, Y, and Z coordinates. For example [4,7,2], [2.1,3.79], or [2,7.4,0]. Any value that is zero can be omitted, as well as commas immediately in front of the right bracket. For example:

[2,2]	is the same as	[2,2,0]
[,,6]	is the same as	[0,0,6]
[5]	is the same as	[5,0,0]
[ ]	is the same as	[0,0,0]

Direction can be entered using any accepted AutoCAD format, including polar and relative coordinates as follows:

Coordinate system	Entry format
Polar	[dist<angle]
Relative	[@ x, y, z]

These options provide the ability to determine locations, distances, and directions within a drawing. For example, to determine a point coordinate value for a location that is 6 units from 2,2,0 at an angle within the XY plane of 45°, the following sequence is used:

```
Command: CAL↵
>> Expression: [2,2,0]+[6<45]↵
(6.24264 6.24264 0.0)
```

In an application of this type, the point answer is returned in parentheses, with spaces to separate the numbers instead of commas.

Calculations can also be performed within the point coordinate specification, as shown in the next sequence:

```
>> Expression: [2+3,2+3,0]+[1,2,0]↵
(6.0 7.0 0.0)
```

A point location can be specified using the "@" symbol. Entering this symbol supplies the current value of the **LASTPOINT** system variable:

```
Command: CAL↵
>> Expression: @↵
```
(*point coordinates*)

<table>
<tr><td>

NOTE

</td><td>

The reference to (*point coordinates*) in the previous command sequence represents the point coordinate values returned by AutoCAD. The actual coordinate values will vary based on user input.

</td></tr>
</table>

Besides entering coordinates at the prompt, you can also specify point coordinates by picking with the cursor. The **CUR** function is used to specify a point picked with the cursor, as shown in the following example:

> Command: **CAL**↵
> \>> Expression: **CUR**↵
> \>> Enter a point: (*pick a point*)
> (*point coordinates*)

This method can also be used as part of a calculation, as shown in the following sequence:

> \>> Expression: **CUR+[1,2]**↵
> \>> Enter a point: (*pick a point*)
> (*point coordinates*)

EXERCISE 7-3

❑ Open a drawing and use the **CAL** command to find the following point coordinates using the shortest entry format:
  ❑ [2,2,0]+[6<30]
  ❑ [4,3,0]+[2,2,0]
❑ Use your cursor to select a point within the **CAL** command.
❑ Use your cursor to pick a point and add 3,2,0.

Using the CAL Command Transparently

The **CAL** command can also be used transparently (within another command). To use the geometry calculator transparently, enter the command as 'CAL (an apostrophe followed by CAL). When the **CAL** command is used transparently, the result is supplied as input to the current prompt. This value is not displayed, however.

The following example uses direct distance entry combined with the geometry calculator to provide the correct length of a line. The line being drawn is 8.0 inches times 1.006:

> Command: **L** *or* **LINE**↵
> Specify first point: (*pick first point*)
> Specify next point or [Undo]: **'CAL**↵ (*drag cursor in appropriate direction*)
> \>> Expression: **8*1.006**↵
> 8.048
> Specify next point or [Undo]: ↵

The calculator evaluates the expression and automatically supplies the result of 8.048 at the Specify next point or [Undo]: prompt. When AutoCAD receives a single numeric value at a point prompt, it is automatically understood as a direct distance entry value. A calculation of this type might be a good way to include a shrinkage allowance for a casting or forging pattern.

❑ Open an existing drawing or use one of your templates.
❑ Use the **CAL** command transparently to draw a line using direct distance entry from a point located at 2,4 to 6×1.0625.
❑ Save the drawing as EX7-4.

Using the Object Snap Modes

Object snap points can also be specified as point coordinates to the geometry calculator. The object snaps provide the accuracy that is often needed when finding points on an object. The following example shows the **Endpoint** object snap mode being used to identify a specific point on an object:

> Command: **CAL**↵
> \>> Expression: **END**↵
> \>> Select entity for END snap: *(pick an object)*
> *(point coordinates)*

This example uses the **Endpoint** object snap to find the end of a line and add the point coordinate of 2 at 45°:

> Command: **CAL**↵
> \>> Expression: **END+[2<45]**↵
> \>> Select entity for END snap: *(pick an object)*
> *(point coordinates)*

You can use the geometry calculator to provide information based on selected points. For example, the following sequence can be used to find the point midway between two points selected with the cursor:

> Command: **CAL**↵
> \>> Expression: **(CUR+CUR)/2**↵
> \>> Enter a point: *(pick a point)*
> \>> Enter a point: *(pick a point)*
> *(point coordinates)*

This same technique can be used with any desired object snap mode. The following example is used to divide the distance between the center of a circle and the endpoint of a line by two:

> Command: **CAL**↵
> \>> Expression: **(CEN+END)/2**↵
> \>> Select entity for CEN snap: *(pick the circle)*
> \>> Select entity for END snap: *(pick the line)*
> *(point coordinates)*

The next sequence starts a line halfway between the center of an existing circle and the endpoint of an existing line, as shown in Figure 7-1:

> Command: **L** *or* **LINE**↵
> Specify first point: **'CAL**↵
> \>> Expression: **(CEN+END)/2**↵
> \>> Select entity for CEN snap: *(pick the circle)*
> \>> Select entity for END snap: *(pick the line)*
> Specify next point or [Undo]:

Figure 7-1.
Finding a point
halfway between
the center of a circle
and the endpoint of
a line.

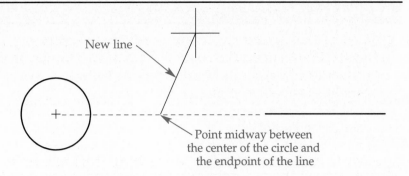

New line

Point midway between
the center of the circle and
the endpoint of the line

The following sequence is used to create a circle with its center located two units along the X axis from the midpoint of an existing line, as shown in Figure 7-2:

Command: **C** *or* **CIRCLE**↵
Specify center point for circle or [3P/2P/Ttr (tan tan radius)]:**'CAL**↵
>> Expression: **MID+[2,0]**↵
>> Select entity for MID snap: *(pick the line object)*
(point coordinates)
Specify radius of circle or [Diameter] <*current*>:

Figure 7-2.
Locating the center
of a circle two units
to the right of the
midpoint of a line.

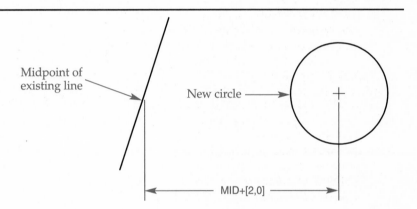

Midpoint of
existing line

New circle

MID+[2,0]

The next sequence determines the centroid (center of mass) of a triangle, defined by picking three endpoints as shown in Figure 7-3:

Command: **CAL**↵
>> Expression: **(END+END+END)/3**↵
>> Select entity for END snap: *(pick first corner of the triangle)*
>> Select entity for END snap: *(pick second corner of the triangle)*
>> Select entity for END snap: *(pick third corner of the triangle)*
(point coordinates)

Figure 7-3.
Locating the center
of mass of a
triangle.

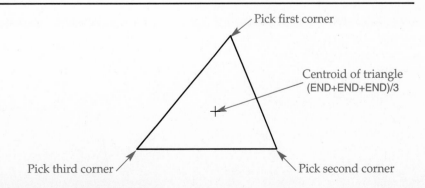

Pick first corner

Centroid of triangle
(END+END+END)/3

Pick third corner

Pick second corner

❑ Open an existing drawing or use one of your templates.
❑ Use the **CAL** command and object snaps as needed to make the following drawings:
  ❑ Use (CEN+END)/2 to draw a line starting halfway between the center of a circle and the endpoint of a line, similar to Figure 7-1.
  ❑ Use MID+[2,0] to draw a circle 2 units on the X axis from the midpoint of a line, similar to Figure 7-2.
  ❑ Draw a triangle and find the center of mass, similar to Figure 7-3.
❑ Save the drawing as EX7-5.

Calculating Distances

There are three basic calculator functions used to calculate distances in a drawing. These are the **DIST**, **DPL**, and **DPP** functions.

The **DIST** function is entered as DIST(P1,P2) where P1 = Point 1 and P2 = Point 2. The **DIST** function performs a simple distance calculation between the two specified points. Similar to all calculator functions, the points can be entered manually or picked. The **DIST** function is used in the following sequence to find a distance between two endpoints of a line:

    Command: **CAL**↵
    >> Expression: **DIST(END,END)**↵
    >> Select entity for END snap: (pick an object)
    >> Select entity for END snap: (pick an object)
    (distance)

The **DPL** function is written as DPL(P,P1,P2) and calculates the perpendicular distance between Point P and a line passing through the Points P1 and P2. See Figure 7-4. The following is an example using **DPL** with the endpoint object snap. The order of selection is P, P1, and then P2:

    Command: **CAL**↵
    >> Expression: **DPL(END,END,END)**↵
    >> Select entity for END snap: (pick an object)
    >> Select entity for END snap: (pick an object)
    >> Select entity for END snap: (pick an object)
    (distance)

Figure 7-4.
Finding the shortest distance between a point and a line.

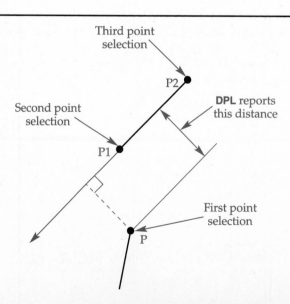

274

The **DPP** function is written as DPP(P,P1,P2,P3). **DPP** functions much like the **DPL** function except it finds the shortest distance between Point P and a plane defined by P1, P2, and P3. See Figure 7-5. The points for **DPP** can be entered manually or picked. The following example shows a calculation of the distance between the point 2,2,6 and 3 points arbitrarily selected on the XY plane:

        Command: **CAL**⏎
        >> Expression: **DPP([2,2,6],CUR,CUR,CUR)**⏎
        >> Enter a point: *(pick a point)*
        >> Enter a point: *(pick a point)*
        >> Enter a point: *(pick a point)*
        6.0

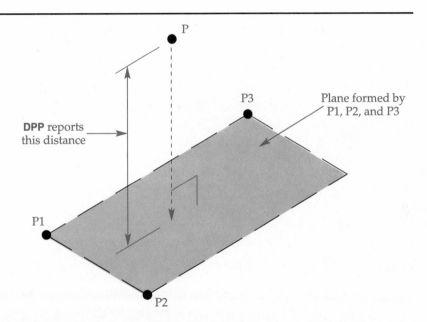

Figure 7-5.
Finding the shortest distance between a point and a plane.

❑ Open an existing drawing or use one of your templates.
❑ Create the following drawings and make the required distance calculations:
    ❑ Draw a line. Find the distance between the ends.
    ❑ Find one-half the length of the line.
    ❑ Draw another line that is not parallel to the first line. Find the perpendicular distance between the endpoint of the second line and the first line.
❑ Save the drawing as EX7-6.

Finding Intersection Points

The **ILL** function locates an intersection point between two nonparallel lines. This function is written as ILL(P1,P2,P3,P4). The intersection of the line containing P1 and P2 with the line containing P3 and P4 is identified. An actual line between P1 and P2 (or P3 and P4) is not necessary. This function finds a hypothetical intersection, acting as though the lines are infinite in length. The following sequence shows the use of the **ILL** function to find the intersection of the lines shown in Figure 7-6:

        Command: **CAL**⏎
        >> Expression: **ILL([2,5,0],[4,6,0],[4,5,0],[2,6,0])**⏎
        (3.0 5.5 0.0)

Figure 7-6.
Finding the point of
intersection
between two
nonparallel lines.

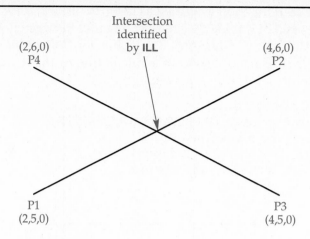

Finding a Point on a Line

The **PLD** function, written as PLD(P1,P2,Dist), finds a point along a line passing through P1 and P2 that is the specified distance from the start point. It is not necessary for an actual line to exist. The following sequence finds a point along a line passing through 0,0 and 3,1 that is 10 units from the start point, as shown in Figure 7-7:

> Command: **CAL.**↵
> \>> Expression: **PLD([ ],[3,1],10).**↵
> (9.48683 3.16228 0.0)

The **PLT** function provides another means of finding a point along a line. Written as PLT(P1,P2,T), this function finds a point along a line passing through P1 and P2. The point is located from the start point based on the T parameter. The *T parameter* is simply a scale factor relative to the distance between P1 and P2. If T=0, the point is P1, if T=1, the point is P2. A T value of .5 identifies the midpoint between P1 and P2, and a T value of 2.0 finds a point twice the length of the line. Figure 7-8 shows several examples.

The following sequence locates a point that is three-quarters of the way along the length of the specified line:

> Command: **CAL.**↵
> \>> Expression: **PLT([ ],[2,2],.75).**↵
> (1.5 1.5 0.0)

Figure 7-7.
Finding a point along a line that is a specified distance from the start point.

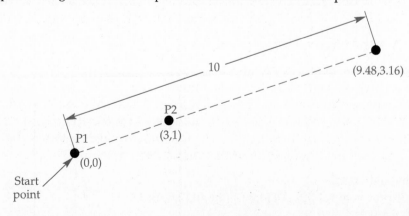

Figure 7-8.
Finding a point
along a line based
on the scale of the
line length.

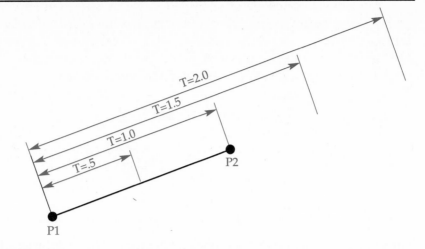

Finding an Angle

The **ANG** function finds the angle between two lines. As with other calculator functions, the lines need not physically exist in the drawing. This function can be entered several different ways, depending on the nature of the angle you are trying to calculate.

To find the angle of a vector from the X axis in the XY plane, enter ANG(*coordinates*). The coordinate values are entered within parentheses. The coordinates can be manually entered or a point can be selected using object snap options. The following shows this method being used to enter the coordinates of a point along the line shown in Figure 7-9A:

    Command: **CAL**↵
    >> Expression: **ANG([1,1,0])**↵
    45.0

If the vector is not known, two points along a line can be used to determine the angle of the line in the XY plane from the X axis. The formula is ANG(P1, P2) as represented in Figure 7-9B and in the following sequence:

    Command: **CAL**↵
    >> Expression: **ANG([2,2],[4,4])**↵
    45.0

You can also calculate an included angle by specifying a vertex and a point on each side. A *vertex* is the intersection of two lines. An *included angle* is the angle formed between the vertex and the sides of the angle. The formula is entered as ANG(VERTEX,P1,P2), Figure 7-9C. The following example determines the angle between two lines, selecting with the **Endpoint** object snap mode:

> Command: **CAL**↵
> \>> Expression: **ANG(END,END,END).**↵
> \>> Select entity for END snap: *(pick vertex)*
> \>> Select entity for END snap: *(pick end of first line)*
> \>> Select entity for END snap: *(pick end of second line)*
> *(angle)*

Figure 7-9.
Finding angles with the **ANG** function. A—Entering a single coordinate returns the angle from horizontal of a line containing 0,0 and the point. B—Entering two coordinates returns the angle from horizontal of a line containing the points. C—Entering three coordinates finds the angle between the formed lines.

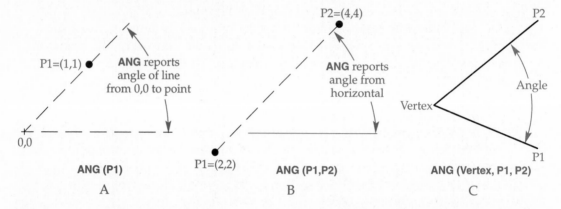

EXERCISE 7-8

❑ Open an existing drawing or use one of your templates.
❑ Create the following drawings and make the required distance calculations:
  ❑ Draw a line using 0,0 as the start point. Do not draw a horizontal line. Use the **ANG** function to determine the angle of the line relative to horizontal.
  ❑ Draw a line at an angle to the XY plane. Use the **ANG** function to determine the angle.
  ❑ Draw an angle with a vertex and two sides similar to Figure 7-9C. Use the **ANG** function to find the included angle.
❑ Save the drawing as EX7-8.

Finding a Radius

You can use the **RAD** function to find the radius of an arc, circle, or 2D polyline arc. The command sequence works like this:

> Command: **CAL**↵
> \>> Expression: **RAD**↵
> \>> Select circle, arc or polyline segment for RAD function: *(select a circle)*
> *(radius)*

You can easily draw objects to match the radius of an existing object using the **RAD** function. The following example uses **RAD** to supply the radius value for a circle to match that of the existing circle, as shown in Figure 7-10:

> Command: **C** *or* **CIRCLE**↵
> Specify center point for circle or [3P/2P/Ttr (tan tan radius)]: *(pick the center point)*
> Specify radius of circle or [Diameter] <*current*>: **'CAL**↵
> \>> Expression: **RAD**↵
> \>> Select circle, arc or polyline segment for RAD function: *(select a circle)*
> *(radius of circle)*

Figure 7-10.
Using the **RAD** function to create a circle equal in diameter to an existing circle.

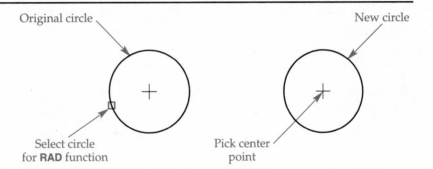

Original circle

New circle

Select circle for **RAD** function

Pick center point

Calculator functions can be combined. For example, suppose you want to draw a new circle that is 25% the size of the original circle, placed in a new position that also needs to be calculated. Look at Figure 7-11 as you follow this command sequence:

> Command: **C** *or* **CIRCLE**↵
> Specify center point for circle or [3P/2P/Ttr (tan tan radius)]: **'CAL**↵
> \>> Expression: **(MID+MID)/2**↵
> \>> Select entity for MID snap: *(pick Line 1)*
> \>> Select entity for MID snap: *(pick Line 2)*
> *(point coordinates)*

Figure 7-11.
Combining calculator functions to revise a circle and place it in a new position.

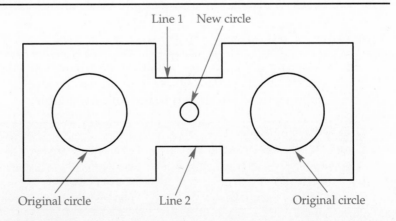

Line 1   New circle

Original circle   Line 2   Original circle

Now, instruct AutoCAD to calculate a new radius that is 25% of the size of the original circle like this:

> Specify radius of circle or [Diameter] <*current*>:'**CAL**↵
> >> Expression: **.25*RAD**↵
> >> Select circle, arc, or polyline segment for RAD function: (*pick one of the original circles*)

The new circle is automatically drawn at the specified location, and at 25% of the size of the original circle.

Another application of the **CAL** command is shown in Figure 7-12, where a new circle is placed 3″ along a centerline from an existing circle. The new circle is 1.5 times larger than the original circle. The following command sequence can be used:

> Command: **C** *or* **CIRCLE**↵
> Specify center point for circle or [3P/2P/Ttr (tan tan radius)]: '**CAL**↵
> >> Expression: **PLD(CEN,END,3.00)**↵
> >> Select entity for CEN snap: (*pick the original circle*)
> >> Select entity for END snap: (*pick near the right end of the centerline*)
> (*point coordinates*)
> Specify radius of circle or [Diameter] <*current*>: '**CAL**↵
> >> Expression: **1.5*RAD**↵
> >> Select circle, arc, or polyline segment for RAD function: (*pick the original circle*)

Figure 7-12.
Copying a circle along a centerline and resizing it.

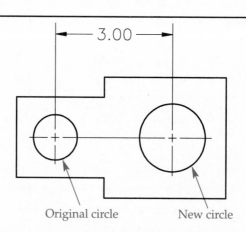

Original circle   New circle

Geometry Calculator Shortcut Functions

To make using the geometry calculator as efficient as possible, some of the most commonly used calculator tasks have shortcuts to reduce your typing requirements. The basic abbreviations are shown in the following table:

Function	Replaces	Description
DEE	DIST(END,END)	Distance between two selected endpoints
ILLE	ILL(END,END,END,END)	Intersection of two lines defined by four selected endpoints
MEE	(END+END)/2	Point midway between two selected endpoints

These functions work exactly the same way as the longer format that you have already learned. Look at each of the shortcut options as you review earlier discussions covering the actual functions used by the shortcuts.

Use the following command sequence to determine the length of a line:

Command: **CAL**↵
>> Expression: **DEE**↵
>> Select one endpoint for DEE: *(pick one end of the line)*
>> Select another endpoint for DEE: *(pick the other end)*
(distance)

The following example shows how to use the **MEE** function to draw a circle at the center of a rectangle, as shown in Figure 7-13:

Command: **C** *or* **CIRCLE**↵
Specify center point for circle or [3P/2P/Ttr (tan tan radius)]:**'CAL**↵
>> Expression: **MEE**↵
>> Select one endpoint for MEE: *(pick one corner of the rectangle)*
>> Select another endpoint for MEE: *(pick the opposite corner of the rectangle)*
(coordinates)
Specify radius of circle or [Diameter] <current>: *(type a radius and press* [Enter] *or pick a radius)*

Figure 7-13.
Centering a circle within a rectangle using the **CAL** command.

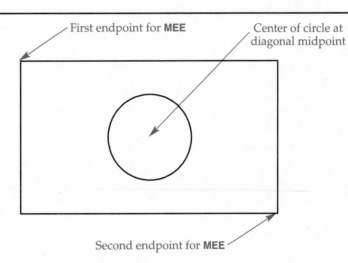

First endpoint for **MEE**

Center of circle at diagonal midpoint

Second endpoint for **MEE**

EXERCISE 7-10

❑ Open an existing drawing or use one of your templates.
❑ Draw a line and then use **DEE** to determine the length.
❑ Draw two intersecting lines and then use the **ILL** function to find the intersection point.
❑ Use the **MEE** function to help you create a drawing similar to Figure 7-13.
❑ Save the drawing as EX7-10.

Using Advanced Math Functions

A number of advanced mathematical functions are also supported by the geometry calculator. These include logarithmic and exponential functions, as well as some data modification and conversion functions. The following table shows each of the advanced math operators supported by the geometry calculator:

Function	Description
ln(x)	Returns the natural log of a number.
log(x)	Returns the base-10 log of a number.
exp(x)	Returns the natural exponent (or antilog) of a number.
exp10(x)	Returns the base-10 exponent of a number.
sqr(x)	Returns a number squared.
sqrt(x)	Returns the square root of a number.
abs(x)	Returns the absolute value (magnitude) of a number.
round(x)	Rounds a number to the nearest integer value.
trunc(x)	Removes the decimal value of a number, returning the integer value.

An example of calculating the square root of 25 is as follows:

Command: **CAL**↵
>> Expression: **SQRT(25)**↵
5.0

Using Trigonometric Functions

When creating precision drawings, you often need to work with distances and angles. The geometry calculator supports several trigonometric functions for the calculations of distances and angles in a drawing. Figure 7-14 shows the basic trigonometric operators and formulas.

The geometry calculator assumes that numeric input indicates degrees unless otherwise specified. This is regardless of the current angular units setting in AutoCAD. To enter angular data as degrees (d), minutes (') and seconds ("), use the format **30d45'15"**. If the minute or second value is zero, it can be omitted from the entry. For example, **42d0'30"** can be written as **42d30"**. However, the degree value must be given, even if it is zero.

Figure 7-14.
The elements of a right triangle and related trigonometric functions.

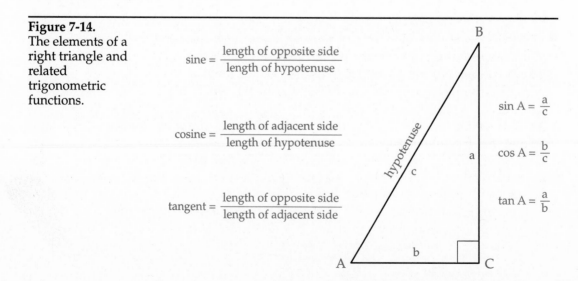

$$\text{sine} = \frac{\text{length of opposite side}}{\text{length of hypotenuse}}$$

$$\text{cosine} = \frac{\text{length of adjacent side}}{\text{length of hypotenuse}}$$

$$\text{tangent} = \frac{\text{length of opposite side}}{\text{length of adjacent side}}$$

$$\sin A = \frac{a}{c}$$

$$\cos A = \frac{b}{c}$$

$$\tan A = \frac{a}{b}$$

To enter a value in radians, use an *r* as a suffix for the number, such as 1.2r. A suffix of *g* indicates that the value is in grads, such as **50.00g**. The geometry calculator output is always decimal degrees, regardless of the angular units style used for the input.

The available trigonometric operators are shown in the following table:

Function	Description
SIN(*angle*)	Returns the sine of the angle.
COS(*angle*)	Returns the cosine of the angle.
TANG(*angle*)	Returns the tangent of the angle.
ASIN(*angle*)	Returns the arcsine of the angle.
ACOS(*angle*)	Returns the arccosine of the angle.
ATAN(*angle*)	Returns the arctangent of the angle.
D2R(*angle*)	Converts from degrees to radians.
R2D(*angle*)	Converts from radians to degrees. (Note: Do not use *r* suffix for this function.)
PI	The constant pi (π, 3.14159…)

To provide an example of using trigonometric functions in the geometry calculator, the following sequence solves for angle *A* in Figure 7-14. The length of side *a* is 4.182 and side *c* is 5.136. Since the length of side *a* divided by the length of side *c* is equal to the sine of angle *A*, the arcsine of *a*/*c* is equal to angle *A*:

```
Command: CAL↵
>> Expression: asin(4.182/5.136).↵
54.5135
```

The returned value of 54.5135 indicates that angle *A* is 54.5135°. Using the information in Figure 7-14 and the geometry calculator, you can quickly solve for missing information needed to complete a drawing.

The constant *pi* (π) is presented in the trigonometry functions table. This constant is also used in circular formulas, such as πR^2 (circular area) or $2\pi R$ (circumference).

EXERCISE 7-11

❑ Open an existing drawing or use one of your templates.
❑ Solve the following math problems with the geometry calculator:
   ❑ Square root of 79.
   ❑ 23 squared.
   ❑ Sine of 30 degrees.
   ❑ Cosine of 30 degrees.
   ❑ Calculate the hypotenuse of a right triangle with side *a* = 6 and side *b* = 2.5.
   ❑ Calculate angle *A* of a right triangle with side *a* = 6 and side *b* = 2.5.
❑ Save the drawing as EX7-11.

Setting and Using Variables with the Geometry Calculator

In AutoCAD, many values are given a special name and stored for access whenever needed. These are called *system variables*, and their values depend on the current drawing or environment. The geometry calculator also has the ability to save values by assigning them to a variable.

A *variable* is a text item that represents a value stored for later use. Calculator variables can store only numeric, point, or vector data. The following example sets a variable named *X* to a value of 1.25:

```
Command: CAL↵
>> Expression: X=1.25↵
1.25
```

The variable can be recalled at a prompt by using the transparent **CAL** command:

> Command: **C** *or* **CIRCLE**↵
> Specify center point for circle or [3P/2P/Ttr (tan tan radius)]: *(pick a center point)*
> Specify radius of circle or [Diameter] <*current*>:'**CAL**↵
> >> Expression: **X**
> 1.25

This extracts the value of the variable *X* (1.25) and uses this as the radius of the circle. The following example sets a variable named *P1* to a user-selected endpoint, then uses *P1* in the operation that follows:

> Command: **CAL**↵
> >> Expression: **P1=END**↵
> >> Select entity for END snap: *(pick an object)*
> *(point coordinate)*
> Command: **L** *or* **LINE**↵
> Specify first point: '**CAL**↵
> >> Expression: **P1**↵
> *(coordinates of P1)*
> Specify next point or [Undo]: ↵

PROFESSIONAL TIP

The variables used by the geometry calculator are actually AutoLISP variables. *AutoLISP* is an easy-to-learn programming language for AutoCAD. An introduction to AutoLISP is given in *AutoCAD and its Applications— Advanced*. For more detailed information on AutoLISP, see *AutoLISP Programming*, also available from Goodheart-Willcox Publisher.

Using AutoCAD System Variables in the Geometry Calculator

The geometry calculator has a specialized function named **GETVAR** that allows you to use values stored in AutoCAD system variables. To retrieve a system variable, type **GETVAR(***variable name***)** at the Expression: prompt. The following example shows the drawing area being increased by multiplying the upper-right limits by 4:

> Command: **LIMITS**↵
> Reset Model space limits:
> Specify lower left corner or [ON/OFF] <0.0000,0.0000>: ↵
> Specify upper right corner <12.0000,9.0000>: '**CAL**↵
> >> Expression: **4*GETVAR(LIMMAX)**↵
> (48.0 36.0 0.0)

If you use the **LIMITS** command, you will see the upper-right value has increased to 48,36.

A complete listing of system variables is available by typing **SETVAR** at the Command: prompt, followed by typing ?. This gives you the Enter variable(s) to list <*>: prompt. The default lists all of the variables:

> Command: **SETVAR**↵
> Enter variable name or [?]: **?**↵
> Enter variable(s) to list <*>: ↵

This opens the **AutoCAD Text Window**, where all the system variables and their settings are listed. Continue pressing [Enter] to see the complete list. Press the [F2] key to return to the graphics window.

INTRODUCTION TO FILTERS

Filters allow you to select any aspect of an object on the screen while "filtering out" other objects, items, or features. A variety of applications for filters are covered in the rest of this chapter and throughout this text where specific applications are discussed. Filters used for layer control were introduced in Chapter 4.

Drawing with X and Y Filters

This discussion involves using the **LINE** command with X and Y filters, which control X and Y coordinates. There is also a Z filter for the Z coordinate, which is used in 3D applications. Enter 0 if prompted for a Z value when working in 2D.

.X

.Y

Suppose you want to construct an isosceles triangle with a height of 2" on a baseline that already exists. Refer to Figure 7-15. First, use this command sequence to establish the base of the triangle:

> Command: **L** *or* **LINE**↵
> Specify first point: **2,2**↵
> Specify next point or [Undo]: **@3<90**↵

Now, place the vertex 2" from the midpoint of the baseline using this sequence:

> Specify next point or [Undo]: **.Y**↵
> of **MID**↵
> of *(pick the baseline)*
> of (need XZ): **@2,0**↵

Finally, complete the triangle with the **Close** option:

> Specify next point or [Undo]: **C**↵
> Command:

Figure 7-15.
Constructing an isosceles triangle using the Y filter.

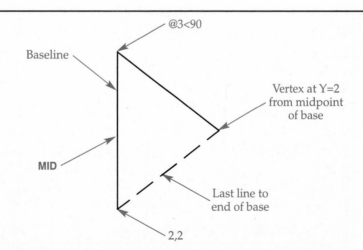

EXERCISE 7-12

❑ Start AutoCAD and use the setup option of your choice.
❑ Use the X and Y filters as previously discussed to assist you in making a drawing similar to Figure 7-15.
❑ Save the drawing as EX7-12.

Earlier in this chapter you learned to construct a circle at the center of a rectangle using the geometry calculator expression (END+END)/2 (or **MEE** shortcut function). The same operation can be performed using X and Y filters. As an example, suppose you want to place the center of a circle at the center of a rectangle, as shown in Figure 7-16. The command sequence is as follows:

Command: **C** *or* **CIRCLE**↵
Specify center point for circle or [3P/2P/Ttr (tan tan radius)]: **.X**↵
of **MID**↵
of *(pick a horizontal line)*
of (need YZ): **MID**↵
of *(pick a vertical line)*
Specify radius of circle or [Diameter] <*current*>: *(specify the radius)*
Command:

In this example, the X value is filtered before the YZ value. However, the same operation can be performed by filtering the Y value first, and then the XZ value.

Figure 7-16.
Centering a circle inside a rectangle using X and Y filters.

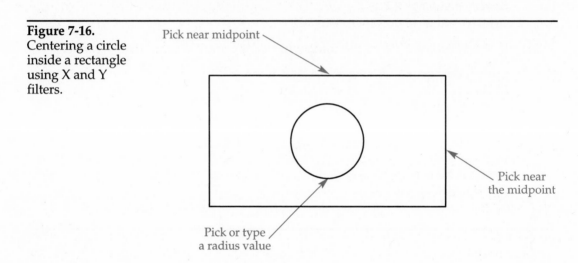

Pick near midpoint

Pick near the midpoint

Pick or type a radius value

Using X and Y Filters to Project Views

If you draw the object shown in Figure 7-17 on a drafting board, you would probably draw the front view first. Then, using drafting instruments, you might project construction lines and points from the front view to complete the right side view.

Filters can be used to perform similar projection operations. The front view of a rectangular object can be drawn very efficiently using the **RECTANG** command. The circle can then be constructed using X and Y filters, as previously described. The command sequence to draw the side view is as follows:

Command: **REC** *or* **RECTANG**↵
Specify first corner point or [Chamfer/Elevation/Fillet/Thickness/Width]: **.Y**↵
of **END**↵
of *(pick near the endpoint of the bottom horizontal line)*
of (need XZ): *(pick a point to set distance between the views)*
Specify other corner point: **@2.5,5**↵
Command:

The rectangle that represents the side view is now complete. Since the side view's lower-left corner is located by filtering the Y value of the front view's lower-right corner, it is aligned orthographically with that view. The @2.5,5 entry locates the upper-right corner of the side view rectangle relative to the filtered point.

AutoCAD and its Applications—Basics

Figure 7-17.
A simple orthographic drawing.

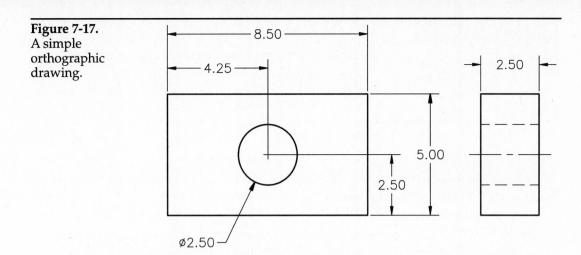

It is also a simple matter to draw the hidden lines that represent the circle seen in the side view. This operation is performed using the object snap modes **Quadrant**, **Nearest**, and **Perpendicular**. First, change the current linetype to Hidden. Then, use the following command sequence. Refer to Figure 7-18.

```
Command: L or LINE↵
Specify first point: .Y↵
of QUA↵
of (pick near the 270° quadrant on the circle)
of (need XZ): NEA↵
of (pick near one of the vertical lines of the side view)
Specify next point or [Undo]: PER↵
of (pick on the opposite vertical line in the side view)
Specify next point or [Undo]: ↵
Command:
```

Now that one of the hidden lines is drawn, you can repeat the procedure to draw the second hidden line. However, an easier way is to use the **OFFSET** command to offset the first hidden line at the required distance.

Figure 7-18.
"Projecting" lines using X and Y filters.

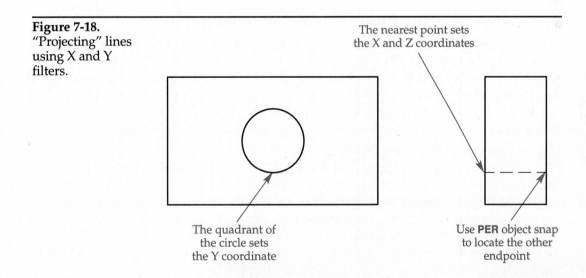

The nearest point sets the X and Z coordinates

The quadrant of the circle sets the Y coordinate

Use **PER** object snap to locate the other endpoint

EXERCISE 7-13

❑ Start AutoCAD and use the setup option of your choice.
❑ Turn off **Grid** and **Snap**.
❑ Draw the front view of the object shown in Figure 7-17 and locate the circle's center using the X and Y filter technique discussed in this chapter.
❑ Construct the right side of the object using the appropriate running object snap modes and X and Y filters.
❑ Save the drawing as EX7-13.

AutoCAD
User's **9**
Guide

CREATING SELECTION SETS

When creating complex drawings, you often need to perform the same editing operation to many objects. For example, assume you have designed a complex metal part with over 40 holes for 1/8" bolts. A design change occurs, and you are notified that 3/16" bolts will be used instead of 1/8" bolts. Therefore, the hole size will also change. You could select and modify each circle individually, but it would be more efficient to create a selection set of all the circles and then modify them simultaneously.

AutoCAD provides two methods of creating selection sets: the **QSELECT** command and the **FILTER** command. The **QSELECT** command is used to create simple selection sets by specifying object types and property values for selection. The **FILTER** command provides additional selection criteria and allows you to save selection sets.

Using Quick Select to Create Selection Sets

QSELECT

Tools
➥ Quick Select...

Properties
window

Quick Select

One way to filter for different objects in a drawing is by using the **QSELECT** command. With **QSELECT**, you can quickly create a selection set based on the filtering criteria you specify. To access **QSELECT**, select **Quick Select...** from the **Tools** pull-down menu, type QSELECT at the Command: prompt, or right-click in the drawing area and choose **Quick Select...** from the shortcut menu. This displays the **Quick Select** dialog box. See Figure 7-19. You can also access the **Quick Select** dialog box by picking the **Quick Select** button in the **Properties** window.

A selection set can be defined in several ways using the **Quick Select** dialog box. You can pick the **Select objects** button and select the objects on screen. You can select a specific object type (such as text, line, or circle) to be selected throughout the drawing. You can also specify a particular property value (such as a color or layer) that objects must possess in order to be selected.

Once the selection criteria is defined, you can use the radio buttons in the **How to apply:** area to include or exclude the defined objects.

Figure 7-19
Selection sets can be defined in the **Quick Select** dialog box.

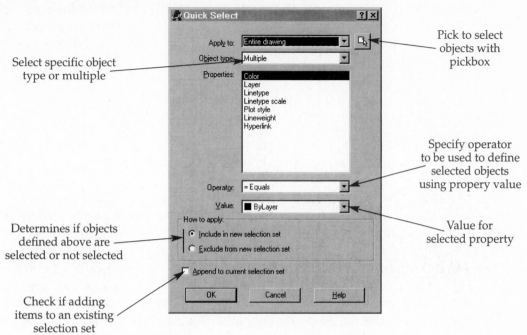

Select specific object type or multiple

Pick to select objects with pickbox

Specify operator to be used to define selected objects using propery value

Value for selected property

Determines if objects defined above are selected or not selected

Check if adding items to an existing selection set

Look at Figures 7-20A and 7-20B as you refer to the following step-by-step example that uses the **Quick Select** command to select objects that are blue:

1. Select **Quick Select...** from the **Tools** pull-down menu to open the **Quick Select** dialog box.
2. In the **Apply to:** drop-down list, select Entire drawing. If you access the **Quick Select** dialog box after a selection set is defined, there is also a Current selection option that allows you to create a subset of the existing set.
3. Under the **Object type:** drop-down list, select Multiple. This will allow you to select any object type. The drop-down list contains all the object types contained in the drawing.
4. In the **Properties:** list, select Color. The items in the **Properties:** list vary depending on which object type is specified.
5. In the **Operator:** drop-down list select = Equals.
6. Under the **Value:** drop-down list select Blue. This drop-down list contains values of the selected property.
7. Under the **How to apply:** area, select the **Include in new selection set** radio button.
8. Pick the **OK** button.

   AutoCAD selects all objects with the color blue, as shown in Figure 7-20B.

   Once a set of objects has been selected, the **Quick Select** dialog box can be used to refine the selection set. Use the **Exclude from new selection set** option to exclude objects, or use the **Append to current selection set** option to add objects. The following procedure refines the selection set to also include black circles:

1. While the initial set of objects is selected, right-click in the drawing area and select **Quick Select...** from the shortcut menu to open the **Quick Select** dialog box.
2. Activate the **Append to current selection set** check box. AutoCAD automatically selects the Entire drawing option in the **Apply to:** drop-down list.
3. Select Circle in the **Object type:** drop-down list, Color in the **Properties:** drop-down list, = Equals in the **Operator:** drop-down list, and Black in the **Value:** drop-down list.
4. In the **How to apply:** area, select the **Include in new selection set** radio button.
5. Pick the **OK** button. The selection now appears as shown in Figure 7-20C.

Figure 7-20.
Creating selection sets with the **Quick Select** dialog box. A—Objects in drawing. B—Selection set containing objects colored blue. C—Circle object added to initial selection set.

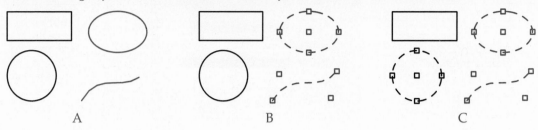

A   B   C

Using Filters to Create a Selection Set

The **FILTER** command is used to create a list of properties that are needed for a specific object to be selected. Filter lists can be created for use at any time. These filter lists are accessed at any Select object: prompt. The **FILTER** command can also be used transparently by typing '**FILTER** at the Select object: prompt.

The **FILTER** command is accessed by typing FI or FILTER. This opens the **Object Selection Filters** dialog box, Figure 7-21.

The three major areas of the **Object Selection Filters** dialog box are the list box, the **Select Filter** area, and the **Named Filters** area. The list box is where the current filter list data is displayed, the **Select Filter** area is used to specify filter criteria, and the **Named Filters** area is used to save filters for future use.

Entering filter data

The **Select Filter** area of the **Object Selection Filters** dialog box is where filter data is entered. The drop-down list and edit boxes can be used to enter the values for the filters. Objects in a drawing can even be selected to develop a filter.

The three edit boxes correspond to X, Y, and Z point coordinates. They are enabled as needed for entering different types of filter information. When the filter drop-down list reads Arc, it refers to an object type. Since no further information is required about the object type, the edit boxes are all disabled.

Setting the filter to Arc Center enables all three edit boxes, which are used to define the center point. When Arc Radius is selected, only the top edit box is enabled because only a single value is required. An example of each of these situations is shown in Figure 7-22.

FILTER
FI

Figure 7-21.
The **Object Selection Filters** dialog box.

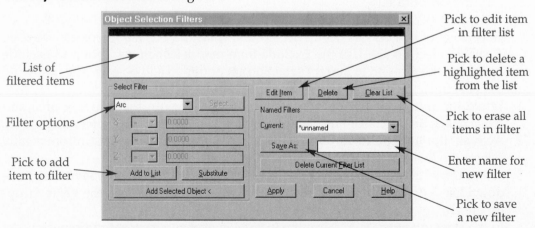

List of filtered items

Filter options

Pick to add item to filter

Pick to edit item in filter list

Pick to delete a highlighted item from the list

Pick to erase all items in filter

Enter name for new filter

Pick to save a new filter

Figure 7-22.
This shows an example of filter items that access the **X:**, **Y:**, and **Z:** edit boxes.

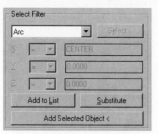

Object filter	Point filter	Distance/length filter
Edit boxes deactivated	All three edit boxes active	One edit box active

For many filter specifications, such as layers, linetypes, and other object properties, the **Select...** button is enabled. The **Select...** button displays the appropriate dialog box for showing the available options. For example, if Color is the specified filter, the **Select...** button displays the standard **Select Color** dialog box. Once the desired filter and value are specified, pick the **Add to List** button to add the new item to the existing filter list.

To use an existing object as a basis for a filter list, pick **Add Selected Object** button. This gives you a Select object: prompt, and once an object is selected, you are returned to the **Object Selection Filters** dialog box. The information from the selected object is placed in the filter list. Since you may not need all of the filter list specifications that result from picking an object, the filter list can now be edited as needed. Editing the filter list is covered later in this section.

To introduce you to selection filters, the following example creates a simple filter list that selects only circle objects.

Command: **FI** *or* **FILTER**⏎

This displays the **Object Selection Filters** dialog box. In the **Select Filter** area, pick the drop-down list to see the selection filter options. From this list, select Circle. To add this specification to the filter list, pick the **Add to List** button. The list box now displays this selection criteria as Object = Circle. This shows that only circle objects will be selected. See Figure 7-23. To use the selection filter, pick the **Apply** button, and the following prompt is issued:

Applying filter to selection.
Select objects: *(window around the objects or type* ALL*)*

Figure 7-23.
Setting the filter so that only circles are selected.

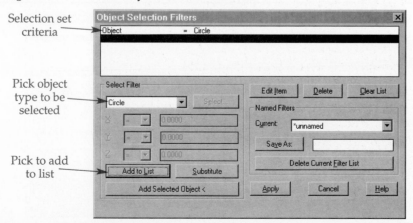

Figure 7-24.
All objects are
filtered out except
for the circles.

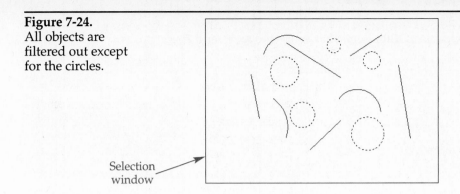

Selection
window

The prompt tells you that the filter is active. In Figure 7-24, a selection window is created around a group of lines, arcs, and circles. Because the filter is set to allow only circle objects, all other object types are filtered out of the selection. AutoCAD reports the number of objects found and the number selected:

> 13 found 8 were filtered out.

To exit the filtered selection and return to a normal selection mode, press [Enter] at the Select objects: prompt. You are then returned to a standard Select objects: prompt, and the filter is no longer applied. You can then make additional selections or complete the command.

> **NOTE**
>
> To remove an item from the filter list, highlight it and pick the **Delete** button. To clear the entire list and start over, pick the **Clear List** button.

Filter lists can be expanded to select only objects with specific properties. The next example creates a filter list that selects only line objects that have a Center linetype. Use the following steps:

1. Enter the **FILTER** command and clear the list box to start a new filter list by picking the **Clear List** button.
2. From the drop-down list in the **Select Filter** area, select Line, then pick the **Add to List** button. This adds the filter Object = Line to the list box.
3. Select Linetype from the drop-down list, then pick the **Select...** button to display the **Select Linetype(s)** dialog box.
4. Select the CENTER linetype, pick the **OK** button, and then pick the **Add to List** button. The **Object Selection Filters** dialog box should appear as shown in Figure 7-25.

Figure 7-25.
Line objects with
Center linetype will
be selected by this
filter.

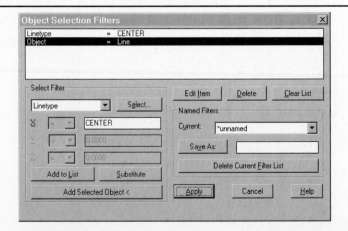

By adding additional filters to the filter list, a filter can be extremely specific when needed. Filters for a specific location or a specific text string can be useful when selecting items in very large, complex drawings.

EXERCISE 7-14

❏ Start AutoCAD and use the setup option of your choice.
❏ Draw a group of lines, arcs, and circles similar to Figure 7-24.
❏ Use the **FILTER** command to create a filter that selects only circles.
❏ Use a selection window around all objects and observe which are selected.
❏ Save the drawing as EX7-14.

Working with relative operators

The term *relative operator* refers to functions that determine the relationship between data items. These relationships include equality, inequality, greater than, less than, and combinations such as greater than or equal to and less than or equal to. Each of the three edit boxes in the **Select Filter** area are preceded by a relative operator drop-down list. An appropriate relative operator can be selected for each data field.

For example, a relative operator can be used to select all arcs that have a radius of 2.5 or greater. To do this, the filter specification is Arc Radius with 2.5 entered in the enabled edit box. Then, select the greater than or equal to symbol (>=) from the relative operator drop-down list. See Figure 7-26.

Figure 7-26.
The greater than or equal to filtering option.

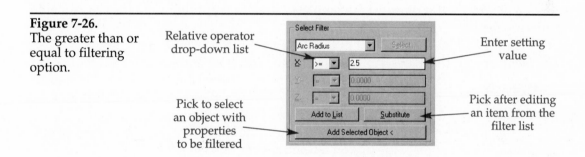

The following chart shows the relative operator functions:

Symbol	Meaning
=	Equal to
!=	Not equal to
<	Less than
<=	Less than or equal to
>	Greater than
>=	Greater than or equal to
×	Equal to any value

Editing the filter list

Editing capabilities are provided that allow you to modify and delete filter list items. If you accidentally enter an incorrect filter specification, you can easily correct it using these steps:

1. Pick the item in the filter list that you need to edit, then pick the **Edit Item** button. The values for the selected specification are then entered in the **Select Filter** area and can be freely edited.
2. Change the values as necessary.
3. Pick the **Substitute** button when finished. The edited filter specification is substituted for the highlighted item. Be sure to pick **Substitute**, and not **Add to List**; otherwise, you end up with two different values for the same filter specification in the filter list.

To remove an item from the filter list, highlight it and select the **Delete** button. Only one filter specification can be deleted at a time using this method. If you need to remove all of the current specifications and start over, pick the **Clear List** button.

Creating named filters

The most powerful feature of CAD is being able to benefit from work you have already done. By reusing previous work instead of repeating the work to produce duplicate results, you increase your efficiency and overall productivity levels.

Complex filter lists can be time-consuming to develop. AutoCAD allows you to name and save filter lists. The **Named Filters** area of the **Object Selection Filters** dialog box is used to create and manage these lists.

When you have created a filter list that you plan to use again, it should be named and saved. When the filter list is completed and tested, follow these steps to name and save the list:

1. Pick the edit box to the right of the **Save As:** button to make it current.
2. Next, enter a short, descriptive name in the edit box. The name for a filter list can be up to 18 characters in length. These named filters are stored in a file named filter.nfl and are available until deleted.
3. Pick the **Save As:** button to save the named filter.

To delete a filter list, make it current by picking the filter name from the **Current:** drop-down list, then pick the button labeled **Delete Current Filter List**.

EXERCISE 7-15

❑ Start AutoCAD and use the setup option of your choice.
❑ Establish the filter that was used in Exercise 7-14 and name it CIRCLE.
❑ Save the drawing as EX7-15.

Using filters on a drawing

Filters can increase productivity, but you must learn to recognize situations when they can be used. Imagine that you have just created the flowchart in Figure 7-27. You are then asked to change all of the text inside the flowchart to a new layer and color for plotting considerations. You could use the **Properties** window and individually select each word on the chart, but you decide to use the **FILTER** command to make the job easier.

The **FILTER** command opens the **Object Selection Filters** dialog box, where you follow these steps:

1. Pick the **Add Selected Object** button. The drawing returns with a Select object: prompt. Pick a text element within one of the boxes.
2. The dialog box returns and displays the characteristics of the text you picked. Highlight items such as Text Position and Text Value, and pick the **Delete** button for each. See Figure 7-28. These filters are not needed because they limit the filter list to specific aspects of the text.

AutoCAD and its Applications—Basics

Figure 7-27.
Original flowchart requiring modification.

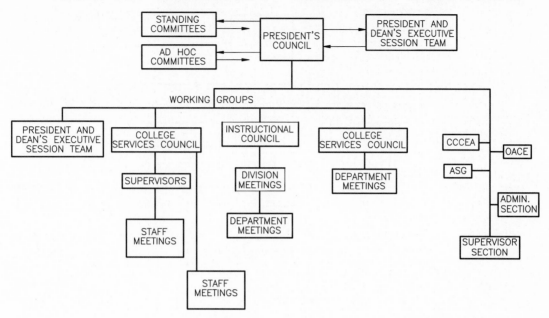

Figure 7-28.
Deleting selection
filters that are too
specific.

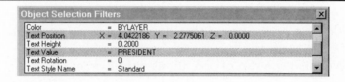

3. Enter a filter name, such as TEXT, in the **Sa̲ve As:** text box and then pick the **Sa̲ve As:** button. TEXT becomes the current filter name.

4. Pick the **Apply** button. The drawing returns and this prompt is given:

> Select object:
> Applying filter to selection.
> Select objects: *(window all drawing text to be included in the selection set)*

The text within the flowchart is now highlighted, and you see this prompt:

> Select objects: Specify opposite corner: 144 found
> 106 were filtered out.
> Select objects: ↵
> Command:

5. The highlighted text returns and the items that were previously highlighted become part of the selection set.

6. At the Command: prompt, enter the **SELECT** command. Enter P when you get the Select objects: prompt. This retrieves the selection set that was previously established with the **FILTER** command. Then use the **Object Properties** toolbar or other editing method to modify the selected text. The revised flowchart is shown in Figure 7-29.

Figure 7-29
Revised flowchart. All text in the flowchart is now red.

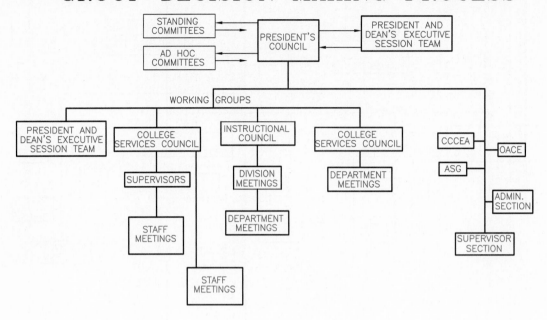

Chapter Test

Answer the following questions on a separate sheet of paper.

1. Identify the command that starts the geometry calculator.
2. Define expression.
3. What is the order of operations within an expression?
4. Give an example of an integer.
5. Give an example of a real number.
6. Show three examples of how the measurement *five feet six inches* can be entered when using the **CAL** command.
7. Give the proper symbol to use for the following math functions:
   A. Addition.
   B. Subtraction.
   C. Multiplication.
   D. Division.
   E. Exponent.
   F. Grouped expressions.
8. Give the expression used to calculate the conversion of 8″ to millimeters.
9. Given the following geometry calculator point coordinate entries, provide the shorter format:
   A. [2,2,0].
   B. [0,0,6].
   C. [5,0,0].
   D. [0,0,0].
10. Show the entry format for the following coordinate systems:
    A. Polar.
    B. Relative.
11. What expression do you enter if you want to use the cursor to specify a point?
12. Give the expression that you would use to find a point that is added to the cursor location at X=1 and Y=2.
13. How do you enter the geometry calculator transparently?
14. Why are object snaps often used when finding points for the geometry calculator?

15. What does AutoCAD recognize when entering object snap instructions in the geometry calculator?
16. Give the expression used to find the distance halfway between the endpoints of two lines.
17. Give the expression used to calculate the distance between the center of two circles.
18. Give the expression used to find the shortest distance from the end of a line to another line with two available endpoints.
19. Give the expression needed to find the distance between the last point used in AutoCAD and the point located at coordinates 4,4,0.
20. Identify the function that is used to find the intersection point between two nonparallel lines.
21. Name the function that is used to find an angle.
22. Give the expression used to identify the included angle when the vertex and sides are available.
23. Provide the function that is used to find the radius of a circle, arc, or 2D polyline.
24. Give the shortcut functions for the following applications:
    A. Distance between two selected endpoints.
    B. Intersection of two lines defined by four selected endpoints.
    C. Point midway between two selected endpoints.
25. Give the function for the following math operations:
    A. Returns a number squared.
    B. Returns the square root of a number.
26. Give an example of the full format for entering degrees, minutes, and seconds in the geometry calculator.
27. Give the trigonometric functions for the following operations:
    A. Returns the sine of angle.
    B. Returns the cosine of angle.
    C. Returns the tangent of angle.
28. Give the function for calculating the constant pi.
29. A _____ is a text item that represents another value that can be accessed later as needed.
30. What is the purpose of X and Y filters?
31. Name the command that allows you to quickly create a selection set based on the filtering criteria that you specify.
32. Identify at least four ways to open the **Quick Select** dialog box.
33. Define filters.
34. How do you enter the **FILTER** command transparently?
35. What happens when you enter the **FILTER** command?
36. What is the purpose of the list box in the **Object Selection Filters** dialog box?
37. What is the purpose of the **Select Filter** area in the **Object Selection Filters** dialog box?
38. What is the purpose of the **Named Filters** area in the **Object Selection Filters** dialog box?
39. What do you do to exit the filtered selection and return to a normal selection mode?
40. How do you remove an item from the filter list?
41. How do you clear the entire filter list and start over again?
42. Name the command that is used to get a Select objects: prompt prior to using the **FILTER** command transparently.
43. Which relative operator is used to select all arcs that have a radius of 4.3 or less?
44. How many characters are allowed in a filter name?
45. If you want to use filters to make changes to the text on your drawing and you pick one of the text objects, the dialog box displays the characteristics of the text you picked. Why is it best to delete items such as Text Position and Text Value?
46. If you add circles to the filter list, what happens when a selection window is placed around a group of lines, arcs, and circles?

47. Identify two ways to specify a linetype in a filter list.
48. Provide the following relative operator symbols:
    A. Not equal to.
    B. Less than.
    C. Less than or equal to.
    D. Greater than.
    E. Greater than or equal to.
    F. Equal to any value.

Drawing Problems

*Use the **CAL** command to calculate the following math problems:*

1. 27.375+15.875
2. 16.0625–7.1250
3. 5 × 17'-8"
4. 48'-0" divided by 16
5. (12.625+3.063)+(18.250–4.375)–(2.625–1.188)
6. 7.25 squared
7. Show the calculation and answer that would be used with the **LINE** command to make an 8" line 1.006 in./in. longer in a pattern to allow for shrinkage in the final casting. Show only the expression and answer.
8. Solve for the deflection of a structural member. The formula is written as $PL^3 / 48EI$, where P = pounds of force, L = length of beam, E = Modulus of Elasticity, and I = moment of inertia. The values to be used are P = 4000 lbs, L = 240", and E = 1,000,000 lbs/in². The value for I is the result of the beam (Width * Height³) / 12, where Width = 6.75" and Height = 13.5".
9. Convert 4.625" to millimeters.
10. Convert 26mm to inches.
11. Convert 65 miles to kilometers.
12. Convert 5 gallons to liters.
13. Calculate the coordinate located at 4,4,0 + 3<30.
14. Calculate the coordinate located at 3+5,1+1.25,0 + 2.375,1.625.
15. Find the square root of 360.
16. What is 3.25 squared?

Given the following right triangle, make the required trigonometry calculations:

17. Length of side *c* (hypotenuse).
18. Sine of angle *A*.
19. Sine of angle *B*.
20. Cosine of angle *A*.
21. Tangent of angle *A*.
22. Tangent of angle *B*.

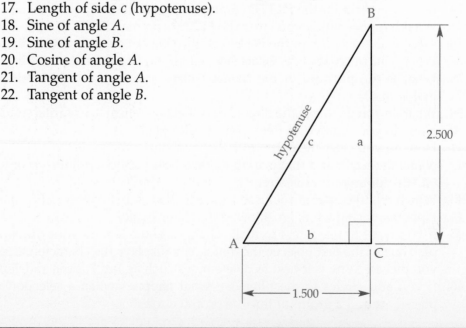

23. Create the following drawing using the **CAL** command and object snap modes as needed to help you. Do not draw dimensions. Save the drawing as P7-23.

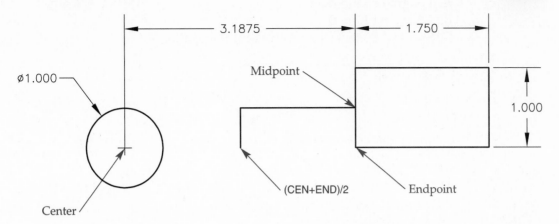

24. Open P7-23 and add the circle as shown below. Save the drawing as P7-24.

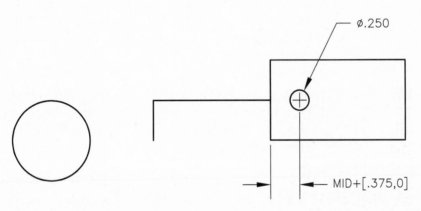

25. Create the following drawing using the **CAL** command and object snap modes as needed to help you. Place the circle with its center at the center of mass of the triangle. Do not draw dimensions. Save the drawing as P7-25.

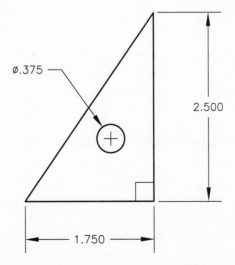

26. Draw the lines shown below using the dimensions given. Do not draw dimensions or labels. Calculate the following and save the drawing as P7-26:
    A. Length of Line A.
    B. Length of Line B.
    C. Shortest distance between Point P and Line B.

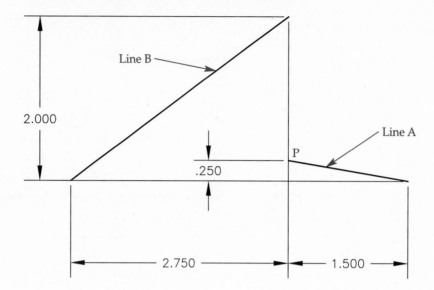

27. Line A has endpoints at 2.88,8.88 and 6.50,6.75. Line B has endpoints at 1.75,7.25 and 6.5,8.5. Determine the point where these lines intersect using the **CAL** command. Then draw the lines and check your solution graphically. Save the drawing as P7-27.

28. Draw the line shown below using the coordinates and dimensions given. Do not draw dimensions or labels. Calculate the coordinate at the other end of the line and the coordinate of a point along the line that is two and one-quarter times the length of the given line. Write your answer and save the drawing as P7-28.

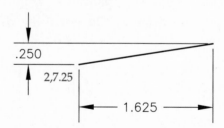

29. Draw the lines shown below. Use the **CAL** command to determine the angle between the lines. Save the drawing as P7-29.

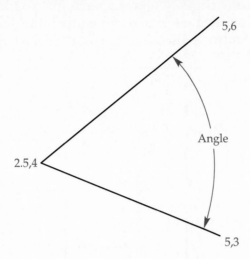

30. Draw a rectangle measuring 3.125 × 5.625. Use the **CAL** command to center a .75 diameter circle in the center of the rectangle. Save the drawing as P7-30.

31. Draw the following object. Then use the **CAL** command to add another circle with a diameter that is 30% of the size of the existing circle. Center the new circle between the midpoints of Line 1 and Line 2. Do not include dimensions. Save the drawing as P7-31.

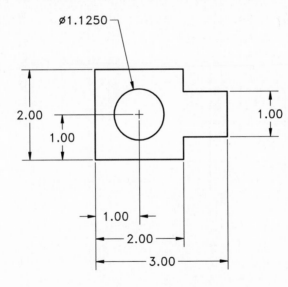

32. Draw the following object. Then use the **CAL** command to create another circle with the same diameter as the existing circle. Place the center of the new circle .5″ above a point that is midway between the center of the existing circle and the midpoint of the right line of the object. Do not include dimensions. Save the drawing as P7-32.

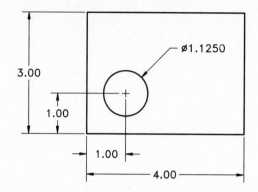

33. Use the X and Y filters to draw an isosceles triangle with a vertical base-line measuring 4.5″ long and 5.75″ high. Save the drawing as P7-33.

34. Draw the object shown below. Then use the **CAL** command to create another circle with a diameter which is 150 percent (1.5X) of the existing circle. Center the new circle 3″ horizontally to the right of the existing circle. Do not dimension the drawing. Save the drawing as P7-34.

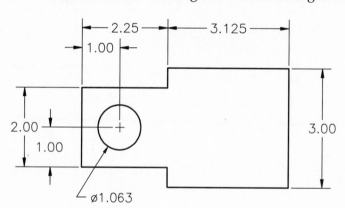

35. Use tracking, object snap modes, and the geometric calculator to draw the following object based on these instructions:
    A. Draw the overall object first, followed by the 10 φ.500 holes.
    B. The B holes are located vertically halfway between the centers of the A holes. The B holes have a diameter one-quarter the size of the A holes.
    C. The B holes that are located horizontally between the A holes are halfway between the centers of the A holes and also have a diameter one-quarter the size of the A holes.
    D. The C holes are located vertically halfway between the A and B holes and have a diameter three-quarters of the B holes.
    E. Draw the rectangles around the circles as shown.
    F. Do not draw dimensions, notes, or labels.
    G. Save the drawing as P7-35.

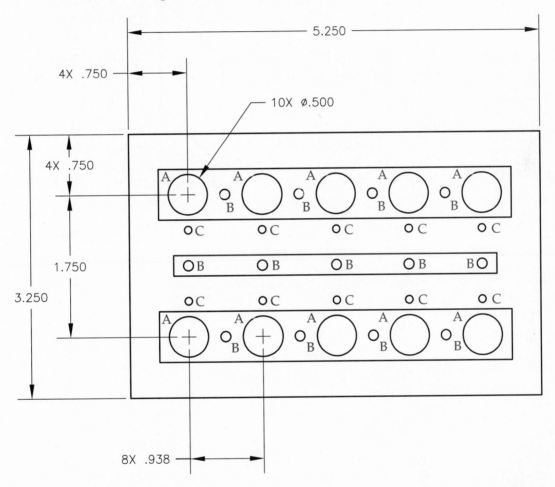

36. Open P7-35. Use a selection filter to erase all circles less than φ.500. Name and save the filter set. Save the drawing as P7-36.

37. Draw the following roof plan. Use the **CAL MEE** option to mirror the roof. Then use the **FILTER** command to change the color of the roof and the linetype to center. Then use the **FILTER** command to change the building outline to a continuous linetype. Do not dimension. Save the drawing as P7-37.

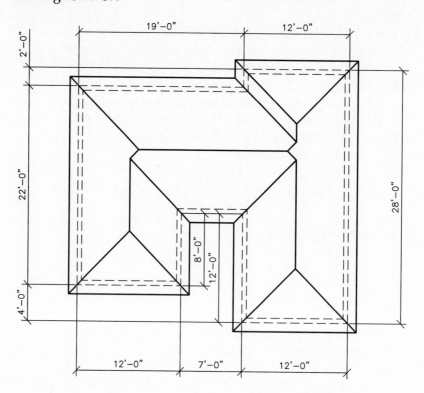

CHAPTER 8

Placing Text on Drawings

Learning Objectives

After completing this chapter, you will be able to:
- Use and discuss proper text standards.
- Use the **DTEXT** or **TEXT** command to display text on the screen while typing.
- Make multiple lines of text with the **MTEXT** command.
- Create text styles using the **Text Style** dialog box.
- Use **AutoCAD DesignCenter** to manage text styles.
- Draw special symbols using control characters.
- Underscore and overscore text.
- Explain the purpose of the Quick Text mode and use the **QTEXT** command.
- Edit existing text.
- Check your spelling.
- Search for and replace material automatically.
- Design title blocks for your drawing template.

Words and notes on drawings have traditionally been added by hand lettering. This is a slow, time-consuming task. Computer-aided drafting programs have reduced the tedious nature of adding notes to a drawing. In computer-aided drafting, lettering is referred to as *text*.

There are advantages of computer-generated text over hand-lettering techniques. When performed by computer, lettering is fast, easier to read, and more consistent. This chapter shows how text can be added to drawings. Also explained is the proper text presentation based on ASME Y14.2M-1992, *Line Conventions and Lettering*.

TEXT STANDARDS

Company standards often dictate how text appears on a drawing. The minimum recommended text height on engineering drawings is .125″ (3mm). All dimension numbers, notes, and other text information should be the same height. Titles, subtitles, captions, revision information, and drawing numbers can be .188″ to .25″ (5 to 6.5mm) high. Many companies specify a .188″, or 5/32″ (5mm), lettering height for standard text. This text size is easy to read even after the drawing is reduced.

Vertical or inclined text may be used on a drawing, depending on company preference. See Figure 8-1. One or the other is recommended, but do not use both. The recommended slant for inclined text is 68° from horizontal. Computer-generated text offers a variety of styles for specific purposes, such as titles or captions. Text on a drawing is normally uppercase, but lowercase letters are used in some instances.

Numbers in dimensions and notes are the same height as standard text. When fractions are used in dimensions, the fraction bar should be placed horizontally between the numerator and denominator using full-size numbers. Fractions can be stacked when using the **MTEXT** command. However, many notes placed on drawings have fractions displayed with a diagonal (/) fraction bar. A dash or space is usually placed between the whole number and the fraction. See Figure 8-2.

Figure 8-1.
Vertical and inclined text.

ABC.. abc.. 123..
ABC.. abc.. 123..

Figure 8-2.
Examples of numbers for different units of measure.

Decimal Inch	Fractional Inch	Millimeter
2.750 .25	$2\frac{3}{4}$ 2 3/4	2.5 3 0.7

SCALE FACTORS FOR TEXT HEIGHT

Scale factors and text heights should be determined before beginning a drawing, and are best incorporated as values within your template drawing files. Scale factors are important because this value is used to make sure that the text is plotted at the proper height. The scale factor is multiplied by the desired plotted text height to get the AutoCAD text height.

The scale factor is always a reciprocal of the drawing scale. For example, if you wish to plot a drawing at a scale of 1/2″ = 1″, calculate the scale factor as follows:

    1/2″ = 1″
    .5″ = 1″
    1/.5 = 2 The scale factor is 2.

An architectural drawing that is to be plotted at a scale of 1/4″ = 1′-0″ has a scale factor calculated as follows:

    1/4″ = 1′-0″
    .25″ = 12″
    12/.25 = 48 The scale factor is 48.

The scale factor of a civil engineering drawing that has a scale of 1″ = 60′ is calculated as follows:

    1″ = 60′
    1″ = (60 × 12)
    720/1 = 720 The scale factor is 720.

If your drawing is in millimeters with a scale is 1:1, the drawing can be converted to inches with the formula 1″ = 25.4mm. Therefore, the scale factor is 25.4. When the metric drawing scale is 1:2, then the scale factor is 1″ = 25.4 × 2, or 1″ = 50.8. The scale factor is 50.8.

After the scale factor has been determined, you should then calculate the height of the AutoCAD text. If the text is to be plotted at 1/8″ (.125″) high, it should be drawn at that height. If the drawing scale is full (1″ = 1″), then the text height is .125″. However, if you are working on a civil engineering drawing with a scale of 1″ = 60′, text drawn at 1/8″ high appears as a dot. Remember that the drawing you are working on is 720 times larger than it is when plotted at the proper scale. Therefore, you must multiply the text height by the 720 scale factor to get text that appears in correct proportion on the screen. If you want 1/8″ high text to appear correctly on a drawing with a 1″ = 60′ scale, calculate the AutoCAD height as follows:

1″ = 60′
1″ = (60 × 12)
720/1 = 720 The scale factor is 720.
text height × scale factor = scaled text height
.125″ × 720 = 90″ The proper text height is 90″.

An architectural drawing with a scale of 1/4″ = 1′-0″ has a scale factor of 48. Text that is to be 1/8″ high should be drawn 6″ high (1/8″ × 48 = 6″).

TEXT COMPOSITION

Composition refers to the spacing, layout, and appearance of the text. With manual lettering, it is necessary to space letters freehand. Spacing is performed automatically with computer-generated text.

Notes should be placed horizontally on the drawing. AutoCAD automatically sets lines of text apart a distance equal to one-half the text height. This helps maintain the identity of individual notes.

The term *justify* means to align the text to fit a given location. For example, left-justified text is aligned along an imaginary left border. Most lines of text are left-justified. Figure 8-3 shows the AutoCAD spacing between lines of left-justified text.

Figure 8-3.
Default spacing between lines of left-justified text.

Text height

1/2 text height

INTERPRET DIMENSIONING A
PER ASME Y14.5M−1994.

AutoCAD provides you with two basic systems for creating text. There is line text for creating single-line text objects, and multiline text for preparing paragraph text. The **DTEXT** (**TEXT**) command is used to create single-line text where the text is entered at the prompt line. The **MTEXT** command is used to create paragraph text that is entered in the **Multiline Text Editor**. Each command is used differently, but the options are similar. Text styles allow you to make the text look the way you want.

Dynamic Text

DTEXT
TEXT
DT

Draw
➡ Text
➡ Single Line Text

The **DTEXT** (dynamic text) command allows you to see the text on the screen as you type. The **DTEXT** command creates single-line text. This means that each line of text is a single text object. **DTEXT** is most useful for text items that require only one line of text. Whenever the text has more than one line or requires mixed fonts, sizes, or colors, multiline text should be used. The **DTEXT** (**TEXT**) commands perform the same function and can be used interchangeably.

The **DTEXT** command can be issued by picking **Single Line Text** from the **Text** cascading menu in the **Draw** pull-down menu, or entering DT, TEXT, or DTEXT at the Command: prompt as follows:

Command: **DT**, **TEXT**, or **DTEXT**↵
Current text style: "Standard" Text height: *current*
Specify start point of text or [Justify/Style]: *(pick a starting point)*
Specify height <*current*>: *(enter a value or press* [Enter]*)*
Specify rotation angle of text <0>: *(enter a value or press* [Enter]*)*
Enter text: *(type text)*↵
Enter text: *(type the next line of text or press* [Enter] *to complete)*
Command:

When the Enter text: prompt appears, a text cursor equal in size to the text height appears on the screen at the text start point. **DTEXT** can be used to enter multiple lines of text simply by pressing [Enter] at the end of each line. The Enter text: prompt is repeated for the next line of text. Press [Enter] twice to exit the **DTEXT** command and keep what you have typed. You can cancel the **DTEXT** command at any time by pressing the [Esc] key. This action erases any incomplete lines of text.

A great advantage of **DTEXT** is that multiple lines of text can be entered. Simply press [Enter] at the end of each line. The text cursor automatically moves to the start point one line below the preceding line. Each line of text is a single object.

While in the **DTEXT** command, the screen crosshairs can be moved independently of the text cursor box. Selecting a new start point completes the line of text being entered and begins a new line at the selected point. Using **DTEXT**, multiple lines of text may be entered anywhere in the drawing without exiting the command. This saves a lot of drafting time. The following are a few aspects of the **DTEXT** command to be aware of:

✓ When you end the **DTEXT** command, the entered text is erased from the screen, then regenerated.

✓ Regardless of the type of justification selected, the cursor box appears as if the text is left-justified. However, when you end the **DTEXT** command, the text disappears and is then regenerated with the alignment you requested.

✓ When you use a control code sequence for a symbol, the control code, not the symbol, is displayed. When you complete the command, the text disappears and is then regenerated showing the proper symbol. Control codes are discussed later in this chapter.

✓ If you cancel the **DTEXT** command, an incomplete line will be deleted.

DTEXT and command line editing

When using the **DTEXT** command, you can do command line editing. The following keys are used to edit the entered material:

- **[↑].** The up arrow key moves backward through previously entered commands, allowing them to become a text entry. You might think of it as moving *up* the list of previous commands.
- **[↓].** After moving backward through any number of previous lines, the down arrow key moves forward again. You might think of this as moving back *down* the list of previously entered commands.
- **[←].** The left arrow key moves the cursor left through the text currently on the command line. Doing this allows you to reposition the cursor to insert text or words that were skipped when entering the text.
- **[→].** After using the left arrow key, the right arrow key moves the typing cursor back to the right.
- **[Home].** Moves the cursor to the home position, which is in front of the first character typed at the command line.
- **[End].** Moves the cursor back to the far right, at the very end of the text typed at the command line.
- **[Insert].** Toggles the command line between Insert mode and Overwrite mode. When in Insert mode, any new text is inserted at the cursor position, and any text existing to the right of the cursor is moved to the right. When in Overwrite mode, new text entered replaces the character at the cursor position.
- **[Page Up].** Does not directly affect the actual command line, but moves the history lines (the lines that show the previous command lines) up whatever number of lines is currently displayed.
- **[Page Down].** Same as the [Page Up] key, except it moves back down the history list.
- **[Delete].** Deletes the character to the right of the text cursor.
- **[Backspace].** Deletes the character to the left of the text cursor.
- **Space bar.** During Insert mode, inserts a space in text at the cursor position. During Overwrite mode, deletes the next character to the right of the cursor position.

The Start point option

After entering the **DTEXT** command, you are given the Specify start point of text or [Justify/Style]: prompt. The default option allows you to select a point on the screen where you want the text to begin. This point becomes the lower-left corner of the text. If you do not like the start point that you pick, you can continue picking until you pick the desired point. After you pick the point, the prompt reads:

Specify Height <*current*>:

This prompt allows you to select the text height. The default value is 0.2000. The previously selected letter height may be displayed as the current value. If you want letters that are .5 unit high, then enter .5. The next prompt is:

Specify rotation angle of text <0>:

The default value for the rotation angle is 0, which places the text horizontally. The values rotate text in a counterclockwise direction. The text pivots about the starting point as shown in Figure 8-4.
The last prompt is:

Enter text:

Type the desired text and press [Enter]. If no other justification is selected, the text is left-justified, as shown in Figure 8-5.

Figure 8-4.
Different rotation
angles for text. The
starting point is
indicated here with
a plus sign.

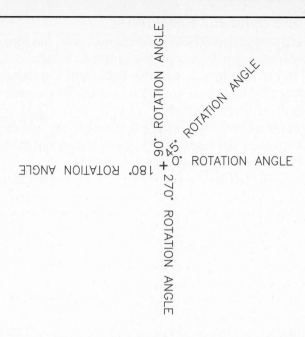

Figure 8-5.
Left-justified text
with the start point
shown.

AUTOCAD LEFT-JUSTIFIED TEXT

NOTE

If the default angle orientation or direction (**ANGBASE** and **ANGDIR** system variables) is changed, the text rotation is affected.

The Justify option

The **DTEXT** command offers a variety of justification options. Left-justification is the default. If you want another option, enter J at the Specify start point of text [Justify/Style]: prompt. When you select the **Justify** option, you can use one of several text alignment options. These options can be seen in the command sequence below, and are explained in the next sections.

Command: **DT**, **TEXT**, *or* **DTEXT**↵
Current text style: "Standard" Text height: 0.2000
Specify start point of text or [Justify/Style]: **J**↵
Enter an option [Align/Fit/Center/Middle/Right/TL/TC/TR/ML/MC/MR/BL/BC/BR]:

- **Align (A).** When this option is selected, you are prompted for two points between which the text string is confined:

    Enter an option
    [Align/Fit/Center/Middle/Right/TL/TC/TR/ML/MC/MR/BL/BC/BR]: **A**↵
    Specify first endpoint of text baseline: *(pick a point)*
    Specify second endpoint of text baseline: *(pick a point)*
    Enter text:

The beginning and endpoints can be placed horizontally or at an angle. AutoCAD automatically adjusts the text width to fit between the selected points. The text height is also changed with this option. The height varies according to the distance between the points and the number of characters. See Figure 8-6.

AutoCAD and its Applications—Basics

Figure 8-6.
Examples of aligned and fit text. In aligned text, the text height is adjusted. In fit text, the text width is adjusted.

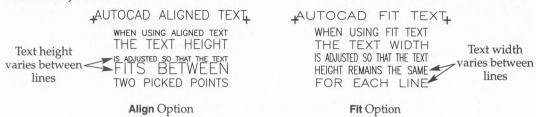

Text height varies between lines

Align Option

Fit Option

Text width varies between lines

PROFESSIONAL TIP

DTEXT is not recommended for aligned text because the text height for each line is adjusted according to the width. One line may run into another.

- **Fit (F).** This option is similar to the **Align** option, except that you can select the text height. AutoCAD adjusts the letter width to fit between the two given points, while keeping text height constant. See Figure 8-6.

    ```
    Enter an option
      [Align/Fit/Center/Middle/Right/TL/TC/TR/ML/MC/MR/BL/BC/BR]: F↵
    Specify first endpoint of text baseline: (pick a point)
    Specify second endpoint of text baseline: (pick a point)
    Specify height <current>: .5↵
    Enter text:
    ```

- **Center (C).** This option allows you to select the center point for the baseline of the text. Enter the letter height and rotation angle after picking the center point. This example uses a .5 unit height and a 0° rotation angle. The prompts appear as follows:

    ```
    Enter an option
      [Align/Fit/Center/Middle/Right/TL/TC/TR/ML/MC/MR/BL/BC/BR]: C↵
    Specify center point of text: (pick a point)
    Specify height <current>: .5↵
    Enter text:
    ```

- **Middle (M).** This option allows you to center text both horizontally and vertically at a given point. The letter height and rotation can also be changed. The command sequence is similar to the sequence for the **Center** option.
- **Right (R).** This option justifies text at the lower-right corner. The point is entered at the End point: prompt. The letter height and rotation can also be entered. The command sequence is similar to the sequence for the **Start point** option. Figure 8-7 compares the **Center**, **Middle**, and **Right** options.

Other text alignment options

There are a number of text alignment options that allow you to place text on a drawing in relation to the top, bottom, middle, left side, or right side of the text. These alignment options are shown in Figure 8-8. These options are shown as abbreviations that correlate to the **DTEXT** prompt line. To use one of these options, type the two letters for the desired option and press [Enter].

Figure 8-7.
Three justification options with start point shown.
A—Using the **Center** text option.
B—Using the **Middle** text option.
C—Using the **Right** text option.

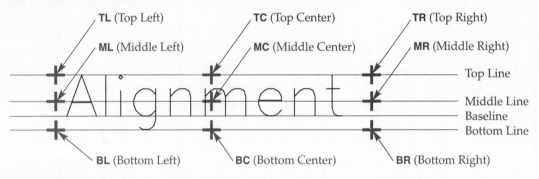

AUTOCAD CENTERED TEXT
A

AUTOCAD MIDDLE TEXT
B

AUTOCAD RIGHT—JUSTIFIED TEXT
C

Figure 8-8.
Using the **TL**, **TC**, **TR**, **ML**, **MC**, **MR**, **BL**, **BC**, and **BR** text alignment options. Notice what the abbreviations stand for.

TL (Top Left)   TC (Top Center)   TR (Top Right)
ML (Middle Left)   MC (Middle Center)   MR (Middle Right)

Top Line
Middle Line
Baseline
Bottom Line

BL (Bottom Left)   BC (Bottom Center)   BR (Bottom Right)

PROFESSIONAL TIP

If you already know which text alignment option you want to use in your drawing, you can enter it at the Specify start point of text or [Justify/Style]: prompt without entering J. Just type the uppercase letter or letters of the desired option and press [Enter].

EXERCISE 8-1

❑ Start AutoCAD and use the setup option of your choice.
❑ Use the **DTEXT** command to type the following multiple lines of text exactly as shown using the **Specify start point** option. Use .25" (6mm) letter height and 0° rotation angle.

> LETTERING HAS TYPICALLY BEEN A SLOW, TIME-CONSUMING TASK. COMPUTER-AIDED DRAFTING HAS REDUCED THE TEDIOUS NATURE OF PREPARING LETTERING ON A DRAWING. IN CAD, LETTERING IS REFERRED TO AS TEXT. COMPUTER-GENERATED TEXT IS FAST, CONSISTENT, AND EASIER TO READ.

❑ Use the **DTEXT** command to type the following information. Each time, change the text option to obtain the format given. Use .5" (12mm) letter height and 0° rotation angle.

> AUTOCAD TEXT LEFT-JUSTIFIED USING THE START POINT OPTION.
> AUTOCAD TEXT RIGHT-JUSTIFIED USING THE RIGHT OPTION.
> AUTOCAD TEXT ALIGNED USING THE ALIGN OPTION.
> AUTOCAD TEXT CENTERED USING THE CENTER OPTION.
> AUTOCAD FIT TEXT USING THE FIT OPTION.
> AUTOCAD TEXT USING THE MIDDLE OPTION.

AutoCAD and its Applications—Basics

❏ Use the **DTEXT** command to type the following information. Each time, change the text option to obtain the format given in each statement. Use .5″ (12mm) letter height and 0° rotation angle.

> AUTOCAD TOP/LEFT OPTION.
> AUTOCAD TOP/CENTER OPTION.
> AUTOCAD TOP/RIGHT OPTION.
> AUTOCAD MIDDLE/LEFT OPTION.
> AUTOCAD MIDDLE/CENTER OPTION.
> AUTOCAD MIDDLE/RIGHT OPTION.
> AUTOCAD BOTTOM/LEFT OPTION.
> AUTOCAD BOTTOM/CENTER OPTION.
> AUTOCAD BOTTOM/RIGHT OPTION.

❏ Save the drawing as EX8-1.

Multiline Text

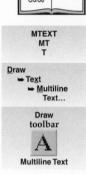

The **MTEXT** command is used to create multiline text objects. Instead of each line being an individual object, all the lines are part of the same object. The **MTEXT** command is accessed by picking the **Multiline Text** button in the **Draw** toolbar, picking **Multiline Text...** in the **Text** cascading menu of the **Draw** pull-down, or entering T, MT, or MTEXT at the Command: prompt.

After entering the **MTEXT** command, AutoCAD asks you to specify the first and second corners of the text boundary. The *text boundary* is a box within which your text will be placed. When you pick the first corner of the text boundary, the cursor changes to a box. Move the box until you have the desired size for your paragraph and pick the opposite corner. See Figure 8-9.

When drawing the boundary window for multiline text, an arrow in the window shows the direction of text flow. While the width of the rectangle drawn provides a limit to the width of the text paragraphs, it does not affect the possible height. The rectangle height is automatically resized to fit the actual text entered. The direction of the flow indicates where the rectangle is expanded if necessary. This is the command sequence:

> Command: **T**, **MT**, *or* **MTEXT**↵
> Current text style: Standard Text height: 0.2000
> Specify first corner: *(pick the first corner)*
> Specify opposite corner or [Height/Justify/Line spacing/Rotation/Style/Width]:
>   *(pick the other corner)*

After picking the text boundary, the **Multiline Text Editor** appears. See Figure 8-10. The **Character** tab is used to enter text, change features (such as font, text height, and color), and copy text. The **Properties** tab is used to change features such as the current text styles, justification, text boundary width, and rotation. The **Line Spacing** tab is used to control line spacing for new or selected multiline text. The **Find/Replace** tab is used to replace selected words with new words.

Figure 8-9.
The text boundary is a box within which your text will be placed. The arrow indicates the direction of text flow.

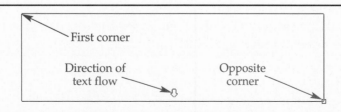

Figure 8-10.
The **Multiline Text Editor** with the **AutoCAPS** shortcut menu activated. Enter text in the text window (shown here highlighted).

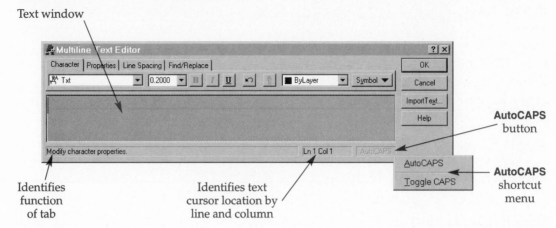

Text window

AutoCAPS button

AutoCAPS shortcut menu

Identifies function of tab

Identifies text cursor location by line and column

In the lower right-hand corner of the **MTEXT** status bar, there is an **AutoCAPS** button. This button controls the caps lock for the **MTEXT** dialog box. One way to turn **AutoCAPS** on or off is to double-click on the **AutoCAPS** button. The second way is to move your mouse to the **AutoCAPS** button and right-click the button. This displays the **AutoCAPS** shortcut menu, shown in Figure 8-10. The **AutoCAPS** option toggles Caps Lock on or off in the **Multiline Text Editor** only. The **Toggle CAPS** option turns Caps Lock on or off globally, identical to the [Caps Lock] key on the keyboard.

To the left of the **AutoCAPS** button, there is a Ln 1 Col 1 message. This means that the text cursor is located at Line 1 Column 1. A *line* is created every time the text cursor moves down. A line can be full of text that you type or can be blank. You can move the text cursor down by pressing the [Enter] key, or by picking with your pointer. A new line is also created when you type to the right boundary and AutoCAD automatically moves the cursor to the next line.

When the text window is filled with text and a new line is added, previous lines begin to be hidden and a scroll bar is displayed at the right. Use the scroll bar to move up and down to access lines in the text window. A column is created every time the text cursor moves to the right. A column is one character wide, whether it is an actual text character or a space.

EXERCISE 8-2

❏ Start AutoCAD and use the setup option of your choice.
❏ Access the **MTEXT** command and create a text boundary that is 4″ (100mm) wide and 2″ (50mm) high.
❏ Pick each of the tabs: **Character**, **Properties**, **Line Spacing**, and **Find/Replace**. Look at the features in each tab and read the message in the lower-left corner.
❏ Type anything you want and press the [Enter] key to watch the line and column number change in the lower-right corner.
❏ Type enough text or press the [Enter] key enough times so the scroll bar is displayed on the right.
❏ Pick the **OK** button when done to see the text displayed on the screen.
❏ Save the drawing as EX8-2.

Modifying character properties with the Multiline Text Editor

The **Multiline Text Editor** is displayed after you define the text boundary. The editing window is the primary feature of this dialog box. There are four tabs in this dialog box, by default the **Character** tab is open. This is where character standards are set and edited. Character standards refer to the content and appearance of the characters in the text object you are editing.

While in the **Multiline Text Editor** there are a number of keystroke combinations that are available. These combinations are as follows:

Keystroke	Function
[↑] [←] [↓] [→]	Arrow keys move the cursor through the text one position in the direction indicated by the arrow.
[Ctrl]+[→] [Ctrl]+[←]	Moves the cursor one word in the direction indicated.
[Home]	Moves the cursor to the start of the current line.
[End]	Moves the cursor to the end of the current line.
[Delete]	Deletes the character immediately to the right of the cursor.
[Backspace]	Deletes the character immediately to the left of the cursor.
[Ctrl]+[Backspace]	Deletes the word immediately to the left of the cursor.
[Ctrl]+[C]	Copy selection to Clipboard. The Clipboard is an internal storage area that temporarily stores information that you copy or cut from a document.
[Ctrl]+[V]	Paste Clipboard contents to the selection or current cursor location.
[Ctrl]+[X]	Cut selection to Clipboard.
[Ctrl]+[Z]	Undo.
[Ctrl]+[Spacebar]	Inserts a nonbreaking space.
[Enter]	Ends the current paragraph, starting a new one on the next line.
[Page Up] [Page Down]	These keys move the cursor up to 28 rows in the indicated direction.
[Ctrl]+[Page Up] [Ctrl]+[Page Down]	These keys move the cursor to the top or bottom of the currently visible page of text.
[Ctrl]+[Home]	Moves the cursor to Line 1, Column 1.
[Ctrl]+[End]	Moves the cursor to the last character position.
[Ctrl]+[A]	Selects all text in the current multiline text object.
[Shift]+[→] [Shift]+[←]	Selects or deselects text. Increases or decreases the selection by one character at a time, depending on the direction indicated.
[Shift]+[↑] [Shift]+[↓]	Selects or deselects text. Increases or decreases the selection by one line at a time, depending on the direction indicated.
[Ctrl]+[Shift]+[→] [Ctrl]+[Shift]+[←]	Selects or deselects text. Increases or decreases the selection by one word at a time, depending on the direction indicated.
[Esc]	Closes the **Multiline Text Editor** and loses any changes made.

PROFESSIONAL TIP

Text can be pasted from any text-based application into the **Multiline Text Editor**. For example, you can copy text from an application like Microsoft® Word, and then paste it into the **Multiline Text Editor**. The pasted text retains its properties. Likewise, text copied or cut from the **Multiline Text Editor** can be pasted into another text based application.

As you move the cursor into the editing window, it changes shape. If you have used other Windows text editors, this is a familiar text cursor shape. Pointing to a character position within the text and pressing the pick button causes the cursor to be placed at the selected location. You can then begin typing or editing as needed. If you begin typing where the text cursor is initially placed, your text begins in the upper-left corner of the text boundary.

Text is selected as it is with most standard Windows text editors. Place the cursor at one end of the desired selection, press and hold the pick button. Drag the cursor until the desired text is highlighted, then release the pick button. Now, any editing operations you perform affect the highlighted text. For example, a copy or cut operation places the highlighted text on the Clipboard. One other way to highlight text is to move your mouse to the word you would like to highlight and double-click it with the pick button. To entirely replace the highlighted text with new text, either paste the new text from the Clipboard or begin typing. The selection is erased and the new text appears in its place.

As you type in the **Multiline Text Editor**, the text cursor moves to the right. When the cursor gets to the end of the text window, the line of text moves to the left, allowing you to continue typing. Notice the scroll bar below the text window. Move the scroll bar to the left or right as needed to uncover hidden text.

Figure 8-11 illustrates the features found in the **Character** tab. Keep in mind that *selected text* refers to text that you have highlighted in the text window:

- **Font list.** A *font* is a family of text characters. Pick the down arrow to open the drop-down list of available text fonts. Picking one of the options allows the selected text to have its font changed. This overrides the font used in the current style. The AutoCAD default text style is named Standard. Txt is the default text font.
- **Font height.** This option allows selected text to have its height changed. This overrides the current setting of the **TEXTSIZE** system variable and the text height set within the text style.
- **Bold.** Pick this button to have the selected text become bold. This only works with some TrueType fonts. The .shx fonts do not have this capability.
- **Italic.** Pick this button to have the selected text become italic. This only works with some TrueType fonts. The .shx style fonts do not have this capability.
- **Underline.** Picking this button underlines selected text.

Figure 8-11.
The **Character** tab.

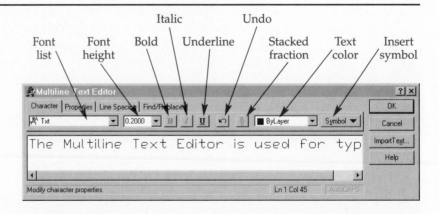

AutoCAD and its Applications—Basics

- **Undo.** Pick this button to undo the previous activity.
- **Stack/Unstack.** This button allows selected text to be stacked vertically or diagonally. To use this feature for drawing a vertically stacked fraction, place a forward slash between the top and bottom items. Then select the text with your pointing device and pick the button. This button is also used for unstacking text that has been previously stacked. You can also use the caret (^) character between text if you want to stack the items without a dividing line. This is called a *tolerance stack.* Typing a number sign (#) between selected numbers results in a diagonal fraction bar. See Figure 8-12.
- **Text color.** The text color is set ByLayer as default, but you can change the text color by picking one of the colors found in the **Text color** drop-down list.
- **Insert symbol.** The **Symbol** button opens the options for inserting symbols. See Figure 8-13. This option allows the insertion of symbols at the text cursor location. The **Non-breaking Space** option keeps two separate words together. The **Other...** option opens the **Unicode Character Map** dialog box, Figure 8-14. To use this dialog box, pick the desired TrueType symbols from the **Font:** drop-down list. The **Next** and **Previous** buttons cycle between the options in the **Subset:** list. The following are the steps for using a symbol or symbols:

1. Pick the desired symbol and then pick the **Select** button. The selected symbol is displayed in the **Characters to Copy:** box.
2. Pick the **Copy** button to have the selected symbol or symbols copied to the Clipboard.
3. Pick the **Close** button to close the dialog box.
4. Back in the **Multiline Text Editor**, place the text cursor where you want the symbols displayed.
5. Move the screen cursor to anywhere inside the text window and right-click to display the **Edit text** shortcut menu.
6. Pick the **Paste** option to have the selected symbols pasted at the text cursor location.

Figure 8-12.
Different types of stack characters.

	Selected text	Stacked text
Vertical fraction	1/2	$\frac{1}{2}$
Tolerance stack	1^2	$\frac{1}{2}$
Diagonal fraction	1#2	½

Figure 8-13.
The **Symbol** menu options.

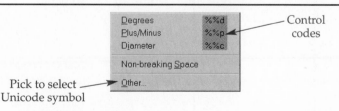

Pick to select Unicode symbol

Control codes

Figure 8-14.
The **Unicode Character Map** dialog box.

Pick to change subset
Pick to select symbol
Pick to copy selected symbol to Clipboard
Selected symbols listed here

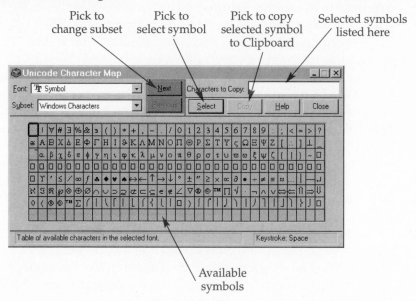

Available symbols

PROFESSIONAL
TIP

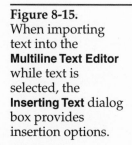

When a symbol in the **Unicode Character Map** dialog box is highlighted, a keyboard shortcut appears on the right side of the status line. Many of these shortcuts involve the [Alt] key and a number, such as Alt+0175. These numbers match the decimal values for ASCII (American Standard Code for Information Interchange) character codes. To enter this symbol in the text window, hold the [Alt] key while typing 0175. Be sure the correct font is selected.

The listing may also specify a Unicode number. If so, the symbol can be entered by typing \U+ followed by the specified number, just as you would to enter a diameter or degree symbol.

- **Import Text... button.** This allows you to import text from an existing text file directly into the **Multiline Text Editor**. The text file can be either a standard ASCII text file or an .rtf (rich text format) file. The imported text becomes a part of the current multiline text object.

  When this option is selected, a standard file dialog box is displayed. Select the text file to be imported. You cannot import a file that is over 16K in size. If you import text while text is selected, the **Inserting Text** dialog box shown in Figure 8-15 appears.

Figure 8-15.
When importing text into the **Multiline Text Editor** while text is selected, the **Inserting Text** dialog box provides insertion options.

Imported text replaces selection
Imported text follows selection
Imported text replaces all text in **Multiline Text Editor**

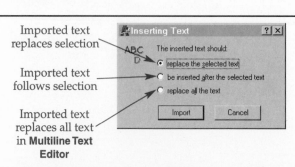

NOTE

The formatting of text within the **Multiline Text Editor** may not always appear exactly as it does in the drawing. This is most commonly true when a substitute font is used for display in the editor. A substitute font may be wider or narrower than the font used in the drawing. AutoCAD automatically reformats the text to fit within the boundary defined in the drawing.

Using the Edit text shortcut menu

The **Edit text** shortcut menu was briefly introduced in the previous discussion. This menu is accessed by right-clicking while the cursor is in the **Multiline Text Editor** text window. Refer to Figure 8-16. The following options are available:

- **Undo.** Select this option to undo the last operation. It may be a cut, paste, or typing operation. Select **Undo** again to bring back the undone operation.
- **Cut.** Pick this option to have the selected text removed from the text window and placed in the Clipboard.
- **Copy.** Use this option to have the selected text copied to the Clipboard.
- **Paste.** This option places text from the Clipboard in the text window at the text cursor location. Text that has been cut, copied, or imported to the Clipboard can be pasted into the text window.
- **Select All.** Pick this option to select and highlight the entire contents of the text window.
- **Change Case.** This option allows you to change the selected text to all uppercase or lowercase characters by picking the related menu item.
- **Remove Formatting.** This option removes text formatting (such as font, height, bold, italic, and underline) that is not part of the original text style from the highlighted text.
- **Combine Paragraphs.** Use this option when you have two or more paragraphs selected and you want them to be one paragraph.

Figure 8-16.
The **Edit text** shortcut menu is accessed by right-clicking while the cursor is in the **Multiline Text Editor** text window.

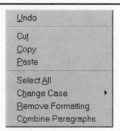

Using the Edit text shortcut menu with stacked text

In addition to the options previously discussed, the **Edit text** shortcut menu has two additional options when stacked characters have been selected: **Stack** or **Unstack** and **Properties**. **Stack** or **Unstack** is used to stack or unstack the selected text. The **Properties** option accesses the **Stack Properties** dialog box. This dialog box, shown in Figure 8-17, has the following features:

- **Upper.** Displays the current text value for the top part of the stack character and allows you to change the value.
- **Lower.** Displays the current text value for the bottom part of the stack character and allows you to change the value.
- **Style.** This option allows you to choose from the **Fraction (Horizontal)**, **Fractional (Diagonal)**, and **Tolerance** styles from the drop-down list.
- **Position.** This option allows you to choose **Bottom**, **Center**, or **Vertical** alignment for your stack character.
- **Text size.** Specifies the size of the stack character by a percentage of the text height.
- **Defaults button.** This drop-down button saves settings as default, or restores the original defaults.
- **AutoStack button.** This button accesses the **AutoStack Properties** dialog box, shown in Figure 8-18. This dialog box contains the following items:
  - **Enable AutoStacking.** Allows you to stack fractions automatically as you type.
  - **Remove Leading Blank.** This option removes a blank between a whole number and a fraction.
  - **Convert it to a diagonal fraction.** This option converts the slash character to a diagonal fraction when AutoStack is on.
  - **Convert it to a horizontal fraction.** This option converts the slash character to a horizontal fraction when AutoStack is on.
  - **Don't show this dialog again; always use these settings.** This option suppresses the display of the **AutoStack Properties** dialog box. The current property settings are maintained.

Figure 8-17.
The **Stack Properties** dialog box.

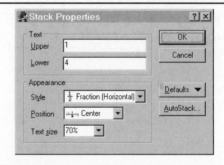

Figure 8-18.
AutoStack Properties dialog box.

Check to activate AutoStacking

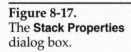

Select style for fractions

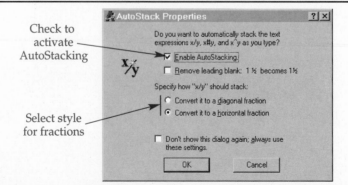

❏ Start AutoCAD and use the setup option of your choice.
❏ Use the **MTEXT** command to create a text boundary that is 4″ (100mm) wide by 2″ (50mm) high.
❏ Type the following text paragraph:

> Entering a paragraph of text is quick and easy with the MTEXT command. The MTEXT command opens the Multiline Text Editor, where text is typed and edited as needed. The MTEXT command is accessed by picking Multiline Text in the Text cascading menu of the Draw pull-down menu, by picking the Multiline Text button in the Draw toolbar, or by entering MTEXT at the Command: prompt.

❏ Use the cursor menu to select the entire paragraph and then change the height to .125 (3mm) and change the font from Txt to Romans.
❏ Select the entire paragraph again and this time change the font to Arial. Now notice that the **Bold** and **Italic** buttons are active. This is because the Arial font is a TrueType font.
❏ Make the word MTEXT bold.
❏ Make the words Multiline Text Editor italic.
❏ Add the following statement to your paragraph:

> The Multiline Text Editor also makes it easy to enter the symbols for degrees (°), plus/minus (±), diameter (∅), greater than (>), and Omega (Ω).

❏ Pick the **OK** button.
❏ Save the drawing as EX8-3.

Using the Properties tab

The **Properties** tab of the **Multiline Text Editor** is shown in Figure 8-19. The following drop-down lists are available:

* **Style.** This drop-down list displays the current text style. Standard is the default text style. Selecting a new style changes all the text in the window. All styles defined in the drawing are listed in the drop-down list. If text styles have not been created, then only the Standard style is listed.
* **Justification.** This drop-down list provides the list of multiline text justification options. See Figure 8-19. There is an icon to the left of each option name that identifies the option. The two-letter abbreviation corresponds to the **DTEXT** command justification options.

    The text is justified in relation to the boundary. Left-justified text is aligned along the left side, center-justified text is centered in the boundary, and right-justified text is aligned with the right side. See Figure 8-20.

    When you are placing the text boundary window, the flow arrow also identifies the justification. The flow arrow points downward for any top-justification

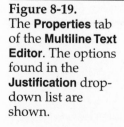

Figure 8-19.
The **Properties** tab of the **Multiline Text Editor**. The options found in the **Justification** drop-down list are shown.

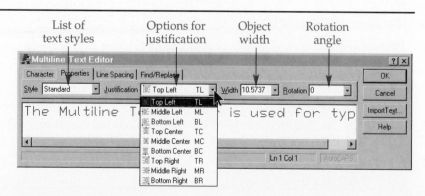

Figure 8-20.
The **MTEXT** justification options.

Top Left
Left Justified

Top Center
Center Justified

Top Right
Right Justified

Middle Left
Left Justified

Middle Center
Center Justified

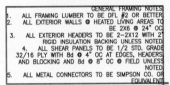

Middle Right
Right Justified

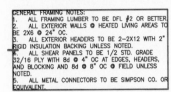

Bottom Left
Left Justified

Bottom Center
Center Justified

Bottom Right
Right Justified

 This symbol represents the insertion point

option. When the text uses any bottom-justification option, the flow is upward so the arrow points upward. When middle-justification, the flow is in *both* directions, so both upward and downward arrows are displayed.

- **Width.** This option has a drop-down list and a text box. The value provided represents the current text boundary width. You can change this value to establish a new width. The **(no wrap)** option deactivates word wrap. When you are typing and reach the end of a line, *word wrap* automatically starts a new line. If you pick the **(no wrap)** option, each line of text continues beyond the right boundary until you press [Enter] to go to the next line.
- **Rotation.** This option has a drop-down list and a text box that allow you to set the rotation angle of the paragraph.

EXERCISE 8-4

❑ Start AutoCAD and use the setup option of your choice.
❑ Use the **MTEXT** command to create a text boundary that is 4″ (100mm) wide by 2″ (50mm) high.
❑ Type the following text paragraph:

> Multiline text is created using the MTEXT command. This provides you with the opportunity to place several lines of text on a drawing and have all of the lines act as one text object. It also gives you the convenience of entering and editing the text in the Multiline Text Editor.

❑ Change the width to 2″ (50mm) and observe the effect.
❑ Change the width back to 4″ (100mm).
❑ Change the justification to a few different options just to see the results. Change the justification back to top left.
❑ Pick the **OK** button.
❑ Save the drawing as EX8-4.

AutoCAD and its Applications—Basics

Using the Line Spacing tab

The **Line Spacing** tab is used to control line spacing for new or selected multiline text. There are two drop-down lists, as shown in Figure 8-21. In the first drop-down list, the options allow you to specify how the spacing between lines of the multiline text is adjusted. The **At Least** option automatically adds spaces between lines based on the height of the character in the line. The **Exactly** option forces the line spacing to be the same for all lines of multiline text within the object.

The second drop-down list provides line spacing increment options. The three options are **Single (1x)**, **1.5 Lines (1.5x)**, and **Double (2x)**. This spacing increment is the vertical distance from the bottom of one line to the bottom of the next line of multiline text.

Using the Find/Replace tab

The **Find/Replace** tab of the **Multiline Text Editor** is used to find and replace text in the current text object. This tab is illustrated in Figure 8-22.

Type the word you want to find in the **Find** text box. Words that were previously entered are found in the drop-down list. Then pick the **Find** button to locate the identified text.

Figure 8-21.
The **Line Spacing** tab of the **Multiline Text Editor**.

Line spacing option

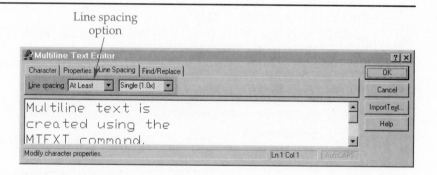

Figure 8-22.
Using the **Find/Replace** tab of the **Multiline Text Editor**. A—Enter the text to find and the replacement text. B—Pick the **Replace** button to replace the selected text.

Text to find Pick to find text Replacement text Pick to replace Select search options

Old text has been replaced

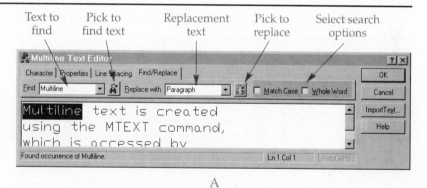

A

B

If you want to replace the text identified in the **Find** text box, enter the replacement text in the **Replace with** text box. In Figure 8-22A, Multiline is to be replaced with Paragraph. Pick the **Replace** button once to find the first occurrence of the word in the **Find** text box. Pick this button again to have the selected text replaced with the new text. Figure 8-22B shows the result of the replacement.

The **Find/Replace** tab also contains two check boxes for search options. If the **Match Case** check box is activated, the search only finds text that matches the specification *exactly*, including specified uppercase and lowercase characters. For example, if this box is unchecked, a search for HELLO finds Hello, hello, and heLLo. The **Whole Word** check box is used to specify a search for a whole word, and not part of another word. For example, if **Whole Word** is not checked, a search for the word the would find those letters wherever they occur—including as part of other words, such as o<u>the</u>r or we<u>ather</u>.

Setting multiline text options at the prompt line

You can set the **MTEXT** options at the Command: prompt. After picking the first boundary corner, select an option. The following command sequence shows an example:

```
Command: T, MT, or MTEXT↵
Current text style: Standard. Text height: 0.2000
Specify first corner: (pick the first boundary corner)
Specify opposite corner or [Height/Justify/Line spacing/Rotation/Style/Width]: H↵
Specify height <0.2000>: .125↵
Specify opposite corner or [Height/Justify/Line spacing/Rotation/Style/Width]: J↵
Enter justification [TL/TC/TR/ML/MC/MR/BL/BC/BR] <TL>: MC↵
Specify opposite corner or [Height/Justify/Line spacing/Rotation/Style/Width]: L↵
Enter line spacing type [At least/Exactly] <At least>: E↵
Enter line spacing factor or distance <1x>: 2x↵
Specify opposite corner or [Height/Justify/Line spacing/Rotation/Style/Width]: R↵
Specify rotation angle <0>: 30↵
Specify opposite corner or [Height/Justify/Line spacing/Rotation/Style/Width]: S↵
Enter style name or [?] <Standard>: ↵
Specify opposite corner or [Height/Justify/Line spacing/Rotation/Style/Width]: W ↵
Specify width: 4↵
```

A value specified in the **Width** option automatically sets the multiline text boundary width and opens the **Multiline Text Editor**.

NOTE The **-MTEXT** command can be used to enter a multiline text object without using the **Multiline Text Editor**. The options at the Command: prompt are identical to the Command: prompt options for the **MTEXT** command. Lines of text are entered at the Mtext: prompt, similar to the entry of dynamic text.

AutoCAD User's Guide 11

AUTOCAD TEXT FONTS

A *font* is a particular letter face design. The standard AutoCAD text fonts are shown in Figure 8-23. These fonts have .shx file extensions.

The Txt font is the AutoCAD default. The Txt font is rather rough in appearance and may not be the best choice for your application, even though Txt requires less time to regenerate than other fonts. The Romans (roman simplex) font is smoother than Txt. It closely duplicates the single-stroke lettering that has long been the standard for most drafting. The complex and triplex fonts are multistroke fonts for drawing titles and subtitles. The gothic and italic fonts are ornamental styles. In addition, AutoCAD provides several standard symbol fonts.

AutoCAD and its Applications—Basics

Figure 8-23.
Standard AutoCAD text and symbol fonts.

	Fast Fonts		Gothic Fonts
Txt	abcdABCD12345	Gothice	abcdABCD12345
Monotxt	abcdABCD12345	Gothicg	abcdABCD12345
		Gothii	abcdABCD12345

Fast Fonts
- Txt: abcdABCD12345
- Monotxt: abcdABCD12345

Simplex Fonts
- Romans: abcdABCD12345
- Scripts: abcdABCD12345
- Greeks: αβχδABXΔ12345
- Italic: abcdABCD12345
- Simplex: abcdABCD12345

Duplex Font
- Romand: abcdABCD12345

Complex Fonts
- Romanc: abcdABCD12345
- Italicc: abcdABCD12345
- Scriptc: abcdABCD12345
- Greekc: αβχδABXΔ12345
- Complex: abcdABCD12345

Triplex Fonts
- Romant: abcdABCD12345
- Italict: abcdABCD12345

Gothic Fonts
- Gothice: abcdABCD12345
- Gothicg: abcdABCD12345
- Gothii: abcdABCD12345

ISO Fonts
- Isocp: abcdABCD12345
- Isocp2: abcdABCD12345
- Isocp3: abcdABCD12345
- Isoct: abcdABCD12345
- Isoct2: abcdABCD12345
- Isoct3: abcdABCD12345

Symbol Fonts
- Syastro: ⚹''⊂⊙♀♀⊕12345
- Symap: ⚹≋○□△12345
- Symath: ←↓∂∇א'|||12345
- Symeteo: |\⌐⎯▲12345
- Symusic: symbols 12345
- GDT: ∠⊥□▱⌒ABCD12345

Several additional AutoCAD fonts provide special alphabets or symbols that are accessed by typing specific keys. This is called *character mapping*. Character mapping for non-Roman and symbol fonts is displayed in Figure 8-24.

TrueType fonts are scaleable and have an outline. *Scaleable* means that the font can be displayed on the screen or printed at any size and still maintain proportion. TrueType fonts have an outline, but they appear filled in the graphics window. When you plot or print, the fonts can be filled or shown as an outline. The **TEXTFILL** system variable controls this appearance. The **TEXTFILL** default is 1, which draws filled fonts. A setting of 0 draws the font outlines.

Figure 8-24.
Character mapping for non-Roman and symbol fonts.

	A	B	C	D	E	F	G	H	I	J	K	L	M	N	O	P	Q	R	S	T	U	V	W	X	Y	Z
Greekc	Α	Β	Χ	Δ	Ε	Φ	Γ	Η	Ι	ϑ	Κ	Λ	Μ	Ν	Ο	Π	Θ	Ρ	Σ	Τ	Υ	∇	Ω	Ξ	Ψ	Ζ
Greeks	Α	Β	Χ	Δ	Ε	Φ	Γ	Η	Ι	ϑ	Κ	Λ	Μ	Ν	Ο	Π	Θ	Ρ	Σ	Τ	Υ	∇	Ω	Ξ	Ψ	Ζ
Syastro	⊙	☿	♀	⊕	♂	♃	♄	♅	Ψ	♇	☽	☌	✳	♌	♉	♈	♊	♋	♍	♎	♏	♐	♑	≈
Symap	○	□	△	◇	☆	+	×	∗	●	■	◢	◀	▼	▶	★	⊢	⊥	⊤	✳	✦	©	✿	△
Symath	א	'	|	‖	±	∓	×	·	÷	=	≠	≡	<	>	≤	≥	∝	∼	√	⊂	∪	⊃	∩	∈	→	↑
Symeteo	·	·	∗	▲	·	▲	∧	∩	∪	·	·	'	S	∼	∞	ℝ	6	—	/	|	\	⎯	/
Symusic	·	↘	♪	♩	○	○	●	#	♮	♭	⊢	—	×	╕	𝄞	𝄢	𝄆	·	·	---	⌐	∧	≂	▽

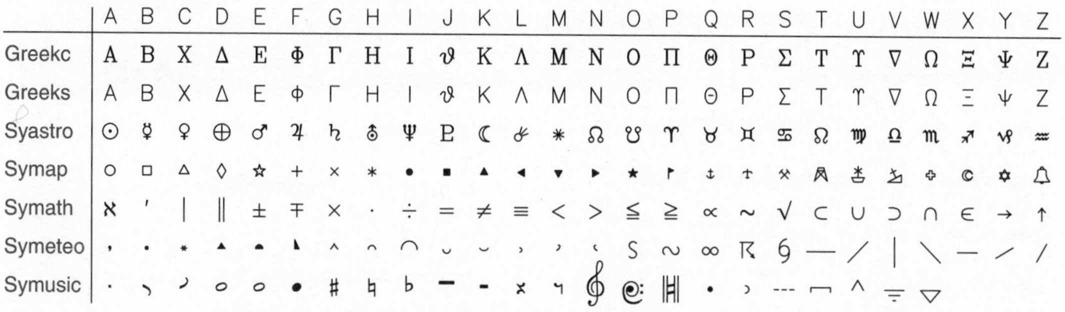

Samples of several TrueType fonts are shown in Figure 8-25. The architect's hand-lettered fonts Stylus BT is an excellent choice for the artistic appearance desired on architectural drawings. Try them and use the one you like the best.

Figure 8-25.
Some of the many TrueType fonts available.

Swiss 721

Regular

swissl (light)	abcdABCD12345
swissli (light italic)	abcdABCD12345
swiss (regular)	abcdABCD12345
swissi (italic)	abcdABCD12345
swissb (bold)	**abcdABCD1234**
swissbi (bold italic)	**abcdABCD12345**
swissk (black bold)	**abcdABCD12345**
swisski (black bold italic)	**abcdABCD12345**

Condensed

swisscl (light)	abcdABCD12345
swisscli (light italic)	abcdABCD12345
swissc (condensed)	abcdABCD12345
swissci (italic)	abcdABCD12345
swisscb (bold)	**abcdABCD12345**
swisscbi (bold italic)	**abcdABCD12345**
swissck (black bold)	**abcdABCD12345**
swisscki (black bold italic)	**abcdABCD12345**

Expanded

swissel (light)	abcdABCD12345
swisse (expanded)	abcdABCD12345
swisseb (bold)	**abcdABCD12345**
swissek (black bold)	**abcdABCD12345**

Outline

swissbo (bold)	abcdABCD12345
swissko (black)	abcdABCD12345
swisscbo (bold condensed)	abcdABCD12345

Monospace 821

monos (monospaced)	abcdABCD12345
monosi (italic)	abcdABCD12345
monosb (bold)	**abcdABCD12345**
monosbi (bold italic)	**abcdABCD12345**

Dutch 801 (serif)

Regular

dutch (regular)	abcdABCD12345
dutchi (italic)	abcdABCD12345
dutchb (bold)	**abcdABCD12345**
dutchbi (bold italic)	**abcdABCD12345**

Expanded

dutcheb (bold)	**abcdABCD12345**

Architect's Hand Lettered

stylus BT	abcdABCD12345

Bank Gothic (all caps)

bgothl (light)	ABCDABCD12345
bgothm (medium)	ABCDABCD12345

Commercial Script

comsc (regular)	abcdABCD12345

Vineta (shadow)

vinet (regular)	**abcdABCD12345**

Commercial Pi

compi (regular)	©®©® ± °'" ●●●-■■

Universal Math

umath (regular)	$\alpha\beta\psi\delta AB\Psi\Delta + - \times \div =$

TrueType and other complex text styles can be very taxing on system resources. This can slow down display changes and increase drawing regeneration time significantly. Use these styles only when necessary. When you must use complex text styles, set your system variables to speed optimized settings.

The **TEXTQLTY** system variable controls how text affects drawing display speeds. Lower values for this variable reduce display quality and speed up display changes. Significant speed increases result from a setting of 0.

AUTOCAD TEXT STYLES

AutoCAD User's Guide 11

Text styles are variations of fonts. A *text style* gives height, width, obliquing angle (slant), and other characteristics to a text font. You may have several text styles that use the same font, but with different characteristics. By default, the Standard text style uses the Txt font with 0.20 height, 0 degrees rotation angle, width of 1, and 0 degrees obliquing angle.

If the **Style** option of the **TEXT** or **DTEXT** command is selected, you can select a previously created text style:

```
Command: DT, TEXT, or DTEXT
Current text style: "Standard" Text height: 0.2000
Specify start point of text or [Justify/Style]: S↵
Enter style name or [?] <current>:
```

Enter the name of an existing style, type ? to see a list of styles, or press [Enter] to keep the existing style. After entering ?, you can type the specific text style(s) to list, or press [Enter] to display all the available text styles. The style name, font file, height, width factor, obliquing angle, and generation of each of the available text styles is then shown in the **AutoCAD Text Window**.

When you are using the **MTEXT** command, the available text styles are provided in the **Style** drop-down list of the **Properties** tab.

EXERCISE 8-5

❑ Start AutoCAD and use the setup option of your choice.
❑ Enter the **DTEXT** command and use the **Style** option to display the available text styles. Look through the list to see what is available. Press the [F2] key to return to the graphics window.
❑ Enter the **MTEXT** command and define a text boundary in order to open the **Multiline Text Editor**. Pick the **Properties** tab. Open the **Style** drop-down list and notice the list of available text styles.
❑ Exit AutoCAD or leave this drawing open for the next exercise.

Selecting and Modifying Text Styles

The **STYLE** command is used to create new text styles and modify or list existing text styles. A *text style* is a set of text characteristics, such as font, height, width, and obliquing angle. The **STYLE** command allows you to customize one of the available fonts to create a new text style.

Access the **STYLE** command by picking **Text Style...** from the **Format** pull-down menu, or by entering ST or STYLE at the Command: prompt. The **STYLE** command opens the **Text Style** dialog box, shown in Figure 8-26. The following describes the features found in this dialog box:

STYLE
ST

Format
➡ Text Style...

- **Style Name area.** Set a new current text style by making a selection from the drop-down list. Use the **New...** button to create a new text style and the **Rename...** button to rename a selected style. If you need to delete a style, use the **Delete** button.
- **Font area.** This area of the **Text Style** dialog box is where you select an available font, style of the selected font, and text height.
  - **Font Name.** This drop-down list is used to access the available fonts. The default font is txt.shx. All .shx fonts are identified with an AutoCAD symbol, while the TrueType fonts have the TrueType symbol.
  - **Font Style.** This drop-down list is inactive unless the selected font has options available, such as bold or italic. None of the .shx fonts have additional options, but some of the TrueType fonts may. For example, the SansSerif font has Regular, Bold, BoldOblique, and Oblique options. Each option provides the font with a different appearance.
  - **Height.** This text box is used to set the text height. The default is 0.0000. This allows you to set the text height in the **DTEXT** command. If you set a value such as .125, then the text height becomes fixed for this text style and you are not prompted for the text height. Setting a text height value other than zero saves time during the command process, but also eliminates your flexibility. ANSI recommended text heights were discussed earlier in this chapter.

Figure 8-26.
The **Text Style** dialog box is used to set the characteristics of a text style.

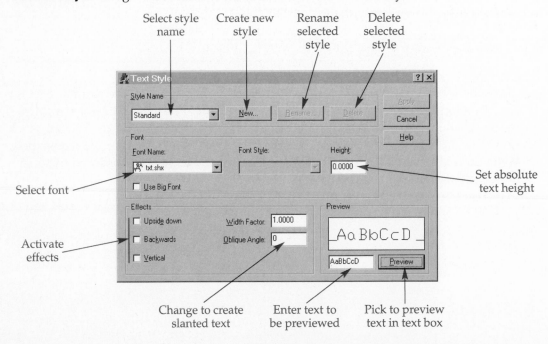

- **Use Big Font.** Asian and other large format fonts (called *Big Fonts*) are activated with this check box. The Big Font is used as a supplement to define many symbols not available in normal font files.
- **Effects area.** This area of the **Text Style** dialog box is used to set the text format. It contains the following options, which are shown in Figure 8-27:
  - **Upside down.** This check box is off by default. When it is checked, the text you draw is placed upside down.
  - **Backwards.** When the box is checked, text that you draw is placed backwards.
  - **Vertical.** This check box is inactive for all TrueType fonts. A check in this box makes .shx text vertical. Text on drawings is normally placed horizontally, but vertical text can be used for special effects and graphic designs. Vertical text works best when the rotation angle is 270°.

Figure 8-27.
Special effects for text styles can be set in the **Text Style** dialog box

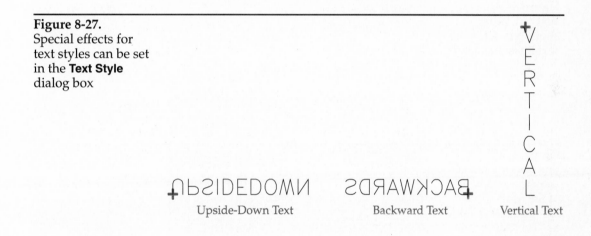

Upside-Down Text   Backward Text   Vertical Text

- **Width Factor.** This text box provides a value that defines the text character width relative to the height. A width factor of 1 is the default. A width factor greater than 1 expands the characters, and less than 1 compresses the characters. See Figure 8-28.

Figure 8-28.
Text width factors are set in the **Text Style** dialog box.

Width Factor	Text
1	ABCDEFGHIJKLM
.5	ABCDEFGHIJKLMNOPQRSTUVWXY
1.5	ABCDEFGHI
2	ABCDEFG

- **Obliquing Angle.** This text box allows you to set an angle at which text is slanted. The zero default draws characters vertically. A value greater than 0 slants the characters to the right, while a negative value slants characters to the left. See Figure 8-29. Some fonts, such as italic.shx, are already slanted.

PROFESSIONAL TIP

Some companies, especially in structural drafting, like to slant text 15° to the right. Also, water features named on maps often use text that is slanted to the right.

- **Preview area.** The image allows you to see how the selected font or style will appear. This is a very convenient way to see what the font looks like before using it in a new style. Figure 8-30 shows previews of various fonts. Specific characters can also be previewed. Simply type the characters in the text box and then pick the **Preview** button.

Figure 8-29.
Text obliquing angles are set in the **Text Style** dialog box.

Obliquing Angle	Text
0	ABCDEFGHIJKLM
15	*ABCDEFGHIJKLM*
–15	ABCDEFGHIJKLM

Figure 8-30.
The **Preview** image shows a sample of the font.
A—The Scripts font.
B—The Gothice font.
C—The Italic font.

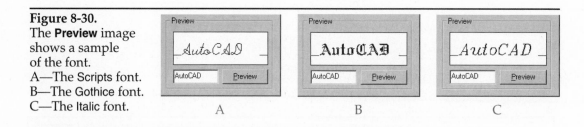

A   B   C

EXERCISE 8-6

❏ Start AutoCAD with the setup option of your choice.
❏ Open the **Text Style** dialog box.
❏ Access the **Style Name** drop-down list just to look through the available options. Select a few of the options that you want to see displayed in the preview image.
❏ Go to the **Font Name** drop-down list and select a few different fonts to see their image in the preview tile. Pick the SansSerif font and then open the **Font Style** drop-down list. Pick each of the options as you watch the preview image change to represent your selection.
❏ Turn the **Upside down** and **Backwards** check boxes on and then off while you watch the preview image.
❏ Change the width factor to 2, .5, and back to 1 while you watch the **Preview** image.
❏ Change the obliquing angle to 15, 30, –15, –30, and then back to 0 while you watch the **Preview** image.
❏ Type your own desired characters in the box to the left of the **Preview** button and then pick the button.
❏ Pick the **Close** button.
❏ Exit AutoCAD or leave this drawing open for the next exercise.

Creating a New Text Style

If you start a new drawing with the AutoCAD default template, the only text style that is available is the Standard style. The Standard text style is based on the txt font, which is not very attractive. This may not suit your needs.

What if you want to create a text style for mechanical drawings that uses the Romans font and characters .125 high? You want to have this available as the most commonly used text on your drawings. You decide to name the style ROMANS-125. This is a name that you can remember, because it uses Romans font characters that are .125" high. It is still a good idea to record the name and details about the text styles you create and keep this information in a log for future reference.

Text style names can have up to 255 characters, including letters, numbers, dashes (–), underlines (_), and dollar signs ($). You can enter uppercase or lowercase letters. The following explains the steps to use to create this text style:

1. Use the **STYLE** command to open the **Text Style** dialog box. Standard is the current style with txt.shx as the font, and a zero text height.
2. Pick the **New...** button. This opens the **New Text Style** dialog box, Figure 8-31A. Notice style1 is in the **Style Name** text box. You can keep a text style name like style1 or style2, but this is not descriptive. Type ROMANS-125 in the box and then pick the **OK** button. See Figure 8-31B. ROMANS-125 is now displayed in the **Style Name** text box of the **Text Style** dialog box.
3. Go to the **Font Name** drop-down list, find romans.shx, and pick it. The font is now romans.shx.
4. Change the value in the **Height** text box to .125. Figure 8-32 shows the work done in Steps 2, 3, and 4.
5. Pick the **Apply** button and then the **Close** button. The new ROMANS-125 text style is now part of your drawing.

Figure 8-31.
The **New Text Style** dialog box.
A—The default entry.
B—A new text style entered.

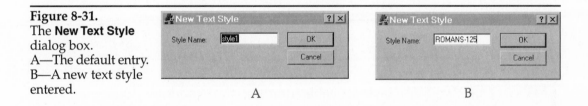

Figure 8-32.
The **Text Style** dialog box showing the changes in the style, font, and height.

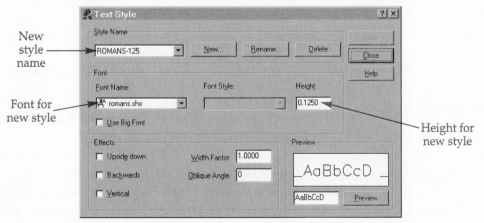

Now, ROMANS-125 is the default style when you use the **DTEXT** or **MTEXT** commands. If you want to create a similar text style for your architectural drawings, you might consider a style name called ARCHITECTURAL-125. For this style, set the font name to Stylus BT and the height to .125.

PROFESSIONAL TIP

You can make the text style name the same as the font name if you wish. In some cases, this is a clear and concise way of naming the style.

EXERCISE 8-7

❑ Start AutoCAD with the setup option of your choice.
❑ Open the **Text Style** dialog box with the **STYLE** command.
❑ Create a text style named ROMANS-125 if you commonly do mechanical drawings, or ARCHITECTURAL-125 if you commonly do architectural drawings.
❑ For ROMANS-125 set the font name to romans.shx and the height to .125.
❑ For ARCHITECTURAL-125 set the font name to Stylus BT and the height to .125.
❑ Pick the **Apply** button and then close the **Text Style** dialog box.
❑ Try out your new text style with the **DTEXT** and **MTEXT** commands.
❑ Create a text style named ROMANS if you commonly do mechanical drawings, or ARCHITECTURAL if you commonly do architectural drawings. For ROMANS set the font name to romans.shx and the height to 0. For ARCHITECTURAL set the font name to Stylus BT and the height to 0.
❑ Pick the **Apply** button and then close the **Text Style** dialog box.
❑ Try out your new text style with the **DTEXT** and **MTEXT** commands.
❑ Save the drawing as EX8-7.

PROFESSIONAL TIP

To save valuable drafting time, add text styles to your template drawings. If only a single text height is needed in the template, set the text height for the style.

Changing, Renaming, and Deleting Text Styles

You can change text style without affecting existing text objects. The changes are applied only to added text using that style.

Existing text styles are easily renamed in the **Text Style** dialog box. Select the desired style name in the **Style Name** text box and pick the **Rename...** button. This opens the **Rename Text Style** dialog box, which is similar to the **New Text Style** dialog box. Change the text style name in the **Style Name** text box and pick the **OK** button.

NOTE

Styles can also be renamed using the **Text styles** option of the **Rename** dialog box. This dialog box is accessed by selecting **Rename...** from the **Format** pull-down menu or by typing RENAME at the Command: prompt.

You can also delete an existing text style in the **Text Style** dialog box by picking the desired style name in the **Style Name** drop-down list followed by picking the **Delete** button. If you try to delete a text style that has been used to create text objects in the drawing, AutoCAD gives you the following message:

> Style is in use, can't be deleted.

This means that there are text objects in the drawing that reference this style. If you want to delete the style, change the text objects in the drawing to a different style. You cannot delete or rename the Standard style.

NOTE	If you change the font and orientation of an existing text style, all text items with that style are redrawn with the new values. This type of change causes an automatic regeneration if the **REGENAUTO** mode is on.

Importing Text Styles from Existing Drawings

The **AutoCAD DesignCenter** can be used to import text styles from existing drawing files. **DesignCenter** allows you to browse through drawing files to find desired text styles then add the needed style into your current drawing file. For a complete introduction to the **AutoCAD DesignCenter**, see Chapter 1.

The **AutoCAD DesignCenter** can be accessed by picking the **AutoCAD DesignCenter** button on the **Standard** toolbar, selecting **AutoCAD DesignCenter** from the **Tools** pull-down menu, typing ADC or ADCENTER at the Command: prompt, or using the [Ctrl]+[2] key combination. See Figure 8-33.

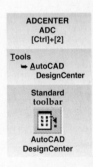

The following procedure is used to import a text style into the current drawing:
1. In the tree view area, locate the existing drawing containing the text style to be copied.
2. Double-click on the file name or pick the minus (–) sign next to it to list the various types of content within the drawing.
3. Pick the Textstyles content in the tree view. This displays the text styles in the palette.
4. Select the text style or text styles to be copied into the drawing. You can then copy the text style in any of the following ways:
   - **Drag and drop.** Move the cursor over the top of the desired text style(s) in the palette, press and hold the pick button on your pointing device, and drag the cursor to the opened drawing. Let go of the pick button and the text style(s) is added to your current drawing file.

Figure 8-33.
The **AutoCAD DesignCenter** allows you to copy a text style from an existing drawing into the current drawing.

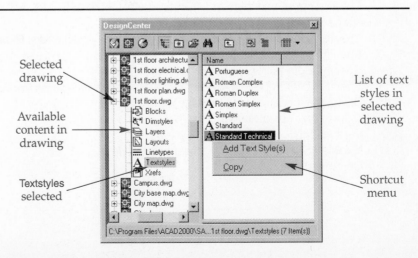

- **Shortcut menu.** Position the cursor over the desired text style in the palette and right-click to open the shortcut menu. See Figure 8-33. Pick the **Add Text Style(s)** option, and the text style is added to your current drawing.
- **Copy and paste.** Use the shortcut menu as described in the previous method, but select the **Copy** option. Move the cursor to the drawing where you want the text style added, then right-click your mouse button and select the **Paste** option from the shortcut menu. The copied text style is added to the current drawing.

PROFESSIONAL TIP To select more than one text style at one time to import into your current drawing file, hold down the [Shift] key and pick the first and last text styles in a group of text styles, or hold down the [Ctrl] key to select multiple text styles individually.

EXERCISE 8-8

❑ Start a new drawing and create four text styles. Save this drawing as EX8-8a and close the drawing.
❑ Open a drawing you created in an earlier chapter that contains only the Standard text style.
❑ Use the **AutoCAD DesignCenter** to insert text styles into the current drawing from EX8-8a by following these instructions:
  ❑ Insert one text style at a time, using each of the three methods to insert each text style.
  ❑ Insert two text styles at the same time. If a duplicate insertion of text styles is inserted, AutoCAD ignores this duplication by giving you this message: Textstyle(s) added. Duplicate definitions will be ignored.
  ❑ Insert all four text styles at the same time.
❑ Save the exercise as EX8-8.

Creating a Text Style at the Prompt Line

A new text style can be created at the prompt line by using the **-STYLE** command. That is a dash (-) entered before STYLE. Everything is done at the prompt line. You may recognize the following prompts from what you have already learned:

```
Command: -STYLE↵
Enter name of text style or [?] <Standard>: ROMANS-125.↵
New style.
Specify full font name or font filename (TTF or SHX) <txt>: ROMANS.↵
Specify height of text <0.0000>: .125↵
Specify width factor <1.0000>: ↵
Specify obliquing angle <0>: ↵
Display text backwards? [Yes/No] <N>: ↵
Display text upside-down? [Yes/No] <N>: ↵
Vertical? <N>: ↵
"ROMANS-125" is now the current text style.
Command:
```

SPECIAL CHARACTERS

Many drafting applications require special symbols for text and dimensions. There are different methods for entering special characters, depending on if you are creating single-line text objects using the **TEXT** or **DTEXT** commands. Drawing symbols when using the **MTEXT** command was explained earlier in this chapter.

In order to draw symbols, AutoCAD requires a control code. The *control code sequence* for a symbol begins with two percent signs (%%). The next character you enter represents the symbol. These control codes are used for single-line text objects that are generated with the **TEXT** or **DTEXT** commands. The following list gives the most popular control code sequences:

Control Code	Description	Symbol
%%D	Degrees symbol	°
%%P	Plus/minus sign	±
%%C	Diameter symbol	Ø

For example, in order to add the note Ø2.75, the control sequence %%C2.75 is used. See Figure 8-34A.

A single percent sign can be added normally. However, when a percent sign must precede another control sequence, %%% can be used to force a single percent sign. For example, suppose you want to type the note 25%±2%. You must enter 25%%%%P2%.

Drawing Underscored or Overscored Text

Text can be underscored (underlined) or overscored by typing a control sequence in front of the line of text. The control sequences are:

    %%O = overscore
    %%U = underscore

For example, the note <u>UNDERSCORING TEXT</u> must be entered as %%UUNDER-SCORING TEXT. The resulting text is shown in Figure 8-34B. A line of text may require both underscoring and overscoring. For example, the control sequence %%O%%ULINE OF TEXT produces the note with both underscore and overscore.

The %%O and %%U control codes are toggles that turn overscoring and underscoring on and off. Type %%U preceding a word or phrase to turn underscoring on. Type %%U after the desired word or phrase to turn underscoring off. Any text following the second %%U then appears without underscoring. For example, <u>DETAIL A</u> HUB ASSEMBLY would be entered as %%UDETAIL A%%U HUB ASSEMBLY.

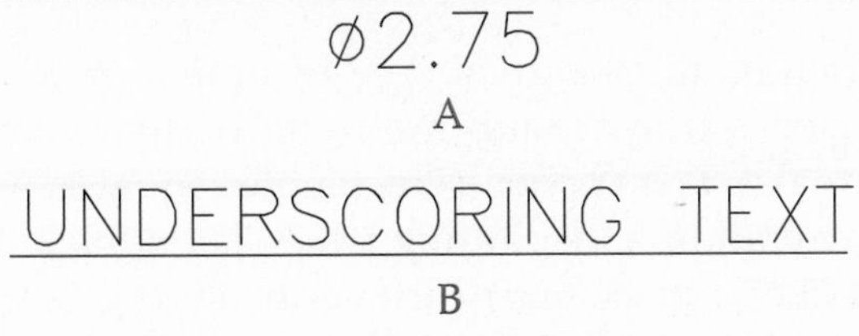

Figure 8-34.
A—The control sequence %%C creates the Ø (diameter) symbol. B—The control sequence %%U underscores text.

Ø2.75

A

<u>UNDERSCORING TEXT</u>

B

Many drafters prefer to underline view labels such as <u>SECTION A-A</u> or <u>DETAIL B</u>. Rather than draw line or polyline objects under the text, use **Middle** or **Center** justification modes and underscoring. The view labels are automatically underlined and centered under the views or details they identify.

Entering Special Characters Using the Unicode System

AutoCAD 2000 supports the Unicode character encoding standard. A *Unicode* font can have up to 65,535 separate characters in a font file, with figures for many different languages. This standard provides support for these languages by allowing the use of characters that are not found on the keyboard. The Unicode standard is active when using either the **MTEXT** or **DTEXT** command.

The Unicode special characters are accessed by typing what is called an *escape sequence*. The prefix \U+ is followed by a four-digit hexadecimal number identifying the symbol. A *hexadecimal* number is a base 16 number, rather than base 10. For example, \U+2205 is the escape sequence for entering a diameter symbol. The following are some examples that are commonly used in drafting technology:

Unicode	Description	Symbol	Example
\U+2205	Diameter symbol	⌀	\U+2205.750 = ⌀.750
\U+00B0	Degree symbol	°	45\U+00B0 = 45°
\U+00B1	Plus/minus symbol	±	2.625\U+00B1.005 = 2.625±.005

EXERCISE 8-9

❏ Start AutoCAD and use the setup option of your choice.
❏ Use the **DTEXT** command and control codes to type the following:

    45°
    1.375±.005
    ⌀3.875
    79%
    <u>UNDERSCORING TEXT</u>

❏ Save the drawing as EX8-9.

AutoCAD User's Guide 8

REDRAWING TEXT QUICKLY

Text often requires a great deal of time to regenerate, redraw, and plot because each character is drawn with many individual vectors (line segments). The Quick Text mode makes text appear as rectangles equal to the height of each text string. This speeds regeneration and plotting time. The Quick Text mode is turned on and off with the **QTEXT** (quick text) command. Figure 8-35 shows a comparison between displays when the Quick Text mode is on and off.

QTEXT

The **QTEXT** command is entered at the Command: prompt. If the last setting was off, the command line appears as follows:

Command: **QTEXT**↵
Enter mode [ON/OFF] <Off>:

Figure 8-35.
Comparison of
Quick Text mode
turned on and off.

Quick Text Mode On

THE QUICK TEXT MODE IS USED TO
SPEED REGENERATION TIME IN
COMPLEX DRAWINGS.

Quick Text Mode Off

Enter ON to activate Quick Text mode and quicken the redraw time. This mode can also be activated by selecting the **Show text boundary frame only** option in the **Display performance** area of the **Display** tab of the **Options** dialog box. This dialog box can be accessed by selecting **Options…** from the **Tools** pull-down menu.

REVISING TEXT WITH DDEDIT

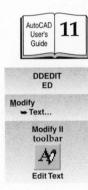

AutoCAD
User's
Guide **11**

DDEDIT
ED

Modify
➥ Text…

Modify II
toolbar

Edit Text

Text editing is accomplished using the **DDEDIT** command. **DDEDIT** is accessed by picking **Text…** in the **Modify** pull-down menu, entering ED or DDEDIT at the Command: prompt, or selecting the **Edit Text** button on the **Modify II** toolbar. The DDEDIT command can also be accessed by selecting the text object, right-clicking, and selecting **Mtext Edit…** or **Text Edit…** from the shortcut menu.

When editing text, AutoCAD first asks you to select an annotation object—any text, leader, or dimension object. If you pick single-line text that was drawn with the **TEXT** or **DTEXT** commands, you get the **Edit Text** dialog box, Figure 8-36. If you pick text that was drawn with the **MTEXT** command, you get the **Multiline Text Editor**. Multiline text is also drawn with the **LEADER** command, which is explained in Chapter 18.

When editing text in either dialog box, if you press [Delete] or [Backspace], the highlighted text disappears and you can enter new text. Pressing the key combination [Ctrl]+[V] to paste the contents of the Clipboard will replace the highlighted text with the new text. If you make a mistake, use the editing keys or press **Cancel** and pick the desired text again. Move the cursor arrow inside the **Text:** text box and pick to remove the highlight around the text. Use the left and right arrow keys to move through the entire line of text, and access the portion of the text that is hidden beyond the limits of the text box. Edit the line of text shown in Figure 8-37 following this procedure:

1. Notice the word inTERPRET should read INTERPRET. To see the beginning of the text, press [Home]. Use the cursor to highlight the letters in by picking and dragging the cursor through the text.
2. Type IN.
3. Notice the word DEMENSIONS is misspelled. Press [Ctrl]+[→] to move to the start of DEMENSIONS. Press [→] once and press [Delete] to delete the E. Now, type in an I, as shown in Figure 8-37B.

Figure 8-36.
The **DDEDIT** command
activates the **Edit Text**
dialog box if the
selected text object
was created with the
DTEXT command.

Edit Text	? X
Text:	This text was created with the DTEXT command.
	OK Cancel Help

Figure 8-37.
Highlight the text
you want to replace.
Then, type the
revised text.

1. inTERPRET DEMENSIONS AND TOLERANCES PER ASME Y14.5–1994
2. REMOVE ALL BURRS AND SHARP EDGES
3. ALL FILLETS AND ROUNDS R.125

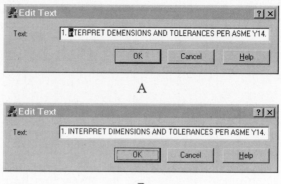

A

B

4. Pick **OK** or press [Enter] to accept the text changes. The revised text is then displayed on your drawing.
5. Press [Enter] or [Esc] to exit the **DDEDIT** command, or enter U to undo the editing if you made a mistake.

NOTE

The examples used in this discussion show how to use the **Edit Text** dialog box to make changes in your text. Spelling is conveniently checked using the **SPELL** command, which is explained later in this chapter.

Editing Techniques

Although it is recommended that you enter text as carefully as possible initially, there are times when you must revise text. The following techniques can be used to help edit text with the **DDEDIT** command:

- **Highlighting in the Text: text box.** Text can be highlighted by moving the cursor arrow to the desired text and picking. Hold the pick button down while you move the cursor across the text to be highlighted. Release the pick button when you have highlighted all of the intended text. If you desire to highlight a single word, move your cursor to the desired word and double-click on it.
- **Removing highlighting in the Text: text box.** Press the [Spacebar], [Delete], or [Backspace] to remove highlighted text.
- **Moving around inside the Text: text box.** Move the cursor arrow inside the **Text:** text box and pick. Then use [←] to move the cursor to the left or [→] to move the cursor to the right.
- **Inserting text.** Type any desired text at the text cursor location. This inserts new text and shifts all existing text to the right.
- **[Backspace].** Pressing [Backspace] when text is not highlighted removes text to the left of the text cursor and moves the text at the right along with the text cursor.
- **Space bar.** Pressing the space bar when text is not highlighted moves all of the text to the right of the text cursor.
- **[←] (left arrow).** Moves the text cursor to the left.
- **[→] (right arrow).** Moves the text cursor to the right.
- **[Ctrl]+[X].** Deletes the entire string of highlighted text.

AutoCAD and its Applications—Basics

❏ Start AutoCAD and use the setup option of your choice.
❏ Use the **DTEXT** command to place the following text:

    3068 SOLID CORE PANELED ENTRY DOOR SC306 ACME DOOR CO.

❏ Use the **DDEDIT** command to change the text to read:

    3'-0" × 6'-8" STEEL FRAME PANELED ENTRY DOOR ER44 CECO ENTRY SYSTEMS.

❏ Turn the Quick Text mode on, then off. Observe the results. Do not forget to use **REGEN** to change the display.
❏ Save the drawing as EX8-10.

CHANGING TEXT WITH PROPERTIES

The **Properties** window can be used to change text. The **Properties** window can be opened by picking the **Properties** button on the **Standard** toolbar, selecting **Properties** from the **Modify** pull-down menu, or typing CH, MO, PROPS, or PROPERTIES at the Command: prompt. You can also open the **Properties** window by selecting the desired text and then right-clicking and selecting **Properties** from the shortcut menu.

You have two options for selecting text to change. You can select the desired text and then display the **Properties** window, or you can display the **Properties** window and then select the desired text. If you display the **Properties** window first, you may need to move the window before you can select the text (if the window covers the text you want to pick). Either way, the **Properties** window is opened, as shown in Figure 8-38.

> PROPERTIES
> CH
> MO
> PROPS
>
> Modify
> ➡ Properties
>
> Standard
> toolbar
>
> Properties

For 2000i Users...

In AutoCAD 2000i, double-click on a text object and the **Properties** window opens automatically.

Figure 8-38.
The **Properties** window shows the properties of the selected text. Note that the properties of text created with the **TEXT** or **DTEXT** command are slightly different than the properties of text created with the **MTEXT** command.

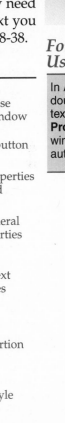

Type of object selected

Pick to close **Properties** window

Quick Select button

Select how properties are listed

Change general object properties

Change text properties

Change insertion point

Change style effects

Notice the top of the window displays Text in the box. This informs you that a text object has been selected. If multiple objects are selected, the drop-down list is used to select which object has its properties displayed.

The **Quick Select** button accesses the **Quick Select** dialog box, which is used for object selection. The **Quick Select** dialog box is discussed in Chapter 7.

The properties of the text object can be displayed on either of the two tabs in the **Properties** window. The **Categorized** tab separates the properties into specific categories. The **Alphabetic** tab lists the properties alphabetically. However, both tabs display the same properties. When the **Categorized** tab is selected, properties are divided into the following categories:

- **General.** These general properties are found in nearly all AutoCAD object types. The general properties include color, layer, linetype, linetype scale, plot style, lineweight, hyperlink, and thickness.
- **Text.** Text properties are common to text and mtext objects. These properties were explained earlier in this chapter.
- **Geometry.** The geometry properties are the X, Y, and Z coordinate of the text insertion point.
- **Misc.** The miscellaneous properties are the **Upside down** and **Backward** effects. These properties are not listed for multiline text objects.

To change a property, pick the property or property setting with the cursor. The property setting can then be edited. For some properties, a pull-down can be used to select other settings. See Figure 8-39.

After you make the desired changes to your text, pick the "X" in the upper-right corner to close the **Properties** window. Then press the [Esc] key twice to deselect the text.

The **Properties** window can also be used to change multiline text. When you select the multiline text to change, the **Properties** window appears with MText identified as the selected object, as shown in Figure 8-40. The properties listed are similar to those listed for a text object. The properties that differ for the two objects are described below:

- **Contents.** Allows you to edit the content or pick the button at the right to open the **Multiline Text Editor**.
- **Direction.** Allows you to specify the horizontal or vertical direction of the multiline text object.
- **Width.** Allows you to specify the width of the multiline text object.
- **Line Space Factor.** Allows you to specify the line spacing factor of the multiline text object.
- **Line Space Style.** Allows you to specify the line spacing style of the multiline text object.

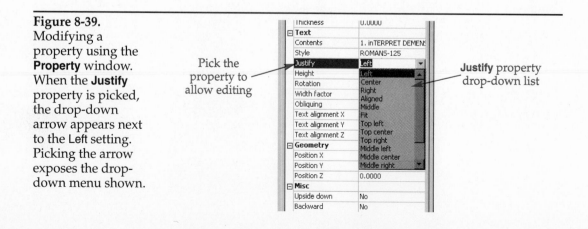

Figure 8-39.
Modifying a property using the **Property** window. When the **Justify** property is picked, the drop-down arrow appears next to the Left setting. Picking the arrow exposes the drop-down menu shown.

Pick the property to allow editing

Justify property drop-down list

AutoCAD and its Applications—Basics

Figure 8-40.
The **Properties** window with an mtext object selected. Note that the list of properties is slightly different than the list for a text object.

Selected object type

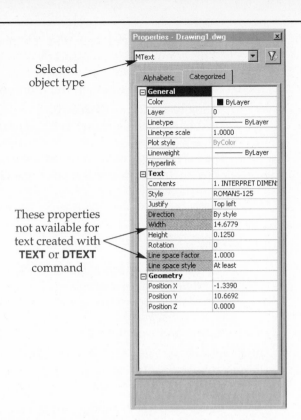

These properties not available for text created with **TEXT** or **DTEXT** command

---

The **CHANGE** command can also be used to modify text objects. This command is accessed by entering -CH or CHANGE at the Command: prompt. Selecting a text object created with the **DTEXT** command results in the following prompts:

Command: **-CH** *or* **CHANGE**↵
Select objects: *(pick text to be changed)*
Select objects: ↵
Specify change point or [Properties]: ↵
Specify new text insertion point <no change>: *(pick a new text location)*
Enter new text style <*existing*>: *(type a new style or accept default)*
Specify new height <*existing*>: *(type a new height or accept default)*
Specify new rotation angle <*existing*>: *(type a new rotation angle or accept default)*
Enter new text <*selected text string*>: *(type a new text or accept default)*
Command:

Text properties can also be changed with the **CHANGE** command. At the Specify change point or [Properties]: prompt, enter P for properties. You will receive the following prompt:

Enter property to change [Color/Elev/LAyer/LType/ltScale/LWeight/Thickness]:

Enter the property you wish to change.

The **CHANGE** command cannot be used to specify a new insertion point for text created with the **MTEXT** command. Also, the thickness and elevation of **MTEXT** objects cannot be changed with this command.

CHECKING YOUR SPELLING

You have been introduced to editing text on the drawing using the **DDEDIT** command and the **Properties** window. You can use these methods to change lines of text and even correct spelling errors. However, AutoCAD has a powerful and convenient tool for checking the spelling on your drawing.

To check spelling, enter SP or SPELL at the Command: prompt or pick **Spelling** from the **Tools** pull-down menu. After entering the command, you are asked to select the text to be checked. You need to pick each line of single-line text or make one pick on multiline text to select the entire paragraph.

The **Check Spelling** dialog box is displayed. See Figure 8-41. The following describes the features found in the **Check Spelling** dialog box:

- **Current dictionary: American English.** The dictionary being used is identified at the top of the dialog box. You can change to a different dictionary by picking the **Change Dictionaries...** button.
- **Current word.** Displays a word that may be spelled incorrectly.
- **Suggestions.** Gives you a list of possible correct spellings for the current word. The highlighted word in the first box is AutoCAD's best guess. Following the highlighted word is a list of other choices. If there are many choices, the scroll bar is available for you to use. If you do not like the word that AutoCAD has highlighted, move the cursor arrow to another word and pick it. The word

Figure 8-41.
The **Check Spelling** dialog box.

Word being questioned

Suggested replacements

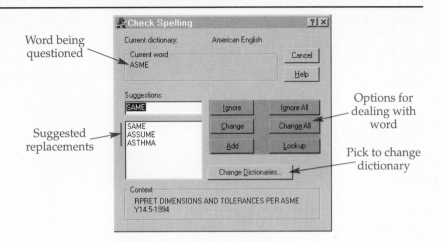

Options for dealing with word

Pick to change dictionary

you pick then becomes highlighted in the list and is shown in the **Suggestions** text box.

- **Ignore.** Pick this button to skip the current word. In Figure 8-41, ASME is not a misspelled word, it just is not recognized by the dictionary. You would select the **Ignore** button and the spell check goes on to the next word.
- **Ignore All.** Pick this button if you want AutoCAD to ignore all words that match the current word.
- **Change.** Pick this button to replace the **Current word** with the word in the **Suggestions** text box.
- **Change All.** Pick this button if you want to replace the **Current word** with the word in the **Suggestions** text box throughout the entire selection set.
- **Add.** Pick this button to add the current word to the custom dictionary. You can add words with up to 63 characters.
- **Lookup.** This button asks AutoCAD to check the spelling of the word you enter in the **Suggestions** text box.
- **Context.** At the bottom of the dialog box, AutoCAD displays the line of text where the current word was found.

Changing Dictionaries

AutoCAD provides you with several dictionaries: one American English, two British English, and two French. There are also dictionaries available for 24 different languages. Pick the **Change Dictionaries...** button to access the **Change Dictionary** dialog box. See Figure 8-42.

The areas of the **Change Dictionary** dialog box are as follows:

- **Main dictionary area.** This is where you can select one of the many language dictionaries to use as the current dictionary. To change the main dictionary, pick the down arrow to access the drop-down list. Next, pick the desired language dictionary from the list. The main dictionary is protected and cannot be added to.
- **Custom dictionary area.** This displays the name of the current custom dictionary, sample.cus by default. You can create your own custom dictionary by entering a new file name with a .cus extension. Words can be added or deleted and dictionaries can be combined using any standard text editor. If you use a word processor such as Microsoft Word or WordPerfect, be sure to save the file as *text only*, with no special text formatting or printer codes.

Figure 8-42.
The **Change Dictionaries** dialog box.

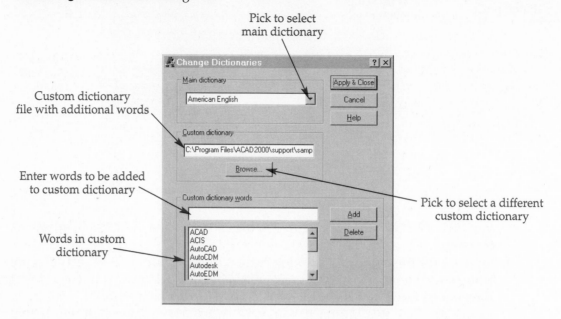

Pick to select
main dictionary

Custom dictionary
file with additional words

Enter words to be added
to custom dictionary

Pick to select a different
custom dictionary

Words in custom
dictionary

PROFESSIONAL TIP

You can create custom dictionaries for various disciplines. For example, when in a mechanical drawing, common abbreviations and brand names might be added to a mech.cus file. A separate file named arch.cus might contain common architectural abbreviations and frequently used brand names.

- **Browse....** Pick this button to access the **Select Custom Dictionary** dialog box.
- **Custom dictionary words area.** Type a word in the text box that you either want to add or delete from the custom dictionary. For example, ASME Y14.5M is custom text used in engineering drafting. Pick the **Add** button to accept the custom word in the text box, or pick the **Delete** button to remove the word from the custom dictionary. Custom dictionary entries may be up to 32 characters in length.

NOTE

The current main and custom dictionaries are stored in the **DCTMAIN** and **DCTCUST** system variables, respectively.

EXERCISE 8-12

❑ Start AutoCAD and use the setup option of your choice.
❑ Use the **MTEXT** command to type a short paragraph of your own choice with spelling errors.
❑ Check the spelling and correct the misspelled words.
❑ Save as EX8-12.

FINDING AND REPLACING TEXT

You can use the **SPELL** command to check and correct the spelling of text in a drawing. If you want to find a piece of text in your drawing and replace it with an alternative piece of text in a single instance or throughout your drawing, you should use the **FIND** command.

To find a string of text in the drawing, enter FIND at the command prompt, pick **Find...** from the **Edit** pull-down menu, or pick the **Find and Replace** button on the **Standard** toolbar. After you enter the command, AutoCAD displays the **Find and Replace** dialog box shown in Figure 8-43.

The **Find and Replace** dialog box contains the following elements:

- **Find text string.** Specify the text string that you want to find in this text box. Enter a string, or choose one of the six most recently used strings from the drop-down list.
- **Replace with.** Specify the text string you want to replace the found text in this text box. Enter a string, or choose one of the most recently used strings from the drop-down list.
- **Search in.** Specify whether to search the entire drawing or only the current selection. If there is a current selection set, **Current selection** is the default value. If there is no current selection set, **Entire drawing** is the default value. Picking the **Select Objects** button closes the dialog box temporarily for you to select objects in your drawing. Press [Enter] to return to the dialog box.
- **Options....** This button displays the **Find and Replace Options** dialog box, in which you can define the type of objects and words that you want to find. See Figure 8-44. The following options are available:
  - **Include area.** This area allows you to specify the type of objects you want to include in the search. By default, all options are selected.
  - **Match Case.** This check box allows you to include the case of the text in **Find text string** as part of the search criteria.
  - **Find Whole Words Only.** This check box allows you to find only whole words that match the text in **Find text string**.

Figure 8-43.
The **Find and Replace** dialog box.

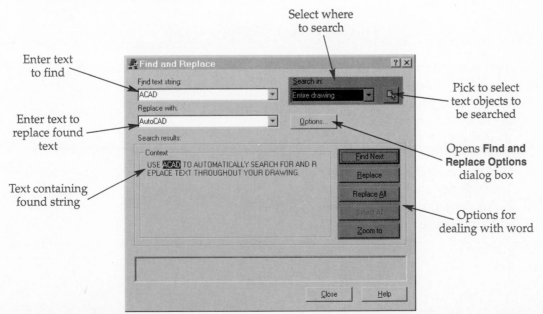

Figure 8-44.
The **Find and Replace Options** dialog box.

Select search options

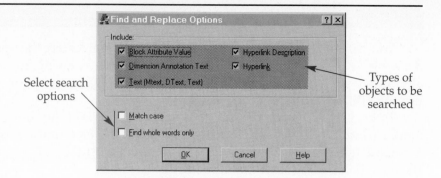

Types of objects to be searched

- **Context.** This area displays and highlights the currently found text string in its surrounding context. If you choose **Find Next**, AutoCAD refreshes the **Context** area and displays the next found text string in its surrounding context.
- **Find/Find Next.** This button allows you to find the text that you enter in **Find text string**. Once you find the first instance of the text, the **Find** button becomes **Find Next** button, which you can use to find the next instance.
- **Replace.** This button allows you to replace found text with the text entered in the **Replace with** text box.
- **Replace All.** This button allows you to find all instances of the text entered in the **Find text string** text box and replace all occurrences with the text in the **Replace with** text box.
- **Select All.** This button allows you to find and select all loaded objects containing instances of the text in **Find text string** text box. This option is available only when searching the **Current selection**. When you choose this button, the dialog box closes and AutoCAD displays a message indicating the number of objects found and selected.
- **Zoom to.** Picking this button displays the area in the drawing that contains the found text.

NOTE

The find and replace strings are saved with the drawing file and may be reused.

ADDITIONAL TEXT TIPS

Text presentation is important on any drawing. It is a good idea to plan your drawing using rough sketches to allow room for text and notes. Some things to consider when designing the drawing layout include:
- ✓ Placement of the views.
- ✓ Arrange text to avoid crowding.
- ✓ Place related notes in groups to make the drawing easy to read.
- ✓ Place all general notes in a common location. Locate notes in the lower-left corner or above the title block when using ANSI standards. Place notes in the upper-left corner when using military standards.
- ✓ Always use the spell checker.

         AutoCAD and its Applications—Basics

Chapter Test

Answer the following questions on a separate sheet of paper.

1. Give the command and inputs required to use the **DTEXT** command to display the following text string: IT IS FAST AND EASY TO DRAW TEXT USING AUTOCAD. The text must be .375 units high, have the default txt font, and fit between two points:
   A. Command: _____
   B. Specify start point of text or [Justify/Style]: _____
   C. Enter an option [Align/Fit/Center/Middle/Right/TL/TC/TR/ML/MC/MR/BL/BC/BR]: _____
   D. Specify first endpoint of text baseline: _____
   E. Specify second endpoint of text baseline: _____
   F. Specify height: _____
   G. Enter text: _____
2. How do you turn on the Quick Text mode if it is currently off using the Command: prompt?
3. List three ways to access the **DTEXT** command.
4. Give the letter you must enter for the following justification options when using the **DTEXT** command:
   A. Left-justified text.
   B. Right-justified text.
   C. Text between two points without regard for text height.
   D. Center the text horizontally and vertically.
   E. Text between two points with a fixed height.
   F. Center text along a baseline.
   G. Top and left horizontal.
   H. Middle and right horizontal.
   I. Bottom and center horizontal.
5. List the **DTEXT** command **Justify** options.
6. How would you specify a text style with a double width factor?
7. How would you specify a text style with a 15° angle?
8. How would you specify vertical text?
9. Give the control sequence required to draw the following symbols when using the **DTEXT** command:
   A. 30°
   B. 1.375 ±.005
   C. Ø24
   D. NOT FOR CONSTRUCTION
10. Why use the Quick Text mode rather than have the actual text displayed on the screen?
11. When setting text height in the **STYLE** command, what value do you enter so text height can be altered each time the **DTEXT** command is used?
12. List a command that lets you alter the location, style, height, and wording of existing single-line text.
13. Identify the command used to revise existing single-line text on the drawing by using the **Edit Text** dialog box.
14. When editing single-line text, how do you remove the character located in front of the text cursor?
15. When using the **Edit Text** dialog box, how do you move the text cursor to the left without removing text characters?
16. When using the **Edit Text** dialog box, how do you remove all of the text to the right of the text cursor?
17. When editing text in the **Text** text box, the flashing vertical bar is called the _____.

18. Determine the AutoCAD text height for text to be plotted .188″ high using a half (1″ = 2″) scale. (Show your calculations.)

19. Determine the AutoCAD text height for text to be plotted .188″ high using a scale of 1/4″ = 1′-0″. (Show your calculations.)

20. What would you do if you just completed editing a line of text and discovered you made a mistake? Assume you are still in the **Edit Text** dialog box.

21. Identify two ways to move around inside the **Text:** box of the **Edit Text** dialog box.

22. What happens when you press the space bar or the [Backspace] key when the text inside the **Text:** text box is highlighted?

23. What happens when you press [Ctrl]+[X] when the text within the **Text:** text box is highlighted?

24. Name the command that lets you make multiline text objects.

25. How does the width of the multiline text boundary affect what you type?

26. What happens if the multiline text that you are entering exceeds or is not as long as the boundary length that you initially establish?

27. What happens when you pick the first corner followed by the other corner of the multiline text boundary?

28. Name the command that you enter if you want to enter multiline text at the prompt line rather than in a text editor.

29. Name two commands that allow you to edit multiline text.

30. How are fractions drawn when using the **DTEXT** command?

31. How do you draw stacked fractions when using the **MTEXT** command?

32. What is the keyboard shortcut for the **DTEXT** command?

33. What does a width factor of .5 do to the text when compared with the default width factor of 1?

34. What do you get when using the **DDEDIT** command on multiline text?

35. What is the keyboard shortcut for the **MTEXT** command?

36. How do you move the text cursor down one line at a time in the **Multiline Text Editor**?

37. What happens when you pick the **Other...** option in the **Symbol** list of the **Character** tab of the **Multiline Text Editor**?

38. Name the internal storage area that temporarily stores information that you copy or cut from a document.

39. When you are in the **Multiline Text Editor**, how do you open the **Edit text** shortcut menu?

40. What is the purpose of the **Width** drop-down list found in the **Properties** tab of the **Multiline Text Editor**?

41. Describe how to find a word or words in a text object and have the word or words replaced with another word or words.

42. Describe how you would create a text style that has the name ROMANS-125_15, uses the romans.shx font, has a fixed height of .125, a text width of 1.25, and an obliquing angle of 15.

43. Name the feature that allows you to move the cursor over the top of the desired text style, in the **AutoCAD DesignCenter**, hold down the pick button, and drag the cursor to the opened drawing.

44. Identify and briefly describe two methods that can be used to import an existing text style from the **DesignCenter** to another drawing when you right-click over the desired text style.

45. Describe the two methods that can be used to select more than one text style at a time to import into your drawing from the **AutoCAD DesignCenter**.

46. Identify three ways to access the AutoCAD spell checker.

47. What is the purpose of the word found in the **Current word** box of the **Check Spelling** dialog box?

48. How do you change the **Current word** if you do not think the word that is displayed in the **Suggestions:** text box of the **Check Spelling** dialog box is the correct word, but one of the words in the list of suggestions is the correct word?
49. What is the purpose of the **Add** button in the **Check Spelling** dialog box?
50. How do you change the main dictionary for use in the **Check Spelling** dialog box?
51. Outline at least five steps that are used to create a new text style with the **Text Style** dialog box.
52. Identify at least four different ways to open the **Properties** window, including all keyboard shortcuts.
53. Describe two ways to select text objects to change when using the **Properties** window.
54. How do you change the text layer in the **Properties** window?
55. Explain how to edit text in the **Properties** window.
56. Name the command that allows you to find a piece of text and replace it with an alternative piece of text in a single instance or for every instance in your drawing.

Drawing Problems

1. Start AutoCAD, use the setup option of your choice, and create text styles as needed. Use the **TEXT** or **DTEXT** command to type the following information. Change the text style to represent each of the four fonts named. Use a .25 unit text height and 0° rotation angle. Save the drawing as P8-1.

   > TXT–AUTOCAD'S DEFAULT TEXT FONT WHICH IS AVAILABLE FOR USE WHEN YOU BEGIN A DRAWING.
   > ROMANS–SMOOTHER THAN TXT FONT AND CLOSELY DUPLICATES THE SINGLE-STROKE LETTERING THAT HAS BEEN THE STANDARD FOR DRAFTING.
   > ROMANC–A MULTISTROKE DECORATIVE FONT THAT IS GOOD FOR USE IN DRAWING TITLES
   > ITALICC–AN ORNAMENTAL FONT SLANTED TO THE RIGHT AND HAVING THE SAME LETTER DESIGN AS THE COMPLEX FONT.

2. Start AutoCAD and use the setup option of your choice and create text styles as needed. Change the options as noted in each line of text. Then use the **DTEXT** command to type the text, changing the text style to represent each of the four fonts named. Use a .25 unit text height. Save the drawing as P8-2.

   > TXT–EXPAND THE WIDTH BY THREE.
   > MONOTXT–SLANT TO THE LEFT –30°.
   > ROMANS–SLANT TO THE RIGHT 30°.
   > ROMAND–BACKWARDS.
   > ROMANC–VERTICAL.
   > ITALICC–UNDERSCORED AND OVERSCORED.
   > ROMANS–USE 16d NAILS @ 10" OC.
   > ROMANT–⌀32 (812.8).

3. Start AutoCAD and use the setup option of your choice. Create text styles with a .375 height with the following font: Arial, BankGothic LtBT, CityBlueprint, Stylus BT, Swis 721 BdOul BT, Vineta BT, Wingdings. Use the **DTEXT** command to type the complete alphabet and numbers 1–10 for the text fonts, all symbols available on the keyboard, and the diameter, degree, and plus/minus symbol. Save the drawing as P8-3.

4. Use the **MTEXT** command to type the following text using a text style with Romans font and .125 text height. The heading text height is .25. Check your spelling. Save the drawing as P8-4.

NOTES:

1. INTERPRET DIMENSIONS AND TOLERANCES PER ASME Y14.5M−1994.
2. REMOVE ALL BURRS AND SHARP EDGES.

CASTING NOTES UNLESS OTHERWISE SPECIFIED:
1. .31 WALL THICKNESS.
2. R.12 FILLETS.
3. R.06 ROUNDS.
4. 1.5°−3.0° DRAFT.
5. TOLERANCES:
   ± 1° ANGULAR
   ±.03 TWO PLACE DIMENSIONS.
6. PROVIDE .12 THK MACHINING STOCK ON ALL MACHINE SURFACES.

5. Use the **MTEXT** command to type the following text using a text style with Stylus BT font and .125 text height. The heading text height is .188. After typing the text exactly as shown, edit the text with the following changes:
   A. Change the \ in item 7 to 1/2.
   B. Change the [in item 8 to 1.
   C. Change the 1/2 in item 8 to 3/4.
   D. Change the ^ in item 10 to a degree symbol.
   E. Check your spelling after making the changes.
   F. Save as drawing P8-5.

COMMON FRAMING NOTES:

1. ALL FRAMING LUMBER TO BE DFL #2 OR BETTER.
2. ALL HEATED WALLS @ HEATED LIVING AREAS TO BE 2 X 6 @ 24" OC.
3. ALL EXTERIOR HEADERS TO BE 2-2 X 12 UNLESS NOTED, W/ 2" RIGID INSULATION BACKING UNLESS NOTED.
4. ALL SHEAR PANELS TO BE 1/2" CDX PLY W/8d @ 4" OC @ EDGE, HDRS, & BLOCKING AND 8d @ 8" OC @ FIELD UNLESS NOTED.
5. ALL METAL CONNECTORS TO BE SIMPSON CO. OR EQUAL.
6. ALL TRUSSES TO BE 24" OC. SUBMIT TRUSS CALCS TO BUILDING DEPT. PRIOR TO ERECTION.
7. PLYWOOD ROOF SHEATHING TO BE \ STD GRADE 32/16 PLY LAID PERP TO RAFTERS. NAIL W/8d @ 6" OC @ EDGES AND 12" OC @ FIELD.
8. PROVIDE [1/2" STD GRADE T&G PLY FLOOR SHEATHING LAID PERP TO FLOOR JOISTS. NAIL W/10d @ 6" OC @ EDGES AND BLOCKING AND 12" OC @ FIELD.
9. BLOCK ALL WALLS OVER 10'-0" HIGH AT MID.
10. LET-IN BRACES TO BE 1 X 4 DIAG BRACES @ 45^ FOR ALL INTERIOR LOAD BEARING WALLS.

6. Open P4-7 and complete the window schedule by entering a text style with the Stylus BT font. Create a layer for the text. Draw the hexagonal symbols in the SYM column. Save the drawing as P8-6.

7. Open P4-8 and complete the door schedule by entering a text style with the Stylus BT font. Create a layer for the text. Draw the circle symbols in the SYM column. Save the drawing as P8-7.

8. Open P4-9 and complete the finish schedule by entering a text style with the Stylus BT font. Save the drawing as P8-8.

9. Open P4-10 and complete the schematic by entering the text using a text style with the Romans font. Create a layer for the text. Save the drawing as P8-9.

10. Open P4-11 and complete the block diagram by entering a text style with the Romans font. Create a layer for the text. Save the drawing as P8-10.

11. Open P5-9 and add text to the circuit diagram. Use a text style with the Romans font. Create a layer for the text. Save the drawing as P8-11.

12. Add title blocks, borders, and text styles to the template drawings you created in earlier chapters. Create a Border layer for the border lines and thick title block lines. Create a Title block layer for thin title block lines and text. Make three template drawings with borders and title blocks for your future drawings. Use the following guidelines:
   A. Prototype 1 for A-size, 8 1/2 × 11 drawings, named TITLEA–MECH.
   B. Prototype 2 for B-size, 11 × 17 drawings, named TITLEB–MECH.
   C. Prototype 3 for C-size, 17 × 22 drawings, named TITLEC–MECH.
   D. Set the following values for the drawing aids:
      Units = three-place decimal
      Grid = .500
      Snap = .250
   E. Draw a border 1/2" from the drawing limits.
   F. Design a title block using created text styles. Place it in the lower-right corner of each drawing. The title block should contain the following information: company or school name, address, date, drawn by, approved by, scale, title, drawing number, material, revision number. See the example on the next page.
   G. Record the information about each template in a log.

R -	CHANGE		DATE	ECN

SPECIFICATIONS

HYSTER COMPANY

THIS PRINT CONTAINS CONFIDENTIAL INFORMATION WHICH IS THE PROPERTY OF HYSTER COMPANY. BY ACCEPTING THIS INFORMATION THE BORROWER AGREES THAT IT WILL NOT BE USED FOR ANY PURPOSE OTHER THAN THAT FOR WHICH IT IS LOANED.

UNLESS OTHERWISE SPECIFIED DIMENSIONS ARE IN ~~INCHES~~ MILLIMETERS AND TOLERANCES FOR:

_____ PLACE DIMS± _____ : _____ PLACE DIMS± _____

ANGLES ± _____ : WHOLE DIMS± _____

DR.		SCALE		DATE	
CK. MAT'L.		CK. DESIGN		REL. ON ECN	
NAME					

MODEL	DWG. FIRST USED	SIMILAR TO

DEPT.	PROJECT	LIST DIVISION	H	PART NO.	R

13. Draw a small parts list (similar to the one shown below) connected to your C-size prototype title block.
    A. Enter PARTS LIST with a style containing a complex font.
    B. Enter the other information using text and the **DTEXT** command. Do not exit the **DTEXT** command to start a new line of text.
    C. Save the drawing as TITLEC-PARTS.
    D. Record the information about the template in a log.

3	HOLDING PINS	12
2	SIDE COVERS	3
1	MAIN HOUSING	1
KEY	DESCRIPTION	QTY

PARTS LIST

UNLESS OTHERWISE SPECIFIED ALL DIMENSIONS IN

INCHES

AND TOLERANCES FOR:

1	PLACE DIMS:	±.1
2	PLACE DIMS:	±.01
3	PLACE DIMS:	±.005
	ANGULAR:	±30'
	FRACTIONAL:	±.1/32
	FINISH:	125? in.

JANE'S
DESIGN

DR:	SCALE:	DATE:	APPD:
JANE	FULL	XX–XX–XX	

MATERIAL:

MILD STEEL

NAME:

XXX–XXXX

FIRST USED ON:	SIMILAR TO:	B	PART NO. 123–321	REV: 0

14. Draw an architectural template for a 17″ × 22″ or 22″ × 34″ sheet size with a title block along the right side similar to the one shown below. Use the same layout and layer instructions given for Problem 12. Save the drawing as ARCH. Record the information about the template in a log.

15. Draw title blocks with borders for your electrical, piping, and general drawings. Use the same instructions provided in Problem 12. The title block can be similar to the one displayed with Problem 12, but the area for mechanical drafting tolerances is not required. Research sample title blocks to come up with your design. Save the templates as ELEC A, ELEC B, PIPE A, PIPE B, or another name related to the drawing type and sheet size.

16. Draw the AND/OR schematic shown below. Save your drawing as P8-17.

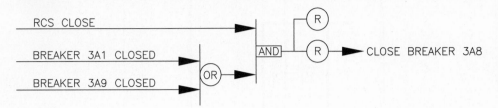

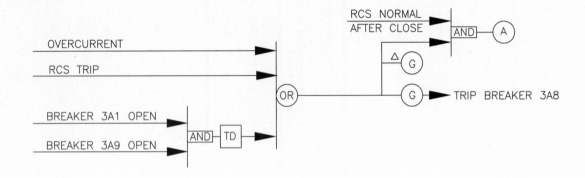

17. Draw the controller schematic shown below. Save your drawing as P8-18.

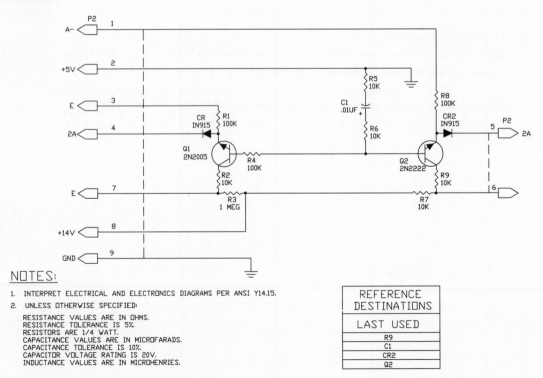

NOTES:

1. INTERPRET ELECTRICAL AND ELECTRONICS DIAGRAMS PER ANSI Y14.15.
2. UNLESS OTHERWISE SPECIFIED:

   RESISTANCE VALUES ARE IN OHMS.
   RESISTANCE TOLERANCE IS 5%.
   RESISTORS ARE 1/4 WATT.
   CAPACITANCE VALUES ARE IN MICROFARADS.
   CAPACITANCE TOLERANCE IS 10%.
   CAPACITOR VOLTAGE RATING IS 20V.
   INDUCTANCE VALUES ARE IN MICROHENRIES.

REFERENCE DESTINATIONS
LAST USED
R9
C1
CR2
Q2

CHAPTER 9

Drawing Display Options

Learning Objectives

After completing this chapter, you will be able to:

■ Explain the differences between the **REDRAW** command and the **REGEN** command.

■ Magnify a small part of the drawing to work on details.

■ Move the display window to reveal portions of the drawing outside the boundaries of the monitor.

■ Create named views that can be recalled instantly.

■ Use the **Aerial View** window.

■ Define the terms model space and paper space.

■ Create multiple viewports in the graphics window.

■ Create 3D viewpoints with the **3DORBIT** and **DVIEW** commands.

■ Control display order.

You can view a specific portion of a drawing using the AutoCAD display commands. The **ZOOM** command allows you to enlarge or reduce the amount of the drawing displayed. The portion displayed can also be moved using the **PAN** command. Panning is like looking through a camera and moving the camera across the drawing. Using the **Aerial View** window, you can locate a particular area of the drawing to view. The **VIEW** command allows you to create and name specific views of the drawing. When further drawing or editing operations are required, the view can be quickly and easily recalled.

Display functions allow you to work in model space or paper space. *Model space* is used for drawing and designing, while *paper space* is used for plotting. Detailed information on the use of model space and paper space to prepare multiview drawings is provided in Chapter 10.

This chapter also discusses the differences between the **REDRAW** and **REGEN** commands. Additionally, using the **REGENAUTO** and **VIEWRES** commands to achieve optimum display speeds and quality is discussed.

REDRAWING AND REGENERATING THE SCREEN

REDRAW
R

View
➡ Redraw

Standard
toolbar

Redraw All

A *blip* is a small cross that is displayed when a point is picked on the screen. See Figure 9-1. These blips are not part of your drawing; they simply stay on the screen until it is redrawn. The **REDRAW** command is used to clean the blips from the screen and refresh objects after editing operations.

Redraw the screen by picking the **Redraw All** button in the **Standard** toolbar, selecting **Redraw** from the **View** pull-down menu, or by entering R or REDRAW at the Command: prompt.

Figure 9-1.
Tiny crosshairs, or blips, appear on the screen when a point is selected.

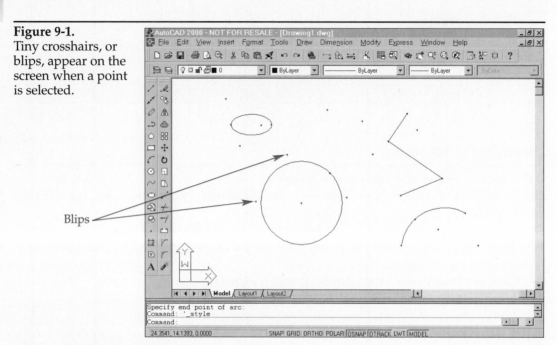

Blips

PROFESSIONAL TIP  Using **REDRAW** every time blips appear will slow your drawing sessions. Redraw the screen only when the blips interfere with the drawing process.

The **REDRAW** command simply refreshes the current screen. To regenerate the screen, the **REGEN** command is used. This command recalculates all drawing object coordinates and regenerates the display based on the current zoom magnification. For example, if you have zoomed in on objects in your drawing and curved edges appear to be straight segments, using **REGEN** will smooth the curves.

REGEN
RE

View
➡ Regen

To access the **REGEN** command, pick **Regen** from the **View** pull-down menu or enter RE or REGEN at the Command: prompt. The screen is immediately regenerated.

Blips are often turned off to eliminate the need for redraws. Blips can be turned on or off by entering the **BLIPMODE** command at the Command: prompt and then entering either ON or OFF as desired.

PROFESSIONAL TIP  Turning **BLIPMODE** off affects the current drawing only. If you want blips to be off in new drawings, turn **BLIPMODE** off in the template drawing.

AutoCAD and its Applications—Basics

The ability to *zoom in* (magnify) a drawing allows designers to create extremely small items, such as the electronic circuits found in a computer. The **ZOOM** command is a helpful tool that you will use often. The different options of the **ZOOM** command are discussed in the next sections.

The **ZOOM** Options

Each of the **ZOOM** options can be accessed by its corresponding button in the **Standard** toolbar, or by selecting the option in the **Zoom** cascading menu from the **View** pull-down menu. All the buttons in the **Zoom** flyout are also found in the **Zoom** toolbar. See Figure 9-2. All **ZOOM** options except **In** and **Out** are available at the Command: prompt:

ZOOM
Z

View
➡ Zoom

> Command: **Z** *or* **ZOOM**↵
> Specify corner of window, enter a scale factor (nX or nXP), or
> [All/Center/Dynamic/Extents/Previous/Scale/Window] <real time>:

The **ZOOM** options are as follows:
- **real time.** The default option allows you to perform realtime zooming. This interactive zooming is discussed later in this chapter.

Figure 9-2.
ZOOM command options.
A—The **Zoom** flyout button on the **Standard** toolbar.
B—The **Zoom** cascading menu.
C—The **Zoom** toolbar contains the same buttons as the **Zoom** flyout.

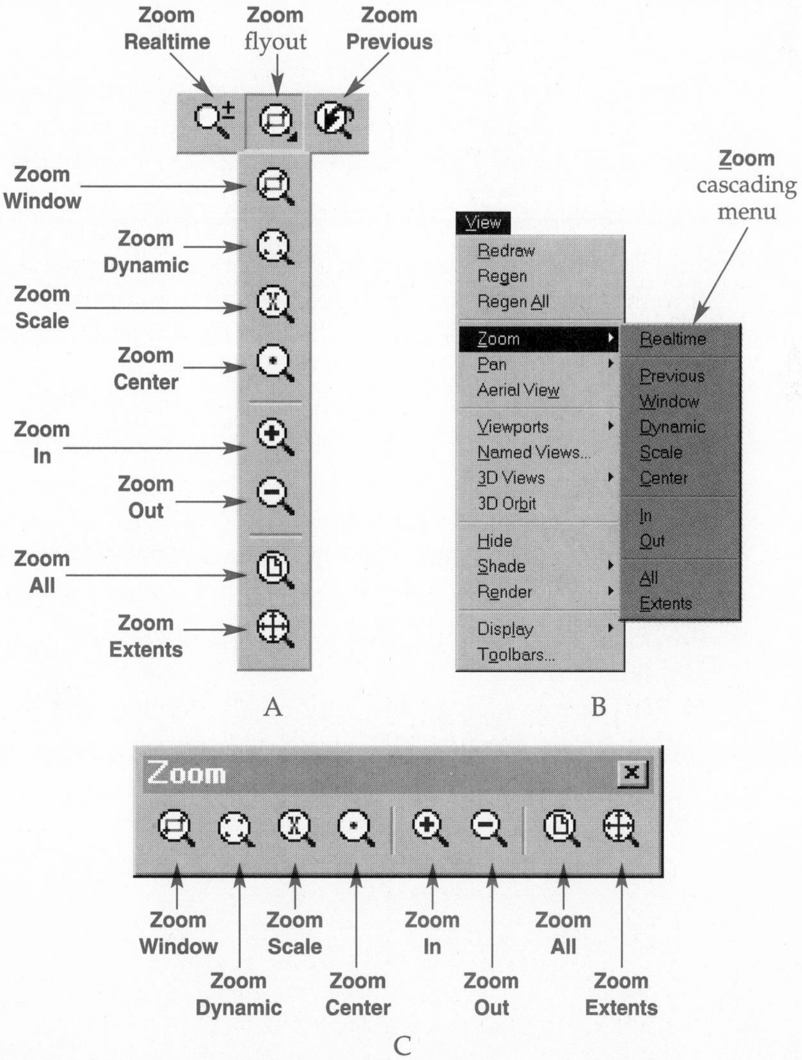

Zoom Realtime Zoom flyout Zoom Previous

Zoom Window
Zoom Dynamic
Zoom Scale
Zoom Center
Zoom In
Zoom Out
Zoom All
Zoom Extents

A

View
Redraw
Regen
Regen All
Zoom ▸
Pan ▸
Aerial View
Viewports ▸
Named Views...
3D Views ▸
3D Orbit
Hide
Shade ▸
Render ▸
Display ▸
Toolbars...

Zoom cascading menu
Realtime
Previous
Window
Dynamic
Scale
Center
In
Out
All
Extents

B

Zoom
Zoom Window
Zoom Dynamic
Zoom Scale
Zoom Center
Zoom In
Zoom Out
Zoom All
Zoom Extents

C

- **All.** Zooms to the edge of the drawing limits. If objects are drawn beyond the limits, the **All** option zooms to the edges of your geometry. Always use this option after you change the drawing limits.
- **Center.** Zoom the center of the display screen to a picked point. If you want to zoom to the center of an area of the drawing and want to magnify the view as well, then pick the center and height of the area in the drawing. Rather than a height, a magnification factor can be entered by typing a number followed by an X, such as 4X. The current value represents the height of the screen in drawing units. Entering a smaller number enlarges the image size, while a larger number reduces it. The command sequence is as follows:

        [All/Center/Dynamic/Extents/Previous/Scale/Window] <real time>: **C**↵
        Specify center point: *(pick a center point)*
        Enter magnification height *<current>*: **4X**↵
        Command:

- **Dynamic.** Allows for a graphic pan and zoom with the use of a view box that represents the screen. This option is discussed in detail later in the chapter.
- **Extents.** Zooms to the extents (or edges) of the geometry in a drawing. This is the portion of the drawing area that contains drawing objects.
- **Window.** Pick opposite corners of a box. Objects in the box enlarge to fill the display. The **Window** option is the default if you pick a point on the screen upon entering the **ZOOM** command.
- **Scale.** The following prompt appears when you select the **Scale** option:

        Enter a scale factor (nX or nXP):

There are two options, **nX** or **nXP**. The **nX** option scales the display relative to the current display. To use this option, type a positive number, then X, and then press [Enter]. For example, enter 2X to magnify the current display "two times." To reduce the display, enter a number less than 1. For example, if you enter .5X, objects appear half as large as they did in the previous display.

The **nXP** option is used in conjunction with model space and paper space. It scales a drawing in model space relative to paper space and is used primarily in the layout of scaled multiview drawings. A detailed discussion of this option is given in Chapter 10.

Both of the **Scale** options can be entered at the initial **ZOOM** command prompt. For example, enter the following to enlarge the current display by a factor of three:

        Command: **Z** *or* **ZOOM**↵
        [All/Center/Dynamic/Extents/Previous/Scale/Window] <real time>: **3X**↵
        Command:

- **Previous.** Returns to the previous display. You can go back ten displays, one at a time.
- **In.** This option is available only on the toolbar and the pull-down menu. It automatically executes a 2X zoom scale factor.
- **Out.** This option is available only on the toolbar and the pull-down menu. It automatically executes a .5X zoom scale factor.

Performing Realtime Zoom

When using the command line, the default option of the **ZOOM** command is **real time**. A *realtime zoom* can be viewed as it is performed. It is activated by pressing [Enter] at the **ZOOM** command prompt line, by picking the **Zoom Realtime** button in the **Standard** toolbar, by picking **Realtime** in the **Zoom** cascading menu in the **View** pull-down menu, or by right-clicking in the drawing area and selecting **Zoom** in the shortcut menu.

Realtime zooming allows you to see the model move on the screen as you zoom. It is the quickest and easiest method for adjusting the magnification of drawings on the screen.

The Zoom cursor (a magnifying glass icon with a plus and minus) is displayed when realtime zoom is executed. Press and hold the left mouse button (pick button) and move the pointer up to zoom in (enlarge) and down to zoom out (reduce). When you have achieved the display you want, release the button. If the display needs further adjustment after the initial zoom, press and hold the left mouse button again and move the pointer to get the desired display. To exit once you are done, press the [Esc] key, the [Enter] key, or right-click to get the shortcut menu and pick **Exit**.

If you right-click while the Zoom cursor is active, a shortcut menu is displayed. See Figure 9-3. This menu appears at the cursor location and contains six viewing options.

- **Pan.** Activates the **Pan Realtime** command. This allows you to adjust the placement of the drawing on the screen. If additional zooming is required, right-click again to display the shortcut menu and pick **Zoom**. In this manner you can toggle back and forth between **Pan** and **Zoom Realtime** to accurately adjust the view. A detailed explanation of the **Pan** command is given later in the chapter.

- **Zoom.** Activates the **Zoom Realtime** command. A check appears to the left of this option if it is active.

- **3D Orbit.** When this is selected, AutoCAD allows you to change your point of view around your drawing. Similar to **Zoom**, this option is used to move around a 3D object. A detailed explanation of **3D Orbit** is provided later in this chapter.

- **Zoom Window.** Activates the **Zoom Window** option and changes the cursor display. See Figure 9-4. You can pick opposite corners of a window but you must press and hold the pick button and drag the window box to the opposite corner, then release the pick button.

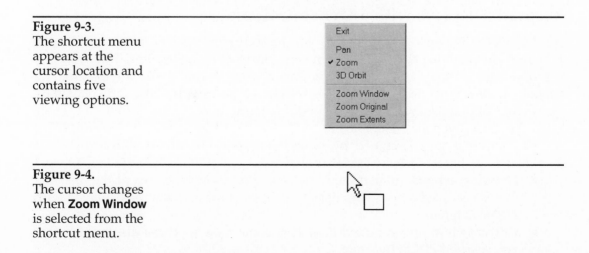

Figure 9-3.
The shortcut menu appears at the cursor location and contains five viewing options.

Figure 9-4.
The cursor changes when **Zoom Window** is selected from the shortcut menu.

- **Zoom Previous.** Restores the previous display before any realtime zooming or panning had occurred. This is a handy function if the current display is not to your liking and it would be easier to start over rather than to make further adjustments.
- **Zoom Extents.** Zooms to the extents of the drawing geometry.

Enlarging with a Window

The **ZOOM Window** option requires that you pick opposite corners of a rectangular window enclosing the area to be zoomed. The first point you pick is automatically accepted as the first corner of the zoom window. After this corner is picked, move the mouse, and a box appears showing the area that will be displayed or zoomed into once the second corner is picked. The box grows and shrinks as you move the pointing device. When the second corner is picked, the center of the window becomes the center of the new screen display. Figure 9-5 shows **ZOOM Window** used on a drawing.

Figure 9-5.
Using the **ZOOM Window** command. A—Select the corners of a window (shown here highlighted). B—The selected window fills the drawing screen. To return to the original view, use the **ZOOM Previous** command.

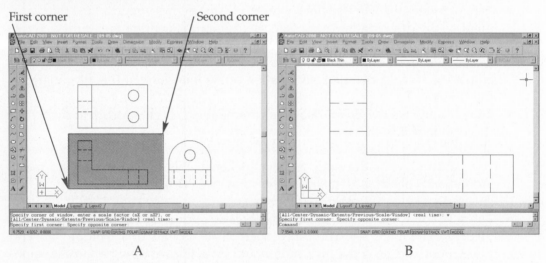

First corner   Second corner

A   B

Accurate Displays with a Dynamic Zoom

The **ZOOM Dynamic** option allows you to accurately specify the portion of the drawing you want displayed. This is done by constructing a *view box*. This view box is proportional to the size of the display area of your screen. If you are looking at a zoomed in view when **ZOOM Dynamic** is selected, the entire drawing is displayed on the screen. To practice with this command, load any drawing into AutoCAD. Then, select the **Zoom Dynamic** command.

The screen is now occupied by three boxes. See Figure 9-6. A fourth box is displayed later. Each box has a specific function:
- **Drawing extents.** (blue dotted line) This box shows the area of the drawing that is occupied by drawing objects. It is the same area that is displayed with **ZOOM Extents**.
- **Current view.** (green dotted line) This is the view that was displayed before you selected **ZOOM Dynamic**.

Figure 9-6.
Features of the
ZOOM Dynamic
command.

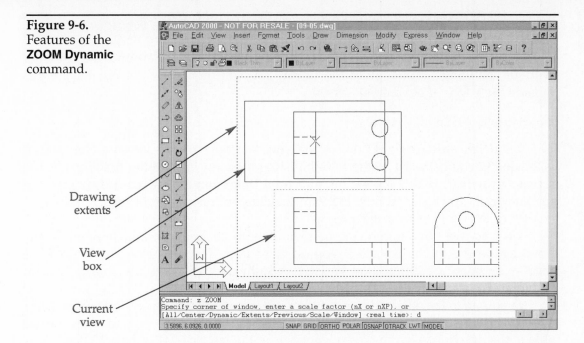

Drawing
extents

View
box

Current
view

- **Panning view box.** (X in the center) Move the pointing device to find the center point of the desired zoomed display. When you press the pick button, the zooming view box appears.
- **Zooming view box.** (arrow on right side) This box allows you to decrease or increase the area that you wish to zoom. Move the pointer to the right and the box increases in size. Move the pointer to the left and the box shrinks. You can also pan up or down with the zooming view box. The only restriction is that you cannot move the box to the left.

The **ZOOM Dynamic** command is not complete until you press [Enter]. If you press the pick button to select the zooming view box, you can resize the viewing area, press the pick button again, and the panning view box reappears. The panning view box can then be repositioned over the area desired. In this manner, you can fine-tune the exact display needed. This is also helpful in defining permanent views, which is discussed later in this chapter.

EXERCISE 9-1

❏ Start AutoCAD and load a drawing from a previous exercise or drawing problem.
   ❏ Enlarge and reduce the drawing using **Zoom Realtime**.
   ❏ Move around the drawing using **Pan Realtime**.
   ❏ Select **ZOOM Window** and enlarge a portion of the drawing.
   ❏ Select **ZOOM Window** again, to move in closer to a detail.
   ❏ Use **ZOOM Previous** to return to the last display.
   ❏ Select **ZOOM Extents** to show only the drawing entities.
   ❏ Select **ZOOM All** to display the entire drawing limits.
   ❏ Select **ZOOM Dynamic**. Maneuver the view box to select a portion of the drawing.
   ❏ Use **ZOOM Dynamic** to enlarge the display.
❏ Save the drawing as EX9-1, then quit the drawing session.

The **PAN** command allows you to move your viewpoint around the drawing without changing the magnification factor. You can then view objects that lie just outside the edges of the display screen.

Performing Realtime Pan

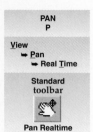

PAN
P

View
➥ Pan
➥ Real Time

Standard toolbar

Pan Realtime

A *realtime pan* allows you to see the drawing move on the screen as you pan. It is the quickest and easiest method for adjusting the view around the drawings on the screen. To activate realtime panning, pick **Real Time** from the **Pan** cascading menu in the **View** pull-down menu, pick the **Pan Realtime** button on the **Standard** toolbar, or enter P or PAN at the Command: prompt.

After starting the command, press and hold the pick button and move the pointing device in the direction you wish to pan. The pan icon of the hand is displayed when a realtime pan is used. A right-click displays the shortcut menu shown in Figure 9-3.

If you pan to the edge of your drawing, a bar is displayed on one side of the hand cursor. The bar correlates to the side of the drawing. For example, if you reach the left side of the drawing, a bar and arrow appear on the left side of the hand. These icons are shown in Figure 9-7.

Figure 9-7.
A bar and arrow appear by the hand cursor when you pan to the edge of the drawing.

Top edge

Left edge

Right edge

Bottom edge

Picking the Pan Displacement

The *pan displacement* is the distance the drawing is moved on the screen. You can pick the displacement by selecting **Point** from the **Pan** cascading menu in the **View** pull-down menu or by entering -P or -PAN at the Command: prompt. The following prompt appears:

Command: **-P** *or* **-PAN**↵
Specify base point or displacement:

You can specify a base point by picking a point or entering absolute coordinates. You are then prompted to select a second point. The display window is moved the distance between the points.

You can also enter the displacement, or the distance the display window is to be moved, by giving coordinates. The coordinates can be either relative or absolute.

Using Pan Presets

The **Pan** cascading menu in the **View** pull-down menu includes four preset directional options: **Left**, **Right**, **Up**, and **Down**. See Figure 9-8. Select one of the options to move the display in the indicated direction.

Figure 9-8.
The **Pan** options can be found in the **Pan** cascading menu of the **View** pull-down menu.

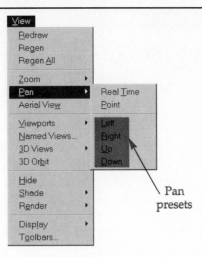

Pan presets

Using Scroll Bars to Pan

The scroll bars found at the bottom and to the right of the drawing area can also be used to pan the display. See Figure 9-9. Pick the arrows at the end of the scroll bar to pan in small increments. Select the scroll bar itself to pan in larger increments. Position the cursor over the box in the scroll bar, pick the left button and hold it, and then move the mouse to see realtime panning in the horizontal or vertical direction.

Figure 9-9.
The drawing window scroll bars can be used for panning operations.

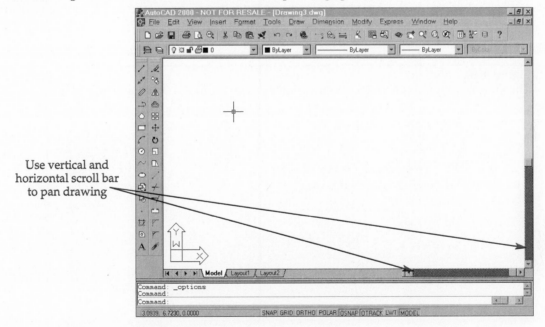

Use vertical and horizontal scroll bar to pan drawing

NOTE

The drawing window scroll bars can be activated and deactivated by selecting the **Display scroll bars in drawing window** option in the **Window Elements** area of the **Display** tab of the **Options** dialog box. To access this dialog box, select **Options...** from the **Tools** pull-down menu.

SETTING VIEW RESOLUTION FOR QUICK DISPLAYS

AutoCAD can save you time on zooming and panning at the expense of display accuracy. Or, AutoCAD can provide a highly accurate display at the expense of zoom and pan speed. The main factor is the view resolution.

The *view resolution* refers to the number of lines used to draw circles and arcs. High resolution values display smooth circles and arcs. Low resolution values display segmented circles and arcs. The view resolution can be set in the **Options** dialog box. To access this dialog box, pick **Options...** from the **Tools** pull-down menu, and then pick the **Display** tab. In the **Display resolution** area in the upper-right corner of the dialog box is the **Arc and circle smoothness:** text box. This contains the current **VIEWRES** setting. See Figure 9-10.

Figure 9-10.
The view resolution (**VIEWRES** value) variable can be set in the **Options** dialog box.

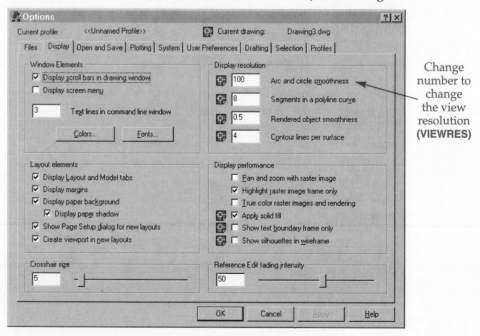

Change number to change the view resolution (**VIEWRES**)

The display smoothness of circles and arcs is controlled by the **VIEWRES** setting. It can vary between 1 and 20000. The default setting is 100, which produces a relatively smooth circle. A number smaller than 100 causes circles and arcs to be drawn with fewer vectors (straight lines). A number larger than 100 causes more vectors to be included in the circles, as shown in Figure 9-11.

It is important to remember that the **VIEWRES** setting is a display function only and has no effect on the plotted drawing. A drawing is plotted using an optimum number of vectors for the size of circles and arcs. In other words, if a circle you draw looks like a polygon in the graphics window before **REGEN** is used, it will look like a circle when the drawing is plotted.

Figure 9-11.
The higher the **VIEWRES** value, the smoother a circle will appear.

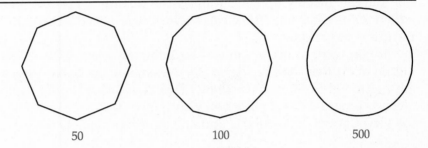

50   100   500

 NOTE
You can change the **VIEWRES** setting by typing VIEWRES at the Command: prompt. A Do you want fast zooms? prompt appears. This prompt is no longer useful, but remains in AutoCAD so programs written for earlier versions will still function properly.

EXERCISE 9-2

❏ Start AutoCAD and load a drawing from a previous exercise or drawing problem.
❏ Adjust the display using each of the following options:
  ❏ Realtime panning.
  ❏ Pan displacement.
  ❏ Pan presets.
  ❏ Drawing window scroll bars.
❏ Access the **Display** tab of the **Options** dialog box and change the **Arc and circle smoothness** to 10. Pick the **OK** button and observe the change in display.
❏ Draw some circles and arcs.
❏ Reset the **Arc and circle smoothness** value to 100.

CREATING YOUR OWN WORKING VIEWS

On a large drawing with a number of separate details, using the **ZOOM** and **PAN** commands can be time-consuming. Being able to quickly specify a certain part of the drawing is much easier. This is possible with the **VIEW** command. It allows you to create named views of any area of the drawing. A view can be a portion of the drawing, such as the upper-left quadrant, or it can represent an enlarged portion. After the view is created, you can instruct AutoCAD to display it at any time.

VIEW
V
DDVIEW

View
➡ Named Views...

View
toolbar

Named Views

Creating Views

The **VIEW** command can be accessed by picking the **Named Views** button in the **View** toolbar, selecting **Named Views...** from the **View** pull-down menu, or entering V, VIEW, or DDVIEW at the Command: prompt. This activates the **View** dialog box. See Figure 9-12.

The **View** dialog box contains the **Named Views** and the **Orthographic & Isometric Views** tabs. The **Named Views** tab is where new views are defined. The **Orthographic & Isometric Views** tab provides preset views around the drawing in AutoCAD.

A list of currently defined views is shown in the **Named Views** tab. If you want to save the current display as a view, pick the **New...** button to access the **New View** dialog box, Figure 9-13. Now, type the desired view name in the **View name:** edit box. The **Current Display** option button is the default. Click **OK** and the view name is added to the list. AutoCAD creates a view from what is currently being displayed in the graphics window.

If you want to use a window to define the view, pick the **Define Window** radio button in the **New View** dialog box, and then pick the **Define View Window** button. You are prompted to Specify first corner. Pick two points to define a window. After the second corner is selected, the **New View** dialog box reappears. Pick the **OK** button and the **View Control** dialog box is updated to reflect the new view.

Figure 9-12.
Select a different view in the **View** dialog box. Create a new view by selecting the **New...** button.

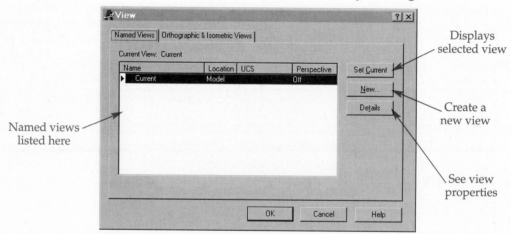

Figure 9-13.
In the **New View** dialog box, name the new view and define the window.

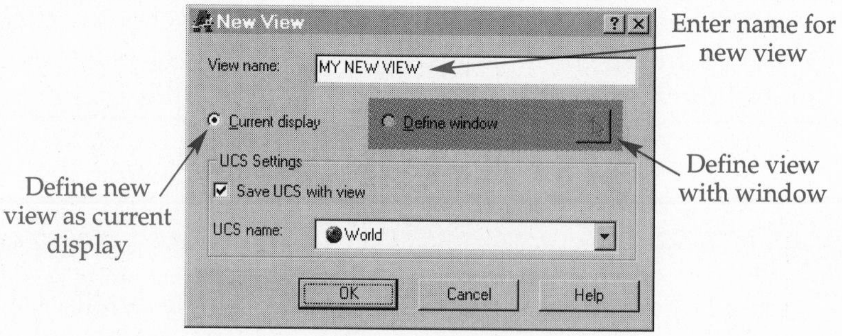

AutoCAD and its Applications—Basics

When creating a view, it is possible to save a named UCS (User Coordinate System) to the particular view being created. The World Coordinate System is the default system in AutoCAD, it determines where the 0,0,0 point is for the X, Y, and Z axes. The UCS command is introduced in Chapter 6 of this text and covered in depth in *AutoCAD and its Applications—Advanced.*

To display one of the listed views, pick its name from the file list in the **Named Views** tab and pick the **Set Current** button. The name of the current view appears in the **Current View:** label below the **Named Views** tab. Now, pick the **OK** button and the screen displays the selected view.

To delete a view displayed in the **View** dialog box, first pick the view name in the list in the **Named Views** tab to highlight it, then right-click the mouse. A shortcut menu appears. Select the **Delete** option in the shortcut menu. The view name is immediately removed from the list. Notice that when a view is highlighted, you can right-click the mouse for other shortcut menu options. You can set a view current with the **Set Current** option, use the **Rename** option to rename a view, delete a view with the **Delete** option, or get a detailed description of the selected view by picking the **Details...** option. Selecting **Details...** opens the **View Details** dialog box, which provides a variety of information about the view. This dialog box can also be accessed by selecting the **Details** button in the **View** dialog box. A discussion of these values related to 3D drawings is given in *AutoCAD and its Applications—Advanced.*

The **Orthographic & Isometric Views** tab in the **View** dialog box allows you to quickly choose a preset view around the drawing. See Figure 9-14. Notice that the icons display the side of the drawing that will be viewed. There are orthogonal views such as Top, Bottom, Front, Back, Left, and Right. Picking any of these icons, then pressing the **Set Current** button changes the view in AutoCAD so that you are looking at your drawing from the selected direction. There are isometric views such as Southwest, Southeast, Northeast, and Northwest. These views can also be selected from the **3D Views** cascading menu in the **View** pull-down menu or from the **View** toolbar. See Figure 9-15. Selecting any of these icons displays a 3D view (isometric) of the drawing. Orthogonal and isometric views are covered in greater depth in *AutoCAD and its Applications—Advanced.*

Figure 9-14.
The **Orthographic & Isometric Views** tab contains six orthographic views and four isometric views.

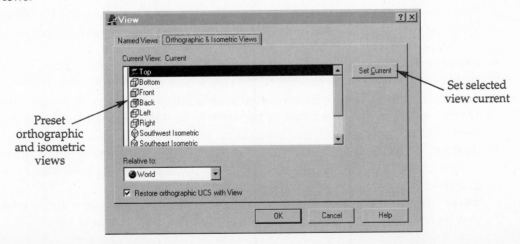

Figure 9-15.
Preset orthographic and isometric views can also be selected in the **3D Views** cascading menu in the **View** pull-down menu or from the **View** toolbar.

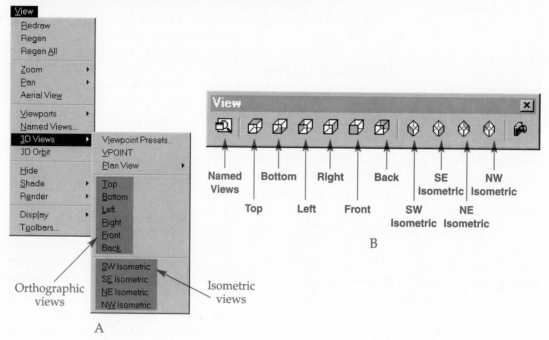

A

B

PROFESSIONAL TIP

Part of your project planning should include view names. A consistent naming system guarantees that all users know the view names without having to list them. The views can be set as part of the template drawings. Then, view names can be placed in a custom screen, or pull-down menu as discussed in *AutoCAD and its Applications—Advanced, AutoCAD 2000.*

Working with Views at the **Command:** Prompt

-VIEW
-V

The **-VIEW** command allows you to create and set views at the Command: prompt. When -V or -VIEW is entered at the Command: prompt, you are presented with the following options:

Enter an option [?/Orthographic/Delete/Restore/Save/Ucs/Window]:

- **?.** This option lists currently defined view names. You are prompted for which views to list. Responding with [Enter] accepts the default and displays all currently defined view names.
- **Orthographic.** This option changes the view to one of the orthographic views that you choose. You are prompted for which orthographic view to display.
- **Delete.** This option removes unneeded views. After selecting this option, you are prompted to enter the name of the view to be deleted. Type the name and press [Enter].
- **Restore.** A saved view can be displayed on the screen using this option. Simply enter the name of the view you want to display at the Enter view name to restore: prompt. The view is then immediately displayed.
- **Save.** This option creates a new view. Enter the new view name at the Enter view name to save: prompt. The current display becomes the new view.

- **UCS.** This option allows you to save the current UCS with any new views you create. You are prompted with Save current UCS with named views? [Yes/No].
- **Window (W).** This option also creates a new view and prompts for a window selection.

USING TRANSPARENT DISPLAY COMMANDS

To begin a new command, you usually need to complete or cancel the current command. Most menu picks automatically cancel the command in progress before initiating the new one. However, some commands function without canceling an active command.

A *transparent command* temporarily interrupts the active command. After the transparent command is completed, the command that was interrupted is resumed. Therefore, it is not necessary to cancel the initial command. Many display commands can be used transparently, including **REDRAW**, **PAN**, **AV**, and several **ZOOM** options.

Suppose that while drawing a line, you need to place a point somewhere off the screen. One option is to cancel the **LINE** command. Then zoom out to see more of the drawing and select **LINE** again. A more efficient method is to use **PAN** or **ZOOM** while still in the **LINE** command. An example of drawing a line to a point off the screen is as follows:

> Command: **L** *or* **LINE**↵
> Specify first point: *(pick a point)*
> Specify next point or [Undo]: *(pick the **Pan** button or enter* 'PAN*)*
> \>\>Press Esc or Enter to exit, or right-click to display shortcut menu. *(pan to the location desired then press* [Enter]*)*
> Resuming LINE command.
> Specify next point or [Undo]: *(pick a point)*
> Specify next point or [Undo]:↵
> Command:

The double prompt (>>) indicates that a command has been put "on hold" while you use a transparent command. The transparent command must be completed before the original command is returned. At that time, the double prompt disappears.

The above procedure is similar when using the **ZOOM** and **-VIEW** commands. When typed at the keyboard, an apostrophe (') is entered before the command. To connect a line to a small feature, enter 'Z or 'ZOOM. To perform a drawing or editing function across different views, use '-V or '-VIEW to restore the desired view.

PROFESSIONAL TIP Both the **Pan** button and **Zoom** button activate commands transparently, but the **Named Views** button does not. To execute a transparent **VIEW** command, you must enter '-V or '-VIEW at the Command: prompt and enter the appropriate option.

When trying to perform a transparent display, you may receive the following message:

> **Requires a regen, cannot be transparent.
> Resuming *current* command.

In this situation, you might try a less dramatic **ZOOM**, **PAN**, or **VIEW** that does not require AutoCAD to regenerate the display.

EXERCISE 9-3

❏ Begin a new drawing or use one of your templates.
❏ Set the drawing limits at 12,9, grid spacing at .5, and snap spacing at .25.
❏ Construct the two arcs shown below.
❏ Window a view of the left arc and name it 1. Restore view 1.
❏ Select the **LINE** command and snap to the top of the arc.
❏ Select **ZOOM Realtime** or **ZOOM Dynamic** transparently. Increase the zooming view box to include both arcs, but do not cause a regeneration.
❏ Extend the line to the top of the other arc. Begin a second line at the bottom of the right arc.
❏ Select **VIEW** transparently and restore view 1. Attach the line to the bottom of the left arc.
❏ Use **ZOOM Realtime** or **ZOOM Dynamic** to show the completed object.
❏ Save the drawing as EX9-3.

VIEW 1

2X R1.0

USING THE AERIAL VIEW

When you work on a large drawing, you can spend a lot of time zooming and panning the graphics window trying to locate a particular detail or feature. One of the most powerful display features in AutoCAD is the **Aerial View** window. **Aerial View** is a navigation tool that lets you see the entire drawing in a separate window, locate the detail or feature you want, and move to it quickly. You can zoom in on an area, change the magnification, and match the view in the graphics window to the one in the **Aerial View** window (or vice versa).

To open the **Aerial View** window, pick **Aerial View** from the **View** pull-down menu or enter AV or DSVIEWER at the Command: prompt. The entire drawing is then displayed in the **Aerial View** window. See Figure 9-16.

The **Aerial View** window initially appears at the lower-right of the graphics window, but can be moved to any convenient location on the screen. To do so, pick the title bar of the **Aerial View** window, hold down the left mouse button, and drag the window to a new location.

AV
DSVIEWER

View
➡ Aerial View

AutoCAD User's Guide 8

Figure 9-16.
The **Aerial View** window (shown here highlighted) is initially in the lower-right corner of the screen.

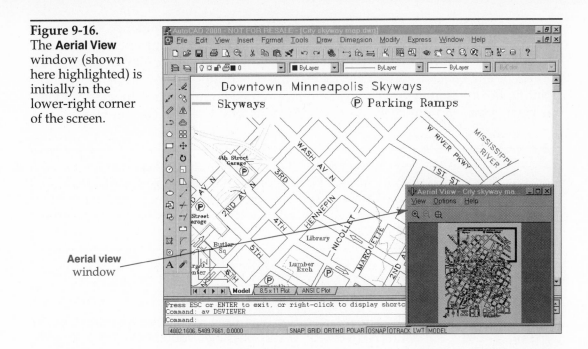

Aerial view window

The menu bar in the **Aerial View** window contains three pull-down menus and three buttons. See Figure 9-17. The buttons provide the same options found in the **View** pull-down menu:

- **Zoom In.** Increases the magnification of the image in the **Aerial View** window.
- **Zoom Out.** Decreases the magnification of the image in the **Aerial View** window.
- **Global.** Displays the entire generated drawing area (the extents of the drawing) in the **Aerial View** window.

The **Options** pull-down menu contains the following aerial viewer options:

- **Auto Viewport.** When on, switching to a different tiled viewport automatically causes the new viewport to be displayed in the aerial view window. When off, AutoCAD will not update the **Aerial View** window to match the active viewport.
- **Dynamic Update.** This causes the **Aerial View** window to update its display after each change in the drawing. Enable this only if your display system is very fast.
- **Realtime Zoom.** Activating this will update the drawing view area as you zoom and pan in the **Aerial View** window.
- **Aerial View Help.** Opens the AutoCAD help to the **Aerial View** section.

Figure 9-17.
The **Aerial View** window has pull-down menus and a toolbar. These contain options for working with the window.

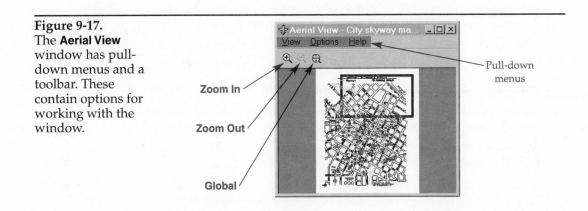

Zoom In

Zoom Out

Global

Pull-down menus

The **Aerial View** window is similar to the **Zoom Dynamic** command. When using the **Aerial View**, the overall drawing can be viewed. There is a current view box that can be resized by pressing the pick button. Moving the pointing device right or left shrinks or enlarges the current view. Press the pick button again and by moving the pointing device around you can pan around in the window. When the desired view has been obtained, right-click and AutoCAD will set that as the current view.

> **NOTE**
>
> You can also right-click inside the **Aerial View** window to get a shortcut menu that accesses the functions described earlier. Best of all, you can use the **Aerial View** zoom and pan functions transparently while a drawing or editing command is in progress.

> **PROFESSIONAL TIP**
>
> Although regeneration has been virtually eliminated with AutoCAD 2000, it is still possible. You should try to avoid regeneration because it slows your work and thought processes. Try the following tips for all your new drawings:
>
> ✓ Set your drawing limits to include a little extra for a border.
> ✓ **ZOOM All**.
> ✓ Create a view named ALL (or a name of your choice) of the entire drawing area.
> ✓ Avoid using **ZOOM All**, **ZOOM Extents**, or **REGEN** again.
> ✓ Create additional views as you need them.
> ✓ Use **Aerial View** whenever possible in place of other display commands. To redisplay the entire drawing without causing a regeneration, restore the view named ALL.
> ✓ Use **ZOOM Realtime** or **ZOOM Dynamic** instead of the other display commands.

EXERCISE 9-4

❏ Start AutoCAD and open the City skyway map.dwg drawing in the Acad2000\ Sample folder.
❏ Activate the **Aerial View** and zoom toward the top of the drawing to include the title of the drawing. Click the left mouse button to resize the window. Click the pick button again to exit the resizing window when the desired window size has been selected.
❏ Move the current view box around until it is toward the top of the drawing.
❏ Zoom out to view the entire map using the **Global** button in the **Aerial View** window.
❏ Resize your **Aerial View** window so it occupies at least one-quarter of your display screen.
❏ Pick the **Zoom In** button in the **Aerial View** window to zoom the **Aerial View** window.
❏ Pick inside the **Aerial View** window to pan around the drawing.
❏ When you are finished experimenting with the **Aerial View**, quit the session without saving.

Model space can be thought of as the *space* where you draw and design in AutoCAD. The term *model* has more meaning when working in 3D, but you can consider any drawing or design as a model, even if it is two-dimensional.

The best way to tell if you are in model space is to look at the UCS (User Coordinate System) icon. Located in the lower-left corner of the screen, this icon represents the current directions of the X and Y coordinates. See Figure 9-18. An introduction of User Coordinate Systems and the UCS icon is given in Chapter 6 of this text and a detailed discussion is in *AutoCAD and its Applications—Advanced*.

Paper space is a *space* you use to lay out a drawing or model to be plotted. Basically, it is as if you place a sheet of paper on the screen, then insert, or *reference*, one or more drawings to the paper. In order to enter paper space, you can pick one of the layout tabs at the bottom of the screen. See Figure 9-19. You can also use the **MODEL** or **PAPER** button on the status bar to switch between model space and paper space. The button displays the current environment, and picking it switches to the other environment.

Figure 9-18.
The UCS icons for model space and paper space.

Model Space   Paper Space

Figure 9-19.
The layout tabs are located at the bottom of the graphic screen window. The **PAPER** button indicates that the paper space environment is active. The button reads **MODEL** when you are working in model space.

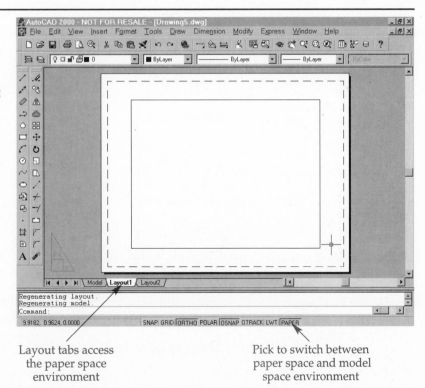

Layout tabs access the paper space environment

Pick to switch between paper space and model space environment

Remember that you should create all your drawings and designs in the **Model** tab, not in the **Layout** tab. Only paper layouts for plotting purposes should be created in the **Layout** tab. To return to model space, pick the **Model** tab.

Do not be confused by model space and paper space. The discussion in Chapter 10 will provide you with a better understanding. Right now, think of these terms in the following manner:

Tab	Environment	Status Bar Button	Activity
Model	Model space	**MODEL**	Drawing and design
Layout	Paper space	**PAPER**	Plotting and printing

TILED VIEWPORTS

The **Model** tab drawing area can be divided into various viewports. These viewports are called *tiled viewports*. Another type of viewports, *floating viewports,* can be created in the **Layout** tab. Tiled viewports are created in model space, floating viewports are created in paper space.

By default, there is only one viewport in the drawing area. Additional viewports can be added. The edges of tiled viewports butt against one another like floor tile. The tiled viewports cannot overlap.

Viewports are different "tiles," or views, into the same drawing. Only one viewport can be active at any given time. The active viewport has a bold outline around its edges. See Figure 9-20.

Figure 9-20.
An example of three tiled viewports in model space. All viewports contain the same objects, but the display in each viewport can be unique.

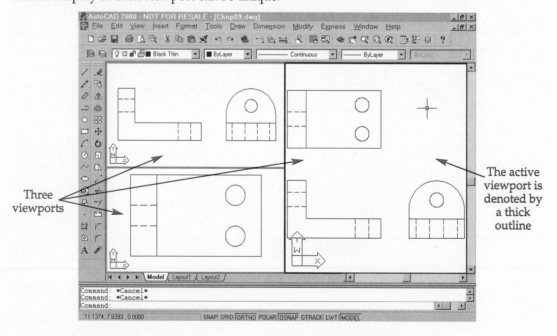

Creating Tiled Viewports

Viewports can be created using the **Viewports** dialog box, Figure 9-21. This dialog box can be accessed by picking the **Display Viewports Dialog** button from either the **Standard**, **Layouts**, or **Viewports** toolbar. You can also enter VPORTS at the Command: prompt, or select **New Viewports...** from the **Viewports** cascading menu in the **View** pull-down menu.

The **New Viewports** tab is shown in Figure 9-21. The **Standard viewports:** list contains many preset viewport configurations. The configuration name identifies the number of viewports and the arrangement or location of the largest viewport. These configurations are shown in Figure 9-22. Select one, and a preview appears in the **Preview** area. Select *Active Model Configuration* to preview the current configuration.

You can name and save a configuration. Enter a name in the **New name:** text box. When you pick the **OK** button, the new named viewport configuration is recorded in the **Named Viewports** tab. Use a descriptive name. For example, if you are going to configure four viewports, you might name this as Four Viewports.

The **Apply to:** drop-down list allows you to specify if the viewport configuration is applied to the graphics window or to the active viewport. Select **Display** to have the configuration applied to the entire drawing area. Select **Current Viewport** to have the new configuration in the active viewport only. See Figure 9-23.

The default setting in the **Setup:** drop-down list is **2D**. When this is selected, all viewports show the top view of the drawing. If the **3D** option is selected, the different viewports display various 3D views of the drawing. At least one viewport is set up with an isometric view. The other viewports have different views, such as a top view or side view. The viewpoint is displayed within the viewport in the **Preview** image. To change a view in a viewport, pick the viewport in the **Preview** image and then select the new viewpoint from the **Change view to:** drop-down list.

VPORTS

View
➡ Viewports
  ➡ New
    Viewports...

Viewports
toolbar

Layouts
toolbar

Standard
toolbar

Display Viewports
Dialog

Figure 9-21.
Specify the number and arrangement of tiled viewports in the **New Viewports** tab of the **Viewports** dialog box.

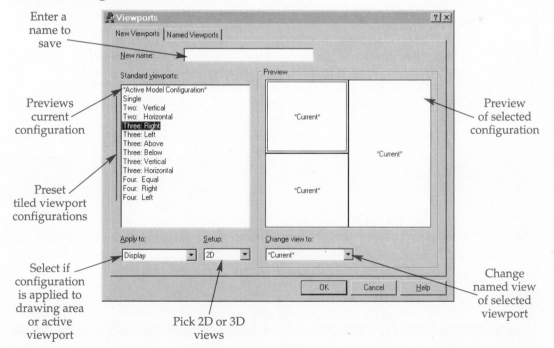

Enter a name to save

Previews current configuration

Preset tiled viewport configurations

Select if configuration is applied to drawing area or active viewport

Pick 2D or 3D views

Preview of selected configuration

Change named view of selected viewport

Figure 9-22.
Preset tiled viewport configurations are available in the **New Viewports** tab of the **Viewports** dialog box.

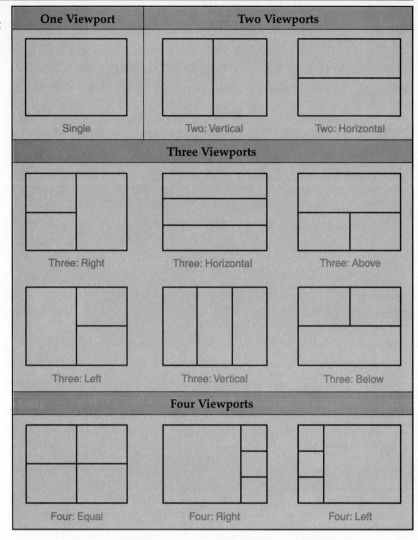

Figure 9-23.
Viewport configurations can be applied to the drawing area or the active viewport. A—Original configuration (Three: Right). B—Use the **Current Viewport** option to create additional viewports within the active viewport. Here, the Two: Vertical configuration is specified for the active viewport.

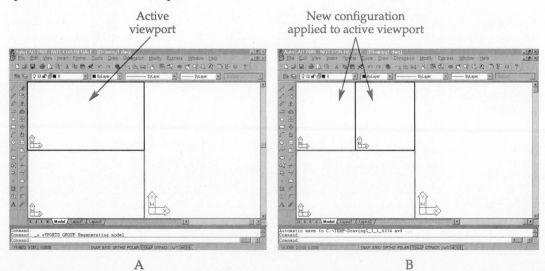

A

B

AutoCAD and its Applications—Basics

The **Named Viewports** tab displays the names of saved viewport configurations and gives you a preview of each. See Figure 9-24. Select the named viewport configuration and pick **OK** to apply it to the drawing area. Named viewport configurations cannot be applied to the active viewport.

You can also select a viewport configuration from the **Viewports** cascading menu in the **View** pull-down menu, shown in Figure 9-25. The following configuration options are available:

- **1 Viewport.** This option replaces the current viewport configuration with a single viewport.
- **2 Viewports.** When you select this option, you are prompted to select a vertical or horizontal arrangement:

Enter a configuration option [Horizontal/Vertical] <Vertical>:

The arrangement you choose is then applied to the active viewport. This configuration does not replace the current viewport configuration.

Figure 9-24.
The **Named Viewports** tab.

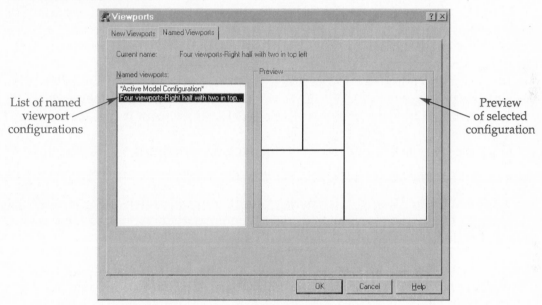

List of named viewport configurations

Preview of selected configuration

Figure 9-25.
The **Viewports** cascading menu in the **View** pull-down menu.

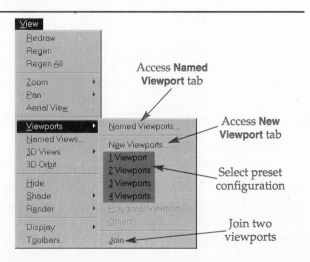

Access **Named Viewport** tab

Access **New Viewport** tab

Select preset configuration

Join two viewports

- **3 Viewports.** The following prompt appears when you select this option:

> Enter a configuration option [Horizontal/Vertical/Above/Below/Left/Right]
> <Right>:

The arrangement you choose is then applied to the active viewport. This configuration does not replace the current viewport configuration.

- **4 Viewports.** This option creates four equal viewports within the active viewport.

NOTE The AutoCAD graphics window can be divided into *tiled viewports*, of which only 64 can be available at one time. You can check this number using the **MAXACTVP** (maximum active viewports) system variable at the Command: prompt.

Once you have selected the viewport configuration and returned to drawing area, move the pointing device around and notice that only the active viewport contains crosshairs. The pointer is represented by an arrow in the other viewports. To make a different viewport active, move the pointer into it and press the pick button.

As you draw in one viewport, the image is displayed in all viewports. Try drawing lines and other shapes and notice how the viewports are affected. Then use a display command, such as **ZOOM**, in the active viewport and notice the results. Only the active viewport reflects the use of the **ZOOM** command.

If you want to join two viewports together, you can do so by picking **Join** from the **Viewports** cascading menu in the **View** pull-down menu. Once **Join** is selected, you are prompted to Select dominant viewport. Select the viewport that has the view you want to keep in the joined viewport.

Once the dominant viewport is selected, you are prompted to Select viewport to join. Select the viewport that you want to join with the active viewport. Once you select a viewport to join, AutoCAD "glues" the two viewports together and retains the dominant view. The two viewports you are joining cannot create an L-shape viewport. In other words, the two edges of the viewports must be the same size in order to join them.

NOTE The **-VPORTS** command can be used to create viewports at the Command: prompt. Enter -VPORTS and the following prompt appears:

> Command: **-VPORTS**↵
> Enter an option
> [Save/Restore/Delete/Join/SIngle/?/2/<3>/4] <3>: ↵

The options are similar to those already discussed.

Uses of Tiled Viewports

Viewports in model space can be used for both 2D and 3D drawings. They are limited only by your imagination and need. See *AutoCAD and its Applications—Advanced* for examples of the tiled viewports in 3D. The nature of 2D drawings, whether mechanical multiview, architectural construction details, or unscaled schematic drawings, lend themselves well to viewports.

EXERCISE 9-5

❑ Start AutoCAD and open the wilhome.dwg drawing from the Acad2000\Sample folder. (wilhome.dwg will be located in this folder if AutoCAD was installed according to suggestions in the *Installation Guide*.)

❑ When the drawing is displayed on the screen, you should see a house floor plan and several elevations. Press the **Model** tab to make model space active. Zoom into various locations to get familiar with the drawing.

❑ Use the **Viewports** dialog box to create three viewports. The large viewport should be on the right.

❑ Use realtime panning to center the drawing in the large viewport. Use realtime zooming to enlarge the drawing to fill the viewport.

❑ In the upper-left viewport, use **ZOOM Window** to find the AQUARIUM elevation in the upper-left corner of the drawing.

❑ Pick the lower-left viewport and zoom in on the Grand Room at the upper-right of the house. Use realtime pan and zoom to locate the entertainment center.

❑ Quit without saving the drawing.

FLOATING VIEWPORTS

AutoCAD User's Guide 15

The layout tabs are used to set up a page to be printed or plotted. The paper space environment is activated when you switch from the **Model** tab to a layout tab. Viewports created in paper space are called floating viewports. These *floating viewports* are actually holes cut into the paper in the layout tab so that the model space drawing can be seen. These viewports are separate objects and can overlap, thus the term "floating viewports," as they can be moved around.

After floating viewports are created, display commands are used to modify the model space "showing through" the viewport. Editing commands such as **MOVE**, **ERASE**, and **COPY** can be used in paper space to modify the viewports.

As you work through the following sections describing floating viewports, be sure a layout tab is selected on your AutoCAD screen.

Creating Floating Viewports

The process of creating floating viewports in paper space is nearly identical to the process of creating tiled viewports in model space. A viewport configuration can be selected from the **Viewports** dialog box, which was discussed earlier in this chapter. Also, the **MVIEW** or **-VPORTS** command options can be used to create single or multiple viewports.

As discussed earlier, when model space is active, the **Viewports** dialog box creates tiled viewports. When paper space is active, it creates floating viewports. This dialog box differs slightly depending on the current environment—model space or paper space. The **Apply to:** drop-down list found in model space becomes the **Viewport spacing:** text box in paper space. Use this setting to specify the space around the edges of the floating viewports. See Figure 9-26.

Figure 9-26.
When paper space is active, the **New Viewports** tab in the **Viewports** dialog box contains the **Viewport spacing:** setting.

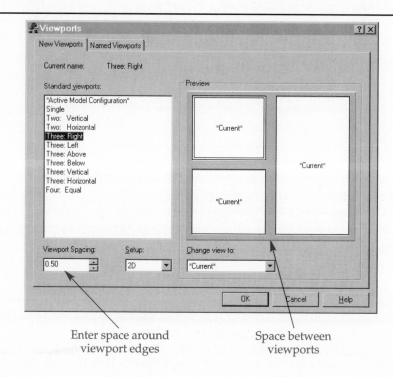

Enter space around viewport edges

Space between viewports

MVIEW
MV
-VPORTS

Floating viewports can also be created using the **-VPORTS** and **MVIEW** commands. These commands are identical when paper space is active. Either command can be typed at the Command: prompt:

Command: **MV**, **MVIEW**, *or* **-VPORTS**↵
Specify corner of viewport or
   [ON/OFF/Fit/Hideplot/Lock/Object/Polygonal/Restore/2/3/4] <Fit>:

The default option is to define a rectangular floating viewport by selecting opposite corners. See Figure 9-27.

The **2**, **3**, and **4** options provide preset viewport configurations similar to the **Viewports** dialog box. These options can also be selected from the **Viewports** cascading menu in the **View** pull-down menu, as was discussed for tiled viewports.

The remaining options are described as follows:
- **ON and OFF.** These options activate and deactivate the model space display within a viewport. When you enter the **OFF** option, you are prompted to select the viewports to be affected. Use the **ON** option to reactivate the viewport.
- **Fit.** This default option creates a single rectangular floating viewport that fills the entire printable area on the sheet.

Figure 9-27.
Creating a rectangular floating viewport using the **MVIEW** command.

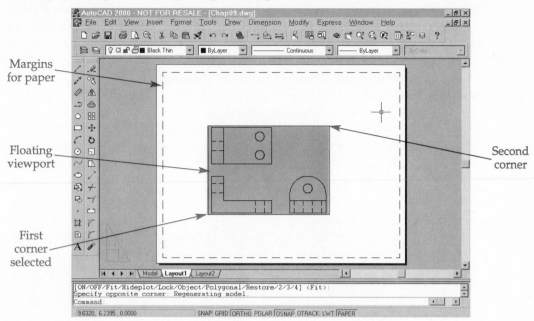

Margins for paper

Floating viewport

First corner selected

Second corner

- **Hideplot.** This option prevents hidden lines in a 3D model from being plotted. This option is covered in greater detail in *AutoCAD and its Applications—Advanced.*
- **Lock.** This option allows you to lock the view in one or more viewports. When a viewport is locked, objects within the viewport can be still edited and new objects can be added, but you are unable to use display commands such as **ZOOM** and **PAN**. This option is also used to unlock a locked viewport.
- **Restore.** Converts saved viewport configurations into individual floating viewports.
- **Object.** Use this option to change a closed object drawn in paper space into a floating viewport. Circles, ellipses, polygons, and other closed shapes can be used as floating viewport outlines. See Figure 9-28. This option can also be accessed by picking the **Convert Object to Viewport** button in the **Viewports**

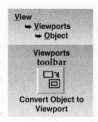

View
→ **Viewports**
  → **Object**

Viewports toolbar

Convert Object to Viewport

Figure 9-28.
Viewports can be created from closed objects. A—Draw the objects in paper space.
B—Objects converted to viewports.

Objects drawn in paper space

Objects converted to floating viewports

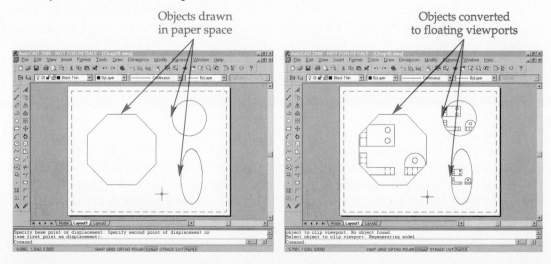

toolbar or by selecting **Object** from the **Viewports** cascading menu in the **View** pull-down menu.

- **Polygonal.** Use this option to draw a floating viewport outline using a polyline. Polylines are discussed in Chapter 15. The viewport shape can be any closed shape composed of lines and arcs. See Figure 9-29. This option can also be accessed by picking the **Polygonal Viewport** button in the **Viewports** toolbar or by selecting **Polygonal Viewport** from the **Viewports** cascading menu in the **View** pull-down menu.

View
→ Viewports
→ Polygonal
Viewport

Viewports
toolbar

Polygonal Viewport

Figure 9-29.
Floating viewports can be a closed shape comprising polylines and polyarcs.

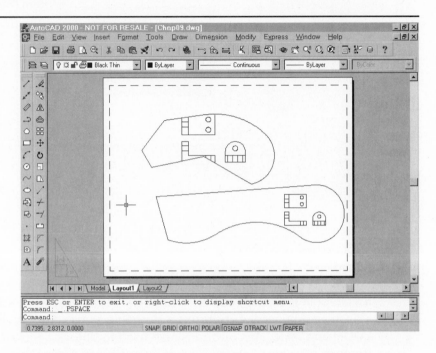

INTRODUCTION TO 3D DISPLAY COMMANDS

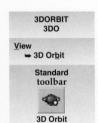

The commands **3DORBIT**, **DVIEW** (dynamic view), and **VPOINT** (viewpoint) are used in 3D drawing. An introduction to the basics of 3D drawing is provided in Chapter 27. However, these display commands are introduced in the next sections.

Using 3DORBIT to Obtain a View

3DORBIT
3DO

View
→ 3D Orbit

Standard
toolbar

3D Orbit

The **3DORBIT** command is a viewing tool that dynamically obtains a new 3D view of your drawing. To access the **3DORBIT** command, select **3D Orbit** from the **View** pull-down menu, pick the **3D Orbit** button from the **Standard** toolbar, or enter 3DO or 3DORBIT at the Command: prompt. If you are realtime zooming or realtime panning, you can right-click and select **3D Orbit** from the shortcut menu.

Once the **3DORBIT** command is accessed, a 3D view appears in the active viewport. The UCS (User Coordinate System) is changed to a shaded 3D icon, and an arcball, which is a circle divided into four quadrants by smaller circles, appears in the middle of the viewport. See Figure 9-30.

The drawing crosshairs also change to a sphere encircled with two lines. By holding down the pick button and moving your pointing device, a 3D view can be obtained. By dragging the pointing device you can see your new viewpoint adjust. It is like walking around your drawing and moving your eye position up, down, and around.

Figure 9-30.
When you activate the **3DORBIT** command, the arcball, shaded UCS icon, and 3D Orbit cursor appear. You can then rotate the objects in 3D space.

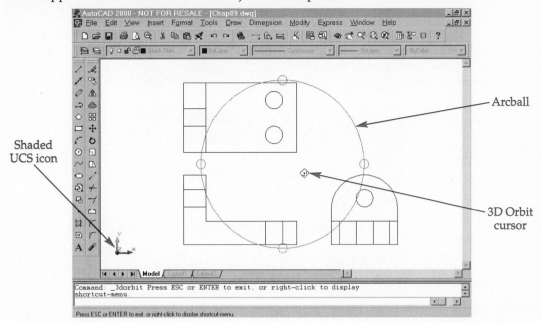

If the cursor is moved over the top of one of the quadrant circles on the arcball, it changes shape, showing you the direction the view can be rotated. If the right mouse button is pressed, a shortcut menu appears so you can use realtime zoom or realtime pan. There are several other options and possibilities with the **3DORBIT** command. The **3DORBIT** command is covered in greater detail in *AutoCAD and its Applications—Advanced.*

Establishing a Dynamic View

When using the **DVIEW** command to view a 3D drawing, you can see the object move as you perform viewing commands such as **ROTATE** and **PAN**. Follow the given example for a brief overview of the **DVIEW** command.

First, open the campus.dwg drawing. This drawing should be in the Acad2000\Sample folder. The drawing that appears is a 3D model of campus buildings. It is displayed in a layout tab for plotting.

Select the **Model** tab and let AutoCAD regenerate the drawing. Select **Plan View** and then **World UCS** from the **3D Views** cascading menu in the **View** pull-down menu. Your display should look like the display in Figure 9-31.

Access the **Viewports** dialog box and select the Three: Right configuration. Next, make the large viewport active by picking anywhere inside it. Then, select **2D Wireframe** from the **Shade** cascading menu in the **View** pull-down menu. This allows viewing of the model in a wireframe view.

Use the **DVIEW** command to create a 3D view of the campus in the large viewport. Proceed as follows:

> Command: **DV** *or* **DVIEW**↵
> Select objects or <use DVIEWBLOCK>: ↵

In order to speed up the **DVIEW** process, press [Enter] at the Select objects or <use DVIEWBLOCK>: prompt. This displays a house that requires less regeneration time than the entire model. Your drawing returns to the screen at the completion of the

Figure 9-31.
Plan view of the campus drawing.

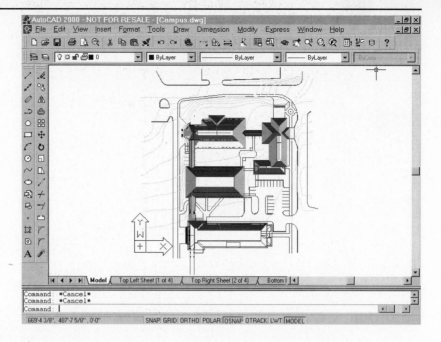

DVIEW command. If you want to work with objects in your drawing on the screen using the **DVIEW** options, use any of the selection methods to select them.

Enter option
[CAmera/TArget/Distance/POints/PAn/Zoom/TWist/CLip/Hide/Off/Undo]: **TA**↵
Specify camera location, or enter angle from the XY plane, or [Toggle (angle in)]
    <-90.00>: **-15**↵
Specify camera location, or enter angle in the XY plane from X axis, or [Toggle
    (angle from)] <-90.00>: **-40**↵
Enter option
[CAmera/TArget/Distance/POints/PAn/Zoom/TWist/CLip/Hide/Off/Undo]: ↵
Command:

Perform a **ZOOM Extents** and your screen should now look like the screen in Figure 9-32.

Figure 9-32.
The view on the right has been set using the **DVIEW** command.

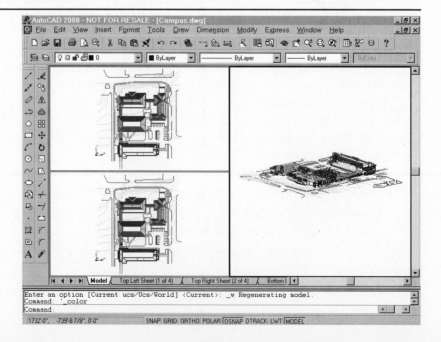

AutoCAD and its Applications—Basics

Try to determine the direction from which you are viewing the campus. Notice in the small viewports that the small parking lot is toward the bottom-right of the screen. Now look at the UCS icon in the large viewport. If it appears that the small parking lot is on the other side of the buildings, that is correct.

There are several other options and possibilities with the **DVIEW** command. You can create a true perspective view by specifying the distance from camera to target. In addition, you can zoom in or away from the object, and clip the front or rear of the screen image. Additional information regarding these options is found in *AutoCAD and its Applications—Advanced, AutoCAD 2000*.

Creating a 3D Viewpoint

The **VPOINT** command allows you to specify the direction from which you will view the object. You can enter XYZ coordinates, or you can visually determine your viewpoint using an *XYZ tripod*. This example uses coordinate entry to determine both viewpoints. Make the upper-left viewport active and enter the following commands:

```
Command: -VP or VPOINT↵
Current view direction: VIEWDIR=0'-0",0'-0", 0'-1"
Specify a view point or [Rotate] <display compass and tripod>: -1,-1,1↵
Regenerating model.
Command:
```

Activate the lower-left viewport and enter the following:

```
Command: -VP or VPOINT↵
Current view direction: VIEWDIR=0'-0",0'-0", 0'-1"
Specify a view point or [Rotate] <display compass and tripod>: 1,-1,1↵
Regenerating model.
Command:
```

The screen should now resemble Figure 9-33.

One advantage of multiple viewports is that each viewport is a separate screen. Therefore, you can display any view of the drawing you wish in each screen. In addition, 3D drawings can appear as either wireframe or solid. A *wireframe* is an object that shows all lines, including those at the back of the object. The views currently on your screen show wireframes. To make an object look more realistic, use the **HIDE** command.

Make the lower-left viewport active and zoom in on the entrance along the right face of the campus area. See Figure 9-34A. Now, use the **HIDE** command to remove hidden lines. This process may take a few minutes depending on the speed of your computer. The hidden lines are removed from the active viewport. See Figure 9-34B.

Figure 9-33.
The **VPOINT**
command is used to
create two different
views in the small
viewports.

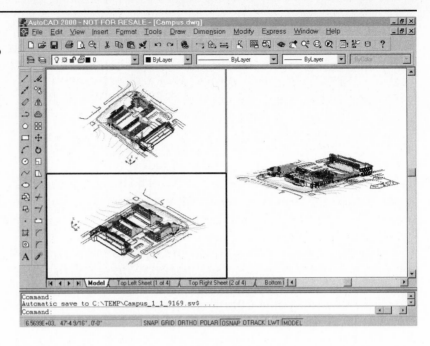

Figure 9-34.
A—Section of building shown as a wireframe. B—Details are clear when hidden lines are removed.

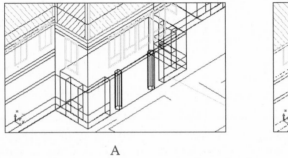

A

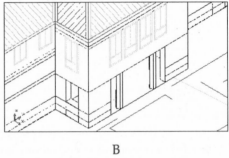

B

NOTE

Entering SHADE at the Command: prompt colors 3D solid faces. To remove the shading or hidden lines from a view, you must pick **2D Wireframe** from the **Shade** cascading menu in the **View** pull down menu. The **SHADE** command is covered in detail in *AutoCAD and its Applications–Advanced, AutoCAD 2000.*

REDRAWING AND REGENERATING VIEWPORTS

Since each viewport is a separate screen, you can redraw or regenerate a single viewport at a time without affecting the others. The **REGEN** (regenerate) command instructs AutoCAD to recalculate all objects in the drawing. This takes considerably longer than a **REDRAW**, especially if the drawing is large. However, **REGEN** can clarify a drawing by smoothing out circles, arcs, ellipses, and splines.

To redraw all viewports, use the **REDRAWALL** command or pick **Redraw** from the **View** pull-down menu. If you need to regenerate all viewports, use the **REGENALL** command or pick **Regen All** from the **View** pull-down menu.

REDRAWALL
RA

View
➥ Redraw

REGENALL
REA

View
➥ Regen All

AutoCAD and its Applications—Basics

Controlling Automatic Regeneration

When developing a drawing, you may use a command that changes certain aspects of the entities. When this occurs, AutoCAD does an automatic regeneration to update the entities. This may not be of concern to you when working on small drawings, but this regeneration may take considerable time on large and complex drawings. In addition, it may not be necessary to have a regeneration of the drawing at all times. If this is the case, set the **REGENAUTO** command to off.

Command: **REGENAUTO**↵
Enter mode [ON/OFF] <*current*>: **OFF** ↵
Command:

Some of the commands that may automatically cause a regeneration are **ZOOM**, **PAN**, **PLAN**, **HIDE**, and **VIEW Restore**.

CONTROLLING THE ORDER OF DISPLAY

AutoCAD has the ability to display both raster and vector images in the graphics window. A *raster image* is composed of dots, or *pixels*, and is also referred to as a *bit map*. Raster images contain no XYZ coordinate values. Objects in a *vector image* (drawing), such as those created in AutoCAD, are given XYZ coordinate values. So, all these objects are composed of points, or *vectors*, connected by straight lines.

Drawings containing both raster and vector images can have objects that overlap each other. For example, in Figure 9-35A the raster image of the **Zoom Previous** button is imported into AutoCAD and overlays the vector image of the text label. In this case the text label should be displayed on top of the raster image. To do this, use the **DRAWORDER** command by picking **Bring Above Object** in the **Display Order** cascading menu of the **Tools** pull-down menu, or enter DR or DRAWORDER at the Command: prompt. The drawing is then displayed and plotted as shown in Figure 9-35B.

The drawing order is the order in which objects are displayed and/or plotted. If an object is moved to the top of the drawing order, it is displayed and plotted first. If one object is moved above another object, it is displayed on top—the text in Figure 9-35B. These order and arrangement functions are handled by the following **DRAWORDER** options:

- **Above object.** The selected object is moved above the reference object.
- **Under object.** The selected object is moved below the reference object.
- **Front.** The selected object is placed to the front of the drawing.
- **Back.** The selected object is placed to the back of the drawing.

DRAWORDER
DR

Tools
➡ Display Order
➡ Bring Above Object

Figure 9-35.
A—An imported raster image obscures part of a vector drawing.
B—The **DRAWORDER** command is used to bring the vector drawing above the raster image.

Zoom Previous

A

Zoom Previous

B

NOTE

See *AutoCAD and its Applications–Advanced, AutoCAD 2000* for more detailed information on the use of raster drawings in AutoCAD.

Chapter Test

Answer the following questions on a separate sheet of paper.

1. What is the difference between the **REDRAW** and **'REDRAW** commands?
2. What are *blips* and how does **REDRAW** affect them?
3. Which command allows you to change the display of blips?
4. Give the proper command option and value to automatically zoom to a 2X scale factor.
5. What is the difference between **ZOOM Extents** and **ZOOM All**?
6. During the drawing process, when should you use **ZOOM**?
7. How many different boxes are displayed during the **ZOOM Dynamic** command?
8. What is a *pan displacement*?
9. When using the **ZOOM Dynamic** option, what represents the current view?
10. What is the purpose of the **PAN** command?
11. Explain how scroll bars can be used to pan the drawing display.
12. How do you access the **PAN** command presets?
13. What is *view resolution*?
14. In which dialog box is circle and arc smoothness set?
15. How do you create a named view of the current screen display?
16. How do you display an existing view?
17. How would you obtain a listing of existing views?
18. How is a transparent display command entered at the keyboard?
19. What is the affect of picking **Global** from the **View** pull-down menu in the **Aerial View** window?
20. What is the function of the **Auto Viewport** option of the **Aerial View** window?
21. Cite several advantages of **Aerial View** over other display commands.
22. Explain the difference between model space and paper space.
23. What type of viewports are created in model space?
24. What type of viewports are created in paper space?
25. What is the purpose of the **Preview** area of the **Viewports** dialog box?
26. Explain the procedures and conditions that need to exist when joining viewports.
27. What commands allow you to create 3D views in a drawing or viewport?
28. How do the **3DORBIT**, **DVIEW**, and **VPOINT** commands differ?
29. Which command regenerates all of the viewports?
30. What is the function of **REGENAUTO**?

Drawing Problems

1. Open the drawing named Oceanarium found in the Acad2000\Sample folder. Perform the following display functions on the drawing:
   A. Select the **Model** tab
   B. **ZOOM Extents.**
   C. Create a view named All.
   D. Zoom in to display the right side of the building.
   E. Create a view of this new window named Rightside.
   F. **ZOOM Previous.**
   G. Use realtime pan and realtime zoom to create a display of the lower-left stair case.
   H. Create a view of this display named West Stair.
   I. Display the view named All.
   J. Save the drawing as P9-1.

2. Load one of your own mechanical template drawings that contains a border and title block. Do the following:
   A. Zoom into the title block area. Create and save a view named Title.
   B. Zoom to the extents of the drawing and create and save a view named All.
   C. Determine the area of the drawing that will contain notes, parts list, or revisions. Zoom into these areas and create views with appropriate names such as Notes, Partlist, and Revisions.
   D. Divide the drawing area into commonly used multiview sections. Save the views with descriptive names such as Top, Front, Rightside, and Leftside.
   E. Restore the view named All.
   F. Save the drawing as P9-2, or as a template.

3. Load one of your own template drawings used for architectural layout that contains a border and title block. Do the following:
   A. Zoom into the title block area. Create and save a view named Title.
   B. Zoom to the extents of the drawing and create and save a view named All.
   C. Determine the area of the drawing that will contain notes, schedules, or revisions. Zoom into these areas and create views with appropriate names such as Notes, Schedules, and Revisions.
   D. Restore the view named All.
   E. Save the drawing as P9-3, or as a template.

4. Open the drawing named City base map. This drawing should be in the Acad2000\Sample folder. Then perform the following:
   A. Make sure the **MODEL** tab is active. Pick **4 Viewports** from the **Viewports** cascading menu in the **View** pull-down menu.
   B. In each viewport, zoom to a different quadrant of the drawing.
   C. Create named views of different parts of the map, such as NorthEast, NorthWest, and SouthEast.
   D. In the upper-right viewport, **ZOOM All** and create a view named All.
   E. Use **3DORBIT** to obtain a 3D view in the upper-right viewport.
   F. Make the upper-left viewport active and split it into four equal viewports.
   G. In each of the new viewports restore your named views from step C.

H. Pick **Join** from the **Viewports** cascading menu in the **View** pull down menu to join the two far-right viewports together. Make the 3D view the dominant view.

I. In the lower-left viewport restore the **All** view.

J. Save the drawing as P9-4 only if required by your instructor.

CHAPTER 10

Layouts, Plotting, and Printing

Learning Objectives

After completing this chapter, you will be able to:

- Print and plot a drawing.
- Set up layouts using title blocks and viewports.
- Create new layouts.
- Manage layouts.
- Select a plotting device and modify a plotting device configuration.
- Explain plot styles, plot style tables, and plot style modes.
- Create and modify plot styles and plot style tables.
- Attach plot style tables to drawings and layouts.
- Assign plot styles to drawings, layers, and objects.
- Select plot settings.
- Calculate scale factors based on drawing scale.
- Create a plot file.
- Plot a group of drawings using the Batch Plot utility.
- Explain keys to efficient plotting.

Often, the end result of the work you perform with AutoCAD will be a plotted drawing. It is far easier for a construction crew in the field to use a printed copy of the drawing rather than using a computer to view the DWG file. Therefore, it is important that you understand the various plotting options available in AutoCAD.

Paper space, model space, the **Model** tab, and layout tabs were all discussed in Chapter 9. Each layout tab can be set to plot different views of the objects using different plotting settings. This allows you to create several different plots using a single drawing.

PLOTTING PROCEDURE

You can create plots from the **Model** tab (model space) and from the layout tabs (paper space). The general procedures for both cases are similar. The following steps are explained later in this chapter:

1. Create the drawing objects in the **Model** tab (model space). If you are creating a layout, create the floating viewports, title block, and other desired items in a layout tab (paper space).
2. Configure the plotting device if it is not already configured.

3. Access the **Page Setup** or **Plot** dialog box and specify values for the plotting settings. Each tab (**Model** and layout) can have its own settings, so each layout can produce a different plot.
4. Plot the drawing.

LAYOUT AND PLOTTING TERMS

It is important to understand the terminology used when discussing model space, paper space, layouts, and plotting. Therefore, this section provides you with a quick overview of the commands and functions that enable you to lay out and plot a drawing. These terms are described in greater detail later in this chapter.

- **Model space.** This is the drawing environment in which the drawing objects are constructed. Model space is active when the **Model** tab is selected. Model space is also activated when you double-click inside a floating viewport in a layout tab.

- **Paper space.** This is the drawing environment used to create plotting layouts, which are arrangements of various objects (such as floating viewports, title blocks, and annotations) on the page to be plotted. Paper space is active by default when a layout tab is selected. If you double-click inside a floating viewport in a layout tab, the viewport becomes active and model space is entered. To switch back to paper space, double-click in an area outside the floating viewport.

- **Layouts.** A layout is the manner in which a drawing is arranged in paper space. A layout may contain a title block, one or more viewports, and annotations. Each drawing can have multiple layouts, and each layout is shown as a tab along the bottom of the drawing area. Each layout can have different page setup and plotting settings.

- **Page setups.** A page setup is the manner in which the drawing is displayed on a sheet of paper in order to create a layout. Most of the aspects of how the drawing is plotted can be established in a page setup, from the plot device to pen settings to scales. These settings can even be saved in the drawing file as a named page setup, which can be recalled each time the drawing is plotted.

- **Layout settings.** These settings are created in the **Page Setup** dialog box and include paper size and drawing units, paper orientation, plot area, plot scale, plot offset, and plot options.

- **Plotters window.** The **Plotters** window allows you to add, delete, configure, and reconfigure plotters. It can be accessed by selecting **Plotter Manager...** from the **File** pull-down menu. When a device is configured, the settings are saved in a PC3 file.

- **Plot styles.** Plot styles contain settings that are applied to objects when they are plotted. A *color-dependent plot style* is applied to all objects with a specific color. A *named plot style* can be assigned to an object or layer.

- **Plot style tables.** A plot style table is a collection of plot styles. There are two types of plot style tables: color-dependent and named. A plot style table can only contain plot styles of a single *plot style mode* (either color-dependent or named). The **Model** tab and each layout tab can have a unique plot style table attached. Only plot styles in the attached plot style table can be used within a tab.

- **Plot Styles window.** The **Plot Styles** window allows you to manage all your plot style table files. From here you can open and edit the plot styles within a plot style table. You can also create new plot style tables.

- **Plot settings.** These settings are created in the **Plot** dialog box and include the same items found in the **Page Setup** dialog box. They control how the drawing is printed on paper. Although this may seem like the last step in the process, plot settings can be created at the beginning of a project and then saved to be used again.
- **Batch Plotting.** Once drawing files have been assigned layouts, page setups, and plot parameters, they can be grouped in *batch list* files using the Batch Plot utility. These files can then be configured to plot off-line or in the background as a group, or "batch," while the user continues with other tasks. Batch plot files are saved with a BP3 extension and can be created without opening a full session of AutoCAD.

LAYOUT SETTINGS

A *layout* shows the arrangement of objects on a sheet of paper for plotting purposes. A layout may include a title block, floating viewports showing your model space drawing, and annotation.

A single drawing can have multiple layouts. Named layouts are displayed as tabs along the bottom of the drawing area. Each layout tab represents a different paper space configuration.

Drawings created with the **Use a Wizard** and **Start from Scratch** setup options have two layouts by default. These are identified by the **Layout1** and **Layout2** tabs below the drawing area. See Figure 10-1. When you pick a layout tab for the first time, the **Page Setup** dialog box for the layout appears. This dialog box allows you to complete a variety of settings for the plotting device and the layout of the drawing on a sheet of paper. This dialog box is discussed later in this chapter. For the time being, select the **OK** button in this dialog box to enter the **Layout1** tab.

Figure 10-1.
A layout is displayed when a layout tab is selected. The layout provides a preview of how the plotted drawing will appear.

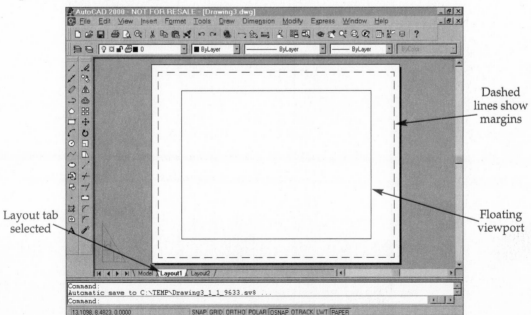

When a layout tab is selected, an image showing a preview of the final printed drawing is shown. The dashed line around the edge of the paper represents the page margins. The solid lines show the outline of a floating viewport. By default, a single viewport is created.

Working in Layout Tabs

A layout can contain many types of objects, including floating viewports, a title block, and notes. Assembling these items in a layout allows you to see exactly what the final plot will look like.

Several settings that affect the display of layouts are contained in the **Layout elements** area of the **Display** tab in the **Options** dialog box. See Figure 10-2. Access this dialog box by selecting **Options...** from the **Tools** pull-down menu. Use the default settings until you are comfortable working with layouts.

Figure 10-2.
Layout display options are found in the **Options** dialog box.

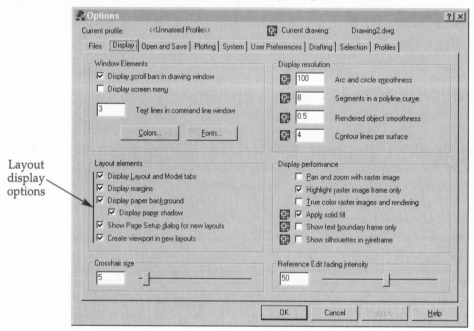

Layout display options

Inserting a title block

Most layouts contain a title block. Title blocks are generally saved in a template file and then inserted as a block when needed. A block is a single object comprising multiple individual objects. See Chapter 23 for a complete discussion on blocks.

It is best to insert a title block into the layout and then save it as a template file. You can then start a new drawing based on the template, and the layout with the title block will already be created.

To insert a title block, select **Block...** from the **Insert** pull-down menu to access the **Insert** dialog box. Pick the **Browse...** button and select the title block drawing to be inserted. Figure 10-3 shows the ANSI A title block inserted into a layout.

NOTE You can also copy a layout containing the title block from an existing drawing using the **AutoCAD DesignCenter**. This is discussed later in this chapter.

Figure 10-3.
The ANSI A title block inserted into the layout. Note that the viewport created by default has been deleted.

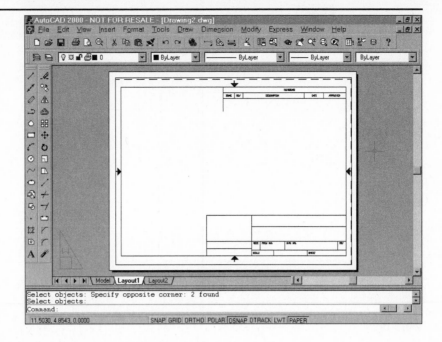

Working with floating viewports

Chapter 9 explained how to create floating viewports in a layout. Once the viewports are created, the display within the viewport must be set to show the correct part of the model space drawing.

Create the floating viewports after the title block has been inserted. This will allow you to position the viewports so they do not interfere with the title block. Floating viewports are created using the **Viewports** dialog box or the **MVIEW** and **-VPORTS** command. This is discussed in Chapter 9.

Figure 10-4 illustrates the following procedure for establishing the display in two floating viewports:

1. Create the first viewport using the **Viewports** dialog box. The model space drawing is visible in the viewport.
2. Create a second viewport.
3. Double-click in the new viewport to enter model space.
4. Use the **XP** option of the **ZOOM** command to scale the drawing. Use realtime panning to display the part of interest in the drawing.
5. Double-click outside of the viewports to activate paper space. Use grips or the **STRETCH** command to resize the viewport.

Using multiple viewports in a layout allows you to illustrate different aspects of the drawing. Using multiple layouts, various types of drawings can be created from a single drawing model. This is a very simple example of the use of floating viewports within a layout. Figure 10-5 shows the viewports created by the **Std. 3D Engineering Views** option available in the Create Layout wizard. The viewports show the three primary orthographic views and an isometric view. The Create Layout wizard is discussed later in this chapter.

CAUTION

If you use zoom to adjust the drawing inside the viewport, the drawing may no longer be to scale. Always use the **ZOOM XP** option as the final step prior to plotting to be certain the drawing is scaled inside the viewport.

Figure 10-4.
These steps illustrate the procedure for adding viewports to a simple layout outlined in the text.

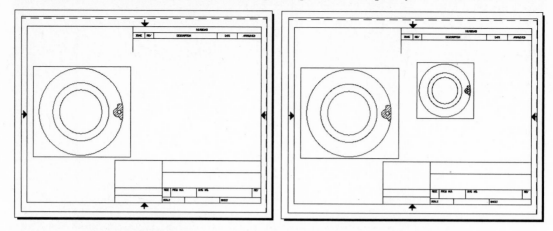

Step 1—Create viewport.   Step 2—Create second viewport.

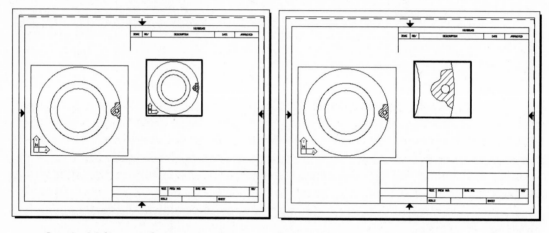

Step 3—Make second viewport active.   Step 4—Zoom and pan display in second viewport.

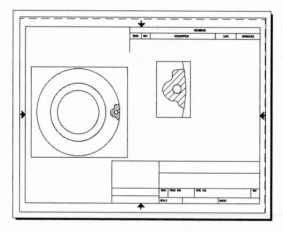

Step 5—Resize viewport.

Figure 10-5.
This example shows the ANSI D title block and the **Std. 3D Engineering Views** viewport configuration. This configuration is available in the Create Layout wizard.

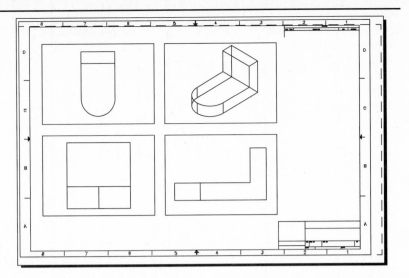

❑ Start a new drawing from scratch.
❑ Create the following layers with the specified properties:

Layer	Color	Linetype
Circle	Blue	Continuous
Line	Red	Hidden
Ellipse	Green	Phantom
Rectangle	Magenta	Dashed

❑ Draw a circle, line, ellipse, and rectangle, each on the appropriate layer.
❑ Perform a **ZOOM Extents**.
❑ Access the **Layout1** tab, cancel the **Page Setup** dialog box, and delete the default viewport.
❑ Create an arrangement of viewports using the Three: Left preset configuration.
❑ Modify the display within the viewports so that all objects are shown in the larger, left viewport, the circle is shown in the top-right viewport, and the ellipse is shown in the lower-right viewport. Double-click in a viewport to make it active.
❑ Save this drawing as EX10-1. It will be used for other Exercises in this chapter.

Managing Layouts

The **LAYOUT** command allows you to manage layouts. To access this command, type LO or LAYOUT at the Command: prompt:

Command: **LO** *or* **LAYOUT**↵
Enter layout option [Copy/Delete/New/Template/Rename/SAveas/Set/?] <set>:

You are prompted to select a **LAYOUT** command option. Some of these options are also available in the **Layouts** toolbars or the **Layout** cascading menu of the **Insert** pull-down menu. You can also position the cursor over a layout tab and right-click to display the layout shortcut menu, Figure 10-6. This shortcut menu also contains many **LAYOUT** command options.

Figure 10-6.
Right-click on a
layout tab to display
the layout shortcut
menu. Many
options for
managing layouts
are available.

<u>N</u>ew layout
From <u>t</u>emplate...
<u>D</u>elete
<u>R</u>ename
<u>M</u>ove or Copy...
Select <u>A</u>ll Layouts
Page <u>S</u>etup...
<u>P</u>lot...

Setting the current layout

The current layout is identified by the highlighted tab at the bottom of the drawing area. To set the current layout, pick the layout tab using the cursor. You can also use the **Set** option of the **LAYOUT** command to specify the current layout.

PROFESSIONAL TIP

If you are selecting options from the layout shortcut menu, you must have the appropriate layout set as current before selecting the command. For example, if you select **Delete** from the layout shortcut menu, the current layout is deleted. If you work at the Command: prompt, the current layout is the default but you can specify a different layout.

Listing layouts

If a drawing has several layouts or layouts with fairly long names, all layout tabs may not be visible. When this is the case, you can use the four buttons to the left of the tab list to view the tabs. See Figure 10-7. The two outer arrows display the left and right ends of the tab list. The inner arrows move the list one tab in the indicated direction. Changing the display of the tab list does not affect the current tab. You still must pick a tab to set it as current.

The **?** option of the **LAYOUT** command can be used to list all layouts within the drawing. After selecting this option, you must switch to the **AutoCAD Text Window** to view the list. To do this, select **Text Window** from the **Display** cascading menu in the **View** pull-down menu or use the [F2] function key.

Figure 10-7.
Use the arrows to select which tabs are displayed.

Move to far   Move to far
left tab   right tab

| ◄◄ | ◄ | ► | ►► | \ Model \ | ANSI A Title Block (portrait) | \ ANSI A Title Block \ | ANSI B T◄ | | | ► |

Move one tab   Move one tab   Pick vertical bar
to the left   to the right   to adjust width
                                                          of tab display

Creating a new layout

There are several methods of creating new layouts. A new layout can be created from scratch, similar to the default layouts created with the **Start from Scratch** and **Use a Wizard** setup options. Layouts can also be copied from existing drawing and template files. Finally, a layout within the drawing can be copied to create a new layout. These methods are described as follows:

- **New layout from scratch.** Use the **New** option of the **LAYOUT** command to create a new layout. You can also create a new layout by selecting **New Layout** from the **Layout** cascading menu in the **Insert** pull-down menu, picking the **New Layout** button in the **Layouts** toolbar, or by right-clicking on a layout tab and selecting **New layout** from the layout shortcut menu. If you select the option from the command line or pull-down menu, the following prompt appears:

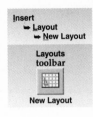

Insert
➥ Layout
➥ New Layout

Layouts
toolbar

New Layout

Enter new Layout name <Layout3>: *(type a name or accept default name)*

The layout name appears on the layout tab. If you use the **New layout** option in the layout shortcut menu, the new layout is created with the default name. You can then use the **Rename** option to change the name.

- **New layout from template.** This option creates a new layout based on a layout stored in an existing drawing or template file. Select this option by using the **Template** option of the **LAYOUT** command, selecting **Layout from Template...** from the **Layout** cascading menu in the **Insert** pull-down menu, or picking the **Layout from Template** button in the **Layouts** toolbar. You can also right-click on a layout tab and select **From template...** in the layout shortcut menu.

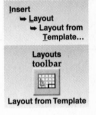

Insert
➥ Layout
➥ Layout from
Template...

Layouts
toolbar

Layout from Template

When you select this option, the **Select File** dialog box is displayed, Figure 10-8A. The Acad2000\Template directory is selected by default. Select the drawing file or template file containing the layout to be copied and pick the **Open** button. If you selected the command option from the shortcut or pull-down menu, the **Insert Layout(s)** dialog box appears. See Figure 10-8B.

Figure 10-8.
Creating a new layout from another drawing or template.
A—Select the drawing or template containing the layout.
B—Highlight the layout(s) to be added to the current drawing.

AutoCAD 2000\Template folder opened by default

Select type of file

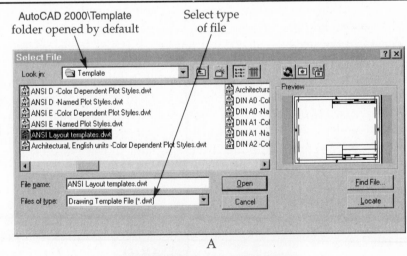

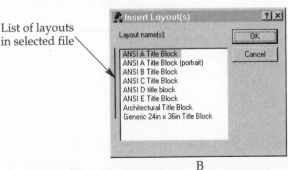

List of layouts in selected file

For 2000i Users...

In AutoCAD 2000i, the **Select File** dialog box from AutoCAD 2000 has been replaced with the **Select Template From File** dialog box, which is identical to the updated **Select File** dialog box. See *Select File* Dialog Box on page 966 for complete details of the dialog box features.

This dialog box lists all layouts in the selected file. Highlight the layout(s) you want to copy and pick the **OK** button.

If you select this option from the command line or use the **Layout from Template** button, the **Insert Layout(s)** dialog box does not appear. Instead, you are prompted to enter the name of the layout to copy.

PROFESSIONAL TIP It is much easier to select layouts to copy using the **Insert Layout(s)** dialog box than it is to enter the name at the Command: prompt. Therefore, use the shortcut menu or pull-down menu to select this **LAYOUT** command option.

- **Copy layout in drawing.** You can create a new layout by copying an existing layout. If you use the **Copy** option of the **LAYOUT** command, enter the name of the layout to copy, then enter the name for the new copy. The current layout is the default layout to copy. If a name for the copy is not entered, AutoCAD uses the current layout name plus a number in parentheses. For example, if the current layout is named **Layout3**, the following prompts appear:

    Command: **LO** *or* **LAYOUT**⏎
    Enter layout option [Copy/Delete/New/Template/Rename/SAveas/Set/?] <set>: **C**⏎
    Enter name of layout to copy <Layout3>: ⏎
    Enter layout name for copy <Layout3 (2)>: ⏎
    Layout "Layout3" copied to "Layout3 (2)".

    You can also copy an existing layout by selecting **Move or Copy...** from the layout shortcut menu. This option provides no opportunity to change the layout to be copied; the current layout tab is copied. When you select this option, the **Move or Copy** dialog box appears, Figure 10-9. Activate the **Create a copy** check box, and then select which layout the new layout tab should be to the left of. The default name is automatically assigned to the new layout. Use the **Rename** option to change it.
- **Using the Create Layout wizard.** You can create a new layout using the Create Layout wizard. To access this wizard, select **Create Layout...** from the **Wizards** cascading menu in the **Tools** pull-down menu. The pages of the wizard allow you to specify a title block, viewports, and many page setup values. These page setup values are discussed later in this chapter.

Figure 10-9.
The **Move or Copy** dialog box is used to reorganize the layout tabs and to copy layout tabs within a drawing. It is accessed through the layout shortcut menu.

Select location of new layout tab

Check to create a copy of the current layout

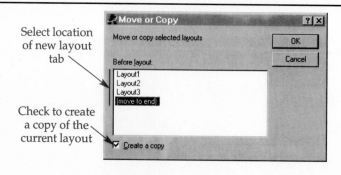

Copying layouts with DesignCenter

Layouts are included as a type of content that can be viewed using the **AutoCAD DesignCenter**. To access **DesignCenter**, select **AutoCAD DesignCenter** from the **Tools** pull-down menu, pick the **AutoCAD DesignCenter** button in the **Standard** toolbar, type ADC or ADCENTER at the Command: prompt, or use the [Ctrl]+[2] key combination.

To copy a layout from an existing drawing or template, first locate the drawing in the **DesignCenter** tree view. Then select Layouts to display the layouts within the drawing. See Figure 10-10. Select the layout(s) to be copied and then use the **Add Layout(s)** or cut and paste options from shortcut menus or drag-and-drop to insert the layouts in the current drawing.

Figure 10-10.
Layouts can be shared between drawings using **DesignCenter**.

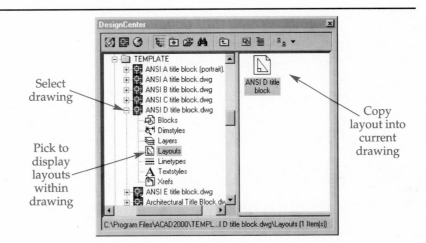

Renaming a layout

The name of the layout appears on its tab. Layouts created by default are named **Layout*n***, where *n* is a number. A layout created by copying another layout has the same name as the initial layout, followed by a number in parentheses. For example, the first copy of **Layout2** is named **Layout2 (1)**.

Layouts are easier to work with when they have a descriptive name. Layouts can be renamed using the **Rename** option of the **LAYOUT** command or by selecting **Rename** from the layout shortcut menu. After the layout has been renamed, the new name is displayed on the tab.

When you select the **Rename** option of the **LAYOUT** command, you are prompted to enter the name of the layout to be renamed. The current layout is provided as a default. Once you have entered the layout name, you are prompted to enter the new layout name.

The **Rename Layout** dialog box appears when you select **Rename** from the layout shortcut menu. If you select this option, you can rename only the current layout. Enter the new name in the text box and pick the **OK** button.

Deleting a layout

When a layout is no longer useful, it can be deleted. You can delete a layout using the **Delete** option of the **LAYOUT** command. You can also delete the active layout by right-clicking and selecting **Delete** from the layout shortcut menu.

When you use the **Delete** option of the **LAYOUT** command, you are prompted to enter the name of the layout to be deleted. The current layout is provided as the default.

If you select **Delete** from the layout shortcut menu, an alert box warns you that the layout will be permanently deleted. Pick the **OK** button to delete the layout.

Saving a layout

The **Saveas** option of the **LAYOUT** command is used to save a single layout as a drawing template or drawing file. The following is the command sequence:

Command: **LO** *or* **LAYOUT**↵
Enter layout option [Copy/Delete/New/Template/Rename/SAveas/Set/?] <set>: **SA**↵
Enter layout to save to template <*current layout*>: *(enter name of layout or accept default)*

After you specify the layout to save, the **Create Drawing File** dialog box appears. You can save the layout in a DWT, DWG, or DXF file. Enter the file name and pick the **SAVE** button. The layout is now saved in the new file.

EXERCISE 10-2

❏ Open EX10-1 if it is not already open.
❏ Rename **Layout1** as **Circle-Ellipse Detail**.
❏ Save and close EX10-1.
❏ Begin a new drawing from scratch.
❏ Delete the **Layout2** layout by right-clicking on the tab and then selecting **Delete** from the layout shortcut menu.
❏ Open **AutoCAD DesignCenter** and copy the **Circle-Ellipse Detail** layout from the EX10-1.dwg drawing file. Close **DesignCenter**.
❏ Create a new layout by copying the **Circle-Ellipse Detail** layout using the **Move or Copy...** option in the layout shortcut menu.
❏ Rename the new layout **Line-Rectangle Detail** and modify the display in the right viewports to show the line and rectangle.
❏ Save this drawing as EX10-2. It will be used for other Exercises in this chapter.

Page Setups for Plotting

A *page setup* contains the settings required to create a finished plot of the drawing. Most of the aspects of how the drawing is plotted can be established in a page setup, from the plot device to pen settings to scales. In fact, the only difference between the **Page Setup** and **Plot** dialog boxes is that the **Page Setup** dialog box does not provide plot preview buttons.

Each layout can have a unique page setup. Therefore, the **Page Setup** dialog box is always tied to the active **Model** tab or layout tab. These settings can even be saved in the drawing file as a named page setup, which can be recalled each time the drawing is plotted. Therefore, the setup becomes a productivity tool since it decreases the amount of time preparing a drawing for plotting.

PAGESETUP

File
➥ Page Setup...

Layouts
toolbar

Page Setup

The settings that compose the page setup are set in the **Page Setup** dialog box. This dialog box is accessed by selecting **Page Setup...** from the **File** pull-down menu, picking the **Page Setup** button in the **Layouts** toolbar, typing PAGESETUP at the Command: prompt, or right-clicking on a layout tab and selecting **Page Setup...** from the layout shortcut menu. The **Page Setup** dialog box is shown in Figure 10-11.

The **Page Setup** dialog box contains two tabs: one for selecting the plot device, and the other for selecting the layout settings. In addition, areas at the top of the dialog box display the current layout name and the current page setup name. The **Layout name** text box is for display only, and shows the name of the current layout. The **Page setup name** text box displays the name of the current page setup.

Figure 10-11.
The **Page Setup** dialog box.

Name of layout

Available tabs

Page setup name

Pick to plot

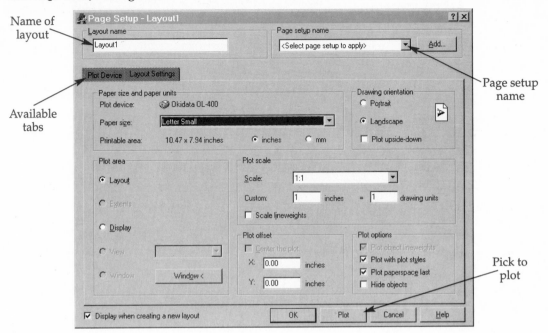

The page setup settings fall into several categories. These areas are discussed in the following sections of the text:

- **Plot device settings.** These settings deal with selecting and configuring the printer or plotter on which the drawing is to be output.
- **Plot style table.** This table contains plot styles. These plot styles determine how an object appears in the plotted drawing. Color, linetype, and lineweight can be determined by an object's plot style, along with line end treatment and fill style.
- **Plot settings.** These settings, which include the paper size and orientation, control what part of the drawing is plotted, as well as the drawing scale and other plotting parameters.

PROFESSIONAL TIP

In the planning stages of your work, create one or more page setups for the drawing and save them in a template drawing.

PLOT DEVICE SELECTION AND MANAGEMENT

Before printing or plotting, make sure that your output device is configured properly, as described in the *AutoCAD Installation Guide*. AutoCAD displays information about the currently configured printer or plotter in the **Plot Device** tab of the **Page Setup** dialog box. See Figure 10-12.

You can use this tab to change many of the printer or plotter specifications. The current device is displayed in the **Plotter configuration** area. When additional devices are configured, you can make a different one current by picking it from the **Name:** drop-down list.

Figure 10-12.
The **Plot Device** tab of the **Page Setup** dialog box.

Select device from list of configured devices

Information about selected device

Select plot style table

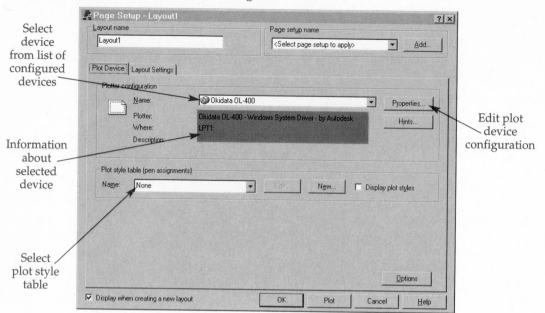

Edit plot device configuration

 NOTE

Add printers and plotters to the list by selecting **Plotter Manager...** in the **File** pull-down menu. This executes the **PLOTTERMANAGER** command and displays the **Plotters** window. Select the Add-A-Plotter Wizard icon to add, modify, and remove printing and plotting devices. See *Appendix D* for information on configuring devices for AutoCAD. When a plotter or printer is installed using the Add-A-Plotter wizard, a PC3 (plot configuration) file is created. This file contains all the settings required for the plotter to function.

Modifying the Plotter Configuration

To change the properties of the current plot device, pick the **Properties...** button in the **Plotter configuration** area. This opens the **Plotter Configuration Editor** dialog box. See Figure 10-13. Three tabs provide access to the plotting device property settings:

- **General tab.** General information about the current plotter is displayed in this tab. The only item you can change is the description.
- **Ports tab.** Use this tab to pick a port to send the plot to, plot to a file, or select AutoSpool. Using AutoSpool, plot files can be sent to a *plot spooler* file, which automatically plots the drawing in the background while you continue to work. See Chapter 6 of the online *AutoCAD Installation Guide* for a step-by-step method of plot spooling.
- **Device and Document Settings tab.** This tab displays a tree list of all the settings applicable to the current plotting device. Clicking on the desired icon enables you to modify specific settings. Items in this list displayed in brackets (< >) can be changed. The Custom Properties item is highlighted by default because it contains the properties most often changed. Pick the **Custom Properties...** button to display the properties dialog box specific to your plotter. Pick the **Save As...** button to save your changes to a PC3 file.

Figure 10-13.
The **Plotter Configuration Editor** dialog box. The **Device and Document Settings** tab is shown here.

Select item to display available settings below

Options available in this area vary depending on selected item in tree view

Use plot configuration files from previous releases

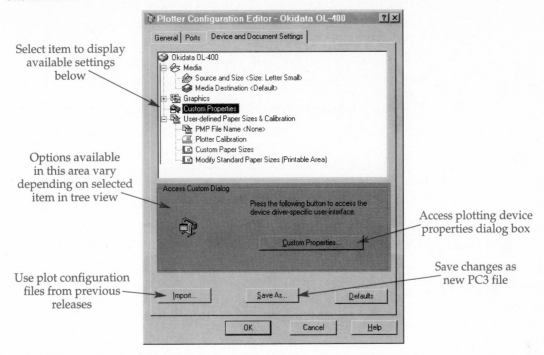

Access plotting device properties dialog box

Save changes as new PC3 file

PROFESSIONAL TIP

It is good practice to create a new PC3 file and preserve the original. If you have old plot configuration files from AutoCAD Release 13 (PCP) or AutoCAD Release 14 (PC2), they can be imported into the current settings by picking the **Import...** button. Settings contained in these two files that can be used by AutoCAD 2000 are plotter name, port information, pen optimization level, paper size, and resolution.

CAUTION

Avoid editing and saving modified PC3 files unless you have been instructed to do so. These files are critical to the proper functioning of your plotter.

Specifying a Plot Style Table

The **Plot style table** area is located in the middle of the **Plot Device** tab of the **Page Setup** dialog box. This area allows you to list and select customized pen assignment files for specialized plotting purposes. Use the default of **None** until you possess a good understanding of plot style tables. Plot style tables are discussed in the following section.

NOTE

If you want to plot a drawing without using a plot style, just pick **None** in the **Plot style table** area of the **Page Setup** dialog box.

PLOT STYLES

The properties of objects in an AutoCAD drawing, such as color, layer, linetype, and lineweight, are used as defaults for plotting. This means that all colors, linetypes, and lineweights will be plotted exactly as they appear in the drawing. But you also have the ability to create multiple plots of the same drawing using different plot style tables. A *plot style table* is a named file that provides complete control over pen settings for plotted drawings.

Plot styles are basically a variety of pen settings that control, among other things, the color, thickness, linetype, line end treatment, and fill style of drawing objects. Plot styles can be assigned to any object or layer.

NOTE In AutoCAD Release 14 a variety of pen parameters were controlled by the **Pen Assignments** dialog box. Most of these features are now managed with the **Plot Style Table Editor** dialog box. Other aspects of plotter functions, such as pen speed, default line width, and optimization, are now stored in the PC3 plotter configuration file.

Plot Style Attributes

By default, objects are drawn without a plot style. When no plot style is applied, objects are plotted according to their assigned properties, such as color, linetype, and lineweight. The finished plot appears identical to the on-screen display.

A plot style is a collection of several properties. When a plot style is assigned to an object, the plot style properties replace the object's properties *for plotting purposes only*. For example, assume a drawing has a layer named Blue, which has blue selected as its color. A line drawn on this layer appears blue on screen. If no plot style is assigned to the line, it will plot as blue also. Now assume a plot style is created with the color red set as one of its properties. This plot style is assigned to the line. The line will now be plotted as red. However, the line still appears blue on screen, because the plot style only takes effect when the object is plotted.

The following properties can be set in a plot style.

* **Color.** A color specified in a plot style will override the object color in the drawing. Use object color is the default setting. This setting plots the object with the same color shown on screen. The following options related to color can also be specified.

- **Dithering.** *Dithering* is the intermingling of dots of various colors to produce what appears to be a new color. Dithering is either enabled or disabled. It is ignored if the plotter does not support it. Dithering may create incorrect linetypes when plotting pale colors or thin lines. It is best to test dithering to see if it produces the best results. Dithering can be used regardless of the object color selected.
- **Convert to Grayscale.** If this option is selected, the object's colors are converted to grayscale if the plotter supports it. If this is not selected, the object colors are used. This option is illustrated in Figure 10-14.
- **Use Assigned Pen Number.** This setting only applies to pen plotters. Available pens range from 1 to 32. The assigned pen number cannot be changed if the plot style color is set to Use object color, or if you are editing a plot style in a color-dependent plot style table. In this case, the value is set to Automatic. If you enter 0 for pen number, the field reads Automatic. AutoCAD selects a pen based on the plotter configuration.
- **Virtual Pen Number.** Pen numbers between 1 and 255 allow non-pen plotters to simulate pen plotters using virtual pens. A 0 or Automatic setting instructs AutoCAD to assign a virtual pen from the AutoCAD Color Index (ACI). See the *AutoCAD Installation Guide* for detailed information on configuring plotters to use virtual pen settings.
- **Screening.** This affects the amount of ink placed on the paper while plotting. A value of 0 produces the color white, and 100 plots the color's full intensity. The effects of screening are shown in Figure 10-15.
- **Linetype.** If you select a plot style linetype, it overrides the object's linetype when plotted. The default value (Use object linetype) plots the object using the linetype displayed on screen. An adaptive adjustment setting adjusts the linetype scale to keep the linetype pattern complete. This is activated by default.
- **Lineweight.** Select a lineweight from this list if you want the plotted lineweight to override the object property in the AutoCAD drawing. The default value is Use object lineweight.

Figure 10-14.
The effects of the Convert to grayscale plot style setting.

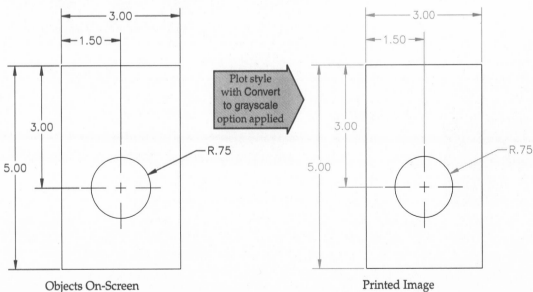

Figure 10-15.
Using the screening
plot style settings.

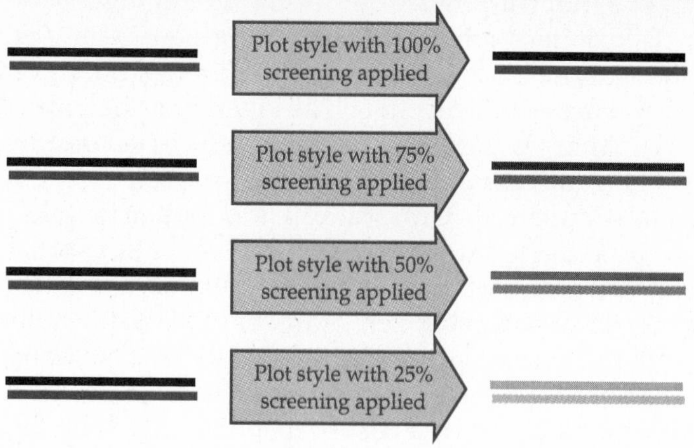

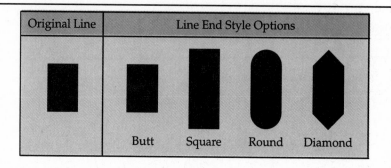

- **Line End Style.** If you select a line end style from this list, the line end style is added to the endpoints when plotted. Figure 10-16 illustrates the end style options. Note that the lines must be relatively thick for the end styles to be noticeable. The default setting is Use object end style.
- **Line Join Style.** If you select a line join style from this list, it overrides the object's line join style when the drawing is plotted. The default setting is Use object join style, but you can select one of the following line end styles: Miter, Bevel, Round, and Diamond.
- **Fill Style.** If you select a fill style from this list, it overrides the object's fill style when the drawing is plotted. The default setting is Use object fill style, but you can select one of the fill styles shown in Figure 10-17.

Figure 10-16.
End line style
options can be
specified within a
plot style.

Original Line	Line End Style Options			
	Butt	Square	Round	Diamond

Figure 10-17.
These fill styles can be set for a plot style.

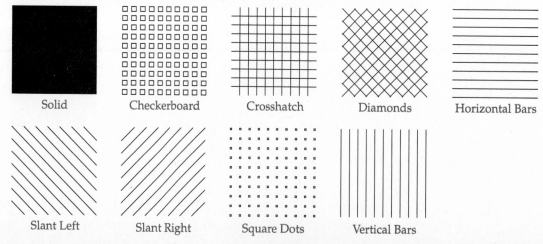

Solid   Checkerboard   Crosshatch   Diamonds   Horizontal Bars

Slant Left   Slant Right   Square Dots   Vertical Bars

Plot Style Modes

There are two plot style modes: color-dependent and named. You can create a *color-dependent plot style* in which each color can be assigned values for the various plotting properties. These settings are saved in a *color-dependent plot style table* file with a CTB extension.

A *named plot style* is assigned to objects. The settings in the named plot style override the object properties when the object is plotted. *Named plot style tables* are saved in a file with an STB extension. These tables allow you to use color properties in the drawing without having the object's color tied to its plotting characteristics. These tables are useful if, for example, you are working on a multiphase project in which different components of the drawing must be highlighted, subdued, or plotted in a specific lineweight or linetype.

Plot Style Tables

AutoCAD is supplied with several plot style tables. Plot style tables are given file names with CTB or STB extensions. These files are saved in the Acad2000\Plot Styles folder. You can also create and save your own customized tables.

To view the available plot style tables, select **Plot Style Manager...** from the **File** pull-down menu or enter STYLESMANAGER at the Command: prompt. The **Plot Styles** window is displayed. See Figure 10-18.

The **Plot Styles** window displays icons for each of the saved plot style tables. There is also an icon to access the Add-A-Plot Style Table wizard. You can double-click on an icon to access the **Plot Style Table Editor** dialog box. This dialog box, which is discussed later in the chapter, is used to edit the plot style table.

Figure 10-18.
Double-click on an icon to edit the plot style table. Select the Add-A-Plot-Style-Table Wizard icon to create a new table.

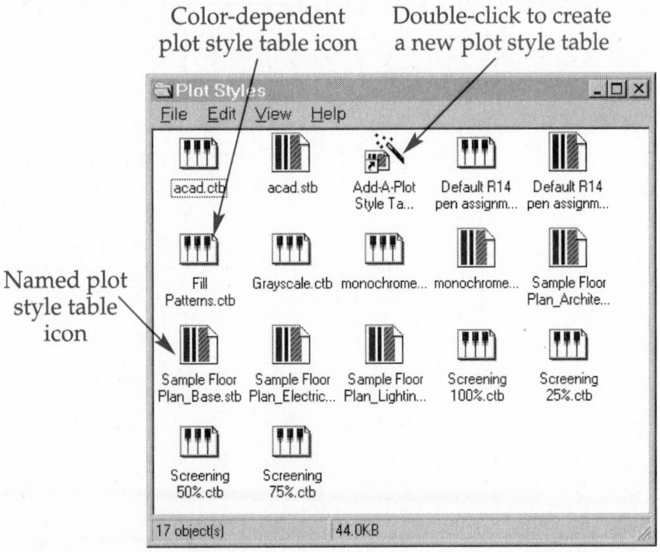

Color-dependent plot style table icon

Double-click to create a new plot style table

Named plot style table icon

Creating a plot style table

Create a named plot style table if you know that components of the drawing or project, such as layouts, layers, and objects, will be plotted at different times using different colors, linetypes, lineweights, or area fills.

Plot style tables are created using the Add-A-Plot Style Table wizard. To access this wizard, select **Add Plot Style Table...** from the **Wizards** cascading menu of the **Tools** pull-down menu. You can also select the Add-A-Plot Style Table Wizard icon in the **Plot Styles** window, which is discussed later in the chapter. The **Add Plot Style Table** wizard is displayed. Read the introductory page and pick **Next** to access the **Begin** page. See Figure 10-19. Four options are available:

- **Start from scratch.** Constructs a new plot style table. The **Browse File** page is skipped with this option because the new plot style table is not based on any existing settings.
- **Use an existing plot style table.** Copies an existing plot style table to be used as a template for a new one. The **Table Type** page is skipped when this option is selected because the plot style mode is determined by the file selected as the template.
- **Use My R14 Plotter Configuration (CFG).** Copies the pen assignments from the acad14.cfg file to be used as a template for a new one. This option should be used if you did not save either a PCP or PC2 file in Release 14.
- **Use a PCP or PC2.** Pen assignments saved previously in a Release 14 PCP or PC2 file are used to make a new plot style table.

After you have selected the beginning plot style table option, press **Next** to go to the **Table Type** page. See Figure 10-20. This page is not displayed if the **Use an existing plot style table** option was selected. Select the **Named Plot Style Table** option to use the named plot style mode, and then pick **Next**.

Select the file on which the plot style table is to be based in the **Browse File** page. Enter the file name in the text box or pick the **Browse...** button to display a **Select File** dialog box. The type of file you select depends on the selected beginning plot style table option. If you are using a CFG file, you must also select the plotter or printer to use.

After selecting the appropriate file, pick the **Next** button to access the **File name** page. See Figure 10-21. Enter a name for the new plot style table. A CTB extension is added to color-dependent plot style tables, and an STB extension is added to named plot style tables.

Once you have entered the plot style table name, pick **Next** to display the **Finish** page, Figure 10-22. Pick the check box at the bottom of the page to attach this plot

---

Figure 10-19.
Select the basis for the plot style table in the **Begin** page of the **Add Plot Style Table** wizard.

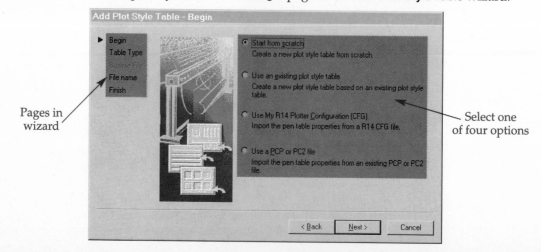

AutoCAD and its Applications—Basics

Figure 10-20.
Select the plot style mode in the **Table Type** page. This page does not appear if the new table is based on an existing plot style table.

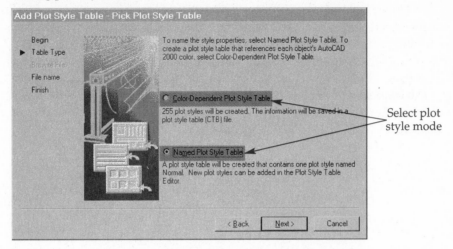

Select plot style mode

Figure 10-21.
Enter the name for the plot style table in the **File name** page.

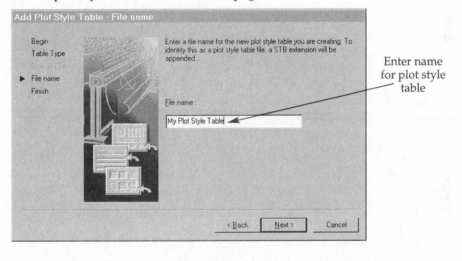

Enter name for plot style table

Figure 10-22.
The **Finish** page allows you to edit the new plot style table immediately and to attach the new table to all new drawings (if the plot style mode matches the setting in the **Options** dialog box).

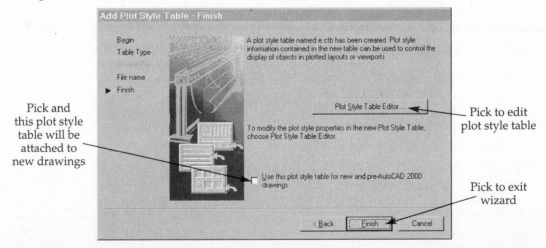

Pick and this plot style table will be attached to new drawings

Pick to edit plot style table

Pick to exit wizard

style table to all new drawings by default. That is, the plot style table will be listed in the **Plot style table area** of the **Page Setup** dialog box. This check box is only available if you are creating a plot style using the mode (color-dependent or named) specified in the **Default plot style behavior for new drawings** area of the **Plotting** tab in the **Options** dialog box. This tab is discussed later in the chapter.

You can edit the new plot style table by selecting the **Plot Style Table Editor...** button, which accesses the **Plot Style Table Editor** dialog box. This is discussed later in the chapter.

Pick **Finish** and the new plot style table is created. The new file is added to the Acad2000\Plot Styles folder and a corresponding icon is added to the **Plot Styles** window.

NOTE

The **Wizards** cascading menu also contains an **Add Named Plot Style Table...** or **Add Color-Dependent Plot Style Table...** option. The plot style mode set for the drawing determines which option is available. The pages in these wizards are identical to the Add-A-Plot Style Table wizard with the following exceptions:

- On the **Begin** page, the **Use an existing plot style table** option is not available.
- There is no **Table Type** page.
- The **Finish** page includes an option to attach the new plot style table to the current drawing.

EXERCISE 10-4

❑ Start a new drawing from scratch.
❑ Use the Add-A-Plot Style Table wizard to create a new color-dependent plot style table called My Color-Dependent Table. Create the table from scratch.
❑ Create a second color-dependent plot style table named My Second C-D Table.
❑ Use the Add-A-Plot Style Table wizard to create a new named plot style table called My Named Table. Create the table from scratch.
❑ Access the **Plot Styles** window to see the icons for the new tables.
❑ Close all drawings and leave AutoCAD open for the next exercise.

Editing a plot style table

Plot style properties are set in the **Plot Style Table Editor** dialog box. To access this dialog box, double-click on the icon for the desired plot style table in the **Plot Styles** window. You can also select the **Edit...** button in the **Plot style table** area of the **Plot Device** tab in the **Page Setup** dialog box.

The **Plot Style Table Editor** dialog box is used to edit both color-dependent and named plot style tables. Color-dependent plot style tables contain 255 preset plot styles—one for each ACI color. A new named plot style table contains one preset plot style, Normal.

The **Plot Style Table Editor** contains three tabs. The **General** tab contains information about the plot style table. See Figure 10-23. Enter a description in the text box. The **Apply global scale factor to non-ISO linetypes and fill patterns** option scales all non-ISO linetypes and fill patterns by the value entered in the **Scale factor** text box.

The **Table View** and **Form View** tabs are used to set the plot style attributes and, for named plot style tables, to create and delete plot styles. These tabs are shown in Figure 10-24.

Figure 10-23.
Information about a plot style table is contained in the **General** tab of the **Plot Style Table Editor** dialog box.

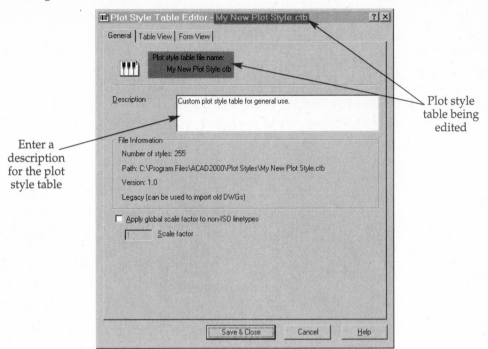

When editing a named plot style table, the Normal plot style is created automatically. This plot style cannot be modified, and is assigned to all layers by default. To create a new plot style, pick the **Add Style** button. In the **Table View** tab, this inserts a new table with the name Style *n* highlighted at the top. Enter a new name. In the **Form View** tab, the **Add Plot Style** dialog box appears. Enter a new name and pick the **OK** button.

If you wish to delete a named plot style, pick the **Delete Style** button in either tab. If the **Form View** tab is displayed, the current style is deleted. If the **Table View** tab is displayed, first select the plot style by picking in the gray bar above the style's name, then pick the **Delete Style** button.

To modify plot style attributes in the **Table View** tab, first use the scroll bar to display the plot style to be edited. Pick the value to be changed and you can modify it with a text box or drop-down list. This editing procedure is similar to changing object properties in the **Properties** window.

The **Form View** tab lists all the attributes in a different format. To view all of the settings for a specific plot style, simply pick the plot style in the **Plot styles:** list box. The properties of the selected plot style are listed in the **Properties** area. Modify the properties using the drop-down lists provided.

Pick the **Save As...** button to change the table name, or pick the **Save & Close** button to save the current file and exit.

Figure 10-24.
Plot style table settings are modified in the **Plot Style Table Editor** dialog box. A—The **Table View** tab for a named plot style table. B—The **Form View** tab for a color-dependent plot style table.

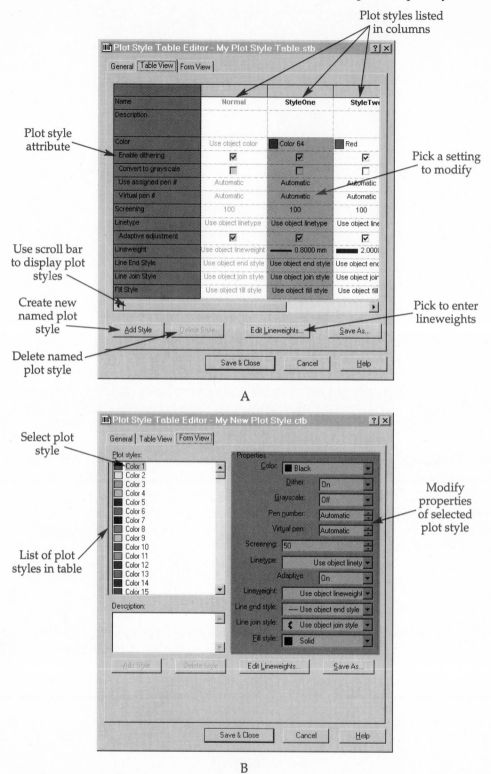

NOTE   Once a plot style table is created, it can be used on new drawings and drawings created in previous releases of AutoCAD.

❑ Start a new drawing from scratch.
❑ Access the **Plot Styles** window and double-click on the My Color-Dependent Table icon.
❑ Use the **Table View** tab to modify the properties of the following plot styles as specified:

Plot Style	Property	New Value
Color 5	Color	Black
	Linetype	Solid
	Lineweight	1.2mm
Color 3	Color	Black
	Linetype	Solid
	Lineweight	1.2mm

❑ Pick the **Save & Close** button.
❑ Edit the My Second C-D Table plot style table using the **Form View** tab. Change the following styles and properties:

Plot Style	Property	New Value
Color 1	Color	Black
	Linetype	Solid
	Lineweight	1.2mm
Color 6	Color	Black
	Linetype	Solid
	Lineweight	1.2mm

❑ Pick the **Save & Close** button.
❑ Double-click on the My Named Table icon in the **Plot Styles** window. Use the **Add Style** button to create two new styles. Assign the following names and properties to the new plot styles:

Plot Style	Property	New Value
Black 100%	Color	Black
	Linetype	Solid
	Lineweight	1.2mm
Black 50%	Color	Black
	Screening	50
	Linetype	Solid
	Lineweight	1.2mm

❑ Pick the **Save & Close** button.
❑ Close the drawing.

Applying Plot Styles

In order to assign plot styles, plot style tables must be specified in the drawing. The **Model** tab and each individual layout tab can be assigned one plot style table each. Only the styles within the attached plot style table can be applied within the layout.

The plot style mode (color-dependent or named) for a drawing is determined when the drawing is first created. The setting is found in the **Plotting** tab of the **Options** dialog box. To access the **Options** dialog box, select **Options...** from the **Tools** pull-down menu or enter OP or OPTIONS at the Command: prompt. You can also right-click in the drawing area and select **Options...** from the shortcut menu. If the **Page Setup** or **Plot** dialog box is open, you can also select the **Options** button in the **Plot Device** tab.

The **Plotting** tab of the **Options** dialog box is shown in Figure 10-25. The plot style mode for new drawings is determined by the setting in the **Default plot style behavior for new drawings** area. By default, the **Use color dependent plot styles** option is selected. When this option is selected, new drawings are set to use only color-dependent plot styles. The default plot style behavior setting can also be set using the **PSTYLEPOLICY** system variable (0 for named plot style mode and 1 for color-dependent mode).

The **Default plot style table** drop-down list can be used to set a default plot style table. When None is selected, objects in the new drawing are plotted based on their on-screen properties. The default plot style table is applied to the **Model** tab and layout tabs in new drawings. However, the plot style table can be changed at any time in the **Page Setup** dialog box.

If you select the **Use named plot styles** option, the drop-down lists below the default plot style table are activated. You can select the default plot styles for layer 0 and for objects. You can select any plot styles from the default plot style table.

The **Add or Edit Plot Style Tables...** button accesses the **Plot Styles** window. This window allows you to edit existing plot style tables and create new plot style tables.

Figure 10-25.
Use the **Plotting** tab of the **Options** dialog box to set default plot style modes and tables for new drawings.

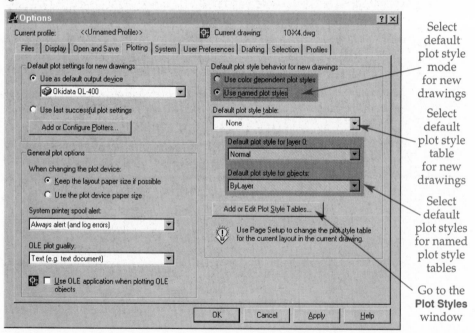

Select default plot style mode for new drawings

Select default plot style table for new drawings

Select default plot styles for named plot style tables

Go to the **Plot Styles** window

Applying color-dependent plot styles

Color-dependent plot style tables contain 255 plot styles—one for each color available in AutoCAD. You cannot add or delete plot styles in a color-dependent table. When you assign a color-dependent plot style table to a layout, the property values set for the plot styles override the on-screen display values during plotting.

Color-dependent plot styles can only be applied to drawings created while the **Use color dependent plot styles** option was selected as the default plot style behavior in the **Options** dialog box. Each of the **Model** and layout tabs can have a different plot style table assigned.

To assign a color-dependent plot style table, access the **Page Setup** dialog box. Select the **Plot Device** tab, and then pick the plot style table from the **Plot style table** drop-down list. See Figure 10-26. The selected plot style table is applied to the active layout or **Model** tab.

Figure 10-26.
Selecting a plot style table for a layout.

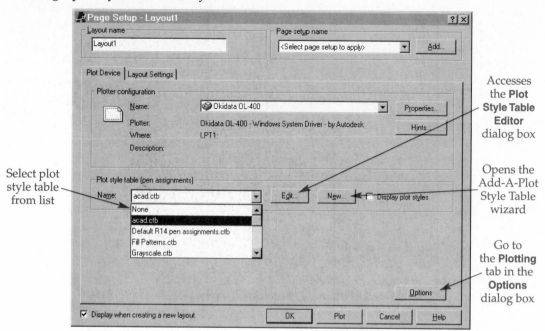

Select plot
style table
from list

Accesses
the **Plot
Style Table
Editor**
dialog box

Opens the
Add-A-Plot
Style Table
wizard

Go to
the **Plotting**
tab in the
Options
dialog box

NOTE	A color-dependent plot style table cannot be attached to layers or objects because they may be composed of a variety of colors. Remember that a color-dependent plot style table should be used only when you want to show all lines of a single color plotted exactly the same.

EXERCISE 10-6

❑ Open EX10-2.
❑ Attach My Color-Dependent Table to the **Circle-Ellipse Detail** layout.
❑ Select **Plot Preview** from the **File** pull-down menu to view the effects of the plot styles. Press the [Esc] key to return to the drawing area.
❑ Attach My Second C-D Table to the **Line-Rectangle Detail** layout. Select **Plot Preview** to see the effects.
❑ Save the drawing as EX10-6 and close.

Applying named plot styles

In order for named plot styles to be used in a drawing, the drawing must have been created with the **Use named plot styles** option selected as the default plot style behavior in the **Options** dialog box. The drawing could also be based on a template with named plot styles.

The **Model** tab and each layout tab can have a named plot style table attached. When you select a plot style table for the **Model** tab, you are also presented the option of selecting the plot style table for all layout tabs. However, each layout tab can have a different plot style table.

Once the named plot style tables have been assigned to the **Model** tab and layout tabs, plot styles can be assigned to objects and layers. A plot style assigned to an object will override a plot style assigned to a layer, just as a color or linetype assigned to an object will override the layer setting.

LAYER
LA

Format
➡ Layer...

Object Properties
toolbar

Layers

Plot styles can be assigned to layers in the **Layer Properties Manager** dialog box, Figure 10-27. To access this dialog box, pick the **Layers** button from the **Object Properties** toolbar, select **Layer...** from the **Format** pull-down menu, or type LA or LAYER at the Command: prompt.

To modify the plot style, pick the current plot style listed for the layer. The **Select Plot Style** dialog box is displayed, Figure 10-28. This dialog box lists the plot styles available in the plot style table attached to the current tab. You can select a different plot style table from the **Active plot style table:** drop-down list. If you select another plot style table, the change is reflected in the **Plot style table** area of the **Page Setup** dialog box. Pick the **Editor...** button to access the **Plot Style Table Editor** dialog box.

Figure 10-27.
Named plot styles can be assigned to layers using the **Layer Properties Manager** dialog box.

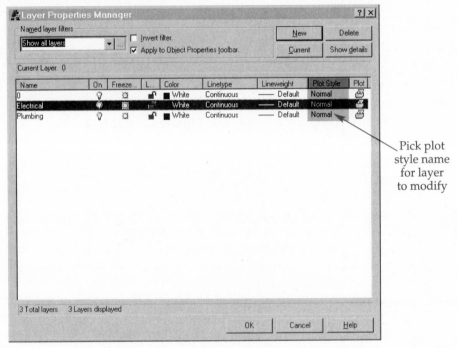

Figure 10-28.
Use the **Select Plot Style** dialog box to select a plot style for a layer.

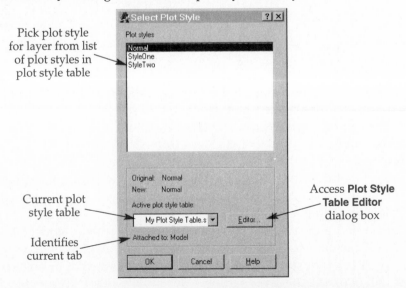

Named plot styles can also be applied to objects. When a plot style is applied to an object, the plot style remains attached to the object in all layout tabs. If the plot style attached to the object is contained in the plot style table attached to the layout tab, the object will be plotted with the plot style settings. However, if the plot style assigned to the object is not found within the plot style table attached to the layout tab, the object is plotted according to its on-screen display settings.

Modifying an object's plot style is similar to modifying an object's layer, color, or linetype. You can select the new plot style from the **Plot Style Control** drop-down list in the **Object Properties** toolbar (Figure 10-29A), or you can use the **Properties** window to change the plot style (Figure 10-29B). Selecting the Other... option accesses the **Select Plot Style** dialog box.

Figure 10-29.
Assigning a new plot style to an object. A—Using the **Plot Style Control** drop-down list in the **Object Properties** toolbar. B—Using the **Properties** window.

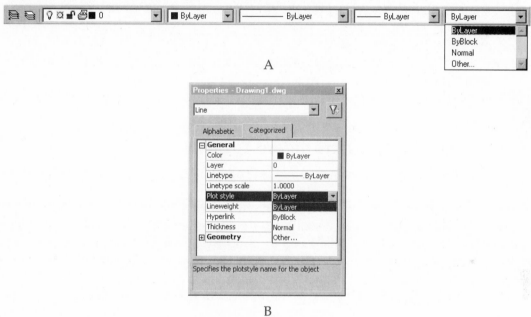

A

B

NOTE

Every AutoCAD object and layer is automatically assigned a plot style. If the current drawing is set to use a named plot style table, the default plot style for objects in the drawing is ByLayer. This means that objects retain the properties of their layer. The default plot style for a layer is Normal. Objects plotted with these settings keep their original properties.

❑ Open EX10-2.
❑ Select all four objects. Right-click and select **Copy** from the shortcut menu. Press [Esc] twice to deselect the objects.
❑ Access the **Plotting** tab of the **Options** dialog box. In the **Default plot style behavior for new drawings** area, select the **Use named plot styles** option.
❑ Close the drawing without saving.
❑ Create a new drawing from scratch.
❑ Right-click in the drawing area and select **Paste** from the shortcut menu. Pick an insertion point.
❑ Perform a **ZOOM Extents**.
❑ Use **AutoCAD DesignCenter** to copy the **Circle-Ellipse Detail** layout and **Line-Rectangle Detail** layout from EX10-2.dwg. Close **DesignCenter**.
❑ Delete the **Layout1** and **Layout2** tabs.
❑ Attach My Named Table plot style table to the **Circle-Ellipse Detail** layout.
❑ Pick the **Model** tab and select None as the plot style table.
❑ Change the plot style property of the circle to Black 100%. Change the plot style property of the ellipse to Black 50%.
❑ Perform a plot preview of the **Model** tab and **Circle-Ellipse Detail** layout and compare the differences.
❑ Save the drawing as EX10-7.

Viewing Plot Style Effects Before You Plot

The display of lineweights in an AutoCAD drawing is controlled by the **LWDISPLAY** system variable. If **LWDISPLAY** is on, lineweights are displayed on screen. Similarly, it is possible to display plot style effects on screen to see how they will appear. To do so, pick the **Display plot styles** check box in the **Plot style table** area of the **Plot Device** tab in the **Page Setup** dialog box. Keep in mind that these two display features can increase the time required to regenerate drawings, and may decrease the performance of AutoCAD.

A quicker method is to use the print preview options, which are discussed later in the text. This displays all lineweights and plot styles exactly as they will appear on the plotted drawing.

PROFESSIONAL TIP

Imported plot settings from PCP and PC2 files are distributed in three different places in AutoCAD 2000.

AutoCAD R14	AutoCAD 2000
Pen assignments	Plot style table
Optimization level/plotter connection	PC3 file
Paper size, plot area, scale, origin, offset	Page setup

This is important if you are involved in a project that requires updating drawings from a previous release of AutoCAD to AutoCAD 2000 format and you wish to retain all of your plot settings.

A majority of the values that must be set prior to plotting can be established and saved in layouts, viewports, layers, plot style tables, and template drawings. If you plan your work well, there should be very little, if anything, you will have to set prior to plotting. Take a look at some of the items required for plotting, and where they can be saved.

Item	Location
Border and title block	Layout
View scales	Viewport (**Zoom XP**)
Text height	Drawing
Object color, lineweight, and end style	Layers and plot style tables
Plot device	Page setup
Plot style table	Page setup
Paper size and drawing orientation	Page setup
Plot scale, area, offset, and options	Page setup

For 2000i Users...

In AutoCAD 2000i, you can add a plot stamp to your printed drawings. Refer to *Adding a Plot Stamp* on page 972 for complete details.

If you prepare for plotting as soon as you begin a new drawing, the act of plotting may mean just a few clicks of your pointing device.

Selecting the desired output device and plot style table was discussed earlier in this chapter. Once these settings are complete, you can specify the plot settings in the **Plot Settings** tab of the **Plot** or **Page Setup** dialog box, Figure 10-30.

Figure 10-30.
The **Plot Settings** tab of the **Plot** (or **Page Setup**) dialog box.

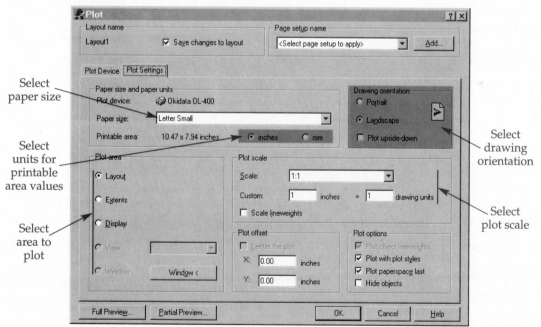

NOTE

The settings discussed in the next sections can be set in either the **Page Setup** or **Plot** dialog boxes. You are not asked for a layout name in the **Page Setup** dialog box since it is tied to a named layout.

Paper Size, Units, and Drawing Orientation

The **Paper size and paper units** area of the **Plot Settings** tab in the **Plot** dialog box controls the paper size. Select the appropriate paper size from the drop-down list. Pick either the **inches** or **mm** radio button to set the units for the paper size specification.

The **Drawing orientation** area of the **Plot** dialog box controls the plot rotation. *Portrait* orients the long side of the paper vertically, and is the standard orientation for most written documents printed on 8.5 × 11 paper. *Landscape* orients the long side of the paper horizontally, and is the default for AutoCAD drawings. If you consider landscape format to be a rotation angle of 0 degrees, the following table should help you determine how to use the **Plot upside-down button** option to achieve several rotation angles.

Orientation Buttons	Rotation Angle
Landscape	0
Portrait	90
Upside-down landscape	180
Upside-down portrait	270

In AutoCAD, the horizontal screen measurement relates to the long side of the paper, the landscape format. However, you might create a drawing, form, or chart in portrait format. This format orients the long side of the plot vertically. AutoCAD rotates plots in 90° increments, as shown in the previous table. Figure 10-31 illustrates the result of a 90° portrait rotation.

Figure 10-31.
The long side of the plot is oriented vertically in a 90° portrait rotation.

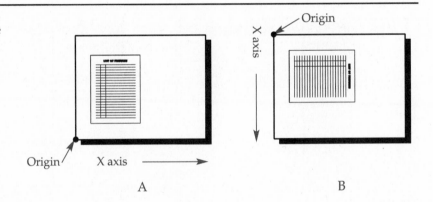

A

B

Plotting Area

The **Plot area** area of the **Plot Settings** tab allows you to choose the portion of the drawing to be plotted, and how it is to be plotted. The five radio button options are described below:

- **Layout/Limits.** The **Layout** option is displayed when plotting a layout. Everything inside the margins of the layout is plotted. The **Limits** option is displayed when plotting the **Model** tab. This option plots everything inside the defined drawing limits.

- **Extents.** The **Extents** option plots only the area of the drawing in which objects are drawn. Before using this option, zoom the extents to include all drawn objects to verify exactly what will be plotted. Be aware that border lines around your drawing (like the title block) may be clipped off if they are at the extreme edge of the screen. This often happens because you are requesting the plotter to plot at the extreme edge of its active area.

- **Display.** This option plots the current screen display.

- **View.** Use this option to plot named views, which were discussed in Chapter 9. This option is disabled if no views have been saved in the drawing. Select the name of the view from the drop-down list. This option is available only when the **Model** tab is current.
- **Window.** This option appears grayed-out until you pick the **Wind_ow...** button. You must define two opposite corners of a window around the portion of the drawing to be plotted.

NOTE If the window you define is too close to an object, some portion of that object may be clipped off in your plot. If this happens, simply adjust the window size the next time you plot. You can prevent these errors by using the plot preview options.

Plot Offset

The **Plot offset** area controls how far the drawing is offset from the lower-left corner of the paper. See Figure 10-32.

The origin of a plotter is the lower-left corner of the plot media. To begin plotting a drawing at that point, leave the values shown in the **X:** and **Y:** text boxes at 0.00. If you want to move the drawing away from the default origin, change the required values in the text boxes. For example, to move the drawing four units to the right and three units above the plotter origin, enter 4 in the **X:** text box, and 3 in the **Y:** text box.

Figure 10-32.
The **Plot offset** area controls how far the drawing is offset from the lower-left corner of the paper.

Pick to have plot centered automatically

Enter offset from lower-left corner

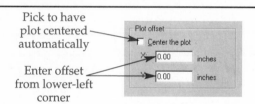

Other Plotting Options

The **Plot options** area of the **Plot** dialog box contains a list of four items that can affect the time and resources required to plot a drawing. Apply these options only when required for the plot by picking the appropriate check box. The following options are available:
- **Plot object lineweights.** Lines having a lineweight other than 0 are plotted using the appropriate thickness. This box is checked by default.
- **Plot with plot st_yles.** All plot styles attached to the drawing and its components are plotted.
- **Plot paperspac_e last.** Paper space objects are plotted first by default. If this box is checked, paper space objects are plotted last. Since there are no paper space objects present in the **Model** tab, this option is available only when plotting from a layout tab.
- **Hide objects.** This option removes hidden lines from objects. When you are plotting from a layout tab, this option affects only objects drawn in paper space. It does not affect any 3D objects within a viewport. To plot objects within viewports with hidden lines removed, you must change the Hide plot property of the viewport. To do this, select the layout tab, pick the viewport, and open the **Properties** window. Pick the Hide plot property and change the setting to yes. See Figure 10-33.

Figure 10-33.
In order to plot objects in a floating viewport with hidden lines removed, the Hide plot setting for the viewport must be yes.

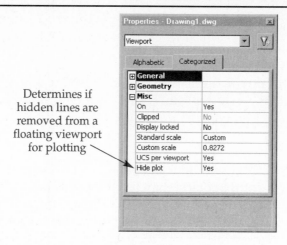

Determines if hidden lines are removed from a floating viewport for plotting

Determining Drawing Scale Factors

The proper scale factor is vitally important because it ensures that text, dimension values, and dimensioning entities (such as arrowheads and tick marks) are plotted at the proper size. The scale factor of the drawing should already be established by the time you are ready to plot and should be an integral part of your template drawings. To obtain the correct text height, the desired plotted text height is multiplied by the scale factor. The scale factor is also used in scaling dimensions.

NOTE Determine the plot scale and scale factor when you begin the drawing. If you find the drawing scale factor does not correspond to the plotting scale, you will need to update dimensions and text.

The scale factor is always the reciprocal of the drawing scale. For example, if you wish to plot a mechanical drawing at a scale of 1/2″ = 1″, calculate the scale factor as follows:

1/2″ = 1″
.5″ = 1″
1 ÷ .5 = 2 *(The scale factor is 2)*

An architectural drawing to be plotted at a scale of 1/4″ = 1′-0″ has a scale factor calculated as follows:

1/4″ = 1′-0″
.25″ = 12″
12 ÷ .25 = 48 *(The scale factor is 48)*

The scale factor of a civil engineering drawing that has a scale of 1″ = 60′ is calculated as follows:

1″ = 60′
1″ = 60 × 12 = 720″ *(The scale factor is 720)*

Once the scale factor of the drawing has been determined, calculate the height of the text in AutoCAD. If text height is to be plotted at 1/8″, it should not be drawn at that height. Remember, all geometry created in AutoCAD should be drawn at full scale.

For example, if you are working on a civil engineering drawing with a scale of 1″ = 60′, the scale factor equals 720. Text drawn 1/8″ high appears as a dot. The full-size civil engineering drawing in AutoCAD is 720 times larger than it will be when plotted at the proper scale. Therefore, you must multiply the text height by 720 in order to get text that appears in correct proportion on the screen. For 1/8″ high text to appear correctly on screen, calculate the AutoCAD text height as follows:

$$1/8'' \times 720$$
$$.125 \times 720 = 90 \text{ (The proper height of the text is 90)}$$

Remember, scale factors and text heights should be determined before beginning a drawing. The best method is to incorporate these as values within your template drawing files.

Scaling the plot

AutoCAD drawing geometry is created at full scale, and the drawing is scaled at the plotter to fit on the sheet size. The **Plot scale** area of the **Plot** dialog box is used to specify the plot scale. The **Scale:** drop-down list contains a selection of 31 different decimal and architectural scales, including Custom and Scaled to Fit. See Figure 10-34. The **Custom:** text boxes allow you to specify the plot scale as a ratio of plotted units to drawing units. An architectural drawing to be plotted at 1/4″ = 1′-0″ can be entered in the text boxes as:

$$1/4'' = 1' \text{ or } .25 = 12 \text{ or } 1 = 48$$

Figure 10-34.
The **Scale:** drop-down list contains a selection of 31 different decimal and architectural scales, including Custom and Scaled to Fit.

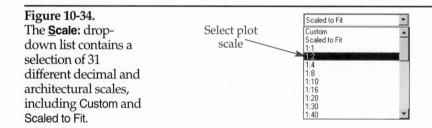

A mechanical drawing to be plotted at a scale of 1/2″ = 1″ can be entered in the text boxes as:

$$1/2'' = 1'' \text{ or } .5 = 1 \text{ or } 1 = 2$$

Pick Scaled to Fit in the **Scale:** drop-down list if you want AutoCAD to automatically adjust your drawing to fit on the paper. This is useful if you have a C-size pen plotter but need to plot a D-size or E-size drawing. However, keep in mind that you may have considerable blank space left on the paper, depending on the size and proportions of your drawing.

The Scaled to Fit option is also useful if you are printing a large drawing on a dot matrix or laser printer that can only use A-size sheets. The drawing is automatically scaled down to fit the size of the printer paper.

Calculating the drawing area and limits

To calculate the available area on a sheet of paper at a specific scale, use this formula:

Scale factor × Media size = Limits

For example, the limits of a B-size (17″ × 11″) sheet of paper at 1/2″ = 1″ scale (scale factor = 2) can be calculated as follows:

$$2 \times 17 = 34 \text{ (X distance)}$$
$$2 \times 11 = 22 \text{ (Y distance)}$$

Thus, the limits of a B-size sheet at the scale of 1/2″ = 1″ are 34,22. The same formula applies to architectural scales. The limits of a C-size architectural sheet (24″ × 18″) at a scale of 1/4″ = 1′-0″ (scale factor = 48) can be determined as follows:

$$48 \times 24 = 1152″$$
$$= 96′ \text{ (X distance)}$$

Use the same formula to calculate the Y distance for the 18″ side of the paper. Refer to the charts in Appendix H to find the limits for common scales on various paper sizes for each drafting field.

CAUTION

Before you plot a drawing, always check the **PSLTSCALE** system variable. This variable controls paper space linetype scaling, and is set to 1 by default. This means that all linetype dash lengths and spaces will be scaled to the paper space scale. For most plotting purposes, **PSLTSCALE** should be set to zero.

If **PSLTSCALE** is set to 1, your viewports can be zoomed to different magnifications and the linetype scale will be the same in all viewports. If **PSLTSCALE** is set to 0, viewports zoomed to varying magnifications will also appear to have differing linetype scales.

Previewing the Plot

Depending on their size and complexity, drawings can require long plotting times. By previewing a plot before it is sent to the output device, you can catch errors, saving material and valuable plot time. This feature is controlled by the **Full Preview…** and **Partial Preview…** buttons at the lower-left corner of the **Plot** dialog box.

If **Partial Preview…** is selected, AutoCAD displays the **Partial Plot Preview** dialog box, shown in Figure 10-35. The outline is the paper size, and the dashed line represents the printable area. The paper dimensions are given for reference. The area the image occupies is called the *effective area*. The effective area dimensions are noted and the outline of this area is filled with a blue hatch pattern. While this preview shows you how the drawing compares to the paper size, the final plot depends on how the printer or plotter is set up.

Figure 10-35.
If **Partial Preview…** is selected, AutoCAD displays the **Partial Plot Preview** dialog box.

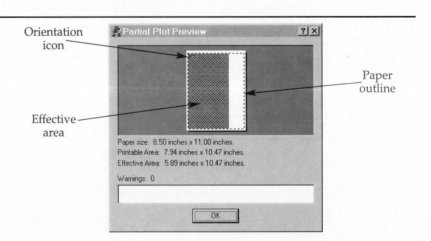

If there is something wrong with the relationship of the display and the paper, AutoCAD gives you messages in the **Warnings:** text box. These warnings give you an opportunity to make corrections and then preview the plot again. You may encounter the following warnings:

- Effective area too small to display.
- Origin forced effective area off paper.
- Plotting area exceeds paper maximum.

Notice the small symbol in the upper-left corner of the effective area in Figure 10-35. This is the *orientation icon*. When the orientation icon appears in the upper-left corner, it indicates the landscape orientation. The icon is in the lower-left corner for a portrait orientation, the lower-right corner for an upside-down landscape orientation, and the upper-right corner for an upside-down portrait orientation.

PROFESSIONAL TIP Rather than using the orientation icon in the **Partial Plot Preview** dialog box to determine the drawing orientation, use the graphic image in the **Drawing orientation** area of the **Plot** dialog box.

Pick the **Full Previe̲w...** button to display the drawing as it will actually appear on the plotted hard copy. The display reflects any plot style tables that have been attached to the drawing. Displaying the full preview takes the same amount of time as a drawing regeneration. Therefore, the drawing size determines how quickly the image is produced.

The drawing is displayed inside a paper outline. The cursor assumes the shape of the zoom icon. Press and hold the pick button as you move the cursor up to enlarge, and down to reduce. Right-click to display the shortcut menu shown in Figure 10-36. It provides several display options, a **Plot** option, and an **Exit** option. The shortcut menu is handy because it allows you to closely examine the drawing before you commit to plotting. You can also press [Esc] or [Enter] to return to the **Plot** dialog box.

Figure 10-36.
Right-click to display the shortcut menu when a plot preview is displayed.

A full preview is also displayed by picking **Plot Previe̲w** in the **F̲ile** pull-down menu. This selection bypasses the **Plot** dialog box.

Before you pick **OK** in the **Plot** dialog box, there are several items you should check:
- ✓ The printer or plotter is plugged in and turned on.
- ✓ The parallel or serial cable to the computer is secure.
- ✓ The pen carousel is loaded and secure, or the pen is in the plotter arm.
- ✓ Pens of proper color and thickness are in correct locations in the pen carousel or rack.
- ✓ The plot media is properly loaded in the plotter and paper grips or clamps are in place.
- ✓ The printer or plotter area is clear for unblocked paper movement.

Once you are satisfied with all plotter parameters and are ready to plot, pick the **OK** button to exit the **Plot** dialog box. AutoCAD then displays the following message on the command line:

Effective plotting area: *(xx)* wide by *(yy)* high
Plotting viewport *n*
Plotting viewport *n*

These are the actual dimensions of the current plotting area. Depending on the type of plotter or printer you are using, one or more dialog boxes may be displayed, showing the drawing name and a meter showing the percentage of the file that has been regenerated and sent to the printer.

Plotting to a File or on the Web

Some computer operating systems allow you to continue working on a drawing while other instructions are being handled by the computer. This capability is called *multitasking* and is a standard feature of the Windows 98, Windows NT, and Unix operating systems. For those operating systems capable of true multitasking, it can be extremely handy to redirect plot output to an external file. This plot file can then be sent directly to a configured plotter while you continue working on a drawing.

Redirecting plot output to a PLT file is good practice if you have only one office or class computer connected to a printer or plotter. This is also the case if your office or school uses a plot spooler. A plot spooler is connected to a plotter and is basically a "smart" disk drive with memory. It reads the PLT file from disk and sends the drawing data to the plotter. A plot spooler removes the need of having a computer connected to the plotter.

Additionally, plot files can be stored in a plot queue on the file server in a networked computer environment. A *plot queue* is a lineup, or list of files, waiting to be plotted. The PLT files can be loaded in the queue and started while users on the network continue doing other work. The Batch Plot utility can also be used to plot a group of PLT files.

If you want to redirect plot output to a file, pick the **Plot to file** check box in the **Plot Device** tab of the **Plot** dialog box. See Figure 10-37. After picking this check box, the note (this file only) is displayed after **Plot to file**. This activates the **File Name:** and **Location:** boxes, which are normally disabled. The location displayed is the path of the current drawing. You can select a previous file location from the drop-down list, or use the **Browse for Folder** or **Browse the Web** dialog box.

Observe that saved plot files are automatically given the extension PLT. The plot file name defaults to the current drawing name, with the addition of either "-model" or "-layout", depending on whether the **Model** tab or a layout tab is current. To provide a different name for the plot file, enter the name in the **File name:** text box and pick **OK**. Pick **OK** to close the dialog box and create the plot file.

From the **Browse the Web** dialog box, you can also save the plot file to a location on the World Wide Web. You must have an Internet browser, such as Netscape or Microsoft Internet Explorer, in order to use this feature. In addition, you must have access to a website using File Transfer Protocol (FTP). With these capabilities, you can copy, move, rename, and delete files and folders found on the Web.

NOTE AutoCAD's Internet features are discussed in detail in *AutoCAD and its Applications, Advanced.*

Figure 10-37.
Use the settings in the **Plot to file** area to create a plot file.

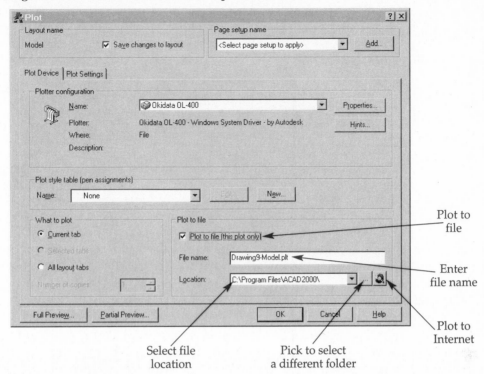

Plot to
file

Enter
file name

Plot to
Internet

Select file
location

Pick to select
a different folder

Additional Plotting Options

The **Plotting** tab of the **Options** dialog box contains general plotting settings, some of which will seldom have to be changed. See Figure 10-38. To access this dialog box, select **Options...** from the **Tools** pull-down menu. This tab provides several general plotting options. The **Default plot style behavior for new drawings** options have been discussed previously. The other areas are discussed briefly here.

- **Default plot settings for new drawings.** The default setting is **Use as default output device**. The device can be selected from the drop-down list. The **Use last successful plot settings** option retains the previous plot settings. Picking the **Add or Configure Plotters** button displays the **Plotters** window.
- **General plot options.** This area allows you to use either the **Keep the layout paper size if possible** option, regardless of the plotter selected, or the **Use the plot device paper size** option. If you choose to keep the layout size, AutoCAD will use the paper size specified in the **Layout Settings** tab of the **Page Setup** dialog box. If this size cannot be plotted, AutoCAD defaults to the size listed in the plotter's PC3 file. These radio buttons reflect the setting of the **PAPERUPDATE** system variable.
  - **System printer spool alert.** If a port conflict occurs during plotting and a drawing is spooled to a system printer, AutoCAD can display an alert and log the error. This drop-down list gives four options for alerting and logging errors.
  - **OLE plot quality.** *OLE* is an acronym for *object linking and embedding* and refers to any text or graphic object that is imported from another software application. This drop-down list allows you to select the type of OLE objects that will be plotted. The **OLEQUALITY** system variable also controls this option.
  - **Use OLE application when plotting OLE objects.** If this check box is activated, applications used to create OLE objects are launched. This may be desirable if you wish to use the OLE software to adjust the quality of the object. This option is also controlled by the **OLESTARTUP** system variable

Figure 10-38.
General plotting settings are found in the **Plotting** tab of the **Options** dialog box.

Select
default
plotter
option

Access
plotters
window

General
plotting
options

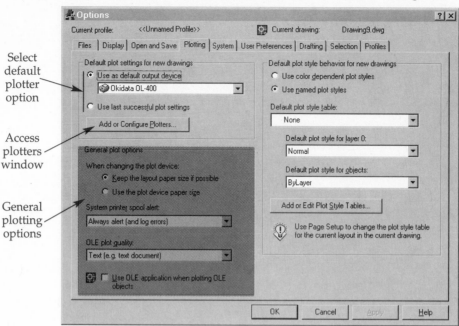

AutoCAD
User's
Guide

16

USING THE BATCH PLOT UTILITY

The Batch Plot utility adds a powerful dimension to printing and plotting. Using this utility, you can create a list of drawings to be printed and then instruct AutoCAD to begin plotting while you return to work on other projects. The Batch Plot utility opens a temporary session of AutoCAD for its purposes, but does not allow you to edit drawings or adjust plot parameters in any way. To use this feature, select Programs from the Windows Start menu, and then select Batch Plot Utility from the AutoCAD menu. See Figure 10-39.

Figure 10-39.
The Batch Plot utility is activated from the Windows desktop.

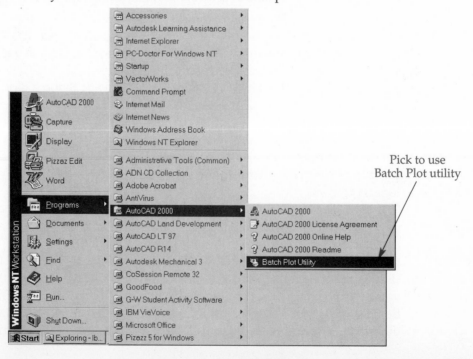

Pick to use
Batch Plot utility

CAUTION Use the Batch Plot utility only if you have previously created all required drawings, layouts, page setups, and PC3 files. Always preview your plots to check for accuracy before saving any of the files. Valuable time may be wasted if you do not plan your plots accurately.

Batch Plot Checklist

Before you use the Batch Plot utility, be sure you have completed the following tasks. Following these guidelines is important if the utility is to run successfully.

✓ Check each drawing to be plotted for accuracy and completeness. If you are plotting a view, display the named view to be plotted before saving the drawing. The default view is plotted by the Batch Plot utility.

✓ Conduct a full preview of the drawing to check for the accuracy of all plot parameters.

✓ Verify the PC3 file if a single plotter is to be used, and carefully check the layout and page setup parameters before creating the batch list.

✓ If more than one drawing is to be plotted using the same plotter, but the drawings have different plot parameters, verify the layouts and page setups to be used for each drawing. If different configurations of the same plot device are to be used, create individual PC3 files before creating the batch list.

✓ If batch drawings will use different devices, carefully check the configurations of each device and save them as PC3 files.

Creating a New Batch Plot List

The **AutoCAD Batch Plot Utility** dialog box is displayed after Batch Plot Utility is selected from the Start menu. See Figure 10-40.

Figure 10-40.
The **AutoCAD Batch Plot Utility** dialog box.

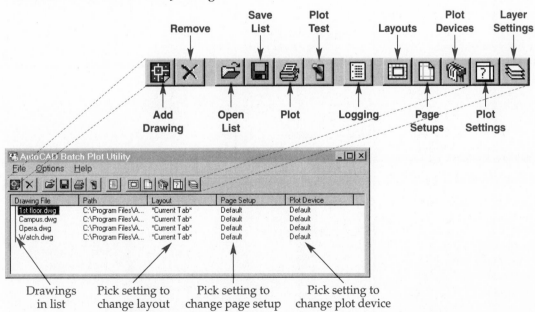

NOTE

In the following discussion, Batch Plot utility commands are selected from the pull-down menus. Most commands can also be selected using the appropriate toolbar buttons. You can also right-click on a selected drawing to display a shortcut menu.

The first step in using the Batch Plot utility is to make a list of the drawings to be plotted using the following steps:

1. Pick **Add Drawing...** from the **File** pull-down menu to add a drawing to the **Drawing File** list. This displays the **Add Drawing File** dialog box, which is a standard file dialog box. Select the desired drawing and pick **OK**.

2. To assign a layout to plot, first pick the drawing name in the **Drawing File** list to highlight it. Next, select **Layouts...** from the **Options** pull-down menu. This displays the **Layouts** dialog box, Figure 10-41. Pick the **Show all layouts** button for a complete list of layouts in the selected drawing. Pick the desired layout(s) and then pick **OK**. The selection is displayed in the **Layout** column.

3. To assign a page setup, first pick the drawing name in the **Drawing File** list to highlight it. Next, select **Page Setups...** from the **Options** pull-down menu. This displays the **Page Setups** dialog box, Figure 10-42. Pick one of the listed page setups or pick the ellipsis (...) button to load page setups from another drawing or template. Pick **OK** to exit. The name is displayed in the **Page Setup** column.

4. Select the plot device in the same manner. Pick the drawing file name, then pick **Plot Devices...** from the **Options** pull-down menu. Select the device you wish to use from the list in the **Plot Devices** dialog box. Pick the **Browse...** button to search for additional PC3 files.

Figure 10-41.
Select the layout(s) to be plotted from the **Layouts** dialog box.

Pick to plot all layouts in drawing

General options

Pick to have layouts listed

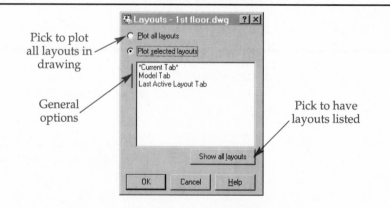

Figure 10-42.
Select the page setup for the drawing in the **Page Setups** dialog box. Pick the ellipsis (...) button to load a page setup from another drawing or template.

Page setups in drawing

Select a drawing or template

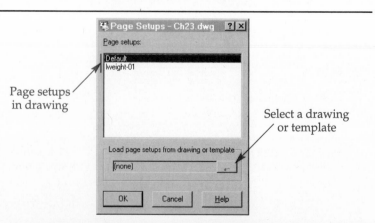

5. Follow the procedure in steps 1 through 4 for all files to be added to the batch plot list.
6. Pick **Save List...** from the **File** pull-down menu to save the completed batch plot list. The **Save Batch Plot List File** dialog box is displayed. Provide a name for the file and pick **Save**. This saves the file with a BP3 file extension. This file is used by the Batch Plot utility to plot your drawings.

PROFESSIONAL TIP Even though a specific page setup and plot device is associated with a drawing, you can still override them in the Batch Plot utility and select page setups from other drawings, or any other PC3 file you have created.

Plotting Specific Layers

The **Layers** button in the **AutoCAD Batch Plot Utility** dialog box allows you to specify which layers you wish to turn off during plotting. Use the following procedure:
1. Select the drawing file name and pick the **Layers** button. This displays the **Plot Settings** dialog box. Be sure the **Layers** tab is current. See Figure 10-43.
2. Select all layers you do not want plotted and pick the **Off** button. Use the standard Windows [Ctrl] and [Shift] key methods for selecting alternate and consecutive items.
3. If you turn off layers that should be plotted, select them and then pick the **On** button.

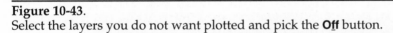

Figure 10-43.
Select the layers you do not want plotted and pick the **Off** button.

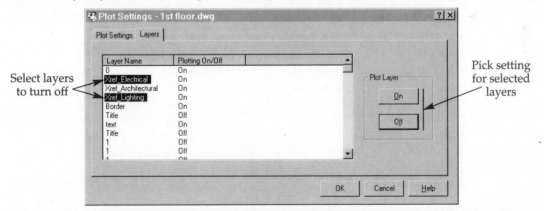

Selecting the Area to Plot

The **Plot Settings** button in the **AutoCAD Batch Plot Utility** dialog box enables you to control the area of the drawing you wish to plot, and the scale with which to plot it. Selecting this button displays the **Plot Settings** tab of the **Plot Settings** dialog box. Three areas in this tab allow you to control what is plotted. See Figure 10-44.
- **Plot Area.** This area provides the same options available in the standard **Page Setup** or **Plot** dialog box, except the **Window** option is not available. When active, the **View** drop-down list shows all named views in the drawing file.

Figure 10-44.
The **Plot Settings** dialog box enables you to control the area of the drawing you wish to plot, and the scale with which to plot it.

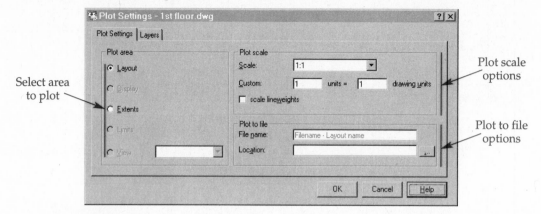

Select area to plot →

Plot scale options

Plot to file options

- **Plot Scale.** Change the plot scale in this area if necessary. If a page setup has not been associated with the selected drawing file, then the plot scale area will reflect the most recent setting in the **Plot** dialog box. If a page setup has been associated with the selected drawing file, then the **Plot Scale** area displays that value. Make it a habit to check this area carefully to ensure that the drawing is plotted at the proper scale.
- **Plot to file.** Enter a file name and location if you wish to have the batch list create a plot file.

Editing a Batch Plot List File

You can open an existing batch plot list file and add or delete files. In addition, you can attach (append) another BP3 file to the current one. These functions are performed in the **AutoCAD Batch Plot Utility** dialog box and are described as follows:
- **Add a drawing to the list.** Pick the **Add Drawing** button and follow steps 1 through 4 as described in the section, Creating a New Batch Plot List.
- **Remove a file from the list.** To remove a file from the current list, highlight the file name and pick the **Remove** button.
- **Append a list to the current one.** Select **Append List...** in the **File** pull-down menu to display the **Append Batch Plot List File** dialog box. Select the desired BP3 file and pick **Open**. The selected file is appended to the end of the current one, and all files are displayed in the list box.

Logging the Batch Plot Process

Logging creates a text file record and an error log of the batch file process. Pick the **Logging** button in the **AutoCAD Batch Plot Utility** dialog box, or pick **Logging...** in the **File** pull-down menu to display the logging options. See Figure 10-45. Plot journal logging and error logging are enabled by default, but can be disabled by picking the **Enable journal logging** or **Enable error logging** check boxes. The default bpjournl.log file and bperror.log files are saved in the Acad2000\Support\Batchplt folder. You can change the names and locations of the log files by entering names in the **File name** text box, or by picking the **Browse...** button to display the **Journal Filename** or **Error Log Filename** dialog boxes.

A record of each batch plot overwrites the previous log file by default. If keeping a record of batch plotting is important, be sure the **Append** radio button is selected. Pick the **Overwrite** radio button if you want only the last batch plotted file to be kept on record.

Figure 10-45.
Logging creates a text file record and an error log of the batch file process.

Location of log file

Replace existing log file

Add text to log file

Add to existing log file

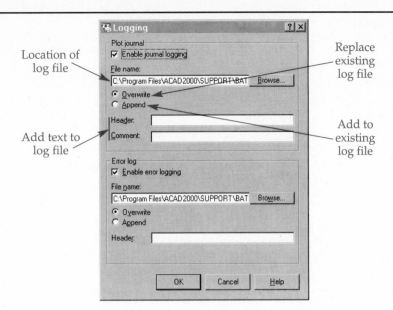

Two options allow you to add lines of text to the log files.

- **Header.** Use this option to add a single line of text to the current log file. The text is the first line printed in the current log file.
- **Comment.** Use this option to add a line of text for each drawing in the file. The text is the first line printed in the log for a specific drawing. A different line of text can be entered for each drawing.

Testing the Batch Plot

The **Plot Test** button in the **AutoCAD Batch Plot Utility** dialog box provides a quick test for your batch plot file without actually plotting the drawings. The results of the test, including any problems that are found, are displayed in the **Plot Test Results** dialog box. A variety of problems can occur, especially if the drawing is being plotted on a different computer than the one it was drawn on. This is common with drawings that contain xref files (see Chapter 24), special fonts, and symbols. Always try to remedy these problems before performing a batch plot. The **PACK** command copies all files associated with a drawing to a selected location. This is found in the **Express** pull-down menu and is available if a full installation of AutoCAD was performed. See Appendix A for information on this and other Express Tools.

Plotting a Batch Plot List

After the batch list is complete, you can choose to close the current session without plotting by picking **Exit** from the **File** pull-down menu. Be sure to save the current list first.

Pick the **Plot** button to begin plotting the list. When the plotting begins, you can open AutoCAD and continue working on other projects, or open any other application while the Batch Plot utility works in the background. A check mark appears next to the drawing name as it is successfully printed. An "X" appears next to drawings that do not plot. Minimize the **AutoCAD Batch Plot Utility** dialog box to remove it from the screen.

PLOTTING HINTS

Plotting can slow down productivity in an office or a classroom if not done efficiently. Establish and follow a procedure for using the plotter, and instruct all drafters, engineers, and other plotter users of the proper operating procedures. Post these in strategic locations.

Planning Your Plots

Planning is again the key word when dealing with plots. In the same way you planned the drawing, you must plan the plot. The following items need to be considered when planning:

✓ Size and type of plotting media, such as bond paper, vellum, or polyester film.
✓ Type of title block.
✓ Location and scale of multiple views.
✓ Origin location, and scale of the drawing.
✓ Color, thickness, and types of pens to be used.
✓ Speed of pens.
✓ Orientation of 3D views.
✓ Portion to be plotted: layout, view, window, display, limits, or extents.

This is only a sample of decisions that should be made before you begin plotting. Remember, the plotter is the funnel that all drawings must go through before they are evaluated, approved, and sent to production or the client. When a bottleneck develops at the plotter, the time savings of a CAD system can be drastically reduced.

PROFESSIONAL TIP

Use preprinted borders and title blocks whenever possible to decrease plotting time. Use block attributes for the title block information that will change with each drawing. A title block with defined attributes can be inserted into any drawing or plotted separately before or after the drawing. This eliminates drawing borders and title blocks every time you create a drawing. Refer to Chapter 25 for a discussion of title block attributes.

Eliminate Unnecessary Plots

The easiest way to eliminate the problems associated with plotting is to eliminate plotting. Make plots *only* when absolutely necessary. This results in time and money savings. A few additional suggestions include the following:

✓ Obtain approvals of designs while the drawings are on screen.
✓ Transfer files or disks for the checker's comments.
✓ Create a special layer with a unique color for markups. Freeze or erase this layer when finally making a plot.
✓ Use a "redlining" software package that enables the checker to review the drawing and apply markups to it without using AutoCAD.
✓ Check drawings on disk. Use a special layer for comments.
✓ Use a printer when check prints are sufficient.
✓ Avoid making plots for backups. Rather, save your drawing files to three different locations, such as the hard disk, a diskette at your workstation, and a diskette at another location. These may also be supplemented with a backup on tape cartridges, optical disks, or other external storage devices.

If You Must Plot...

Industry still exists on a paper-based system. Therefore, it is important that plotters are used efficiently. This means using the plotter only for what is required. Here are a few hints for doing just that.

✓ Ask yourself, "Do I *really* need a plot?" If the answer is an unqualified *yes*, then proceed.
✓ Plan your plot!

✓ Pick the least busy time to make the plot.

✓ If more than one plotter is available, use the smallest, least complex model.

✓ Select the smallest piece of paper possible.

✓ Use the lowest quality paper possible.

✓ Decide on only one pen color and thickness to make the plot.

✓ Use the most inexpensive pen possible.

✓ Use the fastest pen speed to achieve quality without pen skipping.

✓ Use a continuous linetype when possible. Hidden and center linetypes increase plot time significantly and cause pen wear. This is not as much of a factor with penless plotters, such as laser and inkjet devices.

✓ Create batch plot files and use batch plotting at times when plotter and printer use is light.

Producing Quality Plots

When you must plot the highest quality drawing for reproduction, evaluation, or presentation, use your plotter in a manner that does the job right the first time. Keep in mind these points before making that final plot.

✓ Choose the device that will produce the quality of print needed. Select the right tool for the job.

✓ Choose the paper type and size appropriate for the project.

✓ Set pen speeds slow enough to produce good lines without skipping.

✓ If using wet ink pens, select the proper ink for your climate.

✓ Apply the appropriate plot style table for color plotting.

NOTE In Chapters 23 and 24, you will see how details and drawings can be inserted into and referenced from other drawings. When using these techniques with multiple viewports, you must carefully control which layers are displayed in each viewport. This task is handled by the **VPLAYER** command, and with options in the **Layer Properties Manager** dialog box. This is covered in Chapter 24.

Chapter Test

Answer the following questions on a separate sheet of paper.

1. What is paper space?
2. Which drawing environment (space) is active when the **Model** tab is selected?
3. What is a layout?
4. How do you create floating viewports in a layout?
5. When working in a layout tab, how do you activate a viewport in order to zoom or pan the viewport display?
6. List three methods used to create a new layout tab.
7. When creating a new layout from a template, why is it better to select the command option from the shortcut menu rather than using the toolbar button?
8. How can you rename a layout?
9. If all layout tabs are not visible on screen, how do you select a tab that is not currently visible?
10. List the types of files a layout can be saved as.
11. How do you access the **Plotter Configuration Editor** from the **Page Setup** dialog box?
12. List five properties that can be set within a plot style.

---

13. Name the two plot style modes and the file extensions for their plot style tables.
14. What is a plot style table?
15. How do you access the **Plot Styles** window?
16. How do you create a new plot style table?
17. When you create a new color-dependent plot style table, how many plot styles does it contain?
18. When you create a new named plot style table, how many plot styles does it contain?
19. List two ways to access the **Plot Style Table Editor**.
20. What determines the plot style mode for a drawing?
21. Explain how you can specify a plot style table to be attached to all new drawings by default.
22. How does a color-dependent plot style table attached to a layout affect the plotting of the layout?
23. Plot styles of which plot style mode can be attached to layers and objects?
24. Explain how to assign a plot style to a layer.
25. Name two methods of assigning a plot style to an object.
26. What setting is used to have the effect of plot styles displayed in a layout?
27. Calculate the scale factors for drawings with the following scales:
    A. 1/4″ = 1″
    B. 1/8″ = 1′-0″
    C. 1″ = 30′
28. Calculate the drawing limits for the following scales and sheet sizes:
    A. 2″ = 1″ scale, 17 × 11 sheet size
    B. 1/2″ = 1′-0″ scale, 48 × 36 sheet size
    C. 1″= 10′ scale, 36 × 24 sheet size
29. Define *plot file* and explain how it is used.
30. Define *plot queue*.
31. What do you enter in the **Plot** dialog box to make the plotted drawing twice the size of the soft copy drawing?
32. What do you enter to specify a plot scale of 1/4″ = 1′-0″?
33. What system variable controls paper space linetype scaling?
34. Name the pull-down menu where the **Plot...** command is found.
35. How do you add a printer or plotter to the **Plot Device** tab of the **Plot** dialog box?
36. What is the difference between a PC2 file and a PC3 file?
37. How do you save a plot file named PLOT1 to a 3.5″ disk?
38. Identify the two types of paper orientation.
39. List an advantage of the partial preview format.
40. Cite two advantages of the full preview format.
41. Identify at least one disadvantage of the full preview format.
42. What is the purpose of batch plotting?
43. How do you access the **AutoCAD Batch Plot Utility** dialog box?
44. Explain why you should plan your plots.
45. Provide the best method to speed up the plotting process in a classroom or company.
46. Check prints are best generated on a(n) _____.
47. What type of paper and pens should be used for a check plot?
48. What type of paper and pens should be used for a final plot?

For Questions 49–53, specify if the statement is true or false.

49. Plot styles can be added to and deleted from color-dependent plot style tables.
50. Plot styles can be added to and deleted from named plot style tables.
51. The plot style mode of a drawing cannot be changed.
52. A plot style assigned to a layer will override a plot style assigned to an object on the layer when the drawing is plotted.
53. If a drawing has multiple layouts, all layouts must use the same plot style table.

Drawing Problems

1. Create a new B-size decimal template drawing for use with mechanical (machine) parts. Use the following guidelines:
   A. Create a layout with the border and title block.
   B. Establish the appropriate settings to make this a half-scale (1" = 2") drawing.
   C. Create three different text styles: one to plot at 1/8" high, another at 3/16" high, and a third at 1/4" high. Set the text heights and linetype scale according to the values given in the chart in Appendix H.
   D. Save the drawing template as MECH-B-HALF.DWT.

2. Create a new C-size architectural template drawing. Use the following guidelines:
   A. Create a layout with the border and title block. Set units to architectural and set the area to 160' × 120'. Select to work on the drawing without the layout visible.
   B. Establish the appropriate settings to make this a 1/8" = 1'–0" scale drawing.
   C. Create three different text styles: one to plot at 1/8" high, another at 3/16" high, and a third at 1/4" high. Set the text heights and linetype scale according to the values given in the chart in Appendix H.
   D. Save the drawing as ARCH-C-EIGHTH.DWT.

3. Create a new C-size civil engineering template drawing. Use the following guidelines:
   A. Create a layout with the border and title block. Set units to engineering, angle to surveyor, angle measure to east, angle direction to counterclockwise, and set the area to 1000' × 750'. Select to work on the drawing while viewing the layout.
   B. Establish the appropriate settings to make this a 1" = 50' scale drawing.
   C. Create three different text styles: one to plot at 1/8" high, another at 3/16" high, and a third at 1/4" high. Set the text heights and linetype scale according to the values given in the chart in Appendix H.
   D. Save the drawing as CIVIL-C-1=50.DWT.

4. Open one of your drawings from Chapter 8. Plot the drawing on B-size paper using the **Limits** option. Use different color pens for each color in the drawing.

5. Zoom in on a portion of the drawing used for Problem 4 and select the **Display** plotting option. Rotate the plot 90° and fit it on the paper.

6. Using the same drawing used in Problem 4, use the **Window** option. Window a detailed area of the drawing. Plot the drawing to fit the paper size chosen.

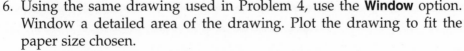

7. Draw the views needed to describe the object completely. Set up appropriate layers, colors, and linetypes. Do not dimension the drawing. Plot from a layout tab using a scale of 1:1. Save the problem as P10-7.

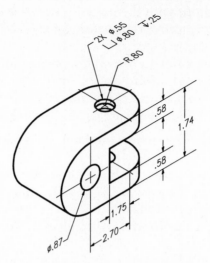

8. Draw the stainless steel stud shown on a B-size sheet at a scale of 2:1 (2 times actual size). Use a template drawing with a single floating model space viewport. Do not dimension the drawing. Be sure that paper space is active before using the **PLOT** command. Save the drawing as P10-8. Set the plot scale at 1:1.

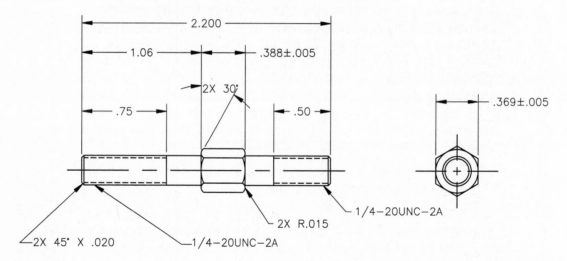

9. Draw the schematic shown on an A-size sheet at full scale. The size of the components is not important, but keep the same proportions as shown. Using color-dependent plot styles, have the equipment (shown in color in the diagram) plot with a lineweight of 0.8mm and 80% screening. Plotted text height should be 1/8″. Save the drawing as P10-9. Plot in paper space at 1:1.

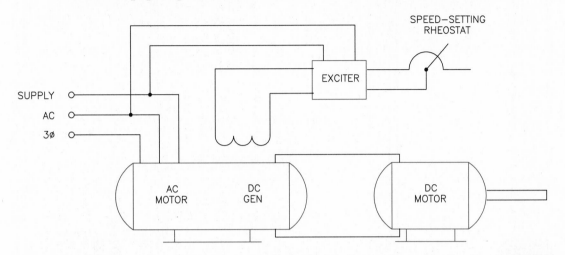

10. Draw the schematic shown on a B-size sheet at full scale. The size of the components is not important, but keep the same proportions as shown. Plotted text height should be 1/8″. Create four layouts with the names and displays as follows:

   A. The **Entire Schematic** layout plots the entire schematic.
   B. The **3 Wire Control** layout plots only the 3 Wire Control diagram.
   C. The **Motor** layout plots the motor symbol and connections in the lower-center of the schematic.
   D. The **Schematic** layout plots schematic without the 3 Wire Control and motor components.

Save the drawing as P10-10. Plot in paper space at 1:1.

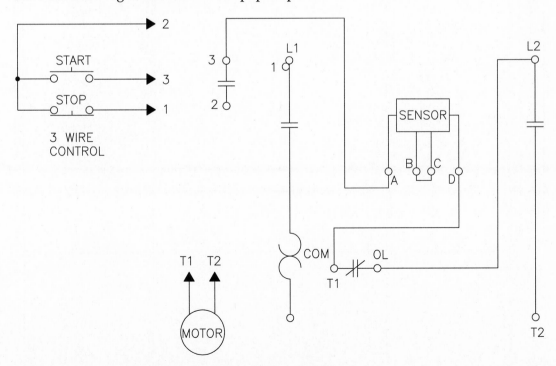

Elevation section. (Steve D. Bloedel)

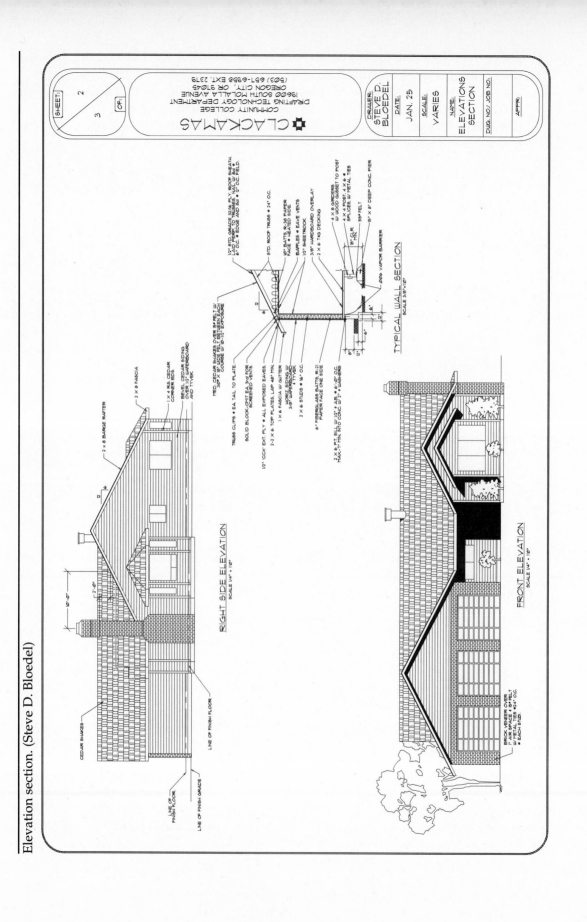

RIGHT SIDE ELEVATION
SCALE 1/4" = 1'0"

FRONT ELEVATION
SCALE 1/4" = 1'0"

TYPICAL WALL SECTION
SCALE 3/8"=1'0"

CHAPTER 11

Basic Editing Commands

Learning Objectives

After completing this chapter, you will be able to:

- Draw chamfers and angled corners with the **CHAMFER** command.
- Use the **FILLET** command to draw fillets, rounds, and other rounded corners.
- Remove a portion of a line, circle, or arc using the **BREAK** command.
- Use the **TRIM** and **EXTEND** commands to edit an object.
- Relocate an object using the **MOVE** command.
- Make single and multiple copies of existing objects using the **COPY** command.
- Draw a mirror image of an object.
- Change the angular position of an object using the **ROTATE** command.
- Use the **ALIGN** command to move and rotate an object simultaneously.
- Change the size of an object using the **SCALE** command.
- Modify the length and height of an object using the **STRETCH** and **LENGTHEN** commands.
- Create selection sets and object groups.

This chapter explains commands and methods for changing a drawing. With manual drafting techniques, editing and modifying a drawing can take hours or even days. AutoCAD, however, makes the same editing tasks simpler and quicker. In Chapter 4 you learned how to draw and erase lines. The **ERASE** command is one of the most commonly used editing commands. You also learned how to select objects by picking with the cursor or using a window box, crossing box, window polygon, crossing polygon, or fence. The items selected are referred to as a *selection set*.

Many of the same selection methods and techniques can be used for the editing commands discussed in this chapter. You will learn how to draw angled and rounded corners. You will also learn how to move, copy, rotate, scale, and create a mirror image of an existing object. These features are found in the **Modify** toolbar and **Modify** pull-down menus. The editing commands discussed in this chapter are basically divided into two general groups—editing individual features of a drawing and editing major portions of a drawing. Commands typically used to edit individual features of a drawing include the following:

- **CHAMFER**
- **FILLET**
- **BREAK**
- **TRIM**
- **EXTEND**
- **LENGTHEN**

The following commands are used to edit entire drawings or major portions of a drawing, though they can also be used to edit individual features:

- **MOVE**
- **COPY**
- **ROTATE**
- **MIRROR**
- **SCALE**
- **STRETCH**
- **CHANGE**
- **GROUP**

DRAWING CHAMFERS

A *chamfer* in mechanical drafting is a small angled surface used to relieve a sharp corner. AutoCAD defines a chamfer as "any angled corner on the drawing." The size of a chamfer is determined by its distance from the corner. A 45° chamfer is the same distance from the corner in each direction, Figure 11-1. Chamfers were introduced in Chapter 5.

CHAMFER
CHA

Modify
➡ Chamfer

Modify
toolbar

Chamfer

Chamfers are drawn between two lines that may, or may not, intersect. Chamfers can also connect polylines, xlines, and rays. The **CHAMFER** command can be accessed by selecting the **Chamfer** button in the **Modify** toolbar, by picking **Chamfer** from the **Modify** pull-down menu, or by typing CHA or CHAMFER at the Command: prompt. The following shows the default values and the options that are available when you enter the **CHAMFER** command:

> Command: **CHA** *or* **CHAMFER.**↵
> (TRIM mode) Current chamfer Dist1 = 0.5, Dist2 = 0.5
> Select first line or [Polyline/Distance/Angle/Trim/Method]:

The current settings are displayed for your reference. Chamfers are established with two distances, or a distance and angle. The default value is 0.5 for both distances. This produces a 45° × 0.5 chamfered corner. The following is a brief description of each **CHAMFER** option:

- **Polyline.** Use this option if you want to chamfer all of the eligible corners on a polyline. The term "eligible" means that the chamfer distance is small enough to work on the corner.
- **Distance.** This option lets you set the chamfer distance for each line from the corner.
- **Angle.** This option uses a chamfer distance on the first selected line and applies a chamfer angle to determine the second line chamfer.
- **Trim.** Enter this to set the **Trim** mode. If **Trim** is on, the selected lines are trimmed or extended as required from the corner before creating the chamfer line. If **No trim** is active, the **Trim** mode is off. In this case, the selected lines are not trimmed or extended and only the chamfer line is added.
- **Method.** This is a toggle that sets the chamfer method to either **Distance** or **Angle**. **Distance** and **Angle** values can be set without affecting each other.

Figure 11-1.
Examples of different chamfers.

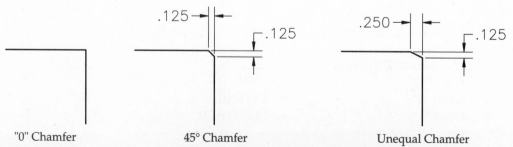

"0" Chamfer   45° Chamfer   Unequal Chamfer

Setting the Chamfer Distance

For 2000i Users...

When setting the chamfer distances in AutoCAD 2000i, you can select the first line to be chamfered immediately after entering the second chamfer distance. In AutoCAD 2000, you must reissue the **CHAMFER** command after setting the chamfer distances.

The chamfer distance must be set before you can draw chamfers. The distances that you set remain in effect until changed. Most drafters set the chamfer distance as exact values, but you can also pick two points to set the distance. The following procedure is used to set the chamfer distance:

Command: **CHA** *or* **CHAMFER**↵
(TRIM mode) Current chamfer Dist1 = 0.5, Dist2 = 0.5
Select first line or [Polyline/Distance/Angle/Trim/Method]: **D**↵
Specify first chamfer distance <0>: *(specify a distance, such as .25)*
Specify second chamfer distance <0.25>: *(press [Enter] for the current distance, or type a new value)*
Command:

Now you are ready to draw chamfers. Enter the **CHAMFER** command and select the first and second lines:

Command: **CHA** *or* **CHAMFER**↵
(TRIM mode) Current chamfer Dist1 = 0.25, Dist2 = 0.25
Select first line or [Polyline/Distance/Angle/Trim/Method]: *(pick the first line)*
Select second line: *(pick the second line)*

After the lines are picked, AutoCAD automatically chamfers the corner. Objects can be chamfered even when the corners do not meet. AutoCAD extends the lines as required to generate the specified chamfer and complete the corner if **TRIMMODE** is on. If **TRIMMODE** is off, AutoCAD does not extend the lines to complete the corner. This is discussed later.

If the specified chamfer distance is so large that the chamfered objects disappear, AutoCAD does not perform the chamfer. Instead, a message such as 2 lines were too short is given. If you want to chamfer additional corners, press [Enter] to repeat the **CHAMFER** command. The results of several chamfering operations are shown in Figure 11-2.

Figure 11-2.
Using the **CHAMFER** command.

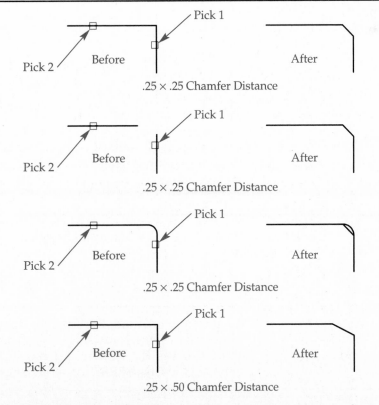

Chamfering the Corners of a Polyline

Polylines are objects that can be made up of many different widths and shapes. Polylines are drawn and edited in Chapters 15 and 16. All corners of a closed polyline can be chamfered at one time. Enter the **CHAMFER** command, select the **Polyline** option, and then select the polyline. The corners of the polyline are chamfered to the distance values set. If the polyline was drawn without using the **Close** option, the beginning corner is not chamfered, as shown in Figure 11-3.

Figure 11-3.
Using the **Polyline** option of the **CHAMFER** command.

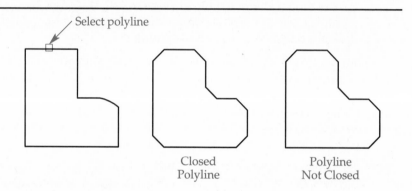

Setting the Chamfer Angle

Instead of setting two chamfer distances, you can set the chamfer distance for one line and an angle to determine the chamfer to the second line. To do this, use the **Angle** option:

Command: **CHA** *or* **CHAMFER**↵
Select first line or [Polyline/Distance/Angle/Trim/Method]: **A**↵
Specify chamfer length on the first line <0>: *(enter a chamfer distance, .5 for example)*
Specify chamfer angle from the first line <0>: *(enter an angle, 45 for example)*
Command:

Now, you are ready to enter the **CHAMFER** command again and draw a chamfer with the **Angle** option, as shown in Figure 11-4. You can see in the following command sequence that distance and angle are now the defaults:

Command: **CHA** *or* **CHAMFER**↵
(TRIM mode) Current chamfer Length = 0.5, Angle = 45.0
Select first line or [Polyline/Distance/Angle/Trim/Method]: *(pick the first line)*
Select second line: *(pick the second line)*
Command:

Figure 11-4.
Using the **Angle** option of the **CHAMFER** command with the chamfer length set at .5 and the angle set at 45°.

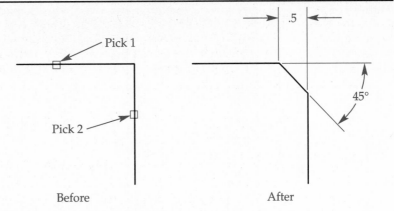

Before   After

EXERCISE 11-1

❑ Begin a new drawing or use one of your templates.
❑ Use the **Distance** option of the **CHAMFER** command to draw the objects shown in Figure 11-1.
❑ Draw the "Before" objects shown in Figure 11-2. Use the **Distance** option to change them to the "After" objects.
❑ Draw the "Before" object shown in Figure 11-4 and then use the **Angle** option of the **CHAMFER** command to create the "After" object.
❑ Save the drawing as EX11-1.

Setting the Chamfer Method

When you set chamfer distances or distance and angle, AutoCAD maintains the setting until you change it. You can set the values for each method without affecting the other. Use the **Method** option if you want to toggle between drawing chamfers by **Distance** and by **Angle**. The default option contains the values that you previously set:

```
Command: CHA or CHAMFER↵
(TRIM mode) Current chamfer Length = 0.5, Angle = 45.0
Select first line or [Polyline/Distance/Angle/Trim/Method]: M↵
Enter trim method [Distance/Angle]: D↵
Select first line or [Polyline/Distance/Angle/Trim/Method]: (pick the first line)
Select second line: (pick the second line)
Command:
```

Setting the Chamfer Trim Mode

You can have the selected lines automatically trimmed with the chamfer, or you can have the selected lines remain in the drawing after the chamfer, as shown in Figure 11-5. To set this, enter the **Trim** option and then select either T for **Trim** or N for **No trim**:

```
Command: CHA or CHAMFER↵
Select first line or [Polyline/Distance/Angle/Trim/Method]: T↵
Enter trim mode option [Trim/No trim] <Trim>: N↵
Select first line or [Polyline/Distance/Angle/Trim/Method]: (pick the first line)
Select second line: (pick the second line)
Command:
```

You can also use the **TRIMMODE** system variable to set **Trim** or **No trim** by typing TRIMMODE at the Command: prompt. A 1 setting trims the lines before chamfering, while a 0 setting does not trim the lines.

Figure 11-5.
Using the **Trim**
option of the
CHAMFER
command.

Before Chamfer	Chamfer with Trim	Chamfer with No Trim

NOTE

The **TRIMMODE** system variable affects both the **FILLET** and **CHAMFER** commands. If the **Polyline** option is used with the **No trim** mode active, any chamfer lines created are not part of the polyline.

PROFESSIONAL TIP

When the **CHAMFER** or **FILLET** command is set to **Trim**, lines that do not connect at a corner are automatically extended and the chamfer or fillet is applied. However, when the **No trim** option is used, these lines are not extended, but the chamfer or fillet is drawn anyway. If you have lines that are drawn short of a corner and want them to connect to the chamfer or fillet, you need to extend them if you draw in the **No trim** mode.

EXERCISE 11-2

❏ Begin a new drawing or use one of your templates.
❏ Draw the "Before" objects shown in Figure 11-5 and then use the **Trim** mode as needed to create the "After" objects.
❏ Save the drawing as EX11-2.

AutoCAD
User's
Guide **9**

DRAWING ROUNDED CORNERS

In mechanical drafting, an inside rounded corner is called a *fillet*. An outside rounded corner is called a *round*. AutoCAD refers to all rounded corners as fillets.

Fillets were introduced in Chapter 5 when drawing filleted corners on rectangles with the **RECTANG** command. The **FILLET** command draws a rounded corner between intersecting and nonintersecting lines, circles, and arcs. To access the **FILLET** command, pick the **Fillet** button on the **Modify** toolbar, select **Fillet** from the **Modify** pull-down menu, or type F or FILLET at the Command: prompt.

Fillets are sized by radius. The default radius is 0.5. A new radius is specified first by typing R on the prompt line for the **Radius** option as follows:

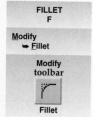

FILLET
F

Modify
➥ Fillet

Modify
toolbar

Fillet

Command: **F** *or* **FILLET**↵
Current settings: Mode = TRIM, Radius = 0.5
Select first object or [Polyline/Radius/Trim]: **R**↵
Specify fillet radius <*current*>: *(type the fillet radius, .25 for example, and press [Enter], or press [Enter] to accept the current value)*

For 2000i Users...

When setting the fillet radius in AutoCAD 2000i, you can select the first line to be filleted immediately after entering the radius. In AutoCAD 2000, you must reissue the **FILLET** command after setting the fillet radius.

Once the fillet radius has been given, repeat the **FILLET** command to fillet the objects. The command sequence shown in Figure 11-6 is as follows:

Command: **F** *or* **FILLET**↵
Current settings: Mode - TRIM, Radius - .25
Select first object or [Polyline/Radius/Trim]: *(pick the first object to be filleted)*
Select second object: *(pick the other object to be filleted)*
Command:

Figure 11-6.
Using the **FILLET** command.

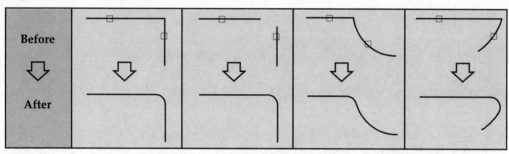

NOTE

The value of the radius for fillets is stored in the **FILLETRAD** system variable. This variable is changed when you enter a new value using the **Radius** option of the **FILLET** command. You can also change **FILLETRAD** at the Command: prompt.

EXERCISE 11-3

❏ Begin a new drawing or use one of your templates.
❏ Draw the "Before" objects shown in Figure 11-6. Use the **FILLET** command as needed to create the "After" objects.
❏ Save the drawing as EX11-3.

Rounding the Corners of a Polyline

Fillets can be drawn at all corners of a closed polyline by selecting the **Polyline** option. The current fillet radius is used with this option. Polylines are fully explained in Chapters 15 and 16. The command sequence shown in Figure 11-7 is as follows:

Command: **F** *or* **FILLET**↵
Current settings: Mode = TRIM, Radius = 0.25
Select first object or [Polyline/Radius/Trim]: **P**↵
Select 2D polyline: *(pick the polyline)*
n lines were filleted
Command:

Figure 11-7.
Using the **Polyline** option of the **FILLET** command.

Select polyline

Closed polyline

Polyline not closed

Before

After

After

AutoCAD tells you how many lines were filleted. Then the Command: prompt returns. If the polyline was drawn without using the **Close** option, the beginning corner is not filleted.

Setting the Fillet Trim Mode

The **TRIMMODE** system variable and the **Trim** option controls whether or not the **FILLET** command trims off object segments that extend beyond the fillet radius point. When the **Trim** mode is active, objects are trimmed. When the **Trim** mode is inactive, the filleted objects are not changed after the fillet is inserted, as shown in Figure 11-8. Use the **Trim** option like this:

> Command: **F** or **FILLET**↵
> Current settings: Mode = TRIM, Radius = 0.25
> Select first object or [Polyline/Radius/Trim]: **T**↵
> Enter Trim mode option [Trim/No trim] <Trim>: **N**↵
> Select first object or [Polyline/Radius/Trim]: *(pick the first object)*
> Select second object: *(pick the second object)*
> Command:

Figure 11-8.
Using the **Trim** option of the **FILLET** command.

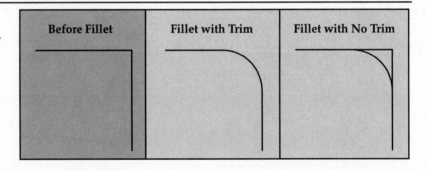

| Before Fillet | Fillet with Trim | Fillet with No Trim |

If the lines to be filleted do not connect at the corner, they are automatically extended when the **Trim** mode is on. However, they are not extended when using **No trim**. If you do not want a separation between the line and the filleted corner, extend the lines to the corner before filleting.

Filleting Parallel Lines

You can also draw a fillet between parallel lines. When parallel lines are selected, a radius is placed between the two lines. In **Trim** mode, a longer line is trimmed to match the length of a shorter line. The radius of a fillet between parallel lines is always half of the distance between the two lines, regardless of the radius setting for the **FILLET** command.

Chamfering and Filleting Objects Together

Line objects (lines, arcs, and circles) can be filleted and chamfered to other line objects or to polyline objects. When the **Trim** option is active and a line object is connected to a polyline, the separate entities (the line, polyline, and filleted corner) become a single polyline. When the **No Trim** option is active, the entities retain their original properties and the fillet or chamfer is a line object. Polylines are discussed in Chapters 15 and 16.

All corners of a single polyline can be edited using the **Polyline** option of the **CHAMFER** or **FILLET** command. A single corner of a polyline can be filleted or chamfered by selecting the polyline on both sides of the corner. However, two separate polylines cannot be chamfered or filleted together. If you attempt this, AutoCAD will respond with a message at the Command: prompt: Cannot chamfer (fillet) polyline segments from different polylines.

For 2000i Users...

AutoCAD 2000i allows you to create a chamfer or fillet between two separate poly-lines.

EXERCISE 11-4

❑ Begin a new drawing or use one of your templates.
❑ Draw a corner similar to the one on the left in Figure 11-8. Make two copies of the object.
❑ Use the **Trim** and **No Trim** options to create the objects shown on the right in Figure 11-8.
❑ Draw two parallel lines with different lengths. Fillet one end of the lines using the **Trim** option. Use the **No Trim** option on the other end.
❑ Save the drawing as EX11-4.

BREAK
BR

Modify
➡ Break

Modify
toolbar

Break

REMOVING A SECTION FROM AN OBJECT

The **BREAK** command is used to remove a portion of a line, circle, arc, trace, or polyline. This command can also be used to divide a single object into two objects. The **BREAK** command can be accessed by picking the **Break** button in the **Modify** toolbar, by picking **Break** in the **Modify** pull-down menu, or by typing BR or BREAK at the Command: prompt.

When using the **BREAK** command, the following prompts appear:

> Command: **BR** *or* **BREAK**↵
> Select object: *(pick the object)*
> Specify second break point or [First point]: *(pick second break point or type* **F**
>   *to select first break point)*

The **BREAK** command requires you to select the object to be broken, the first break point, and the second break point. When you select the object, the point you pick is also used as the first break point by default. If you wish to select a different first break point, type F at the Specify second break point or [First point]: prompt to select the **First point** option. After both break points are specified, the part of the object between the two points is deleted. See Figure 11-9.

The **BREAK** command can also be used to split an object in two without removing a portion. This is done by selecting the same point as both the first and second break points. This can be accomplished by entering @ at the Specify second break point: prompt. The @ symbol repeats the coordinates of the previously selected point.

> Command: **BR** *or* **BREAK**↵
> Select object: *(pick the object)*
> Specify second break point or [First point]: @↵
> Command:

Using break without removing a portion of the object is shown in Figure 11-10.

When breaking arcs or circles, always work in a counterclockwise direction. Otherwise, you may break the portion of the arc or circle that you want to keep. If you want to break off the end of a line or arc, pick the first point on the object. Then pick the second point slightly beyond the end to be cut off, Figure 11-11. When you pick a second point that is not on the object, AutoCAD selects the point on the object nearest to the point you picked.

If you want to break a line from the point of intersection with another line, use the **Intersection** object snap mode as follows:

> Command: **BR** *or* **BREAK**↵
> Select object: *(pick the line)*
> Specify second break point or [First point]: **INT**↵
> of *(move the aperture to the intersection and pick)*
> Command:

The line is now broken between the first point and the point of intersection.

PROFESSIONAL TIP

You may want to turn running object snaps off if they conflict with the points you are trying to pick when using the **BREAK** command. Picking the **OSNAP** button on the status bar is an easy way to temporarily override the running object snaps.

Figure 11-9.
Using the **BREAK** command to break an object. The first pick can be used to select both the object and the first break point.

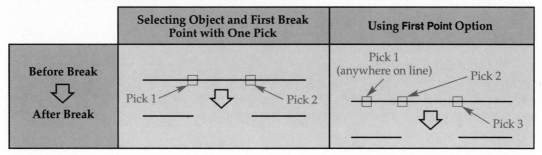

	Selecting Object and First Break Point with One Pick	Using First Point Option
Before Break ⬇ After Break	Pick 1 → ⬇ ← Pick 2	Pick 1 (anywhere on line) Pick 2 ⬇ Pick 3

Figure 11-10.
Using the **BREAK** command to break an object at a single point, without removing any of the object. Select the same point as the first break point and the second break point.

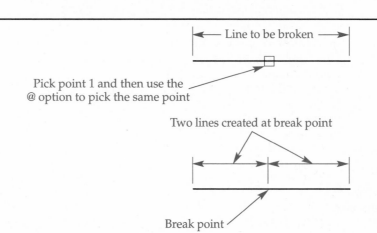

Line to be broken

Pick point 1 and then use the @ option to pick the same point

Two lines created at break point

Break point

EXERCISE 11-5

❏ Begin a new drawing or use one of your templates.
❏ Draw two horizontal lines and use the **BREAK** command to break each line at two points, similar to Figure 11-9.
❏ Draw two horizontal lines and use the **BREAK** command to break each line at one point, similar to Figure 11-10.
❏ Draw two circles and two arcs and break each similar to Figure 11-11.
❏ Save the drawing as EX11-5.

Figure 11-11.
Using the **BREAK** command on circles and arcs.

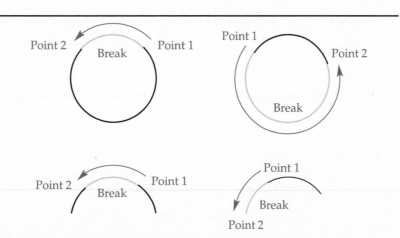

Point 2   Break   Point 1

Point 1   Point 2   Break

Point 2   Break   Point 1

Point 1   Break   Point 2

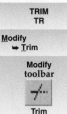

TRIM
TR

Modify
➡ Trim

Modify
toolbar

Trim

For 2000i Users...

In AutoCAD 2000i, you can access the **EXTEND** command while using the **TRIM** command. After selecting the cutting edge, hold the [Shift] key while selecting an object to extend the object to the cutting edge.

The **TRIM** command cuts lines, polylines, circles, arcs, ellipses, splines, xlines, and rays that extend beyond a desired point of intersection. To access the **TRIM** command, pick the **Trim** button in the **Modify** toolbar, pick **Trim** from the **Modify** pull-down menu, or type TR or TRIM at the Command: prompt.

The command requires that you pick a "cutting edge" and the object(s) to trim. The *cutting edge* can be an object that defines the point where the object you are trimming will be cut. A cutting edge can be an object such as a line, arc, or text. If two corners of an object overrun, select two cutting edges and two objects. Refer to Figure 11-12 as you go through the following sequence:

Command: **TR** *or* **TRIM**↵
Current settings: Projection = UCS, Edge = None
Select cutting edges...
Select objects: *(pick first cutting edge)*
Select objects: *(pick second cutting edge)*
Select objects: ↵
Select object to trim or [Project/Edge/Undo]: *(pick the first object to trim)*
Select object to trim or [Project/Edge/Undo]: *(pick the second object to trim)*
Select object to trim or [Project/Edge/Undo]: ↵
Command:

Figure 11-12.
Using the **TRIM** command. Note the cutting edges.

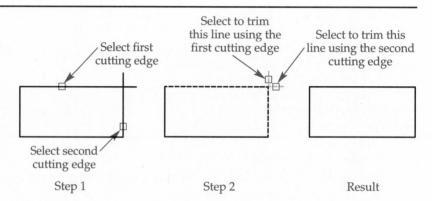

Select to trim this line using the first cutting edge

Select to trim this line using the second cutting edge

Select first cutting edge

Select second cutting edge

Step 1   Step 2   Result

Trimming to an Implied Intersection

An *implied intersection* is the point where two or more objects would meet if extended. Trimming to an implied intersection is possible using the **Edge** option of the **TRIM** command. When you enter the **Edge** option, the choices are **Extend** and **No extend**. When **Extend** is active, AutoCAD checks to see if the cutting edge object will extend to intersect the object to be trimmed. If so, the implied intersection point can be used to trim the object. This does not change the cutting edge object at all. The command sequence for the **TRIM** operation shown in Figure 11-13 is as follows:

Command: **TR** *or* **TRIM**↵
Current settings: Projection = UCS, Edge = None
Select cutting edges...
Select objects: *(pick the cutting edge)*
Select objects: ↵
Select object to trim or [Project/Edge/Undo]: **E**↵
Enter an implied edge extension mode [Extend/No extend]: **E**↵
Select object to trim or [Project/Edge/Undo]: *(pick the object to trim)*
Select object to trim or [Project/Edge/Undo]: ↵
Command:

Figure 11-13.
Trimming to an implied intersection.

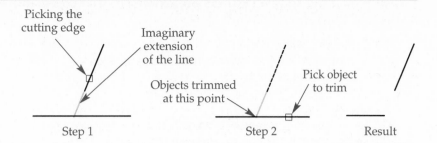

The **Edge** option can also be set using the **EDGEMODE** system variable. **Extend** is active when the **EDGEMODE** is 1. With this setting, the cutting edge object is checked to see if it will extend to intersect the object to be trimmed. The **No extend** option is set when **EDGEMODE** is set to 0. Set the **EDGEMODE** system variable by typing EDGEMODE at the Command: prompt and entering the new value.

Using the Undo Option

The **TRIM** command has an **Undo** option that allows you to cancel the previous trimming without leaving the command. This is useful when the result of a trim is not what you expected. To undo the previous trim, simply type U immediately after performing an unwanted trim. The trimmed portion returns and you can continue trimming other objects:

```
Command: TR or TRIM↵
Current settings: Projection = UCS, Edge = Extend
Select boundary edges...
Select objects: (pick the first cutting edge)
Select objects: ↵
Select object to trim or [Project/Edge/Undo]: (pick the object to trim)
Select object to trim or [Project/Edge/Undo]: U↵
Command has been completely undone.
Select object to trim or [Project/Edge/Undo]: (pick the object to trim)
Select object to trim or [Project/Edge/Undo]: ↵
Command:
```

An Introduction to the Project Mode

In a 3D drawing environment, some lines may appear to intersect, but may not actually intersect. In such a case, using the **Project** option of the **TRIM** command can allow trimming operations. This option is also controlled by the **PROJMODE** system variable. Using AutoCAD for 3D drawing is explained in *AutoCAD and its Applications, Advanced*.

EXTENDING LINES

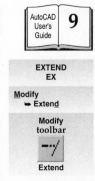

The **EXTEND** command is the opposite of the **TRIM** command. The **EXTEND** command is used to lengthen lines, elliptical arcs, rays, open polylines, and arcs to meet other objects. **EXTEND** does not work on closed polylines because an unconnected endpoint does not exist.

To use the **EXTEND** command, pick the **Extend** button in the **Modify** toolbar, select **Extend** from the **Modify** pull-down menu, or type EX or EXTEND at the Command: prompt. The command format is similar to **TRIM**. You are asked to select boundary edges, as opposed to cutting edges. *Boundary edges* are objects such as lines, arcs, or text to which the selected objects are extended. The command sequence is shown below and illustrated in Figure 11-14:

```
Command: EX or EXTEND↵
Current settings: Projection = UCS, Edge = None
Select boundary edges...
Select objects: (pick the boundary edge)
Select objects: ↵
Select object to extend or [Project/Edge/Undo]: (pick the object to extend)
Select object to extend or [Project/Edge/Undo]: ↵
Command:
```

If there is nothing for the selected line to meet, AutoCAD gives the message No edge in that direction or Entity does not intersect an edge.

Figure 11-14.
Using the **EXTEND** command. Note the boundary edges.

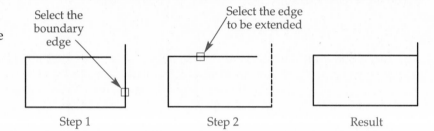

Step 1   Step 2   Result

Extending to an Implied Intersection

You can extend an object to an implied intersection using the **Edge** option in the **EXTEND** command. When you enter the **Edge** option, the choices are **Extend** and **No extend**, just as with the **TRIM** command. When **Extend** is active, the boundary edge object is checked to see if it intersects when extended. If so, the implied intersection point can be used as the boundary for the object to be extended, as shown in Figure 11-15. This does not change the boundary edge object at all.

```
Command: EX or EXTEND↵
Current settings: Projection = UCS, Edge = None
Select boundary edges...
Select objects: (pick the boundary edge)
Select objects: ↵
Select object to extend or [Project/Edge/Undo]: E↵
Enter implied edge extension mode [Extend/No extend] <No extend>: E↵
Select object to extend or [Project/Edge/Undo]: (pick the object to extend)
Select object to extend or [Project/Edge/Undo]: ↵
Command:
```

Figure 11-15.
Extending to an implied intersection.

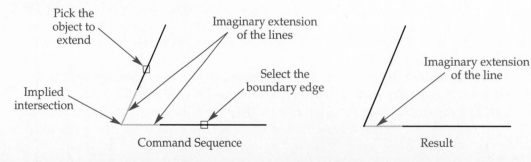

Command Sequence   Result

The **Edge** option can also be set using the **EDGEMODE** system variable as previously discussed with the **TRIM** command.

Using the Undo Option

The **Undo** option in the **EXTEND** command can be used to reverse the previous operation without leaving the **EXTEND** command. The command sequence is the same as discussed for the **TRIM** command.

The **Project** Mode of the **EXTEND** Command

In a 3D drawing, some lines may appear to intersect in a given view, but may not actually intersect. In such a case, you can use the **Project** option or the **PROJMODE** system variable as explained for the **TRIM** command.

PROFESSIONAL TIP

The **TRIM** and **EXTEND** commands have a convenient Smart mode. To use the Smart mode, press [Enter] rather than selecting a cutting or boundary edge. Then, when an object to trim or extend is picked, AutoCAD searches for the nearest intersecting object or implied intersection in the direction of your pick (depending on the **EDGEMODE** setting). AutoCAD then uses this object as the cutting or boundary edge. The object must be visible on the screen, and cannot be a block or xref object. Also, trimming can be done between two actual or implied intersections, but not between a combination of one actual and one implied intersection.

CHANGING LINES AND CIRCLES

The endpoint location of a line or the radius of a circle can be altered using the **CHANGE** command. To access the **CHANGE** command, type -CH or CHANGE at the Command: prompt. The keyboard shortcut is a hyphen (-) typed before CH. You are then prompted to select the objects to change. After the objects are selected, AutoCAD prompts for the change point. The *change point* is the new endpoint or radius location.

The **CHANGE** command also has a **Properties** option. This option can be used to change several properties of the selected object.

PROFESSIONAL TIP

The **CHANGE** command is normally an inefficient command to use. It is easier to relocate line endpoints using grip editing (discussed in Chapter 12). You can modify object properties more easily using the **Properties** window or the **Object Properties** toolbar.

❏ Begin a new drawing or use one of your templates.
❏ Make a drawing similar to the one shown below. Perform the **BREAK**, **TRIM**, and **EXTEND** operations noted.
❏ Save the drawing as EX11-6.

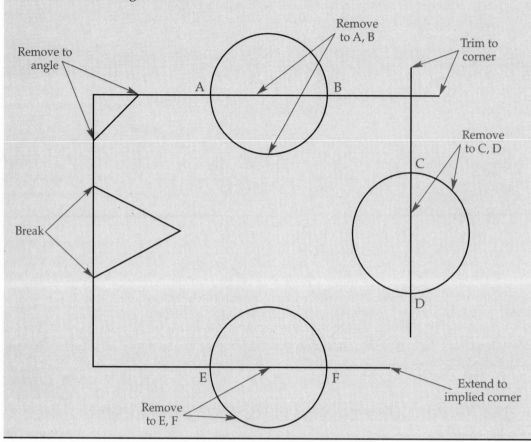

MOVING AN OBJECT

MOVE
M

Modify
➥ Mo**v**e

Modify
toolbar

Move

In many situations, you may find that the location of a view or feature is not where you want it. This problem is easy to fix using the **MOVE** command. You can access the **MOVE** command by picking the **Move** button in the **Modify** toolbar, picking **Mo**v**e** from the **Modify** pull-down menu, or typing M or MOVE at the Command: prompt.

After the **MOVE** command is accessed, AutoCAD asks you to select the objects to be moved. Use any of the selection set options to select the objects. Once the items are selected, the next prompt requests the base point. The *base point* provides a reference point. Most drafters select a point on an object, the corner of a view, or the center of a circle. The next prompt asks for the second point of displacement. This is the new position. All selected entities are moved the distance from the base point to the displacement point.

The following **MOVE** operation relates to the object shown in Figure 11-16. As the base point is picked, the object is automatically dragged into position. This is the command sequence:

Command: **M** *or* **MOVE**↵
Select objects: *(select the object or objects to be moved)*
Select objects: ↵
Specify base point or displacement: *(enter coordinates or pick a point on-screen)*
Specify second point of displacement or <use first point as displacement>: *(establish the new position by typing coordinates or picking a second point on-screen)*
Command:

Figure 11-16.
Using the **MOVE** command. When you select the object to be moved, it becomes highlighted.

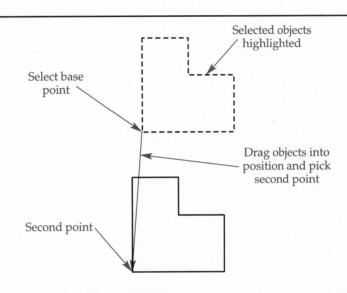

Selected objects highlighted

Select base point

Drag objects into position and pick second point

Second point

Using the First Point as Displacement

In the previous **MOVE** command, you selected a base point and then selected a second point of displacement. The object moved the distance and direction that you specified. You can also move the object relative to the first point. This means that the coordinates you use to select the base point are automatically used as the coordinates for the direction and distance for moving the object. Follow this command sequence to do this:

Command: **M** *or* **MOVE**↵
Select objects: *(select the objects to move)*
Select objects: ↵
Specify base point or displacement: **2,4**↵
Specify second point of displacement or <use first point as displacement>: ↵ *(the object moves a distance and direction equal to the coordinates specified for the base point, which is 2 units in the X direction and 4 units in the Y direction for this example)*
Command:

PROFESSIONAL TIP

Always use object snap to your best advantage with editing commands. For example, suppose you want to move an object to the center point of a circle. Use the **Center** object snap mode to select the center of the circle as the second point of displacement.

COPY
CO

<u>M</u>odify
➥ Copy

Modify
toolbar

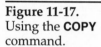

Copy Object

The **COPY** command is used to make a copy of an existing object or objects. To access the **COPY** command, pick the **Copy** button in the **Modify** toolbar, select **Copy** from the **Modify** pull-down menu, or type CO or COPY at the Command: prompt. The command prompts are the same as the **MOVE** command. However, when a second point of displacement is picked, the original object remains and a copy is drawn. The following command sequence is illustrated in Figure 11-17:

Command: **CO** *or* **COPY**↵
Select objects: *(select the objects to be copied)*
Select objects: ↵
Specify base point or displacement, or [Multiple]: *(select base point or enter displacement)*
Specify second point of displacement or <use first point as displacement>: *(pick second point or press* [Enter] *if displacement was specified)*
Command:

Figure 11-17.
Using the **COPY**
command.

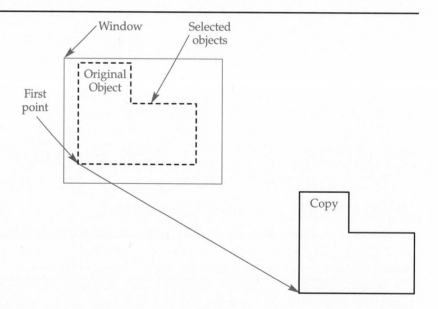

The **COPY** command is similar to the move command. You can either specify a base point and a second point of displacement, or specify a displacement. If you specify a displacement, a copy of the object is made at the specified location.

Making Multiple Copies

To make several copies of the same object, select the **Multiple** option of the **COPY** command by typing M at the Specify base point or displacement, or [Multiple]: prompt. The prompt for a second point repeats. When you have made all the copies needed, press [Enter]. The results are shown in Figure 11-18.

Figure 11-18.
Using the **Multiple** option of the **COPY** command.

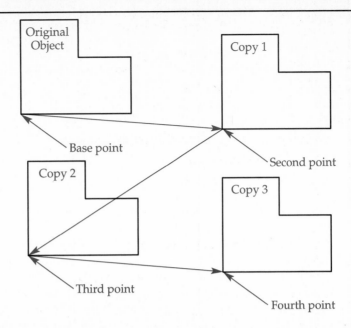

❏ Begin a new drawing or use one of your templates.
❏ Draw a square and an equilateral triangle (equal sides and angles) using the **POLYGON** command.
❏ Move the square to a new location.
❏ Move the triangle by specifying a displacement of 2,4 at the Specify base point or displacement prompt.
❏ Copy the triangle next to the new square position. Leave a small space between the two objects.
❏ Move all features to a new position in the upper-left corner of the screen.
❏ Copy the original triangle by specifying the coordinates 2,4 at the Specify base point or displacement prompt.
❏ Make four copies of the square anywhere on the screen. The new copies should not touch other objects.
❏ Save the drawing as EX11-7.

DRAWING A MIRROR IMAGE OF AN OBJECT

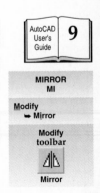

It is often necessary to draw an object in a reflected, or mirrored, position. The **MIRROR** command performs this task. Mirroring an entire drawing is common in architectural drafting when a client wants a plan drawn in reverse.

The **MIRROR** command is accessed by picking the **Mirror** button in the **Modify** toolbar, by selecting **Mirror** in the **Modify** pull-down menu, or by typing MI or MIRROR at the Command: prompt.

Selecting the Mirror Line

When you enter the **MIRROR** command, you select the objects to mirror and then select a mirror line. The *mirror line* is the hinge about which objects are reflected. The objects and any space between the objects and the mirror line are reflected, Figure 11-19.

The mirror line can be placed at any angle. Once you pick the first endpoint, a mirrored image appears and moves with the cursor. Once you select the second mirror line endpoint, you have the option to delete the original objects. Refer to Figure 11-20 and the following command sequence:

Figure 11-19.
When an object is reflected about a mirror line, the space between the object and the mirror line is also mirrored.

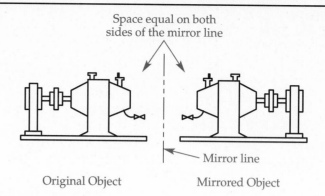

Space equal on both sides of the mirror line

Mirror line

Original Object   Mirrored Object

Command: **MI** *or* **MIRROR**↵
Select objects: *(select objects to be mirrored)*
Select objects: ↵
Specify first point of mirror line: *(pick the first point on the mirror line)*
Specify second point of mirror line: *(pick the second point on the mirror line)*
Delete source objects? [Yes/No] <N>: *(type Y and press [Enter] to delete the original objects, or press [Enter] to accept the default and keep the original objects)*
Command:

Figure 11-20.
Using the **MIRROR** command. You have the option to delete the old objects.

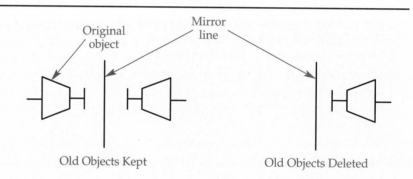

Original object

Mirror line

Old Objects Kept   Old Objects Deleted

❏ Begin a new drawing or use one of your templates.
❏ Draw the half object shown below. Then, complete the entire object using the **MIRROR** command. Do not dimension.
❏ Save the drawing as EX11-8.

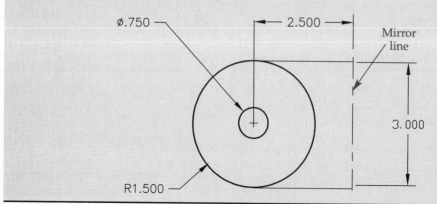

ø.750

2.500

Mirror line

3.000

R1.500

Mirroring Text

Normally, the **MIRROR** command reverses any text associated with the selected object. Backwards text is generally not acceptable, although it is used for reverse imaging. To keep the text readable, the **MIRRTEXT** system variable must be zero. There are two values for **MIRRTEXT**, as shown in Figure 11-21.

- **1.** Text is mirrored in relation to the original object. This is the default value.
- **0.** Prevents text from being reversed.

To draw a mirror image of an existing object and leave the text readable, set the **MIRRTEXT** variable to 0 by typing MIRRTEXT at the Command: prompt and entering the 0. Then, proceed to the **MIRROR** command.

Figure 11-21.
The **MIRRTEXT** system variable options.

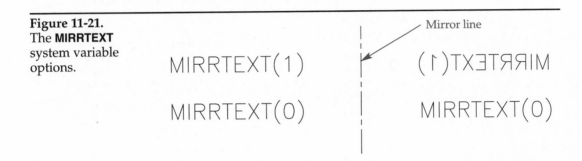

EXERCISE 11-9

❏ Begin a new drawing or use one of your templates.
❏ Make a drawing similar to the "original" object shown below. With the **MIRRTEXT** variable set to 0, mirror the object as shown in the center example.
❏ Mirror the object as required to give the result on the right example.
❏ Save the drawing as **EX11-9**.

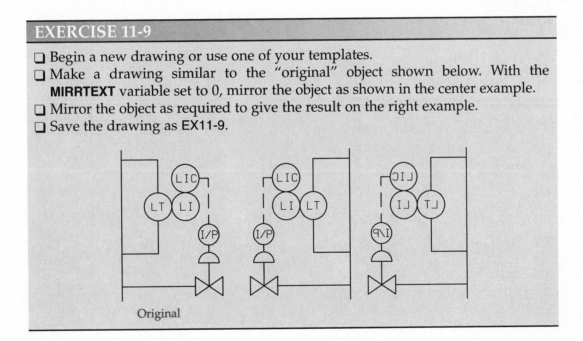

ROTATING EXISTING OBJECTS

ROTATE
RO

Modify
→ Rotate

Modify
toolbar

Rotate

Design changes often require that an object, feature, or view be rotated. For example, the office furniture layout may have to be moved, copied, or rotated for an interior design. AutoCAD allows you to easily revise the layout to obtain the final design.

To rotate selected objects, pick the **Rotate** button on the **Modify** toolbar, pick **Rotate** from the **Modify** pull-down menu, or type RO or ROTATE at the Command: prompt. Objects can be selected using any of the selection set options. Once the objects are selected, pick a base point and enter a rotation angle. A negative rotation angle revolves the object clockwise. A positive rotation angle revolves the object counterclockwise. See Figure 11-22. The **ROTATE** command sequence appears as follows:

    Command: **RO** *or* **ROTATE**↵
    Current positive angle in UCS: ANGDIR = counterclockwise, ANGBASE = 0
    Select objects: *(select the objects)*
    Select objects: ↵
    Specify base point: *(pick the base point or enter coordinates and press [Enter])*
    Specify rotation angle or [Reference]: *(type a positive or negative rotation angle and press [Enter], or pick a point on-screen)*
    Command:

If an object is already rotated and you want a different angle, you can do this in two ways. Both ways involve using the **Reference** option after selecting the object for rotation. The first way is to specify the existing angle and then the new angle, Figure 11-23A:

    Specify rotation angle or [Reference]: **R**↵
    Specify the reference angle <0>: **135**↵
    Specify the new angle: **180**↵

The other method is to pick a reference line on the object and rotate the object in relationship to the reference line, Figure 11-23B:

    Specify rotation angle or [Reference]: **R**↵
    Specify the reference angle <0>: *(pick an endpoint of a reference line that forms the existing angle)*
    Specify second point: *(pick the other point of the reference line that forms the existing angle)*
    Specify the new angle: *(specify a new angle, such as 180, and press [Enter])*

Figure 11-22.
Rotation angles.

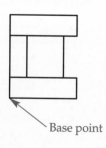
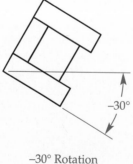

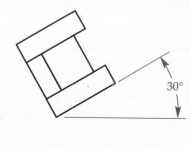

Base point

−30° Rotation

30° Rotation

Figure 11-23.
Using the **Reference** option of the **ROTATE** command. A—Entering reference angles. B—Selecting points on a reference line.

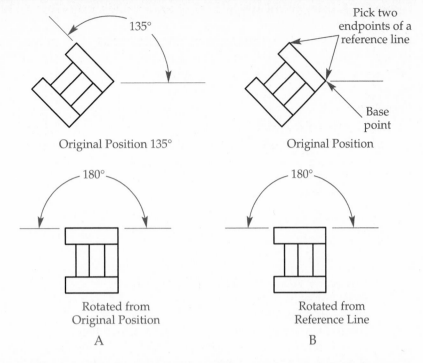

Original Position 135°

Original Position

Rotated from Original Position

Rotated from Reference Line

A

B

PROFESSIONAL TIP

Always use the object snap modes to your best advantage when editing. For example, suppose you want to rotate an object. It may be difficult to find an exact corner without using object snap modes. To select the base point, use the **Endpoint** or **Intersection** mode.

MOVING AND ROTATING AN OBJECT AT THE SAME TIME

AutoCAD User's Guide 9

The **ALIGN** command is primarily used for 3D applications, but it has 2D applications when you want to move and rotate an object. The command sequence asks you to select objects, and then asks for three source points and three destination points. For 2D applications, you only need two source and two destination points. Press [Enter] when the prompt requests the third source and destination points.

The *source points* define a line related to the object's original position. The *destination points* define the location of this line relative to the object's new location.

To access the **ALIGN** command, pick **Align** in the **3D Operation** cascading menu of the **Modify** pull-down menu, or type AL or ALIGN at the Command: prompt. The command sequence is as follows. Refer to Figure 11-24:

ALIGN
AL

Modify
➡ 3D Operation
➡ Align

Figure 11-24. Using the **ALIGN** command to move and rotate a kitchen cabinet layout against a wall.

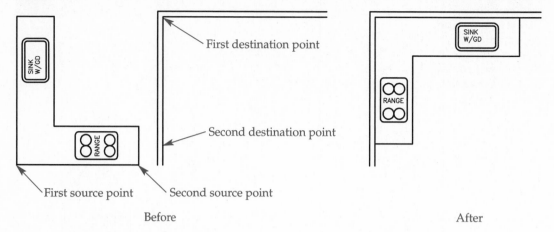

Before   After

Command: **AL** *or* **ALIGN.**↵
Select objects: *(select the objects)*
Select objects: ↵
Specify first source point: *(pick the first source point)*
Specify first destination point: *(pick the first destination point)*
Specify second source point: *(pick the second source point)*
Specify second destination point: *(pick the second destination point)*
Specify third source point or <continue>: ↵
Scale objects to alignment points? [Yes/No] <N>: *(Enter* Y *to scale the object if the distance between the source points is different than the distance between the destination points)*
Command:

EXERCISE 11-11

❑ Begin a new drawing or use one of your templates.
❑ Make a drawing similar to the one shown below. Do not add text or leaders.
❑ Use the **ALIGN** command to move and rotate Part A into position with Part B. S1 is the first source point and S2 is the second source point. D1 is the first destination point and D2 is the second destination point.
❑ Save the drawing as EX11-11.

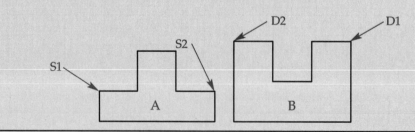

AutoCAD User's Guide **9**

CHANGING THE SIZE OF AN OBJECT

A convenient editing command that saves hours of drafting time is the **SCALE** command. This command lets you change the size of an object or the complete drawing. The **SCALE** command enlarges or reduces the entire object proportionately. If associative dimensioning is used, the dimensions also change to reflect the new size. This is discussed in Chapter 19.

To scale objects, pick the **Scale** button in the **Modify** toolbar, pick **Sca̲le** from the **Modify** pull-down menu, or type SC or SCALE at the Command: prompt. The command sequence is as follows:

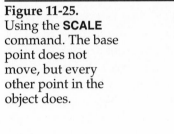
> Command: **SC** *or* **SCALE.**↵
> Select objects: *(select objects to be scaled)*
> Select objects: ↵
> Specify base point: *(select the base point)*
> Specify scale factor or [Reference]:

Specifying the scale factor is the default option. Enter a number to indicate the amount of enlargement or reduction. For example, if you want to double the scale, type 2 at the Specify scale factor or [Reference]: prompt, as shown in Figure 11-25. The chart in Figure 11-26 shows sample scale factors.

Figure 11-25.
Using the **SCALE** command. The base point does not move, but every other point in the object does.

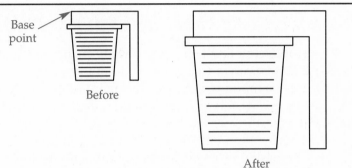

Figure 11-26.
Different scale factors and the resulting sizes.

Scale Factor	Resulting Size
10	10 × bigger
5	5 × bigger
2	2 × bigger
1	Equal to existing size
.75	3/4 of original size
.50	1/2 of original size
.25	1/4 of original size

Using the **Reference** Option

An object can also be scaled by specifying a new size in relation to an existing dimension. For example, suppose you have a shaft that is 2.50″ long and you want to make it 3.00″ long. To do so, use the **Reference** option as follows, as shown in Figure 11-27:

> Specify scale factor or [Reference]: **R**↵
> Specify reference length <1>: **2.5**↵
> Specify new length: **3**↵
> Command:

Figure 11-27.
Using the **Reference** option of the **SCALE** command.

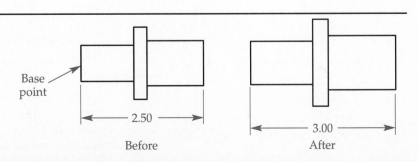

	NOTE	The **SCALE** command changes all dimensions of an object proportionately. If you want to change only the width or length of an object, use the **STRETCH** or **LENGTHEN** command.

AutoCAD
User's
Guide **9**

STRETCHING AN OBJECT

The **SCALE** command changes the length and width of an object proportionately. The **STRETCH** command changes only one dimension of an object. In mechanical drafting, it is common to increase the length of a part while leaving the diameter or width the same. In architectural design, room sizes may be stretched to increase the square footage.

When using the **STRETCH** command, you can select objects with a crossing window or crossing polygon. To use a crossing window, type C at the Select objects: prompt or drag your selection window from right to left.

To access the **STRETCH** command, pick the **Stretch** button in the **Modify** toolbar, pick **Stretch** from the **Modify** pull-down menu, or type S or STRETCH at the Command: prompt. The command sequence is as follows:

> Command: **S** or **STRETCH**↵
> Select objects to stretch by crossing-window or crossing-polygon...
> Select objects: (*select the first corner of a crossing window*)
> Specify opposite corner: (*pick the second corner*)
> Select objects: (*pick additional objects or press* [Enter])

Select only the portion of the object to be stretched, as shown in Figure 11-28. If you select the entire object, the **STRETCH** command works like the **MOVE** command.

STRETCH
S

Modify
➡ Stretch

Modify
toolbar

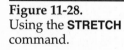

Stretch

Figure 11-28.
Using the **STRETCH** command.

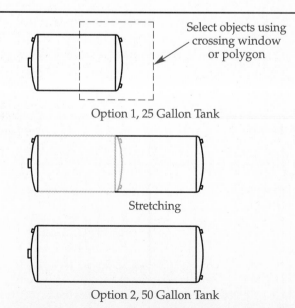

Select objects using crossing window or polygon

Option 1, 25 Gallon Tank

Stretching

Option 2, 50 Gallon Tank

Next, you are asked to pick the base point. This is the point from which the object will be stretched. Then, pick a new position for the base point. As you move the screen cursor, the object is stretched or compressed. When the displayed object is stretched to the desired position, pick the new point. The command sequence after selecting objects is as follows:

Specify base point or displacement: *(pick the base point for the stretch to begin)*
Specify second point of displacement: *(pick the final location of the base point)*
Command:

The example in Figure 11-28 shows the object being stretched. This is a common use of the **STRETCH** command. You can also use the **STRETCH** command to reduce the size of an object.

Using the Displacement Option

The displacement option works the same with the **STRETCH** command as with the **MOVE** and **COPY** commands. After selecting the objects to be stretched, enter a displacement as shown in the following:

Specify base point or displacement: *(enter an X and Y displacement, such as 2,3)*
Specify second point of displacement: ↵
Command:

When you press [Enter] at the Specify second point of displacement: prompt, the object is automatically stretched as you specified with the X and Y coordinates. In this case, the object is stretched 2 units in the X direction and 3 units in the Y direction.

PROFESSIONAL TIP

It may not be common to have objects lined up in a convenient manner for using the **Crossing** selection method with the **STRETCH** command. You should consider using the **Crossing-polygon** selection option to make selecting the objects easier. Also, make sure the **DRAGMODE** variable is turned on so you can watch the object stretch to its new size. If the stretched object is not what you expected, cancel the command with the [Esc] key. The **STRETCH** command and other editing commands discussed in this chapter work well with the Ortho mode on. This restricts the object movement to only horizontal and vertical directions.

EXERCISE 11-13

❑ Begin a new drawing or use one of your templates.
❑ Design and draw a cylindrical-shaped object similar to the tank in Figure 11-28.
❑ Stretch the object to approximately twice its original length.
❑ Stretch the object to about twice its original height.
❑ Save the drawing as EX11-13.

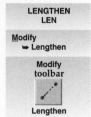

LENGTHEN
LEN

Modify
➥ Lengthen

Modify
toolbar

Lengthen

The **LENGTHEN** command can be used to change the length of objects and the included angle of an arc. Only one object can be lengthened at a time. The **LENGTHEN** command does not affect closed objects. For example, you can lengthen a line, polyline, arc, elliptical arc, or spline but you cannot lengthen a closed polygon or circle.

To access the **LENGTHEN** command, pick the **Lengthen** button in the **Modify** toolbar, pick **Lengthen** from the **Modify** pull-down menu, or type LEN or LENGTHEN at the Command: prompt. When you select an object, AutoCAD gives you the current length if the object is linear, or the included angle if the object is an arc:

> Command: **LEN** *or* **LENGTHEN**⏎
> Select an object or [DElta/Percent/Total/DYnamic]: *(pick an object)*
> Current length: *current*
> Select an object or [DElta/Percent/Total/DYnamic]:

Each option is described below:

- **DElta.** The **DElta** option allows you to specify a positive or negative change in length measured from the endpoint of the selected object. The lengthening or shortening happens closest to the selection point and changes the length by the amount entered. See Figure 11-29.

> Command: **LEN** *or* **LENGTHEN**⏎
> Select an object or [DElta/Percent/Total/DYnamic]: **DE**⏎
> Enter delta length or [Angle] <0.000> *(enter the desired length, .75 for example)*
> Select an object to change or [Undo]: *(pick the object)*
> Select an object to change or [Undo]: *(select another object to lengthen or press* [Enter] *to exit command)*
> Command:

The **Delta** option has an **Angle** suboption that lets you change the included angle of an arc by a specified angle. The command sequence is as follows, as shown in Figure 11-30:

> Command: **LEN** *or* **LENGTHEN**⏎
> Select an object or [DElta/Percent/Total/DYnamic]: **DE**⏎
> Enter delta length or [Angle] <0.000>: **A**⏎
> Enter delta angle <0.000>: *(enter an angle such as* 45)
> Select an object to change or [Undo]: *(pick the arc)*
> Select an object to change or [Undo]: ⏎
> Command:

Figure 11-29.
Using the **Delta** option of the **LENGTHEN** command.

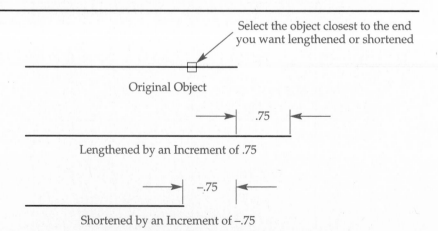

Select the object closest to the end you want lengthened or shortened

Original Object

.75

Lengthened by an Increment of .75

−.75

Shortened by an Increment of −.75

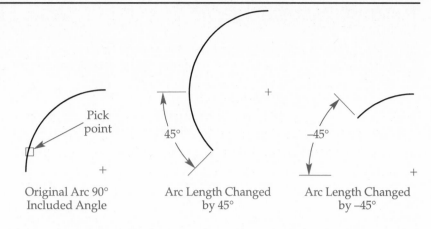

Figure 11-30.
Using the **Angle** suboption of the **LENGTHEN** command's **Delta** option.

Pick point

Original Arc 90°
Included Angle

45°

Arc Length Changed
by 45°

–45°

Arc Length Changed
by –45°

- **Percent.** The **Percent** option allows you to change the length of an object or the angle of an arc by a specified percentage. If you consider the original length 100%, then you can make the object shorter by specifying less than 100% or longer by specifying more than 100%. Look at Figure 11-31 and follow this command sequence:

  > Command: **LEN** or **LENGTHEN**↵
  > Select an object or [DElta/Percent/Total/DYnamic]: **P**↵
  > Enter percent length <100.0>: **125**↵
  > Select an object to change or [Undo]: *(pick the object)*
  > Select an object to change or [Undo]: ↵
  > Command:

- **Total.** The **Total** option allows you to set the total length or angle by the value that you specify. You do not have to select the object before entering one of the options, but doing so lets you know the current length and, if an arc, angle of the object. See Figure 11-32:

  > Command: **LEN** or **LENGTHEN**↵
  > Select an object or [DElta/Percent/Total/DYnamic]: *(pick an object)*
  > Current length: 3.000
  > Select an object or [DElta/Percent/Total/DYnamic]: **T**↵
  > Specify total length or [Angle] <1.000>: *(enter a new length such as 3.75 or A if it is an angle)*
  > Select an object to change or [Undo]: *(pick the object)*
  > Select an object to change or [Undo]: ↵
  > Command:

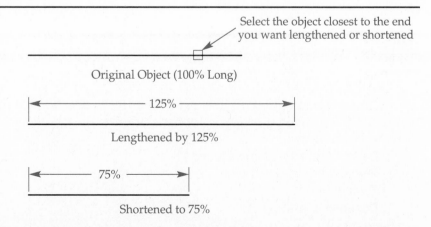

Figure 11-31.
Using the **Percent** option of the **LENGTHEN** command.

Select the object closest to the end you want lengthened or shortened

Original Object (100% Long)

125%

Lengthened by 125%

75%

Shortened to 75%

Figure 11-32.
Using the **Total** option of the **LENGTHEN** command.

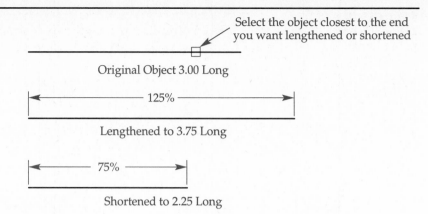

Select the object closest to the end you want lengthened or shortened

Original Object 3.00 Long

125%

Lengthened to 3.75 Long

75%

Shortened to 2.25 Long

- **DYnamic.** This option lets you drag the endpoint of the object to the desired length or angle with the screen cursor. See Figure 11-33. It is helpful to have the grid and snap set to usable increments when using this option. This is the command sequence:

  > Command: **LEN** *or* **LENGTHEN.**⏎
  > Select an object or [DElta/Percent/Total/DYnamic]: **DY**⏎
  > Select an object to change or [Undo]: *(pick the object)*
  > Specify new end point *(move the cursor to the desired length and pick)*
  > Select an object to change or [Undo]: ⏎
  > Command:

Figure 11-33.
Using the **Dynamic** option of the **LENGTHEN** command.

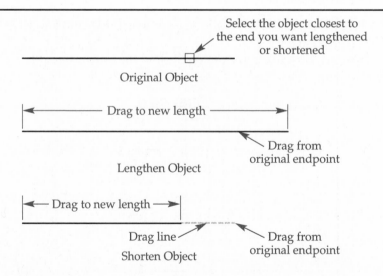

Select the object closest to the end you want lengthened or shortened

Original Object

Drag to new length

Lengthen Object

Drag from original endpoint

Drag to new length

Drag line

Shorten Object

Drag from original endpoint

- ❑ Begin a new drawing or use one of your templates.
- ❑ Use the **LENGTHEN** command and the following options to draw objects similar to the ones specified in the given figure numbers. (Note: Use the **COPY** command to make two copies of each original object, one for lengthening and one for shortening.)
  - ❑ **Delta.** Figure 11-29 and Figure 11-30.
  - ❑ **Percent.** Figure 11-31.
  - ❑ **Total.** Figure 11-32.
  - ❑ **Dynamic.** Figure 11-33.
- ❑ Save the drawing as EX11-14.

> **NOTE**
>
>
> Only lines and arcs can be lengthened dynamically. A spline's length can only be decreased. Splines are discussed in Chapter 16.

SELECTING OBJECTS FOR FUTURE EDITING

Throughout this chapter, you have worked with the basic editing commands by entering the command and then selecting the object to be edited. You can also set up AutoCAD to let you select the object first and then enter the desired editing command. The settings controlling object selection are found in the **Selection** tab of the **Options** dialog box. These settings are discussed in Chapter 12.

The **SELECT** command is used to preselect an object or group of objects for future editing. It is designed to increase your productivity. Often you are working with the same set of objects, moving, copying, or scaling them. Set these aside as a selection set with the **SELECT** command. Then continue to perform another drawing task. To return to those objects set aside, enter P for **Previous** at the Select objects: prompt. Only the last selection set you make can be modified. The command sequences for creating a selection set and then moving it are as follows:

> Command: **SELECT**↵
> Select objects: *(use any method to select an individual object or group of objects)*
> Select objects: *(select additional objects or press* [Enter]*)*
> Command:

This creates a selection set. Later, when you want to move these objects, use the **Previous** option as follows:

> Command: **M** *or* **MOVE**↵
> Select objects: **P**↵ *(this selects the object or group of objects previously selected using the* **SELECT** *command)*
> Select objects: ↵
> Specify base point or displacement: *(pick the base point)*
> Specify second point of displacement: *(pick the new location of the base point)*
> Command:

> **NOTE**
>
>
> The selection set created with the **SELECT** command cannot be accessed with the **Previous** option after another selection set is defined. For example, you use the **SELECT** command and select three circles as a selection set. Then you use the **MOVE** command to move a line. The line you moved would now be selected by the **Previous** option, rather than the circles defined with the **SELECT** command.

EXERCISE 11-15

❑ Begin a new drawing or use one of your templates.
❑ Draw two circles with 1.5" (40mm) radii spaced .25" (6mm) apart.
❑ Use the **SELECT** command to select both circles for future editing.
❑ Draw at least three other small objects.
❑ Use the **COPY** command and the **Previous** option to copy the original two circles to a new location.
❑ Save the drawing as EX11-15.

A group is a named selection set. These selection sets are saved with the drawing and, therefore, exist between multiple drawing sessions. Objects can be members of more than one group and groups can be nested. *Nesting* means placing one group inside of another group.

An object existing in multiple groups creates an interesting situation. For example, if a line and an arc are grouped and then the arc is grouped with a circle, moving the first group moves the line and arc, and moving the second group moves the arc and circle. Nesting can be used to place smaller groups into larger groups for easier editing.

By default, selecting one object within a group causes the entire group to be selected. This setting can be changed in the **Selection** tab of the **Options** dialog box, with the **Object grouping** check box in the **Selection Modes** area.

GROUP
G

The **GROUP** command can be accessed by typing G or GROUP at the Command: prompt. Either of these entry methods displays the **Object Grouping** dialog box shown in Figure 11-34.

There are many elements found in the **Object Grouping** dialog box. The text box displays the **Group Name** and lists whether or not the group is selectable. If a group is selectable, picking any object in it selects the entire group. Making a group nonselectable allows individual objects within the group to be edited.

The **Group Identification** area has several components:

- **Find Name.** This button displays a dialog list of all groups with which an object is associated. When you pick this button, a Pick a member of a group: prompt appears. Once you pick an object, the **Group Member List** dialog box lists any groups with which the object is associated.
- **Highlight.** This button allows a group name to be specified, then highlights all its members in the drawing editor. This allows you to see the parts of the drawing that are identified as the members of that group. Then pick the **Continue** button or press [Enter] to return to the **Object Grouping** dialog box.
- **Include Unnamed.** This check box causes unnamed groups to be listed with named groups. Unnamed groups are given a default name by AutoCAD in the format: *Ax, where x is an integer value that increases with each new group, such as *A6. Unnamed groups can be named later using the **Rename** option.

Figure 11-34.
The **Object Grouping** dialog box. The different elements are shown here highlighted.

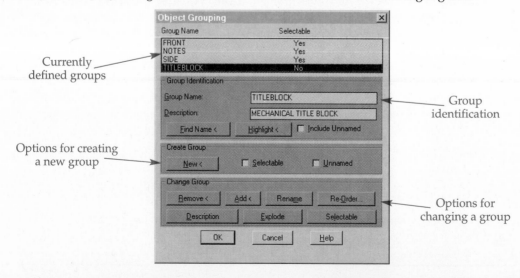

The **Create Group** area contains the options for creating a new group:

- **New.** This button creates a new group from the selected objects using the name entered in the **Group Name:** text box. AutoCAD issues a Select objects for grouping: prompt after you enter a new name in the **Group Name:** text box.
- **Selectable.** A check in this box sets the initial status of the **Selectable** value as Yes for the new group. This is indicated in the **Selectable** list described earlier. No check here specifies No in the **Selectable** list. This can be changed later.
- **Unnamed.** This indicates whether the new group will be named. If this box is checked, AutoCAD assigns its own default name as detailed previously.

The **Change Group** area of the **Object Grouping** dialog box shows the options for changing a group:

- **Remove.** Pick this button to remove objects from a group definition.
- **Add.** This button allows objects to be added to a group definition.
- **Rename.** Pick this button to change the name of an existing group. Unnamed groups can be renamed.
- **Re-Order....** Objects are numbered in the order that they are selected when defining the group. The first object is numbered 0, not 1. This button allows objects to be reordered within the group. For example, if a group contains a set of instructions, you can reorder the instructions to suit the typical steps that are used. The **Order Group** dialog box is displayed when you pick this button. The elements of this dialog box are briefly described as follows:
  - **Group Name.** Displays the name of the selected group.
  - **Description.** Displays the description for the selected group.
  - **Remove from position (0-n).** Position number of the object to reorder, where n is the total number of objects found in the group. You place the desired order in the text box to the right of this and the next two features.
  - **Replace at position (0-n).** Position to which the number is being moved.
  - **Number of objects (1-n).** Displays the number of objects or the range to reorder.
  - **Reverse Order.** Pick this button to have the order of all members in the group reversed.
- **Description.** Updates the group with the new description entered in the **Description:** text box.
- **Explode.** Pick this button to delete the selected group definition, but not the group's objects. The group name is removed and the original group is exploded. Copies of the group become unnamed groups. By selecting the **Include Unnamed** check box, these unnamed groups are displayed and can then be exploded, if needed.
- **Selectable.** Toggles the selectable value of a group. This is where you can change the value in the **Selectable** list.

EXERCISE 11-16

❏ Load AutoCAD and open one of your previous, more complex drawings.
❏ Use the **GROUP** command to name and describe several different elements of the drawing as groups. For example, for views use FRONT, TOP, SIDE, TITLEBLOCK, or NOTES.
❏ Use each element of the **Object Grouping** dialog box to see the effect on the groups that you have named.
❏ Save the drawing as EX11-16.

Chapter Test

Answer the following questions on a separate sheet of paper.

1. Give the command and entries used to draw a .125 × .125 chamfer:
   - A. Command: _____
   - B. Select first line or [Polyline/Distance/Angle/Trim/Method]: _____
   - C. Specify first chamfer distance <*current*>: _____
   - D. Specify second chamfer distance <*previous*>: _____
   - E. Command: _____
   - F. Select first object or [Polyline/Distance/Angle/Trim/Method]: _____
   - G. Select second line: _____

2. Give the command and entries required to produce .50 radius fillets on all corners of a closed polyline:
   - A. Command: _____
   - B. Select first object or [Polyline/Radius/Trim]: _____
   - C. Specify fillet radius <*current*>: _____
   - D. Command: _____
   - E. Select first object or [Polyline/Radius/Trim]: _____
   - F. Select 2D polyline: _____

3. Give the command, entries, and actions required to move an object from Position A to Position B:
   - A. Command: _____
   - B. Select objects: _____
   - C. Select objects: _____
   - D. Specify base point or displacement: _____
   - E. Specify second point of displacement or <use first point as displacement>: _____

4. Give the command and entries needed to make two copies of the same object:
   - A. Command: _____
   - B. Select objects: _____
   - C. Select objects: _____
   - D. Specify base point or displacement, or [Multiple]: _____
   - E. Specify base point: _____
   - F. Specify second point of displacement or <use first point as displacement>: _____
   - G. Specify second point of displacement or <use first point as displacement>: _____

5. Give the command and entries necessary to draw a reverse image of an existing object and remove the existing object:
   - A. Command: _____
   - B. Select objects: _____
   - C. Select objects: _____
   - D. Specify first point of mirror line: _____
   - E. Specify second point of mirror line: _____
   - F. Delete source objects? [Yes/No] <N>: _____

6. Give the command and entries needed to rotate an object 45° clockwise:
   - A. Command: _____
   - B. Select objects: _____
   - C. Select objects: _____

D. Specify base point: _____

E. Specify rotation angle or [Reference]: _____

7. Give the command and entries required to reduce the size of an entire drawing by one-half:

A. Command: _____

B. Select objects: _____

C. Select objects: _____

D. Specify base point: _____

E. Specify scale factor or [Reference]: _____

8. Define the term "displacement" as it relates to the **MOVE** and **COPY** commands.

9. Explain the difference between the **MOVE** and **COPY** commands.

10. List two locations you normally choose as the base point when using the **MOVE** or **COPY** commands.

11. Describe the purpose of the **SELECT** command.

12. What is a selection set?

13. How do you select objects for editing that have previously been picked using the **SELECT** command?

14. How is the size of a fillet specified?

15. Identify the selection method or methods issued by AutoCAD when using the **STRETCH** command.

16. How do you cancel the **STRETCH** command?

17. The **EXTEND** command is the opposite of the _____ command.

18. Name the system variable used to preset the fillet radius.

19. In what direction should you pick points to break a portion out of a circle or arc?

20. Name the command that trims an object to a cutting edge.

21. Name the command associated with boundary edges.

22. The **MOVE**, **COPY**, **TRIM**, **EXTEND**, and **STRETCH** commands are located in the _____ pull-down menu.

23. Name the command that can be used to move and rotate an object simultaneously.

24. Describe the difference between **Trim** and **No trim** when using the **CHAMFER** and **FILLET** commands.

25. What is the purpose of the **Method** option in the **CHAMFER** command?

26. How can you split an object in two without removing a portion?

27. Name the option in the **TRIM** and **EXTEND** commands that allows you to trim or extend to an implied intersection.

28. How do you use the Smart mode with the **TRIM** and **EXTEND** commands?

29. Identify the **LENGTHEN** command option that corresponds to each of the following descriptions:

A. Change a length or arc angle by a percentage of the total.

B. Drag the endpoint of the object to the desired length or angle.

C. Allows a positive or negative change in length from the endpoint.

D. Set the total length or angle to the value specified.

30. Define a group.

31. How do you access the **Object Grouping** dialog box?

32. Describe how you create a new group.

33. Give the keyboard shortcut for the following commands:

A. **CHAMFER**   H. **COPY**

B. **FILLET**   I. **MIRROR**

C. **BREAK**   J. **ROTATE**

D. **TRIM**   K. **ALIGN**

E. **EXTEND**   L. **SCALE**

F. **CHANGE**   M. **LENGTHEN**

G. **MOVE**

Drawing Problems

Use your templates as appropriate for each of the following problems. Start a new drawing for each problem, unless indicated otherwise.

1. Draw Object A using the **LINE** and **ARC** commands. Make sure that the corners overrun and the arc is centered, but does not touch the lines. Then use the **TRIM**, **EXTEND**, and **MOVE** commands to make the object look like Object B. Save the drawing as P11-1.

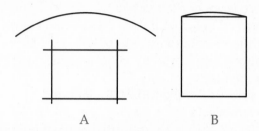

A   B

2. Open drawing P11-1 for further editing (Object A). Using the **STRETCH** command, change the shape to Object B. Make a copy of the new revision. Change the copy to represent Object C. Save the drawing as P11-2.

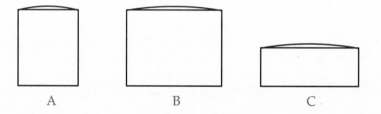

A   B   C

3. Refer to Figure 11-28 in this chapter. Draw and make three copies of the object shown in Option 1. Stretch the first copy to twice its length as shown as Option 2. Stretch the second copy to twice its height. Double the size of the third copy using the **SCALE** command. Save the drawing as P11-3.

4. Draw Objects A, B, and C shown below without dimensions. Then, move Objects A, B, and C to new positions. Select a corner of Object A and the center of Objects B and C as the base points. Save the drawing as P11-4.

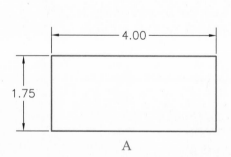

A

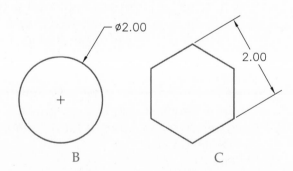

B   C

5. Draw Objects A, B, and C shown in Problem 11-4 at the left side of the screen. Make a copy of Object A two units to the right. Make four copies of Object B three units, center-to-center, to the right using the **Multiple** option. Make three copies of Object C three units, center-to-center, to the right. Save the drawing as P11-5.

6. Draw the object shown using the **ELLIPSE**, **COPY**, and **LINE** commands. The rotation angle of the ellipse is 60°. Use the **BREAK** or **TRIM** command when drawing and editing the lower ellipse. Save the drawing as P11-6.

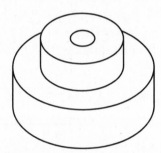

7. Open drawing P11-6 for further editing. Shorten the height of the object using the **STRETCH** command as shown below. Next, add to the object as indicated. Save the drawing as P11-7.

8. Draw Object A. Use the **TRIM** command to help change Object A into Object B. Save the drawing as P11-8.

A   B

9. Draw Object A, without dimensions. Use the **CHAMFER** and **FILLET** commands to your best advantage. Then draw a mirror image as Object B. Now, remove the original view and move the new view so that Point 2 is at the original Point 1 location. Save the drawing as P11-9.

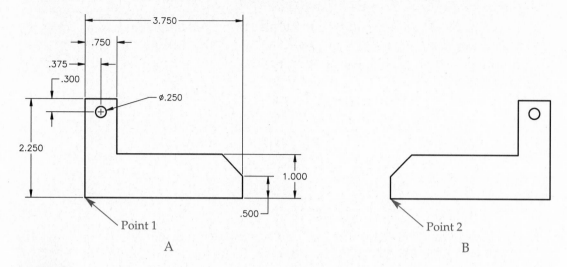

A   B

10. Draw the object shown below, without dimensions. The object is symmetrical; therefore, draw only the right half. Then mirror the left half into place. Use the **CHAMFER** and **FILLET** commands to your best advantage. All fillets and rounds are .125. Save the drawing as P11-10.

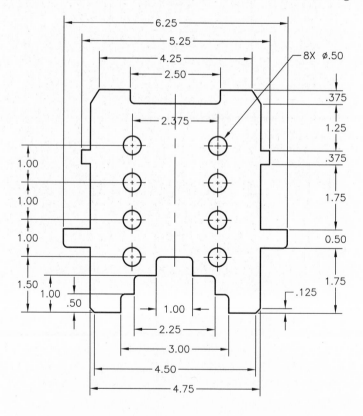

11. Use the **TRIM, OSNAP**, and **OFFSET** commands to assist you in drawing this object. Do not draw centerlines or dimensions. Save the completed drawing as P11-11.

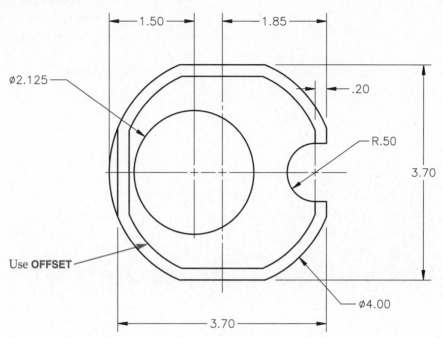

12. Draw the object shown below, without dimensions. Then mirror the right half into place. Use the **CHAMFER** and **FILLET** commands to your best advantage. Save the drawing as P11-12.

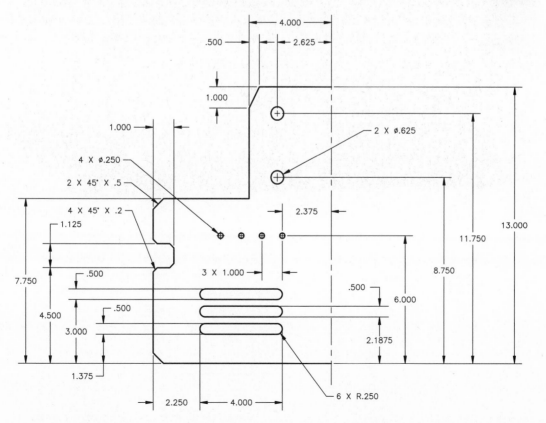

13. Redraw the objects shown below. Then mirror the drawing, but have the text remain readable. Delete the original image during the mirroring process. Save the drawing as P11-13.

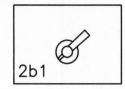

2b1

5a2 4a1 8a1

1b1

11b1

TRANSFER   LTS. HTRS. FANS   2b1   RESET   BYPASS

14. Draw the kitchen cabinet layout shown in view A and the partial floor plan shown at B. Make the cabinet 24″ (600mm) deep and the walls 6″ (150mm) wide. Make the sink and range proportional in size to the given illustration. Use the **ALIGN** command to move and rotate the cabinet layout into the wall location as shown on the right. Save the drawing as P11-14.

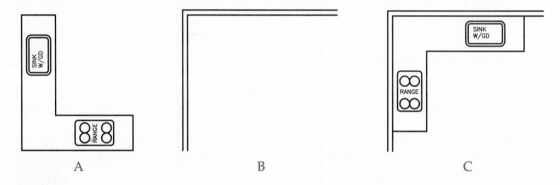

A   B   C

15. Draw the following object without dimensions. Use the **TRIMMODE** setting to your advantage. Save the drawing as P11-15.

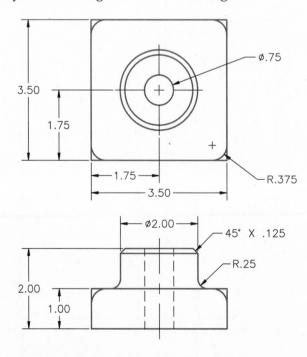

16. Draw the objects shown below. Use the **GROUP** command to name each of the objects with the names below them. Use the object groups to draw the one-line electrical diagram shown below. Use the **Explode** option to edit the symbols at 1 and 2 in the diagram as shown. Save the drawing as P11-16.

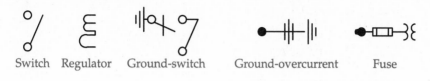

Switch   Regulator   Ground-switch   Ground-overcurrent   Fuse

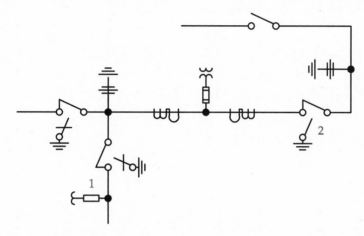

17. Draw the following bracket. Do not include dimensions in your drawing. Use the **FILLET** command where appropriate. Save the drawing as P11-17.

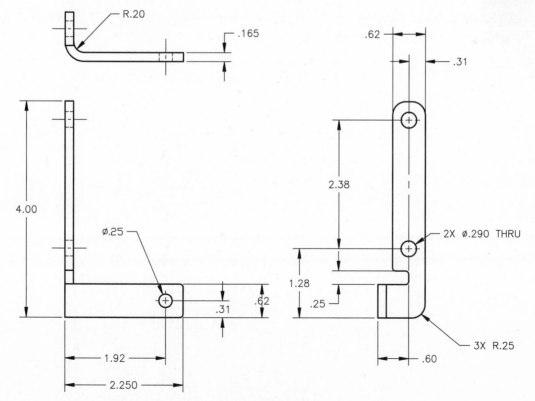

ALL FILLETS AND ROUNDS R.06

18. Draw this refrigeration system schematic. Save the drawing as P11-18.

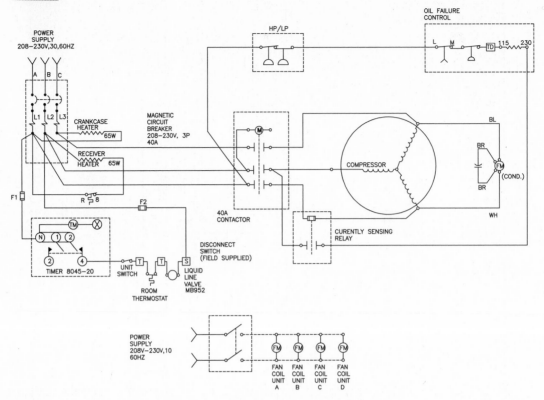

19. Draw this timer schematic. Save the drawing as P11-19.

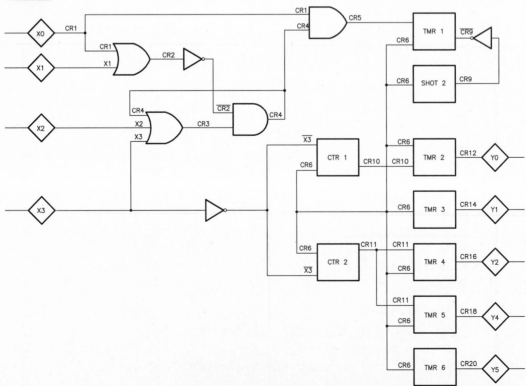

CHAPTER 12

Automatic Editing

Learning Objectives

After completing this chapter, you will be able to:
- Use grips to do automatic editing with the **STRETCH**, **COPY**, **MOVE**, **ROTATE**, **SCALE**, and **MIRROR** commands.
- Identify the system variables used for automatic editing.
- Perform automatic editing with the **Properties** window.
- Use the property painter to match object properties.

In Chapter 11, you learned how to use commands that let you do a variety of drawing and editing activities with AutoCAD. These editing commands give you maximum flexibility and increase productivity. However, this chapter takes editing a step further by allowing you to first select an object and then automatically perform editing operations.

AUTOMATIC EDITING WITH GRIPS

AutoCAD
User's
Guide | 9

"Hold," "grab," and "grasp" are all words that are synonymous with grip. In AutoCAD, *grips* are features on an object that are highlighted with a small box. For example, the grips on a straight line are the endpoints and midpoint. When grips are used for editing, you can select an object to automatically activate the grips. Then, pick any of the small boxes to perform stretch, copy, move, rotate, scale, or mirror operations.

When grips are enabled and there is no command active, a pick box is located at the intersection of the screen crosshairs. You can pick any object to activate the grips. Figure 12-1 shows what grips look like on several different objects. For text, the grip box is located at the insertion point.

You can control grip settings in the **Selection** tab of the **Options** dialog box. The **Options** dialog box is opened by picking **Options...** in the **Tools** pull-down menu or by right-clicking and selecting **Options...** from the shortcut menu. You can access the **Selection** tab of the **Options** dialog box directly by typing GR or DDGRIPS at the Command: prompt. The **Selection** tab in the **Options** dialog box is shown in Figure 12-2.

Notice the two check boxes in the **Grips** area. Pick the **Enable grips** check box to turn grips on or off. This can also be set using the **GRIPS** system variable.

```
DDGRIPS
GR

Tools
 ↳ Options...
```

Figure 12-1.
Grips are placed at
strategic locations
on objects.

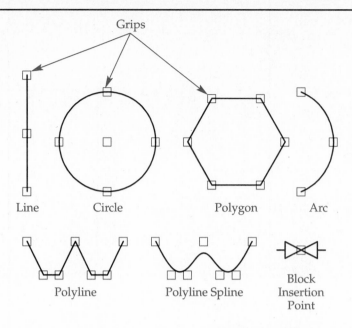

Figure 12-2.
The **Selection** tab of the **Options** dialog box contains grip control settings.

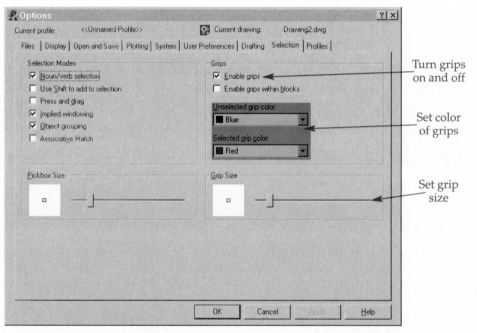

Pick the **Enable grips within blocks** check box to have grips displayed on every subobject of a block. A *block* is a special symbol designed for multiple use. Blocks are discussed in detail in Chapter 23. When this check box is off, the grip location for a block is at the insertion point, as shown in Figure 12-1. Grips in blocks can also be controlled with the **GRIPBLOCK** system variable.

The two color drop-down lists allow you to change the color of grips. The grips displayed when you first pick an object are referred to as *unselected grips* because you have not yet picked a grip to perform an operation. An unselected grip is a square with a color outline. Unselected grips are blue by default and are called "*warm.*"

After you pick a grip it is called a *selected grip*. A selected grip appears as a filled-in square, as shown in Figure 12-3. Selected grips are red by default and are called "hot." If more than one object is selected and they have warm grips, then they are all

AutoCAD and its Applications—Basics

Figure 12-3.
Selected (hot) grips
are filled-in squares.
Unselected (warm)
grips are colored
outlines.

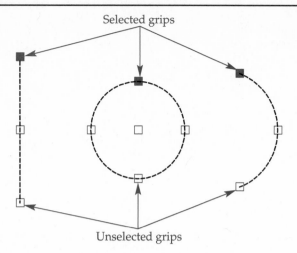

Selected grips

Unselected grips

affected by what you do with the hot grips. Objects that have warm and hot grips are highlighted and are part of the selection set.

You can remove highlighted objects from the selection set by holding down the [Shift] key and picking the object to be removed. The highlighting goes away, but the grips remain. These are called *"cold"* grips. Objects with cold grips are not affected by what you do to objects with warm grips. Return the object with cold grips to the selection set by picking it again. This highlights the object and retains the warm grips.

You can also control grip color with the **GRIPCOLOR** and **GRIPHOT** system variables. **GRIPCOLOR** controls the color of unselected (warm) grips, while **GRIPHOT** regulates the color of selected (hot) grips. When you enter one of these variables, simply set the color number as desired.

The **Grip Size** scroll bar in the **Selection** tab of the **Options** dialog box lets you graphically change the size of the grip box. The sample in the image tile gets smaller or larger as you move the scroll bar. Change the grip size to whatever works best for your drawing. Very small grip boxes may be difficult to pick. However, the grips may overlap if they are too large.

The grip size can be given a numerical value at the command line using the **GRIP-SIZE** system variable. To change the default of 3, enter GRIPSIZE at the Command: prompt and then type a desired size in pixels.

The **Pickbox Size** scroll bar lets you adjust the size of the pick box. The sample in the image tile gets smaller or larger as you move the scroll bar. Stop when you have the desired size. The pick box size is also controlled by the **PICKBOX** system variable, where the desired size is set in pixels.

Using Grips

To activate grips, move the pick box to the desired object and pick. The object is highlighted and the unselected (warm) grips are displayed. To select a grip, move the pick box to the desired grip and pick it. Notice that the crosshairs snap to a grip. When you pick a grip the command line shows the following prompt:

    ** STRETCH **
    Specify stretch point or [Base point/Copy/Undo/eXit]:

This activates the **STRETCH** command. All you have to do is move the cursor to make the selected object stretch, as shown in Figure 12-4. If you pick the middle grip of a line or arc, or the center grip of a circle, the object moves. These are the other options:

- **Base point.** Type B and press [Enter] to select a new base point.
- **Copy.** Type C and press [Enter] if you want to make one or more copies of the selected object.

Figure 12-4.
Using the automatic
STRETCH command.
Note the selected grip.
A—Stretching a line.
B—Stretching a circle.
C—Stretching an arc.

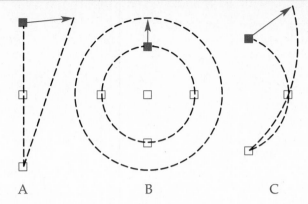

A   B   C

- **Undo.** Type U and press [Enter] to undo the previous operation.
- **eXit.** Type X and press [Enter] to exit the command. The selected (hot) grip is gone, but the unselected (warm) grips remain. You can also use the [Esc] key to cancel the command. Canceling twice removes the selected and the unselected grips and returns the Command: prompt.

You can pick objects individually, or use a window or crossing box. Figure 12-5 shows how you can stretch features of an object after selecting all the objects. Step 1 in Figure 12-5A stretches the first corner and Step 2 stretches the second corner. You can also make more than one grip hot at the same time by holding down the [Shift] key as you pick the grips, as shown in Figure 12-5B. Here are some general rules and guidelines that can help make grips work for you:

✓ Be sure the **GRIPS** system variable is on.
✓ Pick an object or group of objects to activate grips. Objects in the selection set are highlighted.
✓ Pick a warm grip to make it hot.
✓ Make multiple grips hot by holding the [Shift] key while picking warm grips.
✓ If more than one object has hot grips, they are all affected by the editing commands.

Figure 12-5.
Stretching an object. A—Select corners to stretch individually. B—Select several hot grips by holding down the [Shift] key.

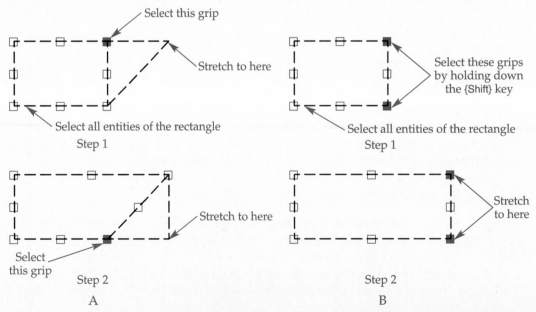

✓ Remove objects from the selection set by holding down the [Shift] key and picking them, thus making the grips cold.

✓ Return objects to the selection set by picking them again.

✓ Remove hot grips from the selection set by pressing the [Esc] key to cancel. Cancel again to remove all grips from the selection set. If you have not yet picked a hot grip, cancel twice at the keyboard. You can also right-click and select **Deselect All** from the shortcut menu to remove all grips.

For 2000i Users...

In AutoCAD 2000i, if no grips are hot, pressing the [Esc] key once deactivates all grips.

PROFESSIONAL TIP When editing with grips, you can enter coordinates to help improve your accuracy. Remember that any of the coordinate entry methods will work.

EXERCISE 12-1

❏ Start a new drawing or use one of your templates.

❏ Draw a line with coordinates X = 2, Y = 4 and X = 2, Y = 7. Draw a circle with the center at X = 5.5, Y = 5.5, with a radius of 1.5. Finally, draw an arc with its center at X = 8.5, Y = 5.5, a start point of X = 9.5, Y = 4, and an endpoint of X = 9.5, Y = 7.

❏ Make sure **GRIPS** is on.

❏ Experiment with the **STRETCH** command using grips by picking the points as follows:

  ❏ Line—Pick the ends first and then the middle to see what happens.

  ❏ Circle—Pick one of the quadrants, and then the center.

  ❏ Arc—Pick the ends and the middle.

  ❏ Line, Circle, Arc—Hold the [Shift] key down and pick an endpoint of the line and arc and a quadrant of the circle.

❏ Make a couple of changes to the pick box size and the grip size and return to the drawing to select objects and work with grips between each change. Decide which pick box and grip size work best for you.

❏ Save the drawing as EX12-1.

You can also use the **MOVE, ROTATE, SCALE**, and **MIRROR** commands to automatically edit objects. All you have to do is pick the object and then select one of the grips. When you see the ** STRETCH ** command, press [Enter] to cycle through the command options:

    ** STRETCH **
    Specify stretch point or [Base point/Copy/Undo/eXit]: ↵
    ** MOVE **
    Specify move point or [Base point/Copy/Undo/eXit]: ↵
    ** ROTATE **
    Specify rotation angle or [Base point/Copy/Undo/Reference/eXit]: ↵
    ** SCALE **
    Specify scale factor or [Base point/Copy/Undo/Reference/eXit]: ↵
    ** MIRROR **
    Specify second point or [Base point/Copy/Undo/eXit]: ↵

As an alternative to pressing [Enter], you can enter the first two characters of the desired command from the keyboard. Type MO for **MOVE**, MI for **MIRROR**, RO for **ROTATE**, SC for **SCALE**, and ST for **STRETCH**.

AutoCAD also allows you to right-click and access a grips shortcut menu, as shown in Figure 12-6. This menu is only available after a grip has been turned into a selected (hot) grip.

Figure 12-6.
The grips shortcut
menu appears when
a grip is selected
and you right-click.

> Enter
>
> Move
> Mirror
> Rotate
> Scale
> Stretch
>
> Base Point
> Copy
> Reference
> Undo
>
> Properties
> Go to URL...
>
> Exit

The shortcut menu allows you to access the five grip editing options without using the keyboard. All you do is pick either **Move**, **Mirror**, **Rotate**, **Scale**, or **Stretch** as needed. Another option in the shortcut menu is **Base Point**. This allows you to select another base point other than the selected (hot) grip. The shortcut menu also provides direct access to the **Copy** option, which is explained later in this chapter. The **Undo** option closes the shortcut menu and returns to the current grip activity.

An added bonus in the grips shortcut menu is the **Properties...** option. Selecting this opens the **Properties** window, where you can change properties of the objects being edited. Selecting the **Exit** option closes the grips shortcut menu and removes the hot grip.

NOTE

When AutoCAD is configured to display a screen menu, the **Move**, **Mirror**, **Rotate**, **Scale**, and **Stretch** automatic editing commands appear in a separate screen menu whenever a grip is selected.

PROFESSIONAL TIP

Many of the conventional AutoCAD editing operations can be performed when warm grips are displayed on screen and the **PICKFIRST** variable is set to 1 (its default value). The editing commands can be selected from the pull-down menus, toolbars, or entered at the Command: prompt. For example, the **ERASE** command can be used to clear the screen of all objects displayed with warm grips by first picking the objects and then selecting the **ERASE** command.

Moving an Object Automatically

If you want to move an object with grips, select the object, pick a grip to use as the base point, and then press [Enter] to cycle through the commands until you get to this prompt:

```
** MOVE **
Specify move point or [Base point/Copy/Undo/eXit]:
```

The selected grip becomes the base point. Then, move the object to a new point by picking the new location. You may want to use an object snap mode or coordinates to place it in a new location. The **MOVE** operation is complete, as shown in Figure 12-7.

AutoCAD and its Applications—Basics

Figure 12-7.
The automatic
MOVE command.
The selected grip
becomes the base
point for the move.

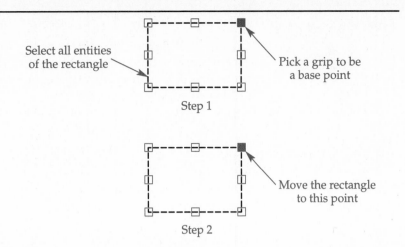

Select all entities
of the rectangle

Pick a grip to be
a base point

Step 1

Move the rectangle
to this point

Step 2

If you accidentally pick the wrong grip or want to have a base point other than the selected grip, type B and press [Enter] for the **Base point** option and pick a new base point.

Copying an Object Automatically

The **Copy** option is found in each of the editing commands. When using the **STRETCH** command, the **Copy** option allows you to make multiple copies of the object you are stretching. Holding down the [Shift] key while performing the first **STRETCH** operation accesses the **Multiple** mode. The prompt looks like this:

    ** STRETCH (multiple) **
    Specify stretch point or [Base point/Copy/Undo/eXit]:↵

The **Copy** option in the **MOVE** command is the true form of the **COPY** command. You can activate the **Copy** option by typing C as follows:

    ** MOVE **
    Specify move point or [Base point/Copy/Undo/eXit]: **C**↵
    ** MOVE (multiple) **
    Specify move point or [Base point/Copy/Undo/eXit]: *(make as many copies as desired*
        *and enter X, press [Esc], or select E**x**it from the grips shortcut menu to exit)*

Holding down the [Shift] key while performing the first **MOVE** operation also puts you in the **Copy** mode. The **Copy** option works similarly in each of the editing commands. Try it with each to see what happens. When you are in the **STRETCH** or **MOVE** commands, you can also access the **Copy** option directly by picking the right mouse button to open the grips shortcut menu.

<table>
<tr><td>**PROFESSIONAL TIP**</td><td>When in the **Copy** option of the **MOVE** command, if you make the first copy followed by holding the [Shift] key, the distance of the first copy automatically becomes the snap spacing for additional copies.</td></tr>
</table>

EXERCISE 12-3

❑ Start a new drawing or use one of your templates.
❑ Use the **RECTANG** command to draw the objects shown at A, B, C, and D below. Do not draw dimensions.
❑ Use the **Copy** option of the **STRETCH** command to make Object A look similar to the example at the right.
❑ Use the **Copy** option of the **STRETCH** command to make Object B look similar to the example at the right. Make two grips hot for this to work.
❑ Use the **Copy** option of the **MOVE** command to make multiple copies to the right of Object C.
❑ Use the **MOVE** command to make multiple copies to the right of Object D while holding down the [Shift] key.
❑ Save the drawing as EX12-3.

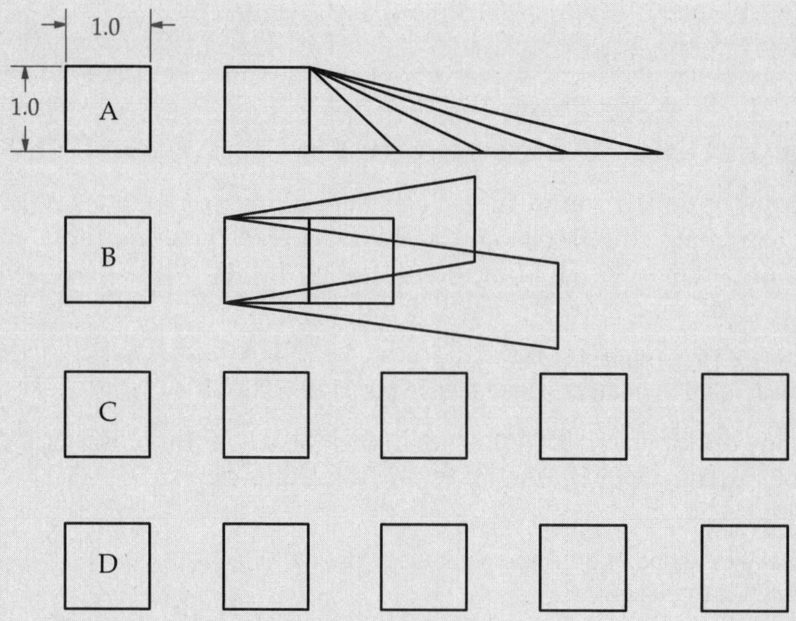

Rotating an Object Automatically

To automatically rotate an object, select the object, pick a grip to use as the base point, and press [Enter] until you see this prompt:

** ROTATE **
Specify rotation angle or [Base point/Copy/Undo/Reference/eXit]:

Now, move your pointing device to rotate the object. Pick the desired rotation point, or enter a rotation angle at the Command: prompt.

Type R and press [Enter] if you want to use the **Reference** option. The **Reference** option may be used when the object is already rotated at a known angle and you want to rotate it to a new angle. The reference angle is the current angle and the new angle is the desired angle. Figure 12-8 shows the **ROTATE** options.

Figure 12-8.
The rotation angle
and **Reference**
option of the
ROTATE command.

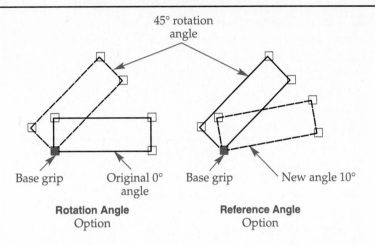

Base grip   Original 0°
        angle   Base grip   New angle 10°

Rotation Angle
Option

Reference Angle
Option

EXERCISE 12-4

- ❏ Start a new drawing or use one of your templates.
- ❏ Use the **RECTANG** command to draw a rectangle similar to the one shown at the left of Figure 12-8. Orient the long sides so they are at 0°.
- ❏ Use grips to rotate the object 45°.
- ❏ Rotate the object again to 20° using the **Reference** option.
- ❏ Save the drawing as EX12-4.

Scaling an Object Automatically

If you want to scale an object with grips, cycle through the editing options until you get this prompt:

> ** SCALE **
> Specify scale factor or [Base point/Copy/Undo/Reference/eXit]:

Move the screen cursor and pick when the object is dragged to the desired size. You can also enter a scale factor to automatically increase or decrease the scale of the original object. You can use the **Reference** option if you know a current length and a desired length.

The selected base point remains in the same place when the object is scaled. Figure 12-9 shows the two **SCALE** options.

Figure 12-9.
The options for the
automatic **SCALE**
command include
the **Scale factor**
option and the
Reference length
option.

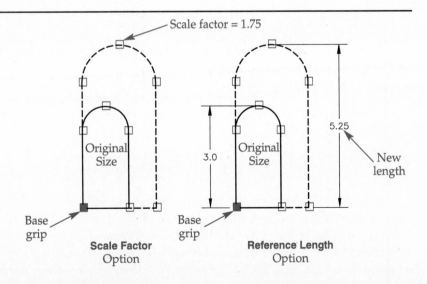

Scale factor = 1.75

Original
Size   3.0   Original
                             Size

5.25

New
length

Base
grip   Base
                   grip

Scale Factor
Option

Reference Length
Option

❑ Start a new drawing or use one of your templates.
❑ Draw an object similar to the original object on the left in Figure 12-9.
❑ Activate grips to make a copy of the object to the right of the original.
❑ Scale the first object using a scale factor of 1.5.
❑ Use the **Reference** option to scale the second object to any height.
❑ Save the drawing as EX12-5.

Mirroring an Object Automatically

If you want to mirror an object using grips, the selected grip becomes the first point of the mirror line. Then press [Enter] to cycle through the editing commands until you get this prompt:

** MIRROR **
Specify second point or [Base point/Copy/Undo/eXit]:

Use the **Base point** option to reselect the first point of the mirror line. Pick another grip or any point on the screen as the second point of the mirror line, Figure 12-10. Unlike the standard **MIRROR** command, the automatic **MIRROR** command does not give you the option to delete the old objects. The old objects are deleted automatically. If you want to keep the original object while mirroring, use the **Copy** option in the **MIRROR** command.

Figure 12-10.
When using the automatic **MIRROR** command, the selected grip becomes the first point of the mirror line and the original object is automatically deleted.

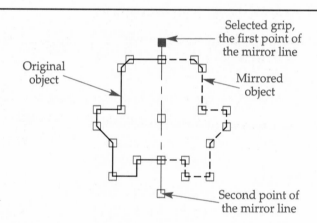

Original object

Selected grip, the first point of the mirror line

Mirrored object

Second point of the mirror line

❑ Start a new drawing or use one of your templates.
❑ Draw a shape similar to the original object in Figure 12-10.
❑ Use grips to mirror the object along the centerline.
❑ Save the drawing as EX12-6.

BASIC EDITING VS. AUTOMATIC EDITING

In Chapter 11 you were introduced to basic editing. Basic editing allows you to first enter a command and then select the desired object to be edited. You can also set system variables to first select the desired objects and then enter the desired command. The automatic editing features discussed in this chapter use grips and related editing commands to edit an object automatically, after first selecting the object.

The **Selection Modes** area of the **Selection** tab in the **Options** dialog box allows you to control the way that you use editing commands. See Figure 12-11. Select or deselect the following options based on your own preferences:

DDSELECT
SE

Tools
➡ Options...

- **Noun/verb selection.** When you first select objects and then enter a command, it is referred to as the *noun/verb* format. The pick box is displayed at the screen crosshairs. A "✓" in this check box means that the noun/verb method is active. The **PICKFIRST** system variable can also be used to set the noun/verb selection. When using the *verb/noun* format, you enter the command before selecting the object. Remove the "✓" from the **Noun/verb selection** check box to enter the command before making a selection.

Figure 12-11.
The **Selection Modes** area of the **Selection** tab in the **Options** dialog box.

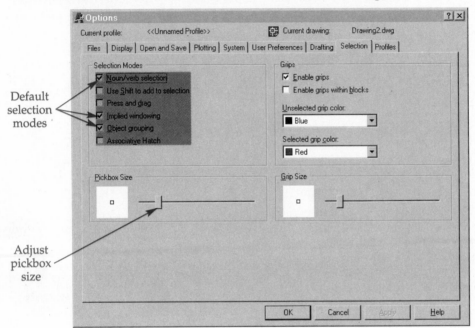

Default selection modes

Adjust pickbox size

> **NOTE**
>
> Some editing commands, such as **FILLET, CHAMFER, DIVIDE, MEASURE, OFFSET, EXTEND, TRIM**, and **BREAK** require that you enter the command before you select the object.

- **Use Shift to add to selection.** When this check box is off, every object or group of objects you select is highlighted and added to the selection set. If you pick this check box, it changes the way AutoCAD accepts objects you pick. For example, if you pick an object, it is highlighted and added to the selection set. However, if you pick another object, it is highlighted and the first one is removed from the selection set. This means that you can only include one object by picking, or one group of objects with a selection window. If you want to add more items to the selection set, you must hold down the [Shift] key as you pick them. Turning on the **PICKADD** system variable does the same thing as turning on this feature.
- **Press and drag.** This is the same as turning on the **PICKDRAG** system variable. With **Press and drag** on, you create a selection window by picking the first corner, then moving the cursor while holding down the pick button. Release the pick button when you have the desired selection window. By default, this

option is off. This means that you need to pick both the first and second corner of the desired selection window.

- **Implied windowing.** By default, this option is on. This means that you can automatically create a window by picking the first point and moving the cursor to the right to pick the second point, or make a crossing box by picking the first point and moving the cursor to the left to pick the second point. This is the same as turning on the **PICKAUTO** system variable. This does not work if **PICKDRAG** is on.
- **Object grouping.** This option controls whether or not AutoCAD recognizes grouped objects as singular objects. When off, the individual elements of a group can be selected for separate editing without having to first explode the group.
- **Associative hatch.** The default is off, which means that if an associative hatch is moved, the hatch boundary does not move with it. Select this toggle if you want the boundary of an associative hatch to move when you move the hatch pattern. It is a good idea to have this on for most applications. Hatches and hatch boundaries are fully explained in Chapter 22.

Setting Object Sorting Methods

The **Object Sorting Methods** area shown in Figure 12-12 appears when you pick the **User Preferences** tab in the **Options** dialog box. The check boxes in the **Object Sorting Methods** area allow you to control the order in which objects are displayed or plotted. The check boxes are explained as follows:

- **Object selection.** Objects selected using a windowing method are placed in the selection set in the order they occur in the drawing database.
- **Object snap.** Object snap modes find objects in the order they occur in the drawing database.
- **Redraws.** Objects are displayed by a **REDRAW** command in the order they occur in the drawing database.
- **Regens.** Objects are displayed by a drawing regeneration in the order they occur in the drawing database.
- **Plotting.** Objects are plotted in the order they occur in the drawing database.

Figure 12-12.
The **User Preferences** tab of the **Options** dialog box.

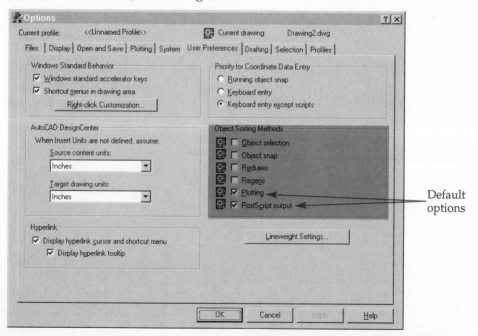

AutoCAD and its Applications—Basics

- **PostScript output.** The **PSOUT** command processes objects in the order they occur in the drawing database. PostScript is a copyrighted page description language that is used in the desktop publishing industry. This is discussed further in *AutoCAD and its Applications—Advanced*. The **PSOUT** command converts an AutoCAD drawing to a PostScript file.

NOTE

Object sorting is also controlled by the **SORTENTS** system variable using bit values.

PROFESSIONAL TIP

Notice in Figure 12-12 that only two of the check boxes are checked. Object sorting takes time and should only be used if the drawing or application software you are using requires object sorting. Turn the **Object selection** sorting on if you want AutoCAD to find the last object drawn when selecting overlapping objects.

EXERCISE 12-7

❑ Start a new drawing, use one of your templates, or open a previous exercise.
❑ Open the **Selection** tab in the **Options** dialog box.
❑ Pick the **User Preferences** tab to see the **Object Sorting Methods** area.
❑ Cancel the dialog box.
❑ Quit the drawing session without saving or keep it open for the next exercise.

USING THE **PROPERTIES** WINDOW

An object or objects can be edited automatically using the **Properties** window. To edit an object using the **Properties** window, pick the **Properties** button from the **Standard** toolbar, pick **Properties** from the **Modify** pull-down menu, or type MO, CH, PROPS, or PROPERTIES at the Command: prompt. You can also toggle the **Properties** window on and off using the [Ctrl]+[1] key combination. If an object or objects have already been selected, you can also access the **Properties** window by right-clicking and selecting **Properties** from the shortcut menu.

The **Properties** window appears as shown in Figure 12-13. The **Properties** window can be docked in the drawing area similar to a toolbar. This was discussed in Chapter 1.

While the **Properties** window is displayed, you can enter commands and continue to work in AutoCAD. You can close the box by picking the "X" in the top right corner.

When you access the **Properties** window without first selecting an object, No selection can be seen in the top drop-down list. This means that AutoCAD does not have any objects selected to modify. The four categories—**General**, **Plot style**, **View**, and **Misc**—list the current settings for the drawing. You can organize the categories alphabetically by selecting the **Alphabetic** tab or by category, by selecting the **Categorized** tab.

Figure 12-13.
The **Properties** window can be used to modify different properties of an object.

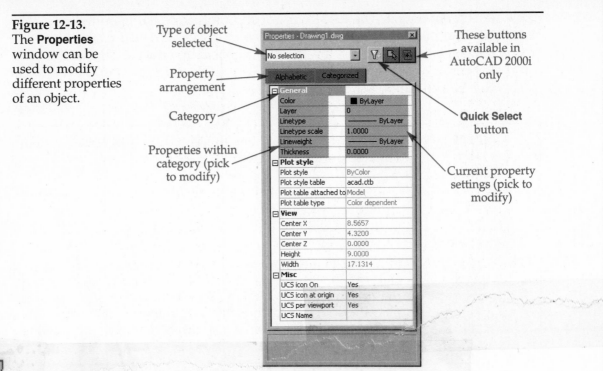

Type of object selected

Property arrangement

Category

Properties within category (pick to modify)

These buttons available in AutoCAD 2000i only

Quick Select button

Current property settings (pick to modify)

For 2000i Users...

In AutoCAD 2000i, the **Properties** window includes two additional buttons. Use the **Select Objects** button to activate the pick box and select objects from the drawing area. The **Toggle value of PICKADD Sysvar** button toggles the **PICKADD** system variable, which is discussed on page 495.

Underneath each category is a list of object properties. For example, in Figure 12-13 the current color is ByLayer. To change a property, pick the property or its current value. Once the property is highlighted, one of the following methods is used to set the new value:

- A drop-down arrow with a list of values.
- A **Pick Point** button allows you to pick a new coordinate location.
- A text box is opened when you select some properties such as the radius of an arc. Entering a new value in this box allows you to change the radius.

Once a property to be modified has been selected, a description of what that property does is shown at the bottom of the dialog box.

In the upper-right portion of the **Properties** window is the **Quick Select** button. This accesses the **Quick Select** dialog box, where you can create object selection sets. The **Quick Select** dialog box is covered in depth in Chapter 7.

Modifying an Object Using the **Properties** Window

The previous discussion introduced you to the **Properties** window. The following explains how to change object properties in the **Properties** window. In order to modify an object, the **Properties** window must be open and an object must be selected. For example, if a circle and a line are drawn, and you need to modify the circle, first pick on the circle to make the grips appear, and then use one of the methods to open the **Properties** window.

The **Properties** window displays the categories that can be modified for the circle. All objects have a **General** category. The **General** category allows you to modify properties such as color, layer, linetype, linetype scale, plot style, lineweight, hyperlink, and thickness. For example, do the following to change the color of the circle:

1. Select the **Color** property in the window by picking on the word **Color**. A drop-down arrow appears to the right of the current color.
2. Select the drop-down arrow and a list of available colors appears.
3. Select the new color. If the desired color is not in the list, then select Other... from the bottom of the list. This displays the **Select Color** dialog box, from which a color can be selected.

Once a color has been selected, the **Properties** window displays the current color for the circle.

A description of each of the properties in the **General** category follows:

- **Color.** Pick this property to display a drop-down arrow from which a color can be selected. At the bottom of the drop-down list is the Other... option which displays the **Select Color** dialog box showing all the colors available.
- **Layer.** Select the desired layer for the object here. Layers are discussed in Chapter 4.
- **Linetype.** Select the desired linetype for the object.
- **Linetype scale.** To change the individual object's linetype, highlight the value and type a new scale value. The linetype scale for an individual object is a multiplier of the **LTSCALE** system variable. This was discussed in Chapter 4.
- **Plot style.** Picking on this property displays a drop-down arrow with various plot styles. Initially only one style is available: ByColor. In order to create a list of plot styles you must create a plot style table. Plotting and plot styles are discussed in Chapter 10.
- **Lineweight.** Select the desired lineweight for the object. Lineweights are discussed in Chapter 4.
- **Hyperlink.** Picking on this property displays a button with three dots. By selecting this button, you can access the **Insert Hyperlink** dialog box. Use this dialog box to add a hyperlink to a graphical object, a description, or a URL address to an object.
- **Thickness.** This property allows you to change the thickness of a 3D object in a text box. Thickness is discussed in Chapter 27.

As stated earlier, all objects have a **General** category. Depending on the type of object that has been selected to modify, other categories are also displayed. See Figure 12-14. One of the most common categories is **Geometry**. Although most objects have a **Geometry** category, the properties within the categories vary, depending on the type of object. Typically, there are three properties that allow you to change the absolute coordinates for the object by specifying the **X**, **Y**, and **Z** coordinates. Pick one of these properties and a pick button is displayed. The button allows you to pick a point in your drawing for the new location. In addition to the pick button, the value for the coordinate can also be changed in a text box.

Figure 12-14.
The **Properties** window with a line object selected. Notice that there are only two categories that can be modified for the line object.

Type of object selected

General properties

Start point and endpoint coordinates

These values cannot be directly modified, but change if endpoints are modified

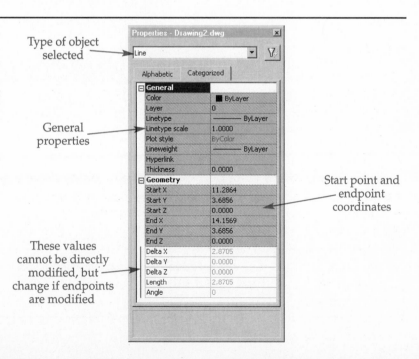

When multiple objects are selected, you can use the **Properties** window to modify all the objects, or you can pick only one of the selected objects to be modified. The drop-down list displays the types of objects selected. See Figure 12-15. Select All to change a properties of all selected objects. Only properties shared by all selected objects are displayed when All is selected. To modify only one object, select the appropriate object type.

When all the changes to the object have been finished, press the [Esc] button on the keyboard to clear the grips and remove the object from the **Properties** window. The object is now displayed in the drawing window with the desired changes.

For example, if you select a circle, two categories appear in the **Properties** window, **General** and **Geometry**. See Figure 12-16. The **Geometry** category displays the current location of the center of the circle by showing three properties: **Center X**, **Center Y**, and **Center Z**. To choose a new center location for the circle, select the appropriate property and pick a new point or type the coordinate values. There are also other properties that can be modified for the circle, such as the **Radius**, **Diameter**, **Circumference**, and **Area**. By changing any of these values, you are modifying the size of the circle.

Figure 12-15.
The **Properties** window with three objects selected. You can edit the objects individually or all together by selecting All (3).

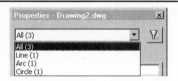

Figure 12-16.
The **Properties** window with a Circle object selected for editing.

Type of object selected

Pick to modify location

Pick button

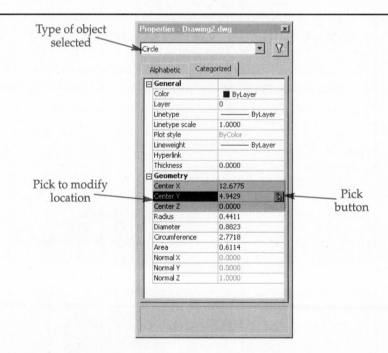

 NOTE The **Properties** window is discussed where appropriate throughout this text.

❑ Start a new drawing, use one of your templates, or open a previous exercise.
❑ Draw a line with endpoint coordinates X = 2, Y = 3, and X = 2, Y = 6.
❑ Draw a circle with a radius of 1.250 and a center location of X = 6, Y = 4.5.
❑ Use the **DTEXT** command with .25 text height to position the word **LINE** below the line and **CIRCLE** below the circle.
❑ Use the **Properties** window to edit the line as follows:
    ❑ Change the start point to X = 6.750, Y = 3.770.
    ❑ Change the endpoint to X = 6.750, Y = 6.750.
❑ Use the **Properties** window to edit the circle as follows:
    ❑ Change the center location to X = 7.125, Y = 5.25.
    ❑ Change the radius to .375.
❑ Change the LINE label to .125″ height and place it above the line.
❑ Change the CIRCLE label to read Circle and justify the middle of it with the center of the circle. Modify the text height to be .375″.
❑ Save the drawing as EX12-8.

PROFESSIONAL TIP

If you are trying to pick an object on top of another, AutoCAD may not pick the one you want. However, AutoCAD picks the last thing you drew if <u>O</u>bject Selection is on in the **Object Sorting Methods** area in the **User Preferences** tab of the **Options** dialog box.

CHANGING THE PROPERTIES OF AN OBJECT AT THE COMMAND PROMPT

Object properties can be changed at the Command: prompt using the **CHANGE** and **CHPROP** commands. Select the **Properties** option of the **CHANGE** command as follows:

Command: **-CH** *or* **CHANGE**↵
Select objects: *(pick the object)*
Select objects: ↵
Specify change point or [Properties]: **P**↵
Enter property to change [Color/Elev/LAyer/LType/ltScale/LWeight/Thickness]:

The following properties can be changed with the **CHANGE** command:
- **Color.** Changes the color of the selected object.
- **Elev.** Used to change the elevation in 3D drawing.
- **Layer.** Changes the layer designation.
- **LType.** Changes the current linetype of a selected object to a linetype that has been loaded using the **LINETYPE** command.
- **ltScale.** Changes the individual object linetype scale.
- **LWeight.** Changes the individual object's lineweight. (Lineweights appear if the **LWT** button in the status bar is selected.)
- **Thickness.** Used to change the thickness in 3D drawing.

The **CHPROP** (change property) command lets you change only properties of an object. It does not allow for a point change, as does the **CHANGE** command. This is the command sequence for **CHPROP**:

Command: **CHPROP**↵
Select objects: *(pick the object)*
Select objects: ↵
Enter property to change [Color/LAyer/LType/ltScale/LWeight/Thickness]:

Except for **Elevation**, the **CHPROP** options are the same as those discussed for the **CHANGE** command.

EXERCISE 12-9

❏ Start a new drawing or use one of your templates.
❏ Draw a vertical line on the left side of the screen, a circle in the middle, and a hexagon on the right side.
❏ Load the CENTER, HIDDEN, and PHANTOM linetypes.
❏ Use the **CHANGE** command to change the line's linetype to CENTER and the hexagon's linetype to PHANTOM.
❏ Use the **CHPROP** command to change the circle's linetype to HIDDEN and the color to red.
❏ Use the **CHPROP** command to change the hexagon color to yellow.
❏ Save the drawing as EX12-9.

EDITING BETWEEN MULTIPLE DRAWINGS

One of the advantages of AutoCAD 2000 is the capability of editing in more than one drawing at a time. This allows you to copy objects from one drawing into another drawing. You can also refer to another drawing to obtain information (such as a distance) while working in a different drawing.

To take a look at how this works, use the **OPEN** command to first open EX12-8. Then use the **OPEN** command again to open EX12-9. Two drawings have now been opened in AutoCAD. In the **Window** pull-down menu, pick **Tile Horizontally**. This "tiles" the two open drawings, Figure 12-17.

Figure 12-17.
Multiple drawings can be tiled to make editing easier.

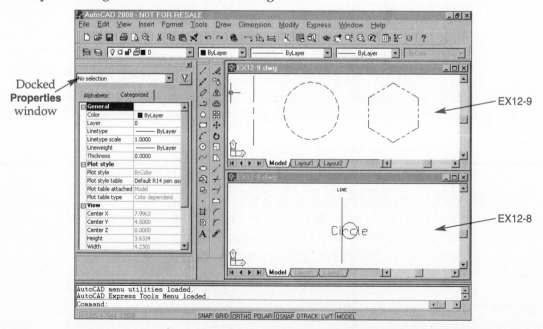

Copying Objects Between Drawings

The Windows function *copy and paste* is used to copy an object from one drawing to another. To use this feature in AutoCAD, the object that you intend on copying must be selected with grips. For example, if you want to copy the circle from drawing EX12-9 into drawing EX12-8, you would first select the circle. Once the circle is selected, right-click to get the shortcut menu shown in Figure 12-18.

The shortcut menu has two options that allow you to copy to the Windows Clipboard:

- **Copy.** This option takes selected objects from AutoCAD and places them on the Windows Clipboard to be used in another application or another AutoCAD drawing.
- **Copy with Base Point.** This option also copies the selected objects to the Clipboard but allows you to specify a base point to position the copied object when it is pasted. When using this option, AutoCAD prompts you to select a base point. Select a logical base point, such as a corner or center point of the object.

Once you have selected one of the two copy options, make the second drawing active by picking inside of the it. Right-click and a shortcut menu is displayed as shown in Figure 12-19. Notice that the copy options remain available, but three paste options

---

Figure 12-18.
Right-click to access this shortcut menu to select one of the copy options.

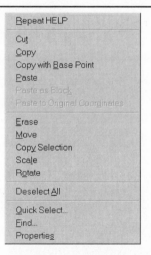

Figure 12-19.
Right-click to access this shortcut menu and select one of the paste options to paste an object from the Clipboard to a drawing.

Paste options

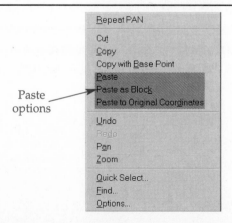

---

have become available below the copy options. The paste options are only available if there is something on the Clipboard. The three options are described below:

- **Paste.** This option pastes any information from the Clipboard into the current drawing. If the **Copy with Base Point** option was used to place objects in the Clipboard, then the objects being pasted are attached to the crosshairs at the specified base point.
- **Paste as a Block.** This option "joins" all objects in the Clipboard when they are pasted into the drawing. The pasted objects act like a block in that they are single objects joined together to form one object. Blocks are covered in Chapter 23. Use the **EXPLODE** command to get the objects to act individually again.
- **Paste to Original Coordinates.** This option pastes the objects from the Clipboard to the same coordinates at which they were located in the original drawing.

You can also copy objects between drawings using a drag-and-drop operations. To do so, first open both drawings and arrange their windows so they are both visible in the drawing area. Select the object to be copied, and then press and hold the pick button. Move the cursor into the other drawing and release the pick button. The object is automatically copied into the second drawing.

EXERCISE 12-10

❑ Open drawings EX12-8 and EX12-9, then tile the drawings horizontally.
❑ Use the **Properties** window to make the circles in both drawings green.
❑ Select the circle from EX12-9.
❑ Right-click and select **Copy with Base Point**. Select the center of the circle as the base point.
❑ Use [CTRL]+[TAB] to make EX12-8 active.
❑ Right-click and select **Paste** from the shortcut menu. Pick a new location for the circle.
❑ Select the line and hexagon in EX12-9 and copy them to the Clipboard.
❑ Use the **Paste as Block** option to paste the objects into the EX12-8 drawing.
❑ Pick either the newly pasted line or the hexagon and notice that they are selected together as a group.
❑ Save the drawing as EX12-10.

MATCHING PROPERTIES

MATCHPROP
MA
PAINTER

Modify
➥ Match Properties

Standard
toolbar

Match Properties

The **MATCHPROP** command allows you to copy properties from one object to one or more objects. This can be done in the same drawing or between drawings. To access the **MATCHPROP** command, select the **Match Properties** button in the **Standard** toolbar, select **Match Properties** from the **Modify** pull-down, or enter MA, MATCHPROP, or PAINTER at the Command: prompt. The following is the prompt sequence:

Command: **MA**, **MATCHPROP**, or **PAINTER.**↵
Select source object: *(pick the object that has the properties you want to paint)*

When you first access the **MATCHPROP** command, AutoCAD prompts you for the source object. The source object is the object that has all the properties you would like to copy to another object or series of objects. Once the source object has been selected, AutoCAD displays the properties it will paint to the destination object. The next prompt reads:

> Current active settings: Color Layer Ltype Ltscale Lineweight Thickness PlotStyle
>   Text Dim Hatch
> Select destination object(s) or [Settings]:

This allows you to pick the objects you want to receive the properties of the source object. If you want the properties painted to all objects in the drawing, type ALL at this prompt.

To change the properties to be painted, access the **Settings** option by typing S and pressing [Enter] as follows:

> Select destination object(s) or [Settings]: **S**↵

The **Property Settings** dialog box now appears, showing the types of properties that can be painted. See Figure 12-20. The following describes the major areas of the **Property Settings** dialog box:

- **Basic Properties.** This area lists the general properties of the selected object. If you do not want the property to be copied, deselect the appropriate check box. All active properties will be transferred to the destination objects.
- **Special Properties.** In addition to general properties, you can also paint over dimension styles, text styles, and hatch patterns. These properties are replaced in the destination object if these check boxes are active.

For example, if you want to paint only the color property and text style of one text object to another text object, uncheck all boxes except the **Color** property check box and the **Text** property check box.

Figure 12-20.
The **Property Settings** dialog box for the **MATCHPROP** command. Select the properties to paint onto a new object.

Properties to be painted to other objects →

Properties particular to specific objects →

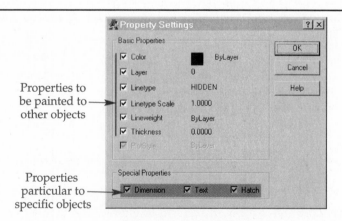

NOTE

To use the **MATCHPROP** command between drawings, select the source object from one drawing and the destination object from another.

PROFESSIONAL TIP

Use the **Partial Open** option in the **Open** command to partially open existing drawings to be used as source objects for copying or property matching. **Partial Open** is discussed in Chapter 3.

❏ Open drawings EX12-9 and EX12-10, then tile the drawings horizontally.
❏ Make the EX12-9 drawing active.
❏ Use the **MATCHPROP** command to paint the color and linetype of the hexagon to the circle you pasted in drawing EX12-10.
❏ Open one of your previous drawings that contains text, such as a Chapter 8 exercise or problem.
❏ Create a new text style different from the text style on the existing drawing. Use the Romand.shx font in the text style, for example. Use the **MATCHPROP** command to change all text to the new text style.
❏ Save the drawing as EX12-11.

Chapter Test

Answer the following questions on a separate sheet of paper.

1. How do you turn grips on and off?
2. Which option of the automatic **ROTATE** command would you use to rotate an object from an existing 60° angle to a new 25° angle?
3. What scale factor is used to scale an object to become three-quarters of its original size?
4. Name the two system variables that control the color of grips.
5. Name the editing commands that can be accessed automatically using grips.
6. When grips are active, how do you cycle through the available automatic commands?
7. Explain the difference between "noun/verb" selection and "verb/noun" selection.
8. Name the system variable that allows you to set the "noun/verb" selection.
9. What does **Use Shift to add to selection** mean?
10. Describe how the **Press and drag** option works.
11. Name the system variable that is used to turn on the **Press and drag** option.
12. Name the system variable that turns on the **Implied windowing** option.
13. Identify two ways to access the **Options** dialog box.
14. Explain two ways to change the pick box size.
15. Explain how you would change the radius of a circle from 1.375 to 1.875 using the **Properties** window.
16. Identify the pull-down menu and the item you pick from this menu to access the **Properties** window.
17. How would you change the linetype of an object using the **Properties** window?
18. Name the command that allows you to change the location of an object or object properties at the command line.
19. Name the command that is used at the command line to change only the properties of an object.
20. How do you change the color of an object using the **Properties** window?
21. How do you access the grips shortcut menu?
22. What is the purpose of the **Base Point** option in the grips shortcut menu?
23. Explain the function of the **Undo** option in the grips shortcut menu.
24. Describe the purpose of the **Properties...** option in the grips shortcut menu.
25. What happens when you choose the **Exit** option in the grips shortcut menu?
26. What command is used to quickly change the properties of objects to match the properties of a different object?
27. What is the purpose of the **Selection** tab found in the **Options** dialog box?
28. How do you change an existing text that reads AutoCAD to read AutoCAD 2000 by using the **Properties** window?

29. Name the option used to have a group of objects joined as a block when they are pasted.
30. When you use the option described in Question 29, how do you separate the objects back into individual objects?

Drawing Problems

Use templates as appropriate for each of the following problems. Use grips and the associated editing commands or other editing techniques discussed in this chapter.

1. Draw the objects shown at A below and then use the **STRETCH** command to make them look like the objects at B. Do not include dimensions. Save the drawing as P12-1.

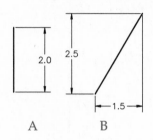 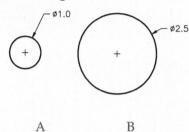 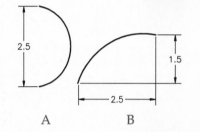

A   B   A   B   A   B

2. Draw the object shown at A below. Then using the **Copy** option of the **MOVE** command, copy the object to the position shown at B. Edit Object A so that it resembles Object C. Edit Object B so that it looks like Object D. Do not include dimensions. Save the drawing as P12-2.

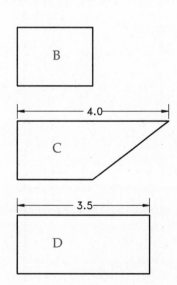

3. Draw the object shown at A below. Then copy the object, without rotating it, to a position below as indicated by the dashed lines. Then, rotate the object 45°. Copy the rotated object at B to a position below as indicated by the dashed lines. Use the **Reference** option to rotate the object at C to 25° as shown. Do not include dimensions. Save the drawing as P12-3.

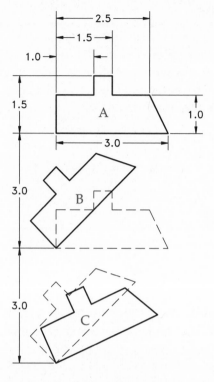

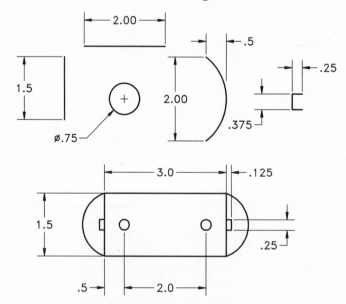

4. Draw the individual objects (vertical line, horizontal line, circle, arc, and "C" shape) at A below using the dimensions given. Then, use grips and the editing commands to create the object shown at B. Do not include dimensions. Save the drawing as P12-4.

5. Use the completed drawing from Problem 12-4. Erase everything except the completed object and move it to a position similar to A below. Copy the object two times to positions B and C. Use the automatic **SCALE** command to scale the object at B to fifty percent of its original size. Use the **Reference** option of the **SCALE** command to enlarge the object at C from the existing 3.0 length to a 4.5 length as shown in C. Do not include dimensions. Save as P12-5.

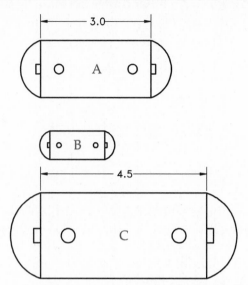

6. Draw the dimensioned partial object shown at A. Do not include dimensions. Mirror the drawing to complete the four quadrants as shown at B. Change the color of the horizontal and vertical parting lines to red and the linetype to **Center**. Save the drawing as P12-6.

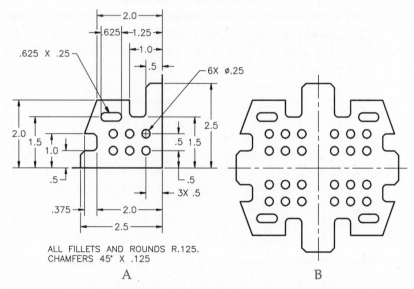

ALL FILLETS AND ROUNDS R.125.
CHAMFERS 45° X .125

A   B

7. Load the final drawing you created in Problem 12-6. Use the **Properties** window to change the circles from a .25 diameter to a .125 diameter. Change the linetype of the slots to Phantom. Be sure the linetype scale allows the linetypes to be displayed. Save the drawing as P12-7.

8. Use the editing commands discussed in this chapter to assist you in drawing the following object. Draw the object within the boundaries of the given dimensions. All other dimensions are flexible. Do not include dimensions in the drawing. Save the drawing as P12-8.

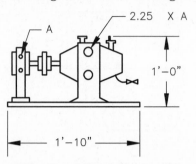

9. Draw the following object within the boundaries of the given dimensions. All other dimensions are flexible. Do not include dimensions. After drawing the object, create a page for a vendor catalog as follows:

- All labels should be ROMAND text centered directly below the view. Use a text height of .125.
- Label the drawing ONE-GALLON TANK WITH HORIZONTAL VALVE.
- Keep the valve the same scale as the original drawing in each copy.
- Copy the original tank to a new location and scale it so that it is two times its original size. Rotate the valve 45°. Label this tank TWO-GALLON TANK WITH 45° VALVE.
- Copy the original tank to another location and scale it so that it is 2.5 times the size of the original. Rotate the valve 90°. Label this tank TWO- AND ONE-HALF GALLON TANK WITH 90° VALVE.
- Copy the two-gallon tank to a new position and scale it so that it is two times this size. Rotate the valve to 22°30′. Label this tank FOUR-GALLON TANK WITH 22°30′ VALVE.
- Left-justify this note at the bottom of the page: Combinations of tank size and valve orientation are available upon request.
- Use the **Properties** window to change all tank labels to ROMANC, .25″ high.
- Change the note at the bottom of the sheet to ROMANS, centered on the sheet using uppercase letters.
- Save the drawing as P12-9.

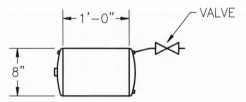

CHAPTER 13

Creating Multiple Objects with Array

Learning Objectives

After completing this chapter, you will be able to:

■ Create an arrangement of objects in a rectangular pattern.
■ Create an arrangement of objects in a circular pattern.

Some designs require a rectangular or circular pattern of the same object. For example, office desks are often arranged in rows. Suppose your design calls for five rows, each having four desks. You can create this design by drawing one desk and copying it 19 times. You can also save the desk as a block and insert it 20 times. However, both of these operations are time-consuming. A quicker method is to use AutoCAD's **ARRAY** command. Using **ARRAY**, you first select the object(s) to be copied. Then, you are prompted to enter the type of arrangement (rectangular or polar).

A *rectangular array* creates rows and columns of the selected items, and you must provide the spacing. A *polar array* constructs a circular arrangement. For a circular array, you must specify the number of items to array, the angle between items, and the center point of the array. Some examples are shown in Figure 13-1.

AutoCAD User's Guide 9

Figure 13-1.
Examples of arrays created with the **ARRAY** command.

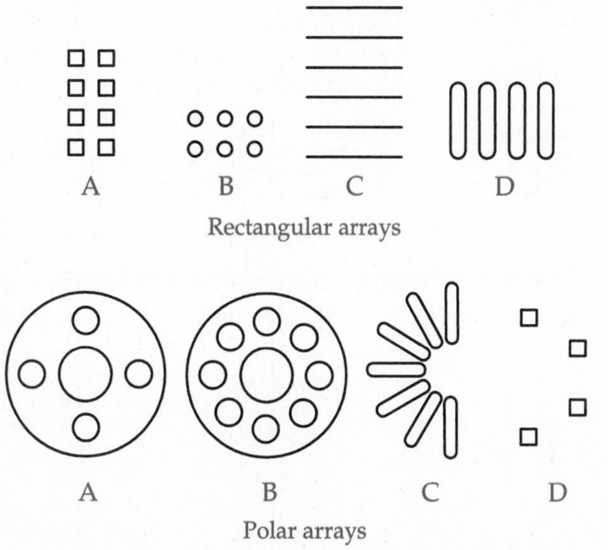

Rectangular arrays

Polar arrays

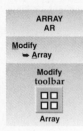

ARRAY
AR

Modify
➥ Array

**Modify
toolbar**

Array

In this chapter, you will experiment with the **ARRAY** command using a .5 unit square. You may want to draw this object now in order to use it as you study the chapter.

You can access the **ARRAY** command by typing AR or ARRAY at the Command: prompt, picking the **Array** button on the **Modify** toolbar, or selecting **Array** from the **Modify** pull-down menu. After you issue the **ARRAY** command, AutoCAD asks you to select objects. Any of the selection set methods, such as **Window** or **Crossing**, are valid. After you select the desired objects, you must specify whether you want a rectangular or polar array. The command sequence is as follows:

> Command: **AR** *or* **ARRAY**⏎
> Select objects: *(select the objects)*
> *n* found
> Select objects: ⏎
> Enter the type of array [Rectangular/Polar] *<current>*: *(type P or press* [Enter]*)*

ARRANGING OBJECTS IN A RECTANGULAR PATTERN

*For 2000i
Users...*

In AutoCAD 2000i, arrays are created using the **Array** dialog box. Refer to **Array** *Dialog Box* on page 974 for more information.

A rectangular array places objects in line along the X and Y axes. You can specify a single row, a single column, or multiple rows and columns. *Rows* are horizontal and *columns* are vertical. AutoCAD reminds you of this by indicating the direction in parentheses: (–––) for rows and (| | |) for columns. The following sequence creates a rectangular pattern of a .5 unit square having 3 rows, 3 columns, and .5 spacing between objects.

> Enter the type of array [Rectangular/Polar] *<current>*: **R**⏎
> Enter the number of rows (–––) <1>: **3**⏎
> Enter the number of columns (| | |) <1>: **3**⏎
> Enter the distance between rows or specify unit cell (–––): **1**⏎
> Specify the distance between columns (| | |): **1**⏎
> Command:

The original object and resulting array are shown in Figure 13-2. When giving the distance between rows and columns, be sure to include the width and height of the object. Figure 13-2 shows how to calculate the distance between objects in a rectangular array.

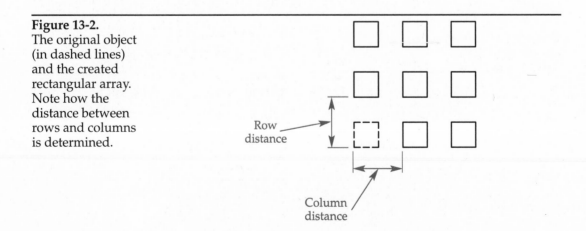

Figure 13-2.
The original object (in dashed lines) and the created rectangular array. Note how the distance between rows and columns is determined.

Row distance

Column distance

AutoCAD allows you to specify the distance separating objects with your pointing device. This distance is called the ***unit cell***. The unit cell distance is the same as the distance between rows and columns. However, it is entered with the pointing device, just like selecting a window. See Figure 13-3. The second point's distance and direction from the first point determines the X and Y spacing for the array.

Enter the distance between rows or specify unit cell (–––): *(pick a corner)*
Specify opposite corner: *(pick the second corner)*

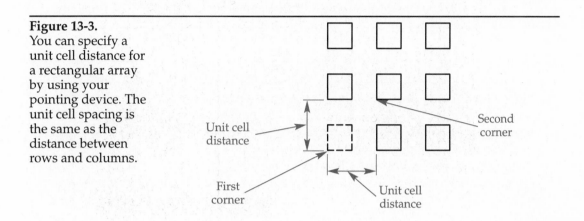

Figure 13-3.
You can specify a unit cell distance for a rectangular array by using your pointing device. The unit cell spacing is the same as the distance between rows and columns.

Figure 13-4 shows how you can place arrays in four directions by entering either positive or negative row and column distance values. The dashed box is the original object. The row and column distance is one unit and the box is .5 units square.

Specifying the unit cell distance can create a quick row and column arrangement in any direction. For example, in Figure 13-5, the second unit cell corner is picked below and to the left of the first corner.

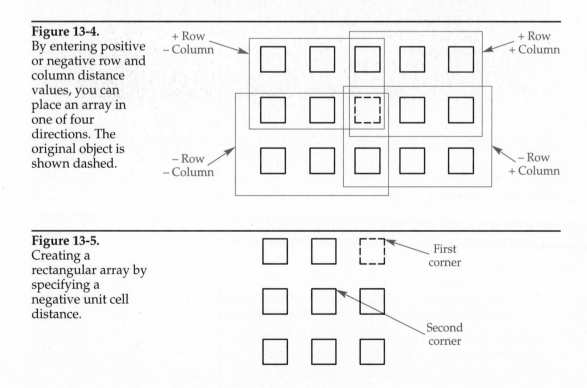

Figure 13-4.
By entering positive or negative row and column distance values, you can place an array in one of four directions. The original object is shown dashed.

Figure 13-5.
Creating a rectangular array by specifying a negative unit cell distance.

EXERCISE 13-1

☐ Start a new drawing or use one of your templates.
☐ Construct the Bill of Materials form shown below using the **LINE** and **ARRAY** commands. Line A is arrayed in nine rows and one column. The distance between rows is given. Line B is arrayed in one row and three columns. The distance between the columns is provided.
☐ Complete the headings using the **DTEXT** command with **Middle** justification.

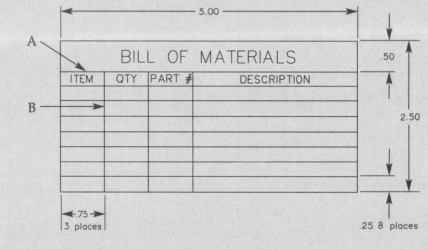

☐ Save the drawing as EX13-1.

ARRANGING OBJECTS AROUND A CENTER POINT

For 2000i Users...

In AutoCAD 2000i, arrays are created using the **Array** dialog box. Refer to **Array** Dialog Box on page 974 for more information.

The **Polar** option of the **ARRAY** command enables you to create a polar array. First, erase everything on your screen except for one .5 unit square. Enter the following command sequence:

> Command: **AR** or **ARRAY**↵
> Select objects: (select the object)
> 1 found
> Select objects: ↵
> Enter the type of array [Rectangular/Polar] <current>: **P**↵
> Specify center point of array: (pick the center point)

Next, AutoCAD requests the number of objects you want in the array. If you know the exact number needed, enter that value. If you would rather specify an angle between items, just press [Enter]. This method is shown in the example below.

> Enter the number of items in the array: ↵
> Specify the angle to fill (+=ccw, −=cw) <360>:

Notice the options represented by +=ccw and −=cw in parentheses. You can array the object in a counterclockwise direction by entering a positive angle value. Numbers entered without the plus sign are positive. Objects can be arrayed clockwise by entering the minus sign before the angle value. Pressing [Enter] at this prompt without entering a value copies the object through 360°. This is the default value.

The final value needed is the angular spacing between the arrayed objects. The sequence is as follows:

> Angle between items: **45**↵

A number entered at this prompt is assumed to be the angle. This prompt is only displayed if you press [Enter] at the Enter the number of items in the array: prompt. If you specify the number of items, AutoCAD calculates the angle for you. The last prompt is:

> Rotate arrayed objects? [Yes/No] <Y> **N**↵

You can have the objects rotated as they are copied around the center point. This keeps the same face of the object always pointing toward the center point. If objects are not rotated as they are copied, they remain in the same orientation as the original object. See Figure 13-6.

Figure 13-6.
Using the **Polar** option of the **ARRAY** command to rotate a square.
A—The square is rotated as it is arrayed.
B—The square is not rotated as it is arrayed.

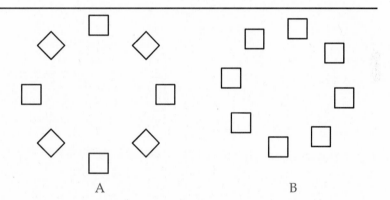

A   B

EXERCISE 13-2

❏ Start a new drawing or use one of your templates.
❏ Create a 360° polar array of five circles.
❏ Copy one of the circles to the side of the polar array.
❏ Create an array with the copied circle. Each circle should be 30° apart, and the array should go through 270°.
❏ Save the drawing as EX13-2 and quit.

Chapter Test

Answer the following questions on a separate sheet of paper.
1. What is the difference between polar and rectangular arrays?
2. What four values should you know before you create a rectangular array?
3. Define the term *unit cell.*
4. Suppose an object is 1.5″ (38mm) wide and you want to create a rectangular array with .75″ (19mm) spacing between objects. What should you specify for the distance between columns?
5. How do you create a rectangular array that is rotated?
6. What values should you know before you create a polar array?

7. Suppose you enter a value for the Enter the number of items in the array: prompt in a polar array. Which of the following values are you *not* required to give?
    A. Angle to fill.
    B. Angle between items.
    C. Center point.
    D. Rotate objects as they are copied.
8. What happens to an object when it is *not* rotated as it is arrayed?
9. How do you specify a clockwise polar array rotation?

Drawing Problems

1. Draw the following object views using the dimensions given. Use **ARRAY** to construct the hole and tooth arrangements. Use one of your templates for the drawing. Do not add dimensions. Save the drawing as P13-1.

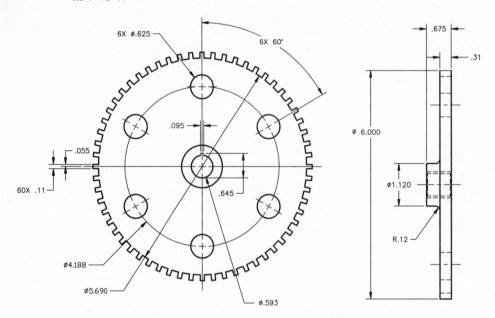

2. You have been given an engineer's sketches and notes to construct a drawing of a sprocket. Create a front and side view of the sprocket using the **ARRAY** command. Place the drawing on one of your templates. Do not add dimensions. Save the drawing as P13-2.

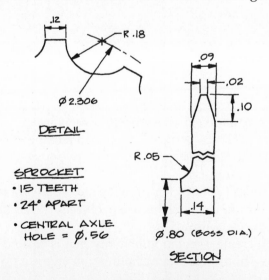

3. The following engineering sketch shows a steel column arrangement on a concrete floor slab for a new building. The steel columns are represented by I-shaped symbols. The columns are arranged in "bay lines" and "column lines." The column lines are numbered 1, 2, and 3. The bay lines are labeled A through G. The width of a bay is 20'-0". Line balloons, or tags, identify the bay and column lines. Draw the arrangement using **ARRAY** for the steel column symbols and the tags. Do not dimension the drawing. The following guidelines will help you.

A. Begin a new drawing named P13-3 or use an architectural template.
B. Select architectural units and specify a 36 × 24 sheet size. Determine the scale required for the floor plan to fit on this sheet size, and specify your limits accordingly.
C. Draw the steel column symbol to the dimensions given.
D. Set the grid spacing at 2'-0" (24").
E. Set the snap spacing at 12".
F. Draw all other objects.
G. Place text inside the balloon tags. Set the running object snap mode to **Center** and use **DTEXT** with **Middle** justification. Make the text height 6".
H. Place a title block on the drawing.
I. Save the drawing as P13-3.

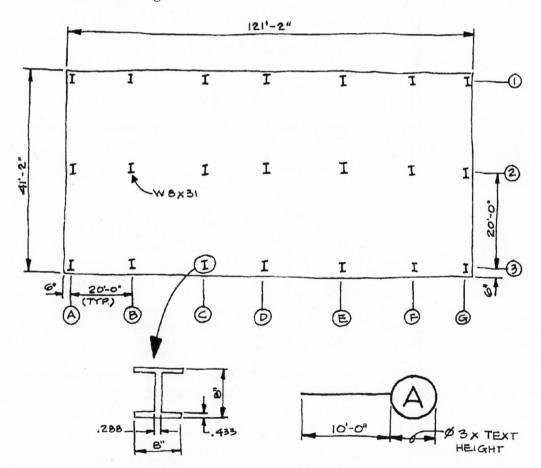

4. The engineering sketch given is a proposed office layout of desks and chairs. One desk is shown with the layout of a chair, keyboard, monitor, and tower-mounted computer (drawn with dotted lines). All of the desk workstations should have the same configuration. The exact sizes and locations of the doors and windows are not important for this problem. Use the following guidelines to complete this problem.

A. Begin a new drawing called P13-4.
B. Choose architectural units.
C. Select a C-size template drawing and be sure to create the drawing in model space. Use the **ZOOM XP** option to display the drawing at a scale that fits the C-size layout.
D. Use the appropriate drawing and editing commands to complete this problem quickly and efficiently.
E. Draw the desk and computer hardware to the dimensions given.
F. Do not dimension the drawing. Plot a paper space layout tab at a one-to-one scale.
G. Save the drawing as P13-4.

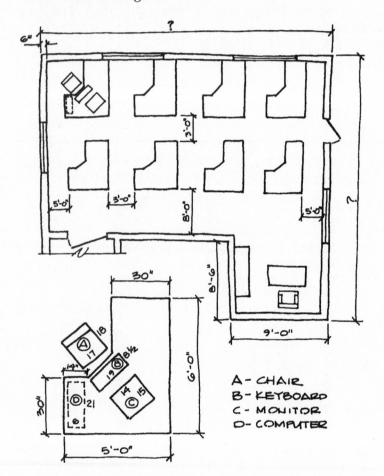

A - CHAIR
B - KEYBOARD
C - MONITOR
D - COMPUTER

CHAPTER 14

Working with AutoCAD Files

Learning Objectives

After completing this chapter, you will be able to:

- Explain the meaning and use of Windows file extensions.
- Select, display, and arrange folders and files in Windows Explorer.
- Manage files and folders using Windows Explorer.
- Search for files and folders using Windows Explorer.
- Copy, move, delete, and rename files using Windows Explorer.
- Format and copy diskettes using Windows Explorer.
- Perform drag-and-drop operations using Windows Explorer.
- Manage critical files using the **Options** dialog box.
- Import and export a variety of file types in AutoCAD.

AutoCAD works with several types of computer files. The files are identified by a three-letter file extension at the end of the file name. Windows® Explorer provides a variety of tools to help you manage these files and the folders where they are stored. This chapter covers many of those functions.

AutoCAD can write drawing files in a variety of formats, many of which are compatible with other popular software applications. You can export the industry standard DXF file for use with other CAD packages or specific applications. Files can also be exported for use in the design and animation software programs 3D Studio VIZ® and 3D Studio MAX®, or for use in the stereolithography process. In addition, you can import several different file types into AutoCAD.

TYPES OF FILE NAMES

Drawing file names can be up to 255 characters long. They can contain letters, numbers, spaces, dollar signs ($), hyphens (-), and underscores (_). When you begin a new drawing, AutoCAD adds a file extension to the end of the file name. This extension is .dwg. If you name a drawing Building 340, AutoCAD adds the extension to create the file as Building 340.dwg. When you open the drawing to edit, you only have to type Building 340. AutoCAD knows to look for that file, plus the .dwg extension. File names are not case-sensitive. This means that you can name a drawing PROBLEM 20-12, but Windows interprets Problem 20-12 as the same file name. See Figure 14-1.

Figure 14-1.
File names are not case sensitive. This alert box appears when you attempt to save as an already existing file.

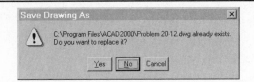

After you edit the Building 340.dwg file and save it again, the original is converted to a backup file. Its file extension is automatically changed to .bak (backup). AutoCAD maintains a current DWG file and one BAK file. If you revise the Building 340 drawing again, the BAK file is erased and the previous DWG file becomes the backup. Only a newly revised drawing is given the .dwg file extension.

Some common file extensions used by AutoCAD and Windows include the following:

AutoCAD	
BAK	Backup copy of a drawing file
DCL	Dialog control language description file
DWG	Drawing file
DWT	Drawing template file
LIN	File containing the linetypes used by AutoCAD
MNU	Menu source file
PAT	Hatch patterns file
PLT	Plot file
Windows	
BMP	Bitmap file
CLP	Windows Clipboard file
COM	Command file
DLL	Dynamic-link library file
EXE	Executable file
INI	Initialization file
WMF	Windows metafile

PROFESSIONAL TIP

Saving backup files is the default behavior of AutoCAD. This feature is controlled by the **Create backup copy with each save** option in the **File Safety Precautions** area of the **Open and Save** tab of the **Options** dialog box. The creation of backup files can be disabled to reduce the amount of time required to save, but this is not advised for most applications. If a drawing file becomes corrupt, a backup file may be the only way to recover data which would otherwise be lost. Recovering lost or damaged drawing data is discussed later in this chapter.

NOTE

Refer to Appendix E, Managing the AutoCAD System, for important information on hard disk structure and management. This information is applicable to any classroom or business application.

INTRODUCTION TO WINDOWS EXPLORER

The Windows Explorer is a program that allows you to manage and display folders and files. It is activated by picking <u>P</u>rograms from the Start menu on the Windows task bar, then selecting Windows Explorer.

NOTE The functions of the Windows Explorer are very similar in Windows 95, Windows 98, and Windows NT. However, there are some minor differences. This chapter is based on the Windows Explorer provided with Windows 98. The material in the chapter is still applicable if you are using a different operating system, but the Exploring window may appear slightly different.

Elements of the Exploring Window

When you use Windows Explorer, all your work is performed using a directory tree. The *directory tree* is a graphic representation of the directory structure and the folders and files it contains. When you start Windows Explorer, the window displays the contents of the current drive. See Figure 14-2. The window is divided in half with a vertical *split bar*. The left half of the window displays the directory tree, and the right half lists the contents of the current folder. You can drag the split bar to the left or to the right to display more or less of the contents in each side of the window.

At the right of the window is a contents list of the folders and files contained in the selected folder. Each folder in this list is also represented with a folder icon. A *file icon* indicating the file type appears next to each file name. There are icons to represent program files (EXE and BAT files), document files (TXT and WRI files), and other types of files.

Figure 14-2.
When you activate Windows Explorer, the Exploring window is displayed.

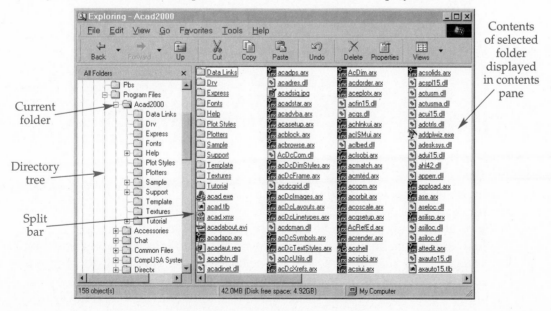

You must first select a file or folder in the Exploring window before you can work with it. When you want to select a file or folder, place the cursor over the desired file or folder icon and pick. More than one file or folder can be selected by pressing and holding the [Shift] key as you pick with your pointing device. The item(s) you select is then highlighted and you can proceed with the desired operation. More information about file and folder selection appears later in this chapter.

Drive icons represent each of the drives on your computer. These are listed below the My Computer icon near the top of the list in the All Folders pane. See Figure 14-3. The text to the right of each icon lists the label and the drive letter for each icon. You can see that the diskette drive (A:) is represented with a different icon than those used for the hard disk (C:).

To work with the contents of one of the available drives, pick the desired drive icon and its contents are displayed in the pane on the right. If you are connected to a network or are using a CD-ROM device, appropriate icons are displayed.

Just below the Exploring window title bar are pull-down menus. The menus displayed depend on your operating system. Many of the commands located in these menus are explored later in this chapter.

Finally, as with all Microsoft Windows applications, the Exploring window can be moved, resized, closed, and reduced to the taskbar at any time. Standard methods are used to perform these activities.

Figure 14-3.
Drive icons are listed under the My Computer icon.

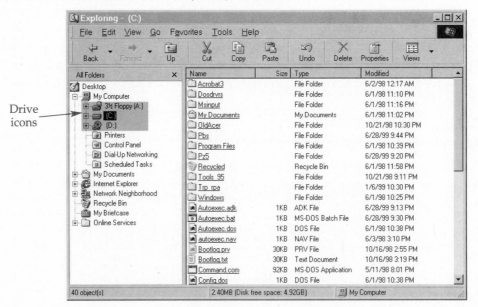

Accessing Windows Explorer Commands

Most commands used in Windows Explorer can be accessed in several ways. Commands can be activated from a toolbar button, pull-down menu, or shortcut menu. Some commands can also be accessed through keyboard shortcuts.

Toolbar buttons enable you to perform a variety of functions quickly. The toolbar display is toggled on and off by selecting Toolbar from the View pull-down menu. A check mark next to a toolbar name indicates that it is active.

Figure 14-4 provides quick identification of the toolbar available in the Windows Explorer operating system. The functions of these buttons are described later in this chapter when applicable.

Figure 14-4.
Many file management options are available in the Windows Explorer toolbar.

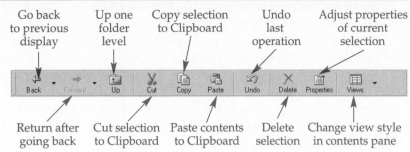

Go back to previous display — Up one folder level — Copy selection to Clipboard — Undo last operation — Adjust properties of current selection

Return after going back — Cut selection to Clipboard — Paste contents to Clipboard — Delete selection — Change view style in contents pane

---

NOTE

The terms *folder* and *directory* are used interchangeably and mean the same thing.

Listing Folders and Files

The Exploring window is initially displayed, similar to the one shown in Figure 14-2. The window is composed of the title bar, pull-down menu bar, standard toolbar, Address text box, Links bar, All Folders pane, the contents pane, and a status bar. The Address text box and Links bars are not active by default.

Folder and device icons in the All Folders pane may be preceded by a small box containing a "+" or a "−" symbol. The + indicates that the folder contains additional folders, or *subfolders*. Picking the + symbol expands the tree to display the next level of folders. You can collapse or hide the display by picking the "−" symbol.

Folders in the All Folders pane are opened with a single pick on the icon. The folder contents are displayed in the contents pane. Folders in the contents pane must be double-clicked to open. The open folder is automatically closed when a new one is selected and opened.

NOTE

When installing AutoCAD, the default location of the AutoCAD 2000 folder is in the Program Files folder. However, the location and name of the AutoCAD 2000 folder can be easily changed during installation and may not agree with the default settings. If you are unsure of the name or location of the AutoCAD folder, ask your instructor or supervisor.

PROFESSIONAL TIP

When the directory tree is expanded to several levels, you can quickly back up to the previous level or branch by picking the Back button or by pressing the [Backspace] key.

The contents of a folder can be viewed in several different ways. These are found in the View pull-down menu. The current display method is indicated by a dot to the left of the name.

- **As Web Page.** Displays each folder or file icon in the currently selected view format, as described below. The left side of the contents pane resembles a Web page layout, and provides capsule information about the current folder or the selected item. Each folder can be customized similar to Web page content. See Figure 14-5A.

- **Large icons.** Displays each folder or file icon in a large format with the file name below it. See Figure 14-5B.
- **Small icons.** Displays each folder or file icon in a small format with the file name to the right side. See Figure 14-5C.
- **List.** Displays a small icon list of file names that fills the height of the list box with multiple columns. Files that do not fit in the box are listed in additional columns to the right. Use the horizontal scroll bar to display them. See Figure 14-5D.
- **Details.** Displays columns of file name, size, type, and last date and time modified. See Figure 14-5E.

Figure 14-5.
There are five different ways to have files listed in the contents pane. A—Web page. B—Large icons. C—Small icons. D—List. E—Details.

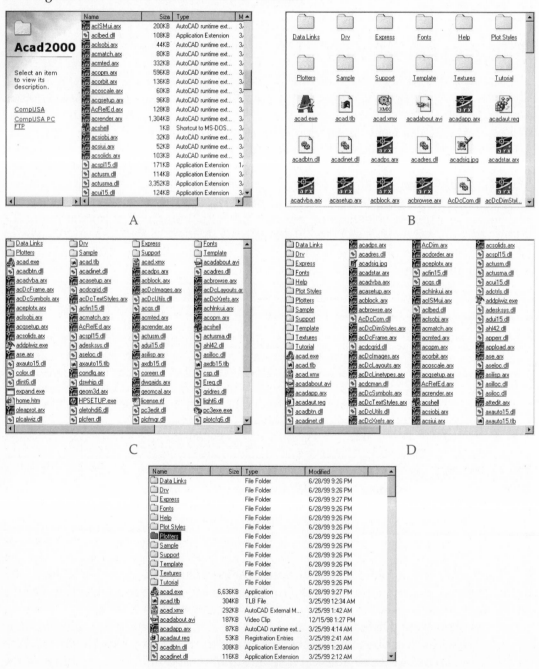

These view options can also be selected using the Views button at the right side of the toolbar. Selecting the Views button toggles through the options. The drop-down arrow displays a list of the options.

PROFESSIONAL TIP Viewing and arranging options can also be selected by right-clicking on any open area of the contents pane and selecting an option from the pull-down menu.

BASIC WINDOWS EXPLORER FUNCTIONS

Before using the Windows Explorer to manage your folders and files, it is best to have a good understanding of how these items are selected and what kinds of actions Windows Explorer is capable of performing.

PROFESSIONAL TIP Windows NT and 98 make extensive use of the right-click on the pointer. Practice using this feature inside windows and dialog boxes or when selecting folders and files. You will find that this method can speed up many operations normally performed by selecting items in the pull-down menus. Right-clicking is discussed where applicable in this chapter.

Selecting Files

When performing functions such as copying, moving, renaming, and deleting, it is first necessary to select the file(s). When files have been selected, they are highlighted. Files can be selected in the following ways:

- Pick the file to select it.
- To select a group of files that are listed together, pick a point that does not highlight a file and hold and drag the pointer to display a dashed selection box similar to an AutoCAD selection window. As the dashed box touches or surrounds the file name, it is highlighted. The selection box should surround or touch all files required. Release the pick button to complete the selection. See Figure 14-6.
- Pick the first file in the list, hold the [Shift] key, then pick the last file in the list. All files between are highlighted.
- Pick the first file, hold the [Ctrl] key, then pick other files that are scattered throughout the list. To deselect one or more currently selected files, press [Ctrl]+[Shift] while picking the files. Pressing the [Ctrl] key while using the window style selection allows multiple windows to be specified. The [Ctrl]+[Shift] combination can also be used with window style selections.
- Press the [Tab] key to activate the contents pane, then use the arrow keys to locate and highlight a single file. This selection method also supports the [Ctrl] and [Shift] key combinations.

Once files have been selected by one or more of the above methods, you can perform the required function.

Figure 14-6.
A group of files that are listed together can be selected by picking and dragging the dashed box so that all files are highlighted.

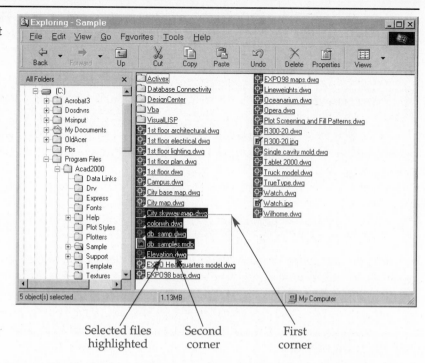

Selected files highlighted   Second corner   First corner

EXERCISE 14-1

❑ Activate the Windows Explorer and insert a diskette that contains drawing files.
❑ Use the Windows Explorer to do the following:
   ❑ Adjust the visibility of the Windows Explorer toolbars to match your preferences.
   ❑ List all files in the Acad2000\Sample folder.
   ❑ List all files on your diskette.
   ❑ View the file list using large icons.
   ❑ View the file list showing all details.
   ❑ Select a group of files from your diskette using the pick and drag method.
❑ Close Windows Explorer.

Selecting Multiple Folders and Files

A consecutive group of items can be selected by picking the first item, then holding the [Shift] key and picking the last item in the group. Two or more consecutive groups can be selected as follows:

1. Pick the first item in a group. Hold the [Shift] key and pick the last item in the group.
2. Press the [Ctrl] key and select the first item in the second group.
3. Press the [Ctrl]+[Shift] keys and pick the last item in the group. This selects the second group.
4. Press the [Ctrl] key and select the first item in the third group.
5. Press the [Ctrl]+[Shift] keys and pick the last item in the group. This selects the third group.
6. Continue in this manner until all groups are selected.

If the number of files or folders you need to select far outnumber those that will remain unselected, use the following technique.

1. Pick Select All from the Edit pull-down menu. This selects all folders and files in the current drive or folder.
2. Deselect the items that you do not want to be part of the selected group by holding down the [Ctrl] key and picking the item(s) you wish to remove.

A second method to use if only a few files or folders are to remain unselected is as follows:

1. Select only the files that are not to be acted on.
2. Pick Invert Selection from the Edit pull-down menu. This automatically deselects the items you picked and selects all remaining items.

The status bar at the bottom of the Exploring window displays the number of objects in the current folder, the total number of bytes in the selected items, and the disk free space if a folder in the left pane is selected. Check the status bar when selecting files to be copied to storage media. You can quickly see if the total file sizes can be accepted by the destination disk.

If you wish to hide the status bar to make more room to display folders and files, pick Status Bar from the View pull-down menu to toggle the status bar off.

Arranging Folder and File Icons

Once you have selected the display that suits your needs, you can quickly arrange the icons by one of four methods. These are selected by picking Arrange Icons from the View pull-down menu.

- **by Name.** Displays icons alphabetically. Folders are always listed first, then files. If a small or large icon view is set, the icons are arranged alphabetically in rows beginning at the upper-left and progressing to the right on each row.
- **by Type.** Displays icons by file type. Folders are always displayed first, then files are listed alphabetically according to the three-letter file extension.
- **by Size.** Files are listed from smallest number of bytes to largest.
- **by Date.** Displays icons by date last modified, most recent first. If small or large icon view is set, the icons are arranged in rows, with most recent on the left.

When icons are displayed in either small or large format, you can choose to move them around and arrange them to suit your needs, or let Windows Explorer arrange them for you. The Auto Arrange option is the default, and icons are automatically arranged in rows and columns. Pick Arrange Icons in the View menu to see this option. A check mark means it is active. Turn this option off by selecting it to remove the check mark. Now you can freely pick and drag icons to new locations. If your arrangement gets too messy, you can align the icons into the nearest rows and columns by picking Line up Icons in the View menu. This option does not produce the compact arrangement that Auto Arrange provides, but merely moves icons to the nearest row and column. Gaps in the arrangement remain.

| NOTE | When the Details option is active, you can automatically reverse the order of listing by picking any one of the column headings in the contents pane. For example, picking Size displays files first from largest to smallest, then folders. Pick Size again to return to the default display of folders first, then files from smallest to largest. Test this feature by picking each of the column headings. |

Launching Applications with Windows Explorer

Many of the files that appear in the Exploring window are associated with application programs. By double-clicking on the file icon or on the file name itself, you can load the file and simultaneously start the application with which it is associated. Consider the portion of the Exploring window shown in Figure 14-7. Double-clicking on the drawing file campus.dwg highlights the file name in the window. AutoCAD is loaded and the campus drawing is opened.

Figure 14-7.
Double-clicking on a DWG file in Windows Explorer starts AutoCAD and loads the selected file into the drawing editor.

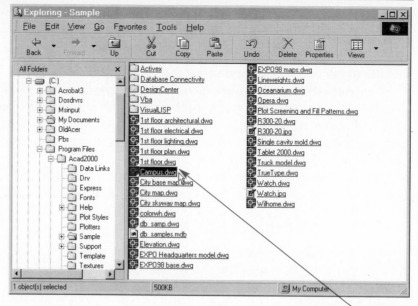

Double-click a DWG file
to start AutoCAD and
open the drawing

Searching for Files

Before you can manage your files and folders, you must locate them. Windows provides a variety of options within Windows Explorer to help you find the items you need. Pick Find, then Files or Folders... in the Tools menu, to begin a search. The Find: All Files dialog box appears. See Figure 14-8.

Conducting a Basic Search

Pick the Name & Location tab if it is not active. This tab requires only two pieces of search data: the file or folder name, and a location from which to begin the search. Use the following procedure to search for a file:

1. Enter the item name in the Named: text box. If prior searches have been conducted, pick the drop-down arrow and select an existing name. Each item you search for is added to this list. If you wish to narrow the search to include the exact format of capital and lower-case characters, pick Case Sensitive from the Options menu.
2. Enter the drive or folder location of the item. Pick the Browse button to access the Browse for Folder dialog box. See Figure 14-9.
3. Pick the Include subfolders check box if you want the search to include all subfolders within the drive or folder location you have chosen.

Figure 14-8.
The Find: All Files dialog box is used to search for files.

Enter name of file

Enter folders to search

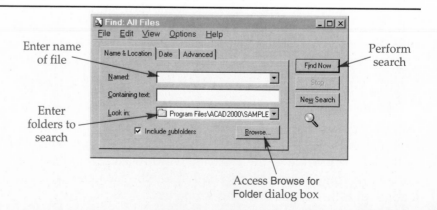

Perform search

Access Browse for Folder dialog box

Figure 14-9.
Pick the Browse
button to search for
the location in a tree
format.

Pick to display
subfolders

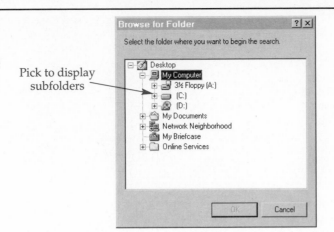

4. Pick the Find Now button to begin the search. If the item you need is found and the search is still proceeding, pick the Stop button.
5. Pick the New Search button, then pick OK to clear the item name and begin a new search.

Additional Search Options

You can refine and narrow your searches by using the two additional tabs in the Find: All Files dialog box. The Date and Advanced tabs allow you to specify a variety of date formats, file types, and sizes in order to focus the search. Consult the Windows Explorer online help for detailed instructions on the use of these options.

EXERCISE 14-2

❑ Insert one of your diskettes in the A: drive and select 3½ Floppy (A:) from the All Folders pane.
❑ Make a folder on the A: drive called CLASSES and another called PROJECTS.
❑ Make two subfolders in the CLASSES folder called CAD-I and CAD-II.
❑ Rename the two subfolders to CAD-1 and CAD-2.
❑ Make two subfolders in the PROJECTS folder called P-100 and P-200.
❑ Copy a group of drawing files from the hard disk to one of the subfolders under either CLASSES or PROJECTS. Extend your selection of drawing files as described in this chapter.
❑ Check the contents pane to verify that the files were copied correctly. Now, delete the subfolder and all the files it contains.
❑ Delete all the folders created in this exercise.

FILE MANAGEMENT WITH WINDOWS EXPLORER

Keep an Exploring window open on your desktop at all times. You will often need to rename, copy, delete, and move files and folders. These management functions are quick and easy using Windows Explorer.

Copying Folders and Files

Copy folders and files using menu selections or accelerator keys as follows:
1. Open the folder you wish to copy from.
2. Select the file to be copied, then pick the Copy button, select Copy from the Edit pull-down menu, press [Ctrl]+[C], or right-click and select Copy from the shortcut menu (Figure 14-10). This copies the file to the Clipboard.

Figure 14-10.
If you right-click
when a file is
selected, this
shortcut menu
allows you to access
Windows Explorer
commands quickly.

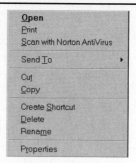

| |
| Open |
| Print |
| Scan with Norton AntiVirus |
| Send To ▶ |
| Cut |
| Copy |
| Create Shortcut |
| Delete |
| Rename |
| Properties |

3. Open the folder or drive you wish to copy to.
4. Pick the Paste button, select Paste from the Edit pull-down menu, press [Ctrl]+[V], or right-click and select Paste from the shortcut menu to paste the file from the Clipboard.

The same steps can be used to copy a folder or a group of files. Use one of the selection methods previously mentioned to highlight the group.

Moving Folders and Files

Moving folders and files is done in the same manner as copying, except that the Cut option is used instead of Copy:
1. Open the folder you wish to move an item from.
2. Select the file to be moved. Pick the Cut button, select Cut from the Edit pull-down menu, press [Ctrl]+[X], or right-click and select Cut from the shortcut menu. This deletes the file and places it in the Clipboard.
3. Open the folder or drive you wish to move the item to.
4. Pick the Paste button, select Paste from the Edit pull-down menu, press [Ctrl]+[V], or right-click and select Paste from the shortcut menu to paste the file from the Clipboard.

Drag-and-drop operations provide faster and easier ways to copy or move files and folders. These options are discussed later in this chapter.

Renaming Folders and Files

Before a folder or file can be renamed it must first be selected. Then proceed in the following manner:
1. Pick Rename from the File pull-down menu or right-click and select Rename from the shortcut menu.
2. Type the new name. Be sure to include the three-letter file extension if it is displayed.
3. Press [Enter] or pick anywhere on the screen.

You can also quickly rename a folder or file without using the Rename command as follows:
1. Pick the file or folder to select it.
2. Pick it again and a blinking cursor appears at the end of the name.
3. Type the new name and press [Enter] or pick anywhere on the screen.

If the files in the contents pane are displayed with the three-letter file extension, you must include the extension when renaming a file. If you omit the extension, a Windows alert informs you that the file may be unusable if the extension is changed. You can avoid this problem by doing the following:

1. Pick Folder Options... in the View pull-down menu.
2. Pick the View tab in the Folder Options dialog box.
3. Pick Hide file extensions for known file types.
4. Pick OK to exit.

By performing this operation, files in the contents pane are displayed without the three-letter extension. Therefore, when you rename a file, Windows automatically retains the file extension. This provides you with a fail-safe manner for renaming files.

Deleting Folders and Files

Windows 95, 98, and Windows NT store all deleted items in the Recycle Bin. Delete folders and files as follows:

1. Select the folder or file(s) to be deleted.
2. Pick the Delete button, select Delete from the File pull-down menu, press the [Delete] key, or right-click and select Delete from the shortcut menu.
3. The Confirm File Delete dialog box asks if you are sure you want to send the file(s) to the Recycle Bin. Pick Yes.

The Recycle Bin is a repository for all deleted files. See Figure 14-11. If for any reason you feel that a file has been deleted by mistake, open the Recycle Bin and remove the file as follows:

1. Display the Windows desktop.
2. Double-click on the Recycle Bin icon to open the Recycle Bin.
3. Select the files you wish to restore.
4. Pick Restore from the File pull-down menu. The files are removed from the Recycle Bin and returned to their original location prior to the deletion.

Figure 14-11.
The Recycle Bin is a repository for all deleted files.

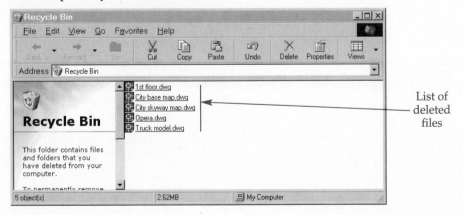

List of deleted files

CAUTION	Empty the Recycle Bin only when you are sure that its contents are no longer needed. Once the Recycle Bin has been emptied, you cannot recover the files.

Viewing the Properties of a File

You can quickly display detailed information about any folder or file as follows:

1. Select the file.
2. Pick Properties from the Edit pull-down menu or right-click and select Properties from the shortcut menu. The Properties dialog box is displayed. See Figure 14-12.

Creating a New Folder

Organizing the files on your hard disk is a very important component of computer system maintenance. It is often desirable to keep block symbols, hatch patterns, and script files in separate subfolders. Once you have created a new folder, you can move and copy files and subfolders to it from other locations on your hard disk.

1. Pick the drive or folder icon where you want the new folder to appear.
2. Pick Folder from the New cascading menu in the File pull-down menu. Alternatively, you can right-click in the contents pane, and then pick New and Folder from the shortcut menu. See Figure 14-13. A New Folder icon and label appear in the contents pane.
3. Type a new name and press [Enter]. The folder is ready to be used.

Avoid saving your files in the AutoCAD program directories or folders. It is best to create new folders for your work. Always check with your instructor or supervisor before creating new folders or performing any disk management function. The same naming conventions used for file names apply to folder names.

Figure 14-12.
The Properties dialog box displays details about the file.

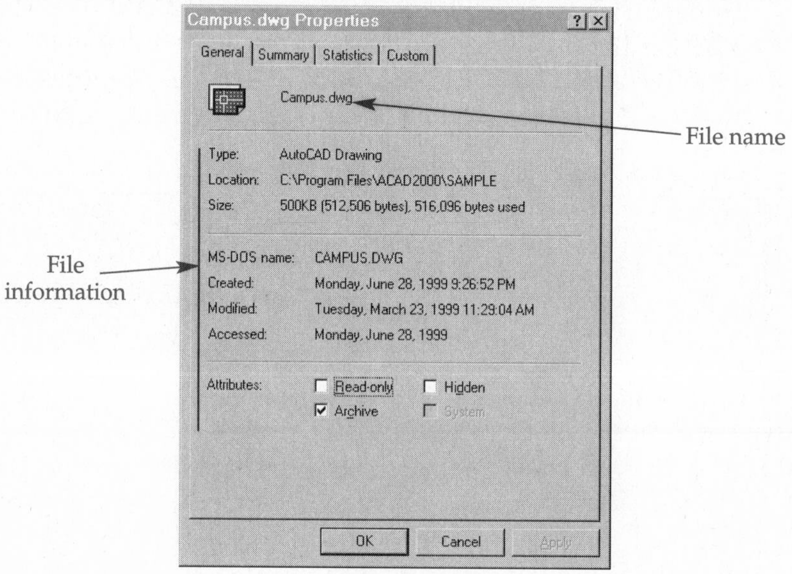
Campus.dwg Properties
General
Summary
Statistics
Custom
Campus.dwg
File name
Type: AutoCAD Drawing
Location: C:\Program Files\ACAD2000\SAMPLE
Size: 500KB (512,506 bytes), 516,096 bytes used
MS-DOS name: CAMPUS.DWG
Created: Monday, June 28, 1999 9:26:52 PM
Modified: Tuesday, March 23, 1999 11:29:04 AM
Accessed: Monday, June 28, 1999
File information
Attributes:
Read-only
Hidden
Archive
System
OK
Cancel
Apply

Figure 14-13.
Right-click in the
contents pane, then
pick New and Folder
from the cursor
menu to quickly
create a new folder.

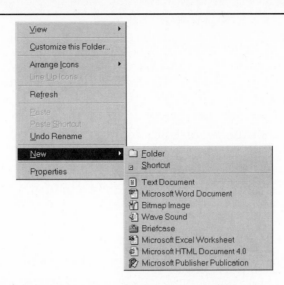

EXERCISE 14-3

❑ Insert one of your diskettes with drawings into the A: drive.
❑ Use the Windows Explorer to do the following:
  ❑ Copy one of your files and rename it using an .old file extension.
  ❑ Change the name of the file in the previous step to test.old.
  ❑ Copy and rename test.old to test-2.old.
  ❑ Delete all files with the .old extension.
  ❑ List the files on the diskette in the A: drive. Check to see whether there are any
    files with the .old extension.
❑ Close the Windows Explorer.

DISK OPERATIONS USING WINDOWS EXPLORER

A variety of disk operations can also be performed with the Windows Explorer.
These operations include formatting, labeling, and copying diskettes. Each of these
functions is located in the shortcut menu that appears after right-clicking on the disk
drive icon, Figure 14-14.

Figure 14-14.
This shortcut menu
appears after right-
clicking on the disk
drive icon.

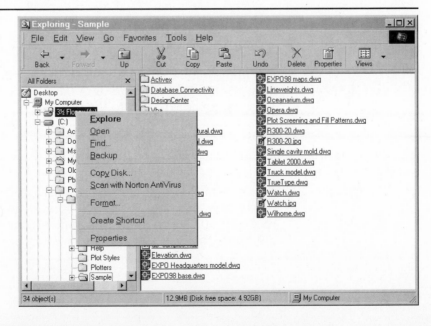

Formatting a Diskette

New diskettes must be formatted before they can be used. Although preformatted diskettes can be purchased, formatting is a process that is useful for thoroughly cleaning a diskette. The formatting process prepares a diskette so information can be copied to it. If the diskette you intend to format has previously been used, Windows Explorer detects this and informs you accordingly before it removes any existing data from the diskette. To format a diskette, do the following:

1. Insert a diskette in the appropriate disk drive.
2. Right-click on the diskette name or icon. Select Format... from the shortcut menu.
3. The Format dialog box then appears, Figure 14-15.
4. Specify the capacity of the diskette to be formatted in the Capacity: list box using the drop-down list.
5. If you want to provide a label for the diskette, enter the desired name in the Label: text box. A label is an identifying name for the diskette. The name is shown in the title bar of the directory window.
6. Pick the Start button to begin formatting the diskette.
7. When the formatting is complete, pick OK.

Figure 14-15.
A—The Windows 98 Format dialog box. B—The Windows NT Format dialog box.

Select capacity
Enter a label

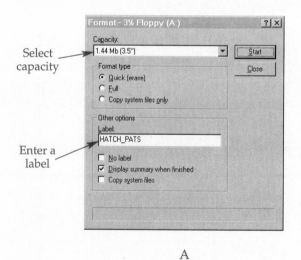

Select capacity
Enter a label

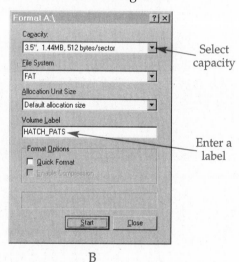

A   B

PROFESSIONAL TIP   Get in the habit of providing a volume label for each diskette you format. Write the volume label name on the adhesive label before attaching it to the diskette.

CAUTION Always use caution when formatting a diskette. Remember that in addition to preparing a new diskette, a full format erases any existing data. Unless you are running a disk recovery utility program, you *cannot* recover information on a diskette that is accidentally formatted.

Windows 98 and Windows NT differ somewhat in the options provided in the Format dialog box. Note the differences in Figure 14-15 as you read the items here.

Windows 98

- **Quick (erase).** Only file names (File Allocation Table, or FAT) are deleted. The diskette is not actually erased and is not checked for bad sectors or corrupt disk medium. The **Quick** option can only be used on diskettes that have been previously formatted.
- **Full.** A full format is the default in NT, but must be selected in 98. This executes a thorough check of the diskette and marks bad sectors, but takes longer than a quick format.
- **Copy system files only.** Makes a bootable disk without formatting.
- **No label.** Deletes current label from the diskette.
- **Display summary when finished.** Displays a dialog box that provides detailed information about the diskette when formatting is complete.
- **Copy system files.** Makes a bootable disk by copying system files, and formats the diskette.

Windows NT

- **File system.** The FAT file system is the standard DOS, Windows 3.x, and Windows 95 File Allocation Table system. When Windows NT is installed, you have the option of partitioning part or all of the hard disk as the NT File System (NTFS). The NTFS option is only available when formatting a hard drive.
- **Allocation Unit Size.** The smallest part of a diskette that is allocated to a file. The default setting is best for most uses.
- **Enable Compression.** Folders and files are compressed when saved to diskette.

Copying a Diskette

Throughout this text you have been advised to always make a backup copy of your AutoCAD drawings on portable storage media such as 3.5" diskettes and Zip disks. It is also a good idea to have a second backup of your original backup. You can easily copy the contents of one diskette to another using Windows Explorer. To copy a diskette, do the following:

1. Insert the source diskette in the drive you want to copy from. If your computer has two drives, you can insert the destination diskette in the second drive. The destination diskette is called the *copy to* diskette.
2. Right-click the drive icon for the source diskette in the All Folders pane.
3. Select Copy Disk... from the shortcut menu. The Copy Disk dialog box appears, Figure 14-16.
4. Labels and icons representing the diskette formats are shown in the Copy Disk dialog box. Select the appropriate icons for the Copy from: and the Copy to: disks.
5. Pick the Start button. A Copy Disk alert asks you to insert the diskette you want to copy from. Insert the proper diskette and pick OK. If you have selected to use two different disk drives, you'll be asked to insert both the source and destination

Figure 14-16.
The Copy Disk dialog box.

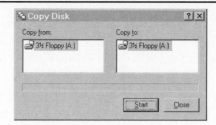

diskettes. If using a single disk drive computer, you will have to switch diskettes when prompted.

6. At the next Copy Disk alert, insert the diskette you want to copy to and pick OK.
7. The contents of the source diskette are then copied to the destination diskette.

 CAUTION The Copy Disk command not only copies, it formats! Therefore, there is no need to spend time formatting a diskette before making a copy. Be certain your destination diskette is blank or only has unneeded files on it.

Protecting Your Diskettes

Dust, heat, cold, magnets, cigarette smoke, and coffee do great damage to your diskettes. Placing your diskette on or near any other electrical or magnetic device can quickly ruin your files. This includes your digitizer tablet! A ringing telephone can even be a dangerous enemy of the diskette because of its magnetic field. Beyond physical damage, you or someone else could write over the files on a diskette, or put files on the wrong diskette, making them difficult or impossible to find.

The easiest way to protect the data on your diskette from accidental erasure is to use the write-protect tab. The write-protect tab is a small, sliding tab located on the bottom side of the diskette. Notice that the write-protect tab is in effect when it is moved toward the edge of the diskette. Use the point of a pen or your fingernail to slide the tab. See Figure 14-17.

When the tab is moved to the write-protect position, you cannot format, save, or copy files to that diskette. However, the files can be read from the diskette. Windows Explorer displays a dialog box with a write-protect error message if you attempt to format or save to a write-protected diskette. If you must use the diskette for writing or formatting purposes, simply move the write-protect tab to the appropriate position.

Figure 14-17.
To prevent your files from being erased, move the write-protect tab to the "read only" position.

Write protect

AutoCAD and its Applications—Basics

❑ Insert one of your blank diskettes into the A: drive.
❑ Use the Format command to format the diskette and label it PROBLEMS.
❑ Copy a drawing file from the Acad2000\Sample folder from the hard disk to the diskette.
❑ Use the Copy Disk command to make a backup copy of the PROBLEMS diskette.

Additional Disk Management Functions

The shortcut menu that is displayed by right-clicking on the diskette drive icon (Figure 14-14) provides several other functions for managing the contents of diskettes. The following list briefly describes these options:

- **Explore.** Changes the current Exploring window to reflect the contents of the diskette.
- **Open.** Opens a separate window that displays all folders and files in the diskette.
- **Find.** Opens the Find: All Files dialog box for the diskette.
- **Create Shortcut.** Allows you to create a shortcut icon on the desktop. When you double-click on this shortcut icon, a 3.5" Floppy window is opened, exactly like the Open command above.
- **Properties.** Opens the Properties dialog box for the diskette. The General tab displays general information about the diskette and provides a text box for naming the diskette. The Tools tab provides three tools that allow you to check the diskette for errors, back up the diskette to a tape drive, and defragment data stored on the diskette. The Compression tab provides information on how much additional storage space can be gained by compressing the diskette. Pick the Compress Drive... button to proceed. Check your *Windows 98* or *Windows NT Users Guide*, or use the Windows online help for additional information on these tools.

NOTE Many software applications place new options on the shortcut menu, so your menu may show additional options that are not listed here.

DRAG-AND-DROP OPERATIONS WITH WINDOWS EXPLORER

The "drag-and-drop" style interface in Windows makes many common Windows Explorer functions faster and easier. Drag-and-drop options are provided for copying, moving, and deleting files and folders. When you drag any file or folder to a new location on the same disk drive, the items are moved to the new location. Dragging an item to a different disk drive creates a copy on the second disk drive. If the default operation is not what you need, you can drag the files or folders using the second mouse button (the right-click button). When you drop the items, a shortcut menu appears listing the available options. For example, the shortcut menu shown in Figure 14-18 is displayed when dragging an item to an alternate location on the same disk drive. Because moving the file is the default operation, the **Move Here** option is shown in bold text. You can select from the other options or pick Cancel. To delete files or folders, you can drag them to the Recycle Bin icon on either the desktop or in the All Folders pane.

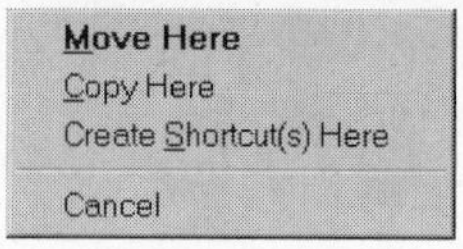

Figure 14-18.
The drag-and-drop
shortcut menu
provides additional
flexibility for drag-
and-drop operations.

Move Here
Copy Here
Create Shortcut(s) Here

Cancel

The Windows Explorer can also be used to dynamically drag-and-drop file icons into the AutoCAD drawing area. This powerful capability allows you to open drawings, insert drawing files as blocks, insert text files as multiline text, and import PostScript and raster files. Drag-and-drop can also be used to load menu, linetype, shape, script, and slide files, as well as AutoLISP and ARX applications

The following table lists the different kinds of drag-and-drop operations that can be used in AutoCAD. Also listed are the required file name extensions, the related AutoCAD commands, and the chapters in this text where additional command information can be found.

Operation	File Extension	Related Command	Related Chapter
Load a linetype file	LIN	**LINETYPE**	Chapter 4
Insert a text file	TXT	**MTEXT**	Chapter 8
Load a shape font	SHP	**COMPILE**	Chapter 8
Insert a drawing file	DWG	**INSERT**	Chapter 23
Open a drawing file	DWG	**OPEN**	Chapter 2
Print a drawing	DWG	**PLOT**	Chapter 10
Load a slide file	SLD	**VSLIDE**	Chapter 28
Run a script file	SCR	**SCRIPT**	Chapter 28
Insert a DXF file	DXF	**INSERT**	Chapter 14
Open a DXF file	DXF	**OPEN**	Chapter 14
Load a DXB file	DXB	**DXBIN**	Chapter 14

Additional files that can be used with drag-and-drop are discussed in *AutoCAD and its Applications—Advanced.* The following table lists those files.

Operation	File Extension	Related Command
Load ADS and ARX applications	EXE, ARX	**XLOAD**
Import a PostScript image	EPS, PS	**PSIN**
Load a menu file	MNU	**MENU**
Insert an AutoLISP routine	LSP	**LOAD**

Dragging and Dropping a Text File

You will learn in Chapter 23 that AutoCAD objects, such as text, can be saved to disk with the **WBLOCK** command and inserted into other drawing files. A text file created with a text editor outside of AutoCAD can also be inserted into a drawing using drag-and-drop if it is saved as a TXT file. To drag a text file into AutoCAD, do the following:

1. Start both AutoCAD and Windows Explorer. Arrange the display windows so that both are visible.
2. In the Exploring window, open the folder that contains the text file you want to insert.
3. Click the text file icon, drag it into the AutoCAD drawing area, and then release the mouse button. The text is inserted in the current text style and on the current layer.

The text file is inserted as an mtext object, and appears with grips. The location of the text can be quickly changed by using the grips.

External text files can be created with Notepad, WordPad, or your own ASCII text editor. Remember that the text file must have a TXT extension. Without this extension, a text file has no association with an application and cannot be inserted.

PROFESSIONAL TIP

If you use the right mouse button when dragging a text file into AutoCAD, a shortcut menu offers additional options. The **Insert here** option produces the same result as a regular drag-and-drop operation. Optionally, you can attach a hyperlink to an existing drawing object or cancel the operation. Using hyperlinks in AutoCAD is discussed in *AutoCAD 2000 and its Applications—Advanced*.

Using Drag-and-Drop to Print a Drawing

You can plot a drawing by dragging the drawing file icon directly to the appropriate printer icon. The drawing file icon you select is opened in the drawing editor using the **FILEOPEN** command. This command allows you to open a file without using a dialog box, regardless of the setting of the **FILEDIA** system variable. To use the **FILEOPEN** command, AutoCAD 2000 must first set Single Document Interface mode active by setting the **SDI** system variable to 1. Once the drawing appears in the drawing area, the **Plot** dialog box is displayed. You can then modify the printing parameters as required and print the drawing. After exiting the **Plot** dialog box, **SDI** is reset to its previous value.

To print a drawing on the system printer using drag-and-drop, do the following:
1. Launch Windows Explorer.
2. Display the Windows desktop and double-click to open My Computer. See Figure 14-19A.
3. Double-click on the Printers folder to display the Printers window. See Figure 14-19B. Arrange the desktop so both the Printers window and Exploring window are visible.
4. In Windows Explorer, select the file you wish to print and drag it to the desired printer icon in the Printers window. Release the mouse button.
5. The AutoCAD program window is moved to the front, the file is opened, and the **Plot** dialog box is displayed.
6. Make any necessary adjustments to the plotting parameters. Pick **OK** to print the drawing.

NOTE

Before you can use this method, you may need to edit the properties of AutoCAD drawing files. This is done by picking Folder Options... from the View pull-down menu in the Windows Explorer to display the Folder Options dialog box. Pick the File Types tab and select AutoCAD Drawing Files from the Registered file types: list, then select the Edit... button. In the Edit File Type dialog box, highlight the print option in the Actions: list and pick the Edit... button to display the Editing action for type: AutoCAD Drawing dialog box. Finally, select the Browse... button next to the Application used to perform action: text box and locate the acad.exe file in the Acad2000 program folder. Pick OK and apply the changes, then exit from the dialog session. Be sure to check with your instructor or system administrator before making any changes to the operating system.

Figure 14-19.
A—The My Computer window. B—Double-click on the Printers folder to display the Printers window.

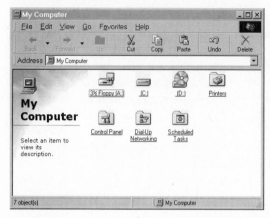

A

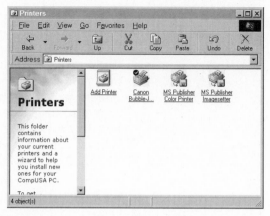

B

PROFESSIONAL TIP

You can place a printer icon on the Windows desktop and avoid having to open the My Computer and Printers windows. Simply create a Windows shortcut by pressing the [Ctrl] key, then picking and dragging the printer icon to a location on the desktop. The label below this icon will change to "Shortcut to…". To change the label, pick the name to highlight it and then pick it again to edit. Type a new name, then press [Enter]. Now when you need to print a document, just drag the file name from Windows Explorer and drop it on the new printer icon.

Dragging and Dropping Drawing Files into AutoCAD

One or more drawing files can be easily opened in AutoCAD using drag-and-drop. It is important to remember that when you want to open a file, you need to drag it to the *title bar* of the AutoCAD 2000 program window.

1. Start both AutoCAD and Windows Explorer.
2. Arrange the display so that both windows are visible.
3. Select any number of drawing files in Windows Explorer.
4. Drag the selected file icons to the title bar of the AutoCAD program window.
5. Each drawing is then opened in a separate drawing window.

Drag-and-drop can also be used to insert any drawing into the current drawing session. This method is very similar to the **INSERT** command discussed in Chapter 23. Like **INSERT**, the drawing you drag-and-drop becomes a block. Therefore, be sure to explode it after insertion, if necessary. To insert a drawing, drag it into the drawing area of the drawing you want to insert it into.

Drawings can only be inserted one at a time. Using the right mouse button when dragging files into the drawing area displays a shortcut menu with the following options:

- **Insert here.** Inserts the drawing the same as a regular drag-and-drop.
- **Open.** Opens the drawing in a new drawing window.
- **Create Xref.** Attaches an external reference to the selected drawing using the drop point as the insertion location and default scale and rotation.
- **Create Hyperlink here.** Creates a hyperlink to the drawing attached to a selected object.
- **Cancel.** Stops the drag-and-drop operation.

AutoCAD and its Applications—Basics

❏ Launch both Windows Explorer and AutoCAD. Arrange the display windows so that both are visible.
❏ Open a directory containing one or more DWG files.
❏ Using the methods described previously, drag one or more drawing file icons on to the AutoCAD program window title bar.
❏ Drag a drawing file icon into a drawing window. Answer the prompts for insertion point, scale, and rotation angle, and then explode the inserted drawing.
❏ Use Notepad to create a simple text file. Make the notes specific to your particular application. Save the file as a TXT file.
❏ Activate the AutoCAD graphics window.
❏ Drag the text file you created with Notepad into the drawing window area.

NOTE This chapter has introduced you to only some of the features within Windows Explorer. Become familiar with *all* the functions offered by this useful tool. By making Windows Explorer an integral part of your daily work, you can greatly increase your productivity.

RECOVERING A DAMAGED DRAWING

A damaged drawing file is one that has been corrupted and cannot be loaded into the AutoCAD drawing editor with the **OPEN** command. Drawings can be corrupted in the following ways:

• A bad or corrupted diskette.
• Running out of disk space during a drawing session.
• Power failures.
• Hardware or software problems.

A valuable resource for recovering lost or damaged drawing data is the backup file. By default, AutoCAD creates a BAK file when you save a drawing—so a BAK file stores the drawing prior to your most recent save operation. A BAK file is also a drawing file, but it uses a different file extension.

AutoCAD does not allow you to open BAK files directly. To open a BAK file, it must be renamed to use a .dwg file extension. Note that Windows Explorer must display file extensions to be able to change them.

When a BAK file does not provide the best solution, AutoCAD provides a method for recovering most damaged files. You can type RECOVER at the Command: prompt, or select **Recover...** from the **Drawing Utilities** cascading menu in the **File** pull-down menu. This displays the **Select File** dialog box. Select the proper folder and file and AutoCAD attempts to recover the damaged drawing. If it is successful, the file is loaded into the drawing editor, and it can be worked on normally. If you do not save the file before exiting AutoCAD, the recovered drawing is lost.

There is also an automatic saving feature in AutoCAD that creates a temporary backup file during a drawing session. This file can be a valuable backup if you find your drawing is corrupted as a result of an improper termination or system crash. By default, AutoCAD names the automatically saved file *DrawingName_n_n_nnnn*.sv$ and saves it in the C:\Temp folder. If you need to use this file, you must rename it as a DWG file in Windows Explorer.

USING THE AUDIT COMMAND

You can perform a diagnostic check on your drawing files with the **AUDIT** command. This checks for and corrects errors. You have the option of fixing errors or leaving them.

```
Command: AUDIT↵
Fix any errors detected? [Yes/No] ⟨N⟩: ↵
 1            Blocks audited
 55           Blocks audited
Pass  1  539       objects audited
Pass  2  539       objects audited
Pass  3  5500      objects audited
Total errors found 0 fixed 0
Command:
```

If you answer no, as in the above example, all errors are listed for your reference, but they are not fixed. To fix errors in the transferred drawing, type Y at the Fix any errors detected? prompt.

AutoCAD displays the errors and notifies you that they are fixed like this:

```
 3            Blocks audited
Pass  1  29        objects audited
Pass  2  14        objects audited
Total errors found 2 fixed 2
```

If the system variable **AUDITCTL** is set to 1 (on), AutoCAD automatically creates an audit report that lists the corrections made. This report is given the same name as the drawing, but has an ADT file extension. The file is placed in the same directory as the drawing. This is an ASCII text file (American Standard Code for Information Interchange). You can open this file and read the information using any ASCII text editor, such as Windows Notepad or WordPad.

Listing the Audit Report

It is not necessary to leave AutoCAD to display the audit report. Simply pick Programs, Accessories, and then Notepad from the Start menu.

To list the audit report, first select Open... from the File menu. Then, select the audit file. Pick OK and the contents of the file are displayed on the screen. After reviewing the file, you can exit Notepad.

UNDERSTANDING AUTOCAD'S TEMPORARY FILES

AutoCAD maintains several temporary files while you are working on a drawing. You might consider these as "worksheets" that AutoCAD opens, much like the notes, references, sketches, and calculations you may have scattered around your desk. These files are created automatically to store portions of the AutoCAD program not currently in use, and for information related to the current drawing file. These files are critical to AutoCAD's operation, and must be maintained and safeguarded properly.

Program Swap Files

AutoCAD uses a virtual memory system. *Virtual memory* is a combination of memory and hard disk space. The main program file for AutoCAD is named acad.exe. It is a very large file—over 6.6MB. If there is not enough room in your computer's physical memory (RAM) to store the program, AutoCAD creates *pages* of the program in free space on your hard disk drive.

A virtual memory system keeps only the part of the program that is currently being used in physical memory. If additional portions of the program are needed, AutoCAD creates a page on the hard disk and writes the least-used portion of the program to that page. The new portion of the program that is requested is written to physical memory. Thus, AutoCAD creates a *paging* system using virtual memory. The least-used pages are written to a page called a *swap file*, and are held there until needed again.

When required, AutoCAD's paging system automatically creates and maintains a swap file. These files are critical to AutoCAD, and must never be deleted while you are in a drawing session. Should you experience an improper termination of AutoCAD, and the drawing file is not saved properly, these swap files may be left open. In that case, the files are no longer of use and can be deleted, but only *after* you have exited AutoCAD.

Temporary Files

The second piece of AutoCAD's virtual memory system is called the *pager*. This works similar to the swap file system, but creates temporary storage space for drawing file information. The entire contents of a small drawing may fit into your computer's physical memory, but as the drawing grows larger, portions of it must be temporarily removed. AutoCAD creates a *page file* for the least-used portion of your drawing, and opens the physical memory for new drawing data. When the drawing data contained in the page file is needed, it is *paged* back into memory. These temporary files are given the file extension of AC$. These are vital files and must never be deleted while working in AutoCAD.

If AutoCAD should terminate improperly, these page files are left open in the temporary files directory—usually C:\Windows\Temp. If AutoCAD is no longer running, the AC$ files left behind are no longer of any use, and can be deleted. Always delete these files with Windows Explorer, and never while you are working in AutoCAD.

Creating a Workspace for Temporary Files

The default workspace for AutoCAD's temporary files is C:\Windows\Temp. You can create a folder on your hard drive and tell AutoCAD to always use that folder for storage of temporary files. Use the following procedure to allocate space for these files.
1. Pick **Options...** in the **Tools** pull-down menu or right-click and select **Options...** from the shortcut menu. This displays the **Options** dialog box.
2. Pick the **Files** tab.
3. Pick the + symbol to the left of Temporary Drawing File Location. The current location is displayed. The default is C:\Windows\Temp in Windows 95/98, and C:\Temp in Windows NT.
4. Pick the current directory (folders) path to select it.
5. Pick the **Browse...** button to display the **Browse for Folder** dialog box.
6. Find the folder you want to use for temporary files and select it. Pick **OK** to exit.

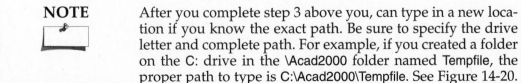

| NOTE | After you complete step 3 above you, can type in a new location if you know the exact path. Be sure to specify the drive letter and complete path. For example, if you created a folder on the C: drive in the \Acad2000 folder named Tempfile, the proper path to type is C:\Acad2000\Tempfile. See Figure 14-20. |

Figure 14-20.
The location of temporary drawing files can be specified in the **Options** dialog box.

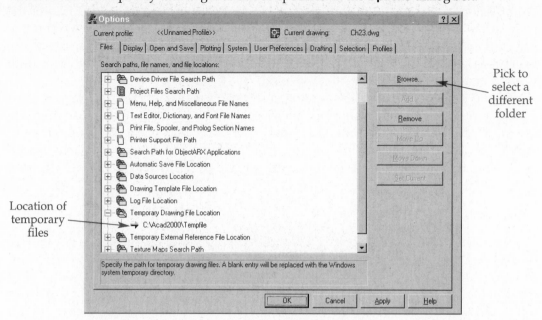

Pick to select a different folder

Location of temporary files

IMPORTING AND EXPORTING FILES

AutoCAD provides you with the ability to work with files other than DWG files. You can import external data into a drawing, or export the current drawing to files that can be used in other programs for rendering, animation, desktop publishing, presentations, stereolithography, and solid modeling. This section provides a brief overview of AutoCAD's capabilities in importing and exporting a variety of different files.

DXF Files

The DXF file format is one of the most commonly used methods for sharing drawing files with CAD applications other than AutoCAD. *DXF* is an acronym for *drawing interchange format*. A DXF file is simply an ASCII text file that defines the objects and settings within a drawing.

You can save an entire drawing or just selected objects as a DXF file using either the **SAVEAS** or **WBLOCK** command. When using **SAVEAS**, select the desired DXF version from the **Save as type:** list. You can save the DXF file to be compatible with AutoCAD 2000 or with previous releases of AutoCAD. See Figure 14-21. Pick the **Options...** button to access the **DXF Options** settings in the **Saveas Options** dialog box. The available options are as follows:

- **ASCII.** Writes the DXF file in a standard ASCII text format.
- **BINARY.** Writes the DXF file using a binary file format. This option can reduce the size of the translated file by 25% or more.
- **Select objects.** Allows selection of specific drawing objects to be saved to the DXF file.
- **Save thumbnail preview image.** Saves a preview image with the file.
- **Decimal places of accuracy (0 to 16).** Specifies the decimal places of precision for ASCII format DXF files.

To write a DXF file using the **WBLOCK** command, specify a file name with a .dxf extension in the **File Name:** field in the **Write Block** dialog box. The **WBLOCK** command automatically creates an AutoCAD 2000 format DXF file.

Figure 14-21.
The **Save Drawing As** dialog box allows you to save a drawing as one of four different forms of DXF file.

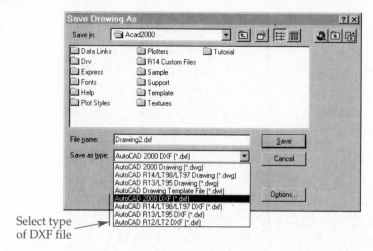

Select type
of DXF file

Existing DXF files can be opened directly with the **OPEN** command, or their contents can be inserted into the current drawing using the **INSERT** command. To access DXF files in the file selection dialog boxes displayed by these commands, specify DXF (*.dxf) in the **Files of type:** list. DXF files only show a preview if they were created with AutoCAD 2000 and the **Save thumbnail preview image** option was used.

DXF applications

There are several applications where you will want to convert an AutoCAD file to DXF format. The most common application is sharing drawings with CAM systems or other CAD systems. Numerical control (NC) programs also use DXF files. The file is used to translate the shape and features of a machine part to code that can be used for lathes, milling machines, and drill presses. In addition, desktop publishing programs use DXF files to translate drawings into images that can be inserted into a page layout. Also, programs that perform stress analysis and calculations often rely on DXF drawings.

Importing a Scanned File

Scanning is the process of creating an electronic file from a hard copy. Scanners reflect light off the hard copy and translate this data into an electronic file. Many scanning programs create a DXB (drawing interchange binary) file after scanning an existing paper drawing with a camera or plotter-mounted scanner. The file created is in binary code. The **DXBIN** command converts this code into drawing data. This drawing data becomes an AutoCAD drawing file with a .dwg extension.

To import a DXB file, pick **Drawing Exchange Binary...** from the **Insert** pull-down menu, or type DXBIN at the Command: prompt. The **Select DXB File** dialog box appears. Select the scanned file and pick the **Open** button. You can then edit the drawing using typical AutoCAD commands. After you enter a file name, it can then be edited and saved as a drawing file.

AutoCAD Release 13 and Release 14 Files

The **SAVEAS** command allows you to save an AutoCAD 2000 drawing file in Release 13 and 14 format. Pick **Save As...** in the **File** pull-down menu to display the **Save Drawing As** dialog box. Pick the **Save as type:** drop-down list to see the types of DWG files that can be saved. See Figure 14-22. You can save the current drawing as a

Figure 14-22.
The **Save Drawing As** dialog box allows you to save a drawing in a format usable by previous releases of AutoCAD.

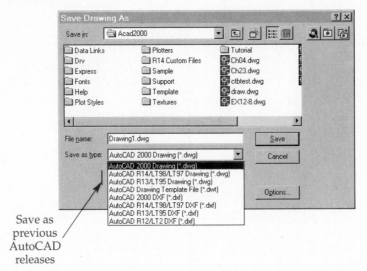

Save as previous AutoCAD releases

Release 13 or Release 14 drawing file, or you can save the drawing as a DXF file compatible with Release 12.

When saving as earlier release drawings, some drawing information specific to AutoCAD 2000 may be lost. Most of this information is restored if the drawing is then reopened in AutoCAD 2000.

3D Studio Files

3D Studio VIZ® and 3D Studio MAX® are Autodesk products that allow you to design, render, and animate 3D models. You can export or import 3D Studio files with AutoCAD 2000. When you type 3DSOUT at the Command: prompt to export a 3D Studio file, you are prompted to select objects. Select all the 3D objects you wish to export and press [Enter]. The **3D Studio Output File** dialog box is displayed. Enter the file name in the **File name:** text box. Press [Enter] or pick **Save** when you are finished. Exporting a 3D Studio file can also be executed using the **EXPORT** command and then picking the **3D Studio (*.3ds)** file type in the **Export Data** dialog box.

You can import an existing 3D Studio file into AutoCAD by selecting **3D Studio...** from the **Insert** pull-down menu. The **3D Studio File Import** dialog box is displayed. Select the appropriate 3DS file from the list and press [Enter]. You can also import a 3D Studio file by typing 3DSIN at the Command: prompt.

Solid Model Files

A *solid* is a 3D object composed of a specific material and possessing unique characteristics related to its shape and composition. These characteristics are called *mass properties*. Solids are created in AutoCAD with one of several commands found in the **Solids** cascading menu of the **Draw** pull-down menu.

The term *solid modeling* refers to the process of constructing a part from one or more 3D solid shapes called *primitives* and performing any necessary editing functions to create the final product. This procedure is discussed in detail in *AutoCAD 2000 and its Applications—Advanced*.

A solid model is frequently used with analyzing and testing software and in part manufacturing. AutoCAD drawings can be converted into a file that can be used for these purposes. To do so, use the **ACISOUT** command. Choose **Export...** from the **File** pull-down menu. Pick **ACIS (*.sat)** in the **Save as type:** drop-down list of the **Export**

Data dialog box. When you pick **OK**, you are prompted to select objects. Use any of the standard selection methods to choose the solid objects, then press [Enter]. If ACISOUT is typed at the Command: prompt, the **Create ACIS File** dialog box is displayed instead of the **Export Data** dialog box. Notice that SAT file is the default setting. Do not change this. Type the file name in the **File name:** text box and press [Enter] or pick **Save**. The SAT file is stored in ASCII format.

Solid model data stored in the SAT file can be read back into AutoCAD using the **ACISIN** command. When you enter this command, the **Select ACIS File** dialog box is displayed. Pick the file from the list, then pick **Open** or press [Enter]. The **ACISIN** command is also activated by picking **ACIS File...** in the **Insert** pull-down menu.

PROFESSIONAL TIP   The ASCII file created by the **ACISOUT** command may be from three to four times smaller than the DWG file. For this reason, it may be efficient to store 3D solid models as SAT files rather than DWG files. When you need to work with the model for any purpose in AutoCAD, simply use the **ACISIN** command. This command creates solid objects from the model data stored in the SAT file.

Stereolithography Files

Stereolithography is a technology where a plastic prototype 3D model is created using a computer-generated solid model, a laser, and a vat of liquid polymer. This technology is also referred to as *rapid prototyping* because a prototype 3D model can be designed and formed in a short amount of time, without using standard manufacturing processes. Most software used to create a stereolithograph can read an STL file. AutoCAD can export a drawing file to the STL format, but *cannot* import an STL file.

After entering the **STLOUT** command, you are prompted to select a single object. Select one object and press [Enter]. You are then asked if you want to create a binary STL file. If you answer no to this prompt, an ASCII file is created. Keep in mind that a binary STL file may be at least five times smaller than the ASCII STL file. After you choose the type of file to create, the **Create STL File** dialog box is displayed. Type the file name in the **File name:** text box and pick **Save** or press [Enter].

Postscript Files

PostScript is a copyrighted page description language developed by Adobe Systems. This language is widely used in the desktop publishing industry. AutoCAD drawing files can be exported to the EPS PostScript file format by typing PSOUT at the Command: prompt. The **Create PostScript File** dialog box is displayed. You can also pick **Export...** from the **File** pull-down menu to display the **Export Data** dialog box. Then, pick **Encapsulated PS (*.eps)** in the file type drop-down list. Type the file name in the **File name:** text box and pick **Save** or press [Enter].

When a PostScript file is selected for export, the **Options...** button is activated. Pick this to view the **Export Options** dialog box. This allows you to fine-tune the content and appearance of the exported EPS file. The use of PostScript files is discussed in detail in *AutoCAD and its Applications—Advanced*.

PostScript files can be imported into AutoCAD by picking **Encapsulated Postscript...** from the **Insert** pull-down menu. The **Select Postscript File** dialog box is displayed. Then, pick **Encapsulated PS (*.eps)**. Type the file name in the **File Name:** text box and pick **Open** or press [Enter].

Additional Files

Three additional files are listed in the **Export Data** dialog box and are defined here.

- **Metafile (.wmf).** A Windows file that contains vector information. It can be scaled and retain its resolution. See *AutoCAD and its Applications—Advanced* for a detailed discussion of metafiles.
- **DXX Extract (.dxx).** An extract file of attribute information contained in a block. This file is created using the **ATTEXT** command, which is discussed in Chapter 25.
- **Bitmap (.bmp).** A *bitmap* is a digital image composed of bits or screen pixels. Also referred to as a *raster image,* it contains no vector information, as does the metafile. Bitmaps are discussed in *AutoCAD 2000 and its Applications—Advanced.*

Chapter Test

Answer the following questions on a separate sheet of paper.

1. What is a file type extension?
2. What types of files are identified by the following extensions?
   A. BAK
   B. LIN
   C. MNU
   D. PLT
   E. BMP
   F. EXE
3. How do you launch Windows Explorer?
4. How do you list all files on the diskette in the A: drive?
5. In the Windows Explorer, how do you open a folder in the All Folders list box to view its files in the contents pane?
6. Using Windows Explorer, how do you select several files that are scattered randomly throughout the file list?
7. What is the procedure for changing a file name?
8. How can a file be moved to a new location?
9. How are files initially deleted?
10. How are files removed from the Recycle Bin to prevent being permanently deleted?
11. What two panes compose the Exploring window?
12. Write the correct path name for a drawing file named houseplan located in the Architectural subfolder, which is a branch of the Projects folder on the C: hard disk drive.
13. How can you select a consecutive group of items?
14. Which AutoCAD command is activated by dragging and dropping a drawing file into AutoCAD?
15. What three-letter file extension is valid when using drag-and-drop to place text in an AutoCAD drawing?
16. What is the purpose of the Exploring window *split bar*?
17. Describe the right-clicking process for creating a new folder.
18. How can 3.5" diskettes be protected to prevent data from being written to them accidentally?
19. How can a damaged file be recovered?
20. What command allows you to run a diagnostic check of a drawing file?
21. What type of memory system does AutoCAD use to create pages of the program on the hard disk?
22. What is the name of the backup drawing file that AutoCAD creates automatically?

23. Define the following abbreviations.
    A. DXF.
    B. DXB.
24. What commands can be used to create a DXF file?
25. What commands can be used to access the contents of an existing DXF file?
26. List some of the programs that can use DXF files.
27. When would you use the **DXBIN** command?
28. Name five types of files that can be imported into AutoCAD.
29. Why might it be more efficient to store solid models in the form of SAT files rather than as drawing files?
30. What is an STL file and what is it used for?

Drawing Problems

Obtain the permission of your instructor or system administrator before creating or deleting folders, formatting or labeling diskettes, deleting files, or using any Windows Explorer command that can alter the structure of the hard disk files and directories.

1. Make backup copies of all your diskettes. Use the Copy command in Windows Explorer. Copy the files in two different ways.
    A. Copy all DWG files to the new diskette. Then copy all BAK files to the new diskette.
    B. Copy a second diskette, or recopy the first diskette.
    C. List the files on your backup diskette. Be sure that files with both .dwg and .bak extensions have been copied. Then rename all files with the .bak extension to have an .old extension.

2. Get a printed listing of the files contained on one diskette. Ask your instructor or supervisor for assistance if you are not familiar with the printer.

3. Load one of your simple drawings into the AutoCAD graphics window. Create a DXF file of the drawing. Generate a printed copy of the contents of the DXF file.

4. This problem involves making new subfolders and copying drawing files to them.
    A. Make your own subfolder under the Acad2000 folder. Name it using your initials.
    B. Make the new subfolder current.
    C. Copy all your drawing files from one 3.5" diskette to the subfolder.
    D. Make a subfolder within your new directory and name it Bak.
    E. Make the Bak subfolder current.
    F. Copy all of your BAK files into the Bak subfolder.
    G. Open a separate window for each of your subfolders.

5. Make a new subfolder of the folder you created in Problem 4. Name the new subfolder Test.
    A. Copy the contents of the Bak subfolder into Test.
    B. Display the contents of the Test subfolder in the contents pane.
    C. Rename one of the files in the Test subfolder to hey.you.
    D. Use the Search command and list all files with a .you file extension.
    E. Copy the hey.you file to the Bak subfolder and rename it who.me.
    F. Use the Search command and list all files with a .me file extension.
    G. Copy who.me to one of your 3.5" diskettes and name it yes.you.
    H. Delete the three files you just created.
    I. Activate the Bak subfolder and delete it and all the files it contains.

6. Format four diskettes in a row without exiting the Format dialog box. Provide volume labels for the diskettes as they are formatted. When all formatting is complete, change the names of each diskette label without formatting the diskettes again.

 7. Use the copy disk option of Windows to make backup copies of all your 3.5″ diskettes that are used for drawing and data file storage. Label the diskettes that are copied with the same labels as the originals, but add a designation that indicates either "backup" or "copy".

 8. Create a diskette that you use only for storage of DXF files. Open your drawing files and save them as DXF files to the diskette. Keep this diskette for backup purposes.

 9. If you have access to a scanner, create a DXB file from an old, hand-drawn print. Import the DXB file using the **DXBIN** command. Compare the new AutoCAD drawing with the original.

 10. Use one of the previous problems to fix errors that may exist in the transferred file using the **AUDIT** command.

CHAPTER 15

Introduction to Polylines and Multilines

Learning Objectives

After completing this chapter, you will be able to:

- Use the **PLINE** command to draw polyline objects.
- Draw objects with the **TRACE** command.
- Explain the functions of the **UNDO** and **REDO** commands.
- Compare the results of using the **FILL** mode on and off.
- Use the **MLINE** command to draw multilines.
- Create your own multiline styles with the **MLSTYLE** command.
- Edit multiline intersections, corners, and vertices.
- Perform drawing tasks with the **SKETCH** command.

Polylines and multilines are two AutoCAD features that provide you with endless possibilities for design and drafting applications. This chapter introduces you to the use of polylines and fully explains how to create drawing features with multilines. You will also see how to sketch freehand with AutoCAD. A complete discussion of editing polylines is provided in Chapter 16.

The term *polyline* is composed of the words "poly" and "line." *Poly* means *many*. A *polyline* is a single object that can be made up of one or more varied-width line segments. Polylines are drawn with the **PLINE** command and its various options. The **TRACE** command, which is similar to the **PLINE** command, is also introduced in this chapter.

Multilines are combinations of parallel lines consisting of individual lines called *elements.* Multilines can have up to 16 individual line elements. You can offset the elements as needed to create a desired pattern for any field of drafting (for example, architectural, schematic, or mechanical drafting). Multilines are drawn using the **MLINE** command and its options.

INTRODUCTION TO DRAWING POLYLINES

The **PLINE** command is used to draw polylines and any related objects made up of line segments. Polylines have advantages over normal lines for the following reasons:

- Polylines can be drawn as thick or tapered lines.
- They have much more flexibility than lines drawn with the **TRACE** command.
- They can be used with any linetype.

- They can be edited using advanced editing features.
- Closed polygons can be drawn.
- The area or perimeter of a polyline object can be determined easily.
- Arcs and straight lines of varying thickness can be joined as single objects.

The **PLINE** command is similar to the **LINE** command. However, there are additional options, and all segments of a polyline are treated as a single object. To draw a polyline, you can pick the **Polyline** button from the **Draw** toolbar, pick **Polyline** from the **Draw** pull-down menu, or type PL or PLINE at the Command: prompt:

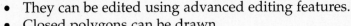

> Command: **PL** *or* **PLINE.**↵
> Specify start point: *(select a point)*
> Current line-width is 0.0000
> Specify next point or [Arc/Close/Halfwidth/Length/Undo/Width]: *(select the next point)*

A line width of 0.0000 produces a line of minimum width. If this is acceptable, you may select the endpoint of the line. If additional line segments are added to the first line, the endpoint of the first line automatically becomes the starting point of the next line. Press [Enter] to end the **PLINE** command and return to the Command: prompt.

Setting the Polyline Width

If it is necessary to change the line width, use the **Width** option after you enter the **PLINE** command and select the first point. The sequence is as follows:

> Command: **PL** *or* **PLINE.**↵
> Specify start point: *(select a point)*
> Current line-width is 0.0000
> Specify next point or [Arc/Close/Halfwidth/Length/Undo/Width]: **W.**↵

When the **Width** option is selected, you are asked to specify the starting and ending widths of the line. The starting width value that you specify becomes the default setting for the ending width. Therefore, to keep the line the same width, press [Enter] at the second prompt. If a tapered line is desired, enter different values for the starting and ending widths.

The following command sequence draws the line shown in Figure 15-1. Notice that the starting and ending points of the line are located at the center of the line.

> Command: **PL** *or* **PLINE.**↵
> Specify start point: **4,4.**↵
> Current line-width is 0.0000
> Specify next point or [Arc/Close/Halfwidth/Length/Undo/Width]: **W.**↵
> Specify starting width <0.0000>: **.25.**↵
> Specify ending width <0.2500>: .↵
> Specify next point or [Arc/Close/Halfwidth/Length/Undo/Width]: **8,4.**↵
> Specify next point or [Arc/Close/Halfwidth/Length/Undo/Width]: .↵
> Command:

Figure 15-1.
A thick polyline drawn using the **Width** option of the **PLINE** command.

Start point (4,4)　　　　　　　　　　　　　　　　　　Endpoint (8,4)

Drawing a Tapered Polyline

Enter different starting and ending widths if you want to draw a tapered polyline, Figure 15-2. In the following example, the starting width is .25 units and the ending width is .5 units:

```
Command: PL or PLINE↵
Specify start point: 4,4↵
Current line-width is 0.0000
Specify next point or [Arc/Close/Halfwidth/Length/Undo/Width]: W↵
Specify starting width <0.0000>: .25↵
Specify ending width <0.2500>: .5↵
Specify next point or [Arc/Close/Halfwidth/Length/Undo/Width]: 8,4↵
Specify next point or [Arc/Close/Halfwidth/Length/Undo/Width]: ↵
Command:
```

The **Width** option of the **PLINE** command can be used to draw an arrowhead. To do so, specify 0 as the starting width and then use any desired ending width.

Figure 15-2.
The **PLINE Width** option can be used to draw a wide tapered polyline.

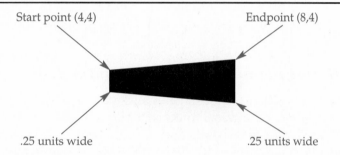

Start point (4,4)   Endpoint (8,4)

.25 units wide   .25 units wide

Using the Halfwidth Option

The **Halfwidth** option of the **PLINE** command allows you to specify the width of the polyline from the center to one side. After picking the first point of the polyline, enter the **Halfwidth** option and specify values for the starting and ending half-widths. Notice that the polyline in Figure 15-3 is twice as wide as the polyline in Figure 15-2.

```
Specify next point or [Arc/Close/Halfwidth/Length/Undo/Width]: H↵
Specify starting half-width <0.0000>: .25↵
Specify ending half-width <0.2500>: .5↵
```

Figure 15-3.
Specifying the width of a polyline with the **Halfwidth** option of the **PLINE** command. Notice that a starting value of .25 produces a polyline width of .5 units, and an ending value of .5 produces a polyline width of 1 unit.

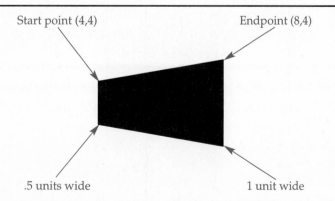

Start point (4,4)   Endpoint (8,4)

.5 units wide   1 unit wide

Using the Length Option

The **Length** option of the **PLINE** command allows you to draw another polyline having the same angle as the previous polyline. After drawing a polyline, reissue the **PLINE** command and pick a starting point. Then, enter the **Length** option and give the desired length:

    Command: **PL** *or* **PLINE**↵
    Specify start point: *(pick a starting point for the first polyline)*
    Current line-width is 0.0000
    Specify next point or [Arc/Close/Halfwidth/Length/Undo/Width]: *(pick an endpoint for the first polyline)*
    Specify next point or [Arc/Close/Halfwidth/Length/Undo/Width]: ↵
    Command: ↵
    PLINE Specify start point: *(pick a starting point for the second polyline)*
    Current line-width is 0.0000
    Specify next point or [Arc/Close/Halfwidth/Length/Undo/Width]: **L**↵
    Specify length of line: *(enter or pick any desired length for the second polyline)*
    Specify next point or [Arc/Close/Halfwidth/Length/Undo/Width]: ↵
    Command:

The second polyline is drawn at the same angle as the previous polyline, and at the length you specify.

Undoing Previously Drawn Polylines

While inside the **PLINE** command, you can use the **Undo** option to erase the last polyline segment drawn. To do so, enter U at the prompt line and then press [Enter]. Each time you use the **Undo** option, another polyline segment is erased. A quick way to go back and correct the polyline while remaining in the **PLINE** command is as follows:

    Specify next point or [Arc/Close/Halfwidth/Length/Undo/Width]: **U**↵
    Specify next point or [Arc/Close/Halfwidth/Length/Undo/Width]:

After you press [Enter], the last polyline segment drawn is automatically removed. However, the cursor remains attached to the end of the polyline segment that was drawn before the undone segment. You can now continue to draw additional polyline segments, or type U and press [Enter] again to undo another segment. You can use the **Undo** option to remove all of the polyline segments up to the first point of the polyline. The segments are removed in reverse order (from the order in which they were drawn).

U
[Ctrl]+[Z]

Edit
➥ **Undo**

Standard
toolbar

Undo

The **U** command (*not* the **Undo** option of the **PLINE** command) works in much the same way. However, the **U** command can be used to undo any previous commands. This is done after a command has been completed by picking the **Undo** button from the **Standard** toolbar, picking **Undo** from the **Edit** pull-down menu, pressing the [Ctrl]+[Z] key combination, or entering U at the Command: prompt. The **U** command can also be activated by right-clicking in the drawing area and selecting **Undo** from the shortcut menu. AutoCAD gives you a message indicating which command was undone:

    Command: **U**↵
    PLINE
    Command:

In this example, the **PLINE** command was the last command undone. You can reissue the **U** command if you wish to undo another previous command. However, you can only undo one command at a time. The **UNDO** command, which features a number of options as compared to the **U** command, is discussed later in this chapter.

Drawing Thick Lines Using the **TRACE** Command

When it is necessary to draw wide lines, the **TRACE** command can be used instead of the **PLINE** command. To use the **TRACE** command, enter TRACE at the Command: prompt. Specify the trace width (stored in the **TRACEWID** system variable) and then select points as you would with the **LINE** command.

TRACE

> Command: **TRACE**↵
> Specify trace width <*current*>: *(enter width)*
> Specify start point: *(select start point)*
> Specify next point: *(select second point)*
> Specify next point: *(select additional points or press* [Enter] *to complete)*
> Command:

When you use the **TRACE** command, objects are made up of *trace segments*. The previous trace segment is not drawn on screen until the next endpoint is specified, because trace segment ends are mitered to fit the next segment. There is no close option with the **TRACE** command.

USING THE **UNDO** COMMAND

AutoCAD User's Guide 4

As mentioned earlier in this chapter, the **UNDO** command is different from the **U** command. The **UNDO** command offers several options that allow you to undo a single command or a number of commands at once. The command sequence is as follows:

> Command: **UNDO**↵
> Enter the number of operations to undo or [Auto/Control/BEgin/End/Mark/Back]:

The default option allows you to designate the number of previous command sequences you wish to remove. For example, if you enter 1, the previous command sequence is removed. If you enter 2, the previous two command sequences are removed. AutoCAD tells you which commands were undone with a message after you press [Enter]:

> Command: **UNDO**↵
> Enter the number of operations to undo or [Auto/Control/BEgin/End/Mark/Back]: **2**↵
> PLINE LINE
> Command:

There are several other types of undo operations that can be performed with the **UNDO** command, depending on the option you select. The **Auto** option can be turned on or off. When this option is on, any commands that are part of a group and used to perform a single operation are removed together. For example, when a command contains other commands, all of the commands in that group are removed as one single command. The **Auto** option is active by default. If it is turned off, each command in a group of commands is treated individually.

The **Control** option allows you to specify how many of the **UNDO** command options you want active. You can even disable the **UNDO** command altogether. To use the **Control** option, enter C after issuing the **UNDO** command:

> Enter the number of operations to undo or [Auto/Control/BEgin/End/Mark/Back]: **C**⏎
> Enter an UNDO control option [All/None/One] <All>: *(enter a control option and press* [Enter]*)*

Selecting the **All** suboption keeps the full range of **UNDO** command options active. This is the default setting. The **None** suboption disables the **U** and **UNDO** commands. When the **U** command is entered, the following prompt appears:

> Command: **U**⏎
> U command disabled. Use UNDO command to turn it on

This prompt indicates how to reactivate the **U** and **UNDO** commands. If you type UNDO at the Command: prompt, the following appears:

> Command: **UNDO**⏎
> Enter an UNDO control option [All/None/One] <All>:

To activate the **UNDO** options, press [Enter] for **All**. You can also enter O for the **One** suboption. This setting limits **UNDO** to one operation only. Now, when you enter the **UNDO** command, you get the following prompt:

> Command: **UNDO**⏎
> Control/<1>: ⏎
> LINE
> Everything has been undone
> Command:

You can type C at the Control/<1>: prompt to redisplay the **Control** suboptions.

PROFESSIONAL TIP

When you use the **UNDO** command, AutoCAD maintains an "undo" file. This file saves previously used **UNDO** commands. All **UNDO** entries saved before disabling **UNDO** with the **Control None** suboption are discarded. This frees up some disk space, and may be valuable information for you to keep in mind if you ever get close to having a full disk. If you want to continue using the **U** and **UNDO** commands to some extent, then you might consider using the **UNDO Control One** suboption. This allows you to keep using the **U** and **UNDO** commands to a limited extent while freeing disk space holding current information about **UNDO**.

The **BEgin** and **End** options of the **UNDO** command are used together to perform several undo operations at once. They allow you to group a series of commands and treat the entire group as a single command. Once the group is defined, the **U** command is then used to remove the commands that follow the **BEgin** option but precede the **End** option.

These options are useful if you can anticipate the possible removal of several commands that are entered consecutively. For example, if you think you may want to undo the next three commands altogether, do the following:

> Command: **UNDO**↵
> Enter the number of operations to undo or [Auto/Control/BEgin/End/Mark/Back]: **BE**↵
> Command: **L** *or* **LINE**↵
> Specify first point: *(pick a point)*
> Specify next point or [Undo]: *(pick an endpoint)*
> Specify next point or [Undo]: ↵
> Command: **PL** *or* **PLINE**↵
> Specify start point: *(pick a point)*
> Current line-width is 0.0000
> Specify next point or [Arc/Close/Halfwidth/Length/Undo/Width]: *(pick an endpoint)*
> Specify next point or [Arc/Close/Halfwidth/Length/Undo/Width]: ↵
> Command: **L** *or* **LINE**↵
> Specify first point: *(pick a point)*
> Specify next point or [Undo]: *(pick an endpoint)*
> Specify next point or [Undo]: ↵
> Command: **UNDO**↵
> Enter the number of operations to undo or [Auto/Control/BEgin/End/Mark/Back]: **E**↵
> Command: **U**↵

The **U** command undoes the three commands that were executed in the previous sequence. Note that the **BEgin** option must precede the command sequence and the **End** option must immediately follow the last command to be undone.

The **UNDO Mark** option allows you to insert a "marker" in the undo file. The **UNDO Back** option then enables you to delete commands "back" to the marker. For example, if you do not want certain work to be undone by the **Back** option, enter the **Mark** option after completing the work:

> Command: **UNDO**↵
> Enter the number of operations to undo or [Auto/Control/BEgin/End/Mark/Back]: **M**↵
> Command:

Then, if you decide to remove any additional work, reissue the **UNDO** command and enter the **Back** option. This will undo everything back to the marker:

> Command: **UNDO**↵
> Enter the number of operations to undo or [Auto/Control/BEgin/End/Mark/Back]: **B**↵

If no marks have been entered, this undoes everything in the entire drawing. AutoCAD questions your choice with the following message:

> This will undo everything. OK? <Y>:

If you want everything that you have drawn and edited to be undone, press [Enter]. If not, enter N or NO and press [Enter], or press the [Esc] key.

PROFESSIONAL
TIP

The **UNDO Mark** option can be used to assist in the design process. For example, if you are working on a project and have completed a portion of the design, you can mark the spot with the **Mark** option and then begin work on the next design phase. If anything goes wrong with this part of the design, you can simply use the **UNDO Back** option to remove everything back to the mark.

AutoCAD
User's
Guide **4**

REDO
[Ctrl]+[Y]

Edit
➥ <u>R</u>edo

**Standard
toolbar**

Redo

REDOING THE UNDONE

The **REDO** command is used to bring back objects that were erased with the **UNDO** and **U** commands. Enter REDO at the Command: prompt, pick **Redo** from the **Edit** pull-down menu, press the [Ctrl]+[Y] key combination, or pick the **Redo** button from the **Standard** toolbar to activate the command.

The **REDO** command works only *immediately* after undoing something. **REDO** does *not* bring back polyline segments that were removed using the **Undo** option of the **PLINE** command.

AutoCAD
User's
Guide **8**

FILLING POLYLINES AND TRACES

In the discussion of the **PLINE** and **TRACE** commands earlier in this chapter, the results were shown as if the objects were solid, or filled in. You can leave traces and polylines filled in, or you can show an outline. These functions are controlled by the **FILL** command, Figure 15-4. The **FILL** command has two optional modes, **ON** and **OFF**.

Command: **FILL**↵
Enter mode [ON/OFF] <*current*>:

Figure 15-4.
Examples of using the **FILL** mode on and off.

FILL On		FILL Off	
Polyline	Trace	Polyline	Trace

The value specified in brackets is the default, or previous setting. When the **FILL** mode is turned on, traces and polylines appear filled after they are drawn. When **FILL** is off, traces and polylines appear as outlines, and the corners are mitered. After turning **FILL** off, enter RE or REGEN at the Command: prompt to have the fill removed.

The **FILL** mode can also be set in the **Apply solid fill** check box in the **Options** dialog box. The check box is located in the **Display performance** area of the **Display** tab in the **Options** dialog box.

PROFESSIONAL TIP

When there are many wide polylines or traces in a drawing, it is best to have the **FILL** mode turned off. This saves time when redrawing, regenerating, or plotting a check copy of the drawing. Turn **FILL** on for the final drawing.

EXERCISE 15-4

❑ Start a new drawing or use one of your templates.
❑ Use the **TRACE** command to draw a 2 unit by 4 unit rectangle with a .125 line width. Draw another rectangle with a .25 line width.
❑ Use the **PLINE** command to draw a 2 unit by 4 unit rectangle with a .125 line width. Draw another rectangle with a .25 line width.
❑ Turn **FILL** off and on and observe the difference.
❑ Use the **REGEN** command with **FILL** on and off, and notice the regeneration speed in each situation. There may not be much difference with a fast computer unless the file starts to become large.
❑ Save the drawing as EX15-4.

DRAWING MULTILINES

AutoCAD User's Guide **6**

Multilines, discussed briefly earlier in this chapter, are objects that can consist of up to 16 parallel lines. The lines in a multiline are called *elements*. The **MLINE** command is used to draw multilines, and a multiline configuration, or style, can be set using the **MLSTYLE** command. The AutoCAD default multiline style has two elements and is called STANDARD.

MLINE
ML

The **MLINE** command is accessed by picking the **Multiline** button from the **Draw** toolbar, picking **Multiline** from the **Draw** pull-down menu, or entering ML or MLINE at the Command: prompt as follows:

Draw
➡ Multiline

Draw toolbar

Multiline

```
Command: ML or MLINE↵
Current settings: Justification = Top, Scale = 1.00, Style = STANDARD
Specify start point or [Justification/Scale/STyle]: 2,2↵
Specify next point: 6,2↵
Specify next point or [Undo]: 6,6↵
Specify next point or [Close/Undo]: 2,6↵
Specify next point or [Close/Undo]: C↵
Command:
```

The **MLINE** command prompts and options are similar to those used with the **LINE** command. As shown in the previous command sequence, you can use the **Close** option at the last prompt to close a polygon. Enter U during the command sequence to undo the previously drawn multiline segment. The object created in the previous example is shown in Figure 15-5. Two lines are drawn because this multiline uses AutoCAD's STANDARD multiline style.

Figure 15-5.
A multiline object created with AutoCAD's STANDARD multiline style.

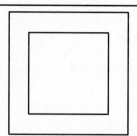

Multiline Justification

Multiline justification determines how the resulting lines are offset, based on the definition points provided. *Definition points* are the points you enter when drawing multilines. The justification can be specified only once during a single **MLINE** command sequence, and it is based on counterclockwise movement. The justification options are **Top**, **Zero**, and **Bottom**.

The **Top** option is set by default. To change the justification, enter J at the first prompt displayed after entering the **MLINE** command. Then, enter the first letter of the desired justification format (T, Z, or B). The results of the three different justification options, using the same point entries, are shown in Figure 15-6. Observe each orientation as you go through the following command sequence:

```
Command: ML or MLINE↵
Current settings: Justification = Top, Scale = 1.00, Style = STANDARD
Specify start point or [Justification/Scale/STyle]: J↵
Enter justification type [Top/Zero/Bottom] <current>: (type T, Z, or B, and press [Enter])
Current settings: Justification = specified value, Scale = 1.00, Style = STANDARD
Specify start point or [Justification/Scale/STyle]: 2,2↵
Specify next point: 6,2↵
Specify next point or [Undo]: 6,6↵
Specify next point or [Close/Undo]: 2,6↵
Specify next point or [Close/Undo]: C↵
Command:
```

Figure 15-6.
Multilines drawn using each of the three justification options. The definition points (represented by plus symbols) are picked in a counterclockwise rotation.

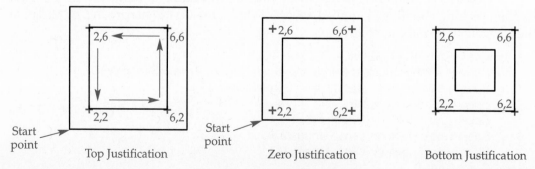

The current multiline justification setting is stored by the **CMLJUST** system variable. You can change the setting by entering 0 for the **Top** option, 1 for the **Zero** option, or 2 for the **Bottom** option.

PROFESSIONAL TIP

As shown in Figure 15-6, the multiline justification options control the direction of the offsets for elements of the current style. The multiline segments in these examples are drawn in a counterclockwise direction. Unexpected results can sometimes occur when using the **MLINE** command, depending on the justification and drawing direction.

EXERCISE 15-5

❏ Start a new drawing or use one of your templates.
❏ Use the **MLINE** command and its justification options to draw three objects similar to the ones shown in Figure 15-6.
❏ Observe the difference between the justification options.
❏ Save the drawing as EX15-5.

Adjusting the Multiline Scale

The **MLINE Scale** option controls the multiplier value for the offset distances specified with the **MLSTYLE** command. The multiplier value is stored by the **CMLSCALE** system variable. The example in the previous section used a scale setting of 1 (the default). When the scale is 1, the distance between multiline elements is equal to 1 times the offset distance. For example, if the offset distance is 0.5, the distance between multiline elements is 0.5 when the multiline scale is 1. If the multiline scale is 2, the distance between multiline elements is 1 (0.5 × 2).

The multiline scale is set to 2 in the next example. A comparison of multilines drawn with different scale settings is shown in Figure 15-7.

```
Command: ML or MLINE↵
Current settings: Justification = Top, Scale = 1.00, Style = STANDARD
Specify start point or [Justification/Scale/STyle]: S↵
Enter mline scale <1.00>: 2↵
```

Figure 15-7.
Multiline scale settings.

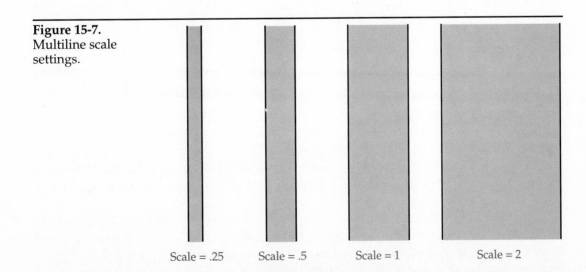

Scale = .25   Scale = .5   Scale = 1   Scale = 2

❑ Start a new drawing or use one of your templates.
❑ Use the **MLINE** command and the **Scale** option to draw three objects similar to the ones shown in Figure 15-7.
❑ Observe the difference between the multiline scales.
❑ Save the drawing as EX15-6.

Setting Your Own Multiline Style

You can specify the current multiline style by using the **STyle** option of the **MLINE** command. However, before a new multiline style can be accessed, it must be saved using the **MLSTYLE** command. To use a multiline style that has been saved, enter ST to access the **STyle** option and then enter the style name as follows:

Command: **ML** *or* **MLINE**↵
Current settings: Justification = Top, Scale = 1.00, Style = STANDARD
Specify start point or [Justification/Scale/STyle]: **ST**↵
Enter mline style name or [?] : **ROAD1**↵
Justification = Top, Scale = 1.00, Style = ROAD1

If you forget the name of the desired multiline style, you can enter ? to access the text window, where the currently loaded multiline styles are listed. See Figure 15-8. If you enter a multiline style that does not exist, the **Load multiline style from file** dialog box is displayed. You can look for the desired multiline file in the acad.mln file library, or pick the **Find File...** button to open the **Browse/Search** dialog box to search other files for the multiline style. (The **Browse/Search** dialog box was discussed in Chapter 3.) If the desired multiline style does not exist, AutoCAD gives you this message:

Multiline style *style name* not found in C:\Program Files\ACAD2000\SUPPORT \acad.mln.
You can use the "MLSTYLE" command to load it from another file.

Figure 15-8.
A list of loaded multiline styles can be displayed by accessing the text window.

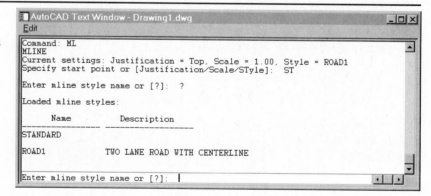

Creating Multiline Styles

Multiline styles are defined using the **MLSTYLE** command. The current style is stored by the **CMLSTYLE** system variable. The **MLSTYLE** command can be accessed by picking **Multiline Style...** from the **Format** pull-down menu. You can also enter MLSTYLE at the Command: prompt.

The **MLSTYLE** command displays the **Multiline Styles** dialog box. This is where multiline styles can be defined, edited, and saved. See Figure 15-9. Styles can be saved to an external file so they can be used in other drawings. The options provided in the **Multiline Style** area of the **Multiline Styles** dialog box are described as follows:

Figure 15-9.
The **Multiline Styles** dialog box is used to define, edit, and save multiline styles.

Pick to save a style to file

Pick to load a style

Image of multiline

Pick to change element properties

Pick to select new current style

Pick to rename a style

Pick to add the style in the **Name:** text box to the current list

Pick to change multiline properties

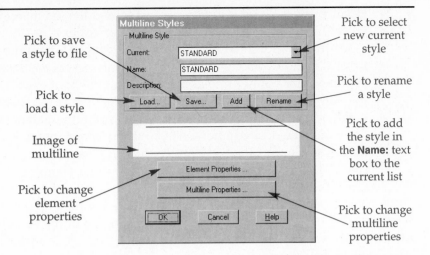

- **Current: text box.** The **Current:** text box makes the specified multiline style current. Specifying a different style changes the setting of the **CMLSTYLE** system variable. Until you create a multiline style, the only style available is STANDARD.
- **Name: text box.** This text box is used to enter the name for a new style.
- **Description: text box.** An optional description of your multiline style may be entered in this text box. This is discussed later in this chapter.
- **Load... button.** This button allows you to load a multiline style from an external multiline definition file.
- **Save... button.** The **Save...** button is used to save a style to a file.
- **Add button.** Pick the **Add** button after entering a multiline style name in the **Name:** text box. This adds the multiline style name to the list of defined styles.
- **Rename button.** Pick this button to rename a multiline style.

The image tile in the center of the **Multiline Styles** dialog box displays a representation of the current multiline elements. The image is updated when a new style is entered.

Using the **Element Properties** Dialog Box

Picking the **Element Properties...** button in the **Multiline Styles** dialog box displays the **Element Properties** dialog box, Figure 15-10. You can create new multiline styles using this dialog box. The features provided are described as follows:
- **Elements: area.** This area of the dialog box displays the current offset, color, and linetype settings for each multiline element. Picking one of the elements highlights the items for modification.
- **Add button.** Pick this button to add a new element to the multiline definition. Doing this adds an element with the following settings: **Offset** = 0.0, **Color** = BYLAYER, and **Ltype** = Bylayer. This allows you to draw a multiline element between the two existing elements.

Figure 15-10.
The **Element Properties** dialog box is used to create multiline styles.

Pick to delete the highlighted element

Pick to add a new element

Pick to select a color

Pick to select a linetype

Defined elements

Enter an offset

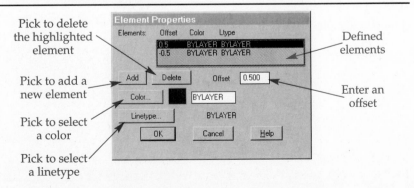

- **Delete button.** Pick this button to delete a highlighted item in the **Elements:** area.
- **Offset text box.** Use this text box to enter either a positive or negative offset value for a highlighted element. Press [Enter] to accept the value you specify.
- **Color... button.** Picking the **Color...** button accesses the **Select Color** dialog box. Pick the color you wish to assign to the highlighted element. After picking **OK**, the new color is displayed in the image tile next to the **Color...** button.
- **Linetype... button.** Pick this button to display the **Select Linetype** dialog box. Then pick the desired linetype from the **Loaded Linetypes** list. Linetypes must be loaded before they can be used (see Chapter 4). After picking **OK**, the selected linetype is listed with the highlighted element.

The results of adding a new element to a multiline definition are shown in Figure 15-11. The color and linetype values are both specified as BYLAYER. Pick **OK** to exit the **Element Properties** dialog box. The current status of the multiline is displayed by the image tile in the **Multiline Styles** dialog box. You can continue in this manner and add up to 16 different elements to the multiline style.

Figure 15-11.
The new element is added to the multiline style.

New element

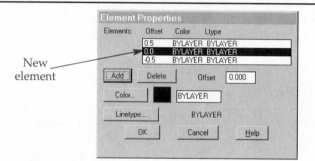

Using the Multiline Properties Dialog Box

The **Multiline Properties** dialog box offers additional options for customizing multiline styles. This dialog box is accessed by picking the **Multiline Properties...** button in the **Multiline Styles** dialog box. See Figure 15-12. You can add caps, segment joints, and background color to multiline elements. The features in the **Multiline Properties** dialog box are described as follows:

- **Display joints check box.** This check box acts as a toggle for the display of joints. *Joints* are lines that connect the vertices of adjacent multiline elements. Joints are also referred to as *miters*. The difference between drawing multilines with joints and without joints is shown in Figure 15-13.

Figure 15-12. The **Multiline Properties** dialog box is used to customize a multiline style.

Activate to display joints

Settings for caps

Check to enable **Fill** settings

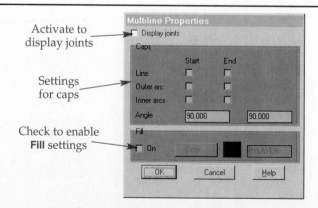

     AutoCAD and its Applications—Basics

Figure 15-13.
Multilines can be drawn with or without displayed joints.

Joints Enabled   Joints Disabled

- **Caps area.** The settings in this area control the placement of caps on multilines. *Caps* are lines connecting the corresponding vertices of the beginning or ending points of the multiline elements. Using the check boxes, caps can be set at the start points, endpoints, or both. Arcs can also be specified. Arcs can be set to connect the ends of the outermost elements only, pairs of interior elements, or both the outer and interior elements. The arcs are drawn tangent to the elements they connect. Specifying outermost arcs to be drawn requires at least two multiline elements.

  You can also change the angle of the caps relative to the direction of the multiline elements by entering new values in the **Angle** text boxes. Several examples of different cap options are shown in Figure 15-14.

- **Fill area.** If the check box labeled **On** is activated, the multiline is filled with a solid fill pattern in the color specified. Pick this check box to activate the **Color...** button. You can leave the color set to BYLAYER or change it by picking the **Color...** button. Examples of multilines drawn with the **Fill** setting on and off are shown in Figure 15-15.

Figure 15-14.
Various cap options used with multilines.

Caps Off   Line Caps On   Outer Arcs On   Inner Arcs On

90° Angle Caps Off   45° Angle Caps Off   45° Angle Line Caps On

Figure 15-15.
The multiline **Fill** setting allows you to draw multilines with a solid fill pattern.

Fill Setting On   Fill Setting Off

Creating and Drawing a Multiline

Now that you have seen how the **MLINE** and **MLSTYLE** commands work, you can create your own multiline style and draw multilines with that style. Suppose you need to draw a multiline for a two-lane road to be used in a mapping project. The following procedure is used to create the style and draw the multiline:

1. Access the **Multiline Styles** dialog box. Pick the **Element Properties...** button and set the following elements in the **Element Properties** dialog box:

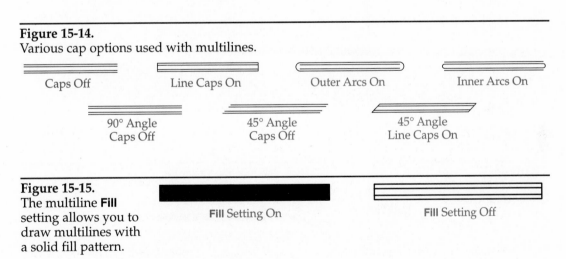

Offset	Color	Ltype
0.25	BYLAYER	BYLAYER
0.0	BYLAYER	CENTER2
−0.25	BYLAYER	BYLAYER

2. Pick **OK**.
3. Pick the **Multiline Properties...** button in the **Multiline Styles** dialog box to display the **Multiline Properties** dialog box. Be sure the **Display joints**, **Caps**, and **Fill** check boxes are not activated, and the entries in the **Angle** text boxes are set to 90°.
4. Pick **OK**.
5. Enter ROAD1 in the **Name:** text box in the **Multiline Style** area of the **Multiline Styles** dialog box.
6. In the **Description:** text box, enter the description TWO LANE ROAD WITH CENTERLINE.
7. Pick the **Save...** button to display the **Save Multiline Style** dialog box.
8. The acad.mln file appears in the **File name:** text box, as shown in Figure 15-16. Pick the **Save** button.
9. Pick the **Load...** button in the **Multiline Styles** dialog box to access the **Load Multiline Styles** dialog box.
10. Pick the ROAD1 multiline style, as shown in Figure 15-17, and then pick **OK**.
11. Pick **OK** to exit the **Multiline Styles** dialog box.
12. Enter the **MLINE** command to draw the ROAD1 multiline.

Figure 15-16.
Use the **Save Multiline Style** dialog box to save the ROAD1 style to the acad.mln file.

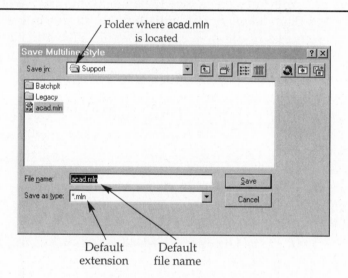

Figure 15-17.
The **Load Multiline Styles** dialog box.

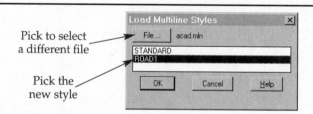

If the ROAD1 multiline style was not set current in the **Multiline Styles** dialog box, use the **MLINE STyle** option to access it. Then, draw the multiline shown in Figure 15-18 using the following command sequence:

```
Command: ML or MLINE.↵
Current settings: Justification = Top, Scale = 1.00, Style = STANDARD
Specify start point or [Justification/Scale/STyle]: ST.↵
Enter mline style name or [?]: ROAD1.↵
Current settings: Justification = Top, Scale = 1.00, Style = ROAD1
Specify start point or [Justification/Scale/STyle]: (enter start point)
Specify next point: (enter endpoint)
Specify next point or [Undo]: ↵
Command:
```

Figure 15-18.
A multiline drawn with the ROAD1 style.

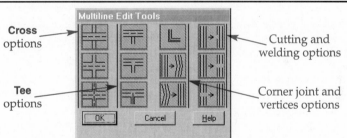

EXERCISE 15-7

❑ Start a new drawing or use one of your templates.
❑ Use the **MLSTYLE** and **MLINE** commands to create the following:
  ❑ A multiline with joints similar to the one shown in Figure 15-13.
  ❑ Multilines with several types of caps similar to those shown in Figure 15-14.
  ❑ A multiline with the **Fill** setting on.
  ❑ A multiline defined with a style similar to that shown in Figure 15-18, but with a different linetype.
❑ Save the drawing as EX15-7.

EDITING MULTILINES

AutoCAD
User's
Guide **9**

The **MLEDIT** command permits limited editing operations for multiline objects. Access this command by picking **Multiline...** from the **Modify** pull-down menu, entering MLEDIT at the Command: prompt, or picking the **Edit Multiline** button in the **Modify II** toolbar. This displays the **Multiline Edit Tools** dialog box, Figure 15-19. Each of the four columns in this dialog box contains three image buttons. The image buttons give you an example of what to expect when using each editing option. These options are described in the following sections.

MLEDIT

Modify
  ↳ **Multiline...**

Modify II
toolbar

Edit Multiline

Figure 15-19. The **Multiline Edit Tools** dialog box has 12 different options. Refer to the text for an explanation of each option.

Editing Intersections

The first (left) column in the **Multiline Edit Tools** dialog box displays three different types of multiline intersections. Picking a button allows you to create the type of intersection shown. The name of the **MLEDIT** option is displayed in the lower-left corner of the dialog box when you pick an image button. The buttons in the first column are shown in Figure 15-20 and described below:

- **Closed Cross.** This option lets you create what is referred to as a *closed cross*. This is where the first multiline selected, called the background, is trimmed, while the second multiline selected, called the foreground, remains unchanged. Note that the trimming is apparent, not actual. This means that the line visibility of the background multiline is changed, but it is still one multiline. The command sequence is as follows:

      Command: **MLEDIT**↵ *(pick the* **Closed Cross** *image button and pick* **OK***)*
      Select first mline: *(pick the foreground multiline)*
      Select second mline: *(pick the background multiline)*

Figure 15-20.
Creating a closed cross, open cross, and merged cross intersection with the **MLEDIT** command.

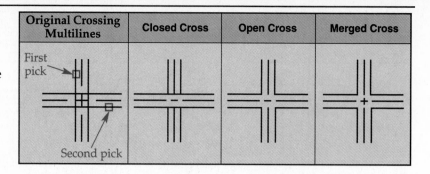

Original Crossing Multilines	Closed Cross	Open Cross	Merged Cross
First pick → Second pick			

The closed cross intersection is drawn. AutoCAD then issues a prompt to let you pick additional multilines for intersection. You can also type U to undo the intersection you have just made. If you undo the intersection, AutoCAD provides the Select first mline: prompt again:

> Select first mline or [Undo]: **U**⏎
> Select first mline: *(pick the foreground multiline)*
> Select second mline: *(pick the background multiline)*
> Select first mline or [Undo]: ⏎
> Command:

- **Open Cross.** Select the **Open Cross** image button to trim all of the elements of the first picked multiline and only the outer elements of the second multiline, as shown in Figure 15-20. The command sequence is the same as that used for the **Closed Cross** option.
- **Merged Cross.** The **Merged Cross** image button allows you to trim all the outer multiline elements while leaving all the interior elements the same. See Figure 15-20.

EXERCISE 15-8

❑ Start a new drawing or use one of your templates.
❑ Use the **MLINE** and **MLEDIT** commands to do the following:
 ❑ Draw three sets of intersecting multilines. Then, use the **Closed Cross** option to edit the first set of multilines, the **Open Cross** option to edit the second set, and the **Merged Cross** option to edit the third set. Use Figure 15-20 as an example.
❑ Save the drawing as EX15-8.

Editing Tees

The image buttons in the second column of the **Multiline Edit Tools** dialog box are used for editing multiline tees. The results of using the **MLEDIT** tee options are illustrated in Figure 15-21. The options are described as follows:

- **Closed Tee.** Pick the **Closed Tee** option to have AutoCAD trim or extend the first selected multiline to its intersection with the second multiline.
- **Open Tee.** The **Open Tee** option is similar to the **Closed Tee** option. It allows you to trim the elements where a trimmed or extended multiline intersects with another multiline. The first pick specifies the multiline to trim or extend and the second pick specifies the intersecting multiline. The intersecting multiline is trimmed and left open where the two multilines join.
- **Merged Tee.** The **Merged Tee** option is similar to the **Open Tee** option. It trims the intersecting multiline after the first multiline is trimmed or extended to the intersecting multiline. However, the interior elements are joined. This creates an open appearance with the outer elements while merging the interior elements.

Figure 15-21.
Using the **MLEDIT** **Tee** options to edit multiline tees.

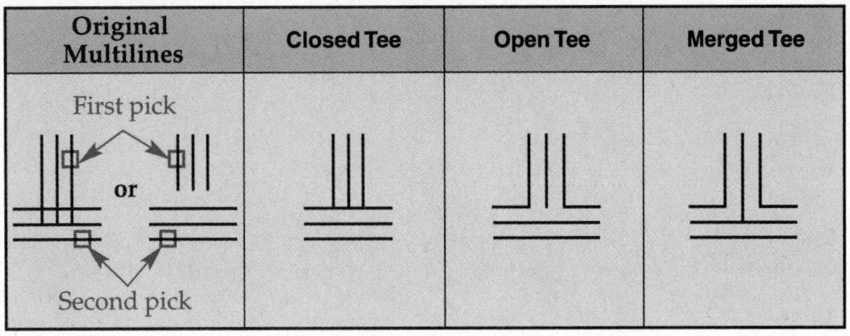

Original Multilines	Closed Tee	Open Tee	Merged Tee
First pick or Second pick			

Editing Corner Joints and Multiline Vertices

The image buttons in the third column of the **Multiline Edit Tools** dialog box provide options for creating corner joints and editing multiline vertices. These options are described as follows:

- **Corner Joint.** This option allows you to create a corner joint between two multilines. The first multiline is trimmed or extended to its intersection with the second multiline, as shown in Figure 15-22.

- **Add Vertex.** This option adds a vertex to an existing multiline at the location you pick, Figure 15-23. The command sequence differs slightly from the sequences used with the other **MLEDIT** options. After you select the **Add Vertex** option and pick **OK**, you are prompted with the following:

  Select mline: *(pick a location on the multiline for the new vertex)*
  Select mline or [Undo]: ↵
  Command:

- **Delete Vertex.** The **Delete Vertex** option allows you to remove a vertex from an existing multiline. The vertex closest to the location you pick is deleted, Figure 15-23.

Figure 15-22.
A corner joint can be created between two multilines using the **MLEDIT** **Corner Joint** option.

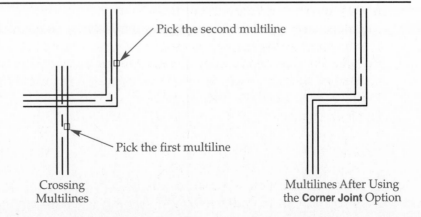

Pick the second multiline

Pick the first multiline

Crossing Multilines

Multilines After Using the **Corner Joint** Option

Figure 15-23.
The **MLEDIT Add Vertex** and **Delete Vertex** options are used to edit multiline vertices.

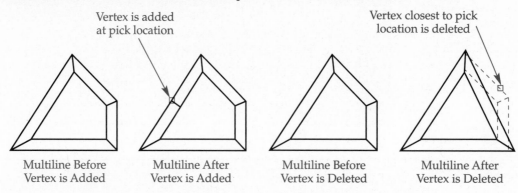

Vertex is added at pick location

Vertex closest to pick location is deleted

| Multiline Before Vertex is Added | Multiline After Vertex is Added | Multiline Before Vertex is Deleted | Multiline After Vertex is Deleted |

EXERCISE 15-10

❑ Start a new drawing or use one of your templates.
❑ Use the **MLINE** and **MLEDIT** commands to do the following:
  ❑ Draw multilines similar to the unedited objects shown in Figure 15-22. Then, use the **Corner Joint** option to create an object similar to the edited example.
  ❑ Draw multilines similar to the unedited objects shown in Figure 15-23. Then, use the **Add Vertex** and **Delete Vertex** options to create objects similar to the edited examples.
❑ Save the drawing as EX15-10.

Cutting and Welding Multilines

The fourth column of image buttons in the **Multiline Edit Tools** dialog box is used for *cutting* a portion out of a single multiline element or the entire multiline, or connecting spaces between multiline elements. AutoCAD refers to the connecting operation as *welding*. The **MLEDIT** cutting and welding options are described as follows:

- **Cut Single.** This option allows you to cut a single multiline element between two specified points, as shown in Figure 15-24. Cutting only affects the visibility of elements, and does not separate a multiline object. The multiline is still a single object. After selecting the **Cut Single** option and picking **OK**, you are prompted with the following:

      Select mline: *(pick a location for the first cutting point on the multiline)*
      Select second point: *(pick a location for the second cutting point)*
      Select mline or [Undo]: ↵
      Command:

- **Cut All.** This option cuts all the elements of a multiline between specified points. See Figure 15-24. The multiline is still a single object, even though it appears to be separated.

- **Weld All.** This option allows you to repair all cuts in a multiline. Select the **Weld All** option, then pick a point on each side of the cut multiline. The multiline is restored to its precut condition.

Figure 15-24.
The **MLEDIT** cutting options allow you to cut single multiline elements or entire multilines between two specified points.

Original Multiline	Cut Single	Cut All
	Pick points	

EXERCISE 15-11

❑ Start a new drawing or use one of your templates.
❑ Use the **MLINE** and **MLEDIT** commands to do the following:
   ❑ Draw multilines similar to those illustrated on the left in Figure 15-24. Then, use the **Cut Single** and **Cut All** options to create objects similar to the edited multilines shown. Then, use the **Weld All** option to restored the multilines to their original conditions.
❑ Save the drawing as EX15-11.

PROFESSIONAL TIP

Multiline objects can be converted to individual line segments by using the **EXPLODE** command. This command is explained in Chapters 17 and 23. The following is a brief look at the **EXPLODE** command sequence:

Command: **X** *or* **EXPLODE**⏎
Select objects: *(pick the object to explode)*
Select objects: ⏎
Command:

SKETCHING WITH AUTOCAD

Sketching is a feature of AutoCAD that allows you to draw objects as if you were sketching with pencil and paper. Sketching is done with the **SKETCH** command. While this command is not commonly used, it does have value for certain applications. The **SKETCH** command is sometimes used when it is necessary to draw a contour that is not defined by geometric shapes or lines. Other examples of applications for freehand sketching in AutoCAD include:
- Contour lines on topographic maps.
- Maps of countries and states.
- Architectural landscape symbols, such as trees, bushes, and plants.
- Graphs and charts.
- Graphic designs, such as those found on a greeting card.
- Short breaks, such as those used in mechanical drafting.

Before using the **SKETCH** command, it is best to turn the Snap and Ortho modes off, because they limit the cursor's movement. Normally, you want total control over the cursor when sketching. When you enter the **SKETCH** command, you are prompted with the following:

Command: **SKETCH**⏎
Record increment <0.1000>:

The *record increment* is the length of each sketch line element generated as you move the cursor. For example, if the record increment is set to 0.1000 (the default value), sketched images consist of lines that are 0.1 units in length. An increment setting of 1 creates sketched line segments 1 unit long. Reducing the increment setting increases the accuracy of your sketched image. However, record increments less than 0.1 consume great amounts of computer storage.

To view the chosen record increment, turn **ORTHO** on and draw a set of stair steps. Each horizontal and vertical element represents the length of the record increment. If **SNAP** is turned on, the record increment then becomes equal to the snap spacing. A comparison of record increments is shown in Figure 15-25. To set a record increment of .1, issue the **SKETCH** command, enter .1, and press [Enter]. Or, press [Enter] to accept the default value. AutoCAD then issues the following prompt:

Pen eXit Quit Record Erase Connect .

This prompt displays the **SKETCH** subcommands. Once you see this prompt, a subcommand can be accessed by entering its corresponding capitalized letter. Pressing the left mouse button activates the **Pen** subcommand.

If you are using a multibutton puck, the buttons on your puck are used to activate the **SKETCH** subcommands. The normal puck buttons for the Snap (4) and Ortho (5) modes remain disabled as long as the **SKETCH** command is active. The following table lists the keyboard entries and puck buttons used to access each subcommand.

Subcommand	Keyboard Entry	Puck Button	Subcommand Function
Pen	P	0	Toggles pen up and down.
Period	"."	1	Draws a line from the endpoint of a sketched line.
Record	R	2	Records sketched lines as permanent.
eXit	X, space bar, or [Enter]	3	Records sketched lines and exits the **SKETCH** command.
Quit	Q or [ESC]	4	Removes all unrecorded objects.
Erase	E	5 ·	Erases all unrecorded objects.
Connect	C	6	Allows connection to the endpoint of a sketched line when pen is up.

Sketched line segments are line objects by default. You can use the **SKPOLY** system variable to create sketched lines that are defined as polyline objects. The settings for the **SKPOLY** system variable are 0 for line objects and 1 for polyline objects.

Figure 15-25.
Record increments used with the **SKETCH** command.

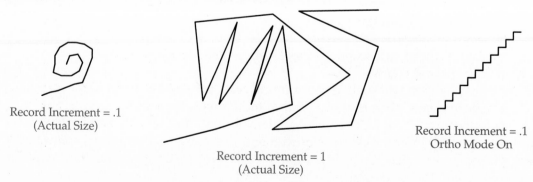

Record Increment = .1
(Actual Size)

Record Increment = 1
(Actual Size)

Record Increment = .1
Ortho Mode On

Drawing Sketched Lines

After entering the **SKETCH** command, actual sketching is done with the **Pen** subcommand. Using this subcommand is similar to sketching with paper and pencil. When the pencil is "down," you are ready to draw. When the pencil is "up," you are thinking about what to draw next or moving to the next location. After issuing the **SKETCH** command, enter P to toggle the pen down and begin sketching. You can also press your left mouse button to move the pen up and down. Move the cursor around to create a line. Enter P again, or press your left mouse button, to toggle the pen up and stop sketching.

PROFESSIONAL TIP 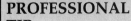 If you do not consider yourself an artist, trace an existing design. Tape the design to a digitizer and move the cursor along the outline of the shape with the pen down. Move the pen up when you want to specify a new sketching location.

Using the **Period (.)** Subcommand

The **Period** subcommand allows you to draw a straight line from the endpoint of the last sketched line to a selected point. This subcommand is accessed by entering a period (.) at the prompt displayed by the **SKETCH** command. Use the following procedure:
1. Complete the segment you are working on and make sure the pen is up.
2. Move the cursor to the desired endpoint.
3. Enter a period (.) or press puck button 1. A straight line is automatically drawn. If **ORTHO** is turned on, only vertical or horizontal lines are drawn.

Using the **Connect** Subcommand

It is common to toggle the pen up to pause from sketching or to make a menu selection. When the pen is up, you can return to the last sketched point and resume sketching by using the **Connect** subcommand. To do so, enter C or press puck button 6. AutoCAD responds with this message:

    Connect: Move to endpoint of line.

Move the cursor to the end of the previously sketched temporary line. As soon as the crosshairs touch the previously drawn line, the pen automatically moves down and you can resume sketching.

Using the **Erase** Subcommand

You can erase line segments while sketching. If you make a mistake, enter E for the **Erase** subcommand, or press puck button 5. The pen may be up or down. If the pen is down, it is automatically raised. AutoCAD responds with the following message:

    Erase: Select end of delete. <Pen up>

Move the cursor to erase any portion of the sketch, beginning from the last point. When finished, enter P or press puck button 0. If you decide not to erase anything, enter E or press puck button 5. AutoCAD returns to the **SKETCH** command prompt after issuing the message Erase aborted.

Recording Sketched Lines

Sketched lines are displayed in color when you first begin to sketch. These lines are referred to as *temporary lines*. Temporary lines become *permanent lines*, and are displayed in their final color, after they are *recorded*. You can record lines and remain in the **SKETCH** command by entering R or pressing puck button 2. You can also record lines and exit the **SKETCH** command by entering X, or by pressing the space bar, [Enter], or puck button 3. AutoCAD responds with a message indicating the number of lines recorded. For example, if you created 32 lines, the message reads 32 lines recorded.

Quitting the **SKETCH** Command

To quit the **SKETCH** command without recording any temporary lines, enter Q, press the [Esc] key, or press puck button 4. This removes all temporary lines and returns you to the Command: prompt.

Managing Storage Space with the **SKETCH** Command

Sketching rapidly consumes computer storage space. A drawing with fine detail, for example, will quickly fill a 3.5" diskette. Therefore, the **SKETCH** command should be used only when necessary. The record increment should be set as large as possible, but at a setting so that the results still appear pleasing. In commercial applications, such as the design of topographical maps, computer storage capacities are designed to accept the required input. A sketch of a rose is shown in Figure 15-26. This drawing nearly filled one high-density 3.5" diskette (1.44MB).

Figure 15-26.
A rose drawn using the **SKETCH** command.
(Courtesy of Susan Waterman)

EXERCISE 15-12

❏ Start a new drawing or use one of your templates.
❏ Use the **SKETCH** command to sketch a bush, tree, or houseplant in plan (top) view.
❏ Save the drawing as EX15-12.

Chapter Test

Answer the following questions on a separate sheet of paper.

1. Give the command and entries required to draw a polyline from Point A to Point B with a beginning width of .500 and an ending width of 0.
   A. Command: _____
   B. Specify start point: _____
      Current line-width is 0.0000
   C. Specify next point or [Arc/Close/Halfwidth/Length/Undo/Width]: _____
   D. Specify starting width <0.0000>: _____
   E. Specify ending width <.500>: _____
   F. Specify next point or [Arc/Close/Halfwidth/Length/Undo/Width]: _____
   G. Specify next point or [Arc/Close/Halfwidth/Length/Undo/Width]: _____

2. Give the command and entries needed to draw two parallel lines, with a center-line in between, zero justification, and a style already saved as ROAD1:
   A. Command: _____
   B. Current settings: Justification = Top, Scale = 1.00, Style = STANDARD
   C. Specify start point or [Justification/Scale/STyle]: _____
   D. Enter mline style name or [?]: _____
   E. Current settings: Justification = Top, Scale = 1.00, Style = ROAD1
   F. Specify start point or [Justification/Scale/STyle]: _____
   G. Enter justification type [Top/Zero/Bottom] <top>: _____
   H. Current settings: Justification = Zero, Scale = 1.00, Style = ROAD1
   I. Specify start point or [Justification/Scale/STyle]: _____
   J. Specify next point: _____
   K. Specify next point or [Undo]: _____

3. How do you draw a filled arrow using the **PLINE** command?
4. Name two commands that can be used to draw wide lines.
5. Which **PLINE** command option allows you to specify the width from the center to one side?
6. What is an advantage of leaving the **FILL** mode turned off?
7. What is the difference between picking <u>U</u>ndo from the <u>E</u>dit pull-down menu and entering the **UNDO** command?
8. Name the command that is used to bring back an object that was previously removed using **UNDO**.
9. Name the **MLINE** command option that establishes how the resulting lines are offset based on the definition points provided.
10. Name the option that controls the multiplier value for the offset distances specified with the **MLINE** command.
11. How do you access the **Multiline Styles** dialog box?
12. Describe the function of the **Add** button in the **Element Properties** dialog box.
13. Describe the function of the **Linetype...** button in the **Element Properties** dialog box.
14. Define *caps.*
15. List the settings in the **Multiline Properties** dialog box that control the options for placing end caps on multilines.
16. Define *joints.*
17. What is displayed when you enter the **MLEDIT** command?
18. How do you access one of the **MLEDIT** options?
19. List the three options that are used for editing multiline intersections with the **MLEDIT** command.
20. Name the **MLEDIT** option in which the intersecting multiline is trimmed and left open after the first multiline is trimmed or extended to its intersection with the intersecting multiline.

21. Name the **MLEDIT** option that allows you to remove a vertex from an existing multiline.
22. Name the **MLEDIT** option that lets you remove a portion from an individual multiline element.
23. Name the **MLEDIT** option that removes all of the elements of a multiline between two specified points.
24. Name the **MLEDIT** option that repairs all cuts in a multiline between two selected points.
25. Explain why the Snap and Ortho modes should be turned off for most sketching applications.

Drawing Problems

1. Use the **PLINE** command to draw the following object with a .032 line width. Do not draw dimensions. Save the drawing as P15-1.

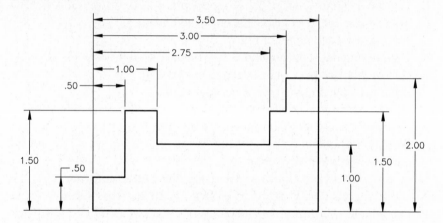

2. Use the **PLINE** command to draw the following object with a .032 line width. Do not draw dimensions. Save the drawing as P15-2.

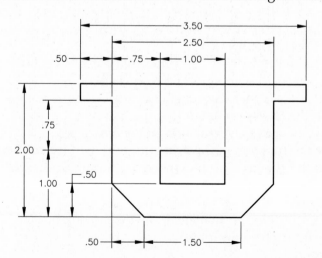

3. Use the **TRACE** command to draw the following object with a .032 line width. Do not draw dimensions.
   A. Turn off the **FILL** mode and use the **REGEN** command. Then, turn on **FILL** and reissue the **REGEN** command.
   B. Observe the difference with **FILL** mode on and off.
   C. Save the drawing as P15-3.

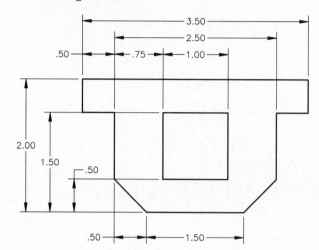

4. Use the **PLINE** command to draw the filled rectangle shown below. Do not draw dimensions. Save the drawing as P15-4.

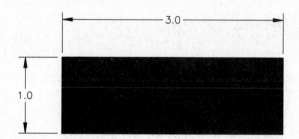

5. Draw the objects shown below. Do not draw dimensions. Then, use the **UNDO** command to remove Object B. Use the **REDO** command to bring Object B back. Save the drawing as P15-5.

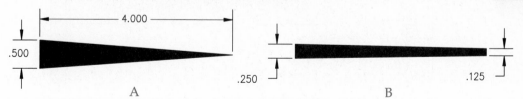

6. Draw the object shown below. Do not draw dimensions. Set decimal units, .25 grid spacing, and .0625 snap spacing. Set the limits to 11,8.5. Save the drawing as P15-6.

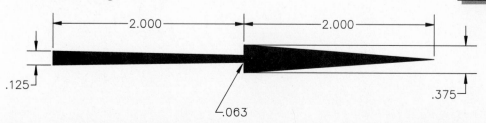

7. Open P4-12 and add the arrowheads. Draw one arrowhead using the **PLINE** command and then use the necessary editing commands to place the rest. Refer to the original problem. Save the drawing as P15-7.

8. Draw the objects shown using the **MLINE** command. Use the justification options indicated with each illustration. Set the limits to 11,8.5, the grid spacing to .50, and the snap spacing to .25. Set the offset for the multiline elements to .125. Do not add text or dimensions. Save the drawing as P15-8.

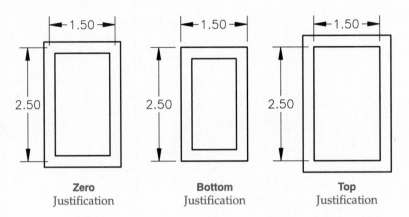

| **Zero** | **Bottom** | **Top** |
| Justification | Justification | Justification |

9. Draw the partial floor plan shown using the multiline commands. Carefully observe how the dimensions correlate with the multiline elements to determine your justification settings. Also, use the appropriate cap and multiline editing options. Set the limits to 88',68', the grid spacing to 24", and the snap spacing to 12", and use architectural units. Make all walls 6" thick. Do not add text or dimensions. Save the drawing as P15-9.

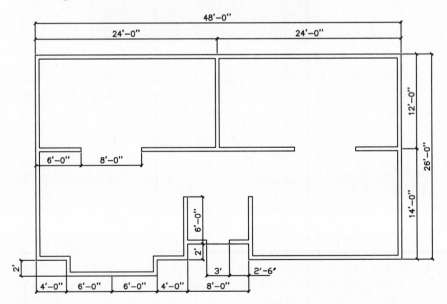

AutoCAD and its Applications—Basics

10. Draw the proposed subdivision map using the multiline commands. The roads are 30' wide. Use a centerline linetype for the center of each road. Adjust the linetype scale as needed. Do not include dimensions. Save the drawing as P15-10.

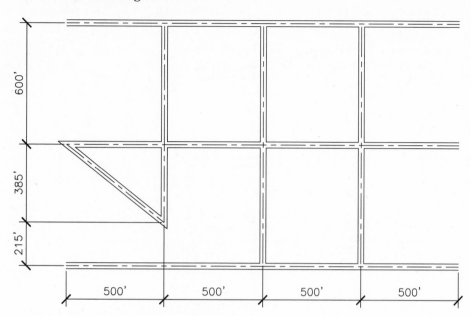

11. Draw the partial floor plan using multilines for the walls. Do not dimension the floor plan. Save the drawing as P15-11.

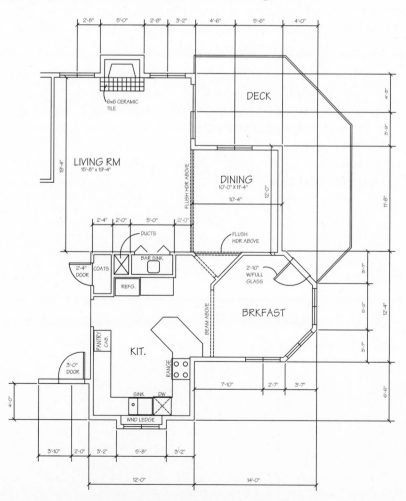

12. Draw the proposed electrical circuit using the multiline commands. Establish a line offset that is proportional to the given layout. Use a phantom linetype for the center of each run. Do not draw the grid, which is provided as a drawing aid. Save the drawing as P15-12.

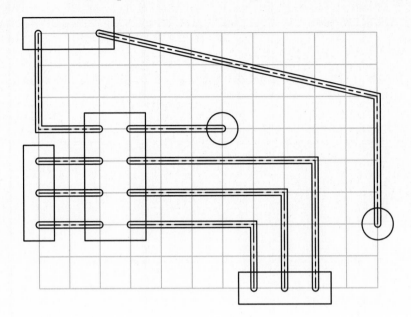

13. Use the **SKETCH** command to sign your name. Save the drawing as P15-13.

14. Use the **SKETCH** command to design the cover of a greeting card. Save the drawing as P15-14.

15. Locate a map of your state and make a photocopy. Tape the copy to your digitizer. Using the **SKETCH** command, do the following:
    A. Trace the outline of the map.
    B. Include all major rivers and lakes.
    C. Save the drawing as P15-15.

Drawing and Editing Polylines and Splines

Learning Objectives

After completing this chapter, you will be able to:

- Use the **PLINE** command to draw polylines and polyarcs.
- Edit existing polylines with the **PEDIT** command.
- Describe the function of each **PEDIT** command option.
- Use the **EXPLODE** command to change polylines into individual line and arc segments.
- Draw and edit spline curves.
- Create a polyline boundary.

The **PLINE** command was introduced in Chapter 15 as a way to draw thick and tapered lines. As you will find, the **PLINE** command can also be used to draw a variety of special shapes, limited only by your imagination. The discussion of the **PLINE** command in Chapter 15 focused on line-related options, such as **Width**, **Halfwidth**, and **Length**. The editing functions were limited to the **ERASE** and **UNDO** commands. This chapter explains how to use the **PLINE** command to create polyline arcs and introduces advanced editing commands for polylines. This chapter also discusses how to convert polylines into smooth curves, and how to create and edit true spline curves.

The **PLINE** command can be accessed by picking the **Polyline** button in the **Draw** toolbar or selecting **Polyline** from the **Draw** pull-down menu. You can also type PL or PLINE at the Command: prompt.

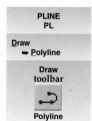

PLINE
PL

Draw
➥ Polyline

Draw
toolbar

Polyline

DRAWING POLYLINE ARCS

AutoCAD
User's
Guide 6

The **Arc** option of the **PLINE** command is similar to the **ARC** command, with the exception that the **PLINE Width** and **Halfwidth** options can be used to set an arc width. The arc width can range from 0 up to the radius of the arc. A polyline arc with different end widths is drawn by accessing the **Width** option and changing the width values. The arc shown in Figure 16-1 was drawn with the following command sequence:

```
Command: PL or PLINE.↵
Specify start point: (pick the first point)
Current line-width is 0.0000
Specify next point or [Arc/Close/Halfwidth/Length/Undo/Width]: W↵
Specify starting width <current>: .1↵
Specify ending width <current>: .4↵
Specify next point or [Arc/Close/Halfwidth/Length/Undo/Width]: A↵
Specify endpoint of arc or [Angle/CEnter/CLose/Direction/Halfwidth/Line/Radius/
    Second pt/Undo/Width]: (pick the arc endpoint)
Specify endpoint of arc or [Angle/CEnter/CLose/Direction/Halfwidth/Line/Radius/
    Second pt/Undo/Width]: ↵
Command:
```

Figure 16-1.
A polyline arc with different starting and ending widths.

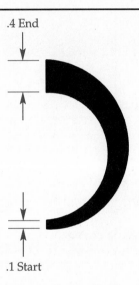

.4 End

.1 Start

Drawing a Continuous Polyline Arc

A polyline arc continued from a previous line or polyline is tangent to the last object drawn. The arc's center is determined automatically, but you can pick a new center. If a straight polyline is continued from a polyline arc, the arc's tangent direction remains the same as that of the previous line, arc, or polyline. This may not be what you want. In this case, it may be necessary to specify a setting with one of the **PLINE Arc** options. These include **Angle**, **CEnter**, **CLose**, **Direction**, **Radius**, and **Second pt** (second point). These options are very similar to the **ARC** command options and are explained in the following sections.

Specifying the Included Angle

The following is an example of using the **Angle** option inside the **PLINE Arc** command sequence to specify an angle for a polyline arc. The object drawn in this sequence is illustrated in Figure 16-2:

```
Specify next point or [Arc/Close/Halfwidth/Length/Undo/Width]: A↵
Specify endpoint of arc or [Angle/CEnter/CLose/Direction/Halfwidth/Line/Radius/
    Second pt/Undo/Width]: A↵
Specify included angle: (specify the included angle, such as 60, and press [Enter])
Specify endpoint of arc or [CEnter/Radius]: (select the arc endpoint)
Specify endpoint of arc or [Angle/CEnter/CLose/Direction/Halfwidth/Line/Radius/
    Second pt/Undo/Width]: ↵
Command:
```

Figure 16-2.
Drawing a polyline
arc with a specified
angle.

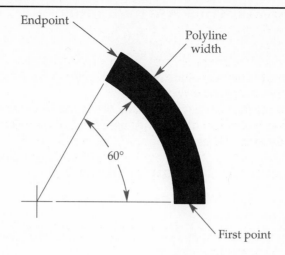

Using the CEnter Option

When a polyline arc is continued from a drawn object, the center point is calculated automatically. You may want to pick a new center point if the polyline arc does not continue from another object or if the center point calculated is not suitable. The **CEnter** option allows you to specify a new center point for the arc. It is used as follows:

> Specify next point or [Arc/Close/Halfwidth/Length/Undo/Width]: **A**↵
>
> Specify endpoint of arc or [Angle/CEnter/CLose/Direction/Halfwidth/Line/Radius/ Second pt/Undo/Width]: **CE**↵ *(notice that two letters, CE, are required for this option)*
>
> Specify center point of arc: *(select the arc center point)*
>
> Specify endpoint of arc or [Angle/Length]: *(select the arc endpoint, or type A or L, and press [Enter])*

If A is entered at this prompt, the next prompt is:

> Specify included angle: *(enter an included angle and press [Enter])*

If L is entered, the next prompt is:

> Specify length of chord: *(enter a chord length and press [Enter])*

Using the Direction Option

The **Direction** option alters the bearing of the arc. It changes the default option of placing a polyline arc tangent to the last polyline, arc, or line. This option can also be entered when you are drawing an unconnected polyline arc. The **Direction** option functions much like the **Direction** option of the **ARC** command. The following is an example of using the **Direction** option inside the **PLINE Arc** command sequence:

> Specify next point or [Arc/Close/Halfwidth/Length/Undo/Width]: **A**↵
>
> Specify endpoint of arc or [Angle/CEnter/CLose/Direction/Halfwidth/Line/Radius/ Second pt/Undo/Width]: **D**↵
>
> Specify the tangent direction for the start point of arc: *(enter a direction in positive or negative degrees, or specify a point on either side of the start point)*
>
> Specify endpoint of the arc: *(select an endpoint)*

Drawing a Polyline Arc by Radius

Polyline arcs can be drawn by giving the arc's radius. Enter the **Radius** option inside the **PLINE Arc** command sequence as follows:

Specify endpoint of arc or [Angle/CEnter/CLose/Direction/Halfwidth/Line/Radius/
    Second pt/Undo/Width]: **R↵**
Specify radius of arc: *(enter the arc radius and press* [Enter]*)*
Specify endpoint of arc or [Angle]: *(pick the arc endpoint or enter* A *to specify an
    included angle)*

Specifying a Three-Point Polyline Arc

A three-point polyline arc can be drawn by using the **Second pt** option. The sequence is as follows:

Specify endpoint of arc or [Angle/CEnter/CLose/Direction/Halfwidth/Line/Radius/
    Second pt/Undo/Width]: **S↵**
Specify second point on arc: *(pick the second point on the arc)*
Specify end point of arc: *(pick the endpoint to complete the arc)*

Using the CLose Option

The **CLose** option saves drafting time by automatically adding the last segment to close a polygonal shape. Using this option inside the **PLINE Arc** command sequence closes the shape with a polyline arc segment, rather than a straight polyline. See Figure 16-3. Notice that CL is entered at the prompt line to distinguish this option from the **CEnter** option:

Specify endpoint of arc or [Angle/CEnter/CLose/Direction/Halfwidth/Line/Radius/
    Second pt/Undo/Width]: **CL↵**

Figure 16-3.
Using the **CLose** option inside the **PLINE Arc** command sequence to close a polygonal shape.

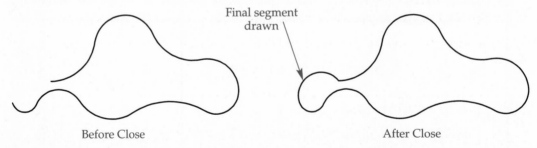

Before Close   After Close

EXERCISE 16-1

❏ Start a new drawing or use one of your templates.
❏ Draw several continuous polyline arcs. Draw at least four segments and use the **CLose** option to close the polyline.
❏ Draw a polyline arc with specified endpoints and a 90° included angle. Then continue from the first arc with another 90° polyline arc.
❏ Draw a polyline arc using two endpoints and a center point.
❏ Specify two endpoints, a center point, and an included angle to draw a polyline arc.
❏ Specify endpoints and a positive direction to draw a polyline arc. Then see how using a negative direction affects the arc.
❏ Specify the endpoints for a 1.5 unit radius polyline arc.
❏ Draw a polyline arc using three specified points.
❏ Save the drawing as EX16-1.

Presetting Polyline Widths

You can preset a constant width for polylines with the **PLINEWID** system variable. This can save you valuable drafting time. To specify a setting, enter PLINEWID at the Command: prompt and enter a new value.

Although objects drawn with the **POLYGON** command are constructed with polylines, they are not affected by the **PLINEWID** system variable. When you are done drawing wide polylines, be sure to set the value of **PLINEWID** to 0.

REVISING POLYLINES USING THE PEDIT COMMAND

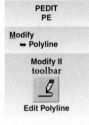

AutoCAD User's Guide 9

Polylines are drawn as single segments. A polyline joined to another polyline might then be joined to a polyline arc. Even though you draw connecting segments, AutoCAD puts them all together. The result is one polyline treated as a single object. When editing a polyline, you must edit it as one object or divide it into its individual segments. These changes are made with the **PEDIT** and **EXPLODE** commands. The **EXPLODE** command is discussed later in this chapter.

The **PEDIT** command is accessed by picking the **Edit Polyline** button from the **Modify II** toolbar, by typing PE or PEDIT at the Command: prompt, or by selecting **Polyline** from the **Modify** pull-down menu. You can also select a polyline and then right-click in the drawing area to display a shortcut menu. Then, choose **Polyline Edit**. The **PEDIT** command sequence is as follows:

> Command: **PE** *or* **PEDIT**⏎
> Select polyline: *(select the polyline)*

PEDIT
PE

Modify
➡ Polyline

Modify II
toolbar

Edit Polyline

You can then use the pick box to select a polyline to be edited. If you use the pick box on a wide polyline, you must place it on the edge of a polyline segment, rather than in the center. If the polyline you want to change was the last object drawn, simply type L for **Last** at the Select polyline: prompt. If the object you select is a line or arc object, the following message is displayed:

> Object selected is not a polyline
> Do you want to turn it into one? <Y>

Entering Y or pressing [Enter] turns the selected object into a polyline. Type N and press [Enter] to leave the object as is.

For 2000i Users...

In AutoCAD 2000i, you can select multiple polylines for editing by using the **Multiple** option at the Select polyline: prompt.

PROFESSIONAL TIP    A group of connected lines and arcs can be turned into a continuous polyline by using the **PEDIT Join** option. This option is discussed later in this chapter.

REVISING A POLYLINE AS ONE UNIT

A polyline can be edited as a single object, or it can be divided into individual segments to revise each segment individually. This section discusses the options for changing the entire polyline. The command sequence is as follows:

> Command: **PE** *or* **PEDIT**⏎
> Select polyline: *(pick a polyline)*
> Enter an option [Close/Join/Width/Edit vertex/Fit/Spline/Decurve/Ltype gen/Undo]: ⏎
> Command:

There is no default option for the **PEDIT** command (you must enter one of the options). Pressing [Enter] returns you to the Command: prompt.

Opening and Closing a Polyline

You may decide that you need to close an open polyline, or that you need to reopen a closed polyline. These functions are performed with the **Open** and **Close** options of the **PEDIT** command.

If you select a polyline that is already closed after issuing the **PEDIT** command, AutoCAD displays the **Open** option along with the other **PEDIT** command options. Enter this option to open the polyline. If you select an open polyline, the **Close** option is displayed instead of the **Open** option. Enter C to close the polyline. Open and closed polylines are shown in Figure 16-4.

The **Open** option is not displayed if you select a polyline that was closed by manually drawing the final segment. It is only available if the polygon was closed using the **Close** option of the **PLINE** command.

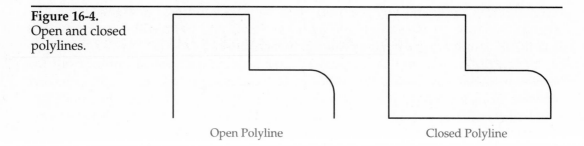

Figure 16-4.
Open and closed polylines.

Open Polyline   Closed Polyline

Joining Polylines to Other Polylines, Lines, and Arcs

Polylines, lines, and arcs that are connected can be joined to create a single polyline by using the **Join** option of the **PEDIT** command. This option works only if the polyline and other existing objects meet *exactly*. They cannot cross, nor can there be any spaces or breaks between the objects. See Figure 16-5. The command sequence to join objects to a polyline and turn them into a single object is as follows:

```
Command: PE or PEDIT↵
Select polyline: (select the original polyline)
Enter an option [Close/Join/Width/Edit vertex/Fit/Spline/Decurve/Ltype gen/Undo]: J↵
Select objects: (select all of the objects to be joined)
Select objects: ↵
n segments added to polyline
Enter an option [Close/Join/Width/Edit vertex/Fit/Spline/Decurve/Ltype gen/Undo]: ↵
Command:
```

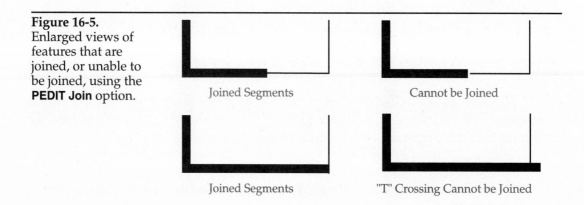

Figure 16-5.
Enlarged views of features that are joined, or unable to be joined, using the **PEDIT Join** option.

Joined Segments   Cannot be Joined

Joined Segments   "T" Crossing Cannot be Joined

Select each object to be joined or group the objects with one of the selection set options. The original polyline can be included in the selection set, but it does not need to be. See Figure 16-6.

Figure 16-6.
Joining a polyline to other connected lines and arcs.

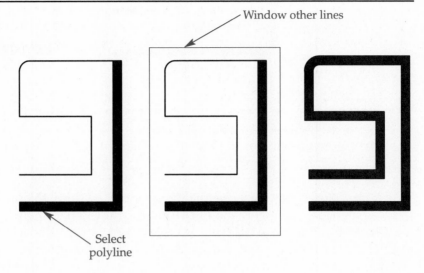

Window other lines

Select polyline

PROFESSIONAL TIP

Once items have been joined into a continuous polyline, the polyline can be closed using the **PEDIT Close** option.

Changing the Width of a Polyline

The **Width** option of the **PEDIT** command allows you to change a polyline width to a new width. The width of the original polyline can be constant, or it can vary. To change a polyline from a .06 width to a .1 width, follow these steps:

    Command: **PE** or **PEDIT**↵
    Select polyline: (pick the polyline)
    Enter an option [Close/Join/Width/Edit vertex/Fit/Spline/Decurve/Ltype gen/Undo]: **W**↵
    Specify new width for all segments: **.1**↵
    Enter an option [Close/Join/Width/Edit vertex/Fit/Spline/Decurve/Ltype gen/Undo]: ↵
    Command:

An unedited polyline and a new polyline after using the **PEDIT Width** option are shown in Figure 16-7.

Circles drawn with the **CIRCLE** command cannot be changed to polylines for editing purposes. Polyline circles can be created by using the **PLINE Arc** option and drawing two 180° arcs, or by using the **DONUT** command. You can change the width of donuts by picking each donut individually and using the **PEDIT Width** option as previously discussed.

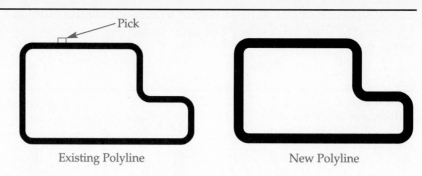

Figure 16-7.
Changing the width
of a polyline.

Pick

Existing Polyline

New Polyline

Editing a Polyline Vertex or Point of Tangency

The **Edit vertex** option of the **PEDIT** command is used to edit polyline vertices and points of tangency. A polyline *vertex* is where straight polyline segments meet and a *point of tangency* is where straight polyline segments or polyline arcs join other polyline arcs. When you enter the **Edit vertex** option, an "X" marker appears on screen at the first polyline vertex or point of tangency. The **Edit vertex** option has 10 additional options, as shown in the following command sequence:

Command: **PE** *or* **PEDIT**↵
Select polyline: *(pick the polyline)*
Enter an option [Close/Join/Width/Edit vertex/Fit/Spline/Decurve/Ltype gen/Undo]: **E**↵
Enter a vertex editing option [Next/Previous/Break/Insert/Move/Regen/Straighten/
   Tangent/Width/eXit] <N>:

The functions of the **Edit vertex** options are explained as follows:
- **Next.** Moves the "X" marker on screen to the next vertex or point of tangency on the polyline.
- **Previous.** Moves the marker to the previous vertex or point of tangency on the polyline.
- **Break.** Breaks a portion out of the polyline.
- **Insert.** Adds a new polyline vertex.
- **Move.** Moves a polyline vertex to a new location.
- **Regen.** Generates the revised version of the polyline.
- **Straighten.** Straightens polyline segments.
- **Tangent.** Specifies a tangent direction for curve fitting when using the **PEDIT Fit** option.
- **Width.** Changes a polyline segment width.
- **eXit.** Returns the **PEDIT** command prompt.

Only the current point identified by the "X" marker is affected by editing functions. In Figure 16-8, the marker is moved clockwise through the points using the **Next** option and counterclockwise using the **Previous** option. If you edit the vertices of a polyline and nothing appears to happen, use the **Regen** option to regenerate the polyline.

Figure 16-8.
Using the **Next** and **Previous** vertex editing options to specify polyline vertices. Note the different positions of the "X" marker.

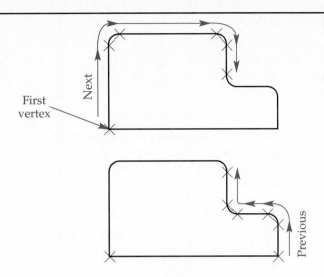

Making Breaks in a Polyline

You can break out a portion of a polyline by using the **Break** option after entering the **Edit vertex** option. First, use the **Next** or **Previous** option to move the "X" marker to the correct vertex, as shown in the following sequence:

> Enter an option [Close/Join/Width/Edit vertex/Fit/Spline/Decurve/Ltype gen/Undo]: **E**↵
> Enter a vertex editing option [Next/Previous/Break/Insert/Move/Regen/Straighten/ Tangent/Width/eXit] <N>: *(press* [Enter] *to move the "X" marker to the position where you want the break to begin)*
> Enter a vertex editing option [Next/Previous/Break/Insert/Move/Regen/Straighten/ Tangent/Width/eXit] <N>: **B**↵

AutoCAD accepts the highlighted vertex as the first break point. The sequence continues as follows:

> Enter an option [Next/Previous/Go/eXit] <N>: *(move the "X" marker to the next or previous vertex)*

Move the marker to the vertex you want to designate as the second break point. Then, enter G for **Go**. This instructs AutoCAD to remove the portion of the polyline between the two selected points. The results of the following command sequence are illustrated in Figure 16-9:

> Enter a vertex editing option
> [Next/Previous/Break/Insert/Move/Regen/Straighten/Tangent/Width/eXit] <N>: **B**↵ *(specifies Point 1)*
> Enter an option [Next/Previous/Go/eXit] <N>: **P**↵ *(specifies Point 2)*
> Enter an option [Next/Previous/Go/eXit] <P>: ↵ *(specifies Point 3)*
> Enter an option [Next/Previous/Go/eXit] <P>: ↵ *(specifies Point 4)*
> Enter an option [Next/Previous/Go/eXit] <P>: **G**↵ *(breaks the polyline between Points 1 and 4)*

Figure 16-9.
Using the **Break** vertex editing option to break out a portion of a polyline.

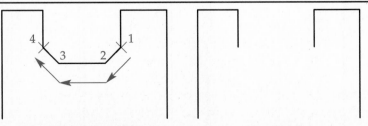

Break Points Specified   New Polyline

Inserting a New Vertex in a Polyline

A new vertex can be added to a polyline using the **Insert** vertex editing option. First, use the **Next** or **Previous** option to locate the vertex next to where you want the new vertex. Refer to Figure 16-10 as you go through the following command sequence:

Enter an option [Close/Join/Width/Edit vertex/Fit/Spline/Decurve/Ltype gen/Undo]: **E**↵
Enter a vertex editing option [Next/Previous/Break/Insert/Move/Regen/Straighten/ Tangent/Width/eXit] <N>: *(move the "X" marker to the desired location)*
Enter a vertex editing option [Next/Previous/Break/Insert/Move/Regen/Straighten/ Tangent/Width/eXit] <N>: **I**↵
Specify location for new vertex: *(pick the new vertex location using your pointing device or enter the coordinates)*
Enter a vertex editing option [Next/Previous/Break/Insert/Move/Regen/Straighten/ Tangent/Width/eXit] <N>: **X**↵

Figure 16-10.
Using the **Insert** vertex editing option to add a new vertex to a polyline.

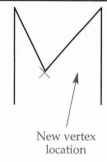

New vertex location

New vertex inserted

Moving a Polyline Vertex

The **Move** vertex editing option enables you to move a polyline vertex to a desired location. This option is similar to the **Insert** option. The "X" marker must first be placed on the vertex you want to move. Then, you can enter the **Move** option and specify the new location. The results of the following sequence are shown in Figure 16-11:

Enter an option [Close/Join/Width/Edit vertex/Fit/Spline/Decurve/Ltype gen/Undo]: **E**↵
Enter a vertex editing option [Next/Previous/Break/Insert/Move/Regen/Straighten/ Tangent/Width/eXit] <N>: *(move the "X" marker to the vertex to be moved)*
Enter a vertex editing option [Next/Previous/Break/Insert/Move/Regen/Straighten/ Tangent/Width/eXit] <N>: **M**↵
Specify new location for marked vertex: *(pick the desired location with your pointing device or enter the coordinates)*
Enter a vertex editing option [Next/Previous/Break/Insert/Move/Regen/Straighten/ Tangent/Width/eXit] <N>: **X**↵

Figure 16-11.
Using the **Move** vertex editing option to place a polyline vertex at a new location.

Existing vertex

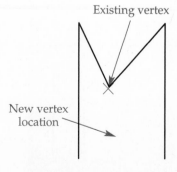
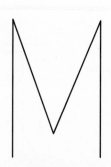

New vertex location

Vertex Moved

Straightening Polyline Segments or Arcs

The **Straighten** vertex editing option allows you to straighten polyline segments or arcs between two points. The command sequence is as follows:

> Enter an option [Close/Join/Width/Edit vertex/Fit/Spline/Decurve/Ltype gen/Undo]: **E**↵
> Enter a vertex editing option [Next/Previous/Break/Insert/Move/Regen/Straighten/Tangent/Width/eXit] <N>: *(move the "X" marker to the first point of the segments to be straightened)*
> Enter a vertex editing option [Next/Previous/Break/Insert/Move/Regen/Straighten/Tangent/Width/eXit] <N>: **S**↵
> Enter an option [Next/Previous/Go/eXit] <N>: *(move the "X" marker to the last point of the segments to be straightened)*
> Enter an option [Next/Previous/Go/eXit] <N>: **G**↵

If the "X" marker is not moved before G is entered, AutoCAD straightens the segment from the first marked point to the next vertex. This provides a quick way to straighten an arc. See Figure 16-12.

Figure 16-12.
The **Straighten** vertex editing option is used to straighten polyline segments.

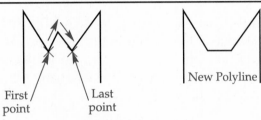

First point   Last point

Straightening Segments

New Polyline

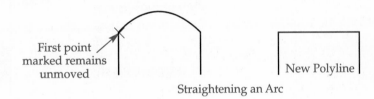

First point marked remains unmoved

Straightening an Arc

New Polyline

PROFESSIONAL TIP

Two AutoCAD express tools can be used when editing polylines. The **Multiple Pedit** and **Polyline Join** tools are available in the **Modify** cascading menu of the **Express** pull-down menu. Express tools are only available if a full installation of AutoCAD was performed. See Appendix A for more information on the express tools.

Changing Polyline Segment Widths

The **Width** vertex editing option is the only option that changes the starting and ending widths of an individual polyline segment. To change a segment width, move the "X" marker to the beginning vertex of the segment to be altered. Then, enter the **Width** option and specify the new width. The command sequence is as follows:

Enter an option [Close/Join/Width/Edit vertex/Fit/Spline/Decurve/Ltype gen/Undo]: **E**↵
Enter a vertex editing option [Next/Previous/Break/Insert/Move/Regen/Straighten/
Tangent/Width/eXit] <N>: *(move the "X" marker to the beginning vertex of the
segment to be changed)*
Enter a vertex editing option [Next/Previous/Break/Insert/Move/Regen/Straighten/
Tangent/Width/eXit] <N>: **W**↵
Specify starting width for next segment <*current width of segment*>: *(enter the
revised starting width and press* [Enter]*)*
Specify ending width for next segment <*revised starting width*>: *(enter the revised
ending width and press* [Enter]*, or press* [Enter] *to keep the width the same as the
starting width)*
Enter a vertex editing option
[Next/Previous/Break/Insert/Move/Regen/Straighten/Tangent/Width/eXit] <N>: **R**↵

Notice that the starting width default value is the current width of the segment to be changed. The ending width default value is the same as the revised starting width. If nothing appears to happen to the segment when you specify the ending width and press [Enter], enter the **Regen** option to have AutoCAD draw the revised polyline. See Figure 16-13.

Figure 16-13.
Changing the width of a polyline segment with the **Width** vertex editing option. Use the **Regen** option to display the change.

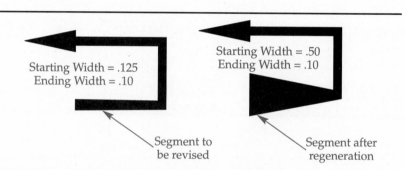

Starting Width = .125
Ending Width = .10

Starting Width = .50
Ending Width = .10

Segment to
be revised

Segment after
regeneration

EXERCISE 16-3

❏ Start a new drawing or use one of your templates.
❏ Draw a polyline with a series of segments. Draw the polyline with at least eight vertices and three arcs.
❏ Issue the **PEDIT** command and enter the **Edit vertex** option. Move the "X" marker around using the **Next** and **Previous** options.
❏ Break the polyline between any three points. Then, undo the breaks.
❏ Insert a new vertex in the polyline.
❏ Move one vertex of the polyline.
❏ Straighten one arc segment or at least three line segments.
❏ Change the starting and ending widths of one segment.
❏ Save the drawing as EX16-3.

AutoCAD and its Applications—Basics

Making Smooth Curves Out of Polylines

In some situations, you may need to convert a polyline into a series of smooth curves. One example of this is a graph. A graph may show a series of plotted points as a smooth curve rather than straight segments. This process is called *curve fitting* and is accomplished using the **PEDIT Fit** option and the **Tangent** vertex editing option.

The **Fit** option allows you to construct pairs of arcs passing through control points. You can specify the control points, or you can simply use the vertices of the polyline. Closely spaced control points produce a smooth curve.

Prior to curve fitting, each vertex can be given a tangent direction. AutoCAD then fits the curve based on the tangent directions that you set. However, you do not need to enter tangent directions. Specifying tangent directions is a way to edit vertices when the **PEDIT Fit** option does not produce the best results.

The **Tangent** vertex editing option is used to edit tangent directions. After entering the **PEDIT** command and the **Edit vertex** option, move the "X" marker to each vertex to be changed. Enter the **Tangent** option for each specified vertex and enter a tangent direction in degrees, or pick a point in the expected direction. The direction you choose is then indicated by an arrow placed at the vertex.

> Enter an option [Close/Join/Width/Edit vertex/Fit/Spline/Decurve/Ltype gen/Undo]: **E**⏎
> Enter a vertex editing option [Next/Previous/Break/Insert/Move/Regen/Straighten/
> Tangent/Width/eXit] <N>: *(move the "X" marker to the desired vertex)*
> Enter a vertex editing option [Next/Previous/Break/Insert/Move/Regen/Straighten/
> Tangent/Width/eXit] <N>: **T**⏎
> Specify direction of vertex tangent: *(specify a direction in positive or negative
> degrees and press [Enter], or pick a point in the desired direction)*

Continue by moving the marker to each vertex that you want to change, entering the **Tangent** option for each vertex and selecting a tangent direction. Once the tangent directions are given for all vertices to be changed, enter the **PEDIT Fit** option.

You can also enter the **PEDIT** command, select a polyline, and then enter the **Fit** option without adjusting tangencies if desired. The polyline shown in Figure 16-14 was made into a smooth curve using the following steps:

> Command: **PE** *or* **PEDIT**⏎
> Select polyline: *(pick the polyline to be edited)*
> Enter an option [Close/Join/Width/Edit vertex/Fit/Spline/Decurve/Ltype gen/Undo]: **F**⏎

If the resulting curve does not look like what you had anticipated, enter the **Edit vertex** option. Then, make changes using the various vertex editing options as necessary.

Figure 16-14.
Using the **PEDIT Fit** option to turn a polyline into a smooth curve.

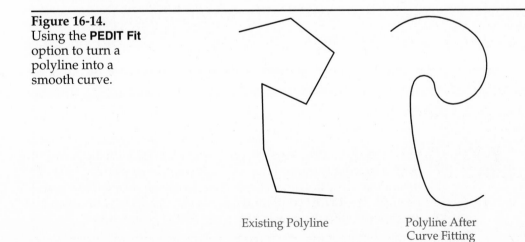

Existing Polyline

Polyline After
Curve Fitting

Using the PEDIT Spline Option

When a polyline is edited with the **PEDIT Fit** option, the resulting curve passes through polyline vertices. The **PEDIT Spline** option also smoothes the corners of a straight-segment polyline. However, this option produces different results. The resulting curve passes through the first and last control points or vertices only. However, the curve *pulls* toward the other vertices (but does not pass through them). The **Spline** option is used as follows:

Command: **PE** *or* **PEDIT**↵
Select polyline: *(pick the polyline to be edited)*
Enter an option [Close/Join/Width/Edit vertex/Fit/Spline/Decurve/Ltype gen/Undo]: **S**↵

The results of using the **Fit** and **Spline** options on a polyline are illustrated in Figure 16-15.

Figure 16-15.
A comparison of polylines edited with the **PEDIT Fit** and **Spline** options.

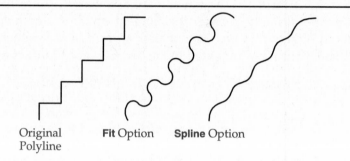

Original Polyline   **Fit** Option   **Spline** Option

Straightening All Segments of a Polyline

The **PEDIT Decurve** option returns a polyline edited with the **Fit** or **Spline** options to its original form. However, the information entered for tangent directions is kept for future reference. You can also use the **Decurve** option to straighten the segments of a polyarc. See Figure 16-16.

Command: **PE** *or* **PEDIT**↵
Select polyline: *(pick the polyline to be edited)*
Enter an option [Close/Join/Width/Edit vertex/Fit/Spline/Decurve/Ltype gen/Undo]: **D**↵

Figure 16-16.
The **PEDIT Decurve** option is used to straighten the curved segments of a polyline.

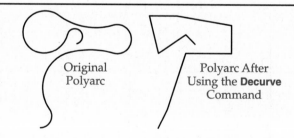

Original Polyarc   Polyarc After Using the **Decurve** Command

PROFESSIONAL TIP

If you make a mistake while editing a polyline, remember that the **Undo** option is available inside the **PEDIT** command. Using the **Undo** option more than once allows you to step backward through each option used. Press [Enter] to return to the Command: prompt. The **UNDO** command can also be used at the Command: prompt to undo the effects of the last **PEDIT** command.

❏ Start a new drawing or use one of your templates.
❏ Draw a polyline with at least five vertices. Make the polyline smooth using the **Fit** option of the **PEDIT** command.
❏ Return the polyline to its original form using the **PEDIT Decurve** option.
❏ Practice with the **Undo** option by first drawing a series of polyline segments. After using the **PEDIT** command to make several changes, use the **Undo** option to return to the original polyline.
❏ Save the drawing as EX16-4.

Changing the Appearance of Polyline Linetypes

The **PEDIT Ltype gen** (linetype generation) option determines how linetypes other than Continuous appear in relation to the vertices of a polyline. For example, when a Center linetype is used and the **Ltype gen** option is disabled, the polyline has a long dash at each vertex. When the **Ltype gen** option is activated, the polyline is generated with a constant pattern in relation to the vertices. The difference between using the **Ltype gen** option off and on is illustrated in Figure 16-17. Also shown are the effects these settings have on spline curves. To turn the **Ltype gen** option on, use the following procedure:

Command: **PE** *or* **PEDIT**↲
Select polyline: *(pick the polyline)*
Enter an option [Close/Join/Width/Edit vertex/Fit/Spline/Decurve/Ltype gen/Undo]: **L**↲
Enter polyline linetype generation option [ON/OFF] <Off>: **ON**↲

You can also change the **Ltype gen** option setting with the **PLINEGEN** system variable. This variable must be set before the desired polyline is drawn (the setting does not affect previously drawn polylines). The settings for the **PLINEGEN** system variable are 0 (off) and 1 (on).

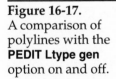

Figure 16-17.
A comparison of polylines with the **PEDIT Ltype gen** option on and off.

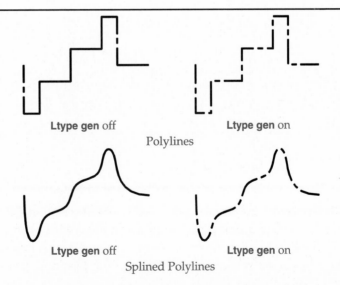

CONVERTING A POLYLINE INTO INDIVIDUAL LINE AND ARC SEGMENTS

EXPLODE
X

Modify
↳ Explode

Modify
toolbar

Explode

A polyline is a single object composed of polyline and polyline arc segments. The **EXPLODE** command allows you to change a polyline into a series of individual lines and arcs. You can then edit each segment individually.

To explode an object, pick the **Explode** button in the **Modify** toolbar, select **Explode** from the **Modify** pull-down menu, or type X or EXPLODE at the Command: prompt. When a wide polyline is exploded, the resulting line or arc is redrawn along the centerline of the original polyline. See Figure 16-18. After the **EXPLODE** command is issued, you are asked to select objects:

> Command: **X** *or* **EXPLODE**↵
> Select objects: *(pick the polyline to be exploded)*
> Select objects: ↵

The **EXPLODE** command removes all width characteristics and tangency information. However, AutoCAD gives you a chance to change your mind by offering this message:

> Exploding this polyline has lost width and tangent information.
> The UNDO command will restore it.

Figure 16-18.
Exploding a wide polyarc.

Existing Polyarc   Exploded Polyarc

EXERCISE 16-5

❑ Start a new drawing or use one of your templates.
❑ Draw a polyline of your own design. Include several different segment widths. Then, explode the polyline and observe what happens.
❑ Restore the original polyline using the **UNDO** command.
❑ Save the drawing as EX16-5.

ADDITIONAL METHODS FOR SMOOTHING POLYLINES

The methods for smoothing polylines that were introduced earlier in this chapter focused on using the **Fit** and **Spline** options of the **PEDIT** command. With the **Fit** option, the resulting *fit curve* passes through the polyline vertices. The **Spline** option creates a *spline curve* that passes through the first and last control points, or vertices. The resulting curve *pulls* toward the other vertices but does not pass through them.

There are also two spline curve options available for smoothing polylines—**Cubic** and **Quadratic**. These options create B-spline curves. A *cubic curve* is extremely smooth. A *quadratic curve* is not as smooth as a cubic curve, but it is smoother than a fit curve. Like a cubic curve, a quadratic curve passes through the first and last control points. The remainder of the curve is tangent to the polyline segments between the intermediate control points, as shown in Figure 16-19.

Figure 16-19.
A comparison of
curves drawn with
the **PEDIT Fit** option
and the **Quadratic**
and **Cubic** spline
curve options.

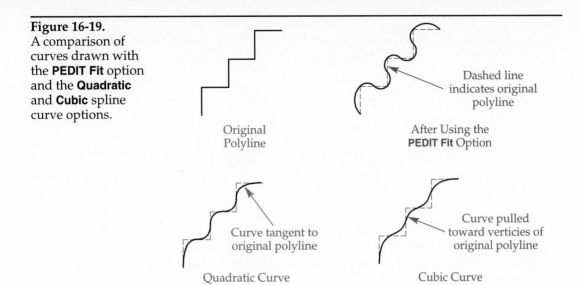

Original
Polyline

Dashed line
indicates original
polyline

After Using the
PEDIT Fit Option

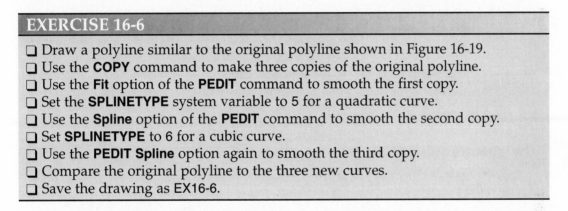

Curve tangent to
original polyline

Quadratic Curve

Curve pulled
toward verticies of
original polyline

Cubic Curve

The **SPLINETYPE** system variable determines whether AutoCAD draws cubic or quadratic curves. The default setting is 6. At this setting, a cubic curve is drawn when using the **Spline** option of the **PEDIT** command. If the **SPLINETYPE** system variable is set to 5, a quadratic curve is generated. The only valid values for **SPLINETYPE** are 5 and 6.

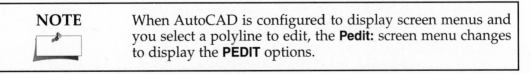

EXERCISE 16-6

❑ Draw a polyline similar to the original polyline shown in Figure 16-19.
❑ Use the **COPY** command to make three copies of the original polyline.
❑ Use the **Fit** option of the **PEDIT** command to smooth the first copy.
❑ Set the **SPLINETYPE** system variable to 5 for a quadratic curve.
❑ Use the **Spline** option of the **PEDIT** command to smooth the second copy.
❑ Set **SPLINETYPE** to 6 for a cubic curve.
❑ Use the **PEDIT Spline** option again to smooth the third copy.
❑ Compare the original polyline to the three new curves.
❑ Save the drawing as EX16-6.

The **SPLINESEGS** system variable controls the number of line segments used to construct spline curves. The **SPLINESEGS** default value is 8, and it can be set at the Command: prompt or in the **Segments in a polyline curve** setting in the **Display** resolution area of the **Display** tab of the **Options** dialog box. This setting creates a fairly smooth spline curve with moderate regeneration time. If you decrease the value, the resulting spline curve is less smooth. If you increase the value, the resulting spline curve is smoother. Although increasing the value above 8 creates a more precise spline curve, it also increases the regeneration time and drawing file size. The relationship between **SPLINESEGS** values and spline curves is shown in Figure 16-20.

NOTE

When AutoCAD is configured to display screen menus and you select a polyline to edit, the **Pedit:** screen menu changes to display the **PEDIT** options.

Figure 16-20.
A comparison of curves drawn with different **SPLINESEGS** system variable settings.

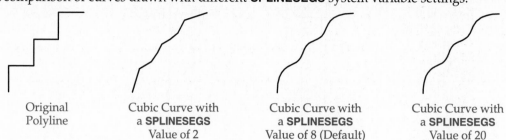

Original
Polyline

Cubic Curve with
a **SPLINESEGS**
Value of 2

Cubic Curve with
a **SPLINESEGS**
Value of 8 (Default)

Cubic Curve with
a **SPLINESEGS**
Value of 20

EXERCISE 16-7

❏ Draw a polyline similar to the original polyline shown in Figure 16-20.
❏ Use the **COPY** command to make three copies of the original polyline.
❏ Set the **SPLINETYPE** system variable to 6 for a cubic curve.
❏ Set the **SPLINESEGS** system variable to 2.
❏ Use the **Spline** option of the **PEDIT** command to smooth the first copy.
❏ Set **SPLINESEGS** to 8.
❏ Use the **PEDIT Spline** option to smooth the second copy.
❏ Set **SPLINESEGS** to 20.
❏ Use the **PEDIT Spline** option to smooth the third copy.
❏ Compare the original polyline to the three new curves and observe the smoothness of each curve.
❏ Save the drawing as EX16-7.

DRAWING CURVES USING THE **SPLINE** COMMAND

The **SPLINE** command is used to create a special type of curve called a nonuniform rational B-spline (NURBS). A NURBS curve is considered to be a true spline. A spline created by fitting a spline curve to a polyline is merely a linear approximation of a true spline and is not as accurate. An additional advantage of spline objects over smoothed polylines is that splines use less disk space.

To access the **SPLINE** command, pick the **Spline** button in the **Draw** toolbar, pick **Spline** from the **Draw** pull-down menu, or type SPL or SPLINE at the Command: prompt. A spline is created by specifying the control points along the curve using any standard coordinate entry method:

SPLINE
SPL

Draw
➥ Spline

Draw
toolbar

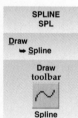

Spline

> Command: **SPL** *or* **SPLINE**↵
> Specify first point or [Object]: **2,2**↵
> Specify next point: **4,4**↵
> Specify next point or [Close/Fit tolerance] <start tangent>: **6,2**↵
> Specify next point or [Close/Fit tolerance] <start tangent>: ↵
> Specify start tangent: ↵
> Specify end tangent: ↵
> Command:

When you have given all of the necessary points along the spline, pressing [Enter] ends the point specification process and allows the start tangency and end tangency to be entered. Specifying the tangents changes the direction in which the spline curve begins and ends. Pressing [Enter] at these prompts accepts the default direction, as calculated by AutoCAD, for the specified curve. The results of the previous command sequence are shown in Figure 16-21.

AutoCAD
User's
Guide **6**

NOTE If only two points are specified along the spline curve, an object that looks like a line is created, but the actual object is still a spline.

Figure 16-21.
A spline drawn with the **SPLINE** command, using the AutoCAD defaults for the start and end tangents.

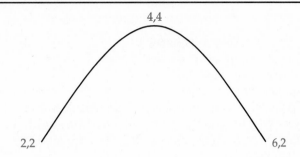

Drawing Closed Splines

The **Close** option of the **SPLINE** command enables you to draw closed splines, Figure 16-22. The command sequence is as follows:

```
Command: SPL or SPLINE↵
Specify first point or [Object]: 2,2↵
Specify next point: 4,4↵
Specify next point or [Close/Fit tolerance] <start tangent>: 6,2↵
Specify next point or [Close/Fit tolerance] <start tangent>: C↵
Specify tangent: ↵
Command:
```

After closing a spline, you are prompted to specify a tangent direction for the start/end point of the spline. Pressing [Enter] accepts the AutoCAD default.

Figure 16-22.
Using the **Close** option of the **SPLINE** command with AutoCAD default tangents to draw a closed spline. Compare this spline to the object shown in Figure 16-21.

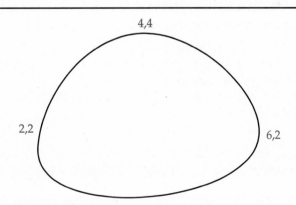

Altering the **Fit Tolerance** Specifications

Different results can be achieved when drawing splines by altering the specifications used with the **Fit Tolerance** option. The outcomes of different settings vary, depending on the configuration of the individual spline object. The setting specifies a *tolerance* within which the spline curves as it passes through the control points.

Specifying the Start and End Tangents

The previous examples using the **SPLINE** command used AutoCAD's default start and end tangents. You can set start and end tangent directions by entering values at the prompts that appear after you pick the points of the spline. The tangency is based on the tangent direction of the selected point. The results of using the horizontal and vertical tangent directions using Ortho mode are shown in Figure 16-23. The following command sequence is used:

```
Command: SPL or SPLINE↵
Specify first point or [Object]: 2,2↵
Specify next point: 4,4↵
Specify next point or [Close/Fit tolerance] <start tangent>: 6,2↵
Specify next point or [Close/Fit tolerance] <start tangent>: ↵
Specify start tangent: (move cursor in tangent direction and press [Enter])
Specify end tangent: (move cursor in tangent direction and press [Enter])
Command:
```

Figure 16-23.
These splines were drawn through the same points but have different start and end tangent directions. The tangent directions, which can be selected using Ortho mode, are shown as arrows.

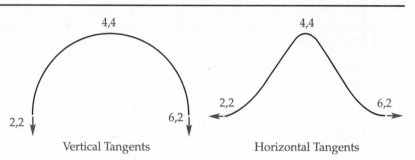

Vertical Tangents   Horizontal Tangents

Converting a Spline-Fitted Polyline to a Spline

A spline-fitted polyline object can be converted to a spline object using the **Object** option of the **SPLINE** command. This option works for either 2D or 3D objects. The command sequence is as follows:

```
Command: SPL or SPLINE↵
Specify first point or [Object]: O↵
Select objects to convert to splines...
Select objects: (pick the spline-fitted polyline)
Select objects: ↵
Command:
```

EXERCISE 16-8

❏ Start a new drawing or use one of your templates.
❏ Draw a spline similar to the one shown in Figure 16-21. Use the AutoCAD default tangents.
❏ Draw a similar spline to the right of the first one using the **Close** option and default tangents.
❏ Draw two splines similar to the objects shown in Figure 16-23. Use Ortho mode for the start and end tangents.
❏ Save the drawing as EX16-8.

The **SPLINEDIT** command allows you to edit spline objects. Several editing options are available. Control points can be added, moved, or deleted to alter the shape of an existing curve. A spline can also be opened or closed. In addition, you can change the start and end tangents.

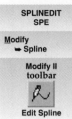

SPLINEDIT
SPE

<u>M</u>odify
➡ Spline

Modify II
toolbar

Edit Spline

To access the **SPLINEDIT** command, pick the **Edit Spline** button from the **Modify II** toolbar, pick **Spline** from the **Modify** pull-down menu, or enter SPE or SPLINEDIT at the Command: prompt. The command sequence is as follows:

    Command: **SPE** *or* **SPLINEDIT**↵
    Select spline: *(pick a spline)*

When you pick a spline, the control points are identified by grips, as shown in Figure 16-24. The command sequence continues with this prompt:

    Enter an option [Fit data/Close/Move vertex/Refine/rEverse/Undo]:

The **SPLINEDIT** command options are described in the following sections.

Figure 16-24.
The control points on a spline are displayed as grips when using the **SPLINEDIT** command.

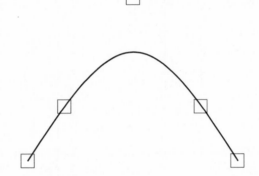

Editing Fit Data

The **Fit data** option of the **SPLINEDIT** command allows spline control points to be edited. Spline control points are called *fit points*. Entering the **Fit data** option gives you the options shown in the following command sequence:

    Command: **SPE** *or* **SPLINEDIT**↵
    Select spline: *(pick a spline)*
    Enter an option [Fit data/Close/Move vertex/Refine/rEverse/Undo]: **F**↵
    Enter a fit data option [Add/Close/Delete/Move/Purge/Tangents/toLerance/eXit] <eXit>:

Each of the **Fit data** options is explained next. See Figure 16-25 for examples of using these options.

- **Add.** This option allows you to add new fit points to a spline definition. When adding, a fit point can be located by picking a point, or you can enter coordinates. Fit points appear as unselected grips. When one is selected, it becomes highlighted along with the next fit point on the spline. You can then add a fit point between the two highlighted points. If the endpoint of the spline is selected, only the endpoint becomes highlighted. If the start point of the spline is selected, the following prompt is issued:

    Specify new point or [After/Before]: <exit>:

    This prompt asks whether to insert the new fit point before or after the existing one. Respond by entering A or B accordingly. When a fit point is added, the spline curve is refit through the added point. See Figure 16-25.

Figure 16-25.
Examples of using the **SPLINEDIT Fit Data** options to edit a spline. Compare the original spline to each of the edited objects.

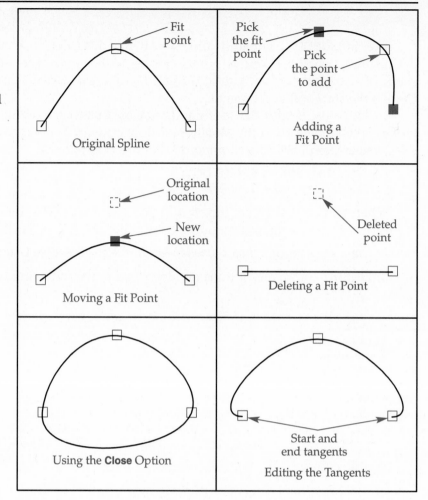

The **Add** option functions in a running mode. This means that you can continue to add points as needed. By pressing [Enter] at a Specify new point <exit>: prompt, you can select other existing fit points. Therefore, points can be added anywhere on the spline.

- **Close/Open.** If the selected spline is open, the **Close** option is displayed. If the spline is closed, the **Open** option is displayed. These options allow you to open a closed spline or close an open spline.
- **Delete.** The **Delete** option allows you to delete fit points as needed. However, at least two fit points must remain. Even when only two points remain, the object is still defined as a spline, not a line. Like the **Add** option, the **Delete** option operates in a running mode, allowing as many deletions as needed. The spline curve is refit through the remaining fit points.
- **Move.** This option allows fit points to be moved as necessary. When the **Move** option is entered, the start point of the spline is highlighted. You can specify a different location simply by picking a new point with your left mouse button. You can also specify other fit points to move. The options are explained as follows:
  - **Specify new location.** This option allows you to move the currently highlighted point to a specified location.
  - **Next.** This option highlights the next fit point. It is activated by pressing [Enter].
  - **Previous.** Entering this option highlights the previous fit point.
  - **Select point.** This option allows you to pick a different fit point to move rather than using the **Next** or **Previous** options.
  - **eXit.** This option returns you to the **Fit Data** option prompt.

- **Purge.** This option lets you remove fit point data from a spline. After using this option, the resulting spline is not as easy to edit. In very complex drawings, such as Geographical Information Systems (GIS) drawings, where many complex splines are created, purging fit point data reduces the file size by simplifying the definition. Once a spline is purged, the **Fit Data** option is no longer displayed by the **SPLINEDIT** command for the purged spline.
- **Tangents.** This option allows editing of the start and end tangents for an open spline and editing of the start tangent for a closed spline. The tangency is set based on the tangent direction of the selected point. You can also use the **System default** option to set the tangency values to the AutoCAD defaults as follows:

  Command: **SPE** *or* **SPLINEDIT**↵
  Select spline: *(pick a spline)*
  Enter an option [Fit data/Close/Move vertex/Refine/rEverse/Undo]: **F**↵
  Enter a fit data option
     [Add/Close/Delete/Move/Purge/Tangents/toLerance/eXit] <eXit>: **T**↵
  Specify start tangent or [System default]: **S**↵
  Specify end tangent or [System default]: **S**↵
  Enter a fit data option
     [Add/Close/Delete/Move/Purge/Tangents/toLerance/eXit] <eXit>: ↵
  Enter an option [Fit data/Close/Move vertex/Refine/rEverse/Undo]: ↵
  Command:

- **toLerance.** Fit tolerance values can be adjusted using this option. The results are immediate, so the fit tolerance can be adjusted as necessary to produce different results.
- **eXit.** Entering this option returns you to the **SPLINEDIT** command option prompt.

Opening or Closing a Spline

The **SPLINEDIT Open** and **Close** options are alternately displayed depending on the current status of the spline object being edited. If the spline is open, the **Close** option is displayed. If the spline is closed, the **Open** option is displayed.

Moving a Vertex

The **SPLINEDIT Move vertex** option allows you to move the fit points of a spline. When you access this option, you can specify a new location for a selected fit point. The options displayed are identical to those used with the **Move** option inside the **SPLINEDIT Fit data** command sequence:

  Command: **SPE** *or* **SPLINEDIT**↵
  Select spline: *(pick a spline)*
  Enter an option [Fit data/Close/Move vertex/Refine/rEverse/Undo]: **M**↵
  Specify new location or [Next/Previous/Select point/eXit] <N>:

You can pick a new location for the highlighted fit point using your left mouse button, or you can enter an option. The **Move vertex** options are explained below:
- **Specify new location.** Allows you to move the currently highlighted point to a specified location.
- **Next.** Highlights the next fit point.
- **Previous.** Highlights the previous fit point.
- **Select point.** Allows you to pick a different fit point to move, rather than using the **Next** or **Previous** options.
- **eXit.** Returns you to the **SPLINEDIT** command prompt.

Smoothing or Reshaping a Section of the Spline

The **SPLINEDIT Refine** option allows fine tuning of the spline curve. Fit points can be added to help smooth or reshape a section of the spline. When you use this option, the fit point data is removed from the spline. The command sequence is as follows:

Command: **SPE** *or* **SPLINEDIT.**↵
Select spline: *(pick a spline)*
Enter an option [Fit data/Close/Move vertex/Refine/rEverse/Undo]: **R.**↵
Enter a refine option [Add control point/Elevate order/Weight/eXit] <eXit>:

Each of the **Refine** options is explained as follows:
- **Add control point.** This option allows you to specify new fit points on a spline as needed.
- **Elevate order.** The *order* of a spline is the degree of the spline polynomial +1. For example, a cubic spline has an order of 4. Elevating the order of a spline causes more control points to appear on the curve for greater control. In Figure 16-26, the control point order of the spline is elevated from 4 to 6. The setting can be from 4 to 26, but it cannot be adjusted downward. For example, if the order is set to 24, the only remaining settings are 25 and 26.

Figure 16-26.
The effects of elevating the order of control points on a spline and increasing the weight of an individual control point.

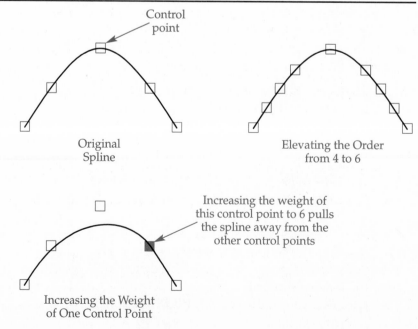

Control point

Original Spline

Elevating the Order from 4 to 6

Increasing the weight of this control point to 6 pulls the spline away from the other control points

Increasing the Weight of One Control Point

- **Weight.** This option allows you to change the *weight* of individual control points. The default setting of 1.0000 can be adjusted to a higher or lower value. When all of the spline control points have the same weight, they all exert the same amount of "pull" on the resulting spline. When a weight value is lessened, the corresponding control point does not pull the spline as close to it as before. Likewise, when a weight value is increased, the control point exerts more pull on the direction of the spline. See Figure 16-26. The weight setting must be positive. The control point selection options of the **Weight** option are the same as those used with the **SPLINEDIT Move vertex** option. You can specify a new weight for the highlighted point by using the **Enter new weight** option, as shown below:

> Enter a refine option [Add control point/Elevate order/Weight/eXit] <eXit>: **W.↵**
> Enter new weight (current = 1.0000) or [Next/Previous/Select point/eXit]
> <N>: *(enter a positive number)*

Reversing the Order of Spline Control Points

The **rEverse** option of the **SPLINEDIT** command allows you to reverse the listed order of the spline control points. This makes the previous start point the new endpoint, and the previous endpoint the new start point. Using this option affects the various control point selection options as a result.

Undoing SPLINEDIT Changes

The **SPLINEDIT Undo** option undoes the previous change made to the spline. You can also use this option to undo changes back to the beginning of the current **SPLINEDIT** command sequence.

Exiting the SPLINEDIT Command

To exit the **SPLINEDIT** command, simply press [Enter] at the **SPLINEDIT** command prompt after making changes. This returns you to the Command: prompt.

EXERCISE 16-10

❑ Start a new drawing or use one of your templates.
❑ Draw a spline similar to the original spline shown in Figure 16-26. Use the AutoCAD default tangents.
❑ Copy the original spline to two locations, similar to the layout in Figure 16-26.
❑ Use the **SPLINEDIT** command on one of the new splines to elevate the order of control points.
❑ Use the **SPLINEDIT** command to increase the weight of one of the control points on the other spline.
❑ Save the drawing as EX16-10.

CREATING A POLYLINE BOUNDARY

When you draw an object with the **LINE** command, each line segment is a single object. You can create a polyline boundary of an area made up of closed line segments using the **BOUNDARY** command. To do so, pick **Boundary...** from the **Draw** pull-down menu, or type BO or BOUNDARY at the Command: prompt.

This displays the **Boundary Creation** dialog box, Figure 16-27. Many of the features in this dialog box are inactive, because they are used for hatching operations. The inactive features are accessed by using the **BHATCH** command. This command is covered in Chapter 22.

Figure 16-27.
The **Boundary Creation** dialog box.

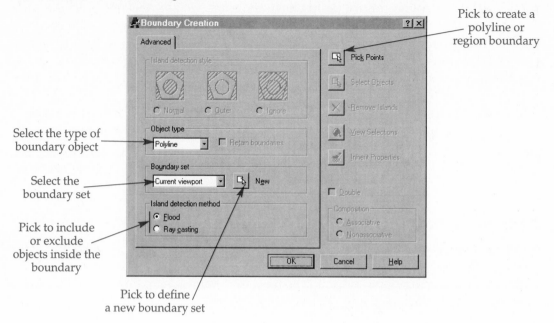

Pick to create a polyline or region boundary

Select the type of boundary object

Select the boundary set

Pick to include or exclude objects inside the boundary

Pick to define a new boundary set

The **Object type** drop-down list contains two options, **Polyline** and **Region**. The **Polyline** option is the default. If set to **Polyline**, AutoCAD creates a polyline around the area. If set to **Region**, AutoCAD creates a closed 2D area. A region may be used for area calculations, shading, or other purposes.

The **Boundary set** drop-down list has the **Current viewport** setting active. A *boundary set* is the portion of the drawing or area that AutoCAD evaluates when defining a boundary. The **Current viewport** option defines the boundary set from everything visible in the current viewport. The **New** button, located to the right of the drop-down list, allows you to define a boundary set. When you pick this button, the **Boundary Creation** dialog box closes and the Select objects: prompt appears. You can then select the objects you want to use to create a boundary set. After you are done, press [Enter]. The **Boundary Creation** dialog box returns with **Existing set** active in the **Boundary set** drop-down list. This means that the boundary set is defined from the objects that you selected.

The **Island detection method** area is used to specify whether objects within the boundary are used as boundary objects. Objects inside a boundary are called *islands*, Figure 16-28. There are two options in the **Island detection method** area. Activate the **Flood** option button if you want islands to be included as boundary objects. Activate the **Ray casting** button if you do not want to include islands as boundary objects.

Figure 16-28.
Objects within a boundary called islands can be included or excluded when defining a boundary set.

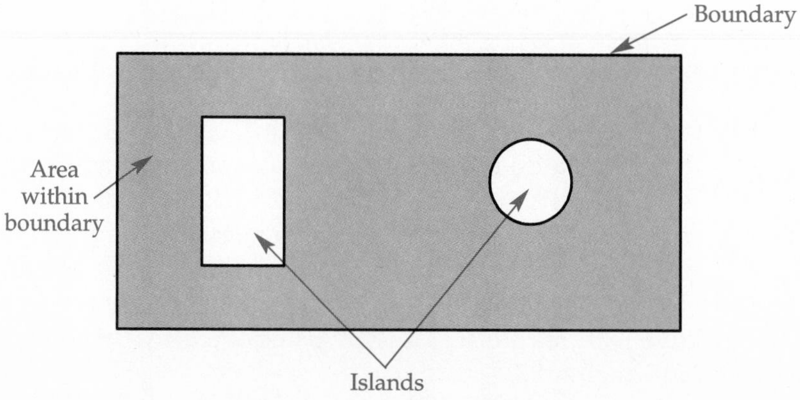

Boundary

Area within boundary

Islands

The only other active feature in the **Boundary Creation** dialog box is the **Pick Points** button, located in the upper-right corner. When you pick this button, the **Boundary Creation** dialog box closes and the Select internal point: prompt appears.

If the point you pick is inside a closed polygon, the boundary is highlighted, as shown in Figure 16-29. If the point you pick is not within a closed polygon, the **Boundary Definition Error** alert box appears. Pick **OK**, close the area in which you want to pick, and try again.

Unlike an object created with the **PEDIT Join** option, a polyline boundary created with the **BOUNDARY** command does not replace the original objects used to create it. The polyline simply *traces* over the defining objects with a polyline. Thus, the separate objects still exist and are *underneath* the newly created boundary. To avoid duplicate geometry, move the boundary to another location on screen, erase the original defining objects, and then move the boundary back to its original position.

Figure 16-29.
When you select a point inside a closed polygon, the boundary becomes highlighted. Boundaries must be closed objects.

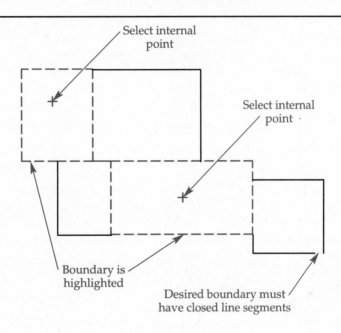

Select internal point

Select internal point

Boundary is highlighted

Desired boundary must have closed line segments

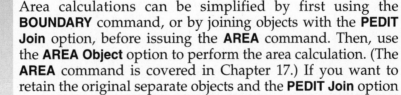

PROFESSIONAL TIP

Area calculations can be simplified by first using the **BOUNDARY** command, or by joining objects with the **PEDIT Join** option, before issuing the **AREA** command. Then, use the **AREA Object** option to perform the area calculation. (The **AREA** command is covered in Chapter 17.) If you want to retain the original separate objects and the **PEDIT Join** option was used, explode the joined polyline. If the **BOUNDARY** command was used, simply erase the polyline boundary.

Chapter Test

Answer the following questions on a separate sheet of paper.

1. Give the command and entries required to create a polyline arc with a starting width of 0 and an ending width of .25. Draw the arc from a known center to an endpoint.
   A. Command: _____
   B. Specify start point: _____
   C. Specify next point or [Arc/Close/Halfwidth/Length/Undo/Width]: _____
   D. Specify starting width: _____
   E. Specify ending width: _____
   F. Specify next point or [Arc/Close/Halfwidth/Length/Undo/Width]: _____
   G. Specify endpoint of arc or [Angle/CEnter/CLose/Direction/Halfwidth/Line/Radius/ Second pt/Undo/Width]: _____
   H. Specify center point of arc: _____
   I. Specify endpoint of arc or [Angle/Length]: _____
   J. Specify endpoint of arc or [Angle/CEnter/CLose/Direction/Halfwidth/Line/Radius/ Second pt/Undo/Width]: _____

2. Give the command and entries required to turn three connected lines into a polyline:
   A. Command: _____
   B. Select polyline: _____
      Object selected is not a polyline. Do you want to turn it into one? <Y>: _____
   C. Enter an option [Close/Join/Width/Edit vertex/Fit/Spline/Decurve/Ltype gen/Undo]: _____
   D. Select objects: _____
   E. Select objects: _____
   F. Select objects: _____
   G. Enter an option [Close/Join/Width/Edit vertex/Fit/Spline/ Decurve/Ltype gen/Undo]: _____

3. Give the command and entries needed to change the width of a polyline from .1 to .25:
   A. Command: _____
   B. Select polyline: _____
   C. Enter an option [Close/Join/Width/Edit vertex/Fit/Spline/Decurve/Ltype gen/Undo]: _____
   D. Specify new width for all segments: _____
   E. Enter an option [Close/Join/Width/Edit vertex/Fit/Spline/Decurve/Ltype gen/Undo]: _____

*For Questions 4 through 10, give the **PEDIT Edit vertex** option that relates to the definition given.*

4. Moves the "X" marker to the next position.
5. Moves a polyline vertex to a new location.
6. Breaks a portion out of a polyline.
7. Generates the revised version of a polyline.
8. Specifies a tangent direction.
9. Adds a new polyline vertex.
10. Returns you to the **PEDIT** command prompt.
11. Which **PEDIT** command options allow you to change the starting and ending widths of a polyline?
12. Why may it appear that nothing happens after you change the starting and ending widths of a polyline?
13. Name the **PEDIT** command option and the vertex editing option used for curve fitting.
14. Which command will remove all width characteristics and tangency information from a polyline?
15. What happens to the screen cursor after you enter the **PEDIT** command?
16. Which two **PEDIT** command options allow you to open a closed polyline and close an open polyline?
17. When you enter the **Edit vertex** option of the **PEDIT** command, where is the "X" marker placed by AutoCAD?
18. How do you move the "X" marker to edit a different polyline vertex?

19. Can you use the **Fit** option of the **PEDIT** command without using the **Tangent** vertex editing option first?
20. Explain the difference between a fit curve and a spline curve.
21. Explain the relationship between a quadratic curve, a cubic curve, and a fit curve.
22. Discuss the appearance of a quadratic curve.
23. What **SPLINETYPE** system variable setting allows you to draw a quadratic curve?
24. What **SPLINETYPE** setting allows you to draw a cubic curve?
25. Name the system variable that can be set to adjust the smoothness of a spline curve.
26. Name the pull-down menu and menu selection used to access the polyline editing options.
27. Explain how you can adjust the way polyline linetypes are generated using the **PEDIT** command.
28. Name the system variable that allows you to alter the way polyline linetypes are generated.
29. Name the command used to create a polyline boundary.
30. Name the command that can be used to create a true spline.
31. How do you accept the AutoCAD defaults for the start and end tangents of a spline?
32. Name the **SPLINE** command option that allows you to turn a spline-fitted polyline into a true spline.
33. Name the command that allows you to edit splines.
34. What is the purpose of the **Add** option used inside the **SPLINEDIT Fit data** command sequence?
35. How many fit points must remain when making deletions to a spline with the **Delete** fit data option?
36. Name the two options that allow you to move the fit points in a spline.
37. What is the purpose of the **SPLINEDIT Refine** option?
38. Identify the **SPLINEDIT** refine option that lets you increase the number of control points appearing on a spline curve for greater control.
39. Name the **SPLINEDIT** refine option that controls the pull exerted by a control point on a spline.
40. How many changes can you undo inside the **SPLINEDIT** command with the **Undo** option?

Drawing Problems

Start a new drawing for each of the following problems. Specify your own units, limits, and other settings to suit each problem.

1. Draw the polyline shown below. Use the **PLINE Arc**, **Width**, and **Close** options to complete the shape. Set the polyline width to 0, except at the points indicated. Save the drawing as P16-1.

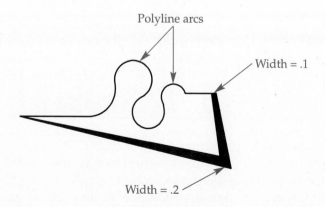

Polyline arcs

Width = .1

Width = .2

2. Draw the two curved arrows shown below using the **PLINE Arc** and **Width** options. The arrowheads should have a starting width of 1.4 and an ending width of 0. The body of each arrow should have a beginning width of .8 and an ending width of .4. Save the drawing as P16-2.

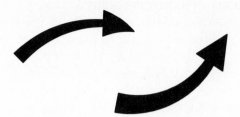

3. Open drawing P16-1 and use the **PEDIT** command to change the object drawn into a rectangle. Use the **PEDIT Decurve** and **Width** options and the **Straighten**, **Insert**, and **Move** vertex editing options. Make a copy of the original object to edit. Save the completed drawing as P16-3.

4. Open drawing P16-2 and make the following changes. Then, save the drawing as P16-4.
   A. Combine the two polylines using the **PEDIT Join** option.
   B. Change the beginning width of the left arrow to 1.0 and the ending width to .2.
   C. Draw a polyline .062 wide similar to Line A below.

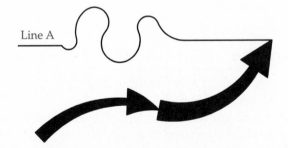

Line A

5. Draw a polyline .032 wide using the following absolute coordinates:

Point	Coordinates	Point	Coordinates	Point	Coordinates
1	1,1	5	3,3	9	5,5
2	2,1	6	4,3	10	6,5
3	2,2	7	4,4	11	6,6
4	3,2	8	5,4	12	7,6

Copy the polyline three times. Use the **PEDIT Fit** option to smooth the first copy. Use the **PEDIT Spline** option to turn the second copy into a quadratic curve. Make the third copy into a cubic curve. Use the **PEDIT Decurve** option to return one polyline to its original form. Save the drawing as P16-5.

6. Use the **PLINE** command to draw a patio plan similar to the one shown in Example A below. Draw the house walls 6″ wide. Copy the drawing three times and use the **PEDIT** command to create the remaining designs shown. Use the **Fit** option for Example B, a quadratic spline for Example C, and a cubic spline for Example D. Change the **SPLINETYPE** system variable as required. Save the drawing as P16-6.

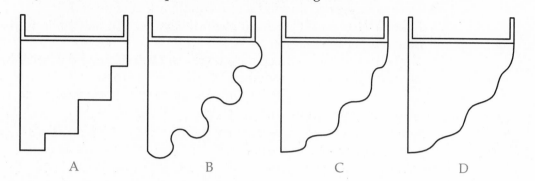

7. Open drawing P16-8 and create four new patio designs. This time, use grips to edit the polylines and create designs similar to Examples A, B, C, and D below. Save the drawing as P16-7.

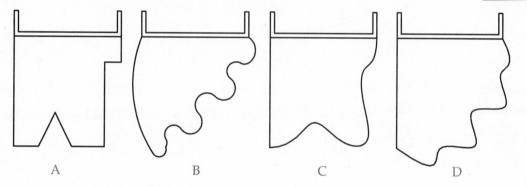

8. Use the **SPLINE** command and other commands such as **ELLIPSE**, **MIRROR**, **OFFSET**, and **PLINE** to design an architectural door knocker similar to the one shown. Use the Gothice text font to place your initials in the center. Save the drawing as P16-8.

9. Use the **SPLINE** command to draw the curve for the cam displacement diagram below. Use the following guidelines and the given drawing to complete this problem:
    A. The total rise equals 2.000.
    B. The total displacement can be any length.
    C. Divide the total displacement into 30° increments.
    D. Draw a half circle divided into 6 equal parts on one end.
    E. Draw a horizontal line from each division of the half circle to the other end of the diagram.
    F. Draw the displacement curve with the **SPLINE** command by picking points where the horizontal and vertical lines cross.
    G. Label the displacement increments along the horizontal scale as shown. Save the drawing as P16-9.

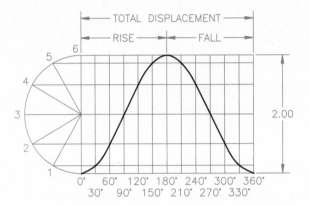

10. Draw a spline similar to the original spline shown below. Copy the spline seven times to create a layout similar to the one given. Perform the **SPLINEDIT** operations identified under each of the seven splines. Save the drawing as P16-10.

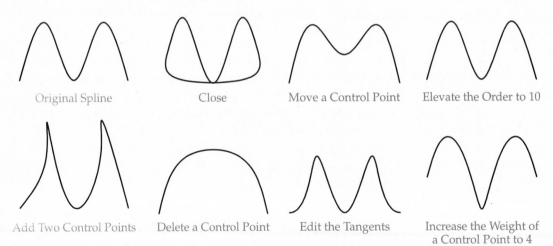

Original Spline   Close   Move a Control Point   Elevate the Order to 10

Add Two Control Points   Delete a Control Point   Edit the Tangents   Increase the Weight of a Control Point to 4

AutoCAD and its Applications—Basics

CHAPTER 17

Obtaining Information about the Drawing

Learning Objectives

After completing this chapter, you will be able to:
■ Use the **AREA** command to calculate the area of an object by adding and subtracting objects.
■ List data related to a single point, object, group of objects, or an entire drawing.
■ Find the distance between two points.
■ Identify a point location.
■ Determine the amount of time spent in a drawing session.

When working on a drawing, you may need to ask AutoCAD for information about the drawing, such as object distances and areas. You can also ask AutoCAD to tell you how much time you have spent on a drawing. The commands that allow you to do this include **AREA**, **DBLIST** (database list), **DIST** (distance), **ID** (identification), **LIST**, **STATUS**, and **TIME**. The **STATUS** command was discussed in Chapter 3 of this text.

These commands are accessed from the **Inquiry** flyout in the **Standard** toolbar and the **Inquiry** cascading menu in the **Tools** pull-down menu. You can also display the **Inquiry** toolbar to access these commands by first picking **Toolbars...** from the **View** pull-down menu and then activating **Inquiry** in the **Toolbars:** list box. See Figure 17-1. Picking the **Mass Properties** button in the **Inquiry** toolbar provides data related to the properties of a region or a 3D object created with solids. This topic is discussed in *AutoCAD and its Applications, Advanced.*

FINDING THE AREA OF SHAPES AND OBJECTS

The most basic function of the **AREA** command is to find the area of any object, circle, polyline, or spline. To select an object, use the **Object** option as follows:

Command: **AA** *or* **AREA**↵
Specify first corner point or [Object/Add/Subtract]: **O**↵
Select objects: *(pick the object)*
Area = *n.nn*, Circumference = *n.nn*
Command:

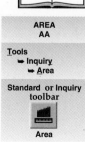

AREA
AA

Tools
→ Inquiry
→ Area

Standard or Inquiry
toolbar

Area

Figure 17-1.
The inquiry commands are grouped together in the **Inquiry** flyout, the **Inquiry** cascading menu in the **Tools** pull-down menu, and the **Inquiry** toolbar.

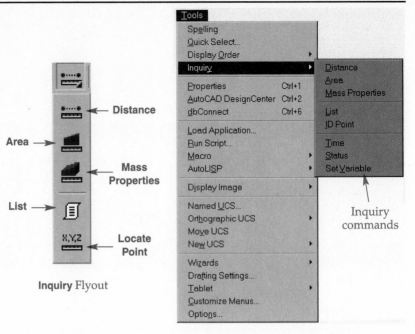

Inquiry Flyout

Inquiry Cascading Menu

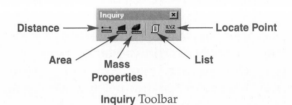

Inquiry Toolbar

The two numeric values represented by *n.nn* indicate the area and circumference of the object. The second value returned by the **AREA** command varies depending on the type of object selected, as shown in the following table.

Object	Value returned
Line	Does not have an area (no value given)
Polyline	Length or perimeter
Circle	Circumference
Spline	Length or perimeter
Rectangle	Perimeter

PROFESSIONAL TIP  AutoCAD gives you the area between three or more points picked on the screen, even if the three points are not connected by lines. The perimeter of the selected points is also given.

Shapes drawn with lines or polylines do not need to be closed for AutoCAD to calculate their area. AutoCAD calculates the area as if a line connects the first and last points.

To find the area of a shape created with the **LINE** command, pick all the vertices of that shape. See Figure 17-2. This is the default mode of the **AREA** command. Setting a running object snap mode such as **Endpoint** or **Intersection** will help you pick the vertices.

Figure 17-2.
Pick all vertices to find the area of an object drawn with the **LINE** command.

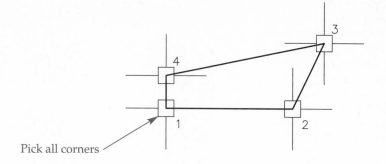

Pick all corners

Command: **AREA**↵
Specify first corner point or [Object/Add/Subtract]: *(pick point 1)*
Specify next corner point or press ENTER for total: *(pick point 2)*
Specify next corner point or press ENTER for total: *(continue picking points until all corners of the object have been selected; then press* [Enter]*)*
Area = *n.nn*, Perimeter = *n.nn*
Command:

Adding and Subtracting Areas

If you enter the **AREA** command and use the **Add** option, you can pick objects drawn with the **PLINE** command. They are then automatically added to calculate the total area. After objects have been added, the **Subtract** option allows you to remove selected areas. Once either of these options is entered, the **AREA** command remains in effect until canceled. You can continue to add or subtract objects and shapes using the **Add** and **Subtract** options.

The next example shows how to use these two options in the same operation. It also shows how objects drawn with the **PLINE** command are easier to pick. Refer to Figure 17-3 as you go through the following sequence:

Command: **AREA**↵
Specify first corner point or [Object/Add/Subtract]: **A**↵
Specify first corner point or [Object/Subtract]: **O**↵
(ADD mode) Select objects: *(pick the polyline)*
Area = 13.7854, Length = 20.1416
Total area = 13.7854
(ADD mode) Select objects: ↵
Specify first corner point or [Object/Subtract]: **S**↵
Specify first corner point or [Object/Add]: **O**↵
(SUBTRACT mode) Select objects: *(pick the first circle)*
Area = 0.7854, Circumference = 3.1416
Total area = 13.0000
(SUBTRACT mode) Select objects: *(pick the second circle)*
Area = 0.7854, Circumference = 3.1416
Total area = 12.2146
(SUBTRACT mode) Select objects: ↵
Specify first corner point or [Object/Add]: ↵

The total area of the object in Figure 17-3, after subtracting the areas of the two holes, is 12.2146. An area value and a length or circumference value are given for each object as it is selected. These values are not affected by the adding or subtracting functions.

Notice in the previous command sequence that if you are finished adding and wish to subtract, you must press [Enter] at the (ADD mode) Select objects: prompt. If you have completed subtracting and wish to add, you must press [Enter] at the (SUBTRACT mode) Select objects: prompt.

Figure 17-3.
To calculate the area of an object drawn with the **PLINE** command, first select the outer boundary of the object using the **AREA** command **Add** option. Then, select the inner boundaries (the circles) using the **AREA** command **Subtract** option. This will calculate the area of the object.

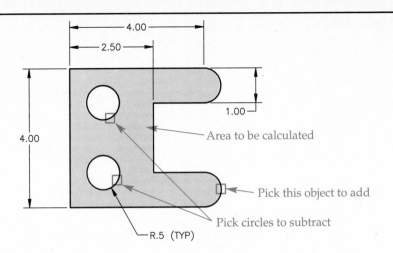

Area to be calculated

Pick this object to add

Pick circles to subtract

R.5 (TYP)

PROFESSIONAL TIP

Calculating area, circumference, and perimeter values of shapes drawn with the **LINE** command can be time-consuming. You must pick each vertex on the object. If you need to calculate areas, it is best to create lines and arcs with the **PLINE** or **SPLINE** command. Then use the **AREA** command **Object** option when adding or subtracting objects.

EXERCISE 17-1

❏ Start a new drawing or use one of your templates.
❏ Draw the objects shown below. Use the dimensions given. The exact locations of the cutout and holes are not important.
❏ Use the **AREA** command to calculate the area of the entire object.
❏ Use the **AREA** command to subtract the areas of the rectangle and the two circles.
❏ Determine the following information:
    1. Area of large rectangle.
    2. Perimeter of large rectangle.
    3. Perimeter of small rectangle.
    4. Circumference of one circle.
    5. Area of large rectangle minus the areas of the three shapes.
❏ Save the drawing as EX17-1. This drawing is used for the next exercise.

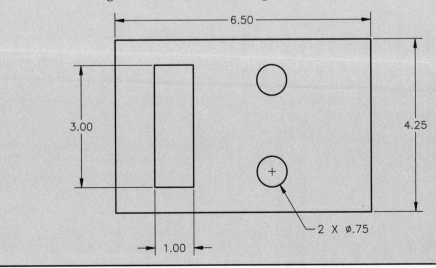

LISTING DRAWING DATA

AutoCAD User's Guide 7

LIST
LI

Tools
➥ Inquiry
➥ List

Standard or Inquiry toolbar

List

The **LIST** command enables you to display data about any AutoCAD object. Line lengths, circle or arc locations and radii, polyline widths, and object layers are just a few of the items you can identify with the **LIST** command. You can select several objects to list. The command sequence is as follows:

> Command: **LI** or **LIST**↵
> Select objects: *(pick one or more objects using any selection method)*
> Select objects: ↵

When you press [Enter], the data for each of the objects picked is displayed in the text window. The following data is given for a line:

> LINE   Layer: *layer name*
>   Space: Model space
>   Handle = *nn*
> from point,   X = *nn.nn*   Y = *nn.nn*   Z = *nn.nn*
>   to point,   X = *nn.nn*   Y = *nn.nn*   Z = *nn.nn*
> Length = *nn.nn*,   Angle in XY Plane = *nn.nn*
>   Delta X = *nn.nn*,   Delta Y = *nn.nn*,   Delta Z = *nn.nn*

The Delta X and Delta Y values indicate the horizontal and vertical distances between the *from point* and *to point* of the line. These two values, along with the length and angle, provide you with four measurements for a single line. An example of the data and measurements provided for two-dimensional lines is shown in Figure 17-4. If a line is three-dimensional, the **LIST** command displays an additional line of information as follows:

> 3D Length = *nn.nn*, Angle from XY Plane = *nn.nn*

The **LIST** command can also be used to determine information about text and multiline text. The data given for text, multiline text, circles, and splines is as follows:

> TEXT   Layer: *layer name*
>   Space: Model space
>   Handle = *nn*
>   Style = *name*
>   Font file = *name*
> start point, X = *n.nn*   Y = *n.nn*   Z = *n.nn*
>   height *n.nn*
>   text *text contents*
>   rotation angle   *nn*
>   width scale factor   *n.nn*
>   obliquing angle   *nn*
>   generation normal

Figure 17-4.
The various data and measurements of a line provided by the **LIST** command.

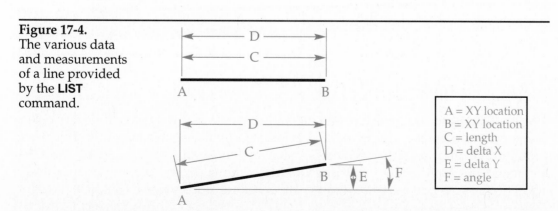

> A = XY location
> B = XY location
> C = length
> D = delta X
> E = delta Y
> F = angle

```
              MTEXT       Layer:    layer name
                          Space:    Model space
                Handle = nn
    Location:     X = n.nn        Y = n.nn        Z = n.nn
    Width:        n.nn
    Normal:       X = n.nn        Y = n.nn        Z = n.nn
    Rotation:     nn
    Text style:   style name
    Text height:  n.nn
    Line spacing: Multiple n.nn = n.nn
    Attachment:   corner of multiline text insertion point
    Flow direction:  direction text is read based on language
    Contents:     multiline text contents


        CIRCLE     Layer:    layer name
                   Space:    Model space
        Handle = nn
              center point,  X = n.nn        Y = n.nn        Z = n.nn
              radius         n.nn
         circumference       n.nn
                  area       n.nn


        SPLINE     Layer:    layer name
                   Space:    Model space
        Handle = nn
                   Length:   n.nn
                    Order:   n.nn
               Properties:   Planar, Non-Rational, Non-Periodic
       Parametric Range:     Start n.nn
                             End n.nn
 Number of control points:   n
          Control Points:    X = n.nn,        Y = n.nn,        Z = n.nn
                             (All XYZ control points listed)
     Number of fit points:   n
               User Data:    Fit Points
                             X = n.nn,        Y = n.nn,        Z = n.nn
                             (All XYZ fit points listed)
        Fit point tolerance: n.nn
```

PROFESSIONAL TIP

The **LIST** command is the most powerful inquiry command in AutoCAD. It provides all the information you need to know about a selected object. Practice listing as many different objects as possible in your drawings. This exercise will help you gain a greater understanding of the different kinds of data stored with each AutoCAD object.

Listing All the Drawing Data

The **DBLIST** (database list) command allows you to list all the data for every object in the current drawing. This command is initiated by typing DBLIST at the Command: prompt. The information provided is listed in the same format used by the **LIST** command. As soon as you enter the **DBLIST** command, the data begins to quickly scroll up the screen in the text window. The scrolling stops when a complete page (or screen) is filled with database information. Press [Enter] to scroll to the end of the next page. Use the scroll buttons to move forward and backward through the listing.

If you find the data you need, press the [Esc] key to exit the **DBLIST** command. You can exit the text window by pressing the [F2] function key.

FINDING THE DISTANCE BETWEEN TWO POINTS

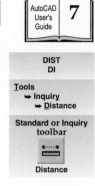

The **DIST** command is used to find the distance between two points. As with the **AREA** command, use object snap modes to accurately pick locations. The **DIST** command provides the distance between the points and the angle of the line. It also gives delta X, Y, and Z dimensions.

```
Command: DI or DIST↵
Specify first point: (select point)
Specify second point: (select point)
Distance = n.nn, Angle in XY Plane = n, Angle from XY Plane = n
Delta X = n.nn, Delta Y = n.nn, Delta Z = n.nn
Command:
```

You can also issue the **DIST** command by clicking the **Distance** button in the **Standard** toolbar or **Inquiry** toolbar. The following sequence is displayed at the Command: prompt:

```
Command: '__dist Specify first point:
```

The apostrophe that appears before dist indicates that this is a transparent command. Transparent commands can be used while you are working within another command. The **ID** command, discussed in the next section, is transparent if accessed from a toolbar or from the **Inquiry** cascading menu.

IDENTIFYING POINT LOCATIONS

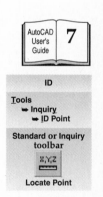

The **ID** command gives the coordinate location of a single point on screen. This command can be used to find the coordinates of the endpoint of a line or the center of a circle. Simply pick the point to be identified when the Specify point: prompt appears. Use the object snap modes for accuracy.

```
Command: ID↵
Specify point: (select the point)
X = nn.nn Y = nn.nn Z = nn.nn
Command:
```

The **ID** command can also help you identify a coordinate location on screen. Suppose you want to see where the point (X = 8.75, Y = 6.44) is located. Enter these numbers at the Specify point: prompt. AutoCAD responds by placing a blip (marker) at that exact location. In order to use this feature, the **BLIPMODE** system variable must be on.

```
Command: ID↵
Specify point: 8.75,6.44↵
X = 8.75 Y = 6.44 Z = 0.00
Command:
```

The **ID** command can also be used to specify a point as the origin for relative coordinates. For example, if you wish to begin drawing a line 10'-6" from the corner of a building on the X axis, issue the **ID** command and pick the corner. Next, enter the **LINE** command and enter the following at the Specify first point: prompt:

Specify first point: **@10'6,0**⏎

When you use the **ID** command, it automatically resets the **LASTPOINT** system variable to the value of the **ID** point. When you include the @ symbol, AutoCAD works from the **LASTPOINT** value. The AutoTrack modes provide similar capabilities with added enhancements. See Chapter 6 for a discussion of the AutoTrack feature.

EXERCISE 17-2

❑ Open EX17-1 if it is not currently on screen.
❑ Use the **LIST** command to display information about one circle and one line on the drawing.
❑ Enter the **DBLIST** command to display information about your drawing.
❑ Press the [Enter] key to display the end of the list and then press the [Esc] key to exit the command.
❑ Use the proper object snap modes to find the following information:
    ❑ Distance between the center points of the two circles.
    ❑ Distance between the center point of the lower circle and the lower-left corner of the large rectangle.
    ❑ Distance between the lower-left and upper-right corners of the large rectangle.
    ❑ Coordinates of the center point of the upper circle.
    ❑ Coordinates of the lower-left corner of the small rectangle.
    ❑ Coordinates of the midpoint of the large rectangle's right side.
    ❑ Location of point (6,4) on your screen.
❑ Save the drawing as EX17-2 and quit.

AutoCAD User's Guide 7

Time

Tools
➥ Inquiry
   ➥ Time

CHECKING THE TIME

The **TIME** command allows you to display the current time, the time related to your drawing, and the time related to the current drawing session. The following information is displayed in the text window when the **TIME** command is entered:

```
Command: TIME⏎
Current time:              Wednesday, February 14, 1999 at 13:39:22:210 PM
Times for this drawing:
  Created:                 Monday, February 12, 1999 at 10:24:48:130 AM
  Last updated:            Monday, February 12, 1999 at 14:36:23:46 PM
  Total editing time:      0 days 01:23:57:930
  Elapsed timer (on):      0 days 00:35:28:650
  Next automatic save in:  0 days 01:35:26:680
Enter option [Display/ON/OFF/Reset]:
```

There are a few things to keep in mind when checking the text window display after issuing the **TIME** command. First, the drawing creation time starts when you begin a new drawing, or when you use the **WBLOCK** command (see Chapter 23). Second, the **SAVE** command affects the Last updated: time. However, when the **QUIT** command is used to end a drawing session and you do not save the drawing, all time in that session is discarded. Finally, you can time a specific drawing task by using the **TIME** command **Reset** option to reset the elapsed timer.

When the **TIME** command is issued, the times shown in the text window are static. This means that none of the times are being updated. You can request an update by using the **Display** option as follows:

Enter option [Display/ON/OFF/Reset]: **D**⏎

When you enter the drawing area, the timer is on by default. If you want to stop the timer, simply enter OFF at the Enter option [Display/ON/OFF/Reset]: prompt. If the timer is off, enter ON to start it again.

If the date and time are incorrect, they can be reset using the Windows Control Panel. Control Panel is accessed by picking Settings in the Start menu, Figure 17-5. The Control Panel allows you to modify certain aspects of your system, such as the colors that appear on your screen and the system time. Double-click on the Date/Time icon, Figure 17-6. This displays the Date/Time Properties dialog box, which you can use to change your system's date and time. See Figure 17-7.

Figure 17-5.
The Control Panel window is accessed by picking Settings in the Start menu.

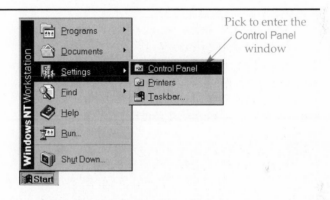

Figure 17-6.
Double-click the Date/Time icon in the Control Panel window to change the system clock settings.

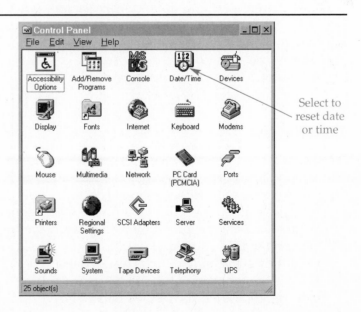

Figure 17-7.
After displaying the Date/Time Properties dialog box, highlight the item to change and enter the new setting.

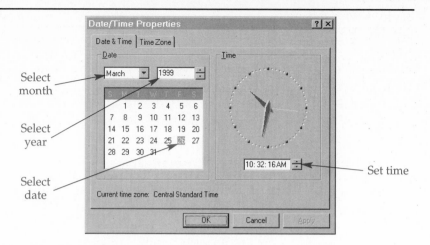

To change the system date and time, do the following:

1. Pick the Date & Time tab if it is not active.
2. Set the date by first picking the correct month from the drop-down list. Set the year by using the up or down arrows. Pick the day by highlighting the correct date shown on the calendar. To change the time, highlight the current time displayed and enter the hour, minutes, and seconds. Use the up and down arrows to specify AM or PM.
3. Pick the OK button and then select Close from the File pull-down menu in the Control Panel window.

It is important that your system date and time settings are always accurate. Date and time changes are recognized by other Windows applications that use the system clock, such as Windows Explorer and Windows Clock. Windows Explorer functions are covered in Chapter 14 of this text.

EXERCISE 17-3

❑ Open any one of your saved drawings.
❑ Enter the **TIME** command and study the information that is displayed.
❑ If the current date and time are incorrect, inform your instructor or supervisor. Then, use Control Panel to set the correct date and time.
❑ Update the **TIME** command display.
❑ Reset the elapsed timer.
❑ Exit AutoCAD without saving your drawing.

Chapter Test

Answer the following questions on a separate sheet of paper.

1. To add the areas of several objects, when do you select the **Add** option?
2. When using the **AREA** command, explain how picking a polyline is different from picking an object drawn with the **LINE** command.
3. What information is provided by the **AREA** command?
4. What is the **LIST** command used for?
5. Describe the meaning of delta X and delta Y.
6. What is the function of the **DBLIST** command?
7. How do you cancel the **DBLIST** command?
8. What are the two purposes of the **ID** command?
9. What information is provided by the **TIME** command?
10. When does the drawing creation time start?
11. It is necessary to exit AutoCAD to reset the date and time. (True/False)

Drawing Problems

1. Draw the object shown below using the dimensions given. Check the time when you enter the drawing area. Draw all the features using the **PLINE** and **CIRCLE** commands. Use the **Object**, **Add**, and **Subtract** options of the **AREA** command to calculate the following measurements:
   A. Area and perimeter of Object A.
   B. Area and perimeter of Object B.
   C. Area and circumference of one of the circles.
   D. Area of Object A minus the area of Object B.
   E. Area of Object A minus the areas of the other three features.
   Enter the **TIME** command and note the editing time spent on your drawing. Save the drawing as P17-1.

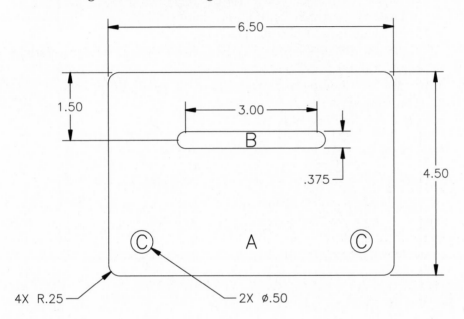

2. Draw the deck shown below using the **PLINE** command. Draw the hexagon using the **POLYGON** command. Use the following guidelines to complete this problem:
   A. Specify architectural units for your drawing. Use 1/2" fractions and decimal degrees. Leave the remaining settings for the drawing units at the default values.
   B. Set the limits to 100',80' and perform a **ZOOM All**.
   C. Set the grid spacing to 2' and the snap spacing to 1'.
   D. Calculate the measurements listed below:
      a. Area and perimeter of Object A.
      b. Area and perimeter of Object B.
      c. Area of Object A minus the area of Object B.
      d. Distance between Point C and Point D.
      e. Distance between Point E and Point C.
      f. Coordinates of Points C, D, and F.
   E. Enter the **DBLIST** command and check the information listed for your drawing.
   F. Enter the **TIME** command and note the total editing time spent on your drawing.
   G. Save the drawing as P17-2.

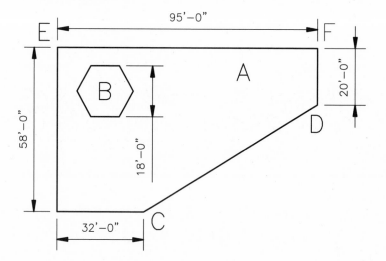

3. The drawing shown on the following page is a view of the gable end of a portion of a house. Draw the house using the dimensions given. Draw the windows as single lines only (the location of the windows is not important). The spacing between the second-floor windows is 3". The width of this end of the house is 16'-6". The length of the roof is 40'. You may want to use the **PLINE** command to assist in creating specific shapes in this drawing. Save the drawing as P17-3. Calculate the following:
   A. Total area of the roof.
   B. Diagonal distance from one corner of the roof to the other.
   C. Area of the first-floor window.
   D. Total area of all second-floor windows, including the 3" space between them.
   E. Siding will cover the house. What is the total area of siding for this end?

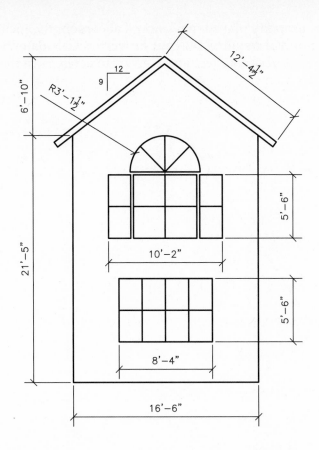

4. The drawing shown below is a side view of a pyramid. The pyramid has four sides. Create an auxiliary view showing the true size of a pyramid face. Using inquiry techniques, calculate the following (save the drawing as P17-4):

A. Area of one side.
B. Perimeter of one side.
C. Area of all four sides.
D. Area of the base.
E. True length (distance) from the midpoint of the base on one side to the apex.

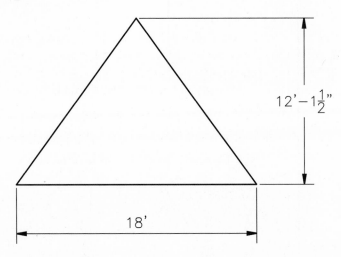

5. Draw the property plat shown below. Label property line bearings and distances only if required by your instructor. Calculate the area of the property plat in square feet and convert to acres. Save the drawing as P17-5.

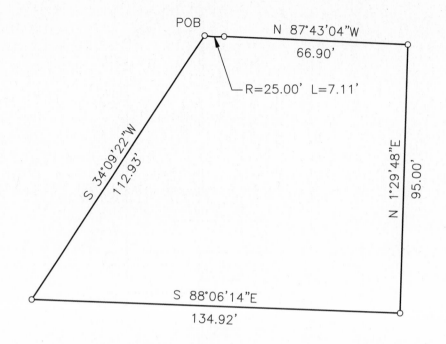

6. Draw the subdivision plat shown below. Label the drawing as shown. Calculate the acreage of each lot and record each value as a label inside the corresponding lot (for example, .249 AC). Save the drawing as P17-6.

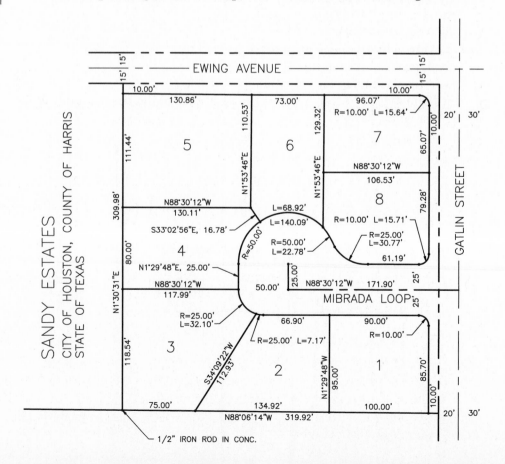

CHAPTER 18

Basic Dimensioning Practices

Learning Objectives

After completing this chapter, you will be able to:

■ Use the dimensioning commands to dimension given objects to ASME and other drafting standards.

■ Control the appearance of dimensions.

■ Add linear, angular, diameter, and radius dimensions to a drawing.

■ Set the appropriate units and decimal places for dimension numbers.

■ Use text size and style consistent with ASME and other professional standards.

■ Use the proper character codes to display symbols with dimension text.

■ Add dimensions to a separate layer.

■ Place general notes on drawings.

■ Draw datum and chain dimensions.

■ Add dimensions for multiple items using the **QDIM** command.

■ Dimension curves.

■ Draw oblique dimensions.

■ Use the **QLEADER** command to draw specific notes with linked leader lines.

■ Dimension objects with arrowless tabular dimensions.

■ Prepare thread symbols and notes.

■ Create and use dimension styles.

■ Create dimension style overrides.

Dimensions are given to describe the size, shape, and location of features on an object or structure. The dimension may consist of numerical values, lines, symbols, and notes. Typical AutoCAD dimensioning features and characteristics are shown in Figure 18-1.

Each drafting field (such as mechanical, architectural, civil, and electronics) uses a different type of dimensioning technique. It is important for a drafter to place dimensions in accordance with company and industry standards. The standard emphasized in this text is ASME Y14.5M-1994, *Dimensioning and Tolerancing*. The *M* in Y14.5M means the standard is written with metric numeric values. ASME Y14.5M-1994 is published by The American Society of Mechanical Engineers (ASME). The standard can be ordered directly from ASME, 345 E. 47th Street, New York, NY 10017. It can also be obtained from the American National Standards Institute (ANSI), 1430 Broadway, New York, NY 10018. This text discusses the correct application of both inch and metric dimensioning.

Figure 18-1.
Dimensions describe size and location. Follow accepted conventions when dimensioning.

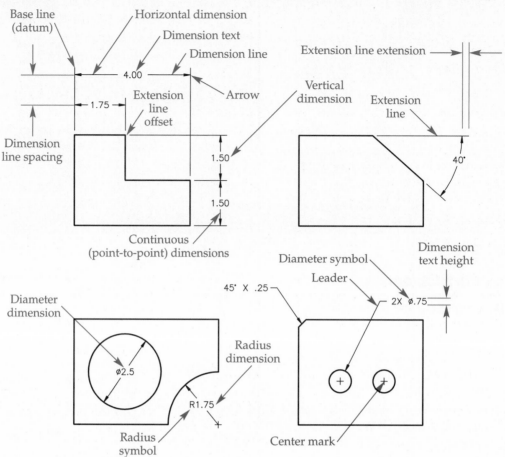

AutoCAD's dimensioning functions provide you with unlimited flexibility. Available commands allow you to dimension linear distances, circles, and arcs. You can also place a note with an arrow and leader line pointing to the feature. In addition to these commands, dimension styles allow you to control the height, width, style, and spacing of individual components of a dimension.

This text covers the comprehensive elements of AutoCAD dimensioning in four chapters. This chapter covers fundamental standards and practices for dimensioning. Chapter 19, *Editing Dimensions*, covers editing procedures for dimensions. Chapter 20, *Dimensioning with Tolerances*, covers dimensioning applications with tolerances. Chapter 21, *Geometric Dimensioning and Tolerancing*, covers geometric dimensioning and tolerancing practices. If you use AutoCAD for mechanical drafting in the manufacturing industry, you may want to study all four dimensioning chapters. If your business is in another field, such as architectural design, you may want to learn the basics covered in Chapters 18 and 19, and skip Chapters 20 and 21.

This chapter will get you started dimensioning immediately with AutoCAD. As you progress, you will learn about dimension settings that can be used to control the way dimensions are presented. You can control things such as the space between dimension lines, the arrowhead size and type, and the text style, height, and position. You will also learn how to create dimension styles that have settings used on the types of drawings done at your company or school.

When you dimension objects with AutoCAD, the objects are automatically measured exactly as you have them drawn. This makes it important for you to draw accurate original objects and features. Use the object snaps to your best advantage when dimensioning.

DIMENSION ARRANGEMENT

Dimensions are meant to communicate information about the drawing. Different industries and companies apply similar techniques for presenting dimensions. The two most accepted arrangements of text are unidirectional and aligned.

Unidirectional Dimensioning

Unidirectional dimensioning is typically used in the mechanical drafting field. The term **unidirectional** means *one direction*. This system has all dimension numbers and notes placed horizontally on the drawing. They are read from the bottom of the sheet.

Unidirectional dimensions normally have arrowheads on the ends of dimension lines. The dimension number is usually centered in a break near the center of the dimension line. See Figure 18-2.

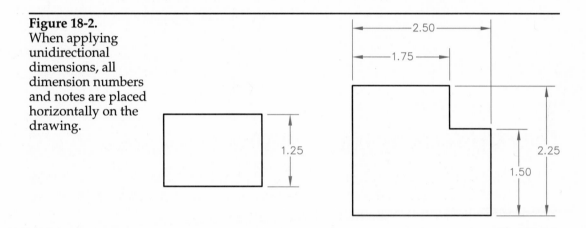

Figure 18-2. When applying unidirectional dimensions, all dimension numbers and notes are placed horizontally on the drawing.

Aligned Dimensioning

Aligned dimensions are typically placed on architectural or structural drawings. The term **aligned** means the dimension numbers are lined up with the dimension lines. The dimension numbers for horizontal dimensions read horizontally. Dimension numbers for vertical dimensions are placed so they are read from the right side of the sheet. See Figure 18-3. Numbers for dimensions placed at an angle read at the same angle as the dimension line. Notes are usually placed so they read horizontally.

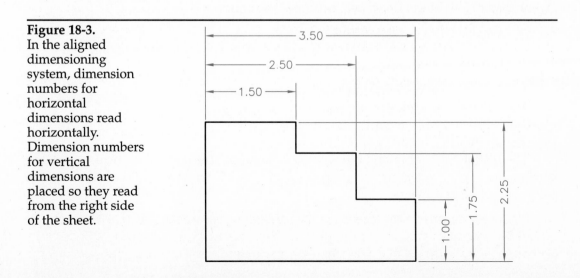

Figure 18-3. In the aligned dimensioning system, dimension numbers for horizontal dimensions read horizontally. Dimension numbers for vertical dimensions are placed so they read from the right side of the sheet.

When using the aligned system, terminate dimension lines with tick marks, dots, or arrowheads. In architectural drafting, the dimension number is generally placed above the dimension line and tick marks are used. See Figure 18-4.

Figure 18-4.
An example of aligned dimensioning in architectural drafting. Notice the tick marks used in place of the arrowheads and the placement of the dimensions above the dimension line.

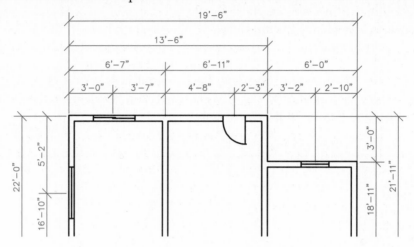

DRAWING DIMENSIONS WITH AUTOCAD

AutoCAD has a variety of dimensioning applications that fall into five fundamental categories: linear, angular, diameter, radius, and ordinate. These applications allow you to perform nearly every type of dimensioning practice needed for your discipline.

DRAWING LINEAR DIMENSIONS

AutoCAD
User's
Guide **12**

DIMLINEAR
DLI

Dimension
➥ Linear

Dimension
toolbar

⊢◄┤

Linear Dimension

Linear means straight. In most cases, dimensions measure straight distances, such as horizontal, vertical, or slanted surfaces. The **DIMLINEAR** command allows you to measure the length of an object and place extension lines, dimension lines, dimension text, and arrowheads automatically. To do this, pick the **Linear Dimension** button in the **Dimension** toolbar, select **Linear** from the **Dimension** pull-down menu, or type DLI or DIMLINEAR at the Command: prompt. The command sequence is as follows:

Command: **DLI** or **DIMLINEAR**↵
Specify first extension line origin or <select object>: (*pick the origin of the first extension line*)
Specify second extension line origin: (*pick the origin of the second extension line*)

The points you pick are the extension line origins. See Figure 18-5. Place the crosshairs directly on the corners of the object where the extension lines begin. Use object snap modes for accuracy.

The **DIMLINEAR** command allows you to generate horizontal, vertical, or rotated dimensions. After selecting the object or points of origin for dimensioning, the following prompt appears:

Specify dimension line location or [Mtext/Text/Angle/Horizontal/Vertical/Rotated]:

Figure 18-5.
Establishing extension line origins. The **Endpoint** or **Intersection** object snap modes are useful in accurately locating the origins.

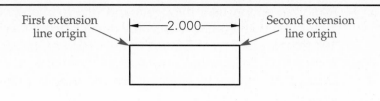

These options are outlined as follows:

- **Specify dimension line location.** This is the default. Simply drag the dimension line to a desired location and pick. See Figure 18-6. This is where preliminary plan sheets and sketches help you determine proper distances to avoid crowding. The extension lines, dimension line, dimension text, and arrowheads are automatically drawn.
- **Mtext.** This option accesses the **Multiline Text Editor** dialog box, Figure 18-7. Here you can provide a specific measurement or text format for the dimension. See Chapter 8 for a complete description of the **Multiline Text Editor**. The chevrons (< >) represent the current dimension value. Edit the dimension text and pick **OK**. For example, the ASME standard recommends that a reference dimension be displayed enclosed in parenthesis. Type an open and closed parenthesis around the chevrons to create a reference dimension. If you want the current dimension value changed, delete the chevrons and type the new value. If you want the chevrons to be part of the dimension text, type the new value inside or next to the chevrons. While this is not an ASME standard, it may be needed for some applications.

Figure 18-6.
Establishing the dimension line's location.

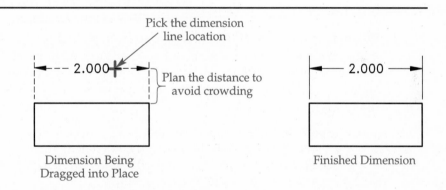

Figure 18-7.
When you use the **Mtext** option, the **Multiline Text Editor** dialog box appears. The chevrons (< >) represent the dimension value AutoCAD has calculated.

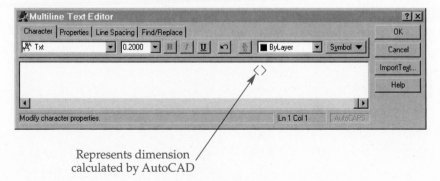

- **Text.** This option uses the command line to change dimension text. This is convenient if you prefer to type the desired text rather than using the **Multiline Text Editor**. The **Text** and **Mtext** options both create multiline text objects. The **Text** option displays the current dimension value in brackets and allows you to accept this value by pressing [Enter], or type a new value. The command sequence works like this:

> Specify dimension line location or
>   [Mtext/Text/Angle/Horizontal/Vertical/Rotated]: **T**↵
> Enter dimension text <2.875>:

Pressing [Enter] accepts the current value. Type a new value, such as a reference dimension (which is displayed in parentheses), as follows:

> Enter dimension text <2.875>: **(<>)**↵

- **Angle.** This option allows you to change the dimension text angle. This option can be used when creating rotated dimensions or for adjusting the dimension text to a desired angle. The sequence is as follows:

> Specify dimension line location or
>   [Mtext/Text/Angle/Horizontal/Vertical/Rotated]: **A**↵
> Specify angle of dimension text: *(enter desired angle)*

- **Horizontal.** This option sets the dimension to a horizontal distance only. This may be helpful when dimensioning the horizontal distance of a slanted surface. The **Mtext**, **Text**, and **Angle** options are available again in case you want to change the dimension text value or angle.
- **Vertical.** This option sets the dimension being created to a vertical distance only. This option may be helpful when dimensioning the vertical distance of a slanted surface. Like the **Horizontal** option, the **Mtext**, **Text**, and **Angle** options are available.
- **Rotated.** This option allows an angle to be specified for the dimension line. A practical application is dimensioning to angled surfaces and auxiliary views. This technique is different from other dimensioning commands because you are asked to provide a dimension line angle. See Figure 18-8. The command sequence looks like this:

> Specify dimension line location or
>   [Mtext/Text/Angle/Horizontal/Vertical/Rotated]: **R**↵
> Specify angle of dimension line <0>: *(enter a value, such as 45, or pick two points on the line to be dimensioned)*

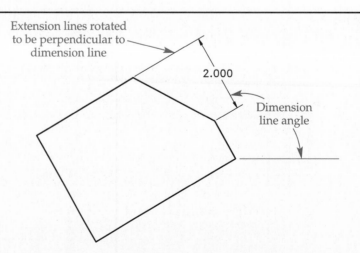

Figure 18-8.
Rotating a dimension for an angled view.

Extension lines rotated to be perpendicular to dimension line

2.000

Dimension line angle

Selecting an Object to Dimension

In the previous discussion, the extension line origins were picked in order to establish the extents of the dimension. Another powerful AutoCAD option allows you to pick a single line, circle, or arc to dimension. This works when you are using the **DIMLINEAR**, **DIMALIGNED**, and **QDIM** commands, which are discussed later. You can use this AutoCAD feature any time you see the Specify first extension line origin or <select object>: prompt. Press [Enter] and select the object being dimensioned. When you select a line or arc, AutoCAD automatically begins the extension lines from the endpoints. If you pick a circle, the extension lines are drawn from the closest quadrant and its opposite quadrant. See Figure 18-9.

Figure 18-9.
AutoCAD can automatically determine the extension line origins if you select a line, arc, or circle.

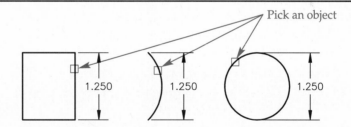

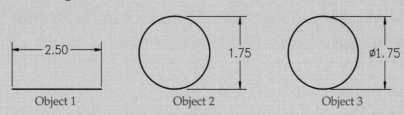

Dimensioning in AutoCAD, like dimensioning on a conventional drafting board, should be performed as accurately and neatly as possible. You can achieve consistently professional results by using the following guidelines:

- Always construct drawing geometry accurately. Never truncate, or round-off, decimal values when entering locations, distances, or angles. For example, enter .4375 for 7/16, rather than .44.
- Set the desired precision level before beginning your dimensioning. Most drawings have varying levels of precision for specific drawing features, so select the most common precision level to start with, and adjust the precision as needed for each dimension. Setting the dimension precision is explained later in this chapter.
- Always use the precision drawing aids to ensure the accuracy of dimensions. If the point being dimensioned does not coincide with a snap point or a known coordinate, use an appropriate object snap override.
- *Never* type a different dimension value than what appears in the brackets. If a dimension needs to change, revise the drawing or dimensioning variables accordingly. The ability to change the dimension in the brackets is provided by AutoCAD so that a different text format can be specified for the dimension. Prefixes and suffixes can also be added to the dimension in the brackets. A typical example of a prefix might be to specify the number of times a dimension occurs, such as 4X 1.750. Other examples of this capability appear later in this chapter.

DIMENSIONING ANGLED SURFACES AND AUXILIARY VIEWS

When dimensioning a surface drawn at an angle, it may be necessary to align the dimension line with the surface. For example, auxiliary views are normally placed at an angle. In order to properly dimension these features, the **DIMALIGNED** command or the **Rotated** option of **DIMLINEAR** can be used.

Using the DIMALIGNED Command

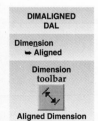
The **DIMALIGNED** command can be accessed by picking the **Aligned Dimension** button on the **Dimension** toolbar, picking **Aligned** in the **Dimension** pull-down menu, or typing DAL or DIMALIGNED at the Command: prompt. The results of the **DIMALIGNED** command are displayed in Figure 18-10. The following shows the command sequence:

Command: **DAL** *or* **DIMALIGNED**↲
Specify first extension line origin or <select object>: (*pick first extension line origin*)
Specify second extension line origin: (*pick second extension line origin*)
Specify dimension line location or [Mtext/Text/Angle]: (*pick the dimension line location*)
Dimension text = 2.250
Command:

Figure 18-10.
The **DIMALIGNED** dimensioning command allows you to place dimension lines parallel to angled features.

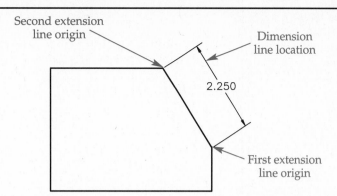

Second extension line origin

Dimension line location

2.250

First extension line origin

- ❏ Start AutoCAD and use one of your templates.
- ❏ Set up the appropriate layers for your drawing elements, including a layer for dimensions.
- ❏ Draw the objects shown below. Object A is a hexagon circumscribed about a 2″ diameter circle. The absolute coordinates for Object B are provided.
- ❏ Use the **DIMALIGNED** command to dimension Object A. Use the **Rotate** option of the **DIMLINEAR** command to dimension Object B.
- ❏ Save the drawing as EX18-3.

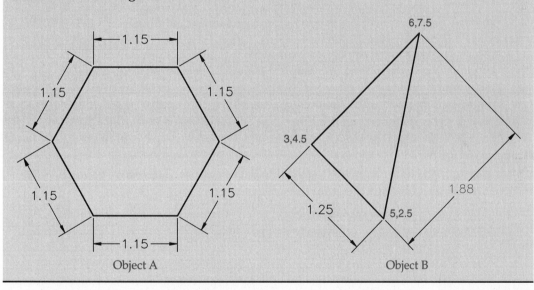

Object A

Object B

DIMENSIONING ANGLES

Coordinate and angular dimensioning are both accepted for dimensioning angles. *Coordinate dimensioning* of angles can be accomplished with the **DIMLINEAR** command. These dimensions locate the corner of the angle, as shown in Figure 18-11.

Angular dimensioning locates one corner with a dimension and provides the value of the angle in degrees. See Figure 18-12. You can dimension the angle between any two nonparallel lines. The intersection of the lines is the angle's vertex. AutoCAD automatically draws extension lines if they are needed.

Figure 18-11.
Coordinate
dimensioning of
angles.

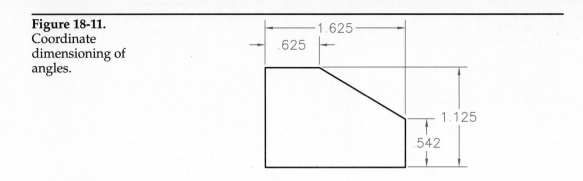

Figure 18-12.
Two examples of drawing angular dimensions.

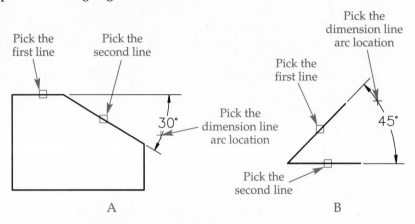

The type of angular unit depends on the criteria set within the dimensions style, which is discussed later in this chapter. The **DIMANGULAR** command is used for the angular method. The **DIMANGULAR** command is accessed by picking the **Angular Dimension** button in the **Dimension** toolbar, picking **Angular** in the **Dimension** pull-down menu, or by entering DAN or DIMANGULAR at the Command: prompt. Refer to Figure 18-12A as you read the following sequence:

Command: **DAN** *or* **DIMANGULAR.**↵
Select arc, circle, line, or <specify vertex>: *(pick the first leg of the angle to be dimensioned)*
Select second line: *(pick the second leg of the angle to be dimensioned)*
Specify dimension arc line location or [Mtext/Text/Angle]: *(pick the desired location of the dimension line arc)*
Dimension text = 30
Command:

The last prompt asks you to pick the dimension line arc location. If there is enough space, AutoCAD places the dimension text, dimension line arc, and arrowheads inside the extension lines. If there is not enough room between extension lines for the arrowheads and numbers, AutoCAD automatically places the arrowheads outside and the number inside the extension lines. If space is very tight, AutoCAD may place the dimension line arc and arrowheads inside and the text outside, or place everything outside of the extension lines. See Figure 18-13.

Figure 18-13.
The dimension line arc location determines where the dimension line arc, text, and arrows are displayed.

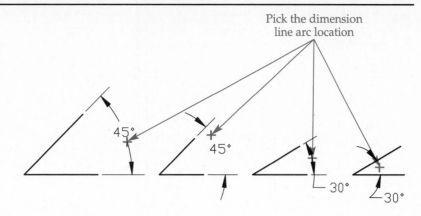

Pick the dimension line arc location

45° 45° 30° 30°

Placing Angular Dimensions on Arcs

The **DIMANGULAR** command can be used to dimension the included angle of an arc. The arc's center point becomes the angle vertex and the two arc endpoints are the origin points for the extension lines. See Figure 18-14. The command sequence is as follows:

> Command: **DAN** or **DIMANGULAR**⌐
> Select arc, circle, line, or <specify vertex>: *(pick the arc)*
> Specify dimension arc line location or [Mtext/Text/Angle]: *(pick the desired dimension line location)*
> Dimension text = 128
> Command:

Figure 18-14.
Placing angular dimensions on arcs.

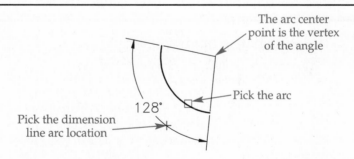

The arc center point is the vertex of the angle

Pick the arc

128°

Pick the dimension line arc location

Placing Angular Dimensions on Circles

The **DIMANGULAR** command can also be used to dimension a portion of a circle. The circle's center point becomes the angle vertex and two picked points are the origin points for the extension lines. See Figure 18-15. The command sequence is as follows:

> Command: **DAN** or **DIMANGULAR**⌐
> Select arc, circle, line, or <specify vertex>: *(pick the circle)*

The point you pick on the circle becomes the endpoint of the first extension line. You are then asked for the second angle endpoint. This becomes the endpoint of the second extension line:

> Specify second angle endpoint: *(pick the second point)*
> Specify dimension arc line location or [Mtext/Text/Angle]: *(pick the desired dimension line location)*
> Dimension text = 85
> Command:

Figure 18-15.
Placing angular
dimensions on
circles.

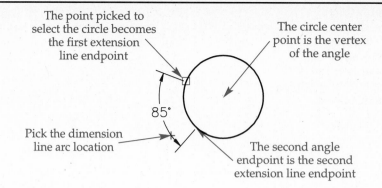

The point picked to
select the circle becomes
the first extension
line endpoint

The circle center
point is the vertex
of the angle

85°

Pick the dimension
line arc location

The second angle
endpoint is the second
extension line endpoint

PROFESSIONAL TIP

Using angular dimensioning for circles increases the number of possible solutions for a given dimensioning requirement, but the actual uses are limited. One professional application is dimensioning an angle from a quadrant point to a particular feature without having to first draw a line to dimension. Another benefit of this option is the ability to specify angles that exceed 180°.

Angular Dimensioning through Three Points

You can also establish an angular dimension through three points. The points are the angle vertex and the two angle line endpoints. See Figure 18-16. To do this, press [Enter] after the first prompt:

Command: **DAN** *or* **DIMANGULAR**⏎
Select arc, circle, line, or <specify vertex>: ⏎
Specify angle vertex: *(pick a vertex point and a "rubberband" connects between the vertex and the cursor to help locate the first point)*
Specify first angle endpoint: *(pick the first endpoint)*
Specify second angle endpoint: *(pick the second endpoint)*
Specify dimension arc line location or [Mtext/Text/Angle]: *(pick the desired dimension line location)*
Dimension text = 60

This method also dimensions angles over 180°.

Figure 18-16.
Angular dimensions
using three points.

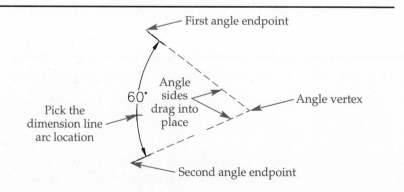

First angle endpoint

Angle
sides
drag into
place

Angle vertex

60°

Pick the
dimension line
arc location

Second angle endpoint

❑ Start AutoCAD and use one of your templates.
❑ Set up the appropriate layers for your drawing elements, including a layer for dimensions.
❑ Use the **LINEAR** and **ANGULAR** dimensioning commands to dimension the object exactly as shown.
❑ Save the drawing as EX18-4.

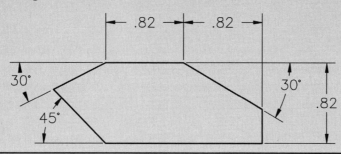

DIMENSIONING PRACTICES

Dimensioning practices often depend on product requirements, manufacturing accuracy, standards, and tradition. Dimensional information includes size dimensions, location dimensions, and notes. Two techniques that identify size and location are chain and datum dimensioning. The method used depends on the accuracy of the product and the drafting field.

Size Dimensions and Notes

Size dimensions provide the size of physical features. They include lines, notes, or dimension lines and numbers. Size dimensioning practices depend on the techniques used to dimension different geometric features. See Figure 18-17. A *feature* is considered any physical portion of a part or object, such as a surface, hole, window, or door. Dimensioning standards are used so an object designed in one place can be manufactured or built somewhere else.

Figure 18-17.
Size dimensions and specific notes.

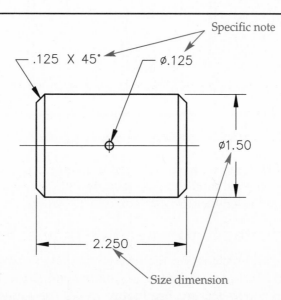

Specific notes and general notes are the two types of notes on a drawing. *Specific notes* relate to individual or specific features on the drawing. They are attached to the feature being dimensioned using a leader line. *General notes* apply to the entire drawing and are placed in the lower-left corner, upper-left corner, or above or next to the title block. Where they are placed depends on company or school practice.

Dimensioning Flat Surfaces and Architectural Features

In mechanical drafting, flat surfaces are dimensioned by giving measurements for each feature. If there is an overall dimension provided, you can omit one of the dimensions. The overall dimension controls the omitted dimension. In architectural drafting, it is common to place all dimensions without omitting any of them. The idea is that all dimensions should be shown to help make construction easier. See Figure 18-18.

Figure 18-18.
Dimensioning flat surfaces and architectural features.

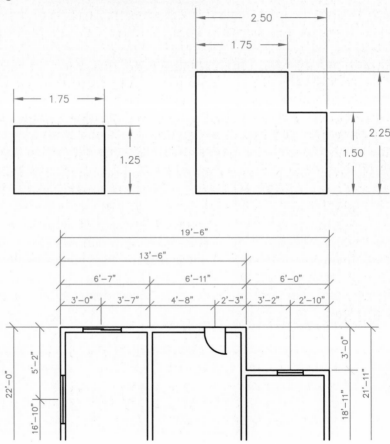

Dimensioning Cylindrical Shapes

Both the diameter and length of a cylindrical shape can be dimensioned in the view where the cylinder appears rectangular. See Figure 18-19. This allows the view where the cylinder appears as a circle to be omitted.

Dimensioning Square and Rectangular Features

Square and rectangular features are usually dimensioned in the views where the length and height are shown. The square symbol can be used preceding the dimension for the square feature. See Figure 18-20. The square symbol must be created as a block and inserted. Blocks are discussed in Chapter 23 of this text.

AutoCAD and its Applications—Basics

Figure 18-19.
Dimensioning
cylindrical shapes.

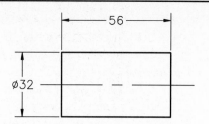

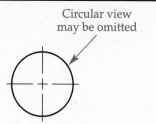

Figure 18-20.
Dimensioning square and rectangular features.

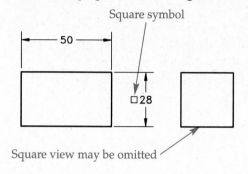

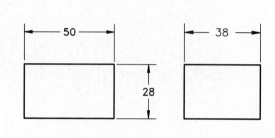

Dimensioning Cones and Hexagonal Shapes

There are two ways to dimension a conical shape. One method is by giving the diameters at both ends and the length. See Figure 18-21. Another method is to give the taper angle and length. Hexagonal shapes are dimensioned by giving the distance across the flats and the length. See Figure 18-22.

Figure 18-21.
Dimensioning conical shapes. These shapes can also be dimensioned with an angle and length.

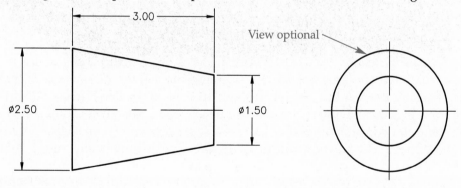

Figure 18-22.
Hexagons are
dimensioned across
their flats with a
length given.

❏ Start AutoCAD and use one of your templates.

❏ Set up the appropriate layers for your drawing elements, including a layer for dimensions.

❏ Draw the objects shown below. Hint: To orient the hexagon as shown, use a six-sided circumscribed polygon. When prompted to enter the radius value, type @.625<0. Use object snap modes, along with X and Y filters, object snap tracking, or construction lines to assist you in drawing the side view of the hexagon.

❏ Dimension the objects exactly as shown using the proper dimensioning commands and techniques.

❏ Save the drawing as EX18-5.

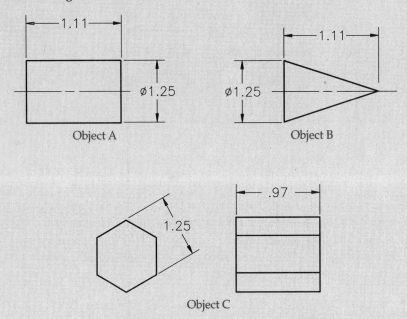

Object A   Object B

Object C

LOCATION DIMENSIONS

Location dimensions are used to locate features on an object. They do not provide the size. Holes and arcs are dimensioned to their centers in the view where they appear circular. Rectangular features are dimensioned to their edges. See Figure 18-23. In architectural drafting, windows and doors are dimensioned to their centers on the floor plan.

Rectangular coordinates and polar coordinates are the two basic location dimensioning systems. *Rectangular coordinates* are linear dimensions used to locate features from surfaces, centerlines, or center planes. AutoCAD performs this type of dimensioning using a variety of dimensioning subcommands. The most frequently used dimensioning command is **DIMLINEAR** and its options. See Figure 18-24.

The *polar coordinate system* uses angular dimensions to locate features from surfaces, centerlines, or center planes. The angular dimensions in the polar coordinate system are drawn using AutoCAD's **DIMANGULAR** command. See Figure 18-25.

Figure 18-23.
Locating circular and rectangular features.

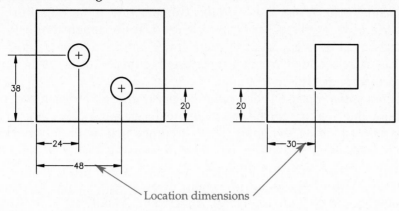

Location dimensions

Figure 18-24.
Rectangular coordinate location dimensions.

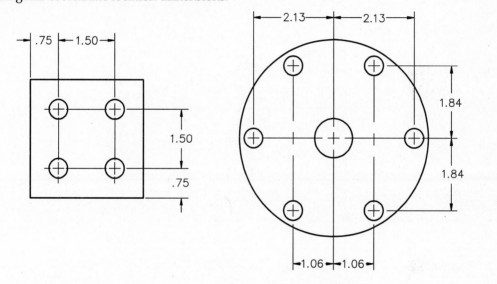

Figure 18-25.
Polar coordinate location dimensions.

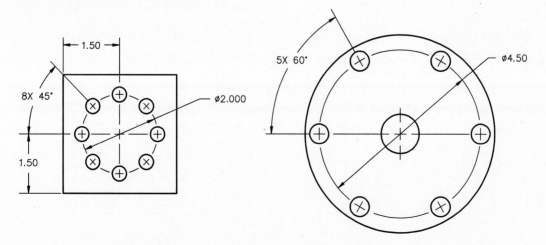

DATUM AND CHAIN DIMENSIONING

With *datum*, or *baseline dimensioning*, dimensions on an object originate from common surfaces, centerlines, or center planes. Datum dimensioning is commonly used in mechanical drafting because each dimension is independent of the others. This achieves more accuracy in manufacturing. Figure 18-26 shows an object dimensioned with surface datums.

Chain dimensioning, also called *point-to-point dimensioning*, places dimensions in a line from one feature to the next. Chain dimensioning is sometimes used in mechanical drafting. However, there is less accuracy than with datum dimensioning since each dimension is dependent on other dimensions in the chain. Architectural drafting uses chain dimensioning in most applications. Figure 18-27 shows an example of chain dimensioning. In mechanical drafting, it is common to leave one dimension blank and provide an overall dimension. Architectural drafting practices usually show dimensions all the way across, plus an overall dimension.

Figure 18-26.
Datum dimensioning.

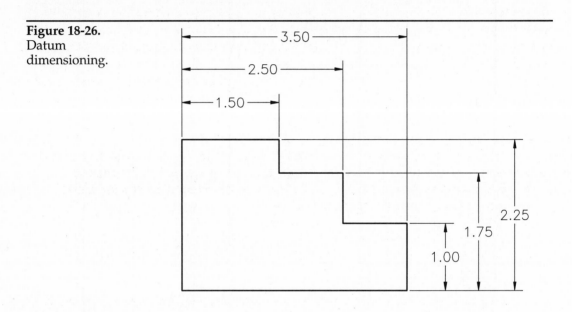

Figure 18-27.
Chain dimensioning.

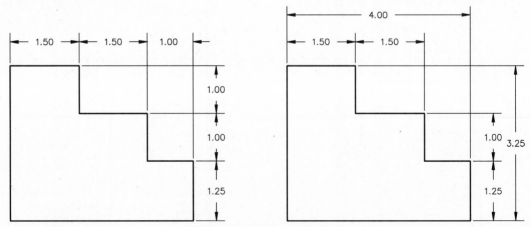

Making Datum and Chain Dimensioning Easy

AutoCAD refers to datum dimensioning as *baseline* and chain dimensioning as *continue*. Datum dimensioning is controlled by the **DIMBASELINE** command, and chain dimensioning is controlled by the **DIMCONTINUE** command. The **DIMBASELINE** and **DIMCONTINUE** commands are used in the same manner. The prompts and options are the same. Use the **Undo** option in the **DIMBASELINE** or **DIMCONTINUE** commands to undo previously drawn dimensions.

Datum dimensions

Datum dimensions are created by picking the **Baseline Dimension** button in the **Dimension** toolbar, picking **Baseline** in the **Dimension** pull-down menu, or by entering either DBA or DIMBASELINE at the Command: prompt. Baseline dimensions can be created with linear, ordinate, and angular dimensions. Ordinate dimensions are discussed later in this chapter.

When you begin a new drawing and enter the **DIMBASELINE** command, AutoCAD asks you to Specify a second extension line origin. Therefore, a dimension must exist before using **Baseline**. AutoCAD will use the most recently drawn dimension as the base dimension, unless you specify a different one. You can add additional datum dimensions to the previous dimension. AutoCAD automatically spaces and places the extension lines, dimension lines, arrowheads, and numbers. For example, to dimension the series of horizontal baseline dimensions shown in Figure 18-28, use the following procedure:

> Command: **DLI** *or* **DIMLINEAR**↵
> Specify first extension line origin or <select object>: *(pick the first extension line origin)*
> Specify second extension line origin: *(pick the second extension line origin)*
> Specify dimension line location or [Mtext/Text/Angle/Horizontal/Vertical/Rotated]: *(pick the dimension line location)*
> Dimension text = 2.000
> Command: **DBA** *or* **DIMBASELINE**↵
> Specify a second extension line origin or [Undo/Select] <Select>: *(pick the next second extension line origin)*
> Dimension text = 3.250
> Specify a second extension line origin or [Undo/Select] <Select>: *(pick the next second extension line origin)*
> Dimension text = 4.375
> Specify a second extension line origin or [Undo/Select] <Select>: ↵
> Select base dimension: ↵
> Command:

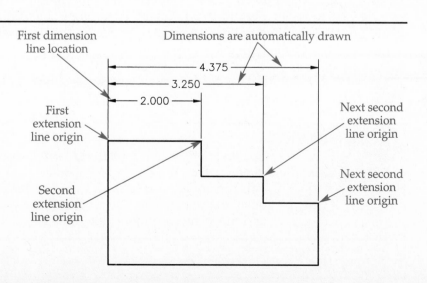

Figure 18-28. Using the **DIMBASELINE** command. AutoCAD automatically spaces and places the extension lines, dimension lines, arrowheads, and numbers.

You can continue to add baseline dimensions until you press [Enter] twice to return to the Command: prompt.

If you want to come back later and add datum dimensions to an existing dimension other than the most recently drawn dimension, you can use the **Select** option by pressing [Enter] at the first prompt. At the Select base dimension: prompt, pick the dimension to serve as the base. Then select the new second extension line origins as described earlier.

When picking an existing dimension to use as the baseline, the extension line nearest the point where you select the dimension is used as the baseline point.

You can also draw baseline dimensions to angular features. First, draw an angular dimension and then enter the **DIMBASELINE** command, or enter the command and pick an existing angular dimension. Figure 18-29 shows angular baseline dimensions.

Figure 18-29.
Using the **DIMBASELINE** command to datum dimension angular features.

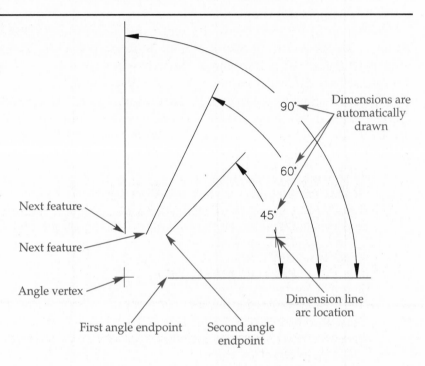

Chain dimensions

DIMCONTINUE
DCO

Dime̲nsion
⟶ Continue

Dimension
toolbar

Continue Dimension

As previously mentioned, when creating chain dimensions you will receive the same prompts and options received while creating datum dimensions. Chain dimensioning is shown in Figure 18-30. Chain dimensions (continue dimensions) are created by picking the **Continue Dimension** button in the **Dimension** toolbar, picking **Continue** in the **Dime̲nsion** pull-down menu, or by entering DCO or DIMCONTINUE at the Command: prompt. Continue dimensions can be created with linear, ordinate, and angular dimensions. Ordinate dimensions are discussed later in this chapter.

PROFESSIONAL TIP	You do not have to use **DIMBASELINE** or **DIMCONTINUE** immediately after a dimension that is to be used as a base or chain. You can come back later and use the **Select** option as previously discussed. Then, select the dimension you want to use and draw the datum or chain dimensions that you need.

Additional symbols are used in dimensions to point out certain features on the drawing. The diameter symbol (⌀) for circles and the radius symbol (R) for arcs are easily drawn. Additional symbols, such as the square symbol (□) for a square feature, can be drawn individually. However, this can be time-consuming. Instead, save the symbol as a block and insert it in the drawing before the dimension text. Storing and inserting blocks is discussed in Chapter 23 of this text.

Another way to place symbols with your dimension text is to create a dimension style that has a text style using the gdt.shx font. Establishing a dimension style with a desired text style is explained later in this chapter. A text style with this font allows you to place commonly used dimension symbols with the lowercase letter keys. When you type a dimension containing a symbol, press the [Caps Lock] key on your keyboard to activate caps lock. By doing this, text is uppercase. When a symbol needs to be inserted, you can press the [Shift] key and the letter that corresponds to the desired symbol.

Often used ASME symbols are shown in Figure 18-32. The letter to the right of each symbol name is the lowercase letter that you press at the keyboard to make the symbol. Additional geometric dimensioning and tolerancing (GD&T) symbols are available by pressing other keyboard keys. GD&T is covered in Chapter 21.

Figure 18-32.
Common dimensioning symbols and how to draw them. The lowercase letter displayed in parentheses with some symbol names is used to place the symbols with your keyboard when using a text style with the gdt.shx font.

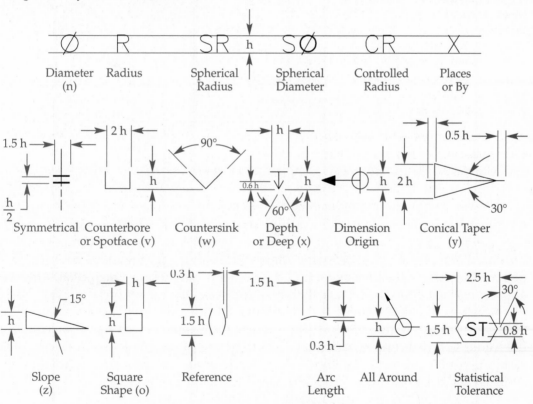

DRAWING CENTER DASHES OR CENTERLINES
IN A CIRCLE OR ARC

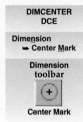
When small circles or arcs are dimensioned, the **DIMDIAMETER** and **DIMRADIUS** commands leave center dashes. If the dimension of a large circle crosses through the center, the dashes are left out. Center dashes and centerlines are drawn by picking the **Center Mark** button in the **Dimension** toolbar, picking **Center Mark** in the **Dimension** pull-down menu, or entering DCE or DIMCENTER at the Command: prompt. The command sequence is as follows:

Command: **DCE** *or* **DIMCENTER.⏎**
Select arc or circle: *(pick the arc or circle)*
Command:

When the circle or arc is picked, center marks are automatically drawn. The size of the center marks, or the amount that the centerlines extend outside the circle or arc, is controlled by the **Center Mark for Circles** area in the **Lines and Arrows** tab of the **Modify Dimension Style** dialog box. Later in this chapter you will see how to control all settings for the display of dimensions using dimension styles. Figure 18-33 shows the difference between drawing center marks and centerlines in arcs and circles.

Figure 18-33.
Arcs and circles displayed with center marks and centerlines.

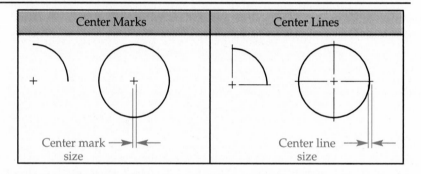

DIMENSIONING CIRCLES

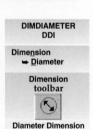
Circles are normally dimensioned by giving the diameter. The ASME standard for dimensioning arcs is to give the radius. However, AutoCAD allows you to dimension either a circle or an arc with a diameter dimension. Diameter dimensions are produced by picking the **Diameter Dimension** button on the **Dimension** toolbar, picking **Diameter** in the **Dimension** pull-down menu, or entering DDI or DIMDIAMETER at the Command: prompt. You are then asked to select the arc or circle.

When using the **DIMDIAMETER** command, a leader line and diameter dimension value are attached to the cursor when you pick the desired circle or arc. You can drag the leader to any desired location and length before picking where you want it. The resulting leader points to the center of the circle or arc just as recommended by the ASME standard. See Figure 18-34. The command sequence is as follows:

Command: **DDI** *or* **DIMDIAMETER.⏎**
Select arc or circle: *(pick the circle)*
Dimension text = 1.250
Specify dimension line location or [Mtext/Text/Angle]: *(pick the dimension line location)*
Command:

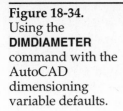

Figure 18-34.
Using the
DIMDIAMETER
command with the
AutoCAD
dimensioning
variable defaults.

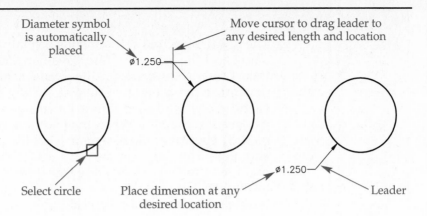

Diameter symbol is automatically placed

Move cursor to drag leader to any desired length and location

Ø1.250

Select circle

Place dimension at any desired location

Ø1.250

Leader

You also have the **Mtext**, **Text**, and **Angle** options that were introduced earlier. Use the **Mtext** or **Text** option if you want to change the text value or the **Angle** option if you want to change the angle of the text.

EXERCISE 18-7

❏ Start AutoCAD and use one of your templates.
❏ Set up the appropriate layers for your drawing elements, including dimensions.
❏ Draw and dimension an object similar to Figure 18-34.
❏ Save the drawing as EX18-7.

Dimensioning Holes

Holes are dimensioned in the view where they appear as circles. Give location dimensions to the center and a leader showing the diameter. Leader lines can be drawn using the **DIMDIAMETER** command as previously discussed. The center mark type and size are controlled in the dimension style, which is discussed later. Multiple holes of the same size can be noted with one hole dimension, such as 2X Ø.50. See Figure 18-35. Use the **Mtext** or **Text** option to create this dimension. The **Angle** option can be used to change the angle of the text numbers, but it is not commonly done.

Figure 18-35.
Dimensioning holes.

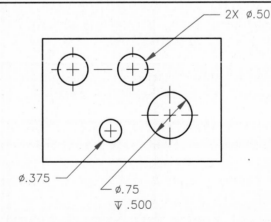

2X Ø.50

Ø.375

Ø.75

▽ .500

The ASME standard recommends a small space between the object and the extension line. This happens when the **Offset from Origin** setting within the dimension style is set to its default or some other desired positive value. This is very useful *except* when providing dimensions to centerlines for the location of holes. When the endpoint of the centerline is picked, a positive value leaves a space between the centerline and the beginning of the extension line. This is not a preferred practice. Change the **Offset from Origin** setting to 0 to remove the gap. Be sure to change back to its positive setting when dimensioning other objects.

Use of the **Dimension Style Manager** dialog box to set this and other dimensioning settings is fully explained later in this chapter.

Dimensioning for Manufacturing Processes

A *counterbore* is a larger diameter hole machined at one end of a smaller hole. It provides a place for the head of a bolt. A *spotface* is similar to a counterbore except that it is not as deep. The spotface provides a smooth recessed surface for a washer. A *countersink* is a cone-shaped recess at one end of a hole. It provides a mating surface for a screw head of the same shape. A note for these features is provided using symbols. First, locate the centers in the circular view. Then, place a leader providing machining information in a note. See Figure 18-36.

Symbols for this type of application can be customized as discussed in Chapter 23. These symbols can also be drawn by creating a dimension style with a text style using the gdt.shx font as explained earlier in this chapter. The symbols and related gdt.shx keyboard letter used to make the symbol are displayed in Figure 18-32.

The **DIMDIAMETER** command gives you multiline text to use during the creation of the dimension. Additional text can be added by editing the dimension text, since it is actually an mtext object.

Figure 18-36.
Dimension notes for machining processes. The symbols can be inserted as blocks, or as lowercase letters when a text style with the gdt.shx font is used.

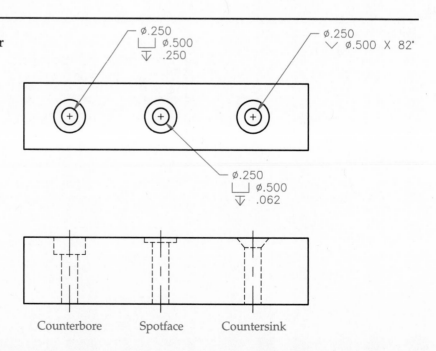

Dimensioning Repetitive Features

Repetitive features refer to many features having the same shape and size. When this occurs, the number of repetitions is followed by an X, a space, and the size dimension. The dimension is then connected to the feature with a leader. See Figure 18-37.

Figure 18-37.
Dimensioning repetitive features (shown in color).

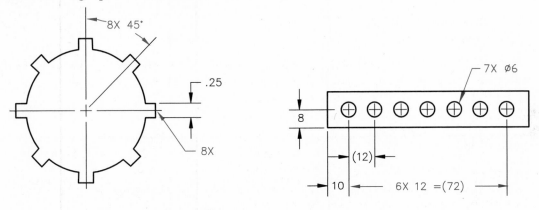

EXERCISE 18-8

❏ Start AutoCAD and use one of your templates.
❏ Set up the appropriate layers for your drawing elements, including dimensions.
❏ Use the proper dimensioning techniques and commands to dimension the objects exactly as shown.
❏ Save the drawing as **EX18-8**.

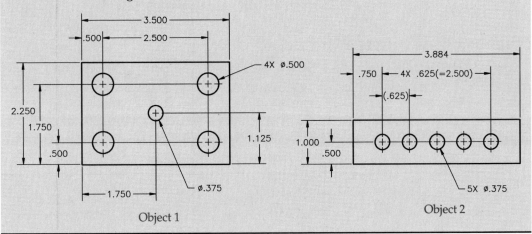

DIMRADIUS
DRA

Dimension
➥ Radius

Dimension
toolbar

Radius Dimension

The standard for dimensioning arcs is a radius dimension. A radius dimension is placed with the **DIMRADIUS** command. Access this command by picking the **Radius Dimension** button on the **Dimension** toolbar, by picking **Radius** in the **Dimension** pull-down menu, or by entering either DRA or DIMRADIUS at the Command: prompt.

When using the **DIMRADIUS** command, you get the Select arc or circle: prompt. A leader line and radius dimension value is attached to the cursor when you pick the desired arc or circle. You can drag the leader to any desired location and length before picking where you want it. The resulting leader points to the center of the arc or circle as recommended by the ASME standard. See Figure 18-38. The command sequence is as follows:

Command: **DRA** or **DIMRADIUS**↵
Select arc or circle: (pick an arc)
Specify dimension line location or [Mtext/Text/Angle]: (drag the leader to a desired location and pick)
Dimension text = 0.750
Command:

As with the previous dimensioning commands, you can use the **Mtext** or **Text** option to change the dimension text or use the **Angle** option to change the angle of the text value.

Figure 18-38.
Using the
DIMRADIUS
command to
dimension arcs with
AutoCAD
dimensioning
defaults.

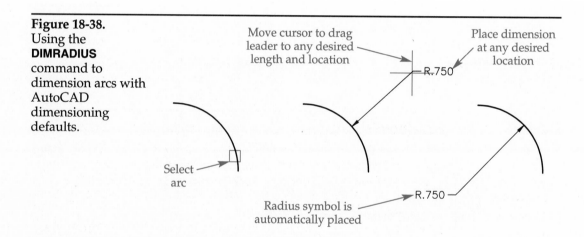

Dimensioning Fillets and Rounds

Small inside arcs are called *fillets*. Small arcs on outside corners are called *rounds*. Fillets are designed to strengthen inside corners. Rounds are used to relieve sharp corners. Fillets and rounds can be dimensioned individually as arcs or in a general note. The general note such as ALL FILLETS AND ROUNDS R.125 UNLESS OTHERWISE SPECIFIED is usually placed near the title block. See Figure 18-39.

Figure 18-39.
Dimensioning fillets
and rounds.

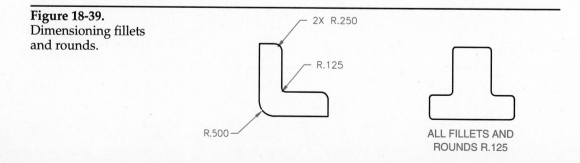

❑ Start AutoCAD and use one of your templates.
❑ Set up the appropriate layers for your drawing elements, including dimensions.
❑ Draw and dimension an object similar to Figure 18-38.
❑ Draw and dimension objects similar to Figure 18-39.
❑ Save the drawing as EX18-9.

Dimensioning Curves

When possible, curves are dimensioned as arcs. When they are not in the shape of a constant-radius arc, they should be dimensioned to points along the curve using the **DIMLINEAR** command. See Figure 18-40.

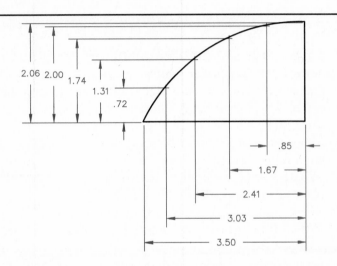

Figure 18-40. Dimensioning curves that do not have a constant radius.

Dimensioning Curves with Oblique Extension Lines

The curve shown in Figure 18-40 is dimensioned using the normal practice, but in some cases, spaces may be limited and oblique extension lines are used. First, dimension the object using the **DIMLINEAR** command as appropriate, even if dimensions are crowded or overlap. See Figure 18-41A.

The .150 and .340 dimensions are to be placed at an oblique angle above the view. The **Oblique** option is accessed by picking **Oblique** in the **Dimension** pull-down menu. Oblique is one of the options found in the **DIMEDIT** command, which is explained in detail in Chapter 19.

After selecting the command, you are asked to select the objects. Pick the dimensions to be redrawn at an oblique angle. In this case, the .150 and .340 dimensions are selected.

```
Command: DIMEDIT↵
Enter type of dimension editing [Home/New/Rotate/Oblique] <Home>: O↵
Select objects: (pick the .150 and .340 dimensions)
Select objects: ↵
```

Next, you are asked for the obliquing angle. Careful planning is needed to make sure the correct obliquing angle is selected. Obliquing angles originate from 0° East and revolve counterclockwise:

```
Enter obliquing angle (press ENTER for none): 135↵
Command:
```

The result is shown in Figure 18-41B.

Figure 18-41.
Drawing
dimensions with
oblique extension
lines.

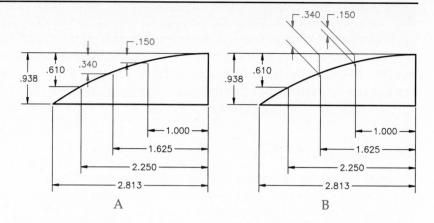

A   B

DRAWING LEADER LINES

The **DIMDIAMETER** and **DIMRADIUS** commands automatically place leaders on the drawing. The **QLEADER** command allows you to begin and end a leader line where you desire. You can also place single or multiple lines of text with the leader. This command is ideal for the following situations:
* Adding specific notes to the drawing.
* When a leader line must be staggered to go around other drawing features. Keep in mind that staggering leader lines is not a recommended ASME standard.
* Where a double leader is required. Drawing two leaders from one note is not a recommended ASME standard.
* When making custom leader lines.
* When drawing curved leaders for architectural applications.

The **QLEADER** command creates leader lines and related notes that are considered complex objects. This command provides you with the flexibility to place tolerances and multiple lines of text with the leader. Some of the leader line characteristics, such as arrowhead size, are controlled by the dimension style settings. Other features, such as the leader format and annotation style, are controlled by the **Settings** option within the **QLEADER** command. *Annotation* is text such as notes and dimensions on a drawing.

QLEADER
LE

Dimension
➥ Leader

Dimension
toolbar

Quick Leader

The **QLEADER** command is accessed by picking the **Quick Leader** button in the **Dimension** toolbar, selecting **Leader** in the **Dimension** pull-down menu, or typing LE or QLEADER at the Command: prompt. The initial prompts look like the **LINE** command, with the Specify from point: and Specify to point: prompts. This allows you to pick where the leader starts and ends.

In mechanical drafting, properly drawn leaders have one straight segment extending from the feature to a horizontal shoulder, which is 1/4″ (6mm) long. While most other fields also use straight leaders, AutoCAD provides the option of drawing curved leaders, which are commonly used in architectural drafting. The command sequence begins like this:

Command: **LE** *or* **QLEADER.**↵
Specify first leader point, or [Settings]<Settings>: *(pick the leader start point)*
Specify next point: *(pick the second leader point, which is the start of the leader shoulder)*
Specify next point: ↵ *(press* [Enter] *and the shoulder is drawn automatically)*
Specify text width <0.0000>: ↵
Enter first line of annotation text <Mtext>: *(enter text)*↵
Enter next line of annotation text: ↵

In this example, AutoCAD automatically draws a leader shoulder in front of the text.

QLEADER Settings

The **Settings** option, available at the beginning of the **QLEADER** command, can be used to give you greater control over the leader and the text associated with the leader. For example, the leader can be set to have the first segment always drawn at a 45° angle and the second segment (or shoulder) always drawn at 0°.

When you select the **Settings** option of the **QLEADER** command, the **Leader Settings** dialog box is displayed. This dialog box has three tabs: **Annotation**, **Leader Line & Arrow**, and **Attachment**. The appearance of the arrow and leader line is determined by the settings in the **Leader Line & Arrow** tab. The settings found in the **Annotation** and **Attachment** tabs determine the appearance of the text portion of the leader.

Leader line and arrow settings

The **Leader Line & Arrow** tab of the **Leader Settings** dialog box is shown in Figure 18-42. The settings in this tab determine the type of arrowhead, type of leader line, angles for leader line and shoulder, and number of requested points.

The **Leader Line** area is used to specify either a line leader (by picking the **Straight** radio button) or spline leader (by selecting the **Spline** radio button). The spline leader is curved, and is commonly used in architectural drafting. Figure 18-43 shows examples of the spline and straight leader lines.

Figure 18-42.
The **Leader Line & Arrow** tab of the **Leader Settings** dialog box.

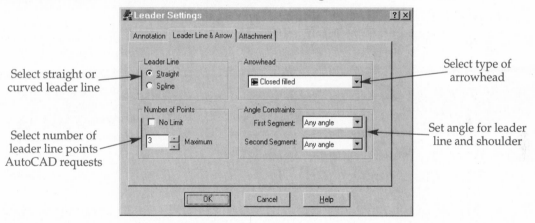

Figure 18-43.
The type of leader line (straight or spline) is set in the **Leader Line & Arrow** tab of the **Leader Settings** dialog box.

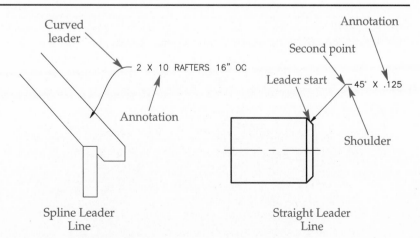

You can also set the maximum number of vertices on the leader line. This is set in the **Number of Points** area. Set the maximum number of vertices in the **Maximum** text box, or select the **No Limit** check box to have no maximum number. After the maximum number is reached, the **QLEADER** command automatically stops drawing the leader and asks for text information. To use less than the maximum number of points, press the [Enter] key at the Specify next point prompt. If the leader is a line object, a value of three for the maximum number of points defines a maximum total of two line segments.

The **Arrowhead** area uses the default value assigned to leaders within the current dimension style. To change the appearance of the arrowhead, open the drop-down list to display the full range of choices. Changing the **Arrowhead** setting creates a dimension style override, discussed later in this chapter.

The first two segments of the leader line can be held to certain angles. These angles are set in the **Angle Constraints** area. The options for each segment are Any angle, Horizontal, 90, 45, 30, or 15. The Ortho mode setting overrides the angle constraints, so it is advisable to turn Ortho mode off while using this command.

PROFESSIONAL TIP The ASME standard for leaders does not recommend a leader line that is less than 15° or greater than 75° from horizontal. Use the **Angle Constraints** settings in the **Leader Settings** dialog box to help maintain these standards.

Leader text settings

The **Annotation** and **Attachment** tabs of the **Leader Settings** dialog box control the way text is used with the leader line. The **Annotation** tab contains settings that specify the type of object used for annotation, additional options for mtext objects, and tools that automatically repeat annotations. The **Attachment** tab has options for specifying the point where the leader line shoulder meets an mtext annotation object.

The **Annotation** tab is shown in Figure 18-44. The **Annotation Type** area determines which type of entity is inserted and attached to the end of the leader line. The following options are available:

- **MText.** This is the default setting, causing a multiline text object to be inserted after the leader lines are drawn. See Figure 18-45A.
- **Copy an Object.** This option allows an mtext, text, block, or tolerance object to be copied from the current drawing and inserted at the end of the current

Figure 18-44.
The **Annotation** tab of the **Leader Settings** dialog box.

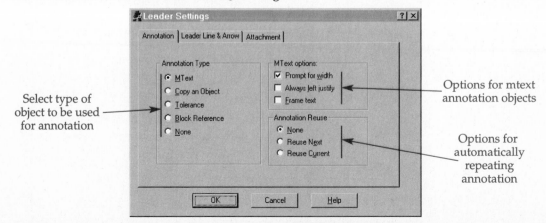

leader line. This is useful when the same note or symbol is required in many places throughout a drawing. After drawing the leader line, the **Select an object to copy:** prompt appears. The selected object is placed at the end of the shoulder. See Figure 18-45B.

- **Tolerance.** This displays the **Geometric Tolerance** dialog box for creation of a feature control frame. See Figure 18-45C. Geometric tolerancing is explained in detail in Chapter 21 of this text.
- **Block Reference.** This option inserts a specified block at the end of the leader. A *block* is a symbol that was previously created and saved. Blocks can be inserted into other drawings. These multiple-use symbols are explained in detail in Chapter 23 of this text. Blocks can be scaled during the insertion process. A special symbol block called Target is inserted in Figure 18-45D.
- **None.** This option ends the leader with no annotation of any kind. See Figure 18-45E. The **None** option can be used as a way to create multiple leaders for a single leader annotation, as shown in Figure 18-46. Multiple leaders are not a recommended ASME standard, but they are used for some applications, such as the leader for welding symbols. The welding symbol shown in Figure 18-46B was created as a block and then inserted using the **Block Reference** annotation option.

You can automatically repeat the previous leader annotation using the options in the **Annotation Reuse** area. The default option is **None**. This allows you to specify the annotation when creating a leader. If you wish to use an annotation repeatedly, select the **Reuse Next** option and then create the first leader and annotation. When you create another leader, the setting automatically changes to **Reuse Current**, and the annotation is inserted automatically. The annotation is repeated for all new leaders until the **Annotation Reuse** setting is changed back to **None**.

Figure 18-45.
The annotation object is selected in the **Annotation** tab of the **Leader Settings** dialog box.

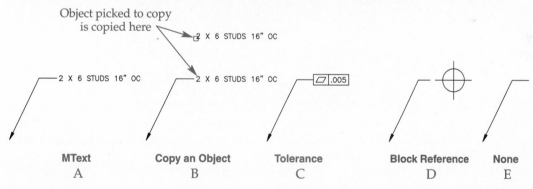

Figure 18-46.
Use the **None** annotation option when drawing multiple leaders.

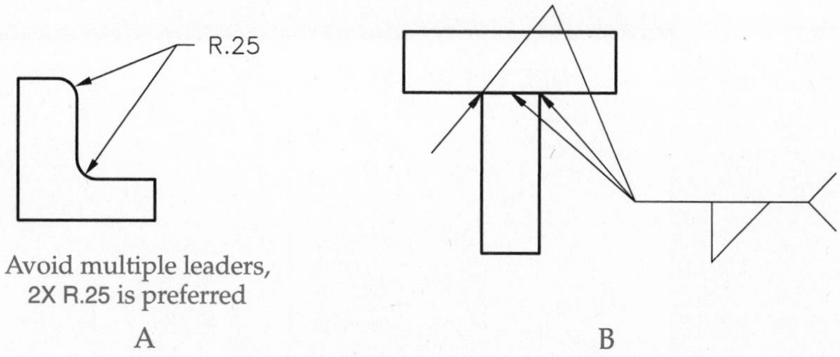

The **MText options** area of the **Annotation** tab is only available if **MText** is selected as the annotation type. These settings can be overridden by selecting the **Mtext** option during the **QLEADER** command. The following options are available:

- **Prompt for width.** If checked, you are prompted to define the size of the mtext box. If this option is not checked, a value of 0 (no text wrapping) is assigned to the mtext box.
- **Always left justify.** Forces the mtext to be left justified, regardless of the direction of the leader line.
- **Frame text.** Creates a box around the mtext text box. The default properties of the frame are controlled by the dimension line settings of the current dimension style.

The **Attachment** tab is only available when the **MText** option is selected in the **Annotation Type** area. This tab contains options that determine how the mtext object is positioned relative to the endpoint of the leader line shoulder. See Figure 18-47. Different options can be specified for mtext to the right of the leader line and mtext to the left of the leader line. These options are shown in Figure 18-48.

The **Underline bottom line** option causes a line to be drawn along the bottom of the mtext box. When this check box is selected, the choices for text on left and right side become grayed-out.

Figure 18-47.
The **Attachment** tab of the **Leader Settings** dialog box determines the location of the mtext annotation relative to the leader line shoulder.

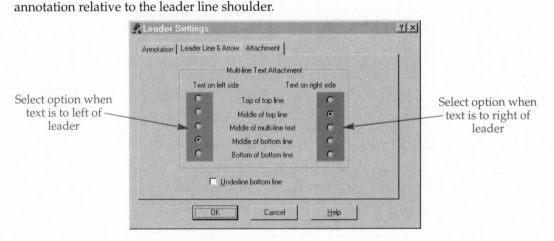

Figure 18-48.
Placement of mtext is controlled by the options in the **Attachment** tab of the **Leader Settings** dialog box.

	Top of Top Line	Middle of Top Line	Middle of Multiline Text	Middle of Bottom Line	Bottom of Bottom Line
Text on Left Side	⌀.250 ⌴⌀.500 ▽.062	⌀.250 ⌴⌀.500 ▽.062	⌀.250 ⌴⌀.500 ▽.062	⌀.250 ⌴⌀.500 ▽.062	⌀.250 ⌴⌀.500 ▽.062
Text on Right Side	⌀.250 ⌴⌀.500 ▽.062	⌀.250 ⌴⌀.500 ▽.062	⌀.250 ⌴⌀.500 ▽.062	⌀.250 ⌴⌀.500 ▽.062	⌀.250 ⌴⌀.500 ▽.062

AutoCAD and its Applications—Basics

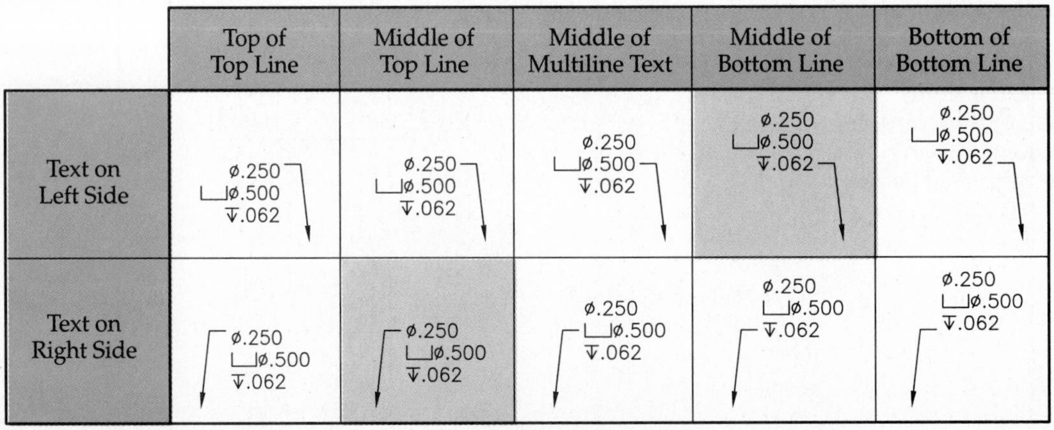

Using the LEADER Command

The **LEADER** command can also be used to draw leaders. This command does not provide the convenience, flexibility, and ability to easily comply with drafting standards as does the **QLEADER** command. The **LEADER** command can only be accessed from the command prompt:

Command: **LEADER**↵
Specify leader start point: *(pick the leader start point)*
Specify next point or [Annotation/Format/Undo] <Annotation>:

The **Annotation** option is the default and is accessed by pressing [Enter]. When this option is selected, the following prompt appears:

Enter first line of annotation text or <options>: *(enter text or press* [Enter] *to access other options)*

Enter the first line of annotation text, then press [Enter]. You can then enter additional lines of text, or press [Enter] again to complete the leader. Press [Enter] before typing the first line of text to access the annotation options shown in the following prompt:

Enter first line of annotation text or <options>: ↵
Enter an annotation option [Tolerance/Copy/Block/None/Mtext] <Mtext>:

These options are identical to the annotation type options available in the **Leader Settings** dialog box.

The **LEADER** command also has the **Format** options that are accessed as follows:

Specify next point or [Annotation/Format/Undo] <Annotation>: **F**↵
Enter leader format option [Spline/STraight/Arrow/None] <Exit>:

The **Spline** option is used for drawing curved leader lines, and the **STraight** option is used for drawing straight leader lines. The **Arrow** option places an arrowhead at the start of leaders, and the **None** option draws leaders without arrows.

The **Undo** option is used to remove the last leader segment that you drew.

Additional leader tools are found in the Express Tools. The **Leader Tools** cascading menu can be accessed by selecting **Dimension** from the **Express** pull-down menu. See Appendix A for Express Tools information.

EXERCISE 18-10

❏ Start AutoCAD and use one of your templates.
❏ Set up the appropriate layers for your drawing elements, including dimensions.
  Use the **QLEADER** command to draw the following:
  ❏ Draw and dimension objects similar to Figure 18-43.
  ❏ Draw multiple leaders with a note similar to Figure 18-46.
  ❏ Experiment by drawing a leader with each of the settings in the **Attachment** tab of the **Leader Settings** dialog box.
❏ Save the drawing as EX18-10.

Dimensioning Chamfers

A *chamfer* is an angled surface used to relieve sharp corners. The ends of bolts are commonly chamfered to allow them to engage the threaded hole better. Chamfers of 45° are dimensioned with a leader giving the angle and linear dimension, or with two linear dimensions. This can be accomplished using the **QLEADER** command. See Figure 18-49.

Chamfers other than 45° must have either the angle and a linear dimension or two linear dimensions placed on the view. See Figure 18-50. The **DIMLINEAR** and **DIMANGULAR** commands are used for this purpose.

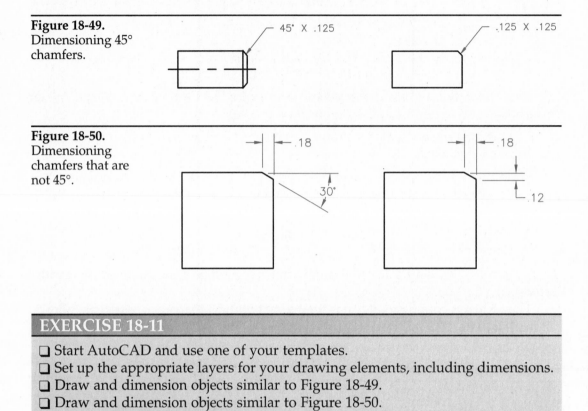

Figure 18-49.
Dimensioning 45° chamfers.

Figure 18-50.
Dimensioning chamfers that are not 45°.

ALTERNATE DIMENSIONING PRACTICES

In industries where computer-controlled machining processes are used, it is becoming common to omit dimension lines. Arrowless and tabular dimensioning are two types of dimensioning that omit dimension lines. Another type, chart dimensioning, involves changing values of a product, and the dimensions are shown in a chart.

Arrowless Dimensioning

Arrowless dimensioning is becoming popular in mechanical drafting. It is also used in electronics drafting, especially for chassis layout. This type of dimensioning has only extension lines and numbers. Dimension lines and arrowheads are omitted. Dimension numbers are aligned with the extension lines. Each dimension number represents a dimension originating from a common point. This starting, or 0, dimension is typically known as a *datum*, or *baseline*. Holes or other features are labeled with identification letters. Sizes are given in a table placed on the drawing. See Figure 18-51.

Figure 18-51.
Arrowless
dimensioning.

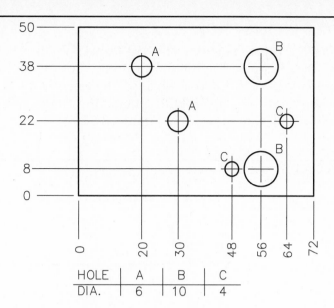

HOLE	A	B	C
DIA.	6	10	4

Tabular Dimensioning

Tabular dimensioning is a form of arrowless dimensioning where dimensions to features are shown in a table. The table gives the location of features from the X axis and Y axis. It also provides the depth of features from a Z axis, when appropriate. Each feature is labeled with a letter or number that correlates to the table. See Figure 18-52.

Figure 18-52.
Tabular dimensioning. (Doug Major)

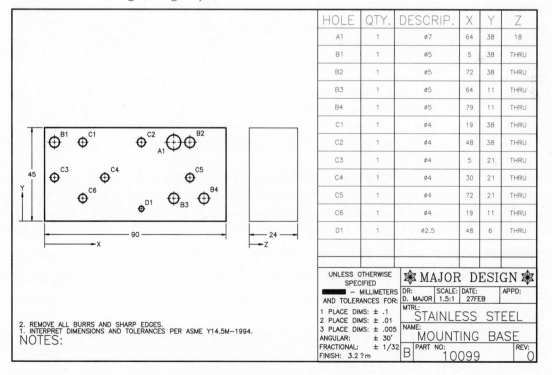

HOLE	QTY.	DESCRIP.	X	Y	Z
A1	1	ø7	64	38	18
B1	1	ø5	5	38	THRU
B2	1	ø5	72	38	THRU
B3	1	ø5	64	11	THRU
B4	1	ø5	79	11	THRU
C1	1	ø4	19	38	THRU
C2	1	ø4	48	38	THRU
C3	1	ø4	5	21	THRU
C4	1	ø4	30	21	THRU
C5	1	ø4	72	21	THRU
C6	1	ø4	19	11	THRU
D1	1	ø2.5	48	6	THRU

UNLESS OTHERWISE SPECIFIED
■■■ – MILLIMETERS AND TOLERANCES FOR:
1 PLACE DIMS: ± .1
2 PLACE DIMS: ± .01
3 PLACE DIMS: ± .005
ANGULAR: ± 30'
FRACTIONAL: ± 1/32
FINISH: 3.2 ?m

✳ MAJOR DESIGN ✳

| DR: D. MAJOR | SCALE: 1.5:1 | DATE: 27FEB | APPD: |

MTRL: STAINLESS STEEL
NAME: MOUNTING BASE

B | PART NO: 10099 | REV: 0

NOTES:
2. REMOVE ALL BURRS AND SHARP EDGES.
1. INTERPRET DIMENSIONS AND TOLERANCES PER ASME Y14.5M–1994.

Chart Dimensioning

Chart dimensioning may take the form of unidirectional, aligned, arrowless, or tabular dimensioning. It provides flexibility in situations where dimensions change as requirements of the product change. The views of the product are drawn and variable dimensions are shown with letters. The letters correlate to a chart where the different options are shown. See Figure 18-53.

Figure 18-53.
Chart
dimensioning.

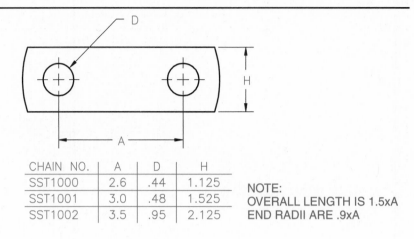

CHAIN NO.	A	D	H
SST1000	2.6	.44	1.125
SST1001	3.0	.48	1.525
SST1002	3.5	.95	2.125

NOTE:
OVERALL LENGTH IS 1.5xA
END RADII ARE .9xA

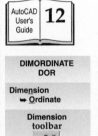

AutoCAD
User's
Guide **12**

DIMORDINATE
DOR

Dime̲nsion
↳ O̲rdinate

Dimension
toolbar

Ordinate Dimension

Drawing Arrowless Dimensions

AutoCAD refers to arrowless dimensioning as *ordinate dimensioning.* These dimensions are done using the **DIMORDINATE** command. This command is accessed by picking the **Ordinate Dimension** button in the **Dimension** toolbar, by picking **Ordinate** in the **Dime̲nsion** pull-down menu, or by entering DOR or DIMORDINATE at the Command: prompt. When using this command, AutoCAD automatically places an extension line and number along X and Y coordinates. Since you are working in the XY plane, it is often best to have Ortho mode on.

The world coordinate system (WCS) 0,0 coordinate has been in the lower-left corner of the screen for the drawings you have already completed. In most cases, this is fine. However, when doing ordinate dimensioning, it is best to have the dimensions originate from a primary datum, which is often a corner of the object. The WCS is fixed; the user coordinate system (UCS), on the other hand, can be moved to any orientation desired.

All ordinate dimensions originate from the current UCS origin. The UCS is discussed in detail in *AutoCAD and its Applications—Advanced, AutoCAD 2000.* In general, the UCS allows you to set your own coordinate system. If you do this, all the Dimension text: prompts display the actual dimensions from the XY coordinates on the object. Move the UCS origin to the corner of the object or the appropriate datum feature by selecting **Mo̲ve UCS** from the **T̲ools** pull-down menu. You are then prompted to specify a new origin point. Use an object snap mode to select the corner of the object or appropriate datum feature. In Figure 18-54A, the UCS is moved to an appropriate location.

Next, if there are circles on your drawing, use the **DIMCENTER** command to place center marks in the circles, as shown in Figure 18-54B. This makes your drawing conform to ASME standards and provides something to pick when dimensioning the circle locations. Now, you are ready to start placing the ordinate dimensions. Enter the **DIMORDINATE** command as follows:

Command: **DOR** *or* **DIMORDINATE.**↵
Specify feature location: *(pick the feature to be dimensioned)*

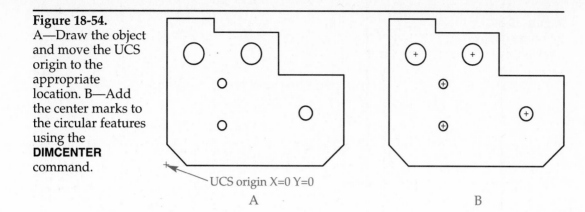

UCS origin X=0 Y=0

A   B

When the Specify feature location: prompt appears, move the screen cursor to the point or feature to be dimensioned. If the feature is the corner of the object, pick the corner. If the feature is a circle, pick the end of the center mark. This leaves the required space between the center mark and the extension line. Zoom in if needed and use the object snap modes. The next prompt asks for the leader endpoint, which actually refers to the extension line endpoint.

> Specify leader endpoint or [Xdatum/Ydatum/Mtext/Text/Angle]: *(pick the endpoint of the extension line)*
> Dimension text = 0.500

If the X axis or Y axis distance between the feature and the extension line endpoint is large, the default axis may not be the desired axis for the dimension. When this happens, use the **Xdatum** or **Ydatum** option to tell AutoCAD the axis from which the dimension originates.

The **Mtext**, **Text**, and **Angle** options are identical to the options available with other dimensioning commands. Pick the leader endpoint to complete the command.

Figure 18-55 shows the ordinate dimensions placed on the object. Notice the dimension text is aligned with the extension lines. Aligned dimensioning is standard with ordinate dimensioning. Finally, complete the drawing by adding any missing lines, such as centerlines or fold lines. Identify the holes with letters and correlate a dimensioning table. See Figure 18-56.

Figure 18-55.
Placing the ordinate dimensions.

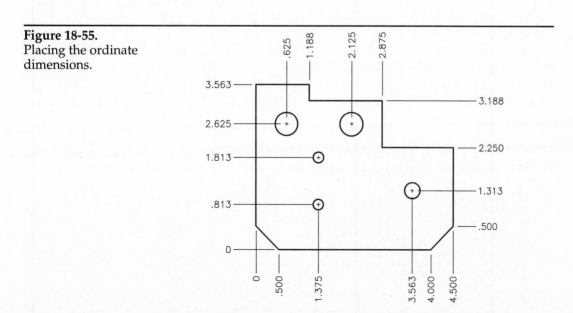

Figure 18-56.
Completing the drawing.

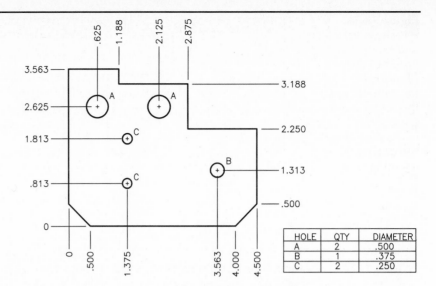

HOLE	QTY	DIAMETER
A	2	.500
B	1	.375
C	2	.250

You can leave the UCS origin at the corner of the object, or move it back to the corner of the screen (WCS) by selecting **World** from the **New UCS** cascading menu in the **Tools** pull-down menu.

PROFESSIONAL TIP

Most ordinate dimensioning tasks work best with Ortho mode on. However, when the extension line is too close to an adjacent dimension number, it is best to stagger the extension line as shown in the following illustration. With Ortho mode off, the extension line is automatically staggered when you pick the offset second extension line point as demonstrated.

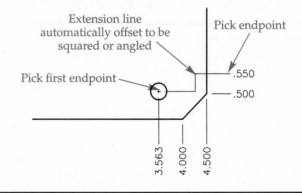

EXERCISE 18-12

❏ Start AutoCAD and use one of your templates.
❏ Set up the appropriate layers for your drawing elements, including dimensions.
❏ Draw and use ordinate dimensioning to dimension the object shown in Figure 18-51.
❏ Save the drawing as EX18-12.

There are many different thread forms. The most common forms are the Unified and metric screw threads. The parts of a screw thread are shown in Figure 18-57.

Threads are commonly shown on a drawing with a simplified representation. Thread depth is shown with a hidden line. This method is used for both external and internal threads. See Figure 18-58.

Figure 18-57.
Parts of a screw thread.

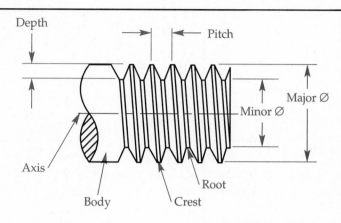

Figure 18-58.
Simplified thread representations.

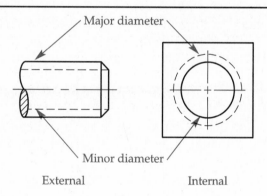

Showing the Thread Note

The view shows the reader that a thread exists, but the thread note gives exact specifications. The thread note for Unified screw threads must be given in the following order:

3/4 - 10UNC - 2A
(1)   (2) (3)   (4) (5)
(1) Major diameter of thread, given as fraction or number.
(2) Number of threads per inch.
(3) Thread series. UNC = Unified National Coarse. UNF = Unified National Fine.
(4) Class of fit. 1 = large tolerance. 2 = general purpose tolerance. 3 = tight tolerance.
(5) A = external thread. B = internal thread.

The thread note for metric threads is displayed in the following order:

M 14 X 2
(1) (2)   (3)
(1) M = metric thread.
(2) Major diameter in millimeters.
(3) Pitch in millimeters.

There are too many Unified and metric screw threads to discuss here. Refer to the *Machinery's Handbook* or a comprehensive drafting text for more information.

The thread note is typically connected to the thread view with a leader. See Figure 18-59. A chamfer is often placed on the external thread. This makes it easier to engage the mating thread.

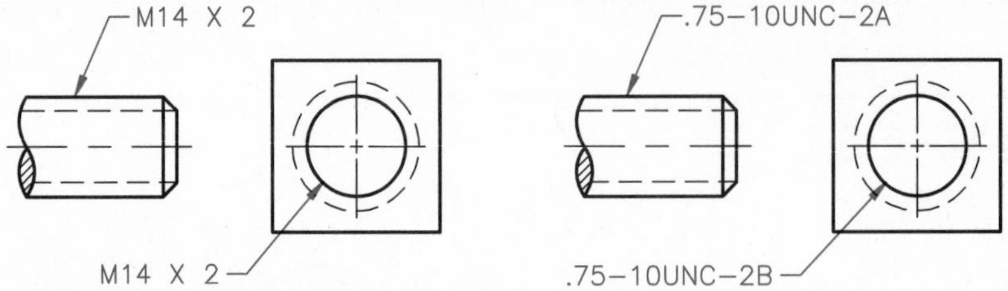

Figure 18-59.
Displaying the thread note with a leader.

M14 X 2

M14 X 2

.75−10UNC−2A

.75−10UNC−2B

EXERCISE 18-13

❑ Start AutoCAD and use one of your templates.
❑ Set up the appropriate layers for your drawing elements, including dimensions.
❑ Draw a simplified representation of an external and internal Unified screw thread. Do the same for a metric screw thread.
❑ Use the **QLEADER** command to label each view. Label the Unified screw thread as 3/4-10UNC-2A and the metric screw thread as M14 X 2.
❑ Your drawing should look similar to Figure 18-59.
❑ Save the drawing as EX18-13.

LAYOUT DIMENSIONING

It is recommended that you use caution when placing associative dimensions on a model space while paper space is active. (Model space and paper space were discussed in Chapters 9 and 10 of this text.) The model space environment is active when the **Model** tab is selected. The paper space environment is active when a layout tab is selected.

Existing dimensions will remain unchanged in a model space viewport when you use editing commands such as **STRETCH, TRIM**, or **EXTEND**, or display commands such as **ZOOM** or **PAN**. To make sure that AutoCAD calculates a scale factor that is compatible between the **Model** and layout tabs, activate the **Scale dimensions to layout (paperspace)** check box in the **Fit** tab of the **Modify Dimension Style** dialog box.

PROFESSIONAL TIP

Dimensions should normally be created with the **Model** tab active. Use caution when dimensioning with a layout tab active. You can create linear dimensions from objects created in the **Model** tab when the layout tab is active, but diameter and radius dimensions cannot be drawn. Also, if you dimension some objects in model space and others in paper space, some of your dimensions will appear in the **Model** tab and others will appear in a layout tab. This situation would force you to juggle dimension variables and switch between tabs frequently. However, there are valid reasons to place items such as drawing notes in a layout tab when they are part of the drawing format.

DIMENSION STYLES

The appearance of dimensions, from the size and the style of the text to the color of the dimension line, is controlled by over 70 different settings. *Dimension styles* are saved configurations of these settings. So far in this chapter, you have used only a few of these settings. The dimension settings that you used were introduced to help you perform specific tasks.

A dimension style is created by changing the dimension settings as needed to achieve the desired dimension appearance for your drafting application. For example, the dimension style for mechanical drafting probably has Romans text font placed in a break in the dimension line, and the dimension lines are capped with arrowheads. See Figure 18-3. The dimension style for architectural drafting may use CityBlueprint or Stylus BT text font placed above the dimension line, and dimension lines are terminated with slashes. See Figure 18-4.

The dimension style can have dimensions based on national or international standards, or may be set up to match company or school applications and standards. The dimensioning practice that you have been doing in this chapter was based on the AutoCAD Standard dimension style. This dimension style uses the AutoCAD default settings and variables.

CREATING DIMENSION STYLES

You might think of dimension styles as the dimensioning standards you use. Dimension styles are usually established for a specific type of drafting field or application. You can customize dimension styles to correspond to drafting standards such as ASME/ANSI, ISO (International Organization for Standardization), MIL (military), architectural, structural, civil, or your own school or company standards.

Dimension styles are created using the **Dimension Style Manager** dialog box. See Figure 18-60. This dialog box is accessed by picking the **Dimension Styles** button in the **Dimension** tool bar, by picking **Dimension Style...** in the **Format** pull-down menu, by picking **Style...** in the **Dimension** pull-down menu, or by entering D, DST, DDIM, DIMSTY, or DIMSTYLE at the Command: prompt.

DIMSTYLE
D
DST
DDIM
DIMSTY

Dimension
➥ Style...
Format
➥ Dimension
Style...

Dimension
toolbar

Dimension Style

Figure 18-60.
The **Dimension Style Manager** dialog box. The Standard dimension style is the AutoCAD default.

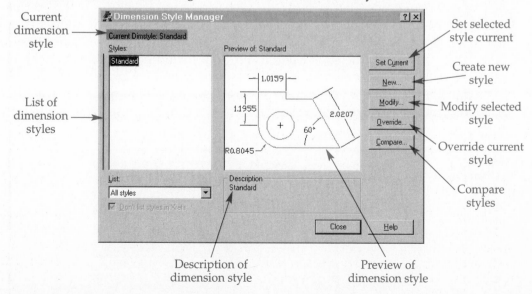

Current dimension style

List of dimension styles

Set selected style current

Create new style

Modify selected style

Override current style

Compare styles

Description of dimension style

Preview of dimension style

The current dimension style, Standard, is noted at the top of the **Dimension Style Manager** dialog box. The **Styles:** box displays the dimension styles found within the current drawing. The **List:** box controls whether all styles or only the styles in use are displayed in the **Styles:** box.

If there are external reference drawings (xrefs) within the current drawing, the **Don't list styles in Xrefs** box can be checked to eliminate xref dependent dimension styles from the **Styles:** box. This is often valuable because xref dimension styles cannot be used to create new dimensions objects. External references are discussed in Chapter 24.

The **Description** box and **Preview of:** image provide information about the selected dimension style. The Standard dimension style is the AutoCAD default. If you change any of the AutoCAD default dimension settings without first creating a new dimension style, the changes are automatically stored in a dimension style override.

The following describes additional options found in the **Dimension Style Manager**:

- **Set Current.** This button makes current the dimension style selected in the **Styles:** box. When a dimension style is current, all new dimensions are created in that style. All existing dimensions are not affected by a change to the current style. Xref dependent dimension styles cannot be set current.

- **New.** Use this button to create a new dimension style. When you pick this button, the **Create New Dimension Style** dialog box is displayed. See Figure 18-61. Pick the **Continue** button to access the **New Dimension Style** dialog box. The following options are available in this dialog box:
  - **New Style Name.** Give your new dimension style a descriptive name, such as Architectural or Mechanical.
  - **Start With.** This option helps you save time by basing the settings for a new style upon an existing dimension style. Xref dimension styles can be selected from this dialog box only if they were displayed in the **Dimension Style Manager**.
  - **Use for.** The choices in this drop-down list are All dimensions, Linear dimensions, Angular dimensions, Radius dimensions, Diameter dimensions, Ordinance dimensions, and Leaders and Tolerances. Use the All dimensions option to create a new dimension style. If you select one of the other options, you create a "substyle" of the dimension style specified in the **Start With:** text box. The settings in the new style are applied to the dimension type selected in this box.

- **Modify.** Selecting this button opens the **Modify Dimension Style** dialog box, which allows you to make changes to the currently selected style. Xref styles cannot be modified.

- **Override.** An *override* is a temporary change to the current style settings. Picking this button opens the **Override Current Style** dialog box. This button is only available for the style listed as current. Including a text prefix for just a few of the dimensions on a drawing is an example of an override. Once an override is created it is made current and is displayed as a branch, called the *child*, of the style from which it is created. The dimension style from which the

---

Figure 18-61.
The **Create New Dimension Style** dialog box. Changes to the AutoCAD default dimension style Standard result in a dimension style override.

Pick to modify new style

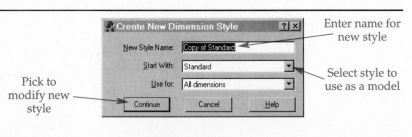

Enter name for new style

Select style to use as a model

AutoCAD and its Applications—Basics

child is created is called the *parent*. The override settings are lost when any other style, including the parent, is selected to become current again.

- **Compare.** Sometimes it is useful to view the details of two styles to determine why one is not behaving as the other. When the **Compare...** button is selected, you can compare two styles by entering the name of one style in the **Compare:** box and the name of the other in the **With:** box. Only the differences between the selected styles are displayed in the **Compare Dimension Styles** dialog box.

The **New Dimension Style**, **Modify Dimension Style**, and the **Override Current Style** dialog boxes have the same tabs. See Figure 18-62. The **Lines and Arrows**, **Text**, **Fit**, **Primary Units**, **Alternate Units**, and **Tolerances** tabs access the settings used for changing the way dimensions are displayed.

An alternative method of setting the dimension variables is to access the variables directly at the Command: prompt. For example, **DIMSCALE** is a system variable that can be used to change the **Use overall scale of:** setting on the **Fit** tab. In this book, the system variables are noted in parenthesis where applicable. The following shows an example of setting the dimension variable for overall scale at the command line:

> Command: **DIMSCALE**↵
> Enter new value for DIMSCALE <*current*>: *(enter a new value)*

Figure 18-62.
The **Lines and Arrows** tab of the **Modify Dimension Style** dialog box.

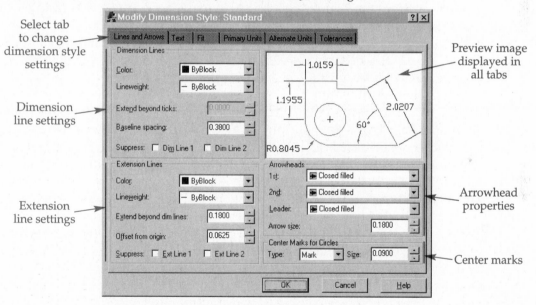

Select tab to change dimension style settings

Dimension line settings

Extension line settings

Preview image displayed in all tabs

Arrowhead properties

Center marks

Using the Lines and Arrows Tab

When the **New** (or **Modify**) button is selected from the **Dimension Style Manager** dialog box, the **New** (or **Modify**) **Dimension Style** dialog box is displayed with six tabs: **Lines and Arrows**, **Text**, **Fit**, **Primary Units**, **Alternate Units**, and **Tolerances**. As adjustments are made to the current dimension style, an image on each tab updates to graphically reflect those changes. The **Lines and Arrows** tab controls all settings for the display of the lines, arrowheads, leaders, and center marks of dimension strings. See Figure 18-62.

The **Dimension Lines** area is used to change the format of the dimension line with the following settings:

- **Color.** (**DIMCLRD**) By default, the dimension line color is assigned to ByBlock, which indicates that the line assumes the currently active color setting of all elements within the dimension object. The ByBlock color setting means that the color assigned to the created block is used for the component objects of the block. All associative dimensions are created as block objects. Blocks are symbols designed for multiple use and are explained in Chapter 23. Associative dimensions are discussed in this chapter and in Chapter 19. If the current entity color is set to ByLayer when the dimension block is created, then it comes in with a ByLayer setting. The component objects of the block then take on the color of the layer where the dimensions are created. If the current object color is an absolute color, then the component objects of the block take on that specific color regardless of the layer where the dimension was created.

- **Lineweight. (DIMLWD)** By default, the dimension line lineweight is assigned to ByBlock, which indicates that the line assumes the currently active lineweight setting of all elements within the dimension object. The ByBlock lineweight setting means that the lineweight assigned to the created block is used for the component objects of the block. If the current object lineweight is set to ByLayer when the dimension block is created, then it comes in with a ByLayer setting. The component objects of the block then take on the lineweight of the layer where the dimensions are created. If the current object lineweight is an absolute lineweight, the component objects of the block take on that specific lineweight regardless of the layer where the dimension was created.

- **Extend beyond ticks. (DIMDLE)** This text box is inactive unless you are using tick marks instead of arrowheads. Architectural tick marks, or oblique arrowheads, are often used when dimensioning architectural drawings. The different settings for arrowhead styles are explained later in this chapter. In this style of dimensioning, the dimension lines often cross over the extension lines. The extension represents how far the dimension line extends beyond the extension line. See Figure 18-63. The 0.00 default is used to draw dimensions that are not extended past the extension lines.

- **Baseline spacing. (DIMDLI)** This text box allows you to change the spacing between the dimension lines of baseline dimensions. The default spacing is .38 units. AutoCAD automatically spaces the dimension lines this distance when you use the **DIMBASELINE** command. The default value is generally too close for most drawings. Try other values to help make the drawing easy to read. Figure 18-64 shows the dimension line spacing.

- **Suppress. (DIMSD1** and **DIMSD2)** This option has two toggles that keep either the first, second, or both dimensions lines and their arrowheads from being displayed. The **Dim Line 1** and **Dim Line 2** check boxes refer to the first and second points picked when the dimension is created. Both dimension lines are displayed by default. The results of using these options are shown in Figure 18-65.

The **Extension Lines** area of the **Lines and Arrows** tab is used to change the format of the extension lines with the following dimension settings:

- **Color. (DIMCLRE)** The color choice made here controls the extension line color. The default value is ByBlock.

- **Lineweight. (DIMLWE)** The lineweight setting controls the lineweight of the extension lines.

Figure 18-63.
Using the **Extend beyond ticks** settings to allow the dimension line to extend past the extension line. With the default value of 0, the dimension line does not extend.

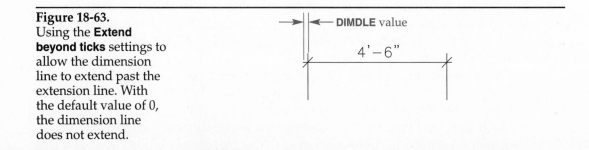

AutoCAD and its Applications—Basics

Figure 18-64.
The **Baseline spacing** setting controls the spacing between dimension lines.

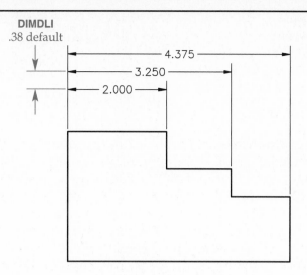

Figure 18-65.
Using the **Dim Line 1** and **Dim Line 2** dimensioning settings.

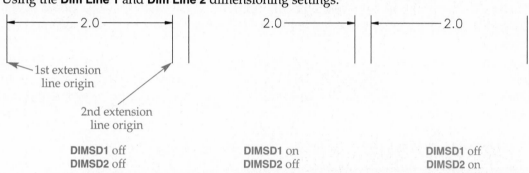

- **Extend beyond dim lines. (DIMEXE)** This text box is used to set the extension line extension, which is the distance the extension line runs past the last dimension line. See Figure 18-66. The default value is 0.18, and an extension line extension of .125 is common on most drawings.
- **Offset from origin. (DIMEXO)** This text box is used to change the distance between the object and the beginning of the extension line. See Figure 18-66. Most applications require this small offset. The default is .0625. It is recommended that a 0.0 setting be used when an extension line meets a centerline.
- **Suppress. (DIMSE1** and **DIMSE2)** This option is used to suppress either the first, second, or both extension lines using the **Ext Line 1** and **Ext Line 2** check boxes. Extension lines are displayed by default. An extension line might be suppressed, for example, if it coincides with an object line. See Figure 18-67.

Figure 18-66.
The extension line extension (**Extend beyond dim lines**) and the extension line offset (**Offset from origin**).

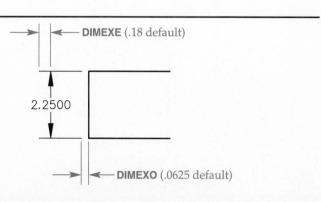

Figure 18-67.
Suppressing
extension lines.

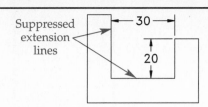

The **Arrowheads** area provides several different arrowhead options and controls the arrowhead size. Use the appropriate drop-down list to select the arrowhead used for the **1st** arrowhead (**DIMBLK1**), **2nd** arrowhead (**DIMBLK2**), and **Leader** arrowhead (**DIMDRBLK**). The default arrowhead is Closed Filled, and other options are shown in Figure 18-68. If you pick a new arrowhead in the **1st:** drop-down list, AutoCAD automatically makes the same selection for the **2nd:** drop-down list. Check your drafting standards before selecting the appropriate arrowhead.

Notice in Figure 18-68 there is no example of the User Arrow... option. This option is used to access an arrowhead of your own design. For this to work, you must first design an arrowhead and save it as a block. Blocks are discussed in Chapter 23 of this text. When you pick the User Arrow... option in the **Arrowheads** list, you get the **Select Custom Arrow Block** dialog box. Type the name of your custom arrow block in the **Select from Drawing Blocks:** text box and then pick **OK** to have the arrow used on the drawing.

When you access the Oblique or Architectural tick arrowhead options, the **Extend beyond ticks:** text box in the **Dimension Lines** area is activated. This allows you to enter a value for a dimension line projection beyond the extension line. The default value is zero, but some architectural companies like to project the dimension line past the extension line by setting this to a desired value.

The **Arrow Size:** text box (**DIMASZ**) allows you to change the size of arrowheads. The default value is .18. An arrowhead size of .125" is common on mechanical drawings. Figure 18-69 shows the arrowhead size value.

Figure 18-68.
Examples of dimensions drawn using the options found in the **Arrowhead** drop-down list.

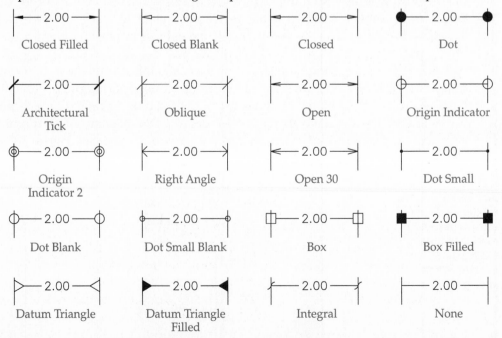

Figure 18-69.
The default arrow
size is .18.

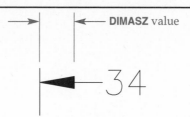

The **Center Marks for Circles** area (**DIMCEN**) of the **Lines and Arrows** tab allows you to select the way center marks are placed in circles and arcs. The **Type:** setting has the following options:

- **None.** Provides for no center marks to be placed in circles and arcs.
- **Mark.** The **Mark** option is used to place only center marks without lines.
- **Line.** This option places center marks and centerlines.

After selecting either the **Mark** or **Line** center mark option, you can place center marks on circles and arcs by using the **DIMCENTER** command. The results of drawing center marks and center lines is shown in Figure 18-33.

The **Size:** text box is used to change the size of the center mark and centerline. The default size is .09. The size specification controls the **Mark** and **Line** options in different ways, as shown in Figure 18-33.

EXERCISE 18-14

❏ Start AutoCAD and use one of your templates.
❏ Open the **Dimension Styles** dialog box and notice Standard as the current dimension style.
❏ Create a new style named Mechanical or Architectural, depending on your area of interest. The new style should be based on the Standard style.
❏ Use the **Lines and Arrows** tab to make the following settings based on your preferred drafting field:

Setting	Architectural	Mechanical
Dimension line spacing	.75	.50
Extension line extension	.18	.125
Extension line offset	.08	.0625
Arrowheads	Architectural Tick, Dot, or Oblique	Closed Filled, Closed Blank, or Open
Arrowhead size	.18	.125
Center	Mark	Line
Center size	.25	.125

❏ Pick **Close.**
❏ Save the drawing as EX18-14.

Using the Text Tab

Changes can be made to dimension text by picking the **Text** tab in the **New** (or **Modify**) **Dimension Style** dialog box. See Figure 18-70.

The **Text Appearance** area is used to set the dimension text style, color, height, and frame. The following explains each of the options:

- **Text style.** (**DIMTXSTY**) The dimension text style uses the Standard text style by default. Text styles must be loaded in the current drawing before they are available for use in dimension text. Pick the desired text style from the drop-down list.

Figure 18-70.
The **Text** tab of the
**Modify Dimension
Style** dialog box.

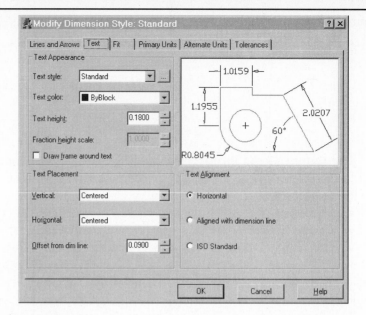

- **Text color. (DIMCLRT)** Pick this button to open the **Select Color** dialog box for changing the color of dimension text. The dimension color default is ByBlock.
- **Text height. (DIMTXT)** The dimension text height is set by entering the desired value in this text box. Dimension text height is commonly the same as the text height found on the rest of the drawing, except for titles, which are larger. The default dimension text height is .18, which is an acceptable standard. Many companies use a text height of .125. The ASME standard recommends text height between .125 and .188. The text height for titles and labels is usually between .18 or .25.
- **Fraction height scale. (DIMTFAC)** This setting controls the height of fractions for Architectural or Fractional unit dimensions. The value in this box is multiplied by the text height value to determine the height of the fraction. A value of 1.0 creates fractions that are the same text height as regular (non-fractional) text, which is the normally accepted standard. A value less than 1.0 makes the fraction smaller than the regular text height.
- **Draw frame around text. (DIMGAP)** If checked, AutoCAD draws a rectangle around the text. The distance between the text and the frame is determined by the setting for the **Offset from dim line** value, which is explained later in this chapter.

The **Text Placement** area of the **Text** tab is used to place the text relative to the dimension line. See Figure 18-71. The preview image changes to represent the selections you make. The **Vertical: (DIMTAD)** drop-down has the following options for the vertical justification:

- **Centered.** This option is the default. It places dimension text centered in a gap provided in the dimension line. This is the dimensioning practice commonly used in mechanical drafting and many other fields.
- **Above.** This is the option generally used for architectural drafting and building construction, in which the dimension text is placed above the dimension line. This places the dimension text horizontally and above horizontal dimension lines and in a gap provided in vertical and angled dimension lines. Architectural drafting commonly uses *aligned dimensioning*, in which the dimension text is aligned with the dimension lines and all text reads from either the bottom or right side of the sheet. An additional setting to provide this is discussed later.
- **Outside.** This option places the dimension text outside the dimension line and either above or below a horizontal dimension line or to the right or left of a vertical dimension line, depending on which way you move the cursor.

- **Suppress arrows if they don't fit inside the extension lines. (DIMSOXD)** This option removes the arrowheads if they do not fit inside the extension lines. Use this with caution, because it can create dimensions that violate standards.

Sometimes it becomes necessary to move the dimension text from its default position. The text can be moved by grip editing the text portion of the dimension. The options in the **Text Placement** area (**DIMTMOVE**) of the **Fit** tab instruct AutoCAD how to handle these grip editing situations. The following options are available:

- **Beside the dimension line. (DIMTMOVE = 0)** When the dimension text is grip edited and moved, the text is constrained to move with the dimension line and can only be placed within the same plane as the dimension line.
- **Over the dimension line, with a leader. (DIMTMOVE = 1)** When the dimension text is grip edited and moved, the text can be moved in any direction away from the dimension line. A leader line is created that connects the text back to the dimension line.
- **Over the dimension line, without a leader. (DIMTMOVE = 2)** When the dimension text is grip edited and moved, the text can be moved in any direction away from the dimension line without a connecting leader.

PROFESSIONAL TIP To return the dimension text to its default position, select the text, right-click to choose the **Dim Text position** shortcut menu option, and then select **Home text**.

The **Scale for Dimension Features** area of the **Fit** tab is used to set the scale factor for all dimension features in the entire drawing. The **Use overall scale of: (DIMSCALE > 0)** sets a multiplier for dimension settings, such as text height and the offset from origin. For example, if the height of the dimensioning text is set to .125 and the value for the overall scale is set to 100, then the dimension text can be measured within the drawing to be 12.5 units (100 × .125). If the drawing is then plotted and the plot scale is set to 1=100, the size of the dimension text on the paper measures .125 units.

Select the **Scale dimensions to layout (paperspace) (DIMSCALE = 0)** option if you are dimensioning in a floating viewport in a layout tab. It allows the overall scale to adjust according to the active floating (paper space) viewport by setting the overall scale equal to the viewport scale factor.

The **Fine Tuning** area of the **Fit** tab provides you with maximum flexibility in controlling where you want to place dimension text. The **Place text manually when dimensioning (DIMUPT)** option gives you control over text placement and dimension line length outside extension lines. The text can be placed where you want it, such as moved to the side within the extension lines, or placed outside of the extension lines.

The **Always draw dim line between ext lines (DIMTOFL)** option forces AutoCAD to place the dimension line inside the extension lines, even when the text and arrowheads are outside. The default application is with the dimension line and arrowheads outside the extension lines. Figure 18-74 shows the difference between checked and unchecked. Forcing the dimension line inside the extension lines is not an ASME standard, but it may be preferred by some companies.

Figure 18-74.
The affects of the **Always draw dim line between ext lines** option of the **Fine Tuning** area of the **Fit** tab.

DIMTOFL = off   DIMTOFL = on

EXERCISE 18-15

❑ Start AutoCAD and use one of your templates.
❑ Open the **Dimension Style Manager** dialog box, pick the **Modify** button, and access the **Text** tab.
❑ Pick each of the **Horizontal** justification options as you watch how the image tile changes with each selection.
❑ Pick each of the **Vertical** justification options as you watch how the image tile changes with each selection.
❑ Access the **Fit** tab. Select the various options and notice how the preview image changes.
❑ Save the drawing as EX18-15.

Using the Primary Units Tab

The following section explains the function of each of the options in the **Primary Units** tab of the **New** (or **Modify**) **Dimension Style** dialog box. See Figure 18-75.

The **Linear Dimensions** area of the **Primary Units** tab is used to set units for linear dimensions. The following discusses each of the setting options:

- **Unit format.** (**DIMLUNIT/DIMALTU**) Select the type of units for dimension text from this drop-down list. The default is Decimal units. A definition and examples of the different units are provided in Chapter 2 of this text.

Figure 18-75.
The **Primary Units** tab of the **Modify Dimension Style** dialog box.

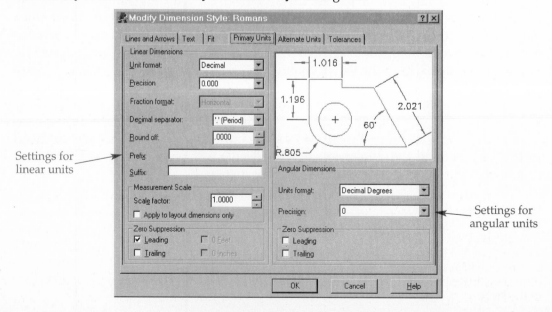

AutoCAD and its Applications—Basics

- **Precision. (DIMDEC/DIMALTD)** This drop-down list allows you to decide how many zeros follow the decimal place when decimal related units are selected. The default is 0.0000, while 0.00 and 0.000 settings are also common in mechanical drafting. When fractional units are selected, the precision values are related to the smallest desired fractional denominator. The default is 1/16", but you can choose other options ranging from 1/256" to 1/2", or 0" if you want no fractional values displayed. A variety of dimension precision can be found on the same drawing.

- **Fraction format. (DIMFRAC)** The options for controlling the display of fractions are Diagonal, Horizontal, and Not Stacked. This choice is only available if the Architectural or Fractional style is selected for the unit format.

- **Decimal separator. (DIMDSEP)** Decimal numbers may use commas, periods, or spaces as separators. The "." (Period) option is the default.

- **Round off. (DIMRND/DIMALTRND)**. This text box is used to have AutoCAD round off all numbers to a specified value. The default is zero, which means that no rounding takes place and all dimensions are placed exactly as measured. If you enter a value of .1, all dimensions are rounded to the closest .1 unit. For example, an actual measurement of 1.188 is rounded to 1.2.

- **Prefix. (DIMPOST/DIMAPOST)** *Prefixes* are special notes or applications placed in front of the dimension text. A typical prefix might be SR3.5 where SR means spherical radius. When a prefix is used on a diameter or radius dimension, the prefix replaces the ∅ or R symbol.

- **Suffix:. (DIMPOST/DIMAPOST)** *Suffixes* are special notes or applications placed after the dimension text. A typical suffix might be 3.5 MAX, where MAX is the abbreviation for maximum. The abbreviation IN. can also be used when one or more inch dimensions are placed on a metric dimensioned drawing, or a suffix of MM on one or more millimeter dimensions are placed on an inch drawing.

PROFESSIONAL TIP

Usually, a prefix or suffix is not used on every dimension in the drawing. A prefix or suffix is normally a special specification and might be used in only a few cases. Because of this, you might set up a special dimension style for these applications or enter them when needed by using the **MText** or **Text** option of the related dimensioning command.

- **Measurement Scale.** This area is used to set the scale factor of linear dimensions. Set the value in the **Scale factor:** text box (**DIMLFAC**). If a value of 1 is set, dimension values are displayed the same as they are measured. If the setting is 2, dimension values are twice as much as the measured amount. For example, an actual measurement of 2 inches is displayed as 2 with a scale factor of 1, but the same measurement is displayed as 4 when the scale factor is 2. Placing a check in the **Apply to layout dimensions only** (**DIMLFAC** < 0) check box makes the linear scale factor active only when dimensioning in a layout tab.

- **Zero Suppression (DIMZIN/DIMALTZ)** This area of the **Primary Units** tab provides four check boxes. The following options are used to suppress leading and trailing zeros in the primary units.
  - **Leading.** This check box is off by default, which leaves a zero on dimension numerals less than one, such as 0.5. This option is used when using metric dimensions as recommended by the ASME standard. Check this box to remove the 0 on decimal units less than one, as recommended by ASME for inch dimensioning. The result is a decimal dimension such as .5.

- **Trailing.** This check box is off by default, which leaves zeros after the decimal point based on the precision setting. This is usually off for inch dimensioning, because the trailing zeros often control tolerances for manufacturing processes. Check this box when doing metric dimensioning because the ASME standard recommends that zeros be removed following decimal metric dimensions.
- **0 Feet.** This check box is on by default, and removes the zero in feet and inch dimensions when there are zero feet. For example, when **0 Feet** is on, a measurement reads 11″. If **0 Feet** is off, the same dimension reads 0′-11″. This option is not available when using the Decimal unit format.
- **0 Inches.** This check box is on by default, and removes the zero when the inch part of feet and inch dimensions is less than one inch, such as 12′-7/8″. If this check box is off, the same dimension reads 12′-0 7/8″. Also, it removes the zero from a dimension with no inch value (a dimension reads 12′ rather than 12′-0″). This option is not available when the unit format is Decimal.

PROFESSIONAL TIP

Any settings you make during the **Quick** or **Advanced** setup or when using the **UNITS** command are not altered by changes made in the **Primary Units** tab.

The **Angular Dimensions** area of the **Primary Units** tab is used to set the desired type of angular units for dimensioning. Angular units were discussed in the section in Chapter 2 on AutoCAD setup and with the **UNITS** command. The setup options and **UNITS** command do not control the type of units used for dimensioning. The following settings are found in this area:

- **Units format.** (**DIMAUNIT**) The default setting is Decimal Degrees and the other options are Deg/Min/Sec, Grads, Radians, and Surveyor. Select the desired option from the drop-down list.
- **Precision.** (**DIMADEC**) Sets the desired precision of the angular dimension numeral display. Select an option from the drop-down list.
- **Zero Suppression.** (**DIMAZIN**) This area of the **Angular Dimensions** area is used to keep or remove leading or trailing zeros on the angular dimension numerals.

Using the Alternate Units Tab

The **Alternate Units** tab of the **Dimension Style** dialog box is used to set alternate units. See Figure 18-76. *Alternate units*, or *dual dimensioning*, have inch measurements followed by millimeters in brackets, or millimeters followed by inches in brackets. Dual dimensioning practices are no longer a recommended ASME standard. ASME recommends that drawings be dimensioned using inch or metric units only. However, the use of alternate units can be used in many other applications.

The **Display Alternate Units** (**DIMALT**) check box must be selected in order to activate the settings on the **Alternate Units** tab. The **Alternate Units** area has many of the same settings found in **Primary Units** tab. The **Multiplier for alt units** (**DIMALTF**) setting is multiplied by the primary unit to establish the value for the alternate unit. 25.4 is the default, because a value in inches is converted to millimeters by multiplying by 25.4. The **Placement** area controls the location of the alternate unit. The two options are **After primary value** and **Below primary value**.

The final tab in the **Modify Dimensions Style** dialog box, **Tolerances**, is discussed in Chapter 20. After completing the information on all tabs, select the **OK** button to return to the **Dimension Style Manager** dialog box. Select **Set Current** to have all new dimensions take on the qualities of your newly created style.

Figure 18-76.
The **Alternate Units** tab of the **Modify Dimension Style** dialog box.

Pick to activate
other settings

Settings for
alternate units

Location of
alternate units

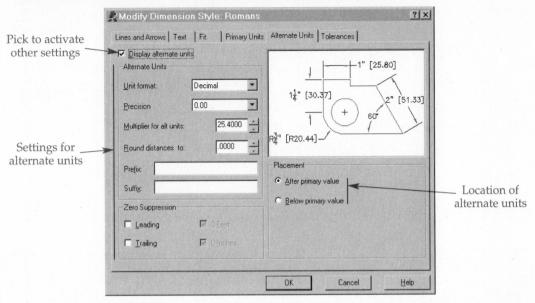

EXERCISE 18-16

❏ Start AutoCAD and use one of your templates.
❏ Open the **Dimension Style Manager** dialog box, select **Modify**, and then pick the **Primary Units** tab.
❏ Set the primary units to three-place decimal.
❏ Create text styles using the ROMANS and Stylus BT text fonts. Access the **Text** tab in the **Modify Dimension Style** dialog box and notice the options in the **Style:** drop-down list.
❏ Set text height at .125 and the **Offset from dim line** to .05.
❏ Draw a dimension 5.625 in length using ROMANS font with the dimension text centered in a gap provided in the dimension line.
❏ Draw another dimension 5.625 using Stylus BT font with the dimension text above the dimension line.
❏ Save the drawing as EX18-16.

MAKING YOUR OWN DIMENSION STYLES

AutoCAD
User's
Guide   **12**

Creating and recording dimension styles is part of your AutoCAD management responsibility. You should carefully evaluate the items contained in the dimensions for the type of drawings you do. During this process, be sure to carefully check company or national standards to verify the accuracy of your plan. Then make a list of features and values for the dimensioning settings you use based on what you have learned in this chapter. When you are ready, use the **Dimension Style Manager** dialog box options to establish dimension styles named to suit your drafting practices.

The following provides two lists of possible dimension style settings. One list is for mechanical manufacturing and the other is for architectural drafting applications. The other settings are AutoCAD defaults.

Setting	Mechanical (Inch)	Architectural
Dimension line spacing	.50	.75
Extension line extension	.125	.18
Extension line offset	.0625	.08
Arrowhead options	Closed Filled, Closed, or Open	Architectural Tick, Dot, Closed Filled, Oblique, or Right Angle
Arrowhead size	.125	.18
Center	Line	Mark
Center size	.25	.25
Text placement	Manually	Manually
Vertical justification	Centered	Above
Text alignment	Horizontal	Aligned with dimension line
Primary units	Decimal (default)	Architectural
Dimension precision	0.000	1/16"
Zero suppression (metric)	Leading Off Trailing On	Leading Off Trailing On
Zero suppression (inch)	Leading On Trailing Off	Leading On Trailing Off
Angles	Decimal Degrees (default)	Deg/Min/Sec
Tolerances	By application	None
Text style	gdt	Stylus BT
Text height	.125	.125
Text gap	.05	.1

EXERCISE 18-17

- ❏ Create your own dimension style settings list for the type of drafting you perform.
- ❏ Open the **Dimension Style Manager** dialog box and change the settings as needed to match the list you created.
- ❏ Save the dimension style with a name that describes the list you made.
- ❏ Save as EX18-17.

PROFESSIONAL TIP

The **Express** pull-down menu includes tools that allow you to import and export dimension style settings. See Appendix A for additional information on the **Dimstyle Export** and **Dimstyle Import** tools. The **AutoCAD DesignCenter** can also be used as a way to copy existing dimensions styles from one drawing to another. Refer to Chapter 1 for information on the **DesignCenter**.

OVERRIDING EXISTING DIMENSIONING VARIABLES

Generally, it is appropriate to have one or more dimensioning variables set to perform specific tasks that relate to your dimensioning practices. However, situations may arise where it is necessary to alter dimensioning variables to modify one or more specific dimensions on the final drawing. For example, assume you have the value for **Offset from origin** (**DIMEXO**) set at .0625, which conforms to ASME standards.

However, in your final drawing, there are three specific dimensions that require a 0 **Offset from the origin** setting. You can pick these three dimensions and alter the **DIMEXO** variable exclusively using the **DIMOVERRIDE** command. The command works like this:

Command: **DOV** *or* **DIMOVERRIDE**↵
Enter dimension variable name to override or [Clear overrides]: **DIMEXO**↵
Enter new value for dimension variable <0.0625>: **0**↵
Enter dimension variable name to override: *(type another variable name to override or press* [Enter])
Select objects: *(select the dimension or dimensions to override)*
Select objects: ↵
Command:

The **DIMEXO** variable automatically changes from .062 to 0 on the three selected dimensions. You can also clear any previous overrides by using the **Clear** option like this:

Command: **DOV** *or* **DIMOVERRIDE**↵
Enter dimension variable name to override or [Clear overrides]: **C**↵
Select objects: *(select the dimension or dimensions to clear an override)*
Select objects: ↵
Command:

PROFESSIONAL TIP

It may be better to use the **Dimension Styles Manager** dialog box rather than the **DIMOVERRIDE** command, depending on the nature of the change. In the dialog box you can pick an existing style, change the variable, then make a new style.

It is also sometimes better to generate a new style, because certain situations require specific dimension styles in order to prevent conflicts with drawing geometry or dimension crowding. For example, if a number of the dimensions in the current drawing all require the same overrides, then generating a new dimension style is a good idea. If only one or two dimensions need the same overrides, using the **DIMOVERRIDE** command may be more productive.

EXERCISE 18-18

❑ Start AutoCAD and use one of your templates.
❑ Create and save dimension style with dimensioning values set as follows:

Arrowhead size = .1
Text offset from dimension line = .05
Dimension line extend beyond ticks = .12
Dimension line baseline spacing = .5
Extension line offset from origin = .06

❑ Make a drawing similar to Figure 18-40.
❑ Use the **QDIM** command with the baseline option to dimension the object.
❑ After completing the entire drawing with the dimensioning values set as required, use the **DIMOVERRIDE** command to change only the **Extension Line offset from origin:** value to 0 on all dimensions except the overall dimensions.
❑ Save the drawing as EX18-18.

USING THE DIMENSIONING MODE

Throughout this chapter, you have been introduced to performing dimensioning tasks by using toolbar buttons, pull-down menus, or by typing commands directly at the Command: prompt. AutoCAD provides you maximum flexibility by providing access to many dialog boxes. These dialog boxes offer you the most visual communication with AutoCAD. The dimensioning practices that have been discussed throughout this chapter can also be accessed at the Command: prompt by putting AutoCAD into the dimensioning mode. Most of the commands that have been introduced can be entered while in the dimensioning mode.

Dimensioning mode is used by entering either DIM or DIM1 at the Command: prompt. The **DIM** command allows you to enter as many consecutive dimensioning commands as you want until you decide to exit the command. The **DIM1** command allows you to use only one dimensioning command before automatically returning you to the Command: prompt. When you enter the **DIM** or **DIM1** command, you are in the dimensioning mode and you get the Dim: prompt:

       Command: **DIM** *or* **DIM1**↵
       Dim:

If you want to leave the dimensioning mode, enter E or EXIT or press the [Esc] key. Dimensioning commands, with names that are different from what you have already learned, are used at the Dim: prompt while you are in the dimensioning mode. Generally, dimensioning commands are entered at the Command: prompt with the DIM prefix. However, the DIM prefix is not used when at the Dim: prompt in the dimensioning mode. The following is a list that shows the AutoCAD commands and their related dimensioning mode commands:

AutoCAD command	Dimensioning mode command	AutoCAD command	Dimensioning mode command
DIMALIGNED	ALIGNED	DIMORDINATE	ORDINATE
DIMANGULAR	ANGULAR	DIMOVERRIDE	OVERRIDE
DIMBASELINE	BASELINE	DIMRADIUS	RADIUS
DIMCENTER	CENTER	DIMSTYLE (Restore)	RESTORE
DIMCONTINUE	CONTINUE	DIMLINEAR (Rotated)	ROTATED
DIMDIAMETER	DIAMETER	DIMSTYLE (Save)	SAVE
DIMEDIT (Home)	HOMETEXT	DIMSTYLE (Status)	STATUS
DIMLINEAR (Horizontal)	HORIZONTAL	DIMEDIT	TEDIT
LEADER	LEADER	DIMEDIT (Rotate)	TROTATE
QLEADER	not available from the dimensioning mode	DIMSTYLE (Apply)	UPDATE
		DIMSTYLE (Variables)	VARIABLES
DIMEDIT (Text)	NEWTEXT	DIMLINEAR (Vertical)	VERTICAL
DIMEDIT (Oblique)	OBLIQUE		

To give you an example of how the **DIM** command works, try drawing a horizontal linear dimension and a couple of datum dimensions similar to Figure 18-28 using the following sequence:

Command: **DIM**↵
Dim: **HOR** *or* **HORIZONTAL**↵
Specify first extension line origin or <select object>: *(pick the first extension line origin)*
Specify second extension line origin: *(pick the second extension line origin)*
Specify dimension line location or [Mtext/Text/Angle]: *(pick the dimension line location)*
Dimension text <2.000>: ↵
Dim: **BASE** *or* **BASELINE**↵
Specify a second extension line origin or [Select] <Select>: *(pick the origin of the next dimension's second extension line)*
Dimension text <3.250>: ↵
Dim: **BASE** *or* **BASELINE**↵
Specify a second extension line origin or [Select] <Select>: *(pick the origin of the next dimension's second extension line)*
Dimension text <4.375>: ↵
Dim: **E** *or* **EXIT**↵
Command:

EXERCISE 18-19

❑ Begin a new drawing or use one of your prototypes.
❑ Use the **DIM1** command to draw an object with dimensions similar to Figure 18-6.
❑ Use the **DIM** command to draw an object with dimensions similar to Figure 18-3.
❑ Save the drawing as EX18-19.

Chapter Test

Answer the following questions on a separate sheet of paper.
1. What are the recommended standard units of measure for mechanical drawings?
2. Name the units of measure commonly used in architectural and structural drafting, and show an example.
3. What is the recommended height for dimension numbers and notes on drawings?
4. Name the pull-down menu where the **Linear**, **Aligned**, and **Radius** dimensioning commands are found.
5. Name the two dimensioning commands that provide linear dimensions for angled surfaces.
6. Name the **DIMLINEAR** option that opens the **Multiline Text Editor** for changing the dimension text.
7. Name the **DIMLINEAR** option that allows you to change dimension text at the prompt line.
8. What is the keyboard shortcut for the **DIMBASELINE** command?
9. What other command can be used to create baseline dimensions?
10. Name at least three modes of dimensioning available through the **QDIM** command.
11. Name the command used to dimension angles in degrees.
12. AutoCAD refers to chain dimensioning as _____.
13. AutoCAD refers to datum dimensioning as _____.
14. The command used to provide diameter dimensions for circles is _____.
15. The command used to provide radius dimensions for arcs is _____.
16. What does the *M* mean in the title of the standard ASME Y14.5M-1994?

17. Does a text style have to be loaded before it can be accessed for use in dimension text?
18. How do you access the **DIMRADIUS** and **DIMDIAMETER** commands from a pull-down menu?
19. How do you place a datum dimension from the origin of the previously drawn dimension?
20. How do you place a datum dimension from the origin of a dimension that was drawn during a previous drawing session?
21. Describe how the **QDIM** command can be used to modify an existing string of dimensions.
22. Oblique extension lines are drawn using the _____ command and by accessing the _____ option.
23. Define annotation.
24. Identify how to access the **QLEADER** command using the following methods:
    A. Toolbar.
    B. Pull-down menu.
    C. Command: prompt.
25. Text placed using the **QLEADER** command is a _____ text object.
26. Describe the purpose of the **Copy an object** option in the **Leader Settings** dialog box.
27. Define arrowless dimensioning.
28. AutoCAD refers to arrowless dimensioning as _____ dimensioning.
29. Name the pull-down menu selection that allows you to draw arrowless dimensions.
30. What is the importance of the user coordinate system (UCS) when doing arrowless dimensioning?
31. Identify the elements of this Unified screw thread note: 1/2-13 UNC-2B.
    A. 1/2.
    B. 13.
    C. UNC.
    D. 2.
    E. B.
32. Identify the elements of this metric screw thread: M 14 X 2.
    A. M.
    B. 14.
    C. 2.
33. How does the arrowhead specified for the dimension style affect the arrowhead used with the **QLEADER** command?
34. Name the dialog box that is used to create dimension styles.
35. Identify at least three ways to access the dialog box identified in Question 34.
36. Define an AutoCAD dimension style.
37. Name the dialog box tab used to control the appearance of dimension lines, extension lines, arrowheads, and center marks.
38. Name the dialog box tab used to control dimensioning settings that adjust the location of dimension lines, dimension text, arrowheads, and leader lines.
39. Name the dialog box tab used to control the dimensioning settings that display the dimension text.
40. Name at least four arrowhead types that are available in the **Lines and Arrows** tab for common use on architectural drawings.
41. Identify the dialog box tab used to control the dimension text location as you place the dimension.
42. Name the area in the **Modify Dimension Style** dialog box in which vertical justification of text can be set.
43. Which option for the vertical justification mentioned in Question 42 is commonly used in mechanical drafting?

44. Define primary units.
45. Given the following dimension text examples, identify if the application is for inch decimal drawings, metric decimal drawings, or architectural drawings:
    A. 12'-6".
    B. 0.5.
    C. .500.

Drawing Problems

Use the startup option of your choice or use one of your templates. Set limits, units, dimension variables, and other parameters as needed. Use the following general guidelines.

A. *Use dimension styles and text fonts that match the type of drawing as discussed in this chapter.*
B. *Use grids and object snap modes to your best advantage.*
C. *Apply dimensions accurately using ASME or other related industry/architectural standards. Dimensions are in inches, or feet and inches unless otherwise specified.*
D. *Set separate layers for dimensions and other features.*
E. *Plot drawings with proper line weights.*
F. *For mechanical drawings, place general notes 1/2" from lower-left corner:*

>   3. UNLESS OTHERWISE SPECIFIED, ALL DIMENSIONS ARE IN INCHES
>   (*or* MILLIMETERS *as applicable*).
>   2. REMOVE ALL BURRS AND SHARP EDGES.
>   1. INTERPRET DIMENSIONS AND TOLERANCES PER ASME Y14.5M-1994.
>   NOTES:

G. *Save each drawing as P18-(problem number).*
1.

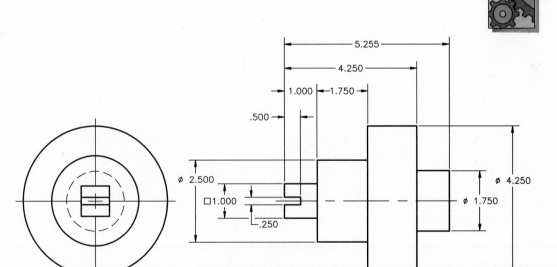

Title: Shaft
Material: SAE 1030

2.

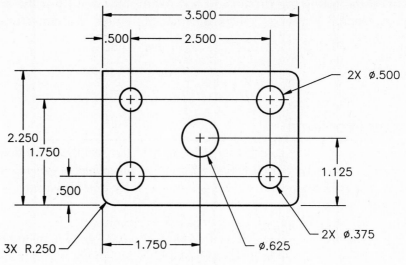

Title: Gasket

3.

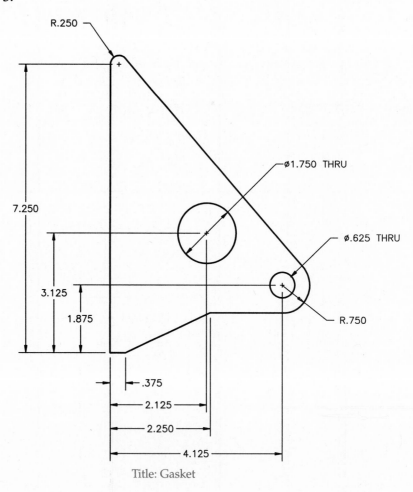

Title: Gasket

4.

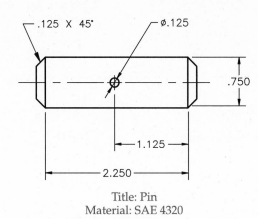

Title: Pin
Material: SAE 4320

5.

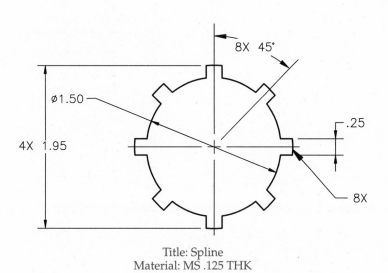

Title: Spline
Material: MS .125 THK

6.

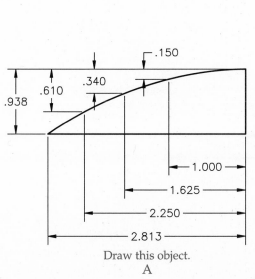

Draw this object.
A

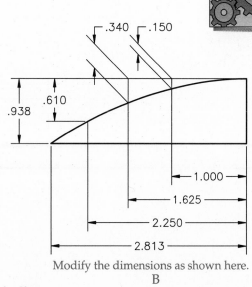

Modify the dimensions as shown here.
B

Title: Shim

7.

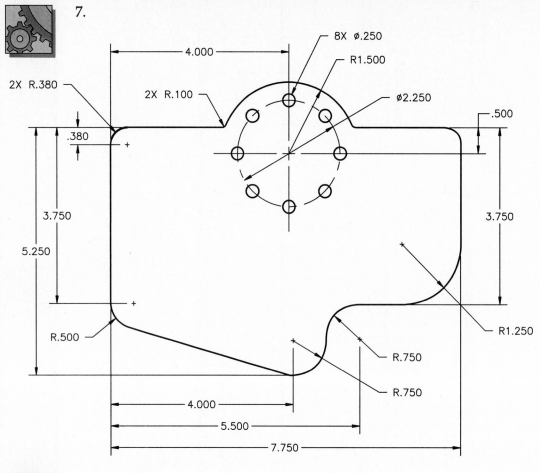

8.

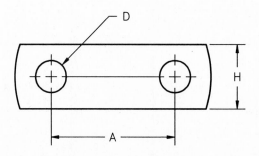

CHAIN NO.	A	D	H
SST1000	2.6	.44	1.125
SST1001	3.0	.48	1.525
SST1002	3.5	.95	2.125

Note:
Overall Length is 1.5xA
end radii are .9xA

Title: Chain Link
Material: Steel

9. Convert the given drawing to a drawing with the holes located using arrowless dimensioning based on the X and Y coordinates given in the table. Place a table above your title block with Hole (identification), Quantity, Description, and Depth (Z-axis).

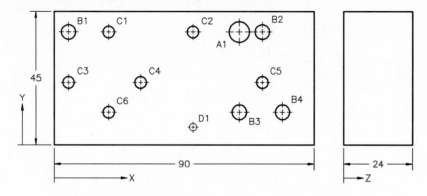

HOLE	QTY.	DESCRIP.	X	Y	Z
A1	1	ø7	64	38	18
B1	1	ø5	5	38	THRU
B2	1	ø5	72	38	THRU
B3	1	ø5	64	11	THRU
B4	1	ø5	79	11	THRU
C1	1	ø4	19	38	THRU
C2	1	ø4	48	38	THRU
C3	1	ø4	5	21	THRU
C4	1	ø4	30	21	THRU
C5	1	ø4	72	21	THRU
C6	1	ø4	19	11	THRU
D1	1	ø2.5	48	6	THRU

Title: Base
Material: Bronze

10.

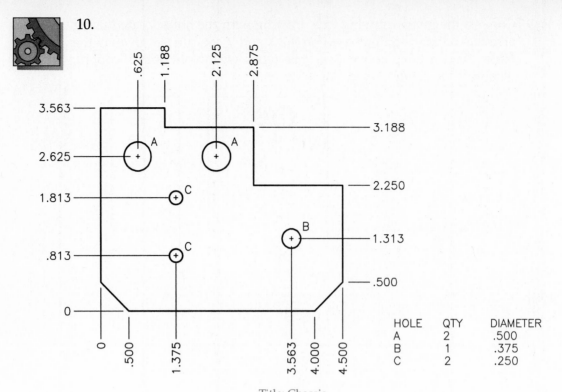

HOLE	QTY	DIAMETER
A	2	.500
B	1	.375
C	2	.250

Title: Chassis
Material: Aluminum .100 THK

11.

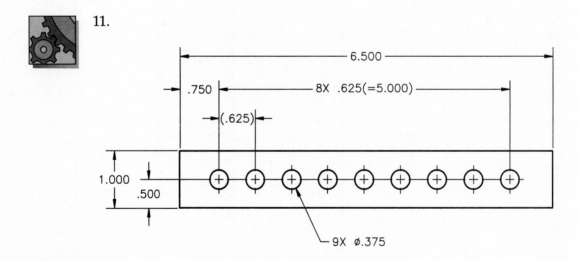

12.

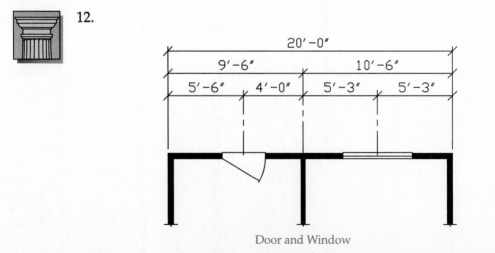

Door and Window

13.

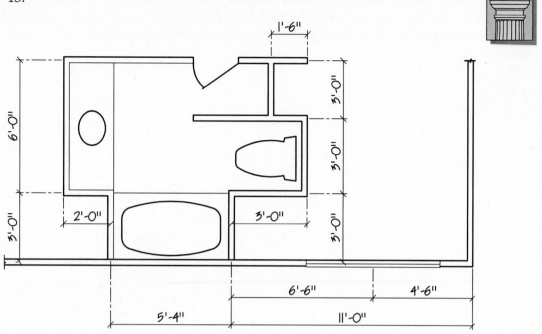

Title: Bathroom Area

14. The overall dimensions are given on the following kitchen drawing. Establish the rest of the dimensions using your own design.

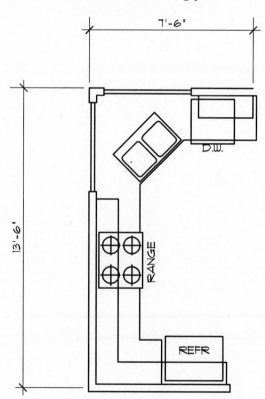

Title: Kitchen Area

Problems 15–17, use the isometric drawing provided to create a multiview drawing for the part. Include only the views necessary to fully describe the object. Dimension according to the ASME standards discussed in this chapter, using a dimension style appropriate for mechanical drafting.

15.

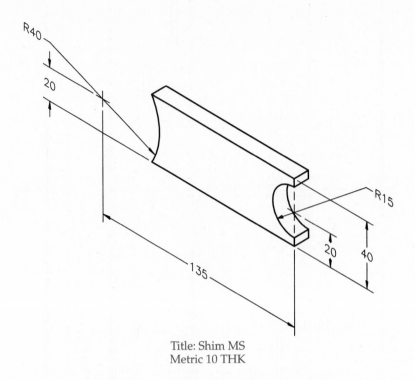

Title: Shim MS
Metric 10 THK

16. Half of the object is removed for clarity. The entire object should be drawn.

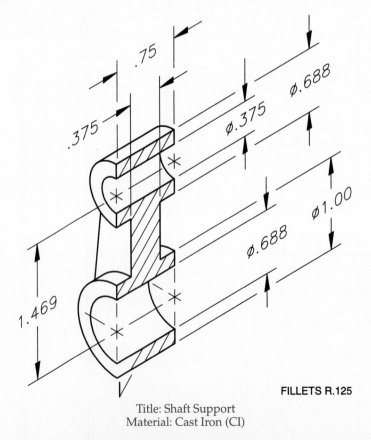

FILLETS R.125

Title: Shaft Support
Material: Cast Iron (CI)

17. Half of the object is removed for clarity. The entire object should be drawn.

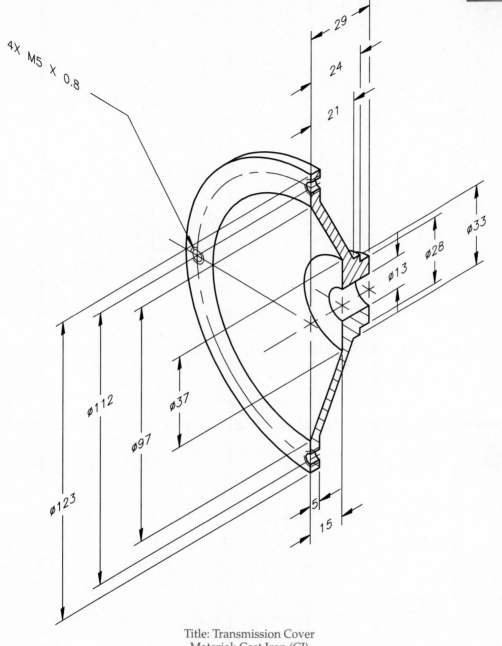

Title: Transmission Cover
Material: Cast Iron (CI)
Metric

18. Draw this floor plan. Size the windows and the doors to your own specifications.

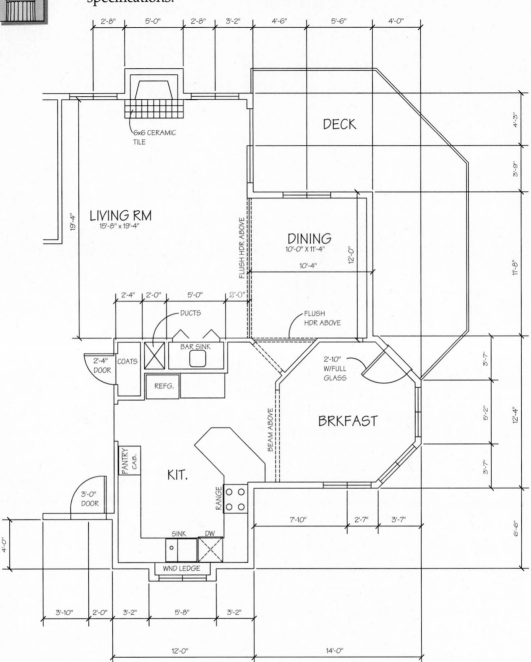

19.

HOLE LAYOUT

KEY	SIZE	DEPTH	NO. REQD
A	⌀.250	THRU	6
B	⌀.125	THRU	4
C	⌀.375	THRU	4
D	R.125	THRU	2

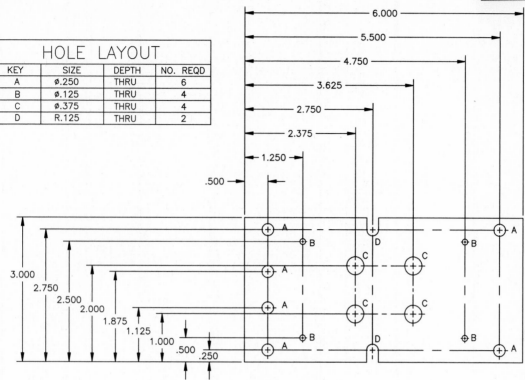

Title: Chassis Base (datum dimensioning)
Material: 12 gage Aluminum

20.

HOLE LAYOUT

KEY	SIZE	DEPTH	NO. REQD
A	⌀.250	THRU	6
B	⌀.125	THRU	4
C	⌀.375	THRU	4
D	R.125	THRU	2

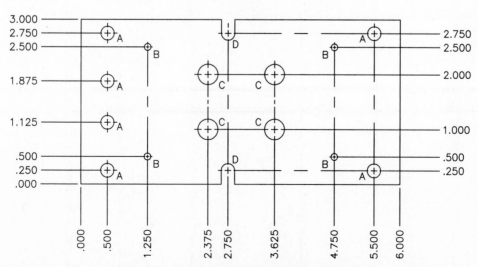

Title: Chassis Base (arrowless dimensioning)
Material: 12 gage Aluminum

21

HOLE LAYOUT

KEY	X	Y	SIZE	TOL
A1	.500	2.750	⌀.250	±.002
A2	.500	1.875	⌀.250	±.002
A3	.500	1.125	⌀.250	±.002
A4	.500	.250	⌀.250	±.002
A5	5.500	2.750	⌀.250	±.002
A6	5.500	.250	⌀.250	±.002
B1	1.250	2.500	⌀.125	±.001
B2	1.250	.500	⌀.125	±.001
B3	4.750	2.500	⌀.125	±.001
B4	4.750	.500	⌀.125	±.001
C1	2.375	2.000	⌀.375	±.005
C2	2.375	1.000	⌀.375	±.005
C3	3.625	2.000	⌀.375	±.005
C4	3.625	1.000	⌀.375	±.005
D1	2.750	2.750	R.125	±.002
D2	2.750	.250	R.125	±.002

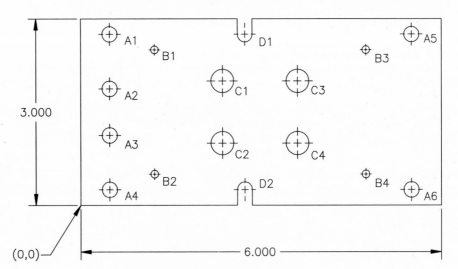

Title: Chassis Base (arrowless tabular dimensioning)
Material: 12 gage Aluminum

22.

HOLE LEGEND

KEY	DIAMETER	DEPTH
A	SEE VIEW A	THRU
B	.500	THRU
C	.594	THRU
D	1.625	THRU
E	.813	THRU
F	SEE VIEW B	THRU
G	.141	THRU

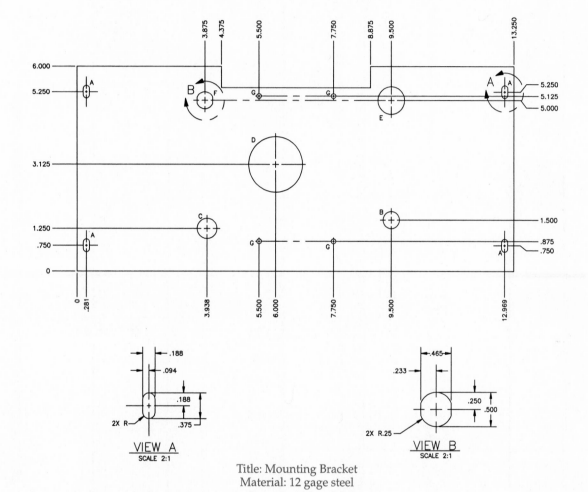

Title: Mounting Bracket
Material: 12 gage steel

VIEW A
SCALE 2:1

VIEW B
SCALE 2:1

23.

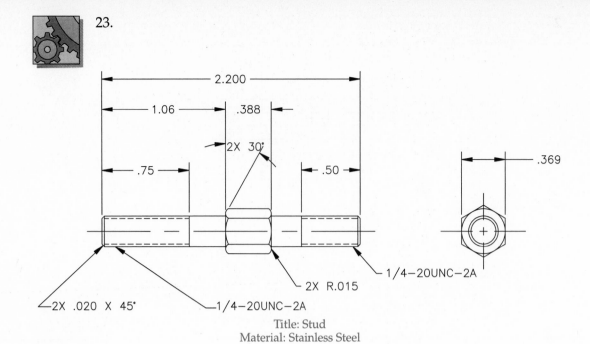

Title: Stud
Material: Stainless Steel

24.

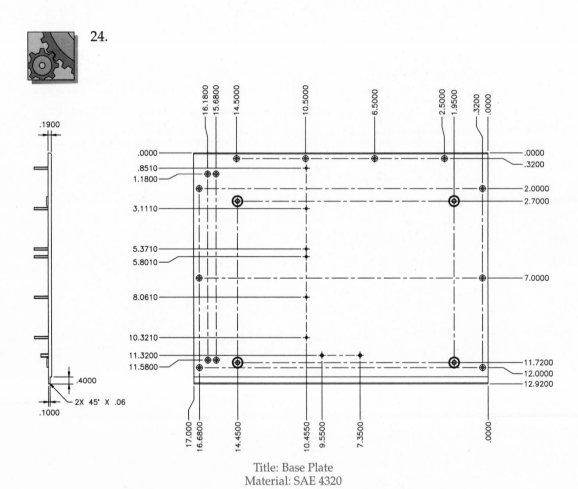

Title: Base Plate
Material: SAE 4320

25.

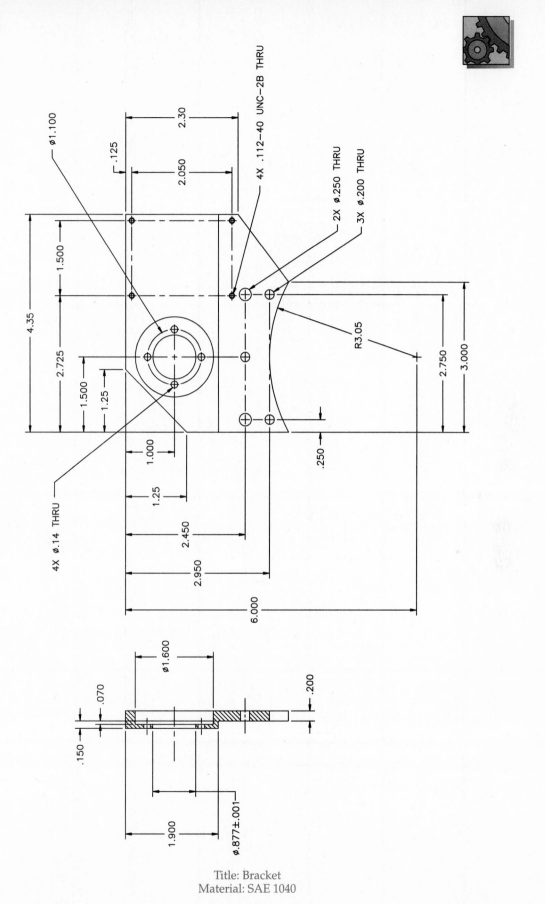

Title: Bracket
Material: SAE 1040

26.

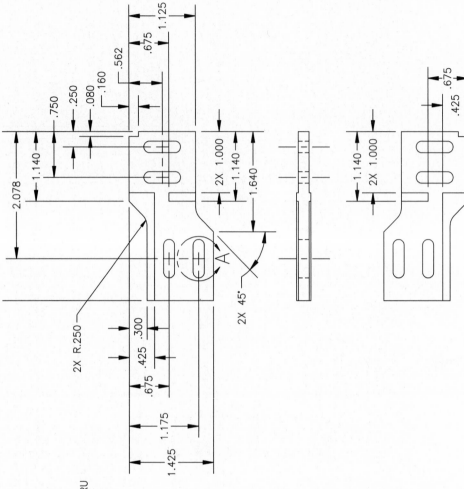

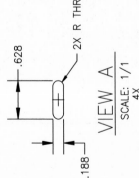

.628

2X R THRU

.188

VIEW A
SCALE: 1/1
4X

Title: Support
Material: Aluminum

CHAPTER 19

Editing Dimensions

Learning Objectives

After completing this chapter, you will be able to:
- Make changes to existing dimensions.
- Update a dimension to reflect the current dimension style.
- Import dimension styles from another drawing.
- Use the **Properties** window to edit individual dimension properties.
- Edit individual elements of associative dimensions.

The tools used to edit dimensions vary from simple erasing techniques to object editing commands. Often, the dimensioned object is edited and the dimensions are automatically updated to reflect the changes. This chapter provides you with a variety of useful techniques for editing dimensions.

SELECTING DIMENSIONS FOR EDITING

In Chapter 4, you were introduced to the **ERASE** command. Among the many selection options used with this command are **Last**, **Previous**, **Window**, **Crossing**, **WPolygon**, **CPolygon**, and **Fence**.

Erasing existing features such as large groups of dimensions often becomes difficult. For example, the objects may be very close to other parts of the drawing. When there are many objects, it is usually time-consuming to erase each one individually. When this situation occurs, the **Crossing**, **CPolygon**, and **Fence** selection options of the **ERASE** command are useful. A comparison of using the **Window** and **Crossing** selection options with the **ERASE** command on a group of dimensions is shown in Figure 19-1. For a review of these techniques, refer to Chapter 4.

Figure 19-1. Using the **Window** and **Crossing** selection options of the **ERASE** command to erase dimensions.

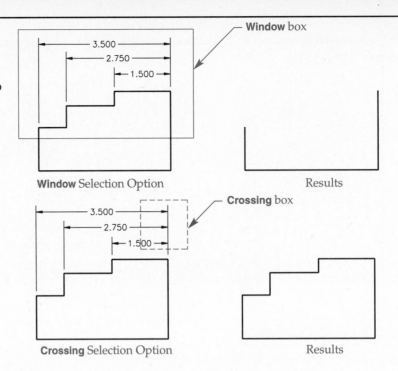

Window Selection Option   Results

Crossing Selection Option   Results

EDITING DIMENSION TEXT VALUES

The **DDEDIT** command can be used to edit existing dimension text. You can add a prefix or suffix to the text, or edit the dimension text format. This is useful when you wish to alter dimension text without creating a new dimension. For example, a linear dimension does not automatically place a diameter symbol with the text value. Using the **DDEDIT** command is one way to locate this symbol on the dimension once it has already been placed in the drawing.

You can access the **DDEDIT** command by picking the **Edit Text** button from the **Modify II** toolbar, picking **Text...** from the **Modify** pull-down menu, or by entering ED or DDEDIT at the Command: prompt. When you enter this command, the following prompt is displayed:

Select an annotation object or [Undo]:

After you select a dimension to edit, the **Multiline Text Editor** is displayed. See Figure 19-2. The two brackets next to the flashing cursor represent the existing dimension text. To add a diameter symbol to the text, pick the **Symbol** button and select **Diameter**. This adds the %%c control code before the brackets and inserts the diameter symbol before the original dimension value. The results of changing an existing dimension in this manner are shown in Figure 19-3.

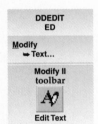

DDEDIT
ED

Modify
➥ Text...

Modify II
toolbar

Edit Text

Figure 19-2.
The **Multiline Text Editor** can be used to edit existing dimension text.

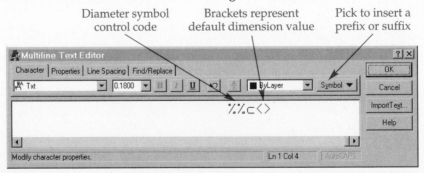

Diameter symbol control code   Brackets represent default dimension value   Pick to insert a prefix or suffix

Figure 19-3.
Using the **DDEDIT** command to add a diameter symbol to an existing dimension. A—Original dimension. B—Diameter symbol added.

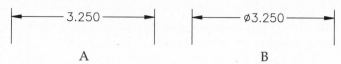

|←——— 3.250 ———→| |←——— ⌀3.250 ———→|

A   B

PROFESSIONAL TIP

You can replace the brackets representing the dimension value with numeric values. However, if the dimension is subsequently stretched, trimmed, or extended, the dimension text value will not change. Therefore, try to leave the default value.

EXERCISE 19-1

❑ Start a new drawing or use one of your templates.
❑ Draw and dimension an object similar to the one shown in the upper-left corner of Figure 19-1.
❑ Make a copy of the object and position it directly below the original object.
❑ Use the **Window** selection option of the **ERASE** command to remove the dimensions of the first object, as shown in the top example of Figure 19-1.
❑ Use the **Crossing** selection option of the **ERASE** command to remove the dimensions of the second object, as shown in the bottom example of Figure 19-1.
❑ Draw an original object and add a dimension similar to the one shown in Figure 19-3A.
❑ Use the **DDEDIT** command to add a diameter symbol to the dimension.
❑ Save the drawing as EX19-1.

EDITING DIMENSIONS WITH THE QDIM COMMAND

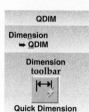

AutoCAD User's Guide **12**

QDIM
Dimension
➡ QDIM

Dimension toolbar

Quick Dimension

The **QDIM** command can be used to perform several different types of dimension editing operations. You can change the arrangement of an existing dimension, add an additional dimension, or remove an existing dimension. The **QDIM** command can be accessed by picking the **Quick Dimension** button from the **Dimension** toolbar, picking **QDIM** from the **Dimension** pull-down menu, or by entering QDIM at the Command: prompt.

The **QDIM** command can also be used to place a new dimension in a drawing. This was discussed in Chapter 18. The **QDIM** command sequence is as follows:

```
Command: QDIM↵
Select geometry to dimension: (pick the dimension to edit)
Select geometry to dimension: ↵
Specify dimension line position, or
[Continuous/Staggered/Baseline/Ordinate/Radius/Diameter/datumPoint/Edit]
    <Continuous>:
```

The **Continuous** and **Baseline** options can be used to change the existing arrangement of a selected group of dimensions. The **Edit** option can be used to add a dimension or remove a dimension from a specified group and then change the arrangement. These options, illustrated in Figure 19-4, are described as follows:

- **Continuous.** This option allows you to change the arrangement of a selected group of dimensions to a continuous arrangement. In continuous dimensioning, or chain dimensioning, dimensions are placed next to each other in a line, or end to end. This was discussed in Chapter 18. An example of this type of dimensioning is shown in Figure 19-4A.

- **Baseline.** This option allows you to create a series of baseline dimensions from an existing dimension arrangement. In baseline dimensioning, dimensions are aligned so that they originate from common features. Baseline dimensions are drawn in Figure 19-4B. In the example shown, the **Baseline** option has been used to change the dimensioning arrangement from continuous to baseline.

- **Edit.** This option allows you to add one or more dimensions to a selected group or remove a dimension and then automatically reorder the group. You can use the **Add** option inside the **Edit** option to add a dimension to an object, or you can use the **Remove** option to remove a dimension. The following command sequence uses the **Edit Add** option to add the dimension shown in Figure 19-4C:

Command: **QDIM**⏎
Select geometry to dimension: *(pick the desired dimensions to change)*
Select geometry to dimension: ⏎
Specify dimension line position, or
[Continuous/Staggered/Baseline/Ordinate/Radius/Diameter/datumPoint/Edit]
  <Baseline>: **E**⏎
Indicate dimension point to remove, or [Add/eXit] <eXit>: **A**⏎
Indicate dimension point to add, or [Remove/eXit] <eXit>: *(pick the location to add the dimension)*
One dimension point added.
Indicate dimension point to add, or [Remove/eXit] <eXit>: ⏎
Specify dimension line position, or
[Continuous/Staggered/Baseline/Ordinate/Radius/Diameter/datumPoint/Edit]
  <Baseline>: *(pick a location for the baseline dimension arrangement)*

The **Edit Remove** option allows you to remove one or more dimensions from the selected group. The remaining dimensions are then automatically reordered after you pick a location for the arrangement.

Figure 19-4.
The **QDIM** command can be used to change existing dimension arrangements and add or remove dimensions.

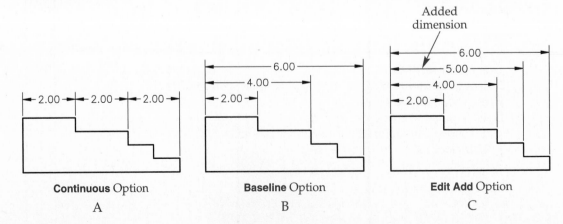

Continuous Option
A

Baseline Option
B

Edit Add Option
C

AutoCAD and its Applications—Basics

❑ Start a new drawing or use one of your templates.
❑ Using Figure 19-4 as an example for this exercise, use the **PLINE** command to draw an object similar to the one shown in Figure 19-4.
❑ Dimension the object as shown with the **DIMLINEAR** and **DIMCONTINUE** commands.
❑ Copy the object and its dimensions to another location in your drawing.
❑ Use the **QDIM** command to change the dimensioning arrangement from continuous to baseline.
❑ Copy the object with the baseline dimensions to another location in your drawing.
❑ Use the **QDIM** command's **Edit Add** option to change the newly copied object and dimensions to an arrangement similar to the one in Figure 19-4C.
❑ Copy the edited object and its dimensions to another location in your drawing.
❑ Use the **QDIM** command's **Edit Remove** option to change the newly copied object and dimensions to an arrangement similar to the one in Figure 19-4B.
❑ Save the drawing as EX19-2.

EDITING DIMENSION TEXT PLACEMENT

AutoCAD User's Guide **12**

The **DIMTEDIT** command allows you to change the placement and orientation of an existing associative dimension text value. An *associative dimension* is one in which all elements of the dimension (including the dimension line, extension lines, arrowheads, and text) act as a single object. Thus, when an associative dimension is selected for editing, the entire dimension is highlighted. Associative dimensioning is controlled by the **DIMASO** system variable, and is active by default.

Good dimensioning practice requires that adjacent dimension text be *staggered*, rather than stacked. As an example, in Figure 19-5, one of the dimensions has been moved to a new location to separate the text elements. This type of dimension editing can be accomplished by using the **DIMTEDIT** command.

To access the **DIMTEDIT** command, pick the **Dimension Text Edit** button from the **Dimension** toolbar, pick one of the options from the **Align Text** cascading menu in the **Dimension** pull-down menu, or enter DIMTEDIT at the Command: prompt. You can also enter TEDIT at the Dim: prompt. After selecting the command, select the dimension to be altered.

DIMTEDIT

Dimension
➥ Align Text

Dimension
toolbar

Dimension Text Edit

If the **DIMASO** system variable was on when the dimension was created, the text of the selected dimension automatically drags with the screen cursor. This allows you to relocate the text with your pointing device. If you pick a point, AutoCAD automatically moves the text and reestablishes the break in the dimension line. You can also select from the options that are displayed on the command line during this sequence:

Specify new location for dimension text or [Left/Right/Center/Home/Angle]:

Figure 19-5. Using the **DIMTEDIT** command to stagger dimension text. A—Original dimension. B—Dimension text moved.

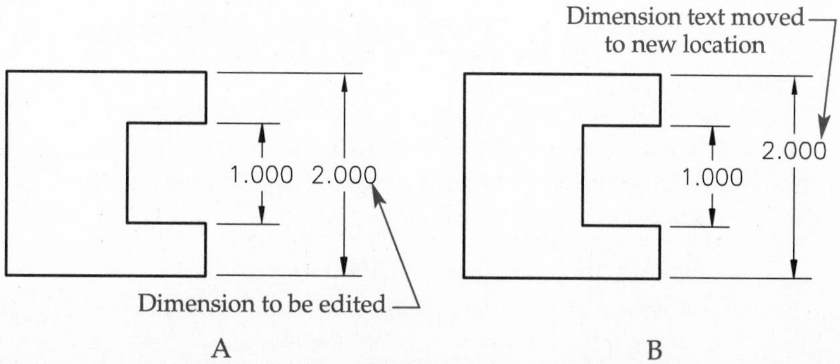

Dimension text moved to new location

1.000   2.000

2.000

1.000

Dimension to be edited

A

B

You can move the text to the left or right, center it, place it at an angle, or move it back to the original position. The options are described as follows:

- **Left.** This option moves horizontal text to the left and vertical text down.
- **Right.** This option moves horizontal text to the right and vertical text up.
- **Center.** This option centers the dimension text on the dimension line.
- **Home.** Text that has been relocated can be moved back to its original position using this option. This can also be accomplished by typing HOM or HOMETEXT at the Dim: prompt.
- **Angle.** This option allows you to place dimension text at an angle. When the **Angle** option is entered, you are asked to specify a rotation angle. The text is then rotated about its middle point.

The results after using each of the **DIMTEDIT** command options are shown in Figure 19-6.

Figure 19-6.
A comparison of the options used with the **DIMTEDIT** command.

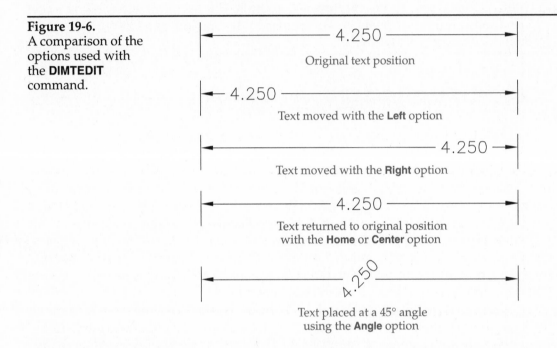

EXERCISE 19-3

❏ Start a new drawing or use one of your templates.
❏ Using Figure 19-6 as an example, draw an object with a dimension similar to the original one given in Figure 19-6. Make four copies of the dimension and position them as shown in the figure. Use the **DIMTEDIT** command options as shown in the figure.
❏ Save the drawing as EX19-3.

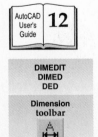

AutoCAD User's Guide 12

DIMEDIT
DIMED
DED

Dimension toolbar

Dimension Edit

USING THE DIMEDIT COMMAND

The **DIMEDIT** command can be used to change the text value, text placement, or extension lines of an existing dimension. You can access the **DIMEDIT** command by picking the **Dimension Edit** button from the **Dimension** toolbar or by entering DED, DIMED, or DIMEDIT at the Command: prompt:

Command: **DED, DIMED,** *or* **DIMEDIT**↵
Enter type of dimension editing [Home/New/Rotate/Oblique] <Home>:

AutoCAD and its Applications—Basics

This command has four options that can be used to edit individual or multiple dimensions. The options are described as follows:

- **Home.** This is the default option. It is identical to the **Home** option of the **DIMTEDIT** command.
- **New.** This option allows you to specify new dimension text and is similar to the **DDEDIT** command. After entering this option, the **Multiline Text Editor** is displayed. Enter a prefix or suffix for the text and pick **OK**. The Select objects: prompt then appears, and any dimensions that are selected assume the new text. This option can also be accessed by typing N or NEWTEXT at the Dim: prompt.
- **Rotate.** This option is used to rotate dimension text. It is similar to the **Angle** option of the **DIMTEDIT** command.
- **Oblique.** This option allows you to change the angle of the extension lines. The **Oblique** option can also be accessed directly by picking **Oblique** from the **Dimension** pull-down menu.

SHORTCUT MENU OPTIONS

If you select a dimension and right-click, a shortcut menu is displayed. See Figure 19-7. The shortcut menu contains the following dimension-specific options:

- **Dim Text position.** The options in this cascading menu automatically move the dimension text.
- **Precision.** These options allow you to easily adjust the number of decimal places displayed in a dimension text value.
- **Dim Style.** This cascading menu allows you to create a new dimension style based on the properties of the selected dimension. You can also change the dimension style of the dimension.

In addition to the **Dim Style** option in the shortcut menu, there are other methods of changing the dimension style of an existing dimension.

Figure 19-7.
Select a dimension and then right-click to access this shortcut menu.

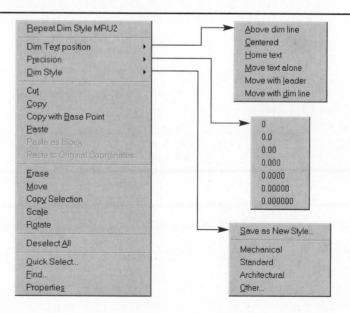

Changing the Dimension Style

So far you have learned how to edit dimension text, text placement, dimension group arrangements, and other elements of existing dimensions. You will often find it necessary to change the dimension style of a dimension. You can also import dimension styles from a separate drawing for use in the current drawing. These methods are discussed in the following sections.

As discussed in Chapter 18, the **Dimension Style Manager** dialog box enables you to create dimension styles by specifying settings for text styles, positioning elements, and other properties. When there are a number of dimension styles used in your drawing, you may need to change the style of an existing dimension to a different style.

A dimension's style can be changed using any of the following methods:

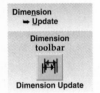

- **Dim Style cascading menu from shortcut menu.** Select the dimension and right-click to access the shortcut menu. Select a new dimension style from the cascading menu.
- **Dim Style Control drop-down list in the Dimension toolbar.** Select the dimension and then select the new dimension style from this drop-down list. See Figure 19-8.
- **Properties window.** Using the **Properties** window to modify dimension properties is discussed later in the text. The **Dim style** property is listed in the **Misc** category.
- **Update** option. The **Update** dimension command changes the style of the selected dimension to the current dimension style. This command can be accessed by picking the **Dimension Update** button in the **Dimension** toolbar, selecting **Update** from the **Dimension** pull-down menu, or typing UP or UPDATE at the Dim: prompt.

Figure 19-8.
The **Dim Style Control** drop-down list in the **Dimension** toolbar can be used to make a dimension style current when you wish to update the style of an existing dimension.

Dim Style Control
drop-down list

PROFESSIONAL TIP

In previous AutoCAD releases, when you modified a dimension style, the changes were not automatically made to existing dimensions of that style. The **Dimension Update** command was used to update those existing dimensions to include the modifications made to the style. In AutoCAD 2000, existing dimensions are automatically updated when a dimension style is modified. Therefore, the **Dimension Update** command is no longer very useful.

The **AutoCAD DesignCenter** can be used to import existing dimension styles from existing drawing files. **DesignCenter** is activated by picking the **AutoCAD DesignCenter** button on the **Standard** toolbar, picking **AutoCAD DesignCenter** from the **Tools** pull-down menu, typing ADC or ADCENTER at the Command: prompt, or using the [Ctrl]+[2] key combination. See Chapter 1 for an introduction to the **AutoCAD DesignCenter**.

Use the following procedure to copy dimension styles from an existing drawing into the current drawing:

1. Locate the drawing from which the dimension styles are to be copied in the tree view of **DesignCenter**.
2. Select the file name to list the various types of content that can be accessed.
3. Select the Dimstyle content. The dimension styles in the drawing are shown in the preview palette. See Figure 19-9.
4. Select the dimension style(s) to be copied. Use the [Ctrl] and [Shift] keys to select multiple items. Right-click to access the shortcut menu and select **Add Dimstyle(s)** to copy the styles to the current drawing. You can also use the **Cut** and **Paste** options from the shortcut menus or a drag-and-drop operation to copy the dimension styles.

Figure 19-9.
Copying dimension styles using **AutoCAD DesignCenter**.

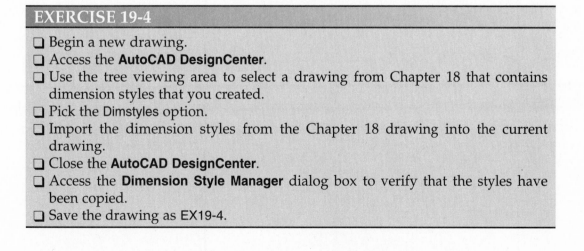

❏ Begin a new drawing.
❏ Access the **AutoCAD DesignCenter**.
❏ Use the tree viewing area to select a drawing from Chapter 18 that contains dimension styles that you created.
❏ Pick the Dimstyles option.
❏ Import the dimension styles from the Chapter 18 drawing into the current drawing.
❏ Close the **AutoCAD DesignCenter**.
❏ Access the **Dimension Style Manager** dialog box to verify that the styles have been copied.
❏ Save the drawing as EX19-4.

PROPERTIES
PROPS
CH
MO
[Ctrl]+[1]

Modify
➡ Properties

Standard
toolbar

Properties

The **Properties** window can be used to change the various text, justification, and formatting properties of selected dimensions. To access this window, pick the **Properties** button on the **Standard** toolbar, select **Properties** from the **Modify** pull-down menu, or enter CH, MO, PROPS, or PROPERTIES at the Command: prompt. You can also use the [Ctrl]+[1] key combination.

NOTE

It is recommended that you review the Chapter 18 sections that cover the creation of dimension styles, because the same procedures used to specify style settings are involved in changing dimension properties with the **Properties** window.

The dimension properties listed in the **Properties** window are broken down into eight categories. See Figure 19-10. To change an existing property or value, access the proper category and pick the property to highlight it. You can then change the corresponding value.

Figure 19-10.
The **Properties** window can be used to edit dimension properties after a dimension has been selected. Shown are the expanded categories listing the properties and current settings.

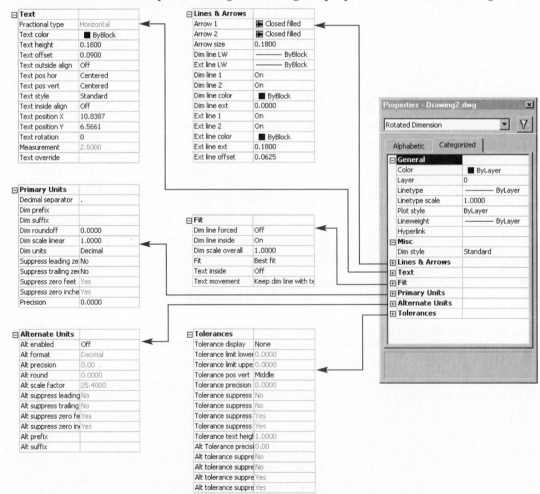

The dimension properties listed in the **Properties** window are based on the dimension style assigned to the text. These are the same settings found on the **Dimension Style Manager** dialog box. Changing one of these settings overrides the dimension style value for the selected dimension. The individual properties are described in Chapter 18.

Dimension style setting can also be modified using the **DIMOVERRIDE** command. To access this command, pick **Override** from the **Dimension** pull-down menu or enter DOV, DIMOVER, or DIMOVERRIDE at the Command: prompt. You are then prompted to type the dimension variable to override, to type the new value for the variable, and to select the dimension(s) to modify.

DIMOVERRIDE
DOV
DIMOVER

Dimension
➡ O**v**erride

PROFESSIONAL TIP

Using the **Properties** window to modify dimension settings is much more efficient than using the **DIMOVERRIDE** command.

EXERCISE 19-5

❏ Start a new drawing or use one of your templates.
❏ Create a dimension similar to the one shown in Figure 19-3B.
❏ Copy the dimension five times for a total of six dimensions.
❏ Using the **Properties** window, edit the first dimension as follows:
   ❏ Change the **Arrow 1** property so that the arrowhead is an architectural tick.
   ❏ Change the **Dim line color** setting to Red.
   ❏ Turn the **Ext line 1** option off.
❏ Edit the second dimension as follows:
   ❏ Change the **Text color** setting to Yellow.
   ❏ Change the **Text height** setting to 0.5000.
❏ Edit the third dimension as follows:
   ❏ Change the **Dim scale overall** setting to 2.000.
❏ Edit the fourth dimension as follows:
   ❏ Change the **Dim units** setting to Fractional.
   ❏ Change the **Precision** setting to 0 1/256.
❏ Edit the fifth dimension as follows:
   ❏ Turn the **Alt enabled** option on.
   ❏ Change the **Alt precision** setting to 0.0000.
❏ Edit the sixth dimension as follows:
   ❏ Change the **Tolerance display** setting to Limits.
   ❏ Change the **Tolerance limit lower** setting to 0.0001.
   ❏ Change the **Tolerance limit upper** setting to 0.0002.
❏ Save the drawing as EX19-5.

USING THE MATCHPROP COMMAND

AutoCAD User's Guide 9

The dimension editing methods presented in this chapter have focused on updating individual dimension properties and changing dimensions to a different dimension style. You can also edit dimensions by matching the properties of one dimension to another in your drawing file with the **MATCHPROP** command. This command allows you to select the properties of one dimension and apply those properties to one or more existing dimensions in your file.

The **MATCHPROP** command can be accessed by picking the **Match Properties** button on the **Standard** toolbar, selecting **M**atch Properties from the **M**odify pull-down menu, or by entering MA or MATCHPROP at the Command: prompt. This command is covered more completely in Chapter 12. The command sequence is as follows:

Command: **MA** *or* **MATCHPROP**↵
Select source object: *(pick the source dimension)*
Current active settings: Color Layer Ltype Ltscale Lineweight Thickness PlotStyle
   Text Dim Hatch
Select destination object(s) or [Settings]: *(pick one or more destination dimensions)*
Select destination object(s) or [Settings]: ↵
Command:

When using the **MATCHPROP** command, the **Dimension** setting must be active for the command to work with dimensions. You can check this after you have selected the source object. When the Current active settings: prompt line appears, Dim should appear with the other settings. (Notice that the **Dimension** setting is active in the previous command sequence.) If this setting does not appear when you are prompted to select a destination object, enter S for the **Settings** option. This displays the **Property Settings** dialog box. Activate the **Dimension** check box in the **Special Properties** area and pick **OK**. You can then select one or more destination dimensions.

After you select the dimensions to change and press [Enter], all of the destination dimensions are updated to reflect the properties of the source dimension.

EXERCISE 19-6

❑ Open drawing EX19-5.
❑ Use the **MATCHPROP** command to match the properties of the first dimension to the remaining dimensions.
❑ Save the drawing as EX19-6.

EDITING ASSOCIATIVE DIMENSIONED OBJECTS

As discussed earlier in this chapter, an associative dimension, which is made up of a group of individual elements, is treated as a single object. When an associative dimension is selected for editing, the entire group of elements is highlighted. If you use the **ERASE** command, for example, you can pick the dimension as a single object and erase all the elements at once.

One benefit of *associative dimensioning* is that it permits existing dimensions to be updated as an object is edited. This means that when a dimensioned object is edited and the dimension is included in the selection set, the dimension value automatically changes to match the edit. The automatic update is only applied if you accepted the default text value during the original dimension placement, or if you kept the value represented by brackets (<>) in the **Multiline Text Editor**. This provides you with an important advantage when editing an associative dimensioned drawing. Any changes to objects are automatically transferred to the dimensions.

Associative dimensioning is controlled by the **DIMASO** dimension variable and is active by default. With the **DIMASO** variable turned on, stretching, trimming, or extending an object also changes the dimensions associated with the object. With the **DIMASO** variable turned off, elements of the dimension are considered separately. Thus, you can edit the dimension line, arrowheads, extension lines, and text as individual items. However, the dimension is not updated when the object is edited.

Associative dimensions drawn with the **DIMALIGNED, DIMANGULAR, DIMDIAMETER, DIMLINEAR, DIMORDINATE,** and **DIMRADIUS** commands are changed when editing commands are used to alter objects. Marks placed by the **DIMCENTER** command remain as unique items and are not affected.

When you stretch an associative dimensioned object, changes to the dimension can be seen dynamically while the dimension and the object are being dragged. This function is controlled by the **DIMSHO** system variable. If **DIMASO** and **DIMSHO** are both turned on, the new dimension text is shown as the dimension is stretched. Both **DIMASO** and **DIMSHO** are active by default.

When a dimensioned object is edited using grips or the **MIRROR, ROTATE,** or **SCALE** commands, the dimensions are also changed if **DIMASO** is on. Angular, linear, and ordinate associative dimensions are all altered by the **STRETCH** command. Only linear associative dimensions are affected by the **EXTEND** and **TRIM** commands. Refer to Chapters 11 and 12 of this text if you need to review the AutoCAD editing commands.

Stretching an Object and Its Dimensions

If you use the **STRETCH** command to stretch an associative dimensioned object, the dimension is automatically updated when the command is completed. After entering the command, select the object and dimension using the **Crossing** or **CPolygon** selection option. Figure 19-11 shows the **Crossing** selection option used to stretch a triangle and its associated dimensions.

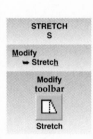

Figure 19-11.
When you stretch an object and an associative dimension, the dimension text is automatically changed to reflect the new value.

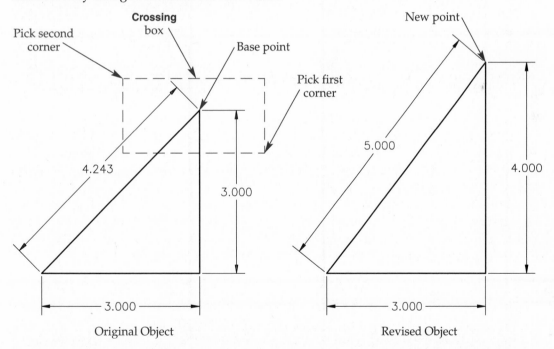

Original Object   Revised Object

Moving Dimension Text

ASME standards advise that adjacent dimensions be staggered. However, AutoCAD centers all dimension text unless you specify otherwise. You can locate dimension text as desired without using automatic horizontal justification by activating the **Place text manually when dimensioning** check box, which is located in the **Fit** tab of the **Modify Dimension Style** dialog box. This function is also controlled by the **DIMUPT** system variable. This variable is turned off by default. See Chapter 18 for more information on user positioned text.

If you wish to relocate existing dimension text, using grips is the fastest way to adjust the text position. This method requires only quick picks and no command entry. Simply pick the dimension, pick the dimension text grip, and then drag the text to the new location. See Figure 19-12A. The **STRETCH** command can also be used to move dimension text within the dimension line. See Figure 19-12B.

The **DIMTEDIT** and **DIMEDIT** commands can also be used to move dimension text. These commands were discussed earlier in this chapter.

Figure 19-12.
Repositioning dimension text. A—Using grips to move dimension text to a different location. B—Using the **STRETCH** command to relocate the text.

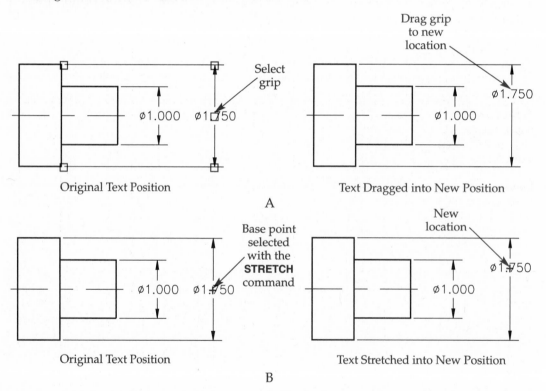

EXERCISE 19-8

❏ Draw an object similar to the original object illustrated in Figure 19-12.
❏ Copy the object and place it below the first object.
❏ Use grips to move the dimension text belonging to the first object. Stagger the text as shown in the example.
❏ Use the **STRETCH** command to move the dimension text of the other object.
❏ Save the drawing as EX19-8.

Extending and Trimming Dimensions

The **EXTEND** command can be used to extend an object and its related dimensions to meet another object. When selecting objects to extend, you must select both the object and the dimension. The dimension text is then automatically updated to reflect the new dimension. See Figure 19-13.

The **TRIM** command can be used to trim dimensioned objects and update the dimensions in one operation. See Figure 19-14. Select the cutting edge and then pick the dimension and objects to be trimmed.

NOTE	The **EXTEND** and **TRIM** commands are discussed in greater detail in Chapter 11.

Figure 19-13.
When you extend objects with an associative dimension, the dimension text is automatically updated to reflect the new value.

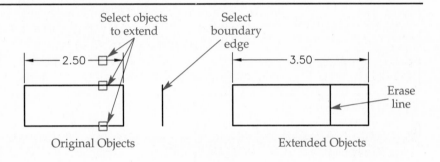

Figure 19-14.
Dimensioned objects and their associative dimensions can be trimmed in one operation using the **TRIM** command.

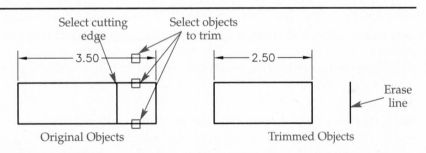

EXERCISE 19-9

❏ Draw objects similar to the original ones shown in Figure 19-13.
❏ Use the **EXTEND** command to edit the objects so that they are similar to the edited example in Figure 19-13.
❏ Draw an object similar to the original object shown in Figure 19-14.
❏ Use the **TRIM** command to edit the object so that it is similar to the edited example in Figure 19-14.
❏ Save the drawing as EX19-9.

MAKING CHANGES TO DIMENSION ELEMENTS

As previously discussed, the component parts of an associative dimension cannot be edited separately because the dimension is treated as one object. However, you can use the **EXPLODE** command to break an associative dimension into its individual elements for editing purposes. Dimensions can also be changed individually or in groups using the **UPDATE**, **HOMETEXT**, and **NEWTEXT** commands. These editing methods are discussed in the following sections.

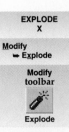

Exploding an Associative Dimension

An associative dimension is treated as one object even though it consists of extension lines, a dimension line, arrowheads, and text. At times, you may find it necessary to edit the individual parts. For example, you may want to erase the text without erasing the dimension line, arrowheads, or extension lines. To do this, you must first explode the dimension using the **EXPLODE** command. Always be careful when exploding dimensions because they may lose their layer assignment.

> **PROFESSIONAL TIP**
>
> Exercise caution when using the **EXPLODE** command on dimensions. An exploded dimension loses its associativity with the associated feature. One way to edit individual dimension properties without removing the associative dimensioning feature is to use the **Properties** window. If you know in advance that you need to work with individual elements of the dimensions in your drawing, turn the **DIMASO** system variable off before you start to dimension. Once a dimension has been exploded or drawn with **DIMASO** off, there is no way to convert it back to an associative dimension.

DIMENSION DEFINITION POINTS

When you draw an associative dimension, the points used to specify the dimension location and the center point of the dimension text are called the *definition points*, or *defpoints*. When a dimension location is redefined, the revised position is based on the definition points. The definition points are located on the Defpoints layer. This layer is automatically created by AutoCAD. The definition points are displayed with the dimension.

Normally, the Defpoints layer does not plot. The definition points are plotted only if the Defpoints layer is renamed. The definition points are displayed when the dimensioning layer is on, even if the Defpoints layer is turned off.

If you select an object for editing and wish to include the dimensions in the edit, then you must include the definition points of the dimension in the selection set. If you need to snap to a definition point only, use the **Node** object snap mode.

Chapter Test

Answer the following questions on a separate sheet of paper.

1. Name at least three selection options that can be used to easily erase a group of dimensions surrounding an object without erasing any part of the object.
2. Explain how you would add a diameter symbol to a dimension text value using the **DDEDIT** command.
3. Which command and option can you use to add a new baseline dimension to an existing set of baseline dimensions?
4. Define *associative dimension*.
5. Name the command that allows you to control the placement and orientation of an existing associative dimension text value.
6. Identify where and how to access the command in Question 5, given the following general locations:
   A. Toolbar.
   B. Command: prompt.

7. Name the command to use if you want to change the text or extension lines of an existing dimension.
8. Identify where and how to access the command in Question 7, given the following general locations:
    A. Toolbar.
    B. Command alias.
9. What happens when you use the **New** option of the **DIMEDIT** command?
10. Name the **DIMEDIT** option that is used to change extension lines to an angle of your choice.
11. What three command options related to dimension editing are available in the shortcut menu accessed when a dimension is selected?
12. Name three methods of changing the dimension style of a dimension.
13. How does the **Dimension Update** command affect selected dimensions?
14. Name three methods of copying dimension styles from the preview palette of the **AutoCAD DesignCenter** into the current drawing.
15. How do you access the **Property Settings** dialog box?
16. Why is it important to have associative dimensions for editing objects?
17. Name the command that can be used to lengthen an object and its dimension to meet another object.
18. Name the command that can be used to trim an object and its dimension to meet another object.
19. What are definition points?
20. On which layer are definition points automatically located by AutoCAD?

Drawing Problems

1. Open P18-1 and edit as follows:
    A. Erase the left side view.
    B. Stretch the vertical dimensions to provide more space between dimension lines. Be sure the space you create is the same between all vertical dimensions.
    C. Stagger the existing vertical dimension numerals if they are not staggered as shown in the original problem.
    D. Erase the 1.750 horizontal dimension and then stretch the 5.255 and 4.250 dimensions to make room for a new datum dimension from the baseline to where the 1.750 dimension was located. This should result in a new baseline dimension that equals 2.750. Be sure all horizontal dimension lines are equally spaced.
    E. Save the drawing as P19-1.

2. Open P18-2 and edit as follows:
    A. Stretch the total length from 3.500 to 4.000, leaving the holes the same distance from the edges.
    B. Fillet the upper-left corner. Modify the 3X R.250 dimension accordingly.
    C. Save the drawing as P19-2.

3. Open P18-4 and edit as follows:
   A. Use the existing drawing as the model and make four copies.
   B. Leave the original drawing as it is, and edit the other four pins in the following manner, keeping the ⌀.125 hole exactly in the center of each pin.
   C. Make one pin with a total length of 1.500.
   D. Create the next pin with a total length of 2.000.
   E. Edit the third pin with a length of 2.500.
   F. Change the last pin to a length of 3.000.
   G. Organize the pins on your drawing in a vertical row ranging in length from the smallest to the largest. You may need to change the drawing limits.
   H. Save the drawing as P19-3.

4. Open P18-5 and edit as follows:
   A. Modify the spline to have 12 projections, rather than eight.
   B. Change the angular dimension, linear dimension, and 8X dimension to reflect the changes.
   C. Save the drawing as P19-4.

5. Open P18-11 and edit as follows:
   A. Stretch the total length from 6.500 to 7.750.
   B. Add two more holes that continue the equally spaced pattern of .625 apart.
   C. Change the 8X .625(=5.00) dimension to read 10X .625(=6.250).
   D. Save the drawing as P19-5.

6. Open P18-13 and edit as follows:
   A. Make the bathroom 8'-0" wide by stretching the walls and vanity that are currently 6'-0" wide. Do this without increasing the size of the water closet compartment. Provide two equally spaced oval sinks where there is currently one.
   B. Save the drawing as P19-6.

7. Open P18-14 and edit as follows:
   A. Make the kitchen 15'-0" deep where it is currently 13'-6".
   B. Stretch the 7'-6" dimension (counter and wall) to 9'-0" and make the wall and cabinet at the refrigerator the same dimension.
   C. Save the drawing as P19-7.

8. Open P18-19 and edit as follows:
   A. Lengthen the part .250 on each side for a new overall dimension of 6.500.
   B. Change the width of the part from 3.000 to 3.500 by widening an equal amount on each side.
   C. Save the drawing as P19-8.

9. Open P18-22 and edit as follows:
   A. Lengthen the mounting bracket equally on both sides to a new overall dimension of 13.500.
   B. Lengthen the A slots from .375 to .500, and lengthen the F slots from .500 to .750 equally on both sides for all slots.
   C. Save the drawing as P19-9.

10. Open P18-23 and edit as follows:
    A. Shorten the .75 thread on the left side to .50.
    B. Shorten the .388 hexagon length to .300.
    C. Save the drawing as P19-10.

CHAPTER 20

Dimensioning with Tolerances

Learning Objectives

■ Define and use dimensioning and tolerancing terminology.
■ Identify different types of tolerance dimensions.
■ Create dimension styles with specified tolerance settings.
■ Prepare drawings with dimensions and tolerances from engineering designs, sketches, and layouts.

This chapter discusses the basics of tolerancing and explains how to prepare dimensions with tolerances for mechanical manufacturing drawings. Chapter 18 introduced you to the creation of dimension styles and explained how to set the specifications for dimension geometry, fit format, primary units, alternate units, and text. Dimensioning for mechanical drafting usually uses the following AutoCAD settings, depending on company practices:

Lines and Arrows

- The dimension line spacing for baseline dimensioning is usually more than the .38 default.
- The extension line extension is .125 and the extension line offset is .0625.
- Arrowheads are closed filled, closed blank, closed, or open.
- A small dot is used on a leader pointing to a surface.
- The centerline option is used for center marks for circles and located arcs. Fillets and rounds generally have no center marks.

Fit Format

- The manually defined format is convenient for flexible text placement.
- The best fit option for text and arrows is common, but other format options work better for some applications.
- Horizontal and vertical justification is usually in centered format.
- Text placement is normally inside and outside horizontal for unidirectional dimensioning.

Primary Units, Text, and Tolerances

- Objects are dimensioned in inches or millimeters.
- The primary units are typically decimal, with the number of decimal places controlled by the feature tolerance.

- Using alternate units for dual dimensioning is not a recommended ASME practice.
- The text is usually placed using the Romans font, a height of .125, and a gap of .0625.
- The tolerance method depends on the application.

TOLERANCING FUNDAMENTALS

A *tolerance* is the total amount that a specific dimension is permitted to vary. A tolerance is not given to values identified as reference, maximum, minimum, or stock sizes. The tolerance may be applied directly to the dimension, indicated by a general note, or identified in the drawing title block. See Figure 20-1.

The *limits* of a dimension are the largest and smallest numerical values that the feature can be. In Figure 20-2A, the dimension is stated as 12.50±0.25. This is referred to as *plus-minus dimensioning*. The tolerance of this dimension is the difference between the maximum and minimum limits. The upper limit is 12.50 + 0.25 (12.75), and the lower limit is 12.50 – 0.25 (12.25). So, if you take the upper limit and subtract the lower limit, the tolerance is .50.

Figure 20-1.
Tolerances can be specified on the dimension, in a general note, or in the drawing title block.

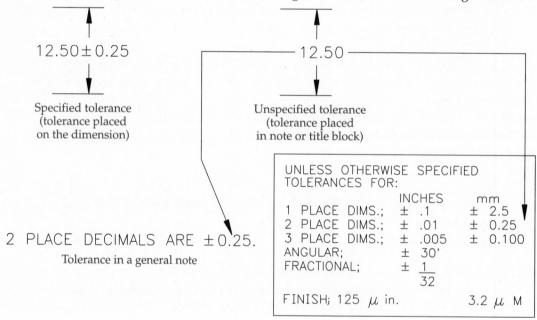

12.50±0.25

Specified tolerance
(tolerance placed
on the dimension)

12.50

Unspecified tolerance
(tolerance placed
in note or title block)

2 PLACE DECIMALS ARE ±0.25.
Tolerance in a general note

UNLESS OTHERWISE SPECIFIED
TOLERANCES FOR:

	INCHES	mm
1 PLACE DIMS.;	± .1	± 2.5
2 PLACE DIMS.;	± .01	± 0.25
3 PLACE DIMS.;	± .005	± 0.100
ANGULAR;	± 30'	
FRACTIONAL;	± $\frac{1}{32}$	

FINISH; 125 μ in.   3.2 μ M

Tolerances in a general note

Figure 20-2.
Examples using plus-minus dimensioning and limits dimensioning.

12.50±0.25

12.75
12.25

Plus-Minus Dimensioning

A

Limits Dimensioning

B

The specified dimension is the part of the dimension where the limits are calculated from. The specified dimension of the feature shown in Figure 20-2 is 12.50. A tolerance on a drawing may be displayed with plus-minus dimensioning, or the limits may be calculated and shown as in Figure 20-2B. Many schools and companies prefer the second method, which is called *limits dimensioning*. This is because the limits are given and calculations are not required.

A *bilateral tolerance* is permitted to vary in both the positive and negative directions from the specified dimension. An *equal bilateral tolerance* has the same variation in both directions. In an *unequal bilateral tolerance,* the variation from the specified dimension is not the same in both directions. See Figure 20-3.

A *unilateral tolerance* is permitted to increase or decrease in only one direction from the specified dimension. See Figure 20-4.

Figure 20-3.
Examples of bilateral tolerances.

$$24 \, ^{+0.08}_{-0.20}$$

Metric

$$.750 \, ^{+.002}_{-.003}$$

Inch

Unequal Bilateral Tolerance

$$24 \pm 0.1$$

Metric

$$.750 \pm .005$$

Inch

Equal Bilateral Tolerance

Figure 20-4.
The variance of a unilateral tolerance is in only one direction from the specified dimension.

$$24 \, ^{0}_{-0.2}$$

$$24 \, ^{+0.2}_{0}$$

Metric

$$.625 \, ^{+.000}_{-.004}$$

$$.625 \, ^{+.004}_{-.000}$$

Inch

ASSIGNING DECIMAL PLACES TO DIMENSIONS AND TOLERANCES

The ASME Y14.5M-1994 standard, *Dimensioning and Tolerancing*, has separate recommendations for the way the number of decimal places is displayed for inch and metric dimensions. Examples of decimal dimension values in inches and metric units are shown in Figures 20-3 and 20-4. The following are some general rules:

Inch Dimensioning

- A specified inch dimension is expressed to the same number of decimal places as its tolerance. Zeros are added to the right of the decimal point if needed. For example, the inch dimension .250±.005 has an additional zero added to the .25 to match the three-decimal tolerance. The dimensions 2.000±.005 and 2.500±.005 both have zeros added to match the tolerance.
- Both plus and minus values of an inch tolerance have the same number of decimal places. Zeros are added to fill in where needed. For example:

$$^{+.005}_{-.010} \quad not \quad ^{+.005}_{-.01}$$

Metric Dimensioning

- The decimal point and zeros are omitted from the dimension when the metric dimension is a whole number. For example, the metric dimension 12 has no decimal point followed by a zero. This rule is true unless tolerance values are displayed.
- When a metric dimension includes a decimal portion, the last digit to the right of the decimal point is not followed by a zero. For example, the metric dimension 12.5 has no zero to the right of the 5. This rule is true unless tolerance values are displayed.
- Both plus and minus values of a metric tolerance have the same number of decimal places. Zeros are added to fill in where needed.
- Zeros are not added after the specified dimension to match the tolerance. For example, both 24±0.25 and 24.5±0.25 are correct. However, some companies prefer to add zeros after the specified dimension to match the tolerance, in which case 24.00±0.25 and 24.50±0.25 are both correct.

AutoCAD
User's
Guide **12**

DDIM
D

F**o**rmat
↦ **Dimension Style...**

**Dimension
toolbar**

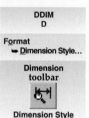

Dimension Style

SETTING PRIMARY UNITS

As discussed in Chapter 18, dimension styles with specified formatting, justification, and text settings can be conveniently created using the **Dimension Style Manager** dialog box. See Figure 20-5. This dialog box is accessed by picking the **Dimension Style** button in the **Dimension** toolbar, picking **Dimension Style...** from the **F**o**rmat** pull-down menu, or entering D or DDIM at the Command: prompt.

Once the **Dimension Style Manager** dialog box is open, pick the **Modify...** button to access the **Modify Dimension Style** dialog box. The **Primary Units** tab is used to set the type of units and precision of the dimension. See Figure 20-6. The **Tolerances** tab allows you to set the tolerance format values. See Figure 20-7.

In the **Linear Dimensions** area of the **Primary Units** tab, the **Precision** drop-down list allows you to specify the number of zeros displayed after the decimal point of the specified dimension. The ASME standard recommends that the precision for the dimension and the tolerance be the same for inch dimensions, but it may be different for metric values as previously discussed. You must set the precision values for the specified dimension and the tolerance dimension separately, even if you want them to be the same. AutoCAD does not automatically do this for you. To set the tolerance

Figure 20-5.
The **Dimension Style Manager** dialog box.

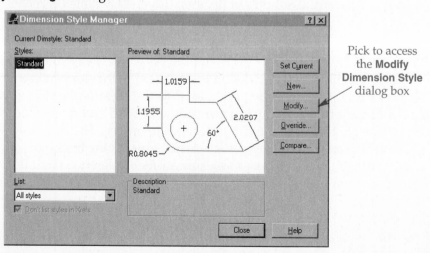

Pick to access
the **Modify
Dimension Style**
dialog box

AutoCAD and its Applications—Basics

Figure 20-6.
Settings for the units and precision of linear dimensions are located in the **Primary Units** tab.

Set the precision for specified dimensions

Settings should match the **Zero Suppression** tolerance format settings in the **Tolerances** tab

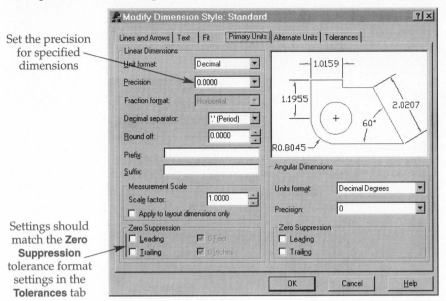

Figure 20-7.
The **Tolerances** tab contains formatting settings for tolerance dimensions.

Select a tolerance method

Set the precision for tolerance dimensions

Settings should match the **Zero Suppression** linear dimension settings in the **Primary Units** tab

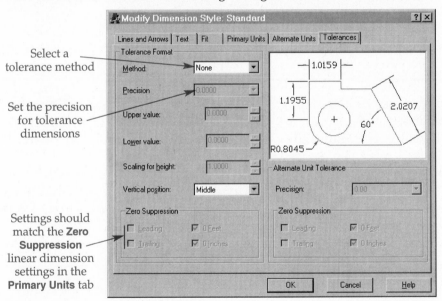

precision, you must first specify a tolerance method using the **Method:** drop-down list in the **Tolerances** tab. Tolerance methods are discussed in the next section of this chapter. Once a method is selected, you can set the tolerance dimension precision by accessing the **Precision** drop-down list. This setting is also controlled by the **DIMTDEC** dimension variable.

Like the precision settings, the **Zero Suppression** settings for linear dimensions in the **Primary Units** tab must be set separately from the **Zero Suppression** tolerance format settings in the **Tolerances** tab. These options were explained in Chapter 18. The settings should be the same. For example, the **Leading** options should be off and the **Trailing** options should be on for metric dimensions. For inch dimensions, the **Leading** options should be on and the **Trailing** options should be off. As is the case with the precision settings, a tolerance method must be selected before the **Zero**

Suppression tolerance format options can be specified. Zero suppression for the tolerance dimension is controlled by the **DIMTZIN** system variable. Zero suppression for the specified dimension is controlled by the **DIMZIN** system variable.

SETTING TOLERANCE METHODS

The **Tolerances** tab can be used to apply a tolerance method to your drawing. Refer to Figure 20-7. The **Method:** drop-down list provides **None** as the default option. This means that no tolerance method is used with your dimensions. As a result, most of the options in this area are disabled. If you pick a tolerance method from the drop-down list, the resulting image in the tab reflects the method selected. The drop-down list options are shown in Figure 20-8. These options are discussed in the following sections.

Figure 20-8.
A tolerance dimensioning method can be selected from the options in the **Method:** drop-down list, located in the **Tolerance Format** area of the **Tolerances** tab.

Select a
tolerance method

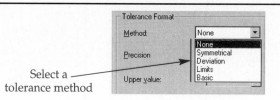

Symmetrical Tolerance Method

The **Symmetrical** tolerance dimensioning option is used to draw dimension text that displays an equal bilateral tolerance in the plus/minus format. When the **Symmetrical** option is selected, the **Upper value:** text box, **Scaling for height:** text box, and **Vertical position:** drop-down list are active, and the preview image displays an equal bilateral tolerance. See Figure 20-9. You can enter a tolerance value in the **Upper value:** text box.

The **Symmetrical** tolerance option can also be set by turning the **DIMTOL** (tolerance) system variable on, turning the **DIMLIM** (limits) system variable off, and setting the **DIMTP** (tolerance plus) and **DIMTM** (tolerance minus) system variables to the same numerical value.

Figure 20-9.
Setting the **Symmetrical** tolerance method option current with an equal bilateral tolerance value of 0.005.

Specified
tolerance
method

Equal
bilateral
tolerance
value

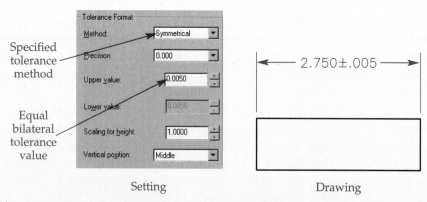

Setting

Drawing

| NOTE | When you turn the **DIMTOL** system variable on, **DIMLIM** is automatically turned off. When you turn **DIMLIM** on, **DIMTOL** is automatically turned off. |

EXERCISE 20-1

❏ Start a new drawing or use one of your templates.
❏ Set the required units, precision, zero suppression, and tolerance method to draw an object with equal bilateral tolerance dimensioning. Draw an object similar to the one shown in Figure 20-9.
❏ Save the drawing as EX20-1.

Deviation Tolerance Method

AutoCAD refers to an unequal bilateral tolerance as a *deviation*. This means that the tolerance deviates (departs) from the specified dimension with two different values. The deviation tolerance method can be set by selecting the **Deviation** option in the **Tolerances** tab. After selecting this option, the **Upper value:** and **Lower value:** text boxes become active so that you can enter the desired upper and lower tolerance values. See Figure 20-10. The preview image in the tab changes to match a representation of an unequal bilateral tolerance.

The **Deviation** option can also be used to draw a unilateral tolerance by entering zero for either the **Upper value:** or **Lower value:** setting. If you are using inch units, AutoCAD includes the plus or minus sign before the zero tolerance. When metric units are used, the sign is omitted. See Figure 20-11.

Figure 20-10.
Setting the **Deviation** tolerance method option current with unequal bilateral tolerance values.

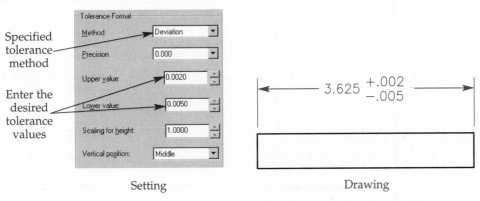

Setting   Drawing

Figure 20-11.
When a unilateral tolerance is specified, AutoCAD automatically places the plus or minus symbol in front of the zero tolerance if English units are used. The symbol is omitted with metric units.

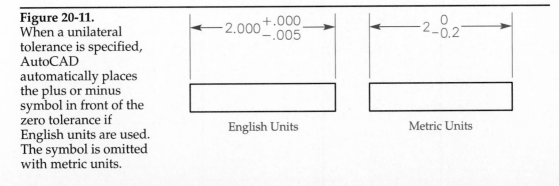

English Units   Metric Units

The **Deviation** tolerance method option can also be set by turning the **DIMTOL** system variable on, turning the **DIMLIM** system variable off, and setting the **DIMTP** and **DIMTM** system variables to different numerical values.

EXERCISE 20-2

❏ Start a new drawing or use one of your templates.
❏ Set the required units, precision, zero suppression, and tolerance method to draw the following:
  ❏ An object with an unequal bilateral tolerance dimension, similar to the one shown in Figure 20-10.
  ❏ An object with a unilateral tolerance dimension, similar to the example shown with English units in Figure 20-11.
  ❏ Change the **MEASUREMENT** system variable to 1. Draw another object and apply the same unilateral dimension used with the previous object. Note the differences.
❏ Save the drawing as EX20-2.

Limits Tolerance Method

As discussed earlier, in limits dimensioning, the tolerance limits are given and no calculations from the specified dimension are required (unlike plus-minus dimensioning). The limits tolerance method can be set by picking the **Limits** method option in the **Tolerances** tab. When this option is set, the **Upper value:** and **Lower value:** text boxes are activated. You can then enter the desired upper and lower tolerance values that are added and subtracted from the specified dimension. The values you enter can be the same or different. See Figure 20-12.

Figure 20-12.
Setting the **Limits** tolerance method option current with specified limits values.

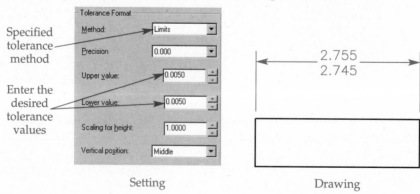

Setting   Drawing

❑ Start a new drawing or use one of your templates.
❑ Set the required units, precision, zero suppression, and tolerance method to draw an object with a limits tolerance dimension. Drawn an object similar to the one shown in Figure 20-12.
❑ Save the drawing as EX20-3.

Basic Tolerance Method

The basic tolerance method is used to draw basic dimensions. A *basic dimension* is considered to be a theoretically perfect dimension and is used in geometric dimensioning and tolerancing, which is covered in Chapter 21. The basic tolerance method can be set by picking the **Basic** option in the **Tolerances** tab. At this setting, the **Upper value:** and **Lower value:** options in the **Tolerance Format** area are disabled because a basic dimension has no tolerance. A basic dimension is distinguished from other dimensions because it has a rectangle placed around it, as shown in Figure 20-13.

Figure 20-13.
The **Basic** tolerance method option is used for basic dimensioning. Basic dimensions are drawn with the text placed inside a rectangle.

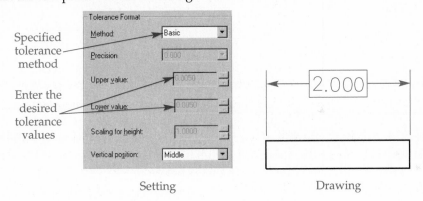

Specified tolerance method

Enter the desired tolerance values

Setting

Drawing

Tolerance Method Review

✓ If your tolerance dimensions do not reflect the level of precision you want, change the precision using the **Precision** drop-down list in the **Tolerance Format** area of the **Tolerances** tab. You can also use the **DIMTDEC** system variable to set the desired value.

✓ Each tolerance method option you pick is represented by an image preview in the **Modify Dimension Style** dialog box.

✓ When drawing inch tolerance dimensions, you should activate the **Leading Zero Suppression** tolerance format option in the **Tolerances** tab. The same option should be activated for linear dimensions in the **Primary Units** tab. You can then properly draw inch tolerance dimensions without placing the zero before the decimal point, as recommended by ASME standards. These settings would allow you to draw a tolerance dimension such as .625±.005.

✓ When drawing metric tolerance dimensions, deactivate the **Leading Zero Suppression** tolerance format option in the **Tolerances** tab, and deactivate the same option for linear dimensions in the **Primary Units** tab. This allows you to place a metric tolerance dimension with the zero before the decimal point, as recommended by ASME standards (for example, a dimension such as 12±0.2).

Tolerance Justification

You can control the alignment, or justification, of symmetrical and deviation tolerance dimensions by accessing the **Vertical position:** drop-down list in the **Tolerance Format** area of the **Tolerances** tab. The **Middle** option centers the tolerance with the specified dimension, and is active by default. This is also the recommended ASME practice. The other justification options are **Top** and **Bottom**. Deviation tolerance dimensions displaying each of the justification options are shown in Figure 20-14. The justification for symmetrical and deviation tolerance dimensions is also controlled by the **DIMTOLJ** system variable.

Figure 20-14.
Examples of the tolerance justification options used with symmetrical and deviation tolerance dimensions.

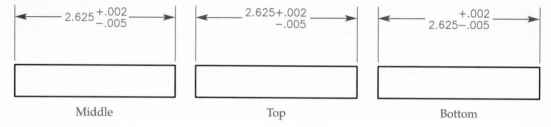

Middle   Top   Bottom

Tolerance Height

You can set the text height of the tolerance dimension in relation to the text height of the specified dimension. This is done by using the **Scaling for height:** text box in the **Tolerance format** area of the **Tolerances** tab. The default is 1.0000, which makes the tolerance dimension text the same height as the specified dimension text. This is the recommended ASME standard. If you want the tolerance dimension height to be three-quarters as high as the specified dimension height, enter .75 in the **Scaling for height:** text box. Some companies prefer this practice to keep the tolerance part of the dimension from taking up additional space. Examples of tolerance dimensions with different text heights are shown in Figure 20-15. The tolerance text height is also controlled by the **DIMTFAC** system variable.

Figure 20-15.
Using different scale settings for the text height of tolerance dimensions.

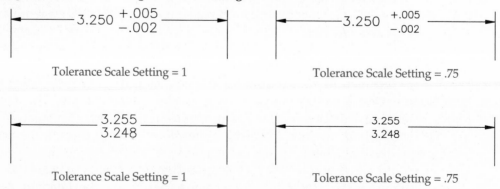

❑ Start a new drawing or use one of your templates.
❑ Set the required units, precision, zero suppression, tolerance method, justification, and height to draw the following:
  ❑ Three dimensioned objects similar to the examples shown in Figure 20-14.
  ❑ Four dimensions similar to the examples shown in Figure 20-15.
❑ Save the drawing as EX20-4.

Chapter Test

Answer the following questions on a separate sheet of paper.
1. Define the term *tolerance*.
2. Give an example of an equal bilateral tolerance in inches and in metric units.
3. Give an example of an unequal bilateral tolerance in inches and in metric units.
4. What are the limits of the tolerance dimension 3.625±.005?
5. Give an example of a unilateral tolerance in inches and in metric units.
6. Which dialog box is used to create dimension styles? How is it accessed?
7. How do you open the **Tolerances** tab?
8. How do you set the number of zeros displayed after the decimal point for a tolerance dimension?
9. What zero suppression settings should be specified for linear and tolerance dimensions when using metric units?
10. What zero suppression settings should be specified for linear and tolerance dimensions when using inch units?
11. What is the purpose of the **Symmetrical** tolerance method option?
12. What is the purpose of the **Deviation** tolerance method option?
13. What is the purpose of the **Limits** tolerance method option?
14. What happens to the preview image in the **Tolerances** tab when a tolerance method option is picked from the **Method:** drop-down list?
15. Name the tolerance dimension justification option recommended by the ASME standard.
16. Explain the results of setting the **Scaling for height:** option to 1 in the **Tolerances** tab.
17. What setting would you use for the **Scaling for height:** option if you wanted the tolerance dimension height to be three-quarters of the specified dimension height?

Drawing Problems

Set the limits, units, dimension style settings, and other parameters as needed for the following problems. Use the guidelines given below.
  A. *Draw and dimension the necessary multiviews for the following drawings to exact size. You must use the proper view for the problems presented in 3D.*
  B. *Apply dimensions accurately using ASME standards. Create dimension styles that suit the specific needs of each drawing. For example, save different dimension styles for metric and inch dimensions.*
  C. *Create separate layers for the views and dimensions.*
  D. *Plot the drawings with 0.6mm object lines and 0.3mm thin lines.*
  E. *Place the following general notes in the lower-left corner of each drawing:*

        3. UNLESS OTHERWISE SPECIFIED, ALL DIMENSIONS ARE IN
            MILLIMETERS. *(or* INCHES *as applicable)*
        2. REMOVE ALL BURRS AND SHARP EDGES.
        1. INTERPRET PER ASME Y14.5M-1994.
        NOTES:

  F. *Save the drawings as P20-1, P20-2, and so on.*

1.

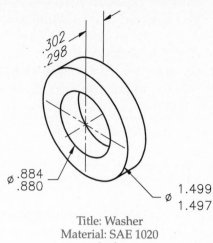

.302
.298

Ø .884
.880

Ø 1.499
  1.497

Title: Washer
Material: SAE 1020
Inch

2.

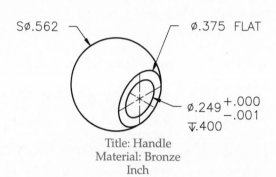

SØ.562

Ø.375 FLAT

Ø.249 +.000
       −.001
↧.400

Title: Handle
Material: Bronze
Inch

3.

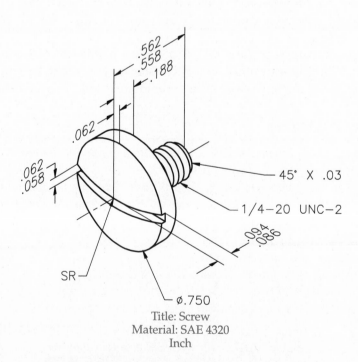

.562
.558

.188

.062

.062
.058

45° X .03

1/4−20 UNC−2

.094
.086

SR

Ø.750

Title: Screw
Material: SAE 4320
Inch

4.

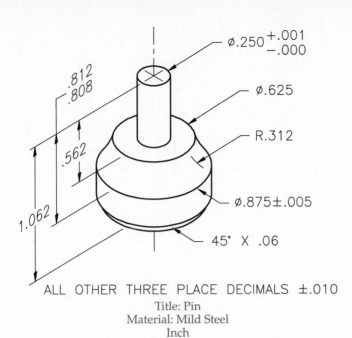

Ø.250 +.001 −.000

Ø.625

R.312

Ø.875±.005

45° X .06

.812 / .808

.562

1.062

ALL OTHER THREE PLACE DECIMALS ±.010

Title: Pin
Material: Mild Steel
Inch

5. This object is shown as a section for clarity. Do not draw a section.

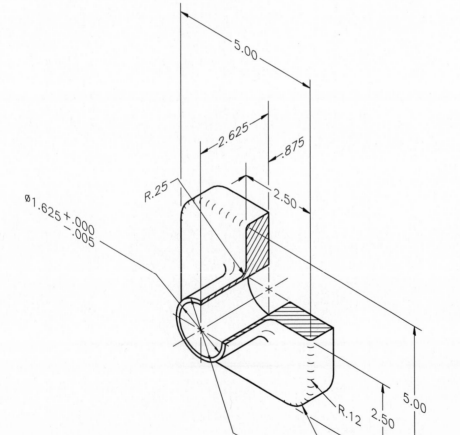

5.00

2.625

.875

2.50

R.25

Ø1.625 +.000 −.005

Ø1.875 +.008 −.000

R.12

R1.00

2.50

5.00

Title: Thrust Washer
Material: SAE 5150
Inch

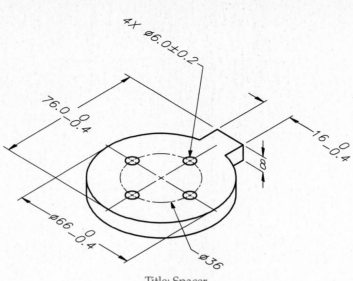

Title: Spacer
Material: Cold Rolled Steel
Metric

7.

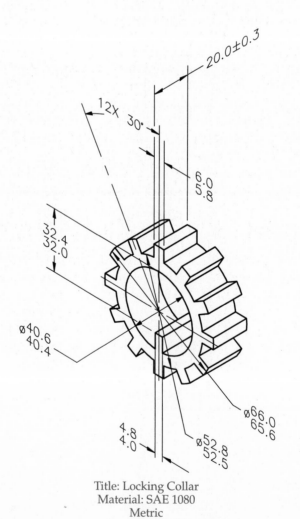

Title: Locking Collar
Material: SAE 1080
Metric

CHAPTER 21

Geometric Dimensioning and Tolerancing

Learning Objectives

After completing this chapter, you will be able to:
- Identify symbols used in geometric dimensioning and tolerancing.
- Use the **TOLERANCE**, **QLEADER**, and **LEADER** commands to create geometric tolerancing symbols.
- Draw and edit feature control frames.
- Draw datum feature symbols.
- Place basic dimensions on a drawing.

This chapter is an introduction to geometric dimensioning and tolerancing (GD&T) principles as adopted by the American National Standards Institute (ANSI) and published by the American Society of Mechanical Engineers (ASME) for engineering and related document practices. The standard is titled ASME Y14.5M-1994, *Dimensioning and Tolerancing*. *Geometric tolerancing* is a general term that refers to tolerances used to control the form, profile, orientation, runout, and location of features on an object.

The drafting applications covered in this chapter use the AutoCAD geometric tolerancing capabilities and additional recommendations to comply with the ASME Y14.5M-1994 standard. This chapter is only an introduction to geometric dimensioning and tolerancing. For complete coverage of GD&T, refer to *Geometric Dimensioning and Tolerancing*, also published by Goodheart-Willcox. Before beginning this chapter, it is recommended that you have a solid understanding of dimensioning and tolerancing standards and AutoCAD applications. This introductory material is presented in Chapters 18 through 20 of this text.

The discussion in this chapter divides the dimensioning and geometric tolerancing symbols into the following five basic types:
- Dimensioning symbols.
- Geometric characteristic symbols.
- Material condition symbols.
- Feature control frames.
- Datum feature symbols.

When you draw GD&T symbols, it is recommended that you use a dimensioning layer so the symbols and text can be plotted as lines that have the same thickness as extension and dimension lines (.01″ or .3mm). The suggested text font is Romans. These practices correspond with the ASME Y14.2M-1992 standard, *Line Conventions and Lettering*.

DIMENSIONING SYMBOLS

Symbols represent specific information that would be difficult and time-consuming to duplicate in note form. Symbols must be clearly drawn to the required size and shape so that they communicate the desired information uniformly. Symbols are recommended by ASME Y14.5M because they are an international language, read the same way in any country. In an international economy, it is important to have effective communication on engineering drawings. Symbols make this communication process uniform. ASME Y14.5M also states that the adoption of dimensioning symbols does not prevent the use of equivalent terms or abbreviations in situations where symbols are considered inappropriate.

Symbols aid in clarity, presentation of the drawing, and reduction of drawing time. Creating and using AutoCAD symbols is covered later in this chapter and in Chapter 23. A sample group of recommended dimensioning symbols is shown in Figure 21-1.

Figure 21-1.
Dimensioning symbols recommended by ASME Y14.5M-1994.

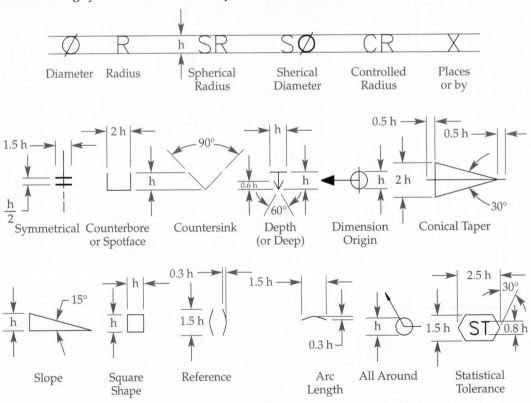

h = Letter height

GEOMETRIC CHARACTERISTIC SYMBOLS

In GD&T, symbols are used to provide specific controls related to the form of an object, the orientation of features, the outlines of features, the relationship of features to an axis, or the location of features. These symbols are known as *geometric characteristic symbols*. Geometric characteristic symbols are separated into five types: form, profile, location, orientation, and runout, as shown in Figure 21-2.

Figure 21-2.
Geometric characteristic symbols recommended by ASME Y14.5M-1994.

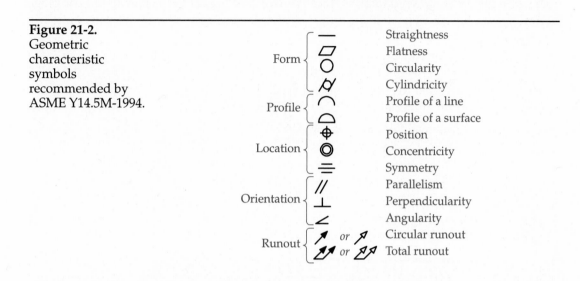

MATERIAL CONDITION SYMBOLS

Material condition symbols are often referred to as *modifying symbols* because they modify the geometric tolerance in relation to the produced size or location of the feature. Material condition symbols are only used in geometric dimensioning applications. The symbols used in a feature control frame to indicate *maximum material condition (MMC)* or *least material condition (LMC)* are shown in Figure 21-3. *Regardless of feature size (RFS)* is also a material condition. However, there is no symbol for RFS because it is assumed for all geometric tolerances and datum references unless MMC or LMC is specified.

Figure 21-3.
Material condition symbols. In ASME Y14.5M-1994, there is no symbol for RFS, since it is assumed unless otherwise specified.

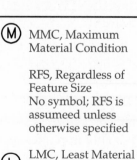

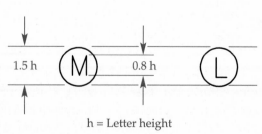

Surface Control, Regardless of Feature Size

Regardless of feature size is assumed as the material condition when there is no material condition symbol following the geometric tolerance in a feature control frame. *Regardless of feature size* means that the geometric tolerances remain the same regardless of the actual produced size. The term *produced size*, when used here, means the actual size of the feature when measured after manufacture.

When a feature control frame is connected to a feature surface with a leader or an extension line, it is referred to as *surface control*. See Figure 21-4. The geometric characteristic symbol shown is straightness, but the applications are the same for any characteristic.

Look at the chart in Figure 21-4 and notice how the possible sizes range from 6.20 (MMC) to 5.80 (LMC). With surface control, perfect form is required at MMC. *Perfect form* means that the object cannot exceed a true geometric form boundary established at maximum material condition. The geometric tolerance at MMC is zero, as shown in the chart. As the produced size varies from MMC in the chart, the geometric tolerance increases until it equals the amount specified in the feature control frame.

Figure 21-4.
The drawing below specifies surface control regardless of feature size. The actual meaning of the geometric tolerance is shown at right.

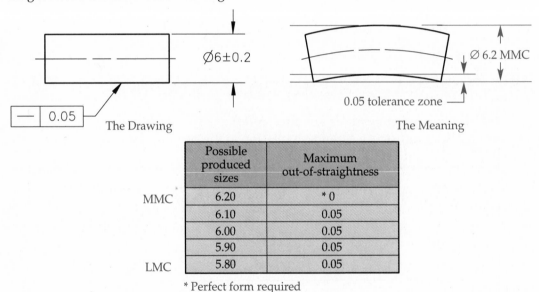

	Possible produced sizes	Maximum out-of-straightness
MMC	6.20	* 0
	6.10	0.05
	6.00	0.05
	5.90	0.05
LMC	5.80	0.05

* Perfect form required

Axis Control, Regardless of Feature Size

Axis control is indicated when the feature control frame is shown with a diameter dimension. See Figure 21-5. Regardless of feature size is assumed. With axis control, perfect form is not required at MMC. Therefore, the specified geometric tolerance stays the same at every produced size. See the chart in Figure 21-5.

Maximum Material Condition Control

If the material condition control is maximum material condition, the symbol for MMC must be placed in the feature control frame. See Figure 21-6. When this application is used, the specified geometric tolerance is held at the maximum material condition produced size. See the chart in Figure 21-6. Then, as the produced size varies from MMC, the geometric tolerance increases equal to the change. The maximum geometric tolerance is at the LMC produced size.

Figure 21-5.
The drawing below specifies axis control regardless of feature size. The actual meaning of the geometric tolerance is shown at right.

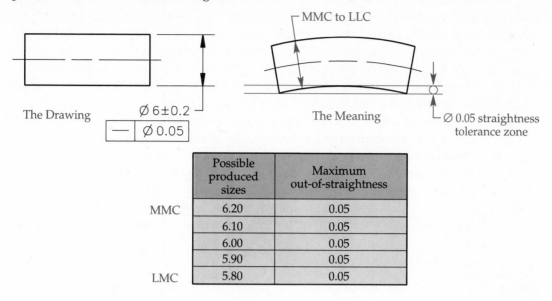

The Drawing

$\varnothing$ 6±0.2

— | $\varnothing$ 0.05

The Meaning

MMC to LLC

$\varnothing$ 0.05 straightness tolerance zone

	Possible produced sizes	Maximum out-of-straightness
MMC	6.20	0.05
	6.10	0.05
	6.00	0.05
	5.90	0.05
LMC	5.80	0.05

Figure 21-6.
A drawing that specifies maximum material condition applied to a feature. The symbol for MMC is shown highlighted.

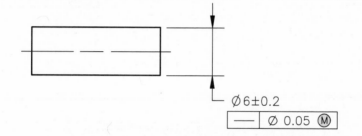

$\varnothing$6±0.2

— | $\varnothing$ 0.05 Ⓜ

	Possible produced sizes	Maximum out-of-straightness
MMC	6.20	0.05
	6.10	0.15
	6.00	0.25
	5.90	0.35
LMC	5.80	0.45

Least Material Condition Control

If the material condition control is least material condition, the symbol for LMC must be placed in the feature control frame. When this application is used, the specified geometric tolerance is held at the least material condition produced size. Then, as the produced size varies from LMC, the geometric tolerance increases equal to the change. The maximum geometric tolerance is at the MMC produced size.

FEATURE CONTROL FRAME

A geometric characteristic, geometric tolerance, material condition, and datum reference (if any) for an individual feature are specified by means of a feature control frame. The *feature control frame* is divided into compartments containing the geometric characteristic symbol in the first compartment, followed by the geometric tolerance. Where applicable, the geometric tolerance is preceded by the diameter symbol, which describes the shape of the tolerance zone, and is followed by a material condition symbol (if other than RFS). See Figure 21-7.

When a geometric tolerance is related to one or more datums, the datum reference letters are placed in compartments following the geometric tolerance. *Datums* are considered theoretically perfect surfaces, planes, points, or axes. When there is a multiple datum reference, both datum reference letters, separated by a dash, are placed in a single compartment after the geometric tolerance. A *multiple datum reference* is established by two datum features, such as an axis established by two datum diameters. Several feature control frames with datum references are shown in Figure 21-8.

Figure 21-7.
Feature control frames containing the geometric characteristic symbol, geometric tolerance, and diameter symbol (as applicable). The material condition symbol is left off for RFS, since it is assumed. Note that the geometric tolerance is expressed as a total, not a plus-minus value.

Geometric tolerance

Geometric characteristic symbol

Geometric characteristic symbol

Geometric tolerance

Diameter symbol

Material condition symbol

Figure 21-8.
Examples of datum references indicated in feature control frames.

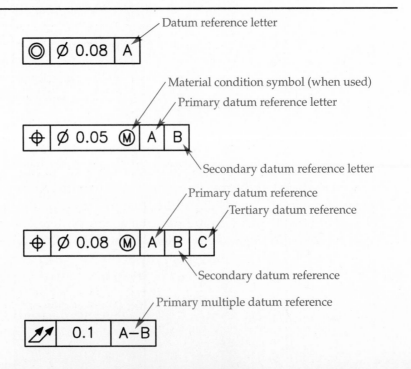

Datum reference letter

Material condition symbol (when used)

Primary datum reference letter

Secondary datum reference letter

Primary datum reference

Tertiary datum reference

Secondary datum reference

Primary multiple datum reference

There is a specific order used to display elements in a feature control frame. See Figure 21-9. Notice that the datum reference letters can be followed by a material condition symbol where applicable.

Figure 21-9.
The order of elements in a feature control frame.

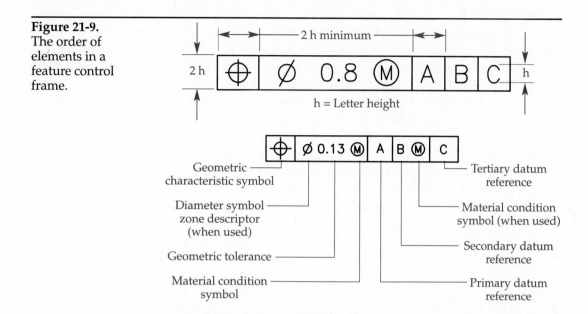

BASIC DIMENSIONS

A *basic dimension* is considered a theoretically perfect dimension. Basic dimensions are used to describe the theoretically exact size, profile, orientation, and location of a feature. These dimensions provide the basis from which permissible variations are established by tolerances on other dimensions, in notes, or in feature control frames. In simple terms, a basic dimension tells you where the geometric tolerance zone or datum target is located.

Basic dimensions are shown on a drawing with a rectangle placed around the dimension text, as shown in Figure 21-10. A general note can also be used to identify basic dimensions in some applications. For example, the note UNTOLERANCED DIMENSIONS LOCATING TRUE POSITION ARE BASIC indicates the dimensions that are basic. The basic dimension rectangle is a signal to the reader to look for a geometric tolerance in a feature control frame related to the features being dimensioned.

Figure 21-10.
Basic dimensions are identified with a rectangle drawn around the text.

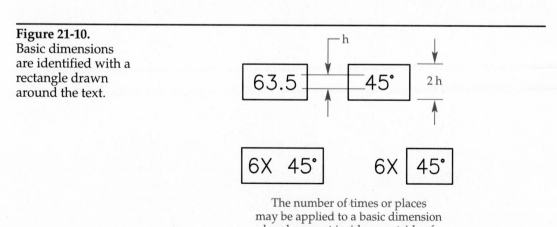

The number of times or places may be applied to a basic dimension by placement inside or outside of the basic dimension symbol

h = Letter height

ADDITIONAL SYMBOLS

Other symbols commonly used in geometric dimensioning and tolerancing are shown in Figure 21-11. These symbols are used for specific applications, and are identified as follows:

- **Free state.** Free state describes distortion of a part after the removal of forces applied during manufacture. The free state symbol is placed in the feature control frame after the geometric tolerance and the material condition (if any), if the feature must meet the tolerance specified while in free state.
- **Tangent plane.** A tangent plane symbol is placed after the geometric tolerance in the feature control frame when it is necessary to control a feature surface by contacting points of tangency.
- **Projected tolerance zone.** A projected tolerance zone symbol is placed in the feature control frame to inform the reader that the geometric tolerance zone is projected away from the primary datum.
- **Between.** The between symbol is used with profile geometric tolerances to identify where the profile tolerance is applied.
- **Statistical tolerance.** The statistical tolerance symbol is used to indicate that a tolerance is based on statistical tolerancing. *Statistical tolerancing* is the assigning of tolerances to related dimensions based on the requirements of statistical process control (SPC). *Statistical process control* is a method of monitoring and adjusting a manufacturing process by using statistical signals. The statistical tolerancing symbol is placed after the dimension or geometric tolerance that requires SPC. See Figure 21-12. When the feature can be manufactured either by using SPC or by using conventional means, both the statistical tolerance with the statistical tolerance symbol and the conventional tolerance must be shown. An appropriate general note should accompany the drawing. Either of the two following notes is acceptable:
- FEATURES IDENTIFIED AS STATISTICAL TOLERANCED SHALL BE PRODUCED WITH STATISTICAL PROCESS CONTROL.
- FEATURES IDENTIFIED AS STATISTICAL TOLERANCED SHALL BE PRODUCED WITH STATISTICAL PROCESS CONTROL, OR THE MORE RESTRICTIVE ARITHMETIC LIMITS.

Figure 21-11.
Additional recommended dimensioning symbols.

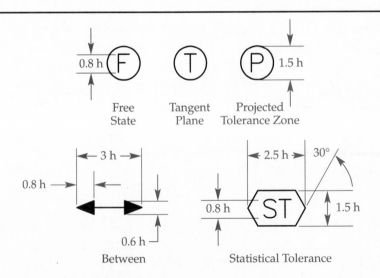

Figure 21-12.
Different ways to apply a statistical tolerance. The statistical tolerance symbol is shown here highlighted.

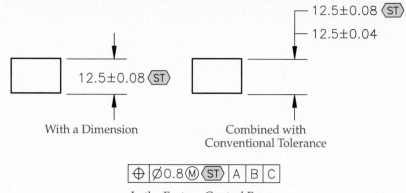

With a Dimension

Combined with Conventional Tolerance

In the Feature Control Frame

DATUM FEATURE SYMBOLS

As discussed previously, datums refer to theoretically perfect surfaces, planes, points, or axes. In this introduction to datum-related symbols, the datum is assumed. In geometric dimensioning and tolerancing, the datums are identified with a **datum feature symbol**.

Each datum feature requiring identification must have its own identification letter. Any letter of the alphabet can be used to identify a datum, except for *I*, *O*, or *Q*. These letters can be confused with the numbers 1 or 0. On drawings where the number of datums exceeds the number of letters in the alphabet, double letters are used, starting with *AA* through *AZ*, and then *BA* through *BZ*. Datum feature symbols can be repeated only as necessary for clarity. In Figure 21-13, the datum feature symbol recommended by ASME Y14.5M-1994 is shown.

The datum feature symbol used in drawings prior to the release of ASME Y14.5M-1994 is distinctively different. The previously used datum feature symbol is shown in Figure 21-14.

Figure 21-13.
The datum feature symbol based on ASME Y14.5M-1994.

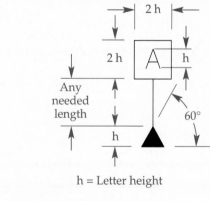

h = Letter height

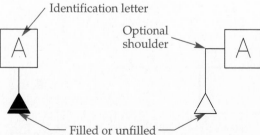

Figure 21-14.
The datum feature
symbol based on
ANSI Y14.5M-1982.
The standard was
revised to ASME
Y14.5M-1994.

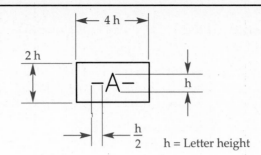

h = Letter height

Applications of the Datum Feature Symbol

When a surface is used to establish a datum plane on a part, the datum feature symbol is placed on the edge view of the surface or on an extension line in the view where the surface appears as a line. See Figure 21-15. A leader line can also be used to connect the datum feature symbol to the view.

When the datum is an axis, the datum feature symbol can be placed on the drawing using one of the following methods. See Figure 21-16.

- The symbol can be placed on the outside surface of a cylindrical feature.
- The symbol can be centered on the opposite side of the dimension line arrowhead.
- The symbol can replace the dimension line and arrowhead when the dimension line is placed outside the extension lines.
- The symbol can be placed on a leader line shoulder.
- The symbol can be placed below, and attached to, the center of a feature control frame.

Elements on a rectangular symmetrical part or feature can be located and dimensioned in relationship to a datum center plane. Datum center plane symbols are shown in Figure 21-17.

Figure 21-15.
Datum feature symbols used to identify datum planes.

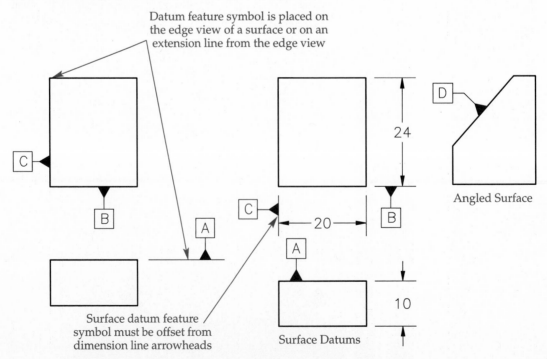

Figure 21-16.
Different methods of using the datum feature symbol to represent the datum axis.

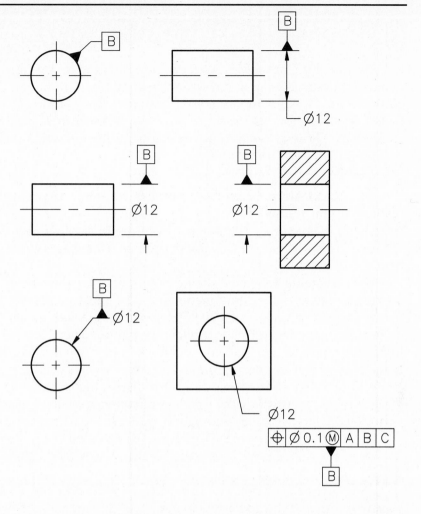

Figure 21-17.
Placing datum center plane symbols. Axis and center plane datum feature symbols must align with, or replace, the dimension line arrowhead. Or, the datum feature symbol must be placed on the feature, leader shoulder, or feature control frame.

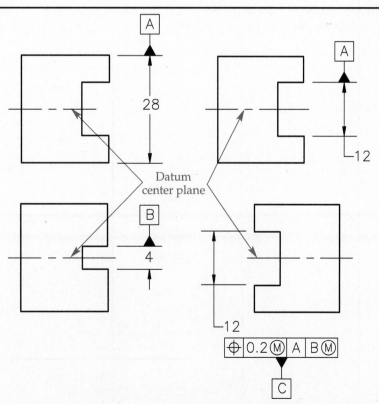

This chapter has given you an introduction to the appearance and use of geometric dimensioning and tolerancing symbols. AutoCAD provides you with the ability to add GD&T symbols to your drawings. The feature control frame and related GD&T symbols can be created using the **TOLERANCE**, **QLEADER**, and **LEADER** commands. These commands are discussed in the following sections.

Using the TOLERANCE Command

TOLERANCE
TOL

Dimension
↳ **Tolerance...**

Dimension toolbar

Tolerance

The **TOLERANCE** command provides tools for creating GD&T symbols and feature control frames. To access this command, pick the **Tolerance** button on the **Dimension** toolbar, pick **Tolerance...** from the **Dimension** pull-down menu, or enter TOL or TOLERANCE at the Command: prompt. This displays the **Geometric Tolerance** dialog box, Figure 21-18.

The **Geometric Tolerance** dialog box is divided into areas containing compartments that relate to the components found in a feature control frame. The compartments, located in each of the five **Tolerance** and **Datum** areas, allow you to specify geometric tolerance and datum reference values. There are two levels in each area that can be used to create a feature control frame. The first, or upper, level is used to make a single feature control frame. The lower level is used to create a double feature control frame. There are also options for displaying a diameter symbol and a modifying symbol. In addition, the **Geometric Tolerance** dialog box allows you to display a projected tolerance zone symbol and value, and part of the datum feature symbol.

Geometric characteristic symbols can be accessed in the **Sym** area, located at the far left of the dialog box. This area has two image tile buttons that can be used to display one or two geometric characteristic symbols. Keep in mind that the corresponding text boxes along the upper row in each area are used for a single feature control frame, and the text boxes in the lower row are used to create a double feature control frame. Picking one of the image tile buttons in the **Sym** area opens the **Symbol** image tile menu, Figure 21-19. Pick a symbol to have it displayed in the **Sym** image

Figure 21-18.
The **Geometric Tolerance** dialog box is used to draw GD&T symbols and feature control frames to desired specifications.

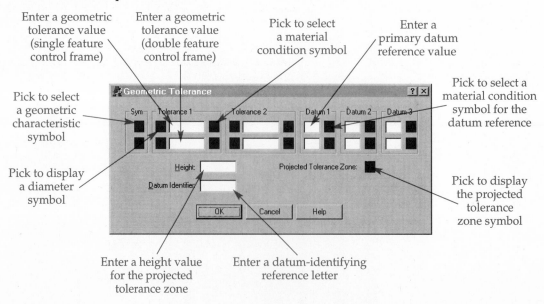

Figure 21-19.
The **Symbol** image tile menu is used to select a geometric characteristic symbol for use in a feature control frame.

Pick the desired symbol

Pick to remove a symbol from the **Sym** area

tile that you selected. After making a selection, the **Geometric Tolerance** dialog box returns. You can pick the same image tile again to select a different symbol, if you wish. To remove a previously selected symbol, pick the blank image tile in the lower-right corner of the **Symbol** image tile menu.

After picking a geometric characteristic symbol, you can enter tolerance or datum values to be used in the feature control frame. The other options and features in the **Geometric Tolerance** dialog box are explained as follows:

- **Tolerance 1 area.** This area allows you to enter the first geometric tolerance value used in the feature control frame. If you are drawing a single feature control frame, enter the desired value in the upper text box. If you are drawing a double feature control frame, enter a value in the lower text box. Double feature control frames, discussed later in this chapter, are used for applications such as unit straightness, unit flatness, composite profile tolerance, composite positional tolerance, and coaxial positional tolerance. After entering a tolerance value in one of the text boxes, you can also add a diameter symbol by picking the image tile to the left of the text box. Pick the diameter image tile again to remove the diameter symbol.

    The image tile to the right of the text box is used to place a material condition symbol. When you pick this image tile, the **Material Condition** image tile menu appears, Figure 21-20. Pick the desired symbol to have it displayed in the image tile you selected. In the example given, an MMC symbol is selected. To remove a selected symbol, pick the blank tile in the **Material Condition** image tile menu. Notice the old RFS symbol in Figure 21-20. This symbol was used in ANSI Y14.5M-1982. It is not used in ASME Y14.5M-1994, because RFS is assumed unless otherwise specified.

    In Figure 21-21, a position symbol is shown in the **Sym** image tile, and 0.5 is entered as the tolerance value in the upper text box in the **Tolerance 1** area. The value is preceded by a diameter symbol and followed by an MMC symbol. Remember that a zero precedes metric decimals, and there is no zero in front of inch decimals.

Figure 21-20.
The **Material Condition** image tile menu. Pick the desired material condition symbol for the geometric tolerance and datum reference as needed. Notice the symbol for RFS is available. This symbol is not used in ASME Y14.5M-1994, but it may be needed when editing older drawings.

Old RFS symbol

Pick the desired symbol

Pick to remove a selected symbol

Figure 21-21.
The **Geometric Tolerance** dialog box with a diameter symbol, geometric tolerance value, and MMC material condition symbol added to the **Tolerance 1** area (shown here highlighted).

The tolerance value, diameter symbol, and material condition symbol are entered

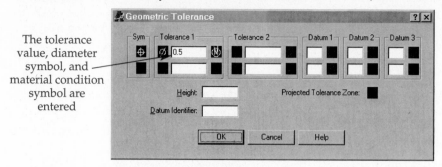

- **Tolerance 2 area.** This area is used for the addition of a second geometric tolerance to the feature control frame. This is not a common application, but it may be used in some cases where there are restrictions placed on the geometric tolerance specified in the first compartment. For example, the second geometric tolerance value may be 0.8 MAX, which means that the specification given in the first compartment is maintained but cannot exceed 0.8 maximum.
- **Datum areas.** The **Datum 1** area is used to establish the information needed for the primary datum reference compartment. Like the **Tolerance** areas, this area offers two levels of text boxes to create single or double feature control frames. You can also specify a material condition symbol for the datum reference by picking the image tile next to the corresponding text box to open the **Material Condition** image tile menu. The **Datum 2** and **Datum 3** areas are used to specify the secondary and tertiary datum reference information. Refer to Figure 21-9 to see how the datum reference and related material condition symbols are placed in the feature control frame.
- **Height: text box.** This text box can be used to specify the height of a projected tolerance zone. The use of a projected tolerance zone in a drawing is discussed later in this chapter.
- **Projected Tolerance Zone: image tile.** This tile can be picked to display a projected tolerance zone symbol in the feature control frame. The projected tolerance zone symbol and the value specified in the **Height:** text box are used together when a projected tolerance zone is applied to the drawing.
- **Datum Identifier: text box.** This text box is used to enter a datum-identifying reference letter to be used as part of the datum feature symbol. An uppercase letter should be entered. If you want to comply with ASME Y14.5M-1994, you need to first design a datum feature symbol and save it as a block. Creating your own dimensioning symbols is discussed later in this chapter, and blocks are discussed in Chapter 23.

After you have entered all the desired information in the **Geometric Tolerance** dialog box, pick **OK**. See Figure 21-22A. The following prompt is then displayed:

Enter tolerance location: *(pick the location for the feature control frame to be drawn)*
Command:

The feature control frame for the given example is shown in Figure 21-22B.

Figure 21-22.
A—When the desired values have been specified in the **Geometric Tolerance** dialog box, pick **OK**. In this example, primary, secondary, and tertiary datum reference values have been added and are shown highlighted along with the geometric tolerance value.
B—The feature control frame created by the values specified in the dialog box.

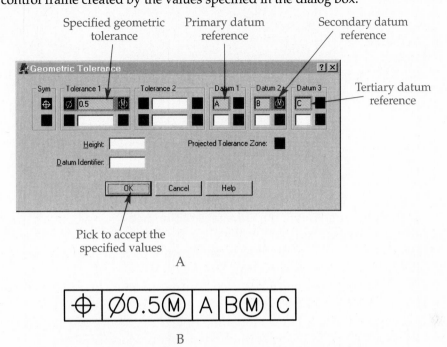

Specified geometric tolerance

Primary datum reference

Secondary datum reference

Tertiary datum reference

Pick to accept the specified values

A

B

EXERCISE 21-1

❑ Start a new drawing or use one of your templates.
❑ Draw the same feature control frames that are displayed in Figures 21-7 and 21-8.
❑ Save the drawing as **EX21-1**.

Using the **QLEADER** and **LEADER** Commands to Place GD&T Symbols

In many cases, leader lines are connected to feature control frames or other GD&T symbols in order to identify toleranced features. The **QLEADER** and **LEADER** commands enable you to draw leader lines and access the dialog boxes used to create feature control frames in one operation. Refer to Chapter 18 for a complete discussion of the **QLEADER** and **LEADER** commands.

The **QLEADER** command can be accessed by picking the **Quick Leader** button from the **Dimension** toolbar, picking **Leader** from the **Dimension** pull-down menu, or by entering LE or QLEADER at the Command: prompt. When you enter this command, the **Settings** option can be used to open the **Leader Settings** dialog box, Figure 21-23. Pick the **Tolerance** option button to connect a feature control frame or datum feature symbol to a leader line. The command sequence is as follows:

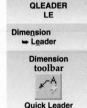

QLEADER
LE

Dimension
➥ Leader

Dimension
toolbar

Quick Leader

Command: **LE** *or* **QLEADER**↵
Specify first leader point, or [Settings] <Settings>: ↵ *(when the* **Leader Settings** *dialog box is displayed, pick the* **Tolerance** *option button and then pick* **OK***)*
Specify first leader point, or [Settings] <Settings>: *(pick the leader start point)*
Specify next point: *(pick the next leader point)*
Specify next point: ↵

Figure 21-23.
The **Leader Settings** dialog box. Activate the **Tolerance** option button when placing a feature control frame with the **QLEADER** command.

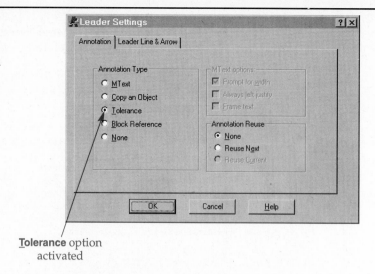

Tolerance option
activated

After pressing [Enter], the **Geometric Tolerance** dialog box is displayed for you to specify the desired settings and values for the feature control frame. Pick the **OK** button when you are ready to have the feature control frame connected to the leader line in your drawing, as shown in Figure 21-24.

The **LEADER** command can also be used to connect a feature control frame to a leader line. After picking a start point and a second leader point, you can use the **Annotation** option to enter a single line of text to go with the leader, or you can access the **Annotation** options. The command sequence is as follows:

> Command: **LEAD** *or* **LEADER**.⏎
> Specify leader start point: *(pick the leader start point)*
> Specify next point: *(pick the next point of the leader)*
> Specify next point or [Annotation/Format/Undo] <Annotation>: ⏎
> Enter first line of annotation text or <options>: ⏎
> Enter an annotation option [Tolerance/Copy/Block/None/Mtext] <Mtext>: **T**⏎

Entering the **Tolerance** annotation option displays the **Geometric Tolerance** dialog box. You can then establish the feature control frame information. When you pick **OK**, the feature control frame is connected to the leader shoulder.

Figure 21-24.
After completing the **QLEADER** command, the constructed feature control frame is connected to the leader line.

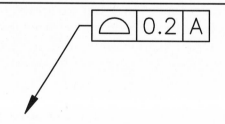

EXERCISE 21-2

❏ Open drawing EX21-1.
❏ Using the **QLEADER** or **LEADER** command, draw the feature control frame shown in Figure 21-24.
❏ Save the drawing as EX21-2.

INTRODUCTION TO PROJECTED TOLERANCE ZONES

In some situations where positional tolerance is used entirely in out-of-squareness, it may be necessary to control perpendicularity and position next to the part. The use of a *projected tolerance zone* is recommended when variations in perpendicularity of threaded or press-fit holes could cause the fastener to interfere with the mating part. A projected tolerance zone is usually specified for a fixed fastener, such as the threaded hole for a bolt or the press-fit hole for a pin. The length of a projected tolerance zone can be specified as the distance the fastener extends into the mating part, the thickness of the part, or the height of a press-fit stud. The normal positional tolerance extends through the thickness of the part.

However, this application can cause an interference between the location of a thread or press-fit object and its mating part. This is because the attitude of a fixed fastener is controlled by the actual angle of the threaded hole. There is no clearance available to provide flexibility. For this reason, the projected tolerance zone is established at true position and extends away from the primary datum at the threaded feature. The projected tolerance zone provides a larger tolerance because it is projected away from the primary datum, rather than within the thread. A projected tolerance is also easier to inspect than the tolerance applied to the pitch diameter of the thread. This is because a thread gauge with a post projecting above the threaded hole can be used to easily verify the projected tolerance zone with a coordinate measuring machine (CMM).

One method for displaying the projected tolerance zone is to place the projected tolerance zone symbol and height in the feature control frame after the geometric tolerance and related material condition symbol. The related thread specification is then connected to the sectional view of the thread symbol. With this method, the projected tolerance zone is assumed to extend away from the threaded hole at the primary datum. See Figure 21-25.

Figure 21-25.
A projected tolerance zone representation with the length of the projected tolerance zone given in the feature control frame. The projected tolerance zone symbol is shown highlighted.

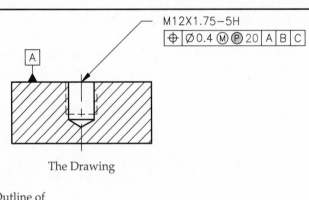

The Drawing

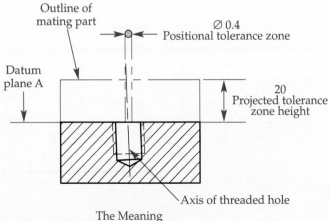

The Meaning

To provide additional clarification, the projected tolerance zone can be shown using a chain line in the view where the related datum appears as an edge and the minimum height of the projection is dimensioned. See Figure 21-26. The projected tolerance zone symbol is shown alone in the feature control frame after the geometric tolerance and material condition symbol (if any). The meaning is the same as previously discussed.

Figure 21-26.
A projected tolerance zone representation with the length of the projected tolerance zone shown with a chain line and a minimum dimension in the adjacent view. The projected tolerance zone symbol is shown highlighted.

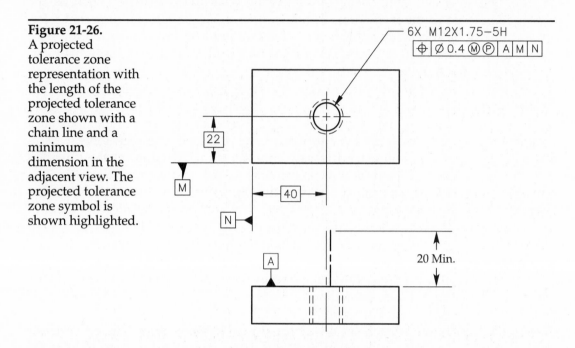

Drawing the Projected Tolerance Zone

You can add projected tolerance zone specifications to a feature control frame using the **Geometric Tolerance** dialog box. Enter the desired geometric tolerance, diameter symbol, material condition symbol, and datum reference as previously discussed. Enter the projected tolerance zone height in the **Height:** text box. Notice that 24 is entered in the **Height:** text box in Figure 21-27. Pick the **Projected Tolerance Zone:** image tile to access the projected tolerance zone symbol. Pick the **OK** button when you are done.

Now follow the screen prompt and place the feature control frame in the desired location. Notice in Figure 21-28 that AutoCAD displays the projected tolerance zone height in a separate compartment below the feature control frame. This representation is in accordance with ANSI Y14.5M-1982. The ASME Y14.5M-1994 convention has no lower compartment, as shown in Figure 21-25.

Figure 21-27.
To add projected tolerance zone specifications to the feature control frame, enter the projected tolerance zone height and symbol in the **Geometric Tolerance** dialog box.

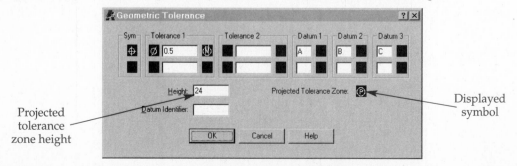

Figure 21-28.
The feature control frame created by the values specified in Figure 21-27. The AutoCAD projected tolerance zone compartment conforms to ANSI Y14.5M-1982 standards. See Figures 21-25 and 21-26 for applications of the projected tolerance zone as recommended by ASME Y14.5M-1994.

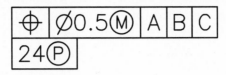

If you want to dimension the projected tolerance zone height with a chain line, then omit the value in the **Height:** text box in the **Geometric Tolerance** dialog box and only pick the **Projected Tolerance Zone:** image tile. This adds a compartment below the feature control frame with only the projected tolerance zone symbol. This representation is in accordance with ANSI Y14.5M-1982, but it does not match the ASME Y14.5M-1994 convention illustrated in Figure 21-26.

EXERCISE 21-3

❑ Open drawing EX21-1.
❑ Draw the feature control frame and projected tolerance zone compartment shown in Figure 21-28.
❑ Save the drawing as EX21-3.

DRAWING A DOUBLE FEATURE CONTROL FRAME

Several GD&T applications require that the feature control frame be doubled in height, with two sets of geometric tolerancing values provided. These applications include unit straightness and flatness, composite positional tolerance, and coaxial positional tolerance.

To draw a double feature control frame, first use the **TOLERANCE** command and create the desired first level of the feature control frame in the **Geometric Tolerance** dialog box as previously discussed. (You can also use the **QLEADER** or **LEADER** command if you are connecting the feature control frame to a leader line.) Next, pick the lower image tile in the **Sym** area. When the **Symbol** dialog box is displayed again, pick another geometric characteristic symbol. This results in two symbols displayed in the **Sym** area. Continue specifying the needed information in the lower-level **Tolerance** and **Datum** area compartments. Sample entries for a double feature control frame are shown in Figure 21-29.

Figure 21-29.
Specifying information for a double feature control frame in the **Geometric Tolerance** dialog box.

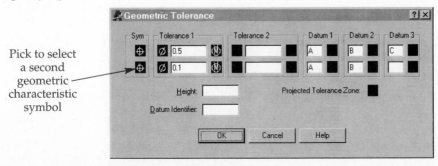

If the two symbols in the **Sym** image tiles are the same, then the double feature control frame is drawn with one geometric characteristic symbol displayed in a single compartment. See Figure 21-30A. This is acceptable if only one geometric characteristic symbol is required for the feature-relating control, but it is inappropriate if you need to display the same geometric characteristic symbol twice. If you are drawing a double feature control frame with different geometric characteristic symbols for a combination control, then the feature control frame must have two separate compartments. See Figure 21-30B.

Figure 21-30.
A—If only one geometric characteristic symbol entered in the **Geometric Tolerance** dialog box is required for display, it is shown once in the first compartment of the double feature control frame. B—If two different symbols are used, they are displayed in separate compartments.

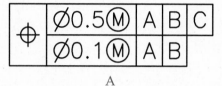
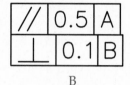

A   B

EXERCISE 21-4

❑ Open drawing EX21-1.
❑ Draw the double feature control frames shown in Figure 21-30.
❑ Save the drawing as EX21-4.

AutoCAD User's Guide 12

DRAWING DATUM FEATURE SYMBOLS

As discussed earlier in this chapter, datums in a drawing are identified by datum feature symbols. You can draw datum feature symbols using the **TOLERANCE**, **QLEADER**, or **LEADER** commands. When you access the **Geometric Tolerance** dialog box, enter the desired datum reference letter in the **Datum Identifier:** text box. See Figure 21-31.

After picking **OK**, place the datum feature symbol at the desired location in your drawing. You can also draw a datum feature symbol connected to a feature control frame by selecting the desired geometric characteristic symbol and entering the necessary information in the **Geometric Tolerance** dialog box. In Figure 21-32, datum feature symbols are shown with and without a feature control frame. Notice that the

Figure 21-31.
Using the **Geometric Tolerance** dialog box to enter a datum-identifying reference letter. This letter is used to create the datum feature symbol.

Specified datum reference letter

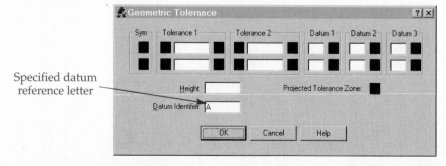

Figure 21-32.
A—A datum feature symbol drawn without a feature control frame.
B—A datum feature symbol drawn with a feature control frame. Note that these symbols do not comply with the ASME Y14.5M-1994 standard.

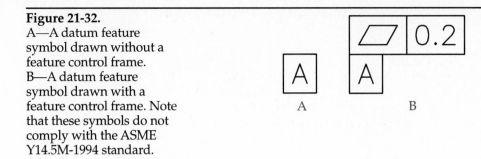

symbols are placed inside squares. This complies with the ANSI Y14.5M-1982 standard, rather than ASME Y14.5M-1994. In order to match the ASME Y14.5M-1994 standard, the symbols need to be drawn as shown in Figure 21-13. One way to do this is to create your own symbols that you can insert as needed. Creating and saving your own symbols for multiple insertion is discussed in Chapter 23.

Before you learn how to create your own symbols, you can modify the symbols shown in Figure 21-32 by establishing a dimension style that uses the **Datum triangle** or **Datum triangle filled** arrowhead type for the leader lines. These leader options are available in the **Leader:** drop-down list in the **Arrowheads** area of the **Lines and Arrows** tab, located in the **Modify Dimension Style** dialog box. Creating dimension styles with the **Dimension Style Manager** and the **Modify Dimension Style** dialog boxes was discussed in Chapter 18.

After creating a dimension style that uses datum triangles for leader arrowheads, enter the **QLEADER** or **LEADER** command to draw a leader segment that connects to the datum feature symbol as shown in Figure 21-33A. This modifies the symbol in Figure 21-32A. Use the object snap modes to help you properly position the leader with the symbol. If you use the **QLEADER** command, pick the leader start point and endpoint, and press [Enter]. Then, press the [Esc] key when prompted for the text width and the annotation text. If you use the **LEADER** command, pick the leader line points, and then use the **None** annotation option to specify no annotation text.

To modify the datum feature symbol shown in Figure 21-32A, you must draw the datum feature symbol, the feature control frame, and the leader line separately. First, draw the datum feature symbol as previously discussed. Then use the **QLEADER** or **LEADER** command to draw a connecting leader segment as shown in Figure 21-33B. Finally, draw the feature control frame and connect it to the datum triangle as shown. The datum feature symbol and the feature control frame can be moved as needed to allow for proper positioning.

Figure 21-33.
A—To draw a datum feature symbol in accordance with ASME Y14.5M-1994, create a dimension style that uses the **Datum triangle** or **Datum triangle filled** leader arrowhead option. Then, use the **QLEADER** or **LEADER** command to connect a leader arrow to the existing symbol. B—If a feature control frame is to be used, the datum feature symbol, leader line, and feature control frame must be drawn separately.

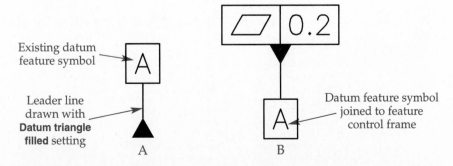

❏ Start a new drawing or use one of your templates.
❏ Draw the datum feature symbol shown in Figure 21-32A.
❏ Modify the symbol to look like the one shown in Figure 21-33A.
❏ Draw the datum feature symbol and feature control frame shown in Figure 21-33B.
❏ Save the drawing as EX21-5.

PROFESSIONAL TIP

Chapter 23 of this text provides a detailed discussion on how to create your own symbol libraries. A *symbol library* is a related group of symbols. It is recommended that you design dimensioning symbols that are not available in AutoCAD, such as the datum feature symbol that is recognized by ASME Y14.5M-1994. This symbol is shown in Figure 21-13.

Your symbol library might include the counterbore, countersink, depth, and other dimensioning symbols illustrated in Figure 21-1. These symbols are easily drawn if you establish a dimension style that uses the gdt.shx font. Chapter 18 explains how to create such a dimension style to help you draw these symbols when needed.

CONTROLLING THE HEIGHT OF THE FEATURE CONTROL FRAME

Referring to Figure 21-9, the height of the feature control frame is shown as twice the height of the text. Text on engineering drawings is generally drawn at a height of .125″ (3mm), which makes the feature control frame height equal to .25″ (6mm). As a result, the distance from the text to the feature control frame should be equal to half the text height. For example, if the height of the drawing text is .125″, the space between the text and the feature control frame should be .0625″ to result in a .25″ high frame.

The distance from the text to the feature control frame is controlled by the **DIMGAP** dimension variable. See Figure 21-34. The default value is .09″. You can change this setting at the command line or by entering a new value in the **Offset from dim line:** text box, located in the **Text Placement** area in the **Text** tab of the **Modify Dimension Style** dialog box. The setting also controls the gap between the dimension line and the dimension text for linear dimensions, and the space between the dimension text and the rectangle for basic dimensions. Basic dimensions are discussed in the next section.

Figure 21-34.
The **DIMGAP** dimension variable setting controls the distance from the text to the feature control frame.

DRAWING BASIC DIMENSIONS

Basic dimensions, discussed earlier in this chapter, can be automatically drawn by accessing the **Text** tab in the **Modify Dimension Style** dialog box. It is recommended that you establish a separate dimension style for basic dimensions, because not all of your dimensions will be basic on a drawing. To use the basic dimensioning feature, activate the **Draw frame around text** check box in the **Text Appearance** area. The resulting image tile displays a drawing with basic dimensions.

As previously discussed, the **Offset from dim line:** setting in the **Text** tab controls the space between the basic dimension text and the rectangle around the dimension. A basic dimension is shown in Figure 21-35.

Figure 21-35.
An AutoCAD basic dimension.

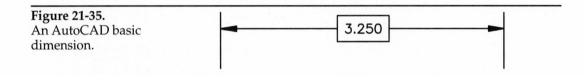

EXERCISE 21-6

❑ Start a new drawing or use one of your templates.
❑ Create a new dimension style named GDT. With the dimension text height set to .125″, change the space between the text and the feature control frame so that it is .0625″, or half the text height.
❑ Use the new dimension style to draw the feature control frame shown in Figure 21-34.
❑ Draw the basic dimension shown in Figure 21-35.
❑ Save the drawing as EX21-6.

EDITING FEATURE CONTROL FRAMES

A feature control frame acts as one object. When you pick any location on the frame, the entire object is selected. You can edit feature control frames using AutoCAD editing commands such as **ERASE**, **COPY**, **MOVE**, **ROTATE**, and **SCALE**. The **STRETCH** command only allows you to move a feature control frame. This effect is similar to the results of using the **STRETCH** command with text objects.

You can edit the values inside a feature control frame by using the **DDEDIT** command. When you enter this command and select the desired frame, the **Geometric Tolerance** dialog box is displayed with all the current values listed. After you make the desired changes and pick **OK**, the feature control frame is shown with the revised information. You can also use the **DDEDIT** command to edit basic dimensions. When you select a basic dimension for editing, the **Multiline Text Editor** is displayed. You can then edit the basic dimension as you would any other dimension.

SAMPLE GD&T APPLICATIONS

This chapter is intended to give you a general overview of GD&T applications and basic instruction on how to draw GD&T symbols using AutoCAD. If you are in the manufacturing industry, you may have considerable use for geometric dimensioning and tolerancing. The support information presented in this chapter may be a review or it may inspire you to learn more about this topic. The drawings in Figure 21-36 are intended to show you some common GD&T applications using the available dimensioning and geometric characteristic symbols.

Figure 21-36.
Examples of typical geometric dimensioning and tolerancing applications using various dimensioning and geometric characteristic symbols.

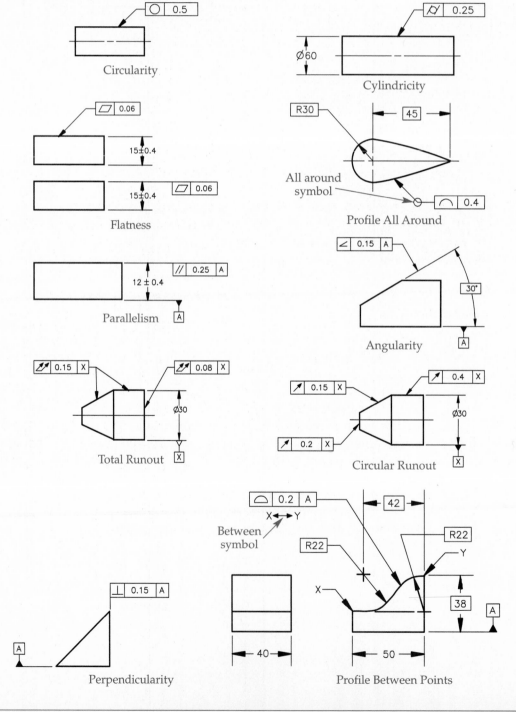

Chapter Test

Answer the following questions on a separate sheet of paper.

1. Identify each of the following geometric characteristic symbols:

   A. —

   B. ⟋⟋

   C. ○

   D. ⟋

   E. ⌒

   F. ⌓

   G. ⊕

   H. ◎

   I. ≡

   J. //

   K. ⊥

   L. ∠

   M. ↗

   N. ⟋↗

2. Identify the parts of the feature control frame shown below:

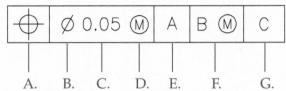

3. Name the current standard for dimensioning and tolerancing that is adopted by the American National Standards Institute and published by the American Society of Mechanical Engineers.
4. Name three commands that can be used to draw a feature control frame.
5. Identify the dialog box that contains settings used to create a feature control frame.
6. How do you access the **Symbol** image tile menu?
7. How do you remove a geometric characteristic symbol from one of the image tiles in the **Sym** area of the **Geometric Tolerance** dialog box?
8. Describe the procedure used to draw a feature control frame connected to a leader line.
9. Describe how to place a projected tolerance zone symbol and height value with the feature control frame.
10. Explain how to create a double feature control frame.
11. Which AutoCAD setting allows you to draw basic dimensions? How is it accessed?
12. Identify the AutoCAD setting that controls the space between the text in a feature control frame and the surrounding frame.
13. Describe how to draw a datum feature symbol without an attached feature control frame. How do you add a leader line with a filled datum triangle to the symbol?
14. Name the command that can be used to edit the existing values in a feature control frame.

Drawing Problems

Create dimension styles that will assist you with the following problems. Draw fully dimensioned multiview drawings. The required number of views depends upon the problem and is to be determined by you. Apply geometric tolerancing as discussed in this chapter. Modify the available AutoCAD drawing applications to comply with ASME Y14.5M-1994 standards. The problems are presented in accordance with ASME Y14.5M-1994.

1. Open drawing P20-5. Edit the drawing by adding the geometric tolerancing applications shown below. If you did not draw P20-5, then start a new drawing and draw the problem now. *Note:* The problem is shown as a cutaway for clarity. You do not need to draw a section. Untoleranced dimensions are ±.02 for two-place decimal precision and ±.005 for three-place decimal precision. Save the drawing as P21-1.

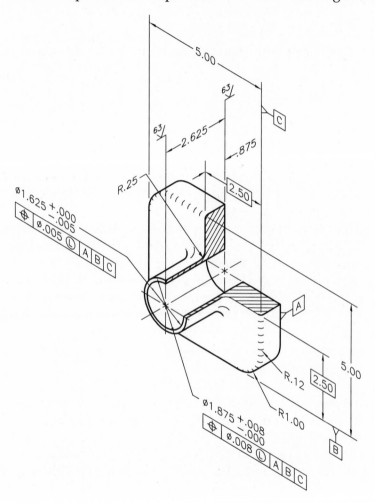

2. Open drawing P20-6. Edit the drawing by adding the geometric tolerancing applications shown below. If you did not draw P20-6, then start a new drawing and draw the problem now. Untoleranced dimensions are ±0.5. Save the drawing as P21-2.

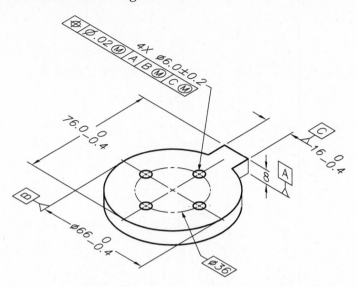

3. Open drawing P20-7. Edit the drawing by adding the geometric tolerancing applications shown below. If you did not draw P20-7, start a new drawing and draw the problem now. Save the drawing as P21-3.

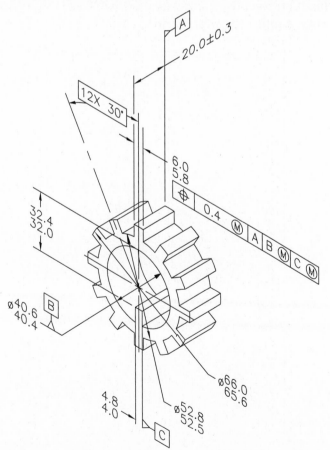

4. Draw the following object as previously instructed. Untoleranced dimensions are ±0.3. Save the drawing as P21-4.

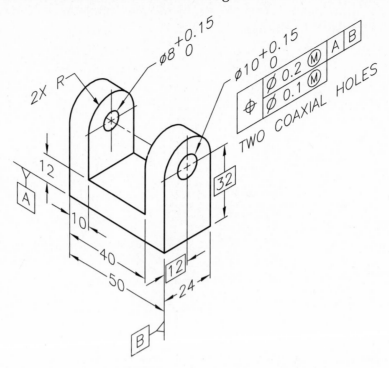

5. Draw the following object as previously instructed. *Note:* The problem is shown with a full section for clarity. You do not need to draw a section. Untoleranced dimensions are ±.010. Save the drawing as P21-5.

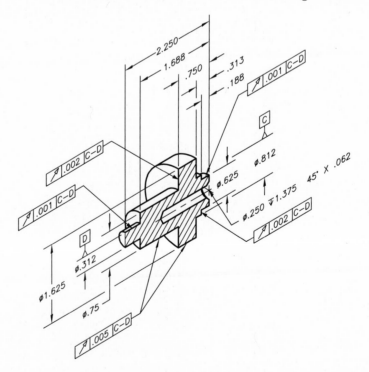

6. Draw the following object as previously instructed. *Note:* The problem is shown with a half section for clarity. You do not need to draw a section. Untoleranced dimensions are ±.010. Save the drawing as P21-6.

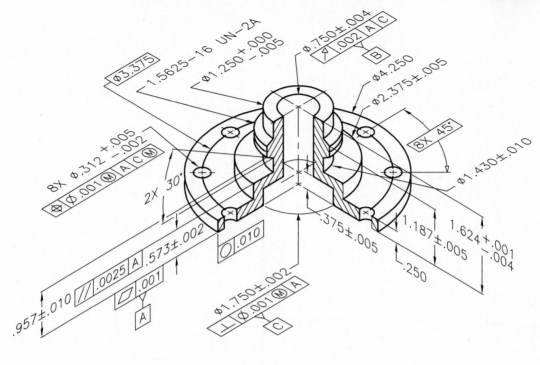

7. Open drawing P18-25. Edit the drawing by adding the geometric tolerancing applications shown below. If you did not draw P18-25, start a new drawing and draw the problem now. Save the drawing as P21-7.

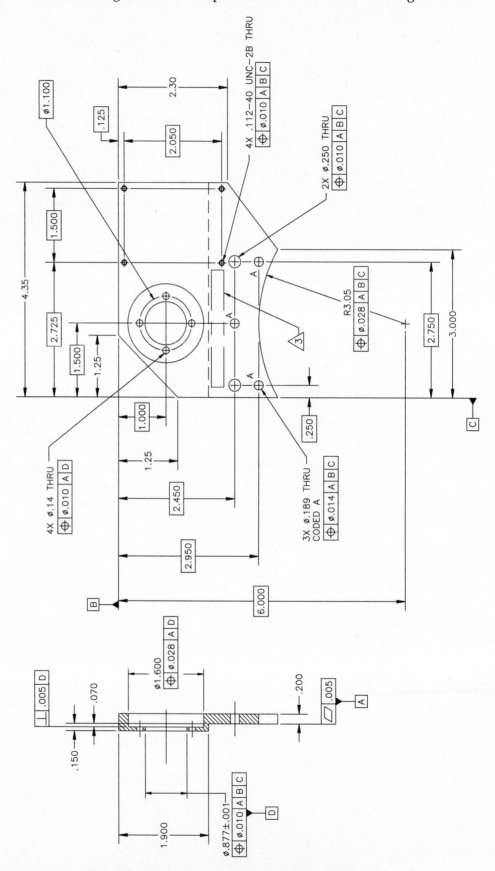

CHAPTER **22**

Drawing Section Views and Graphic Patterns

Learning Objectives

After completing this chapter, you will be able to:

- Identify sectioning techniques.
- Use sections and dimensioning practices to draw objects given in engineering sketches.
- Draw section material using the **BHATCH**, **HATCH**, and **SOLID** commands.
- Prepare graphic displays, such as graphs and logos, using the **BHATCH** and **SOLID** commands.
- Edit existing associative hatch patterns using **HATCHEDIT**.

In mechanical drafting, internal features in multiviews appear as hidden lines. It is poor practice to dimension to hidden lines, but these features must be dimensioned. Therefore, section views are used to clarify the hidden features.

Section views show internal features as if a portion of the object is cut away. They are used in conjunction with multiviews to completely describe the exterior and interior features of an object.

When sections are drawn, a *cutting-plane line* is placed in one of the views to show where the cut was made. The cutting-plane line is the *saw* that cuts through the object to expose internal features. It is drawn with a thick dashed or phantom line in accordance with ASME Y14.2M. The arrows on the cutting-plane line indicate the line of sight when looking at the section view.

The cutting-plane lines are often labeled with letters that relate to the proper section view. A title, such as SECTION A-A, is placed under the view. When more than one section view is drawn, labels continue with B-B through Z-Z. The letters I, O, and Q are not used because they may be confused with numbers.

Labeling multiple section views is necessary for drawings with multiple sections. When only one section view is present and its location is obvious, a label is not needed. Section lines are used in the section view to show where the material has been cut away. See Figure 22-1.

Sectioning is also used in other drafting fields, such as architectural and structural drafting. Cross sections through buildings show the construction methods and materials. See Figure 22-2. The cutting-plane lines used in these fields are often composed of letter and number symbols. This helps coordinate the large number of sections found in a set of architectural drawings.

Figure 22-1.
A three-view
multiview drawing
with a full section
view.

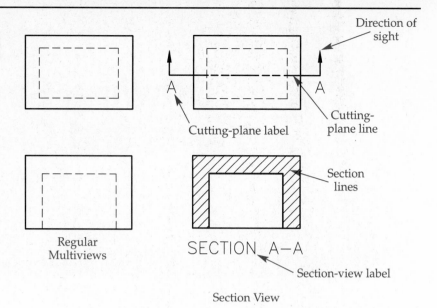

Direction of
sight

A   A

Cutting-plane label

Cutting-
plane line

Regular
Multiviews

Section
lines

SECTION A—A

Section-view label

Section View

Figure 22-2.
An architectural
sectional view.
(Alan Mascord,
Design Associates)

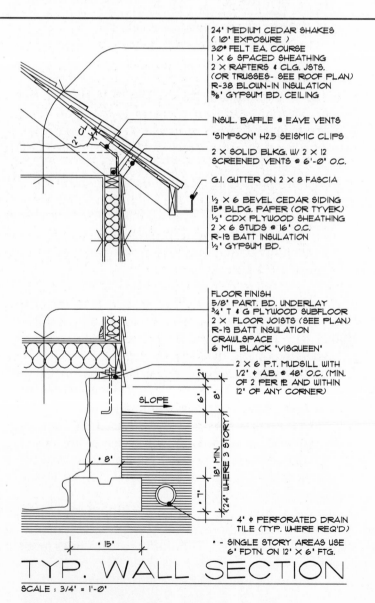

24' MEDIUM CEDAR SHAKES
(10' EXPOSURE)
30# FELT EA. COURSE
1 X 6 SPACED SHEATHING
2 X RAFTERS & CLG. JSTS.
(OR TRUSSES- SEE ROOF PLAN)
R-38 BLOWN-IN INSULATION
⅜' GYPSUM BD. CEILING

INSUL. BAFFLE @ EAVE VENTS

'SIMPSON' H2.5 SEISMIC CLIPS

2 X SOLID BLKG. W/ 2 X 12
SCREENED VENTS @ 6'-0' O.C.

G.I. GUTTER ON 2 X 8 FASCIA

½ X 6 BEVEL CEDAR SIDING
15# BLDG. PAPER (OR TYVEK)
½' CDX PLYWOOD SHEATHING
2 X 6 STUDS @ 16' O.C.
R-19 BATT INSULATION
½' GYPSUM BD.

FLOOR FINISH
5/8' PART. BD. UNDERLAY
¾' T & G PLYWOOD SUBFLOOR
2 X FLOOR JOISTS (SEE PLAN)
R-19 BATT INSULATION
CRAWLSPACE
6 MIL BLACK 'VISQUEEN'

2 X 6 P.T. MUDSILL WITH
1/2' ⌀ A.B. @ 48' O.C. (MIN.
OF 2 PER ⅊ AND WITHIN
12' OF ANY CORNER)

SLOPE

18' MIN.
(24' WHERE 3 STORY)

4' ⌀ PERFORATED DRAIN
TILE (TYP. WHERE REQ'D)

* - SINGLE STORY AREAS USE
6' FDTN. ON 12' X 6' FTG.

TYP. WALL SECTION

SCALE : 3/4' = 1'-∅'

TYPES OF SECTIONS

There are many types of sections available for the drafter to use. The section used depends on the detail to be sectioned. For example, one object may require the section be taken completely through the object. Another may only need to remove a small portion to expose the interior features.

Full sections remove half the object. See Figure 22-1. In this type of section, the cutting-plane line passes completely through the object along a center plane.

Offset sections are the same as full sections, except that the cutting-plane line is staggered. This allows you to cut through features that are not in a straight line. See Figure 22-3.

Figure 22-3.
An offset section.

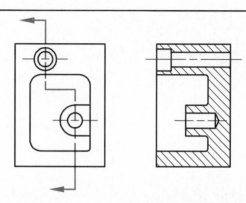

Half sections show one-quarter of the object removed. The term *half* is used because half of the view appears in section and the other half is shown as an exterior view. Half sections are commonly used on symmetrical objects. A centerline is used to separate the sectioned part of the view from the unsectioned portion. Hidden lines are normally omitted from the unsectioned side. See Figure 22-4.

Aligned sections are used when a feature is out of alignment with the center plane. In this case, an offset section will distort the image. The cutting-plane line cuts through the feature to be sectioned. It is then rotated to align with the center plane before projecting into the section view. See Figure 22-5.

Revolved sections clarify the contour of objects that have the same shape throughout their length. The section is revolved in place within the object, or part of the view may be broken away. See Figure 22-6. This section makes dimensioning easier.

Figure 22-4.
A half section.

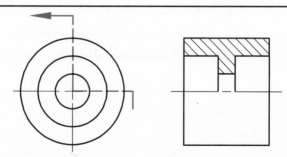

Figure 22-5.
An aligned section.

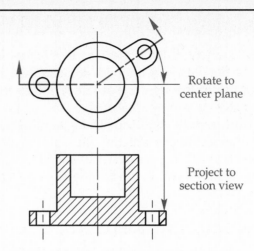

Rotate to
center plane

Project to
section view

Figure 22-6.
A revolved section.

Removed sections serve much the same function as revolved sections. The section view is removed from the regular view. A cutting-plane line shows where the section was taken. When multiple removed sections are taken, the cutting planes and related views are labeled. Drawing only the ends of the cutting-plane lines simplifies the views. See Figure 22-7.

Broken-out sections show only a small portion of the object removed. This section is used to clarify a hidden feature. See Figure 22-8.

Figure 22-7.
Removed sections.

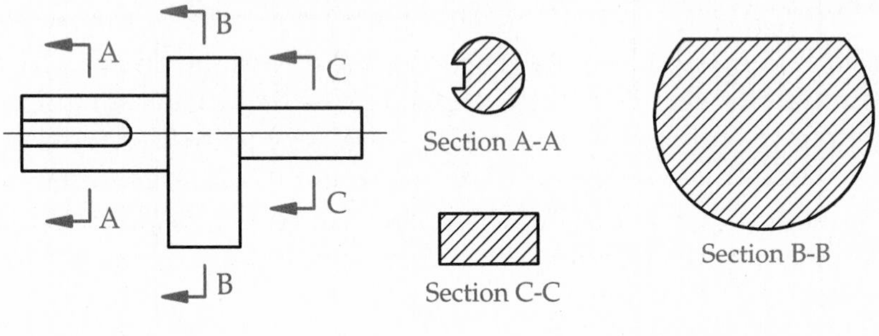

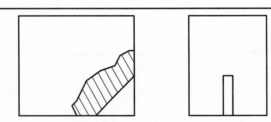

B

A

C

Section A-A

A

C

Section B-B

B

Section C-C

Figure 22-8.
A broken-out
section.

AutoCAD and its Applications—Basics

Section line symbols are placed in the section view to show where material has been cut away. The following rules govern section line symbol usage:

- Section lines are placed at 45° unless another angle is required to satisfy the next two rules.
- Section lines should not be drawn parallel or perpendicular to any other adjacent lines on the drawing.
- Section lines should not cross object lines.
- Avoid section lines placed at angles greater than 75° or less than 15° from horizontal.

Section lines may be drawn using different patterns to represent the specific type of material. Equally-spaced section lines represent a general application. This is adequate in most situations. Additional patterns are not necessary if the type of material is clearly indicated in the title block. Different section line material symbols are needed when connected parts of different materials are sectioned.

AutoCAD has standard section line symbols available. These are referred to as *hatch patterns*. These symbols are located in the acad.pat file. The AutoCAD pattern labeled ANSI31 is the general section line symbol and is the default pattern in a new drawing. It is also used when representing cast iron in a section. The ANSI32 symbol is used for sectioning steel. Other standard AutoCAD hatch patterns are shown in Figure 22-9.

When very thin objects are sectioned, the material may be completely blackened or filled in. AutoCAD refers to this as *solid*. The ASME Y14.2M standard recommends that very thin sections be drawn without section lines or solid fill. When you change to a different hatch pattern, the new pattern becomes the default in the current drawing until it is changed.

Figure 22-9.
Standard AutoCAD hatch patterns. (Autodesk, Inc.)

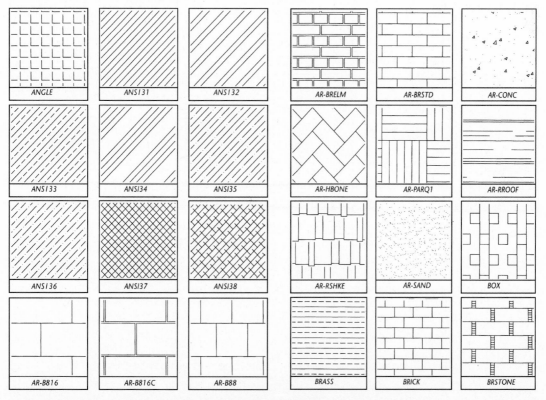

Figure 22-9. *(Continued)*

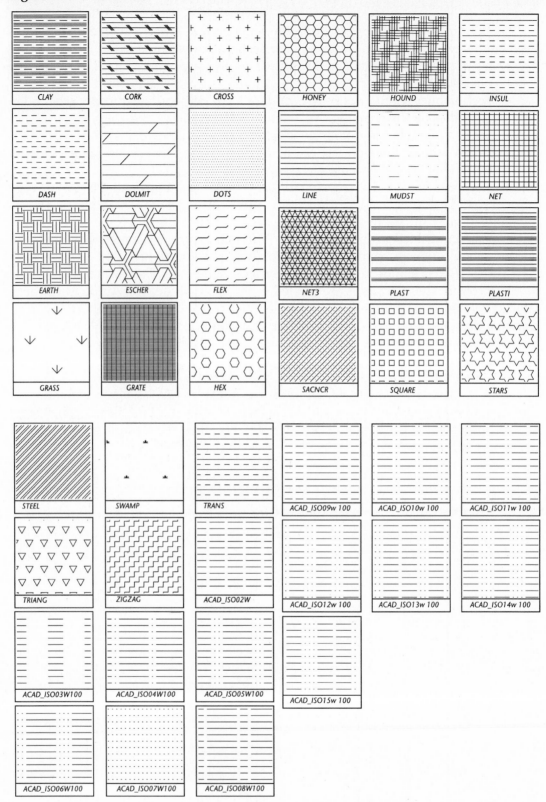

AutoCAD hatch patterns are not limited to sectioning. They can be used as artistic patterns in a graphic layout for an advertisement or promotion. They might also be added as shading on an architectural elevation or technical illustration.

The **BHATCH** command simplifies the hatching process by automatically hatching any enclosed area. Hatch patterns are selected and applied using the **Boundary Hatch** dialog box. Access this dialog box with the **BHATCH** command by picking the **Hatch** button on the **Draw** toolbar, by picking **Hatch...** in the **Draw** pull-down menu, or by entering H or BHATCH at the Command: prompt.

The **Boundary Hatch** dialog box is divided into the **Quick** and **Advanced** tabs. See Figure 22-10. A series of buttons that determine the method of applying the hatch and a **Preview** button are also included.

Figure 22-10.
The **Quick** tab of the **Boundary Hatch** dialog box.

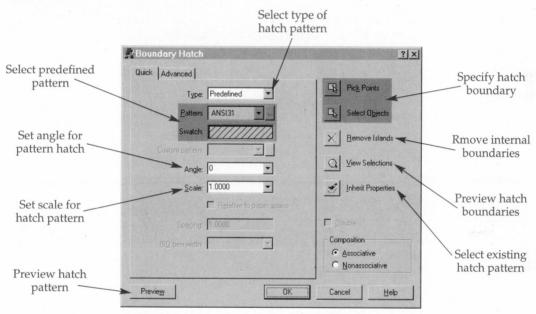

Selecting a Hatch Pattern

The hatch pattern is selected in the **Quick** tab of the **Boundary Hatch** dialog box. The following three categories of hatch patterns are available in the **Type:** drop-down list:

- **Predefined.** These predefined AutoCAD patterns are stored in the acad.pat and acadiso.pat files.
- **User defined.** Selecting this option creates a pattern of lines based on the current linetype in your drawing. You can control the angle and spacing of the lines.
- **Custom.** Specifies a pattern that is defined in any custom PAT file that you have added to the AutoCAD search path. (To use the patterns in the supplied acad.pat and acadiso.pat files, choose Predefined.)

Predefined hatch patterns

AutoCAD has many predefined hatch patterns. These patterns are contained in the acad.pat and acadiso.pat files. To select a predefined hatch pattern, select Predefined

For 2000i Users...

In AutoCAD 2000i, hatch patterns can be selected and inserted directly from **DesignCenter** using a drag-and-drop operation. Refer to *Drag-and-Drop Hatch Patterns*, beginning on page 976.

in the **Type:** drop-down list and then select the predefined pattern. You can select the pattern from the **Pattern:** drop-down list, or you can pick the ellipsis (**...**) button next to the **Pattern:** drop-down arrow to display the **Hatch Pattern Palette** dialog box. See Figure 22-11.

The **Hatch Pattern Palette** provides sample images of the predefined hatch patterns. The hatch patterns are divided among the four tabs: **ANSI**, **ISO**, **Other Predefined**, and **Custom**. Select the desired pattern from the appropriate tab, and pick the **OK** button to return to the **Boundary Hatch** dialog box. The selected pattern is displayed in the **Swatch** tile and listed in the **Pattern:** text box. You can also access the **Hatch Pattern Palette** dialog box by picking the image displayed in the **Swatch** tile.

You can control the angle and scale of any predefined pattern using the **Angle** and **Scale** drop-down lists. For predefined ISO patterns, you can also control the ISO pen width using the **ISO pen width:** drop-down list.

An object can be hatched solid by selecting the SOLID predefined pattern. Figure 22-12 shows examples of solid objects.

Figure 22-11.
The **Hatch Pattern Palette** dialog box can be used to select a predefined or custom hatch pattern.

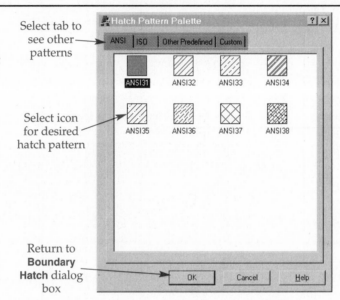

Figure 22-12.
Using the SOLID hatch pattern to make solid objects.

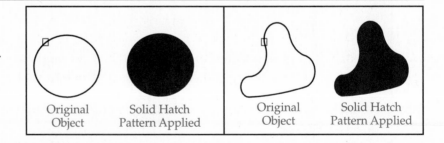

User defined hatch patterns

A user defined hatch pattern is a pattern of lines drawn using the current line-type. The angle for the pattern relative to the X axis is set in the **Angle:** text box, and the spacing between the lines is set in the **Spacing:** text box.

You can also specify double hatch lines by selecting the **Double** check box on the right side of the **Boundary Hatch** dialog box. This check box is only available when User defined is selected in the **Type:** drop-down list. Figure 22-13 shows examples of user defined hatch patterns.

AutoCAD and its Applications—Basics

Figure 22-13.
Examples of different hatch angles and spacing.

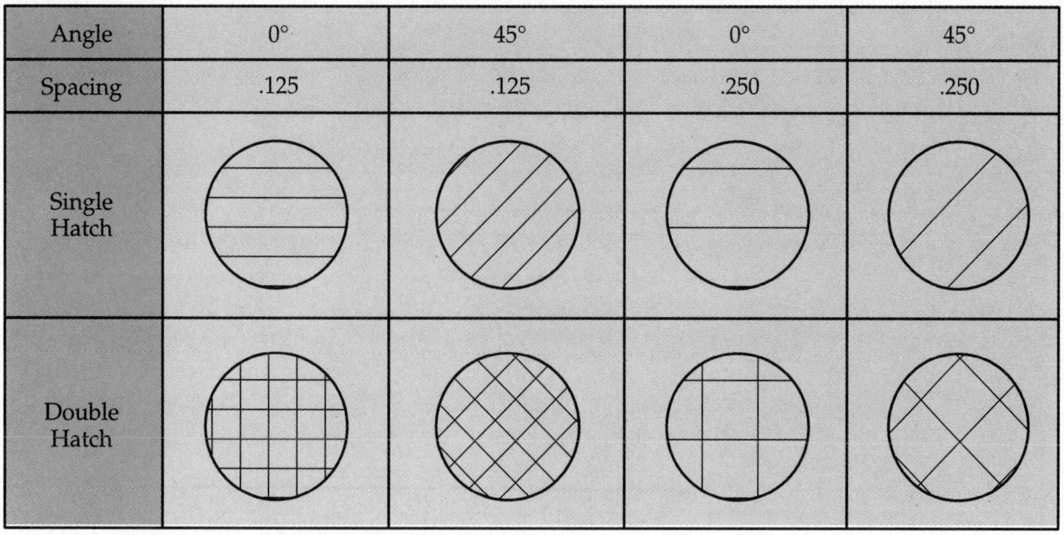

Angle	0°	45°	0°	45°
Spacing	.125	.125	.250	.250
Single Hatch				
Double Hatch				

AutoCAD stores the selected angle in the **HPANG** system variable and the spacing in the **HPSPACE** system variable. AutoCAD stores the setting of the **Double** check box in the **HPDOUBLE** system variable.

Custom hatch patterns

You can create custom hatch patterns and save them in PAT files. When you select **Custom** in the **Type:** drop-down list, the **Custom pattern:** drop-down list is enabled. You can select a custom pattern from this drop-down list, or pick the ellipsis (**...**) button to select the pattern from the **Custom** tab of the **Hatch Pattern Palette** dialog box. You can set the angle and scale of custom hatch patterns, just as you can with predefined hatch patterns.

Selecting an existing pattern

You can specify the hatch pattern by selecting an identical hatch pattern from the drawing. Picking the **Inherit Properties** button allows you to select a previously drawn hatch pattern and use it as the current hatch pattern settings. The prompts looks like this:

> Select associative hatch object: *(pick the desired hatch pattern)*
> Inherited Properties: Name *<hatch name>*, Scale *<hatch scale>*, Angle *<hatch angle>*
> Select internal point: *(pick a point inside the new area to be hatched)*

After the internal point has been picked, the **Boundary Hatch** dialog box is displayed with the settings of the selected pattern.

Hatch Pattern Scale

Predefined and custom hatch patterns can be scaled by entering a value in the **Scale:** text box. The drop-down list contains common scales broken down in .25 increments. The scales in this list start with .25 and go to a scale of 2, although you can type any scale in the text box. AutoCAD stores the selected scale in the **HPSCALE** system variable.

The pattern scale default is 1 (full scale). If the drawn pattern is too tight or too wide, type a new scale. Figure 22-14 shows examples of different scales.

The **Relative to paper space** check box is used to scale the hatch pattern relative to paper space units. Use this option to easily display hatch patterns at a scale appropriate for your layout.

Figure 22-14.
Hatch pattern scale
factors.

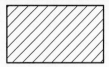 

Scale = 1   Scale = 2   Scale = 3

PROFESSIONAL TIP

When you start AutoCAD with a wizard, the hatch pattern scale factor is automatically set based on the information you provide. The adjusted settings are related to the full scale of the objects you draw. You can leave the settings as established by AutoCAD or you can change them. If you are using a template or starting AutoCAD from scratch, you can set the hatch pattern scale factor to match the drawing size.

Enter a larger scale factor when hatching large areas. This makes your section lines look neater and saves regeneration and plot time. For metric drawings, set the hatch scale to 25.4, because 1″ = 25.4mm.

Selecting Areas to Be Hatched

Areas to be hatched can be selected by one of two methods: picking points or selecting objects. Both of these selection methods are accessed by picking a button in the **Boundary Hatch** dialog box.

Using the **Pick Points** button is the easiest method of defining an area to be hatched. When you pick the button, the drawing returns. Pick a point within the region to be hatched, and AutoCAD automatically defines the boundary around the selected point. The following prompts are displayed:

> Select internal point: *(pick a point inside the area to be hatched)*
> Selecting everything visible…
> Analyzing the selected data…
> Analyzing internal islands…
> Select internal point: *(pick an internal point of another object or* [Enter] *if you are done selecting objects)*

More than one internal point can be selected. When you are finished selecting points, press [Enter] and the **Boundary Hatch** dialog box returns. Then pick the **OK** button, and the feature is automatically hatched. See Figure 22-15.

Figure 22-15.
Defining the hatch boundary by picking a point.

Move the screen cursor
and pick a point inside the
area to be hatched

Selecting the Internal Point   The Results

AutoCAD and its Applications—Basics

When you are at the Select internal point: prompt, you can enter U or UNDO to undo the last selection, in case you picked the wrong area. You can also undo the hatch pattern by entering U at the Command: prompt after the pattern is drawn. However, you can preview the hatch before applying it to save time.

The **Select Objects** button is used to define the hatch boundary if you have items that you want to hatch by picking the object, rather than picking inside the object. See Figure 22-16. These items can be circles, polygons, or closed polylines. This method works especially well if the object to be hatched is crossed by other objects, such as the graph lines that cross the bars in Figure 22-17. Picking a point inside the bar results in the hatch displayed in Figure 22-17A. You can pick inside each individual area of each bar, but this can be time-consuming. If the bars were drawn using a closed polyline, all you have to do is use the **Select Objects** button to pick each bar. See Figure 22-17B.

The **Select Objects** button can also be used to pick an object inside an area to be hatched to exclude it from the hatch pattern. An example of this is the text shown inside the hatch area of Figure 22-18.

Figure 22-16.
Selecting objects to be hatched.

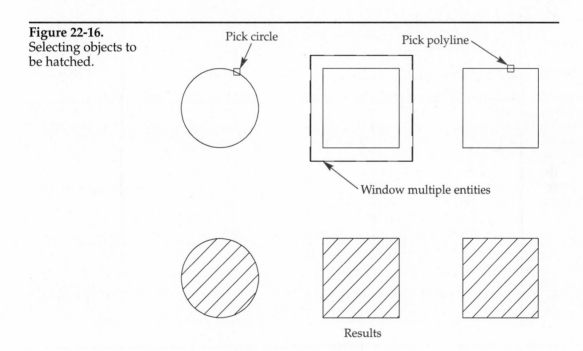

Figure 22-17.
A—Applying a hatch pattern to objects that cross each other using the **Pick Points** button.
B—Applying a hatch pattern to a closed polygon using the **Select Objects** button.

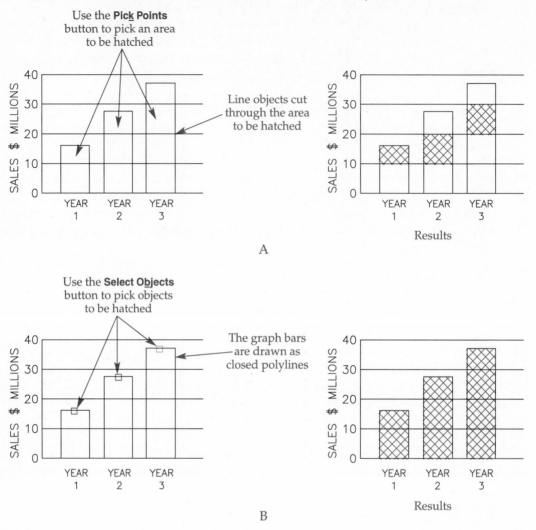

Figure 22-18.
Using the **Select Objects** button to exclude an object from the hatch pattern.

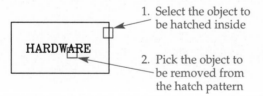

1. Select the object to be hatched inside

2. Pick the object to be removed from the hatch pattern

Results

Islands

Boundaries inside another boundary are known as *islands*. AutoCAD can then either ignore these internal boundary objects and hatch through them or consider them as islands and hatch around them.

When you use the **Pick Points** button to hatch an internal area, islands are left unhatched by default, as shown in Figure 22-19A. However, if you want islands to be hatched, pick the **Remove Islands** button in the **Boundary Hatch** dialog box after selecting the internal point. The graphics window returns with the following prompts:

        Select island to remove: (*pick the islands to remove*)
        ⟨Select island to remove⟩/Undo: ↵

Select the islands to remove and press [Enter] to return to the dialog box. The island objects are now removed from the hatch boundary. See Figure 22-19B.

The **Advanced** tab of the **Boundary Hatch** dialog box allows you to set the island detection style and the island detection method. See Figure 22-20.

The **Island detection style** area is used to specify the method for hatching islands. If no islands exist, specifying an island detection style has no effect. There are three options that allow you to choose the features to be hatched. These options are illustrated by the image tiles in the dialog box. The three style options are:

- **Normal.** This option hatches inward from the outer boundary. If AutoCAD encounters an island, it turns off hatching until it encounters another island. Then the hatching is reactivated. Every other closed boundary is hatched with this option.
- **Outer.** This option hatches inward from the outer boundary. AutoCAD turns hatching off when it encounters an island and does not turn it back on. AutoCAD hatches only the outermost level of the structure and leaves the internal structure blank.
- **Ignore.** This option ignores all islands and hatches everything within the selected boundary.

Figure 22-19.
A—Original objects.
B—Using the **Pick Points** button to hatch an internal area leaves islands unhatched.
C—After picking an internal point, use the **Remove Islands** button and pick the islands. This allows the islands to be hatched.

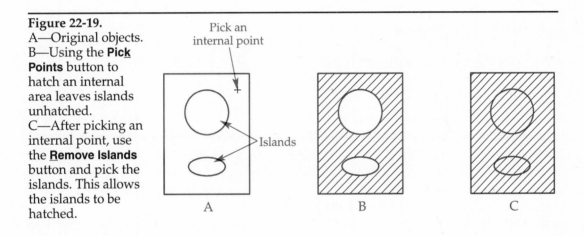

Figure 22-20.
The **Advanced** tab of the **Boundary Hatch** dialog box contains options for island detection and boundary object creation.

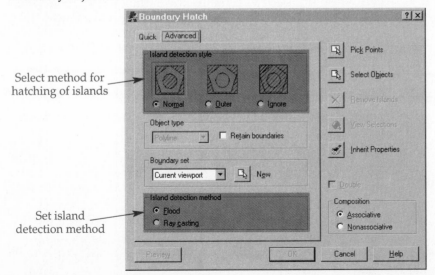

The **Island detection method** area has two options: **Flood** and **Ray casting**. The **Flood** radio button is selected by default. This setting leaves internal objects (islands) unhatched. Pick the **Ray casting** radio button if you want to hatch through islands.

Previewing the Hatch

Before applying a hatch pattern to the selected area, you can use preview tools to be sure the hatch pattern and hatch boundary settings are correct. The following buttons, which are found in the **Boundary Hatch** dialog box, can be used to preview the boundary and hatch pattern:

- **View Selections button.** You can instruct AutoCAD to let you see the boundaries of selected objects. The **View Selections** button is available after picking objects to be hatched. Pick this button and the drawing is displayed with the hatch boundaries highlighted. When you are finished, press [Enter] or the right mouse button to return to the **Boundary Hatch** dialog box.
- **Preview button.** Pick the **Preview** button if you want to look at the hatch pattern before you apply it to the drawing. This allows you to see if any changes need to be made before the hatch is drawn. When using this option, AutoCAD temporarily places the hatch pattern on your drawing and displays <Hit enter or right-click to return to the dialog> at the command line. When finished previewing the hatch, press [Enter] or the right mouse button. The **Boundary Hatch** dialog box is displayed again. Change the hatch pattern, scale, or rotation angle as needed and preview the hatch again. When you are satisfied with the preview of the hatch, pick the **OK** button to have it applied to the drawing.

Hatch Pattern Composition

The **BHATCH** command creates associative hatch patterns by default, but can be set to create nonassociative patterns. *Associative hatch patterns* update automatically when the boundary is edited. If the boundary is stretched, scaled, or otherwise edited, the hatch pattern automatically fills the new area with the original hatch pattern. Associative hatch patterns can be edited using the **HATCHEDIT** command, which is discussed later in this chapter.

The **Composition** area of the **Boundary Hatch** dialog box has **Associative** and **Nonassociative** radio buttons. The **Associative** option is on by default. When selected, the **Nonassociative** option creates a nonassociative hatch that is independent of its boundaries. This means that if you pick only the hatch boundary to edit, the hatch pattern does not change with it. For example, if you pick a hatch boundary to scale, only the boundary is scaled while the pattern remains the same. You need to select both the boundary and the pattern before editing if you want to modify both.

EXERCISE 22-1

❏ Start AutoCAD and use one of your templates with a Hatch layer.
❏ Open the **Boundary Hatch** dialog box. Pick the ellipsis (...) button next to **Pattern:** to view the pattern lists and images. Select several different images to see what happens.
❏ Use the **LINE** command to draw an object similar to the one shown here. The exact dimensions are up to you. Be sure each area of the object is closed.
❏ Use the **BHATCH** command to make a full section of the object, as shown in the right object. Use the ANSI31 hatch pattern.
❏ Draw the bar graph shown in Figure 22-17 without text. Use a closed polyline to draw the graph bars. Use the **Select Objects** option to select the bars for hatching.
❏ Draw the HARDWARE box shown in Figure 22-18. Hatch the area inside the box without hatching the text.

AutoCAD and its Applications—Basics

❑ Use closed polylines to draw the object in Figure 22-19A. Copy the object to a position directly below the original. Use the **Pick Points** option to hatch the object as shown in Figure 22-19B. Use the **Pick Points** button and the **Remove Islands** button to hatch the object as shown in Figure 22-19C.

❑ Preview each hatch pattern before you apply it, to be sure the results are what you expect.

❑ Initiate the **BHATCH** command and pick the **Inherit Properties** button. Pick a hatch pattern on your drawing that is different from the current hatch pattern settings. Notice that the name and settings of the selected pattern becomes current.

❑ Save the drawing as EX22-1.

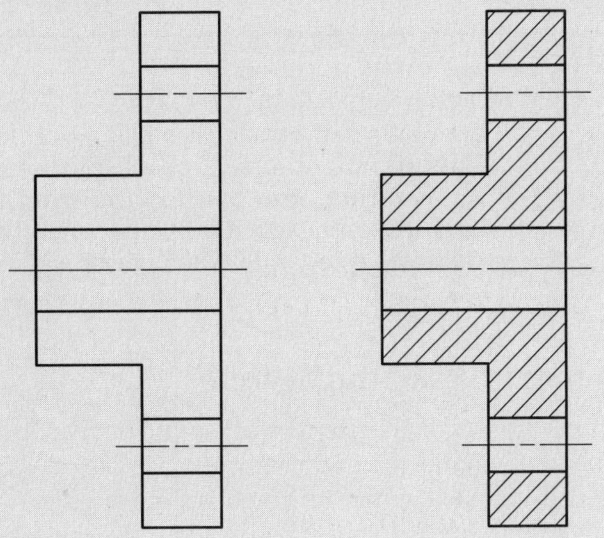

Object to be Hatched   Applied Hatch

Correcting Errors in the Boundary

The **BHATCH** command works well unless you have an error in the hatch boundary. The most common error is a gap in the boundary. This can be very small and difficult to detect, and happens when you do not close the geometry or use object snaps for accuracy. However, AutoCAD is quick to let you know by displaying the **Boundary Definition Error** alert box. See Figure 22-21. Pick the **OK** button and then return to the drawing to find and correct the problem. Figure 22-22 shows an object where the corner does not close. The error is too small to see on the screen, but using the **ZOOM** command reveals the problem. Fix the error and use the **BHATCH** command again.

Another error message occurs when you pick a point outside the boundary area. When this happens, you also get the **Boundary Definition Error** alert. All you have to do is pick **OK** and then select a point inside the boundary you want hatched.

Figure 22-21.
A **Boundary Definition Error** alert box is displayed if problems occur in your hatching operation.

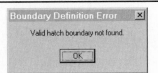

Figure 22-22.
Using the **ZOOM** command to find the source of the hatching error.

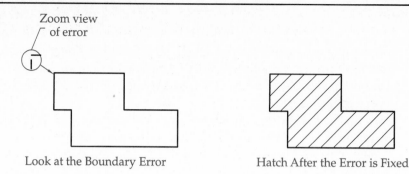

Look at the Boundary Error

Hatch After the Error is Fixed

PROFESSIONAL TIP	When creating an associative hatch, it is best to specify only one internal point per hatch block placement. If you specify more than one internal point in the same operation, AutoCAD creates one hatch object from all points picked. This can cause unexpected results when trying to edit what appears to be a separate hatch object.

Improving Boundary Hatching Speed

In most situations, boundary hatching works with satisfactory speed. Normally, the **BHATCH** command evaluates the entire drawing visible on screen to establish the boundary. This process can take some time on a large drawing.

You can improve the hatching speed and resolve other problems using options found in the **Advanced** tab in the **Boundary Hatch** dialog box. See Figure 22-23.

The drop-down list in the **Boundary set** area specifies what is evaluated when hatching. The default setting is Current viewport. If you want to limit what AutoCAD evaluates when hatching, you can define the boundary area so the **BHATCH** command only considers a specified portion of the drawing. To do this, pick the **New** button. Then at the Select objects: prompt, use a window to select the features of the object to be hatched. This is demonstrated in Figure 22-24.

Figure 22-23.
The **Advanced** tab of the **Boundary Hatch** dialog box provides options to improve hatching efficiency.

Create boundary object around hatch pattern

Default setting

Pick to limit boundary set area

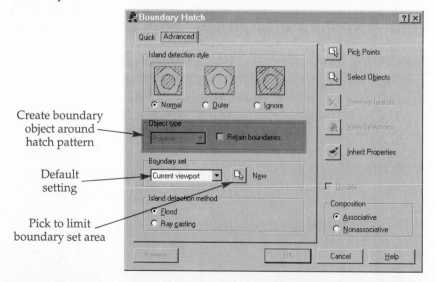

AutoCAD and its Applications—Basics

Figure 22-24.
The boundary set limits the area that AutoCAD evaluates during a boundary hatching operation.

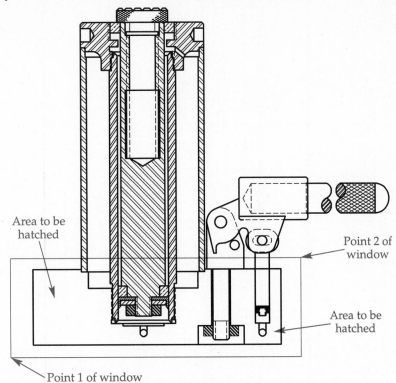

Area to be hatched

Point 2 of window

Area to be hatched

Point 1 of window

After selecting the object(s), the **Boundary Hatch** dialog box returns, displaying the **Advanced** tab. Notice in the **Boundary set** area that the drop-down now displays Existing set as shown in Figure 22-25. The drawing with hatch patterns applied is shown in Figure 22-26.

You can make as many boundary sets as you wish. However, the last one made remains current until another is created. The **Retain boundaries** check box in the **Object type** area can be selected as soon as a boundary set is made. Checking this box allows you to keep the boundary of a hatched area as a polyline, and continues to save these as polylines every time you create a boundary area. The default is no check in this box, so the hatched boundaries are not saved as polylines.

When you use the **BHATCH** command and pick an internal area to be hatched, AutoCAD automatically creates a temporary boundary around the area. If the **Retain boundaries** check box is unchecked, the temporary boundaries are automatically removed when the hatch is complete. However, if you check the **Retain boundaries** check box, the hatch boundaries are kept when the hatch is completed.

When the **Retain boundaries** check box is checked, the **Object type** drop-down list is activated. See Figure 22-27. Notice that the drop-down list has two options: Polyline (the default) and Region. If Polyline is selected, the boundary is a polyline object around the hatch area. If Region is selected, then the hatch boundary is the hatched region. A *region* is a closed two-dimensional area.

Figure 22-25.
When the **Boundary set** area displays Existing set in the drop-down list, AutoCAD only evaluates objects in the boundary for the hatch.

Boundary set

Existing set   New

Figure 22-26.
Results of hatching the drawing in Figure 22-24 after selecting a boundary set.

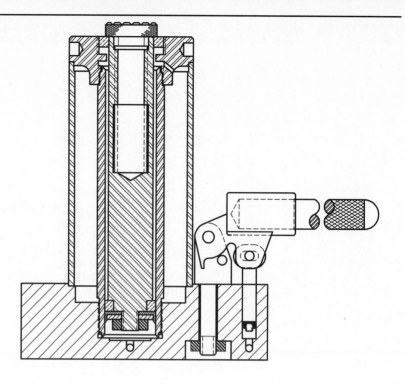

Figure 22-27.
There are two object type options for the boundary. These options are only available if **Re̲tain boundaries** is checked.

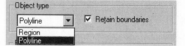

PROFESSIONAL TIP

There are a number of techniques that can help you save time when hatching, especially with large and complex drawings. These include the following:

- Zoom in on the area to be hatched to make it easier for you to define the boundary. When you zoom into an area to be hatched, the hatch process is much faster because AutoCAD does not have to search the entire drawing to find the hatch boundaries.
- Preview the hatch before you apply it. This allows you to easily make last minute adjustments.
- Turn off layers where there are lines or text that might interfere with your ability to accurately define hatch boundaries.
- Create boundary sets of small areas within a complex drawing to help save time.

Using the **HATCH** command at the Command: prompt also allows you to hatch objects. Entering -H (a hyphen followed by H) or HATCH at the Command: prompt displays the following command sequence options:

HATCH
-H

> Command: **-H** *or* **HATCH**↵
> Enter pattern name or [?/Solid/User defined] <ANSI31>:

Entering ? gives you this prompt:

> Enter pattern(s) to list <*>:

You can enter the name or names of specific hatch patterns, or press [Enter] to accept the wildcard (*), which lists all the hatch patterns in the **AutoCAD Text Window**.

To create a user defined hatch pattern, select the **User defined** option. You are then prompted to enter an angle and spacing.

The island detection method can be specified when the hatch pattern is selected. The three style options are Normal (hatches every other feature), Outer (hatches outermost feature area only), and Ignore (ignores all interior features and hatches the entire object). These options were discussed earlier in the chapter.

Any one of the options can be used by typing the desired pattern followed by a comma and the option. For example, entering NET3,O at the Enter pattern name or [?/Solid/User defined] prompt results in the Outer island detection style being used with the Net3 hatch pattern.

After selecting the pattern, you are then asked to define the pattern scale and angle.

> Enter pattern name or [?/Solid/User defined] <ANSI31>: ↵
> Specify a scale for the pattern <1.0000>: ↵
> Specify an angle for the pattern <0>: ↵

The hatch scale can be specified referencing model space, if desired. However, it is much simpler to reference the scale to paper space. This allows the scale factor to be based on the plotted scale of the drawing. To do this, enter XP after the scale. For example, entering 1XP as the scale factor causes AutoCAD to automatically calculate the actual scale required within model space to match the specified value of 1 in paper space:

> Specify a scale for the pattern <1.0000>: **1XP**↵

When you do this, notice that the next use of the **HATCH** command offers the actual pattern scale calculated by AutoCAD as the default. It is not necessary to enter 1XP again since the default value shown is the model space equivalent. Model space and paper space are discussed in detail in Chapters 9 and 10 of this text.

An alternative method of entering values for this prompt is by picking two points in the drawing. AutoCAD then measures the distance and uses it as the scale factor. This method does not allow the **XP** option to be used.

After setting the scale and angle, the following prompt appears:

> Select objects to define hatch boundary or <direct hatch>,
> Select objects:

By default, the area to be hatched is defined by selecting objects. There is no option to define the boundary by selecting an internal point. However, you can press [Enter] at the Select objects: prompt to activate the **direct hatch** option. When using the **direct hatch** option, you define the boundary by selecting points. The following prompts appear:

> Select objects to define hatch boundary or <direct hatch>,
> Select objects: ↵ *(press* [Enter] *to access the* **direct hatch** *option)*
> Retain polyline boundary? [Yes/No] <N>: ↵

The direct hatching option places a polyline boundary around the area to be hatched. You can keep the polyline or delete it based on your response to the Retain polyline boundary? [Yes/No]: prompt. When you pick the first point of the polyline boundary, you get options that are just like the **PLINE** command:

Specify start point: *(pick start point)*
Specify next point or [Arc/Close/Length/Undo]: *(specify corners of boundary)*
Specify next point or [Arc/Close/Length/Undo]: ↵
Specify start point for new boundary or <apply hatch>: *(press* [Enter] *to apply hatch pattern or select another point to define another boundary)*

You can draw another polyline boundary or you can press [Enter] to have the hatch drawn in the boundary you just finished. You do not have to draw a hatch pattern in a predefined area. You can draw a hatch pattern anyplace using the direct hatching method.

NOTE

As previously mentioned, an *associative* pattern is a hatch pattern that is automatically updated when an object is edited. Patterns drawn with the **HATCH** command are *nonassociative*. This means that if you pick only the hatch boundary to edit, the hatch pattern does not change with it.

Making Individual Line Hatch Patterns

When you use the **HATCH** command and draw a hatch pattern using any of the designated hatch names, the pattern is drawn as a block. This means that the entire hatch pattern acts as one object. For example, if you pick one line of the pattern to erase, the entire hatch pattern is erased. You can make each line of the hatch pattern an individual object by typing an asterisk (*) before the hatch pattern name:

Command: **-H** *or* **HATCH**↵
Enter a pattern name or [?/Solid/User defined] <ANSI31>: ***ANSI31**↵

The rest of the command sequence works as previously discussed. Now, each line in the hatch pattern is a single object. This allows you to edit the lines individually. Include all the lines in a selection set if you want to edit them together. The individual line hatch pattern remains as default until changed. Be sure to change it if you want to draw the next hatch pattern as a block. A hatch pattern can also be exploded to create individual lines.

Hatching around Text

AutoCAD automatically places an imaginary box around the text in a hatch boundary. Hatch patterns are not placed inside these imaginary boxes. The text must also be selected as an element of the hatch boundary for this to work properly. An example is the bar graph shown in Figure 22-28. Always place the text before hatching the area. When you are prompted to select objects, pick the object to be hatched and then the text to be hatched around.

The object and the text are picked individually. You can also window both for this to work.

AutoCAD and its Applications—Basics

Figure 22-28.
Hatching around
text.

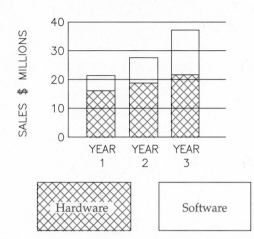

THREE YEAR SALES
PERFORMANCE

EDITING HATCH PATTERNS

You can edit hatch boundaries and hatch patterns with grips and editing commands such as **ERASE**, **COPY**, **MOVE**, **ROTATE**, and **SCALE**. If a hatch pattern is associative, whatever you do to the hatch boundary is automatically done to the associated hatch pattern. As explained earlier, a hatch pattern is associative if the **Associative** radio button in the **Boundary Hatch** dialog box is active.

A convenient way to edit a hatch pattern is by using the **HATCHEDIT** command. You can access this command by picking **Hatch...** in the **Modify** pull-down menu, picking the **Edit Hatch** button on the **Modify II** toolbar, or entering HE or HATCHEDIT at the Command: prompt. The command sequence is as follows:

> Command: **HE** or **HATCHEDIT**↵
> Select associative hatch object: *(pick the hatch pattern to edit)*

When you select a hatch pattern or patterns to edit, the **Hatch Edit** dialog box is displayed. See Figure 22-29. The **Hatch Edit** dialog box has the same features as the **Boundary Hatch** dialog box, except that only the items that control hatch pattern characteristics are available.

The available features work just like they do in the **Boundary Hatch** dialog box. You can change the pattern type, scale, or angle; remove the associative qualities; set the inherit properties of an existing hatch pattern; or use the **Advanced** tab options to edit the hatch pattern. You can also preview the edited hatch before applying it to your drawing.

Figure 22-29.
The **Hatch Edit**
dialog box is used
to edit hatch
patterns. Notice that
only the options
related to hatch
characteristics are
available.

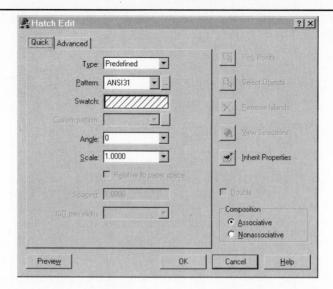

EXERCISE 22-3

❑ Start AutoCAD and use one of your templates that has a Hatch layer.
❑ Draw each of the objects displayed at each of the A positions shown below.
❑ Be sure the hatch pattern is associative.
❑ Copy the objects at the A positions to B and C positions.
❑ Use the **HATCHEDIT** command to change the hatch pattern of the A objects to the
representation found at B and C positions.
❑ Adjust the hatch pattern, scale, angle, and style to obtain the figures shown.
❑ Save as EX22-3.

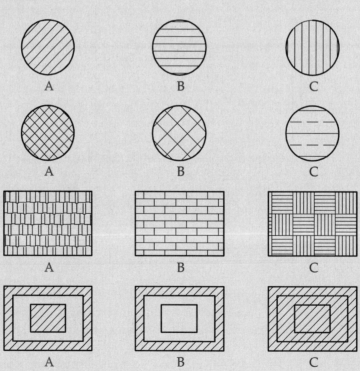

AutoCAD and its Applications—Basics

Editing Associative Hatch Patterns

When you edit an object with an associative hatch pattern, the hatch pattern changes to match the edit. For example, the object in Figure 22-30A is stretched and the hatch pattern matches the new object. When the island in Figure 22-30B is erased, the hatch pattern is automatically revised to fill the area where the island was located. As long as the original boundary is being edited, the associative hatch will update. After you erase the island in Figure 22-30B, a new island cannot be added, because it was not originally calculated to be a part of the hatch boundary.

Figure 22-30.
Editing objects with associative hatch patterns. The hatch pattern changes to match the edit.

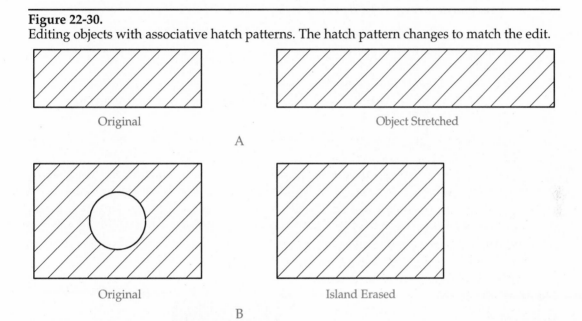

Original   Object Stretched

A

Original   Island Erased

B

EXERCISE 22-4

❏ Start AutoCAD and use one of your templates.
❏ Use the **BHATCH** command to create associative hatch patterns during this exercise.
❏ Draw the original hatched object shown in Figure 22-30A. Copy the object to the right of the original and then use the **STRETCH** command to stretch the copied object into the edited object. NOTE: Try this using grips on the boundary after you use the **STRETCH** command.
❏ Draw the original hatched object with the island shown in Figure 22-30B. Copy the object to the right of the original. Use the **MOVE** command to move the island inside the rectangle. Move the island outside of the rectangle boundary, what happens? Move the island back into the rectangle, then erase the island to see what happens.
❏ Save the drawing as EX22-4.

DRAWING OBJECTS WITH SOLID FILLS

In previous chapters, you have learned that polylines, polyarcs, trace segments, and doughnuts may be filled in solid when **FILL** mode is on. When **FILL** is off, these objects are drawn as outlines only. The **SOLID** command works in much the same manner except that it fills objects or shapes that are already drawn and fills areas that are simply defined by picking points.

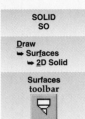

SOLID
SO

Draw
➥ Surfaces
➥ 2D Solid

Surfaces
toolbar

2D Solid

The **SOLID** command is accessed by picking the **2D Solid** button from the **Surfaces** toolbar, picking **2D Solid** from the **Surfaces** cascading menu in the **Draw** pull-down menu, or entering SO or SOLID at the Command: prompt. You are then prompted to select points. If the object to fill solid is rectangular, pick the corners in the numbered sequence shown in Figure 22-31.

Notice that AutoCAD prompts you for another third point after the first four. This prompt allows you to fill in additional parts of the same object, if needed. AutoCAD assumes that the third and fourth points of the previous solid are now points one and two for the next solid. The subsequent points you select fill in the object in a triangular fashion. Continue picking points, or press [Enter] to stop. The following sequence draws the object shown in Figure 22-32.

Command: **SO** or **SOLID**↵
Specify first point: *(pick point 1)*
Specify second point: *(pick point 2)*
Specify third point: *(pick point 3)*
Specify fourth point or <exit>: *(pick point 4 and the rectangular portion is drawn)*
Specify third point: *(pick point 5)*
Specify fourth point or <exit>: ↵
Specify third point: ↵

Different types of solid arrangements can be drawn by altering the numbering sequence. See Figure 22-33. Also, the **SOLID** command can be used to draw filled shapes without prior use of the **LINE**, **PLINE**, or **RECTANG** commands; simply pick the points. Consider using various object snap modes when picking the points of existing geometry.

Figure 22-31.
Using the **SOLID** command. Select the points in the order shown.

Figure 22-32.
The **SOLID** command allows you to enter a second "third point" (point 5 here) after entering the fourth point.

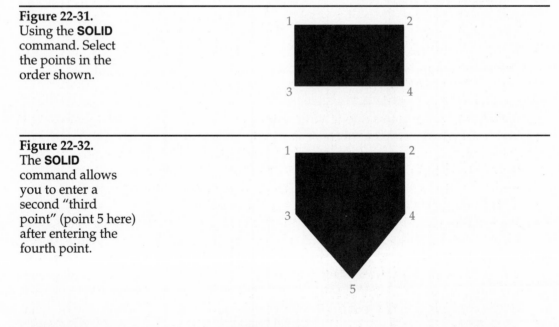

Figure 22-33.
Using a different numbering sequence for the **SOLID** command will give you different results.

EXERCISE 22-5

❏ Start AutoCAD and use one of your templates.
❏ Create a new layer named Solid-Magenta and draw all solids on this layer.
❏ Practice using the **SOLID** command by drawing the objects shown in Figures 22-31, 22-32 , and 22-33.
❏ Save the drawing as EX22-5.

Chapter Test

Answer the following questions on a separate sheet of paper.
For Questions 1–6, name the type of section identified in each of the following statements:
1. Half of the object is removed, the cutting-plane line generally cuts completely through along the center plane.
2. Used primarily on symmetrical objects, the cutting-plane line cuts through one-quarter of the object.
3. The cutting-plane line is staggered through features that do not lie in a straight line.
4. The section is turned in place to clarify the contour of the object.
5. This section is rotated and located from the object. The location of the section is normally identified with a cutting-plane line.
6. Remove a small portion of the view to clarify an internal feature.
7. AutoCAD's standard section line symbols are called _____.
8. In which pull-down menu can you select **Hatch...** to display the **Boundary Hatch** dialog box?
9. Name the command that lets you automatically hatch an enclosed area just by picking a point inside the area.
10. Explain the purpose and function of the ellipsis (...) buttons in the **Boundary Hatch** dialog box.
11. Identify two ways to select a predefined hatch pattern in the **Boundary Hatch** dialog box.
12. Explain how you set a hatch scale in the **Boundary Hatch** dialog box.
13. What command allows you to change a hatch pattern (where all elements of the hatch are one unit) so that each element is an individual entity.
14. Explain how to use an existing hatch pattern on a drawing as the current pattern for your next hatch.
15. Describe the purpose of the **Preview** button found in the **Boundary Hatch** dialog box.
16. What happens if you try to hatch an area where there is a gap in the boundary?
17. How do you limit AutoCAD hatch evaluation to a specific area of the drawing?

18. Define *associative hatch pattern*.
19. How do you change the hatch angle in the **Boundary Hatch** dialog box?
20. Describe the fundamental difference between using the **Pick Points** and the **Select Objects** buttons in the **Boundary Hatch** dialog box.
21. If you use the **Pick Points** button inside the **Boundary Hatch** dialog box to hatch an area, how do you hatch around an island inside the area to be hatched?
22. How do you use the **BHATCH** command to hatch an object with text inside without hatching the text?
23. Name the command that may be used to edit existing associative hatch patterns.
24. How does the **Hatch Edit** dialog box compare to the **Boundary Hatch** dialog box?
25. Explain the three island detection style options.
26. What happens if you erase an island inside an associated hatch pattern?
27. How do you draw a hatch pattern without displaying the boundary?
28. What is the result of stretching an object that is hatched with an associative hatch pattern?
29. Identify three ways to create a solid circle.
30. How do you access the Solid pattern when using the **HATCH** command?

Drawing Problems

For Problems 1–4, use the following guidelines:
A. Use an appropriate template with a mechanical drawing title block.
B. Create separate layers for views, dimensions, and section lines.
C. Place the following general notes 1/2" from the lower-left corner.

> 2. REMOVE ALL BURRS AND SHARP EDGES
> 1. INTERPRET PER ASME Y14.5M-1994
> NOTES:

1. Draw the full section shown on the right. Save the drawing as P22-1.

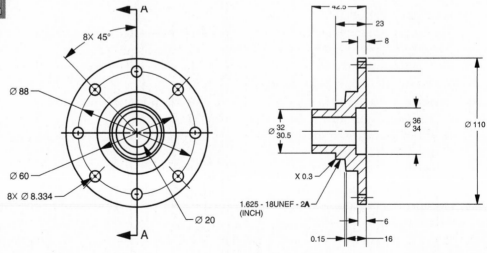

Name: Hub
Material: Cast Iron

2. Draw the half section shown in the center. Add the additional notes: OIL QUENCH 40-45C, CASE HARDEN .020 DEEP, and 59-60 ROCKWELL C SCALE. Save the drawing as P22-2.

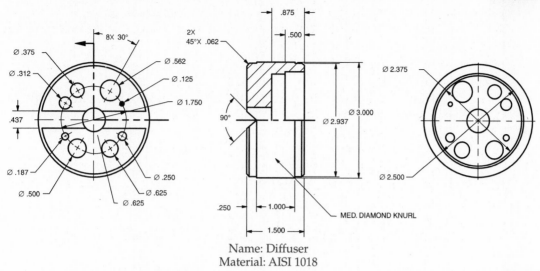

Name: Diffuser
Material: AISI 1018

3. Draw the aligned section shown on the right. Add the additional notes: FINISH ALL OVER 1.63mm UNLESS OTHERWISE SPECIFIED and ALL DIMENSIONS ARE IN MILLIMETERS. Save the drawing as P22-3.

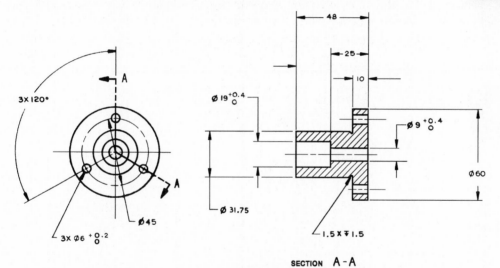

Name: Bushing
Material: SAE 1030

4. Draw the aligned section shown on the right. Add the additional notes: FINISH ALL OVER 1.63mm UNLESS OTHERWISE SPECIFIED and ALL DIMENSIONS ARE IN MILLIMETERS. Save the drawing as P22-4.

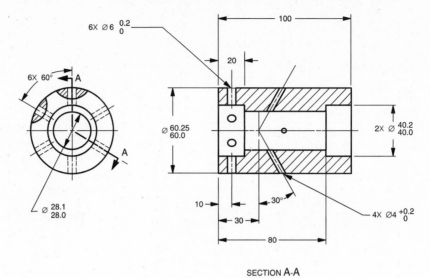

SECTION A-A

Name: Nozzle
Material: Phosphor Bronze

For Problems 5–15, draw the following problems using commands discussed in this chapter and in previous chapters. Use templates that are appropriate for the specific problems. Use text styles that correlate with the problem content. Place dimensions and notes when needed. Make your drawings proportional to the given problems when dimensions are not given. Save each of the drawings as P22-(problem number).

5.

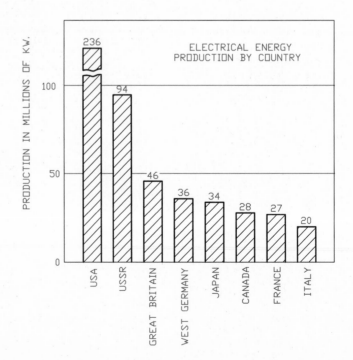

6.

COMPONENT LAYOUT

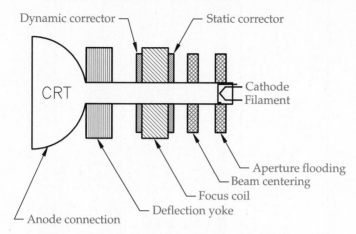

Dynamic corrector — Static corrector

CRT

Cathode
Filament

Aperture flooding
Beam centering
Focus coil
Deflection yoke
Anode connection

7.

SOLOMAN SHOE COMPANY

PERCENT OF TOTAL SALES EACH DIVISION

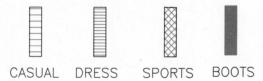

CASUAL   DRESS   SPORTS   BOOTS

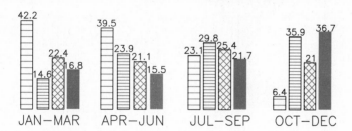

42.2   39.5   35.9   36.7
                    29.8 25.4
        23.9 21.1   21.7   21
   14.6   15.5 23.1
        16.8   6.4

JAN—MAR   APR—JUN   JUL—SEP   OCT—DEC

8.

DIAL TECHNOLOGIES
EXPENSE BUDGET
FISCAL YEAR

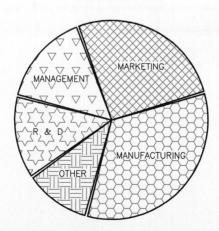

MARKETING

MANAGEMENT

R & D

MANUFACTURING

OTHER

9.

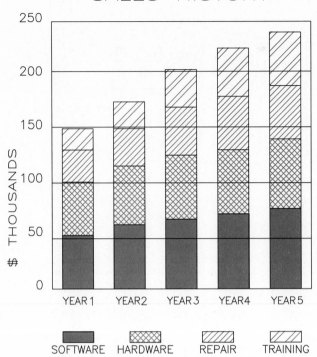

SALES HISTORY

10.

11.

Architectural
Design
Consultants

12.

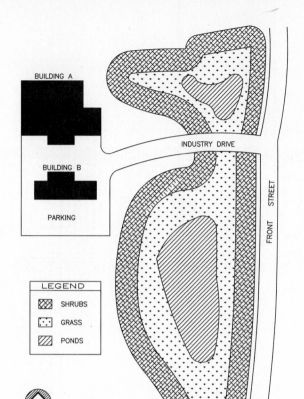

BUILDING A

BUILDING B

PARKING

INDUSTRY DRIVE

FRONT STREET

LEGEND

SHRUBS

GRASS

PONDS

13.

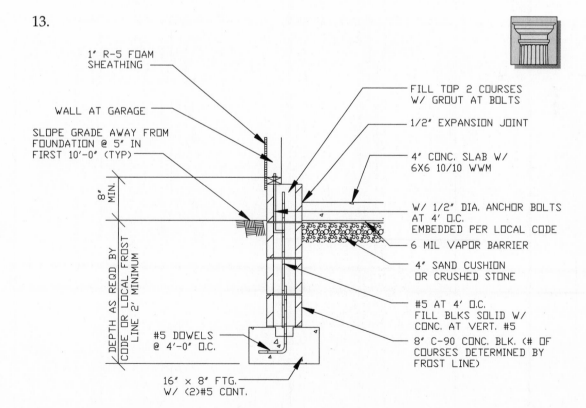

1" R-5 FOAM
SHEATHING

WALL AT GARAGE

SLOPE GRADE AWAY FROM
FOUNDATION @ 5" IN
FIRST 10'-0" (TYP)

8" MIN.

DEPTH AS REQD BY
CODE OR LOCAL FROST
LINE 2' MINIMUM

#5 DOWELS
@ 4'-0" O.C.

16" × 8" FTG.
W/ (2)#5 CONT.

FILL TOP 2 COURSES
W/ GROUT AT BOLTS

1/2" EXPANSION JOINT

4" CONC. SLAB W/
6X6 10/10 WWM

W/ 1/2" DIA. ANCHOR BOLTS
AT 4' O.C.
EMBEDDED PER LOCAL CODE

6 MIL VAPOR BARRIER

4" SAND CUSHION
OR CRUSHED STONE

#5 AT 4' O.C.
FILL BLKS SOLID W/
CONC. AT VERT. #5

8" C-90 CONC. BLK. (# OF
COURSES DETERMINED BY
FROST LINE)

14.

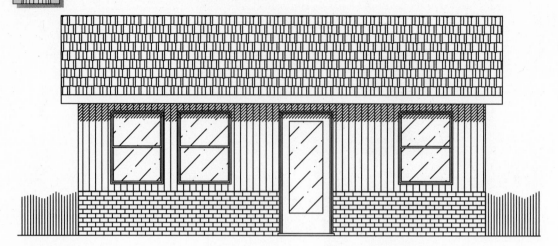

Creating Symbols for Multiple Use

Learning Objectives

After completing this chapter, you will be able to:

- Create and save blocks.
- Insert blocks into a drawing.
- Edit a block and update it in a drawing.
- Insert drawings and blocks into drawings using the **AutoCAD DesignCenter**.
- Create blocks that are saved independent of the drawing.
- Construct and use a symbol library of blocks.

One of the greatest benefits of AutoCAD is its ability to store symbols for future use. These symbols, or *blocks*, can be inserted into a drawing and scaled and rotated in one operation. If a block is edited, drawings containing the block can be updated to include the new version. There are two types of blocks used in AutoCAD. A *block* created with the **BLOCK** command is stored within a drawing. A *wblock* created with the **WBLOCK** command is saved as a separate drawing file and can be used in any drawing. Since any AutoCAD drawing can be inserted into another drawing, a wblock provides *global* access (access to any drawing), as opposed to *local* access (access to the current drawing only). Both types of blocks can be used to create a *symbol library*, which is a related group of symbols.

When a drawing is inserted or referenced, it becomes part of the drawing on screen, but its content is not added to the current drawing file. Any named objects, such as blocks and layers, are referred to as *dependent symbols*. When a dependent symbol is revised, a drawing that references it is automatically updated by AutoCAD the next time it is opened.

CREATING SYMBOLS AS BLOCKS

AutoCAD User's Guide 13

The ability to draw and store symbols is one of the greatest time-saving features of AutoCAD. The **BLOCK** command is used to create a symbol and keep it within a specific drawing file. The block can then be inserted as many times as needed into the drawing in which it was defined. A pre-drawn block created with the **WBLOCK** command can be inserted as many times as needed into *any* drawing. Upon insertion, both types of blocks can be scaled and rotated to meet the drawing requirements.

Constructing Blocks

A block can be any shape, symbol, view, or drawing that you use more than once. Before constructing a block, review the drawing you are working on. This is where a sketch of your drawing can be useful. Look for any shapes, components, notes, and assemblies that are used more than once. These can be drawn once and then saved as blocks.

Existing drawings can also be used as blocks. This can be done two different ways:
- Use the **BASE** command to assign an insertion point to the drawing to be used as a block.
- Use the **INSERT** command to insert the existing drawing into the drawing you are working on.

These two methods are discussed later in this chapter.

PROFESSIONAL TIP

Blocks that vary in size from one drawing to the next should be drawn to fit inside a one-unit square. It does not matter if the object is measured in feet, inches, or millimeters. This makes it easy to scale the symbol later when you insert it into a drawing.

Drawing the Block Components

Draw a block as you would any other drawing geometry. If you want the block to have the color and linetype of the layer it will be inserted on, be sure to set layer 0 current before you begin drawing the block. If you forget to do this and draw the objects on another layer, simply use the **Properties** window or **Object Properties** toolbar to place all the objects on layer 0 before using the **BLOCK** command.

When you finish drawing the object, determine the best location on the symbol to use as an insertion point. When you insert the block into a drawing, the symbol is placed with its insertion point on the screen cursor. Several examples of commonly used blocks with their insertion points highlighted are shown in Figure 23-1.

If it is important that the block maintains a specific color and linetype regardless of the layer it is to be used on, be sure to set the color and linetype before drawing the objects. On the other hand, if the block can assume the current color and linetype when the block is inserted into a drawing, set the current object color and linetype to ByBlock.

Figure 23-1.
Common drafting symbols and their insertion points for placement on drawings. The insertion points are shown as colored dots.

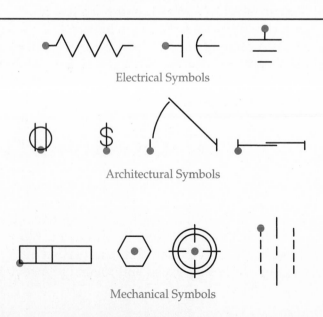

Electrical Symbols

Architectural Symbols

Mechanical Symbols

AutoCAD and its Applications—Basics

To set the color to ByBlock, pick ByBlock in the **Color Control** drop-down list of the **Object Properties** toolbar. You can also pick **Color…** from the **Format** pull-down menu to access the **Select Color** dialog box. Pick the **ByBlock** button in the **Logical Colors** area, Figure 23-2.

To set the linetype to ByBlock, pick ByBlock in the **Linetype Control** drop-down list of the **Object Properties** toolbar. Or, pick **Linetype…** from the **Format** pull-down menu to display the **Linetype Manager** dialog box. Pick ByBlock in the **Linetype** list and then pick the **Current** button. See Figure 23-3.

Once the current color and linetype are both set to ByBlock, you can create blocks. A block created with these settings assumes the current color and linetype when it is inserted into a drawing, regardless of the current layer setting.

Figure 23-2.
After picking **Color…** from the **Format** pull-down menu to display the **Select Color** dialog box, pick the **ByBlock** button to have the block assume the current color when it is inserted into a drawing.

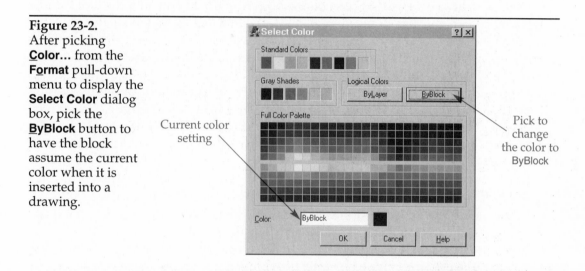

Figure 23-3.
To set the ByBlock linetype current, pick ByBlock in the **Linetype** list of the **Linetype Manager** dialog box and then pick the **Current** button.

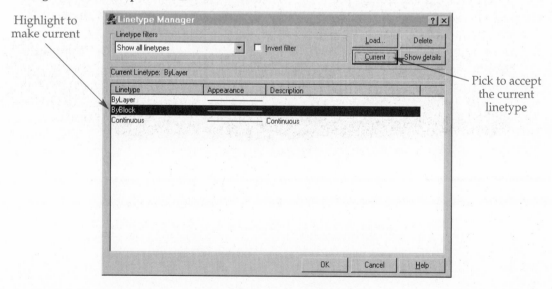

BLOCK.⌐
BMAKE or B.⌐

Draw
➥ Block
Make...

Draw
toolbar

Make Block

Creating Blocks

When you draw a shape or symbol, you have not yet created a block. To save your object as a block, pick the **Make Block** button in the **Draw** toolbar, pick **Make...** from the **Block** cascading menu in the **Draw** pull-down menu, or enter B, BLOCK, or BMAKE at the Command: prompt. Any one of these methods displays the **Block Definition** dialog box, Figure 23-4. The process for creating a block is as follows:

1. In the **Name:** text box, enter a name for the block, such as PUMP. The name cannot exceed 255 characters. It can include numbers, letters, and spaces, as well as the dollar sign ($), hyphen (-), and underscore (_).

2. In the **Objects** area, pick the **Select objects** button to use your pointing device to select objects for the block definition. The drawing area returns and you are prompted to select objects. Select all the objects that will make up the block. Press [Enter] when you are done. The **Block Definition** dialog box reopens, and the number of objects selected is shown in the **Objects** area. If you want to create a selection set, use the **Quick Select** button to define a filter for your selection set.

3. In the **Objects** area, specify whether to retain, convert, or delete the selected objects. If you want to keep the selected objects in the current drawing (in their original state), pick the **Retain** radio button. If you want to replace the selected objects with one of the blocks you are creating, pick the **Convert to block** radio button. If you want to remove the selected objects after the block is defined, pick the **Delete** radio button.

4. In the **Base point** area, enter the coordinates for the insertion base point or pick the **Pick point** button to use your pointing device to select an insertion point.

5. In the **Description:** text box, enter a textual description to help identify the block for easy reference, such as This is a vacuum pump symbol.

6. In the **Preview icon** area, specify whether to create an icon from the block definition. The purpose of the icon is to provide a preview image when using the **AutoCAD DesignCenter**. The **AutoCAD DesignCenter** is discussed later in this chapter. You may want icons for your most important blocks, but you can have an icon for every block if you wish. To omit an icon from the block definition, pick the **Do not include an icon** radio button. To save an icon with the block definition, pick the **Create icon from block geometry** radio button. An image of the icon is then displayed to the right.

7. Use the **Insert units:** drop-down list to specify the type of units the **AutoCAD DesignCenter** will use when inserting the block.

8. After you have finished defining the block, pick **OK**.

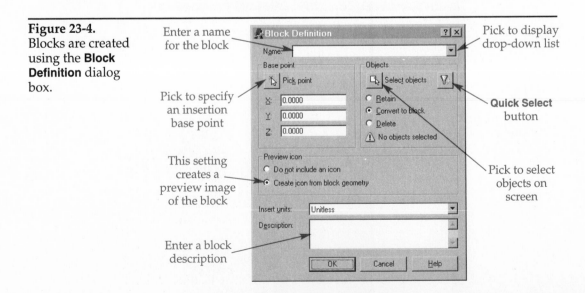

Figure 23-4.
Blocks are created using the **Block Definition** dialog box.

Enter a name for the block

Pick to specify an insertion base point

This setting creates a preview image of the block

Enter a block description

Pick to display drop-down list

Quick Select button

Pick to select objects on screen

The **Convert to block** radio button is active by default. If you select the **Delete** option and then decide that you want to keep the original geometry in the drawing after you have defined the block, you can enter the **OOPS** command. This returns the original objects to the screen, whereas entering U at the Command: prompt or picking the **Undo** button from the **Standard** toolbar removes the block from the drawing.

To verify that the block was saved properly, access the **Block Definition** dialog box. Pick the **Name:** drop-down list button to display a list of all blocks in the current drawing, Figure 23-5. The block names are organized in numerical and alphabetical order. If there are more than six blocks in your drawing, a scroll bar appears to the right of the list so that you can access the remaining blocks.

The **-BLOCK** command can also be used to create new blocks and list existing blocks. Access this command by typing **-B** or **-BLOCK** at the Command: prompt. When the **-BLOCK** command is entered, the options in the **Block Definition** dialog box are presented as prompts on the command line. To display a list of block names, use the **?** option as follows:

-BLOCK
-B

Command: **-B** *or* **-BLOCK**↵
Enter block name or [?]: **?**↵
Enter block(s) to list <*>:

Press [Enter] to list all of the blocks in the current drawing. The following information is then displayed in the **AutoCAD Text Window**:

Defined blocks.
  "PUMP"

User Blocks	External References	Dependent Blocks	Unnamed Blocks
1	0	0	0

This listing reports each block name, as well as the different types of blocks and the number of each type in the drawing. When you create a block, you have actually created a *block definition*. Therefore, the first entry in the block listing is that of *defined* blocks. *User blocks* are those created by you. *External references* are drawings referenced with the **XREF** command. (External references are discussed in Chapter 24.) Blocks that reside in a referenced drawing are called *dependent blocks*. *Unnamed blocks* are objects such as associative dimensions and hatch patterns.

Try stepping through the process of creating a block again. Draw a one-unit square and name it PLATE. See Figure 23-6. After creating the block, be sure to confirm that the PLATE block was saved by using the **-BLOCK** command.

Figure 23-5.
A list of blocks in the current drawing is accessed by picking the **Name:** drop-down list button in the **Block Definition** dialog box.

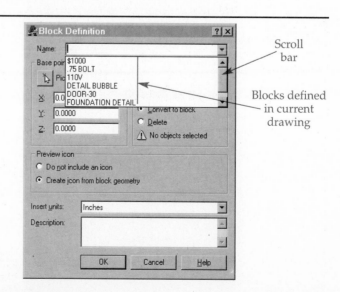

Figure 23-6.
The procedure for drawing a one-unit square and defining it as a block. A—Draw the block. B—Pick the insertion base point. C—Select the square using the **Window** selection option or any other suitable option.

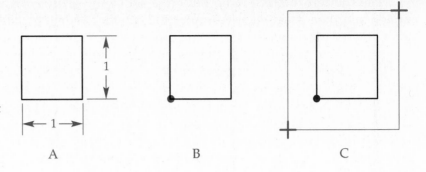

A
B
C

PROFESSIONAL TIP

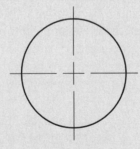

Blocks can be used when creating other blocks. Suppose you design a complex part or view that will be used repeatedly. You can insert existing blocks into the view and then save the entire object as a block. This is called *nesting*, where larger blocks contain smaller blocks. The larger block must be given a different name. Proper planning and knowledge of all existing blocks can speed up the drawing process and the creation of complex parts.

EXERCISE 23-1

❑ Start a new drawing or use one of your templates. Specify decimal units.
❑ Set layer 0 current. Draw a circle with a one-unit diameter and add centerlines as shown below.
❑ Create a block of the circle and centerlines and name it CIRCLE.
❑ Pick the center of the circle as the insertion base point.

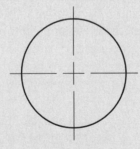

❑ Save the drawing as EX23-1.

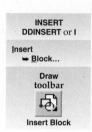
Once a block has been created, it is easy to insert it into a drawing. First, determine a proper size and rotation angle for the block. Blocks are normally inserted on specific layers, so set the proper layer *before* inserting the block. Once a block has been inserted into a drawing, it is referred to as a ***block reference***.

Inserting Blocks

Blocks are placed on your drawing with the **INSERT** command. Enter I, INSERT, or DDINSERT at the Command: prompt, pick the **Insert Block** button from the **Draw** toolbar, or pick **Block...** from the **Insert** pull-down menu. This accesses the **Insert** dialog box, Figure 23-7.

INSERT
DDINSERT or I

Insert
→ Block...

Draw
toolbar

Insert Block

Figure 23-7.
The **Insert** dialog box allows you to select and prepare a block for insertion. Select the block you wish to insert from the drop-down list or enter the block name in the **Name:** text box.

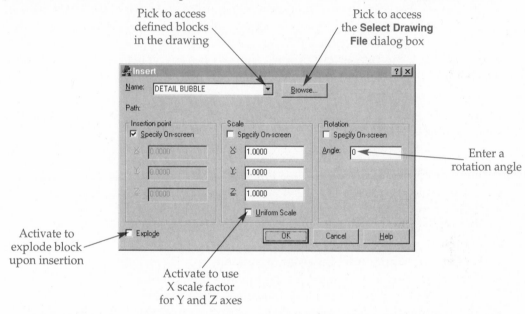

Pick the **Name:** drop-down list button to access the defined blocks in the current drawing. Highlight the name of the block you wish to insert. If the list of block names is long, use the scroll bar to display additional blocks. You may also enter the name of the block in the **Name:** text box. Once the desired block has been chosen, you must specify the insertion location, scale, and rotation angle. You can also specify whether to explode the block upon inserting it. The option buttons and other features in the **Insert** dialog box are described as follows:

- **Browse... button.** Pick this button to display the **Select Drawing File** dialog box and select a drawing file for insertion into the current drawing.
- **Insertion point area.** If the **Specify On-screen** check box is activated, you can pick an insertion point on screen and insert the block dynamically. If you wish to insert the block using absolute coordinates, disable the check box and enter the coordinates in the **X:**, **Y:**, and **Z:** text boxes. Entering coordinates in this manner is referred to as using *preset values*. If preset values are used, the block is immediately inserted at the specified coordinates when you pick **OK**.

- **Scale area.** The **Scale** area allows you to specify scale values for the block in relation to the X, Y, and Z axes. By default, the **Specify On-screen** check box is inactive. This causes the block to be inserted at a one-to-one scale once the insertion point has been selected. If you want to be prompted for the scale at the command line when inserting the block, activate the **Specify On-screen** check box. If the check box is inactive, you can enter scale values in the **X:**, **Y:**, and **Z:** text boxes. If you activate the **Uniform Scale** check box, you can simply specify a scale value for the X axis. The same value is then used for the Y and Z axes when the block is inserted.
- **Rotation area.** The **Rotation** area allows you to insert the block at a specified angle. By default, the **Specify On-screen** check box is inactive and the block is inserted at an angle of zero. If you want to use a different angle, enter a value in the **Angle:** text box. If you want to be prompted for the rotation angle at the command line when inserting the block, activate the **Specify On-screen** check box.
- **Explode check box.** When a block is created, it is saved as a single object. Therefore, it is defined as a single object when inserted in the drawing, no matter how many objects were used to create the block. Activate the **Explode** check box if you wish to explode the block into its original objects for editing purposes. If you explode the block upon insertion, it will assume its original properties, such as its original layer, color, and linetype.

When you pick the **OK** button, prompts appear for any values defined as **Specify On-screen** in the **Insert** dialog box. If you are specifying the insertion point on-screen, the following prompt appears:

Specify insertion point or [Scale/X/Y/Z/Rotate/PScale/PX/PY/PZ/PRotate]: *(pick the point to insert the block)*

If you select one of the options, the new value will override any setting in the **Insert** dialog box. The following options are available:
- **Scale.** This option affects the overall scale of the X, Y, and Z axes.
- **X.** Entering this option affects only the X scale factor.
- **Y.** Entering this option affects only the Y scale factor.
- **Z.** Entering this option affects only the Z scale factor.
- **Rotate.** This option sets the rotation angle.
- **PScale.** This option allows you to preview the scale of the X, Y, and Z axes. You are then prompted to enter the actual scale factors.
- **PX.** This option allows you to preview the scale of the X axis. You are then prompted to enter the actual scale factor.
- **PY.** This option allows you to preview the scale of the Y axis. You are then prompted to enter the actual scale factor.
- **PZ.** This option allows you to preview the scale of the Z axis. You are then prompted to enter the scale factor.
- **PRotate.** This option is used to preview the rotation angle. You are then prompted to enter the actual rotation angle.

If you are specifying the scale factor, the following prompt appears:

Enter X scale factor, specify opposite corner, or [Corner/XYZ] <1>: *(pick a point, or enter a value for the scale)*

Moving the cursor scales the block dynamically as it is dragged. If you want to scale the block visually, pick a point when the object appears correct. If you enter an X scale factor or press [Enter] to accept the default scale value, you are then prompted with the following:

Enter Y scale factor <use X scale factor>: *(enter a value or press [Enter] to accept the same scale specified for the X axis)*
Specify rotation angle <0>: *(pick a point, enter a value for the rotation angle and press [Enter], or press [Enter] to accept the default angle)*

The X and Y scale factors allow you to stretch or compress the block to suit your needs. This is why it is a good idea to draw blocks to fit inside a one-unit square. It makes the block easy to scale because you can enter the exact number of units for the X and Y dimensions. If you want the block to be three units long and two units high, respond with the following:

Enter X scale factor, specify opposite corner, or [Corner/XYZ] <1>: **3**↲
Enter Y scale factor <use X scale factor>: **2**↲

Notice that the prompt for the Y scale factor allows you to accept the X scale factor for Y by simply pressing [Enter]. The object shown in Figure 23-8 was given several different X and Y scale factors using the **INSERT** command.

Figure 23-8.
A comparison of different X and Y scale factors used for inserting the PLATE block.

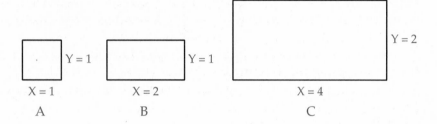

A   B   C

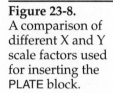

PROFESSIONAL TIP

A block's rotation angle can also be based on the current UCS. If you want to insert a block at a specific angle based on the current UCS or an existing UCS, be sure the proper UCS is active. Then insert the block and use a rotation angle of zero. If you decide to change the UCS later, any inserted blocks retain their original angle.

Block Insertion Options

It is possible to create a mirror image of a block by simply entering a negative value for the scale factor. For example, entering -1 for both the X scale factor and the Y scale factor mirrors the block to the opposite quadrant of the original orientation specified and retains the original size. Different mirroring techniques are shown in Figure 23-9. The insertion point is indicated by a dot.

Figure 23-9.
Negative and positive scale factors have different effects when used to insert a block.

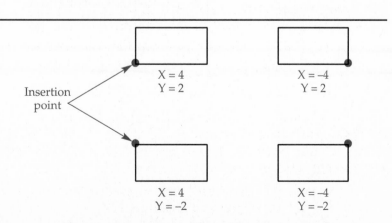

An approximate dynamic scaling technique is made possible by using the **Corner** option inside the **INSERT** command sequence. You can size the block dynamically as you move the cursor if the **DRAGMODE** system variable is set to **Auto**. Use the **Corner** option as follows:

Enter X scale factor, specify opposite corner, or [Corner/XYZ] <1>: **C**↵
Specify opposite corner: *(move the cursor to change the size of the block and pick a point or enter absolute coordinates)*

If you pick a point on screen, be sure to pick a point above and to the right of the insertion point to insert the block as drawn. Picking a corner point below or to the left of the insertion point generates a mirror image such as those shown in Figure 23-9.

In addition to the scaling options previously discussed, a block that is scaled during insertion can be classified as a *real block*, a *schematic block*, or a *unit block*. A ***real block*** is one that is drawn at a one-to-one scale. It is then inserted into the drawing using 1 for both the X and Y scale factors. Examples of real blocks could include a car design, a bolt, or a pipe fitting. See Figure 23-10A.

A ***schematic block*** is a block that is originally drawn at a one-to-one scale. It is then inserted into the drawing using the scale factor of the drawing for both the X and Y scale values. Examples of schematic blocks could include notes, detail bubbles, or section symbols. See Figure 23-10B.

Unit blocks are also originally drawn at a one-to-one scale. There are three different types of unit blocks. One example of a *1D unit block* is a 1″ line object that is turned into a block. A *2D unit block* is any object that can fit inside a 1″ × 1″ square. A *3D unit block* is any object that can fit inside a 1″ cube. To use a unit block, insert the block and determine the individual scale factors for each axis. For example, a 1D unit block could be inserted at a scale of 4, which would turn the line into a 4″ line. A 2D unit block could be assigned different scale factors for the X and Y axes, such as 48 for the X axis and 72 for the Y axis. See Figure 23-10C. A 3D unit block could be inserted at different scales for the X, Y, and Z axes.

Figure 23-10.
A—Real blocks, such as this car, are drawn at a one-to-one scale and inserted using a scale factor of 1 for both the X and Y axes. B—A schematic block is inserted using the scale factor of the drawing for the X and Y axes. C—A 2D unit block can be inserted at different scales for the X and Y axes.

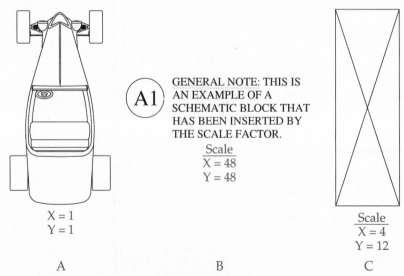

❏ Open EX23-1 if it is not currently on your screen.
❏ Draw a 1 × 1 square on layer 0 and define it as a block named PLATE.
❏ Insert the PLATE block into the drawing. Enter an X scale factor of 6 and a Y scale factor of 4.
❏ Insert the CIRCLE block twice into the drawing as shown. The small circle is one unit in diameter and the large circle is 1.5 units in diameter.
❏ Make a block of the entire drawing and name it PLATE-1. Pick the lower-left corner as the insertion point.
❏ Insert the PLATE-1 block into your drawing and enter a scale of –1, –1. Also during insertion, rotate the object 45°.

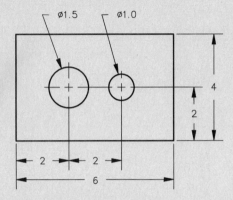

❏ Save the drawing as EX23-2.

The Effects of Layers on Blocks

Blocks retain the property characteristics of the layer(s) on which they were drawn. In Chapter 4, you learned that all objects in AutoCAD are created in ByLayer mode by default. This means that the object color and linetype properties are dictated by the layer on which objects are created. For example, suppose the CIRCLE block was drawn on layer 1 with the color red and a dashed linetype. When inserted, the block appears red and dashed, no matter what layer it is inserted on. If different colors, linetypes, or even layers are used in a block, they also remain the same when the block is inserted on a different layer. Therefore, a block defined in ByLayer mode retains its properties when inserted into a drawing (or another drawing, if the block was saved as a drawing file). If the layers included in the inserted block do not exist in the drawing, AutoCAD automatically creates them.

For a block to assume the property characteristics of the layer it is inserted on, it must be created on layer 0. Suppose you create the CIRCLE block on layer 0 and insert it on layer 1. The block becomes part of layer 1 and thus assumes the color and linetype of that layer. Exploding the CIRCLE block returns the objects back to layer 0 and to the original color and linetype assigned to layer 0.

An exception occurs if objects within the block are drawn using an explicit color or linetype; in other words, the objects are not drawn using the default ByLayer mode. In this case, the exploded CIRCLE block objects would retain their original properties.

Changing the Layer, Color, and Linetype of a Block

If you insert a block on the wrong layer, or if you wish to change the color or linetype properties of the block, you can use the **Properties** window to modify it. Select the block to modify, and its properties are listed. See Figure 23-11. Notice that Block Reference is now specified in the drop-down list. You can now modify the selected block.

To modify the layer of the selected block, pick **Layer** in the **General** category. A drop-down arrow appears, allowing you to access the layer you want to use for the block. Once the new layer has been selected, pick the X at the upper right of the **Properties** window to close the window. The block is now changed to the proper layer.

You may also want to change the color or linetype of a block. If the block was originally created on layer 0, it will assume the color and linetype of the current layer when it is inserted. If it was created on another layer, it will retain its original color and linetype.

If you wish to change the color or linetype of an inserted block, you can access the **Properties** window and select the corresponding property in the **General** section after selecting the block. Select the desired color or linetype from the corresponding drop-down list.

Figure 23-11.
The **Properties** window allows you to change the layer, color, linetype, and other properties of a block.

Type of object

Insertion point

Scale factors

Block name

Rotation angle

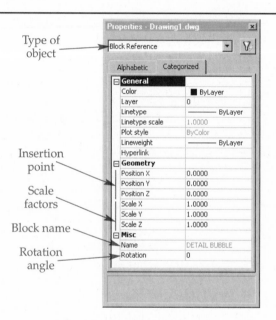

PROFESSIONAL TIP

If you want to change the properties of several blocks, you can use the **Quick Select** dialog box to create a selection set of block reference objects. Once the blocks are selected, change the properties using the **Properties** window or **Object Properties** toolbar. The Quick Select dialog box is discussed in Chapter 7.

Inserting Multiple Copies of a Block

The features of the **INSERT** and **ARRAY** commands are combined using the **MINSERT** (multiple insert) command. This method of inserting and arraying blocks saves time and disk space. To access the **MINSERT** command, type MINSERT at the Command: prompt.

An example of an application using the **MINSERT** command is the arrangement of desks on a drawing. Suppose you want to draw the layout shown in Figure 23-12. First, specify architectural units and set the limits to 30',22'. Draw a 4' × 3' rectangle and save it as a block named DESK. The arrangement is to be three rows and four columns. Make the horizontal spacing between desks 2', and the vertical spacing 4'. Use the following command sequence:

> Command: **MINSERT**↵
> Enter block name or [?]: <current>: **DESK**↵
> Specify insertion point or [Scale/X/Y/Z/Rotate/PScale/PX/PY/PZ/PRotate]: *(pick a point)*
> Enter X scale factor, specify opposite corner, or [Corner/XYZ] <1>: ↵
> Enter Y scale factor <use X scale factor>: ↵
> Specify rotation angle <0>: ↵
> Enter number of rows (---) <1>: **3**↵
> Enter number of columns (|||) <1>: **4**↵
> Enter distance between rows or specify unit cell (---): **7'**↵
> Specify distance between columns (|||): **6'**↵

The resulting arrangement is shown in Figure 23-12. The complete pattern takes on the characteristics of a block, except that an array created with the **MINSERT** command cannot be exploded. Since the array cannot be exploded, you can use the **Properties** window to modify the number of rows and columns, change the spacing between objects, or change the layer, color, or linetype properties. If the initial block is rotated, all arrayed objects are also rotated about their insertion points. If the arrayed objects are rotated about the insertion point while using the **MINSERT** command, all objects are aligned on that point.

Figure 23-12.
To create an arrangement of desks using the **MINSERT** command, first create a block named DESK.

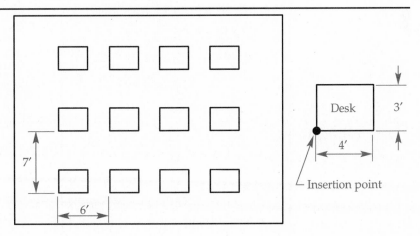

As an alternative to the previous example, if you were working with different desk sizes, a 2D unit block may serve your purposes better than an exact size block. To create a 5' × 3'-6" (60" × 42") desk, for example, insert a one-unit square block using either the **INSERT** or **MINSERT** command, and enter the following for the X and Y scale factors:

Enter X scale factor, specify opposite corner, or
   [Corner/XYZ] <1>: **60↵**
Enter Y scale factor <use X scale factor>: **42↵**

A 2D unit block can be used in this manner for a variety of objects.

EXERCISE 23-3

❑ Start a new drawing or use one of your templates. Specify architectural units and set the limits to 80',60'. Then, perform a **ZOOM All**.
❑ Draw the chair shown below and save it as a block named CHAIR.
❑ Use the **MINSERT** command twice to create the theater arrangement. The sides of the chairs should touch. Each row on either side of the aisle should have 10 chairs. The spacing between rows is 4'. The width of the center aisle is 5'.
❑ Consider where you should insert the first chair to obtain the pattern.

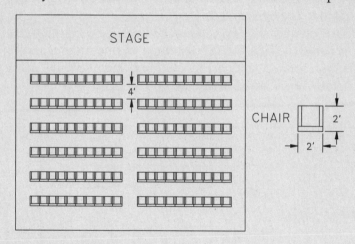

❑ Save the drawing as EX23-3.

Inserting Entire Drawings

The **INSERT** command can be used to insert an entire drawing file into the current drawing. To do so, enter the **INSERT** command and pick the **Browse...** button in the **Insert** dialog box to access the **Select Drawing File** dialog box. You can then select a drawing file to insert, as discussed earlier in this chapter.

When one drawing is inserted into another, the inserted drawing becomes a block reference. As a block, it may be moved to a new location with a single pick. The drawing is inserted on the current layer, but it does not inherit the color, linetype, or thickness properties of that layer. You can explode the inserted drawing back to its original objects if desired. Once exploded, the drawing objects revert to their original layers. A drawing that is inserted brings any existing block definitions, layers, linetypes, text styles, and dimension styles into the current drawing.

By default, every drawing has an insertion point of 0,0,0. (This is the insertion point used for a drawing file when you insert it into the current drawing.) If you want to change the insertion point of the drawing you need to insert, you can use the **BASE** command. Pick **Base** from the **Block** cascading menu in the **Draw** pull-down menu, or enter BASE at the Command: prompt as follows:

BASE

Draw
→ Block
   Base

     Command: **BASE**↵
     Enter base point <0.0000, 0.0000, 0.0000>: *(pick a point or enter new coordinates)*

The new base point now becomes the insertion point for the drawing.

PROFESSIONAL TIP

When working on a drawing, it is common practice in industry to refer to other drawings to check features or dimensions. In many instances, the prints are not available and must be produced. You can avoid such delays by using the **INSERT** command. When you need to reference another drawing, simply insert it into your current drawing. When you are done checking the features or dimensions you need, simply use the **UNDO** command to undo the **INSERT** operation or erase the inserted drawing.

EXERCISE 23-4

❏ Open EX23-2.
❏ If your drawing does not have a Red layer, create one and set it current.
❏ Draw a 6 × 4 rectangle. Insert two of the CIRCLE blocks into the rectangle, both one unit in diameter. Make a new block of this drawing and name it PLATE-2.
❏ Erase all objects on screen and set the 0 layer current. Insert both the PLATE-1 and PLATE-2 blocks.
❏ The PLATE-2 block should appear red because it was created on the Red layer. The PLATE-1 block should be black.
❏ Set the Red layer current and insert the PLATE-1 block. It should appear red because it was created on layer 0 and assumes the color of the layer on which it is inserted.
❏ Enter the **BASE** command. Choose an insertion point below and to the left of the objects on screen.
❏ Save the drawing as EX23-4.
❏ Start a new drawing named PLATES.
❏ Insert drawing EX23-4 into your new drawing. The insertion point used is the one you established using the **BASE** command.
❏ Enter any editing command and select a line on one of the PLATE blocks. The entire drawing should be highlighted, since the drawing is actually one large block.
❏ Save the drawing again as EX23-4.

Using the AutoCAD DesignCenter

Blocks or drawing files can be readily located and previewed before they are inserted using the **AutoCAD DesignCenter**. You can easily insert blocks or entire drawings into your current drawing using the "drag and drop" capability of **DesignCenter**. You can also browse through existing drawings for blocks, show images of blocks and drawings, and display other information about saved blocks or files.

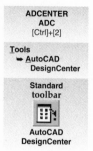

ADCENTER
ADC
[Ctrl]+[2]

Tools
➡ AutoCAD
DesignCenter

Standard toolbar

AutoCAD
DesignCenter

To access **DesignCenter**, pick the **AutoCAD DesignCenter** button in the **Standard** toolbar, select **AutoCAD DesignCenter** from the **Tools** pull-down menu, enter ADC or ADCENTER at the Command: prompt, or use the [Ctrl]+[2] key combination. The drawing that is currently open is highlighted in the **Tree View** area of the **DesignCenter**. The preview palette, located on the right side of the **DesignCenter** window, contains icons identifying the different types of content in the current drawing. See Figure 23-13. The same icons are listed under the highlighted drawing file in the **Tree View** area. You can pick any of these icons to list information about the corresponding content.

Figure 23-13.
The **AutoCAD DesignCenter** is used to search for existing blocks and drawing files for insertion into the current drawing.

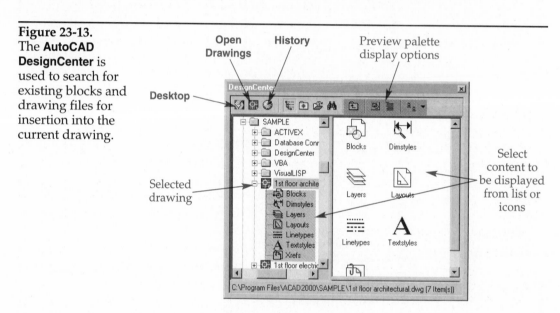

Use the **Desktop**, **Open Drawings**, and **History** buttons to display the hierarchy of files and folders on your computer and network drives, view the contents of open drawings, or list the last twenty files or Internet locations viewed. The following describes each of these features:

- **Desktop.** Displays the hierarchy of files and folders on your computer and network drives, including My Computer and Network Neighborhood.
- **Open Drawings.** Displays all drawings currently open in the AutoCAD session, including drawings that are minimized.
- **History.** Displays the last twenty drawings, files, or locations to which you connected using the **Browse the Web** dialog box. The history is saved from session to session.

To view the blocks that belong to a drawing, click on the Blocks icon in the "tree" area or double-click the Blocks icon in the preview palette. Use the **Preview**, **Description**, and **Views** buttons to display different types of information for a block or drawing. See Figure 23-14. The following explains each of these features:

- **Preview.** Displays a preview of the selected block at the bottom of the palette. If there is no preview image saved with the selected item, the preview area is empty.
- **Description.** Displays a text description of the selected item at the bottom of the palette. The description shown is the information that you added when creating the block. If a preview image is also displayed, the description is displayed below it.

Figure 23-14.
Use the
DesignCenter to find
the block to be
inserted into the
current drawing.

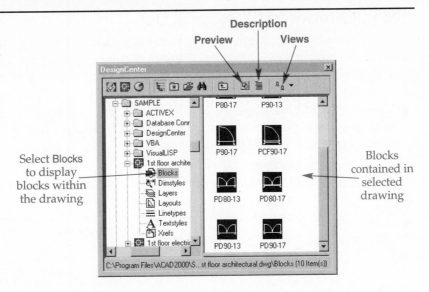

Select Blocks
to display
blocks within
the drawing

Blocks
contained in
selected
drawing

- **Views.** Provides different display formats for the block loaded in the palette. You can select the **View** button to cycle through display formats. Display formats include: **Large icons**, **Small icons**, **List**, and **Details**.

Once the desired block has been found, use the drag and drop feature to insert it into the current drawing. To use drag and drop, move the cursor over the top of the block in the **Preview Palette**, press and hold down the pick button on your pointing device, and drag the cursor to the opened drawing. Release the pick button and the block is inserted into the drawing. The block is inserted into the drawing based on the type of inserted units specified when creating the block. For example, if the original block was a 1″ × 1″ square, and the inserted units specified were feet when the block was created, then the block will be a 12″ × 12″ square when it is inserted from the **AutoCAD DesignCenter**.

To insert a whole drawing using **DesignCenter**, select the directory in which the drawing resides. Any drawings in the selected directory show up in the **Preview Palette**. Use the drag and drop feature to insert them into the current drawing. In addition to inserting blocks and drawings, **DesignCenter** can insert dimension styles, layers, layouts, linetypes, text styles, and xrefs.

EDITING BLOCKS

AutoCAD 2000 gives you the ability to edit blocks in the current drawing. This is referred to as *in-place reference editing*. This allows you to make minor changes to blocks, wblocks, or drawings that have been inserted in the current drawing. Wblocks and inserted drawings can be edited without the need to open the original file. In-place editing allows you to edit blocks without the need to explode and redefine the block. In-place editing cannot be used on blocks that have been inserted into a drawing with the **MINSERT** command.

If you do not use in-place reference editing, blocks must first be broken into their original components before they can be edited. Two methods can be used to break blocks apart. The first method is called *asterisk insertion*, and is done at the time of insertion. The second method uses the **EXPLODE** command, which can be done at any time.

Editing Blocks In-Place

REFEDIT

Modify
➥ In-place Xref and
   Block Edit
➥ Edit Reference

You can edit a block in-place by using the **REFEDIT** command. This command is accessed by typing **REFEDIT** at the Command: prompt, using the **Refedit** toolbar, or by picking **In-place Xref and Block Edit** and **Edit Reference** in the **Modify** pull-down menu.

Display the **Refedit** toolbar by right-clicking on any displayed toolbar button, then pick **Refedit**. See Figure 23-15. The button on the left of the toolbar is **Edit Block or Xref**. Use this button to access the **REFEDIT** command from the toolbar.

When you use the **REFEDIT** command, you get this prompt:

Command: **REFEDIT**↵
Select reference: *(select the block to edit)*

Figure 23-15.
The **Refedit** toolbar.

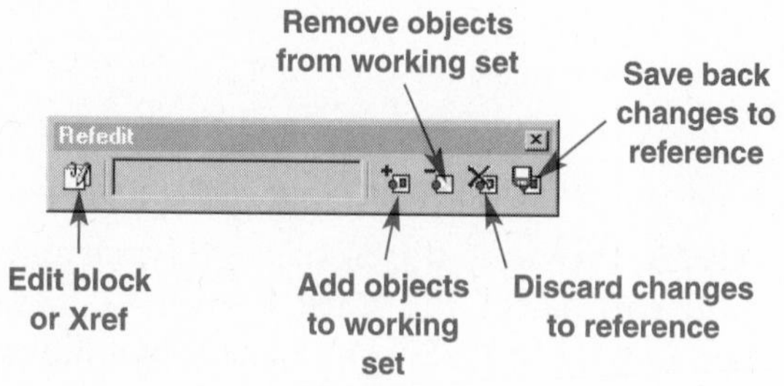

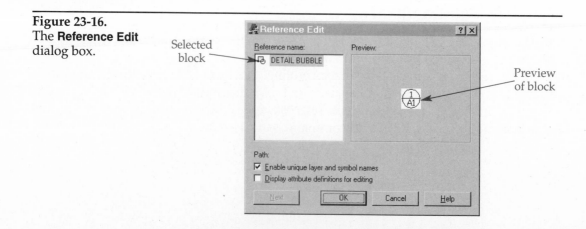

Now the **Reference Edit** dialog box is displayed. See Figure 23-16. The following explains the features of the **Reference Edit** dialog box:

- **Reference name.** This displays the name of the selected block and any references nested within the selected block. Figure 23-17 shows a block nested within the selected block.
- **Preview.** An image of the selected block is displayed here. You can cycle through nested blocks by picking the reference name or by using the **Next** button. The preview images changes to display the currently selected block.
- **Enable unique layer and symbol names.** This check box controls layer and symbol names of objects extracted from the reference. If this check box is selected, layer and symbol names are given a prefix such as $#$.
- **Display attribute definitions for editing.** If this check box is selected, the block attributes and attribute definitions are available for editing. The attributes of the original block reference are unchanged when your changes are saved to the block being edited. The edited attribute definitions only take effect in future insertions of the edited block. Attributes are explained in detail in Chapter 25.
- **Next.** Pick this button to cycle through block references that are available for selection.
- **OK.** Pick the **OK** button after selecting the desired block from the tree view.

Figure 23-16.
The **Reference Edit** dialog box.

Figure 23-17.
Nested blocks are shown in the tree view of the **Reference Edit** dialog box.

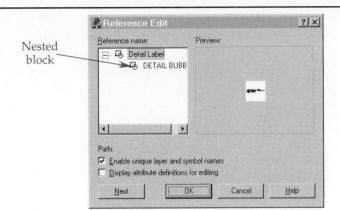

Nested block

After you pick the **OK** button, the **Refedit** toolbar is displayed and you get the following prompt:

Select nested objects: *(select the objects in the block to edit)*

Pick all objects in the block to be edited, then press [Enter].

Select nested objects: ↵
n items selected
Use REFCLOSE or the Refedit toolbar to end reference editing session.
Command:

If multiple insertions of the same block are displayed, be sure to pick the one you originally selected.

When the Command: prompt is available, all the objects in the drawing are grayed out, except the objects you selected. Now use any drawing or editing commands to alter the object as desired. Pick the **Save back changes to reference** button in the **Refedit** toolbar. Pick **OK** at the AutoCAD alert shown in Figure 23-18 if you want to continue with the save. Changes to the edited block are displayed immediately. The changes also affect other insertions of the same block and future insertions of the block.

Objects that are selected for editing are referred to as the *working set* and appear brighter than other objects. Objects that are not a part of the working set are faded. The percent of fading is controlled in the **Display** tab of the **Options** dialog box. A maximum of 90% fading is allowed, and the default is 50%. See Figure 23-19. This value is controlled by the **XFADECTL** variable. Enter a value in the **Reference Edit fading intensity** text box in the lower-right corner, or move the slider.

Objects that are added to the drawing during the edit can be removed from the working set. These additional buttons on the **Refedit** toolbar are described below.

- **Add objects to working set.** Any object that is drawn during the in-place edit is automatically added to the working set. Additional existing objects can be added with this feature. If an object is added to the working set, it is removed from the host drawing. The **REFSET** command allows you to add to or remove objects from the working set.

Figure 23-18.
This dialog box appears after editing the selected objects within the block and picking the **Save back changes to reference** button.

Figure 23-19.
Set the amount of fading in the **Reference Edit fading intensity** area of the **Display** tab of the **Options** dialog box.

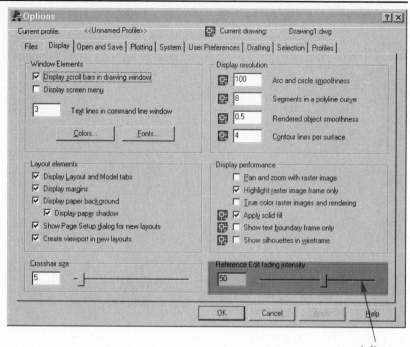

Adjust intensity of fading

- **Remove objects from the working set.** Use this feature to remove objects from the working set. When an object is removed from the set it appears faded. If an object is removed from the working set, it is added to the host drawing.
- **Discard changes to reference.** Pick this if you want to exit the reference edit function without saving changes to the object. The **REFCLOSE** command allows you to save or discard changes to the working set, and closes reference editing.

The **REFEDIT** command can also be used in the command window by typing **-REFEDIT** at the Command: prompt. This is the command sequence:

Command: **-REFEDIT**⏎
Select reference: *(select the block to change)*

At the next prompt, type O and press [Enter] to accept the currently highlighted reference, or press [Enter] to use the **Next** option:

Select nesting level [Ok/Next] <Next>: ⏎
Select nesting level [Ok/Next] <Next>: O⏎
Select nested objects: *(select objects within the block to edit)*
Display attribute definitions [Yes/No] <No>: *(type Y or [Enter] for No)*
Use REFCLOSE or the Refedit toolbar to end reference editing session.
Command: *(use drawing and editing commands as needed to edit the block)*

Use the **Save back changes to reference** button on the **Refedit** toolbar as previously discussed, or type the **REFCLOSE** command and use one of its options. The **Save** option is used as follows:

Command: **REFCLOSE**⏎
Enter option [Save/Discard reference changes] <Save>: ⏎

The AutoCAD alert box is displayed. Use OK to accept the changes.

Exploding a Block during Insertion

If you wish to edit the individual objects of a block at the time of insertion, you can insert a block and explode it in a single operation. This is accomplished by picking the **Explode** check box in the **Insert** dialog box, as discussed earlier in this chapter. If you are using the **-INSERT** command, enter an asterisk (*) before the block name as follows:

```
Command: -INSERT↵
Enter block name or [?] <current>: *PLATE-1↵
Specify insertion point for block: (pick a point)
Specify scale factor for XYZ axes: (specify the scale and press [Enter])
Specify rotation angle <0>: ↵
```

The inserted geometry is not part of a block. It consists of individual objects that have their original properties and can be edited.

Using the EXPLODE Command

The **EXPLODE** command is used to break apart any existing block, polyline, or dimension. To access this command, pick the **Explode** button in the **Modify** toolbar, select **Explode** from the **Modify** pull-down menu, or type X or EXPLODE at the Command: prompt as follows:

```
Command: X or EXPLODE↵
Select objects: (pick the block)
Select objects: ↵
```

When the block is exploded, the component objects are quickly redrawn. The individual objects can now be changed individually. To see if the **EXPLODE** command worked properly, select any object that was formerly part of the block. Only that object should be highlighted. If so, the block was exploded properly.

EXPLODE
X

Modify
➡ Explode

Modify
toolbar

Explode

NOTE

You can explode a block that was scaled using different X, Y, and Z values when it was inserted. This type of block is technically a *nonuniformly* scaled block. Versions of AutoCAD prior to Release 13 did not allow exploding of such blocks.

If you know in advance that you want a block to be exploded, remember to pick the **Explode** check box in the **Insert** dialog box for this to happen automatically upon insertion of the block.

Redefining Existing Blocks

A situation can arise where you discover that the original definition of a block must be edited. This is an easy process, even if you have placed the block on a drawing many times. To redefine an existing block, follow this procedure:

1. Insert the block to be redefined anywhere in your drawing.
2. Make sure that you know where the insertion point of the block is located.
3. Explode the inserted block using the **EXPLODE** command.
4. Edit the block as needed.
5. Recreate the block definition using the **BLOCK** command.
6. Give the block the same name and the same insertion point it originally had.
7. Select the objects to be included in the block.
8. Pick **OK**. When a message from AutoCAD appears and asks if you want to redefine the block, pick **Yes**.
9. When the **BLOCK** command is complete, all insertions of the block are updated.

A common mistake is to forget to use the **EXPLODE** command before redefining the block. When you try to create the block again with the same name, an alert box indicating the block references itself is displayed. This means you are trying to create a block that already exists. Once you press the **OK** button, the alert box disappears and the **Block Definition** dialog box is redisplayed. Press the **Cancel** button, explode the block to be redefined, and try again.

NOTE

You can also redefine existing blocks using the **-BLOCK** command instead of the **Block Definition** dialog box. This command was covered earlier in this chapter. After the block has been inserted and exploded, and the necessary changes have been made, issue the **-BLOCK** command. Enter the same block name, enter Y or YES to redefine the block, pick the same insertion point, and select the revised objects. Finally, press [Enter] to redefine the block.

Understanding the Circular Reference Error

As described in the previous example, when you try to redefine a block that already exists (using the same name), AutoCAD informs you that the block references itself. The concept of a block *referencing itself* may be a little difficult to grasp at first without fully understanding how AutoCAD works with blocks. A block can be composed of any objects, including other blocks. When using the **BLOCK** command to incorporate an existing block into a new block, AutoCAD must make a list of all the objects that compose the new block. This means that AutoCAD must refer to any existing block definitions that are selected to be part of the new block. If you select an instance, or reference, of the block being redefined as a component object for the new definition, a problem occurs. You are trying to redefine a block name using a previous version of the block with the same name. In other words, the new block refers to a block of the same name, or *references itself*.

For example, assume you create a block named BOX that is composed of four line objects in the shape of a square, and insert it. You then decide that the block needs to be changed so that it contains a small circle in the lower-left corner. If the original BOX block is exploded, all that is left are the four line objects. After drawing the required circle, you can enter the **BLOCK** command and recreate a block named BOX by selecting the four lines and the circle as the component objects. Redefining a block destroys the old definition and creates a new one. Any blocks with the same name are redefined with the updated changes. Make sure you want to redefine the block before agreeing to do so. Otherwise, give the block a new name. The correct way to redefine a block is shown in Figure 23-20.

Alternately, assume you do not explode the block, but still draw the circle and try to redefine the block. By selecting the BOX block *and* the circle, a new block named BOX would now be a block reference of the BOX block with a circle. The old block definition of BOX has not been destroyed, but a new definition has been attempted. Thus, AutoCAD is trying to define a new block named BOX by using an instance of the BOX block. This is referred to as a *circular reference*, and is what is meant by a block referencing itself. See Figure 23-20.

Figure 23-20.
A—The correct procedure for redefining a block. B—Redefining a block that has not first been exploded creates an invalid circular reference.

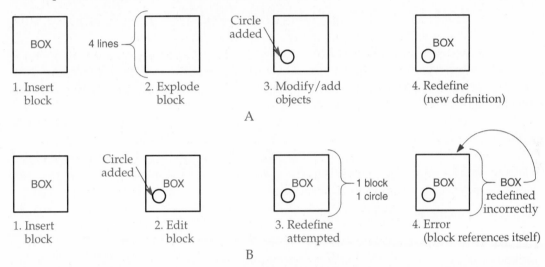

CREATING A BLOCK FROM A DRAWING FILE

You can create a block from any existing drawing. This allows you to avoid redrawing the object as a block, thus saving time. Remember, if something has already been drawn, try to use it as a block rather than redrawing it. Use the **-INSERT** command in the following manner to define a block named BOLT from an existing drawing file named fastener.dwg:

> Command: **-INSERT**↵
> Enter block name or [?]: <*current*>: **BOLT=FASTENER**↵
> Specify insertion point or [Scale/X/Y/Z/Rotate/PScale/PX/PY/PZ/PRotate]: *(press the* [Esc] *key)*

The drawing is not inserted on screen because the command is canceled. However, a block named BOLT is saved and added to the drawing file, and it can be used in the same manner as any other block.

The same procedure is possible using the **Insert** dialog box. Using the **Browse...** button, select the fastener file. The selected file is then displayed in the **Name:** text box. Use this text box to change the name from fastener to BOLT and pick **OK**. The file can be inserted into the drawing, or you can press the [Esc] key to exit the command. A block named BOLT has now been created from the file and can be used as desired.

CREATING PERMANENT GLOBAL BLOCKS

Blocks created with the **BLOCK** command can only be used in the drawing in which they were made. However, you may want to use blocks on many different drawings without having to redraw them. The **WBLOCK** (write block) command allows you to create a drawing (.dwg) file out of a block. You can also use the **WBLOCK** command to create a global block from any object (it does not have to be first saved as a block). The resulting drawing file can then be inserted as a block into any drawing.

There are several ways to use the **WBLOCK** command. To see how the first method works, open drawing EX23-1. Convert the CIRCLE block to a permanent block by making it a separate drawing file using the following procedure:

Command: **W** *or* **WBLOCK**↵

The **Write Block** dialog box appears, Figure 23-21. This dialog box is similar to the **Block Definition** dialog box. Pick the **Block:** option button, then select the CIRCLE block from the drop-down list in the **Source** area. Enter the name of the wblock, HOLE, in the **File name:** text box. Specify where you want to save the wblock by picking the button next to the

---

Figure 23-21.
Using the **Write Block** dialog box to create a wblock from an existing block. The wblock is saved as a drawing file with a .dwg extension.

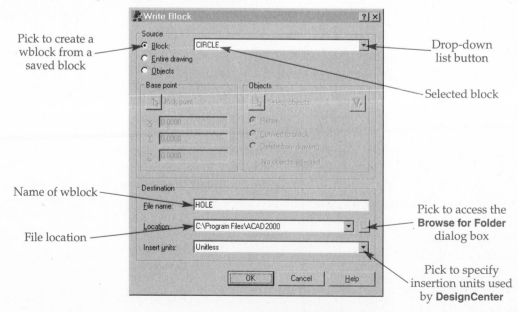

Location: drop-down list (if the path shown is not the desired location). Picking this button displays the **Browse for Folder** dialog box. If you want to insert the block at a specific unit size when using the **AutoCAD DesignCenter**, select the type of units in the **Insert units:** drop-down list, as discussed earlier in this chapter. When you are finished, pick **OK**.

The above sequence wrote a new block, with the name HOLE, to a drawing file on disk. You can now use the **INSERT** command to insert the wblock into the current drawing or any other drawing.

NOTE

When another drawing is inserted into the current drawing, the referenced drawing acts as a block. It is a single object and its individual components cannot be edited unless the block is exploded.

When you access the **Write Block** dialog box and select a block from the drop-down list, AutoCAD assumes the new drawing file will have the same name and lists it in the **File name:** text box. Decide whether to use the name of the selected block for the drawing file or enter a new name.

Creating a New Wblock

Suppose you want to create a wblock from a shape you have just drawn, but you have not yet made a block. The following sequence is used to save a selected object as a drawing file. First, enter the **WBLOCK** command and select the **Objects** option button in the **Write Block** dialog box (it is active by default). Pick the **Select objects** button to select the objects for the drawing file. Next, pick the **Pick point** button to select the insertion point. You can also enter coordinates in the **X:**, **Y:**, and **Z:** text boxes. Then give the file a name in the **File name:** text box. If the path shown in the **Location:** text box is not where you want to save the file, access the **Browse for Folder** dialog box by picking the button next to the drop-down arrow. Select the type of units that the **AutoCAD DesignCenter** will use to insert the block in the **Insert units:** drop-down list. When you are through, pick **OK**. See Figure 23-22.

Figure 23-22.
Using the **Write Block** dialog box to create a wblock from selected objects without first defining a block.

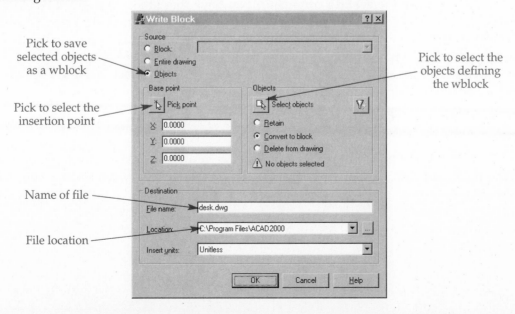

This sequence is the same as that used with the **BLOCK** command. However, the wblock is saved to disk as a drawing file, *not* as a block in the current drawing. Be sure to specify the correct file path in the **Location:** text box when using the **Write Block** dialog box. A drawing file named desk that is to be saved in the blocks folder on the C: hard drive, for example, would be saved as c:\blocks\desk. If you want to save the drawing file on a diskette in the A: drive, enter the file name A:desk in the **File name:** text box.

Storing a Drawing as a Wblock

An entire drawing can also be stored as a wblock. To do this, pick the **Entire drawing** option button in the **Write Block** dialog box. Give the wblock a name in the **File name:** text box. To specify a location for the new drawing file, access the **Browse for Folder** dialog box or accept the path displayed in the **Location:** text box. Select the type of units the **AutoCAD DesignCenter** will use to insert the block in the **Insert units:** drop-down list, and pick **OK** when you are through.

In this case, the whole drawing is saved to disk as if you had used the **SAVE** command. The difference is that all unused blocks are deleted from the drawing. If the drawing contains any unused blocks, this method reduces the size of a drawing considerably.

PROFESSIONAL TIP

Using the **Entire drawing** wblock option is a good way to remove named objects that are unused in your drawing to reduce the file size. Use this routine when you have completed a drawing and decide that the unused blocks, layers, styles, and objects are no longer needed. The **PURGE** command can also be used to remove any unused layers, linetypes, text styles, dimension styles, multiline styles, blocks, and shapes. But the process is slower than using the **Entire drawing** wblock option. The **PURGE** command is discussed later in this chapter.

Inserting a Drawing File with the **Select Drawing File** Dialog Box

When you use the **INSERT** command, you have the option to insert a block *or* a wblock. Picking the **Browse...** button in the **Insert** dialog box activates the **Select Drawing File** dialog box. You can then scroll through the files in any folder, or on another drive, and pick the file name you need. This was discussed earlier in this chapter.

If you enter the **-INSERT** command, you can access the **Select Drawing File** dialog box by entering a tilde (~) when prompted for the block name as follows:

Command: **-INSERT**↵
Enter block name or [?]: *<current>*: **~**↵

You can use the tilde character whenever any AutoCAD command prompt requests a file name. One of several dialog boxes is then displayed so that you may select a file.

❏ Open drawing EX23-2.
❏ Create a wblock named PLATE-1 using the existing block of the same name.
❏ Use Windows Explorer to list your drawing files. Be sure plate-1.dwg is listed.
❏ Start a new drawing or use one of your templates.
❏ Insert the plate-1 drawing file into the current drawing.
❏ Save the drawing as EX23-7.

Revising an Inserted Drawing

You may find that you need to revise a drawing file that has been used in other drawings. If this happens, you can quickly update any drawing in which the revised drawing is used. For example, if a drawing file named pump was used several times in a drawing, simply enter the **-INSERT** command, and type an equal sign (=) after the block name to update all of the references to the pump drawing:

Command: **-INSERT**↲
Enter block name or [?]: *<current>*: **PUMP=**↲
Block "pump" already exists. Redefine it? [Yes/No] <N>: **Y**↲
Block "pump" redefined
Regenerating model.
Specify insertion point or [Scale/X/Y/Z/Rotate/PScale/PX/PY/PZ/PRotate]: *(press the* [Esc] *key)*

All of the pump references are automatically updated, and by pressing the [Esc] key to cancel the command, no new insertions of the pump drawing are made.

Suppose you had inserted a drawing file named fastener into your current drawing, but then saved it as a block and named it screw. Now you have decided to revise the fastener drawing. The screw block can be updated using the **-INSERT** command as follows:

Command: **-INSERT**↲
Enter block name or [?]: *<current>*: **SCREW=FASTENER**↲
Block "screw" already exists. Redefine it? [Yes/No] <N>: **Y**↲
Block "screw" redefined
Regenerating model.
Specify insertion point or [Scale/X/Y/Z/Rotate/PScale/PX/PY/PZ/PRotate]: *(press the* [Esc] *key)*

PROFESSIONAL TIP

If you work on projects in which inserted drawings may be revised, it may be more productive to use reference drawings instead of inserted drawing files. Reference drawings are used with the **XREF** command, which is discussed in Chapter 24. All referenced drawings are automatically updated when a drawing file that contains the externally referenced material is loaded into AutoCAD.

For 2000i Users...

AutoCAD 2000i includes several symbol libraries that can be accessed from the **AutoCAD Today** window. Refer to *Symbol Libraries* on page 963 for more information.

As you become proficient with AutoCAD, you will want to start constructing symbol libraries. A *symbol library* is a collection of related shapes, views, and symbols that are used repeatedly in drawings. You may eventually want to incorporate symbols into your screen and tablet menus. This is discussed in detail in *AutoCAD and its Applications— Advanced*. First, you need to know where symbols (blocks and drawing files) are stored and how they can be inserted into different drawings.

Blocks vs Separate Drawing Files

As discussed earlier, the main difference between the **BLOCK** and **WBLOCK** commands is that a block is saved with the drawing in which it is created and the **WBLOCK** command saves the block as a separate drawing file. A complete drawing file occupies considerably more disk space than a block. Also, a drawing file can contain many blocks; once the drawing file is inserted into the current drawing, all the blocks in the drawing file are also inserted into the drawing.

If you decide to use blocks, each person in the office or class must have a copy of the drawing that contains the blocks. This is often done by creating the blocks in a template file or a separate drawing file. If drawing files are used, each student or employee must have access to the files.

Using 3.5" Diskettes

Diskettes are good to use for temporarily storing backup copies of drawing and data files. They also allow you to transport files from one workstation to another in the absence of a network or modem. However, avoid making diskettes the primary means for storing symbols, especially if you have sufficient room on the hard disk, optical, or network server drives. Inserting and removing diskettes from a disk drive is tedious and time-consuming, because it takes more time for the computer to access the diskettes. If you must adopt this method, follow these guidelines:

- Create all symbols as separate drawing files.
- Assign one person to initially create the symbols for each specialty.
- Follow class or company symbol standards.
- Print a hard copy of the symbol library. Include a representation of the symbol, its insertion point, any other necessary information, and where it is located. A sample is shown in Figure 23-23. Provide all users of the symbols with a copy of the listing.
- Save one group of symbols (drawing files) per diskette. For example, individual diskettes may contain the following types of symbols:
  - ✓ Electronic
  - ✓ Electrical
  - ✓ Piping
  - ✓ Mechanical
  - ✓ Structural
  - ✓ Architectural
  - ✓ Landscaping
  - ✓ Mapping
- Use the following methods to label diskettes:
  - ✓ In Windows Explorer, right-click on the 3½ Floppy (A:) icon. This activates a shortcut menu. Select Properties to access the 3½ Floppy (A:) Properties dialog box. Type a label in the Label: text box of the General tab, and pick OK.
  - ✓ Use stick-on labels to identify all diskettes. Write on each label before attaching it. Use the same name as the volume label.

Figure 23-23.
A printed copy of piping flow diagram blocks used for template drawings in a symbol library. Each colored dot indicates the insertion point, and is not part of the block.

PIPING FLOW DIAGRAM SYMBOLS

GATEVALVE	CHECKVALVE	GLOBEVALVE	CONTROLVALVE	SAFETYVALV–R	SAFETYVALV–L
PUMPR–TOP	PUMPR–DN	PUMPR–UP	PUMPL–UP	PUMPR–DN	PUMPR–TOP
INSTR–LOC	INSTR–PAN	TRANS	INSTR–CON	DRAIN	VENT

- Copy the symbol diskettes and provide a copy for each workstation in the class or office.
- Keep backup copies of all symbol diskettes in a secure place.
- When symbols are revised, update all copies of diskettes containing the edited symbols.
- Inform all users of any changes to saved symbols.

Using the Hard Disk Drive

The local or network hard disk drive is one of the best places to store a symbol library. It is easily accessed, quick, and more convenient to use than diskettes. Symbols saved to a hard disk drive should be created with the **WBLOCK** command, just as they are with diskettes. The drawing files can be saved in the current folder (usually Acad2000) or in another folder. If drawing files are stored in the Acad2000 folder, they are easier to find. However, storing symbols in separate folders keeps the Acad2000 folder uncluttered and easy to manage. A good idea is to create a Blocks folder for storing your blocks, as shown in Figure 23-24.

Figure 23-24.
An efficient way to store blocks saved as drawing files is to set up a Blocks folder containing folders for each type of symbol on the hard drive.

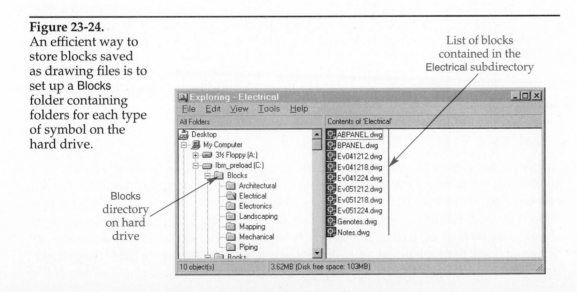

List of blocks contained in the Electrical subdirectory

Blocks directory on hard drive

If a symbol is saved as a file, you must search for its folder the first time the symbol is inserted. After its initial insertion, the drawing file is saved as a block definition in the current drawing, and it can be accessed by entering its file name.

Drawing files are saved on the hard disk drive using the same systematic approach used with diskettes. These additional guidelines also apply:

- All workstations in the class or office should have folders with the same names.
- One person should be assigned to update and copy symbol libraries to all workstation hard drives.
- Drawing files should be copied onto each workstation's hard drive from a master diskette or network server.
- The master diskettes and backup diskettes of the symbol libraries should be kept in separate locations.

Copying a Symbol Library into a New Drawing

A symbol library of blocks that is part of a drawing can be copied into a new drawing file. The incoming blocks are not displayed, they are only included as definitions in the drawing file. This allows you to use blocks created on one drawing without also having to use the drawing. The process is easy. If the drawing pipeflow.dwg saved on the diskette in the A: drive contains the needed blocks, use the **-INSERT** command as follows:

Command: **-INSERT**↵
Enter block name or [?] <*current*>: **A:PIPEFLOW**↵
Specify insertion point or [Scale/X/Y/Z/Rotate/PScale/PX/PY/PZ/PRotate]: (*press the* [Esc] *key to cancel the command*)

After pressing the [Esc] key, the drawing is not inserted on screen, but the blocks are now included with your new file. Check this by entering the **BLOCK** command and accessing the named objects listed in the **Name:** drop-down list in the **Block Definition** dialog box. The blocks that were in the pipeflow drawing are now defined in the new drawing.

You can also use the **Insert** dialog box to copy a symbol library of blocks into the current drawing. After accessing the **Insert** dialog box, pick the **Browse...** button to display the **Select Drawing File** dialog box. Access the **Look in:** drop-down list and pick the 3½ Floppy (A:) icon to select the desired drawing file.

Another way to insert a drawing file is to use the **AutoCAD DesignCenter**. Browse the folders for the appropriate drawing file, then select the drawing in the preview palette and drag and drop it into the current drawing.

 NOTE | If a symbol library is saved as a template file, it cannot be inserted into another drawing. However, a symbol library template is beneficial when starting a new drawing in which the symbols are to be used. For example, when starting a new mechanical drawing, a mechanical template that contains a mechanical symbol library would be helpful.

Creating a Symbol Library Listing

After deciding which method of using symbols as blocks is best for you, create a symbol library listing. Distribute it to anyone who will be using the symbols. The list can be a pen or printer plot of the symbol libraries in each drawing file. These lists should be updated when revisions are made to symbols. A copy on 8.5" × 11" paper should be given to all users. A larger copy of the list should be placed on a wall or bulletin board. Examples of symbol library lists used in engineering offices are shown in Figure 23-25 and Figure 23-26.

Figure 23-25.
Shown are instrumentation loop diagram symbols. (Willamette Industries, Inc.)

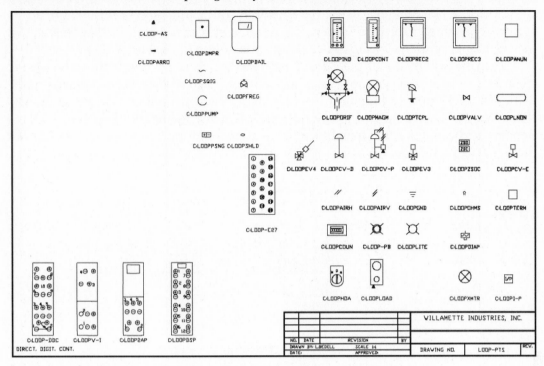

Figure 23-26.
Shown are isometric piping symbols. (Willamette Industries, Inc.)

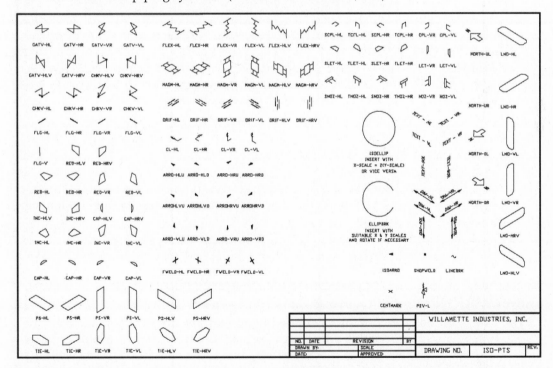

RENAME
REN

Format
➥ Rename...

Blocks can be renamed using the **RENAME** command. Access this command by selecting **Rename...** from the **Format** pull-down menu or entering REN or RENAME at the Command: prompt. This displays the **Rename** dialog box, Figure 23-27.

To change the name of the CIRCLE block to HOLE, select Blocks from the **Named Objects** list. A list of block names defined in the current drawing then appears in the **Items** list. Pick circle to highlight it in the list. When this name appears in the **Old Name:** text box, enter the new block name HOLE in the **Rename To:** text box. Pick the **Rename To:** button and the new block name appears in the **Items** list. Pick **OK** to exit the **Rename** dialog box.

Figure 23-27.
The **Rename** dialog box allows you to change the name of a block and other named objects.

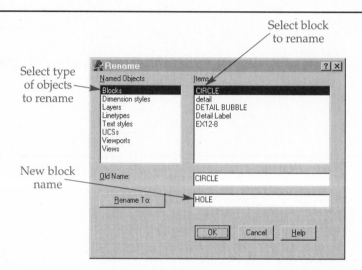

Select type of objects to rename

Select block to rename

New block name

NOTE

Since AutoCAD does not permit the renaming of layer 0 or the Continuous linetype, these two named objects do not appear in the **Items** list in the **Rename** dialog box.

NOTE

The **-RENAME** command can be used to rename blocks, layers, views, and other named objects at the Command: prompt.

PROFESSIONAL TIP

Several block-related Express Tools are available for use. The **Extended Clip**, **Copy Nested Entities**, **Trim to Block Entities**, **Extend to Block Entities**, and **List Xref/Block Entities** tools are found in the **Express** pull-down menu and the **Express** toolbars. These tools are only available if a full AutoCAD installation was performed. See Appendix A for Express Tools information.

As discussed in the previous section, a block is a named object. In many drawing sessions, not all of the named objects in a drawing are used. For example, your drawing may contain several layers, text styles, and blocks that are not used. Since these objects occupy disk space, it is good practice to delete or *purge* the unused objects with the **PURGE** command.

To access the **PURGE** command, pick **Purge** from the **Drawing Utilities** cascading menu in the **File** pull-down menu, or enter PU or PURGE at the Command: prompt. The command sequence allows you to display each of the unused named objects one at a time and decide whether to delete or save them. You can also specify a named object by entering the option corresponding to the type of object to be purged. Use the **PURGE** command in the following manner to delete a block named LINESPEC:

> Command: **PU** *or* **PURGE**⏎
> Enter type of unused objects to purge
> [Blocks/Dimstyles/LAyers/LTypes/Plotstyles/SHapes/textSTyles/Mlinestyles/All]: **B**⏎
> Enter name(s) to purge <*>: ⏎
> Verify each name to be purged? [Yes/No] <Y>: ⏎
> Purge block "linespec"? <N> **Y**⏎

The **PURGE** command lists all unused blocks individually and gives you the option to answer yes or no. The **All** option can be used to delete all unused named objects. This is a good way to clean up a drawing after it is completed, but it is slower than using the **Entire drawing** wblock option in the **Write Block** dialog box, as discussed earlier in this chapter.

<table>
<tr><td>PURGE
PU</td></tr>
<tr><td>File
➥ Drawing
Utilities
➥ Purge</td></tr>
</table>

For 2000i Users...

In AutoCAD 2000i, the **PURGE** command accesses the **Purge** dialog box. Refer to *Purge Dialog Box* on page 978 for additional information.

Chapter Test

Answer the following questions on a separate sheet of paper.

1. Define *symbol library*.
2. Which color and linetype settings should be used if you want a block to assume the current color and linetype when it is inserted into a drawing?
3. When should a block be drawn to fit inside a one-unit square, and what type of block is this called when it is inserted?
4. A block name can be _____ characters long.
5. What are two ways to access a listing of all blocks in the current drawing?
6. Describe the term *nesting* in relation to blocks.
7. How do you preset block insertion variables using a dialog box?
8. Describe the effect of entering negative scale factors when inserting a block.
9. Why would the **Corner** option be used when scaling a block during insertion?
10. What properties do blocks drawn on a layer other than layer 0 assume when inserted?
11. Why would you draw blocks on layer 0?
12. What is a limitation of an array pattern created with the **MINSERT** command?
13. What is the purpose of the **BASE** command?
14. Explain the difference between the **Scale** and **PScale** preset options used with the **INSERT** command.
15. Identify the two methods that allow you to break an inserted block into its individual objects for editing purposes.
16. Suppose you have found that a block was incorrectly drawn. Unfortunately, you have already inserted the block 30 times. How can you edit all of the blocks quickly?
17. What is the primary difference between blocks created with the **BLOCK** and **WBLOCK** commands?

18. After entering the **-INSERT** command, what would you enter when prompted for a block name to define a block named RESISTOR from an existing drawing file named electrical.dwg?

19. Explain two ways to remove all unused blocks from a drawing.

20. Suppose you revise a drawing named desk. However, this drawing had been inserted several times into another drawing and saved as a block named DESK2. How would you update the DESK2 insertions?

21. Why is it best to save symbol libraries to a hard disk drive rather than using diskettes?

22. What advantage is offered by having a symbol library of blocks in a single drawing, rather than using wblocks?

23. Give the command and entries needed to insert all of the blocks from a drawing named a:struct-1 into the current drawing.
    A. Command: _____
    B. Enter block name or [?] <*current*>: _____
    C. Specify insertion point or [Scale/X/Y/Z/Rotate/PScale/PX/PY/PZ/PRotate]: _____

24. What is the purpose of the **PURGE** command?

25. Name the capability of the **AutoCAD DesignCenter** that allows you to easily insert a block into a drawing.

26. Identify the **AutoCAD DesignCenter** feature that displays the hierarchy of files and folders on your computer and network drives.

27. This **DesignCenter** feature displays all currently open drawings.

28. Name the **DesignCenter** feature that displays an image of the selected block at the bottom of the palette.

29. Identify the **DesignCenter** feature that gives a text description of the selected object at the bottom of the palette.

30. Give the dimensions of a block when it is inserted from the **DesignCenter** if the original block was a 1″ × 1″ square and the inserted units were specified in feet.

Drawing Problems

1. Create a symbol library for one of the drafting disciplines listed below, and then save it as a template or drawing file. Then, after checking with your instructor, draw a problem using the library. If you save the symbol library as a template, start the problem with the template. If you save it as a drawing file, start a new drawing and insert the symbol library into it.

   Specialty areas you might create symbols for include:
   - Mechanical (machine features, fasteners, tolerance symbols).
   - Architectural (doors, windows, fixtures).
   - Structural (steel shapes, bolts, standard footings).
   - Industrial piping (fittings, valves).
   - Piping flow diagrams (tanks, valves, pumps).
   - Electrical schematics (resistors, capacitors, switches).
   - Electrical one-line (transformers, switches).
   - Electronics (IC chips, test points, components).
   - Logic diagrams (AND gates, NAND gates, buffers).
   - Mapping, civil (survey markers, piping).
   - Geometric tolerancing (feature control frames).

   Save the drawing as P23-1 or choose an appropriate file name, such as ARCH-PRO or ELEC-PRO.

2. Display the symbol library created in Problem 1 on screen and print a hard copy. Put the printed copy in your notebook as a reference.

3. Open P13-3 from Chapter 13. The sketch for this drawing is shown below. Erase all copies of the symbols that were made, leaving the original objects intact. These include the steel column symbols and the bay and column line tags. Then do the following:

   A. Make blocks of the steel column symbol and the tag symbols.
   B. Use the **MINSERT** command or the **ARRAY** command to place the symbols in the drawing.
   C. Dimension the drawing as shown in the sketch.
   D. Save the drawing as P23-3.

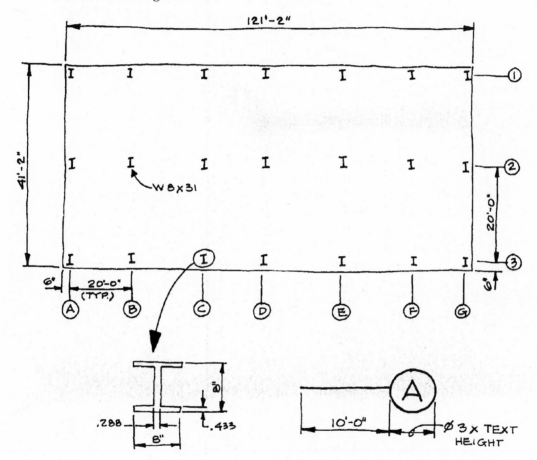

Problems 4–8 represent a variety of electrical schematics, piping flow diagrams, and logic diagrams created using symbols as blocks. Create each drawing as shown (the drawings are not drawn to scale). The symbols should first be created as blocks or wblocks and then saved in a symbol library using one of the methods discussed in this chapter. Place a border and title block on each drawing. Save the drawings as *P23-4*, *P23-5*, and so on.

4.

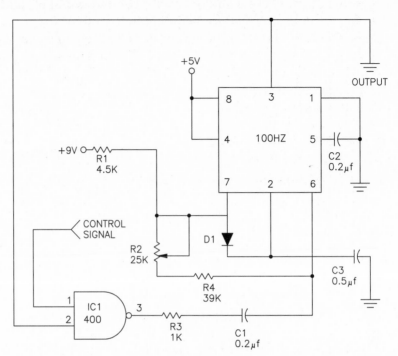

Integrated Circuit for Clock

5.

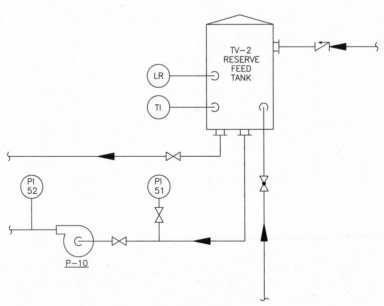

Piping Flow Diagram

6.

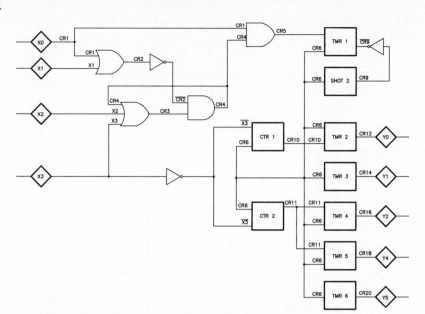

Logic Diagram of Marking System

7. Open P13-4 from Chapter 13. The sketch for this drawing is shown below. Erase all of the desk workstations except one. Then do the following:

A. Create a block of the workstation.

B. Insert the block into the drawing using the **MINSERT** command.

C. Dimension one of the workstations as shown in the sketch.

D. Save the drawing as P23-7.

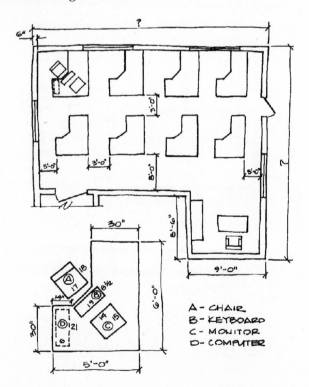

A - CHAIR
B - KEYBOARD
C - MONITOR
D - COMPUTER

Problems 8–12 are presented as engineering sketches. They are schematic drawings created using symbols and are not drawn to scale. The symbols should first be drawn as blocks and then saved in a symbol library. Place a border and title block on each of the drawings.

8. The drawing shown is a logic diagram of a portion of a computer's internal components. Create the drawing on a C-size sheet. Save the drawing as P23-8.

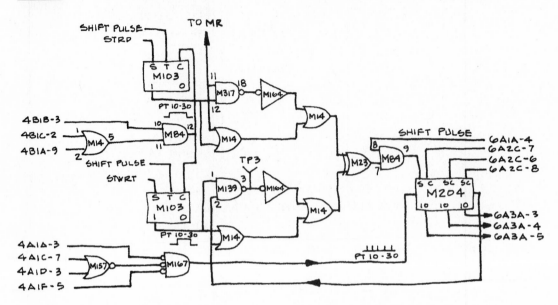

9. The drawing shown is a piping flow diagram of a cooling water system. Create the drawing on a B-size sheet. Look closely at this drawing. Using blocks and the correct editing commands, it may be easier to complete than you think. Draw the thick flow lines with polylines. Save the drawing as P23-9.

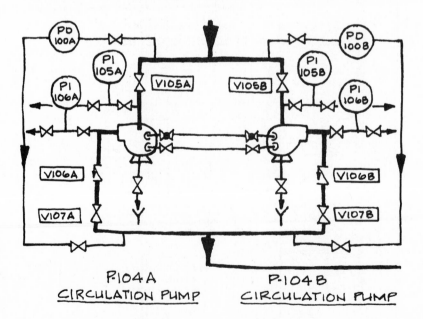

10. The drawing shown is the general arrangement of a basement floor plan for a new building. The engineer has shown one example of each type of equipment. Use the following instructions to complete the drawing:
    A. Create the drawing on a C-size sheet.
    B. All text should be 1/8″ high, except the text for the bay and column line tags, which should be 3/16″ high. The line balloons for the bay and column lines should be twice the diameter of the text height.
    C. The column and bay line steel symbols represent wide-flange structural shapes, and should be 8″ wide × 12″ high.
    D. The PUMP and CHILLER installations (except PUMP #4 and PUMP #5) should be drawn per the dimensions given for PUMP #1 and CHILLER #1. Use the dimensions shown for the other PUMP units.
    E. TANK #2 and PUMP #5 (P-5) should be drawn per the dimensions given for TANK #1 and PUMP #4.
    F. Tanks T-3, T-4, T-5, and T-6 are all the same size, and are aligned 12′ from column line A.
    G. Plan this drawing carefully and create as many blocks as possible to increase your productivity. Dimension the drawing as shown, and provide location dimensions for all equipment not shown in the engineer's sketch.
    H. Save the drawing as P23-10.

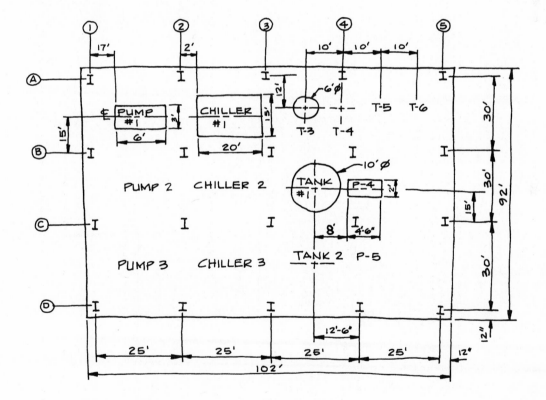

11. The drawing saved as P23-10 must be revised. The engineer has provided you with a sketch of the necessary revisions. It is up to you to alter the drawing as quickly and efficiently as possible. The dimensions shown on the sketch below *do not* need to be added to the drawing; they are provided for construction purposes only. Revise P23-10 so that all chillers and the four tanks reflect the changes. Save the drawing as P23-11.

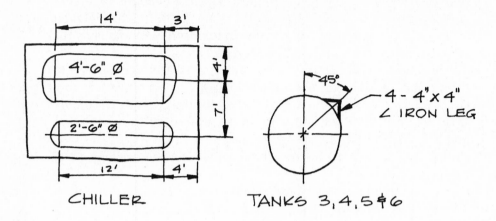

12. The piping flow diagram shown is part of an industrial effluent treatment system. Draw it on a C-size sheet. Eliminate as many bends in the flow lines as possible. Place arrowheads at all flow line intersections and bends. The flow lines should not run through any valves or equipment. Use polylines for the thick flow lines. Save the drawing as P23-12.

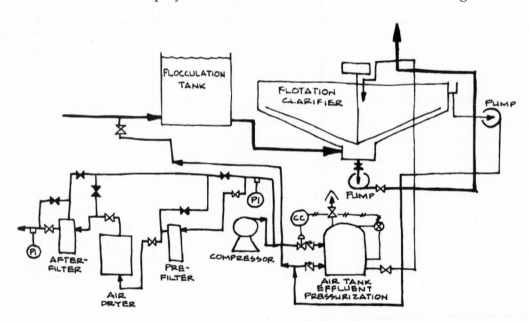

CHAPTER 24

External References

Learning Objectives

After completing this chapter, you will be able to:

■ Define the function of external references.
■ Reference an existing drawing into the current drawing using the **XREF** command.
■ Bind external references and selected dependent objects to a drawing.
■ Use the **AutoCAD DesignCenter** to attach external references.
■ Edit external references in the current drawing.
■ Use external references to create a multiview layout.
■ Control the display of layers in viewports using the **Layer Properties Manager** dialog box.

When you create multiple objects in a drawing by copying them, the drawing file grows in size. This is because AutoCAD must maintain a complete description of the geometry of each copied object. On the other hand, when you use a block to represent multiple objects, AutoCAD maintains only one description of the block's geometry. All other instances of the block are recorded as X, Y, and Z coordinates, and AutoCAD refers to the original block definition to obtain the block's data. The size of a drawing is decreased considerably if blocks are used rather than copied objects. Blocks and wblocks, or inserted drawings, were discussed in Chapter 23.

AutoCAD enables you to go even further in your efforts to control the size of drawing files and maximize efficiency with the **XREF** command. This command allows you to incorporate, or *reference*, one or more existing drawings into the current drawing without adding them to the contents of the current file. This procedure is excellent for applications in which existing base drawings or complex symbols and details must be shared by several users, or are used often. This chapter discusses the **XREF** command and illustrates how it can be used to create a multiview layout with a variety of scale values.

USING REFERENCE DRAWINGS

Any machine or electrical appliance contains a variety of subassemblies and components. These components are assembled to create the final product. The final product occupies a greater amount of space and weighs more than any of the individual parts. In the same way, a drawing composed of a variety of blocks and inserted drawings grows much larger and occupies more disk space than the individual symbols and components.

AutoCAD allows you to *reference* existing drawings to the master drawing you are currently working on. When you externally reference (xref) a drawing, the drawing's geometry is not added to the current drawing (unlike the geometry of inserted drawing files), but it is displayed on screen. This makes for much smaller files. It also allows several people in a class or office to reference the same drawing file, with the assurance that any revisions to the reference drawing will be displayed in any drawing where it is used.

The **XREF** command is used to reference other drawing files into the master drawing. To access this command, pick the **External Reference** button from either the **Reference** or **Insert** toolbar, pick **Xref Manager...** from the **Insert** pull-down menu, or enter XREF or XR at the Command: prompt. This displays the **Xref Manager** dialog box, Figure 24-1. This dialog box is a complete management tool for your external references.

XREF
XR

Insert
➡ X**r**ef Manager...

Reference or Insert
toolbar

External Reference

Reference drawings can be used in two basic ways:

- To construct a drawing using predrawn symbols or details, a method similar to the use of blocks.
- Before plotting, to lay out a drawing composed of multiple views or details, using existing drawings. This technique is discussed later in the chapter.

Benefits of External References

One of the most important benefits of using xrefs is that whenever the master drawing is opened, the latest versions of the xrefs are displayed. If the original externally referenced drawings are modified between the time you revise the master and the time you open and plot it, all revisions are automatically reflected. This is because AutoCAD reloads each xref whenever the master drawing is loaded.

There are other significant advantages to using xrefs. They can be nested, and you can use as many xrefs as needed for any drawing. This means that a detail referenced to the master drawing can be composed of smaller details that are themselves xrefs. You can also attach other xrefs to the referenced drawing and have such updates automatically added to the master drawing when it is opened.

Figure 24-1.
The **Xref Manager** dialog box provides access to all options for externally referenced files.

Pick to attach
an external reference
to current drawing

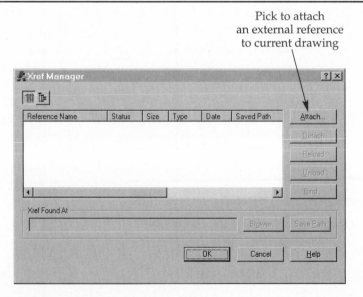

Attaching an External Reference to the Current Drawing

Using the **XREF** command is similar to using the **INSERT** command. A referenced drawing that is inserted into the current drawing is said to be *attached*. To attach the reference to the current drawing, enter the **XREF** command and pick the **Attach...** button in the **Xref Manager** dialog box. This displays the **Select Reference File** dialog box. This is a standard file dialog box with a drawing preview area and a **Find File...** option. Use this dialog box to access the appropriate folder and select the desired drawing file to attach. Pick **Open** when you are finished.

Once a file to attach has been specified, the **External Reference** dialog box is displayed, Figure 24-2. This dialog box is used to indicate how and where the reference is to be placed in the current drawing. The name and path of the currently selected xref are shown in the upper-left corner of the dialog box. To change the drawing to be attached, pick the **Browse...** button and select the new file in the **Select Reference File** dialog box. When attaching an xref, pick the **Attachment** option in the **Reference Type** area. This option is active by default. Working with the **Overlay** option is discussed later in this chapter.

If there is more than one external reference already in the current drawing, you can attach another copy of an xref by picking the **Name:** drop-down list arrow. You can also attach an existing xref by highlighting the desired reference name in the **Xref Manager** dialog box and picking the **Attach...** button.

The lower portion of the **External Reference** dialog box contains the options for the xref insertion location, scaling, and rotation angle. The text boxes in the **Insertion point** area allow you to enter 2D or 3D coordinates for insertion of the xref if the **Specify On-screen** check box is inactive. Activate this check box if you wish to specify the insertion location on screen. Scale factors for the xref can be set in the **Scale** area. By default, the X, Y, and Z scale factors are set to 1. You can enter new values in the corresponding text boxes, or activate the **Specify On-screen** check box to display scaling prompts on the command line. The rotation angle for the inserted xref is 0 by default. You can specify a different rotation angle in the **Angle:** text box, or activate the **Specify On-screen** check box if you wish to be prompted at the command line.

Figure 24-2.
The **External Reference** dialog box is used to specify how an external reference is placed in the current drawing.

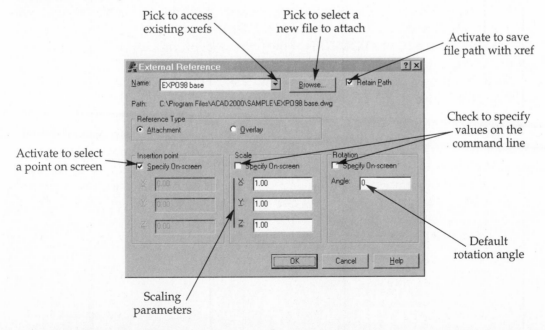

The **Retain Path** check box offers the option of saving the file path location with the external reference. When the path is not included, AutoCAD looks only in the Support File Search Path locations specified in the **Files** tab of the **Options** dialog box to find the referenced file. Saving the path location can be helpful when exchanging drawings with other sites that use different path structures.

> **NOTE**
>
> AutoCAD also searches for xref files in all paths of the current project name. These paths are listed under the Project Files Search Path in the **Files** tab of the **Options** dialog box. You can create a new project as follows:
>
> 1. Pick Project Files Search Path to highlight it, and then pick the **Add...** button.
> 2. Enter a project name if desired.
> 3. Pick the plus sign icon (+), and then pick the word Empty.
> 4. Pick the **Browse...** button and locate the folder that is to become part of the project search path. Then pick **OK**.
>
> Complete the project search path definition by entering the **PROJECTNAME** system variable and specifying the same name that is used in the **Options** dialog box.

In the example given in Figure 24-2, the file Acad2000\Sample\EXPO98 base.dwg is selected for attachment. Because the **Specify On-screen** check box in the **Insertion point** area is activated, the dialog box disappears when you pick **OK**. The xref is attached to your cursor and you are prompted for the insertion point. You can use any valid point specification option, including object snap modes.

As you can see, the options for attaching an xref are essentially the same as those used when inserting a block. Both commands function in a similar manner, but the internal workings and results are different. Remember that externally referenced files are not added to the current drawing file's database, as are inserted drawings. Therefore, using external references helps keep your drawing file size to a minimum.

Attaching Xrefs with **AutoCAD DesignCenter**

AutoCAD DesignCenter provides a quick method for attaching external references to the current drawing. To access **DesignCenter**, pick the **AutoCAD DesignCenter** button on the **Standard** toolbar, select **AutoCAD DesignCenter** from the **Tools** pull-down menu, type ADC or ADCENTER at the Command: prompt, or use the [Ctrl]+[2] key combination.

ADCENTER
ADC
[Ctrl]+[2]

Tools
➥ **AutoCAD DesignCenter**

Standard toolbar

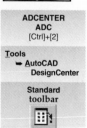

AutoCAD DesignCenter

Use the following procedure to attach an xref to the current drawing:

1. Find the folder containing the drawing to be attached using the tree view in the left pane of **DesignCenter**. Display the contents of the folder in the preview palette.
2. Once the drawing is displayed in the preview palette, you can attach it as an xref using either of two methods. Right-click on the file and select **Attach as xref...** from the shortcut menu, or drag-and-drop the drawing into the current drawing area *using the right mouse button* and select **Attach as xref...** from the shortcut menu displayed.
3. The **External Reference** dialog box is displayed. Enter the appropriate values and pick **OK**.

Overlaying the Current Drawing with an External Reference

There are many situations in which you may want to see what your drawing looks like with another drawing overlaid on it. Overlaying the current drawing with an external reference file allows you to temporarily view the xref without attaching it. This is accomplished by activating the **Overlay** option button in the **External Reference** dialog box after selecting an xref.

The difference between an overlaid xref and an attached xref is related to the way in which nested xrefs are handled. *Nesting* occurs when an externally referenced file is referenced by an xref file that has been attached to the current drawing. The xref file that is attached is known as the *parent xref*. When an xref is overlaid, any nested xrefs that it contains are displayed if the xrefs were *attached*, but not if they were *overlaid*. In other words, any nested overlays are not carried into the master drawing with the parent xref.

Detaching, Reloading, and Unloading

As discussed earlier, each time you open a master drawing containing an attached xref, the xref is also loaded and appears on screen. This attachment remains permanent until you remove or *detach* it. This is done by highlighting the reference name in the **Xref Manager** dialog box and picking the **Detach** button. When you detach an externally referenced file, all instances of the xref are erased, and all referenced data is removed from the current drawing. All xrefs nested within the detached file are also removed. The actual detachment does not occur until you press **OK** and close the dialog box. This is helpful if you accidentally detach an xref, because you can simply press **Cancel** to prevent the detachment and return to the drawing.

There may be situations where you need to update or *reload* an xref file in the master drawing. For example, if an externally referenced file is edited by another user while the master drawing is open, the version on disk may be different than the version currently displayed. To update the xref, highlight the reference name in the **Xref Manager** dialog box and pick the **Reload** button. This forces AutoCAD to read and display the most recently saved version of the drawing.

When you need to temporarily remove an xref file without actually detaching it, you can *unload* the xref. To do so, highlight the reference name in the **Xref Manager** dialog box and pick the **Unload** button. When an xref is unloaded, it is not displayed or regenerated, and AutoCAD's performance is increased. To display the xref again, access the **Xref Manager** dialog box and pick the **Reload** button.

Using the Xref Manager Dialog Box

In addition to attaching xref files, you can use the **Xref Manager** dialog box to access current information about any referenced file in the master drawing. Each of the labeled columns in this dialog box lists information, Figure 24-3. The file names in the **Reference Name** column can be displayed either in list view or tree view. The list view display mode is active by default. It can be activated by picking the **List View** button, located at the upper-left corner of the dialog box, or by pressing the [F3] key. The labeled columns displayed in list view are described as follows:

- **Reference Name.** This column lists the names of all existing external references.
- **Status.** This column describes the current status of each xref. The xref status can be classified as one of the following:
  - **Loaded.** The xref is attached to the drawing.
  - **Unloaded.** The xref is not displayed or regenerated.
  - **Unreferenced.** The xref has nested xrefs that are not found or are unresolved. An unreferenced xref is not displayed.
  - **Not Found.** The xref file was not found in valid search paths.
  - **Unresolved.** The xref file is missing or cannot be found.

Figure 24-3.
Additional information on referenced files is displayed in the **Xref Manager** dialog box.

Pick to display
Tree View

List View
active

Listed
xrefs

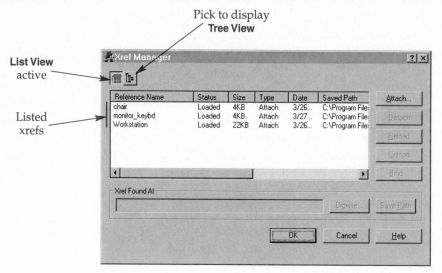

- **Orphaned.** The parent of the nested xref was unloaded or cannot be found.
- **Reload.** The xref is marked to be reloaded. Loading and unloading both occur after the dialog box is closed.
- **Unload.** The xref is marked to be unloaded.
- **Size.** The file size for each xref is listed in this column.
- **Type.** This column indicates whether the xref was attached or referenced as an overlay.
- **Date.** The last modification date for the file being referenced is indicated in this column.
- **Saved Path.** This column lists the path name saved with the xref. If only a file name appears here, the path has not been saved.

To quickly see a listing of your externally referenced files that shows nesting levels, pick the **Tree View** button or press the [F4] key. See Figure 24-4. In the tree view display mode, the drawing is indicated with the standard AutoCAD 2000 drawing file icon, and xrefs appear as a sheet of paper with a paper clip. Nesting levels are shown in a format that is similar to the arrangement of folders. The xref icon can take on different appearances, depending on the current status of the xref. An xref whose status is unloaded will have an icon that is grayed out. A question mark indicates that the file was not found. An upward arrow shown with the icon means the xref has just been reloaded, and a downward arrow means the xref has just been unloaded.

Figure 24-4.
The tree view display mode shows nested xref levels and the status of each xref.

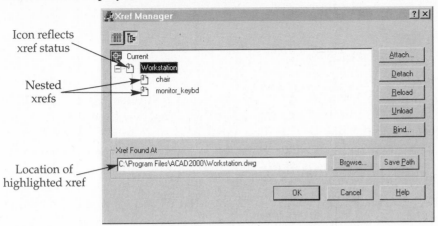

Icon reflects xref status

Nested xrefs

Location of highlighted xref

Updating the Xref Path

As previously discussed, a file path saved with an externally referenced file is displayed in the **Saved Path** column of the **Xref Manager** dialog box. If an xref file is not found in the **Saved Path** location when the master drawing is opened, AutoCAD searches along the *library* path, which includes the current drawing folder and the Support File Search Path locations set in the **Files** tab of the **Options** dialog box. If a file with a matching name is found, it is resolved. In such a case, the **Saved Path** location differs from where the file was actually found. You can check this in the **Xref Manager** dialog box by highlighting an xref name and then comparing the path listed in the **Saved Path** column with the listing in the **Xref Found At** area. To update the **Saved Path** location, pick the **Save Path** button.

When a referenced drawing has been moved and the new location is not on the library path, its status is indicated as Not Found. You can update the path to refer to the new location by selecting the **Browse...** button in the **Xref Found At** area. Using the **Select new path** dialog box, go to the new folder and select the desired file. Then, press **Open** to update the path. When you pick **OK**, the xref is automatically reloaded into the drawing.

Binding an External Reference

An externally referenced file can be made a permanent part of the master drawing as if it had been inserted with the **INSERT** command. This is called *binding* an xref. Binding is useful when you need to send the full drawing file on disk to a plotting service, or to a client.

Before an xref is bound, all dependent objects in the externally referenced file, such as blocks, dimension styles, layers, linetypes, and text styles, are named differently by AutoCAD. When an xref is attached to the master drawing, dependent objects are renamed so that the xref name precedes the actual object name. The names are separated by a vertical bar symbol (|). For example, prior to binding, a layer named Notes within an externally referenced drawing file named Title comes into the master drawing as Title|Notes. This is done to distinguish the xref-dependent layer name from the same layer name in the master drawing. When an xref file is bound to the master drawing, the dependent objects are renamed again to reflect that they have become a permanent part of the drawing. There are different renaming methods, depending on the type of binding that is performed.

To bind an xref using the **Xref Manager** dialog box, highlight the xref to bind and select the **Bind...** button. This displays the **Bind Xrefs** dialog box, which contains the **Bind** and **Insert** option buttons. See Figure 24-5.

Figure 24-5.
The **Bind Xrefs** dialog box allows you to specify how the xref is incorporated into the master drawing.

The **Insert** option brings the xref into the drawing as if you had used the **INSERT** command. All instances of the xref are converted to normal block objects. Also, the drawing is entered into the block definition table, and all named objects such as layers, blocks, and styles are incorporated into the master drawing as named in the xref. For example, if an xref named PLATE is bound and it contains a layer named OBJECT, the xref-dependent layer PLATE|OBJECT becomes the locally defined layer OBJECT. All other xref-dependent objects are stripped of the xref name, and they assume the properties of the locally defined objects with the same name. The **Insert** binding option provides the best results for most purposes.

PROFESSIONAL TIP  Try the express tool named **PACK** to save all files associated with a drawing to a location of your choice. The express tools are available if a full installation of AutoCAD was performed. See Appendix A of this text for more information on this command.

The **Bind** option also brings the xref in as a native part of the master drawing and converts all instances of the xref to blocks. However, the xref name is kept with the names of all dependent objects, and the vertical line in each of the names is replaced with two dollar signs with a number in between. For example, a layer named Title|Notes is renamed Title0Notes when the xref is bound using the **Bind** option. The number inside the dollar signs is automatically incremented if a local object definition with the same name exists. For example, if Title0Notes already exists in the drawing, the layer is renamed to Title1Notes. In this manner, unique names are created for all xref-dependent object definitions that are bound. Any of the named objects can be renamed as desired using the **RENAME** command.

In some cases, you may only need to incorporate one or more specific named objects from an xref into the master drawing, rather than the entire xref. If you only need selected items, it can be counterproductive to bind an entire drawing. In this case, you can bind only the named objects you select. This technique is covered later in this chapter.

Clipping an External Reference

A frequent need with externally referenced files is to display only a specific portion of a drawing. AutoCAD allows you to create a boundary that displays a subregion of an external reference. All geometry occurring outside the border is invisible. Objects that are partially within the subregion appear to be trimmed at the boundary. Although these objects appear trimmed, the referenced file is not changed in any way. Clipping is applied to selected instances of an xref, and not to the actual xref definition.

AutoCAD and its Applications—Basics

The **XCLIP** command is used to create and modify clipping boundaries. To access the **XCLIP** command, pick the **External Reference Clip** button from the **Reference** toolbar, pick **X̲ref** from the **Clip** cascading menu in the **Modify** pull-down menu, or enter XC or XCLIP at the Command: prompt. The prompt sequence for creating a rectangular boundary for an xref is as follows:

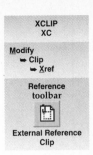

XCLIP
XC

Modify
➡ Clip
  ➡ X̲ref

Reference
toolbar

External Reference
Clip

> Command: **XC** *or* **XCLIP**↵
> Select objects: *(select any number of xref objects)*
> Select objects: ↵
> Enter clipping option
> [ON/OFF/Clipdepth/Delete/generate Polyline/New boundary] <New>: ↵

The Select objects: prompt allows you to select any number of xrefs to be clipped. Then press [Enter] to accept the default **New boundary** option. This option allows you to select the clipping boundary. The other options of the **XCLIP** command include the following:

- **ON and OFF.** The clipping feature can be turned on or off as needed by using these options.
- **Clipdepth.** This option allows a front and back clipping plane to be defined. The front and back clipping planes define what portion of a 3D drawing is displayed. An introduction to 3D drawing techniques is given in Chapter 27 of this text. Clipping of 3D models is discussed in *AutoCAD and its Applications—Advanced*.
- **Delete.** To remove a clipping boundary completely, use this option.
- **generate Polyline.** This option allows you to create a polyline object to represent the clipping border of the selected xref.

After the **New boundary** option is selected, the **XCLIP** command sequence continues as follows:

> Specify clipping boundary:
> [Select polyline/Polygonal/Rectangular] <Rectangular>: *(press [Enter] to create a rectangular boundary)*
> Specify first corner: *(pick the first corner)*
> Specify opposite corner: *(pick the other corner)*

An example of using the **XCLIP** command is illustrated in Figure 24-6. Note that the geometry outside of the clipping boundary is no longer displayed after the command is completed. A clipped xref can be edited just like an unclipped xref. The clipping boundary moves with the xref. Note also that nested xrefs are clipped according to the clipping boundary for the parent xref.

If you do not wish to create a rectangular clipping boundary after selecting an xref, there are two other options for defining a boundary. These options are described as follows:

- **Select polyline.** This option allows you to select an existing polyline object as a boundary definition. The border can be composed only of straight line segments, so any arc segments in the selected polyline are treated as straight line segments. If the polyline is not closed, the start and end points of the boundary are connected.
- **Polygonal.** This option allows an irregular polygon to be drawn as a boundary. This option is similar to the **WPolygon** selection option, and allows a fairly flexible boundary definition.

The clipping boundary is invisible by default. The boundary can be displayed by setting the **XCLIPFRAME** system variable to 1.

Figure 24-6.
A clipping boundary is used to clip selected areas of an xref. A—Using the **Rectangular** boundary selection option. B—The clipped xref.

Rectangular
clipping boundary

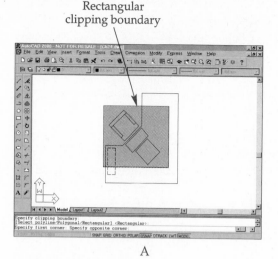
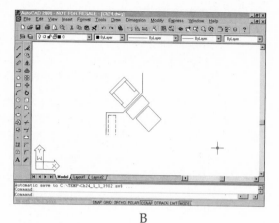

A   B

PROFESSIONAL TIP

If a drawing will be used as an external reference, it is good practice to save the file with spatial and layer indexes. *Spatial* and *layer indexes* are lists that organize objects by their location in 3D space and their layer name. These lists help improve the performance of AutoCAD when referencing drawings with frozen layers and clipping boundaries. Layers that are frozen are not loaded when demand loading is enabled, and any areas outside clipping boundaries are also not loaded. (Demand loading is discussed in the next section.)

You can create spatial and layer indexes using the **Save Drawing As** dialog box. The procedure is as follows:

1. Pick the **Options...** button, and make sure the **DWG Options** tab is active in the **Saveas Options** dialog box.
2. In the **Index type:** drop-down list, pick the type of index required. The default option is **None**.
3. Pick **OK**, and then save the drawing.

Using Demand Loading

Demand loading controls how much of an external reference file is loaded when it is attached to the master drawing. When demand loading is enabled, the only portion of the xref file loaded is the part necessary to regenerate the master drawing. This improves performance and saves disk space because the entire xref file is not loaded. For example, any data on frozen layers, as well as any data outside of clipping regions, is not loaded.

Demand loading is enabled by default. To check or change the setting, open the **Open and Save** tab of the **Options** dialog box. The three demand loading options are found in the **Demand load Xrefs:** drop-down list in the **External References (Xrefs)** area. The options are described as follows:

- **Enabled**. When this option is active, demand loading is turned on. While the drawing is being referenced, the xref file is kept open and other users cannot edit the file.
- **Disabled.** Enabling this option turns off demand loading.
- **Enabled with copy.** When this option is active, demand loading is turned on, and other users can edit the original drawing because AutoCAD uses a copy of the referenced drawing.

NOTE

Two additional settings in the **Open and Save** tab of the **Options** dialog box control the effects of changes made to xref-dependent layers and in-place reference editing. (Reference editing is discussed later in this chapter.) The settings are controlled by check boxes in the **External References (Xrefs)** area. Each option is explained as follows:

- **Retain changes to Xref layers.** This option allows you to keep all changes made to the properties and states of xref-dependent layers. Any changes to layers take precedence over the layer settings in the xref file. The edited properties are retained even if an xref is reloaded. The **VISRETAIN** system variable also controls this function. It is set to 1 and is active by default.
- **Allow other users to Refedit current drawing.** This option controls whether the current drawing can be edited in place by others while it is open and when it is referenced by another file. (In-place editing, or reference editing, is discussed later in this chapter.) This option is active by default and is controlled by the **XEDIT** system variable.

PROFESSIONAL TIP

When an xref is loaded, a write lock is placed on the original file to prevent other users from changing the xref. This is because demand loading is enabled by default. The file is kept open in case you need to thaw a layer or change the clipping and therefore need to access more of the xref drawing data. Because the file is kept open, it is locked and cannot be edited by anyone else.

Demand loading speeds the process of resolving xrefs, and in most cases is best left on. However, if you disable demand loading, the xref file is loaded entirely into the master drawing and can be opened or edited as desired by other users on the network. Also, if the **Enabled with copy** demand loading option is active, as discussed earlier, the source file can be edited because AutoCAD uses a copy of the file. To update an xref after the source file has been changed, use the **Reload** option in the **Xref Manager** dialog box.

As discussed earlier, binding allows you to make all dependent objects in an xref file a permanent part of the master drawing. Dependent objects include named items such as blocks, dimension styles, layers, linetypes, and text styles. Before binding, you cannot directly use any dependent objects from a referenced drawing in the master drawing. For example, a layer that exists only in a referenced drawing cannot be made current in the master drawing. The same applies for text styles.

When a drawing is referenced to the master drawing, all dependent named objects are renamed. As discussed previously, before binding, all xref-dependent layer names are given the name of the referenced drawing, followed by the vertical bar symbol (|), and then the name of the layer. This naming convention enables you to quickly identify which layers belong to a specific referenced drawing. In Figure 24-7, the **Layer Properties Manager** dialog box shows how layer names in the master drawing are distinguished from those belonging to different xref files.

There may be cases where you wish to individually bind an xref-dependent named object, such as a layer or block, rather than the entire xref file. After a permanent bind is created, the dependent object can be used in the master drawing. When you do not wish to bind the entire drawing, you can select individual items to bind using the **XBIND** command.

To access the **XBIND** command, pick the **External Reference Bind** button from the **Reference** toolbar, pick **Object** from the **Modify** pull-down menu and then pick **Bind...** from the **External Reference** cascading menu, or enter XB or XBIND at the Command: prompt. This displays the **Xbind** dialog box, Figure 24-8. This dialog box allows you to select individual xref-dependent objects for binding.

The three xrefs shown are indicated by the AutoCAD drawing file icons. Notice that a plus sign (+) icon is shown in the box to the left of each icon. You can click the plus sign to expand the listing and display the contents of the xref file. The object

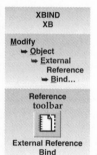

XBIND
XB

Modify
➥ Object
➥ External
Reference
➥ Bind...

Reference
toolbar

External Reference
Bind

Figure 24-7.
Xref-dependent layer names in the master drawing are preceded by the xref drawing name and the vertical bar symbol (|).

Externally
referenced
drawing
layer names

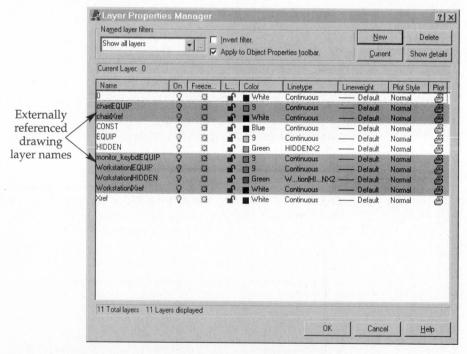

Figure 24-8.
The **Xbind** dialog box is used to individually bind xref-dependent objects to the master drawing.

Referenced
drawings in
master
drawing

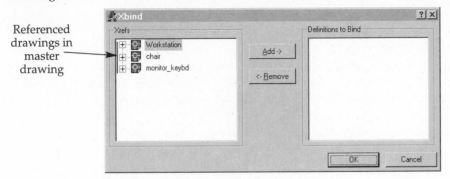

groups belonging to the Workstation xref file are shown in Figure 24-9. Each group is identified by a representative icon.

To select an individually named object from a group, you must first expand the group listing by clicking on the plus sign next to the corresponding icon. In Figure 24-10, the xref-dependent dimension styles, layers, and text styles have been accessed for individual selection. To select an object for binding, highlight it and pick the **Add** button. The names of all objects selected and added are displayed in the **Definitions to Bind** list on the right. Each name appears with the xref name prefix and the vertical bar symbol. When all desired objects have been selected, pick the **OK** button. A message displayed at the command line indicates how many objects of each type were bound.

When an individual dependent object is bound to the master drawing, it is automatically renamed. This was discussed earlier in this chapter. Individual objects that are bound using the **XBIND** command are renamed in the same manner as objects that

Figure 24-9.
Clicking the plus sign next to the AutoCAD drawing file icon identifying each xref file expands the listing to show the object groups for individual object selection and binding.

Object
groups

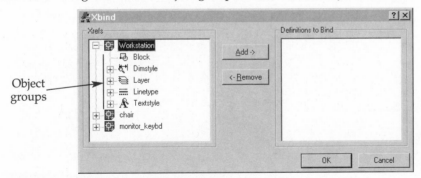

Figure 24-10.
To display the xref-dependent objects within an object group, click on the plus sign next to the appropriate group icon.

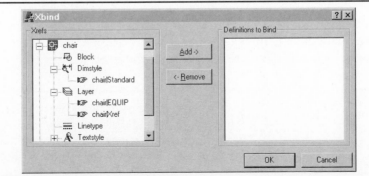

are bound using the **Bind** option in the **Bind Xrefs** dialog box. The renaming method consists of replacing the vertical bar symbol in the object name with two dollar signs and a number, typically 0. For example, after binding, a layer named a-new-door belonging to the xref named XREF1 would be named xref1$0$a-new-door.

In addition to being renamed, a bound layer can also be assigned a linetype that was not previously defined in the master drawing. An automatic bind is performed so that the required linetype definition can be referenced by the new layer. A new linetype name, such as xref1$0$hidden, is created for the linetype. In similar fashion, a previously undefined block may be automatically bound to the master drawing as a result of binding layers, linetypes, or nested blocks.

As discussed earlier, bound objects can be renamed as desired. This is done using the **RENAME** command.

NOTE

You can instruct AutoCAD to create and maintain a log file of the attaching, detaching, and reloading functions used in any drawing containing xrefs. Simply set the **XREFCTL** system variable to 1. At this setting, AutoCAD creates an XLG file having the same name as the current drawing, and the file is saved in the same folder. Each time you load a drawing that contains xrefs, or use the attaching, detaching, or reloading options provided by the **XREF** command, AutoCAD appends information to the log file. A new heading, or title block, is added to the log file each time the related drawing file is opened. The log file provides the following information:

- The drawing name, plus the date, time, and type of each xref operation.
- The nesting level of all xrefs affected by the operation.
- A list of xref-dependent objects affected by the operation, and the names of the objects added to the drawing.

You can also create a general log file of all activity while in AutoCAD. In the **Options** dialog box, open the **Open and Save** tab. In the **File Safety Precautions** area, activate the **Maintain a log file** check box. A log file will be created in the folder that is specified under the Log File Location in the **Files** tab of the **Options** dialog box. After exiting AutoCAD, you can view the log file in ASCII text format using Windows Notepad or any text editor.

EDITING REFERENCE DRAWINGS

New to AutoCAD 2000 is the ability to edit reference drawings *in place*, or within the master drawing. This function, called *reference editing*, allows any user to edit referenced and nested reference drawings inside the master drawing when it is open. Any changes can then be saved to the original xref drawing without exiting the master drawing. This method negates the need to open the original file for editing.

NOTE

In-place reference editing is best suited for minor revisions. Larger revisions should be done inside the original drawing. Making major changes with in-place editing can decrease the performance of AutoCAD because additional disk space is used.

The **REFEDIT** command is used to edit externally referenced drawings in place. To issue this command, pick the **Edit block or Xref** button from the **Refedit** toolbar, pick **Edit Reference** from the **In-place Xref and Block Edit** cascading menu in the **Modify** pull-down menu, or enter REFEDIT at the Command: prompt.

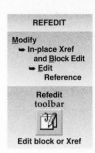
Command: **REFEDIT**↵
Select reference:

This prompt asks you to select a reference to edit. After you make a selection, the **Reference Edit** dialog box is displayed, Figure 24-11. A preview of the selected xref is shown in the **Preview:** panel, and the name of the file is highlighted. In the example shown, one of the chairs in the Workstation reference drawing has been selected.

In the **Path:** area, the check box labeled **Enable unique layer and symbol names** is active by default. This option controls the naming of selected layers and objects that are *extracted*, or temporarily removed from the drawing, for editing purposes. If this check box is selected, layer and object names are given the prefix $*n*$, with *n* representing an incremented number. This is similar to the renaming method used when an xref is bound.

If the selected xref file contains other references, the **Reference name:** area lists all nested xrefs in tree view. In the example given, chair is a nested xref in the Workstation xref. If you pick the drawing file icon next to chair in the tree view, an image preview is displayed. See Figure 24-12. If there are additional nested xrefs, you can pick the

---

Figure 24-11.
The **Reference Edit** dialog box lists the name of the selected reference drawing and displays an image preview. In this example, the chair xref was selected.

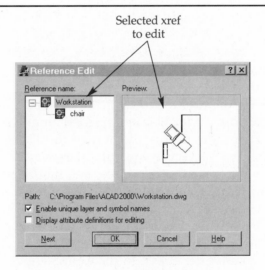

Selected xref
to edit

Figure 24-12.
The **Preview:** panel displays the chair xref after it is selected in tree view.

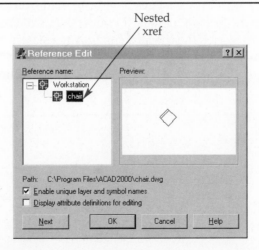

Nested
xref

Next button to cycle through them. Pick **OK** after selecting the xref to edit. The following prompt is then displayed:

Select nested objects:

This prompt asks you to pick objects that belong to the previously selected xref. Pick all lines and any other geometry of the object to be edited, and then press [Enter]. The nested objects that you select make up the *working set*. If multiple instances of the same xref are displayed, be sure to pick objects from the one you originally selected.

After you are done selecting nested objects, the **Refedit** toolbar is displayed. See Figure 24-13. This toolbar displays the name of the selected reference drawing and is left on screen for the remainder of the reference editing session. You can use the toolbar to add objects to the working set, remove objects from the working set, and save or discard changes to the original xref file. The editing functions provided by the toolbar buttons are described as follows:

- **Add objects to working set.** Any object that is drawn during the in-place edit is automatically added to the working set. Additional existing objects can also be added to the working set by using this button. If an object is added to the working set, it is extracted, or removed, from the host drawing. The **REFSET** command allows you to add objects to the working set, or remove objects, during the in-place edit.
- **Remove objects from working set.** This button allows you to remove selected objects from the working set. When a previously extracted object is removed, it is added back to the host drawing.
- **Discard changes to reference.** Pick this button if you wish to exit the reference editing session without saving changes.
- **Save back changes to reference.** Pick this button if you wish to save the editing changes and exit the reference editing session. You can also save or discard changes and end the session by using the **REFCLOSE** command.

After you define the working set, it appears differently from the rest of the drawing. All nonselected objects are faded, or grayed out, Figure 24-14A. The objects in the working set appear in the normal display mode. The nonselected objects are displayed at a percentage of the normal display. The percentage of fading is 50% by default and can be changed by accessing the **Display** tab in the **Options** dialog box. Enter a value in the **Reference Edit fading intensity** text box in the lower-right corner, or move the slider. A maximum fading value of 90% is allowed. This value is also controlled by the **XFADECTL** system variable.

Once the working set has been defined, you can use any drawing or editing commands to alter the object. In the example given in Figure 24-14A, the chair has been selected from the workstation so that arms can be added.

Once the necessary changes have been made, pick the **Save back changes to reference** button from the **Refedit** toolbar. If you wish to exit the reference editing session without saving changes, pick the **Discard changes to reference** button. If you save changes, pick **OK** when AutoCAD asks if you wish to continue with the save and redefine the xref. All instances of the xref are then immediately updated. See Figure 24-14B.

Figure 24-13.
The **Refedit** toolbar is used to perform reference editing functions.

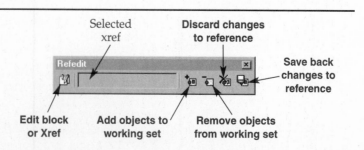

Selected xref

Discard changes to reference

Save back changes to reference

Edit block or Xref

Add objects to working set

Remove objects from working set

Figure 24-14.
Reference editing.
A—Objects in the
drawing that are not
a part of the
working set are
grayed out during
the reference editing
session. B—All
instances of the xref
are immediately
updated after
reference editing.

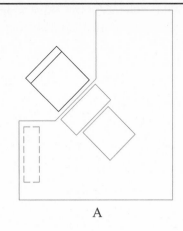
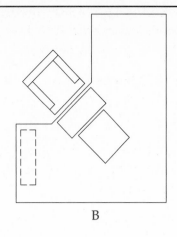

A   B

CAUTION

All reference edits made in this manner are saved back to the original drawing file, and will affect any master drawing that references the file when the master is opened. For this reason, it is critically important that external references be edited only with the permission of your instructor or supervisor.

USING XREFS IN MULTIVIEW LAYOUTS

Multiview mechanical drawings and architectural construction drawings often contain sections and details drawn at different scales. These sections and details can be created as separate drawing files and then attached as xrefs to a master drawing. By controlling the display of layers within viewports, you can create a multiview layout.

The following general procedure is used to create a multiview layout using external references:

1. Create the drawings and details to be displayed in the multiview drawing as separate drawing files.
2. Begin a new master drawing based on a template containing a title block.
3. Make a layer for referenced drawings and a layer for viewports.
4. Create viewports in a layout tab.
5. Use the **XREF** command to reference one drawing into each viewport. Adjust the display within the viewports using the **XP** option of the **ZOOM** command. Control the drawing display within the viewports using the **Layer Properties Manager** dialog box.

These steps are explained in more detail in the following sections.

Layouts

Creating a multiple viewport layout requires a basic understanding of the two designing environments in AutoCAD: model space and paper space. *Model space* is the environment in which you draw and design. When the **Model** tab is selected, model space is active. Model space is also accessed by double-clicking inside a floating viewport in a layout tab. All drawings and models should be created in model space.

Paper space is the environment you use when you wish to create a layout of the drawing prior to plotting. By default, paper space is active when a layout tab is selected. One powerful aspect of using paper space is that you can create a layout of several different drawings and views, each with different scales. You can even mix 2D and 3D views in the same paper space layout.

Model space and paper space were discussed in Chapter 9, and a thorough explanation of layouts was provided in Chapter 10. Review those chapters if you are having difficulty understanding these concepts.

Viewports

The most important visualization aspect involved in creating a multiview layout is to imagine that the sheet of paper you are creating will contain several cutouts *(viewports)* through which you can see other drawings *(models)*. See Figure 24-15.

As you know, objects and designs should be created at full-size in model space. If you are designing a machine part, you are probably using decimal units. If you are designing a house, you are using architectural units.

When creating a multiview layout of multiple drawings, double-click inside a viewport to make it active and then *reference* (insert) the drawing to be displayed. This procedure will be explained later in this chapter.

Now, imagine the C-size paper is hanging up in front of you, and the first viewport is cut 12″ wide and 12″ high. You want to display the floor plan of a house inside the opening. If you then place the full-size model of the floor plan directly behind the C-size paper, the house will extend many feet beyond the edges of the paper. How can you place the drawing within the viewport? You know the floor plan should be displayed inside the viewport at a scale of 1/4″ = 1′-0″. The scale factor of 1/4″ = 1′-0″ is 48. Therefore, you need to move the floor plan model away from the C-size paper until it is 1/48 (reciprocal of 48) the size it is now. When you do that, the entire floor plan fits inside the viewport you cut. This is accomplished with the **XP** (times paper space) option of the **ZOOM** command, which is discussed later. See Figure 24-16.

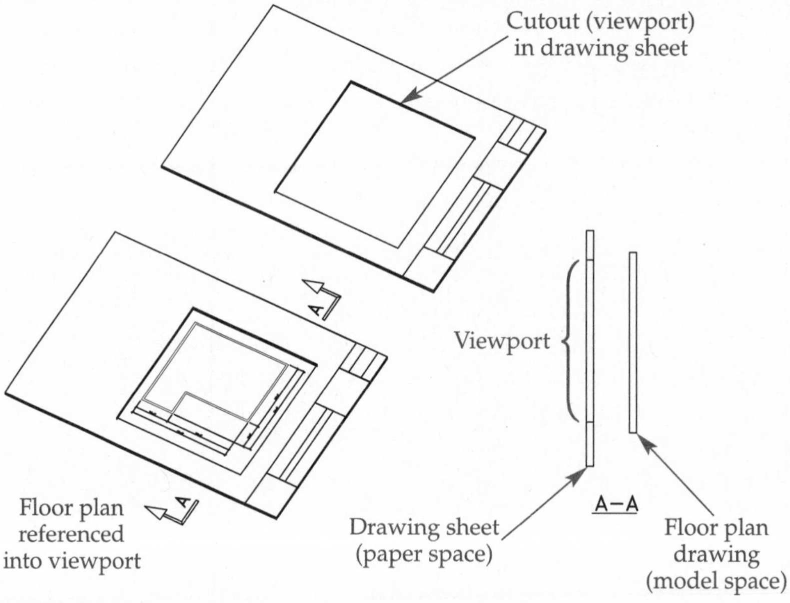

Figure 24-15.
Views of other drawings can be seen through viewports cut into paper space.

Cutout (viewport) in drawing sheet

Viewport

Floor plan referenced into viewport

Drawing sheet (paper space)

A–A

Floor plan drawing (model space)

Figure 24-16.
A floor plan placed inside a viewport.

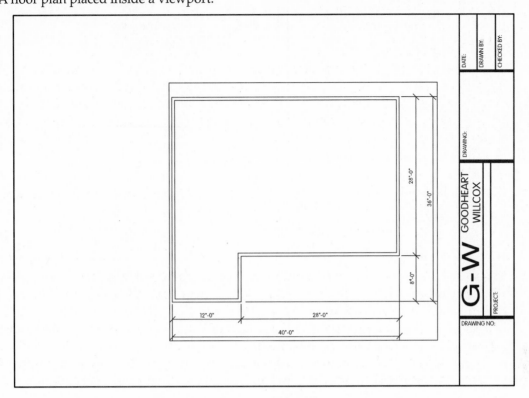

Constructing a Multiview Drawing

Now that you have a good idea of the multiview plotting process, the following example leads you through the details of the procedure. This example uses a house floor plan, a stair detail, and a footing detail. This drawing is *not* among the sample drawings furnished with AutoCAD. Instead, the drawing is based on Exercise 24-1. Complete Exercise 24-1 before working through the example.

EXERCISE 24-1

❑ If you wish to work along at your computer with the following example of multiview drawing construction, complete this exercise before reading further. It is not necessary to complete this exercise in order to understand the process discussed in the following example, but it may assist you in quickly grasping the concepts of the procedure.

❑ The three drawings shown below—the floor plan, stair detail, and footing detail—should be created for this exercise. They are highly simplified for the purpose of this exercise and explanation, and should not be regarded as complete representations of actual designs. Exact dimensions are not necessary, because the purpose of this exercise is to illustrate the creation of a multiview drawing. You may simplify the drawings further to speed up the exercise.

❑ Each drawing should be created, named, and stored separately with different names. Do not put a border or title block on the drawings. The names are shown in the following table:

(Continued on the following page)

FLOOR.DWG		STAIR.DWG		FOOTING.DWG	
Layer	**Color**	**Layer**	**Color**	**Layer**	**Color**
Wall	White	Wall	Yellow	Floor	Green
Dimen	Cyan	Floor	White	Foot	White
Notes	Red	Stair	Green	Dimen	Cyan
		Foot	White	Notes	Red
		Dimen	Cyan	Earth	Yellow
		Notes	Red		

❏ Use the following scales and scale factors when constructing each of the drawings.

> FLOOR.DWG: 1/4″ = 1′-0″ (Scale factor = 48)
> STAIR.DWG: 3/8″ = 1′-0″ (Scale factor = 32)
> FOOTING.DWG: 3/4″ = 1′-0″ (Scale factor = 16)

The scale factors are important when setting the **DIMSCALE** dimensioning variable, and when establishing text height. Remember to multiply the plotted text height, such as .125, by the scale factor, such as 48, to get the text height to use in AutoCAD (.125 × 48 = 6). The scale factor is also used with the **ZOOM XP** command and viewport scale discussed later in the text.

❏ Save the drawings to a hard disk folder, preferably not in the \Acad2000 folder. Check with your instructor or supervisor before creating or using hard disk space. Save backup copies on a diskette.

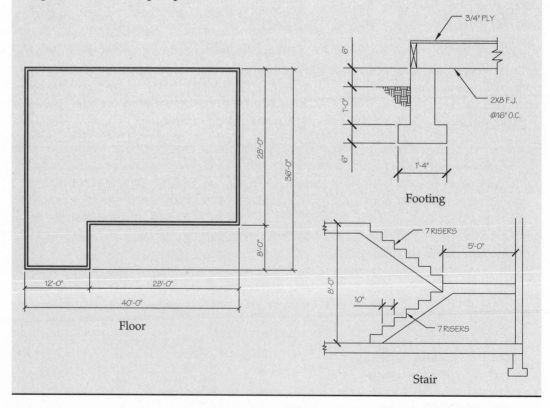

Floor

Footing

Stair

Initial Drawing Setup

The first aspect of drawing setup is to place a border and title block on the screen. These items are created in the layout tab. They should be the proper size for the plot you wish to make. This can be accomplished in one of the following ways, depending on the depth of your preparation:

- Draw a border on a separate layer, then draw a title block.
- Draw a border and insert a predrawn title block.
- Open or insert a predrawn standard border and title block template containing all constant text and attributes for variable information. The Architectural, english units template drawing is a D-size sheet, but is appropriate for this example. It contains one viewport, which shows as a thin line just inside the left border line. Erase this viewport before creating a new one.

The method you use is not of primary importance for this example, but it is always best to use existing borders and title blocks to maximize efficiency and consistency.

PROFESSIONAL TIP   This initial setup phase is unnecessary if your school or company uses preprinted border and title block sheets. You might use a *phantom* border and title block sheet on the screen for layout purposes, and to add additional information to the title block. This phantom information can be frozen before plotting.

When setting up a drawing, first display a paper space layout, then set the units and limits to match the type of drawing you are creating. Be sure the extents of your border and title block match the maximum active plotting area, or *clip limits* of your plotter. This example uses a standard architectural C-size sheet (18″ × 24″), and assumes that the plotter's active area is .75″ less along the top and bottom and 1.25″ less on the sides, for a total plotting area of 16.5″ × 21.5″.

NOTE   Use the page setup options to accurately create an appropriate layout based on your specific plotter or printer and available paper sizes. Settings selected in the **Page Setup** dialog box are immediately reflected in the selected layout. See Chapter 10 for information on the **Page Setup** dialog box.

Set the units and limits for the new layout as follows (if you do not use a template or page setup):

1. Pick a layout tab.
2. Set the following in the **Drawing Units** dialog box:
   - Architectural units.
   - Units precision = 1/2″.
   - System of angle measure = Decimal degrees.
   - Angle precision = 0.
   - Direction for angle 0 = East.
   - Angles measured counterclockwise.
3. Set the drawing limits to 26,20.
4. Pick **Zoom all** button from the **Standard** toolbar.

The upper-right corner limit of 26,20 provides additional space on the screen outside the paper limits.

Creating New Layers

The border and title block should be on a separate layer, so you may want to create a new layer called Border or Title and assign it a separate color. Be sure to make this new layer current before you draw the border.

At this point, you can set an appropriate snap grid and visible grid values. If you wish to use an existing border and title block, insert it now. The template drawing should include proper grid and snap settings.

One of the principle functions of this example is to use existing drawings of the house floor plan, stairs, and footing. These drawings will not become a part of our new drawing, but they will be *referenced* to the current drawing in order to save drawing file space. Therefore, you should also create a new layer for these drawings and name it Xref. Assign the Xref layer the color of 7.

The referenced drawings will fit inside viewports. These viewports can be any shape and are given the object name of viewport. Therefore, they can be edited like any other AutoCAD object. Create a layer called Viewports for these entities and assign it a color.

The layers of any existing drawings that you reference (xref) into your new drawing remain intact. Therefore, you do not have to create additional layers unless you want to add information to your drawing.

If you do not have an existing C-size architectural border and title block, you can draw a border at this time. Make the Border layer current and draw a polyline border using the **RECTANG** command at the dimensions of 16.5″ × 21.5″. Draw a title block if you wish. Your screen should look similar to Figure 24-17.

Figure 24-17.
The border and title block in paper space.

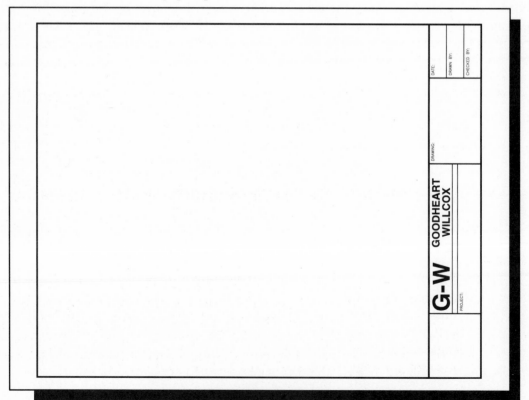

Creating Viewports

The process of creating viewports is completed in a paper space layout because viewports are *cut* out of the paper. When creating a drawing in a layout, your screen represents a sheet of paper. You will now create an opening through which you can view a referenced drawing.

Methods of creating viewports are explained in Chapter 9. For this example, you can select the **Single Viewport** button in the **Viewports** toolbar to create each viewport. Be sure to set the Viewports layer current before creating the viewport. This allows them to be turned off for plotting. Select two points to create a 12″ × 12″ viewport positioned as shown in Figure 24-18.

At this point, you can continue creating as many viewports as required. However, this example continues the process and references a drawing into the new viewport.

Figure 24-18.
A viewport added to the border and title block in paper space.

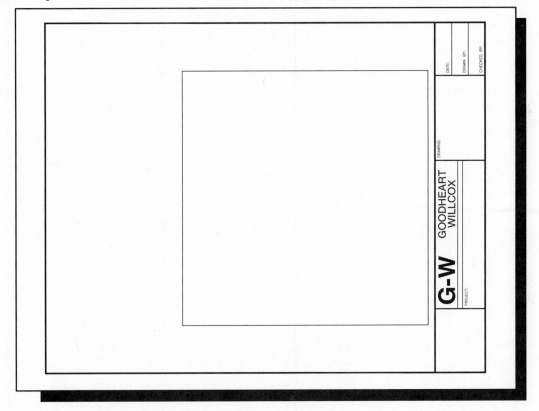

Placing Views in the Drawing

A viewport has now been created into which you can insert a view of the 2D or 3D model (drawing) that has been previously created. In this case, we will reference the drawing of the floor plan named Floor. Instead of using the **INSERT** command, which combines an existing drawing with the new one, use the **XREF** command so that AutoCAD creates a *reference* to the Floor drawing. This allows the size of the new drawing to remain small because the Floor drawing has not been combined with it.

The following procedure allows you to enter model space, reference an existing drawing to the new one, and **ZOOM** to see the referenced drawing.

1. If the layout tab is active, double-click inside the viewport to activate model space within the viewport.

2. Set the Xref layer current.
3. Pick **E<u>x</u>ternal Reference...** from the **<u>I</u>nsert** pull-down menu. The **Select Reference File** dialog box is displayed. See Figure 24-19.
4. Select floor.dwg in the dialog box, and pick the **OK** button.

The **External Reference** dialog box is displayed. See Figure 24-20. Set the insertion point to 0,0,0 values, the X, Y, and Z scale to 1.0, and the rotation angle to 0. Pick the **OK** button and perform a **ZOOM Extents**. Your drawing should now resemble the one shown in Figure 24-21.

All layers on the referenced drawing are added to the new drawing. These layers can be distinguished from existing layers because the drawing name is automatically placed in front of the layer name and separated by a vertical bar symbol (I). This naming convention is shown in the **Layer Control** drop-down list on the **Object Properties** toolbar and in the **Layer Properties Manager** dialog box.

Figure 24-19.
The **Select Reference File** dialog box.

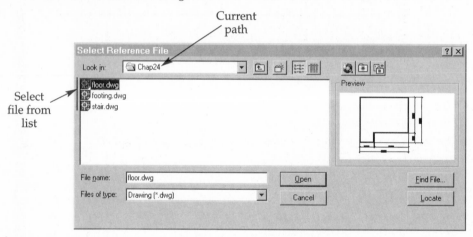

Figure 24-20.
Insertion point, scale, and rotation are set in the **External Reference** dialog box.

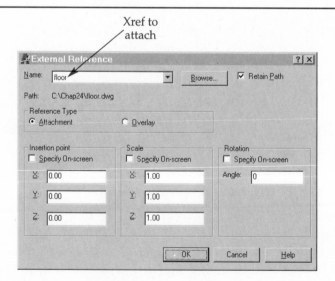

Figure 24-21.
The floor plan is referenced into the first viewport.

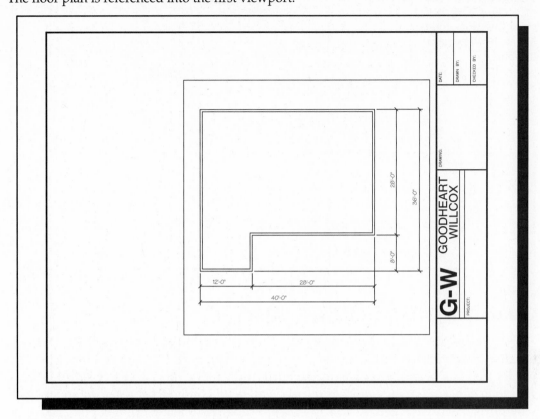

Scaling a Drawing in a Viewport

When a drawing has been referenced and placed in a viewport, it is ready to be scaled. After using the **Extents** option of the **ZOOM** command, the referenced drawing fills the viewport. However, this does not imply that the drawing is displayed at the correct scale.

The scale factor of each view of the multiview drawing is an important number to remember; it is the number used to size your drawing in the viewport. The scale factor is used in conjunction with the **XP** option of the **ZOOM** command, or can be selected in the **Viewports** toolbar. Since the intended final scale of the floor plan on the plotted drawing is to be 1/4" = 1'-0", the scale factor is 48, or 1/48 of full size. A detailed discussion of determining scale factors is given in Chapter 10.

Be sure you are still in the model space environment within the viewport. Enter the following:

> Command: **Z** *or* **ZOOM**↵
> Specify corner of window, enter a scale factor (nX or nXP), or
> [All/Center/Dynamic/Extents/Previous/Scale/Window] <real time>: **1/48XP**↵

The scale can also be set by picking 1/4" = 1' from the scale drop-down list in the **Viewports** toolbar. See Figure 24-22. The drawing may not change much in size, depending on the size of the viewport. Also, keep in mind that the viewport itself is an object that can be moved or stretched if needed. Remember to change to paper space when editing the size of the viewport. If part of your drawing extends beyond the edge of the viewport after applying the scale, simply use grips or the **STRETCH** command to change the size of the viewport.

Figure 24-22.
The scale can be set by picking 1/4″ = 1′ from the drop-down list in the **Viewports** toolbar.

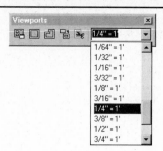

PROFESSIONAL TIP

You can use any display command inside a viewport. If a drawing is not centered after scaling, simply use **PAN** to move it around. If lines of a drawing touch a viewport edge, those lines will not be visible if the viewport layer is frozen or turned off.

Controlling Viewport Layer Visibility

If you create another viewport, the floor plan will immediately fill it. This is because a viewport is just a window through which you can view a drawing or 3D model that has been referenced to the current drawing. One way to control what is visible in subsequent viewports is to freeze all layers of the Floor drawing in any new viewports that are created. Access the **Layer Properties Manager** dialog box and set all layers from the Floor xref to be frozen in new viewports by picking the icons in the **New VP Freeze** column. See Figure 24-23. When the snowflake icon appears in this column, the layer is not displayed in any new viewports.

Figure 24-23.
The snowflake and rectangle icon indicates a frozen layer in a viewport. The sun replaces the snowflake when the layer is thawed.

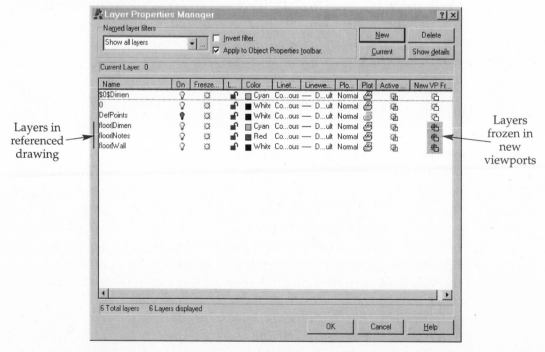

Layers in referenced drawing

Layers frozen in new viewports

The frozen or thawed status in the current viewport is controlled by the icons in the **Active VP Freeze** column.

Creating Additional Viewports

The previous example of creating a viewport and referencing a drawing to it is the same process that is used to create the additional two viewports in our example. In this case, two viewports are created before using the **XREF** command. If you know the number, size, and location of all viewports needed on a multiview drawing, it may save time to create them all at once.

Now that the floor plan layers will be frozen in new viewports, the other two viewports can be created. Use the following procedure:
1. Double-click outside the viewport to activate paper space.
2. Set the Viewports layer current.
3. Draw a viewport to the dimensions shown in Figure 24-24 using the **Polygonal Viewport** button in the **Viewports** toolbar.
4. Draw a third viewport 6" wide and 5" high.
   The final arrangement of the three viewports is shown in Figure 24-25.

Now that the viewports are complete, you can begin referencing the remaining two drawings. The following procedure uses **AutoCAD DesignCenter** to reference the Stair drawing:
1. Set the current layer to Xref, and double-click in the lower-left viewport to make model space active.
2. Activate **AutoCAD DesignCenter**. Locate the folder that contains the stair.dwg file files and pick it. Files contained in the selected folder are displayed in the palette view.
3. Right-click on the stair.dwg file and select **Attach as Xref...** from the shortcut menu. See Figure 24-26. The **External Reference** dialog box is displayed. Use 0,0,0 for the insertion point, 1.0 for the scale, and 0 for the rotation angle.
4. Press [Ctrl]+[2] to temporarily dismiss **DesignCenter**.
5. The scale factor for the stair drawing is 32. Use the **ZOOM** command and enter 1/32XP to scale the drawing correctly.

Figure 24-24.
Draw this polygonal
viewport.

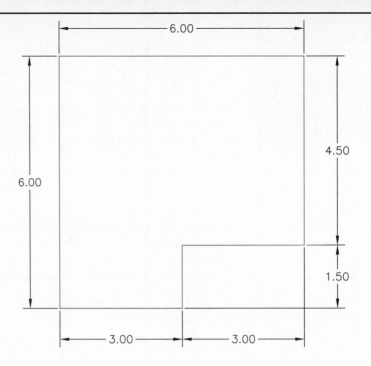

Figure 24-25.
Two additional viewports are placed and sized in the drawing.

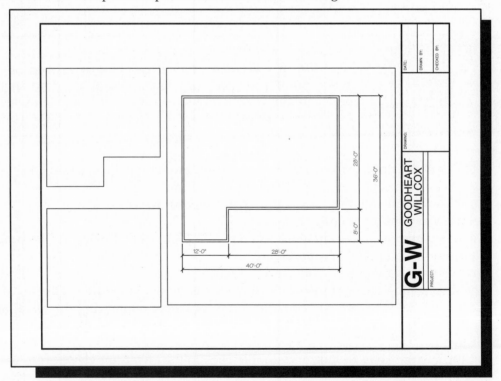

Figure 24-26.
Attaching a
reference drawing
using **AutoCAD**
DesignCenter.

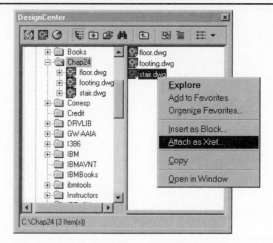

The drawing now appears as shown in Figure 24-27. Notice that the stair drawing is shown in all three viewports. Use the **Layer Properties Manager** dialog box to freeze the stair layers in selected viewports using the following procedure:

1. Pick the large viewport to make it active.
2. Open the **Layer Properties Manager** dialog box.
3. Select all layers that begin with the name of the referenced drawing you wish to freeze in the active viewport. In this case, all layers that begin with STAIR are selected.
4. Pick the sun icon in the **Active VP Freeze** column of one of the selected layers. All selected icons change to a snowflake. Pick **OK**. The stair drawing is now removed from the large viewport.

Repeat this procedure to freeze stair layers in the upper-left viewport.

Figure 24-27.
The reference drawing stair is displayed in all viewports. Use the **Layer Properties Manager** dialog box to restrict its visibility.

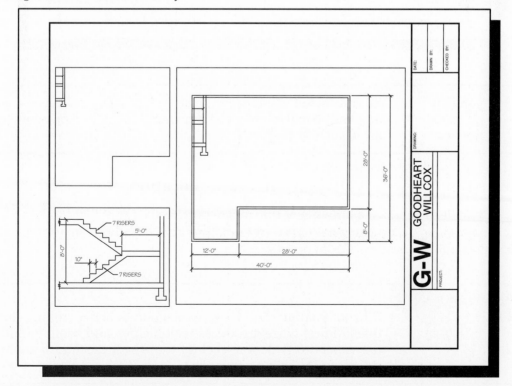

The final drawing can now be inserted into the last viewport. Prepare the third view by following these steps:

1. Double-click in the upper-left viewport.
2. Set the Xref layer current.
3. Attach the footing drawing as an xref using one of the methods explained earlier in this chapter.
4. Freeze the Footing layers in the other two viewports.
5. Use the **ZOOM** command and enter 1/16XP.

The drawing should now appear as shown in Figure 24-28.

Figure 24-28.
The new drawing is completed by referencing the footing.

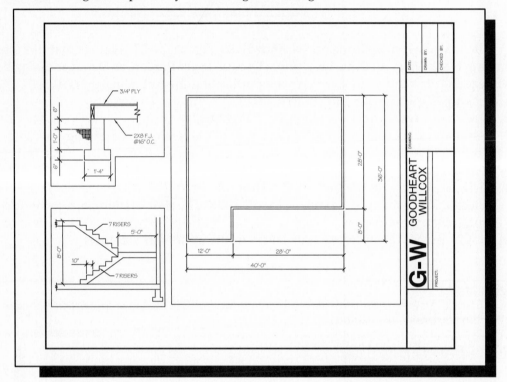

NOTE	Be sure to set the current layer to Xref when referencing a drawing so that the inserted drawing is not placed on another layer, such as Viewports.

Adjusting Viewport Display, Size, and Location

If you need to adjust a drawing within a viewport, first be sure that model space is current. Then, pick the desired viewport to make it active, and use an appropriate display command, such as **ZOOM** or **PAN**.

PROFESSIONAL TIP 	When a floating model space viewport is active, rolling the IntelliMouse wheel produces realtime pan and zoom within the viewport. A double-click of the wheel executes a zoom extents in the active viewport.

The entire viewport can be moved to another location, but you must first activate the paper space layout. Pick the viewport border to display its grips. An object inside the viewport is not selected when picked because those objects are in model space. After selection, adjust the location of the viewports.

Changing viewport shape and size

Paper space viewport shape and size can be quickly changed using the **VPCLIP** command. This command can also be accessed by selecting the **Clip Existing Viewport** button in the **Viewports** toolbar. A viewport can be clipped by either selecting an existing shape that has been drawn or by drawing a new polygon. Use the following procedure to change the shape of a viewport.

1. Activate a paper space layout. Pick the **Clip Existing Viewport** button in the **Viewports** toolbar.
2. Select the outline of the viewport to be resized.
3. Select the new clipping object, such as a circle that has been previously drawn over the current viewport. The old viewport is deleted.

The **Delete** option of the **VPCLIP** command enables you to delete a viewport that was previously clipped. It prompts you to select the clipping object, which is the new shape that was drawn to clip the old viewport. After selecting the viewport and pressing [Enter], the original viewport is restored and the clipped version is deleted.

Locking the viewport scale

Once a drawing has been scaled properly inside a viewport, it is important to avoid using zoom again prior to plotting. AutoCAD 2000 provides a viewport locking feature that helps prevent inadvertent zooms. To lock the display in a viewport, access the **Properties** window and then select the viewport from paper space. Change the Display locked property to yes. Repeat the procedure for all viewports you wish to lock.

Adding notes and titles

There are two ways in which titles and notes can be added to a multiview drawing. The first method is to add the notations to the original drawing. In this manner, all titles and notes are referenced to the new drawing. This is the best system to use if the titles, scale label, and notes will not change.

However, titles may change. You may want to be sure that all titles of views are the same text style, or you might want to add a special symbol. This is easily completed after the drawings are referenced. The most important thing to remember is that the paper space layout must be active to add text. You can use new and existing text styles to add titles and notes to a drawing using the **DTEXT** or **MTEXT** command. See Figure 24-29.

Removing viewport outlines

The viewport outlines can be turned off for plotting purposes, as shown in Figure 24-29. Open the **Layer Properties Manager** dialog box and click on the plot icon for the appropriate layer. A red circle and diagonal slash is placed over the symbol, indicating that this layer will not plot.

NOTE	If you freeze the Viewports layer and a box still surrounds one of the views, you are probably still in model space. Remember that a box outlines the current viewport in model space. Enter PS at the Command: prompt or pick the **Model** button on the status bar to enter paper space and the outline disappears.

Figure 24-29.
The completed drawing with titles added and viewport outlines turned off.

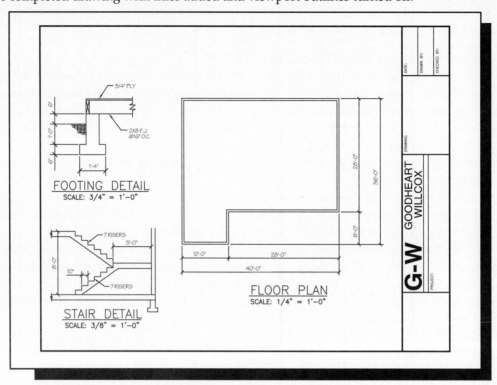

Plotting a Multiview Drawing

You have already taken care of scaling the views when you referenced them and used the **ZOOM XP** command. The drawing that now appears on your screen in paper space can be plotted at full scale, 1=1, with the **PLOT** command.

Using the **PLOT** command in this manner is a simple procedure, but only if you planned your drawing at the start of the project. The process of creating a properly scaled multiview layout will go smoothly if you have planned the project. Review the following items, and keep them in mind when starting any drawing or design project—especially one that involves the creation of a multiview paper space layout.

- Determine the size of paper to be used.
- Determine the type of title block, notes, revision blocks, parts lists, etc., that will appear on the drawing.
- Prepare a quick sketch of the view layouts and their plotted scales.
- Determine the scales to be used for each viewport.
- Establish proper text styles and heights based on the drawing scale factors.
- Set the **DIMSCALE** variable using the proper scale factor when creating drawings in model space.

There is no substitute for planning a project before you begin. It may seem like an unnecessary expense of time, but it will save time later in the project, and may help you become more productive in all your work.

EXERCISE 24-2

❑ Use the template method to recall the border and title block drawing you used in Exercise 24-1. Name the drawing EX24-2.
❑ Create layers for referenced drawings (Xref) and viewports (Viewport).
❑ Select a paper space layout tab.
❑ Create an arrangement of three viewports on the Viewport layer. Leave space in the upper-right corner for an additional viewport.
❑ **ZOOM** to display the open area in the upper-right corner of the drawing.
❑ Create a single viewport in the current screen display.
❑ Reference the floor drawing used in Exercise 24-1 into one of the viewports in the group of three viewports. Be sure the Xref layer is current.
❑ Save the drawing as EX24-2.

Chapter Test

Answer the following questions on a separate sheet of paper.
1. When inserting an xref, how does the **Overlay** option differ from the **Attach** option?
2. What effect does the use of referenced drawings have on drawing file size?
3. When are xrefs updated in the master drawing?
4. Why would you want to bind a dependent symbol to a master drawing?
5. What does the layer name WALL0NOTES mean?
6. Name the system variable that controls the creation of the xref log file.
7. What are spatial and layer indexes and what function do they perform?
8. What keyboard strokes can be used to display or dismiss the **AutoCAD DesignCenter**?
9. What command is used to edit external references in place?
10. What is the function of the **VPCLIP** command?
11. What is the purpose of locking a viewport?
12. Your drawings should be created in what *space*?
13. Why would you want to reference one drawing to another rather than insert it?
14. Indicate the command and value you would use to specify a 1/2″ = 1′-0″ scale inside a viewport.
15. How do you freeze all layers of a referenced drawing inside any new viewports?
16. Do you need to be in paper space or model space in order to resize a viewport?
17. Explain why you should plan your plots.

Drawing Problems

1. Open one of your dimensioned drawings from Chapter 19. Construct a multiview layout and generate a plot on C-size paper.
   A. Create four viewports of equal size, separated by 1" of empty space.
   B. Select each viewport and display a different view of the drawing.
   C. Plot the drawing and be sure to use the scale of 1 = 1.
   D. Save the drawing as P24-1.

2. Open one of your dimensioned drawings from Chapter 19. Construct a multiview layout and generate a plot on C-size or B-size paper. Create a single viewport and plot at the scale of 1:1.

3. Open one of your dimensioned drawings from Chapter 20. Construct a multiview layout and generate a plot on C-size or B-size paper. Create a single viewport and plot at the scale of 1:1.

4. Open one of your dimensioned drawings from Chapter 21. Construct a multiview layout and generate a plot on C-size or B-size paper. Create a single viewport and plot at the scale of 1:1.

5. Open one of your drawings from Chapter 22. Construct a multiview layout and generate a plot on C-size or B-size paper. Create a single viewport and plot at the scale of 1:1.

6. Open one of your drawings from Chapter 23. Construct a multiview layout and generate a plot on C-size or B-size paper. Create a single viewport and plot at the scale of 1:1.

CHAPTER 25

Assigning Attributes and Generating a Bill of Materials

Learning Objectives

After completing this chapter, you will be able to:

- Assign visible or hidden attributes to blocks.
- Edit attributes defined for existing blocks.
- Create a template file for the storage of block attribute data.
- Extract attribute values to create a bill of materials.

Blocks become more useful when written information is provided with them. It is even more helpful to assign information that is either visible (displayed) or hidden. From this data, a list very similar to a bill of materials can be requested and printed.

Written or numerical values assigned to blocks are called *attributes* by AutoCAD. Attribute information can be *extracted* from the drawing, in addition to being used as text. Several blocks with attributes are shown in Figure 25-1.

The creation, editing, and extraction of attributes can be performed with dialog boxes that are displayed by the **ATTDEF**, **ATTEDIT**, **PROPERTIES**, and **ATTEXT** commands. You can also define, manage, and extract attributes at the command line by using the **-ATTDEF**, **ATTDISP**, and **-ATTEXT** commands. This chapter introduces these commands and discusses how they are used to create textual information for drawing symbols and extract data for a bill of materials.

The **ATTDEF** (attribute define) command allows you to create attribute text and specify how it is displayed. The **ATTDISP** (attribute display) command governs which attributes are displayed. You can selectively or collectively edit attributes using the **ATTEDIT**(attribute edit) command. Using the **ATTEXT** (attribute extract) command, you can extract attributes from a drawing in a list or report form.

NOTE   A command line version of a command that displays a dialog box is distinguished by entering a dash, or hyphen, in front of the command. For example, the command line version of the **ATTDEF** dialog box command is **-ATTDEF**.

Figure 25-1.
Examples of blocks with defined attributes.

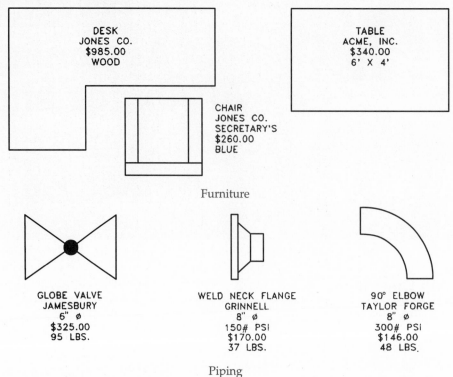

Furniture

Piping

ASSIGNING ATTRIBUTES TO BLOCKS

The first step in defining attributes for a block is to decide what information about the block is needed. In most cases, the name of the object should be your first attribute. This could be followed by other attribute items, such as the manufacturer, type, size, price, and weight. After you determine which attributes to assign, decide how you should be prompted to enter a value for each attribute. A typical prompt, for example, might be What is the size?

Suppose you are drawing a valve symbol for a piping flow diagram. You might want to list all the product-related data along with the symbol. The number of attributes needed is limited only by the project requirements.

Once the symbol is drawn, you can use the **ATTDEF** (attribute define) command to assign attributes. To access this command, pick **Define Attributes...** from the **Block** cascading menu in the **Draw** pull-down menu, or enter ATT or ATTDEF at the Command: prompt. This displays the **Attribute Definition** dialog box, Figure 25-2.

This dialog box is divided into four areas. Each area allows you to set the specific aspects of an attribute. The four areas, their components, and other features in the **Attribute Definition** dialog box are described as follows:

- **Mode area.** Use this area to specify any of the attribute modes you wish to set. The following is a description of each mode option:
  - **Invisible.** If you want the attribute to be shown with the inserted block, leave the **Invisible** check box inactive. If you activate this check box, the attribute will not be displayed when the block is inserted.
  - **Constant.** If you decide the value of the attribute should always be the same, activate the **Constant** check box. This means that all future uses of the block will display the same attribute value (and you will not be prompted for a new value). If you wish to use different attribute values for inserted blocks, leave this check box inactive.

Figure 25-2.
Attributes can be assigned to blocks using the **Attribute Definition** dialog box.

Select one · or more attribute modes

Select the insertion point

Enter an attribute tag, prompt, and value

Specify the text settings

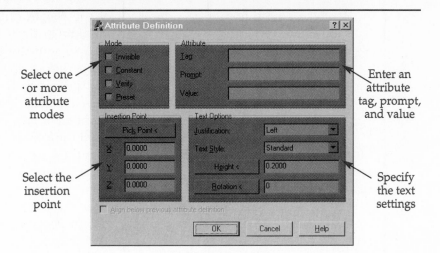

- **Verify.** Activate the **Verify** check box if you want a verification prompt to ask you whether the specified attribute value is correct when you insert the block. If you do not wish to be prompted for verification, leave this check box inactive.
- **Preset.** If you want all attributes to assume preset values during the insertion of a block, activate the **Preset** check box. This option disables all attribute prompts during a block insertion. Default values are used instead. Leave this check box inactive if you wish to display the normal prompts.

If you do not activate any of the attribute options, the display on the command line will be in **Normal** mode. This means that you will be prompted to enter values for all attributes, and they will be visible when inserted with a block.

- **Attribute area.** This area lets you assign a tag, prompt, and value to the attribute in the corresponding text boxes. The entries in these text boxes can contain up to 256 characters. If the first character in an entry is a space, start the string with a backslash (\). If the first character is a backslash, begin the entry with two backslashes (\\). Each option is described as follows:
  - **Tag: text box.** Use this text box to enter the name, or tag, of the attribute. You must enter a name or number. Any characters can be used, except spaces and exclamation marks. All text is displayed in uppercase.
  - **Prompt: text box.** Use this text box to enter a prompt statement that you want AutoCAD to prompt you with when the block is inserted. For example, if Size is specified as the attribute tag, you might enter What is the valve size? or Enter valve size: as the insertion prompt. If the **Constant** attribute mode is set, this option is inactive.
  - **Value: text box.** The entry in this text box is used as a *default* attribute value when the block is inserted, unless you change it at the insertion prompt. You do not have to enter anything in this text box. You might decide to enter a message regarding the type of information needed, such as 10 SPACES MAX or NUMBERS ONLY. The default value is displayed in chevrons (< >) when you are prompted for the attribute value.
- **Text Options area.** This area allows you to specify the justification, style, height, and rotation angle for attribute text. The options in this area are described as follows:
  - **Justification:.** You can use the **Justification:** drop-down list to select a justification option for the attribute text. The default option is Left.
  - **Text Style:.** To specify a text style for the attribute, access the **Text Style:** drop-down list to display all of the text styles in the current drawing. The default style is Standard.

- **Height.** Use the text box to the right of the **Height** button to specify the height of the attribute text. Selecting the **Height** button temporarily returns you to the drawing area and allows you to indicate the text height by picking points on screen. Once the points are picked, the dialog box returns and the corresponding height is shown in the text box.
- **Rotation.** To specify a rotation angle for the attribute text, enter an angular value in the text box next to the **Rotation** button. This button and the text box work in the same manner as the **Height** button and text box.
- **Insertion Point area.** This area is used to select the location, or insertion point, for the attribute. Selecting the **Pick Point** button temporarily returns you to the drawing area and allows you to pick a point on screen. Once the insertion point is picked, the dialog box returns and the point is indicated by the coordinates in the **X:**, **Y:**, and **Z:** text boxes. You can also enter your own coordinates in these text boxes to specify an insertion point.
- **Align below previous attribute definition check box.** When you first access the **Attribute Definition** dialog box, this check box is grayed out. After you create a block attribute, you can press [Enter] to reissue the **ATTDEF** command and create another attribute. When the **Attribute Definition** dialog box is redisplayed, the **Align below previous attribute definition** check box can be activated. If you want the next attribute to be placed below the first with the same justification, pick this check box. When you do this, the **Text Options** and **Insertion Point** areas become inactive.

When you are finished defining the attribute, pick **OK**. The attribute tag is then placed on screen. If you set the attribute mode to **Invisible**, do not be dismayed; this is the only time the tag appears. When the block is inserted, you are prompted for information based on how you defined the attribute.

Once you have created attributes for an object, you can use the **BLOCK** or **WBLOCK** command to define the object as a block. Blocks were discussed in Chapter 23. When creating the block, be sure to select all of the objects and attributes that go with the block. If you use the **Block Definition** or **Write Block** dialog box, it is recommended that you deactivate the **Retain** check box. When the block is created, the selected objects should disappear, as well as the attributes. If any attributes remain on screen, undo the command and try again, making sure that all of the attributes are selected.

NOTE Attributes can be defined at the Command: prompt using the **-ATTDEF** command. To access this command, enter -ATT or -ATTDEF at the Command: prompt. The command sequence then provides all the options found in the **Attribute Definition** dialog box.

AutoCAD User's Guide **13**

EDITING ATTRIBUTE DEFINITIONS

Occasionally you may need to change certain aspects of text attributes *before* they are included in a block or wblock definition. If you only want to change the tag, prompt, or default value assigned to a text attribute, you may do so quickly using the **DDEDIT** command. To access the **DDEDIT** command, pick the **Edit Text** button on the **Modify II** toolbar, select **Text...** from the **Modify** pull-down menu, or enter ED or DDEDIT at the Command: prompt. The **DDEDIT** command allows you to select only one attribute definition at a time. The command sequence is as follows:

DDEDIT
ED

Modify
➡ Text...

Modify II
toolbar

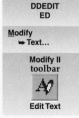

Edit Text

Command: **ED** *or* **DDEDIT**↵
Select an annotation object or [Undo]: *(select one attribute definition to change)*

The **Edit Attribute Definition** dialog box is displayed, Figure 25-3. Revise the **Tag:**, **Prompt:**, or **Default:** values as required in the corresponding text boxes. When you are done making changes, pick **OK** to close the dialog box. The **DDEDIT** command prompt remains on the command line, should you want to select another object or undo the changes you made. When you are finished, press [Enter] to end the command.

Figure 25-3.
The **Edit Attribute Definition** dialog box is used to change the tag, prompt, or default value of an attribute.

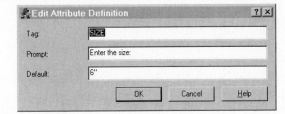

Using the Properties Window

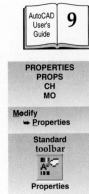

The **Properties** window provides expanded editing capabilities for attribute text. To activate this window, pick the **Properties** button on the **Standard** toolbar, pick **Properties** from the **Modify** pull-down menu, or enter CH, MO, PROPS, or PROPERTIES at the Command: prompt. You can also select the attribute text to be edited before accessing the window by using your pointing device to activate grips on the attribute. Then, right-click and select **Properties** from the shortcut menu to display the **Properties** window.

After a text attribute is selected, Attribute appears in the text box near the top of the window. The **Categorized** tab separates the properties and defined values of an attribute into four groups: **General**, **Text**, **Geometry**, and **Misc**. See Figure 25-4. These groups list all aspects of the attribute and enable you to change their values.

You can change the color, linetype, layer, or thickness of the selected attribute in the **General** section. The attribute tag, prompt, and default value entries are listed in the **Text** section. You can select **Tag**, **Prompt**, or **Value** to change the corresponding values. There are also options to change the text style, justification, height, rotation

Figure 25-4.
The **Properties** window can be used to modify attributes.

Selected object to edit

Pick to change the attribute tag

Pick to change an attribute mode setting

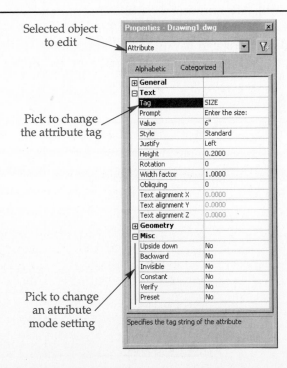

angle, width factor, and obliquing angle in the **Text** section. You can change the insertion point of the text attribute in the **Geometry** section by using the **Position** options to enter new coordinates. Additional text options are available in the **Misc** section.

Perhaps the most powerful feature of the **Properties** window for editing attributes is the ability to change the attribute modes that were originally defined. As discussed earlier, an attribute may be defined with the **Invisible**, **Constant**, **Verify**, or **Preset** modes active. Remember that the **Constant** mode assumes the values of an attribute will remain unchanged. Therefore, no prompt is defined for the attribute and no prompt is presented when the attribute is inserted with the block.

To revise the attribute definition for normal prompting, select **Constant** in the **Misc** section and pick Yes from the drop-down list. Then, select **Prompt** in the **Text** section and enter a prompt. If you want to turn on the **Verify** or **Preset** modes, or change an attribute from visible to invisible, select the appropriate option in the **Misc** section and pick Yes in the corresponding drop-down list.

NOTE

Attribute definitions can also be modified using the **CHANGE** command. Enter -CH or CHANGE at the Command: prompt and select the attribute. You are then prompted to modify the insertion point, text style, height, rotation angle, tag, prompt, and default value.

INSERTING BLOCKS WITH ATTRIBUTES

When you use the **INSERT** command to place a saved block with attributes in your drawing, you are prompted for additional information after the insertion point, scale factors, and rotation angle are specified. The prompt statement that you entered with the **ATTDEF** command appears, and the default attribute value appears in brackets. Accept the default by pressing [Enter], or provide a new value. The attribute is then displayed with the block.

Attribute prompts may be answered using a dialog box if the **ATTDIA** system variable is set to 1 (on). After issuing the **INSERT** command and entering the insertion point, scale, and rotation angle of a block, the **Enter Attributes** dialog box appears. See Figure 25-5. This dialog box can list up to eight attributes. If the block has more than eight attributes, you can display the next page of attributes by clicking the **Next** button.

Figure 25-5.
The **Enter Attributes** dialog box allows you to enter or change attribute definitions when a block is inserted.

Accept or change the existing attributes

Pick to display the next page of attributes

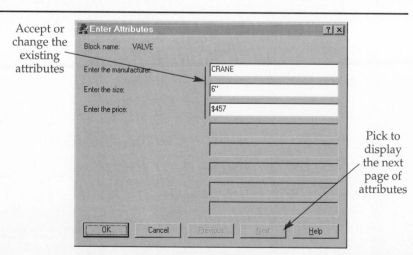

Responding to attribute prompts in a dialog box has distinct advantages over answering the prompts on the command line. With the dialog box, you can see at a glance whether all the attribute values are correct. To change a value, simply move to the incorrect value and enter a new one. You can quickly move forward through the attributes and buttons in the **Enter Attributes** dialog box by using the [Tab] key. Using the [Shift]+[Tab] key combination cycles through the attributes and buttons in reverse order. When you are finished, pick **OK** to close the dialog box. The inserted block with attributes then appears on screen.

PROFESSIONAL TIP

Set the **ATTDIA** system variable to 1 in your template drawings to automatically activate the **Enter Attributes** dialog box whenever you insert a block with attributes.

EXERCISE 25-1

❑ Start a new drawing using your A-size or B-size architectural template.
❑ Draw the valve symbol shown.

GATE
CRANE
6"
$457

❑ Assign the attributes listed in the table below using the **ATTDEF** command.

Tag	Prompt	Value	Mode
Type	*(None)*	GATE	Constant
Mfr.	Enter the valve manufacturer:	CRANE	Invisible
Size	Enter the size:	6"	Normal and preset
Price	Enter the price:	$457	Invisible and Verify

❑ Create a block or wblock the object. Include the valve symbol and the attributes in the block definition and name it VALVE.
❑ Use the **INSERT** command to insert the VALVE block into your drawing. Enter new values for the attributes if you wish. You should be prompted twice for the price if the **Verify** mode was set properly (if you are not using the **Enter Attributes** dialog box).
❑ Save the drawing as EX25-1.

Attribute Prompt Suppression

Some drawings may use blocks with attributes that always retain their default values. In this case, there is no need to be prompted for the attribute values when inserting a block. You can turn off the attribute prompts by setting the **ATTREQ** system variable to 0.

After making this setting, try inserting the VALVE block. Notice that none of the attribute prompts appear. The **ATTREQ** system variable setting is saved with the drawing. To display attribute prompts again, change the setting back to 1.

Part of your project and drawing planning should involve the setting of system variables such as **ATTREQ**. Setting **ATTREQ** to 0 before using blocks can save time in the drawing process. Always remember to set **ATTREQ** back to 1 when you want to use the prompts instead of accepting defaults. When anticipated attribute prompts are not issued, you should check the current **ATTREQ** setting and adjust it if necessary.

Controlling the Display of Attributes

Attributes are intended to contain valuable information about the blocks in your drawings. This information is normally not displayed on screen or during plotting. The principal function of attributes is to generate materials lists and to speed accounting. In most cases, you can use the **DTEXT** and **MTEXT** commands to create specific labels or other types of text. To control the display of attributes on screen, use the **ATTDISP** (attribute display) command. This command can be accessed by picking **Attribute Display** from the **Display** cascading menu in the **View** pull-down menu, or by entering ATTDISP at the Command: prompt:

Command: **ATTDISP**↵
Enter attribute visibility setting [Normal/ON/OFF] <Normal>:

The command options are described as follows:
- **Normal.** This option displays attributes exactly as you created them. This is the default setting.
- **ON.** This option displays *all* attributes, including those defined with the **Invisible** mode.
- **OFF.** This option suppresses the display of all attributes.

After attributes have been drawn, defined with blocks, and checked for correctness, hide them by entering the **Off** option of the **ATTDISP** command. If attributes are left on, they clutter the screen and lengthen regeneration time. In a drawing where attributes should be visible but are not, check the current setting of **ATTDISP** and adjust it if necessary.

AutoCAD
User's
Guide **13**

ATTEDIT
ATE
DDATTE

Modify
➥ Attribute
➥ Single...

Modify II
toolbar

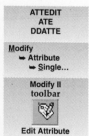

Edit Attribute

CHANGING ATTRIBUTE VALUES

As discussed earlier, you can freely edit attribute definitions using the **Properties** window or the **DDEDIT** command before they are included in a block definition. However, once the block is created, the attributes are part of it and any changes must be performed with the **ATTEDIT** (attribute edit) command. This command allows you to change attribute values after selecting a single block reference with attributes. To access the **ATTEDIT** command, pick the **Edit Attribute** button on the **Modify II** toolbar, select **Single...** from the **Attribute** cascading menu in the **Modify** pull-down menu, or enter ATE, ATTEDIT, or DDATTE at the Command: prompt.

After selecting the block reference to be edited, the **Edit Attributes** dialog box is displayed. This dialog box is identical to the **Enter Attributes** dialog box shown in Figure 25-5. To edit an attribute value, highlight the desired attribute and make the necessary changes. The edited changes are shown with the block.

❏ Open drawing EX25-1.

❏ Insert the VALVE block into your drawing three times. Accept the default attribute values. Align the blocks vertically as shown below.

❏ Issue the **ATTDISP** command and enter the **On** option to display all attributes.

❏ Use the **ATTEDIT** command to change the attribute values to those listed in the table below. Assume the blocks are numbered 1 to 3, from top to bottom.

	1	2	3
Type	GATE	GATE	GATE
Mfr.	CRANE	POWELL	JENKINS
Size	4″	8″	10″
Price	$376	$563	$837

❏ Save the drawing as EX25-2.

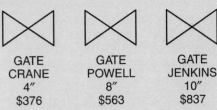

GATE   GATE   GATE
CRANE   POWELL   JENKINS
4″   8″   10″
$376 $563 $837

Using FIND to Edit Attributes

One of the quickest ways to edit attributes is with the **FIND** command. Pick the **Find and Replace** button in the **Standard** toolbar to access the **Find and Replace** dialog box. You can then search the entire drawing for an attribute, or you can search a selected group of objects. The **Find and Replace** dialog box is discussed in detail in Chapter 8.

PROFESSIONAL TIP

If you know that specific attributes may need to be changed in the future, make a group out of them. Use the **GROUP** command, select all the attributes, and give the group a name. Then, after picking the **Select objects** button in the **Find and Replace** dialog box, type G at the command prompt and enter the name of the group. All objects in that group are selected.

Editing Attribute Values and Properties at the Command Line

The **ATTEDIT** command allows you to edit attribute values in a dialog box by selecting blocks one at a time. You can also edit several block attributes at once, edit attributes individually, or change attribute properties by answering prompts on the command line. This type of attribute editing is done using the **-ATTEDIT** command. To access this command, pick **Attribute** from the **Modify** pull-down menu and then select **Global**, or enter -ATE or -ATTEDIT at the Command: prompt:

Command: **-ATE** *or* **-ATTEDIT**↵
Edit attributes one at a time? [Yes/No] <Y>:

-ATTEDIT
-ATE

Modify
➥ Attribute
    ➥ Global

This prompt asks if you want to edit attributes individually. Pressing [Enter] at this prompt allows you to select any number of different block attributes for individual editing. AutoCAD lets you edit them all, one at a time, without leaving the command. It is also possible to change the same attribute on several insertions of the same block. If you enter the **-ATTEDIT** command and respond with No, you may change specific letters, words, and values of a single attribute. This lets you change all other insertions, or instances, of the same block, and is known as *global editing*. For example, suppose a block named with the attribute RESISTOR was inserted on a drawing in 12 locations. However, you misspelled the attribute as RESISTER. If you enter the **-ATTEDIT** command and specify No when asked whether to edit attributes individually, you can edit the attribute *globally*.

Each **-ATTEDIT** editing technique allows you to determine the exact block and attribute specifications to edit. The following prompts appear after you specify individual or global editing:

```
Enter block name specification <*>:
Enter attribute tag specification <*>:
Enter attribute value specification <*>:
```

To selectively edit attribute values, respond to each prompt with the correct name or value. You are then prompted to select one or more attributes. Suppose you receive the following message after entering an attribute value and selecting an attribute:

```
0 found
```

You have picked an attribute that was not specified correctly. It is often quicker to press [Enter] at each of the three specification prompts and then *pick* the attribute you need to edit.

Editing Several Insertions of the Same Attribute

A situation may occur where a block having a wrong or misspelled attribute is inserted several times. For example, in Figure 25-6, the VALVE block was inserted three times with the manufacturer's name specified as CRANE. Unfortunately, the name was supposed to be POWELL. To change the attribute for each insertion, enter the **-ATTEDIT** command and specify global editing. Respond to the prompts in the following manner:

```
Command: -ATE or -ATTEDIT↵
Edit attributes one at a time? [Yes/No] <Y>: N↵
Performing global editing of attribute values.
Edit only attributes visible on screen? [Yes/No] <Y>: ↵
Enter block name specification <*>: ↵
Enter attribute tag specification <*>: ↵
Enter attribute value specification <*>: ↵
Select Attributes: (pick CRANE on each of the VALVE blocks and press [Enter] when
    completed)
3 attributes selected.
Enter string to change: CRANE↵
Enter new string: POWELL↵
```

After pressing [Enter], each of the CRANE attributes on the blocks selected is changed to the new value POWELL.

Figure 25-6.
Using the global editing technique with the **-ATTEDIT** command allows you to change the same attribute on several block insertions.

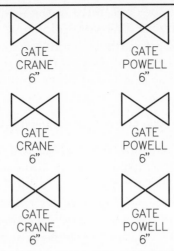

GATE CRANE 6"   GATE POWELL 6"

GATE CRANE 6"   GATE POWELL 6"

GATE CRANE 6"   GATE POWELL 6"

Existing Blocks   After Global Editing

EXERCISE 25-3

❑ Open drawing EX25-1.
❑ Insert the VALVE block into your drawing in three locations.
❑ Issue the **ATTDISP** command and set the attribute display to **On**.
❑ Enter the **-ATTEDIT** command and specify global editing. Change the name of the manufacturer from CRANE to POWELL on each of the blocks. Then, reenter the command and change the price from $457 to $487.
❑ Save the drawing as EX25-3.

PROFESSIONAL TIP

Use care when assigning the **Constant** mode to attribute definitions. The **-ATTEDIT** command displays 0 found if you attempt to edit an inserted block attribute with a **Constant** mode setting. The inserted block must then be exploded and redefined. Assign the **Constant** mode only to attributes you know will not change.

Editing Different Attributes One at a Time

Compared to individual editing, global editing is a quicker and more precise method of changing identical block attribute values. On the other hand, individual editing allows you to change any value on any block attribute in one sequence. Several different attributes and text strings can be changed in order without leaving the **-ATTEDIT** command. After you enter this command and respond Yes to edit attributes one at a time, press [Enter] at the three specification options and select the attributes. Press [Enter] when you are finished. The following prompts then appear:

(*n*) attributes selected.
Enter an option [Value/Position/Height/Angle/Style/Layer/Color/Next] <N>:

Along with this prompt, an "X" marker appears on screen at the first attribute selected. This marker indicates the attribute that is being edited. The order that AutoCAD uses to highlight attributes to edit is the same order in which you selected them. The default command option is **Next**. Pressing [Enter] causes the "X" marker to move to the next attribute in sequence. If you enter a different option and make a change, the marker does not move to the next attribute automatically. It remains in case you want to enter a different option and make another change to the attribute. The individual attribute editing options are described as follows:

- **Value.** This option allows you to change any part of the existing attribute value or enter a new value. The following prompt is displayed when you enter this option:

  Enter type of value modification [Change/Replace] <R>:

  Pressing [Enter] indicates you want to replace the attribute. AutoCAD then requests a new attribute value. You can also change any part of the attribute by entering the **Change** option. AutoCAD responds with Enter string to change: and Enter new string: prompts. A *string* is any sequence of consecutive characters. Enter any successive portion of the existing text string (using uppercase or lowercase characters as needed), and then enter the new text string.
- **Position.** This option allows you to specify a new text insertion point for the attribute value.
- **Height.** This option allows you to change the current text height of the attribute.
- **Angle.** You can use this option to specify a different rotation angle for the attribute.
- **Style.** Enter this option to specify a new attribute text style.
- **Layer.** This option allows you to change the current layer assigned to the attribute.
- **Color.** This option allows you to change the current color assigned to the attribute.

Individual attribute editing can be used to correct misspelled words, replace words, or change other attribute information or properties. In Figure 25-7, two of the attributes assigned to the block were changed. The manufacturer was changed from POWELL to CRANE, and the price was changed from $565 to $556. Suppose these are the only two attributes to be edited. The entire command sequence is as follows:

```
Command: -ATTEDIT↵
Edit attributes one at a time? [Yes/No] <Y>: ↵
Enter block name specification <*>: ↵
Enter attribute tag specification <*>: ↵
Enter attribute value specification <*>: ↵
Select Attributes: (select the two attributes and press [Enter])
2 attributes selected. (the "X" marker appears at POWELL, the first attribute
    selected)
Enter an option [Value/Position/Height/Angle/Style/Layer/Color/Next] <N>: V↵
Enter type of value modification [Change/Replace] <R>: ↵
Enter new attribute value: CRANE↵
Enter an option [Value/Position/Height/Angle/Style/Layer/Color/Next] <N>: (press [Enter]
    to move the "X" marker to the next attribute, $565)
Enter an option [Value/Position/Height/Angle/Style/Layer/Color/Next] <N>: V↵
Enter type of value modification [Change/Replace] <R>: C↵
Enter string to change: 65↵
Enter new string: 56↵
Enter an option [Value/Position/Height/Angle/Style/Layer/Color/Next] <N>: (press [Enter]
    to exit the -ATTEDIT command and have the final change take place)
```

The completed attribute edit is shown in Figure 25-7C.

Figure 25-7.
Several attributes can be selected and edited individually inside the same **-ATTEDIT** command sequence. The attributes to be changed are indicated with the "X" marker.

GATE
POWELL
6"
$565

A

GATE
CRANE
6"
$565

B

GATE
CRANE
6"
$556

C

PROFESSIONAL TIP

When creating blocks that contain attributes, add as many attributes as will be needed. If you do not have values for some of them, simply enter TO COME as the value, or a similar value to remind you that information is needed. Adding an attribute to a block is much more time-consuming than changing an attribute value with the **-ATTEDIT** or **ATTEDIT** command.

Redefining a Block and its Attributes

You may encounter a situation in which an existing block and its associated attributes must be revised. You may need to delete existing attributes, or add new ones, in addition to revising the geometry of the block itself. This could normally be a time-consuming task, but it is made easy with the **ATTREDEF** command. To access this command, enter AT or ATTREDEF at the Command: prompt. You are then prompted to select the attribute to be redefined.

When redefining a block and its attributes, a copy of the existing block must be exploded prior to using the **ATTREDEF** command, or completely new geometry must be used. If this is not done, the following error message will be displayed:

New block has no attributes.

Once you explode the existing block, or draw new geometry, you can use the **ATTREDEF** command. The sequence is as follows:

Command: **AT** or **ATTREDEF**↵
Enter name of the block you wish to redefine: *(enter the block name and press* [Enter]*)*
Select objects for new Block...
Select objects: *(select the block geometry and all new and existing attributes and press* [Enter]*)*
Specify insertion base point of new Block: *(pick the insertion base point)*

After you pick the insertion point, all existing instances of the redefined block and attributes will be immediately updated. If any of the old attributes were omitted from the redefined block, they will not be included in the new version.

Editing a Block and Attributes with the REFEDIT Command

All objects within a block, including attributes, can be edited using the **REFEDIT** command. The reference editing process used for block attributes is similar to that used for blocks and referenced drawings (blocks and external references were discussed in Chapters 23 and 24). The originally defined attributes can be displayed during the edit, and they can be edited. You can also make changes to the original drawing geometry of the block without first exploding the block. The resulting changes can then be saved back to the block, or they can be discarded. Changes to

---

REFEDIT

Modify
➥ In-place Xref
and Block Edit
➥ Edit
Reference

Refedit
toolbar

Edit block or Xref

attributes in the edited block do not affect current instances of the block, and will only take effect for subsequent insertions.

To access the **REFEDIT** command, pick the **Edit block or Xref** button from the **Refedit** toolbar, pick **Edit Reference** from the **In-place Xref and Block Edit** cascading menu in the **Modify** pull-down menu, or enter REFEDIT at the Command: prompt:

Command: **REFEDIT**↵
Select reference:

After you select a block, or *reference*, with attributes, the **Reference Edit** dialog box is displayed. The selected block is highlighted in the **Reference name:** list, and an image of the block is displayed in the **Preview:** tile. To enable attribute editing, activate the **Display attribute definitions for editing** check box and pick **OK**. This allows you to display the attributes and make them available for editing. You are then prompted with the following:

Select nested objects:

To edit the block attributes, pick any part of the drawing geometry belonging to the block. You can also select any other individual objects that are part of the block for editing purposes. Press [Enter] when you are finished selecting objects. Any objects you select become part of the *working set* and are subsequently displayed with the *original* attribute definitions. The assigned attribute values are made invisible, and any unselected objects in the drawing are shown faded to distinguish them from the working set. You can now make changes to the selected drawing geometry, or you can choose to edit the attributes only. To change an attribute definition or an assigned value, enter the **DDEDIT** command and select the attribute. Then, edit the attribute in the **Edit Attribute Definition** dialog box, as described earlier in this chapter. Once you are finished editing all attributes, press [Enter] to exit the **DDEDIT** command, and pick the **Save back changes to reference** button in the **Refedit** toolbar (this toolbar is displayed as long as you are inside the **REFEDIT** command sequence). When a message from AutoCAD asks you whether you want to save the changes and redefine the block, pick **OK**.

Changes made to block attribute values will show up in subsequent uses of the block (any existing references of the block are not updated). However, if a change is made in the above manner to the default value of an attribute defined with the **Constant** mode active, all existing instances of the attribute will be changed when the changes are saved back to the block.

Using the -REFEDIT Command

The **-REFEDIT** command allows you to change block attributes during a reference editing session by answering prompts on the command line. The same editing options used with the **REFEDIT** command are available. The sequence is as follows:

Command: **-REFEDIT**↵
Select reference: *(select the block containing the attributes to edit and press* [Enter]*)*
Select nesting level [Ok/Next] <Next>: **O**↵
Select nested objects: *(select any individual objects contained within the reference that you wish to edit, or select any part of the reference to access attribute editing and press* [Enter]*)*
(n) items selected
Display attribute definitions [Yes/No] <No>: **Y**↵
Use REFCLOSE or the Refedit toolbar to end reference editing session.
Command:

You can now use the **DDEDIT** command to edit the attribute definitions and assigned values. You can also use any other command to edit any selected drawing geometry of the block. When you are through, pick the **Save back changes to reference** button in the **Refedit** toolbar, and then pick **OK** to accept the changes and redefine the block. You can also use the **REFCLOSE** command to exit the reference editing session as follows:

```
Command: REFCLOSE↵
Enter option [Save/Discard reference changes] <Save>: ↵
```

Pick **OK** when you are asked whether to save the changes to the block definition.

USING ATTRIBUTES TO AUTOMATE DRAFTING DOCUMENTATION

So far you have seen that attributes are extremely powerful tools for assigning textual information to drawing symbols. However, attributes may also be used to automate any detailing or documentation task that requires a great deal of text. Such tasks include the creation of title block information and revision block data, as well as the generation of a parts list or list of materials.

Attributes and Title Blocks

After a drawing is completely drawn and dimensioned, it is then necessary to fill out the information used in the drawing title block. This is usually one of the more time-consuming tasks associated with drafting documentation, and it can be efficiently automated by assigning attributes. The following guidelines are suggested:

1. The title block format is first drawn in accordance with industry or company standards. You can use one of the title block formats provided by the **LAYOUT** or **MVSETUP** commands, as discussed in Chapters 10 and 24, or you may create your own. Use the correct layer(s), and be sure to include your company or school logo in the title block. If you work in an industry that produces items for the federal government, also include the applicable FSCM code in the title block. A typical A-size title block drawn in accordance with the ASME Y14.1 *Drawing Sheet Size and Format* standard is illustrated in Figure 25-8.

NOTE The FSCM (Federal Supply Code for Manufacturers) is a five-digit numerical code identifier applicable to any organization that produces items used by the federal government. It also applies to government activities that are responsible for the development of certain specifications, drawings, or standards that control the design of items.

---

2. After drawing the title block, create a separate layer for the title block attributes. By placing the attributes on a separate layer, you can easily suppress the title block information by freezing the layer that contains the attributes. This can greatly reduce redraw and regeneration times. When you are ready to plot the finished drawing, simply thaw the frozen layer.

Figure 25-8.
A title block sheet must adhere to applicable standards. This title block is for an A-size sheet and adheres to the ASME Y14.1 *Drawing Sheet Size and Format* standard.

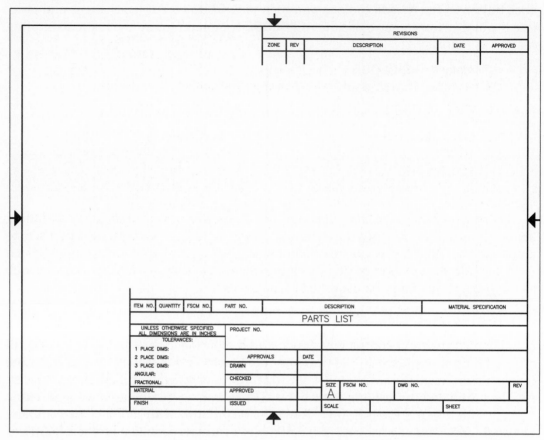

Figure 25-9.
Attributes should be defined for each area of the title block.

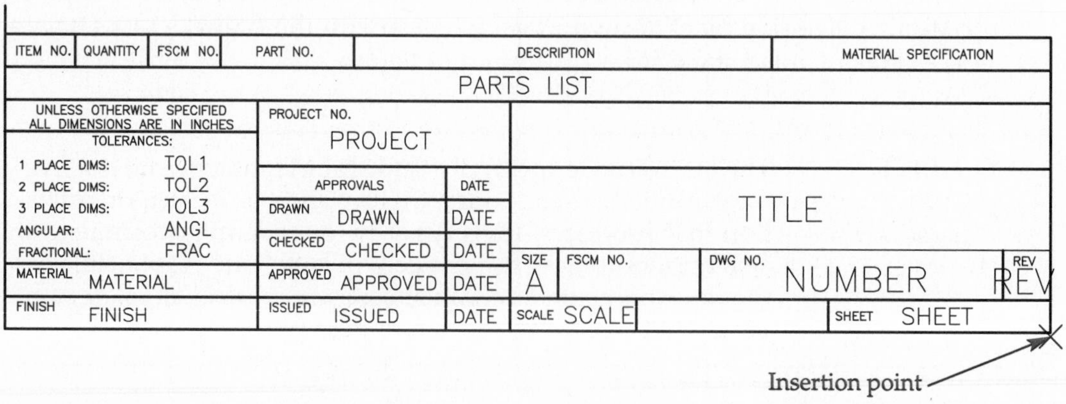

3. Define attributes for each area of the title block. As you create the attributes, determine the appropriate text height and justification modes for each definition. Attributes should be defined for the drawing title, drawing number, drafter, checker, dates, drawing scale, sheet size, material, finish, revision letter, and tolerance information. See Figure 25-9. Include any other information that may be specific to your organization or application.

4. Assign default values to the attributes wherever possible. As an example, if your organization consistently specifies the same overall tolerances on drawing dimensions, the tolerance attributes can be assigned default values.

AutoCAD and its Applications—Basics

Once you have defined each attribute in the title block, the **WBLOCK** command can be used to save the drawing as a file to disk so that it can be inserted into a new drawing. You can also use the **BLOCK** command to create a block of the defined attributes within the current file, which can then be saved as a template or wblock file. Both methods are acceptable and are explained as follows:

- **WBLOCK method.** The **WBLOCK** command saves a drawing file to disk so that it can be inserted into any drawing that is currently open. Be sure to use 0,0 as the insertion point for the title block. Drawings used in this manner should be given descriptive names. An A-size title block, for example, could be named TITLEA or FORMATA. To utilize the wblock file, begin a new drawing and insert the template drawing. After locating and scaling the drawing, the attribute prompts are displayed. If the **ATTDIA** system variable is set to 1, all of the attributes can be accepted or edited in the **Enter Attributes** dialog box. When you pick **OK** to close the dialog box, the attributes are placed in the title block. This method requires that you begin with a new drawing, and that you know the information requested by the attribute prompts. Remember, should you enter information that is incorrect, it can be altered using the **ATTEDIT** command.

- **BLOCK method.** If you use the **BLOCK** command, you can use the **Block Definition** dialog box to create a block of the defined attributes in the title block. When you select the objects for the block, be sure to select *only* the defined attributes you have created. Do not select the headings of the title block areas, or any of the geometry in the title block. When you pick the insertion base point, select a corner of the title block that will be convenient to use each time this block is inserted into a drawing. The point indicated in Figure 25-9 shows an appropriate location for the insertion base point. Finally, activate the **Delete** option button in the **Block Definition** dialog box so that the attribute definitions will be removed from the title block (when you insert the block later, the attribute values will be inserted where the attribute definitions were located). You can also place the attribute definitions on a separate layer and freeze it so that the original attributes will not be displayed. The current drawing now contains a block of defined attributes for use in the title block.

    If you save the drawing as a template file and begin a new drawing using the template, the title block data can be entered at any time during the creation of the new drawing. To do so, issue the **INSERT** command, enter the name of the block in the **Insert** dialog box, and pick the proper insertion base point. The attribute prompts are then either displayed on the command line or in a dialog box, depending on the value of the **ATTDIA** system variable.

Regardless of the method used, title block data can be entered quickly and accurately without the use of text commands. If the attributes are entered using the **Enter Attributes** dialog box, all the information can be seen at once, and mistakes can be corrected quickly. Attributes can be easily edited at a later date if necessary. The attribute text height or location can be changed with the **-ATTEDIT** command, and attribute values can be changed with the **ATTEDIT** command. The completed title block after insertion of the attribute block is shown in Figure 25-10.

Figure 25-10.
The title block after insertion of the attributes. When the drawing is complete, dates and approvals can be added with the **ATTEDIT** command provided attributes have been previously defined.

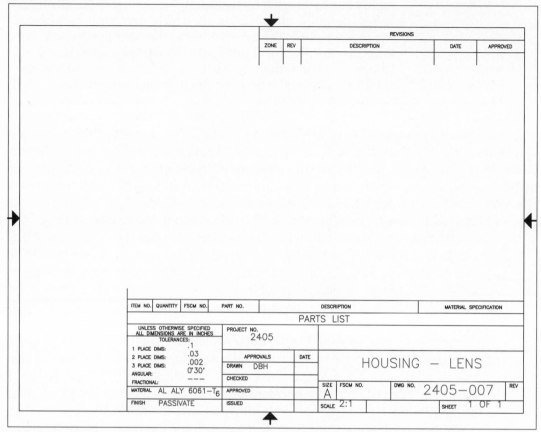

Attributes and Revision Blocks

It is almost certain that a detail drawing will require revision at some time in the use of a product. Typical changes that occur include design improvements and the correction of drafting errors. The first time that a drawing is revised, it is usually assigned the revision letter A. If necessary, revision letters continue with B through Z, but the letters I, O, and Q are not used, because they might be confused with numbers.

Title block formats include an area specifically designated to record all drawing changes. This area is normally located at the upper-right of the title block sheet, and is commonly called the *revision block*. The revision block provides space for the revision letter, a description of the change, the date, and approvals. These items are entered in columns. A column for the zone is optional, and need only be added if applicable. *Zones* appear in the margins of a title block sheet and are indicated by alphabetical and numeric entries. They are used for reference purposes the same way reference letters and numbers are used to identify a street or feature on a road map. Although A-size and B-size title blocks may include zones, they are rarely needed.

Block attributes provide a handy means of completing the necessary information in a revision block. Refer to Figure 25-11 as you follow these steps:

1. First, create the drawing geometry for the revision block using the appropriate layer(s).
2. Define attributes that describe the zone (optional), revision letter, description of change, date, and change approval on a separate layer.
3. Use left-justified text for the change description attribute, and middle-justified text for the remainder of the attributes.

Figure 25-11.
The revision block consists of lines and defined attributes. The border lines must be drawn as part of the block, and the upper-left corner is used as the insertion point.

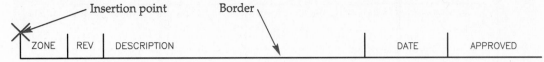

4. Use the **WBLOCK** command to save the revision block and attributes as a drawing file. Use a descriptive name such as REVBLK or REV. Keep in mind that each line of the parts list or revision block has its own border lines. Therefore, the borders must be saved with the attributes. Use the upper-left endpoint of the revision block as the insertion point.

Now, after a drawing has been revised, simply insert the revision block at the correct location. If the **ATTDIA** system variable is set to 1, you can answer the attribute prompts in the **Enter Attributes** dialog box. After providing the change information, pick the **OK** button and the completed revision block is automatically added to the title block sheet. See Figure 25-12.

Figure 25-12.
The completed revision block after it is inserted into the drawing.

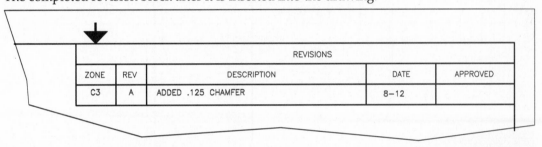

Attributes and Parts Lists

Assembly drawings require a parts list, or list of materials, that provides information about each component of the assembly or subassembly. This information includes the quantity, FSCM code (optional), part number, description, and item number for each component. In some organizations, the parts list is generated as a separate document, usually in an 8 1/2″ × 11″ format. In other companies, it is common practice to include the parts list on the face of the assembly drawing. Whether they are created as a separate document or as part of the assembly drawing itself, parts lists provide another example of how attributes may be used to automate the documentation process.

Refer once again to the title block in Figure 25-8. Observe the section specifically designated for a parts list, located just above the title block area. Now, consider the example illustrated in Figure 25-13 as you follow these guidelines:

1. First, create a parts list block using the appropriate drawing layer(s).
2. On a separate layer, define attributes that describe the quantity, FSCM code (optional), part number, item description, material specification, and item number for the components of an assembly drawing.
3. Use left-justified text for the item description attribute and middle-justified text for the other attributes.
4. Use the **WBLOCK** command to save the parts list block to disk with a descriptive name, such as PL for parts list or BOM for bill of materials. You can also use the **BLOCK** command to create a block of the parts list in the current drawing. Use the lower-left endpoint of the parts list block as the insertion point, as shown in Figure 25-13.

Figure 25-13.
The parts list block is drawn with defined attributes and the insertion point located at the lower-left endpoint.

QTY	FSCM	PART_NO.	ITEM_DESC.		MATL_SPEC.	ITEM

Insertion point

Now, after an assembly drawing has been completed, simply insert the parts list block into the drawing at the correct location. If the **ATTDIA** system variable is set to 1, you can answer the attribute prompts in the **Enter Attributes** dialog box. After providing the necessary information, click **OK** and the completed parts list block is automatically added to the title block sheet. See Figure 25-14. Repeat the procedure as many times as required for each component of the assembly drawing.

From the preceding examples, you can see that block attributes are powerful objects. Their applications are virtually endless. Can you think of any other drafting procedures that could be similarly automated?

Figure 25-14.
The completed parts list block after it is inserted into the drawing.

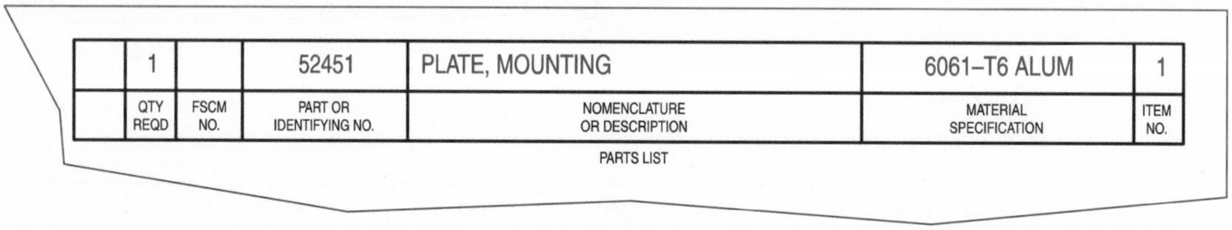

1		52451	PLATE, MOUNTING	6061–T6 ALUM	1
QTY REQD	FSCM NO.	PART OR IDENTIFYING NO.	NOMENCLATURE OR DESCRIPTION	MATERIAL SPECIFICATION	ITEM NO.

PARTS LIST

PROFESSIONAL TIP

A truly integrated CAD environment continually seeks out new methods to automate the drafting and design process. In such organizations, the *electronic geometry* embodied in a CAD file is the original, or master, document. If you work in a supervisory capacity, you are probably authorized to *sign off* completed drawings, or approve revised drawings. How can you *electronically* add your signature to an AutoCAD drawing? Consider using the following procedure.

- Set the **SKPOLY** system variable to 1 to draw polylines when you use the **SKETCH** command. Use the **SKETCH** command to reproduce your signature. Sketching your name is a little difficult with a pointing device, but it can be reasonably accomplished with a bit of practice.
- Use the **PEDIT** command to *tweak* the signature into a more acceptable representation of your handwriting.
- Use the **WBLOCK** command to save a file of your signature to a diskette. Keep the diskette in your briefcase or store it in a secure location. Do not store your signature block on a computer hard drive or a network drive where anyone can access it.
- When you need to approve a drawing, simply insert and scale your signature block as required in the correct location.

AutoCAD provides a method for listing attributes associated with any specified block. You can tabulate block information by creating a special *template file*. This file is a list of attributes that can be used in a bill of materials by third-party packages, or in databases. The file is used with drawings that contain specific blocks and attributes you wish to list. After the template file is completed, the **ATTEXT** command can be used to create an *extract file* that allows AutoCAD to find and list the attributes specified in the template file. This extract file can be opened to display the attributes on screen, or you can print the file.

Creating a Template File

You often need to be selective when listing blocks and attributes. In most cases, only certain types of attribute data need to be extracted from a drawing. This requires guidelines for AutoCAD to use when sorting through a drawing for attribute information. The guidelines for picking out specific attributes from blocks are specified in the template file. This file is then used by AutoCAD to list the attributes when you create an extract file. The template file is a simple text file and can be created using database, word processing, or text editor programs.

In addition to listing attributes, the template file can be designed to list information about certain block characteristics. These include the following:

- **Name.** The block name.
- **Level.** The block nesting level.
- **X.** The X coordinate of the block insertion point.
- **Y.** The Y coordinate of the block insertion point.
- **Z.** The Z coordinate of the block insertion point.
- **Layer.** The name of the layer the block is inserted on.
- **Orient.** The rotation angle of the block.
- **Number.** The number of block insertions made.
- **Handle.** A unique identifier for the block.
- **XSCALE.** The insertion scale factor for the X axis.
- **YSCALE.** The insertion scale factor for the Y axis.
- **ZSCALE.** The insertion scale factor for the Z axis.
- **XEXTRUDE.** The X value of the block extrusion direction.
- **YEXTRUDE.** The Y value of the block extrusion direction.
- **ZEXTRUDE.** The Z value of the block extrusion direction.

The template file that lists the block attribute data can be written using a database program or a text editing program such as Windows Notepad. An example template file is given below. This file could be used to extract information from the valve symbols in Exercise 25-2.

```
BL:NAME      C010000
BL:LAYER     C005000
BL:X         N008002
BL:Y         N008002
BLANK        C004000
MFR          C010000
SIZE         C008000
PRICE        C010000
```

The first four items in the left column beginning with BL: specify block characteristics, such as the name of the block and its layer. The last three items in the left column specify block attributes and correspond to the defined attribute tags used for Exercise 25-2. The item BLANK is placed in the file to provide spacing between the

BL:Y and MFR entries. There would be no line space inserted between these two items if this entry were omitted.

All of the items in the right column begin with C or N. The C indicates that *character* information is to be extracted from an attribute, and N represents *numeric* information. If a character other than a number is included in an attribute, use C instead of N. Notice that the PRICE attribute uses C. Although the price attribute consists of numerical information, the dollar symbol ($) is used in front of the price and needs to be identified as a character.

The first three numbers after the C or N indicate the number of spaces allotted for the attribute. For example, there are ten spaces allotted to the MFR attribute. The next three digits specify the number of decimal places in the attribute. The X and Y insertion coordinate locations, for example, have been assigned two decimal places. The information included in a template file is detailed in Figure 25-15.

Figure 25-15. Block attribute data is specified in a template file using numeric and character entries.

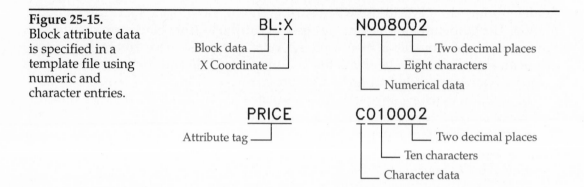

PROFESSIONAL TIP

Your application determines which properties need to be included in the template file. Template files can be created for different groups or departments of a company. The following table lists possible attributes for a desk in the left column. Listed across the top of the next four columns are several different departments in a company. Each **X** indicates which attribute is to be included in the corresponding department's template file.

Attribute	Shipping	Purchasing	Accounting	Engineering
Manufacturer		X	X	
Size	X	X		X
Price		X	X	
Weight	X			X
Color		X		X
Material	X	X		X

❑ This exercise guides you through the construction of a template file for the drawing EX25-2. Use Windows Notepad to create the file.

❑ Open drawing EX25-2.

❑ Pick the Start button on the Windows taskbar. Pick Programs in the Start menu and then pick Accessories. Then, pick Notepad.

❑ Enter the following text at the flashing vertical cursor located at the top left of the Notepad window. You may use either the [Tab] key or the space bar to insert spaces between the columns:

BL:NAME	C010000
BL:LAYER	C005000
BL:X	N008002
BL:Y	N008002
BLANK	C004000
MFR	C010000
SIZE	C008000
PRICE	C010000

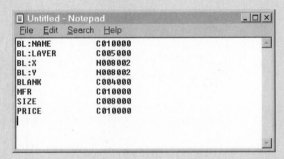

❑ When you are through entering text, your screen should appear as shown above.

❑ Select Save As... from the File pull-down menu, and save the file with the name EX25-4. Notepad automatically adds the .txt extension to the file name.

❑ Select Exit from the File pull-down menu to exit Notepad and return to AutoCAD.

Extracting Block Attribute Data

AutoCAD provides three different formats for listing extracted information in a drawing file. The DXF format is related to programming and is the most complex. See the *AutoCAD 20000 DXF Reference* for information on the DXF format. The other two file formats—SDF and CDF—can be used with a variety of other programs. The *SDF (Space Delimited Format)* is the easiest for the average user to interpret. It means that the different *fields*, or groups of extracted data, are separated by spaces. The *CDF (Comma Delimited Format)* uses commas instead of spaces to separate fields.

The **ATTEXT** command enables you to perform attribute extraction. To issue this command, enter ATTEXT or DDATTEXT at the Command: prompt. This displays the **Attribute Extraction** dialog box, Figure 25-16. Select the desired file format, such as SDF, by clicking the appropriate radio button in the **File Format** area. If you want specific blocks in the extract file, click the **Select Objects** button, and use any selection method to pick the blocks. If you do not select objects, all blocks in the drawing (as specified by the template file) will be used.

Next, pick the **Template File...** button to select a file from the **Output File** dialog box, Figure 25-17. Pick **Open** when you are done, and the **Attribute Extraction** dialog box is redisplayed. The output file, or extract file, can be selected by clicking the **Output File...** button. This redisplays the **Output File** dialog box. If you wish to have the extracted attributes saved in an existing file, select the extract file from the list of

ATTEXT
DDATTEXT

Figure 25-16.
The **ATTEXT**
command activates
the **Attribute**
Extraction dialog box.

Pick to
select specific
blocks

Select the
file format

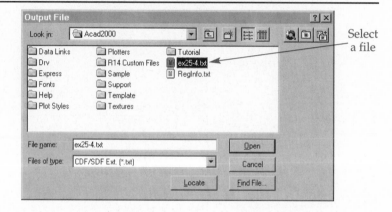

Figure 25-17.
The **Output File**
dialog box allows
you to select a
template file and an
extract file.

Select
a file

folders and files. To save the extracted attributes to a new file, enter a new file name in the **File name:** text box. The current drawing name is the default (AutoCAD automatically appends the .txt extension to the file name). Be sure the extract file name you enter is slightly different from the template file name—for example, EX25-4a. If you use the same name, your original template file will be deleted.

Pick **Save** after specifying the file name, and then pick **OK** in the **Attribute Extraction** dialog box. If all goes well, a message from AutoCAD reports that you have *n* records in extract file. The number of records listed in the file is based on the number of blocks containing the extracted attributes.

The extract file can be displayed on screen by opening the file in Windows Notepad. An example of the extract file in SDF format and CDF format are shown in Figure 25-18. Of the three formats discussed, the CDF format appears to be the most cumbersome. However, the CDF format (as well as the SDF format) may be used with database software. Decide which format is most suitable for your application. Regardless of the extract file format chosen, you may print the file from Windows Notepad by selecting Print from the File pull-down menu.

NOTE

Attribute extraction can also be performed at the command line by using the **-ATTEXT** command. The same options used with the **ATTEXT** command are available. When you are prompted to specify an extract file format, you can also select specific blocks to include in the extract file. You can then specify the template and extract files you wish to use.

AutoCAD and its Applications—Basics

Figure 25-18.
Extract files
displayed in
Windows Notepad.
A—SDF format.
B—CDF format.

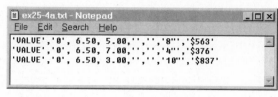

A

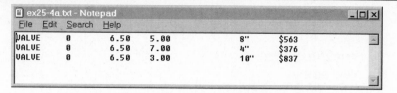

B

PROFESSIONAL TIP

The bill of materials listing discussed in this chapter is a basic list of each block's selected attributes. As you become familiar with AutoCAD, customize it to meet your needs. Study magazines devoted to AutoCAD and read the *AutoCAD User's Guide*. You will find numerous software packages that generate specialized bills of material containing information on quantities and totals, rather than just a list of blocks.

EXERCISE 25-5

❑ Open EX25-2.
❑ Enter the **ATTEXT** command and specify the SDF file format in the **Attribute Extraction** dialog box.
❑ Enter the template file name EX25-4. Enter EX25-4a for the extract file name and pick **OK**.
❑ Enter Windows Notepad and open the extract file to display the bill of materials on screen.

Chapter Test

Answer the following questions on a separate sheet of paper.

1. Define an *attribute*.
2. Explain the purpose of the **ATTDEF** command.
3. Define the function of the following four **ATTDEF** modes:
   A. Invisible
   B. Constant
   C. Verify
   D. Preset
4. What attribute information does the **ATTDEF** command request?
5. Identify the three commands that may be used to edit attributes before they are included within a block.
6. Which command allows you to change an existing attribute from **Visible** to **Invisible**?
7. List the three options for the **ATTDISP** command.
8. What is meant by *global* attribute editing?

9. How does individual attribute editing differ from global editing?
10. Identify the purpose of the following two prompts in the global attribute editing routine.
    A. String to change:
    B. New string:
11. List the different aspects of the attribute that you can change when you edit attributes one at a time.
12. Which command allows you to use a dialog box to create attributes?
13. Explain the function of the **DDATTE** command.
14. How does editing an attribute with **DDEDIT** differ from using the **Properties** window?
15. What purpose does the **ATTREQ** system variable serve?
16. To enter attributes using the dialog box, you must set the **ATTDIA** system variable to _____.
17. When created, a drawing extract file is given this file extension.
18. How is character and numerical data specified in a template file?
19. How do you create a template file?
20. Define all aspects of each of the following template file entries.
    A. BL:X. _____
    B. N006002. _____
    C. PRICE. _____
    D. C010003. _____
21. Describe the difference between CDF and SDF attribute extract formats.

Drawing Problems

1. Start AutoCAD and start a new drawing. Draw the structural steel wide flange shape using the dimensions given. Do not dimension the drawing. Create attributes for the drawing using the information given. Make a block of the drawing and name it W12X40. Insert the block once to test the attributes. Save the drawing as P25-1.

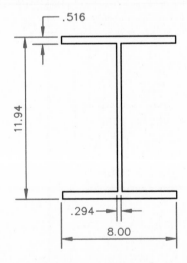

Attributes		
Steel	W12 × 40	Visible
Mfgr	Ryerson	Invisible
Price	$.30/lb	Invisible
Weight	40 lbs/ft	Invisible
Length	10'	Invisible
Code	03116WF	Invisible

2. Load the drawing in Problem 1 (P25-1) and construct the floor plan shown using the dimensions given. Dimension the drawing. Insert the block W12X40 six times as shown. Required attribute data is given in the chart below the drawing. Enter the appropriate information for the attributes as you are prompted for it. Note the steel columns labeled 3 and 6 require slightly different attribute data. You can speed the drawing process by using **ARRAY** or **COPY**. Save the drawing as P25-2.

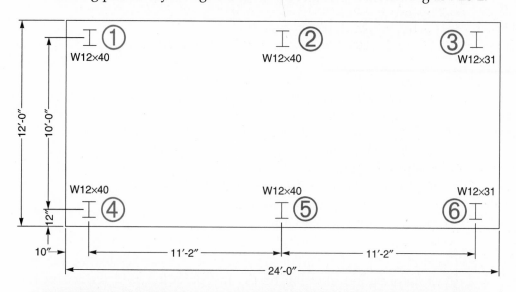

	Steel	Mfgr	Price	Weight	Length	Code
Blocks ①, ②, ④, & ⑤	W12 × 40	Ryerson	$.30/lb	40 lbs/ft	10'	03116WF
Blocks ③, & ⑥	W12 × 31	Ryerson	$.30/lb	31 lbs/ft	8.5'	03125WF

3. Load Problem 2 (P25-2) into the drawing editor. Create a template file for use in extracting the data from structural steel blocks inserted in Problem 2. Use the following information in your template file:

Item	Characters	Decimal Places
Block name	8	0
Steel	8	0
Mfgr	20	0
Price	12	0
Weight	9	0
Length	6	1
Code	8	0

Use the **ATTEXT** command to create a listing of the attribute information. When using **ATTEXT**, give the extract file a slightly different name than the template file. If not, your template file will be converted into the extract file.

4. Select a drawing from Chapter 23 and create a bill of materials for it using the template file method and the **ATTEXT** command. The template file should list all the attributes of each block in the drawing. Use the SDF format to display the file. Display the file in the Windows Notepad.

5. Create a drawing of the computer workstation layout in the classroom or office in which you are working. Provide attribute definitions for all the items listed here.
   - Workstation ID number
   - Computer brand name
   - Model number
   - Processor chip
   - Amount of RAM
   - Hard disk capacity
   - Video graphics card brand and model
   - CD ROM speed
   - Date purchased
   - Price
   - Vendor's phone number
   - Add other data as you see fit

   Generate an extract file for all the computers in the drawing.

6. Open one of your template drawings. Define attributes for the title block information, revision block, and parts list as described in this chapter. **WBLOCK** the entire drawing to disk using 0,0 as the insertion base point. Repeat the procedure for other templates.

CHAPTER 26

Isometric Drawing

Learning Objectives

After completing this chapter, you will be able to:
- Describe the nature of isometric and oblique views.
- Set an isometric grid.
- Construct isometric objects.
- Create isometric text styles.
- Demonstrate isometric and oblique dimensioning techniques.

Being able to visualize and draw three-dimensional shapes is a skill that every drafter, designer, and engineer should possess. This is especially important in 3D modeling. However, there is a distinct difference between drawing a view that *looks* three-dimensional and creating a *true* 3D model.

A 3D model can be rotated on the display screen to view from any angle. The computer calculates the points, lines, and surfaces of the objects in space. Three-dimensional models are introduced in Chapter 27. This chapter focuses on creating views that *look* three-dimensional, using some special AutoCAD functions and two-dimensional coordinates and objects.

PICTORIAL DRAWING OVERVIEW

The word *pictorial* means "like a picture." It refers to any realistic form of drawing. Pictorial drawings show height, width, and depth. Several forms of pictorial drawings are used in industry today. The least realistic is *oblique*. However, this is the simplest type. The most realistic, but also the most complex, is *perspective*. *Isometric* drawing falls midway between the two as far as realism and complexity are concerned.

Oblique Drawings

An oblique drawing shows objects with one or more parallel faces having true shape and size. A scale is selected for the orthographic, or front faces. Then, an angle for the depth (receding axis) is chosen. The three types of oblique drawings are *cavalier*, *cabinet*, and *general*. See Figure 26-1. These vary in the scale of the receding axis. The receding axis is drawn at half scale for a cabinet view and at full scale for a cavalier. The general oblique is normally drawn with a 3/4 scale for the receding axis.

Figure 26-1.
The three types of oblique drawings differ in the scale of the receding axis.

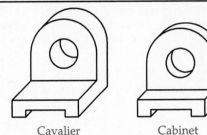

Cavalier   Cabinet   General

Isometric Drawings

Isometric drawings are more realistic than oblique drawings. The entire object appears as if it is tilted toward the viewer. The word *isometric* means equal measure. This equal measure refers to the angle between the three axes (120°) after the object has been tilted. The tilt angle is 35°16′. This is shown in Figure 26-2. The 120° angle corresponds to an angle of 30° from horizontal.

NOTE   When constructing isometric drawings, remember that lines parallel in the orthogonal views must be parallel in the isometric view.

The most appealing aspect of isometric drawing is that all three axis lines can be measured using the same scale. This saves time, while still producing a pleasing pictorial representation of the object. This type of drawing is produced when you use Isometric Snap mode, discussed later.

Closely related to isometric drawing is *dimetric* and *trimetric*. These forms of pictorial drawing differ from isometric in the scales used to measure the three axes. Dimetric drawing uses two different scales, and trimetric uses three scales. Using different scales is an attempt to create *foreshortening*. This means the lengths of the sides appear to recede. The relationship between isometric, dimetric, and trimetric drawings is illustrated in Figure 26-3.

Figure 26-2.
An object is tilted 35°16′ to achieve an isometric view having 120° between the three axes. Notice how the highlighted face corresponds to each view.

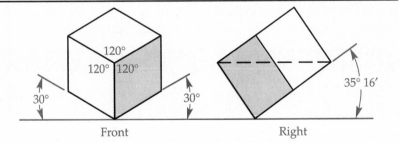

Front   Right

Figure 26-3.
Isometric, dimetric, and trimetric differ in the scales used to draw the three axes. The isometric shown here has the scales represented as one. You can see how the dimetric and trimetric scales vary.

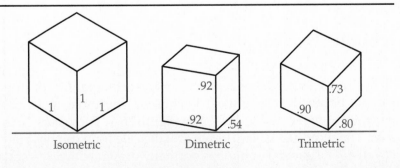

Isometric   Dimetric   Trimetric

Perspective Drawing

The most realistic form of pictorial drawing is perspective. The eye naturally sees objects in perspective. Look down a long hall and notice that the wall and floor lines seem to converge in the distance at an imaginary point. That point is called the *vanishing point*. The most common types of perspective drawing are *one-point* and *two-point*. These forms of pictorial drawing are often used in architecture. They are also used in the automotive and aircraft industries. Examples of one-point and two-point perspectives are shown in Figure 26-4. A perspective of a 3D model can be produced in AutoCAD using the **DVIEW** and **3DORBIT** commands. See *AutoCAD and its Applications—Advanced* for complete coverage of **DVIEW** and **3DORBIT**.

Figure 26-4.
An example of one-point and two-point perspective.

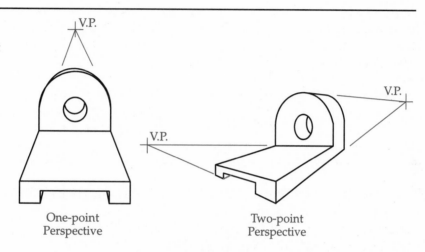

One-point
Perspective

Two-point
Perspective

ISOMETRIC DRAWING

The most common method of pictorial drawing used in industry is isometric. These drawings provide a single view showing three sides that can be measured using the same scale. An isometric view has no perspective and may appear somewhat distorted. Isometric axes are drawn at 30° to horizontal. See Figure 26-5.

The three axes shown in Figure 26-5 represent the width, height, and depth of the object. Lines that appear horizontal in an orthographic view are placed at a 30° angle. Lines that are vertical in an orthographic view are placed vertically. These lines are parallel to the axes. Any line parallel to an axis can be measured and is called an *isometric line*. Lines not parallel to the axes cannot be measured and are called *nonisometric lines*. Note the two nonisometric lines in Figure 26-5.

Figure 26-5.
Isometric axes layout. Lines not parallel to any of the three axes are called nonisometric lines.

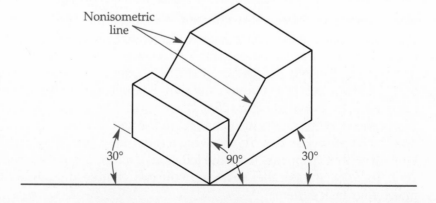

Nonisometric line

30° 90° 30°

Circular features shown on isometric objects must be oriented properly or they appear distorted. The correct orientation of isometric circles on the three principle planes is shown in Figure 26-6. These circles appear as ellipses on the isometric object. The small diameter (minor axis) of the ellipse must always align on the axis of the circular feature. Notice that the centerline axes of the holes in Figure 26-6 are parallel to one of the isometric planes.

A basic rule to remember about isometric drawing is that lines parallel in an orthogonal view must be parallel in the isometric view. AutoCAD's **ISOPLANE** feature makes that task, and the positioning of ellipses, easy.

Figure 26-6.
Proper isometric circle (ellipse) orientation on isometric planes. The minor axis always aligns with the axis centerline.

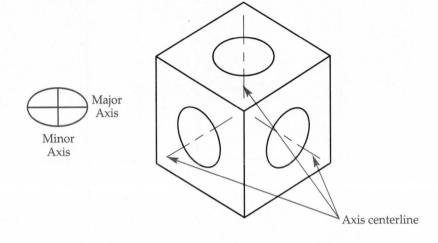

Major Axis

Minor Axis

Axis centerline

> **PROFESSIONAL TIP**
>
> If you are ever in doubt about the proper orientation of an ellipse in an isometric drawing, remember that the minor axis of the ellipse must always be aligned on the centerline axis of the circular feature. This is shown clearly in Figure 26-6.

Setting for Isometric Drawing

AutoCAD User's Guide 7

DSETTINGS
DS
SE
DDRMODES
RM

Tools
➥ Drafting
   Settings...

You can quickly set your isometric variables in the **Drafting Settings** dialog box. To access this dialog box, enter DS, SE, DSETTINGS, RM, or DDRMODES at the Command: prompt, or select **Drafting Settings...** from the **Tools** pull-down menu. This dialog box can also be accessed by right-clicking the **Snap** or **Grid** status bar button and then selecting **Setting...** from the shortcut menu. The **Snap and Grid** tab of this dialog box contains options for isometric drawing. See Figure 26-7.

To activate the isometric snap grid, pick the **Isometric snap** radio button in the **Snap type & style** area. Notice that the **Grid X spacing** and **Snap X spacing** edit boxes are grayed-out. Since X spacing relates to horizontal measurements, it is not used in the isometric mode. You can only set the Y spacing for grid and snap in isometric. Be sure to pick the **Snap On (F9)** and **Grid On (F7)** check boxes if you want Snap and Grid modes to be activated. Select the **OK** button and the grid dots on the screen change to the isometric orientation, as shown in Figure 26-8. If your grid dots are not visible, turn the grid on.

Notice the crosshairs also change and appear angled. This aids you in drawing lines at the proper angles. Try drawing a four-sided surface using the **LINE** command. Draw it so that it appears to be the left side of a box in an isometric layout. See Figure 26-9. To draw nonparallel surfaces, you can change the angle of the crosshairs to make your task easier.

Figure 26-7.
The **Drafting Settings** dialog box allows you to pick settings needed for isometric drawing.

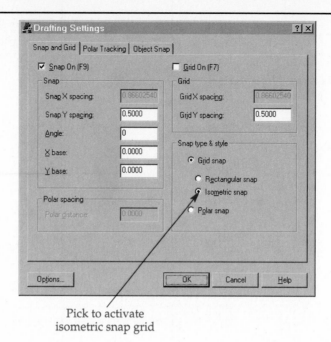

Pick to activate
isometric snap grid

Figure 26-8.
An example of an isometric grid setup in AutoCAD.

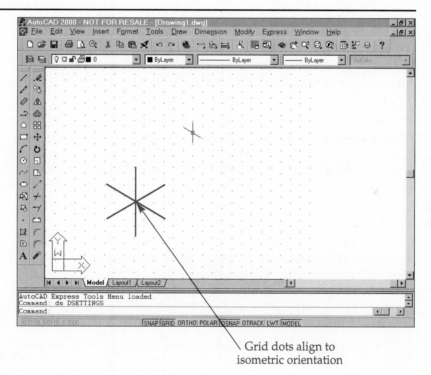

Grid dots align to
isometric orientation

Figure 26-9.
A four-sided object
drawn with the
LINE command can
be used as the left
side of an isometric
box.

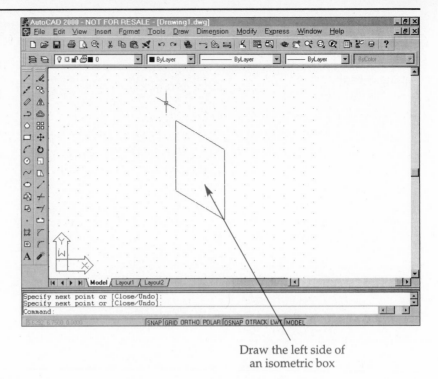

Draw the left side of
an isometric box

To turn off the Isometric mode, pick the **Rectangular snap** button in the **Snap type & style** area. The Isometric mode is turned off and you are returned to the drawing area when you pick the **OK** button.

NOTE

You can also set the Isometric Snap mode at the Command: prompt with the **SNAP** command. Type SNAP or SN, select the **Style** option, and then type I to select **Isometric**.

AutoCAD
User's
Guide
7

Changing the isometric crosshairs orientation

Drawing an isometric shape is possible without ever changing the angle of the crosshairs. However, the drawing process is easier and quicker if the angles of the crosshairs align with the isometric axes.

Whenever the isometric snap style is enabled, simply press the [F5] key or the [Ctrl]+[E] key combination and the crosshairs immediately change to the next plane. AutoCAD refers to the isometric positions as *isoplanes*. The isoplanes are displayed on the prompt line as a reference. The three crosshair orientations and their angular values are shown in Figure 26-10.

Figure 26-10.
The three isometric
crosshair positions
can be changed
using the [F5]
function key, the
[Ctrl]+[E] key
combination, or
using the **ISOPLANE**
command.

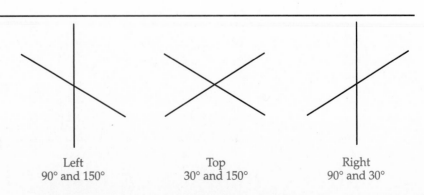

Left
90° and 150°

Top
30° and 150°

Right
90° and 30°

AutoCAD and its Applications—Basics

Another method to toggle the crosshair position is with the **ISOPLANE** command. Enter ISOPLANE at the Command: prompt as follows:

Command: **ISOPLANE**⏎
Current isoplane: Right
Enter isometric plane setting [Left/Top/Right/] <*current*>: ⏎

Press [Enter] to toggle the crosshairs to the next position. The command line displays the new isoplane setting. You can toggle immediately to the next position by pressing [Enter] at the Command: prompt to repeat the **ISOPLANE** command and pressing [Enter] again. To specify the plane of orientation, type the first letter of that position.

The **ISOPLANE** command can also be used transparently while in another command to toggle between isoplanes. For example, suppose that you start to draw a line and then realize you are in the left isoplane and need to be in the top isoplane. The procedure to use is as follows:

Command: **LINE**⏎
Specify first point: **'ISOPLANE**⏎
Current isoplane: Top
>>Enter isometric plane setting [Left/Top/Right] <*current*>: **R**⏎
Current isoplane: Right
Resuming LINE command.
Specify first point: (*continue with command*)

PROFESSIONAL TIP The quickest way to change the isoplane is to press the [F5] function key or press the [Ctrl]+[E] key combination.

The crosshairs are always in one of the isoplane positions when the isometric snap style is in effect. An exception occurs during a display or editing command when a multiple selection set method (such as a window) is used. In these cases, the crosshairs change to the normal vertical and horizontal positions. At the completion of the display or editing command, the crosshairs automatically revert to their former isoplane orientation.

EXERCISE 26-1

❏ Use one of your templates to begin a new drawing.
❏ Set the grid spacing at .5.
❏ Use the **Drafting Settings** dialog box to activate Isometric Snap mode. Specify .25 vertical spacing.
❏ Use the **LINE** command to draw the objects shown. Do not dimension the objects.
❏ Change the **ISOPLANE** orientation as needed.
❏ Save the drawing as EX26-1.

Isometric Ellipses

ELLIPSE
EL

Draw
→ Ellipse
→ Axis, End

Draw
toolbar

Ellipse

Placing an isometric ellipse on an object is made easy using AutoCAD. An ellipse is positioned automatically to the current isoplane setting. To use the **ELLIPSE** command, pick the **Ellipse** button on the **Draw** toolbar, select **Axis, End** from the **Ellipse** cascading menu in the **Draw** pull-down menu, or enter EL or ELLIPSE at the Command: prompt. Once the **ELLIPSE** command is initiated, the following prompts appear:

> Specify axis endpoint of ellipse or [Arc/Center/Isocircle]: I↵
> Specify center of isocircle: *(pick a point)*
> Specify radius of isocircle or [Diameter]:

Do not select the **Center** option; this method does not allow you to create isocircles. Instead, select **Isocircle**, pick the center point, and then select the radius or diameter.

Always check the isoplane position before locating an ellipse on your drawing. You can dynamically view the three positions that an ellipse can take. Enter the **ELLIPSE** command, pick the **Isocircle** option, and press [F5] to toggle the crosshair orientation. See Figure 26-11. The ellipse rotates each time you toggle the crosshairs.

The isometric ellipse is a true ellipse. If selected, grips are displayed at the center and four quadrant points. This simplifies the editing process. See Figure 26-12.

Figure 26-11.
The orientation of an isometric ellipse is determined by the crosshair orientation.

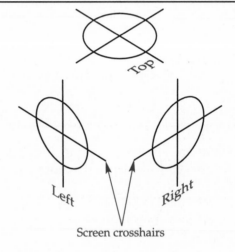

Screen crosshairs

PROFESSIONAL TIP

Prior to drawing isometric ellipses, it is good practice to first place a marker at the ellipse center point. A good technique is to draw a point using an easily visible point style at the center. This is especially useful if the ellipse does not fall on grid or snap points.

CAUTION

It may be tempting to resize or otherwise adjust an isometric ellipse or arc by selecting one of the grips. Keep in mind that as soon as you resize an isometric ellipse in this manner, its angular value has changed and it is no longer isometric. If you rotate an isometric ellipse while Ortho mode is on, it will not appear in a proper isometric plane. You *can* rotate an isometric ellipse, but be sure to enter a value of 120° if you want it to rotate from one of the isometric planes to another.

Figure 26-12.
An isometric ellipse
has grips at its four
quadrant points and
its center.

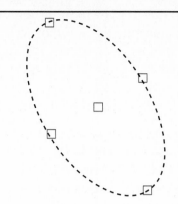

EXERCISE 26-2

❑ Open EX26-1 if this drawing is not already on your screen.
❑ Select the **ELLIPSE** command to place an ellipse on the three sides of the object.
❑ Draw the numbered ellipses in the following manner:
  ❑ Pick a radius of .5 using the cursor to draw Elipse 1.
  ❑ Enter a radius of .75 at the keyboard to draw Elipse 2.
  ❑ Enter D and then a diameter of .6 at the keyboard to draw Elipse 3.
❑ The finished drawing should look like the example given below.
❑ Save the drawing as EX26-2.

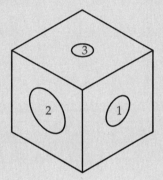

Constructing Isometric Arcs

The **ELLIPSE** command can also be used to draw an isometric arc of any included angle. To construct an isometric arc, use the **Arc** option of the **ELLIPSE** command. To access the **Arc** option, pick the **Ellipse** button on the **Draw** toolbar and then enter A, enter EL or ELLIPSE at the Command: prompt and then enter A, or select **Arc** from the **Ellipse** cascading menu in the **Draw** pull-down menu. Once the **Arc** option is initiated, the following prompts appear:

> Specify axis endpoint of elliptical arc or [Center/Isocircle]: I↵
> Specify center of isocircle: *(pick the center of the arc)*
> Specify radius of isocircle or [Diameter]: *(pick the radius or type a value and press* [Enter]*)*
> Specify start angle or [Parameter] *(pick a start angle or type a value and press* [Enter]*)*
> Specify end angle or [Parameter/Included angle]: *(pick an end angle or type an included angle value and press* [Enter]*)*
> Command:

A common application of isometric arcs is drawing fillets and rounds. Once a round is created isometrically, the edge (corner) of the object sits back from its original, unfilleted position. See Figure 26-13A. You can draw the complete object first, then trim away the excess after locating the fillets. You can also draw the isometric arcs and then the connecting lines. Either way, the center point of the ellipse is a critical feature, and should be located first. The arc at the upper left was drawn first, then copied to the upper back position using grips. Use Ortho mode to help quickly draw 90° arcs.

The next step is to move the original edge to its new position. This is tangent to the isometric arcs. You can do this by snapping the line to the quadrant point of the arc. See Figure 26-13B. Notice the grips on the line and on the arc. The endpoint of the line is snapped to the quadrant grip on the arc. The final step is to trim away the excess lines and upper right arc. The completed feature is shown in Figure 26-13C.

Rounded edges, when viewed straight on, cannot be shown as complete-edge lines that extend to the ends of the object. Instead, a good technique to use is a broken line in the original location of the edge. This is clearly shown in the figure in Exercise 26-3.

Figure 26-13.
Rounds can be drawn with the **Arc** option of the **ELLIPSE** command.

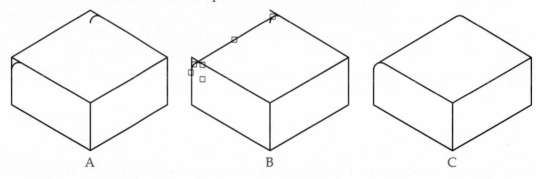

A   B   C

EXERCISE 26-3

❏ Load AutoCAD and begin a new drawing named EX26-3.
❏ Set the grid spacing at .5.
❏ Set the Isometric Snap mode and specify a .25 vertical spacing.
❏ Use the **LINE** command and draw the object shown below. Do not dimension the object.
❏ Fillets and rounds are all .25 radius.
❏ Change the isoplane as needed, and use the **ELLIPSE** command and **Arc** option to complete the object.
❏ Save the drawing as EX26-3.

2.0

Indicates
the edge or
corner

1.75

2.25

Figure 26-14.
Isometric text
applications. The
text shown here
indicates the ISO
style used and the
angle used.

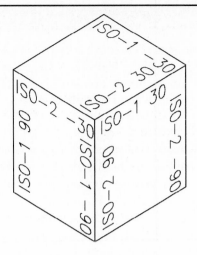

Creating Isometric Text Styles

Isometric text should appear to lie in one of the isometric planes. Drafters and artists occasionally neglect this aspect of pictorial drawing and it shows on the final product. Text should align with the plane that it applies to. This involves creating new text styles.

Figure 26-14 illustrates possible orientation of text on an isometric drawing. Text may be located on the object or positioned away from it as a note. These examples were created using only two text styles. These text styles are based on styles that use an obliquing angle of either 30° or –30°. The labels refer to the style numbers given in the chart below. The angle indicates the rotation angle entered when using one of the **TEXT** commands. For example, ISO-2 90 means that the ISO-2 style was used and the text was rotated 90°. This technique can be applied to any font.

Name	Font	Obliquing Angle
ISO-1	Romans	30°
ISO-2	Romans	–30°

EXERCISE 26-4

❏ Use one of your templates to begin a new drawing.
❏ Create one text style to label the angled (nonisometric) surface of the wedge. See the illustration below.
❏ Create a second style to label the front of the wedge.
❏ Save the drawing as EX26-4.

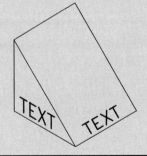

ISOMETRIC DIMENSIONING

An important aspect of isometric dimensioning is to place dimension lines, text, and arrowheads in the proper plane. Remember these guidelines:

- ✓ Extension lines should always extend the plane being dimensioned.
- ✓ The heel of the arrowhead should always be parallel to the extension line.
- ✓ Strokes of the text that would normally be vertical should always be parallel with the extension lines or dimension lines.

These techniques, as well as a dimensioned isometric part, are shown in Figure 26-15. AutoCAD does not automatically dimension isometric objects. You must first create isometric arrowheads and text styles. Then, manually draw the dimension lines and text as they should appear in each of the three isometric planes. This is time-consuming when compared to dimensioning normal 2D drawings.

You have already learned how to create isometric text styles. These can be set up in an isometric template drawing if you draw isometrics often. Examples of arrows for the three isometric planes are shown in Figure 26-16.

Arrowheads can be drawn with the **PLINE** or **LINE** commands or filled-in with a solid hatch pattern or the **SOLID** command. Every arrowhead does not need to be drawn individually. First, draw two isometric axes, as shown in Figure 26-17A. Then, draw one arrowhead like the one shown in Figure 26-17B. Use the **MIRROR** command to create additional arrows. As you create new arrows, move them to their proper plane. Save each arrowhead as a block in your isometric template or prototype. Use names that are easy to remember.

Figure 26-15.
A dimensioned isometric part. Note the text and arrowhead orientation in relation to the extension lines.

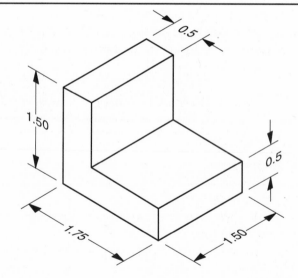

Figure 26-16.
Examples of arrowheads in each of the three isometric planes.

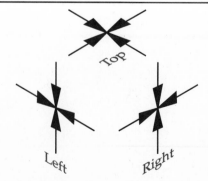

Figure 26-17.
Creating isometric arrowheads. A—Draw the two isometric axes for arrowhead placement. B—Draw the first arrowhead on one of the axis lines. Then, mirror the arrowhead to create others.

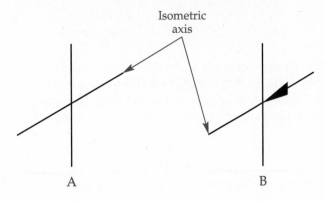

Oblique Dimensioning

AutoCAD User's Guide **12**

AutoCAD has a way to semiautomatically dimension isometric and oblique lines. First, the dimensions must be drawn using any of the linear dimensioning commands. Figure 26-18A illustrates an object dimensioned using the **DIMALIGNED** and **DIMLINEAR** commands. Then, use the **DIMEDIT** command's **Oblique** option to rotate the extension lines. See Figure 26-18B.

To access the **Oblique** option, enter DED or DIMEDIT at the Command: prompt and then enter O for Oblique. You can also select **Oblique** from the **Dimension** pull-down menu. When prompted, select the dimension and enter the obliquing angle.

Figure 26-18A shows numbers by each dimension. The following list gives the obliquing angle required for each numbered dimension in order to achieve the finished drawing shown in Figure 26-18B.

Figure 26-18.
The **OBLIQUE** dimensioning command requires that you select an existing dimension and enter the desired obliquing angle. Refer to the text for the angles represented by the circled numbers.

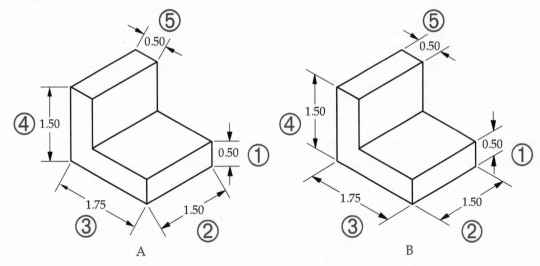

Dimension	Obliquing Angle
1	30°
2	−30°
3	30°
4	−30°
5	30°

This technique creates suitable dimensions for an isometric drawing and is quicker than the previous method discussed. Keep in mind that the oblique method does not rotate the arrows so that the arrowhead heels are aligned with the extension lines. It also does not draw the dimension text aligned in the plane of the dimension.

Chapter Test

Write your answers in the spaces provided.
1. The simplest form of pictorial drawing is _____.
2. How does isometric drawing differ from oblique drawing?
3. How do dimetric and trimetric drawings differ from isometric drawings?
4. The most realistic form of pictorial drawing is _____.
5. What values must be set in the **Drafting Settings** dialog box to set Isometric Snap mode with a spacing of 0.2?
6. What function does the **ISOPLANE** command perform?
7. Which pull-down menu contains the command to access the **Drafting Settings** dialog box?
8. What factor determines the orientation of an isometric ellipse?
9. Name the command and option used to draw an isometric ellipse.
10. Which text style setting allows you to create text that can be used on an isometric drawing?
11. What command and two options must you select in order to draw isometric arcs?
12. On what parts of an isometric circle are grips located?
13. Can grips be used to correctly resize an isometric circle? Explain your answer.
14. What technique does AutoCAD provide for dimensioning isometric objects?

Drawing Problems

Create an isometric template drawing. Use the template to construct the isometric drawings in Problems 1–10. Items that should be set in the template include grid spacing, snap spacing, ortho setting, and text size. Save the template as isoproto.dwt. Save the drawing problems as P26-(problem number).

1.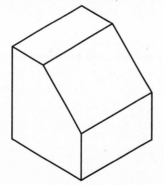

2.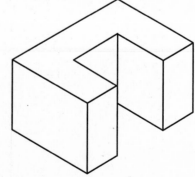

3.

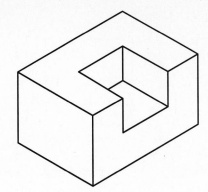

4.

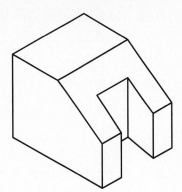

5.

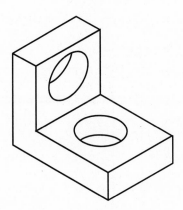

6.

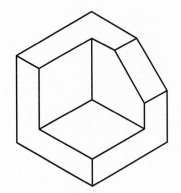

7.

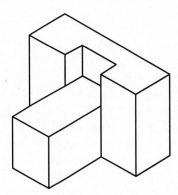

8.

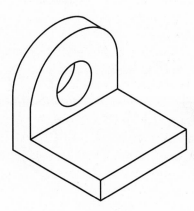

9.

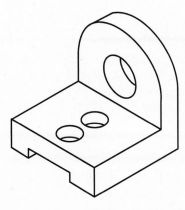

10.

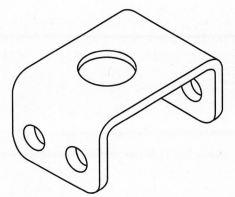

For Problems 11–14, create isometric drawings using the views shown.

11.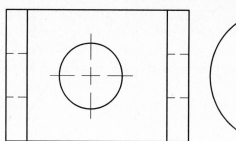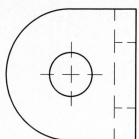

12.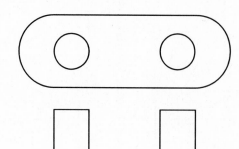

13.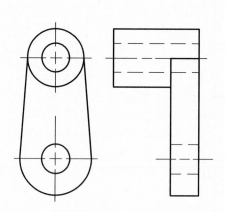

14.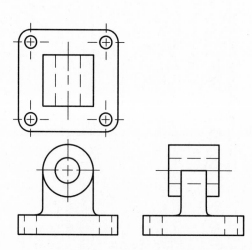

15. Construct a set of isometric arrowheads to use when dimensioning isometric drawings. Load your isometric template drawing. Create arrowheads for each of the three isometric planes. Save each arrowhead as a block. Name them with the first letter indicating the plane: T for top, L for left, and R for right. Also number them clockwise from the top. See the example for the right isometric plane. Save the template again when finished.

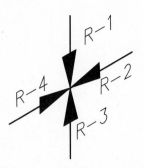

16. Create a set of isometric text styles like those shown in Figure 26-14. Load your template drawing and make a complete set in one font. Make additional sets in other fonts if you wish. Enter a text height of 0 so that you can specify the height when placing the text. Save the template again when finished.

17. Begin a new drawing named P26-17 using your template. Select one of the following problems to dimension: Problem 5, 7, 8, or 9. When adding dimensions, be sure to use the proper arrowhead and text style for the plane that you are working in. Save the drawing when completed.

18. Create an isometric drawing of the switch plate. Select a view that displays the features of the object. Do not include dimensions. Save the drawing as P26-18.

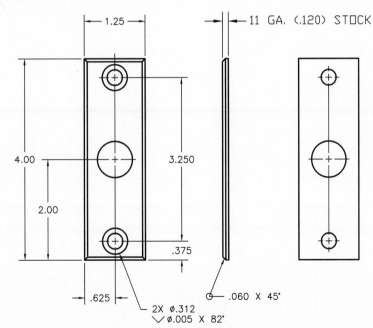

19. Create an isometric drawing of the retainer. Select a view that displays the features of the object. Do not include dimensions. Save the drawing as P26-19.

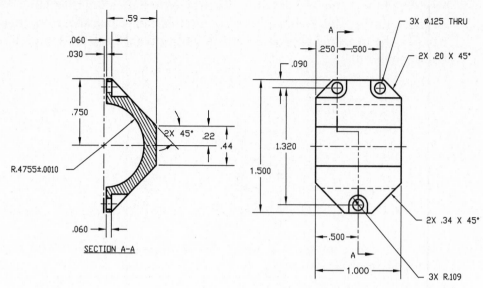

CHAPTER 27

Introduction to Three-Dimensional Drawing

Learning Objectives

After completing this chapter, you will be able to:
- Describe the nature and function of rectangular 3D coordinate systems.
- Use the "right-hand rule" of 3D visualization.
- Construct wireframe and 3D face objects.
- Display 3D objects at any desired viewpoint.

Computers are especially suited to handle information about points in space. However, in order for computer software to accept and use this information, the drafter or designer must first have good 3D visualization skills. These skills include the ability to see an object in three dimensions and to visualize it rotating in space. These skills can be obtained by using 3D techniques to construct objects, and by trying to picture two-dimensional sketches and drawings as 3D models.

This chapter provides an introduction to several aspects of 3D drawing and visualization. A thorough discussion of 3D drawing, visualization, and display techniques is provided in *AutoCAD and its Applications—Advanced*.

RECTANGULAR 3D COORDINATES

A computer can draw lines because it knows the X and Y values of the endpoints. The line does not really exist in the computer, only the points do. When drawing in 3D, you define the third dimension with a third coordinate measured along the Z axis. A computer can only draw lines in 3D if it knows the X, Y, and Z coordinate values of each point on the object.

Compare the 2D coordinate system to the 3D system in Figure 27-1. Note that the positive values of Z in the 3D system come up from the XY plane of a 2D drawing. Consider the surface of your screen as the new Z plane. Anything behind the screen is negative Z and anything in front of the screen is positive Z.

The object in Figure 27-2A is a 2D drawing showing the top view of an object. The XY coordinate values of each point are shown. To convert this object to its three-dimensional form, Z coordinate values are given to each vertex, or corner. In Figure 27-2B, the object is shown pictorially with the XYZ values of each point listed.

Figure 27-1.
A comparison of 2D and 3D coordinate systems.

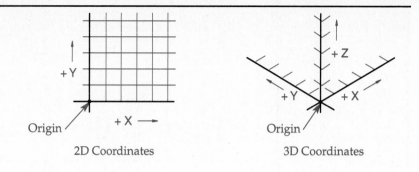

2D Coordinates   3D Coordinates

Figure 27-2.
Each vertex of a 3D object must have an X, Y, and Z value.

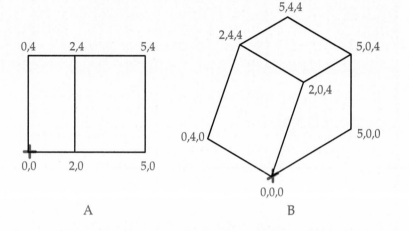

A   B

This same object could have been drawn using negative Z coordinates. In this case, the object would extend behind the screen. Although the sign of the Z value makes no difference to AutoCAD, it is easier to work with positive values.

Study the nature of the 3D coordinate system. Be sure you understand Z values before you begin constructing 3D objects. It is important that you visualize and plan your design when working with 3D constructions.

Three-dimensional objects can be drawn in AutoCAD using a rectangular coordinate system or two additional coordinate systems—spherical and cylindrical. These two systems enable you to work with point locations using distances and angles in order to draw a variety of shapes. For a complete discussion of spherical and cylindrical coordinate systems, please refer to *AutoCAD and its Applications—Advanced*.

EXERCISE 27-1

❏ Study the multiview sketch below.
❏ Given the 3D coordinate axes, freehand sketch the object pictorially. Each tick mark is one unit. Use the correct dimensions as given in the multiview drawing.
❏ When you complete the freehand sketch, draw the object in AutoCAD with the **LINE** command by entering XYZ coordinates for each point.

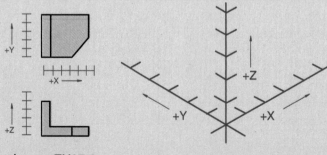

❏ Save the drawing as EX27-1.

         AutoCAD and its Applications—Basics

Most shapes drawn with AutoCAD are extruded shapes. *Extruded* means that a 2D shape is given a base elevation and a thickness. The object then rises up, or "extrudes," to its given thickness. The **ELEV** command controls the base elevation and thickness of shapes. This command does not allow you to draw, it merely sets the base elevation and thickness for the next objects drawn.

> **NOTE**
>
> The current elevation is the level on which the next objects will be drawn. Therefore, if you set the elevation at 2.0, and then draw the bottom of a machine part, the bottom of that part is now sitting at 2.0 units above zero elevation. On the other hand, the *thickness* setting is the value that determines the height of the next object you draw. Therefore, if you want to draw a part 2.0 units high, with the bottom of the part resting on the zero elevation plane, set the elevation to 0.0 and the thickness to 2.0.

The process of drawing a rectangular box four units long by three units wide by two units high begins with the **ELEV** command. The sequence is as follows:

 Command: **ELEV**↵
 Specify new default elevation <0.0000>: ↵
 Specify new default thickness <0.0000>: **2**↵
 Command:

After pressing [Enter], nothing happens on screen. Now use the **LINE** command to draw the top view of the rectangular box. Although it appears that you are drawing four lines, you are actually drawing planes. Each plane has a thickness that you cannot see.

Before you display the 3D construction, use the following guidelines to add a hexagon and circle to the object, as shown in Figure 27-3. The hexagon should sit on top of the rectangle and extend three units above. The circle should appear to be a hole through the rectangle. Since the circle and rectangle have the same elevation, there is no need to use the **ELEV** command.

Before drawing the hexagon, set the base elevation to the top surface of the rectangle and then set the thickness (height) of the hexagon feature. Use the **ELEV** command as follows:

 Command: **ELEV**↵
 Specify new default elevation <0.0000>: **2**↵
 Specify new default thickness <2.0000>: **3**↵
 Command:

Figure 27-3.
A hexagon and circle are added to the rectangle using the command sequences given in the text.

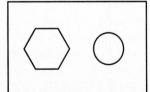

You can now draw the hexagon. The bracketed numbers after each prompt in the previous sequence reflect the current values. A value of 2 is entered for the elevation because the hexagon sits on top of the rectangle, which is two units thick. This is where the hexagon starts. A value of 3 is assigned to the thickness (height) of the hexagon because the hexagon extends 3 units above its starting point.

After drawing the hexagon, set the elevation and thickness for the circle. Reissue the **ELEV** command and proceed as follows:

> Command: **ELEV**↵
> Specify new default elevation <2.0000>: **0**↵
> Specify new default thickness <3.0000>: **2**↵
> Command:

Next, draw the circle to the right of the hexagon. The object is now ready to be viewed in 3D.

PROFESSIONAL TIP Keep in mind that a "hole" drawn using the **ELEV** and **CIRCLE** commands is not really a hole to AutoCAD. It is a cylinder with solid ends. This becomes clear when you display the objects in a 3D view with hidden lines removed.

Some 3D Drawing Hints

✓ Erasing a line drawn with the **ELEV** thickness set to a value other than zero erases an entire plane.

✓ Shapes drawn using the **LINE** and **ELEV** commands are open at the top and bottom.

✓ Circles drawn after using the **ELEV** command are closed at the ends.

✓ The **PLINE** and **TRACE** commands give thickness to lines and make them appear as walls in 3D view.

THE RIGHT-HAND RULE

Before we discuss viewing a 3D drawing, it is worthwhile to review a good technique for 3D visualization. Once you understand the following procedure, viewing a 3D object oriented in AutoCAD's rectangular coordinate system should be relatively easy.

The *right-hand rule* is a graphic representation of positive coordinate values in the three axis directions of a coordinate system. The UCS (User Coordinate System) is based on this concept of visualization. This rule requires that you use the thumb, index finger, and middle finger of your right hand and hold them open in front of you, as shown in Figure 27-4.

Although this may seem a bit unusual to do (especially if you are sitting in the middle of a school library or computer lab), it can do wonders for your understanding of the nature of the three axes. It can also help in understanding how the UCS can be rotated about each of the axis lines, or fingers.

Imagine that your thumb represents the X axis, your index finger is the Y axis, and your middle finger is the Z axis. Hold your hand in front of you and bend your middle finger so it is pointing directly at you. Now you see the plan view. The positive X axis is pointing to the right and the positive Y axis is pointing up. The positive Z axis comes toward you, and the origin of this system is the palm of your hand.

Figure 27-4.
Try positioning
your hand as shown
to understand the
relationship of the
X, Y, and Z axes.

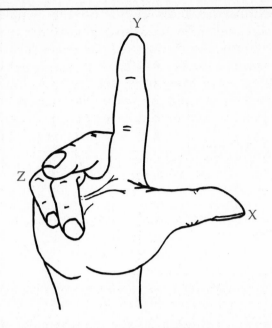

This concept can be visualized even better if you are sitting at a computer and the AutoCAD drawing area is displayed. If the UCS icon is not displayed in the lower-left corner of the screen, turn it on as follows:

Command: **UCSICON**↵
Enter an option [ON/OFF/All/Noorigin/ORigin] <*current*>: **ON**↵

Now orient your right hand as shown in Figure 27-4 and position it next to the UCS icon on screen. Your thumb and index finger should point in the same directions as the X and Y axes, respectively, on the UCS icon. Your middle finger will be pointing out of the screen.

When you use the **VPOINT** command (as discussed later in this chapter), a tripod appears on the screen. It is composed of three axis lines identified as X, Y, and Z. When you see this tripod, you should be able to understand the visual relationship of the right-hand rule. See Figure 27-5.

Figure 27-5.
A comparison of 3D viewing techniques using the UCS icon, the right-hand rule, and the tripod associated with the **VPOINT** command.

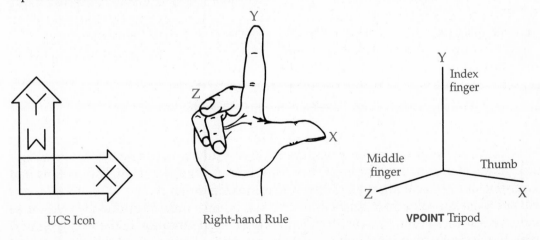

UCS Icon   Right-hand Rule   **VPOINT** Tripod

The right-hand rule can also be used to eliminate confusion when the UCS is rotated to odd angles. The UCS can be rotated to any position. The coordinate system can rotate on any one of the three axis lines, just as a wheel rotates on an axle. Therefore, if you want to rotate the X plane, keep your thumb stationary, and turn your hand toward or away from you. If you wish to rotate the Y plane, keep your index finger stationary and turn your hand to the left or right. When rotating the Z plane, you must keep your middle finger stationary and rotate your entire arm.

If you discover that your 3D visualization skills are weak or that you are having trouble using the UCS icon, don't be afraid to use the right-hand rule. It is a useful technique for improving your 3D visualization skills.

The ability to rotate the UCS around one or more of the three axes can become confusing if proper techniques are not used to visualize the rotation angles. A complete discussion of these techniques is provided in *AutoCAD and its Applications—Advanced*.

DISPLAYING 3D DRAWINGS

Once you have drawn a 3D object in plan view, you should change your point of view so that the object can be seen in three dimensions. The **VPOINT** command allows you to display the current drawing at any angle. It may be easier to understand the function of this command as establishing your position relative to the object.

Imagine that you can position yourself at a coordinate location in 3D space in relation to the object. The **VPOINT** command allows you to provide AutoCAD with XYZ viewing coordinates using your eyes, so the object can be positioned properly. The **VPOINT** command can be accessed by picking **3D Views** from the **View** pull-down menu and then selecting **VPOINT**, or by entering VPOINT at the Command: prompt. Several preset viewpoints can also be selected by picking the appropriate button in the **View** toolbar, Figure 27-6.

VPOINT

View
➥ 3D Views
   VPOINT

Command: **VPOINT**⏎
Current view direction: VIEWDIR=0.0000,0.0000,1.0000
Specify a view point or [Rotate] <display compass and tripod>:

Figure 27-6.
The **View** toolbar contains several preset viewpoints that can be selected by picking the appropriate button.

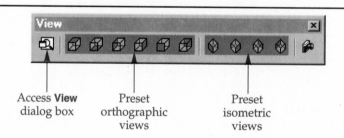

Access **View** dialog box

Preset orthographic views

Preset isometric views

The three coordinate values are the XYZ coordinates of the current viewpoint. The values shown above represent the coordinates for the plan view. This means that your line of sight is along the positive Z axis looking down on the XY plane. You can change these coordinates to select different viewpoints. Since it is difficult to visualize a numerical viewpoint, you can display a graphic representation of the XYZ axes and pick the desired viewpoint with your pointing device. To do so, simply press [Enter] at the **VPOINT** command prompt. This activates the **VPOINT** axes display, Figure 27-7.

Figure 27-7.
The **VPOINT** axes display enables you to position your line of sight in relation to the object.

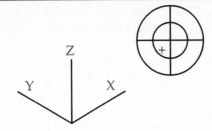

As you move the pointing device, notice what happens on screen. The XYZ coordinate tripod moves and the small set of crosshairs near the concentric circles also moves. The concentric circles represent a compass. When the crosshairs are inside the small circle, you are viewing the object from above. When the crosshairs are located between the two circles, you are viewing the object from below.

The easiest way to locate the viewpoint is to move the cursor while observing the movement of the XYZ tripod. Pick the location where you are satisfied with the appearance of the axes. It may take some practice. Remember that in the top, or plan view, the X axis is horizontal, the Y axis is vertical, and the Z axis comes out of the screen. As you move the tripod, keep track of where the crosshairs are located inside the compass. Compare their position to that of the tripod.

Move the tripod until it is positioned as the one shown in Figure 27-8. Then, press your left mouse button. The resulting display should resemble the object that was drawn with the command sequences earlier in this chapter.

The number of viewpoints you can select is endless. To get an idea of how the **VPOINT** tripod and compass display relates to the viewpoint, see the examples in Figure 27-9. It can be hard to distinguish top from bottom in wireframe views. Therefore, the viewpoints shown in Figure 27-9 are all from above the object, and the **HIDE** command has been used to clarify the views. Use the **VPOINT** command to try each of these 3D views on your computer.

When you are ready to return to the World Coordinate System plan view, use the **PLAN** command. To access the **PLAN** command, enter PLAN at the Command: prompt, or select **3D Views** from the **View** pull-down menu, select **Plan View**, and then select **World UCS**, as shown in Figure 27-10. The command sequence is as follows:

```
Command: PLAN↵
Enter an option [Current ucs/Ucs/World]: <Current>: W↵
Regenerating model.
Command:
```

Figure 27-8.
Using the **VPOINT** command to establish a 3D view for the previously drawn object.

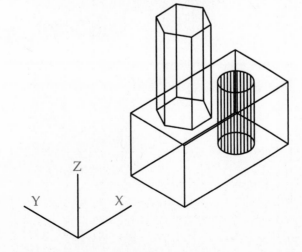

Figure 27-9.
Examples of different viewpoint locations and their related coordinate axes positions.

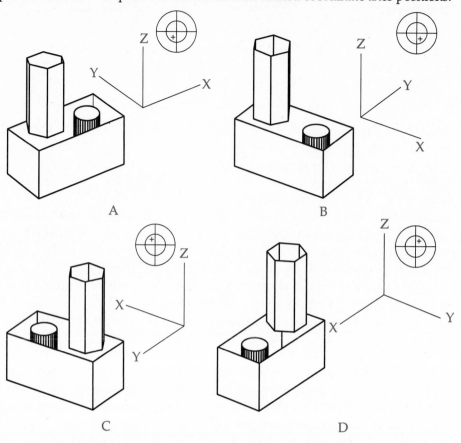

A

B

C

D

Figure 27-10.
The **PLAN** command can be accessed through the **View** pull-down menu.

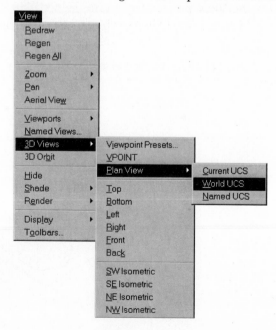

As an alternative to the **PLAN** command, you can also enter the XYZ coordinates for the plan view using the **VPOINT** command:

```
Command: VPOINT↵
Current view direction: VIEWDIR=-2.4227,-2.8555,1.8552
Specify a view point or [Rotate] <display compass and tripod>: 0,0,1↵
Regenerating model.
Command:
```

Either method automatically performs a **ZOOM Extents** operation that fills the drawing area with your original top view. You can use the **ZOOM All** option to redisplay the original drawing limits.

EXERCISE 27-2

❏ Start a new drawing or use one of your templates.
❏ Set the grid spacing to .5 and the snap spacing to .25.
❏ Set the elevation at 0 and the thickness at 2.
❏ Using the **LINE** command, draw a 2 × 3 unit rectangle.
❏ Add a 180° arc to each end of the rectangle.
❏ Set the elevation at 2 and the thickness at 3.
❏ Draw a 1-unit diameter circle in the center of the rectangle.
❏ Use the **VPOINT** command to display the 3D view of your drawing. Display it from three viewpoints using the coordinate axes tripod.
❏ Save the drawing as EX27-2.

Creating Extruded 3D Text

Text added on the plan view is displayed in 3D when you use the **VPOINT** command. However, the displayed text has no thickness, and rests on the zero elevation plane. You can give text thickness and change the elevation by using the **Properties** window. Select the text to change by activating grips on the text, and then highlight the value next to **Thickness** in the **General** category. You can then enter a new thickness value. Examples of 3D text before and after using the **HIDE** command are shown in Figure 27-11.

Figure 27-11.
Examples of applying thickness to text in a 3D view with and without the **HIDE** command.

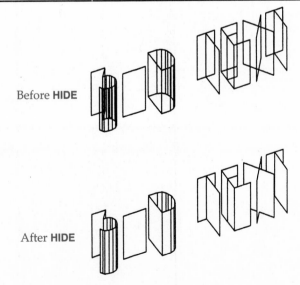

Before **HIDE**

After **HIDE**

AutoCAD User's Guide 17

Removing Hidden Lines in 3D Displays

The displays shown in Figures 27-8 and 27-11 are wireframe representations, where all edges and vertices are visible. A wireframe view can be confusing because features that are normally hidden from view are fully displayed. The best way to mask all features that would normally be hidden is to use the **HIDE** command.

Use the **HIDE** command only after you have selected a 3D viewing angle. To access this command, pick the **Hide** button in the **Render** toolbar, select **Hide** from the **View** pull-down menu, or enter HI or HIDE at the Command: prompt:

HIDE
HI

<u>View</u>
 ➡ <u>Hide</u>

Render
toolbar

Hide

Command: **HI** *or* **HIDE**↵
Regenerating model.
Command:

The size and complexity of the drawing and the speed of your computer determines how long you must wait for the lines to be hidden. The final display of the object in Figure 27-8 is shown in Figure 27-12 with hidden lines removed.

The view in Figure 27-12 may not look exactly as you expected. You probably expected the rectangle to appear solid with a circle in the top representing a hole. Think back to the initial construction of the rectangle. When drawn in the plan view, it consisted of four lines, or planes. It was not drawn with a top or bottom, just four sides. Then you placed a hexagon sitting at the same elevation as the top of the box, and a cylinder inside. That is what appears in the "hidden lines removed" display.

The features that compose the object in Figure 27-12 are shown individually in Figure 27-13. The objects are shown both as wireframes and with hidden lines removed.

To redisplay the wireframe view, simply select another viewpoint or enter REGEN and press [Enter]. A regeneration displays all lines of the objects.

Figure 27-12.
Hidden lines can be removed using the **HIDE** command after a 3D viewing angle has been selected.

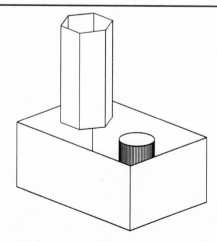

Figure 27-13.
Individual features of the object in Figure 27-12 shown in wireframe views and with hidden lines removed.

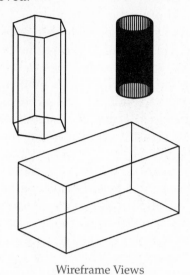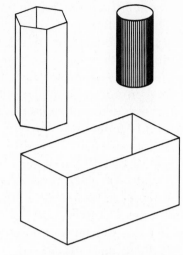

Wireframe Views   Hidden Lines Removed

3D CONSTRUCTION TECHNIQUES

AutoCAD User's Guide **18**

Three-dimensional objects can be drawn in three basic forms—wireframes, surface models, and solid models. The following section discusses the construction of wireframes, and the use of 3D faces to apply a surface to the wireframe. A *wireframe construction* is just that; it is an object that looks like it was made of wire. You can see through it.

There are not a lot of practical applications for wireframe models unless you are an artist designing a new object using coat hangers. Wireframe models are hard to visualize because it is difficult to determine the angle of view and the nature of the surfaces. For example, compare the two objects in Figure 27-14.

Surface modeling, on the other hand, is more easily visualized. A surface model looks more like the real object. Surface models can be used to imitate solid models, and most importantly, can be used for shading and rendering models. These shaded and rendered models can then be used in any number of presentation formats, including slide shows, black and white or color prints, walk-through animation, or animation recorded to videotape.

Figure 27-14.
A wireframe object is harder to visualize than the surface model. (Autodesk, Inc.)

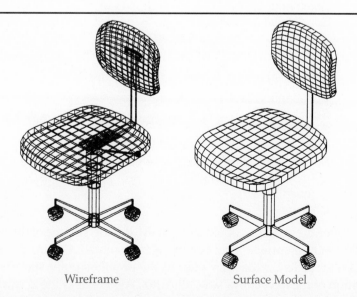

Wireframe   Surface Model

A surface model can also be exported from AutoCAD for use in animation and rendering software, such as Autodesk's 3D Studio MAX® or 3D Studio VIZ®. In addition, surface models are the basis for the construction of composite 3D models, often called *virtual worlds*, which are used in the field of virtual reality.

On the other hand, *solid modeling* more closely represents the design of an object using the materials from which it is to be made. This type of 3D design involves using primitive solid shapes, such as boxes, cylinders, spheres, and cones to construct an object. These shapes are added together and subtracted from each other to create a finished product. The solid model can then be shaded, rendered, and more importantly, analyzed to determine mass, volume, moments of inertia, and centroid location. Some third-party programs allow you to perform finite element analysis on the model.

Before constructing a 3D model, you should determine the purpose of your design. What will the model be used for—presentation, analysis, or manufacturing? This helps you determine which tools you should use to construct the model. The discussions and examples in this chapter provide an introductory view of the uses of wireframes, 3D faces, and basic surfaced objects in order to create 3D constructions. Further study of surface and solid modeling techniques is covered in *AutoCAD and its Applications—Advanced*.

CONSTRUCTING WIREFRAMES AND 3D FACES

Wireframes can be constructed using the **LINE**, **PLINE**, **SPLINE**, and **3DPOLY** commands. AutoCAD provides a number of methods to use, but one particularly useful method involves filters. A *filter* is an existing point, or vector, in your drawing file. When using a filter, you instruct AutoCAD to find the coordinate values of a selected point. Then, you supply the missing value, which can be any X, Y, or Z coordinate, or a combination of coordinates. Filters can be used when working in two-dimensional space or when using a pictorial projection established with the **VPOINT** command.

Using Filters to Create 3D Wireframe Objects

When using the **LINE** command, you must know the XYZ coordinate values of each corner on the object. To draw a 3D object, first decide the easiest and quickest method using the **LINE** command. One technique is to draw the bottom surface. Then, make a copy at the height of the object. Finally, connect the upper and lower corners with lines. The filters can be used with the **COPY** command, or with activated grips in order to copy. From the plan view, step through the process in the following manner:

> Command: **LINE**↵
> Specify first point: **3,3**↵
> Specify next point or [Undo]: **@4,0**↵
> Specify next point or [Undo]: *(continue picking points to construct the box)*

Next, copy the shape up to the height of 3 units.

> Command: **COPY**↵
> Select objects: *(select the box using a window or crossing box)*
> Select objects: ↵
> Specify base point or displacement, or [Multiple]: *(pick a corner of the box)*
> Specify second point of displacement or <use first point as displacement>: **.XY**↵
> of *(pick the same corner)*
> of (need Z): **3**↵
> Command:

Since the shape is copied straight up, the top surface of the box has the same XY values as the bottom surface. That is why .XY was entered as the second point of displacement. This filter picks up the XY values of the previous point specified and applies them to the location of the new copy. Now, all AutoCAD needs is the Z value, which it requests.

Check your progress by looking at the object using the **VPOINT** command. Enter the coordinates given below. Your display should look like that in Figure 27-15.

```
Command: VPOINT↵
Current view direction: VIEWDIR=0.0000,0.0000,1.0000
Specify a view point or [Rotate] <display compass and tripod>: 1,-2,.5↵
Regenerating model.
Command:
```

Finish the object in the pictorial view using the **LINE** command and object snaps. Your drawing should look like the one shown in Figure 27-16.

Figure 27-15.
A partially constructed box using the **LINE** command and filters.

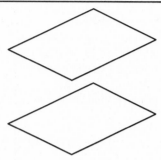

Figure 27-16.
A completed box drawn with the **LINE** command, displayed at a 3D viewing angle.

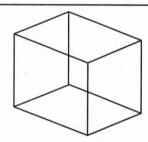

EXERCISE 27-3

❑ Start a new drawing or use one of your templates.
❑ Set the grid spacing at .5, the snap spacing at .25, and the elevation at 0.
❑ Draw the object below to the dimensions indicated.
❑ Use the **LINE** and **COPY** commands to construct the object.
❑ Construct the top and bottom planes in the plan view. Connect the vertical lines in a 3D view.

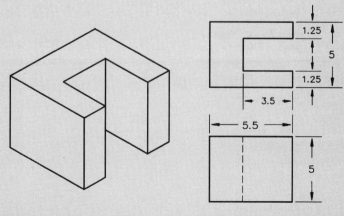

❑ Save the drawing as EX27-3.

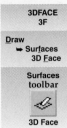
Constructing 3D Faces

Surfaces that appear solid are called *3D faces*. They can be made with the **3DFACE** command. Its prompt structure is similar to that of the **SOLID** command, but you can specify points in either a clockwise or counterclockwise manner. A 3D face must have at least three corners, but it cannot have any more than four corners. To access the **3DFACE** command, pick the **3D Face** button in the **Surfaces** toolbar, pick **3D Face** from the **Surfaces** cascading menu in the **Draw** pull-down menu, or enter 3F or 3DFACE at the Command: prompt.

Draw the previously drawn box again, beginning with the bottom face (set the elevation at 0). Then draw the top face. Draw the bottom face using the following command sequence:

Command: **3F** *or* **3DFACE**↵
Specify first point or [Invisible]: *(pick a point)*
Specify second point or [Invisible]: *(pick a point)*
Specify third point or [Invisible] <exit>: *(pick a point)*
Specify fourth point or [Invisible] <create three-sided face>: *(pick a point)*
Specify third point or [Invisible] <exit>: ↵
Command:

Notice that after you placed the fourth point, a line automatically connected it to the first point. A prompt then asks for the third point again if you want to continue to draw additional faces. Press [Enter] to end the command.

The 3D face can be copied using steps similar to those taken to copy the surface drawn with the **LINE** command. Remember to use filters for copying.

PROFESSIONAL TIP

When moving or copying objects in 3D space, it can simplify matters to use the displacement option to specify positioning data. This allows you to specify the X, Y, and Z movement simultaneously. For example, to copy the 3D face to a position 3 units above the original location on the Z axis, use the following command sequence:

Command: **COPY**↵
Select objects: *(pick the 3D face)*
Select objects: ↵
Specify base point or displacement, or [Multiple]: **0,0,3**↵
Specify second point of displacement or <use first point as displacement>: ↵

If you press [Enter] when prompted for the second point of displacement, the X,Y,Z values previously entered are used as a relative displacement instead of a base point. In this example, the object is copied to a position that differs from the original by 0 units on the X axis, 0 units on the Y axis, and +3 units on the Z axis. To copy an object +1 unit on the X axis, –4 units on the Y axis, and +2 units on the Z axis, the displacement value would be 1,–4,2.

Finally, the four sides of the box are drawn. First, set a viewpoint to display both 3D faces:

Command: **VPOINT**⏎
Current view direction: VIEWDIR=0.0000,0.0000,1.0000
Specify a view point or [Rotate] <display compass and tripod> **-1,-1,.75**⏎
Regenerating model.
Command:

The drawing should now look like the one shown in Figure 27-17. Zoom in if the view is too small. Complete the box using the **3DFACE** command and pick the points as numbered in Figure 27-17.

Command: **3F** *or* **3DFACE**⏎
Specify first point or [Invisible]: *(pick point 1)*
Specify second point or [Invisible]: *(pick point 2)*
Specify third point or [Invisible] <exit>: *(pick point 3)*
Specify fourth point or [Invisible] <create three-sided face>: *(pick point 4)*
Specify third point or [Invisible] <exit>: ⏎
Command:

The first face is complete. Now draw the remaining faces in the same manner. The finished box should appear similar to that shown in Figure 27-18.

How does a 3D face object differ from objects drawn using the **ELEV** and **LINE** commands? For comparison, Figure 27-19 shows boxes drawn using the **ELEV**, **LINE**, and **3DFACE** commands with hidden lines removed by the **HIDE** command.

Figure 27-17.
The top and bottom 3D faces of a box. The numbers indicate the order in which to pick points when using the **3DFACE** command to draw the sides.

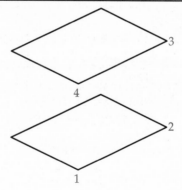

Figure 27-18.
A completed 3D face object appears to be a wireframe construction before using the **HIDE** command.

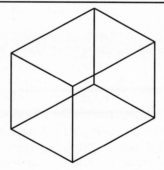

Figure 27-19.
A comparison of boxes drawn with the **ELEV**, **LINE**, and **3DFACE** commands, with hidden lines removed.

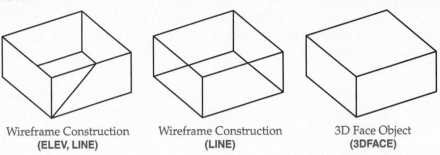

Wireframe Construction
(ELEV, LINE)

Wireframe Construction
(LINE)

3D Face Object
(3DFACE)

EXERCISE 27-4

❏ Start a new drawing or use one of your templates.
❏ Set the grid spacing at .5, the snap spacing at .25, and the elevation at 0.
❏ Use the **3DFACE** command to construct the object shown to the dimensions given.
❏ Draw the bottom of the object in the plan view. Draw the two end faces, the two top angled surfaces, and the front and rear V-shaped surfaces in a 3D view. Remember that a 3D face cannot have more than four corners, so each V-shaped surface must be made of two 3D faces.
❏ Use the **HIDE** command when you complete the object.

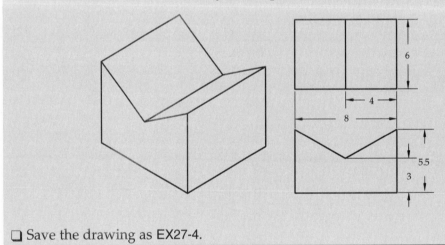

❏ Save the drawing as EX27-4.

CONSTRUCTING 3D SURFACE MODELED OBJECTS

AutoCAD provides several predrawn 3D objects for design purposes. These objects can be quickly placed in your drawing by specifying a location and basic dimensions. Many of the predrawn 3D objects can be selected from the **Surfaces** toolbar. They can also be selected from the **3D Objects** dialog box, which is accessed by selecting **3D Surfaces...** from the **Surfaces** cascading menu in the **Draw** pull-down menu. See Figure 27-20.

Notice the list box to the left of the dialog box. The names listed correspond to the objects shown. An object can be selected by picking either the name or the image. When selected, the image and the name are highlighted.

3D

Draw
➡ Surfaces
    3D Surfaces

Figure 27-20.
A—The **3D Objects** dialog box displays a group of 3D surface modeled objects for use. B— The same objects can be drawn using the **Surfaces** toolbar.

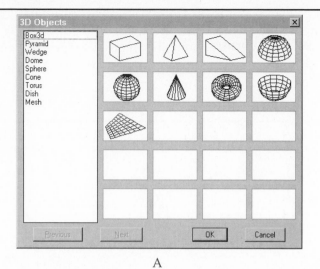

B

A

You can also access the predrawn 3D objects by entering the **3D** command. When you issue this command, the available objects are listed on the command line:

Command: **3D**↵
Enter an option
[Box/Cone/DIsh/DOme/Mesh/Pyramid/Sphere/Torus/Wedge]: *(enter the option for the desired object)*

Regardless of how a 3D object is selected, you are then prompted for a location point. The remaining prompts request various sizes, such as the length, width, height, diameter, and radius, and other specifications, such as the number of longitudinal and latitudinal segments. For example, the **3D** command sequence for the **Dome** option is as follows:

Command: **3D**↵
Enter an option
[Box/Cone/DIsh/DOme/Mesh/Pyramid/Sphere/Torus/Wedge]: **DO**↵
Specify center point of dome: *(pick a point)*
Specify radius of dome or [Diameter]: *(enter a radius or pick on the screen)*
Enter number of longitudinal segments for surface of dome <16>: ↵
Enter number of latitudinal segments for surface of dome <8>: ↵

The object is drawn in the plan view, as shown in Figure 27-21A. Use the **VPOINT** command to produce a 3D view of the object, and use the **HIDE** command to remove hidden lines. The illustration in Figure 27-21B provides an explanation of longitudinal and latitudinal segments. *Longitudinal* refers to an east-west measurement, and *latitudinal* means north-south.

Figure 27-21.
A—The plan view of a dome. B— Longitudinal segments are measured east-west, and latitudinal segments are measured north-south.

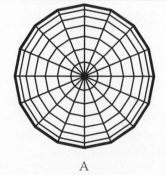

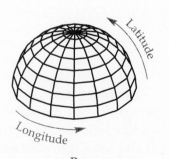

A

B

The objects provided in the **3D Objects** dialog box are easy to draw and fun to work with. Remember that if the current display is a plan view and you draw 3D objects, you must use the **VPOINT** command in order to see a 3D view. The illustrations in Figure 27-22 show the dimensions required to construct the predrawn 3D objects provided by AutoCAD.

Figure 27-22.
The dimensions shown are required to draw AutoCAD's 3D surface modeled objects.

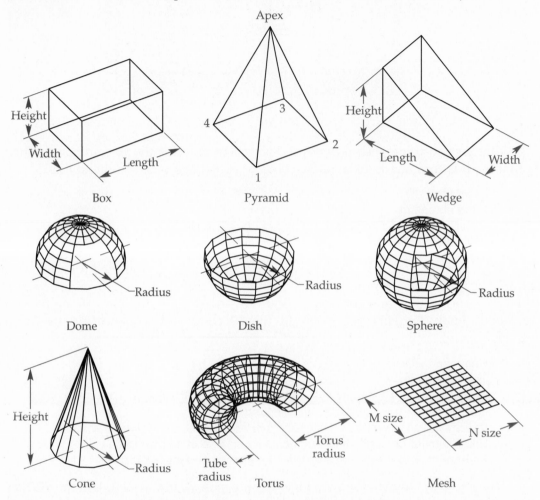

INTRODUCTION TO ENGINEERING LAYOUTS

The **MVSETUP** command can be used to create a paper space layout of four floating model space viewports of any 3D model. The standard engineering drawing views (top, front, and right side) are automatically created. In addition, a pictorial view is placed in the upper-right corner. This view appears in isometric format.

The **MVSETUP** command is actually an AutoLISP routine that provides you with a variety of useful options for constructing paper space layouts. The use of **MVSETUP** with 2D drawing layout was discussed in Chapter 10.

When **MVSETUP** is used to create a standard engineering layout from a 3D model, a step-by-step procedure must be followed in order to achieve properly aligned views. The following is a general outline of the required steps. It is assumed that the 3D model has already been constructed in model space.

1. Use the **MVSETUP** options to establish drawing limits and layers. Create a paper space border and title block layout with the **Title block** option.
2. Establish paper space viewports with the **MVSETUP Create** option using the **Standard Engineering** option.
3. Use the **Scale** and **Align** options to adjust the size and placement of each view within its viewport.
4. Complete the views by adding dimensions and notes, and revise any solid lines that should appear as hidden lines.

A detailed discussion of **MVSETUP** and the creation of a standard engineering drawing layout is provided in *AutoCAD and its Applications—Advanced*.

Chapter Test

Answer the following questions on a separate sheet of paper.
1. When looking at the screen, in which direction does the Z coordinate project?
2. Which command allows you to give objects thickness?
3. If you draw a line after setting a thickness, what have you actually drawn?
4. What is the purpose of the right-hand rule?
5. According to the right-hand rule, name the coordinate axes represented by the following fingers:
   A. Thumb.
   B. Middle finger.
   C. Index finger.
6. What is the purpose of the **VPOINT** command?
7. When the **VPOINT** command's tripod is displayed, what do the concentric circles represent?
8. How are you viewing an object when the small set of crosshairs is inside the small circle in the **VPOINT** command display?
9. How do you create extruded 3D text?
10. What is the function of the **HIDE** command?
11. Define "point filters."
12. How do you access one of AutoCAD's predrawn 3D shapes?

Drawing Problems

1. Draw the object shown below using the **ELEV** command. Display the object in two different views. Use the **HIDE** command on one view. Save the drawing as P27-1.

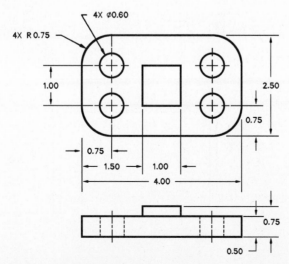

2. Choose Problem 4, 5, or 6 from Chapter 26 and draw it as a wireframe using the **LINE** command. Display the drawing with the **VPOINT** command in four different views. Save the drawing as P27-2.

3. Open drawing P27-2. Use the **3DFACE** command to create faces on the entire part. Display the part in four different views. Save the revised drawing as P27-3.

*For Problems 4-6, draw the objects in 3D form. Use the **LINE** and **3DFACE** commands. Can you create 3D blocks for use in these drawings? Display the drawings from three different viewpoints. Use the **HIDE** command for one of the views. Save the drawings as P27-4, P27-5, and P27-6.*

4.

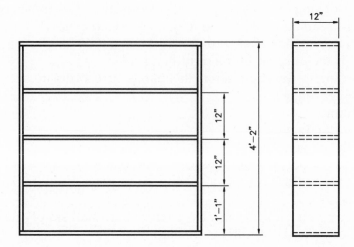

5.

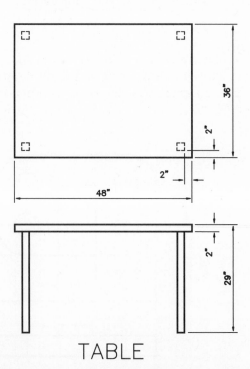

TABLE

6.

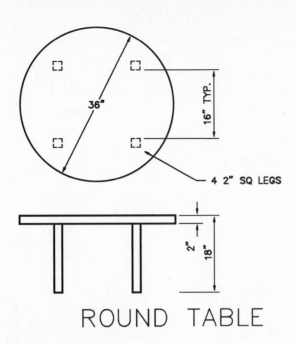

ROUND TABLE

7. Construct a 3D model of the table shown.
   A. Use any 3D construction techniques required.
   B. Use the dimensions given.
   C. Alter the design of the table to include rounded tabletop corners or rounded feet. Try replacing the rectangular feet shown with spheres.
   D. Use the **HIDE** command to remove hidden lines.
   E. Plot the table both in wireframe form and with hidden lines removed.

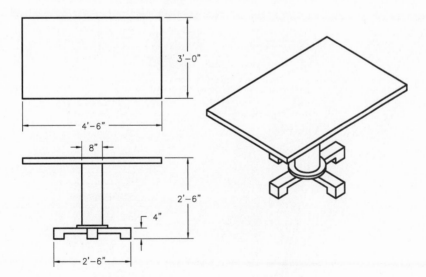

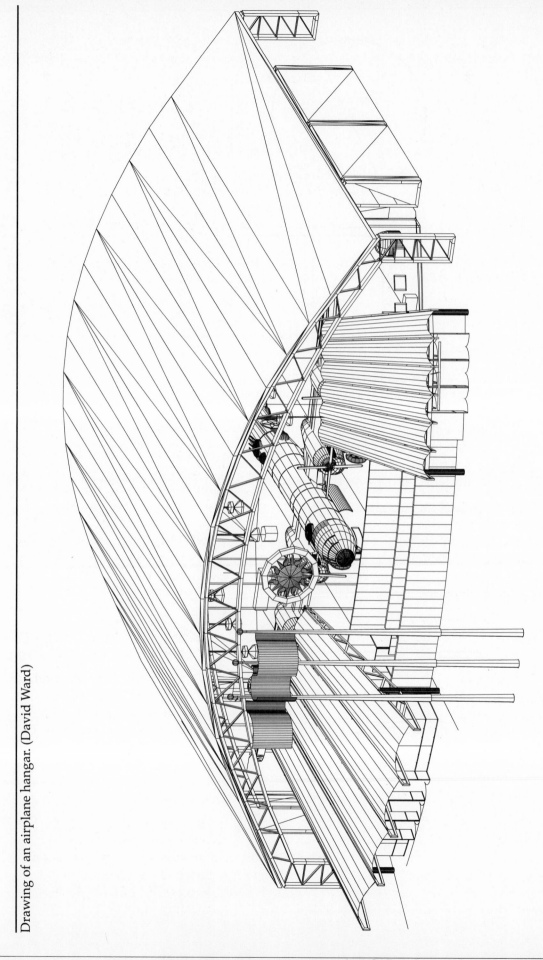

Drawing of an airplane hangar. (David Ward)

CHAPTER 28

External Commands, Script Files, and Slide Shows

Learning Objectives

After completing this chapter, you will be able to:

- Edit the acad.pgp file.
- Use a text editor to create script files.
- Create a continuous slide show of existing drawings.
- Use the **SLIDELIB** command to create a slide library.

This chapter introduces you to the use of scripts. A *script* is a series of commands and variables listed in a text file. When the script file is activated by AutoCAD, the entire list of commands is performed without additional input from the user. One useful script is a continuous slide show. It is excellent for client presentations, demonstrations, and grading drawings.

Word processing and text editor programs can be used to write scripts. There are three tools available under the Windows 98 and NT operating systems for writing ASCII (American Standard Code for Information Interchange) text files: the MS-DOS EDIT text editor, Windows Notepad, and Windows WordPad.

USING TEXT EDITORS

The more experienced you become with AutoCAD, the more you will want to alter the program to suit your specific needs. Most of these alterations are done with a text editor program. While the Windows-supplied Notepad editor is quite capable of performing many of the text editing tasks appropriate for AutoCAD, it cannot accommodate files that exceed 50K (50,000 bytes) in size. However, Notepad is satisfactory for creating simple text files.

Word Processors

Many AutoCAD users rely on full-fledged word processing programs to create their text files. These word processing files should be saved in ASCII format so they are readable by AutoCAD. There are dozens of word processing programs commercially available. The Windows WordPad program is a word processor included with Microsoft Windows. Like Notepad, WordPad may be accessed by picking Accessories in the Program menu. See Figure 28-1.

Figure 28-1.
Both the Notepad text editor and Windows WordPad word processor can be accessed from the Accessories menu.

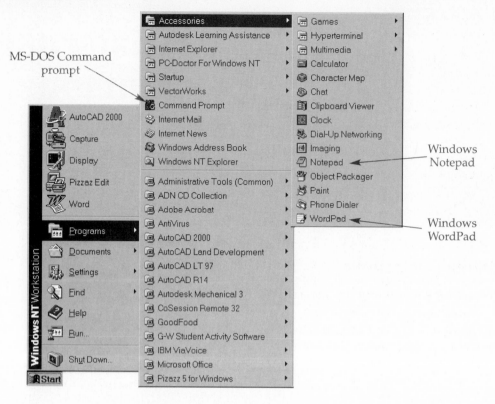

Other Windows-compatible programs you might be familiar with include WordPerfect and Microsoft Word. These are excellent tools for producing written documentation, but exceed what is needed to create text files for AutoCAD. If you choose to use a word processor, save the document as a text file. This prevents the inclusion of special formatting codes.

Programmer's Text Editors

The best type of text editor, however, is a programmer's editor. There are a wide variety of inexpensive yet powerful text editors. These programs are designed for creating the type of file needed to customize AutoCAD. The Norton Editor and Text Pad are examples of excellent programmer's editors.

Programmer's editors are recommended over word processors because of their design, size, function, ease of use, and price.

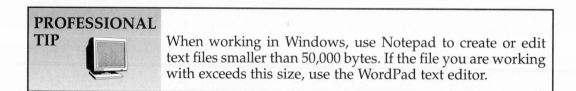

PROFESSIONAL TIP When working in Windows, use Notepad to create or edit text files smaller than 50,000 bytes. If the file you are working with exceeds this size, use the WordPad text editor.

EXTERNAL COMMANDS—THE MS-DOS COMMAND PROMPT

One of the greatest advantages in using Microsoft Windows is the ability to have an application open in one window while working in another window. This capability allows you to edit a text file with Notepad (or another Windows-based text editor) without exiting AutoCAD. Since many of the text files you create will be designed while running AutoCAD, this is a particularly handy feature.

However, there are times when it may be convenient to run a non-Windows application without exiting AutoCAD. This capability is provided with the Windows application called MS-DOS Command Prompt. You can access MS-DOS Command Prompt in the Programs menu. See Figure 28-1. This selection opens the MS-DOS Command Prompt window. See Figure 28-2.

Even though MS-DOS Command Prompt is a Windows application, you can issue a DOS command or run a non-Windows application at the DOS prompt. You can verify for yourself that MS-DOS Command Prompt is a Windows application by pressing the [Alt]+[Tab] key combination to activate the Windows Task List. Also, observe that MS-DOS Command Prompt defaults to the C:\ directory. If necessary, change to the appropriate directory or drive to run your application. You have the option to display the DOS prompt in a window by pressing [Alt]+[Enter].

You can leave the MS-DOS Command Prompt window open or minimize it for later use. By pressing the [Alt]+[Tab] key combination, you can switch back to the Windows application you were running before you invoked MS-DOS Command Prompt. This action does not close MS-DOS Command Prompt. When you are ready to exit MS-DOS Command Prompt, simply type EXIT and press [Enter] or pick the close button.

Figure 28-2.
Pressing [Alt]+[Enter] toggles the MS-DOS Command Prompt window between a window and a full-screen display.

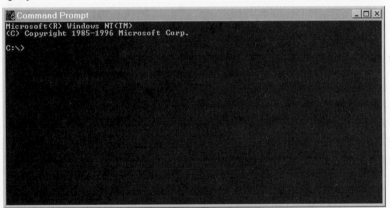

PROFESSIONAL TIP

Be sure to save your AutoCAD drawing before using MS-DOS Command Prompt. This will ensure that no work is lost in case your computer should "hang" or "crash" while you are temporarily exited from AutoCAD. Keep in mind that certain DOS commands should not be used when running the MS-DOS Command Prompt. These commands include UNDELETE and CHKDSK with the /F switch. Also, never use disk-compression and optimization programs in the MS-DOS Command Prompt window.

External commands invoke functions that are not part of AutoCAD. Each of these external commands are defined in a file called acad.pgp (program parameters). This file is placed in the Acad2000\Support folder during the AutoCAD installation procedure. A portion of the acad.pgp file is shown in the Notepad in Figure 28-3.

The Windows Notepad can be initiated directly from AutoCAD. Enter the following to open acad.pgp in Notepad:

Command: **NOTEPAD**⏎
File to edit: **\PROGRAM FILES\ACAD2000\SUPPORT\ACAD.PGP**⏎

Figure 28-3.
The acad.pgp file opened in Notepad.

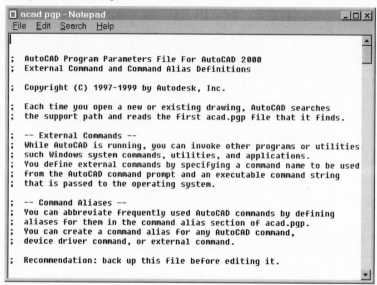

The directory folder path of Program Files\Acad2000\Support is the default name location used when AutoCAD is installed. If the name of the AutoCAD folder was changed, be sure to enter the correct directory name at the prompt above. The Windows Notepad is then opened and the acad.pgp file is displayed.

AutoCAD contains eleven external commands in the acad.pgp file, beginning with **CATALOG**. See Figure 28-4. The first word on each line is the command name typed at AutoCAD's Command: prompt to execute the external command. The second word represents the DOS command or program to be executed. Notice that typing EDIT at the Command: prompt runs the MS-DOS EDIT text editor. Each field in the EDIT entry is separated by a comma and is defined as follows:

- **EDIT.** The command typed at the AutoCAD Command: prompt.
- **START EDIT.** The command or program name executed after the external command name is typed. This is the name that would normally be entered at the DOS prompt or Windows command line to run the text editor. Instructions on how to edit the acad.pgp file for purposes of running your favorite text editor are provided later in this chapter.
- **9.** This bit flag value specifies the way the program starts. The meanings of the bit values are explained in the acad.pgp file.
- **File to edit:.** This is the prompt that appears after the command is typed.

Figure 28-4.
External commands are defined in the acad.pgp file.

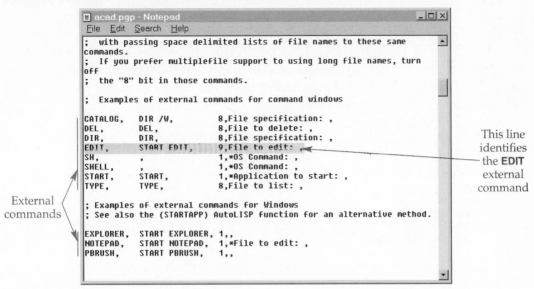

External commands

This line identifies the **EDIT** external command

The SH and SHELL Commands

The **SH** and **SHELL** entries in the acad.pgp file perform a function similar to the MS-DOS Command Prompt application discussed earlier in this chapter. When you enter SH or SHELL on the AutoCAD command line, the following prompt appears:

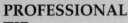

OS Command: *(enter an external command or press* [Enter]*)*

You may enter only one external command at the OS Command: prompt. When the command is completed, you are automatically returned to the AutoCAD graphics window. If you press [Enter] at the OS Command: prompt, you are presented with the DOS prompt in an MS-DOS shell window titled AutoCAD Shell Active. Thus, pressing [Enter] performs much the same function as MS-DOS Command Prompt. As with MS-DOS Command Prompt, when you are ready to exit the AutoCAD shell, type EXIT and press [Enter].

PROFESSIONAL TIP

The **SH** or **SHELL** command can be used to delete a file or do a directory listing from within AutoCAD. If you choose to perform a directory listing, use the command form DIR/P to scroll the directory one page at a time. As with MS-DOS Command Prompt, be careful using certain DOS commands and exit Windows before using any hard disk utility programs.

Command Aliases

AutoCAD allows you to abbreviate command names. This feature is called *command aliasing*. A list of predefined aliases furnished with AutoCAD can be displayed by viewing the contents of the acad.pgp file. You can do this by loading the file into Notepad or another text editor. Scroll down past the list of external commands and you will see the list of command aliases. This is an extensive list containing over 170 aliases. An example of some command aliases is provided here. See Appendix I for the complete listing.

```
A,    *ARC
C,    *CIRCLE
CO,   *COPY
DV,   *DVIEW
E,    *ERASE
L,    *LINE
LA,   *LAYER
LT,   *LINETYPE
M,    *MOVE
P,    *PAN
PL,   *PLINE
R,    *REDRAW
T,    *MTEXT
Z,    *ZOOM
```

You can easily create your own aliases by editing this file. For example, if you want to add an alias **PP** for the **PLOT** command, enter the following below the **PLINE** command in the acad.pgp file:

```
PP,   *PLOT
```

Be sure to include the asterisk since it indicates to AutoCAD that this is an alias. Save the Notepad file. The revised acad.pgp file will not work until you open a new drawing, which reloads the acad.pgp file. You can also reload the acad.pgp file by entering the **REINIT** command. This displays the **Re-initialization** dialog box shown in Figure 28-5. Pick the **PGP File** check box in this dialog box, and then pick **OK** to reinitialize the acad.pgp file so that your new command alias will work.

Figure 28-5.
The **Re-initialization** dialog box.

Check to reload the acad.pgp file

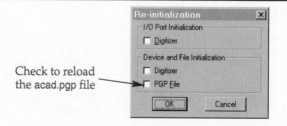

 NOTE

The **Re-initialization** dialog box can also be used if you have one of your serial ports, such as COM1, configured for both a plotter and a digitizer. If you change the cable from plotter to digitizer, pick the **Digitizer** check boxes in both areas of the dialog box to reinitiate the digitizer.

Editing the ACAD.PGP File

There are several tools available to edit the acad.pgp file. The Windows Notepad, MS-DOS EDIT, or another text editor may be used. The easiest editing method is with the Windows Notepad.

PROFESSIONAL TIP

Always make backup copies of AutoCAD text files before editing them. Should you "corrupt" one of these files through incorrect editing techniques, simply delete that file and restore the original.

The acad.pgp file can be easily altered to specify your personal text editor instead of EDIT. For this example, we will use an editor called TE. If you are currently running AutoCAD, use the **NOTEPAD** external command to open the acad.pgp file in Windows Notepad.

> Command: **NOTEPAD**↵
> File to edit: **\PROGRAM FILES\ACAD2000\SUPPORT\ACAD.PGP**↵

The acad.pgp file is displayed in Notepad. You may use any of the text editing keys to move the flashing text cursor around the screen. These keys include the left, right, up, and down arrows, as well as the [Home], [Page Up], [Page Down], [Insert], [Delete], and [End] keys. You can also move the text cursor with your pointing device. Use the down arrow key or your pointing device to move the text cursor to the line labeled:

> EDIT,   START EDIT,   9,File to edit: ,

Remove the word EDIT in both places using the [Backspace] or [Delete] keys, and replace it with the word TE (the name of your text editor). When you are done, the acad.pgp file should appear as shown in Figure 28-6. Entering TE at the AutoCAD Command: prompt now initiates the text editor TE.

To save the edited file, activate the pull-down menus at the top of the screen. Select Save from the File pull-down menu. To return to AutoCAD press [Alt]+[Tab] to display the Task List, then tab through the icons to highlight AutoCAD and release the [Alt] key.

Figure 28-6.
The word EDIT is replaced with TE to specify a different external text editor.

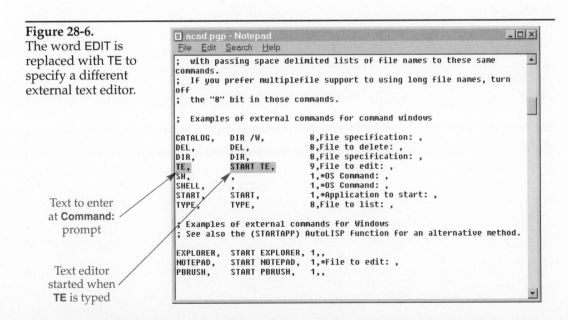

Text to enter at **Command:** prompt

Text editor started when **TE** is typed

If you try using the new text editor command in AutoCAD now, it will not work. This is because AutoCAD is still using the original version of the acad.pgp file. You must re-initialize the acad.pgp file with the **REINIT** command before the **TE** command can function properly.

EXERCISE 28-1

❑ Load AutoCAD and open Windows Notepad.
❑ Use Windows Notepad to edit the acad.pgp file as described in the previous text. Make sure that you have a backup copy of acad.pgp before making your changes.
❑ Save the file, exit Notepad, and use the **REINIT** command.
❑ Test the new command.

CREATING SCRIPT FILES TO AUTOMATE AUTOCAD

A *script file* is a list of commands that AutoCAD executes in sequence without input from the user. Scripts enable nonprogrammers to automate AutoCAD functions. Scripts can be used for specific functions, such as plotting a drawing with the correct **PLOT** command values and settings, or creating a slide show. A good working knowledge of AutoCAD commands is needed before you can confidently create a script file.

When writing a script file, use one command or option per line in the text file. This makes the file easier to fix if the script does not work properly. A return is specified by pressing [Enter] after typing a command. If the next option of a command is a default value to be accepted, press [Enter] again. This leaves a blank line in the script file, which represents pressing [Enter].

The following example shows how a script file can be used to plot a drawing. At your computer, enter these files with Notepad or another text editor. The file extension of the script name must be .scr. Also, place the file in the Acad2000 folder.

Creating a Plotting Script

In Chapter 10, you learned that you can save plotter settings for a specific drawing in the form of a named page setup. This eliminates setting all the plot values each time you plot the same drawing. You can automate this process by including all of the plot values in a script file. If you have drawings that will always be plotted with the same settings, use script files to plot them.

PROFESSIONAL TIP 	Use the **-PLOT** command when writing a script file. This runs the plot script from the command line and enables you to provide text entry to answer all questions for plot setup.
	If a script file is used in the manner discussed here, you can simply execute the script file, then continue your work without having to go through the **Plot** dialog box.

The following script file plots a B-size drawing. The contents of the script file are shown in the left column, and a description of each line is given to the right. This script file is named civil240-b.scr. The "civil" indicates a civil engineering drawing, the "240" is the scale factor, and "b" is the paper size. A comment can be inserted in a script file to provide information to the reader. Simply place a semicolon as the first character on the line and AutoCAD will not process that line. For example, the first line in the following script is a comment for information only:

; Plots a B-size drawing on the HP 1120C DeskJet printer. *(comment only)*
-plot   *(executes command line version of the **PLOT** command)*
y *(Yes to begin detailed plot configuration)*
Layout1 *(plot Layout1)*
   (Enter accepts default plotter)
   (Enter accepts default paper size)
I *(plots in inches)*
L *(plots landscape format)*
N *(does not plot upside-down)*
E *(plots extents of drawing)*
1:1   *(plots at scale of 1:1)*
.02,.02 *(coordinates for plotting xy offset from lower-left corner)*
N *(do not plot with plot styles)*
. *(indicates "none" for plot style name)*
Yes   *(plot with lineweights)*
N *(do not scale lineweights)*
N *(do not plot paper space last)*
N *(do not remove hidden lines)*
N *(do not write the plot to a file)*
N *(do not save changes to layout)*
Y *(proceed with plot)*

Figure 28-7 shows how the script file appears in the Windows Notepad.

To run the script, select **Run Script...** from the **Tools** pull-down menu or enter SCR or SCRIPT at the Command: prompt. Then select the file name civil240-b.scr from the **Select Script File** dialog box. See Figure 28-8. Then sit back and watch the script run.

All the commands, options, and text screens associated with the commands in the script are displayed in rapid succession on the screen. If the script stops before completion, a problem has occurred. Flip the screen to the **AutoCAD Text Window** ([F2]) to determine the last command executed. Return to your text editor and correct the problem. Most often, there are too many or too few returns. Another problem is spaces at the end of a line. If you suspect these errors, retype the line.

Figure 28-7.
The civil240-b.scr script file as it appears in the Windows Notepad.

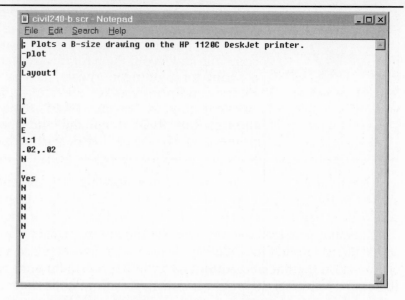

Figure 28-8.
The **Select Script File** dialog box.

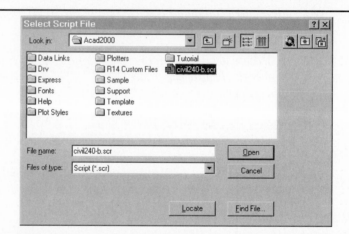

EXERCISE 28-2

❑ Use one of your templates and create a new drawing named scrptest.
❑ Use the **DTEXT** command to write your name in the lower-right corner.
❑ Save the drawing, but do not exit AutoCAD.
❑ Use Notepad to write a script file named test.scr. The script file should do the following:
  ❑ Draw a circle at coordinates 4,4 with a radius of 1.
  ❑ Change the current color to green.
  ❑ Draw a doughnut centered on the circle with an inside diameter of 2.5 and an outside diameter of 2.8.
❑ Switch back to AutoCAD and run test.scr.
❑ If the script file does not run to completion, use Notepad to correct it. Run the script file again until it works.

AutoCAD and its Applications—Basics

A *slide* in AutoCAD, similar to a slide in photography, is a snapshot of the drawing area display. Because of its nature, it cannot be edited or plotted. Slides can be viewed one at a time or as a continuous show. This is why slides are excellent for demonstrations, presentations, displays, and evaluation procedures.

You can create an impressive portfolio using a slide show. A *slide show* is a group of slides that are displayed at preset intervals. The slide show is controlled by a script file, which is a list of commands similar to the previous script examples. Each slide is displayed for a specific length of time. The show can be continuous or a single pass.

Making and Viewing Slides

Creating slides is easy. First display the drawing for which you need a slide. You might display the entire drawing or zoom to a specific area or feature. AutoCAD creates a slide of the current screen display. Make as many slides of one drawing as you want. For each, use the **MSLIDE** command and provide a file name for the slide. Do not enter a file type, as AutoCAD automatically attaches an .sld file extension. If **FILEDIA** is set to 1, a dialog box appears. Use **MSLIDE** at the Command: prompt as follows:

Command: **MSLIDE**↵

The **Create Slide File** dialog box is displayed. This is the standard file dialog box. Pick the drive and folder in which the file is to be stored, enter the name in the **File name:** text box, and pick the **Save** button.

Slide names should follow a pattern. Suppose you are making slides for a class called cad1. File names such as cad1sld1 and cad1sld2 are appropriate. If working on project #4305 for the Weyerhauser Company, you might name the slide to reflect the client name or project number, such as weyersld1 or 4305sld1.

PROFESSIONAL TIP To create a slide file at the highest resolution, set **VIEWRES** to its maximum value of 20000 and execute a regeneration before using the **MSLIDE** command. After making the slide, restore **VIEWRES** to its previous value.

Viewing a slide is as simple as making one. Enter VSLIDE at the Command: prompt to initiate the **VSLIDE** command.

Command: **VSLIDE**↵

The **Select Slide File** dialog box appears. Pick the slide you want to display and pick **OK**. The slide is displayed in the graphics window.

PROFESSIONAL TIP Keep the Acad2000 folder free of drawing, slides, and AutoLISP files. This speeds the computer's access to AutoCAD files. Create a separate folder for slides or save slides on a diskette. If using diskettes, be sure to give the appropriate file name when creating slides.

❏ Load any one of your drawings into the drawing editor.
❏ Create a slide of the entire drawing, using an appropriate file name.
❏ Make slides of two more drawings. Use similar naming techniques.
❏ View each of the slides as they are created.
❏ These slides are required to complete the next exercise.

Writing a Slide Show Script File

A slide show script file contains only two or three commands. This depends on whether it is a single pass or continuous show. A slide show script file typically contains the following commands:

- **VSLIDE.** This command is used to display a slide. The name of the slide follows the command. If the slide name is preceded by an asterisk (*), the slide is preloaded and displayed at the following **VSLIDE** command. This second command is not followed by a slide name, since the slide is already preloaded.
- **DELAY.** Any slide file can be displayed for up to approximately 33 seconds using this command. Delays are given in milliseconds. A delay of four seconds is written as DELAY 4000.
- **RSCRIPT.** This command is used at the end of a continuous script file. It causes the script to repeat.

A slide show begins with the creation of a script file using a text editor. The following script uses four slides. Each appears for three seconds and the script repeats. Notice that the next slide is preloaded while the previous one is viewed.

The show.scr script file is shown as it would be entered in the Windows Notepad, Figure 28-9. Also, do not forget that when using slide files on diskettes, include the disk drive letter and path in front of the file name, such as A:cad1sld2. Use this method with each **VSLIDE** command.

Figure 28-9.
The show.scr script file as it appears in the Windows Notepad.

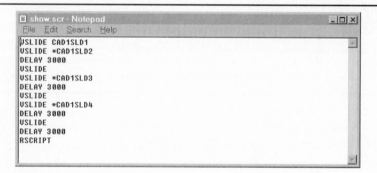

```
VSLIDE CAD1SLD1
VSLIDE *CAD1SLD2
DELAY 3000
VSLIDE
VSLIDE *CAD1SLD3
DELAY 3000
VSLIDE
VSLIDE *CAD1SLD4
DELAY 3000
VSLIDE
DELAY 3000
RSCRIPT
```

Viewing the Slide Show

SCRIPT
SCR

Tools
➥ Run Script...

The slide show is started by entering SCR or SCRIPT at the Command: prompt or by picking **Run Script...** from the **Tools** pull-down menu. Select the script file name show.scr from the **Select Script File** dialog box.

The show begins and the commands in the script file are displayed at the Command: prompt as the slides appear. To stop the show, press the [Backspace] key. You can then work on a drawing, use DOS commands, or work with a text editor on another script file. When finished, resume the slide show where it left off by entering RESUME. Any script file can be interrupted and restarted in this manner.

If your slide show encounters an error and fails to finish the first time through, do not panic. Take the following steps to "debug," or correct, problems in your script file.

1. Run the script to see where it crashes (quits working).
2. Check the command line for the last command that was executed.

3. Look for error messages, such as:
   - **Can't open slide file** *xxxxx*. This indicates an incorrect slide file name.
   - *xxxxx* **Unknown command.** A command may be spelled incorrectly or a space may be left at the end of the line.
   - **Requires an integer value.** The delay value is not all numerical characters, or there may be a space at the end of the line.
4. Correct the problem in the script file and save the file.
5. Test the script.

The most common errors are misspelled commands and spaces at the end of lines. If you suspect there is a space at the end of a line, it is best to delete the line and retype it. If you use Notepad, it is easy to see if a space exists. The flashing cursor, when placed at the end of a line, does not rest on the last character.

EXERCISE 28-4

❏ Create a script file named EX28-4. Use Notepad or your own text editor. It is not necessary to be in the AutoCAD drawing editor to create the script file.
❏ Include the three slides created in Exercise 28-3. If these slides have not been created, make slides of any three of your drawings.
❏ Delay each slide for two seconds.
❏ Make the show run continuously.
❏ Run the slide show. Correct any errors and run it again until it recycles without failing.

CREATING AND USING SLIDE LIBRARIES

AutoCAD User's Guide **24**

In addition to being displayed in slide shows, slide files are also used to create image tile menus. Image tile menus are groups of slides or vector images displayed in a dialog box. Examples are the 3D surfaces displayed after selecting **3D Surfaces...** from the **Surfaces** cascading menu in the **Draw** pull-down menu. Constructing image tile menus is discussed in *AutoCAD and its Applications—Advanced*.

Creating a Slide Library

To create a slide library, you must use a utility program called slidelib.exe, which operates from the DOS prompt. By default, the slidelib.exe utility program is installed in the Acad2000\Support folder. Be sure to include this path when using the utility.

The slidelib.exe program can be used to create slide libraries in two ways. The first method involves listing the slides and their folder location after entering the **SLIDELIB** command. For example, suppose you have four slides of pipe fittings in the \Pipe subdirectory of the Acad2000 folder. Compile these files in a slide library called PIPE in the following manner:

```
Command: SH↵
OS Command: SLIDELIB PIPE↵
SLIDELIB 1.2 (3/8/89)
(C) Copyright 1987-1989, 1994, 1995 Autodesk, Inc.
   All Rights Reserved
\program files\acad2000\pipe\90elbow↵
\program files\acad2000\pipe\45elbow↵
\program files\acad2000\pipe\tee↵
\program files\acad2000\pipe\cap↵
 ↵
 ↵
Command:
```

After entering the last slide, press [Enter] three times to end the **SLIDELIB** command. The new slide library file is saved as pipe.slb.

The second way to use **SLIDELIB** is to first create a list of the slides you will eventually want in the library. Do this with Notepad. This method allows you to accumulate slides over a period of time. Then, when you are ready to create the slide library, the list is prepared. For example, a list of those same pipe fittings is entered in a file called pipe.txt. The list appears in Notepad as follows:

```
90ELBOW
45ELBOW
TEE
CAP
```

After completing the list of slides to include, use the **SLIDELIB** command. The **SLIDELIB** command needs to find the pipe.txt file and use it to create a slide library called pipe.slb. This can all be handled with one entry at the DOS prompt. First, you must shell out of AutoCAD:

```
Command: SH↵
OS Command: SLIDELIB PIPE PIPE.TXT↵
Command:
```

The screen flashes briefly and the AutoCAD graphic window is redisplayed. To see the results, obtain a listing of all SLB files and look for pipe.slb.

Viewing Slide Library Slides

The **VSLIDE** command also is used to view slides contained in a slide library. First change **FILEDIA** to 0. Then provide the library name plus the slide name in parentheses as follows:

```
Command: FILEDIA
New value for FILEDIA ⟨1⟩: 0

Command: VSLIDE↵
Enter name of slide file to view: PIPE(90ELBOW)
```

Use the **REDRAW** command to remove the slide from the screen to display the previous drawing.

Making a Slide Show Using the Slide Library

The advantage of using a slide library for a slide show is that you do not need to preload slides. A slide show of the four slides in the pipe.slb file would appear as follows:

```
VSLIDE PIPE(90ELBOW)
DELAY 1000
VSLIDE PIPE(45ELBOW)
DELAY 1000
VSLIDE PIPE(TEE)
DELAY 1000
VSLIDE PIPE(CAP)
DELAY 1000
REDRAW
```

The **REDRAW** command at the end of the slide show clears the screen and replaces the previous display. An **RSCRIPT** command instead of **REDRAW** repeats the show continuously.

Chapter Test

Answer the following questions on a separate sheet of paper.

1. What precautions should you take when using a word processor to create text files for AutoCAD?
2. How do you activate Windows Notepad from the AutoCAD Command: prompt, and what is the name of the file that allows you to do it?
3. What is the maximum file size (in bytes) that can be handled by the Windows Notepad?
4. How do you open the MS-DOS Command Prompt window?
5. If you edit the acad.pgp file from within AutoCAD, what must you do for the new file definitions to take effect?
6. Describe external commands.
7. Commands located in the acad.pgp file are executed by _____.
8. Name the parts of a command listing found in the acad.pgp file.
9. What is a command alias, and how would you write one for the **POLYGON** command?
10. Define *script file*.
11. Why is it a good idea to put one command on each line of a script file?
12. List two common reasons why a script file might not work.
13. What two commands allow you to make and view slides?
14. What file extension is assigned to slide files?
15. Explain why it is a good idea to keep slide files in a separate folder other than the Acad2000 folder.
16. List the three commands used when writing a slide show.
17. To stop a slide show, press the _____ key.
18. How do you begin a slide show that has been stopped?
19. Briefly explain the two methods used to create a **SLIDELIB** file.
20. Suppose you want to view a slide named VIEW1, which is in a slide library file called VIEWS. How must you enter its name at the Enter name of slide file to view: prompt?
21. What is the principal difference between a slide show script file written for a slide library and one written for a group of slides?

Problems

1. If you use a text editor or word processor other than MS-DOS EDIT or Notepad, create a new command in the acad.pgp file that loads the text editor.

2. Create a new command for the acad.pgp file that activates the Windows Clock.

3. Write a script file called notes.scr that does the following:

   A. Executes the **TEXT** command.
   B. Selects the **Style** option.
   C. Enters a style name.
   D. Selects the last point using the "@" symbol.
   E. Enters a text height of .25.
   F. Enters a rotation angle of 0.
   G. Inserts the text: NOTES:.
   H. Selects the **TEXT** command again.
   I. Enters location coordinates for first note.

J. Enters a text height of .125.

K. Enters a rotation angle of 0.

L. Inserts the text: 1. INTERPRET DIMENSIONS AND TOLERANCES PER ASME Y14.5.

M. Enters an [Enter] keystroke.

N. Inserts the text: 2. REMOVE ALL BURRS AND SHARP EDGES.

O. Enters [Enter] twice to exit the command.

Immediately before this script file is used, select the **ID** command and pick the point where you want the notes to begin. That point will be the "last point" used in the script file for the location of the word NOTES:. The script file, when executed, should draw the following:

NOTES:
1. INTERPRET DIMENSIONS AND TOLERANCES PER ASME Y14.5.
2. REMOVE ALL BURRS AND SHARP EDGES.

4. Create a slide show of your best AutoCAD drawings. This slide show should be considered as part of your portfolio for potential employers. Place all of the slides and the script file on a floppy disk. Make two copies of the portfolio disk on separate diskettes. Keep the following guidelines in mind:

A. Do not delay slides longer than 5 seconds. You can always press the [Backspace] key to view a slide longer.

B. One view of a drawing is sufficient unless the drawing is complex. If so, make additional slides of the drawing's details.

C. Create a cover slide or title page slide that gives your name.

D. Create an ending slide that says THE END.

5. Create a slide show that illustrates specific types of drawings. For example, you might make a slide show for dimensioned mechanical drawings or for electrical drawings. These specialized slide shows in your portfolio are useful if you apply for a job in a specific discipline. Store all slide shows on the same disk. Identify slide shows by their content as follows:

mech.scr—Mechanical
arch.scr—Architectural
pipe.scr—Piping
struct.scr—Structural
elect.scr—Electrical or Electronics
map.scr—Mapping
civil.scr—Civil

6. Create a script file to plot your most frequently used drawing. Use the following guidelines to write the script:

A. Run a trial plot of the drawing first. Record all of the keystrokes required to plot the drawing correctly.

B. Check the results of the trial plot to be sure that the use of pens and the location of the drawing on the paper is correct.

C. Write the script file using the exact keystrokes you recorded.

D. Test the script and note where problems occur.

E. Fix the problems in the script file and test the script until it runs properly.

Appendix A
AutoCAD 2000i Features and Express Tools

This appendix has two distinct parts. The first half of the appendix discusses some of the features new for AutoCAD 2000i. The second half of the appendix provides a brief introduction to the Express Tools available in AutoCAD 2000.

AUTOCAD 2000i FEATURES

The following sections provide additional discussion on some of the new features introduced in AutoCAD 2000i. Most new features are discussed within the text chapters. However, the following topics require additional coverage.

Getting Help in AutoCAD 2000i

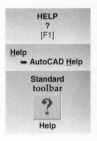

HELP
?
[F1]

Help
➥ AutoCAD Help

Standard
toolbar

?

Help

The format of the AutoCAD help system in AutoCAD 2000i is different from the format used in AutoCAD 2000. To access AutoCAD help, pick the **Help** button in the **Standard** toolbar, select **AutoCAD Help** from the **Help** pull-down menu, enter ? or HELP at the Command: prompt, or press the [F1] key.

The **AutoCAD Help** window consists of two frames, Figure A-1. The left frame, which has five tabs, is used to locate help topics. The right frame displays the selected help topics. In addition to the two frames, the following buttons are located in the **AutoCAD Help** window:
*   **Hide/Show.** This button controls the visibility of the left frame. When you pick **Hide**, the left frame disappears, the show button replaces the **Hide** button, and the buttons appear above the right frame. Pick the **Show** button to view the left frame.
*   **Back.** Pick this button to view the previously displayed help topic.
*   **Print.** If you want to print a help topic, pick this button. Then, you must specify if you want to print the selected help topic or the selected heading and subtopics.
*   **Options.** This button contains a menu with a variety of items. Pick **Hide tabs** to remove the left frame. Use **Forward** and **Back** to navigate help topics. Select **Home** to return to the Getting Information help topic. Pick **Stop** to stop a help topic that is being loaded. **Refresh** regenerates the help topic. **Internet Options...** accesses the Windows **Internet Options** dialog box.

Locating help topics

The left frame is used to navigate through the help documentation to find the desired help topic. This frame has five tabs. Each tab provides a different method of finding help topics.

The **Contents** tab lists each of the help documents within the AutoCAD help system. The following documents are available:

- **Getting Information.** Provides a general introduction to the help system.
- **User's Guide.** This is the most useful help area for most AutoCAD users. The User's Guide contains many "chapters" explaining how various tasks are accomplished using AutoCAD. New AutoCAD users should explore the User's Guide to become comfortable using it.
- **Command Reference.** Contains an alphabetical listing of commands, system variables, and command aliases, along with information on utilities and standard libraries.
- **Express Tools.** This topic links to the Express Tools section of the Autodesk Point A Web site. Express Tools are discussed later in this appendix.
- **Installation Guide.** Contains information for installing and configuring AutoCAD.
- **Driver and Peripheral Guide.** Describes techniques of installing and configuring pointing devices, printers/plotters, and external databases.
- **Customization Guide.** Provides direction in customizing the AutoCAD environment, aliases, and menus, along with an introduction to programming languages.
- **Visual LISP, AutoLISP, and DXF.** Provides access to four documents used for advanced customization and programming:
  - AutoLISP Reference
  - Visual LISP Developer's Guide
  - Visual LISP Tutorials
  - DXF Reference
- **ActiveX and VBA.** Provides access to three documents used for advanced customization and programming:
  - ActiveX and VBA Developer's Guide
  - ActiveX and VBA Reference
  - Connectivity Automation Reference
- **Support Assistance.** This item includes a collection of support items. When you have a question or encounter an issue with which you need assistance, review the issues in the relevant topic area with Support Assistance.

When you first view the **Contents** tab, the ten help documents are listed. A small plus symbol and a closed book symbol precede each document name. These symbols indicate that the document is condensed. To expand the document, pick the plus sign or double-click on the document name. This expands the documents, and subtopics are listed. If a subtopic has a plus symbol, it can also be expanded to reveal subtopics within the subtopic. When a topic is picked, the right frame shows the help topic.

The **Index** tab provides an alphabetical listing of the general topics addressed in the AutoCAD help system. Type in the topic and the index list automatically finds the corresponding index entry. Double-click on the item in the index list to access the **Topics Found** dialog box. This dialog box lists the help topics related to the selected index entry, along with the help document in which the topic is located. Double-click on a help topic to display it in the right frame.

The **Search** tab can be used to search for specific words or phrases. Type the search entry into the **Type in the word(s) to search for:** text box. Pick the arrow button next to the text box to select the AND, OR, NEAR, and NOT search operators. After typing the search entry, pick the **List Topics** button to list all topics containing the search entry. Double-click on a listed help topic (or select the topic and pick the **Display** button) to have the topic displayed in the right frame.

The **Favorites** tab can be used to list help topics for future reference. To save a help topic, display the topic in the right frame, access the **Favorites** tab, and then pick the **Add** button. The topic is listed in the **Topics:** window. When you want to access this topic in the future, simply access the **Favorites** tab and select the topic from the list. This is much easier than navigating through the **Contents** tab to find a help topic. Use the **Remove** button to delete help topics from the **Favorites** tab.

You can sort help topics by posing a question or phrase in the **Query** tab. First, use the **List of component(s) to search** drop-down list to select the help document(s) most likely to contain the desired help information. Normally, the User's Guide or Command Reference contains help topics on basic issues. Then, type the question you want answered in the **Type in a question** text box. You can also enter phrases. Press [Enter] and hyperlinks to help topics are listed in the window. Pick a hyperlink to display the help topic in the right frame.

Help topic features

In addition to text content, help topics displayed in the right frame provide navigational features. See Figure A-1. Help topics have forward and back arrows in their title bars. Pick an arrow to display the previous or next help topic within the help document.

Figure A-1.
The **AutoCAD Help** window.

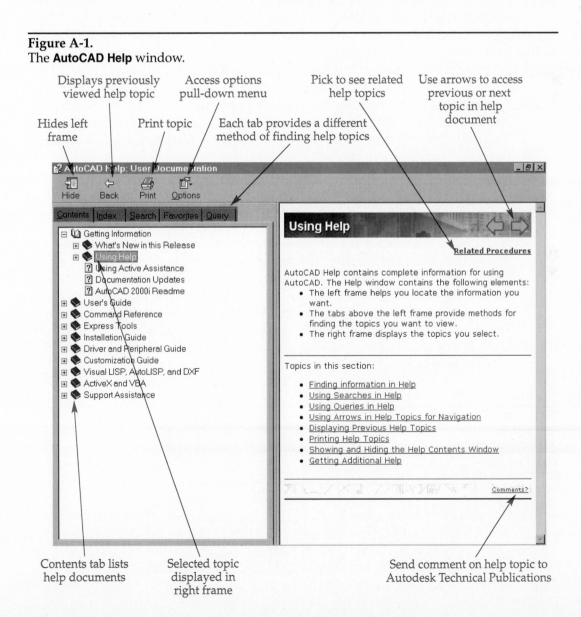

Displays previously viewed help topic

Access options pull-down menu

Pick to see related help topics

Use arrows to access previous or next topic in help document

Hides left frame

Print topic

Each tab provides a different method of finding help topics

Contents tab lists help documents

Selected topic displayed in right frame

Send comment on help topic to Autodesk Technical Publications

Many topics also have a **Related Procedures** link. Pick the link to display a shortcut menu listing related topics. Pick an item from the shortcut menu to access the corresponding help topic. Some help topics include a **See also...** link, which accesses related topics.

Some help topics include a **Display all hidden text on this page** link. Pick this link to display additional text on the help topic. These are often found in Command Reference help topics. After displaying hidden text, the link changes to a **Collapse all hidden text on this page** link. Pick this link to hide the text that had been hidden.

Finally, each help topic contains a **Comments?** link. If you wish to send a comment regarding the help topic to Autodesk Technical Publications, pick this link. Type the comment in the dialog box that appears and pick the **Send Comment** button. Note that these comments are not intended to serve as technical support.

Active Assistance

Assist

Help
↪ Active
   Assistance

Standard
toolbar

Active Assistance

By default, **Active Assistance** is activated when AutoCAD is loaded. It can be activated and deactivated by picking the **Active Assistance** button in the **Standard** toolbar, selecting **Active Assistance** from the **Help** pull-down menu, typing ASSIST at the Command: prompt, or right-clicking on the **Active Assistance** icon in the Windows task bar and picking **Show Active Assistance** or **Exit**.

The **Active Assistance** window is shown in Figure A-2. It provides brief help information for the active command or dialog box. When you enter a command, the **Active Assistance** window displays content related to the command. As its name suggests, the **Active Assistance** window remains active as you work in AutoCAD.

Right-click in the **Active Assistance** window to display the **Active Assistance** shortcut menu. This menu includes the following options:

- **Home.** This options displays the Using Active Assistance topic in the window. This topic provides brief descriptions of the **Active Assistance** window and its options.
- **Back.** Displays the previous topic.
- **Forward.** Returns to the topic displayed prior to using the **Back** option. This option is only enabled after the **Back** option is used.
- **Print.** Prints the displayed topic.
- **Hover help.** This option is only available when a dialog box is displayed on-screen. If hover help is active, the **Active Assistance** window displays a help topic for the specific dialog box item on which the cursor rests. By default, hover help is not selected, and a single topic is displayed for a dialog box.
- **Settings.** Pick **Settings...** to access the **Active Assistance Settings** dialog box. See Figure A-3. The settings at the top of the dialog box allow you to specify if the **Active Assistance** window is displayed when AutoCAD is launched and if hover help is enabled.

Figure A-2.
The **Active Assistance** window provides brief information on the active command or dialog box.

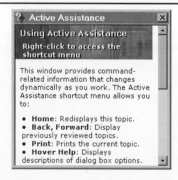

Figure A-3.
Display of the **Active Assistance** window is controlled by the settings in the **Active Assistance Settings** dialog box.

Display when AutoCAD is launched

Activate hover help

Select when **Active Assistance** window is displayed

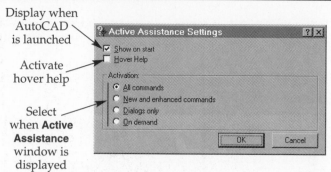

The four options in the **Activation** area control when the **Active Assistance** window is displayed. The **All commands** option has the **Active Assistance** window open at all times. The **New and enhanced commands** option displays the window for commands new for AutoCAD 2000i. The **Dialogs only** option opens the window when a dialog box is accessed. When **On demand** is selected, you must use the **ASSIST** command to open the window.

AutoCAD Today Window

The **AutoCAD Today** window appears when you first open AutoCAD. It can also be opened by picking the **Today** button in the **Standard** toolbar, selecting **Today** from the **Help** pull-down menu, or entering TODAY at the Command: prompt. You can close or minimize the window.

The **AutoCAD Today** window is divided into two sections, Figure A-4. The top section, called **My Workplace**, has two areas:

- **My Drawings area.** This area can be used to open an existing drawing, create a new drawing, or access a symbol library. These functions are discussed below.
- **Bulletin Board area.** This area allows messages to be shared between a group of networked AutoCAD users. A CAD manager could use the bulletin board to send messages to all drafters working on the network.

The lower section of the **AutoCAD Today** window, called **The Web**, provides a direct link to the Autodesk Point A Web site. The Point A Web site provides news, resources, and other services related to design industries. You can customize your Point A access to address a single design discipline, such as architecture, land development, or manufacturing. In addition, Point A is a source of software updates and provides links to resource materials.

Opening drawings

The **Open Drawings** tab in the **My Drawings** area is used to open an existing drawing file. A list of recently opened files is provided. Use the **Select how to begin:** drop-down list to select how the list is sorted. There are four options (see Figure A-5):

- **Most Recently Used.** Files are listed in the order of their last use. Therefore, the last file opened is listed first.
- **History (by Date).** Files are arranged according to the day or week in which they were opened.
- **History (by Filename).** Files are arranged alphabetically. Pick a letter to display the file names that begin with that letter.
- **History (by Location).** Arranges files according to the folders in which they are stored. Pick a folder name to display the files contained within it.

If you want to select a drawing file to open using the **Select File** dialog box, pick the **Browse...** link in the **My Documents** area. The **Select File** dialog box is discussed on page 966.

Figure A-4.
The **AutoCAD Today** window allows you to access saved drawing files and templates, share messages within a network, and access customized information from the Autodesk Point A Web site.

Pick this tab to open an existing drawing

Pick this tab to create a new drawing

Pick this tab to access symbol libraries

Transmit messages within a network

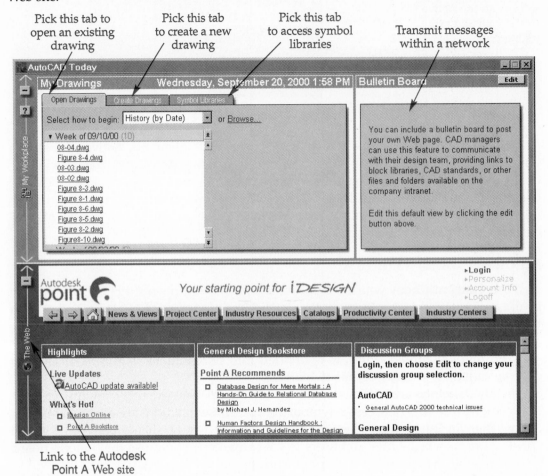

Link to the Autodesk Point A Web site

Figure A-5.
Previously opened files can be sorted in one of four methods. A—Files listed according to when they were previously used. B—Files sorted by the day or week during which they were opened. C—Files sorted alphabetically. D—Files sorted by location.

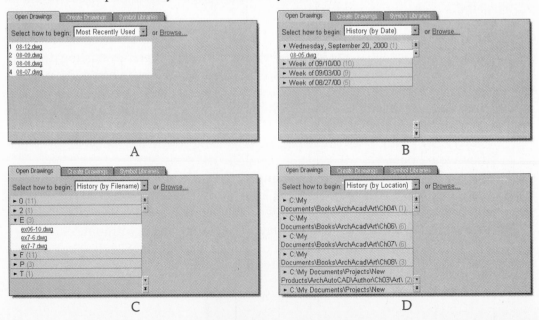

AutoCAD and its Applications—Basics

Creating drawings

In AutoCAD 2000i, new drawings are created using the **Create Drawings** tab in the **My Drawings** area of the **AutoCAD Today** window. To create a new drawing, pick the **New** button from the **Standard** toolbar, select **New** from the **File** pull-down menu, enter NEW at the Command: prompt, or use the [Ctrl]+[N] key combination. The **AutoCAD Today** window appears, with the **Create Drawings** tab selected.

The **Create Drawings** tab provides three methods for creating a new drawing. The method is selected in the **Select how to begin:** drop-down list. The following options are illustrated in Figure A-6:

- **Template.** Use this option to start a new drawing based on an existing template. Recently used templates are listed first, followed by an alphabetical listing. See page 72 for further discussion of starting a drawing using a template.
- **Start from Scratch.** This option is identical to **Start from Scratch** option in AutoCAD 2000, which is fully discussed on page 76.
- **Wizards.** After selecting this option, you can pick either **Quick Setup** or **Advanced Setup**. Pick **Quick Setup** to access the **Quick Setup** wizard, which is discussed beginning on page 65. Pick **Advanced Setup** to access the **Advanced Setup** wizard, which is discussed beginning on page 69.

Symbol libraries

The **Symbol Libraries** tab provides access to the symbol libraries provided with AutoCAD 2000i. Sixteen symbol libraries are listed in the tab. See Figure A-7.

Each symbol library has a corresponding drawing file located in the AutoCAD 2000i\Sample\DesignCenter folder. The symbols composing the library are saved as blocks within the drawing files.

When you select a symbol library from the **Symbol Library** tab, the **AutoCAD Today** window is minimized. The AutoCAD window becomes active and **DesignCenter** is displayed with the Blocks content of the drawing file for the selected symbol library

Figure A-6.
Access the three startup options from the drop-down list in the **Create Drawings** tab.
A—Template. B—Start from Scratch. C—Wizards.

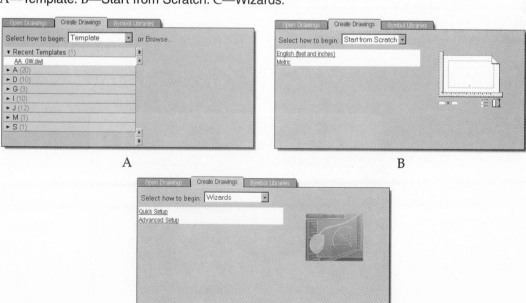

Figure A-7.
Select a symbol
library to access
the blocks in
DesignCenter.

List of symbol
libraries

Pick to modify
or add symbol libraries

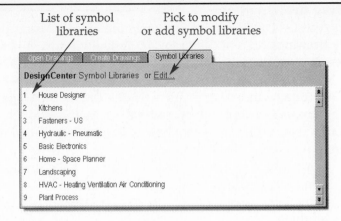

shown. You can now insert symbols from **DesignCenter** into an open drawing. Inserting symbols from **DesignCenter** is discussed on page 814.

The **Edit** link in the **Symbol Libraries** tab is used to modify the list of available symbol libraries. Pick **Edit** to access the **Edit DesignCenter Symbol Libraries** dialog box. See Figure A-8. Select the name of the symbol library to be modified from the **Symbol libraries** list. To move the symbol library's position in the list, use the **Move up** or **Move down** button. To delete a symbol library, pick the **Remove link** button.

In addition, you can add your own custom symbol libraries to the **Symbol Libraries** tab. To do so, use the following procedure:

1. Create a drawing file containing blocks of each of the symbols in the library. Creating blocks is discussed on page 799.
2. After saving the drawing file, pick the **Add link** button in the **Edit DesignCenter Symbol Libraries** dialog box. Pick the drawing file from the **Select DWG to Add As Symbol Library** dialog box.
3. The drawing file name is set as the symbol library name. You can modify the symbol library name in the **Library name** text box.
4. Pick the **OK** button and the new symbol library is included in the **Symbol Libraries** tab.

Figure A-8.
Use the **Edit DesignCenter Symbol Libraries** dialog box to organize the list of symbol libraries and to add new libraries.

Name of selected
library

Add new
library

Specify drawing
file for selected
library

Select library name
to be modified
or moved

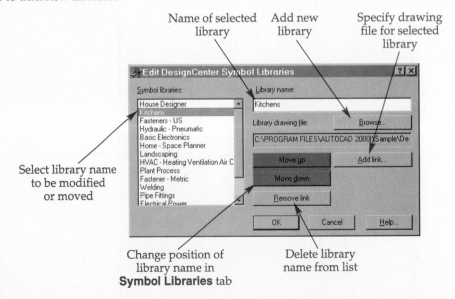

Change position of
library name in
Symbol Libraries tab

Delete library
name from list

Deactivating the AutoCAD Today Window

The **AutoCAD Today** window of AutoCAD 2000i replaces the **Startup** and **Create New Drawing** dialog boxes found in AutoCAD 2000. However, if you prefer not to use the **AutoCAD Today** window, you can customize AutoCAD to use the **Startup** and **Create New Drawing** dialog boxes instead. This setting is found in the **System** tab of the **Options** dialog box.

To access the **Options** dialog box, pick **Options...** from the **Tools** pull-down menu, type OP or OPTIONS at the Command: prompt, or right-click in the drawing area and pick **Options...** from the shortcut menu. In the **System** tab, the **General Options** area includes a **Startup:** drop-down list. See Figure A-9. Pick the drop-down area to select from the following options:

- **Show TODAY startup dialog.** While this option is selected, the **AutoCAD Today** window is activated when AutoCAD is launched or when a new drawing is created.
- **Show traditional startup dialog.** While this option is selected, the **Startup** dialog box appears when AutoCAD is launched and the **NEW** command accesses the **Create New Drawing** dialog box. The **AutoCAD Today** window can still be activated using the **TODAY** command.
- **Do not show a startup dialog.** While this option is selected, no dialog box is displayed when AutoCAD is launched, and the **NEW** command requires command line entry.

Figure A-9.
The drop-down list controls when and if the **AutoCAD Today** window or traditional **Startup** dialog box is displayed.

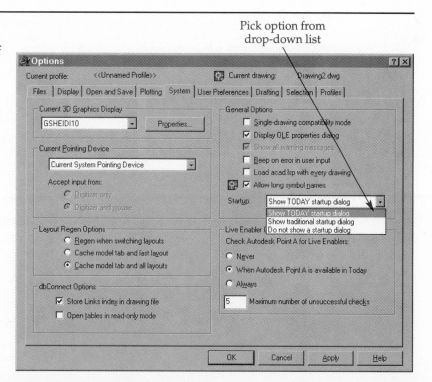

Pick option from drop-down list

Select File Dialog Box

The **Select File** dialog box in AutoCAD 2000i has some features that are not available in the AutoCAD 2000 **Select File** dialog box. This discussion focuses on these additional features. The features identical to those in AutoCAD 2000 are discussed beginning on page 107.

The **Select File** dialog box is shown in Figure A-10. The Places List provides instant access to certain folders. The following buttons are available:

- **History.** Pick this button to list drawing files opened recently from the **Select File** dialog box.
- **Desktop.** Pick this button to list the files, folders, and drives located on your desktop.
- **My Documents.** Displays the files and folders contained in the My Documents folder.
- **Favorites.** Displays files and folders located in the Windows\Favorites folder.
- **Buzzsaw.** Pick this button to display projects on the Buzzsaw Web site. Buzzsaw.com is designed for the building industry. After setting up a project hosting account, users can access project drawings from the Web site. This allows the various companies involved in the construction process to have instant access to the drawing files.
- **RedSpark.** Pick this button to display project accounts on the RedSpark Web site. RedSpark.com is similar to Buzzsaw.com, but is designed for the manufacturing industry.
- **FTP.** Displays available FTP (file transfer protocol) sites. To add or modify the listed FTP sites, select **Add/Modify FTP Locations** from the **Tools** menu in the **Select File** dialog box.

Figure A-10.
The **Select File** dialog box.

966

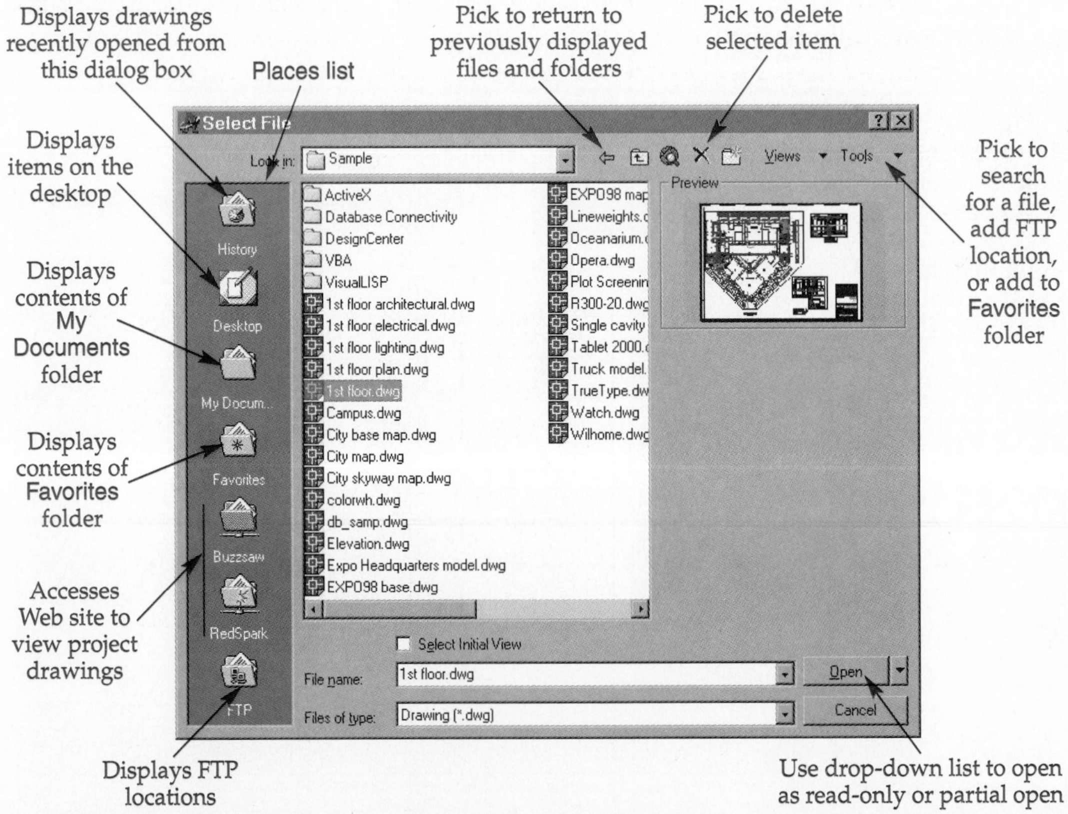

There are two more new features in the AutoCAD 2000i **Select File** dialog box. The **Back** button displays the files and folders that were previously displayed in the dialog box. The **Delete** button causes the selected file or folder to be deleted.

The following table lists items that function the same in AutoCAD 2000i as in AutoCAD 2000, but have been relocated in the **Select File** dialog box:

	Select File Dialog Box Location	
Item	**AutoCAD 2000**	**AutoCAD 2000i**
Views	Buttons	**Views** pull-down menu
Partial open	Button	**Open** drop-down list
Partial load	Button	**Open** drop-down list
Read-only	Check box	**Open** drop-down menu
Add to **Favorites** folder	Button	**Tools** pull-down menu

Finding files

You can search for files from the **Select File** dialog box by picking **Find...** in the **Tools** menu. This accesses the **Find** dialog box, which is shown in Figure A-11. If you know the file name for the drawing, enter it in the **Named** text box. If you do not know the name, you can use wildcard characters (such as *) to narrow the search.

Choose the type of file from the **Type** drop-down list. You can search for DWG, DXF, or DWT files from the **Find** dialog box. If you are searching for another type of file, use the Windows Explorer search tool.

A search can be completed more quickly if you do not search the entire hard drive. If you know the folder in which the file is located, specify the folder in the **Look in** text box. Pick the **Browse** button to select a folder from a dialog box. Select the **Include subfolders** check box if you want the subfolders within the selected folder to be searched.

You can also search for files based on when they were last modified. The **Date Modified** tab provides options to search for files modified within a certain number of days or months, or within a specified time period. This option is very useful if you wish to list all drawings modified within a specific week or month.

Figure A-11.
Use the **Find** dialog box to locate drawing files.

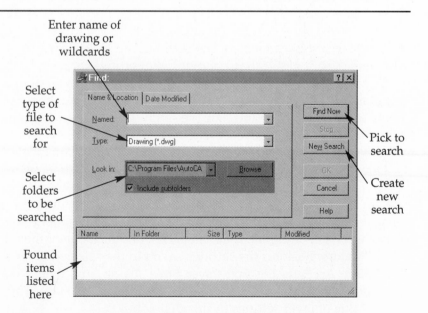

Enter name of drawing or wildcards

Select type of file to search for

Select folders to be searched

Found items listed here

Pick to search

Create new search

❑ Use the **OPEN** command to access the **Select File** dialog box.
❑ Pick each of the buttons in the Places List and observe the folders and files listed in the window.
❑ Use the **Find** tool to find all DWG files in the Program Files\AutoCAD 2000i folder. Be sure to search all subfolders.
❑ Use the **Find** tool to find all DWG files in the Program Files\AutoCAD 2000i folder that were modified in the past three months.

Layer States

Layer settings, such as on/off, frozen/thawed, and locked/unlocked, determine whether or not a layer is displayed, plotted, and editable. The status of layer settings for all layers in the drawing can be saved as a named *layer state*. Once a layer state is saved, the settings can be reset by selecting the layer state.

For example, a basic architectural drawing uses the layers shown in Figure A-12. From this drawing file, three different drawings are plotted: a floor plan, a plumbing plan, and an electrical plan. The following chart shows the layer settings for each of the three drawings:

	Floor Plan	Plumbing Plan	Electrical Plan
0	Off	Off	Off
Dimension-Electrical	Frozen	Frozen	On
Dimension-Floor Plan	On	Frozen	Frozen
Dimension-Plumbing	Frozen	On	Frozen
Electrical	Frozen	Frozen	On
Floor Plan Notes	On	Frozen	Frozen
Plumbing	Frozen	On	Frozen
Title Block	On	Locked	Locked
Walls	On	Locked	Locked
Windows and Doors	On	Frozen	Frozen

Each of the three groups of settings can be saved as an individual layer state. Once the layer state is created, the settings can be restored by simply restoring the layer state. This is easier than changing the settings for each layer individually.

To save a layer state, first set the layer settings you wish to save. Then, pick the **Save state...** button to access the **Save Layer States** dialog box. See Figure A-13. Enter a name for the layer state and pick the settings and properties to be saved. Only saved settings and properties are reset when the layer state is restored. For this example, the three layer states (with settings) shown in Figure A-14 are created.

Once a layer state is saved, it can be restored at any time. By restoring a layer state, the layer settings are automatically changed to match the settings saved in the layer state. To restore a layer state, pick the **Restore state...** button in the **Layer Properties Manager** dialog box. This accesses the **Layer States Manager** dialog box, Figure A-15. Select a layer state from the **Layer states** list and pick one of the following buttons:

- **Restore.** Restores the settings saved in the selected layer state.
- **Edit.** Accesses the **Edit Layer State** dialog box, where you can select which settings and properties are saved in the layer state. You cannot change the value of layer settings in this dialog box.
- **Rename.** Allows you to rename the layer state.

Figure A-12.
Layers for a basic architectural drawing.

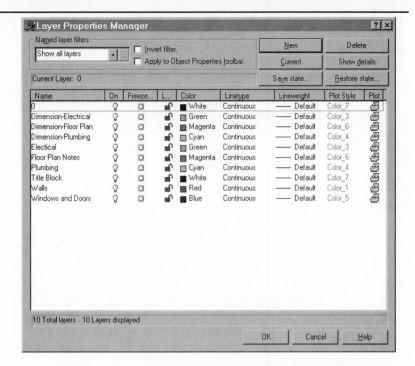

Figure A-13.
Only selected settings and properties are saved in the layer state. Those settings that are not saved are not reset when the layer state is restored.

Enter name for layer state

Pick layer settings and properties to be saved in the layer state

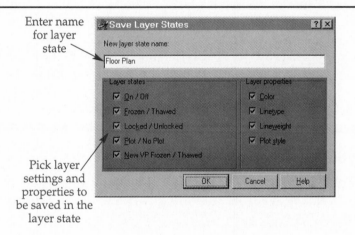

Figure A-14.
The layer states and saved layer settings.

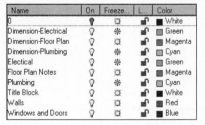

Floor Plan

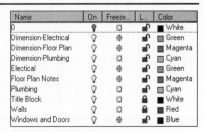

Plumbing Plan

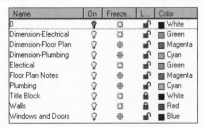

Electrical Plan

Figure A-15.
Use the **Layer States Manager** dialog box to restore, modify, import, or export existing layer states.

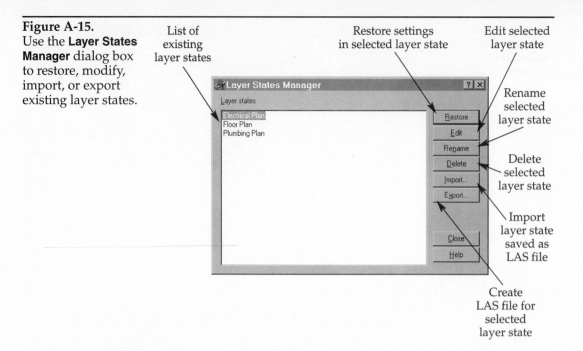

List of existing layer states

Restore settings in selected layer state

Edit selected layer state

Rename selected layer state

Delete selected layer state

Import layer state saved as LAS file

Create LAS file for selected layer state

- **Delete.** Deletes the selected layer state.
- **Export.** Layer states can be saved as LAS files and imported into other drawings. This allows you to share layer states between drawings containing identical layers. Pick this button to access a standard file selection dialog box, where you can specify a name and location for the LAS file.
- **Import.** Accesses a standard file selection dialog box, where you can select an LAS file containing an existing layer state. Imported layer states are listed in the **Layer states** list in the **Layer State Manager**. Select the imported layer state and pick the **Restore** button to have the settings restored.

Specifying Rectangle Dimensions

AutoCAD 2000i provides a **Dimensions** option for the **RECTANGLE** command. The option is available after the first corner of the rectangle is picked:

> Command: **REC** *or* **RECTANGLE**↵
> Specify first corner point or [Chamfer/Elevation/Fillet/Thickness/Width]: *(pick first corner point)*
> Specify other corner point or [Dimensions]:

Enter D to access the **Dimensions** option. You are then prompted to enter the length and width of the rectangle. In the following example, a 5 × 3 rectangle is specified:

> Specify other corner point or [Dimensions]: **D**↵
> Specify length for rectangles <0.0000>: **5**↵
> Specify width for rectangles <0.0000>: **3**↵
> Specify other corner point or [Dimensions]: *(move crosshairs to desired quadrant and pick point)*

After specifying the length and width, the Specify other corner point or [Dimensions]: prompt is displayed. If you wish to change the dimensions, select the **Dimensions** option. If the dimensions are correct, you can specify the other corner point to complete the rectangle. When using the **Dimensions** option, the second corner point determines which of four possible rectangles is drawn. See Figure A-16.

Figure A-16.
When using the **Dimensions** option of the **RECTANGLE** command, the orientation of the rectangle relative to the first corner point is determined by the second corner point.

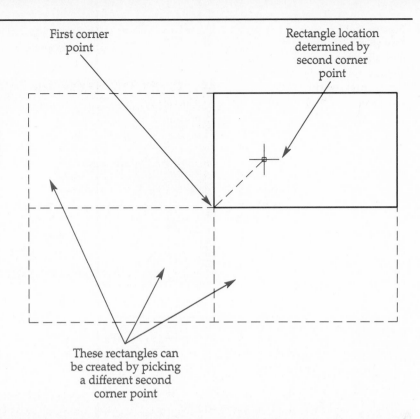

First corner point

Rectangle location determined by second corner point

These rectangles can be created by picking a different second corner point

---

EXERCISE A-2

❑ Use the **AutoCAD Today** window to start a new drawing from scratch.
❑ Use the **Dimensions** option of the **RECTANGLE** command to draw a rectangle 6 units wide and 4 units high. Make the first corner point the lower-left corner of the rectangle.
❑ Create a second rectangle using the lower-right corner of the first rectangle as the first corner point. Use the **Dimensions** option to make the rectangle 3.5 units wide and 7 units high. Position the rectangle so that the first corner is the upper-left corner.
❑ Save the drawing as EXA-2.

Modifying the UCS Icon

The appearance of the UCS icon can be changed in AutoCAD 2000i using the settings in the **UCS Icon** dialog box. See Figure A-17. This dialog box is accessed by selecting **UCS Icon** and then **Properties…** from the **Display** cascading menu in the **View** pull-down menu or by entering UCSICON followed by P (for the **Properties** option) at the Command: prompt.

The **UCS Icon** dialog box allows you to modify three characteristics of the UCS icon:

* **Style.** Select either a 2D or 3D icon in the UCS icon style area. You can also specify the line width as 1, 2, or 3 pixels. If the **3D** style is selected, the **Cone** option is available.
* **Size.** The **UCS icon size** area contains a text box and a slider. The value in the text box is the size of the UCS icon expressed as a percentage of the viewport size. Modify this value by entering a new value in the text box or by adjusting the slider.
* **Color.** Use the drop-down lists in the **UCS icon color** area to set the color of the UCS icon. Notice that different colors can be set for the **Model** tab and **Layout** tab.

Figure A-17.
The **UCS Icon** dialog box allows you to change the appearance of the UCS icon.

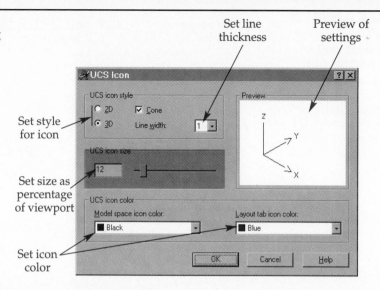

Set line thickness

Preview of settings

Set style for icon

Set size as percentage of viewport

Set icon color

EXERCISE A-3

❑ Access the **UCS Icon** dialog box and modify the following settings:
  ❑ Line width = 3
  ❑ UCS icon size = 25
  ❑ Model space color = Magenta
❑ Pick **OK** to view the changes.
❑ Access the **UCS Icon** dialog box again and change the UCS icon size to 5. Pick **OK** to view the changes.
❑ Reset the default UCS icon settings.

Adding a Plot Stamp

In AutoCAD 2000i, you can add a plot stamp to your drawings. A plot stamp is specific text information included on a printed or plotted drawing. A plot stamp may include information such as the drawing name or the date and time the drawing was printed.

In the **Plot** dialog box, the **Plot Stamp** area in the **Plot Device** tab allows you to activate and modify the plot stamp. See Figure A-18. If the **On** check box is activated, a plot stamp is printed on the drawing. You can also specify the items to be included in the plot stamp by picking the **Settings...** button. This accesses the **Plot Stamp** dialog box, which is shown in Figure A-19.

Specify the information to be included in the plot stamp in the **Plot stamp fields** area of the **Plot Stamp** dialog box. The following items can be included:
- Drawing name
- Layout name
- Date and time
- Login name
- Device name
- Paper size
- Plot scale

You can create additional plot stamp items in the **User defined fields** area. For example, you could add a field for the client name, the project name, or the contractor who will be using the drawing.

The **Preview** area provides a preview of the location and orientation of the plot stamp. The preview does not show the actual plot stamp text.

Figure A-18.
Activate the plot stamp in the **Plot** dialog box. Pick the **Settings...** button to access the **Plot Stamp** dialog box.

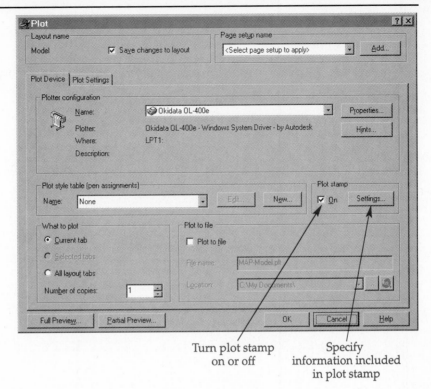

Turn plot stamp
on or off

Specify
information included
in plot stamp

Figure A-19.
Use the **Plot Stamp** dialog box to specify the information included in the plot stamp. You can save plot stamp settings as PSS files.

Select items to be
included in plot stamp

Pick to add
new fields

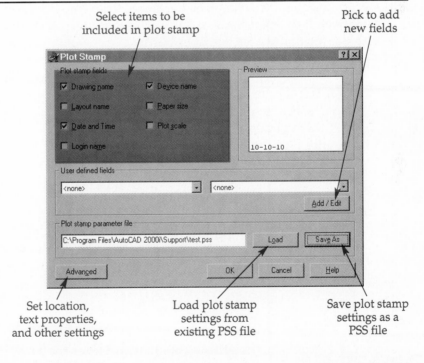

Set location,
text properties,
and other settings

Load plot stamp
settings from
existing PSS file

Save plot stamp
settings as a
PSS file

Plot stamp settings can be saved in a PSS (plot stamp parameter) file. If you load an existing PSS file, the settings saved in the file are automatically set in the **Plot Stamp** dialog box.

Additional plot stamp options are set in the **Advanced Options** dialog box. To access this dialog box, pick the **Advanced...** button in the **Plot Stamp** dialog box. The **Advanced Options** dialog box is shown in Figure A-20. The following options are available:

- **Location.** Pick the corner where the plot stamp begins from the drop-down list. If you want the plot stamp to print upside-down, pick the **Stamp upside-down** check box.

Figure A-20.
Specify the plot stamp location, orientation, text font and size, and units in the **Advanced Options** dialog box.

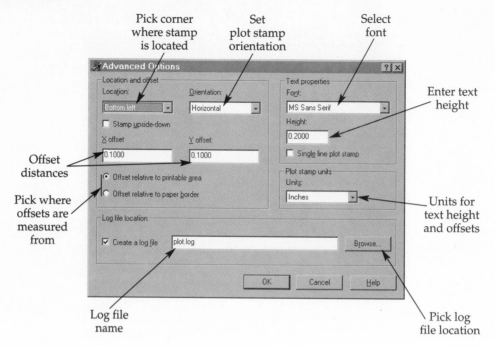

- **Orientation.** Pick Horizontal or Vertical from the drop-down list.
- **Offset.** Set offset distance and pick where the offset distances are measured from (printable area or paper border).
- **Text properties.** Specify the text font and height. Pick the **Single line plot stamp** check box if you want the plot stamp constrained to a single line. If this check box is not checked, the plot stamp will be printed in two lines.
- **Units.** Select the plot stamp units. The plot stamp units can be different from the drawing units.
- **Log file.** Pick the check box to create a log file of plotted items. Specify the name of the log file in the text box. Pick **Browse...** to specify the location of the log file.

NOTE

The log file settings are independent of the plot stamp settings. Thus, you can produce a log file without creating a plot stamp or have a plot stamp without producing a log file.

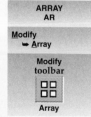
ARRAY
AR

Modify
➡ Array

Modify
toolbar

Array

Array Dialog Box

In AutoCAD 2000i, the **ARRAY** command accesses the **Array** dialog box. To access this dialog box, pick the **Array** button in the **Modify** toolbar, select **Array...** from the **Modify** pull-down menu, or enter AR or ARRAY at the Command: prompt.

All input needed to create the array is specified in the **Array** dialog box. See Figure A-21. Use the **Rectangular Array** and **Polar Array** radio buttons to specify the type of array. Pick the **Select Objects** button to return to the AutoCAD window and pick the objects to be included in the array.

For rectangular arrays, enter the number of rows and columns in the text boxes. To set the offset distance, you can pick the **Pick Both Offsets** button to return to the drawing and specify a unit cell. If you set the row and column offsets separately, you

Figure A-21.
The **Array** dialog box options for a rectangular array.

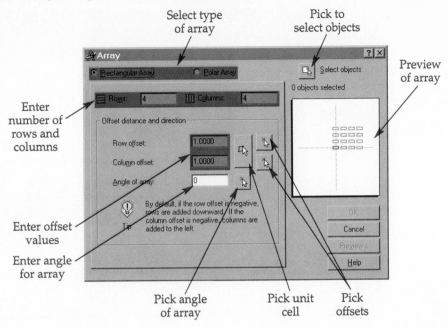

Select type
of array

Pick to
select objects

Enter
number of
rows and
columns

Enter offset
values

Enter angle
for array

Preview
of array

Pick angle
of array

Pick unit
cell

Pick
offsets

can either pick the **Specify Offset** button to specify the offset on-screen, or you can enter the offset in the appropriate text box.

In AutoCAD 2000i, you can also create an angled rectangular array. Enter the angle in the **Angle of array** text box, or pick the **Pick Angle of Array** button to specify the angle with the crosshairs. The column and row alignments are rotated, not the objects. See Figure A-22.

When you select the **Polar Array** radio button, a different panel of options appears. See Figure A-23. To specify the center point, enter values in the text boxes or pick the center point on-screen. Select the desired option from the **Method** drop-down list, and specify the required options. In AutoCAD 2000i, you can specify the center point of the selected objects by picking the **More...** button. This allows you to adjust the objects position relative to the polar array circle.

Figure A-22.
Rectangular arrays can be arranged using the **Angle of Array** setting.

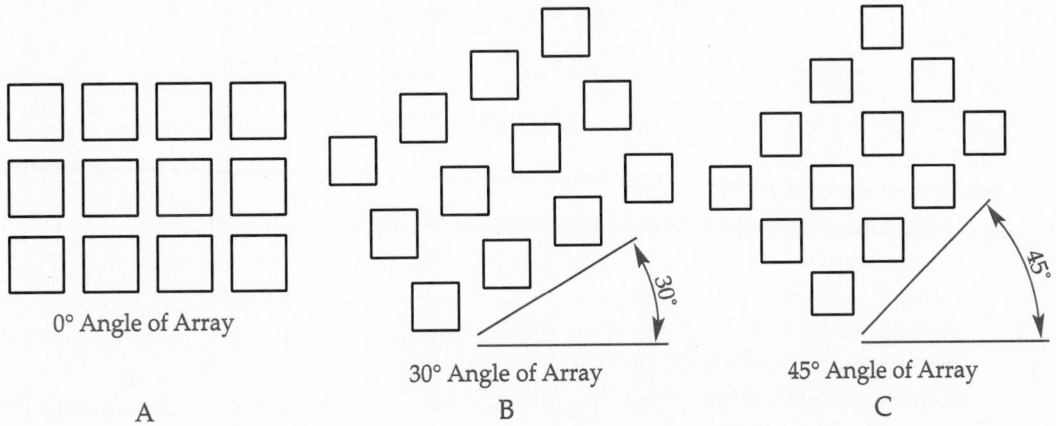

0° Angle of Array

A

30°

30° Angle of Array

B

45°

45° Angle of Array

C

Figure A-23.
The **Array** dialog box options for a polar array.

Select center
point of array

Select
method

Enter
values for
selected
methods

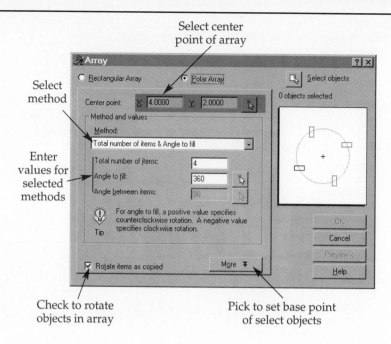

Check to rotate
objects in array

Pick to set base point
of select objects

NOTE   Refer to Chapter 13 for a complete discussion of the array settings.

Drag-and-Drop Hatch Patterns

In AutoCAD 2000i, hatch patterns can be inserted into a drawing from **DesignCenter** using a drag-and-drop operation. This provides a very convenient method of adding hatch patterns to drawings.

Hatch patterns are stored in PAT (pattern) files. In order to drag-and-drop hatch patterns, you must first activate **DesignCenter** and then select a PAT file. Once the PAT file is selected, the hatch patterns it contains are shown in the preview palette. See Figure A-24.

NOTE   AutoCAD includes two PAT files: acad.pat and acadiso.pat. Both are located in the AutoCAD 2000i\Support folder.

Pick a hatch pattern in the preview palette to display a preview of the pattern. Use one of the following three methods to transfer a hatch pattern from **DesignCenter** into the active drawing:

- **Drag-and-drop.** Pick the hatch pattern from **DesignCenter** and hold the mouse button. Move the cursor into the active drawing, and a hatch pattern symbol is displayed under the cursor, Figure A-25A. Place the cursor within the area to be hatched, and then release the pick button. The hatch is applied automatically. See Figure A-25B.
- **Boundary Hatch dialog box.** Right-click on a hatch pattern in **DesignCenter** and select **BHATCH...** from the shortcut menu to access the **Boundary Hatch** dialog box. The selected hatched pattern is displayed automatically. Specifying hatch pattern properties and locations using the **Boundary Hatch** dialog box is explained beginning on page 773.

Figure A-24.
Pick a PAT file in **DesignCenter** to display the hatch patterns in the preview palette.

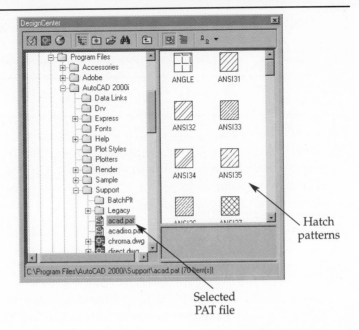

Hatch patterns

Selected PAT file

Figure A-25.
When a hatch pattern is selected in the preview palette, a preview image appears. A—The hatch pattern symbol appears under the cursor during the drag-and-drop and paste operations. B—The hatch pattern added to the drawing.

Selected hatch pattern

Hatch pattern symbol under cursor

Inserted hatch pattern

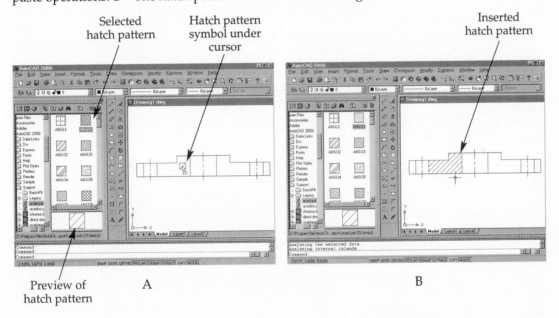

Preview of hatch pattern

A

B

- **Copy and paste.** Hatch patterns can also be inserted using a copy and paste operation. Right-click on the hatch pattern in **DesignCenter** and pick **Copy** from the shortcut menu. Move the cursor into the active drawing, right-click, and select **Paste** from the shortcut menu. The hatch pattern symbol is displayed beneath the cursor. Pick within the area to be hatched, and the hatch pattern is automatically applied.

When hatch patterns are inserted from **DesignCenter**, the angle, scale, and island detection settings match the settings of the previous hatch pattern. If you wish to change these settings after inserting the hatch pattern, use the **HATCHEDIT** command. The **HATCHEDIT** command is explained on page 787.

EXERCISE A-4

❑ Draw an object similar to the object shown in Figure A-25A.
❑ Using **DesignCenter**, display the hatch patterns available in the acad.pat file.
❑ Use the drag-and-drop method to apply the ANSI31 hatch pattern to the four sections that requires hatching.
❑ Save the drawing as EXA-4.

Purge Dialog Box

In AutoCAD 2000i, the **PURGE** command accesses the **Purge** dialog box, Figure A-26. To access this dialog box, select **Purge...** from the **Drawing Utilities** cascading menu in the **File** pull-down menu or type PU or PURGE at the Command: prompt.

Select the appropriate radio button at the top of the dialog box to view content that can be purged or to view content that cannot be purged.

Before purging, select the **Confirm each item to be purged** check box to have an opportunity to review each item before it is deleted. If you wish to purge nested items, pick the **Purge nested items** check box.

If you want to purge only some items, use the tree view to locate and highlight the items, and then pick the **Purge** button. If you want to purge all unused items, pick the **Purge All** button.

Figure A-26.
The **Purge** dialog box.

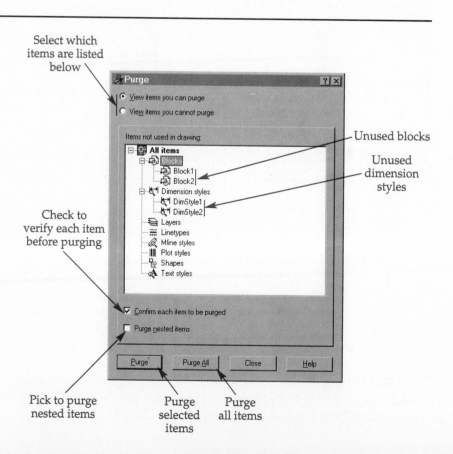

Select which items are listed below

Unused blocks

Unused dimension styles

Check to verify each item before purging

Pick to purge nested items

Purge selected items

Purge all items

If you wish to work with the **PURGE** command at the Command: prompt, enter -PURGE. This provides the same prompt displayed in AutoCAD 2000. Refer to page 831 for further discussion.

EXPRESS TOOLS

For 2000i Users...

Express Tools are not provided with AutoCAD 2000i but can be downloaded from the Autodesk Point A Web site. The Express Tools discussed in this text are those provided with AutoCAD 2000.

When you select a full custom installation, an **Express** pull-down menu is provided. See Appendix D for information on how to install the Express Tools. The following section covers the Express toolbars and pull-down menu. The commands shown in parentheses are the command line entry equivalents.

Express Standard Toolbar

The buttons on the toolbar named **Express Standard** toolbar are described as follows. See Figure A-27.

- **Multiple Entity Stretch. (MSTRETCH)** Multiple entities can be selected using a crossing polygon or window. Pick a base point and the subsequent stretch affects all selected entities.
- **Move Copy Rotate. (MOCORO)** Multiple entities can be selected and then moved, copied, rotated, or scaled about a selected base point.
- **Extended Trim. (EXTRIM)** A powerful command that asks for a polyline, line, circle, or arc for a cutting edge. Next, pick the side to trim on and all lines are automatically trimmed on that side.
- **Multiple Pedit. (MPEDIT)** Performs polyline edit functions on multiple polylines at the same time.
- **Wipeout. (WIPEOUT)** Fills an enclosed area, such as a polyline, with the background color.
- **Revision Cloud. (REVCLOUD)** Creates a series of connected polyline arcs to form a cloud-shaped entity used to surround a revised area on a drawing.
- **Pack 'n Go. (PACKNGO)** Copies all files that are associated with a drawing to any location that you choose. These files include xrefs, fonts, shapes, etc. A text file report is also copied to the location directory.
- **Super Hatch. (SUPERHATCH)** Superhatch works much like the hatch command, but it allows you to use an image, block, xref, or wipeout object as a hatch pattern.
- **Toggle Frames. (TFRAMES)** The frames for both images and wipeouts are toggled on and off using this command.
- **Show URLs. (SHOWURLS)** Shows all embedded URLs (Uniform Resource Locator) in a drawing. Allows editing of URLs.

Figure A-27.
The **Express Standard Toolbar**.

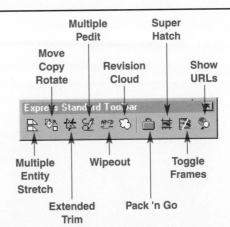

Express Block Tools

The buttons on the **Express Block Tools** toolbar are described as follows. See Figure A-28.

- **Copy Nested Entities. (NCOPY)** Copies entities that are nested inside a block or xref.
- **Trim to Block Entities. (BTRIM)** Blocks or xref objects can be used as cutting edges to trim intersecting entities.
- **Extend to Block Entities. (BEXTEND)** Blocks or xref objects can be used as boundary edges to which other entities can be extended.
- **List Xref/Block Entities. (XLIST)** Pick a nested entity in a block or xref to list the object, block name, layer, color, and linetype.
- **Extended Clip. (CLIPIT)** Enables you to select a polyline, wipeout, circle, or arc to use as a clipping edge, which then becomes the frame for a selected image, xref, or block. This allows you to create views and details that appear in circular or irregular-shaped frames.
- **Global Attribute Edit. (GATTE)** Globally changes attribute values for all insertions of a specific block.
- **Explode Attributes to Text. (BURST)** Explodes blocks, converting attribute values to text objects.

Figure A-28.
The **Express Block Tools** toolbar.

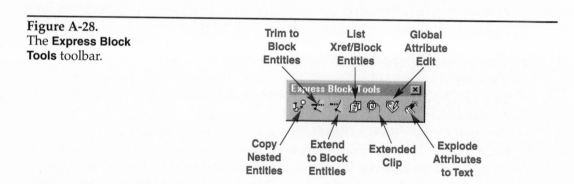

Express Text Tools

The buttons on the **Express Text Tools** toolbar are described as follows. See Figure A-29.

- **Text Fit. (TEXTFIT)** Changes existing text length to fit between new ending and starting points. Text height remains the same.
- **Text Mask. (TEXTMASK)** Hides (masks) all objects behind the selected text. Works with the **WIPEOUT** Express Tool to create a frame around the text that is selected or offset from the text a specified distance.
- **Explode Text. (TXTEXP)** Explodes text into lines and arcs. Thickness and elevation can then be assigned to the resulting entities.
- **Arc Aligned Text. (ARCTEXT)** Text can be placed along an arc.

Figure A-29.
The **Express Text Tools** toolbar.

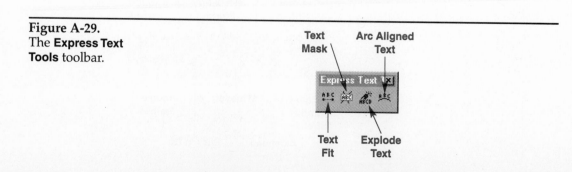

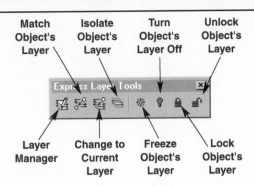

Match Object's Layer | Isolate Object's Layer | Turn Object's Layer Off | Unlock Object's Layer

Layer Manager | Change to Current Layer | Freeze Object's Layer | Lock Object's Layer

Express Layer Tools

The buttons on the **Express Layer Tools** toolbar are described as follows. See Figure A-30.

- **Layer Manager. (LMAN)** Layers can be frozen, thawed, on, or off. These layer states can be saved in an LAY file, much the same as a viewport configuration file.
- **Match Object's Layer. (LAYMCH)** The layer of a selected object can be changed to match the layer of another selected entity.
- **Change to Current Layer. (LAYCUR)** The layers of one or more objects can be changed to the current layer.
- **Isolate Object's Layer. (LAYISO)** One or more selected layers can be isolated by turning all unselected layers off.
- **Freeze Object's Layer. (LAYFRZ)** The layer(s) of selected objects are frozen.
- **Turn Object's Layer Off. (LAYOFF)** The layer(s) of selected objects are turned off.
- **Lock Object's Layer. (LAYLCK)** The layer of a selected object is locked.
- **Unlock Object's Layer. (LAYULK)** The layer of a selected object is unlocked.

Express Pull-Down Menus

The same commands listed in the previous Express Tools toolbars sections are also located in the **Express** pull-down menu. See Figure A-31. Additional commands in the cascading menus of the **Express** pull-down menu that are not found in the Express Tools toolbars are listed here.

Layers cascading menu

- **Layer Merge. (LAYMRG)** Merges all selected objects with a target layer.
- **Layer Delete. (LAYDEL)** Immediately deletes the layer of a selected object.
- **Turn All Layers On. (LAYON)** Turns all layers in the drawing on.
- **Thaw All Layers. (LAYTHW)** Thaws all layers in the drawing.

Text cascading menu

- **Remote Text. (RTEXT)** Remote text (rtext) objects display as normal text or mtext objects do, but the source for the text is either an ASCII text file or the value of a DIESEL expression. You can edit an rtext object with **RTEDIT.**
- **Unmask Text. (TEXTUNMASK)** Removes mask from text that has been masked with the **TEXTMASK** command.
- **Convert Text to Mtext. (TXT2MTXT)** Converts one or more lines of text to mtext.

Dimension cascading menu

- **Leader Tools**
  - **Attach Leader to Annotation. (QLATTACH)** Attaches leader line to mtext, tolerance, or block reference object. Both objects can then be moved together without changing the arrowhead location.

Figure A-31.
The **Express** pull-down and cascading menus.

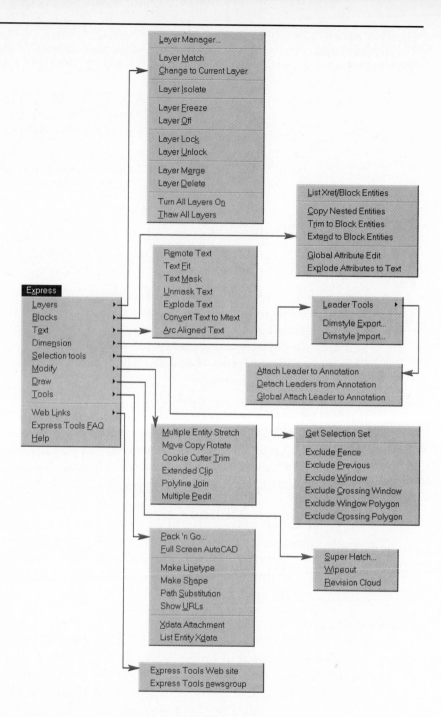

- **Detach Leaders from Annotation.** (**QLDETACHSET**) Detaches leader line from mtext, tolerance, or block reference object.
- **Global Attach Leader to Annotation.** (**QLATTACHSET**) Globally attaches leader lines to mtext, tolerance, or block reference objects.
- **Dimstyle Export.** (**DIMEX**) All settings in a named dimension style can be exported to a file with a .dim file extension.
- **Dimstyle Import.** (**DIMIM**) Imports dimension styles saved in a .dim file.

Selection tools cascading menu

- **Get Selection Set.** (**GETSEL**) Creates a selection set of entities selected on one or more layers.
- **Exclude Fence.** (**EXF**) The **Fence** selection option is used in this command to remove (exclude) objects from the selection set. All objects that are not crossed by the fence are included in the selection set.

- **Exclude Previous. (EXP)** Objects in the previous selection set are removed from the selection set, and all others are included in it.
- **Exclude Window. (EXW)** Objects totally inside the selected window are not included in the selection set.
- **Exclude Crossing Window. (EXC)** Objects touched by the crossing window are not included in the selection set.
- **Exclude Window Polygon. (EXWP)** Objects totally inside the selected window polygon are not included in the selection set.
- **Exclude Crossing Polygon. (EXCP)** Objects totally inside the selected crossing polygon are not included in the selection set.

Modify cascading menu
- **Polyline Join. (PLJOIN)** Joins two or more polylines whose ends do not exactly meet. You are prompted for a selection set of polylines and a fuzz distance. The fuzz distance is the maximum distance that two endpoints of individual polylines can be separated but still be joined.

Tools cascading menu
- **Full Screen AutoCAD. (FULLSCREEN)** Removes the pull-down menus from the display. Move the cursor to the top of the screen and pick to display the pull-down menus again.
- **Make Linetype. (MKLTYPE)** Enables command line entry of code to create a new linetype.
- **Make Shape. (MKSHAPE)** Enables command line entry of code to create a new shape by selecting existing geometry.
- **Path Substitution. (REDIRMODE)** Find and replace directory names for styles, xrefs, images, and rtext.
- **Xdata Attachment. (XDATA)** Extended entity data (xdata) can be attached to a selected entity.
- **List Entity Xdata. (XDLIST)** Lists the xdata attached to an entity.

Appendix B
AutoCAD 2000 System Requirements

This appendix lists the system requirements for AutoCAD 2000. It is intended to be used as a guide for configuring the AutoCAD system that best meets your needs. Your local authorized AutoCAD dealer will provide you with detailed information about system configuration options, and assist you in selecting the platform, peripherals, and companion programs that are right for you. See the AutoCAD 2000 *Installation Guide* for detailed information on peripheral configurations and settings.

SOFTWARE AND HARDWARE REQUIREMENTS

The following software and hardware is required to run AutoCAD 2000. Optional software and hardware is noted as such:

Software

- Windows 98, Windows 95, or Windows NT 4.0 operating system

Memory

- 64MB RAM (32MB minimum)
- 130MB of free hard-disk space
- 64MB of disk swap space (minimum)
- 50MB of free disk space in your system folder

Hardware

- Pentium 133 or better (or a compatible processor)
- 1024 × 768 VGA video display (800 × 600 VGA video display minimum)
- 4X CD-ROM drive for initial installation only
- Windows video display driver
- Pointing device (mouse or digitizer with Wintab driver)
- IBM-compatible parallel port
- For international single-user and student-locked versions only: IBM-compatible parallel port and hardware lock
- Serial port (for digitizers and some plotters)
- Printer or plotter
- Sound card for multimedia learning

3D Graphics

AutoCAD uses the Autodesk Heidi® 3D graphics system and supports dynamically loadable Heidi 3D Display Drivers. These drivers are linked into AutoCAD at run time and allow AutoCAD to take advantage of 3D graphics hardware.

Internet Connectivity

- Modem (if Internet is accessed by network, not required)
- *WHIP!*® Browser Accessory. Drawing web format (DWF) files are designed to be viewed on the Internet or company intranets using a Web browser. You can use the *WHIP!* Browser Accessory 4.0 to view DWF files created with AutoCAD 2000. *WHIP!* is available as a Netscape Navigator® plug-in and as a Microsoft Internet Explorer ActiveX® control. *WHIP!* is installed if you install Internet Tools with AutoCAD. You can also download *WHIP!* from the Web. For information about downloading and using *WHIP!*, see the following Web site:

    http://www.autodesk.com/products/autocad/whip/whip.htm

    To download the plug-in, see the following FTP site:

    ftp://ftp.autodesk.com/pub/component_technologies/whip/whip2.exe

- Microsoft Internet Explorer 3.0 or later, or Netscape Navigator 3.0 or later (one is required if you plan to use Internet Tools)
- TCP/IP or IPX protocol. If you are a system administrator planning to install AutoCAD on a network, you must have either the TCP/IP or IPX protocol installed and functioning on the computers running AutoCAD.

Plotters

A complete list of supported plotters is provided in Chapter 6 of the AutoCAD 2000 *Installation Guide*

Appendix C
Glossary of Computer Terms

This appendix lists and defines some of the most commonly used terms in computer applications. It is intended as a reference for AutoCAD users who wish to review related hardware and software terminology. For a complete list of computer system components required to run AutoCAD, see Appendix B.

A

Accelerator board: A *graphics card* designed to increase the speed and power of the graphics processing duties of a computer. An accelerator board has its own microprocessor (CPU) and relieves the computer's CPU of some of the processing work. Accelerator boards may allow resolution of up to 1600 × 1200 and up to 16.7 million colors. Many industrial applications need high-end graphics accelerator boards because of the complexity of the models, renderings, and animations.

B

Bitmap: A representative image consisting of rows and columns of dots, also known as a *raster image*. The number of dots in a bitmap defines the resolution of the image. A bitmap has no dimensional values. Many paint and draw programs create bitmap images and files. In AutoCAD, *vector images* are produced. Vector images are based on XYZ coordinate locations.

C

Card: A thin plate, commonly known as a *board*, on which a variety of electronic chips are mounted. Also known as a *printed circuit board*, a card can be inserted into a computer to perform a variety of functions, from increasing the power of the computer's graphics to running other peripheral devices.

CD-ROM: A thin, plastic, optical disk that stores data and is read with a CD-ROM player using a laser. The average CD holds about 600 megabytes of information.

CD-ROM drive: A device used to play or read CD-ROMs.

Chip: A very small piece of silicon on which entire integrated electronic circuits are embedded. There are many different types of chips used in computer applications. *Microprocessor chips* run the computer, while *memory chips* temporarily store working information before it is saved to a storage device.

CPU: The abbreviation for *central processing unit*. The CPU is the heart of the computer. In personal computers, it is a microprocessor chip that handles all of the system's calculations.

D

Digitizer tablet: The drawing board of the CAD workstation. A plastic or paper menu overlay containing AutoCAD commands and drawing symbols is commonly placed over the tablet. Items can be selected directly from the menu using a puck or stylus without looking at the screen. Movement of the pointing device is recorded and displayed on screen as the cursor position.

Display device: See *monitor.*

F

Floppy disk: A form of storage media commonly known as a *diskette.* A 3.5" disk can be formatted for either IBM/DOS compatible systems, or for Macintosh systems. The 3.5" disk drive is the standard for new computers. Diskettes hold up to 1.44MB of information and are enclosed in a hard plastic shell that protects them from damage.

Function keys: The individual keys on a keyboard labeled [F1] through [F10] (or [F12]). In AutoCAD, the function keys are used to immediately perform commands and specific operations that would otherwise have to be entered or selected using a pointing device. Each of the function keys is discussed in Chapter 1 of this text.

G

Graphics card: A *board* that controls graphics processing and the resolution of the computer monitor. Accelerator cards, or boards, can be inserted to allow the computer to process graphics faster and with higher resolution.

H

Hard disk drive: A sealed unit that contains one or more metal disks, or platters, used to read and write computer data. Hard disks have a much greater storage capacity than floppy disks, and are measured in megabytes and gigabytes. Common hard disk sizes are 1 gigabyte (1GB) to more than 10 gigabytes (10GB). A small light on the front of the computer indicates when the hard disk drive is being accessed. Before AutoCAD can be used, it must be installed onto the hard disk drive from a CD-ROM.

Hardware: The physical pieces of equipment, such as the microcomputer, monitor, keyboard, printer or plotter, and diskettes used in computer-aided drafting and design.

K

Keyboard: An input device that resembles a standard typewriter keyboard with additional keys located to the left, right, and top. The exact location and number of function keys (numbered [F1] through [F10] or [F12]) varies from one model to another. The keyboard can be used to enter AutoCAD commands or precise coordinate values.

M

Monitor: A computer display output device that resembles a small television. Common monitor sizes are 15", 17", 19", and 21" (measured diagonally).

Mouse: A computer input device used to select items, perform cursor movement, and specify point locations on screen. A *mechanical mouse* has a roller ball on the bottom. The movement of the roller on any flat surface is sent to the computer and displayed as the movement of the screen cursor. Unlike a stylus or puck, a mouse can be lifted and moved to another position without affecting the location of the screen cursor.

An *optical mouse* uses a special reflective pad with grid lines. As the mouse is moved across the grid, a laser detects the movement and indicates the cursor location on screen. The optical mouse must remain on the pad in order to work.

N

Network: A group of several connected computers that communicate with each other. Complex networks may have hundreds of computers or terminals working from a central computer called a *server*. Each workstation on the network still requires a CPU, an input device, and a display device.

O

Optical drive: A disk drive that reads information from optical disks. The most popular optical drives use disks that are about the same size as standard magnetic 3.5" floppy disks, but thicker. While optical disks typically store up to 256MB per disk (512MB compressed), there are optical drives that store more than 4GB (gigabyte) of data. Optical drives provide the reliability of optical media without the cost or vulnerability of magnetic media. Some types of optical disks can be rewritten with new data as required, just like magnetic floppies. They are also faster and more reliable for backups than magnetic tape drives.

P

Page: A portion of the program or current drawing file that is kept in random access memory (RAM), or paged out to the hard disk for temporary storage.

Peripheral: A hardware device connected to the computer, such as a keyboard, monitor, printer, plotter, digitizer, modem, or scanner.

Pixel: A value used to measure screen resolution. Pixel means *picture element*. A pixel appears as a dot on screen, but it is actually a tiny rectangle. The display of a monitor is composed of horizontal rows and vertical columns of pixels. See *resolution*.

Plotter: A device used to output paper and film drawings. A plotter uses felt tip, ball-point, or wet ink pens, inkjets, or pencils to place lines on paper. A *raster plotter*, such as an inkjet plotter, prints an entire row of the image at a time as the paper advances. A *pen plotter* constantly moves around the paper, drawing each vector separately. Plotting is covered in Chapters 4 and 10 of this text.

Pointing device: An input device that is used to move the screen cursor, specify point locations, and select commands. Items can be selected from the screen or a digitizer tablet menu. Commonly used pointing devices include the mouse, trackball, multibutton puck, and pen-shaped stylus. The puck and stylus are used in conjunction with a digitizer. The use of a digitizer tablet menu is discussed in Appendix M.

Printer: An output device that receives images and text from a computer for placement on paper. Laser printers can output images with resolution up to 1200 dpi (dots per inch). Some inkjet printers can output images with resolution up to 720 dpi. Many printers and plotters use the same technology, such as inkjet printing. Often, the only difference is in the size of the device.

Puck: A multibutton input device used with a digitizer tablet. A puck may have as many as 16 buttons. A set of small crosshairs in the puck serves as the pick point for this device. As the bottom surface of the puck slides on the digitizer surface, the movement controls the position of the screen cursor. One of the puck buttons, the pick button, is used to enter points and select menu commands. All the other buttons can be programmed to suit the user.

R

RAM: The abbreviation for *random access memory*. RAM is made up of a group of data-holding blank chips and refers to the ability of the computer to randomly store and search for data in this area of memory. The chips are similar to empty storage boxes. When AutoCAD is loaded, the program files are placed into the computer's RAM. If your computer has a large amount of RAM, most of AutoCAD's files can be placed in the computer's memory. Some (or all) data in a drawing may also be initially placed in the computer's memory.

Resolution: The display quality of images on screen. The amount of resolution in an image determines how smooth or jagged the text and objects appear. Resolution is measured in *pixels*. A typical display resolution is 800×600, meaning the image can display 800 pixels, or dots, horizontally, and 600 dots vertically. High-resolution monitors can display a resolution of 1024×768, or higher.

S

Serial port: A socket or connector where a peripheral device, such as a modem or mouse, is plugged into the computer.

Server: A central computer that serves a network of computers or terminals. The hard disk drives in the server are normally large-capacity drives. Servers need to store a variety of software, and still have plenty of space for the numerous files created by computer users attached to the network. The network server can also store drawing files that may be needed by users in order to complete new drawings.

Storage device: Any drive or peripheral device that is used to save computer files. Common storage devices include floppy disk drives, hard disk drives, and CD-ROM drives.

Storage media: Any device used to store computer data, such as a floppy disk, hard disk, or CD-ROM.

Stylus: A pen-shaped pointing device used in conjunction with a digitizer tablet. A stylus is connected to the digitizer by a cable. When the point of the stylus is pressed down on the digitizer surface, a slight click can be felt and heard. This indicates that a point or menu item at the cursor's position on screen has been selected.

Swap file: A file containing the least-used portions, or pages, of a program on the hard disk. Swap files are used to store data that is not being currently used in physical memory. Pages stored in a swap file are held there until needed again.

T

Trackball: A pointing device that enables you to move the screen cursor by rolling a ball. A trackball requires only the amount of table space needed for it to sit on (the only part that is rotated is the ball). A variety of trackballs are available, but most have two or three buttons, much like a mouse.

V

Virtual memory: A memory system that uses a combination of RAM and hard disk space. A virtual memory system keeps only the part of the program that is being currently used in physical memory. If additional portions of the program are needed, AutoCAD creates a *page* on the hard disk and writes the least-used portion of the program to that page. See *swap file.*

Appendix D

Installation, Configuration, and User Profiles

Before you can use AutoCAD, it must be installed onto the hard disk and then configured to work with your specific hardware. The configuration procedure should be used only once, unless equipment is upgraded or new peripherals are added. To use two or more different menu systems, you can create multiple user profiles. These are discussed later.

Before installing AutoCAD, follow these preparation and setup steps:
- Have Microsoft Windows 98, 95, or NT 4.0 installed and running.
- Determine the hard disk drive and folder to install AutoCAD in.

These steps require only a few minutes and can prevent problems later.

INSTALLING AUTOCAD

Installing AutoCAD is a simple process, but it does require that you are somewhat prepared before beginning. First, be sure that you have enough hard disk space for the program files.

A typical installation of AutoCAD requires approximately 172MB of hard disk space and a full installation requires approximately 195MB. The setup process warns you if there is not enough disk space to install the files you have selected. Approximate hard disk storage areas required for some of the components are as follows:

Files	Disk Space
Full installation	195MB
Typical installation	172MB
Compact installation	86.9MB
Custom installation	varies
Program files	87.8MB
Internet Tools	1.5MB
Fonts	5.4MB
Samples	20.1MB
Dictionaries	512KB
Database	8.4MB
Batch plotting	448KB
Texture maps	13.5MB
VBA Support	7.8MB
Express Tools	6MB
Tutorials	1MB
Plot Lessons	42.4MB

In an effort to run smoothly through the setup process, know the following information before starting:

- AutoCAD serial number_____.
- CD Key_____.
- Disk drive on which to install AutoCAD_____.
- Portion of the AutoCAD files to install_____.
- Dealer's name_____.
- Dealer's telephone number_____.

You are now ready to install the software. Insert the CD into the ROM drive and pick **Run...** from the **Start** menu. The **Run** dialog box is displayed, and a blinking cursor appears in the **Open:** text box. Enter the name of the drive in which you inserted the CD, followed by SETUP—for example, D:\SETUP. Enter the appropriate letter for the disk drive you are using. See Figure D-1. Click the **OK** button, or press [Enter]. The AutoCAD setup program begins.

Figure D-1.
Access the Run dialog box and enter the name of the drive in which you inserted the installation CD.

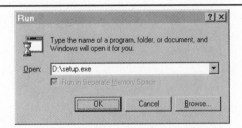

The first screen is the **Installation Menu**. Pick the **Install AutoCAD 2000** option. You can install the **AutoCAD 2000 Migration Assistance** after AutoCAD is installed, or at a later date. Pick **OK** to continue. The next screen is the **Welcome** dialog box. You are strongly urged to close all open applications to insure a smooth installation of AutoCAD. Pick Next to continue.

If a registered version of AutoCAD is found on your system, the **Setup Choices** dialog box is displayed. Pick the **Reinstall** button. If no version of AutoCAD is found, the Software License Agreement page is displayed. Select your country of residence then pick **I Accept**, then the **Next** button.

If you accept the license agreement terms, you are asked to enter the serial number and CD key. See Figure D-2. These numbers are located on a label attached to the CD jewel box, and on the registration card sent with the product.

The next screen requests personal information. Enter the information requested, and use the [Tab] key to move between the text box fields. See Figure D-3. Errors in the serial number can be corrected by picking the **Back** button. Pick the **Next** button when you are finished. Your personal information is redisplayed, and you are given a chance to change your mind or correct anything you enter by picking the **Back** button.

If AutoCAD Release 14 is detected on your system, the **Upgrade Options** page displays the path to the version of AutoCAD found. You can choose to either **Install in a separate folder** or **Upgrade AutoCAD**. If you upgrade, the new version replaces the previous version. If you want to preserve your customized files from the previous version, be sure that the **Migrate previous installation's settings** box is checked.

The **Destination Location** page is displayed next, and the default folder name of C:\Program Files\Acad2000 is given. This folder will contain all installed AutoCAD files. If you wish to change the folder name, pick the **Browse...** button and select or enter the name of the new folder. Pick the **Next** button if you accept the default name of Program Files\Acad2000. If the folder does not exist, you are asked if you want it created. Pick **Yes** to continue.

Figure D-2.
Provide the information needed for the **Serial Number:** and **CD Key:** text boxes.

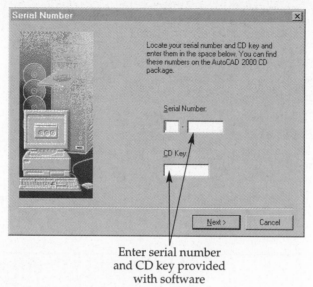

Enter serial number
and CD key provided
with software

Figure D-3.
Enter personal information.

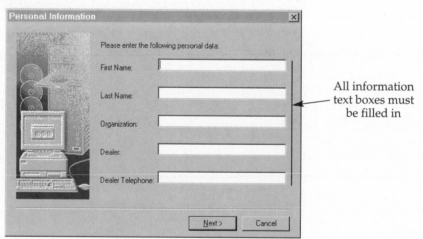

All information
text boxes must
be filled in

The next screen provides four choices for the amount of files that are installed onto your hard disk. See Figure D-4. If hard disk space is a concern to you, choose the **Compact** button. This installation requires 86.9MB of hard disk space. The space available on your hard disk is displayed at the bottom of the dialog box. If you are unsure about which components to install, but have plenty of hard disk space, choose the **Typical** button. Since this button is the default, pressing [Enter] selects the typical installation. The Express Tools are automatically installed with a full installation. You can always do a custom installation later and install the Express Tools.

 NOTE   Regardless of the type of installation you select, you can always run the setup program again later and choose additional components to install.

Figure D-4.
Pick the type of installation you prefer.

Select type of installation →

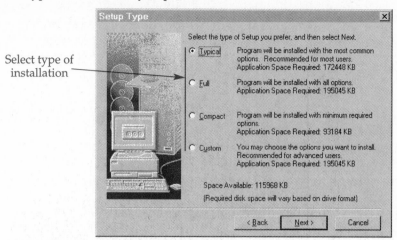

After selecting the installation type, the setup program informs you that it is checking for hard disk space. Then you are asked to select a folder name from a list, or accept the default name in the **Program Folders:** text box. Pick **Next** to continue.

On the next page, Windows Notepad will be assigned as the default text editor unless you pick the **Assign Editor** button to change it.

The final display indicates the components that you have selected for installation. If you wish to change this, pick the **Back** button. Otherwise pick **Next**.

The installation begins, and will take a few minutes, depending on the components of the program you selected for installation and the speed of your CD ROM drive. When the installation is complete, you are given the opportunity to install the AutoCAD Migration Assistance. This is a collection of tools to assist you in upgrading from a previous version. Follow the on-screen instructions to install these files.

After all program components have been installed, you are asked if you want to restart the computer. If you wish to use AutoCAD right away, it is suggested that you pick the default button, **Yes, I want to restart my computer now**.

CONFIGURING AUTOCAD

Configuring AutoCAD for peripheral devices such as plotters, printers, display devices, and digitizers is a simple process. For example, upon installation, AutoCAD finds and uses the current pointing device and system printer. These become the default devices until they are changed.

If you wish to add a new plotter, use the following steps.
1. Pick **Options...** from the **Tools** pull-down menu, then pick the **Plotting** tab.
2. Pick the **Use as default output device** drop-down list to display a list of supported printing and plotting devices.
3. Select the appropriate device from the list. Pick the **OK** button.
4. If your plotter is not listed, pick the **Add or configure Plotters...** button.
5. In the **Plotters** window, double-click on the Add-A-Plotter Wizard icon. Follow the instructions to select and configure your plotter
6. Enter the port name, such as COM1, and press [Enter].
7. When you complete the wizard, close the **Plotters** window and pick the **Add or configure Plotters...** button again. The new printer is added to the list in the **Options** dialog box.

Use the same procedure to select a new pointing device. Pick the **System** tab in the **Options** dialog box, select the appropriate device from the list in the **Current Pointing Device** area and answer the remaining questions to configure the device.

Video display boards (graphics cards), usually come with special drivers that are supplied on a diskette. Always consult the documentation provided with your video card for instructions on how to install special drivers.

EXPRESS TOOLBARS

When you select a full installation, four additional toolbars are displayed on your screen: **Express Block Tools**, **Express Standard Toolbar**, **Express Text Tools**, and **Express Layer Tools**. They also appear if you select **Express** and **Batch Plotting** in a custom installation. In addition to the four toolbars, an **Express** pull-down menu is also provided. Refer to Appendix A of this text for detailed information about these toolbars and pull-down menu.

These bonus utilities are provided by Autodesk on an *as-is* basis, which means that they may contain bugs. These utilities are usually AutoLISP routines or ARX applications that may provide some measure of productivity, but are often new and not fully tested. They are provided for users to experiment with and may eventually, in future releases, become features of AutoCAD. You can access extensive, detailed help for the Express tools by picking **Help...** from the **Express** pull-down menu. In addition you are provided access to the Express Tools FAQ (frequently asked questions), the Express Tools Web site, and the Express Tools newsgroup.

PROFESSIONAL TIP

Many of the express tools that are included in the toolbars and pull-down menu can provide the user with greater flexibility and productivity. Take the time to explore these tools as you work. Excellent on-line help including sample exercises is provided by picking **Help...** from the **Bonus** pull-down menu.

AutoCAD User's Guide **3**

CREATING MULTIPLE-USER PROFILES

A *profile* is a group of settings and values relevant to a particular user or function. The **Profiles** tab of the **Options** dialog box allows you to change the settings and values for a variety of devices and functions to match your needs. All of your preferences can be saved in a *user profile*. Multiple profiles can be saved by a single user for different applications, and several users can create individual profiles to avoid conflict.

PROFESSIONAL TIP

The use of profiles should be emphasized in a school setting or in a company where more than one person will be using the same computer. The intention is that each user can establish the settings to their liking, and then save those settings in a file. Then, regardless of who used the computer previously, and how they may have changed the preferences, it is simply a matter of importing your profile to reset all the preferences.

What is a user profile?

A user profile should not be confused with settings found in a drawing. Template files are used to save settings relating to a drawing session, such as units, limits, object snap settings, drawing aids, grip settings, dimension styles, and text styles. A profile is used to save settings related to the performance and appearance of the software and hardware. A profile can be composed of, but is not limited to, the following settings and values:

- Temporary drawing file location
- Template drawing file location
- Text display format
- Arc and circle smoothness
- Start-up dialog box display
- Minutes between automatic saves
- File extension for temporary files
- AutoCAD screen menu display
- Colors and fonts for AutoCAD screen
- Type of pointer and length of crosshairs
- Type of printer or plotter

Creating a User Profile

A profile can be created and then modified as you determine certain settings and values that work best for you. For example, say you decide you like the pointer crosshairs to extend to the edges of the graphics window, you often use the **Inquiry** toolbar, and you prefer the graphics window background color to be gray. Use the following steps to first establish the settings.

1. Pick **Toolbars...** in the **View** pull-down menu to display the **Toolbars** dialog box.
2. Pick the **Inquiry** check box. The **Inquiry** toolbar is displayed. Pick **OK** to exit.
3. Pick **Options...** from the **Tools** pull-down menu to display the **Options** dialog box.
4. Pick the **Display** tab and set the **Crosshair size** to 100.
5. Pick the **Colors...** button in the **Window Elements** area.
6. In the **Window Element:** drop-down list, pick Model tab background.
7. Select More... from the **Color:** drop-down list. Pick the gray color swatch in the **Select Color** dialog box, then pick the **Apply & Close** button to exit.

Your preferences have now been set as shown in Figure D-5. Next, these settings must be saved in a profile or else they will be lost when AutoCAD is closed. Use the following steps to save the settings to a file:

1. Pick the **Profiles** tab in the **Options** dialog box, Figure D-6.
2. Pick the **Add to List...** button, then enter a name and description in the **Add Profile** dialog box. Pick the **Apply & Close** button to exit.
3. Pick the **Export...** button, then select a folder location for the new file, enter a file name, and pick **Save**. Note that the file is given an .arg extension.
4. In order to apply the profile the next time you run AutoCAD, it must be imported and displayed in the profile list box. Pick the **Import...** button, select the proper ARG file, and then pick **Open**.
5. The imported file is displayed in the list. Select the file to highlight it, then pick the **Set Current** button.

All the settings in your profile are applied while the **Options** dialog box is still open. Therefore, you can select any of the profiles and set them current to see what the settings look like. Of course, all profile settings are not visible, such as temporary file locations and current printer. Additional buttons in the **Profiles** tab are described here.

- **Rename.** Displays the **Change Profile** dialog box. Select the profile you wish to rename first, then enter a new name in the **Profile name:** text box.
- **Delete.** Displays an AutoCAD alert box asking if you want to delete the profile. Pick **Yes** and the selected profile is deleted.
- **Reset.** Resets the selected profile to the default AutoCAD settings.

Figure D-5.
Setting to be saved as a user profile assigned to the drawing.

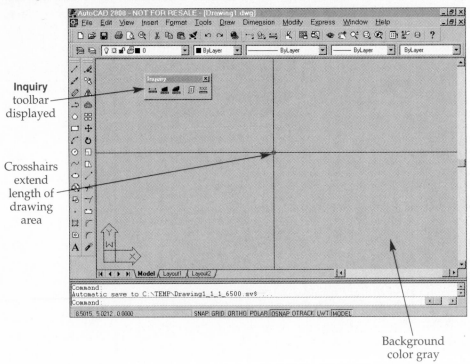

Inquiry toolbar displayed

Crosshairs extend length of drawing area

Background color gray

Figure D-6.
The **Profiles** tab of the **Options** dialog box allows you to create and manage user profiles.

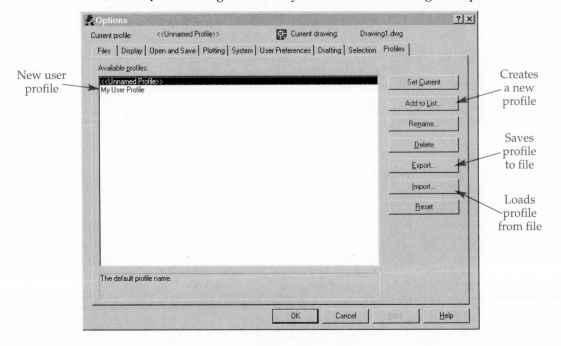

New user profile

Creates a new profile

Saves profile to file

Loads profile from file

AutoCAD and its Applications—Basics

Appendix E

Managing the AutoCAD System

Any business—be it a bakery or engineering firm—relies on structure, organization, and standard procedures. A business lacking in one of these areas does not operate efficiently.

Computer systems can be used within the company structure for organization and procedure, or computers can contain the structural and organizational procedures themselves. In either case, the method in which computer systems are managed greatly affects the operation of the entire company.

Effective management of an AutoCAD system in a school or business means paying careful attention to the following items:

✓ The structure and makeup of the hard disk and mass storage devices.
✓ The location of all files and drawings.
✓ Storage procedures for student or employee drawing files.
✓ Drawing file backup procedures.
✓ The types of template drawings used for specific projects.
✓ The use and location of symbol libraries and reference drawings.
✓ The use and location of special screen and digitizer tablet menus.
✓ Drawing file creation procedures and naming conventions.
✓ Creation and distribution methods for new symbols and menus.
✓ Updating methods for software and hardware.
✓ Hardware maintenance.

Effective procedures and management techniques must be practiced by all students or employees. In addition, any personnel should look for ways that standards can be improved and revised for greater efficiency. In this text, read the section in Chapter 1 on using drawing standards and the section in Chapter 23 on creating and using symbol libraries.

MANAGEMENT PROCEDURES

One of your goals as an AutoCAD user should be to keep the computer system as efficient as possible. This means being organized and knowledgeable of school or company standards. You should also be aware of who has the authority to manage the system, and follow the system manager's guidelines.

If you are the system manager, develop standards and procedures, relay them to system users, and distribute up-to-date documentation, symbol libraries, menus, and standards. Revise standards as needed and distribute them to all users. In addition, incorporate software updates in a consistent and timely manner. Make the maintenance of hardware a priority.

The System Manager

One or two people, depending on the size of the department or company, should be assigned as system manager. The manager has control over all functions of the computer system, and is in charge of preventing inconsistencies in procedure, drawing format, and file storage. The manager is responsible for the following:

- The scheduled use of computers.
- The structure of hard disk directories.
- Administration of the network server and user access to its files.
- The appearance and function of start-up menus and network log-in procedures.
- Implementation of file naming techniques.
- File storage and backup procedures.
- Drawing file access.
- The creation of symbol libraries.
- The development and distribution of written standards.
- Software and hardware upgrading.
- Hardware hygiene and maintenance.

When tasks are delegated, such as the creation of symbol libraries, be sure to include accurate sketches or drawings. Check and approve final drawings before distributing them to users.

Developing Operating Standards and Procedures

The basis of system management is that everyone performs his or her job using the same procedures, symbols, and drawing techniques. A department that operates smoothly is probably using standards such as the following:

- File naming conventions.
- Methods of file storage that identify the location and name.
- File backup methods.
- Standard drawing sheet sizes and title blocks.
- Template drawings.
- The creation of blocks and symbols.
- Standard dimensioning techniques.
- Standard usage of layers, colors, linetypes, and text styles.
- Color schemes for plotting, and plot styles.
- The creation of screen and tablet menus.
- Organized storage of printed or plotted drawings.

Take the time initially to study the needs of your school or company. Meet with other department managers and users to determine the nature of their drawings. Always gain input from people who use the system and avoid making blanket decisions on your own.

Once needs have been established, develop a plan for implementing the required standards and procedures. Assign specific tasks to students or employees. Assemble the materials as they are completed and distribute the documentation and procedures to all users.

When developing procedures, begin with start-up procedures and work through the drawing process. Develop template drawings for specific types of projects first. The final aspects of system development should be the creation of screen and tablet menus and custom programs.

The hard disk drive is the heart of the AutoCAD computer system. It is the storage center for AutoCAD and other programs you use. In addition, it may hold hundreds of additional files, including drawings, templates, custom programs, slides, menu files, script files, and text files. The manner in which you work with the hard disk and arrange its contents can affect your productivity and drawing efficiency. Take time to assess the needs of your school or company and then organize your hard disk drives accordingly.

File Maintenance

The integrity of saved files must be protected by everyone who works with the system. Procedures for file maintenance must be documented. Files of every type, including DWG, DWT, SLD, BAT, LSP, MNU, and BAK files, must have a secure storage area. Any hard disk directories, diskettes, optical discs, and magnetic tape storage areas must be kept clean of nonessential files. File maintenance procedures should include the following documentation:

- Location of essential AutoCAD files.
- Location of backup AutoCAD files.
- Printed contents of all hard disk directories for each workstation.
- Location and contents of all template drawings, supplemented with printed listings.
- Location and contents of all custom programs and associated menus.
- Location of all user files, including templates, drawings, slides, and text files.

Regardless of what you store on the hard disk, have a plan for it. Drawings should not be saved in the Acad2000 folder. Users should not be allowed to save files in the root directory. Decide on the nature of the hard disk structure and then stick to it. Make sure that all users are informed by documenting and distributing the standard procedures accordingly. Place copies of the procedures at each workstation.

Files to be used in conjunction with AutoCAD should be located in subfolders of the Acad2000 folder. Possible uses for subfolders include drawings, AutoLISP files, drivers, slides, and user folders. The individual files should reside within the subfolders. The subfolders of Acad2000 in Figure E-1 are those that are automatically created when AutoCAD is installed. If you plan to store files within the AutoCAD folder tree, plan on creating new subfolders with names such as Drawings, Lisp, and Scripts. When specific types of files are kept in their own subfolders, file maintenance is easier.

Your hard disk planning should take into account future software. New programs should be installed in their own folders on the hard disk, and the files should be managed in the same fashion as the AutoCAD files. An example of a well-planned and closely managed hard disk structure is shown in Figure E-2.

Maintaining Symbol Libraries and Menus

The development of symbol libraries and customized menus is one of the primary concerns of managing an AutoCAD system. In AutoCAD, symbols are created as *blocks*. See Chapter 23 of this text for a full discussion on drawing and saving block symbols.

Figure E-1.
Specific subfolders in the Acad2000 folder are for files that are used with AutoCAD. These subfolders are automatically created when AutoCAD is installed.

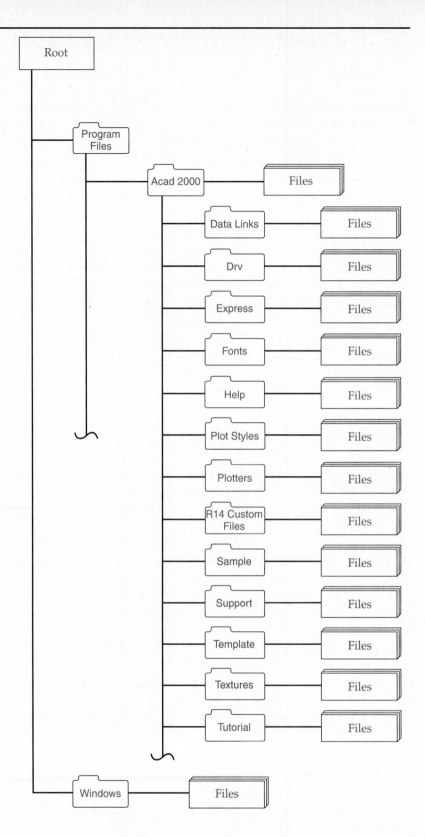

Figure E-2.
The folder structure of a well-managed hard disk appears clean and organized.

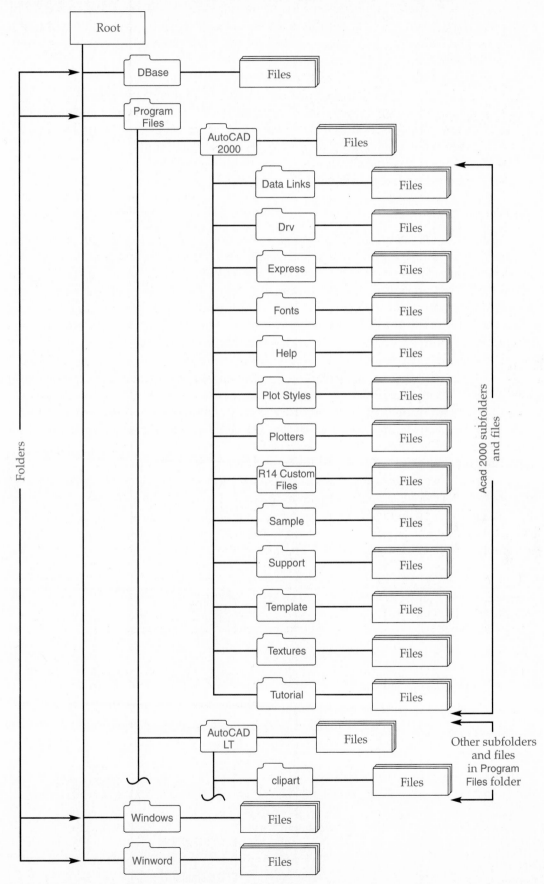

Symbols must be consistent and up-to-date. User menus must also be consistent throughout the department or company. A vital aspect of maintaining standards and consistency is establishing a method for updating symbol libraries and menus. This task should be given to certain students or employees, with the results distributed to all users. The following guidelines should be used for developing and maintaining symbol libraries and selection menus:

- Establish drawing standards for the creation of symbols.
- Develop a symbol naming convention and storage system.
- Post a printed copy of all symbol libraries with their names and locations listed.
- Practice standards for the creation and maintenance of custom menus and toolbars.
- Assign the use of custom menus to specific departments.
- Make revisions to custom menus when necessary.
- Revise upgraded menus on all hard disks.

Network Systems

There is an increasing need for drawing symbol consistency, accurate project time accounting, instant communication between coworkers, and data security. This has led to the popularity of *network systems*. A **network** is nothing more than several connected computers that communicate with each other. Complex networks have hundreds of computers or terminals working from a central computer called a **server**. Each workstation on the network still requires a CPU, an input device, and a display device. A diagram of a typical network system is shown in Figure E-3.

The hard disk drives in the server are normally large-capacity drives. They need to store a variety of software, and still have plenty of space for numerous files created by the computer users attached to the network. The network server can also store drawing files that may be needed by users in order to complete new drawings. For example, a base drawing of the walls of a structure can be stored on the server. When a student or employee needs to work on a new drawing of the plumbing or electrical layout of the structure, he or she can simply load the base drawing from the server into a networked computer and begin working. In most cases, the base drawing is preserved in its original form and a different name is given to the new drawing. AutoCAD provides a function that automatically locks a drawing when someone *checks it out* of the network. This means that only one person can work on a drawing at any given time, thus preventing several people from making different changes to the drawing.

Figure E-3.
A layout of a typical computer network system.

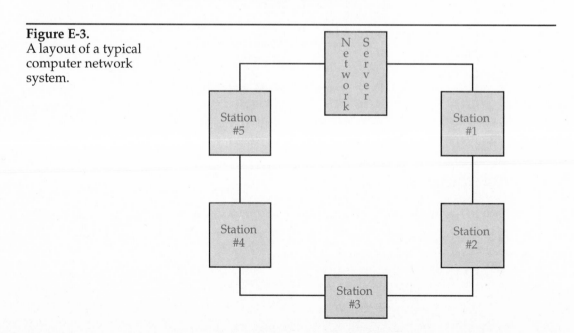

Maintaining the Software

Software upgrades and releases are issued regularly. If you purchase upgrades, converting to new versions should be smooth and have little, if any, effect on production. Establish a procedure for upgrading all computers in the classroom or office. Inform all users of changes by providing a printed listing of new features. If you work for a company, schedule professional upgrade training for managers and employees at an authorized Autodesk Training Center (ATC) or an authorized Autodesk dealer. For information on the nearest ATC or AutoCAD dealer, call 1-800-964-6432. You can also get valuable training information on the World Wide Web at http://www.autodesk.com.

Maintaining the Management System

All systems require continuous maintenance to function efficiently. Always enable users to contribute to the function of the system. Foster creativity by inviting suggestions. Meet with users and managers on a regular basis to learn what is functioning well and what is not. Remember, the system will function efficiently if a majority of those using it enjoy working with the system, and are encouraged to contribute to its growth and development.

Appendix F

The Ergonomic Workstation

Ergonomics is the science of adapting the work environment to suit the needs of the worker. Since the advent of computers in the workplace in the early 1980s, an increasing number of work-related injuries and afflictions have been reported. By far, the most common of these are repetitive motion disorders (also called repetitive stress or strain). Carpal tunnel syndrome is probably the most well-known of these. Most injuries and disorders related to computer work are the result of the sedentary nature of the work, and the fast, repetitive motions of the hands and fingers on the keyboard and pointing devices.

Most disorders of this nature can be prevented to some extent by proper workstation configuration, good posture, and frequent exercises. Figure F-1 shows a piece of ergonomic equipment for the computer workstation. Review the following checklist, and try to adhere to as many of the suggestions as possible. As is often the case, a small adjustment of equipment, or the investment of a few extra dollars, can prevent unnecessary future injuries and lost productivity.

- ✓ Obtain a good chair with proper back support, height, and tilt adjustment.
- ✓ Use adaptive devices such as forearm supports, wrist and palm rests, and keyboard drawers to help maintain a level wrist position in relation to the keyboard and pointing device.
- ✓ Avoid resting your wrists on a table while typing, and use a light stroke on the keys.
- ✓ Investigate the variety of ergonomic keyboards on the market and test for comfort and efficiency. (See website addresses at the end of this appendix.)
- ✓ Position the equipment and supplies of your workstation for ease of use and access. Use a document holder to keep documents at eye level.
- ✓ The screen should be placed 18″ to 30″ away from the eyes, and the top of the display screen should be at eye level.
- ✓ Lighting should not produce a glare on the screen.
- ✓ Provide under-desk space so feet can be placed on a tilted footrest, or at minimum, flat on the floor.
- ✓ Take short breaks throughout the day.
- ✓ Practice refocusing your eyes, and engaging in stretching exercises for hands, arms, shoulders, and neck on a regular basis.

Figure F-1.
The forearm supports provide relief from muscle tension for computer operators and assist in the prevention of repetitive motion disorders. This design was created with AutoCAD. (MyoNetics Inc.)

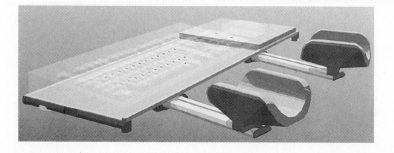

✓ Be aware of how your body feels, especially any changes you feel in your shoulders, arms, wrists, and hands.

✓ Consult your doctor if you notice any numbness, aching, or tingling in your hands, wrists, or arms.

COMFORT IN YOUR WORKSPACE

Sitting in the same position for a long time causes fatigue. Properly arranging your workspace and improving your posture are two highly effective ways to reduce the strain and potential injuries associated with frequent computer use.

Workspace Arrangement

An ergonomically correct workstation will add comfort to the job and help avoid serious injuries. A good chair is essential. The backrest and seat should provide firm support and adjust independently. The front of the seat should be curved to relieve pressure on the thighs. Keep thighs parallel to the floor. Rest your feet flat on the floor or on a footrest.

Use a light touch on the keyboard, keeping your hands and fingers relaxed. Your forearms should be parallel to the floor and your wrists in a neutral, comfortable position. Maintain about a 90° angle in the bend of your elbows.

The monitor should be adjusted so the top of the screen is at eye level, or slightly below. Place the monitor 20" to 24" (50 cm to 60 cm) in front of you, about an arm's length from the screen. Position the monitor to minimize glare from overhead lights, windows, or other light sources. If necessary, turn off lights or use less intense light-bulbs. Close curtains or blinds to block sunlight through windows. Change the brightness and contrast controls on the monitor as needed throughout the day. An antiglare filter placed over the screen is also an alternative.

Posture and Exercise

No matter how comfortable or ergonomically correct your workstation is, you are still at risk for repetitive stress injuries. That is why you need to develop ergonomically sound work habits that include posture awareness and simple exercises. Repetitive stress injuries often develop slowly, over months or even years. You may not even be aware that an injury is developing until the pain becomes intense. These simple practices can help you avoid various types of injuries and disorders associated with using computers every day.

- **Maintain good posture.** The single best thing you can do is work on your posture. Computer users tend to tilt their shoulders and chin toward the screen. Don't allow your head to project forward. This places too much strain on the neck and shoulders. Also, avoid leaning on the armrests of the chair. Instead, type with the entire arm.

  Awareness is the key to maintaining good posture. Sit up straight! It is old-fashioned advice, but it applies more than ever in today's computerized workplace.

- **Get up from your desk.** Sitting for hours at a computer workstation without breaks puts tremendous stress on several areas of your body, including your neck, back, arms, wrists, and legs. Make a habit of getting out of your seat at least once every hour, even if it is only for a few minutes. If you can, walk outside during your break and get some fresh air. You'll return to your workstation feeling refreshed.

- **Practice periodic stretching and exercises.** When most of what you are doing all day is sitting still, moving only your fingers and eyes, the muscles in the rest of your body can become stiff and sore from lack of use. Taking a few moments to stretch periodically throughout the day can relax stiff joints and muscles, helping to avoid problems associated with prolonged muscular stress. Many simple stretching activities can be done right at your workstation without even leaving your seat.
- **Give your eyes a break.** You can greatly reduce eye strain with this simple practice: Every 15 minutes or so, look away from the computer screen and focus on something 20 feet or more away from you.

Several Internet sites provide useful information about preventing repetitive stress injures. Go to www.tifaq.com for answers to the most frequently asked questions about ergonomics and computer use injuries. It also has links to other useful websites, such as 3M Company's self-help site showing exercises that can be done without leaving your workstation. A good resource for college students by college students is www.eecs.harvard.edu/rsi. To learn about cutting-edge accessories including ergonomically designed keyboards, go to ergo.human.cornell.edu.

AutoCAD System Variables

The following listing shows the AutoCAD system variables that can be stored within a drawing or template file. The value of each of these variables is written into the file when the drawing is saved, so the next time the drawing is opened, the values remain the same. Setting the values for most of these variables can be done by entering the variable name or by using the **SETVAR** command. Some variable values are derived by AutoCAD from the current condition of the drawing or the drawing environment, and cannot be directly set. These are referred to as *read-only* variables.

Each of the listings in this appendix provides a brief description of the system variable and the default setting when no specific drawing is referenced. The symbol ($\mathcal{O}$) indicates the variable is read-only. System variables with names in color are available in AutoCAD 2000i only.

VARIABLES SAVED IN DRAWING

Variable Name	Default Value	Description
ANGBASE	0.0000	Sets base angle to 0 relative to current UCS.
ANGDIR	0	Specifies counterclockwise or clockwise angle measurement.
ATTMODE	1	Display mode for block attributes.
AUNITS	0	Format for angular units.
AUPREC	0	Precision of angular units.
BACKZ	$\mathcal{O}$	Controls back clipping plane offset from the target plane.
CECOLOR	"BYLAYER"	Color of newly created objects.
CELTSCALE	1.0000	Individual object linetype scaling for new objects.
CELTYPE	"BYLAYER"	Linetype for newly created objects.
CELWEIGHT	"BYLAYER"	Lineweight setting for new objects.
CHAMFERA	0.5000	First chamfer distance.
CHAMFERB	0.5000	Second chamfer distance.
CHAMFERC	1.0000	Chamfer length.
CHAMFERD	0.0000	Chamfer angle.
CLAYER	"0"	Currently active layer.
CMLJUST	0	Current multiline justification.
CMLSCALE	1.0000	Scale factor for multiline features.
CMLSTYLE	"STANDARD"	Current multiline style name.
CPLOTSTYLE	"BYLAYER"	Current plot style setting for new objects.
CTAB		Identifies the **Model** tab or a specific layout tab as current.
CVPORT	2	Identification number of current viewport.
DIMADEC	0	Decimal places for angular dimensions.
DIMALT	off	Enables or disables alternate units dimensioning.
DIMALTD	2	Decimal places for alternate units dimensions.
DIMALTF	25.4000	Alternate units dimension scale factor.

Variable Name	Default Value	Description
DIMALTRND	0.00	Rounding value for alternate dimension units.
DIMALTTD	2	Decimal places for alternate units tolerance values.
DIMALTTZ	0	Zero suppression for alternate units tolerance values.
DIMALTU	2	Units format for alternate units dimensions.
DIMALTZ	0	Zero suppression for alternate units dimension values.
DIMAPOST	""	Prefix/suffix for alternate units dimensions.
DIMASO	on	Toggles associative dimensioning.
DIMASZ	0.1800	Dimension line and arrowhead size.
DIMATFIT	3	Controls placement of text and arrowheads when there is insufficient space between the extension lines.
DIMAUNIT	0	Unit format for angular dimension values.
DIMAZIN	0	Controls zero suppression for angular dimensions.
DIMBLK	""	Block type to use for both arrowheads.
DIMBLK1	""	Block type to use for first arrowhead.
DIMBLK2	""	Block type to use for second arrowhead.
DIMCEN	0.0900	Controls placement of center marks or centerlines.
DIMCLRD	0	Dimension line, arrowhead, and leader line color.
DIMCLRE	0	Dimension extension line color.
DIMCLRT	0	Dimension text color.
DIMDEC	4	Decimal places for dimension values.
DIMDLE	0.0000	Dimension line extension beyond extension lines.
DIMDLI	0.3800	Incremental spacing between baseline dimensions.
DIMDSEP	"."	Specifies a single character to use as a decimal separator for decimal unit dimensions.
DIMEXE	0.1800	Extension line distance beyond dimension line.
DIMEXO	0.0625	Distance from origin points to extension lines.
DIMFRAC	0	Controls the fraction format used for architectural and fractional dimensions.
DIMGAP	0.0900	Gap size between dimension line and dimension text.
DIMJUST	0	Horizontal justification of dimension text.
DIMLDRBLK	0	Controls the type of arrowhead used for leaders.
DIMLFAC	1.0000	Scale factor for linear dimension values.
DIMLIM	off	Toggles creation of limits-style dimension text.
DIMLUNIT	0	Specifies units for all non-angular dimensions.
DIMLWD	BYBLOCK	Lineweight value for dimension lines.
DIMLWE	BYBLOCK	Lineweight value for extension lines.
DIMPOST	""	Prefix/suffix for primary units dimension values.
DIMRND	0.0000	Rounding value for dimensions.
DIMSAH	off	Toggles appearance of arrowhead blocks.
DIMSCALE	1.0000	Global dimension feature scale factor.
DIMSD1	off	Toggles suppression of first dimension line.
DIMSD2	off	Toggles suppression of second dimension line.
DIMSE1	off	Toggles suppression of first extension line.
DIMSE2	off	Toggles suppression of second extension line.
DIMSHO	on	Controls dynamic update of dimensions while dragging.
DIMSOXD	off	Suppresses dimension lines outside extension lines.
DIMSTYLE	⌒	Name of current dimension style.
DIMTAD	0	Sets text placement relative to dimension line.
DIMTDEC	4	Decimal places for primary units tolerance values.

Variable Name	Default Value	Description
DIMTFAC	1.0000	Scale factor for fractional or tolerance text size.
DIMTIH	on	Orientation of text inside extension lines.
DIMTIX	off	Toggles forced placement of text between extension lines.
DIMTM	0.0000	Lower tolerance value for tolerance dimensions.
DIMTMOVE	0	Controls the format of dimension text when it is moved.
DIMTOFL	off	Toggles forced dimension line creation.
DIMTOH	on	Orientation of text outside extension lines.
DIMTOL	off	Toggles creation of appended tolerance dimensions.
DIMTOLJ	1	Vertical justification for dimension tolerance text.
DIMTP	0.0000	Upper tolerance value for tolerance dimensions.
DIMTSZ	0.0000	Controls size of dimension line tick marks drawn instead of arrowheads.
DIMTVP	0.0000	Vertical position of text above or below dimension line.
DIMTXSTY	"STANDARD"	Text style used for dimension text.
DIMTXT	0.1800	Size of dimension text.
DIMTZIN	0	Zero suppression for primary units tolerance values.
DIMUPT	off	Controls user placement of dimension line and text.
DIMZIN	0	Zero suppression for primary units dimensions.
DISPSILH	0	Toggles display of wireframe silhouette curves.
DWGCODEPAGE	~	**SYSCODEPAGE** value when drawing was created.
ELEVATION	0.0000	Current 3D elevation relative to current UCS.
EXTMAX	~	Upper-right extents of drawing.
EXTMIN	~	Lower-left extents of drawing.
EXTNAMES	1	Specifies the naming parameters for named objects.
FACETRES	0.5000	Smoothness of shaded objects and objects with hidden lines removed.
FILLETRAD	0.5000	Current fillet radius setting.
FILLMODE	1	Toggles fill for solid objects.
FRONTZ	~	Front clipping plane offset from the target plane.
GRIDMODE	0	Toggles display of grid.
GRIDUNIT	0.5000, 0.5000	Current grid spacing in drawing units.
HANDLES	~	Provides support for applications requiring handle access.
HYPERLINKBASE	""	File path specified for all relative hyperlinks in the drawing.
INDEXCTL	0	Controls creation and saving of layer and spatial indexes.
INSBASE	0.0000, 0.0000, 0.0000	Insertion point set by **BASE** command.
INSUNITS	0	Drawing units specified when inserting an object from the **AutoCAD DesignCenter**.
ISOLINES	4	Number of isolines per surface on 3D objects.
LENSLENGTH	~	Length of lens in millimeters for perspective view.
LIMCHECK	0	Toggles active limit checking for object creation.
LIMMAX	12.0000, 9.0000	Upper-right drawing limits.
LIMMIN	0.0000, 0.0000	Lower-left drawing limits.
LOGFILENAME	~	Specifies path and name for the log file.
LTSCALE	1.0000	Current global linetype scale factor.
LUNITS	2	Current display format for linear units.
LUPREC	4	Current linear units precision value.
LWDISPLAY	0	Controls the display of lineweights within the **Model** tab and each individual layout tab.
MAXACTVP	64	Maximum number of active model space viewports.

Variable Name	Default Value	Description
MEASUREMENT	0	Sets drawing units as English or metric.
MIRRTEXT	1	Toggles mirroring technique for text objects.
OLESTARTUP	0	Controls loading of the source application of an embedded OLE object when plotting.
ORTHOMODE	0	Toggles orthogonal drawing control.
PDMODE	0	Current point object display mode.
PDSIZE	0.0000	Current point object display size.
PELLIPSE	0	Controls the object type created with **ELLIPSE**.
PLINEGEN	0	Toggles linetype generation along a polyline.
PLINEWID	0.0000	Current polyline width value.
PROJECTNAME	""	Assigns a project name to the current drawing.
PROXYGRAPHICS	1	Specifies whether images of proxy objects are saved in the drawing.
PSLTSCALE	1	Paper space linetype scale factor.
PSTYLEMODE	✐	Specifies the current plot style mode.
PUCSBASE	""	The base UCS defining the origin and orientation of orthographic UCS settings in paper space only.
QTEXTMODE	0	Toggles **Quick Text** display mode.
REGENMODE	1	Toggles automatic drawing regeneration.
SHADEDGE	3	Controls edge shading during rendering.
SHADEDIF	70	Sets ratio of diffuse reflective light to ambient light.
SKETCHINC	0.1000	Current **SKETCH** record increment value.
SKPOLY	0	Toggles creation of polyline objects by **SKETCH**.
SNAPANG	0	Snap/grid rotation angle in current viewport.
SNAPBASE	0.0000, 0.0000	Snap/grid origin point in current viewport.
SNAPISOPAIR	0	Isometric plane for current viewport.
SNAPMODE	0	Toggles snap mode.
SNAPSTYL	0	Current snap style.
SNAPUNIT	0.5000, 0.5000	Snap spacing for current viewport.
SORTENTS	96	Controls object sort order operations.
SPLFRAME	0	Toggles display of frames for spline-fit polylines.
SPLINESEGS	8	Current number of segments generated for each spline.
SPLINETYPE	6	Current type of spline generation by **PEDIT**.
SURFTAB1	6	Tabulations generated for **RULESURF** and **TABSURF**, and mesh density in the M direction for **REVSURF** and **EDGESURF**.
SURFTAB2	6	Mesh density in the N direction for **REVSURF** and **EDGESURF**.
SURFTYPE	6	Surface fitting type performed by **PEDIT Smooth**.
SURFU	6	Surface density for **PEDIT Smooth** in the M direction.
SURFV	6	Surface density for **PEDIT Smooth** in the N direction.
TARGET	✐	Location of target point in current viewport.
TDCREATE	✐	Local time and date the current drawing was created.
TDINDWG	✐	Total editing time for the current drawing.
TDUCREATE	✐	Universal time and date the current drawing was created.
TDUPDATE	✐	Local time and date of the last update and save.
TDUSRTIMER	✐	User time elapsed.
TDUUPDATE	✐	Universal time and date of the last update and save.
TEXTSIZE	0.2000	Default height of text drawn in current style.
TEXTSTYLE	"STANDARD"	Current text style name.

Variable Name	Default Value	Description
THICKNESS	0.0000	Current 3D solid thickness.
TILEMODE	1	Sets the **Model** tab or last layout tab current.
TRACEWID	0.0500	Current width for **TRACE** objects.
TREEDEPTH	3020	Maximum number of branches for tree-structured spatial index.
TSTACKALIGN	1	Sets the vertical justification of stacked text.
TSTACKSIZE	70	The stacked text character height, expressed as a percentage of the text's current height.
UCSBASE	"World"	The UCS defining the origin and orientation of orthographic UCS settings.
UCSFOLLOW	0	Toggles automatic change to plan view of current UCS.
UCSICON	3	Controls the display of the UCS icon.
UCSNAME	✍	Name of the current UCS for the current space.
UCSORG	✍	Origin point for the current UCS for the current space.
UCSVP	1	Controls the independence of UCS settings in active viewports in relation to the UCS of the current viewport.
UCSXDIR	✍	X direction for the current UCS for the current space.
UCSYDIR	✍	Y direction for the current UCS for the current space.
UNITMODE	0	Current units display format.
VIEWCTR	✍	Center point location for current view in current viewport.
VIEWDIR	✍	Viewing direction of the current view in current viewport.
VIEWMODE	✍	Current viewing mode for the current viewport.
VIEWSIZE	✍	Height of the current view in the current viewport.
VIEWTWIST	✍	View twist angle for current viewport.
VISRETAIN	1	Controls visibility of layers in xref files.
VSMAX	✍	Upper-right corner of the current viewport virtual screen.
VSMIN	✍	Lower-left corner of the current viewport virtual screen.
WORLDVIEW	1	Controls automatic change of UCS for **DVIEW** and **VPOINT**.
XCLIPFRAME	0	Controls visibility of xref clipping boundaries.
XEDIT	1	Controls the reference editing capability of the current drawing when it is referenced by another drawing.

The following listing shows the AutoCAD system variables that are saved with the AutoCAD configuration. These variables are not associated with, or saved in, the drawing file. The values will be the same in the next drawing session as they are when you leave the current drawing. The default values shown here represent the values existing prior to AutoCAD's initial configuration. The symbol (✍) indicates that the variable is read-only.

VARIABLES SAVED IN REGISTRY

Variable Name	Default Value	Description
ACADLSPASDOC	0	Controls whether the acad.lsp file is loaded into every drawing, or just the first one opened in a single session.
APBOX	0	Turns the AutoSnap aperture box on or off.
APERTURE	10	Object snap target aperture height.
ATTDIA	0	Controls use of **Command:** prompt or dialog box.
ATTREQ	1	Use attribute defaults or request values from user.

Variable Name	Default Value	Description
AUDITCTL	0	Toggles the creation of an audit report (ADT) file.
AUTOSNAP	63	Controls display of the AutoSnap marker, tooltip, and magnet.
BLIPMODE	0	Controls display of marker blips.
CMDDIA	1	Enables or disables dialog boxes for a variety of commands.
COORDS	1	Controls dynamic coordinate updating.
CPROFILE	✑	Name of current profile.
CURSORSIZE	5	Controls the size of the screen cursor crosshairs as a percentage of the full screen size.
DCTCUST	""	Current custom dictionary file name and path.
DCTMAIN	(varies by country)	Main dictionary file name.
DEFLPLSTYLE	""	Default plot style for new layers.
DEFPLSTYLE	"BYLAYER"	Default plot style for new objects.
DELOBJ	1	Controls deletion of objects used to create other objects.
DEMANDLOAD	3	Specifies if and when AutoCAD demand loads a third-party application (if the drawing contains custom objects created in that application).
DRAGMODE	2	Controls display of object dragging.
DRAGP1	10	Sets regen-drag input sampling rate.
DRAGP2	25	Sets fast-drag input sampling rate.
DWGCHECK	0	Indicates whether a drawing was last edited using an application other than AutoCAD.
FILEDIA	1	Enables or disables file dialog boxes.
FONTALT	"simplex.shx"	Font file to be used when specified file is not found.
FONTMAP	"acad.fmp"	Font mapping file to be used.
GRIPBLOCK	0	Controls the assignment of grips within block objects.
GRIPCOLOR	5	Color of nonselected grips.
GRIPHOT	1	Color of selected grips.
GRIPS	1	Toggles availability of grip editing modes.
GRIPSIZE	3	Size of grip box in pixels.
IMAGEHLT	0	Controls the highlighting level for raster images.
INETLOCATION	"www.autodesk.com/ acaduser"	Internet location used by **BROWSER**.
INSUNITSDEFSOURCE	0	Drawing units specified for source content that is inserted into the current drawing.
INSUNITSDEFTARGET	0	Drawing units to be used in the current drawing when inserting content.
ISAVEBAK	1	Controls creation of a BAK file when saving.
ISAVEPERCENT	50	Determines amount of wasted space allowed in a drawing.
LAYOUTREGENCTL	3	Specifies how the display list is updated for model and layout tabs
LISPINIT	1	Controls preservation of AutoLISP functions from one drawing to another.
LOGFILEMODE	0	Specifies whether text window contents are written to a log file.
LOGFILEPATH	"C:\Acad2000\acad.log"	Path used for the log files created for all drawings in a single session.
LWDEFAULT	25	Default lineweight value assigned to objects.
LWUNITS	1	Drawing units used for displayed lineweights.
MAXSORT	200	Maximum number of symbol or block names sorted by listing commands.

Variable Name	Default Value	Description
MBUTTONPAN	1	Support level for the third button or wheel on a pointing device.
MEASUREINIT	0	Sets initial drawing units as English or metric
MENUCTL	1	Toggles screen menu switching in response to commands.
MTEXTED	"INTERNAL"	Name of text editor for editing **MTEXT** objects.
OFFSETGAPTYPE	0	Specifies how polylines are offset when a gap is created by the offset value.
OLEHIDE	0	Controls the display of OLE objects in AutoCAD.
OLEQUALITY	1	Default quality level for embedded OLE objects.
OSMODE	0	Current object snap mode bit value.
OSNAPCOORD	2	Controls whether typed coordinates override object snap settings.
PAPERUPDATE	0	Controls display of a warning during plotting when the specified paper size differs from the default used by the plotter.
PICKADD	1	Toggles additive selection of objects.
PICKAUTO	1	Toggles automatic windowing during selection process.
PICKBOX	3	Object selection pick box height in pixels.
PICKDRAG	0	Controls the selection window drawing method.
PICKFIRST	1	Controls the object selection and command entry sequence.
PICKSTYLE	1	Controls group and associative hatch selection.
PLINETYPE	2	Specifies whether AutoCAD uses optimized polylines.
PLOTROTMODE	1	Controls the orientation of plots.
PLQUIET	0	Controls display of plot-related dialog boxes and nonfatal errors resulting from batch plotting and scripts.
POLARADDANG	""	Stores user-defined polar angles
POLARANG	90	Specifies the polar tracking angl
POLARDIST	0.0000	Snap increment use
POLARMODE	1	Specifies control settings for polar tracking.
PROJMODE	1	Controls the projection mode for **TR**
PROXYNOTICE	1	Controls display of a notice when a pro
PROXYSHOW	1	Controls displa
PROXYWEBSEARCH	1	Specifies how AutoCAD checks
PSPROLOG	""	Name for prolog section read from ac
PSQUALITY	75	Controls rendering quality and fill on
PSTYLEPOLICY	1	Controls the association between the c object and its plot style.
RASTERPREVIEW	1	Toggles saving of drawin
REMEMBERFOLDERS	1	Sets default path for **Look in** list in sta dialog box
RTDISPLAY	1	Controls the display of raster objec zooming or panning.
SAVEFILE	⌒	Current automa
SAVEFILEPATH	"C:\TEMP\"	Folder path used for all automatic save drawing session.
SAVETIME	120	Automatic save in
SDI	0	Enables or disables the Multiple D (MDE).
SHORTCUTMENU	11	Controls the availability of shortcut m **Edit**, and **Command** modes.

Variable Name	Default Value	Description
SNAPTYPE	0	Snap style defined for the current viewport.
STARTUPTODAY	1	Determines whether **AutoCAD Today** window or **Startup** dialog box is enabled
TEXTFILL	1	Controls fill for TrueType fonts.
TOOLTIPS	1	Toggles display of toolbar tooltips.
TRACKPATH	0	Controls the display of AutoTracking alignment paths.
TREEMAX	10000000	Limits maximum number of nodes in spatial index tree.
TRIMMODE	1	Controls object trimming for **FILLET** and **CHAMFER**.
UCSAXISANG	90	The default angle used when a UCS is rotated around one of its axes.
UCSORTHO	1	Specifies whether the related orthographic UCS setting is restored when restoring an orthographic view.
UCSVIEW	1	Specifies whether the current UCS is saved when a named view is created.
WHIPARC	0	Controls the smoothness of circles and arcs.
WHIPTHREAD	3	Determines which operations use multithread processing
XFADECTL	50	Controls the fading level for nonselected objects during reference editing.
XLOADCTL	1	Controls xref demand loading.
XLOADPATH	""	Path for storage of temporary copies of demand-loaded xref files.
XREFCTL	0	Controls creation of external reference log (XLG) files.
ZOOMFACTOR	10	Controls the incremental change that occurs when zooming backward or forward with the IntelliMouse wheel.

The following listing shows the AutoCAD system variables that are not saved when different values are assigned. These variables revert to default values when you open an existing drawing or start a new one. Many of these variables are read-only, and reference information specific to the drawing or operating system. Other variables that are not saved are used to change standard features of AutoCAD, and are restored to default values in subsequent editing sessions to avoid unexpected results in common drafting procedures. Many of the variables listed here are commonly referenced or set when customizing. The symbol (ᘓᨆ) indicates the variable is read-only.

VARIABLES NOT SAVED

Variable Name	Default Value	Description
ACADPREFIX	ᘓᨆ	Current support directory search path.
ACADVER	ᘓᨆ	Current AutoCAD version number, including patch level.
ACISOUTVER	40	Controls version of files created using the **ACISOUT** command.
AFLAGS	0	Current attribute flags settings.
AREA	ᘓᨆ	The last area calculated by **AREA**, **LIST**, or **DBLIST**.
BINDTYPE	0	Controls naming of xrefs when they are bound or edited in place.
CDATE	ᘓᨆ	Current date and time, presented as a real number.
CHAMMODE	0	Current chamfer method.
CIRCLERAD	0.0000	Default circle radius value.

Variable Name	Default Value	Description
CMDACTIVE	⌁	Indicates what type of command is active.
CMDECHO	1	Controls echo of prompts and commands during the AutoLISP (command) function.
CMDNAMES	⌁	Name of the currently active command(s).
COMPASS	0	Controls visibility of 3D compass in current viewport.
DATE	⌁	Current Julian date, with the time represented as a fraction in a real number.
DBMOD	⌁	Drawing modification status.
DIASTAT	⌁	Exit method of the last dialog box session.
DISTANCE	⌁	Last distance calculated by **DIST**.
DONUTID	0.5000	Default inside diameter for donuts.
DONUTOD	1.0000	Default outside diameter for donuts.
DWGNAME	⌁	Name of current drawing.
DWGPREFIX	⌁	Directory path for current drawing.
DWGTITLED	⌁	Indicates if current drawing has been named.
EDGEMODE	0	Cutting and boundary edge determination method for **TRIM** and **EXTEND**.
EXPERT	0	Suppression level of warnings and double-check prompts.
EXPLMODE	1	**EXPLODE** support for nonuniformly scaled blocks.
FACETRATIO	0	Specifies the faceting aspect ratio for cylindrical and conic ACIS solids.
FULLOPEN	⌁	Specifies if the current drawing is partially open.
HIDEPRECISION	0	Controls the precision of hiding and shading operations.
HIGHLIGHT	1	Toggles highlighting of selected objects.
HPANG	0	Current default hatch pattern angle.
HPBOUND	1	Object type created by **BHATCH** and **BOUNDARY**.
HPDOUBLE	0	Toggles double hatching for user-defined patterns.
HPNAME	"ANSI31"	Current default hatch pattern name.
HPSCALE	1.0000	Current default hatch pattern scale.
HPSPACE	1.0000	Current hatch pattern line spacing for user-defined patterns.
INSNAME	""	Default block name for **INSERT**.
LASTANGLE	⌁	Last arc angle entered or drawn.
LASTPOINT	0.0000, 0.0000, 0.0000	Last entered UCS coordinates for current space.
LASTPROMPT	⌁	The last text displayed at the command line, including user input.
LOCALE	⌁	ISO language code for the current running version of AutoCAD.
LOGINNAME	⌁	Currently configured user name.
MAXOBJMEM	0	Specifies virtual memory parameters.
MENUECHO	0	Controls level of menu echo.
MENUNAME	⌁	Currently loaded menu file name and path.
MODEMACRO	""	Displays a text string or text written in DIESEL on the status line.
NOMUTT	0	Controls the suppression of messages that are normally displayed.
OFFSETDIST	1.0000	Default offset distance value.
PERIMETER	⌁	Last perimeter value calculated by **AREA**, **LIST**, or **DBLIST**.
PFACEVMAX	⌁	Maximum number of vertices per face.
PLATFORM	⌁	Current operating system.

Variable Name	Default Value	Description
POLYSIDES	4	Default number of sides for **POLYGON**.
POPUPS	∽	Support level of display driver for pull-down menus.
PRODUCT	"AutoCAD"	Returns name of product
PROGRAM	"acad"	Returns name of program
PSVPSCALE	0	View scale factor used for new viewports.
REFEDITNAME	∽	Indicates whether reference editing is active and specifies the reference file name.
RE-INIT	0	Reinitializes the digitizer, digitizer port, and acad.pgp file.
SAVENAME	∽	Default drawing file save name.
SCREENBOXES	∽	Number of available boxes in the screen menu area.
SCREENMODE	∽	Current graphics/text state of the AutoCAD display.
SCREENSIZE	∽	Current viewport size in pixels.
SHPNAME	""	Default shape file name.
SOLIDCHECK	1	Enables or disables solid validation for the current drawing session.
SYSCODEPAGE	∽	System code page specified in acad.xmf.
TABMODE	0	Enables or disables tablet mode.
TEMPPREFIX	∽	Directory name for placement of temporary files.
TEXTEVAL	0	Controls evaluation method for text strings.
TEXTQLTY	50	Resolution of text outlines for TrueType fonts.
TSPACEFAC	1	Controls the line spacing distance for multiline text as a factor of the text height.
TSPACETYPE	1	Specifies the line spacing used for multiline text.
UNDOCTL	∽	Current status of the **UNDO** command.
UNDOMARKS	∽	The number of **UNDO** marks that have been placed.
WMFBKGND	1	Controls the transparency of the background display of AutoCAD objects when they are output to a Windows metafile, copied to the Clipboard, or dragged and dropped into other applications.
WMFFOREGND	0	May modify the color of objects exported as Windows metafiles or copied to the Clipboard
WORLDUCS	∽	Specifies whether the current UCS is the same as the WCS.
WRITESTAT	∽	Controls the read-only or write status of a drawing.

Drawing Sheet Sizes, Settings, and Scale Parameters

Prototype Drawing Sheet Parameters			
Drawing Scale	D-size (34″ × 22″) Drawing Limits	C-size (22″ × 17″) Drawing Limits	B-size (17″ × 11″) Drawing Limits
1″ = 1″	34,22	22,17	17,11
1/2″ = 1″	68,44	44,34	34,22
1/4″ = 1″	136,88	88,68	68,44
1/8″ = 1″	272,176	176,136	136,88
1″ = 1′-0″	408,264	264,204	204,132
3/4″ = 1′-0″	544,352	352,272	272,176
1/2″ = 1′-0″	816,528	528,408	408,264
3/8″ = 1′-0″	1088,704	704,544	544,352
1/4″ = 1′-0″	1632,1056	1056,816	816,528
3/16″ = 1′-0″	2176,1408	1408,1088	1088,704
1/8″ = 1′-0″	3264,2112	2112,1632	1632,1056
3/32″ = 1′-0″	4352,2816	2816,2176	2176,1408
1/16″ = 1′-0″	6528,4224	4224,3264	3264,2112

Prototype Drawing Scale Parameters			
Drawing Scale	Dimension Scale (DIMSCALE)	Linetype Scale (LTSCALE)	Inversion Scale of Border & Parts List Blocks
1″ = 1″	1	.5	1 = 1
1/2″ = 1″	2	1	1 = 2
1/4″ = 1″	4	2	1 = 4
1/8″ = 1″	8	4	1 = 8
1″ = 1′-0″	12	6	1 = 12
3/4″ = 1′-0″	16	8	1 = 16
1/2″ = 1′-0″	24	12	1 = 24
3/8″ = 1′-0″	32	16	1 = 32
1/4″ = 1′-0″	48	24	1 = 48
3/16″ = 1′-0″	64	32	1 = 64
1/8″ = 1′-0″	96	48	1 = 96
3/32″ = 1′-0″	128	64	1 = 128
1/16″ = 1′-0″	192	96	1 = 192

Architectural Sheet Size and Settings

Paper size (in)	Approx. drawing area	Scale	Actual sheet limits	Approx. drawing limits	Text height 1/8"	Text height 1/4"	Scale factor	Ltscale
A 12 × 9	10 × 7.5	1″ = 1′–0″ 1/2″ = 1′–0″ 1/4″ = 1′–0″ 1/8″ = 1′–0″	12′ × 9′ 24′ × 18′ 48′ × 36′ 96′ × 72′	10′ × 7.5′ 20′ × 15′ 40′ × 30′ 80′ × 60′	1.5 3.0 6.0 12.0	3.0 6.0 12.0 24.0	12 24 48 96	6 12 24 48
B 18 × 12	16 × 11	1″ = 1′–0″ 1/2″ = 1′–0″ 1/4″ = 1′–0″ 1/8″ = 1′–0″	18′ × 12′ 36′ × 24′ 72′ × 48′ 144′ × 96′	16′ × 11′ 32′ × 20′ 64′ × 40′ 128′ × 80′				
C 24 × 18	22 × 16	1″ = 1′–0″ 1/2″ = 1′–0″ 1/4″ = 1′–0″ 1/8″ = 1′–0″	24′ × 18′ 48′ × 36′ 96′ × 72′ 192′ × 144′	22′ × 16′ 44′ × 32′ 88′ × 64′ 176′ × 28′				
D 36 × 24	34 × 22	1″ = 1′–0″ 1/2″ = 1′–0″ 1/4″ = 1′–0″ 1/8″ = 1′–0″	36′ × 24′ 72′ × 48′ 144′ × 96′ 288′ × 192′	34′ × 22′ 68′ × 44′ 136′ × 88′ 272′ × 176′				
E 48 × 36	46 × 34	1″ = 1′–0″ 1/2″ = 1′–0″ 1/4″ = 1′–0″ 1/8″ = 1′–0″	48′ × 36′ 96′ × 72′ 192′ × 144′ 384′ × 288′	46′ × 34′ 92′ × 68′ 184′ × 136′ 368′ × 272′				

Mechanical Sheet Size and Settings

Paper size (in)	Approx. drawing area	Scale	Actual sheet limits	Approx. drawing limits	Text height 1/8"	Text height 1/4"	Scale factor	Ltscale
A 11 × 8.5	9 × 7	2″ = 1″ 3/4″ = 1″ 1/2″ = 1″ 1/4″ = 1″	5.5 × 4.25 14.67 × 11.33 22 × 17 44 × 34	4.5″ × 3.5″ 12″ × 9.33″ 18″ × 14″ 36″ × 28″	.0625 .167 .25 .5	.125 .33 .5 1.0	.5 1.33 2 4	.25 .67 1 2
B 17 × 11	15 × 10	2″ = 1″ 3/4″ = 1″ 1/2″ = 1″ 1/4″ = 1″	8.5 × 5.5 22.67 × 14.67 34 × 22 68 × 44	7.5″ × 5″ 20″ × 13.33″ 30″ × 20″ 60″ × 40″				
C 22 × 17	20 × 15	2″ = 1″ 3/4″ = 1″ 1/2″ = 1″ 1/4″ = 1″	11 × 8.5 29.33 × 14.67 44 × 34 88 × 68	10″ × 7.5″ 26.67″ × 20″ 40″ × 30″ 80″ × 60″				
D 34 × 22	32 × 20	2″ = 1″ 3/4″ = 1″ 1/2″ = 1″ 1/4″ = 1″	17 × 11 45.33 × 29.33 68 × 44 136 × 88	16″ × 10″ 42.67″ × 26.67″ 64″ × 40″ 128″ × 80″				
E 44 × 34	42 × 32	2″ = 1″ 3/4″ = 1″ 1/2″ = 1″ 1/4″ = 1″	22 × 17 58.67 × 45.33 88 × 68 176 × 136	21″ × 16″ 56″ × 42.67″ 84″ × 64″ 168″ × 128″				

Civil Sheet Size and Settings								
Paper size (in)	Approx. drawing area	Scale	Actual sheet limits	Approx. drawing limits	Text height		Scale factor	Ltscale
					1/8"	1/4"		
A 11 × 8.5	9 × 7	1" = 10' 1" = 20' 1" = 30' 1" = 50'	110' × 85' 220' × 170' 330' × 255' 550' × 425'	90' × 70' 180' × 140' 270' × 210' 450' × 350'	15 30 45 75	30 60 90 150	120 240 360 600	60 120 180 300
B 17 × 11	15 × 10	1" = 10' 1" = 20' 1" = 30' 1" = 50'	170' × 110' 340' × 220' 510' × 330' 850' × 550'	150' × 100' 300' × 200' 450' × 300' 750' × 500'				
C 22 × 17	20 × 15	1" = 10' 1" = 20' 1" = 30' 1" = 50'	220' × 170' 440' × 340' 660' × 510' 1100' × 850'	200' × 150' 400' × 300' 600' × 450' 1000' × 750'				
D 34 × 22	32 × 20	1" = 10' 1" = 20' 1" = 30' 1" = 50'	340' × 220' 680' × 440' 1020' × 660' 1700' × 1100'	320' × 200' 640' × 400' 960' × 600' 1600' × 1000'				
E 44 × 34	42 × 32	1" = 10' 1" = 20' 1" = 30' 1" = 50'	440' × 340' 880' × 680' 1320' × 1020' 2200' × 1700'	420' × 320' 840' × 640' 1260' × 960' 2100' × 1600'				

Metric Sheet Size and Settings								
Paper size (mm)	Approx. drawing area	Scale	Actual paper limits (mm)	Approx. drawing limits (mm)	Text height		Scale factor	Ltscale
					1/8″	1/4″		
A4 297 × 210	277 × 190	1 = 2	594 × 420	554 × 380	.25	.5	50.8	1
		1 = 5	1485 × 1050	1385 × 950	.625	1.25	127	2
		1 = 10	2970 × 2100	2770 × 1900	1.25	2.5	254	5
		1 = 20	5940 × 4200	5540 × 3800	2.5	5	508	10
		1 = 50	14850 × 10500	13850 × 9500	6.25	12.5	1270	25
		1 = 100	29700 × 21000	27700 × 19000	12.5	25	2540	50
A3 420 × 297	400 × 277	1 = 2	820 × 594	780 × 554				
		1 = 5	2100 × 1485	2000 × 1385				
		1 = 10	4200 × 2970	4000 × 2770				
		1 = 20	8400 × 5940	8000 × 5540				
		1 = 50	21000 × 14850	20000 × 13850				
		1 = 100	42000 × 29700	40000 × 27700				
A2 594 × 420	577 × 400	1 = 2	1188 × 840	1148 × 800				
		1 = 5	2970 × 2100	2870 × 2000				
		1 = 10	5940 × 4200	5740 × 4000				
		1 = 20	11880 × 8400	11480 × 8000				
		1 = 50	29700 × 21000	28700 × 20000				
		1 = 100	59400 × 42000	57400 × 40000				
A1 841 × 594	801 × 554	1 = 2	1682 × 1188	1642 × 1148				
		1 = 5	4205 × 2970	4105 × 2870				
		1 = 10	8410 × 5940	8210 × 5740				
		1 = 20	16820 × 11880	16420 × 11480				
		1 = 50	42050 × 29700	41050 × 28700				
		1 = 100	84100 × 59400	82100 × 57400				
A0 1189 × 841	1149 × 801	1 = 2	2378 × 1682	2338 × 1642				
		1 = 5	5945 × 4205	5845 × 4105				
		1 = 10	11890 × 8410	11690 × 8210				
		1 = 20	23780 × 16820	23380 × 16420				
		1 = 50	59450 × 42050	58450 × 41050				
		1 = 100	118900 × 84100	116900 × 82100				

Command Aliases

Command	Alias	Command	Alias
3DARRAY	3A	DIMSTYLE	D,DST
3DFACE	3F	DIST	DI
3DORBIT	3DO, ORBIT	DIVIDE	DIV
3DPOLY	3P	DONUT	DO
ADCENTER	ADC	DRAWORDER	DR
ALIGN	AL	DSETTINGS	DS, SE
APPLOAD	AP	DTEXT	DT
ARC	A	DVIEW	DV
AREA	AA	ELLIPSE	EL
ARRAY	AR	ERASE	E
ATTDEF	ATT	EXPLODE	X
-ATTDEF	-ATT	EXPORT	EXP
ATTEDIT	ATE	EXTEND	EX
-ATTEDIT	-ATE, ATTE	EXTRUDE	EXT
BHATCH	BH, H	FILLET	F
BLOCK	B	FILTER	FI
-BLOCK	-B	GROUP	G
BOUNDARY	BO	-GROUP	-G
-BOUNDARY	-BO	HATCH	-H
BREAK	BR	HATCHEDIT	HE
CHAMFER	CHA	HIDE	HI
CHANGE	-CH	IMAGE	IM
CIRCLE	C	-IMAGE	-IM
COLOR	COL	IMAGEADJUST	IAD
COLOR	COLOUR	IMAGEATTACH	IAT
COPY	CO	IMAGECLIP	ICL
DBCONNECT	DBC	IMPORT	IMP
DDEDIT	ED	INSERT	I
DDGRIPS	GR	-INSERT	-I
DDRMODES	RM	INSERTOBJ	IO
DDUCS	UC	INTERFERE	INF
DDUCSP	UCP	INTERSECT	IN
DDVPOINT	VP	LAYER	LA
DIMALIGNED	DAL	-LAYER	-LA
DIMANGULAR	DAN	-LAYOUT	LO
DIMBASELINE	DBA	LENGTHEN	LEN
DIMCENTER	DCE	LINE	L
DIMCONTINUE	DCO	LINETYPE	LT, LTYPE
DIMDIAMETER	DDI	-LINETYPE	-LT, -LTYPE
DIMEDIT	DED	LIST	LI, LS
DIMLINEAR	DLI	LTSCALE	LTS
DIMORDINATE	DOR	LWEIGHT	LINEWEIGHT, LW
DIMOVERRIDE	DOV	MATCHPROP	MA
DIMRADIUS	DRA	MEASURE	ME

(Continued on next page)

(Continued from previous page)

Command	Alias
MIRROR	MI
MLINE	ML
MOVE	M
MSPACE	MS
MTEXT	MT, T
-MTEXT	-T
MVIEW	MV
OFFSET	O
OPTIONS	OP, PR
OSNAP	OS
-OSNAP	-OS
PAN	P
-PAN	-P
-PARTIALOPEN	PARTIALOPEN
PASTESPEC	PA
PEDIT	PE
PLINE	PL
PLOT	PRINT
POINT	PO
POLYGON	POL
PREVIEW	PRE
PROPERTIES	CH, MO, PROPS
PROPERTIESCLOSE	PRCLOSE
PSPACE	PS
PURGE	PU
QLEADER	LE
QUIT	EXIT
RECTANGLE	REC
REDRAW	R
REDRAWALL	RA
REGEN	RE
REGENALL	REA
REGION	REG
RENAME	REN
-RENAME	-REN
RENDER	RR
REVOLVE	REV
ROTATE	RO
RPREF	RPR

Command	Alias
SCALE	SC
SCRIPT	SCR
SECTION	SEC
SETVAR	SET
SHADE	SHA
SLICE	SL
SNAP	SN
SOLID	SO
SPELL	SP
SPLINE	SPL
SPLINEDIT	SPE
STRETCH	S
STYLE	ST
SUBTRACT	SU
TABLET	TA
THICKNESS	TH
TILEMODE	TI
TOLERANCE	TOL
TOOLBAR	TO
TORUS	TOR
TRIM	TR
UNION	UNI
UNITS	UN
-UNITS	-UN
VIEW	V
-VIEW	-V
VPOINT	-VP
WBLOCK	W
-WBLOCK	-W
WEDGE	WE
XATTACH	XA
XBIND	XB
-XBIND	-XB
XCLIP	XC
XLINE	XL
XREF	XR
-XREF	-XR
ZOOM	Z

Appendix J
Drafting Standards and Related Documents

The following is a list of ANSI/ASME drafting standards or related documents. They are ANSI/ASME adopted, unless another standard developing organization, such as ANSI/NFPA, is indicated. The ANSI/ASME standards are available by contacting:

The American National Standards Institute
11 West 42nd Street
New York, NY 10036
or
The American Society of Mechanical Engineers
345 East 47th Street
New York, NY 10017

Abbreviations
Y1.1-1989, *Abbreviations for Use on Drawings and in Text*

Charts and graphs (Y15)
Y15.1M-1979 (R1993), *Illustrations for Publication and Projection*
Y15.2M-1979 (R1986), *Time-Series Charts*
Y15.3M-1979 (R1986), *Process Charts*

Dimensions
B4.1-1967 (R1994), *Preferred Limits and Fits for Cylindrical Parts*
B4.2-1978 (R1994), *Preferred Metric Limits and Fits*
B4.3-1978 (R1994), *General Tolerances for Metric Dimensioned Products*
B4.4M-1981 (R1994), *Inspection of Workpieces*
B32.1-1952 (R1994), *Preferred Thickness for Uncoated, Thin, Flat Metals (Under 0.250/in.)*
B32.2-1969 (R1994), *Preferred Diameters for Round Wire-0.500 Inches and Under*
B32.3M-1984 (R1994), *Preferred Metric Sizes for Flat Metal Products*
B32.4M-1980 (R1994), *Preferred Metric Sizes for Round, Square, Rectangle, and Hexagon Metal Products*

B32.5-1977 (R1994), *Preferred Metric Sizes for Tubular Metal Products Other Than Pipe*
B32.6M-1984 (R1994), *Preferred Metric Equivalents of Inch Sizes for Tubular Metal Products Other Than Pipe*
B36.10M-1996, *Welded and Seamless Wrought Steel Pipe*
B36.19M-1985 (R1994), *Stainless Steel Pipe*

Drafting standards
Y14.1-1995, *Decimal Inch Drawing Sheet Size and Format*
Y14.1M-1995, *Metric Drawing Sheet Size and Format*
Y14.2M-1992, *Line Conventions and Lettering*
Y14.3M-1994, *Multiview and Sectional View Drawings*
Y14.4M-1989 (R1994), *Pictorial Drawings*
Y14.5M-1994, *Dimensioning and Tolerancing*
Y14.5.1-1994, *Mathematical Definition of Y14.5*
Y14.5.2, *Certification of GD&T Professionals*
Y14.6-1978 (R1993), *Screw Thread Representation*

Y14.6aM-1981 (R1993), *Screw Thread Representation (Metric Supplement)*
Y14.7.1-1971 (R1993), *Gear Drawing Standards-Part 1-Spur, Helical, Double Helical, and Rack*
Y14.7.2-1978 (R1994), *Gear and Spline Drawing Standards-Part 2-Bevel and Hypoid Gears*
Y14.8M-1996, *Castings and Forgings*
Y14.13M-1981 (R1992), *Mechanical Spring Representation*
Y14.18M-1986, *Optical Parts*
Y14.24M-1989 (R1996), *Types and Applications of Engineering Drawings*
Y14.32.1M-1994, *Chassis Frames Passenger Car and Light Truck—Ground Vehicle Practices*
Y14.34M-1996 (R1993), *Parts Lists, Data Lists, and Index Lists*
Y14.35M-1992, *Revision of Engineering Drawings and Associated Documents*
Y14.36M-1996, *Surface Texture Symbols*

Graphic symbols

Y32.2-1975, *Electrical and Electronic Diagrams*
Y32.2.3-1949 (R1994), *Pipe Fittings, Valves, and Piping*
Y32.2.4-1949 (R1993), *Heating, Ventilating, and Air Conditioning*
Y32.2.6-1950 (R1993), *Heat/Power Apparatus*
Y32.4-1977 (R1994), *Plumbing Fixture Diagrams Used in Architectural and Building Construction*
Y32.7-1972 (R1994), *Railroad Maps and Profiles*
Y32.9-1972 (R1989), *Electrical Wiring and Layout Diagrams Used in Architecture and Building*
Y32.10-1967 (R1994), *Fluid Power Diagrams*
Y32.11-1961 (R1993), *Process Flow Diagrams in the Petroleum and Chemical Industries*
Y32.18-1972 (R1993), *Mechanical and Acoustical Elements as Used in Schematic Diagrams*

ANSI/AWS A2.4-91, *Symbols for Welding, Brazing, and Nondestructive Examination*
ANSI/IEEE 200-1975 (R1989), *Reference Designations for Electrical and Electronics Parts and Equipment*
ANSI/IEEE 315-1975 (R1989), *Electrical and Electronics Diagrams (Including Reference Designation Class Designation Letters)*
ANSI/IEEE 623-1976 (R1989), *Grid and Mapping Used in Cable Television Systems*
ANSI/ISA S5.1-1984 (R1992), *Instrumentation Symbols and Identification*
ANSI/NFPA 170-1991, *Public Fire Safety Symbols*

Letter symbols

Y10.1-1972 (R1988), *Glossary of Terms Concerning Letter Symbols*
Y10.3M-1984, *Mechanics and Time-Related Phenomena*
Y10.4-1982 (R1988), *Heat and Thermodynamics*
Y10.11-1984, *Acoustics*
Y10.12-1955 (R1988), *Chemical Engineering*
Y10.17-1961 (R1988), *Greek Letters Used as Letter Symbols for Engineering Math*
Y10.18-1967 (R1977), *Illuminating Engineering*
ANSI/IEEE 260-1978 (R1992), *SI Units and Certain Other Units of Measurement*

Metric system

SI-1, *Orientation and Guide for use of SI (Metric) Units*
SI-2, *SI Units in Strength of Materials*
SI-3, *SI Units in Dynamics*
SI-4, *SI Units in Thermodynamics*
SI-5, *SI Units in Fluid Mechanics*
SI-6, *SI Units in Kinematics*
SI-7, *SI Units in Heat Transfer*
SI-8, *SI Units in Vibration*
SI-9, *Metrification of Codes and Standards SI (Metric) Units*
SI-10, *Steam Charts, SI (Metric) and U.S. Customary Units*

Some of these standards are, and may in the future be, under review. Information in this appendix is subject to change. Some standards may be out of print. Out of print codes and standards are available from *Global Engineering Documents* (800) 645-7732, and *Document Engineering Co.* (800) 645-7732.

Drafting Symbols

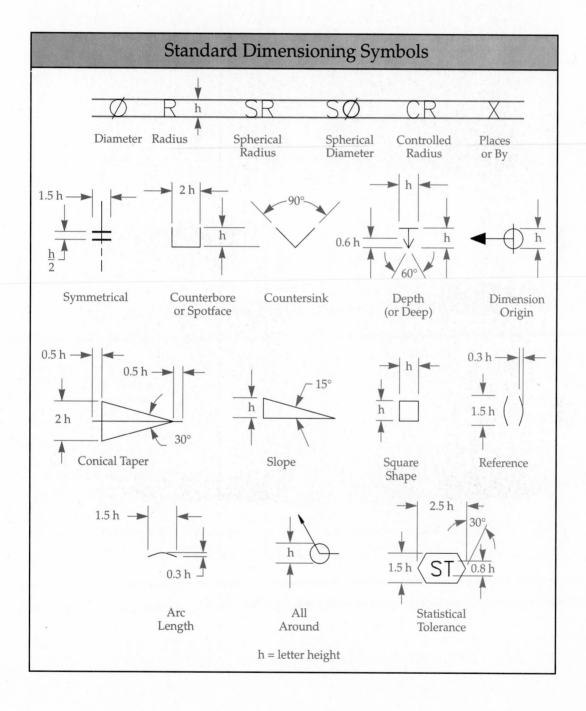

Standard Dimensioning Symbols

Ø R h SR SØ CR X

Diameter Radius Spherical Radius Spherical Diameter Controlled Radius Places or By

Symmetrical — 1.5 h, h/2

Counterbore or Spotface — 2 h, h

Countersink — 90°

Depth (or Deep) — h, 0.6 h, 60°

Dimension Origin — h

Conical Taper — 0.5 h, 0.5 h, 2 h, 30°

Slope — 15°, h

Square Shape — h, h

Reference — 0.3 h, 1.5 h, ( )

Arc Length — 1.5 h, 0.3 h

All Around — h

Statistical Tolerance — 2.5 h, 30°, 1.5 h, 0.8 h, ST

h = letter height

Geometric Dimensioning and Tolerancing Symbols

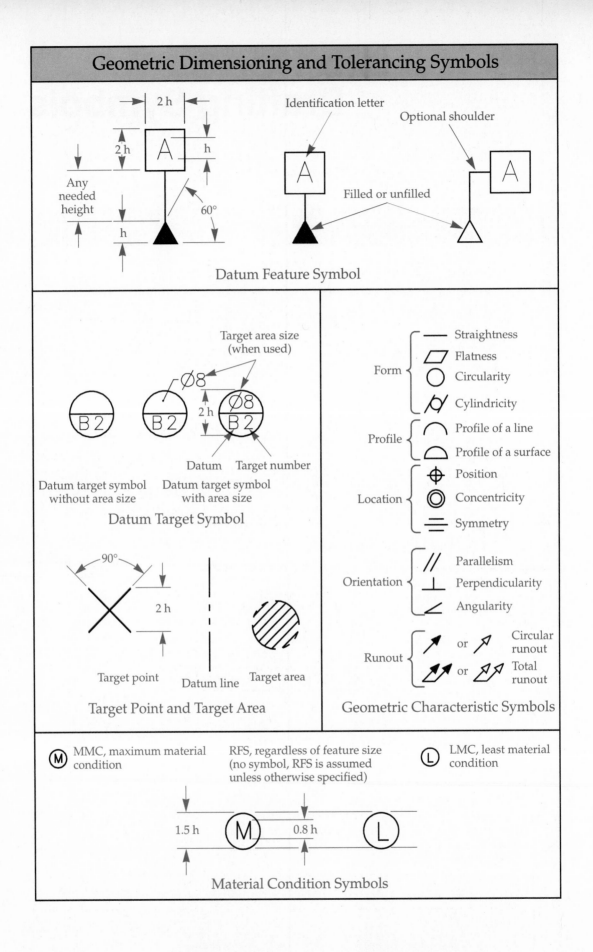

Datum Feature Symbol

Identification letter

Optional shoulder

Filled or unfilled

2 h

2 h

h

Any needed height

h

60°

Target area size (when used)

Ø8

2 h

Ø8

Datum   Target number

Datum target symbol without area size

Datum target symbol with area size

Datum Target Symbol

90°

2 h

Target point

Datum line

Target area

Target Point and Target Area

Straightness

Flatness

Circularity

Cylindricity

Form

Profile of a line

Profile of a surface

Profile

Position

Concentricity

Symmetry

Location

Parallelism

Perpendicularity

Angularity

Orientation

Circular runout

Total runout

Runout   or   or

Geometric Characteristic Symbols

Ⓜ MMC, maximum material condition

RFS, regardless of feature size (no symbol, RFS is assumed unless otherwise specified)

Ⓛ LMC, least material condition

1.5 h   Ⓜ   0.8 h   Ⓛ

Material Condition Symbols

Geometric Dimensioning and Tolerancing Symbols

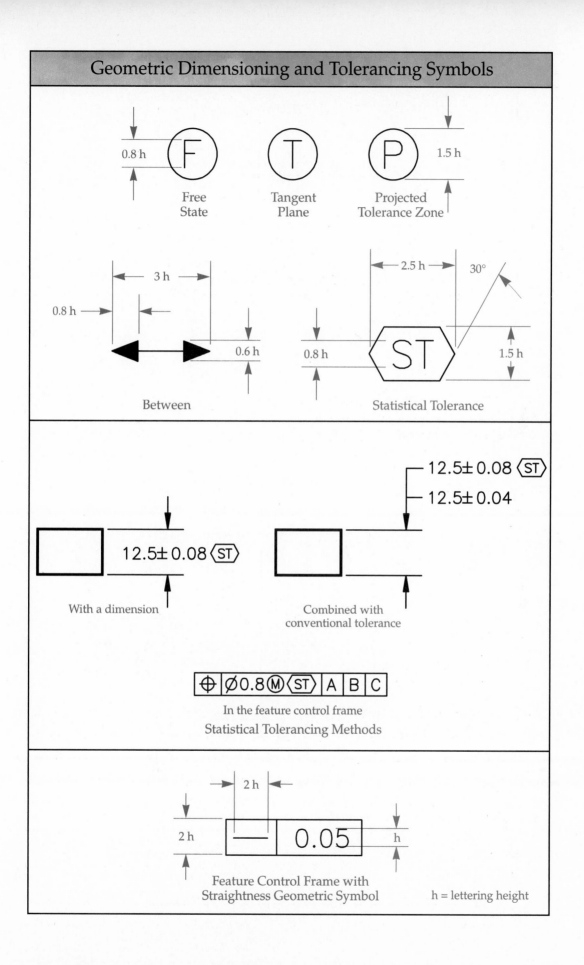

Free State

Tangent Plane

Projected Tolerance Zone

0.8 h

1.5 h

3 h

0.8 h

0.6 h

Between

2.5 h

30°

0.8 h

ST

1.5 h

Statistical Tolerance

12.5± 0.08 〈ST〉

12.5± 0.04

12.5± 0.08 〈ST〉

With a dimension

Combined with conventional tolerance

⊕ │ Ø0.8Ⓜ〈ST〉│ A │ B │ C

In the feature control frame

Statistical Tolerancing Methods

2 h

2 h

— │ 0.05

h

Feature Control Frame with Straightness Geometric Symbol

h = lettering height

Geometric Dimensioning and Tolerancing Symbols

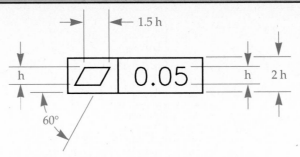

Feature Control Frame with the Flatness
Geometric Characteristic Symbol

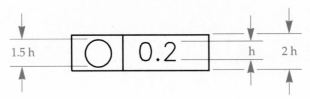

Feature Control Frame with Circularity
Geometric Characteristic Symbol

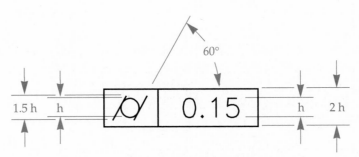

Feature Control Frame with Cylindricity
Geometric Characteristic Symbol

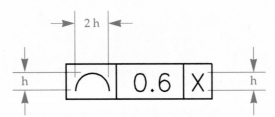

Feature Control Frame with Profile
of a Line Geometric Characteristic
Symbol and a Datum Reference   h = lettering height

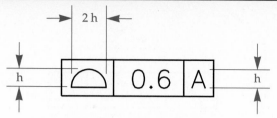

Feature Control Frame with Profile
of a Surface Geometric Characteristic
Symbol and a Datum Reference

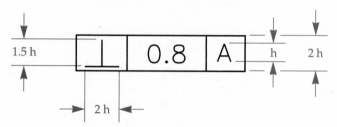

Feature Control Frame with
Parallelism Geometric Characteristic
Symbol and a Datum Reference

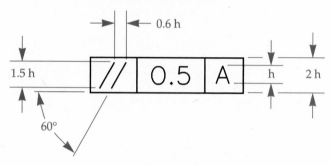

Feature Control Frame with
Perpendicularity Geometric Characteristic
Symbol and a Datum Reference

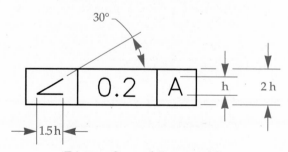

Feature Control Frame with
Angularity Geometric Characteristic
Symbol and a Datum Reference

h = lettering height

Geometric Dimensioning and Tolerancing Symbols

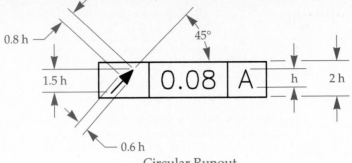

Circular Runout

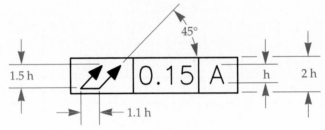

Total Runout

Runout symbols may be drawn open or filled

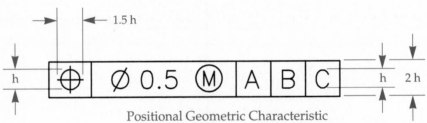

Positional Geometric Characteristic
Symbol and Tolerance in a Feature Control
Frame with Three Datum References

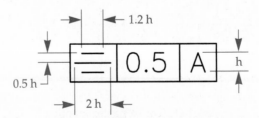

Feature Control Frame with Symmetry
Geometric Characteristic
Symbol and a Datum Reference

h = lettering height

Single Line Piping Symbols

Name	Screwed			Buttwelded		
	Left Side	Front	Right Side	Left Side	Front	Right Side
90° Elbow						
45° Elbow						
Tee						
45° Lateral						
Cross						
Cap						
Concentric Reducer						
Eccentric Reducer						
Union						
Coupling						

Common Symbols for Electrical Diagrams

Amplifier

Antenna, General

Antenna, Dipole

Antenna, Dipole

Antenna, Counterpoise

Battery, Long Line Positive

Multicell Battery

Capacitor, General

Capacitor, Polarized

Circuit Breaker

Ground

Chassis Ground

Connectors, Jack and Plug

Engaged Connectors

Triod with Directly Heated Cathode and Envelope Connection to Base Terminal

Capacitor, Variable

Pentode Using Elongated Envelope

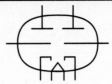

Twin Triode Using Elongated Envelope

Voltage Regulator, also, Glow Lamp

Phototube

Inductor, Winding, Reactor, General

Magnetic Core Inductor

Adjustable Inductor

Balast Lamp

Fluorescent, 2-Terminal Lamp

Incandescent Lamp

Microphone

Receiver, Earphone

Resistor, General

Resistor, Adjustable

Resistor, Variable

Transformer, General

Transformer, Magnetic Core

Shielded Transformer, Magnetic Core

Auto-Transformer, Adjustable

Common Architectural Symbols

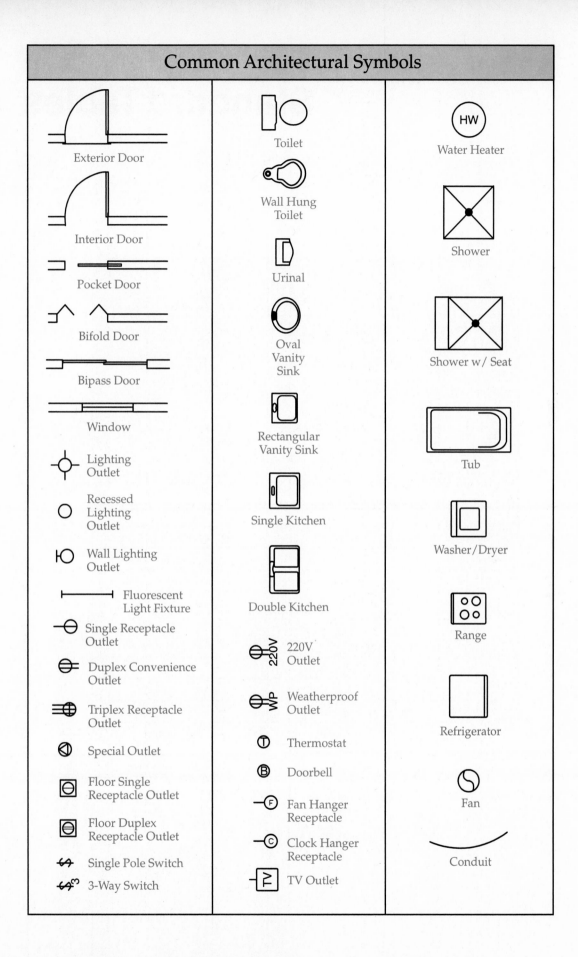

Exterior Door

Interior Door

Pocket Door

Bifold Door

Bipass Door

Window

Lighting Outlet

Recessed Lighting Outlet

Wall Lighting Outlet

Fluorescent Light Fixture

Single Receptacle Outlet

Duplex Convenience Outlet

Triplex Receptacle Outlet

Special Outlet

Floor Single Receptacle Outlet

Floor Duplex Receptacle Outlet

Single Pole Switch

3-Way Switch

Toilet

Wall Hung Toilet

Urinal

Oval Vanity Sink

Rectangular Vanity Sink

Single Kitchen

Double Kitchen

220V Outlet

Weatherproof Outlet

Thermostat

Doorbell

Fan Hanger Receptacle

Clock Hanger Receptacle

TV Outlet

Water Heater

Shower

Shower w/ Seat

Tub

Washer/Dryer

Range

Refrigerator

Fan

Conduit

Solutions to Triangles

$A + B + C = 180°$ $S = \dfrac{a+b+c}{2}$	Right	Oblique	
Have	**Want**	**Formulas for Right**	**Formulas for Oblique**
abc	A	$\tan A = a/b$	$1/2A = \sqrt{(s-b)(s-c)/bc}$
	B	$90° - A$ or $\cos B = a/c$	$\sin 1/2B = \sqrt{(s-a)(s-c)/a \times c}$
	C	$90°$	$\sin 1/2C = \sqrt{(s-a)(s-b)/a \times b}$
	Area	$a \times b/2$	$\sqrt{s \times (s-a)(s-b)(s-c)}$
aAC	B	$90° - A$	$180° - (A + C)$
	b	$a \cot A$	$a \sin B/\sin A$
	c	$a/\sin A$	$a \sin C/\sin A$
	Area	$(a^2 \cot A)/2$	$a^2 \sin B \sin C/2 \sin A$
acC	A	$\sin A = a - c$	$\sin A = a \sin C/c$
	B	$90° - A$ or $\cos B = a/c$	$180° - (A + C)$
	b	$\sqrt{c^2 - a^2}$	$c \sin B/ \sin C$
	Area	$1/2a \sqrt{c^2 - a^2}$	$1/2 ac \sin B$
abC	A	$\tan A = a/b$	$\tan A = a \sin C/b - a \cos C$
	B	$90° - A$ or $\tan B = b/a$	$180° - (A + C)$
	c	$\sqrt{a^2 - b^2}$	$\sqrt{a^2 + b^2 - 2ab \cos C}$
	Area	$a \times b/2$	$1/2ab \sin C$

Rutland Tool and Supply Co., Inc.

Fraction, Decimal, and Metric Equivalents

INCHES		MILLI-METERS	INCHES		MILLI-METERS
FRACTIONS	DECIMALS		FRACTIONS	DECIMALS	
	.00394	.1	$\frac{15}{32}$	.46875	11.9063
	.00787	.2		.47244	12.00
	.01181	.3	$\frac{31}{64}$	.484375	12.3031
$\frac{1}{64}$	.015625	.3969	$\frac{1}{2}$	.5000	12.70
	.01575	.4		.51181	13.00
	.01969	.5	$\frac{33}{64}$	.515625	13.0969
	.02362	.6	$\frac{17}{32}$	.53125	13.4938
	.02756	.7	$\frac{35}{64}$	.546875	13.8907
$\frac{1}{32}$	.03125	.7938		.55118	14.00
	.0315	.8	$\frac{9}{16}$	.5625	14.2875
	.03543	.9	$\frac{37}{64}$	.578125	14.6844
	.03937	1.00		.59055	15.00
$\frac{3}{64}$	.046875	1.1906	$\frac{19}{32}$	.59375	15.0813
$\frac{1}{16}$	.0625	1.5875	$\frac{39}{64}$	.609375	15.4782
$\frac{5}{64}$	.078125	1.9844	$\frac{5}{8}$	.625	15.875
	.07874	2.00		.62992	16.00
$\frac{3}{32}$	.09375	2.3813	$\frac{41}{64}$	.640625	16.2719
$\frac{7}{64}$	.109375	2.7781	$\frac{21}{32}$	.65625	16.6688
	.11811	3.00		.66929	17.00
$\frac{1}{8}$	.125	3.175	$\frac{43}{64}$	.671875	17.0657
$\frac{9}{64}$	.140625	3.5719	$\frac{11}{16}$	.6875	17.4625
$\frac{5}{32}$	.15625	3.9688	$\frac{45}{64}$	.703125	17.8594
	.15748	4.00		.70866	18.00
$\frac{11}{64}$	.171875	4.3656	$\frac{23}{32}$	.71875	18.2563
$\frac{3}{16}$	.1875	4.7625	$\frac{47}{64}$	.734375	18.6532
	.19685	5.00		.74803	19.00
$\frac{13}{64}$	.203125	5.1594	$\frac{3}{4}$	.7500	19.05
$\frac{7}{32}$	.21875	5.5563	$\frac{49}{64}$	.765625	19.4469
$\frac{15}{64}$	.234375	5.9531	$\frac{25}{32}$	.78125	19.8438
	.23622	6.00		.7874	20.00
$\frac{1}{4}$	.2500	6.35	$\frac{51}{64}$	.796875	20.2407
$\frac{17}{64}$	.265625	6.7469	$\frac{13}{16}$	.8125	20.6375
	.27559	7.00		.82677	21.00
$\frac{9}{32}$	.28125	7.1438	$\frac{53}{64}$	.828125	21.0344
$\frac{19}{64}$	.296875	7.5406	$\frac{27}{32}$	.84375	21.4313
$\frac{5}{16}$	.3125	7.9375	$\frac{55}{64}$	.859375	21.8282
	.31496	8.00		.86614	22.00
$\frac{21}{64}$	.328125	8.3344	$\frac{7}{8}$	.875	22.225
$\frac{11}{32}$	.34375	8.7313	$\frac{57}{64}$	.890625	22.6219
	.35433	9.00		.90551	23.00
$\frac{23}{64}$	.359375	9.1281	$\frac{29}{32}$	.90625	23.0188
$\frac{3}{8}$	.375	9.525	$\frac{59}{64}$	.921875	23.4157
$\frac{25}{64}$	.390625	9.9219	$\frac{15}{16}$	.9375	23.8125
	.3937	10.00		.94488	24.00
$\frac{13}{32}$	.40625	10.3188	$\frac{61}{64}$	.953125	24.2094
$\frac{27}{64}$	.421875	10.7156	$\frac{31}{32}$	.96875	24.6063
	.43307	11.00		.98425	25.00
$\frac{7}{16}$	.4375	11.1125	$\frac{63}{64}$	.984375	25.0032
$\frac{29}{64}$	.453125	11.5094	1	1.0000	25.4001

Chord Length—Segments of Circles

Length of arc (l=radians), height of segment (h), length of chord (c), and area of segment (A) for angles from 1 to 180 degrees and radius = 1. For other radii, multiply the values given for distance by the radius, and the values given for the area by r², the square of the radius. The values in the table can be used for U.S. customary or metric units.

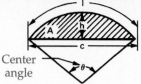

Center angle

Center Angle θ, Degrees	l	h	c	Area of Segment A	Center Angle θ, Degrees	l	h	c	Area of Segment A	Center Angle θ, Degrees	l	h	c	Area of Segment A
1	0.01745	0.00004	0.01745	0.00000	61	1.065	0.1384	1.015	0.09502	121	2.112	0.5076	1.741	0.6273
2	0.03491	0.00015	0.03490	0.00000	62	1.082	0.1428	1.030	0.09958	122	2.129	0.5152	1.749	0.6406
3	0.05236	0.00034	0.05235	0.00001	63	1.100	0.1474	1.045	0.10428	123	2.147	0.5228	1.758	0.6540
4	0.06981	0.00061	0.06980	0.00003	64	1.117	0.1520	1.060	0.10911	124	2.164	0.5305	1.766	0.6676
5	0.08727	0.00095	0.08724	0.00006	65	1.134	0.1566	1.075	0.11408	125	2.182	0.5383	1.774	0.6813
6	0.10472	0.00137	0.10467	0.00010	66	1.152	0.1613	1.089	0.11919	126	2.199	0.5460	1.782	0.6950
7	0.12217	0.00187	0.12210	0.00015	67	1.169	0.1661	1.104	0.12443	127	2.217	0.5538	1.790	0.7090
8	0.13963	0.00244	0.13951	0.00023	68	1.187	0.1710	1.118	0.12982	128	2.234	0.5616	1.798	0.7230
9	0.15708	0.00308	0.15692	0.00032	69	1.204	0.1759	1.133	0.13535	129	2.251	0.5695	1.805	0.7372
10	0.17453	0.00381	0.17431	0.00044	70	1.222	0.1808	1.147	0.14102	130	2.269	0.5774	1.813	0.7514
11	0.19199	0.00460	0.19169	0.00059	71	1.239	0.1859	1.161	0.14683	131	2.286	0.5853	1.820	0.7658
12	0.20944	0.00548	0.20906	0.00076	72	1.257	0.1910	1.176	0.15279	132	2.304	0.5933	1.827	0.7803
13	0.22689	0.00643	0.22641	0.00097	73	1.274	0.1961	1.190	0.15889	133	2.321	0.6013	1.834	0.7950
14	0.24435	0.00745	0.24374	0.00121	74	1.292	0.2014	1.204	0.16514	134	2.339	0.6093	1.841	0.8097
15	0.26180	0.00856	0.26105	0.00149	75	1.309	0.2066	1.218	0.17154	135	2.356	0.6173	1.848	0.8245
16	0.27925	0.00973	0.27835	0.00181	76	1.326	0.2120	1.231	0.17808	136	2.374	0.6254	1.854	0.8395
17	0.29671	0.01098	0.29562	0.00217	77	1.344	0.2174	1.245	0.18477	137	2.391	0.6335	1.861	0.8546
18	0.31416	0.01231	0.31287	0.00257	78	1.361	0.2229	1.259	0.19160	138	2.409	0.6416	1.867	0.8697
19	0.33161	0.01371	0.33010	0.00302	79	1.379	0.2284	1.272	0.19859	139	2.426	0.6498	1.873	0.8850
20	0.34907	0.01519	0.34730	0.00352	80	1.396	0.2340	1.286	0.20573	140	2.443	0.6580	1.879	0.9003
21	0.36652	0.01675	0.36447	0.00408	81	1.414	0.2396	1.299	0.21301	141	2.461	0.6662	1.885	0.9158
22	0.38397	0.01837	0.38162	0.00468	82	1.431	0.2453	1.312	0.22045	142	2.478	0.6744	1.891	0.9314
23	0.40143	0.02008	0.39874	0.00535	83	1.449	0.2510	1.325	0.22804	143	2.496	0.6827	1.897	0.9470
24	0.41888	0.02185	0.41582	0.00607	84	1.466	0.2569	1.338	0.23578	144	2.513	0.6910	1.902	0.9627
25	0.43633	0.02370	0.43288	0.00686	85	1.484	0.2627	1.351	0.24367	145	2.531	0.6993	1.907	0.9786
26	0.45379	0.02563	0.44990	0.00771	86	1.501	0.2686	1.364	0.25171	146	2.548	0.7076	1.913	0.9945
27	0.47124	0.02763	0.46689	0.00862	87	1.518	0.2746	1.377	0.25990	147	2.566	0.7160	1.918	1.0105
28	0.48869	0.02970	0.48384	0.00961	88	1.536	0.2807	1.389	0.26825	148	2.583	0.7244	1.923	1.0266
29	0.50615	0.03185	0.50076	0.01067	89	1.553	0.2867	1.402	0.27675	149	2.601	0.7328	1.927	1.0428
30	0.52360	0.03407	0.51764	0.01180	90	1.571	0.2929	1.414	0.28540	150	2.618	0.7412	1.932	1.0590
31	0.54105	0.03637	0.53448	0.01301	91	1.588	0.2991	1.427	0.2942	151	2.635	0.7496	1.936	1.0753
32	0.55851	0.03874	0.55127	0.01429	92	1.606	0.3053	1.439	0.3032	152	2.653	0.7581	1.941	1.0917
33	0.57596	0.04118	0.56803	0.01566	93	1.623	0.3116	1.451	0.3123	153	2.670	0.7666	1.945	1.1082
34	0.59341	0.04370	0.58474	0.01711	94	1.641	0.3180	1.463	0.3215	154	2.688	0.7750	1.949	1.1247
35	0.61087	0.04628	0.60141	0.01864	95	1.658	0.3244	1.475	0.3309	155	2.705	0.7836	1.953	1.1413
36	0.62832	0.04894	0.61803	0.02027	96	1.676	0.3309	1.486	0.3405	156	2.723	0.7921	1.956	1.1580
37	0.64577	0.05168	0.63461	0.02198	97	1.693	0.3374	1.498	0.3502	157	2.740	0.8006	1.960	1.1747
38	0.66323	0.05448	0.65114	0.02378	98	1.710	0.3439	1.509	0.3601	158	2.758	0.8092	1.963	1.1915
39	0.68068	0.05736	0.66761	0.02568	99	1.728	0.3506	1.521	0.3701	159	2.775	0.8178	1.967	1.2084
40	0.69813	0.06031	0.68404	0.02767	100	1.745	0.3572	1.532	0.3803	160	2.793	0.8264	1.970	1.2253
41	0.71558	0.06333	0.70041	0.02976	101	1.763	0.3639	1.543	0.3906	161	2.810	0.8350	1.973	1.2422
42	0.73304	0.06642	0.71674	0.03195	102	1.780	0.3707	1.554	0.4010	162	2.827	0.8436	1.975	1.2592
43	0.75049	0.06958	0.73300	0.03425	103	1.798	0.3775	1.565	0.4117	163	2.845	0.8522	1.978	1.2763
44	0.76794	0.07282	0.74921	0.03664	104	1.815	0.3843	1.576	0.4224	164	2.862	0.8608	1.981	1.2934
45	0.78540	0.07612	0.76537	0.03915	105	1.833	0.3912	1.587	0.4333	165	2.880	0.8695	1.983	1.3105
46	0.803	0.0795	0.781	0.04176	106	1.850	0.3982	1.597	0.4444	166	2.897	0.8781	1.985	1.3277
47	0.820	0.0829	0.797	0.04448	107	1.868	0.4052	1.608	0.4556	167	2.915	0.8868	1.987	1.3449
48	0.838	0.0865	0.813	0.04731	108	1.885	0.4122	1.618	0.4669	168	2.932	0.8955	1.989	1.3621
49	0.855	0.0900	0.829	0.05025	109	1.902	0.4193	1.628	0.4784	169	2.950	0.9042	1.991	1.3794
50	0.873	0.0937	0.845	0.05331	110	1.920	0.4264	1.638	0.4901	170	2.967	0.9128	1.992	1.3967
51	0.890	0.0974	0.861	0.05649	111	1.937	0.4336	1.648	0.5019	171	2.985	0.9215	1.994	1.4140
52	0.908	0.1012	0.877	0.05978	112	1.955	0.4408	1.658	0.5138	172	3.002	0.9302	1.995	1.4314
53	0.925	0.1051	0.892	0.06319	113	1.972	0.4481	1.668	0.5259	173	3.019	0.9390	1.996	1.4488
54	0.942	0.1090	0.908	0.06673	114	1.990	0.4554	1.677	0.5381	174	3.037	0.9477	1.997	1.4662
55	0.960	0.1130	0.923	0.07039	115	2.007	0.4627	1.687	0.5504	175	3.054	0.9564	1.998	1.4836
56	0.977	0.1171	0.939	0.07417	116	2.025	0.4701	1.696	0.5629	176	3.072	0.9651	1.999	1.5010
57	0.995	0.1212	0.954	0.07808	117	2.042	0.4775	1.705	0.5755	177	3.089	0.9738	1.999	1.5184
58	1.012	0.1254	0.970	0.08212	118	2.059	0.4850	1.714	0.5883	178	3.107	0.9825	2.000	1.5359
59	1.030	0.1296	0.985	0.08629	119	2.077	0.4925	1.723	0.6012	179	3.124	0.9913	2.000	1.5533
60	1.047	0.1340	1.000	0.09059	120	2.094	0.5000	1.732	0.6142	180	3.142	1.0000	2.000	1.5708

Area Equivalents

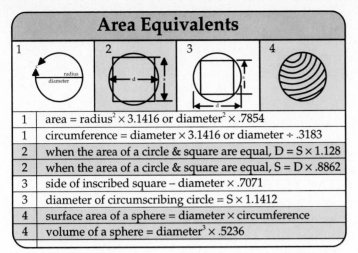

1	area = radius^2 × 3.1416 or diameter^2 × .7854
1	circumference = diameter × 3.1416 or diameter ÷ .3183
2	when the area of a circle & square are equal, D = S × 1.128
2	when the area of a circle & square are equal, S = D × .8862
3	side of inscribed square – diameter × .7071
3	diameter of circumscribing circle = S × 1.1412
4	surface area of a sphere = diameter × circumference
4	volume of a sphere = diameter^3 × .5236

Equivalents

Fahrenheit and Celcius

$$°F = (1.8 × °C) + 32$$
$$°C = (°F − 32) ÷ 1.8$$

Weight

1 gram = .03527 oz (av.)
1 oz = 28.35 grams
1 kilogram = 2.2046 pounds
1 pound = .04536 kilograms
1 metric ton = 2,204.6 pounds
1 ton (2000) lbs in U.S.) = 907.2 kg.

Volume

1 U.S. quart = 0.946 liters
1 U.S. gallon = 3.785 liters
1 liter = 1.0567 U.S. quarts
1 liter = .264 U.S. gallons

Length Conversions

multiply	by	to obtain
Inches	25.4	Millimeters
Feet	304.8	Millimeters
Inches	2.54	Centimeters
Feet	30.48	Centimeters
Millimeters	.03937008	Inches
Centimeters	.3937008	Inches
Meters	39.37008	Inches
Millimeters	.003280840	Feet
Centimeters	.03280840	Feet
Inches	.0254	Meters

Square Area Conversions

multiply	by	to obtain
Millimeters	.00001076391	Feet
Millimeters	.00155003	Inches
Centimeters	.1550003	Inches
Centimeters	.001076391	Feet
Inches	645.16	Millimeters
Inches	6.4516	Centimeters
Inches	.00064516	Meters
Feet	.09290304	Meters
Feet	929.0304	Centimeters
Feet	92,903.04	Millimeters

Rutland Tool and Supply Co., Inc.

Appendix M

Configuring the Digitizer

Digitizing is the process of transferring information from a digitizing tablet into the computer. In AutoCAD, a pointing device can be used with a *digitizing tablet*, or *digitizer*, to select commands and enter data for drawings. A digitizer provides an alternative to using keyboard entry or on-screen commands. You can also use a digitizer to convert existing paper drawings into AutoCAD drawing files.

A digitizer consists of a plastic surface, called a *tablet*, a mounted plastic overlay known as a *tablet menu*, and a pointing device, such as a puck or stylus, for picking locations on the tablet. Digitizers range in size from 6" square to 44" × 60". Many schools and companies use 12" square digitizers to input commands from standard and custom tablet menus.

To use a digitizer, it must first be configured by digitizing the tablet menu, also known as a *template*. The tablet menu contains most of the commands available in AutoCAD. Some commands are accompanied by small symbols, or icons, that indicate the function of the command.

A standard tablet menu is provided by AutoCAD. Tablet menus may also be customized for specific applications. The following sections explain how to install a digitizer and configure a common tablet menu orientation.

INSTALLING AND SETTING UP THE DIGITIZER

Most systems are installed with a mouse to use as a pointing device. If you are using your digitizer as the sole pointing device for all your Windows applications, you will require a driver called WINTAB. The WINTAB driver configures a digitizer to act as a mouse for Windows-based applications, but permits you to use the tablet screen pointing area and menus when running AutoCAD. You must install the WINTAB driver as your system pointing device in Windows before starting AutoCAD and configuring the digitizer. (The digitizer must work correctly in Windows before it can work in AutoCAD.) WINTAB drivers are supplied by the digitizer tablet manufacturers, not by Autodesk. Most drivers can be downloaded from on-line services.

Once the digitizer and the appropriate driver software has been installed, you can start AutoCAD and set the pointing device and its driver. To do so, access the **Options** dialog box. This is done by picking **Options...** from the **Tools** pull-down menu.

When the **Options** dialog box is displayed, pick the **System** tab. The appropriate driver for your digitizer can be selected from the drop-down list in the **Current Pointing Device** area. If Windows NT, Windows 98, or Windows 95 automatically set up the pointing device, the **Current System Pointing Device** is specified as the active driver. If the WINTAB driver has been installed and Windows has been correctly configured for its use, you can select the **Wintab Compatible Digitizer ADI 4.2** option. Selecting this option activates the two **Accept input from:** option buttons. Pick **Digitizer only** or **Digitizer and mouse** as appropriate and press the **OK** button.

> **NOTE** For additional information on setting up the digitizer pointing device, refer to the AutoCAD 2000 *Installation Guide* and Appendix D of this text.

CONFIGURING THE TABLET MENU

To use a tablet menu, the digitizer must first be configured for the specific menu you have. When you initially configure AutoCAD to recognize a digitizer, the *entire* surface of the tablet represents the screen pointing area. The **TABLET** command allows you to configure the digitizer to recognize the tablet menu separately. This includes telling AutoCAD the exact layout of the menu areas and the size and position of the screen pointing area.

As discussed earlier, a standard tablet menu, or template, is supplied with AutoCAD. See Figure M-1. This tablet menu presents commands in related groups.

You can use this template to configure the tablet menu, or you can set up your own configuration. Like the AutoCAD screen menus, a tablet menu can be customized. Referring to Figure M-1, notice the empty space above the menu areas. This space is available for adding commands or symbols to aid picking and inserting functions. Customizing tablet menus is discussed in *AutoCAD and its Applications—Advanced.*

Figure M-1.
The AutoCAD standard tablet menu. A drawing of the menu is provided in the Sample folder of the Acad2000 file folder. (Autodesk, Inc.)

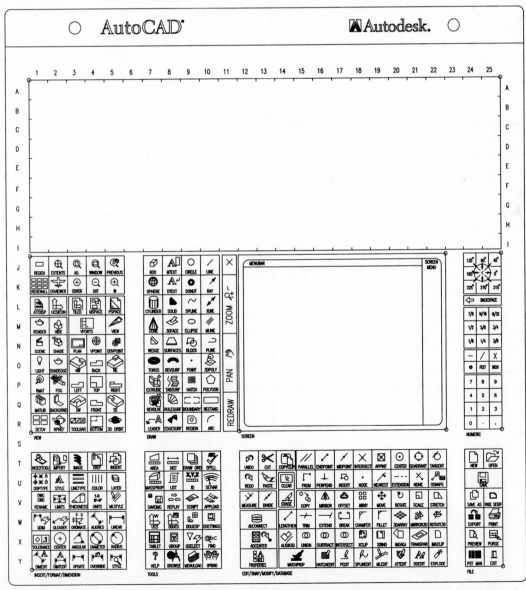

The AutoCAD tablet menu drawing file is found in the Sample folder of the Acad2000 file folder. Open the file named Tablet 2000.dwg to display the template shown in Figure M-1. You can use this template to configure the tablet menu by printing or plotting it full size. The template can be printed on a durable material such as polyester film, or it can be output on paper and covered with clear plastic film for protection. The template can then be mounted to your digitizer tablet for configuration purposes.

After the template is mounted, you can use the **TABLET** command to tell AutoCAD the layout of the tablet menu. When you issue this command, you are prompted for the number of menu areas, three corner points for each area, and the number of columns and rows in each area. The screen pointing area is defined by picking two opposite corners. Referring to Figure M-1, three corners of each menu area are marked with small donuts. As you go through the following example, look at Figure M-2. It illustrates how the standard AutoCAD tablet menu is configured and shows the donuts marking each of the menu area corner points.

Figure M-2.
The four menu areas and the screen pointing area in the AutoCAD standard template are specified by picking the corner points represented by small donuts. (Autodesk, Inc.)

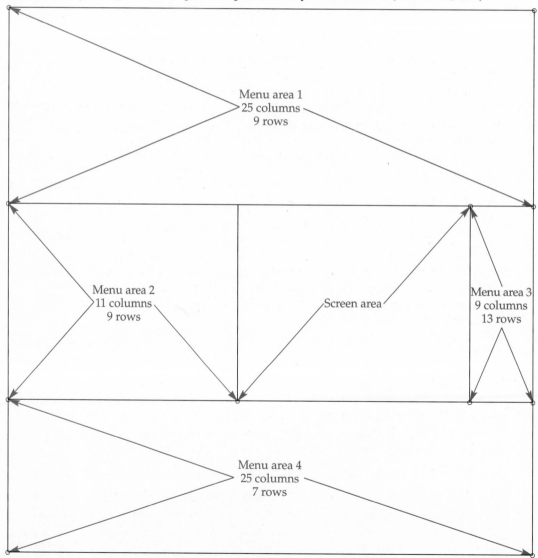

After entering the **TABLET** command, enter CFG for the **Configure** option. This option can be accessed directly by picking **Configure** from the **Tablet** cascading menu of the **Tools** pull-down menu. The sequence is as follows:

Command: **TA** *or* **TABLET**↵
Option (ON/OFF/CAL/CFG): **CFG**↵
Enter number of tablet menus desired (0-4) <0>: **4**↵
Do you want to realign tablet menu areas? <N> **Y**↵
Digitize upper left corner of menu area 1: *(pick the donut at the upper-left corner of area 1)*
Digitize lower left corner of menu area 1: *(pick the next point)*
Digitize lower right corner of menu area 1: *(pick the next point)*
Enter the number of columns for menu area 1(*n - nnnn*)<25>: ↵
Enter the number of rows for menu area 1(*n - nnnn*)<9>: ↵

You have now given AutoCAD the location of menu area 1 and specified the number of command boxes that are available. The command continues with menu areas 2, 3, and 4:

Digitize upper left corner of menu area 2: *(pick the donut at the upper-left corner of area 2)*
Digitize lower left corner of menu area 2: *(pick the next point)*
Digitize lower right corner of menu area 2: *(pick the next point)*
Enter the number of columns for menu area 2(*n - nnnn*)<11>: ↵
Enter the number of rows for menu area 2(*n - nnnn*)<9>: ↵
Digitize upper left corner of menu area 3: *(pick the donut at the upper-left corner of area 3)*
Digitize lower left corner of menu area 3: *(pick the next point)*
Digitize lower right corner of menu area 3: *(pick the next point)*
Enter the number of columns for menu area 3(*n - nnnn*)<9>: ↵
Enter the number of rows for menu area 3(*n - nnnn*)<13>: ↵
Digitize upper left corner of menu area 4: *(pick the donut at the upper-left corner of area 4)*
Digitize lower left corner of menu area 4: *(pick the next point)*
Digitize lower right corner of menu area 4: *(pick the next point)*
Enter the number of columns for menu area 4(*n - nnnn*)<25>: ↵
Enter the number of rows for menu area 4(*n - nnnn*)<7>: ↵

Next, you must locate the opposite corners of the screen pointing area:

Do you want to specify the Floating Screen Pointing Area? <N>: **Y**↵
Do you want the Floating Screen Pointing Area to be the same size as the Fixed
    Screen Pointing Area? <Y>: *(enter Y or N; if you enter Y, digitize the lower-left
    and upper-right corners of the floating screen pointing area when prompted)*
The F12 key will toggle the Floating Screen Pointing Area ON and OFF.
Would you like to specify a button to toggle the Floating Screen
    Area? <N>: *(enter Y or N)*
Command:

If you choose to use a digitizer puck button as the floating screen area toggle, press the button of your choice. Use a button other than the pick button.

The tablet menu configuration is saved in the acad2000.cfg file, which is located in the Acad2000 folder. The system reads this file when loading AutoCAD to determine what kind of equipment you are using. It also determines which menu is current. Use this same process when configuring the tablet for custom menus.

As discussed earlier, a digitizer can be used to convert existing hard copy drawings into AutoCAD drawing files. Most companies do not have the time to convert existing drawings to electronic files because they rely on the CAD system for new product drawings. A more common way to convert existing drawings is to use a scanner, which sends a light or camera over the drawing to transfer the image to the computer. This technique is called *scanning* and is discussed in a later section of this appendix. There are businesses, however, that digitize existing drawings for other companies. These commercial operations use large format digitizers for D-size and E-size drawings.

When a company begins converting to CAD, the normal procedure is to have a manual drafting group and a CAD group. Selected new drawings are created on the computer. This situation may continue until the full capabilities of CAD are realized. Manual drafters remain important because older drawings are often revised in the original format.

There comes a time when a company must make a decision to convert existing paper drawings to CAD drawing files. This problem is not confined to paper drawings. Sometimes it is necessary to convert one type of computer-generated drawing to another CAD system. This might be done with a translation program.

In some situations, the only solution is to redraw the existing drawings with AutoCAD. Time may be saved by digitizing the existing drawing, depending on the type of drawing. A digitizer large enough to accommodate the largest drawing is best, but large drawings can also be digitized on small digitizers, if necessary.

Configuring the Tablet Menu for a Drawing

Before digitizing a drawing, you must configure the tablet, even if it was previously configured for another application. This is done to utilize the maximum area on the tablet. The procedure is similar to the tablet menu configuration previously discussed. To configure the tablet for a drawing, enter the **TABLET** command and use the **Configure** option. The sequence is as follows:

> Command: **TA** *or* **TABLET**↵
> Option (ON/OFF/CAL/CFG): **CFG**↵

Next, AutoCAD asks for the number of tablet menus. Since the entire tablet is used when digitizing an existing drawing, there are no menu areas. Type 0 and press [Enter]. When asked if you want to respecify the screen pointing area, enter Y. Then pick the lower-left corner and the upper-right corner. If your digitizer has proximity lights, watch them as you do this. One of the lights is on when the puck is in the screen pointing area; it turns off when the puck leaves the area. Move the pointing device slowly to the extreme corners until you find the location where the light comes on. This helps you gain use of the entire screen pointing area when digitizing. See Figure M-3. The prompt sequence is as follows:

> Enter number of tablet menus desired (0-4) <0>: ↵
> Do you want to respecify the Fixed Screen Pointing Area? <N>: **Y**↵
> Digitize lower left corner of Fixed Screen Pointing Area: *(pick the lower-left corner of the pointing area)*
> Digitize upper right corner of Fixed Screen Pointing Area: *(pick the upper-right corner of the pointing area)*
> Do you want to specify the Floating Screen Pointing Area?<N> **N**↵
> Command:

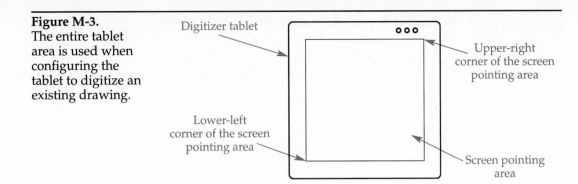

Figure M-3.
The entire tablet area is used when configuring the tablet to digitize an existing drawing.

Digitizer tablet

Upper-right corner of the screen pointing area

Lower-left corner of the screen pointing area

Screen pointing area

Preparing the Drawing

After the tablet has been configured, attach the drawing to the tablet using drafting tape. The drawing does not need to be exactly square on the screen pointing area, but it should be flat. A plot plan attached to a digitizer tablet is shown in Figure M-4. The drawing setup also requires that you specify the same drawing parameters that you would use for a normal drawing. To prepare the drawing for digitizing, enter the drawing limits, units, and other settings to reflect those used with the drawing. Use the following guidelines:

- Set the limits to correlate with the drawing dimensions.
- Set the drawing units to correspond with the type of drawing you are transferring.
- Set the grid and snap to a convenient value.
- Specify the drawing origin using the **UCS** command.

Figure M-4.
The drawing to be digitized is placed flat on the tablet.

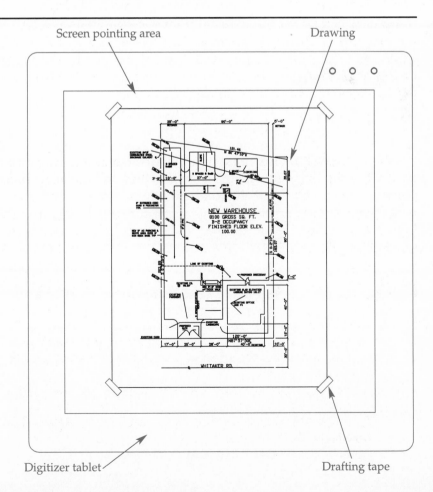

Screen pointing area

Drawing

Digitizer tablet

Drafting tape

Calibrating the Tablet and Digitizing the Drawing

The next step in digitizing a drawing is calibrating the tablet. *Calibrating* is a method of digitizing points to align the drawing with the tablet. The number of points that you digitize during calibration determines how accurately the existing drawing coordinates are transferred to the computer. This is called *transformation*. The different types of transformation are described as follows:

- **Orthogonal.** During calibration, you must enter a minimum of two coordinates to define an area. This is the most basic type of calibration and is known as *orthogonal transformation*. Two points work well if the existing drawing is dimensionally accurate. A dimensionally accurate drawing normally has stable length and width measurements, and angles are not distorted.
- **Affine.** In this type of transformation, three coordinates are selected for calibration. This is necessary when lines are generally parallel, but the horizontal dimensions are stretched in relationship to the vertical dimensions.
- **Projective.** Four calibration points are used in projective transformation. When the existing drawing has stretched or has been distorted to the point where parallel lines tend to converge, then the calibration of four points may be necessary.
- **Multiple point.** In some cases, more than four points may be necessary for calibration. AutoCAD calculates the relationship between the points with accuracy proportional to the number of points digitized. However, nine points are usually the maximum number of points needed, since additional points tend to slow down the transformation process without improving the accuracy.

The **CAL** option of the **TABLET** command allows you to calibrate the drawing with the tablet. The pick button of the digitizer puck is used to select points. After each point is picked, AutoCAD prompts for X,Y coordinate values. Enter the required coordinates, repeating the process for all the points selected.

PROFESSIONAL TIP

When selecting points for calibration, choose locations that are as accurate as possible. For example, in mapping applications, pick property corners or benchmarks. In mechanical drafting, use datums on the drawing. Select points that are distributed in a wide area around the drawing. In addition, the points should be in a triangular relationship, rather than in a straight line.

NOTE

Be sure to look straight down on the target point if you are digitizing points using a puck with crosshairs. Looking through the puck viewing glass at an angle results in inaccurate point selection.

The following example is used to calibrate the plot plan. Orthogonal transformation is sufficient because the existing drawing is very accurate. When you enter the **CAL** option of the **TABLET** command, the tablet mode is turned on and the screen cursor no longer appears.

Command: **TA** *or* **TABLET**↵
Option (ON/OFF/CAL/CFG): **CAL**↵

You are then prompted to digitize two points on the drawing and give the coordinates of each point. The two points may be anywhere, but they are usually the endpoints of a vertical line. Drafters often pick two points on an object on the left side of the drawing, such as the west property line on a plot plan. This begins the orientation of the digitizer in relation to the object as you work from left to right. Look at the existing drawing to be digitized in Figure M-5 as you follow these prompts:

> Digitize point #1: *(pick the lower-left property corner where you set the UCS origin)*
> Enter coordinates for point #1: *(enter **0,0** and press* [Enter] *to coincide with the UCS origin)*
> Digitize point #2: *(pick the north end of the west property line)*

Figure M-5.
To calibrate the drawing with the tablet, carefully select two points and provide the coordinates of the points.

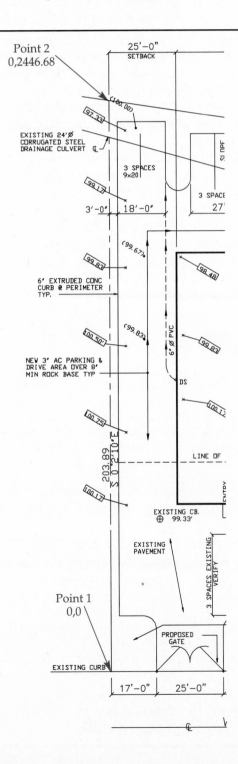

Enter the length of the property line relative to the first point (X = 0, Y = 203.89' or 2446.68") when entering the coordinates for the second point:

Enter coordinates for point #2: **0,2446.68.**↵

Pressing [Enter] for the third point request automatically makes AutoCAD use the orthogonal transformation format:

Digitize point #3 (or press ENTER to end): ↵

Now that the existing drawing has been calibrated to the tablet, it is ready to be digitized. Reissue the **TABLET** command and turn the tablet mode on:

Command: **TA** *or* **TABLET**↵
Option (ON/OFF/CAL/CFG): **ON**↵

The screen cursor returns for you to use AutoCAD commands to draw lines and other features. Use the **LINE** command to draw the property boundaries by picking each property corner. Use the **Close** option for the last line. The resulting property boundaries are shown in Figure M-6.

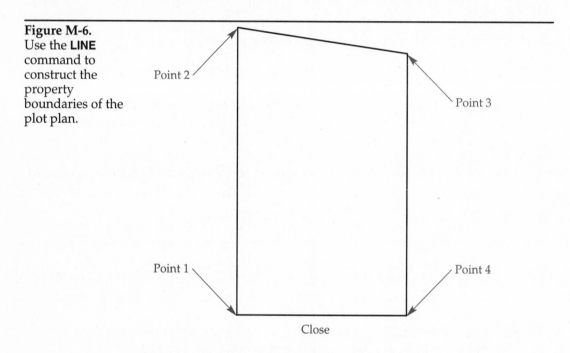

Figure M-6.
Use the **LINE** command to construct the property boundaries of the plot plan.

Point 2

Point 3

Point 1

Point 4

Close

Proceed by digitizing the buildings, roads, walkways, utilities, and other features using commands such as **LINE**, **PLINE**, **ARC**, and **CIRCLE**. Dimension the plot plan using the necessary dimensioning commands and use the **DTEXT** command to add notes.

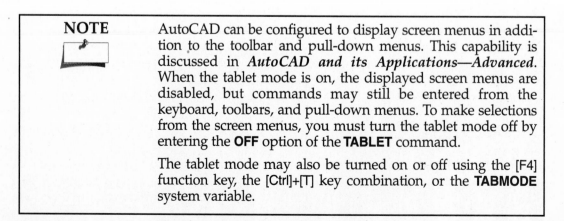

NOTE

AutoCAD can be configured to display screen menus in addition to the toolbar and pull-down menus. This capability is discussed in *AutoCAD and its Applications—Advanced*. When the tablet mode is on, the displayed screen menus are disabled, but commands may still be entered from the keyboard, toolbars, and pull-down menus. To make selections from the screen menus, you must turn the tablet mode off by entering the **OFF** option of the **TABLET** command.

The tablet mode may also be turned on or off using the [F4] function key, the [Ctrl]+[T] key combination, or the **TABMODE** system variable.

The plot plan example in the previous discussion used two calibration points successfully because the existing drawing was very accurate. Three or more points may be digitized to help provide greater accuracy. The same example could be used to illustrate three-point calibration. The third point would be specified as another property line corner, forming a triangular relationship between the points.

When three points are digitized, AutoCAD calculates the relationship between orthogonal, affine, and projective transformations. When AutoCAD is finished making the calculations, a listing displayed in the **AutoCAD Text Window** provides you with this information:

3 calibration points			
Transformation type:	Orthogonal	Affine	Projective
Outcome of fit:	success	exact	impossible
RMS Error:	6.324		
Standard deviation:	2.941		
Largest residual:	9.726		
At point:	2		
Second-largest residual:	8.975		
At point:	1		

The elements in this listing can be interpreted as follows:

- **Outcome of fit**.
  - **Success.** AutoCAD was successful in calibrating the points. The calculation results for an orthogonal transformation are given.
  - **Exact.** There were exactly enough points for AutoCAD to complete the transformation.
  - **Impossible.** AutoCAD was not given enough points to provide a projective transformation.
  - **Failure.** If this message is displayed, there may have been enough calibration points, but AutoCAD was unable to complete a transformation because of collinear or coincident points.
  - **Canceled.** This message may appear as a result of a projective transformation.
- **RMS Error.** *RMS* means *root mean square*, which is a calculation of the accuracy of the calibration points. The smaller the number, the closer it is to a perfect fit.
- **Standard deviation.** This value indicates how much deviation exists among the accuracy of the points. If this value is near zero, then the points have nearly the same degree of accuracy.
- **Largest residual.** This value estimates the worst error you might have in the digitized points, and tells you at which point this occurs.
- **Second largest residual.** This value gives the next least accurate calculation among the calibration points.

Digitizing Large Drawings

The drawing you plan to digitize may be too large for your tablet. This requires you to divide the drawing into sections that fit the tablet area. For example, a large drawing can be divided into four sections. During calibration, establish the coordinates of the boundaries for each section. See Figure M-7. The coordinates of each section are labeled and shown with dots for reference.

Next, tape the portion labeled as SECTION 1 to the tablet and calibrate the tablet to the coordinates 1,1 and 1,8. Follow by digitizing this section.

Proceed by placing the portion labeled as SECTION 2 on the tablet. Calibrate the tablet to the coordinates 10.5,1 and 10.5,8. Then, digitize the portion.

Next, place the portion labeled as SECTION 3 on the tablet. Calibrate the tablet to the coordinates 1,8 and 1,16, and then digitize the portion. Finally, place the SECTION 4 portion on the tablet. Calibrate the tablet to the coordinates 10.5,8 and 10.5,16, and digitize the portion. The entire drawing has now been digitized.

Figure M-7.

Dividing a large drawing into sections for digitizing. Label the sections and the coordinates of the points defining the sections.

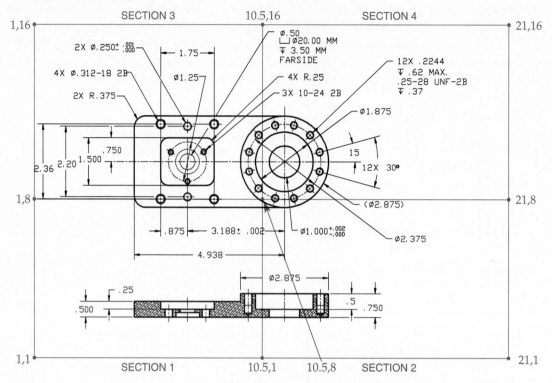

SCANNING EXISTING DRAWINGS

As discussed earlier, scanning is a commonly used method to transfer existing drawings into AutoCAD. Using a scanner is similar to taking a photograph of the drawing. One advantage of scanning over digitizing drawings manually is that the entire drawing—including dimensions, symbols, and text—is transferred to the computer. A disadvantage is that some drawings, when scanned, require extensive editing to make them presentable.

The scanning process picks up images from the drawing. What appears to be a dimension, for example, is only a graphic representation of the dimension, not an *entity*. If you want the dimensional information to be technically accurate, the dimensions must be edited and redrawn.

After the drawing is scanned, the image is sent to a raster converter that translates information to digital or vector format. A *raster* is an electron beam that generates a matrix of pixels. As you learned previously, pixels make up the drawing image on the display screen. A raster editor is then used to display the image for editing.

Companies using scanners can, in many cases, reproduce existing drawings more efficiently than companies that digitize drawings. Scanners transfer drawings from paper, vellum, film, or blueline prints and convert the hard copy image into a raster data file. When an existing drawing has been transferred to the computer, it becomes an AutoCAD drawing and can be edited as necessary.

Index

DXF files, 538, 544–545
  opening, 112
  saving as, 107
DXX files, 548

E

EDGEMODE system variable, 455, 457
Edit Attribute Definition dialog box, 877
Editing objects
  aligning, 465–466
  arraying, 511–515
  block attributes, 876–878, 880–887
  blocks, 810, 815–820
  breaking, 452–453
  chamfers, 444–448
  changing properties, 497–502
  copying, 460–461
  determining area, 613–616
  dimensions, 705–720
  extending, 455–457
  fillets, 448–451
  hatch patterns, 787–789
  lengthening, 470–473
  listing information, 617–618
  mirroring, 461–463
  moving, 458–459
  multilines, 567–571
  polylines, 585–598
  rotating, 464–465
  scaling, 466–468
  splines, 601–605
  stretching, 468–469
  trimming, 454–455
  using grips, 485–494
  viewports, 868–869
  xrefs, 852–855
Effective area, 426
Electrical symbols, 1032
Element Properties dialog box, 563
ELEV command, 921–922
ELLIPSE command, 202–207, 908–910
Ellipses, 202–207
Ellipsis (...) buttons, 37
Elliptical arcs, 205–207
Endpoint object snap mode, 222–223
Enter Attribute dialog box, 878
Entity, 139
EPS files, 538, 547
ERASE command, 139–146
Ergonomics, 1004–1006
Escape key ([Esc]), 56
EXE files, 520, 538
EXIT command, 116
Exiting AutoCAD, 116
EXPLODE command, 596, 719–720, 819
Explorer. *See* Windows Explorer

Exploring window. *See* Windows Explorer
EXPORT command, 546–548
Exporting files, 544–548
  3DS files, 546
  BMP files, 548
  DXF files, 544–545
  DXX files, 548
  EPS files, 547
  SAT files, 546–547
  STL files, 547
  WMF files, 548
Express pull-down menu, 31
Express Tools, 56, 979–983, 994
EXTEND command, 455–457
Extended Intersection object snap mode,
  225–226
Extension lines, 123, 672–673
Extension object snap mode, 227
Extension paths, 220, 227
External commands, 943–945
External Reference dialog box, 841–842
External references, 839–870
  benefits of using, 840
  binding, 845–846
  binding depending objects, 850–852
  clipping, 846–848
  creating with **AutoCAD DesignCenter**, 842
  demand loading, 848–849
  detaching, 843
  editing, 852–855
  overlaying, 843
  paths, 845
  reloading, 843
  unloading, 843
  used in layouts, 855–870
Extract files, 893
Extracting attributes, 893–897

F

Feature control frame, 742–743
  double, 755–756
  editing, 759
  height, 758
Features, 639
Fence selection option, 145
File names, 519–520
FILEDIA system variable, 101–102
FILEOPEN command, 539
Files
  arranging, 527
  copying, 529–530
  deleting, 530
  listing, 523–525
  managing, 999–1002
  moving, 530
  renaming, 530

G

H

M

P

3D Orbit

3D Pan   3D Orbit   3D Swivel   3D Adjust   Back Clip
Clip Planes   On/Off

3D Zoom   3D Continuous   3D Adjust   Front Clip
Orbit   Distance   On/Off

Inquiry

Distance   Mass   Locate
Properties   Point

Area   List

Refedit

Edit block   Reference name   Add objects   Discard changes
or Xref   display   to working set   to reference

Remove objects   Save back
from working set   changes
to reference

Insert

Insert   Image   OLE
Block   Object

External   Import
Reference

Reference

External   External   External Reference   Image   Image   Image
Reference   Reference Clip   Clip Frame   Attach   Adjust   Transparency

External   External   Image   Image   Image   Image
Reference   Reference   Clip   Quality   Frame
Attach   Bind

Shade

2D   Hidden   Gouraud   Gouraud Shaded,
Wireframe   Shaded   Edges On

3D   Flat   Flat Shaded,
Wireframe   Shaded   Edges On

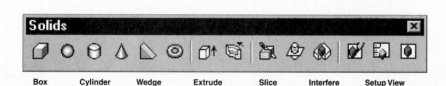

Render

Hide   Scenes   Materials   Mapping   Fog   Landscape   Render
Edit   Preferences

Render   Lights   Materials   Background   Landscape   Landscape   Statistics
Library   New   Library

Layouts

New   Page
Layout   Setup

Layout from   Display
Template   Viewports
Dialog

Solids

Box   Cylinder   Wedge   Extrude   Slice   Interfere   Setup View

Sphere   Cone   Torus   Revolve   Section   Setup   Setup Profile
Drawing

Solids Editing

Union   Intersect   Move   Delete   Taper   Color   Color   Clean   Shell
Faces   Faces   Faces   Faces   Edges

Subtract   Extrude   Offset   Rotate   Copy   Copy   Imprint   Separate   Check
Faces   Faces   Faces   Faces   Edges

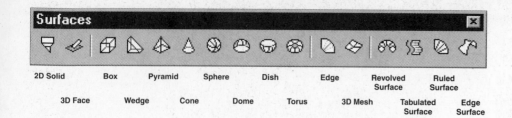

Surfaces

2D Solid   Box   Pyramid   Sphere   Dish   Edge   Revolved Surface   Ruled Surface

3D Face   Wedge   Cone   Dome   Torus   3D Mesh   Tabulated Surface   Edge Surface

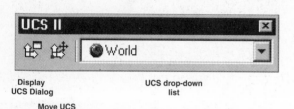

UCS

UCS   UCS Previous   Object UCS   View UCS   Z Axis Vector UCS   X Axis Rotate UCS   Z Axis Rotate UCS

Display UCS Dialog   World UCS   Face UCS   Origin UCS   3-Point UCS   Y Axis Rotate UCS   Apply UCS

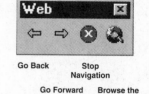

Web

Go Back   Stop Navigation

Go Forward   Browse the Web

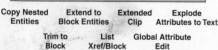

UCS II

Display UCS Dialog   UCS drop-down list

Move UCS Origin

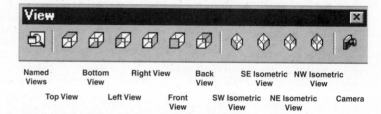

View

Named Views   Bottom View   Right View   Back View   SE Isometric View   NW Isometric View

Top View   Left View   Front View   SW Isometric View   NE Isometric View   Camera

Viewports

Display Viewports Dialog   Polygonal Viewport   Clip Existing Viewport   Viewports drop-down list

Single Viewport   Convert Object to Viewport

Zoom

Zoom Window   Zoom Scale   Zoom In   Zoom All

Zoom Dynamic   Zoom Center   Zoom Out   Zoom Extents

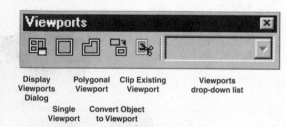

Express Block Tools

Copy Nested Entities   Extend to Block Entities   Extended Clip   Explode Attributes to Text

Trim to Block Entities   List Xref/Block Entities   Global Attribute Edit

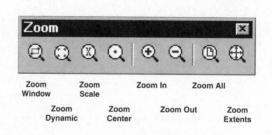

Express Layer Tools

Layer Manager   Change to Current Layer   Freeze Object's Layer   Lock Object's Layer

Match Object's Layer   Isolate Object's Layer   Turn Object's Layer Off   Unlock Object's Layer

Express Standard Toolbar

Multiple Entity Stretch   Extended Trim   Wipeout   Pck 'n Go   Toggle Frames

Move Copy Rotate   Multiple Pedit   Revision Cloud   Super Hatch   Show URLs

Express Text

Text Fit   Explode Text

Text Mask   Arc Aligned Text